Biology

This book is dedicated to the African elephant, the largest living land mammal, which was placed on the endangered species list in October 1989.

Biology

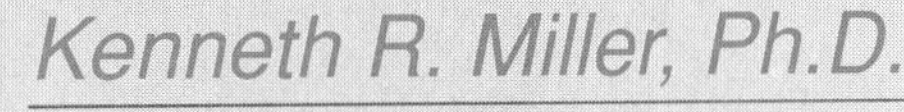
Kenneth R. Miller, Ph.D.

Professor of Biology
Brown University
Providence, Rhode Island

Joseph Levine, Ph.D.

Science Writer and Consultant
Former Assistant Professor of Biology
Boston College
Boston, Massachusetts

Prentice Hall
Englewood Cliffs, New Jersey
Needham, Massachusetts

COMPONENTS OF THE BIOLOGY PROGRAM

Student Text and Annotated Teacher's Edition
Laboratory Manual and Annotated Teacher's Edition
Teacher's Resource Book
Study Guide and Annotated Teacher's Edition
Computer Test Bank with DIAL-A-TEST™ Service
Biology Color Transparencies
Biology Wall Posters
Biotechnology Workbook and Solutions Manual
Biology Courseware
Biology Videos
Biology File

The illustration on the cover depicts a group of African elephants.

Photo credits begin on page Reference 64.

FIRST EDITION

ISBN 0-13-081241-2

13 14 15 16 17 18 19 20

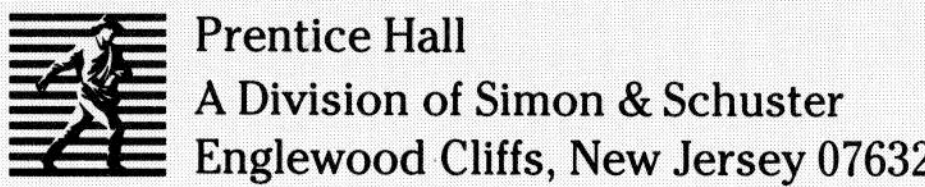
Prentice Hall
A Division of Simon & Schuster
Englewood Cliffs, New Jersey 07632

STAFF CREDITS

Editorial	Harry Bakalian, Pamela E. Hirschfeld, Maureen Grassi, Robert P. Letendre, Elisa Mui Eiger, Christine A. Portante
Art Direction	AnnMarie Roselli
Production	Elizabeth Torjussen, Marjorie MacLeay, Lisa Meyerhoff, Cleasta Wilburn
Photo Research	Libby Forsyth
Marketing	Paul P. Scopa, Victoria Willows
Manufacturing	Laura Sanderson, Denise Herckenrath
Consultants	Linda Grant *National Science Consultant* Sharon Pope *National Social Studies and Cross Curriculum Consultant*

Contributing Writers

Stephanie Baron
Biology Teacher
San Diego Unified School District
San Diego, California

Pamela Cunningham
Former Biology Teacher
Hazlet, New Jersey

Linda Densman
Biology Teacher
and Secondary Science Consultant
Hurst-Euless-Bedford
Independent School District
Hurst, Texas

Kathy French
Biology Teacher
Hurst-Euless-Bedford
Independent School District
Bedford, Texas

Janis W. Lariviere
Biology Teacher
Anderson High School
Austin, Texas

Marcia Mungenast
Science Writer
Upper Montclair, New Jersey

Theresa Flynn Nason
Science Writer
Voorhees, New Jersey

Sylvia Neivert
Science Writer
San Diego, California

Renate Otterbach
Gifted and Talented
Educational Specialist
Wichita Falls, Texas

Denise DiRienzo-Skalecky
Biology Teacher
Bishop Ford Central Catholic
High School
Brooklyn, New York

Evan Silberstein
Biology Teacher
Spring Valley High School
Spring Valley, New York

Myrna Silver
Environmental Science
and Physics Teacher
J. J. Pearce High School
Richardson, Texas

College Reviewers

Michael J. Balick, Ph.D.
Director, Institute of Economic Botany
New York Botanical Garden
Bronx, New York

Marvin Druger, Ph.D.
Professor of Biology
Syracuse University
Syracuse, New York

Mary-Jane Gething, Ph.D.
Professor of Biochemistry
University of Texas
Southwestern Medical Center
Dallas, Texas

Paul E. Hertz, Ph.D.
Chairman, Department of Biological
Sciences
Barnard College
New York, New York

Cheryl L. Mason, Ph.D.
Assistant Professor of Biology
San Diego State University
San Diego, California

Laurence D. Mueller, Ph.D.
Associate Professor of Ecology
and Evolutionary Biology
University of California
Irvine, California

Ada Olins, Ph.D.
Biological Researcher
Department of Biology
Oak Ridge National Laboratory
Oak Ridge, Tennessee

John Penick, Ph.D.
Science Education Center
University of Iowa
Iowa City, Iowa

Kenneth Sebens, Ph.D.
Marine Science Center
Northeastern University,
Nahant, Massachusetts

Jerry W. Shay, Ph.D.
Associate Professor
Department of Cell Biology
and Neuroscience
University of Texas
Southwestern Medical Center
Dallas, Texas

Judy Snyder, Ph.D.
Department of Biology
Denver University
Boulder, Colorado

Susan Speece, Ed.D.
Biology Department Chairperson
Anderson University
Anderson, Indiana

Secondary Reviewers

Tod Anderson
Science Teacher
L. V. Stockard Middle School
Dallas, Texas

Leslie Ferry Bettencourt
Biology Teacher
Lincoln Senior High School
Lincoln, Rhode Island

William A. Feddeler
Science Educator
Warren Consolidated Schools
Warren, Michigan

Steve Ferguson
Biology Teacher
and Department Chairman
Lee's Summit High School
Lee's Summit, Missouri

Larry Flammer
Biology Teacher and Science Supervisor
Campbell Union High School District
San Jose, California

Emile Hamberlin, Ph.D.
Science Instructor
DuSable High School
Chicago, Illinois

Frank R. Johns
Biology Teacher
Lake Placid High School
Lake Placid, New York

Dwight Kertzman
Biology Teacher
and Department Chairman
Booker T. Washington High School
Tulsa, Oklahoma

Priscilla J. Lee
Science Department Chairperson
Venice High School
Los Angeles Unified School District
Los Angeles, California

Mary Grace Lopez
Biology Teacher
W. B. Ray High School
Corpus Christi, Texas

Warren D. Maggard
Biology Teacher
and Department Chairman
South Oldham High School
Crestwood, Kentucky

Della M. McCaughan
Science Department Chairperson
Biloxi High School
Biloxi, Mississippi

Jarvis VNC Pahl
Biology Teacher
Etiwanda High School
Etiwanda, California

Sr. John Ann Proach, C.S.B.
Biology Teacher
and Science Chairperson
Bishop Conwell High School
Levittown, Pennsylvania

Therese A. Scott
Biology Teacher
Sam Houston High School
Arlington ISD
Arlington, Texas

Norma B. Trevino
Biology Teacher
Foy H. Moody Health
and Science Center
Corpus Christi, Texas

Gary J. Vitta
Assistant to the Superintendent
West Essex Regional Schools
North Caldwell, New Jersey

Glenna Wilkoff
Science Chairperson
John Hay High School
Cleveland, Ohio

Reading Consultant

Larry Swinburne, Director
Swinburne Readability Laboratory

Contents

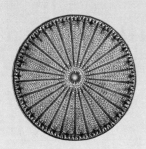

Chapter 14 *Evolution: How Change Occurs* **290–317**

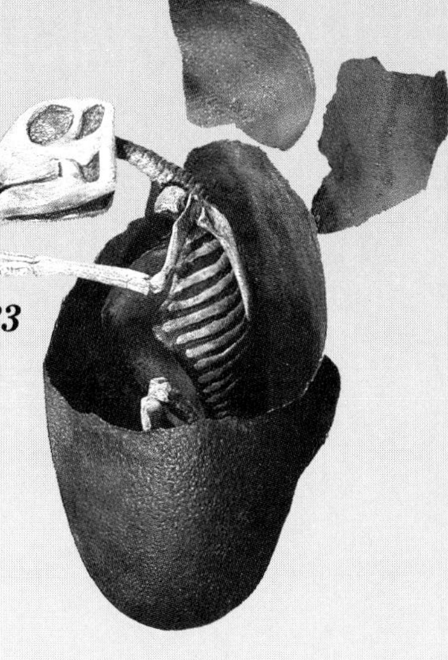

Chapter 15 *Classification Systems* **318–333**

UNIT 5 *Life on Earth: Monerans, Protists, and Fungi* **336–429**

Chapter 16 *The Origin of Life* **338–353**

Chapter 17 *Viruses and Monerans* **354–379**

Chapter 18 *Protists* **380–405**

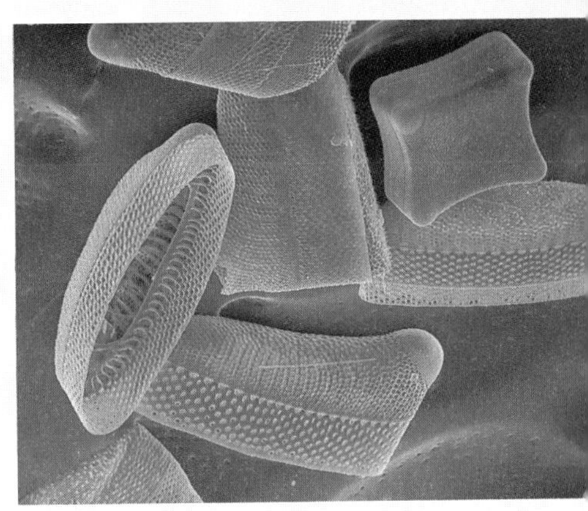

Chapter 19 *Fungi* **406–427**

UNIT 6 *Life on Earth: Plants* 430–551

UNIT 7 *Life on Earth: Invertebrate Animals* 552–675

UNIT 8 *Life on Earth: Vertebrate Animals* 676–805

UNIT 9 *Human Biology* 806–1003

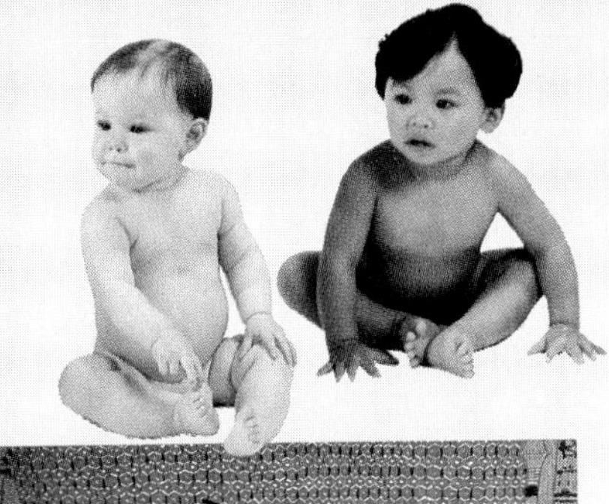

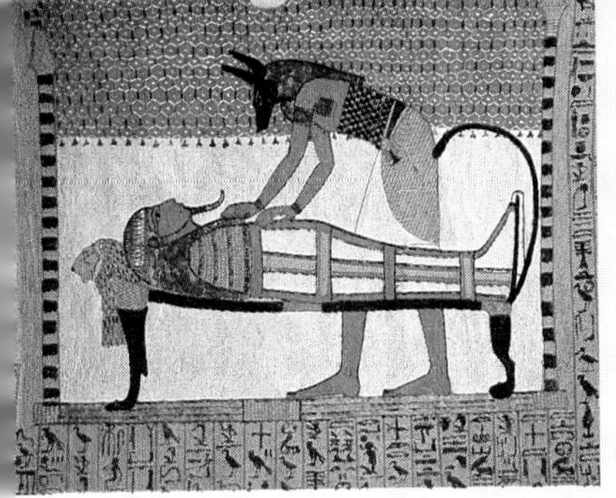

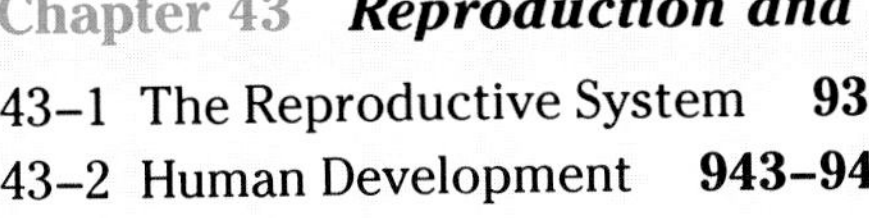

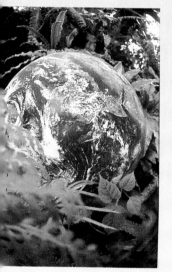

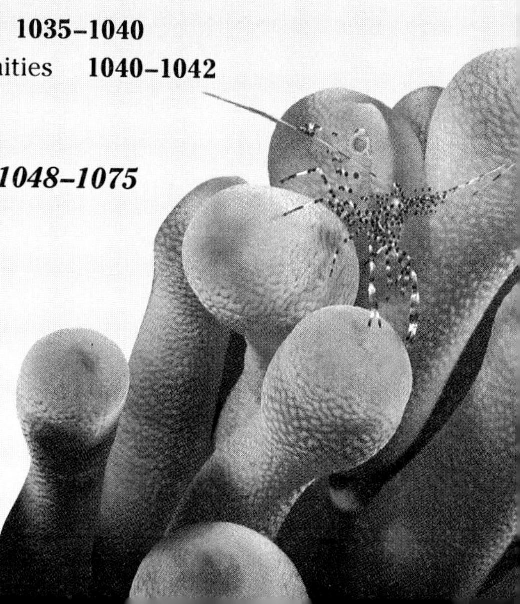

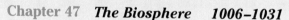

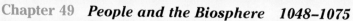

Reference Section

Features

Problem Solving in Biology

Science, Technology, and Society: Breakthroughs

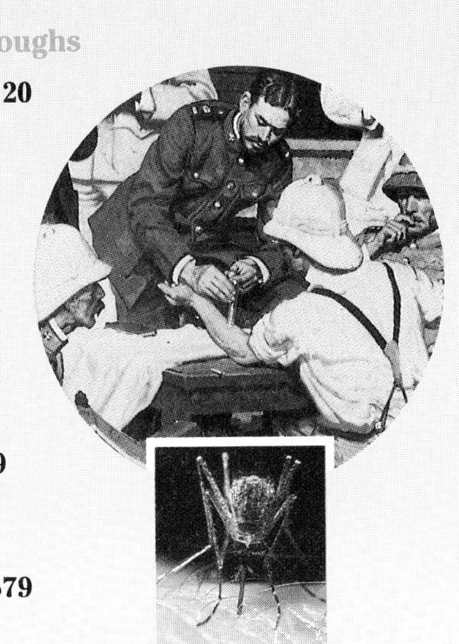

Science, Technology, and Society: Applications

Science, Technology, and Society: Issues

Laboratory Investigations

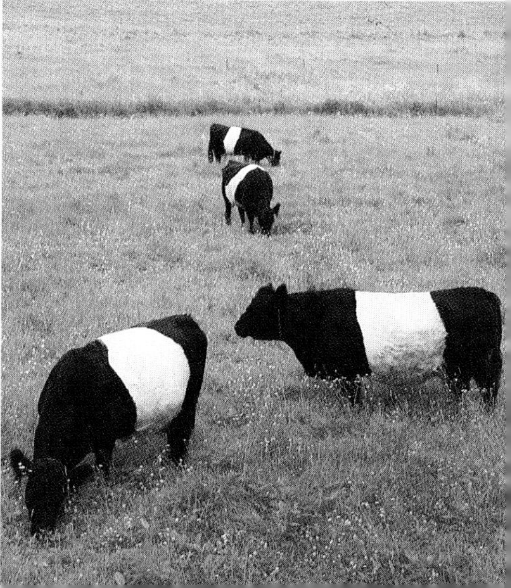

Welcome!

You are about to enter a wonderfully exciting, and sometimes unbelievable, world—the world of living things. In the pages of this textbook you will come to understand the nature of life as we know it today. You will also gain an appreciation of the scientific process that has resulted in the body of knowledge we know as biology.

Your journey through biology will be guided in large part by your teacher and this textbook. There is much to learn between these covers! Great care has been taken to write and present the concepts of biology in a way that makes your learning easier.

But you have an important role to play in the process—to learn to use your textbook effectively. The following pages illustrate some of the features that were designed with you, the student, in mind.

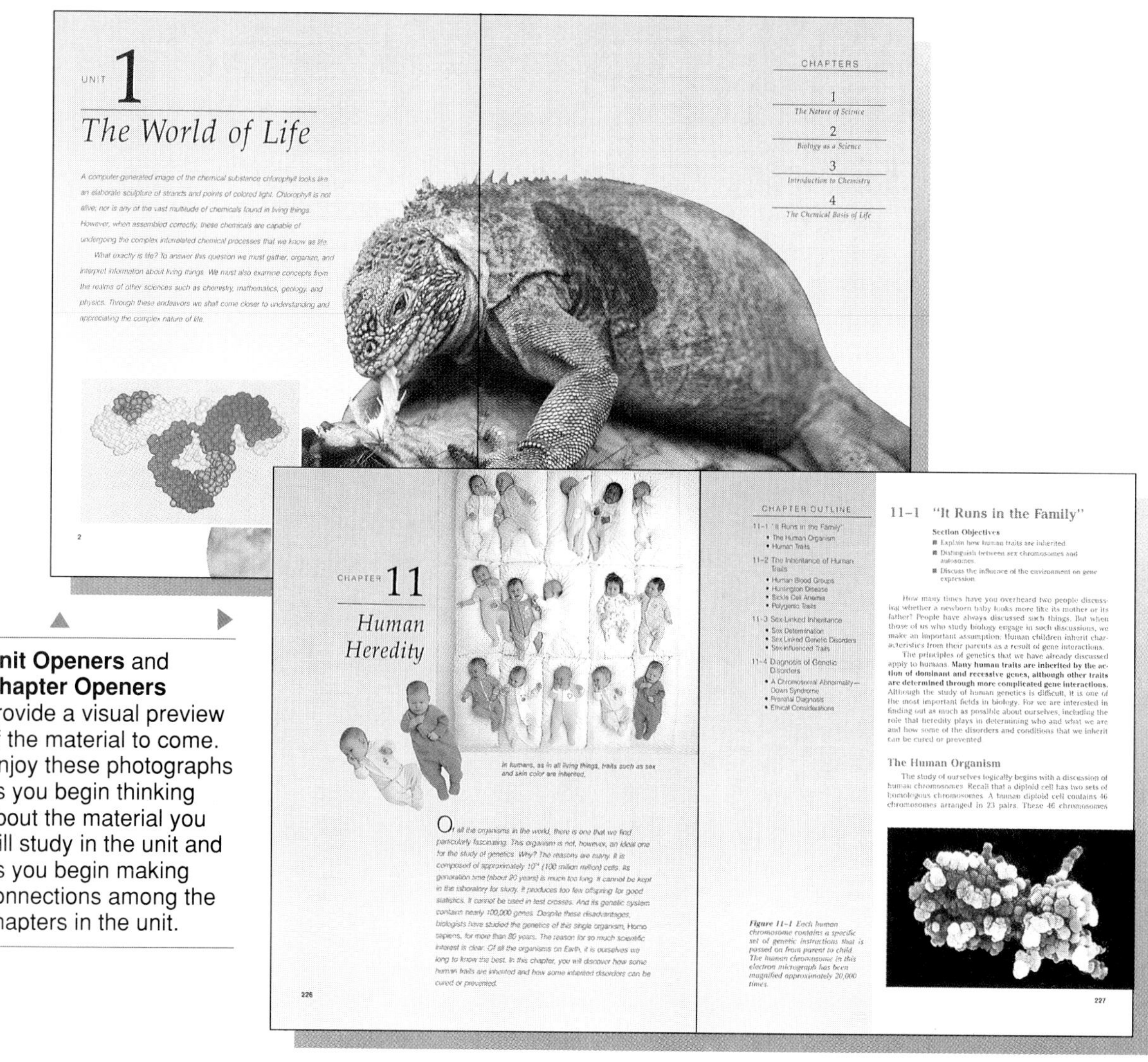

UNIT 1

The World of Life

A computer-generated image of the chemical substance chlorophyll looks like an elaborate sculpture of strands and points of colored light. Chlorophyll is not alive; nor is any of the vast multitude of chemicals found in living things. However, when assembled correctly, these chemicals are capable of undergoing the complex interrelated chemical processes that we know as life.

What exactly is life? To answer this question we must gather, organize, and interpret information about living things. We must also examine concepts from the realms of other sciences such as chemistry, mathematics, geology, and physics. Through these endeavors we shall come closer to understanding and appreciating the complex nature of life.

2

CHAPTERS

1 *The Nature of Science*

2 *Biology as a Science*

3 *Introduction to Chemistry*

4 *The Chemical Basis of Life*

CHAPTER 11

Human Heredity

In humans, as in all living things, traits such as sex and skin color are inherited.

Of all the organisms in the world, there is one that we find particularly fascinating. This organism is not, however, an ideal one for the study of genetics. Why? The reasons are many. It is composed of approximately 10^{14} (100 million million) cells. Its generation time (about 20 years) is much too long. It cannot be kept in the laboratory for study. It produces too few offspring for good statistics. It cannot be used in test crosses. And its genetic system contains nearly 100,000 genes. Despite these disadvantages, biologists have studied the genetics of this single organism, Homo sapiens, for more than 80 years. The reason for so much scientific interest is clear. Of all the organisms on Earth, it is ourselves we long to know the best. In this chapter, you will discover how some human traits are inherited and how some inherited disorders can be cured or prevented.

226

CHAPTER OUTLINE

11–1 "It Runs in the Family"
- The Human Organism
- Human Traits

11–2 The Inheritance of Human Traits
- Human Blood Groups
- Huntington Disease
- Sickle Cell Anemia
- Polygenic Traits

11–3 Sex-Linked Inheritance
- Sex Determination
- Sex-Linked Genetic Disorders
- Sex-Influenced Traits

11–4 Diagnosis of Genetic Disorders
- A Chromosomal Abnormality—Down Syndrome
- Prenatal Diagnosis
- Ethical Considerations

Figure 11–1 Each human chromosome contains a specific set of genetic instructions that is passed on from parent to child. The human chromosome in this electron micrograph has been magnified approximately 20,000 times.

11–1 "It Runs in the Family"

Section Objectives
- Explain how human traits are inherited.
- Distinguish between sex chromosomes and autosomes.
- Discuss the influence of the environment on gene expression.

How many times have you overheard two people discussing whether a newborn baby looks more like its mother or its father? People have always discussed such things. But when those of us who study biology engage in such discussions, we make an important assumption: Human children inherit characteristics from their parents as a result of gene interactions.

The principles of genetics that we have already discussed apply to humans. **Many human traits are inherited by the action of dominant and recessive genes, although other traits are determined through more complicated gene interactions.** Although the study of human genetics is difficult, it is one of the most important fields in biology. For we are interested in finding out as much as possible about ourselves, including the role that heredity plays in determining who and what we are and how some of the disorders and conditions that we inherit can be cured or prevented.

The Human Organism

The study of ourselves logically begins with a discussion of human chromosomes. Recall that a diploid cell has two sets of homologous chromosomes. A human diploid cell contains 46 chromosomes arranged in 23 pairs. These 46 chromosomes

227

Unit Openers and **Chapter Openers** provide a visual preview of the material to come. Enjoy these photographs as you begin thinking about the material you will study in the unit and as you begin making connections among the chapters in the unit.

The **Chapter Outline** represents the major divisions found in the chapter. Read the outline in order to familiarize yourself with the organization and content of the chapter.

Skim the section using the subsection titles and the visuals with their captions. Then as you read more carefully, focus on the **Section Objectives** and the boldfaced **Key Idea.** These features will enhance your ability to organize the material you read.

41–2 Blood

Section Objectives

- List the functions of blood.
- Describe the components of blood.
- Discuss the role of platelets in blood clotting.

The function of the circulatory system is to transport material in a fluid medium throughout the body. This fluid medium is called **blood**. Blood is a type of liquid connective tissue that has many functions. **Blood transports nutrients, dissolved gases (oxygen and carbon dioxide), enzymes, hormones, and waste products; blood regulates body temperature, pH, and electrolytes (ions in solution that conduct electric current); blood protects the body from invaders; and blood restricts the loss of fluid.**

Although blood is referred to as the river of life, the human body contains only 4 to 6 liters of this precious fluid—only 8 percent of the total mass of the body. Approximately 55 percent of blood is made up of a fluid portion called **plasma**. The remaining 45 percent consists of a cellular portion.

Blood Plasma

Plasma is a straw-colored fluid that is 90 percent water and 10 percent dissolved fats, salts, sugars, and proteins called plasma proteins. The plasma proteins, which perform a number of vital functions, are divided into three types: albumins, globulins, and fibrinogen. Albumins help regulate osmotic pressure. Globulins include antibodies that help fight off infection. Fibrinogen is responsible for the ability of blood to clot, a process that will be discussed in more detail later in the chapter. Nutrients, hormones, and waste products are also carried in the plasma.

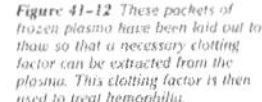

Figure 41–12 These pockets of frozen plasma have been laid out to thaw so that a necessary clotting factor can be extracted from the plasma. This clotting factor is then used to treat hemophilia.

Blood Cells

The cellular portion of the blood includes several types of highly specialized cells and cell fragments. They are red blood cells, white blood cells, and platelets.

RED BLOOD CELLS **Red blood cells,** or erythrocytes (eh-RIHTH-roh-sights), are the most numerous of the blood cells. One microliter of blood contains approximately 5 million red blood cells.

Red blood cells are biconcave, or shaped so that they are narrower in the center than along the edges. These cells are produced from cells in the bone marrow that gradually become filled with hemoglobin, forcing out their nucleus and other organelles. Thus mature red blood cells do not have a nucleus. Hemoglobin is the iron-containing protein that carries oxygen from the lungs to the tissues of the body. Hemoglobin gives the red blood cells their characteristic color.

Red blood cells normally stay in circulation for approximately 120 days before they are destroyed by special white

905

As you read each section, complete the **Chapter Outline** by filling in the details. The handwritten outline you see below is an example of how Section 41–2 might be completed.

CHAPTER OUTLINE

41-1 The Circulatory System
- The Heart
- How the Heart Works
- The Heartbeat
- Blood Vessels
- Pathways of Circulation
- Blood Pressure
- The Lymphatic System

41-2 Blood
- Blood Plasma
- Blood Cells

41-3 The Excretory System
- The Kidneys
- Control of Kidney Function

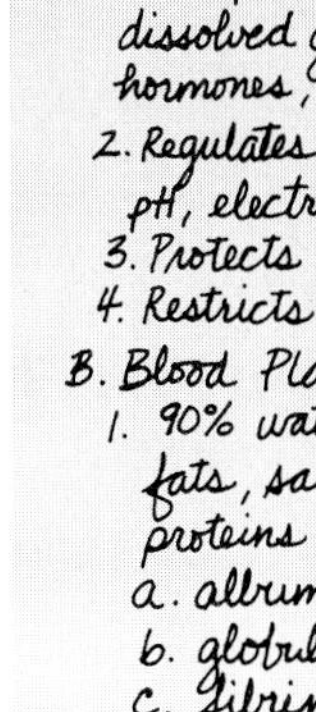

II Blood
A. Function of blood
1. Transports nutrients, dissolved gases, enzymes, hormones, wastes
2. Regulates body temperature, pH, electrolytes
3. Protects body
4. Restricts fluid loss
B. Blood Plasma
1. 90% water, 10% dissolved fats, salts, sugars, proteins
a. albumins
b. globulins
c. fibrinogens
C. Blood Cells
1. Red blood cells
2. White blood cells
3. Platelets and blood clotting

Figure 41–13 The large yellow objects in this photograph are the smallest types of white blood cells. The two red flattened objects are red blood cells.

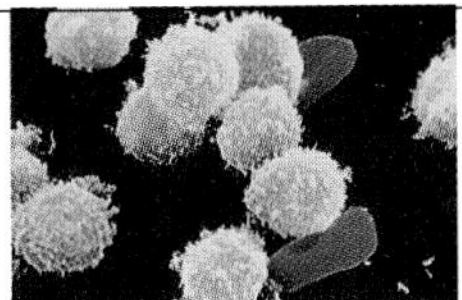

blood cells in the liver and the spleen. At this moment, red blood cells in your body are dying at a rate of about 2 million per second. To replace them, new red blood cells are being formed in the bone marrow at the same rate.

WHITE BLOOD CELLS **White blood cells,** or leukocytes (LOO-koh-sights), are outnumbered by red blood cells almost 500 to 1. White blood cells are produced in the bone marrow, are larger than red blood cells, almost colorless, and do not contain hemoglobin. Unlike red blood cells, white blood cells have a nucleus and can live for many months or years.

The main function of white blood cells is to protect the body against invasion by foreign cells or substances. What enables white blood cells to do this job is, in part, their ability to move out into the surrounding tissue like amebas. Some white blood cells can destroy bacteria and foreign cells by phagocytosis (large particles are taken inside a cell and digested). Others make special proteins called antibodies (globulin-type plasma proteins). Still others release special chemicals that help the body fight off disease and resist infection.

White blood cells respond quickly to infection. Physicians are often able to detect the presence of a serious infection by counting the number of white blood cells in the blood. When an infection such as appendicitis occurs, the number of white blood cells may increase from 10,000 to 30,000 per microliter.

Figure 41–14 When a red blood cell is about 120 days old, its life draws to a close. Here a special type of white blood cell engulfs and destroys an aging red blood cell.

PLATELETS AND BLOOD CLOTTING **Platelets** are not cells; rather, they are tiny fragments of other cells. Platelets are formed when small pieces of cytoplasm are pinched off the large cells called megakaryocytes (mehg-uh-KAHR-ee-oh-sights), which are found in the bone marrow. One microliter of blood contains between 250,000 and 400,000 platelets. The life span of a platelet is approximately 5 to 9 days.

Platelets play an important role in preventing the loss of blood by beginning a chain of reactions that result in blood clotting. When you cut or scratch yourself, blood will flow from

906

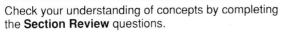

Figure 41–15 This electron micrograph shows the three types of blood cells that make up the cellular portion of the blood. The three large furry objects are white blood cells, the tiny spherical objects in the foreground are platelets, and the beret-shaped object is a red blood cell.

Platelets help the clotting process by clumping together and forming a plug at the site of a wound and then releasing proteins called clotting factors. These proteins start a series of chemical reactions that are extremely complicated. In one reaction, a clotting factor called thromboplastin (thrahm-boh-PLAS-tihn) converts prothrombin, which is found in the plasma of blood, into thrombin. Thrombin is an enzyme that converts the soluble plasma protein fibrinogen into a sticky meshwork of fibrin filaments that stop the bleeding by producing a clot.

The clotting process is extremely complex, and every step of it must go smoothly if a clot is to form. If one of the clotting factors is missing or defective, the clotting process does not work. A serious genetic disorder known as hemophilia results from defects in one of the clotting factor genes. Because they lack one of the clotting factors, hemophilia sufferers may bleed uncontrollably from even small cuts or scrapes. People suffering from hemophilia are given transfusions of clotting factors and platelets in order to treat their disorder.

The clotting of blood is not always a good thing. Sometimes a small clot will form in an unbroken blood vessel, blocking the flow of blood to the cells. If this happens in the brain, brain cells may begin to die, causing a stroke. A stroke may result in the loss of motor functions, such as speech or muscle control, or in death.

Figure 41–16 In the clotting process, a network of fibrin threads forms over a wound, trapping the blood cells.

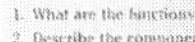

41–2 SECTION REVIEW

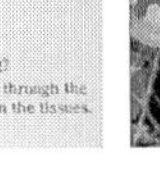

1. What are the functions of blood?
2. Describe the components of blood.
3. What role do platelets play in blood clotting?
4. Infections sometimes block the flow of fluid through the lymphatic system, causing severe swelling in the tissues. Explain why this happens.

907

Check your understanding of concepts by completing the **Section Review** questions.

Although you will be studying biology for only one year, you will need to be scientifically literate all your life. Use **Problem Solving in Biology** to further develop thinking skills you will find necessary in all areas of learning.

PROBLEM SOLVING IN BIOLOGY

WHAT IS IT?—ANALYZING FUNCTION THROUGH FORM

Imagine yourself a world famous invertebrate biologist who is often called upon to describe the habits of newly discovered organisms by comparing their structures to other animals you know. One day specimens belonging to the same species are brought into your laboratory, and you are asked to describe the animal's habits as best you can.

Some of the specimens are larvae that closely resemble one another, although none looks like the adult specimens. These larvae have a tough dark-brown exoskeleton, six legs with tips flattened like canoe paddles, and gills supplied with many tracheal tubes. Larval mouthparts look like a collection of butcher knives—sharp and menacing.

Adult specimens have two pairs of wings and six legs. Their brightly colored exoskeleton is covered with a thick, waxy coating. They have well-developed tracheal tubes spread throughout their body. Two of their mouthparts are relatively sharp, but the rest are blunt and clearly adapted for grinding and pulverizing food. You can tell from samples at the end of the gut that these animals excrete their nitrogenous wastes in the form of uric acid.

Practice your expertise in identifying unknown animals by answering the following questions about this imaginary creature.

1. To what phylum and class does this species probably belong?
2. Describe the probable life cycle of this animal. What sorts of specimens of this species would help you confirm your hypothesis about how this organism develops?
3. Where do you think the larvae live? Explain your answer.
4. What type of food do the larvae probably eat? Explain your reasoning.
5. What sorts of food do the adults probably eat? What evidence leads you to this conclusion?
6. Could the adults of this species survive in dry habitats? Why or why not?

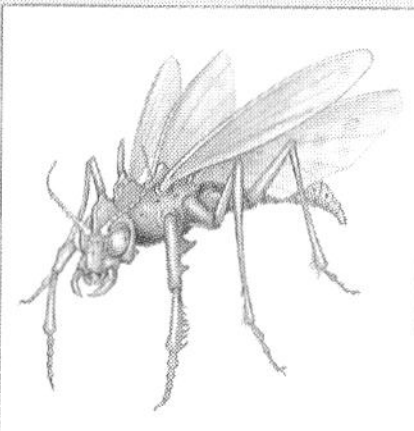

What can you infer from your examination of this mysterious (a fictitious) creature?

SCIENCE, TECHNOLOGY, AND SOCIETY ISSUE

Do Your Cells Belong to You?

In 1976, John Moore was diagnosed as having hairy cell leukemia. With this rare form of cancer, a person has too many B lymphocytes that develop tiny whiskerlike projections. B lymphocytes are white blood cells responsible for making antibodies, which are substances that help the body fight off certain diseases.

At the recommendation of his doctor, Moore had his enlarged spleen removed by physicians at the University of California at Los Angeles (UCLA) Medical Center. Normally, the spleen, an organ located near the stomach, filters out worn out or damaged blood cells. But in a person suffering from hairy cell leukemia, the spleen becomes filled with cancerous cells and can no longer perform its function. In addition, the healthy spleen cells are destroyed. Removal of the spleen is not a cure, but it helps return the number of blood cells to normal.

Whiskerlike projections on white blood cells are characteristic of a person who has hairy cell leukemia.

What Moore did not know until later, however, was that a portion of his spleen was saved and used by researchers to isolate and grow cells in culture—cells that produce a substance that may prove useful against cancer or AIDS. In 1984, UCLA obtained a patent for the cells and their products. One of these products was mass produced by a biotechnology company. The genetically engineered drug was then sold by a pharmaceutical firm. The development [...] ceeding well

. . . that is, until Moore sued UCLA, his doctor, and others for patenting and profiting from parts of his body!

In response to the suit, UCLA and the doctor have claimed that Moore signed two consent forms. One form gave UCLA permission to remove Moore's spleen, a procedure that obviously saved his life. The other gave UCLA all rights to Moore's cells and any future product that might be developed from them. The doctor further stated that Moore gave up claims to his spleen tissue—tissue that was worthless, even dangerous, to him. It was through the application of scientific knowledge that this poisoned tissue was turned into something of value.

In 1988, Moore's case went to trial in California. The court ruled that a person has all legal rights to cells and tissues removed during surgery and later used in scientific research. For now, the ruling stands.

But this is a very complicated issue whose impact may be far reaching. Many researchers believe that this ruling will interfere with new research and raise the cost of its progress. They are also convinced that it will discourage people from donating tissues and organs because of fear that researchers may profit from them. At the heart of the issue is this question: Do people have the right to control the use of their cells even though it might delay or prevent a medical breakthrough?

105

Use **Science, Technology, and Society** to further apply the biology you are learning and the thinking skills you are developing to evaluate current topics in your world.

LABORATORY INVESTIGATION

EXPLORING MEALWORM BEHAVIOR

PROBLEM

How do mealworms respond to their environment?

MATERIALS *(per person)*

aluminum foil	lamp (or sunlight)
150-mL beaker	10 mealworms
dry cereal	petri dish
small paintbrush	ruler
compass	scissors
cellophane tape	sheet of unlined paper
dissecting tray	

PROCEDURE

1. Use the scissors to cut a sheet of paper to fit into the bottom of the dissecting tray.
2. Find the exact center of the paper. Use a compass to draw a circle with a 2.5-cm radius at the center of the sheet of paper. Use the ruler to find the centers of the two longest edges of the paper. Mark these two points. Connect the points with a straight line.
3. Place the sheet of paper in the bottom of the dissecting tray. Tape the sheet of paper to the tray along all edges of the paper.
4. Place 10 mealworms into a 150-mL beaker.
5. Put a petri dish under one edge of the dissecting tray to raise it about 1 cm. Place the mealworms into the circle in the center of the tray.
6. Observe the mealworms' behavior for 10 minutes. Note whether they crawl uphill or downhill. Observe what they do when they reach the edge of the tray. Record your observations. Remove the mealworms from the tray.
7. Place a piece of aluminum foil over half of the tray. Line up one edge of the foil with the line you drew down the center of the paper. Shine the lamp directly over the tray. Place the mealworms back in the circle. Observe the mealworms' behavior for 10 minutes. Record your observations.
8. Remove the aluminum foil. Place a small handful of dry cereal in one corner of the tray. Brush the mealworms back into the circle. Observe the mealworms' behavior for 10 minutes. Record your observations.

OBSERVATIONS

1. How many mealworms remained within the circle in the tilted dissecting tray? How many climbed uphill? How many climbed downhill?
2. In response to light, how many mealworms remained within the circle? How many crawled under the aluminum foil? How many crawled into the light?
3. When cereal was placed in the dissecting tray, how many mealworms remained within the circle? How many crawled into the cereal? How many did not?
4. What did the mealworms do when they reached the edge of the tray?

ANALYSIS AND CONCLUSIONS

1. Do mealworms prefer to climb uphill or downhill? How might this behavior be adaptive?
2. Do mealworms prefer to be in light or in shade? How might this be adaptive behavior?
3. Do mealworms prefer to be in or out of the cereal? How might this behavior be adaptive?
4. How is the mealworms' behavior at the edge of the tray adaptive?

780

Experience biology as a process as well as a body of knowledge. Think about the scientific approach not only as you conduct **Laboratory Investigations** but as you read about the scientific discoveries of others.

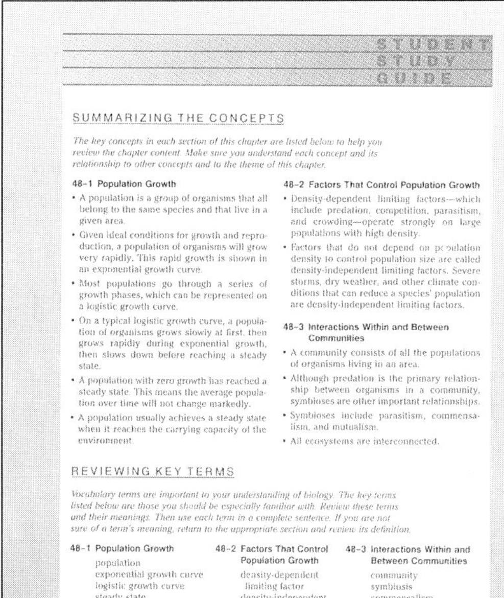

STUDENT STUDY GUIDE

SUMMARIZING THE CONCEPTS

The key concepts in each section of this chapter are listed below to help you review the chapter content. Make sure you understand each concept and its relationship to other concepts and to the theme of this chapter.

48–1 Population Growth

- A population is a group of organisms that all belong to the same species and that live in a given area.
- Given ideal conditions for growth and reproduction, a population of organisms will grow very rapidly. This rapid growth is shown in an exponential growth curve.
- Most populations go through a series of growth phases, which can be represented on a logistic growth curve.
- On a typical logistic growth curve, a population of organisms grows slowly at first, then grows rapidly during exponential growth, then slows down before reaching a steady state.
- A population with zero growth has reached a steady state. This means the average population over time will not change markedly.
- A population usually achieves a steady state when it reaches the carrying capacity of the environment.

48–2 Factors That Control Population Growth

- Density-dependent limiting factors—which include predation, competition, parasitism, and crowding—operate strongly on large populations with high density.
- Factors that do not depend on population density to control population size are called density-independent limiting factors. Severe storms, dry weather, and other climate conditions that can reduce a species' population are density-independent limiting factors.

48–3 Interactions Within and Between Communities

- A community consists of all the populations of organisms living in an area.
- Although predation is the primary relationship between organisms in a community, symbioses are other important relationships.
- Symbioses include parasitism, commensalism, and mutualism.
- All ecosystems are interconnected.

REVIEWING KEY TERMS

Vocabulary terms are important to your understanding of biology. The key terms listed below are those you should be especially familiar with. Review these terms and their meanings. Then use each term in a complete sentence. If you are not sure of a term's meaning, return to the appropriate section and review its definition.

48–1 Population Growth
population
exponential growth curve
logistic growth curve
steady state
carrying capacity

48–2 Factors That Control Population Growth
density-dependent limiting factor
density-independent limiting factor

48–3 Interactions Within and Between Communities
community
symbiosis
commensalism
mutualism

The key concepts in each section of a chapter are listed in **Summarizing the Concepts** to help you review the chapter content. Make sure you understand each concept and its relationship to other concepts and to the theme of the chapter.

Vocabulary terms are important to your understanding of biology. The key terms listed in **Reviewing Key Terms** are those you should be especially familiar with. Review the terms and their meanings. Then use each term in a complete sentence. If you are not sure of a term's meaning, return to the appropriate section and review its definition.

Test your knowledge of the facts presented in the chapter by answering the **Content Review** questions. These facts form the basis of fundamental concepts.

Evaluate your understanding of the concepts by answering the **Concept Mastery** questions.

Apply your factual knowledge and your concept understanding by answering the **Critical and Creative Thinking** questions.

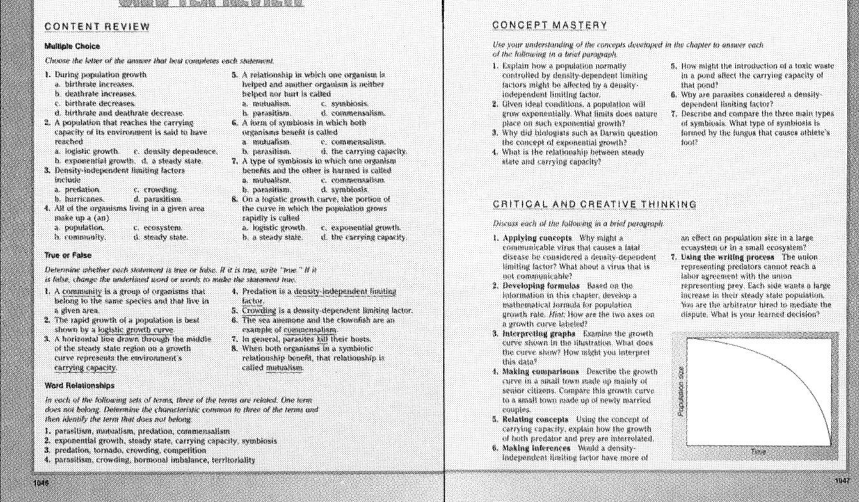

CHAPTER REVIEW

CONTENT REVIEW

Multiple Choice

Choose the letter of the answer that best completes each statement.

1. During population growth
   a. birthrate increases.
   b. deathrate increases.
   c. birthrate decreases.
   d. birthrate and deathrate decrease.
2. A population that reaches the carrying capacity of its environment is said to have reached
   a. logistic growth. c. density dependence.
   b. exponential growth. d. a steady state.
3. Density-independent limiting factors include
   a. predation. c. crowding.
   b. hurricanes. d. parasitism.
4. All of the organisms living in a given area make up a (an)
   a. population. c. ecosystem.
   b. community. d. steady state.
5. A relationship in which one organism is helped and another organism is neither helped nor hurt is called
   a. mutualism. c. symbiosis.
   b. parasitism. d. commensalism.
6. A form of symbiosis in which both organisms benefit is called
   a. mutualism. c. commensalism.
   b. parasitism. d. the carrying capacity.
7. A type of symbiosis in which one organism benefits and the other is harmed is called
   a. mutualism. c. commensalism.
   b. parasitism. d. symbiosis.
8. On a logistic growth curve, the portion of the curve in which the population grows rapidly is called
   a. logistic growth. c. exponential growth.
   b. a steady state. d. the carrying capacity.

True or False

Determine whether each statement is true or false. If it is true, write "true." If it is false, change the underlined word or words to make the statement true.

1. A community is a group of organisms that belong to the same species and that live in a given area.
2. The rapid growth of a population is best shown by a logistic growth curve.
3. A horizontal line drawn through the middle of the steady state region on a growth curve represents the environment's carrying capacity.
4. Predation is a density-independent limiting factor.
5. Crowding is a density-dependent limiting factor.
6. The sea anemone and the clownfish are an example of commensalism.
7. In general, parasites kill their hosts.
8. When both organisms in a symbiotic relationship benefit, that relationship is called mutualism.

Word Relationships

In each of the following sets of terms, three of the terms are related. One term does not belong. Determine the characteristic common to three of the terms and then identify the term that does not belong.

1. parasitism, mutualism, predation, commensalism
2. exponential growth, steady state, carrying capacity, symbiosis
3. predation, tornado, crowding, competition
4. parasitism, crowding, hormonal imbalance, territoriality

1046

CONCEPT MASTERY

Use your understanding of the concepts developed in the chapter to answer each of the following in a brief paragraph.

1. Explain how a population normally controlled by density-dependent limiting factors might be affected by a density-independent limiting factor.
2. Given ideal conditions, a population will grow exponentially. What limits does nature place on such exponential growth?
3. Why did biologists such as Darwin question the concept of exponential growth?
4. What is the relationship between steady state and carrying capacity?
5. How might the introduction of a toxic waste in a pond affect the carrying capacity of that pond?
6. Why are parasites considered a density-dependent limiting factor?
7. Describe and compare the three main types of symbiosis. What type of symbiosis is formed by the fungus that causes athlete's foot?

CRITICAL AND CREATIVE THINKING

Discuss each of the following in a brief paragraph.

1. **Applying concepts** Why might a communicable virus that causes a fatal disease be considered a density-dependent limiting factor? What about a virus that is not communicable?
2. **Developing formulas** Based on the information in this chapter, develop a mathematical formula for population growth rate. *Hint:* How are the two axes on a growth curve labeled?
3. **Interpreting graphs** Examine the growth curve shown in the illustration. What does the curve show? How might you interpret this data?
4. **Making comparisons** Describe the growth curve in a small town made up mainly of senior citizens. Compare this growth curve to a small town made up of newly married couples.
5. **Relating concepts** Using the concept of carrying capacity, explain how the growth of both predator and prey are interrelated.
6. **Making inferences** Would a density-independent limiting factor have more of an effect on population size in a large ecosystem or in a small ecosystem?
7. **Using the writing process** The union representing predators cannot reach a labor agreement with the union representing prey. Each side wants a large increase in their steady state population. You are the arbitrator hired to mediate the dispute. What is your learned decision?

1047

Your enjoyment and understanding of *Biology* by Kenneth Miller and Joseph Levine will be enhanced if you follow the suggestions presented here. We hope you will keep our three R's of biology in mind as you journey through the world of living things:

Relevance—to connect biology with your everyday life.
Respect—to develop a high regard for the environment.
Responsibility—to help you make informed decisions.

ABOUT THE AUTHORS

Kenneth R. Miller was born in 1948 in Rahway, New Jersey. He attended the public schools there and graduated from Rahway High School in 1966. He was already interested in science—often experimenting with a chemistry set in his basement and winning second prize in a science fair with a project on *Euglena*. Miller attended Brown University on a scholarship to study biology and earned his degree in 1970. He was awarded a National Defense Education Act fellowship and earned a Ph.D. in biology at the University of Colorado in 1974. After teaching at Harvard University for six years, he is now Professor of Biology at Brown University in Providence, Rhode Island, where he teaches courses in general biology and cell biology.

Miller is a cell biologist whose research specialty is the structure of biological membranes. His most recent work involves electron microscope studies of photosynthetic membranes from plants and photosynthetic microorganisms. He has published more than 43 scientific papers in journals such as *Nature, The Journal of Cell Biology,* and *Scientific American*. Miller is also an editor for two scientific journals and has written and lectured on educational issues in biology. He serves as Chairman of the Education Committee of the American Society for Cell Biology.

Along with his wife, Jody, and two daughters, Miller lives on a small farm in Rehoboth, Massachusetts. He coaches Little League softball, is a competitor in the masters' swimming program, and enjoys bicycling.

Joseph S. Levine was born in 1951 in Mount Vernon, New York, and graduated from Mount Vernon High School in 1969. He earned a Bachelor's degree from Tufts University, a Master's degree from the Boston University Marine Program in Woods Hole, and a Ph.D. from Harvard in 1980. He taught at Boston College for six years and was awarded a fellowship in Science Broadcast Journalism at WGBH-TV in Boston.

Levine currently works independently in several aspects of public science education. He has published articles in magazines ranging from *Science* to *Smithsonian* and has written two books on aquatic subjects. While at WGBH, he co-produced the prime-time television program *Science Gazette*, as well as science features for National Public Radio's *Morning Edition* and *All Things Considered.* Working with the NOVA staff, he assembled a proposal for an eight-hour series on molecular biology entitled *Life: Cracking the Code*, which is now in production. He has also designed exhibit programs for major public aquaria in Texas, New Jersey, and Florida, as well as an AIDS-awareness exhibit for the California Museum of Science and Industry.

Levine lives in Boston, where his century-old home occupies as much of his time as he allows. There, he gardens and collects tropical fishes, as he has since he was a child. Levine also enjoys bicycling, windsurfing, and skiing, and he treasures rare opportunities to scuba dive or to hike through wilderness areas.

TO THE STUDENT

Dear Reader:

We wrote this book so that you would have the opportunity to read about the science of biology. We hope that you will come away well-informed and enlightened about the living world around us. But we had a second goal as well: to convey some of the wonder and excitement felt by those who have been lucky enough to be involved in scientific work.

Science is not a dehumanized process carried out in white-walled laboratories. It is a human activity, subject to all the faults and frailties of our species. But most of all, there is a secret that scientific institutions and textbooks have often managed to conceal: **Science is fun!** Despite the constant frustrations of delicate equipment, difficult observations, and complicated experiments, scientists *enjoy* what they do.

The openness of science means that everything is subject to proof, and many of today's widely held ideas may have to be abandoned in the future. Scientific textbooks seem to be full of information—almost as if everything interesting has already been observed, measured, and cataloged. Wrong! Many people in the nineteenth century believed that science had progressed about as far as it could and that everything from then on would just involve filling in the details. Yet nearly everything in this book is based on discoveries in the twentieth century, and much of it from just the last ten years. Has biology solved all of its important scientific problems? Of course not!

We believe that our present knowledge represents only a fraction of what the world holds for us to discover. Quite frankly, the interesting work is just beginning—and nothing would reward us more than knowing that a few of you who have used this book might decide to come along for the ride.

KENNETH R. MILLER
JOSEPH S. LEVINE

UNIT 1

The World of Life

A computer-generated image of the chemical substance chlorophyll looks like an elaborate sculpture of strands and points of colored light. Chlorophyll is not alive; nor is any of the vast multitude of chemicals found in living things. However, when assembled correctly, these chemicals are capable of undergoing the complex interrelated chemical processes that we know as life.

What exactly is life? To answer this question we must gather, organize, and interpret information about living things. We must also examine concepts from the realms of other sciences such as chemistry, mathematics, geology, and physics. Through these endeavors we shall come closer to understanding and appreciating the complex nature of life.

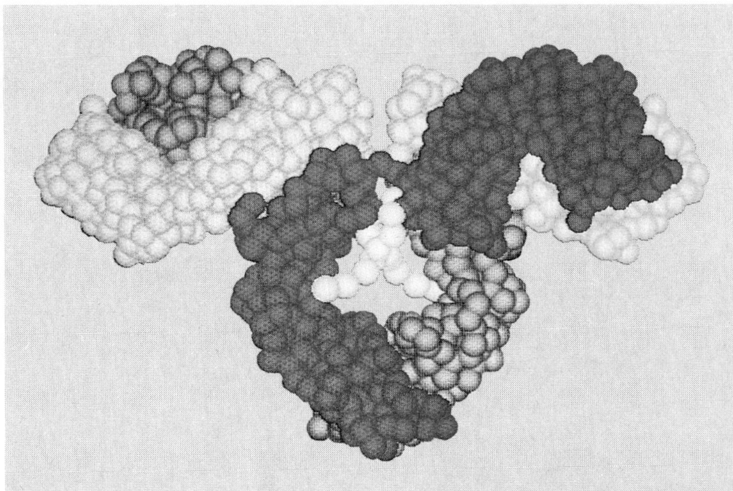

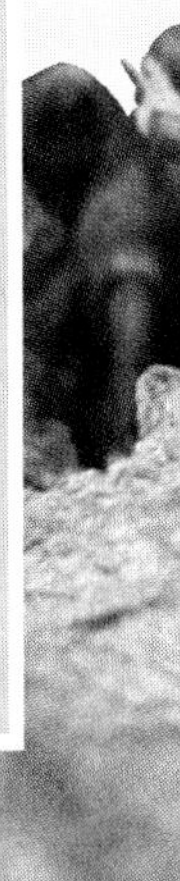

CHAPTERS

CHAPTER 1

The Nature of Science

Storks flying south to their winter home in Kenya

Toward the end of August, you may have taken a walk through your neighborhood. That neighborhood may be one of buildings and pavement, lawns and trees, fields and pasture, or even sand and cactus. Such walks often inspire questions. Why do days get shorter at this time of year? Why does grass stop growing in the fall? Why do some plants flower in spring and others in autumn? How do geese know when to fly south for the winter? How do they even know which way is south?

Like yourself, scientists ask themselves similar questions about their world. Sometimes they find answers—as you do. Sometimes the answer remains to be discovered. And sometimes there is no answer. The important point is not finding the answer but asking the question. For making observations and asking questions is at the very heart of the process known as science.

CHAPTER OUTLINE

1–1 What Is Science?

Section Objective

- Identify the main goal of science.

Asking questions about the world around us is part of human nature. How did life begin? Where did plants and animals come from? Why do animals behave as they do? Every culture in the world has tried to answer these questions—often through myths and legends.

The Pitjendara tribe of central Australia, for example, finds answers to questions about nature on an enormous mound of stone called Ayer's Rock. The rock, which towers more than 300 meters above the flat desert around it, has been carved by centuries of exposure to wind and rain. Erosion has etched gullies and caverns into the rock, and has produced striking formations on its surface. See Figure 1-1.

According to the Pitjendara, the images etched on Ayer's Rock tell stories that depict the adventures, the loves, and the battles of ten enormous creatures. The rock contains the likenesses of two snakes, Liru and Kunia. The Pitjendara believe that the two snakes fought an epic battle that created many features on the southern face of Ayer's Rock. Elsewhere on the rock, a sand-lizard man left his mark digging for water. Through these and other stories, the Pitjendara explain the formation of the world and the processes of birth, life, and death.

The stories of the rock also detail the connections between the tribe and animals important in their everyday lives: snakes,

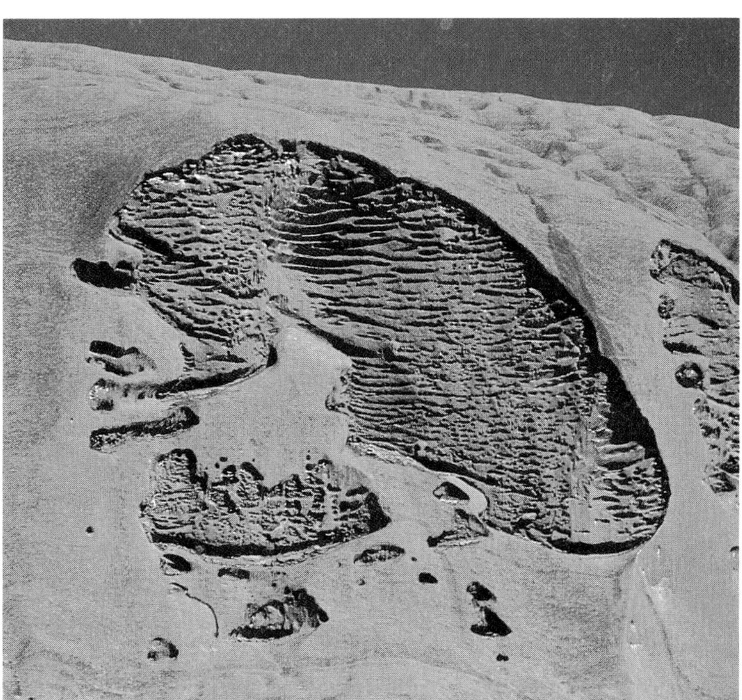

Figure 1–1 *To the Pitjendara, these etchings on Ayer's Rock represent the human brain.*

Figure 1–2 *Ayer's Rock in central Australia is the largest individual rock in the world. Why might people who live their entire lives in this area develop myths and legends about Ayer's Rock?*

Figure 1–3 *These stone statues were created by people living on Easter Island in the Pacific Ocean. The statues may well represent the Easter Islanders' belief that the first humans hatched from eggs brought to Earth by a bird-man.*

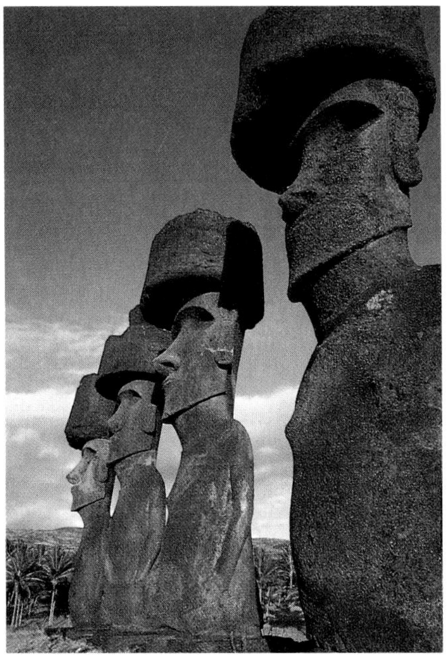

desert lizards, and kangaroos. The stories even explain the origins of dreams. We might say that the rock provides the Pitjendara with answers that other societies seek through a process known as science.

People like the Pitjendara live their entire lives in a single culture. Thus, they often find it difficult to imagine that their particular stories about the world might be in error. Today, however, we can visit and read about many cultures. And when we assemble stories from around the globe, it becomes obvious that all these stories cannot be true.

Is there some other way to explain the world around us? One way is to assume that all events in nature have natural causes. We can then try to arrange a series of observations or tests to learn what those causes are. **Science** is the word that we apply to this process. **The goal of science is to understand the world around us**. There are, however, many important fields of human endeavor that study the world around us but are not considered sciences. Such fields include language, history, art, music, and philosophy. The character that distinguishes science from nonscience is an approach known as the scientific method.

1–1 SECTION REVIEW

1. What is the goal of science?
2. Compare the study of science with the study of literature. How do they differ? How are they similar?

1–2 The Scientific Method

Section Objectives

- Describe the steps in the scientific method.
- Compare a control setup and an experimental setup.
- Identify the basic units of length, mass, volume, and temperature in the metric system.

The simplest definition of the **scientific method** was offered by biologist Claude Villee. He called it "Organized common sense." That is exactly what science should be. **In practice, the scientific method consists of several steps:**

- **Observing and stating a problem**
- **Forming a hypothesis**
- **Testing the hypothesis**
- **Recording and analyzing data**
- **Forming a conclusion**
- **Replicating the work**

To the true scientist, however, the scientific method is more a frame of mind—a frame of mind that involves curiosity. For without curiosity about nature, there would be no interest in why the sun appears to rise and set, why the seasons change, or why a snake sheds its skin. Another important characteristic of the scientific spirit is the refusal to accept an explanation without evidence or proof. This "prove it!" attitude encourages scientists to investigate phenomena and to develop new explanations and ideas.

Observing and Stating a Problem

The process of science starts with an observation. For example, we might notice that the leaves of maple trees turn bright red and yellow in autumn. As curious scientists, we would then be interested in discovering why this color change takes place.

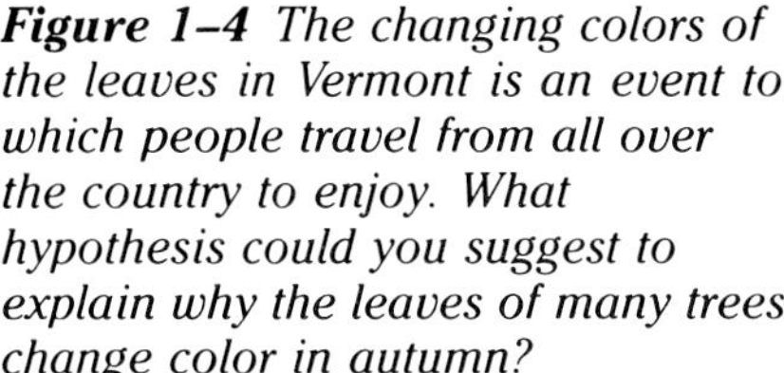

Figure 1–4 *The changing colors of the leaves in Vermont is an event to which people travel from all over the country to enjoy. What hypothesis could you suggest to explain why the leaves of many trees change color in autumn?*

Forming a Hypothesis

We proceed to gather information that helps us generate a **hypothesis**. A hypothesis is a possible explanation, a preliminary conclusion, or even a guess about some event in nature. For example, we can observe that maple leaves change color when the air gets colder. We might then hypothesize that color changes in maples are related to changes in temperature.

Testing the Hypothesis

Next we must test our hypothesis. Some hypotheses may be tested simply through further observation. As you will discover in Chapter 13, Charles Darwin spent most of his life in the field observing nature to test his hypotheses about evolution. Most hypotheses, however, must be tested by experiments. The "autumn leaves" hypothesis falls into this category.

Our observations indicate that leaves change color in the autumn. And our hypothesis is that the color change is related to changes in temperature. We must now perform a test to find out if this is a correct explanation. One experiment we might do is to take a small maple tree growing in a pot and place it in a growth chamber during the month of July. We would lower the temperature to typical autumn levels, about 14°C during the daytime and 3°C at night. If our hypothesis is correct, we might see the leaves begin to change color almost immediately.

Suppose we ran this experiment and the leaves did change color. Would we know for certain that changes in temperature alone were responsible for the color change? After all, there are many differences between the tree in our experiment and a tree in the woods. Did the leaves on our tree turn red because the tree was planted in a small pot? Or because the light inside the growth chamber was different from natural light?

These uncertainties point out the need for a more complicated experiment using at least two trees. We should choose two similar trees and pots of the same size, water the trees at the same time, and place them in identical chambers. We should then conduct an experiment in which one chamber is kept at normal summer temperatures while the other chamber is cooled to autumn temperatures.

Why must we go to the trouble of observing a second tree? This two-part test represents what is called a controlled experiment. Controlled experiments allow researchers to isolate and test the effects of a single factor, or experimental **variable**. In this case, the treatment of the first tree serves as our **control setup** by testing the effects of the pot and growth chamber. The treatment of the second tree, our **experimental setup**, is identical to the control setup in every respect except one—the variable of temperature. See Figure 1-5. Now if we observe a difference between the experimental setup and the control setup, we can be more certain that it is due to the lower temperatures in the experimental chamber.

Figure 1–5 *Whenever possible, an experiment should have both a control setup and an experimental setup. Which part of the experiment contains the variable? What is the variable in this experiment?*

Recording and Analyzing Data

If we were actually to perform this experiment, we would keep careful records of observations and information, or **data**. In this case, such data might include the time it took for each leaf to change color, the total number of leaves on each tree that changed color or fell off, and so on. We might arrange our data in the form of tables and graphs, such as those shown in Figure 1–6. You can see why researchers use these visual representations of experimental data to analyze their results.

EXPERIMENTAL SETUP: Autumn Temperatures											
Day	1	3	5	7	9	11	13	15	17	19	21
Number of Green Leaves	50	50	50	49	49	48	48	48	48	47	47

CONTROL SETUP: Spring Temperatures											
Day	1	3	5	7	9	11	13	15	17	19	21
Number of Green Leaves	50	50	49	49	49	49	49	47	47	47	47

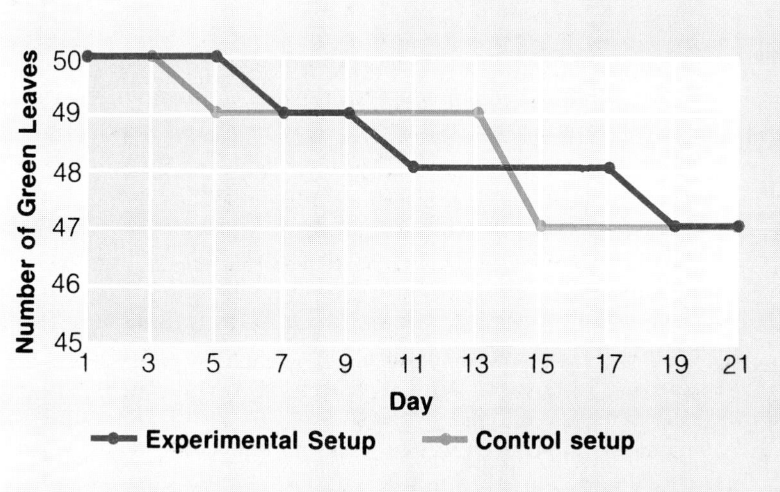

Figure 1–6 Information gathered from an experiment is usually organized in data tables (top). Then the data may be graphed in order to provide a visual representation that is easy to interpret (bottom). Using the data tables and the graph, what conclusions can you reach about the autumn leaves hypothesis?

Forming a Conclusion

If we find that the leaves on our experimental tree change color and those on the control tree do not, we may decide that we have confirmed our original hypothesis: Cold temperatures cause leaves to change color. If the leaves of neither tree change color or if the leaves of both trees change color, we might reject the hypothesis as wrong and start all over with a new idea. This is often the case in science because many guesses about the natural world prove incorrect. But this is also the way science advances, for it points the way to further experiments. If the leaves on neither tree change color, for example, it is possible that temperature alone is not responsible. Perhaps trees also respond to changes in the length of day, decreases in rainfall, or the action of strong winds. These new hypotheses suggest additional experiments that expand our understanding.

Although such experiments are probably impossible for you to perform yourself, scientists have been able to do them and have arrived at an answer to our original hypothesis: Do the colder temperatures of autumn cause a color change in the leaves of maple trees? If you have examined the data in Figure 1–6, you know part of their conclusion: Colder temperatures alone do not cause the color change. Scientists now know that colder temperatures combined with a change in the length of day both play a role in the color change in maple leaves. In addition, many scientists believe that a biological clock within the maple tree also plays a role. But how does this biological clock work? And what chemical triggers the clock? These are questions that as yet remain unanswered. If you should choose to pursue biology as a career, perhaps you will consider these questions once again.

Replicating the Work

The best scientific experiments can be replicated, or reproduced. In other words, it must be possible for either the original experimenter or other researchers to duplicate, or reproduce, the experimental results. Reproducibility in science takes many forms. We might want to replicate the experiment ourselves several times. Or we might want to put several trees in each growth chamber. Such actions would assure us that our results were not due to chance.

Another form of reproducibility is the replication of work by others. If interesting results come from an experiment, a researcher will publish a report of the work in a scientific journal. The report must contain enough detail so that other scientists can copy the experiment precisely to see if the same results continue to occur.

Hypotheses and Theories

When a hypothesis is tested and confirmed often enough that it is unlikely to be disproved by future tests, it may become worthy of being called a **theory**. In scientific usage, the word theory means a great deal more than it does in common speech. Scientific theories are not just hunches or hypotheses. They are powerful, time-tested concepts that make useful and dependable predictions about the natural world.

The Scientific Method—An Everyday Experience

Because many experiments discussed in this book were performed by people called scientists, you might think that science is a special process used only by certain people and useful only under special circumstances. That is not true at all. We all use the scientific method every day!

Let's suppose, for example, that a car will not start. A mechanic will form and test hypotheses about the problem. Perhaps the battery is dead. One experiment would be to crank the starter to see what happens. If the starter motor works but the car still doesn't turn over, it could be that the car is out of gas. A glance at the fuel gauge would test that idea. Again and again, the mechanic would apply the scientific method until the problem is solved. The same technique can find a fault in an electrical circuit or balance a load of laundry in a washing machine. Remember, science is just organized common sense.

A Universal Language—The Metric System

Science works best when scientists everywhere read each other's papers, check each other's experiments, and argue about what those experiments mean. Because most experiments involve measurements, researchers need a universal system of measurement in which to present their findings. **Scientists use the metric system of length, volume, mass, and temperature when describing experiments and data.** The **metric system** is a decimal system based on certain standards and scaled on multiples of 10. The metric system is also known as the International System of Units, or SI.

Figure 1–7 *The metric system is easy to use because it is based on units of ten. How many centimeters are there in 100 meters?*

COMMON METRIC UNITS

Length	**Mass**
1 meter (m) = 100 centimeters (cm)	1 kilogram (kg) = 1000 grams (g)
1 meter = 1000 millimeters (mm)	1 gram = 1000 milligrams (mg)
1 meter = 1,000,000 micrometers (μm)	1000 kilograms = 1 metric ton(t)
1 meter = 1,000,000,000 nanometers (nm)	
1 meter = 10,000,000,000 angstroms (Å)	
1000 meters = 1 kilometer (km)	
Volume	**Temperature**
1 liter (L) = 1000 milliliters (mL) or 1000 cubic centimeters (cm^3)	0°C = freezing point of water 100°C = boiling point of water
kilo- = one thousand	micro- = one millionth
centi- = one hundredth	nano- = one billionth
milli- = one thousandth	

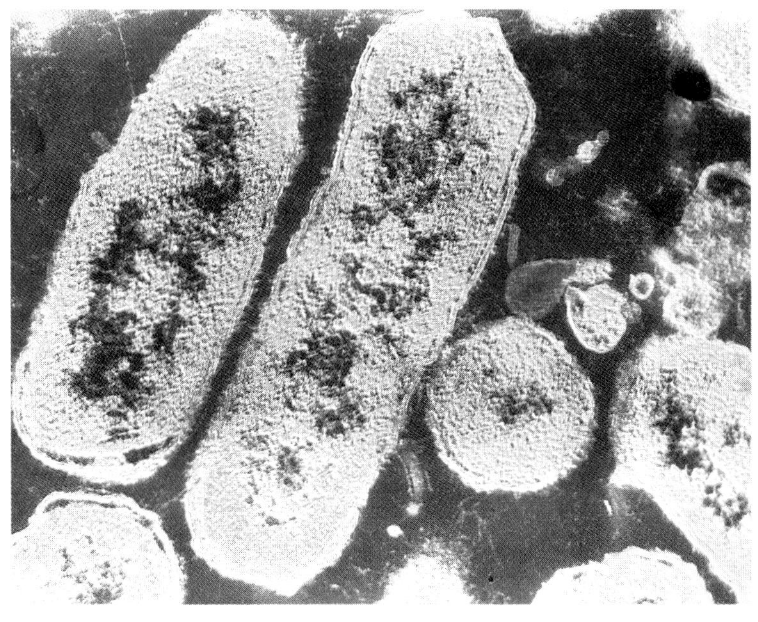

Figure 1–8 Which unit of length would you use to measure this tall African giraffe (left)? This microscopic bacterium (right)?

LENGTH The basic unit of length in the metric system is the **meter** (m). One meter is roughly equivalent to 39.4 inches, a little longer than a yard. To measure objects and distances much larger or smaller than a meter, the metric system uses units larger or smaller than a meter by multiples of 10. A centimeter (cm) is 1/100 of a meter—about the width of the nail on your pinky. As you may have guessed, the prefix *centi-* means one hundredth. A millimeter (mm) is 1/1000 of a meter. The prefix *milli-* means one thousandth. Even smaller units of length—such as those used to describe living cells, pieces of cells, and molecules—are shown in Figure 1–7 on page 11. To measure distances much greater than a meter, scientists use a unit called the kilometer (km). One kilometer contains 1000 meters. What does the prefix *kilo-* mean?

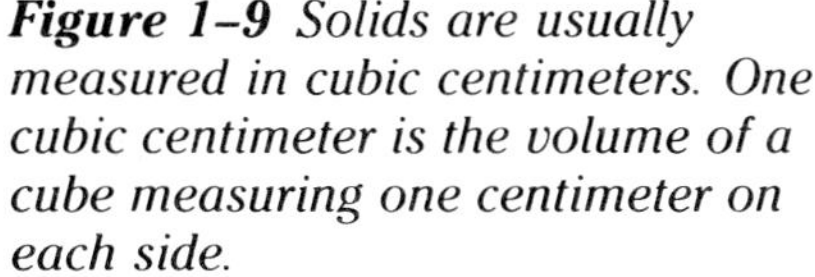

Figure 1–9 Solids are usually measured in cubic centimeters. One cubic centimeter is the volume of a cube measuring one centimeter on each side.

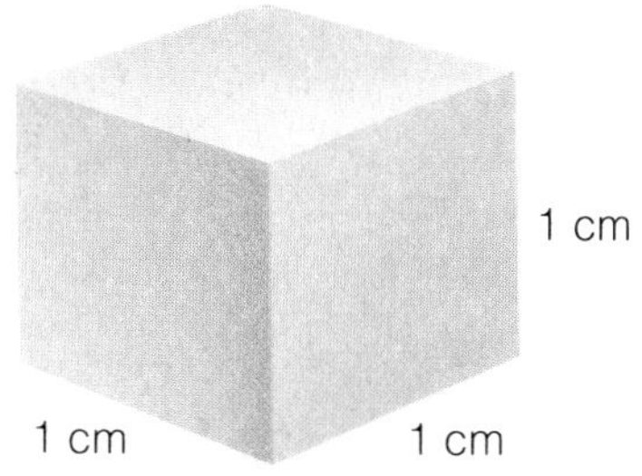

VOLUME Volume is the amount of space an object occupies. The basic metric units of volume are the **liter** (L) for liquids and the **cubic centimeter** (cc, or cm^3) for solids. A liter contains slightly more liquid than a quart. To measure small volumes of liquids, scientists use fractions of a liter called milliliters (mL). There are 1000 milliliters in a single liter. A cubic centimeter is the volume of a solid that measures 1 cm by 1 cm by 1 cm. Keep in mind that 1 milliliter is equal in volume to 1 cubic centimeter, or 1 mL = 1 cc.

MASS AND WEIGHT **Mass** is a measure of the amount of matter in an object. **Weight** is a measure of the pull of gravity on that mass. In outer space, the weight of an object may vary with its position, but its mass always remains the same. On Earth's surface, however, an object's mass and weight can

Figure 1–10 The African elephant is among the largest land creatures ever to walk the Earth (left). The harvest field mouse is one of the smallest mammals on Earth (right). What unit would you use to measure the mass of the elephant? The harvest mouse?

usually be considered constant and are often used interchangeably. The basic metric unit scientists use to describe mass is the **kilogram** (kg). One kilogram is equal to approximately 2.2 pounds. The mass of small objects is measured in grams (g). One gram is 1/1000 of a kilogram. How many milligrams (mg) are there in a gram? In a kilogram?

TEMPERATURE The metric system measures temperature using the **Celsius** (SEHL-see-uhs) **scale** (°C). On this scale, water freezes at 0°C and boils at 100°C. Each Celsius degree, therefore, represents exactly 1/100 of the temperature range between the freezing and boiling points of water. Normal human body temperature is about 37°C, and comfortable room temperature is about 21°C.

Figure 1–11 You can see by the way this chameleon walks lightly across the hot road that temperature has an effect on almost all living things. Scientists measure temperature in degrees Celsius.

1–2 SECTION REVIEW

1. List each step in the scientific method.
2. Define hypothesis. Compare a hypothesis and a theory.
3. What is the only difference between a control setup and an experimental setup?
4. Must the steps in the scientific method always be followed in the same order? Explain your answer.
5. If an experiment does not confirm the hypothesis it was designed to test, has that experiment "failed"?

PROBLEM SOLVING IN BIOLOGY

DIMENSIONAL ANALYSIS

Many times in science you will need to convert one unit of measurement to another. For example, you might be given a problem in kilometers but need the answer in centimeters. The process of converting one unit to another is called dimensional analysis.

Dimensional analysis involves determining three important facts: in what unit your measurement is given, in what unit it should be expressed, and what relationship between the units will allow you to make the conversion. The relationship between the units is called a conversion factor. A conversion factor expresses an exact relationship between the original unit and the desired unit. It is a fraction whose value is 1. For example,

$$\frac{60 \text{ minutes}}{1 \text{ hour}} \text{ or } \frac{1 \text{ liter}}{1000 \text{ milliliters}}$$

Although the numerator (top) of the fraction and the denominator (bottom) of the fraction are different, their actual values are the same. You see that 60 minutes equals 1 hour and 1 liter equals 1000 milliliters.

Any number can be multiplied by 1 without changing its value. Multiplying a measurement by a conversion factor, then, does not change the value of the measurement. This means that you can convert the given unit to the desired unit by multiplying by an appropriate conversion factor. You must, however, choose the correct form of the conversion factor. The unit to be converted must cancel out and the desired unit remain. Thus, the denominator of the conversion factor must contain the same unit as the one given to enable them to be canceled. Similarly, the numerator must contain the unit to be in the answer.

The following example shows how a typical dimensional analysis problem is solved.

Sample Problem Your friend runs 2500 meters while you run 3 kilometers. Using kilometers, which one of you has run a longer distance?

Step 1: Determine the given unit and the desired unit.

given: meters
desired: kilometers

Step 2: Find the relationship between the units and consider the possible conversion factors.

1000 meters = 1 kilometer
therefore:

$$\frac{1 \text{ kilometer}}{1000 \text{ meters}} = 1 \textit{ or } \frac{1000 \text{ meters}}{1 \text{ kilometer}} = 1$$

Step 3: Choose the conversion factor whose denominator has the same units as your given value.

$$\frac{1 \text{ kilometer}}{1000 \text{ meters}} = 1$$

Step 4: Write the original value next to the conversion factor with a multiplication sign between them. Cancel like terms (shown in red).

$$2500 \cancel{\text{ meters}} \times \frac{1 \text{ kilometer}}{1000 \cancel{\text{ meters}}}$$

Step 5: Multiply the resulting equation.

$$2500 \times \frac{1 \text{ kilometer}}{1000} =$$

$$\frac{2500 \text{ kilometers}}{1000} = 2.5 \text{ kilometers}$$

Your friend has run 2.5 kilometers and you have run 3 kilometers. You have run the longer distance!

Practice Problems

Now try your hand at some dimensional analysis problems. You may choose to use a calculator or computer to do the arithmetic calculations.

1. In order to compare the results of several experiments, you need to have all your data in the same unit. Convert the following measurements to the same unit.

16 kilograms	0.002 kilograms
888 grams	155 milligrams

2. A recipe calls for 300 milliliters of water. You add 0.25 liters. Have you put in too much, too little, or the right amount?
3. Determine which of the following measurements is largest: 1800 centimeters, 2.1 meters, 0.0017 kilometers.
4. You are told that you need a jar with a volume of at least 150 cm^3. The label on the jar you find says 0.16 liters. Can you use it?
5. Calculate the number of seconds in 1 year. Then calculate the number of seconds in a decade.

1–3 Science: "Facts" and "Truth"

Section Objectives

- Relate the process of science and change.
- Identify successful study habits.

Scientific knowledge is a constantly changing body of observations. Many "scientific facts" of the past are now known to be false. For much of human history, for example, people "knew" that the Earth was flat, that the sun revolved around the Earth, and that rain fell through holes in heaven from a huge water tank in the sky. Those were the "facts" of an earlier time.

Now, of course, we "know" that the Earth is round (more or less), that the Earth and other planets revolve around the sun, and that rain falls from clouds made of water vapor. These are the scientific "facts" of today—the best explanations of the world around us that scientists have developed so far.

But new discoveries will be made. New theories will be born. Without a doubt, some of what you learn this year will have to be changed one day. Yet this does not mean that science has failed. On the contrary, it means that science continues to succeed in advancing our understanding of the world. Science is not a collection of eternal truths. Rather, it is a process, a way of looking at and understanding the world. And science will continue to change as long as humans wonder about the universe.

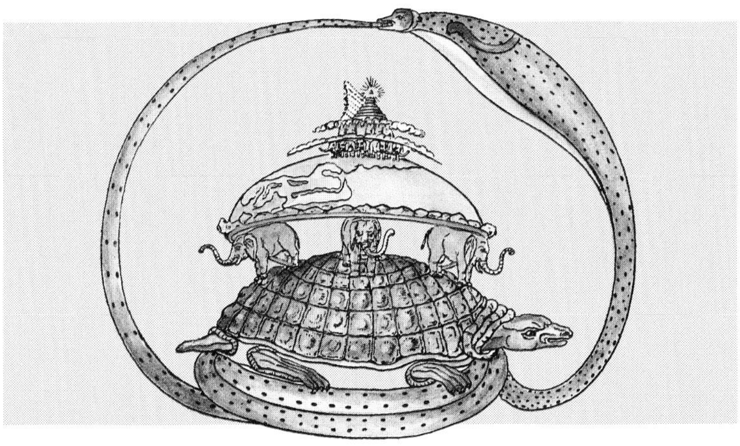

Figure 1–12 *As knowledge grows, facts can change. This print depicts a Hindu legend that tells that the Earth is supported by three elephants resting on the back of a giant tortoise.*

Figure 1–13 *The giant panda (top, left), the white rhinoceros (top, right), and the mountain gorilla (bottom) all look very different. So it might seem that the best way to study these animals is to memorize individual facts about each one. However, if you organize them as a group of mammals, then you will find it easier to learn about them. For all mammals share certain characteristics, no matter how different they may appear. These three particular mammals have another important thing in common —they are endangered species.*

How to Study Science

We, as scientists, sincerely hope that you will find your study of science to be both interesting and rewarding. For an understanding of science is essential to all of us in today's high-tech world. To make your learning easier and more enjoyable, we suggest you study science in a special way. First, do not try to memorize the contents of this book as a list of separate facts. Learning science this way will only make the process more difficult than it needs to be. Isolated facts will show little connection with each other in your mind. It will be as though you wrote each fact on a separate index card and then shuffled dozens of index cards together.

It makes much more sense to arrange facts you need to know in groups according to subject. As you read this book, work at understanding, rather than just memorizing, the topics we talk about. When you study the parts of the cell, for example, don't just memorize their names. Think about what each part does. Remember how each part works with other parts within the cell as a whole. Learning this way is like organizing the index cards of facts into groups that have meaning for you. Then when you need a particular fact, you can look for it under its proper subject heading. That will make it much easier to remember what you need.

Second, remember that science is a process. In addition to learning the scientific facts of today, try to appreciate the process of discovery. Try to see the thinking behind the experiments we describe. Try to understand the kinds of questions scientists ask as they struggle to make sense out of the world. Follow along as we describe the discovery of genes and the development of evolutionary theory. If you can learn to think the way scientists think, you will get a lot more than facts from this course. You will develop the ability to understand the process of science and to be at home in a world that will change constantly throughout your life.

Science and Human Values

An important goal in science is to be objective. But scientists are no different from the rest of us when it comes to emotions or personal opinions. Scientists, after all, are people too—people with likes, dislikes, and occasional biases.

In today's world, scientists have important things to say about questions that are raised regarding health, society, and the environment. Shall we build a nuclear power plant? Dam a river? Develop forest lands into homesteads? Should chemical wastes be buried, burned, or dumped at sea? Are there ways to use chemical wastes for our benefit? Should certain experiments involving humans be forbidden? All of these questions rely on science for at least part of their answers.

But scientific data can be misinterpreted or misapplied by scientists who want to prove a particular point. And decisions made by scientists with personal prejudices may or may not be in the public interest. What this means to you is that understanding science is even more important today than ever before. If enough people understand the nature of science, the dangers posed by misinterpreted or misleading information will be reduced.

Figure 1–14 *No doubt about it—we live in a high-tech world. Computers are now used to show the chemical structure of molecules such as human protein (left). Advances in physics, such as superconductors (right), may revolutionize the ways in which we travel and transmit electricity. As a citizen, you will have to make important decisions about the role of science in society. In order to do this, you must be able to read, understand, and evaluate scientific information.*

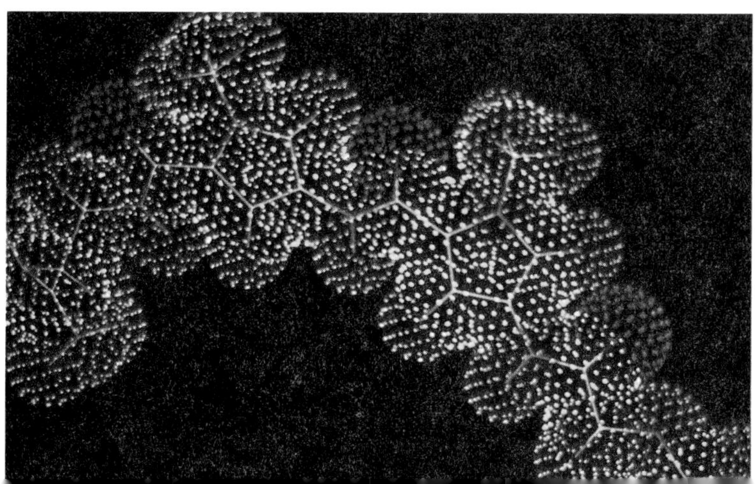

Luckily, men and women of science are taking action. Biologists, chemists, and physicists are speaking out about safety problems involved with nuclear power. Biologists and chemists are warning of the dangers posed by too many chemicals in food and water. And biologists are describing the serious threat to our environment posed by acid rain. We will touch on these and other matters in this book, and we hope that you will keep track of such issues, both in your local community and in the world at large.

1–3 SECTION REVIEW

1. Science will not sit still and allow itself to be memorized. You cannot "learn" biology, stick it away in some mental closet, and pull it out years later. Why is this the case?
2. What is the best way to study science? Why?
3. Why is it important that everyone understand the process of science and the nature of scientific facts?

Section Objective

- Identify and apply proper rules when working in the laboratory.

1–4 Safety in the Laboratory

Biology does not happen in books or in scientists' minds. Biology is most alive and exciting where the experiments that test hypotheses actually take place—in the laboratory and in the field. That is why your course in biology will probably include several laboratory exercises. Only in the laboratory can you perform experiments to learn about the process of science at first hand. Only in the laboratory can you see, touch, and manipulate living systems to understand them more thoroughly.

In the laboratory—as in any place where there are chemicals, flames or heating elements, hot liquids, and electricity—it is important to follow certain basic safety precautions. These precautions are not directed only at you as students. Scientists with many years' experience know that laboratory safety is of prime importance. The experiments you will carry out this year have been tried and tested many times. When properly performed, they are both interesting and educational. However, if laboratory materials are handled carelessly, accidents can happen.

Figure 1–15 *What important safety precautions are these students taking while working in the laboratory?*

The single most important rule for you in the laboratory is simple: Always follow your teacher's instructions and the textbook directions exactly. If you are in doubt about what to do, always ask first. Use Figure 1–16 to familiarize yourself with safety symbols and the rules of laboratory safety. Read the rules and make certain that you understand them. If you are not sure that you understand a rule completely, ask your teacher to explain it.

LABORATORY SAFETY: RULES AND SYMBOLS

Glassware Safety 

1. Whenever you see this symbol, you will know that you will be working with glassware that can easily be broken. Take particular care to handle such glassware safely. And never use broken glassware.
2. Never heat glassware that is not thoroughly dry. Never pick up any glassware unless you are sure it is not hot. If it is hot, use heat-resistant gloves.
3. Always clean glassware thoroughly before putting it away.

Fire Safety 

1. Whenever you see this symbol, you will know that you will be working with fire. Never use any source of fire without wearing safety goggles.
2. Never heat anything—particularly chemicals—unless instructed to do so.
3. Never heat anything in a closed container.
4. Never reach across a flame.
5. Always use a clamp, tongs, or heat-resistant gloves to handle hot objects.
6. Always maintain a clean work area, particularly when using a flame.

Heat Safety 

Whenever you see this symbol, you will know that you should put on heat-resistant gloves to avoid burning your hands.

Chemical Safety 

1. Whenever you see this symbol, you will know that you will be working with chemicals that could be hazardous.
2. Never smell any chemical directly from its container. Always use your hand to waft some of the odors from the top of the container toward your nose—and only when instructed to do so.
3. Never mix chemicals unless instructed to do so.
4. Never touch or taste any chemical unless instructed to do so.
5. Keep all lids closed when chemicals are not in use. Dispose of all chemicals as instructed by your teacher.
6. Immediately rinse with water any chemicals, particularly acids, off your skin and clothes. Then notify your teacher.

Eye and Face Safety 

1. Whenever you see this symbol, you will know that you will be performing an experiment in which you must take precautions to protect your eyes and face by wearing safety goggles.
2. Always point a test tube or bottle that is being heated away from you and others. Chemicals can splash or boil out of the heated test tube.

Sharp Instrument Safety 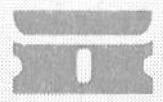

1. Whenever you see this symbol, you will know that you will be working with a sharp instrument.
2. Always use single-edged razors; double-edged razors are too dangerous.
3. Handle any sharp instrument with extreme care. Never cut any material toward you; always cut away from you.
4. Notify your teacher immediately if you are cut in the lab.

Electrical Safety 

1. Whenever you see this symbol, you will know that you will be using electricity in the laboratory.
2. Never use long extension cords to plug in an electrical device. Do not plug too many different appliances into one socket or you may overload the socket and cause a fire.
3. Never touch an electrical appliance or outlet with wet hands.

Animal Safety 

1. Whenever you see this symbol, you will know that you will be working with live animals.
2. Do not cause pain, discomfort, or injury to any animal.
3. Follow your teacher's directions when handling animals. Wash your hands thoroughly after handling animals or their cages.

Figure 1–16 *You will see these safety symbols in the Laboratory Investigations in this textbook and in your Laboratory Manual. Make sure you understand the meaning of each symbol. If you are not sure what a symbol means, ask your teacher.*

1–4 SECTION REVIEW

1. What is the most important general rule to follow when working in the laboratory?
2. Where is the nearest fire extinguisher located in your laboratory or classroom?
3. What sort of instruments might you be more likely to find in a biology laboratory than in a chemistry laboratory?

SCIENCE, TECHNOLOGY, AND SOCIETY BREAKTHROUGH

The Odd Couple: A Messy Lab and a Keen Mind

Some of us professional scientists, despite our efforts, aren't very neat workers in the lab. Oh, sure, we can keep things sterile when they need to be. But as a rule, some of us are a little messy and disorganized. Does that fit in science? Does it match our description of the scientific method? It may not match, but the messy scientist is in good company. One messy scientist was a man named Alexander Fleming.

History records at least two of Fleming's sloppy mistakes. The first was in 1922. He was suffering from a bad cold and accidentally allowed a few drops from his runny nose to drip on a plate of bacteria he was growing. Instead of discarding the dish, Fleming watched it for days. What happened? Lo and behold—the bacteria died! Fleming had discovered lysozyme, a chemical in tears and mucus that helps protect the body against bacteria.

More important work followed. Six years later, Fleming was growing more bacteria. He saw that some of his plates had been contaminated with a greenish mold (*Penicillium*) that grows on bread. Once again Fleming's sloppiness was to blame. But his careful eye and keen mind made something of the event. He saw a clear spot on the culture dish, indicating that the bacteria near the mold had died. The mold was making something that was killing the bacteria. That something turned out to be a chemical that has saved millions of lives: penicillin. Science works that way. It is a very human enterprise—one that even has room for us messy scientists!

Section Objective

- Compare planet Earth to a spaceship traveling through the universe.

1–5 The Spaceship Called Earth

Seen by astronauts from space, Earth is incredibly beautiful. It shines blue, white, and purple against the black, airless void. Since the beginning of human history, poets have written about the beauty of Earth. Artists have created paintings of Earth's magnificent wilderness lands and wild animals. Today, scientists from several fields are warning us that we must learn to protect our planet and preserve its living treasures. Our species has rapidly developed the ability to change the Earth much for the better and much for the worse. We have saved many species from extinction. At the same time, we have destroyed hundreds of other species. We have made gardens bloom in deserts and can now feed more people than ever before. But we have also turned fertile land into dust bowls. We have tremendously increased human life spans and can treat or cure many diseases that were once fatal. Yet we have also manufactured chemicals that once seemed useful but now threaten our health and the health of other species.

Earlier in human history, the Earth seemed to be without end. There were always new wildernesses to settle, new resources to use, and plenty of places to dump our garbage. Now we know that there is limited land—and limited amounts of clean air, water, and other resources. There are also a limited number of places we can use as trash heaps. **The Earth is no longer a planet without end. It is more like a giant spaceship with a living cargo, carrying limited amounts of vital supplies.**

As you read this book, you will learn about the basis of life and about the process by which life has evolved. You will take a tour through the kingdoms of the different kinds of organisms with whom we share our planet. You will learn just how closely all forms of life on Earth are connected. We hope you will also learn how important it is to preserve that life. More than ever before in history, we must work to protect our environment against destruction. Properly applied, science can provide us with the knowledge and tools we need to meet this challenge. We think you will agree that the joys of a ride on spaceship Earth are more than worth the responsibilities we have as its most powerful passengers.

1–5 SECTION REVIEW

1. How does our modern view of Earth's resources differ from older impressions?
2. What are some of the great successes of human endeavors on Earth? What are some of the failures?

Figure 1–17 *Humans have changed the Earth both for the better and for the worse. Vaccines help to prevent many diseases that were once fatal. Modern farming methods can now feed more people than ever before. At the same time, however, we have seen numerous species of living things destroyed by the actions of humans. And we have allowed toxic wastes to seep into our soil and waterways.*

LABORATORY INVESTIGATION

INTERPRETING A CONTROLLED EXPERIMENT

PROBLEM

What effect does the amount of water given to seeds have on the rate of seed germination?

MATERIALS *(per group)*

200 mustard seeds
3 petri dishes with covers
2 50-mL beakers
graduated cylinder
glass-marking pencil

PROCEDURE 

Part A

1. In this investigation you will determine whether the amount of water given to mustard seeds has an effect on the number of seeds that germinate, or sprout. Before you begin, propose a hypothesis predicting the effect that varying amounts of water might have on mustard seed germination. The steps that follow will help you test your hypothesis.
2. Place 50 mustard seeds in each of two petri dishes.
3. Using the graduated cylinder, pour 5 mL of water into one petri dish. Then pour 30 mL of water into the other petri dish. Cover each petri dish. Use the glass-marking pencil to indicate the volume of water in each.
4. Set both petri dishes aside for 48 hours. After 48 hours, count the number of seeds in each petri dish that have begun to germinate. Record your observations in a data table similar to the one shown here.

Part B

1. Place 50 mustard seeds in each of the two beakers.
2. Using the graduated cylinder, pour 5 mL of water into one beaker and 30 mL of water into the other. Cover each beaker with the top or bottom of the remaining petri dish. Then, using the glass-marking pencil, indicate on the cover the volume of water in each beaker.
3. Set the beakers aside for 48 hours. After 48 hours, count the number of seeds in each beaker that have begun to germinate and record your results in your data table.

OBSERVATIONS

Type of Container	Volume of Water	
	5 mL	30 mL
Petri dish		
Beaker		

1. Did the mustard seeds float in any of the containers? If so, were these seeds more likely to germinate?
2. In which container did the germinated seeds have the longest roots?

ANALYSIS AND CONCLUSIONS

1. How did the number of germinated seeds in the petri dishes compare to the number of germinated seeds in the beakers?
2. Did the amount of water in the petri dishes appear to affect the number of germinated seeds? Did these results confirm your hypothesis?
3. Did the amount of water in the beakers appear to affect the number of germinated seeds? Did these results confirm your original hypothesis?
4. Sometimes the results of different parts of an experiment provide different interpretations. When this occurs, scientists often look to see if a hidden variable, which might affect the overall results of an investigation, was introduced. What hidden variable might account for the results you observed in the petri dishes and in the beakers? (*Hint:* Other than water, what substance may have played a role in your experiment?)

STUDENT STUDY GUIDE

SUMMARIZING THE CONCEPTS

The key concepts in each section of this chapter are listed below to help you review the chapter content. Make sure you understand each concept and its relationship to other concepts and to the theme of this chapter.

1–1 What Is Science?

- Science is a process that uses observations and tests to identify the causes of events in nature.

1–2 The Scientific Method

- The main steps in the scientific method are observing and stating a problem, forming a hypothesis, testing the hypothesis through observation or experimentation, recording and analyzing data, forming a conclusion, and replicating the work.
- A hypothesis is a possible explanation about a particular event in nature.
- In order to ensure that the results of an experiment were due to the variable being tested, scientists must run both an experimental setup and a control setup.
- When a hypothesis has been tested and confirmed many times, it may then be considered a theory that can make dependable predictions about nature.
- The metric system is the system of measurement used by scientists all over the world.
- Although mass and weight are considered interchangeable on the surface of the Earth, mass is actually a measure of the amount of matter in an object and weight is a measure of the pull of gravity on that object.

1–3 Science: "Facts" and "Truth"

- Successful science study habits involve relating facts to each other and to the underlying concepts being discussed rather than simply memorizing a list of facts.

1–4 Safety in the Laboratory

- Always follow all written instructions or instructions from your teacher whenever working in the science laboratory.

1–5 The Spaceship Called Earth

- Planet Earth can be compared to a giant spaceship carrying a living cargo and limited amounts of food, water, and other resources.

REVIEWING KEY TERMS

Vocabulary terms are important to your understanding of biology. The key terms listed below are those you should be especially familiar with. Review these terms and their meaning. Then use each term in a complete sentence. If you are not sure of a term's meaning, return to the appropriate section and review its definition.

1–1 What Is Science?

science

1–2 The Scientific Method

scientific method
hypothesis
variable
control setup
experimental setup
data
theory
metric system
meter
liter
cubic centimeter
mass
weight
kilogram
Celsius scale

CHAPTER REVIEW

CONTENT REVIEW

Multiple Choice

Choose the letter of the answer that best completes each statement.

1. A proposed solution or explanation of a scientific event in nature is called a
   a. conclusion. c. control setup.
   b. hypothesis. d. theory.
2. The factor being tested in an experiment is the
   a. data. c. variable.
   b. hypothesis. d. theory.
3. The metric system is based or scaled on powers of
   a. 10. c. 1000.
   b. 100. d. none of these.
4. The basic unit of length in the metric system is the
   a. meter. c. millimeter.
   b. kilometer. d. centimeter.
5. The basic unit of mass in the metric system is the
   a. gram. c. liter.
   b. kilogram. d. pound.
6. A cubic centimeter is equivalent to a
   a. liter. c. milligram.
   b. gram. d. milliliter.
7. Which of the following relationships between an object on Earth and that same object on the moon is true?
   a. mass changes; weight remains the same
   b. neither mass nor weight changes
   c. both mass and weight change
   d. weight changes; mass remains the same
8. If you see the symbol of a flask in a laboratory experiment, you are being cautioned to
   a. put on goggles.
   b. take extra care with glassware.
   c. make sure your measurements are very precise.
   d. use heat-resistant gloves.

True or False

Determine whether each statement is true or false. If it is true, write "true." If it is false, change the underlined word or words to make the statement true.

1. Recorded observations are called <u>data</u>.
2. The <u>control experiment</u> is that part of the experiment without the variable.
3. A kilometer contains 1000 <u>centimeters</u>.
4. A <u>milliliter</u> contains 1000 cubic centimeters.
5. The prefix *centi-* means <u>one hundred</u>.
6. In science, facts <u>never</u> change.
7. The goal of <u>science</u> is to understand the world around us.
8. The <u>kilogram</u> is the unit of mass you would use to measure objects smaller than a gram.

Word Relationships

Replace the underlined definition with the correct vocabulary word.

1. <u>The ability to reproduce results</u> is an important part of any experiment.
2. After observing an event in nature, a scientist may develop a <u>possible explanation or a preliminary conclusion</u> regarding the cause of that event.
3. The liter is a measure of <u>the amount of space an object occupies</u>.
4. Scientists often measure length in <u>hundredths of a meter</u>.
5. <u>The amount of matter in an object</u> can be measured in milligrams.

CONCEPT MASTERY

Use your understanding of the concepts developed in the chapter to answer each of the following in a brief paragraph.

1. Why is it important to have only one variable in an experiment?
2. Scientists throughout the world use a standard system of measurement. Why is a standard measurement system necessary?
3. Why must science textbooks be revised every few years?
4. Compare planet Earth to a giant spaceship.
5. Describe the approach that separates the process of science from other fields of study.
6. Which metric unit would you use to measure each of the following:
   a. volume of a glass of milk
   b. length of your textbook
   c. mass of a mouse
   d. temperature of the Gulf of Mexico
   e. mass of a killer whale
   f. volume of a marble

CRITICAL AND CREATIVE THINKING

Discuss each of the following in a brief paragraph.

1. **Designing an experiment** How would you use the scientific method to find the best place in your class to grow African violets?
2. **Making predictions** Develop a time line in which you predict some of the important advances that may occur in science during the next century.
3. **Interpreting diagrams** Examine the illustration of a control setup and an experimental setup. What is the variable in this experiment? Why?

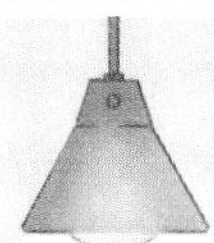
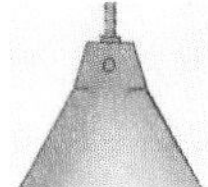

4. **Recognizing fact and opinion** Suppose your friends believe that astrology is a science. How would you convince them that they are wrong?
5. **Relating concepts** The French biologist Louis Pasteur once said, "Chance favors only the mind that is prepared." Explain this statement by relating it to the process of science.
6. **Using the writing process** You have been elected to the Senate. The most important issue that has to be resolved is whether the United States will convert to the metric system. Write a 3-minute speech detailing your reasons for adopting or rejecting the metric system.
7. **Using the writing process** The year is 2050. Write a help-wanted ad that will encourage high school graduates to volunteer for a 2-year mission to planet Mars. The main task of the graduates will be as technicians helping out in various scientific experiments. All graduates will be trained before the mission begins.

CHAPTER 2

Biology as a Science

Without any prior knowledge about trees, it would be difficult for an observer walking through a winter forest to know whether these trees were living or nonliving.

How do you tell whether something is alive? With some living things, it's easy. You could check for breathing, or a pulse, or a response to a pinch or a poke. But such tests would not work for all living things. Is moss growing on a rock alive? How about rust spreading over a piece of metal? If you came upon a tree in the middle of winter when its leaves were gone, how would you tell whether the tree was living or dead?

What we are really asking in such questions is simple. We would like to know what distinguishes life from nonlife. The answer to such questions, however, is not always that clear. So we shall do the next best thing to providing the answer. In this chapter we shall list the characteristics that living things share.

CHAPTER OUTLINE

2–1 Characteristics of Living Things
- Living Things Are Made Up of Cells
- Living Things Reproduce
- Living Things Grow and Develop
- Living Things Obtain and Use Energy
- Living Things Respond to Their Environment

2–2 Biology: The Study of Life
- Branches of Biology
- Tools of a Biologist
- Laboratory Techniques of a Biologist

2–1 Characteristics of Living Things

Section Objectives

- List and describe the characteristics of living things.
- Define homeostasis.

Making up a list of the characteristics of living things is not as easy as it might sound. In fact, scientists have argued for centuries over the basic characteristics that separate life and nonlife. Some of these arguments are still unresolved. For example, in Chapter 17 you will discover that the line between life and nonlife becomes blurred when we consider whether or not viruses are living things.

Despite these arguments, there do seem to be some generally accepted characteristics common to all living things. **We can state with some confidence that all living things**

- **Are made up of one or more units called cells**
- **Reproduce**
- **Grow and develop**
- **Obtain and use energy**
- **Respond to their environment**

It will help in our understanding of living things to consider each of these characteristics in detail.

Living Things Are Made Up of Cells

Living things are made up of small self-contained units called cells. Each cell is a collection of living matter enclosed by a barrier that separates the cell from its surroundings. Most cells can perform all the functions we associate with life.

Cells are remarkably diverse. A single cell by itself can form an entire living organism. Organisms consisting of only a

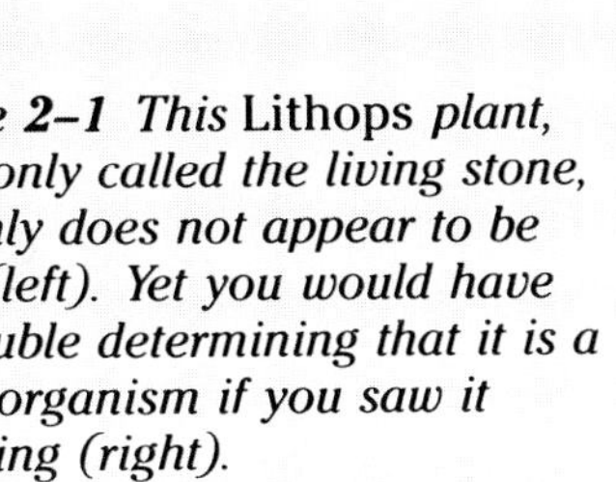

Figure 2–1 *This* Lithops *plant, commonly called the living stone, certainly does not appear to be alive (left). Yet you would have no trouble determining that it is a living organism if you saw it flowering (right).*

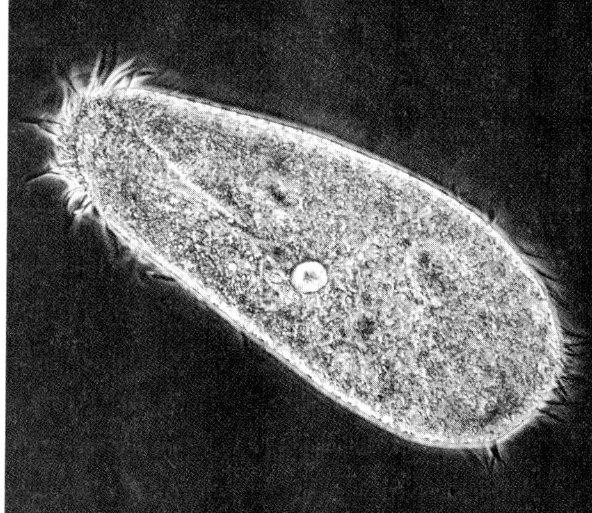

Figure 2–2 Biologists classify organisms as unicellular or multicellular. This unicellular protozoan (left) is a single-celled organism, whereas the multicellular tree sloth (right) is made up of trillions of cells.

single cell are called **unicellular**. See Figure 2–2. (The Latin prefix *uni-* means one, so unicellular means single-celled.) Most of the organisms you are familiar with, such as dogs and trees, are **multicellular**. (The Latin prefix *multi-* means many, so multicellular means many-celled.) Multicellular organisms contain hundreds, thousands, even trillions of cells or more. We will discuss cells in more detail in Chapter 5.

Cells are never formed by nonliving things. They are found in nonliving matter only if that matter was once alive. Wood, for example, is made up largely of the walls that separated individual cells in the living tree.

Living Things Reproduce

Living things can reproduce, or produce new organisms of the same type. Because all individual organisms eventually die, reproduction is necessary if a group of similar organisms (what we will later call a species) is to survive.

There are two basic kinds of reproduction: sexual and asexual. **Sexual reproduction** requires that two cells from different individuals unite to produce the first cell of a new organism. See Figure 2–3. You are reading this textbook because a cell from your mother united with a cell from your father to form that first cell that would grow and develop into you. Most familiar organisms—from maple trees to birds and bees—reproduce sexually. In **asexual reproduction**, a single organism can reproduce without the aid of another. (The prefix *a-* means without, so asexual means without sex.) Asexual reproduction can be very simple: Some single-celled organisms merely divide in two to form two organisms.

Figure 2–3 Orangutans, as well as all other animals, reproduce sexually. In sexual reproduction, one cell from each parent unites to form the first cell of the new organism.

Living Things Grow and Develop

All living things, at one stage or another in their lives, are capable of growth. An acorn, when it sprouts, produces roots, stems, a trunk, and leaves that continue to grow for years. As it grows, the plant takes in substances from the air and soil and

Figure 2–4 All living things grow and develop. Usually growth simply means getting larger, not changing form. But that is not always the case. This caterpillar (left) will grow and develop into an adult Cecropia moth (right).

transforms these substances into living tissue. And long after the tree stops getting larger, it continues to add new material to replace existing parts that wear out.

A snowball, on the other hand, may seem to "grow" if you roll it over fresh snow. But a snowball grows bigger only if someone adds new snow onto its surface. A snowball won't grow bigger by just sitting there. And it certainly cannot change liquid water or solid ice into new snow from which it can grow larger.

During growth, most living things go through a cycle of change called development. The single cell that starts an organism's life divides and changes again and again to form the many and varied cells of an adult organism. You are probably well aware of growth and development since you are now in the midst of one of the most intense spurts of growth and development that you will ever encounter in your life.

As development continues, organisms experience a process called aging. During aging, an organism becomes less efficient at the process of life. The ability to reproduce comes to an end. For virtually all organisms, death is the inevitable end of the life span of every individual. Death, too, is a process of change that separates living and nonliving things.

Living Things Obtain and Use Energy

Living things obtain energy from their environment, or their surroundings, and use that energy to grow, develop, and reproduce. All organisms require energy to build the substances that make up their cells. Any process in a living thing that involves putting together, or synthesizing, complex substances from simpler substances is called **anabolism** (uh-NAB-uh-lihz-uhm).

Plants obtain their energy from sunlight in a process called photosynthesis, which you will study in Chapter 6. (The prefix *photo-* refers to light, and the suffix *-synthesis* means put together. Thus photosynthesis means put together with light.)

Figure 2–5 According to this chart, what is the maximum life span of a blue whale?

MAXIMUM LIFE SPANS

Organism	Life Span
Adult mayfly	1 day
Marigold	8 months
Mouse	1–2 years
Dog	17 years
Blue whale	100 years
Tortoise	152 years
Bristlecone pine	5500 years

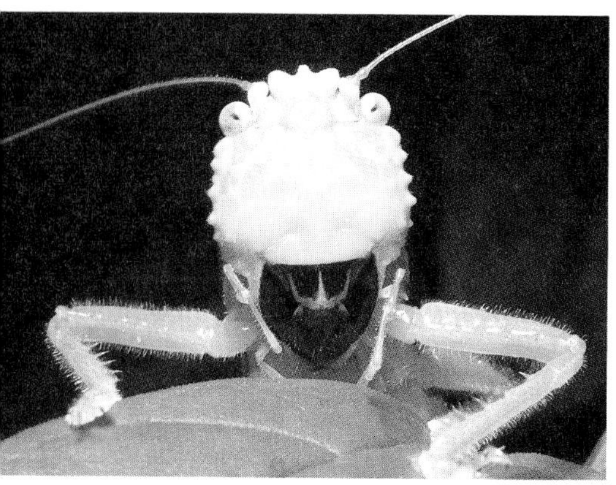

Figure 2–6 This katydid obtains the energy it needs to live from the food it eats. How does the green plant the katydid is munching on obtain its energy?

Animals cannot perform photosynthesis. Animals take in energy in the form of food. Food is broken down during a process called digestion, which you will study in Chapter 39. The final breakdown of complex substances into simpler ones, usually resulting in the release of energy, is called **catabolism** (kuh-TAB-uh-lihz-uhm).

Living things must practice both anabolism and catabolism at the same time, just as a business or a household must take some money in as income and pay some money out as expenses. The total sum of all chemical reactions in the body—the balance of anabolism and catabolism—is called **metabolism**.

Living Things Respond to Their Environment

Living things respond to their environment. Such responses can be rapid, usually through changes in behavior, or slow, usually through changes in metabolic processes or through growth. Anything in the environment that causes an organism to react is called a stimulus. Organisms react to many stimuli, including light, temperature, odor, sound, gravity, heat, water, and pressure. What stimuli are you responding to at this very moment?

The ability of living things to react to stimuli is known as irritability. (No, that does not mean that living things are grouchy. At least not all the time!) Both plants and animals exhibit irritability and can react to a variety of stimuli. Plants, however, usually respond to stimuli more slowly than animals. Plant leaves and stems, for example, grow toward light and away from the pull of gravity. Plant roots, on the other hand, respond to gravity by growing down into the soil.

In general, living things respond to stimuli in ways that improve their chances for survival. **The process by which organisms respond to stimuli in ways that keep conditions in their body suitable for life is called homeostasis**. (The prefix

Figure 2–7 Living things respond to stimuli from their environment. What stimuli is the bat responding to? What will be the logical response of the frog?

Figure 2–8 *This Australian reptile, called the frilled dragon, is basking on a rock in the sun. How does this behavior of the reptile help it achieve homeostasis? What might the reptile do if its body overheats?*

homeo- means similar or same. The suffix *-stasis* means standing or stopping.) **Homeostasis** (hoh-mee-oh-STAY-sihs) refers to an organism's ability to maintain constant or stable conditions that are necessary for life. Just as a thermostat in your home turns on the heat when it gets down to a certain temperature, your body has a thermostat that maintains a constant internal temperature. If you get too hot, you sweat and cool off. And if you sweat for a long time, the resulting thirst persuades you to replace the water your body has lost.

You might point out that nonliving things also respond to the environment. However, the responses of nonliving things are purely mechanical (like a spring that jumps when compressed and released) and are not related to survival.

2–1 SECTION REVIEW

1. List and describe five characteristics that separate living and nonliving things.
2. Compare sexual reproduction and asexual reproduction.
3. Define metabolism, using the terms catabolism and anabolism in your definition.
4. Try to think of a nonliving thing that satisfies each characteristic of living things. Does any nonliving thing have all the characteristics of life?

2–2 Biology: The Study of Life

Section Objectives

- Compare the different branches of biology.
- Describe the different types of microscopes and their limits of resolution.
- Discuss the advantages and disadvantages of different types of microscopes.

Quite literally, biology means the study of life. (The prefix *bio-* means life, and the suffix *-logy* means study of.) Biology, then, is the science that seeks to understand, explain, and even control the living world. Biology, like any other science, advances by observing the world, asking questions, and forming hypotheses that can be tested by experiment. **A biologist is anyone who uses the scientific method to study living things.**

Branches of Biology

The broad field of biology contains many branches, or divisions. Some divisions are quite general: zoologists study animals (the prefix *zoo-* means animal); botanists work with plants (the Greek prefix *botanikos-* means green plants); and microbiologists work with microscopic organisms (the prefix *micro-* means small). Other subdivisions of biology are more focused. Paleontologists, for example, work with extinct organisms (the prefix *paleo-* means ancient), and ethologists study animal behavior (the prefix *ethos-* means custom).

In the course of this textbook we will examine many fields of biology. Here, we can begin our investigation by considering examples of the types of questions that are asked by different kinds of biologists.

QUESTIONS AT THE MOLECULAR LEVEL Some biologists study life at the molecular level. Molecular biologists, for example, may study the basic chemical units of life. Molecular geneticists investigate the workings of DNA, the molecule that controls heredity and directs all the activities of the cell. Other researchers might study the effects of drugs on molecules in cells in order to understand why entire organisms react to those drugs as they do.

QUESTIONS AT THE CELLULAR LEVEL Some biologists study questions that deal with organisms at the cellular level. Cell biologists, for example, might study the way normal cells become cancer cells when exposed to radiation or to the chemicals found in cigarette smoke. Or they might try to explain how a single cell divides and changes to form all the cell types in an

Figure 2–9 *Biology is filled with terms that may seem unfamiliar to you but are actually quite simple. Many scientific terms are derived from Latin or Greek words that may be added in front of another word as a prefix or after another word as a suffix. Using this chart, determine the meaning of the word cytology.*

Prefix	Meaning	Prefix	Meaning	Suffix	Meaning
anti–	against	**herb–**	pertaining to plants	**–cyst**	pouch
arth–	joint, jointed	**hetero–**	different	**–derm**	skin, layer
auto–	self	**homeo–**	same	**–gen**	producing
bio–	related to life	**macro–**	large	**–itis**	inflammation
chloro–	green	**micro–**	small	**–logy**	study
cyto–	cell	**multi–**	consisting of many units	**–meter**	measurement
di–	double	**osteo–**	bone	**–osis**	condition, disease
epi–	above	**photo–**	pertaining to light	**–phase**	stage
exo–	outer, external	**plasm–**	forming substance	**–phage**	eater
gastro–	stomach	**proto–**	first	**–pod**	foot
hemo–	blood	**syn–**	together	**–stasis**	stationary condition

adult organism. Other cell biologists might study how cells communicate with nearby cells.

Figure 2–10 Many bird species have elaborate courtship (mating) behaviors. These albatross are exhibiting a form of courtship behavior called sky pointing. What type of biologist might study courtship behavior?

QUESTIONS AT THE MULTICELLULAR LEVEL Going beyond individual cells, some biologists study multicellular organisms. Zoologists, for example, might be interested in the changes within animals that tell them when to sleep or eat or even when to mate. Paleontologists might try to explain how certain animals changed over time, or evolved. Ethologists might ask why the males of a particular kind of organism are more brightly colored than the females.

QUESTIONS AT THE POPULATION LEVEL Some biologists even go beyond individual organisms in their studies. These biologists are interested in groups of organisms that make up populations and how such populations interact with their environment. Some ecologists, for example, might want to know how the construction of a new road or dam, or the cutting down of forests, will affect nearby plant and animal life. Other ecologists might be concerned with the effects of pesticides or industrial wastes on organisms that live in our waterways.

QUESTIONS AT THE GLOBAL LEVEL Many biologists take a more worldwide view of biology and are concerned with organisms and their environment on a global scale. Global ecologists, for example, might try to estimate the effects on the Earth's climate of burning coal and oil. Or they might try to explain why the fishing off New England is excellent one year and poor the next.

Whether studying questions at the molecular level, the global level, or any level in between, biologists are making important contributions. They are both studying and trying to preserve the wonderful things that are alive on planet Earth—not just for their own use, but for the use of those who will live on this planet after us.

By now it may appear as if biology is a field strictly for scientists with a long list of college degrees. It is true that most biologists do have a bachelor's degree and often go on to graduate school. But it is just as true that anyone can be a biologist. The only real qualifications are hard work, energy, and curiosity. A biologist must be curious about life and have the energy to ask questions in a scientific way—and then try to answer those questions. As you will read in this textbook, many of the greatest names in the history of biology were amateurs, meaning that they did not practice science as a "job." Such people include Charles Darwin, who established the theory of evolution, and Gregor Mendel, who discovered the basic units of heredity. Today other amateurs, including high school and college students, continue to make important contributions to scientific research and the science of biology. No license is required!

Figure 2–11 These Japanese citizens are taking part in an antipollution march in Tokyo. The effects of air pollution on health are among the global questions biologists often try to assess.

Tools of a Biologist

To accomplish their diverse goals, biologists may choose to use a wide variety of tools. In the laboratory, biologists may use pipettes and graduated cylinders to measure and transfer liquids. Solids, on the other hand, are usually measured on mechanical or electronic balances. Many experiments are performed inside enclosures, called hoods, that protect researchers from dangerous fumes or help to control contamination.

In almost all areas of biology, the computer has become an invaluable tool that can be used to perform complex tasks and analyze quantities of data. Many tools, however, are more specific to the type of biological work being undertaken. Global ecologists, for example, may use orbiting satellites to provide detailed maps of the temperature, moisture content, or vegetation of large areas. We shall discuss many more tools and the ways in which they are used throughout this textbook.

Figure 2–12 *This diagram is of a typical compound light microscope. What is another word for the eyepiece?*

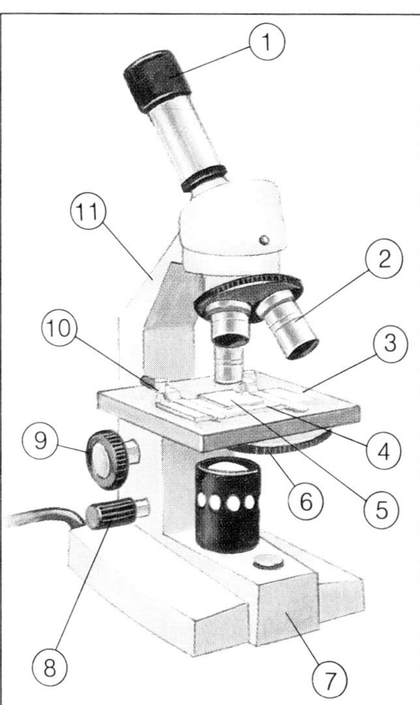

Compound Light Microscope

1. Ocular lens (eyepiece)
2. Objective lens 3. Stage
4. Glass slide 5. Coverslip
6. Diaphragm (regulates light intensity)
7. Base
8. Fine adjustment knob
9. Coarse adjustment knob
10. Stage clips
11. Arm

When you think of biology, there is probably one tool that comes to mind above all others. For almost all biologists need to examine organisms or parts of organisms that are too small to be seen with the unaided eye. **To study small organisms, researchers have developed several kinds of microscopes. Microscopes are instruments that produce larger-than-life images, pictures, or even videotapes.**

THE COMPOUND LIGHT MICROSCOPE The most familiar microscope to high school students is the **compound light microscope**. A typical compound light microscope is shown in Figure 2–12.

Compound light microscopes are important to biologists because they allow them to observe many kinds of cells and single-celled organisms while they are still alive. That is, an organism does not have to be killed to be observed under a compound light microscope.

To use a compound light microscope, you sandwich the object to be viewed between a transparent glass slide and a thin cover slip. This sandwich is then placed on the stage of the microscope so that light passing through it travels through two lenses. The lens at the bottom of the microscope tube, which is closest to the specimen being observed, is called the objective lens. The lens at the top of the microscope tube, through which you look, is called the ocular lens. When you look through the ocular lens in a compound light microscope, you may see an image of the object magnified up to 1000 times.

LIMITS OF RESOLUTION There are limits to what we can see with the compound light microscope. As we increase the magnifying power of a light microscope, we see more and more detail—up to a certain point. Beyond that point, called the **limit of resolution**, objects get blurry and detail is lost. For standard light microscopes, the limit of resolution is about 0.2 micrometers. (A typical cell is about 10 micrometers across.)

When the limit of resolution was first discovered, many people thought that if microscopes were made better, this problem would disappear. However, even a "perfect" microscope will have a limit of resolution. The reason for this has to do with the way light behaves. When light passes through a tiny opening or a lens, it is diffracted, or scattered in a way that makes it hard to form a clear image. When we look at something in the compound light microscope at 1000 times magnification, we have enlarged it just enough to see the limit of resolution of the best light microscopes we can make.

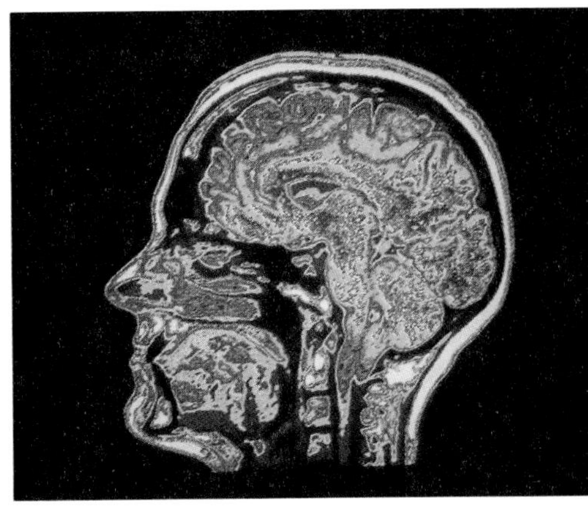

Figure 2–13 *Modern science has provided biologists with many tools unknown in centuries past. This image of a patient's brain was made by a medical scanner called a nuclear magnetic resonance scanner (NMR). What sort of tools do you think biologists will be using a century from now?*

USING A COMPOUND LIGHT MICROSCOPE There are objects—such as dust, feathers, and pollen grains—that can be seen in the light microscope without any special preparation. But many cells and cell parts are so similar in appearance to their surroundings that they cannot be easily seen through the microscope. Researchers have developed several techniques to make such objects visible.

Many specimens are stained before they are observed under a microscope. Stains are used to color cells or parts of cells to make them clearly visible. Some stains color everything in a cell, whereas others color only a part of the cell. One such special stain, known as Feulgen, turns DNA a beautiful pinkish color. Some stains, which "stick" only to certain compounds, can be made to glow in the dark to highlight specific cell parts.

Because many stains kill living cells, special types of light microscopes that do not require staining are used to observe living specimens. Examples of these are the phase contrast microscope, the dark field microscope, and the Nomarski microscope. Each uses a different property of light rays to improve the contrast (clarity) of the image. See Figure 2–14.

ELECTRON MICROSCOPES Although light microscopes are very useful, their limit of resolution restricts their usefulness for studying very small objects such as viruses and individual molecules. Is there a way to see things smaller than light

Figure 2–14 *Notice the variations in this image of an alga as seen through a Nomarski microscope (left), a dark field microscope (center), and a phase contrast microscope (right).*

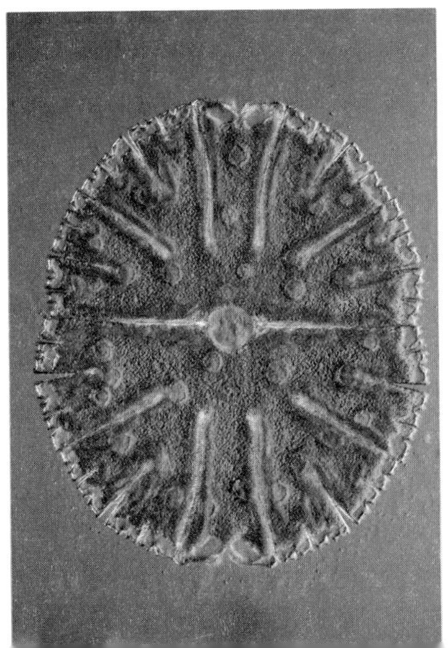

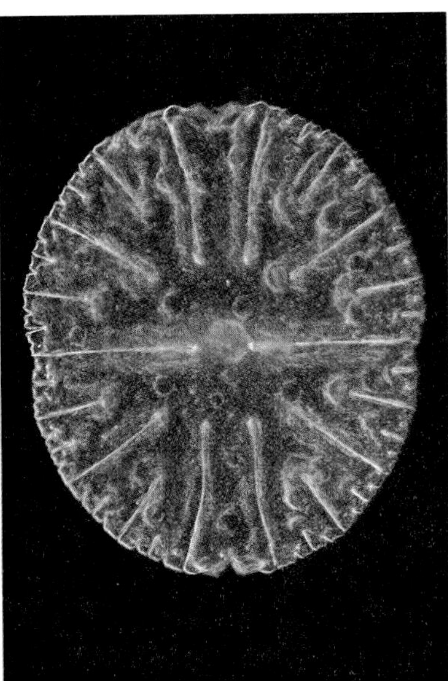

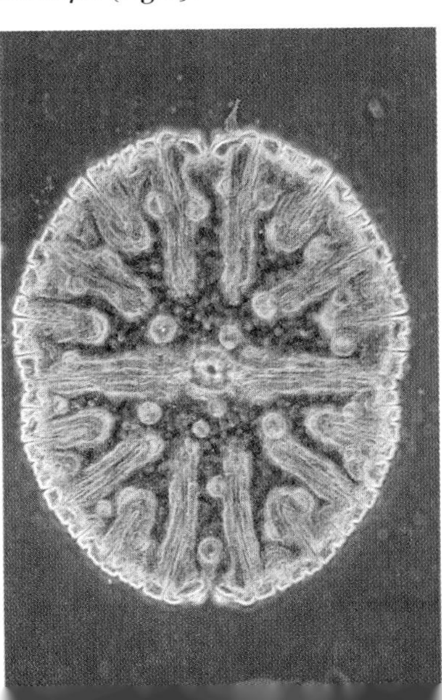

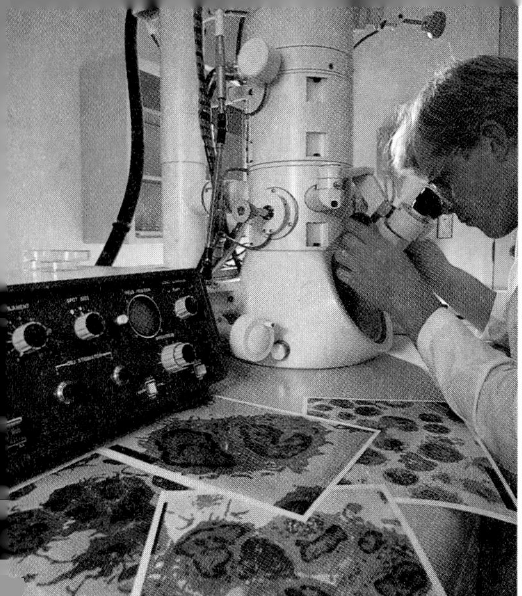

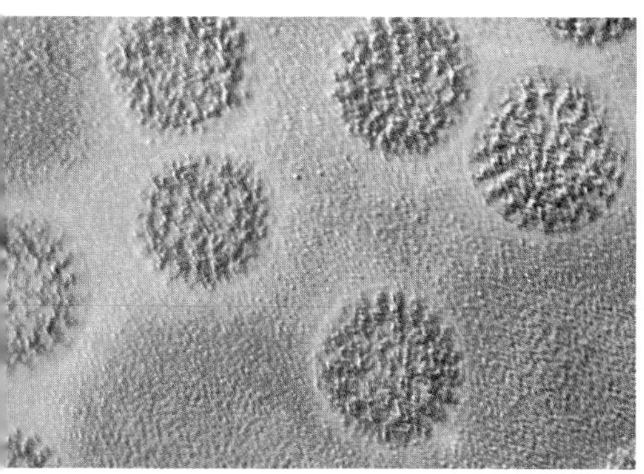

Figure 2–15 *A transmission electron microscope (TEM) sends a beam of electrons through an object to produce an image (top). This image of viruses, which has had color added by a computer, was taken through a TEM (bottom).*

can reveal? Indeed, there is. In the 1920s, physicists in Germany realized that electromagnets could bend streams of electrons in much the same way that glass lenses bend beams of light. They then learned to use electromagnets to build devices called electron microscopes. These same physicists used electromagnets to bend electrons to produce another tool you are probably familiar with: television.

The limit of resolution of electron microscopes is about 1000 times finer than the light microscope. There are several different types of electron microscopes.

Transmission electron microscopes (TEMs) shine a beam of electrons at a sample and then magnify the image of that sample onto a fluorescent screen at the bottom of the microscope. The electron beam can also be used to expose photographic film to produce a permanent image of the specimen. See Figure 2–15.

Scanning electron microscopes (SEMs) get their name from a pencillike beam of electrons that scans back and forth across the surface of a specimen. Electrons that bounce off the specimen are picked up by detectors that provide the information to form an image on a television screen. Rather than showing details inside living things, SEMs show realistic (and often dramatic) three-dimensional pictures of their surfaces. See Figure 2–16.

LIMITATIONS OF ELECTRON MICROSCOPES Electron microscopes are extremely useful when studying very small organisms and parts of organisms. But they do present one serious drawback. Because of the nature of electrons, specimens must be placed in a vacuum, or a chamber from which all the air has been removed. Specimens for TEM work must also be stained with special chemicals, treated with other chemicals, and then cut into very thin slices. Specimens for SEM work do not need to be sliced; but like specimens for TEMs, they must be placed in a vacuum. As you can conclude, in either case the living cells must be killed before they can be observed under an electron microscope.

Figure 2–16 *A scanning electron microscope (SEM) bounces electrons off the surface of an object to form an image. This image of bacteria, which has been colored green through the use of a computer, was taken by using an SEM.*

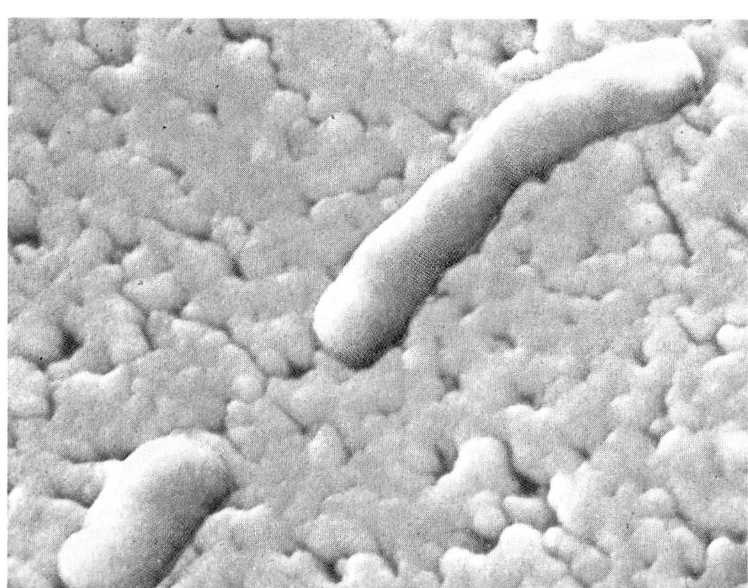

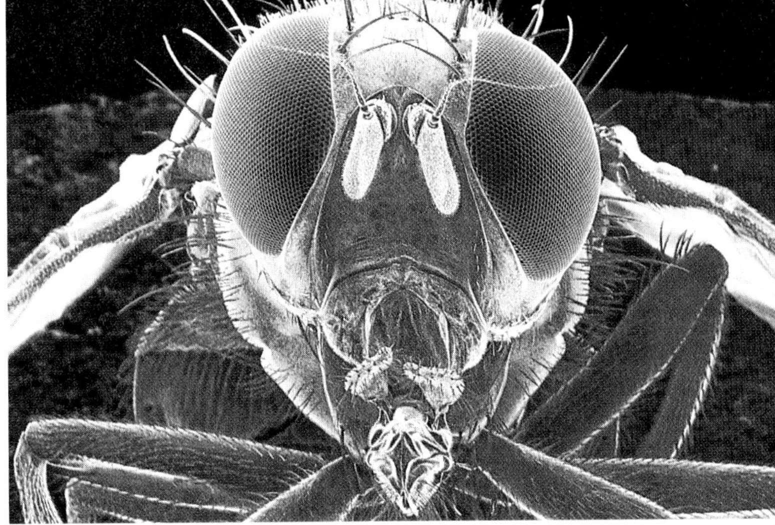

Figure 2–17 *On this fruit fly (left), notice the two large red structures, which are the eyes. Then look at the head of the fruit fly as seen through a compound light microscope, magnified 60 times (right). The two rounded structures on each side of the head are the eyes. A scanning electron microscope produced this detailed three-dimensional image of the eye of the fruit fly (bottom).*

WHICH MICROSCOPES ARE BETTER? All the microscopes we have discussed do different things. The light microscope allows us to observe living cells but it cannot make the tiniest details visible. TEMs reveal innermost details of the cell interior but only after the cell has been killed, sectioned, and stained. SEMs allow us to study the surfaces of objects in three-dimensional detail. All types of microscopes, therefore, provide us with different glimpses of what living cells are like. No one microscope is better than the rest. Each is a tool to be used, when appropriate, by a working biologist.

Laboratory Techniques of a Biologist

You have already read about the laboratory technique called staining, in which parts of a cell are stained so that they appear more visible under a microscope. Throughout this textbook, we will discuss many other laboratory techniques used by biologists. But it will be helpful now for you to learn about some common laboratory techniques.

Figure 2–18 *Blood samples are placed into a centrifuge in order to separate the various components of the blood.*

CENTRIFUGATION Suppose a scientist wants to study one particular part of a cell or the same cell part from many similar cells. How can parts of a cell be obtained? One method is called centrifugation (sehn-trihf-yoo-GAY-shuhn). See Figure 2–18. One common centrifugation technique is to place the cells under study in a blender to break them apart. Breaking apart cells in a blender is called cell fractionation. The broken bits of cells are then placed in a liquid in a tube. The tube is inserted into a centrifuge, which is a device that can spin the tube up to 20,000 times per minute. While spinning, the cell parts begin to separate—with the heaviest parts settling near the bottom of the tube and the lightest parts rising toward the top. A scientist can then remove the specific part of the cell to be studied by selecting the appropriate layer.

MICRODISSECTION Another way to remove parts of a cell, as well as to insert material into a living cell, is a technique called microdissection. In this process, special tools that are so small they can be used only by looking through a microscope are used to dissect or remove specific parts of a cell. In the same way, substances can be added to a living cell.

CELL CULTURES Sometimes scientists want to study a particular kind of cell but to do so they need large numbers of that exact cell. To obtain many identical copies of that cell, the scientist might prepare a cell culture. In this technique, a single cell is placed in a dish that contains the nutrients the cell needs. The cell is allowed to reproduce so that in time an entire population is grown from that single original cell.

2–2 SECTION REVIEW

1. List four branches of biology. What sorts of questions might researchers in each branch study?
2. What type of research could be performed only by using a compound light microscope?
3. Name an advantage and a disadvantage of each type of microscope.
4. Compare a TEM and an SEM. What type of information does each provide?
5. How does the resolution of a microscope affect the observations made by a microbiologist?
6. It has been said that many great discoveries lie in wait for the tools needed to make them. What does this statement mean to you? If possible, include an example in your answer.

SCIENCE, TECHNOLOGY, AND SOCIETY **BREAKTHROUGH**

Yellow Fever: The Scientific Method in Action

Near the turn of the century, American soldiers stationed in the vicinity of Havana, Cuba, began to die in great numbers. They died not from enemy bullets but from a disease known as yellow fever. At one point, more soldiers died from the disease than from fighting in the Spanish-American War that had brought them to Cuba in the first place! The situation became so serious that the United States sent a commission headed by Dr. Walter Reed.

At first, people thought the disease was spread by contact with infected individuals or through infected materials such as bedsheets and clothing. So they boiled the clothes and sheets of sick people before using them again and prevented other soldiers from coming into contact with the infected soldiers. But none of these measures was of any help.

One Cuban doctor, Carlos Finlay, believed that the disease was spread by mosquitoes, which were plentiful in Cuba. Reed did not immediately agree, but he devised what turned out to be a terrifying experiment to test Finlay's hypothesis. Ideally, Reed would have used animals for his experiment. But because no animals that could contract yellow fever were available, the lives of several extraordinarily brave human beings were put at risk.

The commission assembled two groups of volunteers. One group spent twenty difficult, anxious days wearing the filthy clothing of yellow fever patients, sleeping in their soiled sheets, and eating from plates they had used. During this time, however, they were completely screened in and thereby protected from mosquitoes. Not one of these soldiers contracted yellow fever.

The second group of volunteers used only fresh clothing and linens and remained totally isolated from yellow fever patients. These volunteers, however, allowed themselves to be bitten by mosquitoes that had previously bitten yellow fever patients. Because members of the commission thought it unfair to ask others to take a risk they would not take themselves, three of them participated in this group. (Reed himself wanted to take part, but his associates would not let him.) Many of the volunteers in the second group, including all three doctors from the commission, developed yellow fever. One of them, Dr. Jesse Lazear, died.

Reed's experiment had risked human lives—and had cost one. But it had tested an idea and had proved that mosquitoes carried the infection. As a result, war was declared against the mosquito. In ninety days, Havana was completely free of yellow fever. This courageous example of the scientific method in action saved the lives of thousands of people who might have died from the disease.

Walter Reed's discovery of the way in which yellow fever was spread saved countless lives. But most scientists would not necessarily agree that humans should be used in such experiments. Are there diseases so dangerous that finding a cure or treatment is worth placing humans at risk? Or is no discovery worth the cost in human lives? What about only using volunteers, as Reed did? What about only using people with fatal diseases? These are difficult questions to consider. There may not be a right or wrong answer. What is your opinion on this issue?

LABORATORY INVESTIGATION

USING A COMPOUND MICROSCOPE

PROBLEM

What is the proper procedure for using a compound microscope?

MATERIALS *(per group)*

compound microscope	light thread
glass slide	scissors
coverslip	medicine dropper
dark thread	

PROCEDURE 

1. Study Figure 2–12 on page 34 and the Appendix on the use of a microscope at the back of this book until you know the names and functions of each part of the microscope.
2. The magnification of the eyepiece, or ocular lens, is written on the eyepiece. In general, the eyepiece magnifies 10 times.
3. Now find the low-power objective lens and the high-power objective lens. The magnification of each objective lens is written on the lens. In most microscopes, the low-power lens magnifies 10 times and the high-power lens magnifies 43 times. The total magnifying power of the microscope is found by multiplying the magnification of the eyepiece by the objective lens being used.
4. Cut a piece of dark thread about 1 cm long. Do the same with light thread. Place the threads on a clean glass slide so that the threads cross each other at right angles.
5. Use the medicine dropper to place a drop of water on the threads. Then touch one edge of a coverslip to the drop of water and lower the coverslip over the threads.
6. Place the slide on the stage, using the stage clips to hold the slide in position.
7. Position the low-power objective over the slide so that the objective is just above the top of the slide. **CAUTION:** *Never allow the objective to touch the slide.*
8. Look through the eyepiece. Adjust the mirror and the diaphragm so that the field is bright.
9. If the threads are out of focus, use the coarse adjustment knob to raise the objective lens until the threads are clearly seen. Then use the fine adjustment knob to sharpen the focus.
10. Adjust the slide so that the place where the threads cross is in the center of your field of vision.
11. After you have viewed the slide under low power, raise the body tube of the microscope so that the objective is well clear of the lens. Rotate the high-power objective into place above the slide, making sure the objective does not touch the slide. Lower the high-power objective until it is just above the slide.
12. Again, use the coarse adjustment knob to raise the objective until the threads are in focus. Then use the fine adjustment knob to sharpen the focus.
13. Move the slide to the left, to the right, forward, and back. Note the direction the threads appear to move each time you move the slide.

OBSERVATIONS

1. What happens to the brightness when the magnification is changed from low power to high power?
2. When you use the fine adjustment knob, how many threads are in focus at a time?
3. When you move the slide in any direction, how do the threads appear to move?

ANALYSIS AND CONCLUSIONS

1. Why is it important to raise the body tube before rotating the high-power lens into place?
2. Would you be able to see the threads if they were larger and thicker? Explain your answer.

STUDENT STUDY GUIDE

SUMMARIZING THE CONCEPTS

The key concepts in each section of this chapter are listed below to help you review the chapter content. Make sure you understand each concept and its relationship to other concepts and to the theme of this chapter.

2–1 Characteristics of Living Things

- All living things are made up of one or more cells.
- All living things reproduce, either sexually or asexually.
- Living things grow and develop, using energy and raw materials they obtain from the environment.
- Anabolism is any chemical process in a living thing in which complex substances are built up, or synthesized, from less complex substances.
- Catabolism refers to chemical reactions in living things in which complex substances are broken down into simpler ones.
- The sum total of anabolism and catabolism is called metabolism.
- Living things respond to stimuli from their environment. Stimuli include heat, light, water, sound, odor, and pressure.
- To survive, living things must keep conditions in their bodies relatively stable. Homeostasis refers to an organism's ability to maintain constant conditions within its body.

2–2 Biology: The Study of Life

- Different branches of biology deal with questions at the molecular level, cellular level, multicellular level, population level, and global level.
- Biologists use a wide variety of tools; in particular, various types of microscopes.
- The compound light microscope is used to examine living things. It uses light passing through an object to create a magnified image of that object.
- At some point, called the limit of resolution, the object being magnified loses clarity and becomes blurred.
- Electron microscopes use electrons, rather than light, to produce magnified images. To prepare a specimen for viewing under the electron microscope, the specimen must be killed.

REVIEWING KEY TERMS

Vocabulary terms are important to your understanding of biology. The key terms listed below are those you should be especially familiar with. Review these terms and their meanings. Then use each term in a complete sentence. If you are not sure of a term's meaning, return to the appropriate section and review its definition.

2–1 Characteristics of Living Things

unicellular
multicellular
sexual reproduction
asexual reproduction
anabolism
catabolism
metabolism
homeostasis

2–2 Biology: The Study of Life

compound light microscope
limit of resolution
transmission electron microscope
scanning electron microscope

CHAPTER REVIEW

CONTENT REVIEW

Multiple Choice

Choose the letter of the answer that best completes each statement.

1. Single-celled organisms are also called
a. multicellular. c. unicellular.
b. bacteria. d. viruses.

2. Reproduction that involves the union of cells from two parents is called
a. asexual reproduction.
b. irritability.
c. cell division.
d. sexual reproduction.

3. Chemical reactions in an organism that build, or synthesize, complex molecules from less complex molecules are called
a. metabolism. c. catabolism.
b. anabolism. d. digestion.

4. The ability of an organism to maintain constant conditions within the body is called
a. irritability. c. metabolism.
b. homeostasis. d. stimulus.

5. The branch of biology concerned with animal behavior is
a. microbiology. c. botany.
b. zoology. d. ethology.

6. To observe the surface features of a bacterium, you would use a
a. compound light microscope.
b. scanning electron microscope.
c. magnifying lens.
d. transmission electron microscope.

7. To observe living organisms in a drop of water, you would use a
a. compound light microscope.
b. scanning electron microscope.
c. magnifying lens.
d. transmission electron microscope.

8. To observe the internal features of a bacterium, you would use a
a. compound light microscope.
b. scanning electron microscope.
c. magnifying lens.
d. transmission electron microscope.

True or False

Determine whether each statement is true or false. If it is true, write "true." If it is false, change the underlined word or words to make the statement true.

1. <u>Few</u> cells can perform all the functions we associate with life.

2. Plants obtain their energy from sunlight in a process called <u>metabolism</u>.

3. <u>Stimuli</u> include heat, light, pressure, and temperature.

4. Pipettes are used to transfer <u>solids</u> from one container to another.

5. The lens at the top of a compound light microscope is called the <u>objective</u> lens.

6. Compound light microscopes are used to observe <u>living</u> organisms.

7. In a <u>transmission electron microscope</u>, the image is magnified onto a fluorescent screen at the bottom of the microscope.

8. Surface features of very small organisms are best viewed using a <u>dark field microscope</u>.

Word Relationships

In each of the following sets of terms, three of the terms are related. One term does not belong. Determine the characteristic common to three of the terms and then identify the term that does not belong.

1. unicellular, multicellular, cell wall, single-celled
2. temperature, pressure, irritability, gravity
3. zoology, botany, chemistry, ecology
4. ocular lens, electron beam, objective lens, glass slide
5. SEM, compound light microscope, limit of resolution, TEM

CONCEPT MASTERY

Use your understanding of the concepts developed in the chapter to answer each of the following in a brief paragraph.

1. List and describe the basic characteristics of living things.
2. Compare sexual reproduction with asexual reproduction.
3. What is irritability? Give three examples of a stimulus and a possible response in humans.
4. Discuss the importance of cell-staining techniques in the study of living things.
5. Describe the way a transmission electron microscope produces an image.
6. No one microscope is better than another. Each type has an important role to play in biological research. Do you agree or disagree with these statements? Explain your answer.

CRITICAL AND CREATIVE THINKING

Discuss each of the following in a brief paragraph.

1. **Relating concepts** Why is biology considered a science?
2. **Making generalizations** List the attributes you think scientists should possess in order to be successful in their work.
3. **Applying concepts** How would you decide if an object were living or not?
4. **Making inferences** Why might biologists consider metabolism to be the single most important characteristic of life?
5. **Relating cause and effect** An organism's response to a stimulus can be a method of protection. How do these 3 stimuli-response situations protect the organism?
   a. Pulling a hand away from a hot iron
   b. Squinting in a bright light
   c. Producing tears if dirt gets in the eyes
6. **Making comparisons** Compare the growth of an icicle with the growth of a living thing.
7. **Identifying relationships** Which characteristic of living things is important to the survival of the species rather than to the organism itself? Explain your answer.
8. **Using the writing process** You are a biologist and have the opportunity to travel back in time to study an extinct species of your choice. You may take just one modern tool for your study. Which tool would you choose and why?
9. **Using the writing process** If microscopes could talk, what stories would they tell? Write a microscope story. (*Hint:* First decide if you are a compound light microscope or an electron microscope.)

CHAPTER 3

Introduction to Chemistry

An understanding of life—in all its glorious forms—depends upon an understanding of the atomic nature of matter.

For many years, biology was a science that respected a fundamental distinction between the living and the nonliving worlds. Biologists studied organisms; physicists and chemists studied materials. In the twentieth century, however, this distinction has begun to fade. Biologists have gradually realized that a complete description of life must begin at the atomic level and then work up through the complex chemistry of the living cell. Indeed, one of the great scientific stories of this century is the manner in which the boundaries between biology and the physical sciences have become blurred. Biologists now appreciate that the starting point for an understanding of the nature of life is an understanding of the atom. In this chapter, you will do exactly as biologists have done—you will learn about the atomic structure of living and nonliving matter.

CHAPTER OUTLINE

3–1 Nature of Matter

Section Objectives

- Identify several important properties of matter.
- Compare physical and chemical properties.

What are living things made of? Are there special substances that are found in living things but not in nonliving material? Is there a special "spirit" or "essence" that living things possess? Does life have a physical and chemical basis that we can hope to understand and describe in the same way we do something that is not alive, like an automobile engine or a calculator? To answer these questions, we must first examine the world around us . . . a world made up of matter and energy.

Properties of Matter

Matter is all around us. Almost everything we see, touch, taste, or smell is matter. And all forms of matter have properties, or characteristics, by which they are identified.

Certain properties of matter are **physical properties**. Two very important physical properties are used by scientists to define matter: Matter is anything that has mass and volume. Mass is the quantity of matter in an object. Volume is the amount of space matter takes up.

Mass is related to another important property of matter: weight. An object has weight because it has mass, but mass and weight are not the same thing. Weight is a measure of the force of gravity on an object. The greater the mass of an object, the greater the force of gravity on it, and the greater its weight. Thus we can say that the weight of an object is directly proportional to its mass.

Figure 3–1 *The physical properties of matter are often all you need to observe in order to tell substances apart. Because of their physical properties, the rose and the cactus are easily distinguishable.*

Figure 3–2 What physical properties would you use to distinguish coal from sugar? Do these two substances have any physical properties in common?

Matter has other physical properties. These include color, odor, shape, texture, taste, and hardness. You know from experience that a lump of coal has a certain color, texture, and hardness. A lump of sugar has a different color, texture, and hardness. It even has a special taste. Two other important physical properties are melting point and boiling point. **Physical properties of matter can be observed and measured without permanently changing the identity of the matter.**

Matter has **chemical properties** also. **Chemical properties describe a substance's ability to change into another new substance as a result of a chemical change.** A chemical change is a process in which a substance is permanently altered. When a chemical change is completed, it is difficult, if not impossible, to reverse the process and get the starting material back. When coal burns, it undergoes a chemical change with oxygen to form other gases. Once a lump of coal has burned, it is no longer coal. And the gases produced cannot be converted back to coal. The chemical properties of a substance are determined by learning what sorts of chemical reactions the substance can undergo.

Phases of Matter

Ice, liquid water, and water vapor may seem very different to you. Certainly they have different appearances and uses. But actually they are all made of exactly the same substance in different states. These states are called **phases**. Phase is an important physical property of matter. Ice is the solid phase of water. Liquid water is the liquid phase. And water vapor is the gas phase.

The change from one phase of matter to another is a physical change because the substance is not altered. Water, regardless of its phase, is still water. Physical and chemical changes

Figure 3–3 Chemical properties describe how a substance changes into other new substances as a result of a chemical change. What chemical changes can you identify in these photographs of a rusty nut and bolt (left), a fireworks display (center), and a delicious meal grilling on the barbecue (right)?

are common in the world around us. And because living things, including ourselves, are made of matter, an understanding of these physical and chemical changes is important to biology.

Figure 3–4 Phase is an important physical property of matter. Here you see water in its three phases: solid, liquid, and gas.

3–1 SECTION REVIEW

1. Define the following terms: mass, weight, volume.
2. Compare a physical property and a chemical property. A physical change and a chemical change.
3. Using a piece of paper as an example, distinguish between the physical and chemical properties of matter.

3–2 Composition of Matter

Section Objectives

- Describe the structure of an atom.
- Compare elements and compounds.
- Discuss the uses of radioactive isotopes.

Nearly 3000 years ago, the Greek philosopher Democritus challenged his students with a series of questions regarding the nature of matter. He picked up a small piece of salt, divided it into two fragments, and asked his students if each half was still salt. They said it was, and Democritus agreed. Could each half, he then asked, be divided into smaller and smaller pieces forever? Or was there a limit to the number of times a piece of matter could be divided? Democritus surprised his students with this novel idea by further arguing that there must be a tiny elementary particle that one could no longer divide and still call salt. He believed that all forms of matter were made up of basic, indivisible particles. He called these elementary particles **atoms**. The word atom comes from the Greek word *atomos*, meaning unable to be cut.

The approach of Democritus was philosophical rather than experimental. In part, this means that he was content to think about the problem but go no further. Scientists, however, must go further. They will speculate much as Democritus did, but then they will think of a way to test their ideas in an experiment. In the last 200 years, scientists have carefully studied Democritus' concept of the atomic nature of matter and have concluded that he was basically right. We now know that matter is indeed made up of small particles—not because it makes philosophical sense but because the evidence proves it. But we also now know that the atom itself is divisible and that particles smaller than the atom do exist!

Figure 3–5 This photograph of uranium atoms was taken with a scanning transmission electron microscope (STEM). The small dots are individual atoms. The larger patches are clusters of 2 to 20 atoms.

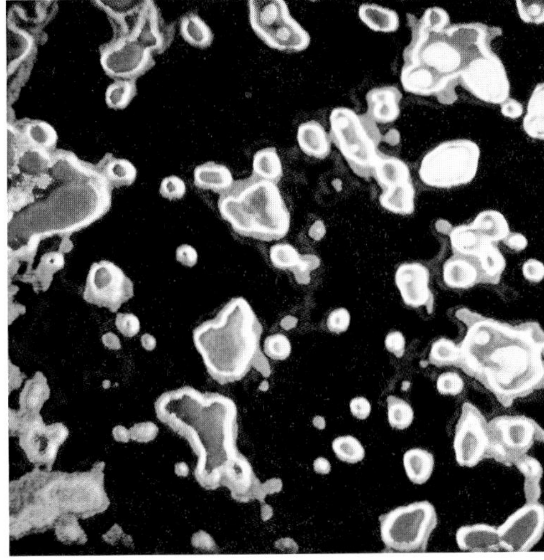

The Atom

The basic unit of matter is the atom. Atoms are very, very small. Indeed, 100 million atoms placed side by side would form a row only 1 centimeter long—about the width of your pinky! Despite its extremely small size, the atom contains many

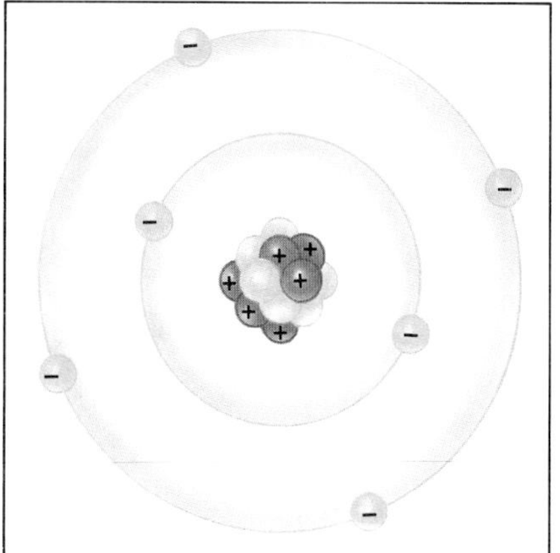

Figure 3–6 This artist's conception of an atom shows the nucleus, with its protons and neutrons, and the series of energy levels, with their electrons, that surround it (top). The illustration shows an atom of the element carbon (bottom).

smaller particles, known as subatomic particles. Scientists know about the existence of at least 200 different kinds of subatomic particles. The three principal subatomic particles are the proton, neutron, and electron.

ATOMIC STRUCTURE The center of the atom is called the **nucleus**. Although the nucleus is about a hundred thousand times smaller than the entire atom, it makes up 99.9 percent of the mass of the atom. The nucleus contains two different kinds of subatomic particles held together by special atomic forces. One of these particles is the **proton**. The proton is a positively charged particle. The other particle found in the nucleus is the **neutron**. The neutron is an electrically neutral particle. It has no charge at all. The proton and neutron are nearly equal in mass (1 atomic mass unit, or amu).

In addition to protons and neutrons, the atom contains another kind of subatomic particle called the **electron**. The electron is a negatively charged particle with a mass about 2000 times less than that of either the proton or neutron (1/1836 amu). Under normal circumstances, the number of negatively charged electrons in an atom is equal to the number of positively charged protons. Therefore, the atom as a whole is neutral; it is neither negatively nor positively charged.

Electrons are not found in the nucleus. They travel at high speeds throughout the atom in a series of distinct **energy levels**, or orbits, that surround the nucleus. The existence of electrons in distinct energy levels is very important in determining the chemical properties of an atom, as you will learn shortly.

ATOMIC NUMBER AND MASS NUMBER The number of protons in the nucleus of an atom is called the **atomic number**. The atomic number identifies an atom. Atoms of the same substance have the same atomic number. But atoms of different substances have different atomic numbers. Thus the atomic number of an atom of a substance is a unique quantity. An atom of hydrogen, which has only 1 proton, has an atomic number of 1. All hydrogen atoms—but only hydrogen atoms—have an atomic number of 1. Helium, with 2 protons in the nucleus of

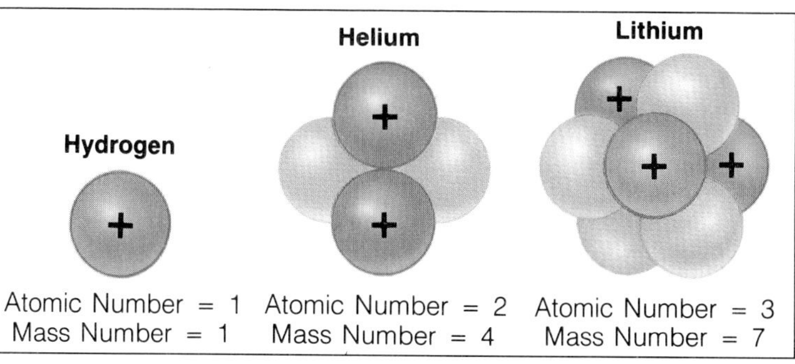

Figure 3–7 The nuclei of hydrogen, helium, and lithium atoms all contain protons. Those of helium and lithium atoms also contain neutrons. Yet hydrogen, helium, and lithium are very different elements. Why?

every atom, has an atomic number of 2. Uranium has an atomic number of 92. How many protons are in a uranium atom?

Although all subatomic particles contribute to the mass of an atom, protons and neutrons are much more massive than electrons. This explains why most of the mass of an atom is concentrated in the nucleus. Scientists often refer to the total number of protons and neutrons in the nucleus as the **mass number**. Hydrogen has a mass number of 1 because the only particle in the nucleus of a hydrogen atom is a proton. A helium atom has 2 protons and 2 neutrons in the nucleus. So the mass number of helium is 4.

Chemical Elements

As you read before, every substance in the world is made up of atoms. **Some substances, known as elements, consist entirely of one type of atom**. At present, scientists have identified 109 different **elements**. Of these 109 elements, 90 types are found in nature. The remaining 19 have been artificially produced by physicists using very special laboratory equipment. Each element can be represented by a chemical symbol. A chemical symbol is a shorthand way of representing an element. Each symbol consists of one or two letters, usually taken from the element's name. For example, the symbol for the element iodine is I. The symbol for hydrogen is H; for carbon, C. Scientists often use the Latin name of an element to create its symbol. For example, the symbol for lead is Pb, from the Latin word *plumbus*. You may recognize that word as the source for the English word plumbing, reflecting the fact that water pipes were once made of lead. Figure 3–8 lists some common elements and their symbols.

Most of the chemical elements are solids. Common examples include carbon, sulfur, phosphorus, sodium, calcium, and potassium. Some elements—such as oxygen, nitrogen, and chlorine—are gases. Only a few elements are liquids. Mercury and bromine are the most common examples.

ISOTOPES As you read, each element has an atomic number that is determined by the number of protons in the nucleus of its atoms. The atomic number of an element never changes. This means that the number of protons in the nucleus of every atom of the element is always the same. However, the number of neutrons can vary from one atom of the element to the next. For example, the most common form of hydrogen has 1 proton and no neutrons in its nucleus. Another form of hydrogen, sometimes known as deuterium, has 1 proton and 1 neutron in its nucleus. And a third form, tritium, has 1 proton and 2 neutrons in its nucleus. Although they have different mass numbers, each form of hydrogen has an atomic number of 1, a single proton in the nucleus, and a single electron. Each form is hydrogen. Atoms of the same element that have the

ELEMENTS IN THE HUMAN BODY

Element	Symbol	Mass (%)
Oxygen	O	65.0
Carbon	C	18.5
Hydrogen	H	9.5
Nitrogen	N	3.3
Phosphorus	P	1.0
Sulfur	S	0.3
Sodium	Na	0.2
Magnesium	Mg	0.1
Silicon	Si	trace
Fluorine	F	trace

Figure 3–8 *This chart shows some of the elements in the human body, their symbol, and their percentage by mass. Which element makes up the greatest percentage? Which elements are found in only trace quantities?*

Figure 3–9 The three isotopes of hydrogen are protium, deuterium, and tritium. Which isotope contains 2 neutrons? What is the atomic number of each isotope?

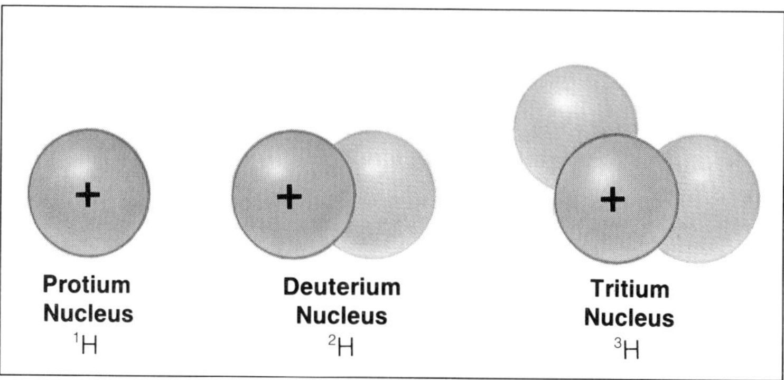

same number of protons but different numbers of neutrons are known as **isotopes** of that element.

Isotopes of an element are represented by adding the number that indicates the mass number of that isotope to the atomic symbol. Thus, ordinary hydrogen is ^{1}H, deuterium is ^{2}H, and tritium is ^{3}H.

RADIOACTIVE ISOTOPES The nuclei of some atoms are unstable and will from time to time break down, releasing matter and/or energy that we call radiation. Atoms that emit radiation are said to be radioactive. Many elements have at least one radioactive isotope. All the isotopes of elements with atomic numbers greater than 83 are radioactive.

Figure 3–10 Radioactive isotopes can be used as tracer elements to produce images such as this axial section through a normal brain (top) and this image of the heart (bottom).

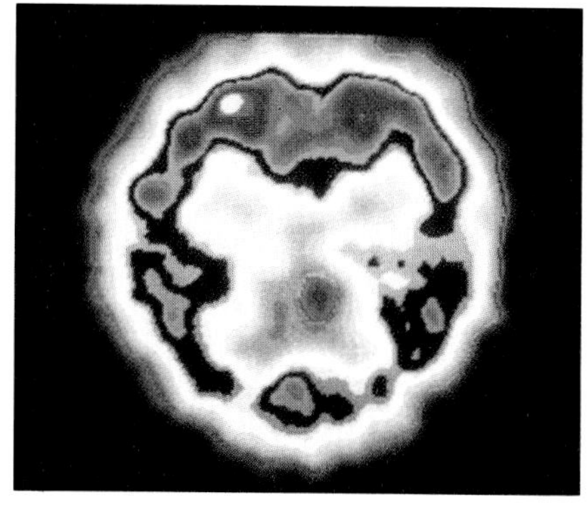

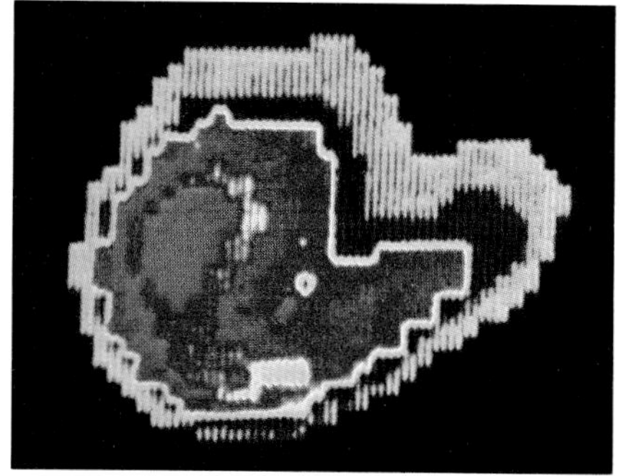

Radioactive isotopes have many practical uses. They are used to study living organisms, to diagnose and treat diseases, to sterilize foods, and to measure the ages of certain rocks.

Radioactive isotopes are frequently used as tracers. A tracer is a radioactive element whose pathway through the steps of a chemical reaction can be followed. An example of a tracer is phosphorus-32.

The nonradioactive element phosphorus is used in small amounts by both plants and animals. If phosphorus-32 is given to an organism, the organism will use the radioactive phosphorus just as it does the nonradioactive phosphorus. However, the path of the radioactive element can be traced, allowing scientists to learn how plants and animals use phosphorus.

Tracers are extremely valuable in diagnosing diseases. Radioactive iodine, iodine-131, can be used to study the function of the thyroid gland, which absorbs iodine. Sodium-24 can be used to detect diseases of the circulatory system. Iron-59 can be used to study blood circulation.

Radioactive isotopes are also used to treat certain diseases. When administered carefully and in the proper amounts, radiation can kill cancer cells with minimal damage to healthy tissue. Cobalt-60 is used extensively in cancer radiation treatments. Carbon-14 has been used to treat brain tumors.

Radioactive isotopes can also be used to kill bacteria that cause food to spoil. Radiation is used to preserve the food that astronauts eat while on the moon and in orbit.

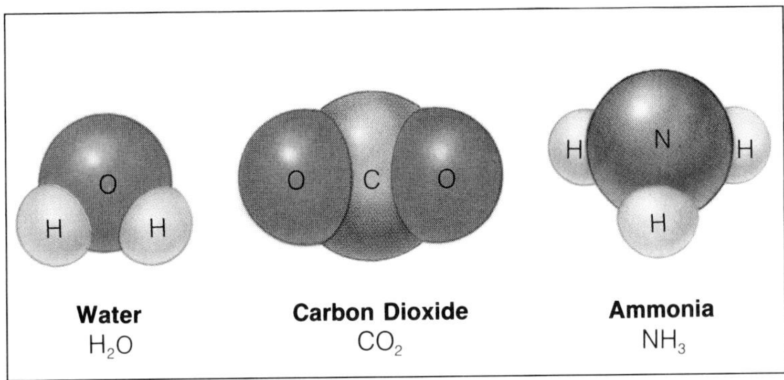

Figure 3–11 *As you can see from this diagram, compounds are made of two or more different atoms combined in definite proportions. The chemical formula for each compound indicates the elements that make up the compound and the number of atoms of each element.*

Another use of radioactive isotopes is in measuring the ages of certain rocks and the fossils they may contain. This use has increased our understanding of the evolution of life on Earth.

One of the difficulties in using radioactive materials is that these substances must be handled with great care. Radiation can damage or kill living things. So it is important that proper safety precautions be taken whenever radioactive isotopes are used. And it is also important that you be aware of and concerned about radioactive materials in the environment.

Chemical Compounds

When elements combine to form substances consisting of two or more different atoms, chemical compounds are produced. A chemical **compound** involves the combination of two or more different atoms in definite proportions. Most materials in the living world are compounds.

Just as elements are represented by chemical symbols, so too are compounds represented by a kind of shorthand. A chemical compound is represented by a chemical formula. A chemical formula consists of the chemical symbols for the elements that make up the compound. Water, which contains 2 atoms of hydrogen and 1 atom of oxygen, has the chemical formula H_2O. Table salt, made of sodium and chlorine, has the formula NaCl. What elements are present in the compound sulfuric acid, whose chemical formula is H_2SO_4?

3–2 SECTION REVIEW

1. Describe the structure of an atom. What is meant by atomic number? Mass number?
2. What is an element? How are elements represented?
3. What is an isotope? What are some uses of radioactive isotopes?
4. How is a compound different from an element?

Section Objectives

- Explain how electron arrangement determines an atom's reactivity.
- Describe the two types of chemical bonds.

3–3 Interactions of Matter

Chemical compounds are formed by the interactions of individual atoms. These interactions involve the combining of atoms of elements in a process known as **chemical bonding**. Chemical bonds are formed in very definite ways. The atoms combine according to certain rules. Such rules are determined by the number of electrons that surround the atomic nucleus—more specifically, the electrons found in the outermost energy level.

Each energy level in an atom can hold only a certain number of electrons. The first, or innermost, energy level can hold only 2 electrons. The second energy level can hold 8 electrons, as can the third when it is an outermost energy level. Figure 3–12 illustrates the arrangement of electrons in the first three energy levels.

When the outermost energy level of an atom contains the maximum number of electrons, the level is full, or complete. Atoms that have filled outermost energy levels are very stable, or unreactive. Such atoms usually do not combine with other atoms to form compounds. They do not form chemical bonds.

In order to achieve stability, an atom will either gain, lose, or share electrons. In other words, an atom will bond with another atom if the bonding gives both atoms complete outermost energy levels.

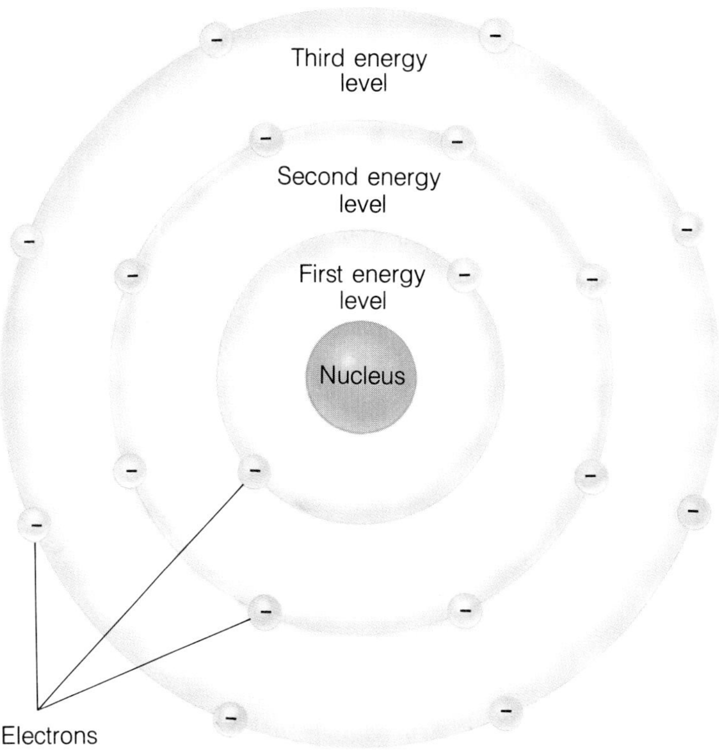

Figure 3–12 *Each energy level in an atom can hold only a certain number of electrons. When the outermost energy level is holding its maximum number of electrons, it is complete, and the atom is stable.*

Ionic Bonds

One way a complete outermost energy level can be achieved is by the transfer of electrons from one atom to another. A bond that involves a transfer of electrons is called an **ionic bond**. An ionic bond, or electron-transfer bond, gets its name from the word **ion**, which means charged particle. Ions are formed when an ionic bond occurs.

A sodium atom has only 1 electron in its outermost energy level, so it can lose that electron very easily. The loss of an electron from a sodium atom produces a sodium ion (Na^+), which has a positive charge. Similarly, chlorine needs only 1 electron to fill its outermost energy level, so it grabs an extra electron easily—possibly from a nearby sodium atom. The addition of an electron to a chlorine atom produces a negatively charged chloride ion (Cl^-). These two ions, now oppositely charged, have a strong attraction for each other—much like opposite poles of a magnet. The strong attraction between oppositely charged ions that have been formed by the transfer of electrons holds the ions together in an ionic bond.

Covalent Bonds

A chemical bond formed by the sharing of electrons is known as a **covalent bond**. By sharing electrons, each atom

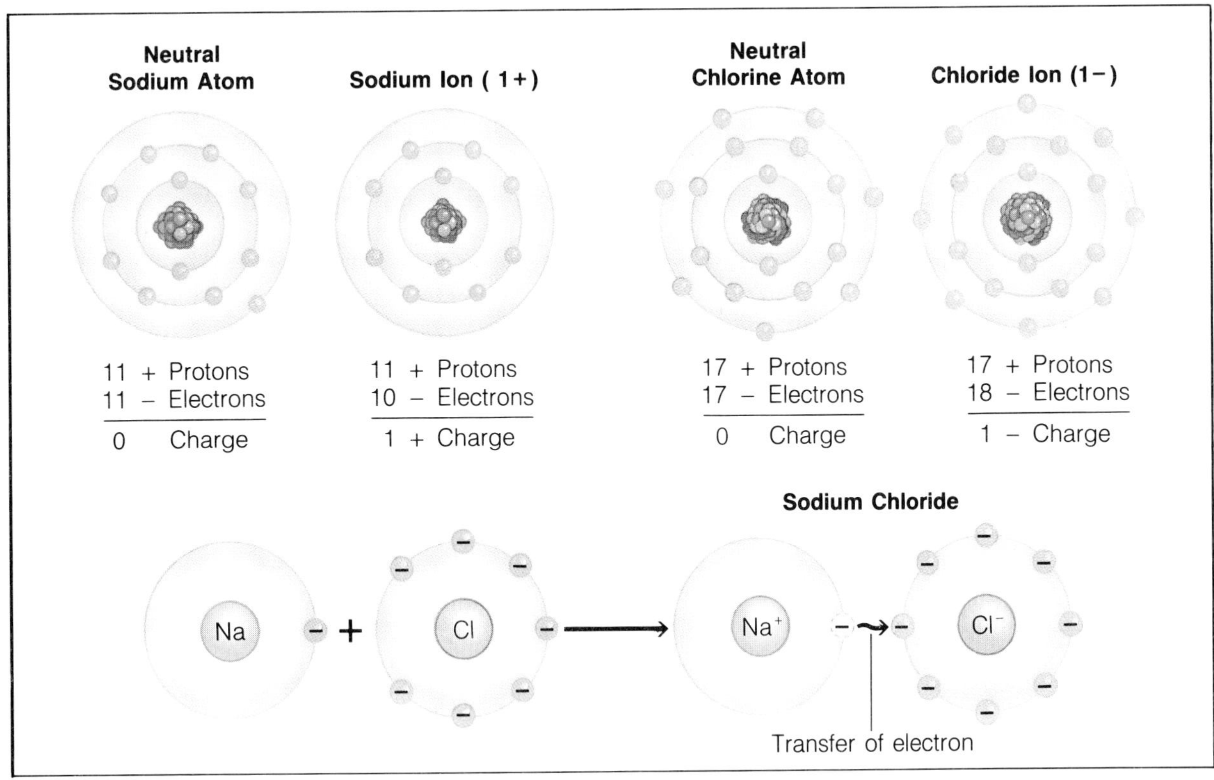

Figure 3–13 *The formation of a positive sodium ion involves the loss of an electron by a sodium atom. The formation of a negative chloride ion involves the gain of an electron by a chlorine atom. The transfer of an electron produces oppositely charged ions that are strongly attracted and held together in an ionic bond. Because only the electrons in the outermost energy level are involved in bonding, only this level has been shown in the bottom diagram.*

fills up its outermost energy level. So the shared electrons are in the outermost energy level of both atoms at the same time. This produces a strong bond that is characteristic of most of the chemicals found in living organisms.

Covalent bonds can be single, double, or triple, depending on the number of electrons that are shared in the bond. The covalent bond between hydrogen and oxygen in water (H_2O) is a single bond. A single pair of electrons is shared between the oxygen atom and each of the 2 hydrogen atoms. In the compound carbon dioxide (CO_2), the carbon atom shares two pairs of electrons, or a total of 4 electrons, with each of the oxygen atoms in the compound. The carbon-oxygen bond in carbon dioxide is a double bond.

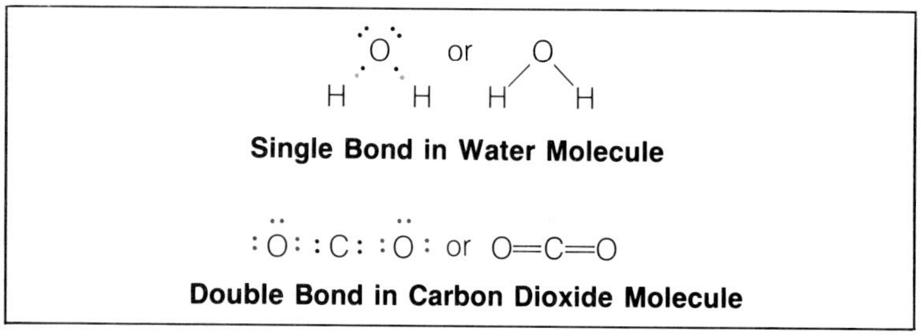

Figure 3–14 *The bonding in molecules can be represented by electron-dot formulas and by structural formulas. An electron-dot formula shows the electron pairs involved in the bonding. A single bond involves one pair of electrons; a double bond involves two. In a structural formula, a dash (–) is used to represent a pair of shared electrons, or a single bond. How is a double bond represented?*

$$H\!:\!\ddot{\underset{\cdot\cdot}{O}}\!:\!H \quad \text{or} \quad H{-}O{-}H$$

Single Bond in Water Molecule

$$:\ddot{O}::C::\ddot{O}: \quad \text{or} \quad O{=}C{=}O$$

Double Bond in Carbon Dioxide Molecule

In a covalent bond, a relatively small number of atoms are involved in the sharing of electrons. The combination of atoms that results forms a separate unit called a **molecule**. A molecule is the smallest particle of a covalently bonded compound. In addition to water and carbon dioxide, some other common covalent compounds are sugar ($C_6H_{12}O_6$) and ammonia (NH_3).

Regardless of the type of bond formed, atoms change their physical and chemical properties when they form a compound. For example, sodium is a silvery metal that reacts explosively with water. Chlorine is a poisonous greenish gas, which was responsible for the deaths of many soldiers in World War I. Neither element in its pure form can be used by your body. Yet they combine to form sodium chloride (NaCl), or table salt, a solid that dissolves easily in water, is not poisonous, and is essential to most living things. It also tastes great on a pretzel!

Figure 3–15 *A covalent bond involves the sharing of electrons. How many double bonds are there in a molecule of carbon dioxide?*

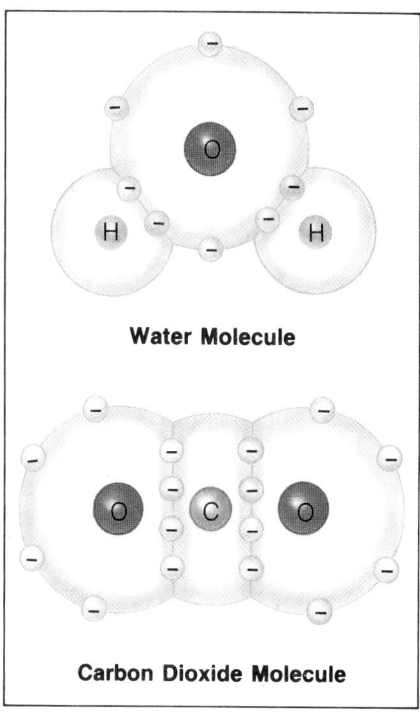

3–3 SECTION REVIEW

1. Describe the arrangement of electrons in the first three energy levels.
2. Compare an ionic bond to a covalent bond.
3. An oxygen atom has 6 electrons in its outermost energy level. A hydrogen atom has 1. Describe how the covalent bonds in the water molecule enable each atom to achieve a complete outermost energy level and, therefore, stability.

SCIENCE, TECHNOLOGY, AND SOCIETY BREAKTHROUGH

A Do-It-Yourself Poison

Each year they cause more than $5 billion in damage to crops and livestock. They are a threat to human health because they can transmit certain diseases. And in order to eliminate them, poisonous substances that may endanger our health as well as the health of our environment must be used. What are these pests who have created economic, environmental, and safety problems? Insects!

Farmers and gardeners use insecticides to protect their plants and animals against insects. Insecticides are compounds that kill insects in a variety of ways. Some kill insects that eat the chemical compounds. Others kill insects upon contact. Certain insecticides produce lethal vapors and gases. Still others kill by infecting insects with deadly diseases.

Although many insecticides are effective in the battles against insect infestation, they often have profound effects on the environment and other living things. Until recently, people had to balance the benefits of insecticide use against possible damage to planet Earth. Now a new class of insecticides that affect only their target and pose little danger to us has been developed.

Scientists working at the State University of New York at Stony Brook combined polysterols—special compounds manufactured by plants—with the element fluorine to produce a new group of compounds called 29-fluorophytosterols. These compounds are harmless to most organisms—ourselves included! But inside an insect's body, special chemicals called enzymes can act on the fluorophytosterols and break them down to produce fluoroacetate, a deadly poison. For insects unfortunate enough to have the special enzymes, this new class of insecticide spells doom!

In and of themselves, 29-fluorophytosterols are harmless, presenting little danger to most living things. But the chemical composition and bodily processes of insects render these compounds deadly! By applying a knowledge of basic chemistry to the workings of living systems, scientists were able to develop exactly the compound they sought: a safe and effective insecticide.

3–4 Chemical Reactions

Section Objectives

- Identify the substances involved in a chemical reaction.
- Describe the role of energy in chemical reactions.

You have learned that two types of bonds can exist between atoms and that compounds with different chemical and physical properties can be formed by the transfer or sharing of electrons. Whenever a chemical bond is formed, a chemical change takes place. Any process in which a chemical change occurs is known as a **chemical reaction**.

Chemical reactions occur all the time and are very much a part of your daily life. Some chemical reactions occur slowly, such as the combination of iron and oxygen to form rust. Others occur quickly. When hydrogen gas is ignited in the presence of oxygen, the reaction is rapid and explosive.

In any chemical reaction there are always two kinds of substances: the substances that are present before the change and the substances that are formed by the change. The elements or

Figure 3–16 *Chemical reactions are many and varied. Here you see two examples: the heating of ammonium dichromate (top) and the decaying of apples (bottom). A chemical reaction always involves a change in the properties and in the energy of the substances involved.*

compounds that enter into a chemical reaction are known as reactants. The elements or compounds produced by a chemical reaction are known as products.

A chemical reaction can be described by using a shorthand method known as a chemical equation. In a chemical equation, symbols and formulas are used to represent reactants and products. And an arrow, which is read "yields," shows the direction of the reaction. Let us use the chemical reaction involving the combination of hydrogen and oxygen to form water to illustrate a chemical equation.

$$\underset{\text{oxygen}}{O_2} + \underset{\text{hydrogen}}{2H_2} \rightarrow \underset{\text{water}}{2H_2O}$$

Chemical reactions are reversible. In principle, any chemical reaction can run in either direction. For example, it is possible for the reaction we have just described to run in reverse.

$$\underset{\text{water}}{2H_2O} \rightarrow \underset{\text{oxygen}}{O_2} + \underset{\text{hydrogen}}{2H_2}$$

This generally does not occur however. Why? Because there is an important difference between the two chemical reactions. When oxygen gas and hydrogen gas burn to form water vapor, an enormous amount of energy is released in the form of heat, light, and sound. But water, on the other hand, does not spontaneously decompose to form hydrogen gas and oxygen gas. In fact, the only convenient way to drive the reaction in this direction is to run an electric current through the water to decompose it. Thus, in one direction the reaction produces energy; in the other direction, it requires energy.

Chemists have learned that the most important factor in determining whether a reaction will occur is the flow of energy. Chemical reactions that release energy will occur spontaneously. Chemical reactions that require energy will not occur without a source of energy.

What significance does this have for you and the other living things that share your world? All living things carry on both kinds of reactions in order to stay alive. The energy needed to grow tall, to read, to think, and even to dream comes from chemical reactions that occur in your body when you digest the food you eat. In the following chapters, you will explore these reactions and the flow of energy necessary for life.

3–4 SECTION REVIEW

1. What is a chemical reaction? A chemical equation?
2. What is a reactant? A product?
3. Describe the role of energy in chemical reactions.
4. Why is it important that energy-absorbing and energy-releasing reactions take place in living things?

PROBLEM SOLVING IN BIOLOGY

STRUCTURAL FORMULAS

Molecules are too small to be seen, yet we draw their pictures anyway. The reason for doing this is simple: In living things, a great many important things happen at the molecular level, and we need a way of representing these events. How shall we draw these pictures of molecules? And once drawn, what do they mean? Let's begin by considering glucose, a simple sugar.

One way to represent glucose is to write its molecular formula:

$$C_6H_{12}O_6$$

This formula tells us how many atoms of each element are in a molecule of glucose. But it does not indicate how the atoms are arranged. To do that, we need to draw a structural formula for the glucose molecule:

```
        H
        |
    H—C—OH
        |
        C————O
  H   / |      \   H
  |  /  H       \  |
  C                C
  | \  OH    H  /  |
 OH  \  |    | /   OH
        C————C
        |    |
        H    OH
```

Chemists often try to simplify structural formulas. One way of doing this is to leave nearly all of the carbons out of the picture. However, everybody knows they're still there! Now the molecule looks like this:

```
        CH2OH
        |
       /————O
  H   / |     \   H
  |  /  H      \  |
  |                |
  | \  OH    H  /  |
 HO  \  |    | /   OH
        |————|
        |    |
        H    OH
```

Sometimes chemists draw the same molecule in an even simpler fashion, like this:

```
      CH2OH
      |
      /————O
     /      \
    |        |
     \      /
      ————
          |
```

Each drawing is useful because it provides important information. For example, we can see that the glucose molecule is folded to form a ring and that the -OH groups (hydroxyl groups) project from one side or the other of that ring into space. None of the structural formulas, however, actually looks like a real molecule of glucose:

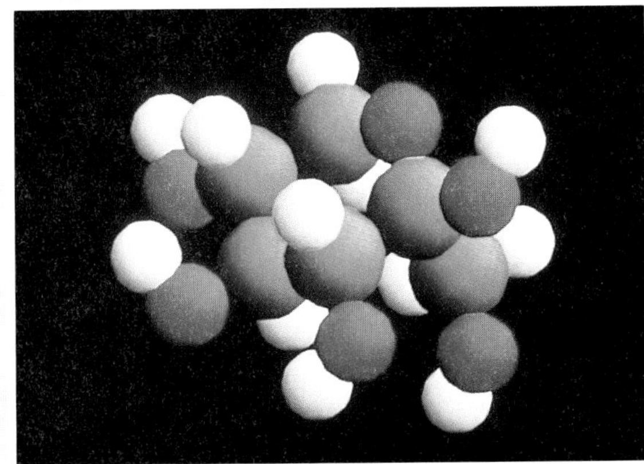

The key idea to remember about chemical formulas and structural formulas is that they are representations. Representations are useful and informative. They help us to visualize things that are hard to explain.

Now try your hand at drawing structural formulas for the following compounds: CH_4 methane; CCl_2F_2 Freon; $C_2H_4(OH)_2$ ethylene glycol or antifreeze; C_2H_6 ethane.

LABORATORY INVESTIGATION

IDENTIFYING ELEMENTS BY DENSITY

PROBLEM

How do the densities of different elements compare?

MATERIALS *(per group)*

aluminum metal
zinc metal
unknown metal sample
graduated cylinder
balance

PROCEDURE 

1. Density is mass per unit volume. In this laboratory investigation, you will measure the density of two elements, zinc and aluminum. Copy the data table shown below onto a separate sheet of paper to record your observations.
2. Using a balance, measure the mass of a small sample of aluminum metal (about 40 g). Record the mass in the data table.
3. Measure the volume of the aluminum metal using the following procedure: Fill a 100-mL graduated cylinder halfway with water and record the initial volume in your data table. Put the aluminum metal into the graduated cylinder. This will cause the water level to rise. Record the final volume of water. Find the volume of the aluminum by subtracting the initial volume of the water from the final volume of the water. Record the result.
4. Calculate the density of the aluminum by dividing the aluminum's mass by its volume: $D = M/V$. Record the result.
5. Find the density of a small sample of zinc metal by measuring its mass and volume according to the same procedure you used for aluminum.
6. Measure the density of an unknown sample of metal. Use your results to determine whether the unknown metal is aluminum or zinc.

OBSERVATIONS

1. How do the densities of aluminum and zinc compare?
2. What are some observable properties of aluminum and zinc?

ANALYSIS AND CONCLUSIONS

1. Is the unknown metal aluminum or zinc? How do you know?
2. Is density a physical or a chemical property? How can you tell?
3. Can density be used to help identify elements? Explain your answer.

Element	Mass (g)	Volume (mL)			Density (g/mL)
		Initial	Final	Metal	
Aluminum					
Zinc					
Unknown					

STUDENT STUDY GUIDE

SUMMARIZING THE CONCEPTS

The key concepts in each section of this chapter are listed below to help you review the chapter content. Make sure you understand each concept and its relationship to other concepts and to the theme of this chapter.

3–1 Nature of Matter

- Two important properties—mass and volume—are used to define matter.
- Physical properties of matter can be observed and measured without permanently changing the identity of the matter. Chemical properties describe a substance's ability to change into another new substance as a result of a chemical change.

3–2 Composition of Matter

- The basic unit of matter is the atom. The nucleus of the atom contains positively charged protons and electrically neutral neutrons. Energy levels outside the nucleus contain negatively charged electrons.
- The number of protons in the nucleus of an atom is called the atomic number.
- Substances that consist entirely of one type of atom are called elements. Atoms of the same element that have the same number of protons but different numbers of neutrons are called isotopes.
- A chemical compound consists of two or more different atoms chemically combined in definite proportions.

3–3 Interactions of Matter

- The combining of atoms of elements is known as chemical bonding. An ionic bond involves a transfer of electrons between atoms. A covalent bond involves the sharing of electrons.

3–4 Chemical Reactions

- In any chemical reaction, reactants combine to yield products.
- Although chemical reactions are reversible in principle, they occur spontaneously only in the direction that produces energy.

REVIEWING KEY TERMS

Vocabulary terms are important to your understanding of biology. The key terms listed below are those you should be especially familiar with. Review these terms and their meanings. Then use each term in a complete sentence. If you are not sure of a term's meaning, return to the appropriate section and review the definition.

3–1 Nature of Matter
physical property
chemical property
phase

3-2 Composition of Matter
atom
nucleus
proton
neutron
electron
energy-level
atomic number
mass number
element
isotope
compound

3-3 Interactions of Matter
chemical bonding
ionic bond
ion
covalent bond
molecule

3-4 Chemical Reactions
chemical reaction

CHAPTER REVIEW

CONTENT REVIEW

Multiple Choice

Choose the letter of the answer that best completes each statement.

1. Substances that enter into a chemical reaction are known as
   a. reactants. c. products.
   b. catalysts. d. isotopes.
2. Two important physical properties used to define matter are
   a. taste and smell.
   b. mass and volume.
   c. weight and boiling point.
   d. mass and freezing point.
3. The nucleus of an atom contains
   a. electrons and protons.
   b. electrons and neutrons.
   c. protons, electrons, and neutrons.
   d. protons and neutrons.
4. A substance consisting of two or more different elements chemically combined is a(an)
   a. molecule.
   b. crystal.
   c. compound.
   d. isotope.
5. An atom with an atomic number of 8 has
   a. 8 protons.
   b. 4 protons plus 4 neutrons.
   c. 4 protons plus 4 electrons.
   d. 4 neutrons plus 4 electrons.
6. Which is true of carbon-12 and carbon-14?
   a. They have the same number of neutrons.
   b. They have the same number of protons.
   c. They have the same mass number.
   d. They are isotopes of different elements.
7. A shorthand way of representing an element is a chemical
   a. formula.
   b. reaction.
   c. property.
   d. symbol.
8. Radioactive isotopes are used
   a. as tracers.
   b. to diagnose disease.
   c. to treat disease.
   d. to do all of these.

True or False

Determine whether each statement is true or false. If it is true, write "true." If it is false, change the underlined word or words to make the statement true.

1. <u>Chemical properties</u> describe a substance's ability to undergo a chemical change.
2. The sharing of electrons is characteristic of <u>ionic</u> bonds.
3. Any process in which a chemical change occurs is known as a chemical <u>formula</u>.
4. The number of protons in the nucleus of an atom is called the <u>mass number</u>.
5. Chemical reactions that <u>absorb</u> energy will occur spontaneously.
6. The amount of space an object takes up is known as <u>weight</u>.
7. Atoms that have <u>complete</u> outermost energy levels are said to be very stable.
8. The positively charged subatomic particle is the <u>electron</u>.

Word Relationships

In each of the following sets of terms, three of the terms are related. One term does not belong. Determine the characteristic common to three of the terms and then identify the term that does not belong.

1. energy level, proton, nucleus, neutron
2. oxygen, sodium, carbon dioxide, mercury
3. solid, mass, liquid, gas
4. 2, second energy level, 8, third energy level
5. molecule, electron transfer, covalent bond, water
6. color, phase, ability to burn, texture
7. products, physical change, reactants, yields
8. Democritus, atom, divisible particle, Greek philosopher

CONCEPT MASTERY

Use your understanding of the concepts developed in the chapter to answer each of the following in a brief paragraph.

1. Describe two important differences between physical and chemical properties.
2. Identify each of the following changes as either a physical change or a chemical change:
   a. melting butter
   b. boiling water
   c. digesting food
   d. baking brownies
   e. exploding TNT
   f. dissolving sugar
   g. burning fuel oil
3. Describe the subatomic particles found in the atom. Be sure to include their charge, mass, and location in your description.
4. What is the atomic number of an element? What is its significance?
5. Nitrogen-14 and nitrogen-15 are isotopes of the element nitrogen. Describe how atoms of these isotopes differ from each other.
6. What is a radioactive isotope? Describe three uses of radioactive isotopes.

CRITICAL AND CREATIVE THINKING

Discuss each of the following in a brief paragraph.

1. **Relating facts** Explain why the use of radioactive isotopes has both advantages and disadvantages.
2. **Developing a model** Draw a diagram of the electron arrangement for the following elements based on their atomic number: lithium (3), carbon (6), fluorine (9), magnesium (12), phosphorus (15), argon (18).
3. **Identifying patterns** Explain why the element neon, with an atomic number of 10, is unreactive.
4. **Synthesizing concepts** Explain the role of energy in chemical reactions.
5. **Applying concepts** A basic principle of electricity is "like charges repel and opposite charges attract." How does the organization of particles in an atom illustrate this principle? How does it refute it?
6. **Using the writing process** The time is 3000 years ago. The Greek philosopher Democritus has proposed that all matter is made up of atoms. Write a brief speech supporting or refuting the concept of indivisible atoms.

CHAPTER 4

The Chemical Basis of Life

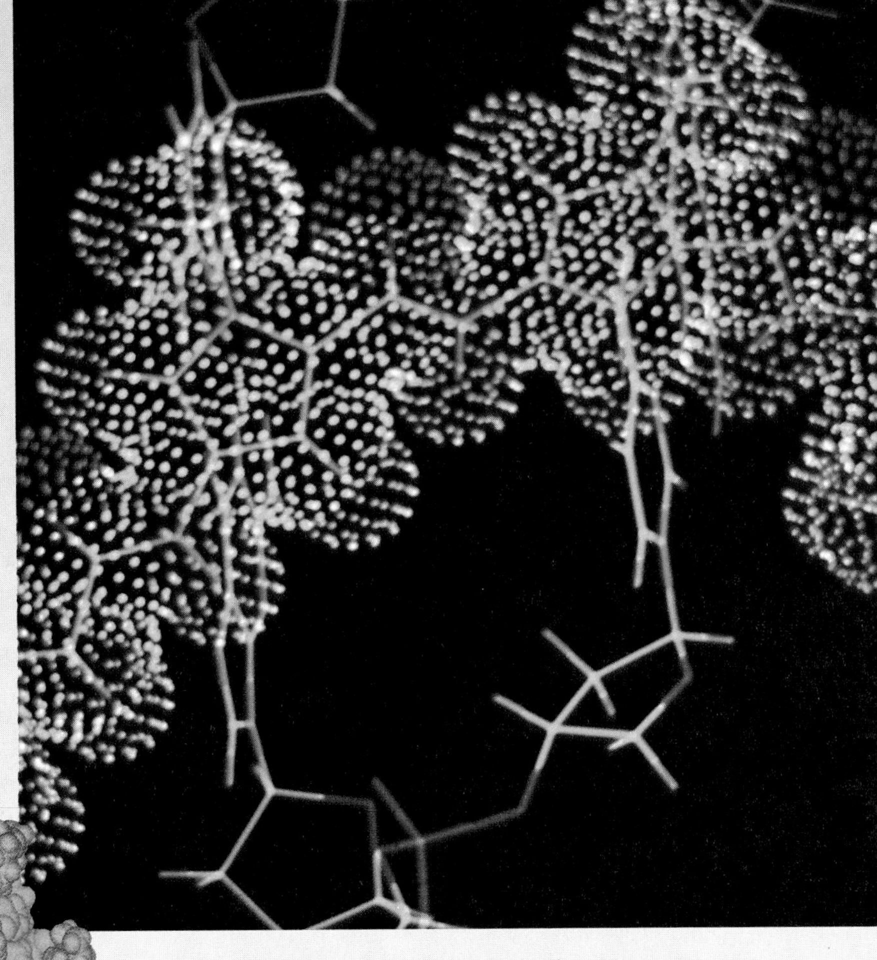

A variety of important chemical substances are combined in specific ways to produce protein molecules, which are among the basic compounds of life.

There are no special elements found in living things. In fact, the molecules that make up a living cell do not, in and of themselves, have the property of life. Yet there can be no doubt that certain elements organized into a variety of molecules do indeed account for life. How, you might ask, is this possible? In a way, we will spend the rest of this book searching for an answer, an answer that will remain incomplete in the end. For life itself is not completely understood. But we can begin. And one way to start is by understanding life not as the property of one particular molecule but as something made possible by a large group of molecules. In this chapter you will learn about the molecules that give life to you and to all other organisms on Earth.

CHAPTER OUTLINE

4–1 Water
- Mixtures
- Solutions
- Suspensions

4–2 Chemical Compounds in Living Things
- Inorganic Compounds
- Organic Compounds
- Polymerization

4–3 Compounds of Life
- Carbohydrates
- Lipids
- Proteins
- Enzymes
- Nucleic Acids

4–1 Water

Section Objectives

- List some important properties of water.
- Describe the nature of mixtures, solutions, and suspensions.
- Define acids, bases, neutralization, and pH scale.

Someone once said that if there is magic on this planet, then it is to be found in water. Water? To most of us, water is so ordinary that it is of little interest and certainly does not seem magical. Yet how wrong we are!

Water is one of the few naturally occurring compounds that is liquid at the temperatures found on much of the Earth's surface. Unlike most other materials, water expands slightly as it makes the phase change from liquid to solid. This explains why ice floats at the surfaces of lakes and rivers rather than sinking to the bottom—a situation that might be disastrous for fish and plant life, to say nothing of the sport of skating!

Water is a most unusual molecule, with physical and chemical properties found in no other material. Water covers more than 75 percent of the Earth's surface and is the most abundant compound in nearly all living organisms.

The most important property of the water molecule is that due to an uneven distribution of electrons, it is slightly

Figure 4–1 The importance of water to all living things cannot be denied—whether it's as a vital body fluid or as home to penguins in Antarctica. The Earth and its inhabitants cannot survive without water. Every attempt must be made to preserve this resource necessary to life.

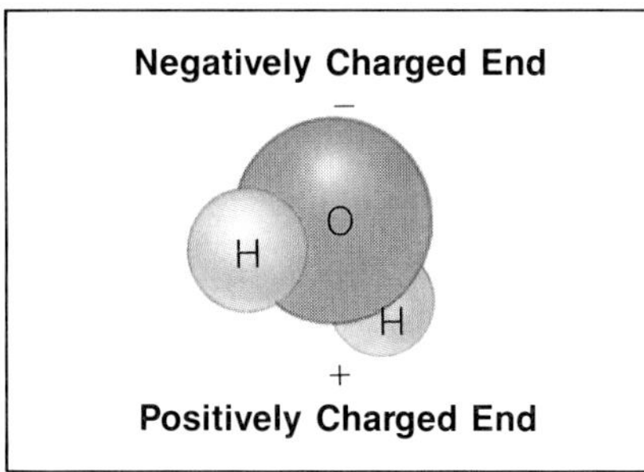

Figure 4–2 *The polarity of a water molecule explains why water is able to dissolve thousands of substances —whether they be ionically or covalently bonded. Which end of a water molecule is positive? Negative?*

charged on each end. See Figure 4–2. In this way, each water molecule is like a little magnet, with one pole near the nucleus of the oxygen atom and the other pole near the nuclei of the two hydrogen atoms. This polarity produces a strong attraction between individual water molecules and between water molecules and other charged molecules.

Mixtures

The slight charges of water molecules make them especially good at forming **mixtures**. A mixture is a substance composed of two or more elements or compounds that are mixed together but not chemically combined. Salt and pepper stirred together constitute a mixture. So do sugar and sand. Unlike chemical compounds, the substances that make up mixtures can be added in varying amounts and are not linked by chemical bonds.

Earth's atmosphere is a mixture of gases; soil is a mixture of individual solid particles; and living things are in part com-

Figure 4–3 *By combining powdered iron (top) with powdered sulfur (center), an iron-sulfur mixture is formed. But because the substances making up this mixture are not linked by chemical bonds, they can be separated easily by a magnet (bottom). The gold miner can separate heavy pieces of gold from rock, sand, and dirt by shaking the mixture in a pan of water and letting the gold settle to the bottom (right).*

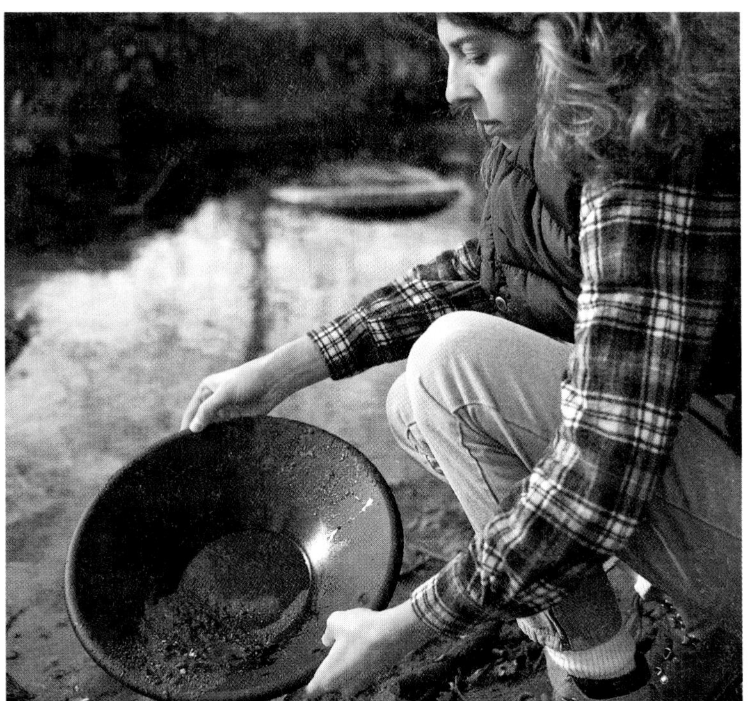

posed of mixtures involving water. The mixtures that are made with water can be of two important types: solutions and suspensions.

Solutions

If a cube of sugar is placed in a glass of warm water, the movement of the water molecules gradually breaks off single molecules from the sugar cube. These sugar molecules then become dispersed in the water and the sugar dissolves. See Figure 4–4. Before long, the sugar cube has completely disappeared and the sugar molecules are uniformly spread throughout the water, forming a **solution**. The sweet taste of the solution tells us that the sugar is still there. The sugar has undergone a physical but not a chemical change in forming a solution with water.

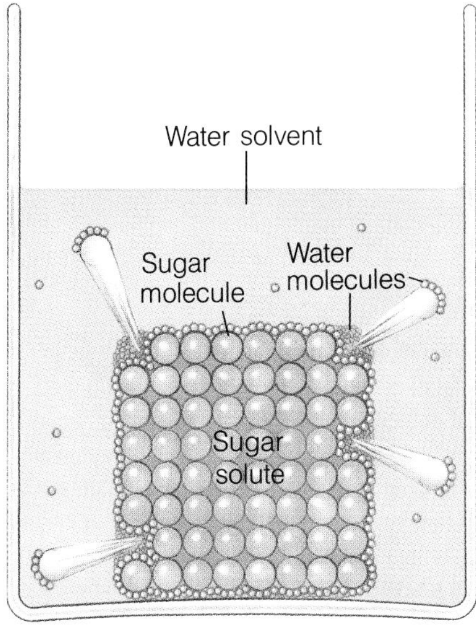

Figure 4–4 *The solution process first involves the separation of solute particles from the surface of the solid solute. Then the solute molecules enter the solution. Finally, the solute molecules are attracted to the solvent molecules.*

You have probably made solutions of water and many other materials, such as sugar, salt, tea, and cocoa. In these solutions, water is the **solvent**, or substance that does the dissolving. The substance that is dissolved—salt or tea, for example—is the **solute**. All solutions consist of a solvent and a solute. Without exaggeration, water is the greatest solvent in the world. This distinction is due largely to the charges at either end of the water molecule, which attract water molecules to other molecules whether they are positively or negatively charged.

ACIDS When ionically bonded compounds dissolve in water, they often dissociate, or break apart, into individual ions. Common table salt (sodium chloride) is a good example.

$$\underset{\textbf{sodium chloride}}{\mathbf{NaCl}} \rightarrow \underset{\textbf{sodium ion}}{\mathbf{Na^+}} + \underset{\textbf{chloride ion}}{\mathbf{Cl^-}}$$

The dissociation of sodium chloride produces the positive sodium ion (Na^+) and the negative chloride ion (Cl^-). Many other compounds follow this general pattern when they dissolve in water. One group of compounds, however, deserves special attention. Consider the following dissociation reaction:

$$\underset{\textbf{hydrochloric acid}}{\mathbf{HCl}} \rightarrow \underset{\textbf{hydrogen ion}}{\mathbf{H^+}} + \underset{\textbf{chloride ion}}{\mathbf{Cl^-}}$$

At first glance this compound dissociates in the same way that salt does. Just like salt, it produces a chloride ion (Cl^-). But the hydrogen ion (H^+) that is produced is very different from the sodium ion (Na^+). The H^+ is the most chemically reactive ion known. It is a single proton, lacking any electrons. This absence of electrons enables the hydrogen ion to attack the chemical bonds in a wide variety of molecules.

Compounds that release hydrogen ions into solution are known as **acids**, and we know HCl as hydrochloric acid. Can you name some other examples of acids?

Figure 4–5 *Hydrochloric acid, HC1, is a strong acid present in the stomach that aids in the process of digestion. Here you see a fiber optic endoscopic image of the stomach lining.*

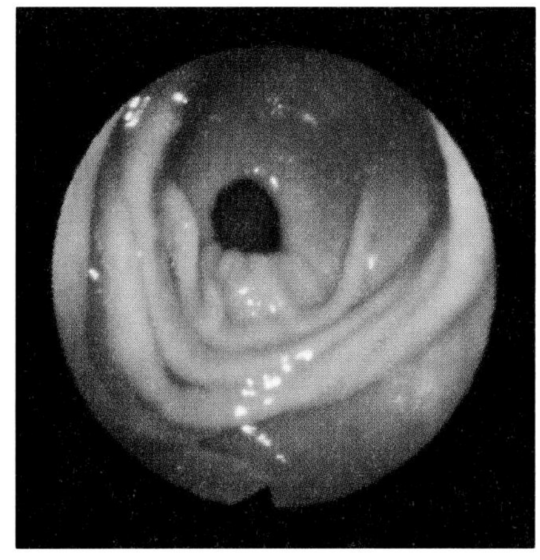

BASES **Bases** are compounds that release hydroxide ions (OH^-) into solution. Sodium hydroxide is an example of a base.

$$\underset{\text{sodium hydroxide}}{\mathbf{NaOH}} \rightarrow \underset{\text{sodium ion}}{\mathbf{Na^+}} + \underset{\text{hydroxide ion}}{\mathbf{OH^-}}$$

Strong acids and bases are highly reactive chemical compounds. They can attack and break a variety of chemical bonds, thus making them potentially dangerous to living tissue.

NEUTRALIZATION AND pH Mixing a strong acid and a strong base results in a reaction in which hydrogen ions and hydroxide ions react to form water. This type of reaction is called a **neutralization reaction**. Can you guess the reason for this name?

$$\underset{\text{hydrogen ion}}{\mathbf{H^+}} + \underset{\text{hydroxide ion}}{\mathbf{OH^-}} \rightarrow \underset{\text{water}}{\mathbf{H_2O}}$$

If the quantities of acid and base being mixed are in perfect balance, the neutralized solution that results is neither acid nor base. The concentrations of hydrogen ions and hydroxide ions are equal. The relative concentrations of hydrogen ions and hydroxide ions in a solution is an important indicator of the properties of the solution. A measurement system known as the **pH scale** indicates the relative concentrations of these two ions. See Figure 4–6.

The pH scale ranges from 0 to 14. Pure water, in which the concentrations of H^+ and OH^- ions are equal, has a pH value of 7.0. Acids have pH values of less than 7. Strong acids, such as those that help digest food in the stomach, have pH values of 1 to 3. Bases have pH values greater than 7. Strong bases, like ammonia or lye, have high pH values, ranging from 11 to 13. The pH values within most cells range from 6.5 to 7.5. These near-neutral values are maintained by dissolved compounds that help prevent sharp, sudden swings of pH, which might cause damaging chemical changes within living tissues.

Figure 4–6 On the pH scale, 7 is neutral, acids are between 0 and 7, and bases are between 7 and 14. A difference of 1 between consecutive numbers on the scale is actually a difference of 10 times the relative strengths of the acids or bases. What cleaner is more basic? What body fluid is most acidic?

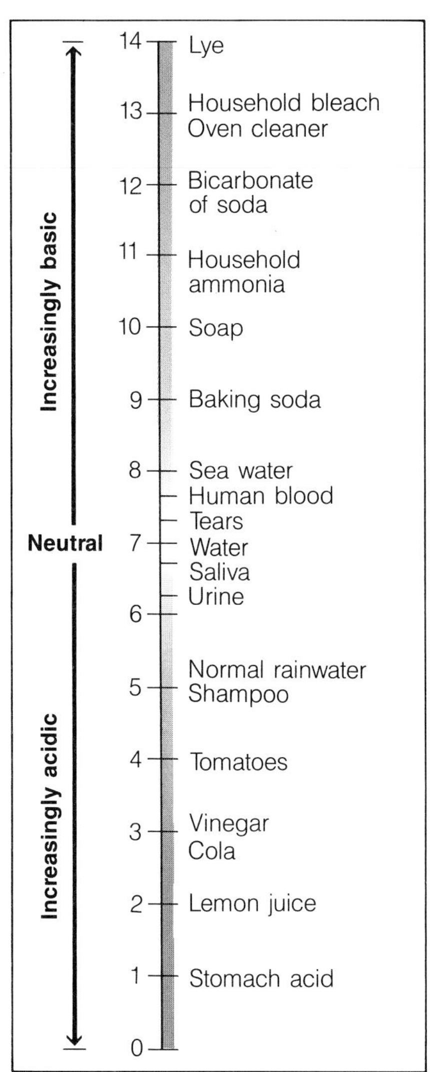

Suspensions

Some materials do not break into individual molecules when placed in water but still form pieces so small that they will not settle to the bottom of a container. The movement of water molecules keeps these small particles suspended. Such mixtures of water and nondissolved material are known as **suspensions**.

In living things, both solutions and suspensions are very important. A perfect example is the blood that circulates through your body. Blood, as you might have guessed, is mostly water. In that water are many dissolved compounds, including salt. So blood is a solution. But blood is also a suspen-

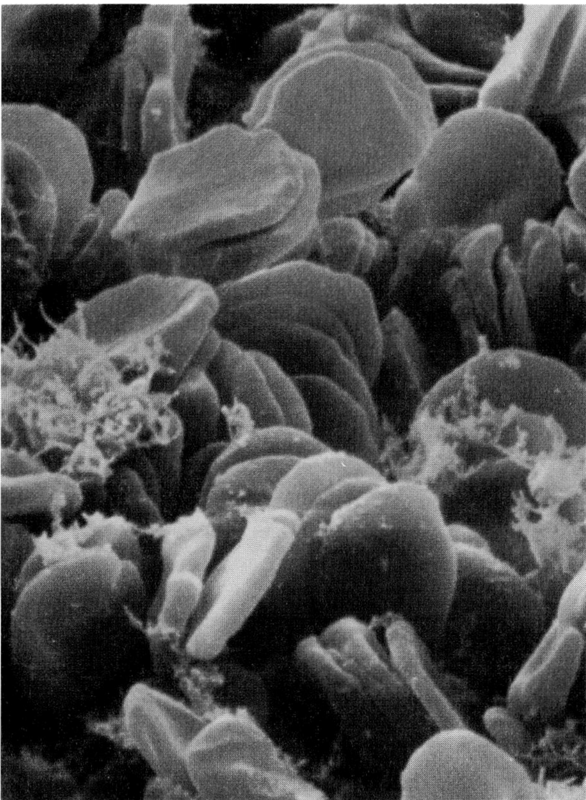

Figure 4–7 Mixtures of water and nondissolved material are called suspensions. Oil and water (left) is a common suspension. Perhaps less familiar to you is the suspension circulating through your body—blood! Blood contains clotting structures, living cells, and other particles, all suspended in a solution of water and other dissolved compounds (right).

sion. It contains tiny structures that aid in clotting, as well as living cells and other suspended particles. See Figure 4-7. These components do not dissolve in blood. Instead, they form a suspension that circulates through the body—an extremely vital suspension made possible by the most important molecule found in living things: water.

4-1 SECTION REVIEW

1. What are some important properties of water? What property accounts for its being the best solvent?
2. What is a mixture? What are two important types of mixtures? How do these two types differ?
3. What is a solution? A solvent? A solute?
4. Describe two important differences between acids and bases.
5. What is a neutralization reaction? Give an example.
6. Hydrogen fluoride (HF) is dissolved in pure water. Predict whether the pH of the solution will be greater than or less than 7.0.

Section Objectives

- Identify the four most abundant elements in living things.
- Compare inorganic compounds and organic compounds.
- Describe the properties that make carbon unique.
- Explain the importance of polymerization.

4–2 Chemical Compounds in Living Things

Although the Earth's crust contains 90 naturally occurring chemical elements, only 11 of these elements are common in living organisms. Another 20 are found in trace amounts. Just four elements—carbon, nitrogen, oxygen, and hydrogen—make up 96.3 percent of the total weight of the human body. **In varying combinations, the elements carbon, hydrogen, oxygen, and nitrogen make up practically all the chemical compounds in living things**. To make the study of these and all other chemical compounds easier, scientists have divided them into two groups: **organic compounds**, which contain carbon, and **inorganic compounds**, which do not.

Inorganic Compounds

Inorganic compounds are primarily those compounds that do not contain carbon. One exception to this definition is carbon dioxide, which although it does contain carbon is an inorganic compound. The natural world is dominated by such compounds. Water is inorganic, as are the minerals that make up most of the sand, soil, and stone of the Earth's landmasses.

Living things contain a great many inorganic compounds, ranging from water to carbon dioxide to calcium phosphate, a mineral from which bones are formed. The group of compounds known as salts that help to balance the pH of the blood are largely inorganic.

Figure 4–8 *A carbon atom contains 6 protons, 6 neutrons, and 6 electrons. What is the arrangement of these 6 electrons?*

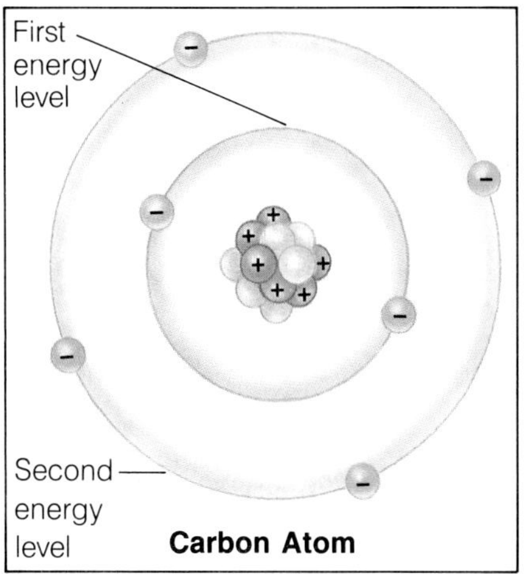

Organic Compounds

Organic compounds are carbon-containing compounds. A special branch of chemistry called organic chemistry deals with the chemistry of carbon and its more than 2 million compounds. Why is carbon so special?

Carbon is a unique element because of its remarkable ability to form covalent bonds that are strong and stable. You will recall that covalent bonds involve the sharing of electrons. Carbon has 6 electrons, 2 in the first energy level and 4 in the second. So only 4 of the 8 positions in its outermost energy level are filled. This means that carbon can form four single covalent bonds. The simplest compound that can be formed from carbon is methane, CH_4. Carbon can also form covalent bonds with oxygen, nitrogen, phosphorus, and sulfur atoms. The ability to bond easily and form compounds with these common elements would be enough to make carbon an interesting element. But there's more!

Carbon can form chains of almost unlimited length by bonding to other carbon atoms. The bonds between carbon atoms in these straight chains can be single, double, or triple covalent bonds—or combinations of these bonds. No other element can equal carbon in this respect. These chains can be closed on themselves to form rings. The ring structures may include single or double bonds, or a mixture of both. This gives even more variety to the kinds of molecules that carbon can form. See Figure 4-9.

Figure 4–9 *Because of its remarkable ability to form a variety of covalent bonds, carbon is an unparalleled element. Here you see some of the different types and arrangements of carbon bonds.*

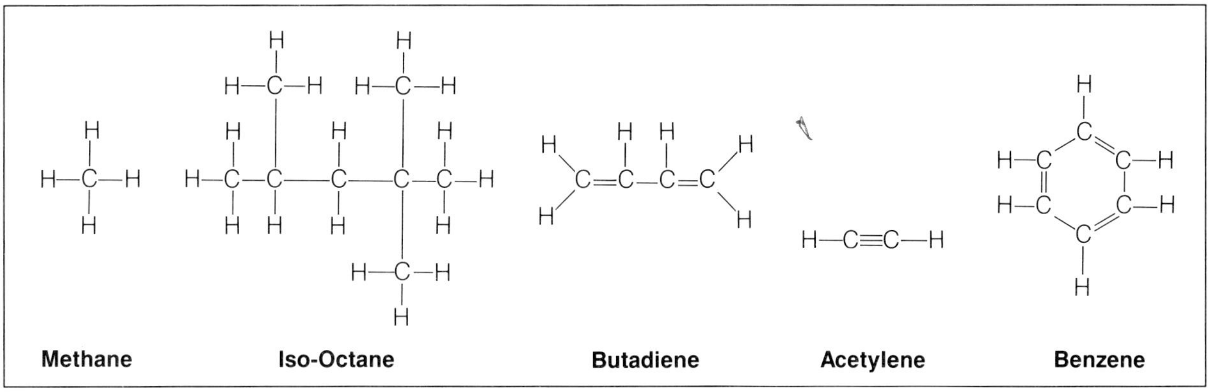

Methane | Iso-Octane | Butadiene | Acetylene | Benzene

Polymerization

Many carbon-based compounds are formed by a chemical process known as **polymerization**, in which large compounds are constructed by joining together smaller compounds. The smaller compounds, or **monomers**, are joined together by chemical bonds to form **polymers**. Many polymers are so large that they are called **macromolecules**. As used here, the prefix *macro-* means giant.

Polymerization provides a way to form complex molecules by joining monomers together. The chemical diversity that polymerization allows living things is similar to the diversity that our alphabet allows us. Although there are only 26 letters in the alphabet, our ability to join them together (polymerize them) to form words gives us an almost infinite variety of possible words (molecules).

Figure 4–10 *A polymer is made up of a series of monomers.*

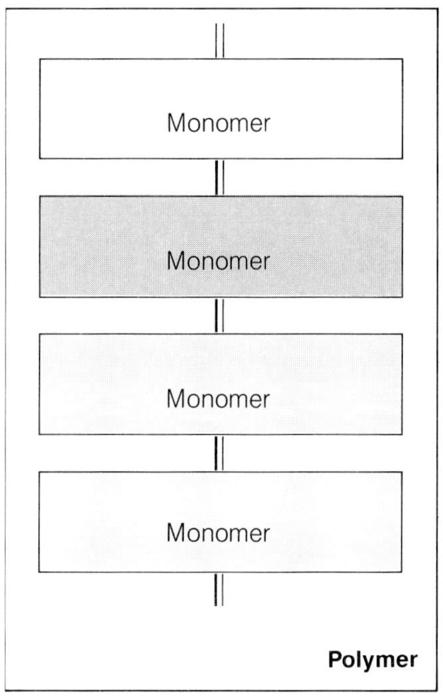

4–2 SECTION REVIEW

1. What is an inorganic compound? An organic compound?
2. Is the chemical composition of the human body similar to the composition of the Earth's crust? Explain your answer.
3. What special properties of carbon make it such an important compound in living things?
4. Describe the process of polymerization.

Section Objectives

- Identify the four groups of organic compounds found in living things.
- Describe the structure and function of each group of compounds of life.
- Explain how enzymes work and why they are important to living things.

4–3 Compounds of Life

The number of possible organic compounds is almost limitless. Fortunately, however, it is possible to classify many important organic compounds found in living things into four groups. **The four groups of organic compounds found in living things are carbohydrates, lipids, proteins, and nucleic acids.** By knowing the characteristics of just these groups, you will know a great deal about the chemistry of living things.

Carbohydrates

Although you may not realize it, you are probably quite familiar with the group of organic compounds known as **carbohydrates**. Carbohydrates, you see, are the molecules that we often call sugars. Carbohydrates contain carbon, hydrogen, and oxygen atoms in an approximate ratio of 1:2:1 (C:H:O). The simplest carbohydrates are called **monosaccharides**, meaning single sugars. Examples of monosaccharides include glucose, galactose, and fructose. Glucose is the sugar green plants produce during the food-making process. Galactose is found in milk. And fructose, the sweetest of these simple sugars, is found in fruits. The formula for all three of these simple sugars is $C_6H_{12}O_6$. What makes them different from one another is the arrangement of the individual atoms. See Figure 4–11.

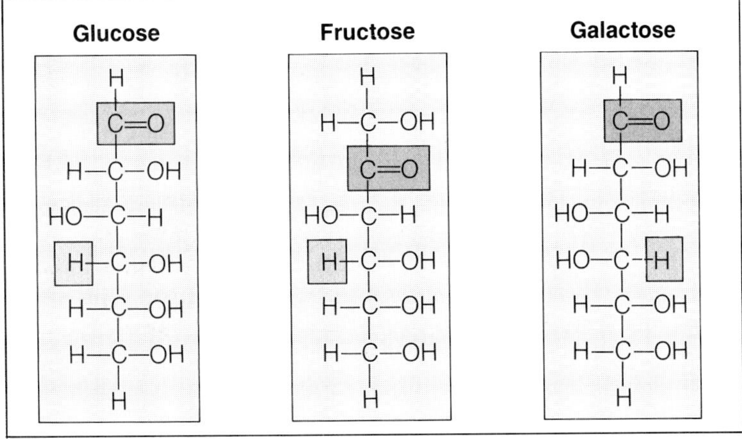

Figure 4–11 Glucose, fructose, and galactose are single sugars, or monosaccharides. Sugars form a group of organic compounds known as carbohydrates. The formula for all three of these single sugars is $C_6H_{12}O_6$. What makes them different from one another?

Sugars are important to living things because they contain a great deal of energy. This energy is stored in the chemical bonds that make up the carbohydrate molecules. When the chemical bonds are broken, the energy is released. Nearly all organisms use glucose as one of their basic energy sources. In Chapter 6, you will learn how the energy from sugar molecules is used by living things.

DEHYDRATION SYNTHESIS Complex carbohydrates are made by a process of polymerization in which two or more

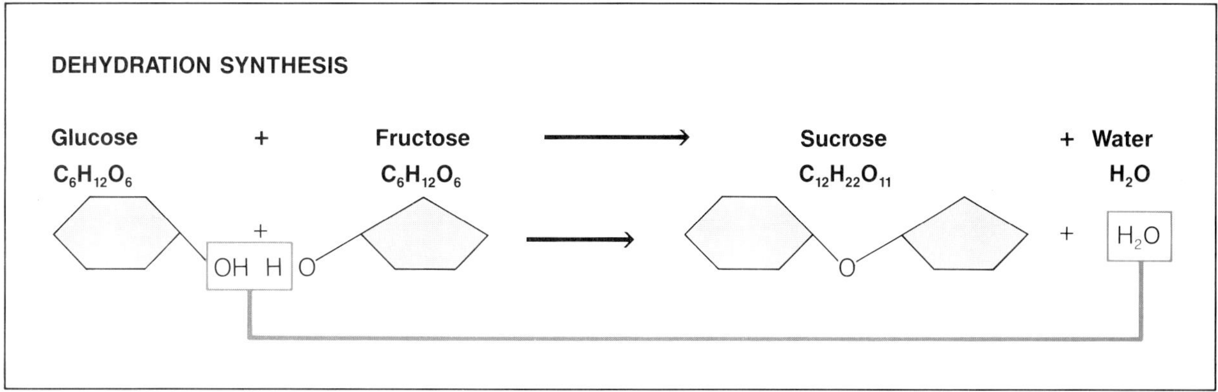

Figure 4–12 The dehydration synthesis of a molecule of glucose and a molecule of fructose produces a molecule of sucrose and a molecule of water. What type of sugar is sucrose?

monosaccharides are combined to form larger molecules. The chemical bond that links two simple sugars is formed between the -OH groups present in each molecule. As you can see from Figure 4–12, one OH from one molecule combines with the H of the OH from the other molecule. When the bond is complete, a molecule of water is removed from the two monosaccharides. Because of the loss of water, the joining of two sugars is known as **dehydration synthesis**. Dehydration means loss of water, and synthesis means putting together.

The compound formed from the joining of two single sugars in dehydration synthesis is called a **disaccharide**, or double sugar. Ordinary table sugar, or sucrose ($C_{12}H_{22}O_{11}$), is a disaccharide. Other disaccharides include maltose (malt sugar) and lactose (milk sugar).

POLYSACCHARIDES Very large molecules can be formed by joining together many monosaccharide units. Such compounds are known as **polysaccharides**. Polysaccharides are the form in which living things store excess sugar. One important polysaccharide is starch. Plants store excess sugar in the form of starch, which is present in potatoes and bread. Starch is a very large molecule formed by joining together hundreds of glucose molecules. Animals store their excess sugar in the form of glycogen in the liver and muscles. Glycogen is an even larger molecule consisting of hundreds or even thousands of glucose molecules. Glycogen is sometimes called animal starch. Do you see why? Because they are polymers of single sugars, both starch and glycogen help store energy in living things. Another polysaccharide is cellulose, which is found only in plants. Cellulose helps to support a plant by giving it strength and rigidity. Cellulose is the major component of wood. As such, it is often used as a building material or a printing material. The page upon which these words are printed is made principally of cellulose.

Figure 4–13 Cellulose fibers (top) are extremely strong and thus able to support the enormous mass of these giant sequoia trees (bottom).

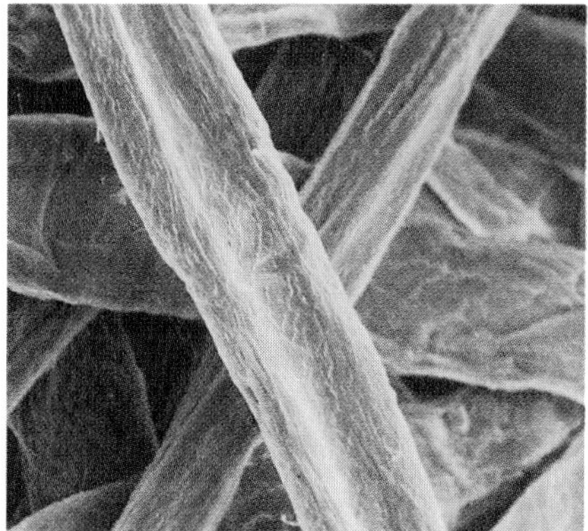

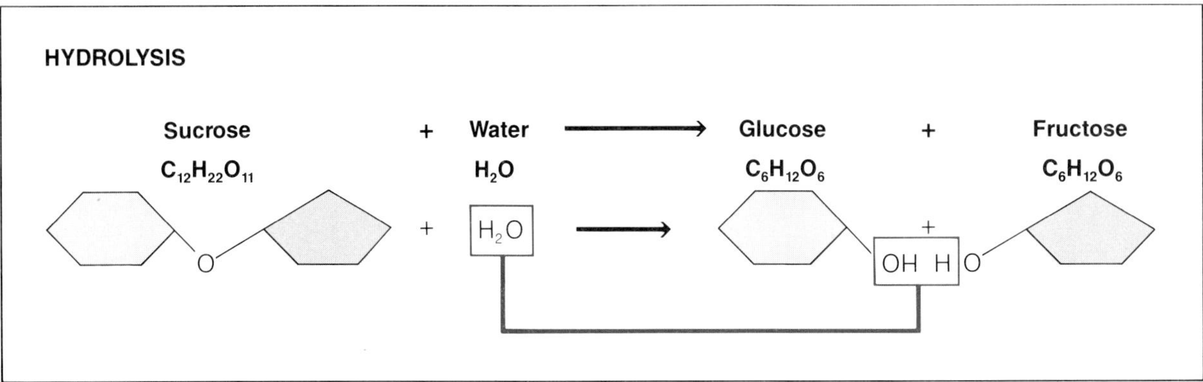

Figure 4–14 *The hydrolysis of a molecule of sucrose produces a molecule of glucose and a molecule of fructose.*

HYDROLYSIS When polysaccharides are split apart to again form monosaccharides, the dehydration synthesis reaction is reversed. This reverse reaction is known as **hydrolysis**. Hydrolysis, which means water splitting, is an appropriate name because a molecule of water is consumed by the chemical reaction that splits the bond between adjacent monosaccharides. Figure 4–14 illustrates the hydrolysis reaction.

Lipids

Lipids are organic compounds that are waxy or oily. Lipids have three major roles in living organisms. Like carbohydrates, lipids can be used to store energy. Lipids are used to form biological membranes. And certain lipids are used as chemical messengers. The common names by which we know lipids are fats, oils, and waxes. Generally, fats and waxes are solid at room temperature, whereas oils are liquid.

Many important lipids are formed from combinations of fatty acids and glycerol. Fatty acids are long chains of hydrogen and carbon atoms that have a carboxyl group attached at one

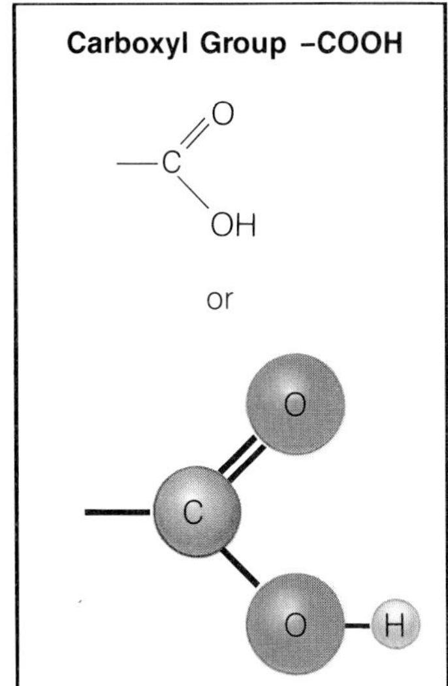

Figure 4–15 *Lipids are organic compounds that are most familiar as fats, oils, and waxes (right). Many lipids are formed from fatty acids and glycerol. All fatty acids contain long chains of carbon and hydrogen atoms to which a carboxyl group is attached. A carboxyl group consists of 1 carbon atom, 1 hydrogen atom, and 2 oxygen atoms (left).*

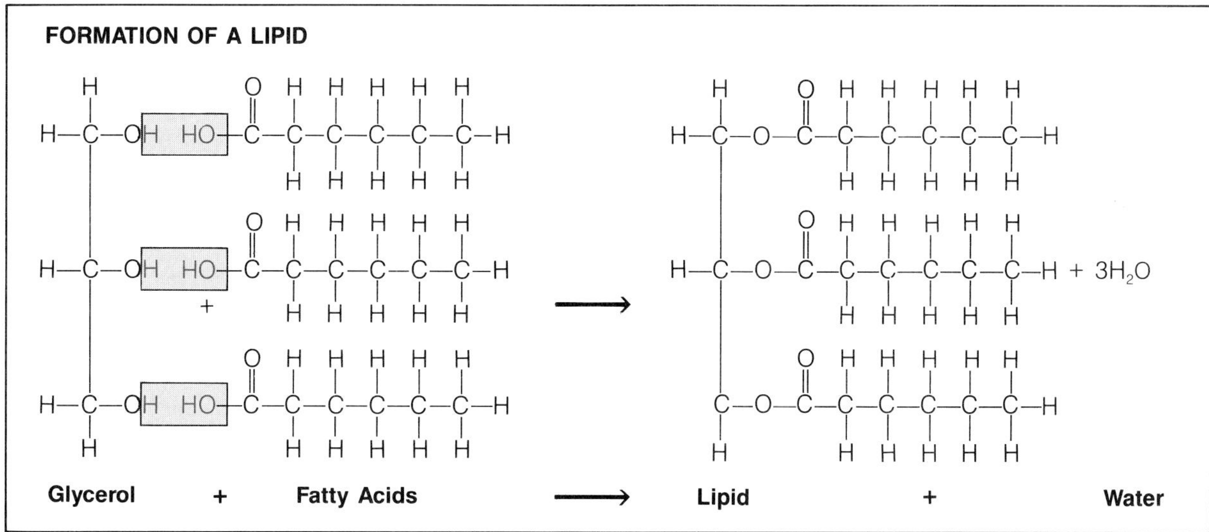

Figure 4–16 The formation of a lipid involves the combination of three fatty-acid molecules with one glycerol molecule. What type of chemical reaction is taking place here?

end. A carboxyl group is a chemical group consisting of one carbon atom, one hydrogen atom, and two oxygen atoms (-COOH). See Figure 4-15. Glycerol, which is an organic alcohol, contains three carbon atoms, each of which is attached to a hydroxyl (-OH) group. Many lipids are formed by the attachment of two or three fatty acids to glycerol. Figure 4-16 shows how fatty acids combine with glycerol to form a lipid. Can you recognize the chemical reaction that is responsible for the formation of the lipid?

SATURATED AND UNSATURATED LIPIDS If every carbon atom in a fatty acid chain is joined to another carbon atom by a single bond, the fatty acid is said to be saturated because it contains the maximum number of hydrogen atoms. If a pair of carbon atoms is joined by a double bond, the fatty acid is said to be unsaturated. Because of the double bond, it does not contain the maximum number of hydrogen atoms. If a fatty acid contains several double bonds, it is said to be polyunsaturated. Figure 4–18 on page 74 shows an example of each of these types of fatty acids.

Lipids made from saturated fatty acids are called saturated fats. Such fats are commonly found in meats and most dairy products. Lipids made from polyunsaturated fatty acids are called polyunsaturated fats. If that term seems familiar, it should. Polyunsaturated fats tend to be liquid at room temperature and are used in many cooking oils, such as sesame, peanut, and corn oil. Including polyunsaturated fats in the diet may help to prevent heart disease, a connection we will explore more completely in Chapter 41.

Both plants and animals use lipids as a means of storing energy. Because lipids contain far fewer oxygen atoms than carbohydrates do, they have less mass per unit of chemical energy than carbohydrates. In other words, when lipids are

Figure 4–17 Animals use lipids as a means of storing energy. When black bears retreat to their dens in late autumn, they lie down and cease to move, eat, drink, and eliminate wastes for about 5 months. Burning up nearly 4000 calories per day, a bear's metabolism operates at 50 to 80 percent its normal rate. The energy the bear needs comes primarily from its stored lipids.

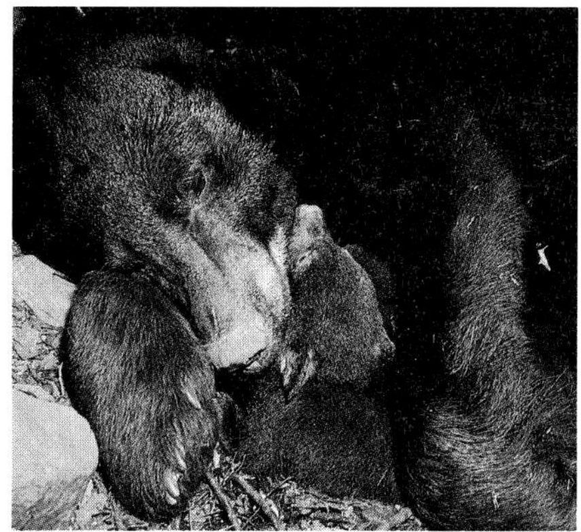

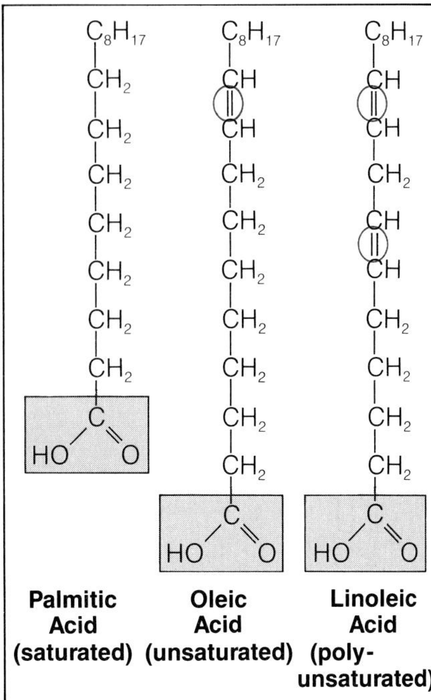

Figure 4–18 Palmitic acid is a saturated fatty acid. Why is oleic acid unsaturated? Why is linoleic acid polyunsaturated?

Figure 4–19 All amino acids have an amino group (-NH_2) on one end and a carboxyl group (-COOH) on the other. They differ in a region of the molecule known as an R group.

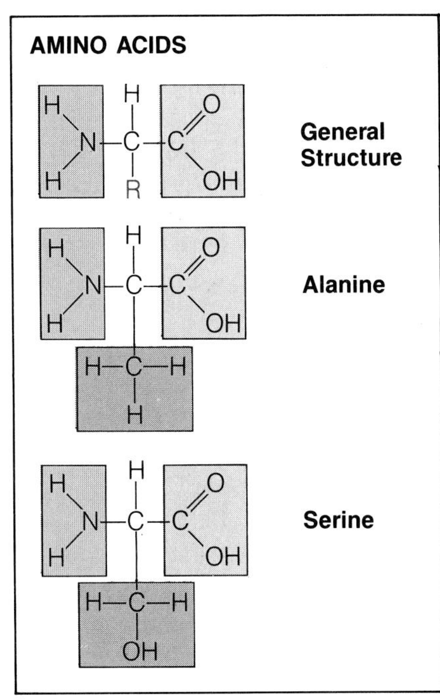

broken down, they produce more energy gram for gram than carbohydrates do.

STEROLS AND PHOSPHOLIPIDS Two other kinds of lipids are particularly important in living organisms. They are sterols and phospholipids. One of the most common sterols is a molecule called **cholesterol**. Cholesterol is an important part of many cells, but excessive cholesterol in the diet is a risk factor in heart disease. Sterol lipids play a number of important roles in building cells and carrying messages from one part of the body to another. We will learn more about sterols later in this textbook.

Phospholipids are molecules consisting of parts that dissolve well in water and parts that do not dissolve well in water. The portions of a phospholipid molecule that do not dissolve in water are oily. What happens to a molecule made of two very different parts? When phospholipid molecules are mixed with water, they may form small balloonlike structures known as liposomes. Each liposome is formed from a double layer, or bilayer, of lipid molecules. A liposome forms spontaneously, or without any outside help. It forms merely by the attraction of the oily parts of the lipid molecules for each other and by the attraction of the other parts of the lipid molecules for the surrounding water. The ability to form bilayers spontaneously is an important property of lipids that enables them to play a key role in forming cell membranes.

Proteins

Proteins are organic compounds that contain nitrogen in addition to carbon, hydrogen, and oxygen. Proteins are polymers of **amino acids**. An amino acid has an amino group (-NH_2) on one end and a carboxyl group (-COOH) on the other. These groups can form covalent bonds with each other. As a result of these bonds, very long chains of amino acids can be put together. All amino acids have a similar chemical structure, but they differ in a region of the molecule known as an R group. See Figure 4–19. There are more than 20 different amino acids, each of which contains a different R group.

PEPTIDES The covalent bond that joins two amino acids is known as a **peptide bond**. A molecule of water is lost when a peptide bond is formed between two amino acids. This reaction is another example of dehydration synthesis. A dipeptide is two amino acids joined by a peptide bond. A tripeptide contains three amino acids. And, as you might expect, a polypeptide is a long chain of amino acids.

PROTEIN STRUCTURE A complete protein contains one or more polypeptide chains and may contain a few other chemical groups that are important to its proper function. Proteins

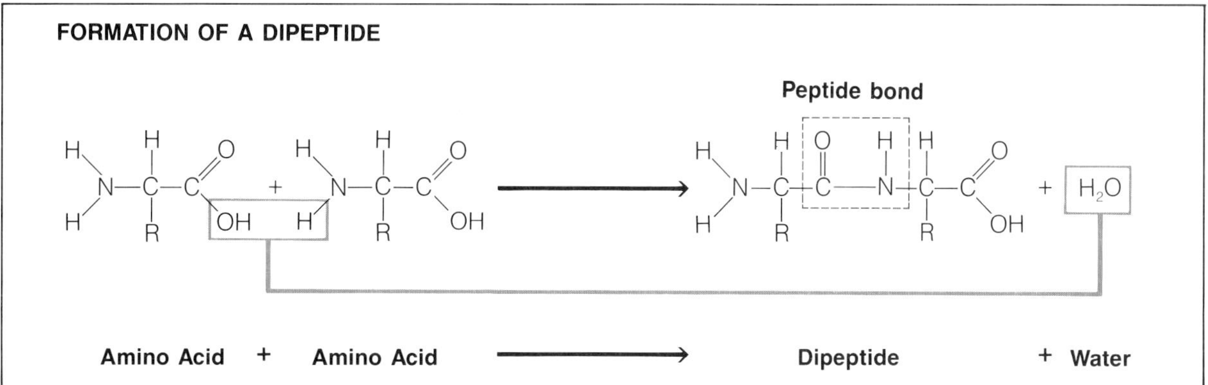

Figure 4-20 Peptide bonds—which result in the formation of dipeptides, tripeptides, and polypeptides—form during the dehydration synthesis of amino acids.

have numerous roles: They help to carry out chemical reactions; they pump small molecules in and out of cells; and they are even responsible for the ability of cells to move. The functions of proteins are at the very center of life itself.

Enzymes

Chemical reactions make life possible. Hundreds of chemical reactions are involved in a process as simple as digesting a chocolate bar. If these chemical reactions proceeded too slowly, not only would the chocolate bar remain in the stomach for a long time, but the ordinary activities of life would come to a halt as well. Since this is not the case, some substances in the body must be responsible for speeding up the process.

A substance that speeds up the rate of a chemical reaction is called a **catalyst**. Catalysts are not changed by the reactions

Figure 4–21 Proteins are found in a variety of substances. These photographs show some of the more common proteins: collagen used in tennis racket strings (top, left), keratin in a peacock feather (top, right), silk from a spider's web (bottom, left), and human hair (bottom, right).

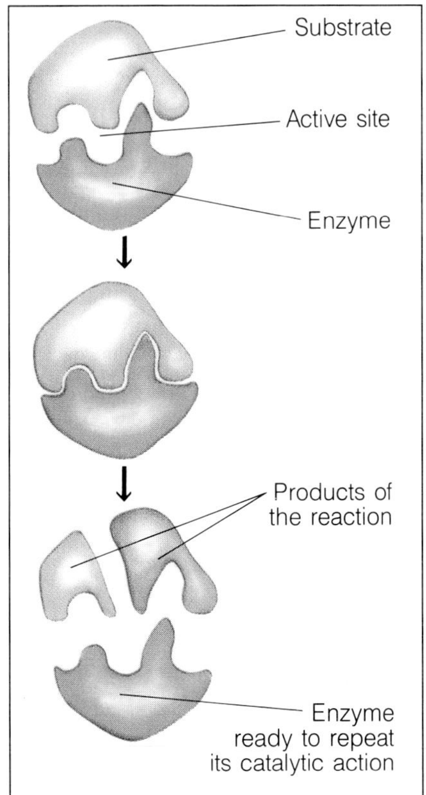

Figure 4–22 *In the lock-and-key hypothesis of enzyme action, an enzyme and its substrate bind at a region known as the active site in a manner similar to the way in which two pieces of a jigsaw puzzle fit together. What is the role of an enzyme?*

Figure 4-23 *Nucleic acids are polymers of nucleotides, which are molecules built up from three basic parts: a special 5-carbon sugar, a phosphate group, and a nitrogenous base.*

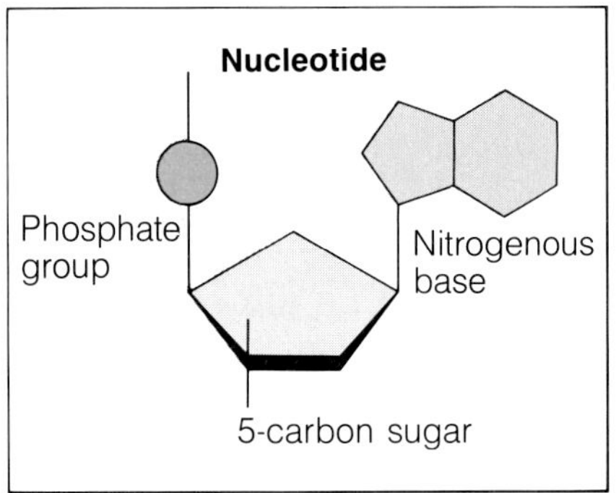

they promote, and therefore they are not used up during the reaction. Catalysts work by lowering the "start-up" energy of a reaction. Chemists often seek catalysts that will speed up reactions important to industry. Living organisms have gone the industrial chemist one better—they contain their own special catalysts, which are known as **enzymes**.

With a few exceptions, enzymes are proteins. Understanding their function is an important part of the study of proteins. Simple cells may have as many as 2000 different enzymes, each one catalyzing a different reaction. An enzyme may accelerate a reaction by a factor of 10^{10}—that is, making it happen 10,000,000,000 times faster! Thus a reaction that might take as long as 1500 years without an enzyme can be completed in just 5 seconds!

Enzymes speed up a reaction by binding to the reactants, which, as you may recall, are the substances that enter into a chemical reaction. The reactants that are affected by an enzyme are known as **substrates**. Substrates bind to enzymes at a region known as the **active site**.

The way in which a chemical reaction is catalyzed varies from one enzyme to another. An enzyme can catalyze a reaction by holding two substrates in positions in which they can react with each other. Or an enzyme can catalyze a reaction by twisting a substrate molecule slightly so that a chemical bond is weakened and broken.

Enzymes are very specific. A particular enzyme can catalyze only one particular chemical reaction involving specific substrates. Scientists theorize that this has something to do with the shape of the enzyme's active site. In fact, the fit between an enzyme's active site and its substrate is often compared to that of a lock and key.

Enzymes are important in regulating chemical pathways, synthesizing materials needed by cells, releasing energy, and transferring information. You will discover that enzymes are involved in digestion, respiration, reproduction, vision, movement, thought, and even in the making of other enzymes.

Nucleic Acids

Nucleic acids are large complex organic molecules composed of carbon, oxygen, hydrogen, nitrogen, and phosphorus atoms. Nucleic acids are polymers of individual monomers known as **nucleotides**. Nucleotides are molecules built up from three basic parts: a special 5-carbon sugar, a phosphate group, and a molecule generally known as a nitrogenous base. See Figure 4–23. Individual nucleotides can be linked together by covalent bonds to form a polynucleotide. There are two basic kinds of nucleic acids: **ribonucleic acid (RNA)**, which contains the sugar ribose, and **deoxyribonucleic acid (DNA)**, which contains the sugar deoxyribose. Despite their name, nucleic acids are not strongly acidic.

Nucleic acids store and transmit the genetic information that is responsible for life itself. How they do this, and how that information is decoded and transferred, is a fascinating story that we will leave for Chapter 7.

4–3 SECTION REVIEW

1. What are the four groups of organic compounds found in living things? Give an example of each.
2. Distinguish between monosaccharides, disaccharides, and polysaccharides.
3. What are lipids? How are they important to living things?
4. Describe the structure of a protein.
5. What is an enzyme? What is its function in living things?
6. Describe the structure and function of nucleic acids. What are two important nucleic acids?

SCIENCE, TECHNOLOGY, AND SOCIETY BREAKTHROUGH

The Structure of Proteins

Although proteins are among the largest of all macromolecules, it is sometimes possible to determine their detailed structure, including the position of every atom. This is done with the aid of a technique called X-ray crystallography.

The first, and often the trickiest, step in the procedure is to grow small crystals of a protein—often no larger than a grain of salt (0.1 mm). These protein crystals are then placed in a finely tuned beam of X-rays. As the X-rays pass through the crystal, they are scattered in a pattern that is recorded on film and then analyzed by computers. These X-ray scattering patterns contain enough information to allow scientists to build a complete model of the protein. The accompanying photograph, showing the arrangement of proteins on the surface of a common cold virus, was obtained by this technique. X-ray crystallography is a powerful scientific tool that enables us to visualize protein structure and understand the biological activities of complex molecules.

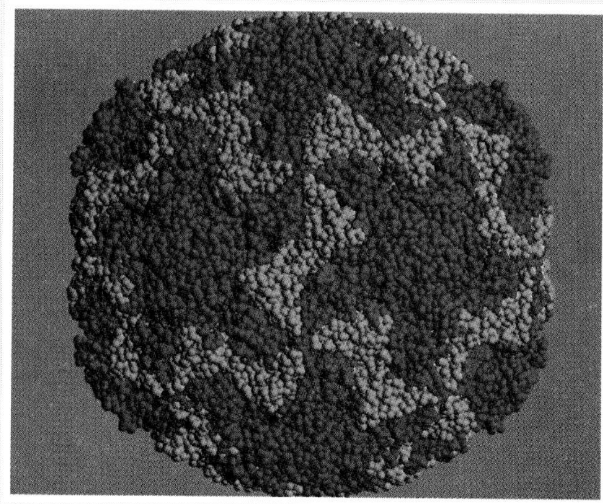

TESTING ENZYME ACTIVITY

PROBLEM

How does pH influence the activity of the enzyme catalase?

MATERIALS *(per group)*

5 125-mL flasks	0.1 M hydrochloric acid
graduated cylinder	3% hydrogen peroxide
petri dish	liver puree (catalase)
3 medicine droppers	small piece of raw beef liver
stirring rod	glass-marking pencil
hydrion (pH) papers	safety goggles
0.1 M sodium hydroxide	

PROCEDURE

1. Prepare an appropriate data table on a separate sheet of paper.
2. Put on safety goggles. Put a small piece of raw liver in an open petri dish. Using a medicine dropper, put a drop of hydrogen peroxide on the liver. **CAUTION:** *Hydrogen peroxide can be irritating to skin and eyes. If you spill any on yourself or your clothes, wash it off immediately.* Observe what happens. Liver contains the enzyme catalase, which breaks down hydrogen peroxide formed in cells. When hydrogen peroxide is broken down by catalase, bubbles of oxygen gas are released.
3. Using the glass-marking pencil, number the flasks from 1 through 5. With a clean medicine dropper, put 10 drops of water in flask 1. Using a graduated cylinder, measure out 5 mL of hydrochloric acid and add it to the water in the flask. **CAUTION:** *When diluting an acid, always pour the acid into the water.* Rinse the dropper and the cylinder.
4. Prepare the following solutions for the remaining flasks. Use procedures similar to those used in step 3. Flask 2: 10 drops of hydrochloric acid added to 5 mL of water. Flask 3: 5.5 mL of water only. Flask 4: 10 drops of sodium hydroxide added to 5 mL of water. Flask 5: 5 mL of sodium hydroxide added to 10 drops of water.
5. Using the stirring rod, put a drop of the solution from flask 1 on a piece of hydrion paper to measure the solution's pH. Record the results in the data table. Repeat the procedure for the solutions in flasks 2, 3, 4, and 5.
6. Using the clean graduated cylinder, add 5 mL of hydrogen peroxide to each flask. Look for bubbles. Identify the amount of activity in each flask by assigning it a number from 0 to 3, when 0 means no bubbles, 1 means few bubbles, and 3 means many bubbles.
7. Rinse out the five flasks thoroughly. Repeat steps 3 through 5.
8. Using a clean medicine dropper, add 5 drops of liver puree to each solution and mix well by swirling the flask.
9. Using the clean graduated cylinder, add 5 mL of hydrogen peroxide to each flask. Identify the amount of activity in each flask from 0 to 3, as you did in step 6.

OBSERVATIONS

1. What happened when hydrogen peroxide was added to each flask without liver puree?
2. What happened when hydrogen peroxide was added to each flask with liver puree?
3. In which flask(s) was the bubble activity greatest? What was the pH of the solution(s)?

ANALYSIS AND CONCLUSIONS

1. What is the purpose of the flasks without liver puree?
2. At what pH does catalase function best? How do you know?
3. If a strong acid has a pH of 1, a strong base, 14, and water, 7, does catalase work best in an acid, base, or neutral environment? Explain.
4. What conclusions can you draw about the pH in body cells?
5. Predict ways in which pH affects the chemical reactions in living cells.

STUDENT STUDY GUIDE

SUMMARIZING THE CONCEPTS

The key concepts in each section of this chapter are listed below to help you review the chapter content. Make sure you understand each concept and its relationship to other concepts and to the theme of this chapter.

4–1 Water

- Water is the most abundant compound in the majority of living organisms.
- A mixture is a substance composed of two or more compounds mixed together but not chemically combined.
- A solution consists of a solvent and solute.
- Compounds that release hydrogen ions (H^+) in solution are acids. Those that release hydroxide ions (OH^-) are bases.

4–2 Chemical Compounds in Living Things

- The four most abundant elements in living things are carbon, hydrogen, oxygen, and nitrogen.
- Inorganic compounds are primarily those that do not contain carbon. Organic compounds contain carbon.
- Polymerization is the process in which polymers are made by joining monomers.

4–3 Compounds of Life

- The four groups of organic compounds found in living things are carbohydrates, lipids, proteins, and nucleic acids.
- The polymerization of two monosaccharides to form a disaccharide occurs as a result of dehydration synthesis. Hydrolysis is the reverse reaction.
- Lipids are important sources of energy and compounds of biological membranes.
- Proteins are polymers of amino acids.
- Enzymes are, with a few exceptions, proteins. Enzymes are catalysts.
- Nucleic acids are polymers of nucleotides.

REVIEWING KEY TERMS

Vocabulary terms are important to your understanding of biology. The key terms listed below are those you should be especially familiar with. Review these terms and their meanings. Then use each term in a complete sentence. If you are not sure of a term's meaning, return to the appropriate section and review its definition.

4–1 Water

mixture
solution
solvent
solute
acid
base
neutralization reaction
pH scale
suspension

4–2 Chemical Compounds in Living Things

organic compound
inorganic compound
polymerization
monomer
polymer
macromolecule

4–3 Compounds of Life

carbohydrate
monosaccharide
dehydration synthesis
disaccharide
polysaccharide
hydrolysis
lipid
cholesterol
protein
amino acid
peptide bond
catalyst
enzyme
substrate
active site
nucleic acid
nucleotide
ribonucleic acid (RNA)
deoxyribonucleic acid (DNA)

CHAPTER REVIEW

CONTENT REVIEW

Multiple Choice

Choose the letter of the answer that best completes each statement.

1. The most abundant compound in most living things is
a. carbon dioxide. c. sodium chloride.
b. water. d. hydrochloric acid.

2. A strong acid has a pH of
a. 14. c. 5.
b. 7. d. 2.

3. Which group of elements combine to form practically all the chemical compounds in living things?
a. carbon, hydrogen, oxygen, nitrogen
b. carbon, hydrogen, phosphorus, nitrogen
c. carbon, sodium, chlorine, oxygen
d. sulfur, phosphorus, carbon, oxygen

4. Proteins are polymers of
a. fatty acids. c. sterols.
b. amino acids. d. nucleic acids.

5. The region on an enzyme to which a substrate binds is called the
a. catalyst. c. active site.
b. activated complex. d. carboxyl group.

6. The function of nucleic acids is related to
a. energy release.
b. enzyme formation.
c. transmission of genetic information.
d. catalyzing chemical reactions.

7. When phospholipid molecules are mixed with water, they form small balloonlike structures called
a. liposomes. c. lysosomes.
b. vacuoles. d. dipeptides.

8. The polysaccharide found only in plants is
a. glucose. c. cholesterol.
b. glycogen. d. cellulose.

True or False

Determine whether each statement is true or false. If it is true, write "true." If it is false, change the underlined word or words to make the statement true.

1. A mixture of oil and vinegar is an example of a <u>solution</u>.
2. Compounds that release hydrogen ions into solution are known as <u>bases</u>.
3. Compounds that contain carbon are called <u>organic</u> compounds.
4. The simplest carbohydrates are called <u>disaccharides</u>.
5. A common sterol whose excessive intake is related to heart disease is <u>cholesterol</u>.
6. Individual monomers of nucleic acids are known as <u>nucleotides</u>.
7. Including <u>saturated</u> fats in the diet may help to prevent heart disease.
8. Polysaccharides are split apart to form monosaccharides in a reaction called <u>hydrolysis</u>.

Word Relationships

In each of the following sets of terms, three of the terms are related. One term does not belong. Determine the characteristic common to three of the terms and then identify the term that does not belong.

1. solution, suspension, solute, solvent
2. monosaccharide, starch, glycogen, cellulose
3. fats, oils, waxes, proteins
4. substrate, enzyme, active site, nucleic acid

CONCEPT MASTERY

Use your understanding of the concepts developed in the chapter to answer each of the following in a brief paragraph.

1. Explain how the polarity of water molecules makes water the best solvent.
2. Compare solutions and suspensions.
3. Describe the properties of carbon that make carbon compounds so numerous.
4. Explain why the formation of a lipid molecule is a dehydration synthesis reaction. Use a diagram to help explain your answer.
5. Distinguish between a saturated, unsaturated, and polyunsaturated fatty acid.
6. Explain the importance of enzymes to living things. Be sure to include the following terms in your answer: catalyst, substrate, active site, "start-up energy," lock and key.

CRITICAL AND CREATIVE THINKING

Discuss each of the following in a brief paragraph.

1. **Applying concepts** One of the digestive juices in the human stomach is hydrochloric acid (HCl). Sometimes an excess of the acid causes stomach discomfort. In such a case, a person might take an antacid such as magnesium hydroxide ($Mg(OH)_2$). Explain why this substance works to relieve the discomfort. What reaction is taking place?
2. **Identifying patterns** Explain why the name carbohydrate is an indication of the chemical composition of any sugar.
3. **Relating facts** Give two reasons why dehydration synthesis and hydrolysis are opposite chemical reactions.
4. **Applying concepts** Relate the structure of a phospholipid to the property that makes it so important in forming cell membranes.
5. **Developing a model** Materials generally dissolve more quickly in a solvent if its temperature is increased. Why do you think this is so?
6. **Identifying relationships** Describe the role that polymerization plays in the formation of carbohydrates, proteins, and nucleic acids.
7. **Applying concepts** The chemical process by which a saturated fat is converted to an unsaturated fat is called dehydrogenation. Explain why this is an appropriate name.
8. **Relating concepts** Despite their name, many amino acids actually raise the pH of a solution in which they are dissolved. How could this be true?
9. **Using the writing process** At the yearly convention of chemical compounds, a great debate is raging. The organic compounds, represented by the carbohydrates, claim they are the most important compounds in living things. The inorganic compounds, championed by water molecules, claim that life could not exist without them. Write a 5-minute speech in which you take the side of the organic or the inorganic compounds. Or, as an alternative, you may file a minority report in which you argue both sides are incorrect.
10. **Using the writing process** Write a short story entitled, "The Day Ice Stopped Floating."

Textbook Illustrator

Textbook illustrators create the artwork that accompanies the information in a textbook. Their illustrations serve to express ideas and clarify explanations contained in the text.

To become a textbook illustrator, a person needs only general art classes and artistic ability, but many artists obtain preparation beyond high school at specialized art schools. Furthermore, some illustrators choose areas such as medical or scientific art that require training in biology or the physical sciences.

To receive additional information write to the Association of Medical Illustrators, 2692 Huguenot Springs Rd., Midlothian, VA 23113.

Biology Teacher

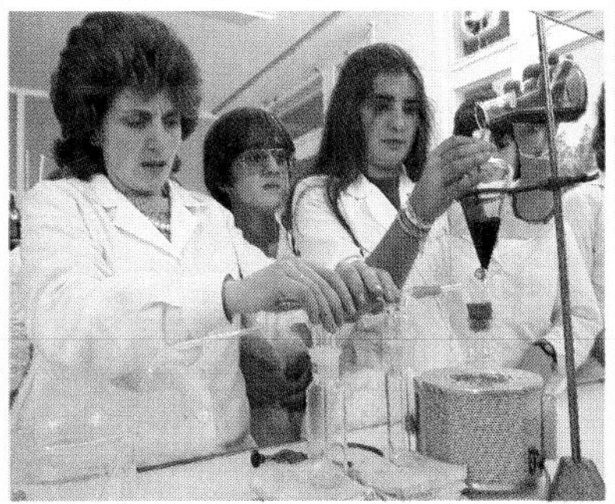

Biology teachers help students explore the complex world of living things. By presenting topics through lectures, demonstrations, laboratory work, and field trips, they help students learn the importance of the scientific method and the value of research. Biology teachers also monitor the progress of individual students by evaluating assignments and exams.

To become a biology teacher, a Bachelor's degree with courses in biology and education is required. In addition, experience as a student teacher is necessary to obtain a state teaching license.

For more information write to the National Association of Biology Teachers, 11250 Roger Bacon Dr., Reston, VA 22090.

Biochemist

Biochemists study chemical processes within living things. They use highly complex equipment to better understand life processes such as growth, reproduction, and metabolism. Some biochemists study the effects of different chemicals on the human body, whereas others develop methods to help doctors diagnose and treat disease.

Biochemists must have a Bachelor's degree in chemistry or biochemistry and an advanced degree in a particular area of biochemistry.

For information about this career write to the American Society of Biological Chemists, 9650 Rockville Pike, Bethesda, MD 20014.

HOW TO FIND OUT ABOUT CAREERS

School and community libraries are a good source of information about different types of jobs and careers. There you will find a number of sources that not only define specific job titles but also describe the nature of the work, educational and training requirements, the employment outlook for that field, working conditions, and other necessary information. Two such publications are the Occupational Outlook Handbook, *published by the United States government, and* The Encyclopedia of Careers and Vocational Guidance.

In addition, many corporations provide career information to interested students. Your school counseling office may have information about some of these companies.

FROM THE AUTHORS

Both of us agree that the first two chapters in this unit were among the hardest to write. Why? Because they have a big job to do. They must teach you not about a specific series of facts, but about an entire way of looking at the world. For biology is much more alive, much more challenging, and much more important than a list of facts could ever be.

Both of us are young as scientists go, but we have seen many changes in biology from the time we studied it in high school. As far as we're concerned, that's just as well. Anything that stays the same long enough can become boring. But biology is always changing fast enough that we never get a chance to get bored—or even to catch our breath. Every year or two, we have to throw out our lecture notes and many of our old ideas. New discoveries regularly force us to completely change the way we think about part of our field. It's a lot of work but also a lot of fun. Because by studying biology, we learn not only about the living world around us, but about the workings of one of the most fascinating parts of that world—the human mind.

Kenneth R Miller   Joe Levine

UNIT 2

Cells: The Basic Unit of Life

Don't be fooled by the inactivity of these polar bears. Even at rest, their bodies are alive with action. Millions of tiny internal factories are busily taking in raw materials, distributing them to specialized departments, shipping the products where they are needed, and disposing of wastes. What are these wondrous little factories? They are the fundamental units of all living organisms—cells.

Every cell is a highly organized structure that is responsible for the form and function of an organism. Some organisms consist of only one cell. Others consist of trillions of cells organized into complex organ systems. But regardless of size or shape, all organisms begin as just a single cell.

Only by understanding the complexity of life at the cellular level can we begin to understand the marvels of living things: why organisms behave as they do, how they develop and reproduce, and how they are affected by environmental factors.

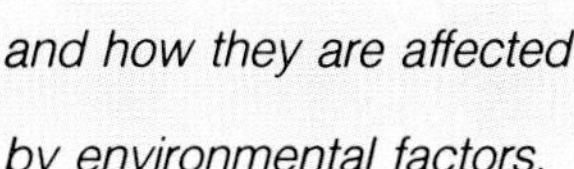

CHAPTERS

CHAPTER 5

Cell Structure and Function

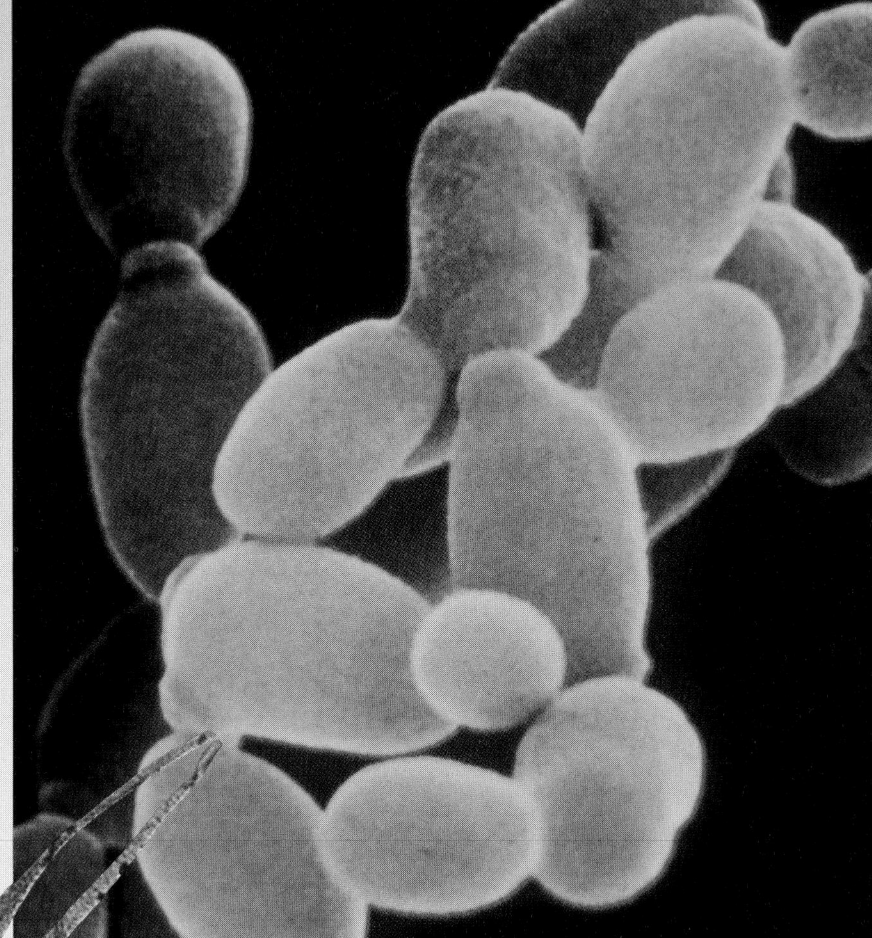

The microscope enabled scientists to discover that all living things are made up of cells. The spherical objects in the large photograph are single-celled yeasts; the branched object in the small photograph is a human nerve cell.

More than 100,000,000,000,000 cells are found in an adult human! We have about 155,000 cells in every square centimeter of our skin, about 30 billion cells in our brain, and about 20 trillion red blood cells in our blood. Many microscopic organisms, including bacteria, consist of just a single cell. Despite our complexity, we begin our lives as single cells.

Cells are the "atoms" of biology, the fundamental units of living organisms. Just as the atom is the smallest unit of an element, the cell is the smallest unit of an organism that can reasonably be thought of as alive. Questions concerning life—from ecology to behavior, from evolution to reproduction—must be partly answered at the level of the cell. The cell is the key to biology because it is at this level that a collection of water, salts, macromolecules, and membranes truly springs to life. In this chapter we shall begin our study of cells by looking into the various parts of the cell.

CHAPTER OUTLINE

5-1 The Cell Theory

Section Objectives

- List the contributions of van Leeuwenhoek, Hooke, Schleiden, Schwann, and Virchow to the development of the cell theory.
- State the cell theory.

Each of us, at one time or another, has tried to look closely at something. You may have picked up a coin and tried to read the initials of its designer, cut closely into the coin's surface. You may have tried to read the details on the face of a stamp, or stared at a blade of grass until the tiniest detail was clear.

Such curiosity led early investigators to examine living things under lenses and microscopes in the hope of getting a better glimpse of their structure. Little by little, their findings led to the most fundamental of all discoveries about the nature of living things: All living things are made of **cells**. Cells are the basic units of structure and function in living things.

The first lenses were used in Europe hundreds of years ago by merchants who needed to determine the quality of cloth. They used their magnifying lenses to examine the quality of the thread and the precision of the weave in a bolt of cloth. From these simple glass lenses, combinations of lenses were put together. In Holland in the early 1600s, two useful instruments were constructed. One was the telescope, which enabled people to see objects at a distance. The telescope made the distant stars in the sky visible. The other instrument, the microscope, made the very small objects in nature visible.

The person who is given credit for developing the first microscope was Anton van Leeuwenhoek (LAY-vuhn-hook), a

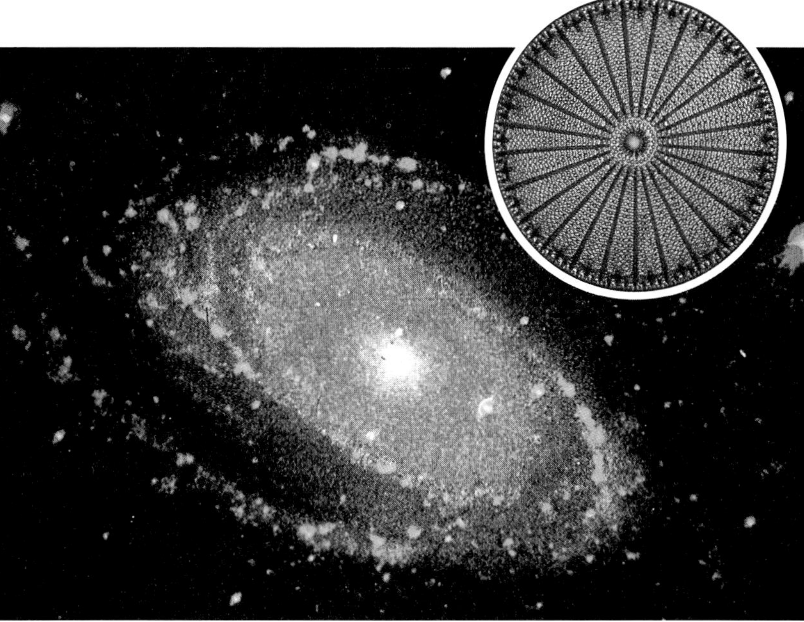

Figure 5–1 *The invention of the telescope enabled astronomers to study distant objects such as this spiral galaxy. The microscope, on the other hand, opened up the world of the very small to biologists. Before the invention of the microscope, a microscopic alga, such as this diatom, could not have been observed.*

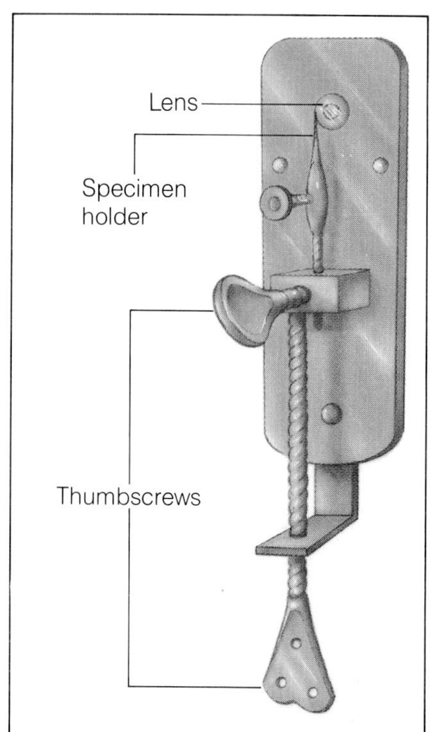

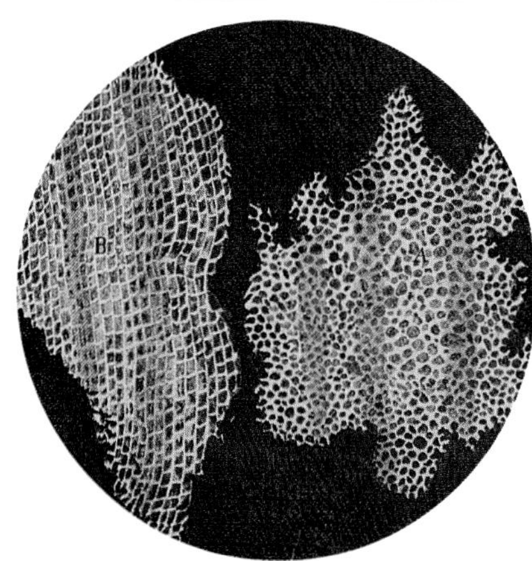

Figure 5–2 *Van Leeuwenhoek's simple microscope (top) could magnify objects a few hundred times. Robert Hooke made this drawing of cork cells (bottom) using a microscope that he built. Hooke, however, was not looking at living cells; what he saw were the cell walls that surround living cork cells.*

Dutch biologist. His invention enabled him to see things that no one had ever seen before. He could see tiny living organisms whose world consisted of a drop of water. Van Leeuwenhoek carefully observed the tiny living things in pond water and made detailed drawings of each kind of organism.

Van Leeuwenhoek's work interested other people in building microscopes. Before long, pioneers in several countries were experimenting with these new instruments. One such person was the Englishman Robert Hooke, who used one of his microscopes to look at thin slices of plant stems, wood, and pieces of cork. Looking at the cork, Hooke saw that it was composed of thousands of tiny chambers. He called these chambers cells because they reminded him of the small rooms called cells in a monastery.

Unfortunately, Hooke was not looking at living cells. He was looking at the nonliving outer walls of what had once been living plant cells. Nonetheless, Hooke's discovery was significant because it opened up the study of cells.

Gradually over the next 200 years, other scientists began to discover that cells were not only found in plants but in other living things too. In 1833, Robert Brown, a Scottish scientist, observed that many cells seemed to have a dark structure near the center of the cell. We now call this structure the nucleus. Five years later, German botanist Matthias Schleiden stated that all plants are made of cells. The next year, Theodor Schwann discovered that all animals are made of cells too. In 1855, Rudolf Virchow, a German physician, added one more element to the developing theory of cells. Based on research, he stated that all cells arise from the division of preexisting cells.

Today, the observations and conclusions of these scientists are summarized into the **cell theory**. The cell theory forms the basic framework in which biologists have tried to understand living things ever since. **The cell theory states:**

- **All living things are composed of cells.**
- **Cells are the basic units of structure and function in living things.**
- **All cells come from preexisting cells.**

5–1 SECTION REVIEW

1. When Hooke first used the term cell, did he intend it to apply to living material? Explain your answer.
2. What contributions did van Leeuwenhoek, Hooke, Schleiden, Schwann, and Virchow make to the development of the cell theory?
3. What role did the invention of the microscope play in the development of the cell theory?

5–2 Cell Structure

Section Objectives

- Identify and give the function of the three basic structures of most cells.
- Compare the structure of the cell membrane and the cell wall.
- Distinguish between prokaryotes and eukaryotes.

There is enormous variety in the size and shape of different cells. The smallest cells, belonging to a group of organisms known as *Mycoplasma* (migh-koh-PLAZ-muh), are only about 0.2 micrometers in diameter. A micrometer is equal to one millionth of a meter. *Mycoplasma* are so small that they often are beyond the resolving power of light microscopes. Larger cells include the giant ameba *Chaos chaos*, which is about 1000 micrometers in diameter. Larger still are the yolks of bird eggs, which are actually single cells containing stored food for the developing bird. For the most part, cells are between 5 and 50 micrometers in diameter. Physical limits on the flow of information through the cell and on the flow of materials into and out of the cell prevent most cells from being much larger than this.

Despite differences in size and shape, there are certain structures that are common to most cells. **The cells of animals, plants, and related organisms have three basic structures: the cell membrane, or outer boundary of the cell; the nucleus, or control center; and the cytoplasm, or material between the cell membrane and the nucleus.** Let's examine a typical plant cell and an animal cell to learn about some of these basic structures.

Figure 5–3 *This diagram shows a typical animal cell. Note that the structures shown are not to scale. (This is true of almost all cell diagrams.) Most structures have been enlarged so that they can be clearly seen. In addition, some structures are more extensive or more numerous in an actual cell than they are in this diagram.*

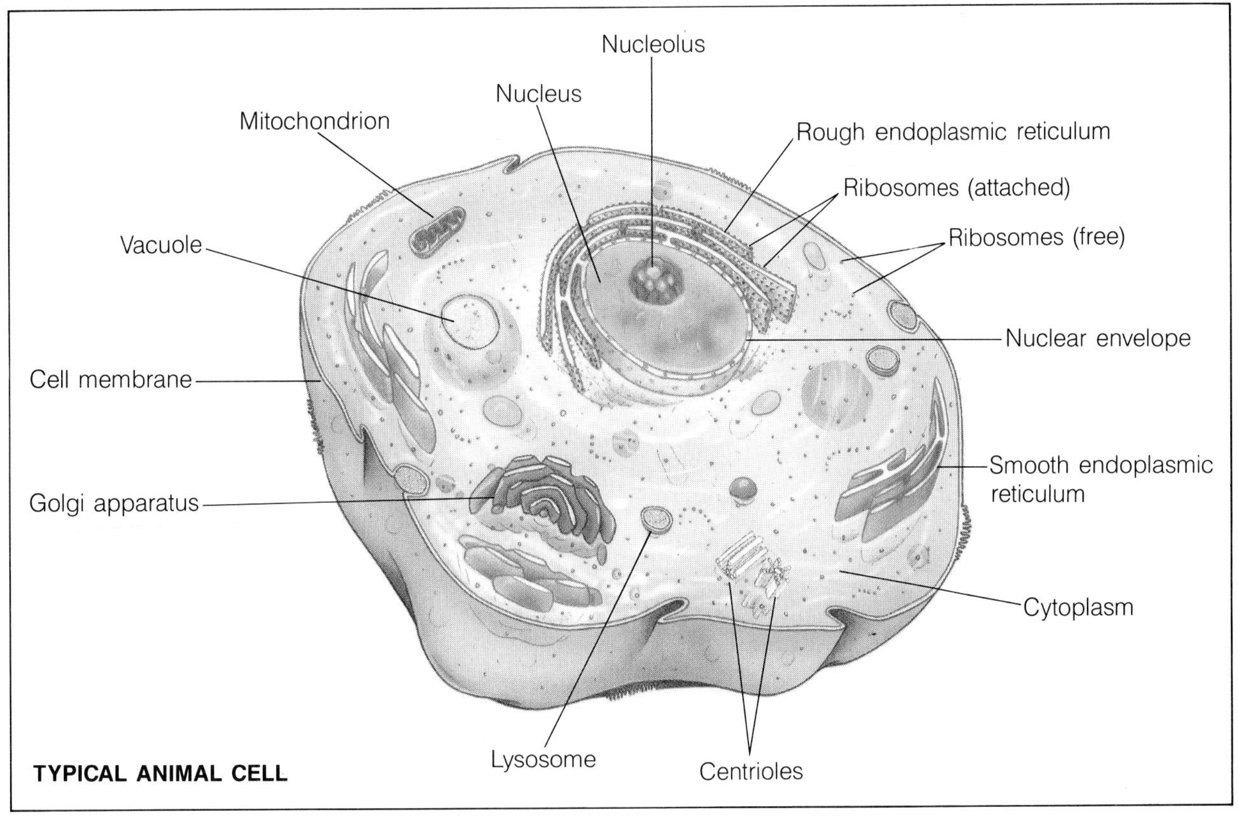

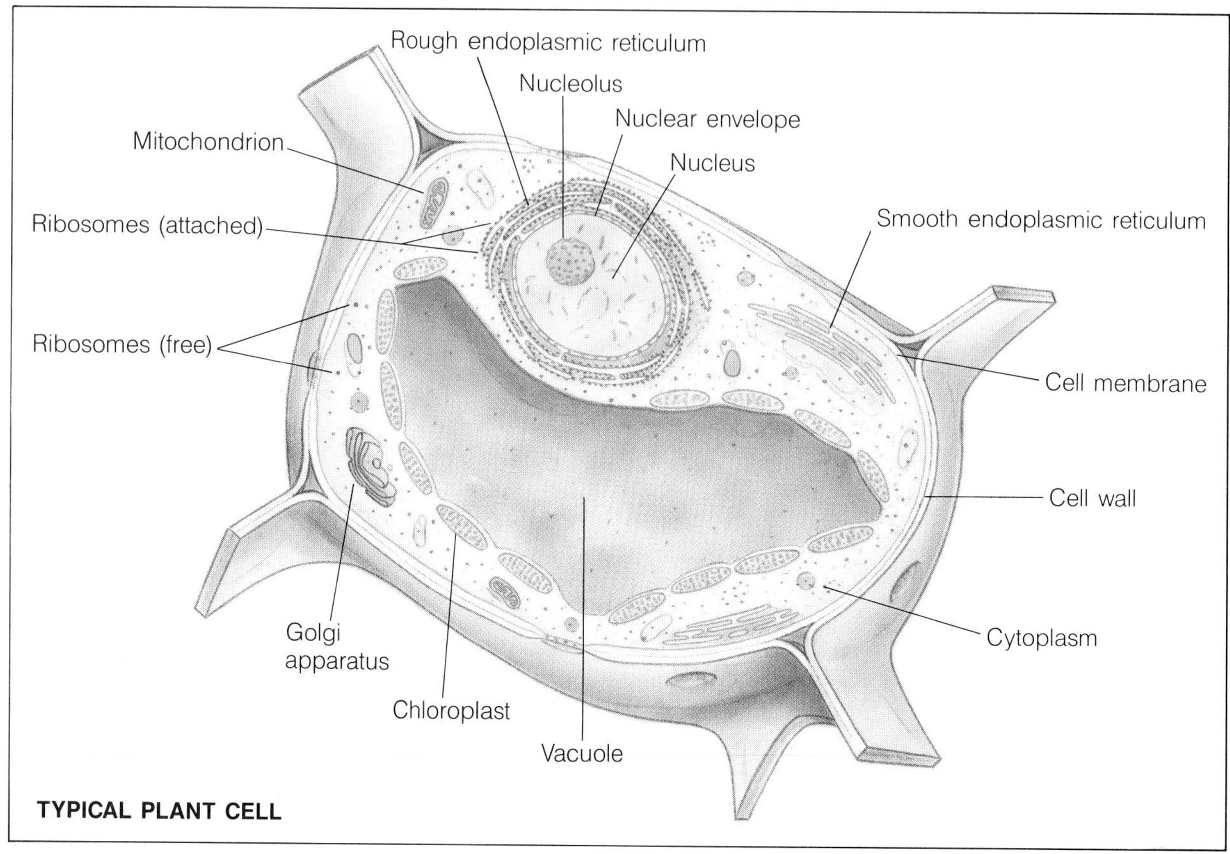

Figure 5–4 *A typical plant cell is shown in this diagram. What is the outer boundary of a plant cell called?*

Cell Membrane

All cells are separated from their surroundings by a **cell membrane**. The cell membrane regulates what enters and leaves the cell and also aids in the protection and support of the cell.

In a way, the cell membrane is similar to the walls that surround a house. As these walls help to protect the house from what is outside, so the cell membrane seals off the cell from its outside environment. But if you lived inside the house, you would still want to receive messages, fuel, and power from outside. So telephone, gas, and electric lines would have to be able to pass through the walls of the house. You would also want to bring in food and take out the trash. Thus doors would be needed. The needs of a cell are similar. It must communicate with other cells, take in food and water, and eliminate wastes. All of these processes take place through the cell membrane.

The cell membrane is composed of several kinds of molecules. The most important of these are the lipids. A double layer of lipid molecules, known as a bilayer, forms the basic unit from which cell membranes are constructed. You can see the structure of the cell membrane in Figure 5–5.

Proteins and carbohydrates are also associated with the cell membrane. Some proteins stick to the surface of the lipid

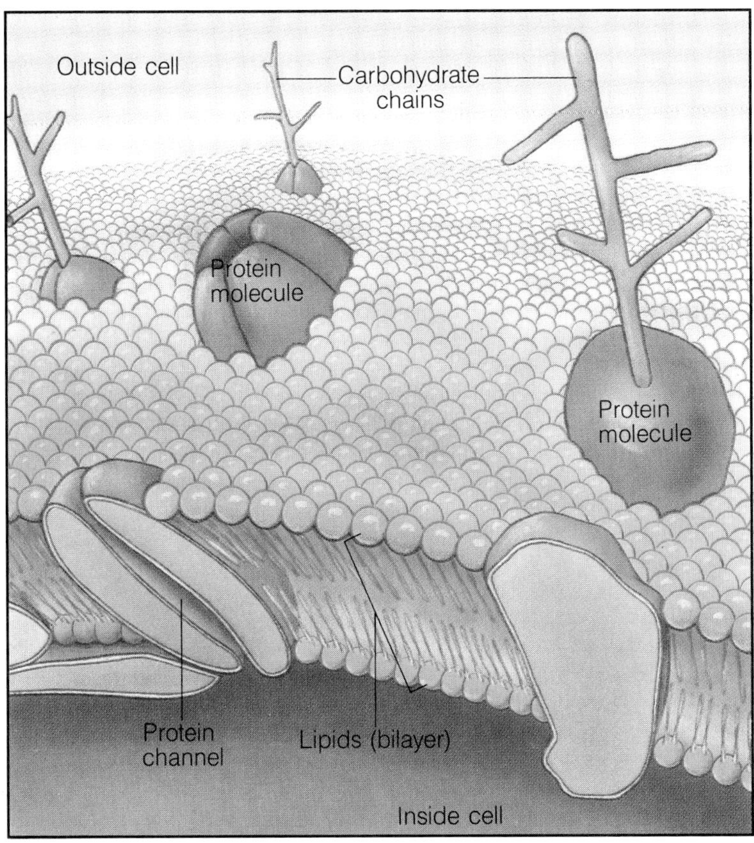

Figure 5–5 According to a widely accepted model of membrane structure called the fluid-mosaic model, cell membranes are formed from double layers of lipids (bilayers) in which proteins are embedded. Some of the proteins form channels that allow certain molecules to pass into and out of the cell. Others resemble small pumps that push molecules from one side of the membrane to the other.

bilayer, whereas others are free to move around within the layer. Some of the free-moving proteins act as channels through which molecules can pass. Others act like small pumps, actively pushing molecules from one side of the membrane to the other. The carbohydrates are attached to proteins or lipids at the membrane surface. Many of these carbohydrates act like chemical identification cards, allowing cells to recognize and interact with each other.

Cell Wall

In organisms such as plants, algae, and some bacteria, the cell membrane is surrounded by a **cell wall**. In other words, the cell wall lies outside the cell membrane. The cell wall helps to protect and support the cell. Because the cell wall is very porous, water, oxygen, carbon dioxide, and other substances can pass through easily.

If we looked at an electron micrograph of a plant cell, we would discover that the cell wall is made up of two or more layers. These layers form in a series of steps. The first layer to form develops where two plant cells meet. See Figure 5–6. This layer contains a gluey substance, called pectin, that helps hold the cells together. Each of the cells then forms a primary cell

Figure 5–6 The primary cell wall forms the outer boundary of plants, algae, and some bacteria. The secondary cell wall, however, generally forms only in woody stems.

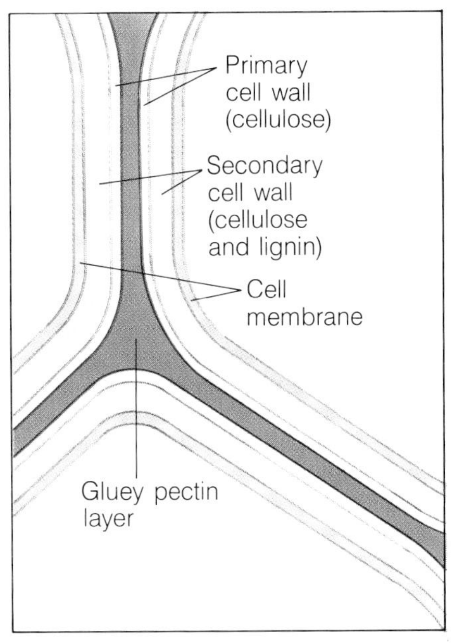

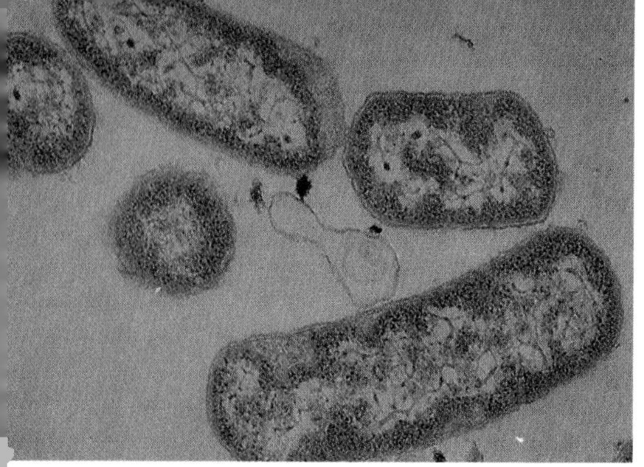

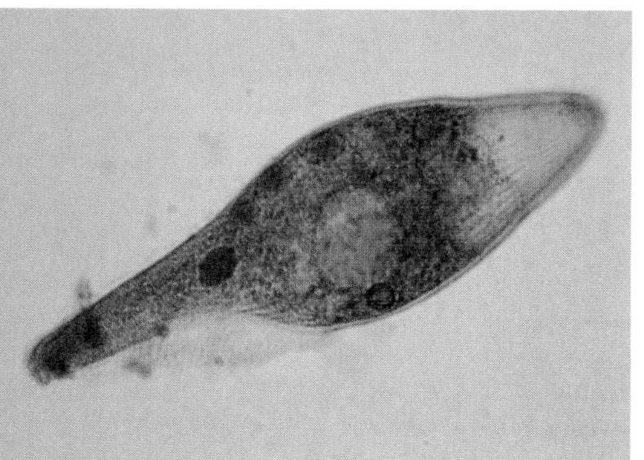

Figure 5–7 *One way of classifying living things is by the presence or absence of a nucleus. Prokaryotes, such as bacteria, do not have a nucleus (top). Eukaryotes, such as a blepharisma, contain a nucleus surrounded by a nuclear envelope (bottom).*

wall on its side of this gluey layer. The primary cell wall is made up of cellulose, a fibrous material. Cellulose fibers make the cell wall elastic, so that it can stretch as the cell grows.

In plants that have woody stems, another layer, called the secondary cell wall, develops. This wall is composed of cellulose and lignin (LIHG-nihn). Lignin makes cellulose more rigid. Wood consists mainly of secondary cell walls.

Nucleus

In many cells we can see a large dark structure, called the **nucleus**, which was first described by Robert Brown. Not all cells have nuclei. Small unicellular organisms known as bacteria, as well as several other kinds of organisms, do not have nuclei. The presence of a nucleus has been used by scientists to divide cells into two general categories: eukaryotic (yoo-kahr-ee-AHT-ihk) cells, those that have a nucleus, and prokaryotic (proh-kahr-ee-AHT-ihk) cells, those that do not have a nucleus.

Organisms made up of eukaryotic cells are commonly known as **eukaryotes** (yoo-KAHR-ee-ohts). The animals and plants that we see around us are eukaryotes. Those organisms, such as bacteria, that are made up of prokaryotic cells are known as **prokaryotes** (pro-KAHR-ee-ohts). The distinction between prokaryotes and eukaryotes is a basic one, and we will return to it many times as we consider the diversity of living things. In fact, scientists consider this distinction far more important than the distinction between plant and animal cells!

Many of the scientists who first examined cells under a microscope suspected that the nucleus was doing something important. What could it be? The nucleus has been found to be the information center of the cell and contains DNA (deoxyribonucleic acid). The instructions for making thousands of different molecules are found in the nucleus. These instructions are decoded and executed by a process that we will discuss in Chapter 7. The nucleus also directs all the activities that occur in a living cell.

NUCLEAR ENVELOPE The nucleus of a eukaryotic cell is generally 2 to 5 micrometers in diameter. Surrounding the nucleus are two membranes that form the **nuclear envelope**. These two membranes form the boundary around the nucleus. In the nuclear envelope are dozens of nuclear pores, or small openings. The molecules that move in and out of the nucleus pass through the nuclear pores.

NUCLEOLUS Most nuclei contain a small region called the **nucleolus** (noo-KLEE-uh-luhs) that is made up of RNA (ribonucleic acid) and proteins. The nucleolus is the structure in which ribosomes are made. Ribosomes, as you will soon learn, aid in the production of proteins within the cell.

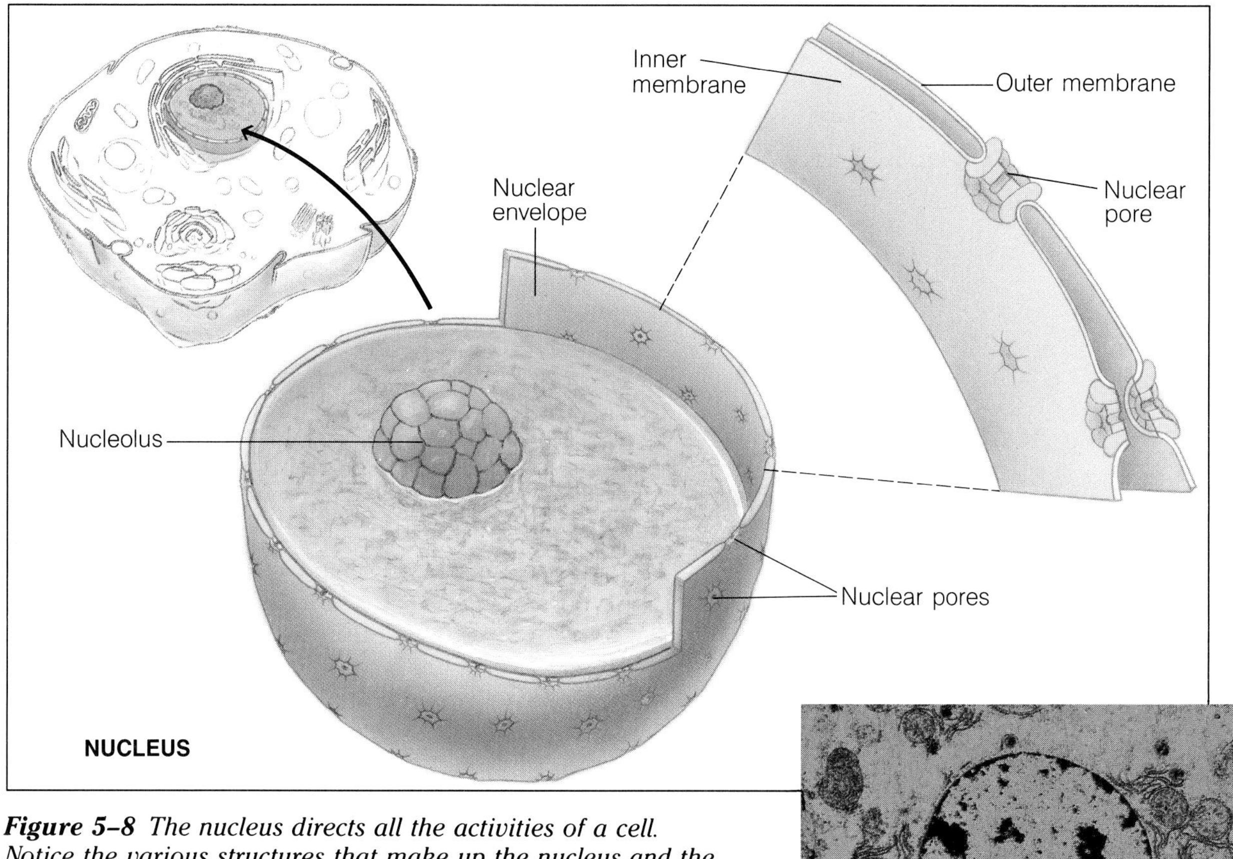

Figure 5–8 The nucleus directs all the activities of a cell. Notice the various structures that make up the nucleus and the appearance of the nucleus viewed through a transmission electron microscope.

CHROMOSOMES The DNA in the nucleus of eukaryotic cells is attached to special proteins and forms large structures called **chromosomes**. Chromosomes contain the genetic information that must be passed to each new generation of cells.

Cytoplasm

Because the nucleus sits in the center of many eukaryotic cells, we can divide the space within a cell into two compartments: the nucleus and the **cytoplasm**. The cytoplasm is the area between the nucleus and the cell membrane. The cytoplasm contains many important structures that we shall discuss in the next section.

5–2 SECTION REVIEW

1. What are the three basic structures found in most cells?
2. What is the function of the cell membrane?
3. Distinguish between a prokaryote and a eukaryote. Why is this distinction important to scientists?

Section Objectives

- Define organelle.
- Describe the functions of the cytoplasmic organelles.
- Compare a plant cell and an animal cell.

5–3 Cytoplasmic Organelles

Even in the low-power images that we can produce with the light microscope, it is clear that there are structures inside the cytoplasm of the cell. The structures in the cytoplasm are generally called **organelles** (or-guh-NEHLZ). **An organelle is a tiny structure that performs a specialized function in the cell.** Each organelle (little organ) has a special job that helps maintain the cell's life. Let's look at some of the organelles that are found in plant and animal cells.

Mitochondria and Chloroplasts: Power Stations

All living things require a reliable source of energy. On the Earth that source is usually the sun or food substances. The **mitochondrion** (might-oh-KAHN-dree-uhn; plural: mitochondria) and the **chloroplast** are key organelles that change energy from one form to another. Mitochondria change the chemical energy stored in food into compounds that are more convenient for the cell to use. Chloroplasts trap the energy of sunlight and convert it into chemical energy. The reactions that take place in both of these organelles are closely related, and we will examine them in more detail in Chapter 6.

The mitochondrion contains two special membranes. The outer membrane surrounds the organelle, and the inner membrane has many folds that increase the surface area of the mitochondrion.

Figure 5–9 *Mitochondria are the powerhouses of the cell. They provide the cell with the energy it needs to survive. Note the structure of a mitochondrion in the diagram and in the electron micrograph.*

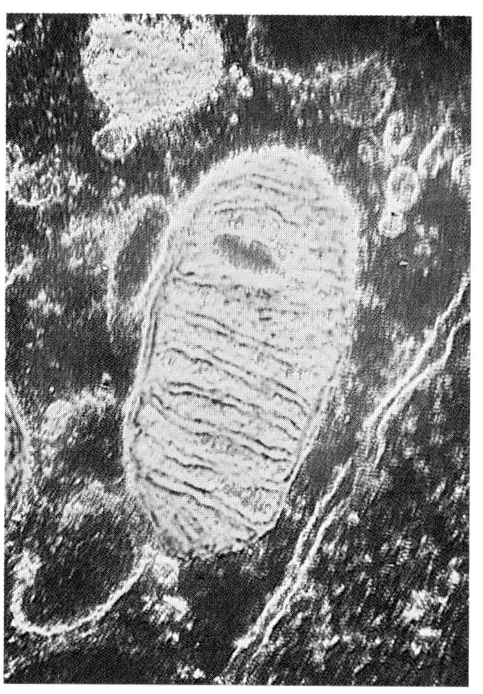

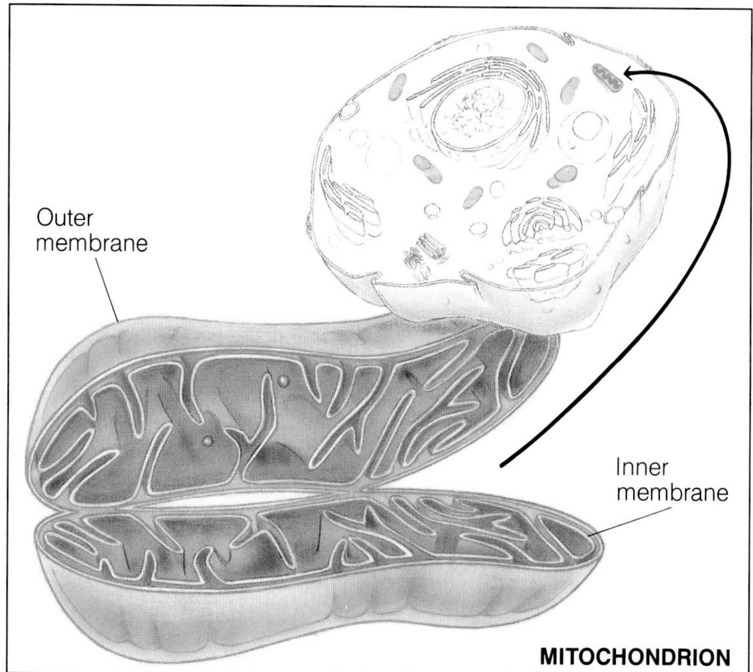

The structure of the chloroplast is similar. It is surrounded by two envelopelike membranes and contains a third kind of membrane, where the radiant energy of the sun is actually changed into chemical energy. Chloroplasts are found only in plant cells and algae. As we will see later, both mitochondria and chloroplasts have a degree of independence from the rest of the cell. This has led to some discussion that they may be descended from independent organisms.

Ribosomes: Protein Factories

Ribosomes are the structures in which proteins are made. Cells that are active in protein synthesis are often crowded with ribosomes. Ribosomes are composed of RNA and protein. Some ribosomes are attached to membranes; some are found free in the cytoplasm. Ribosomes are among the smallest of organelles. They are no larger than 25 nanometers in diameter. A nanometer is equal to one billionth of a meter.

Endoplasmic Reticulum and Golgi Apparatus: Manufacturers and Shippers

Many cells are filled with a complex network of channels known as the **endoplasmic reticulum** (ehn-doh-PLAZ-mihk rih-TIHK-yuh-luhm), or ER. The endoplasmic reticulum transports materials through the inside of the cell. There are two types of endoplasmic reticulum. In the smooth endoplasmic reticulum (smooth ER), the walls of the channels look smooth

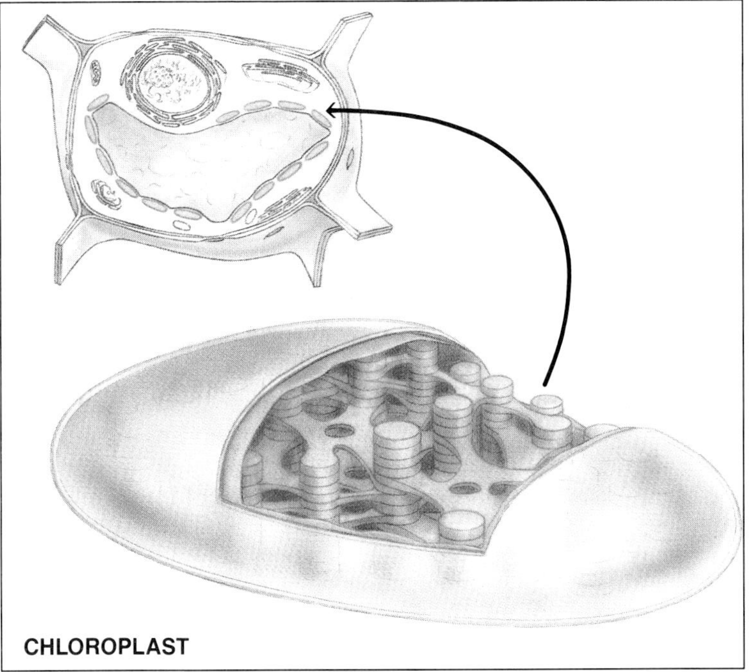

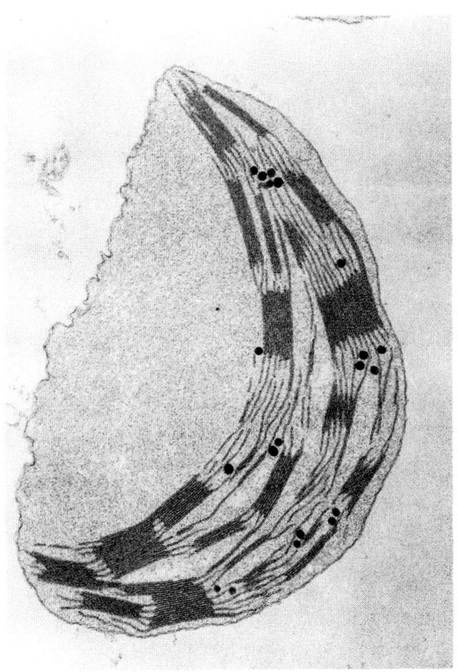

Figure 5–10 *Chloroplasts are organelles that use the radiant energy of sunlight to produce the chemical energy organisms need to survive. Notice the envelopelike membranes within the chloroplasts.*

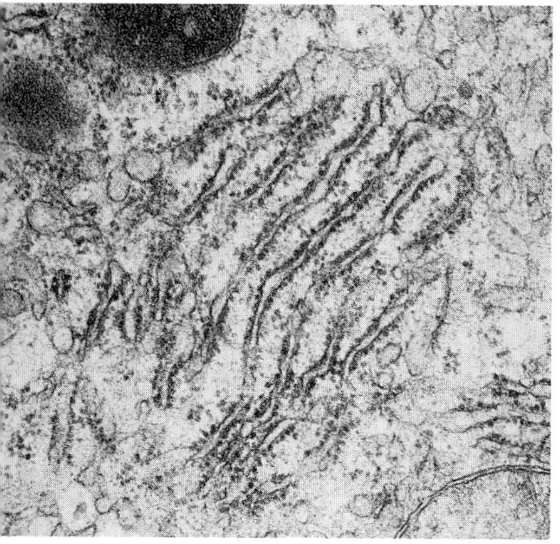

Figure 5–11 The endoplasmic reticulum is actually a series of channels that transport materials throughout the cell. Which type of endoplasmic reticulum has ribosomes attached to its surface?

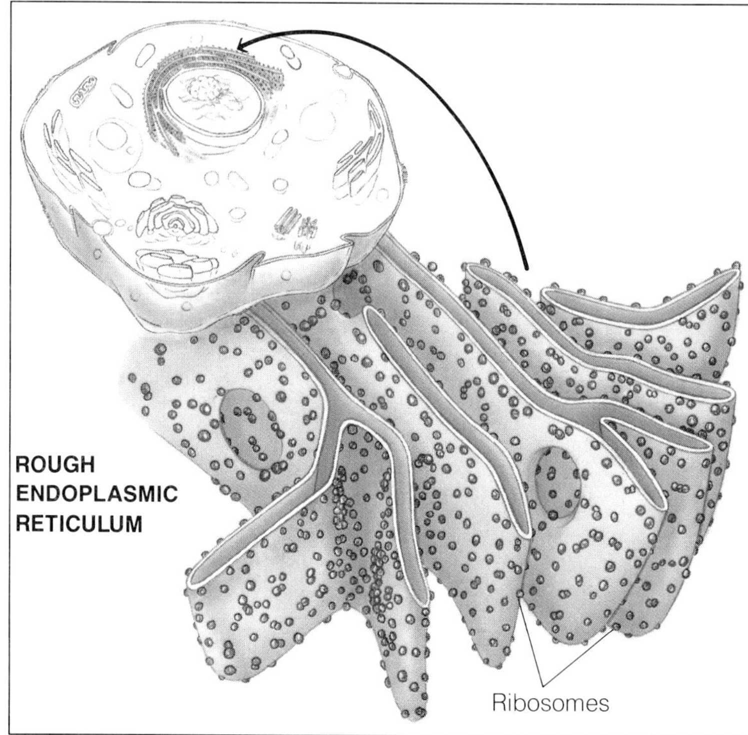

and are not studded with particles or granules. In some cells, special enzymes and chemicals are stored in the smooth endoplasmic reticulum.

The other form of endoplasmic reticulum is involved in the synthesis of proteins. This form is called the rough endoplasmic reticulum (rough ER) because the ribosomes that are stuck to its surface give it a rough appearance. Newly made proteins are inserted into the rough ER, where they may be chemically modified. Many proteins that are released, or exported, from the cell are synthesized on the rough ER.

Like automobiles to which enthusiasts attach chrome panels and hood ornaments, proteins often are modified by special enzymes that attach carbohydrates and lipids to them. In most cases, the proteins are first moved into special compartments known as the **Golgi apparatus**, because they were discovered by the Italian scientist Camillo Golgi. The Golgi apparatus looks like a flattened stack of membranes piled one upon the other, not unlike a stack of pancakes. After modification in the Golgi apparatus, the proteins may then be released from the cell or take up positions in other parts of the cell. Put another way, the Golgi apparatus modifies, collects, packages, and distributes molecules made at one location of the cell and used at another.

Figure 5–12 The Golgi apparatus modifies proteins by attaching carbohydrates or lipids to the proteins. The modified proteins can then be transported from one part of the cell to another.

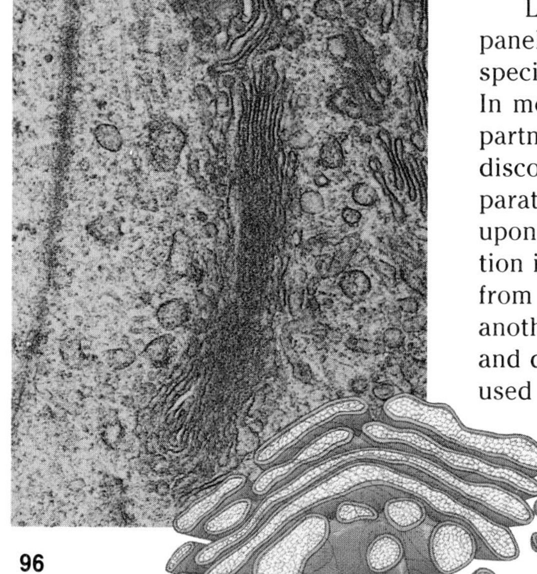

Lysosomes: Cleanup Crews

Some white blood cells in your blood are capable of swallowing whole bacteria. Other cells, such as the single-celled ameba, are capable of engulfing clumps of yeast, sugar, and even tiny pieces of bread. Many cells will seem to engulf microscopic particles of food, foreign material, or even other cells. This process is called endocytosis (ehn-doh-sigh-TOH-sihs). Endocytosis is a way in which materials that are too large to pass through the cell membrane get into the cell.

When a cell encircles a particle, the cell membrane forms a pocket around the foreign material. The foreign material must now be digested, or broken down. That is the job of the **lysosomes** (LIGH-suh-sohmz). Lysosomes are small membrane-bordered structures that contain chemicals and enzymes necessary for digesting certain materials in the cell. Lysosomes are formed by the Golgi apparatus. Plant cells do not have lysosomes.

Lysosomes are also involved in breaking down organelles that have outlived their usefulness. In a way, lysosomes can be thought of as the cell's cleanup crews. As such, lysosomes perform vital functions. Why do you think human diseases that cause the lysosomes to work improperly, such as Tay-Sachs disease and possibly cystic fibrosis, can be serious and even fatal?

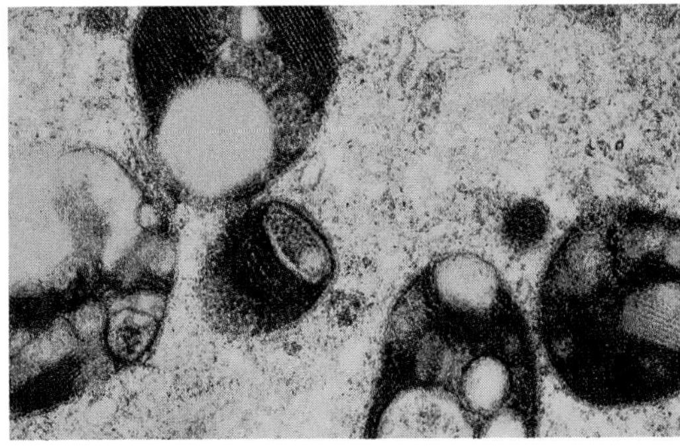

Figure 5–13 *These spherical organelles are lysosomes that have been magnified approximately 95,000 times. Lysosomes contain enzymes that can digest other organelles that have outlived their usefulness. For this reason, lysosomes are thought of as the cell's cleanup crews.*

Vacuoles and Plastids: Storage Tanks

Many cells contain saclike structures, called **vacuoles** (VAK-yoo-ohlz), that store materials such as water, salts, proteins, and carbohydrates. In many plant cells there is a single large central vacuole filled with liquid. The pressure of the liquid-filled vacuole in these cells makes it possible for plants to grow quickly and to support heavy structures such as leaves and flowers. Why do you think a plant that has lost a large amount of water will begin to wilt?

Plastids are plant organelles that may take many forms, one of which is the chloroplast, an organelle we have already mentioned. Many plastids are involved in the storage of food and pigments. Some examples of plastids are leukoplasts (LOO-koh-plasts), which store starch granules, and chromoplasts (KROH-muh-plasts), which store pigment molecules. The red color in the skin of a ripe tomato comes from pigments produced in chromoplasts.

Figure 5–14 *The large saclike structure in this leaf cell is a vacuole, which has been magnified approximately 16,000 times. Vacuoles act as cellular storage tanks and may hold water, salts, proteins, and carbohydrates.*

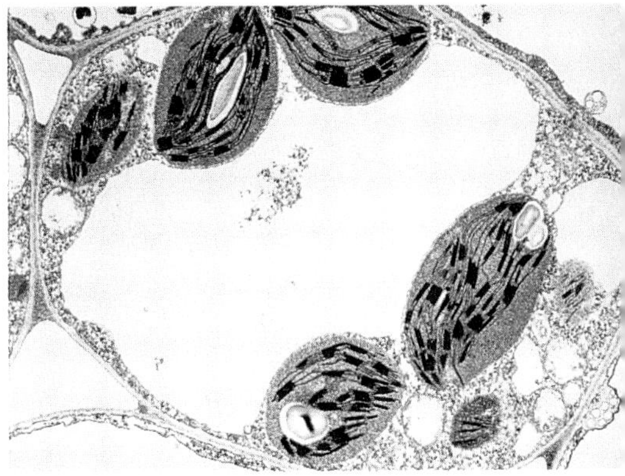

Cytoskeleton: Framework

Cells are found in a bewildering variety of shapes: some round, some cubical, some long and slender. In addition, most cells are capable of some type of movement. Even stationary cells can move the organelles around inside of them. How do they accomplish such motion? And what allows cells to keep their unusual shapes?

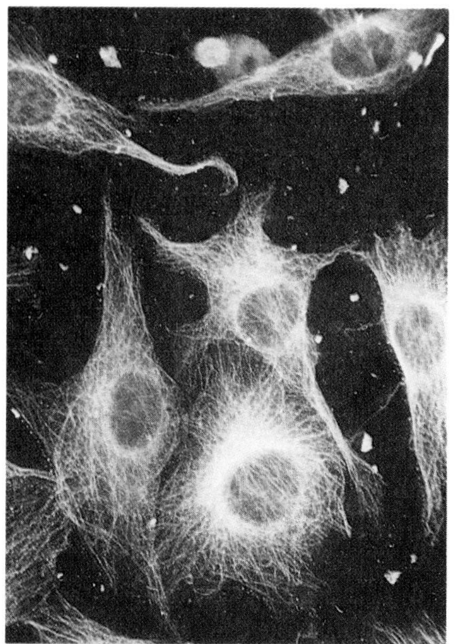

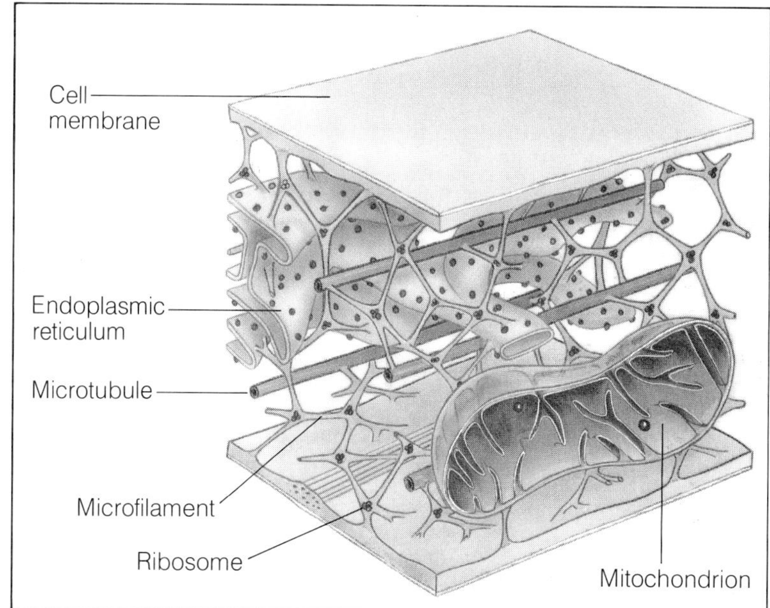

Figure 5–15 *This diagram shows the cytoskeleton of the cell. Notice that the endoplasmic reticulum, mitochondria, and ribosomes are all held in place by the microfilaments and microtubules that form the cytoskeleton. The photograph shows the actual microtubules that make up the cytoskeleton.*

Not too many years ago, scientists were content to suggest that the cytoplasm was filled with a material, called protoplasm, that gave the cell many unique properties. As we have learned more about the composition of the cell, the idea of "protoplasm" has lost acceptance. In its place, biologists have uncovered a framework known as the **cytoskeleton**. The cytoskeleton is composed of a variety of filaments and fibers that support cell structure and drive cell movement.

One of the main components of the cytoskeleton are microtubules, hollow tubules made out of proteins. Microtubules provide support for cell shape, help move organelles through the cell, and play a special role in cell division by forming centrioles (SEHN-tree-ohlz). Centrioles are found in animal cells and many other eukaryotic cells but not in plant cells.

In some cells, the microtubules support hairlike projections from the cell surface known as cilia (SIHL-ee-uh; singular: cilium) and flagella (fluh-JEHL-uh; singular: flagellum). Cilia are short threadlike structures that help unicellular organisms move. They also aid in the movement of substances along the cell's surface. Flagella are longer whiplike structures that help unicellular organisms move about. Cilia and flagella contain nine pairs of microtubules arranged around a pair in the center. These microtubules are linked to each other, and the bridges that connect them generate the force to produce motion.

Another principal component of the cytoskeleton are microfilaments—long, thin fibers that function in the movement and support of the cell. They also permit movement of the cytoplasm within the cell. This is called cytoplasmic streaming. The proteins that make up microfilaments are also found in muscle cells, which are specialized for contraction.

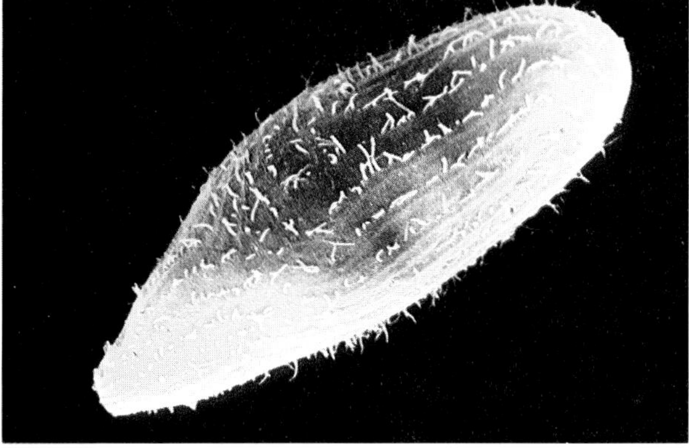

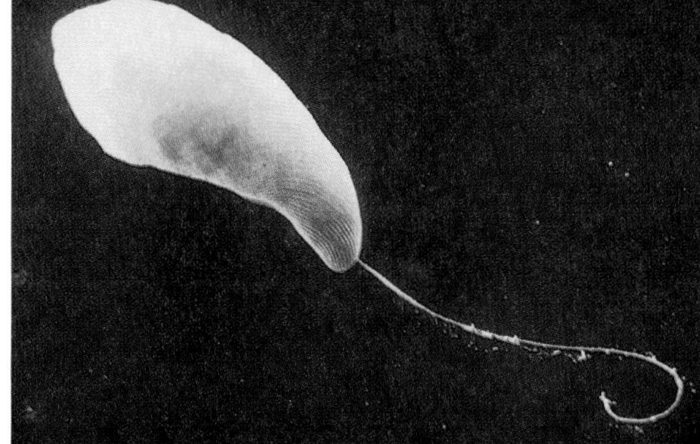

Figure 5–16 *The microtubules of the cytoskeleton support hairlike projections called cilia and flagella. Cilia, such as those on this single-celled organism (left), are short threadlike structures that help the cell move about by beating back and forth. Flagella, such as the one on the single-celled* Euglena *(right), help the cell move by beating in a whiplike fashion.*

5–3 SECTION REVIEW

1. What are organelles? Give two examples of organelles.
2. How do lysosomes function to digest particles?
3. How are mitochondria and chloroplasts similar? How are they different?
4. What components make up the cytoskeleton?

5–4 Movement of Materials Through the Cell Membrane

Section Objectives

- Explain the processes of diffusion and osmosis.
- Compare active and passive transport.
- Describe endocytosis, phagocytosis, pinocytosis, and exocytosis.

Each individual cell exists in a liquid environment. Even the cells of multicellular organisms such as a maple tree or a human are bathed in liquid. The cells of our bodies are bathed in a liquid that was once part of blood. The presence of a liquid environment makes it easier for materials such as food, oxygen, and water to move into and out of the cell. There are several ways in which materials enter and leave the cell.

Diffusion

Although the cell membrane is a barrier, it must not be too effective. Materials must pass into and out of the cell. How is this movement accomplished?

We know that molecules move constantly, colliding with one another and tending to spread out randomly through space. This random motion results in the tendency of molecules to move from a region where they are more numerous to a region where they are less numerous. In other words, molecules move from an area of higher concentration to an area of lower concentration.

The driving force behind the movement of many substances across the cell membrane is called **diffusion** (dih-FYOO-zhuhn). **Diffusion is the process by which molecules of a substance move from areas of higher concentration of that substance to areas of lower concentration.**

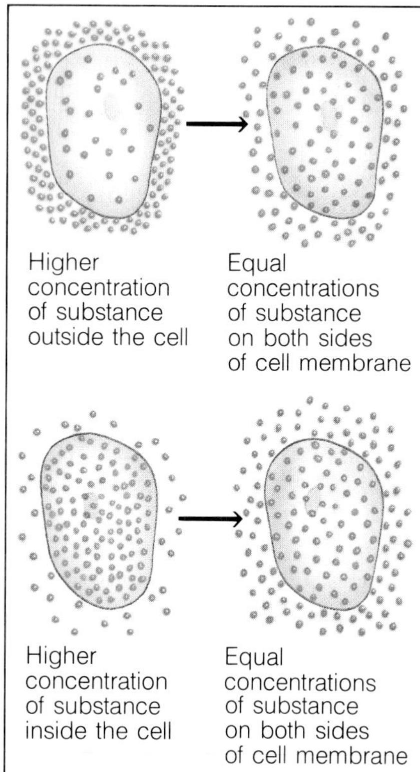

Figure 5–17 *Diffusion is the movement of the molecules of a substance from areas where they are more concentrated to areas where they are less concentrated. What point has been reached when the concentration of a substance is equal on both sides of a cell membrane?*

What factors determine whether diffusion occurs across a membrane? If two substances are present in unequal amounts on either side of a membrane, each substance will tend to move toward the area of lower concentration until equilibrium is reached. See Figure 5–17. Equilibrium occurs when the concentrations of the substances on both sides of the membrane are the same. At this point, we may say that an equilibrium point for each substance has been reached. Individual molecules continue to move rapidly between the two sides at equilibrium, but because roughly equal numbers of molecules move in each direction, there is no further change in concentration.

Another important factor that determines whether diffusion occurs across a membrane is permeability (per-mee-uh-BIHL-uh-tee). If a particular substance is able to diffuse across a membrane, then we say that the membrane is permeable to that substance. A membrane is said to be impermeable to those things that cannot pass across it. As you might expect, biological membranes are permeable to some things and impermeable to others. Therefore, we can describe most biological membranes as **selectively permeable**.

Osmosis

Although compounds that are able to dissolve in the lipid bilayer of the cell membrane pass through the membrane easily, most other molecules do not. There is, however, one important exception to that rule: water. Water molecules pass through most cell membranes very rapidly. The fact that water molecules can pass through membranes so easily has important consequences for the cell.

The diffusion of water molecules through a selectively permeable membrane is called **osmosis** (ahs-MOH-sihs). If a membrane separates two solutions, in which direction will the water molecules move? To answer this question, let us suppose that we place a concentrated sugar solution on one side of a selectively permeable membrane and a dilute sugar solution on the other. As you have just learned, water will pass through the membrane by diffusion from the area of high water concentration to the area of low water concentration. In which direction is that?

Look at Figure 5–18. On the side of the membrane with the concentrated sugar solution, fewer water molecules will strike the membrane because they will be crowded out by the sugar molecules. Thus, this side is the area of low water concentration. On the side of the membrane with the dilute sugar solution, more water molecules will strike the membrane. This side is the area of high water concentration. As a result, more water moves through the membrane from the side that has the low sugar concentration to the side that has the high sugar concentration than moves through in the opposite direction. This results in a net movement of water from the side with the dilute

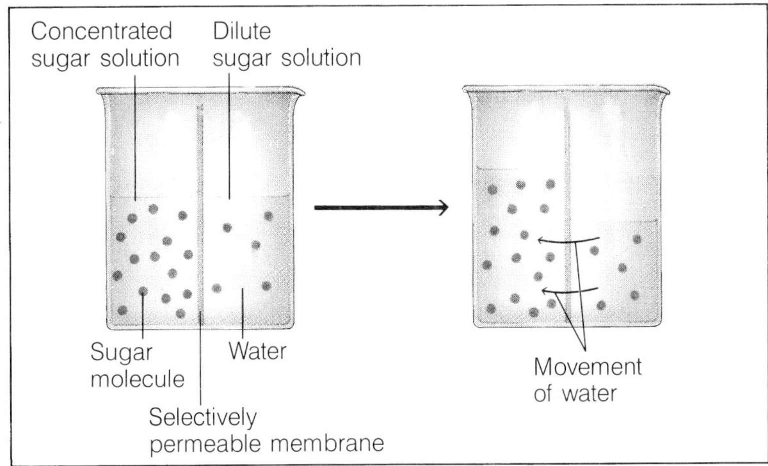

Figure 5–18 Osmosis is the diffusion of water molecules through a selectively permeable membrane from an area of greater concentration of water to an area of lesser concentration of water. In this diagram, there are more water molecules on the side containing the dilute sugar solution. As a result, the water molecules move to the side containing the concentrated sugar solution. Osmosis continues until equilibrium is reached.

sugar solution to the side with the concentrated sugar solution.

The force exerted by osmosis, or osmotic pressure, tends to move water across membranes from a more dilute solution into a more concentrated solution. If, however, two solutions contain exactly the same amount of dissolved material, there is no osmotic pressure across a membrane separating them because the concentrations of dissolved materials are in equilibrium.

Osmotic pressure can cause serious problems for a cell. Because the cytoplasm is filled with salts, sugars, proteins, and other molecules, it will almost always have a much lower concentration of water than is found in fresh water. Therefore, there should be a net movement of water into a typical cell if it is surrounded by fresh water. If water moves in freely, the volume of a cell will increase until the cell becomes swollen and bursts like an overinflated balloon.

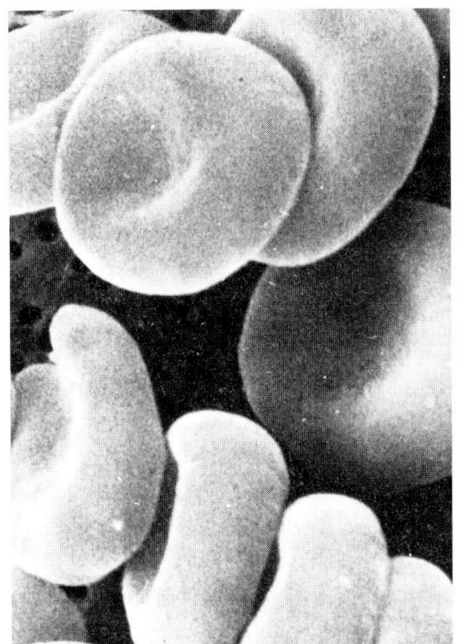

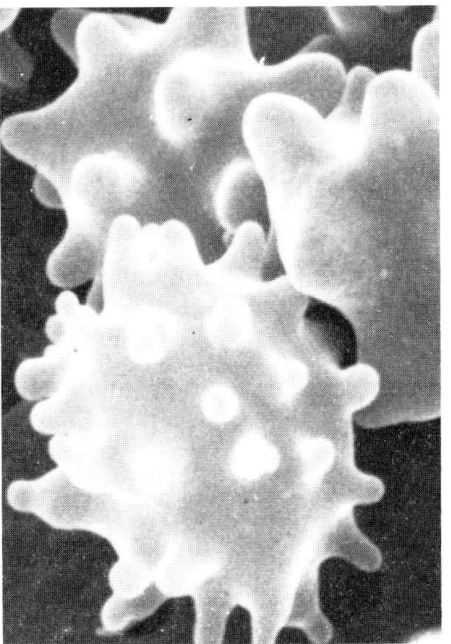

Figure 5–19 Normal red blood cells (left) will shrink if too much water leaves the cells due to osmosis (center). If too much water enters the cells during osmosis, the red blood cells will swell (right).

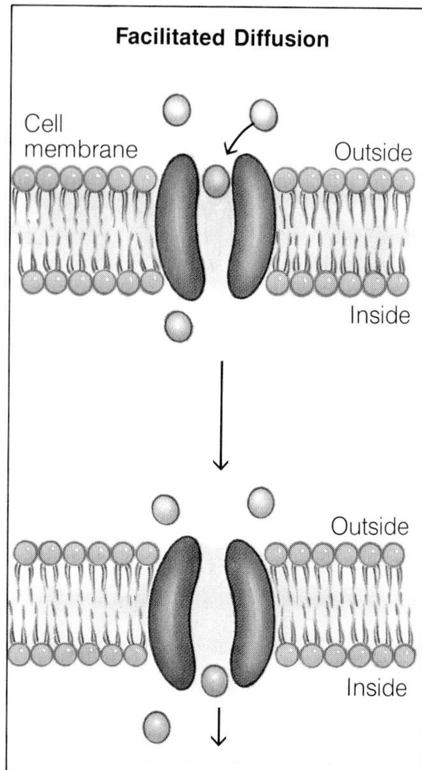

Figure 5–20 *Most molecules that do not dissolve in the lipid bilayer of the cell membrane cannot pass through by diffusion. One way of getting such molecules into the cell is by facilitated diffusion. This process, which does not require any energy, uses a carrier molecule to transport a substance into the cell through the cell membrane.*

The structure of the lipid bilayer makes cell membranes freely permeable to water. Cells deal with the problem of osmotic pressure in a variety of ways.

In some instances, the cells of many organisms do not come in contact with fresh water. Instead, the cells are bathed in fluids, such as blood, that have concentrations of dissolved materials roughly equal to the cells themselves.

Other cells, such as plant cells and bacteria, deal with osmotic pressure in another way. They are surrounded by cell walls that prevent the cells from expanding, even under tremendous osmotic pressure. However, the increased osmotic pressure makes the cells extremely vulnerable to injuries to the cell wall.

Still other cells employ a mechanism to pump out the water that is forced in by osmosis. For example, some unicellular organisms have a structure called a contractile (kuhn-TRAK-tihl) vacuole. By contracting rhythmically, the contractile vacuole pumps water out of the cell.

Facilitated Diffusion

Osmosis and diffusion are forms of passive transport across the cell membrane because energy is not needed for these processes. Some materials, including alcohols and small lipids, can pass directly through the membrane because they can dissolve in the lipid bilayer. But many molecules are transported across a membrane in the direction of lowest concentration by a carrier protein. This process is called **facilitated diffusion**. In red blood cells, for example, a carrier protein in the cell membrane transports glucose from one side of the membrane to the other. The glucose-transporter protein facilitates, or helps in, the diffusion of glucose.

Although facilitated diffusion is fast, specific, and does not require energy, it is still driven by diffusion. Therefore, a net movement of material across a cell membrane by facilitated diffusion can occur only if a concentration difference exists across that membrane.

Active Transport

Active transport is an energy-requiring process that enables material to move across a cell membrane against a concentration difference. There are two types of active transport.

In one type, individual molecules are carried through membrane-associated pumps. Special transport macromolecules that exist in the cell membrane move molecules across the membrane. Among the molecules that are transported are calcium, potassium, and sodium ions. Normally they are not able to diffuse across the membrane. The molecular pumps that carry out this transport require chemical energy, thus making this process a form of active transport. All cells that have been

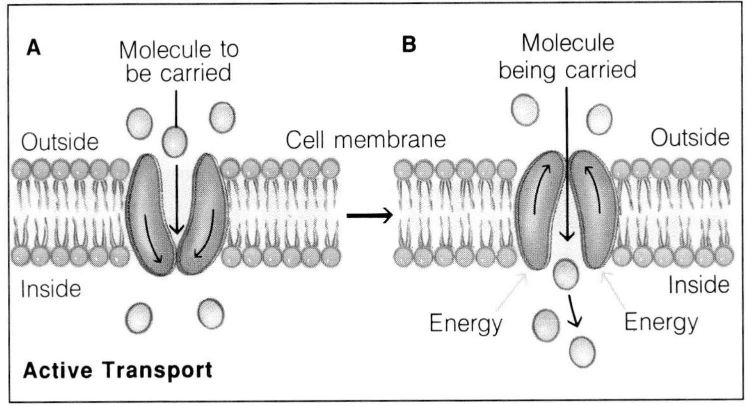

Figure 5–21 *Very often a substance must pass through the cell membrane even if the concentration of that substance is greater inside the cell than it is outside the cell. In such cases, the cell must expend energy in a process called active transport. In one form of active transport, energy is used to change the shape of the cell membrane and to actively pull the substance through the membrane into the cell.*

studied seem to transport at least a few molecules in this way. The use of energy in these systems enables cells to concentrate molecules, even when the normal forces of diffusion might tend to move those molecules in the opposite direction.

In the second type of active transport, large amounts of material are transported through movements of the cell membrane. One of these movements is called endocytosis. As you may remember, endocytosis is the process of taking material into the cell by means of infoldings, or pockets, of the cell membrane. The pocket that results breaks loose from the outer portion of the cell membrane and forms a vacuole within the cytoplasm. Large molecules, clumps of food, and even whole cells can be taken up in this way.

When large particles are taken into the cell by endocytosis, the process is called phagocytosis (fayg-oh-sigh-TOH-sihs). In phagocytosis, extensions of cytoplasm surround and engulf large particles. Amebas use this method of taking in food.

In a process similar to endocytosis, many cells take up liquid from the surrounding environment in a similar way. Tiny pockets form along the cell membrane, fill with liquid, and pinch off to form vacuoles within the cell. This process is known as pinocytosis (pighn-oh-sigh-TOH-sihs).

Figure 5–22 *Another form of active transport is called phagocytosis. During phagocytosis, a large particle is surrounded by pockets of the cell membrane (right). Once the particle is surrounded, the pocket breaks away from the cell membrane and forms a vacuole within the cell. Amebas are one type of organism that takes in food and other materials through phagocytosis (left).*

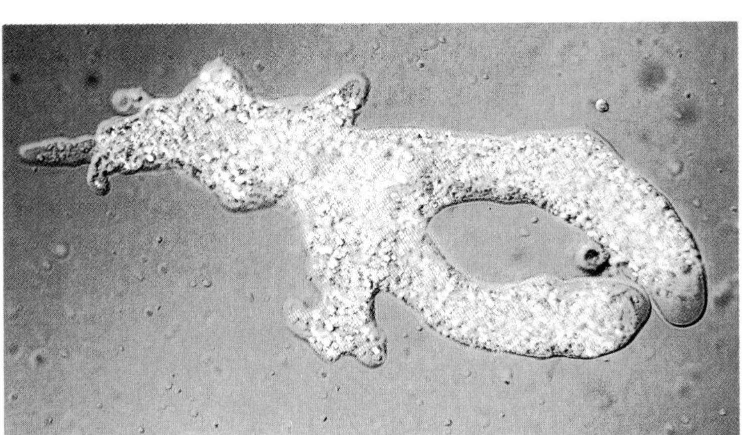

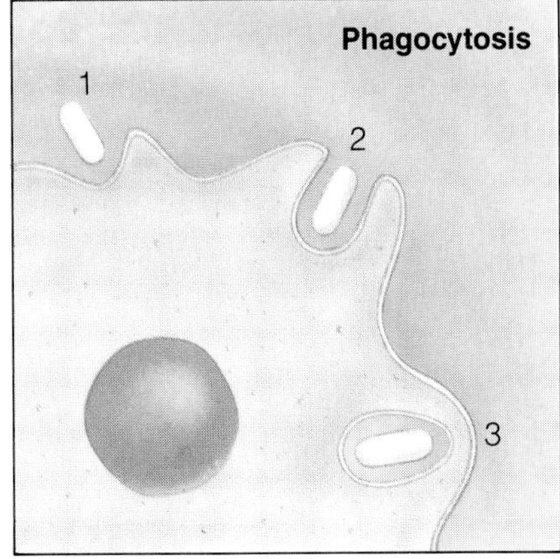

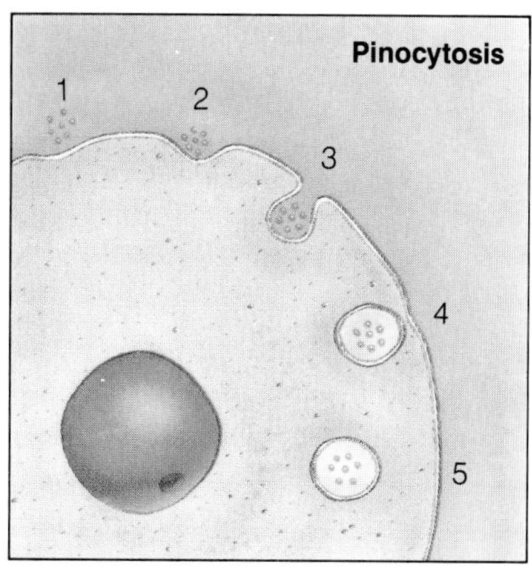

Figure 5–23 *Like phagocytosis, pinocytosis is a form of active transport. In pinocytosis, however, cells take in liquids rather than solid particles.*

As you might expect, cells are also capable of sending material out of the cell. The removal of water by means of a contractile vacuole is one example of this kind of active transport. When other large molecules are removed from the cell, the process is generally known as exocytosis (ehk-soh-sigh-TOH-sihs). As exocytosis occurs, the membrane surrounding the material fuses with the cell membrane, forcing the contents out of the cell.

5–4 SECTION REVIEW

1. What is diffusion?
2. Why is osmosis a form of diffusion?
3. Molecules that are soluble in lipids tend to move across cell membranes more quickly than those that are not. Based on this information, what could you conclude about the structure of the cell membrane?
4. The red blood cell contains a higher concentration of K^+ ions than does the liquid that surrounds it. Are K^+ ions most likely to be moved across the membrane by facilitated diffusion or active transport? Explain.

Section Objective

- Relate cell specialization to cell structure.

5–5 Cell Specialization

Cell specialization is one of the key characteristics of cells in a multicellular organism. **By cell specialization, we mean that cells are often uniquely suited to perform a particular function within the organism.** For example, some cells are specialized to move. Some cells are specialized to react to their environment—the world around them. Some cells are specialized to make certain products. We will now look briefly at three cells, each specialized for a different function.

Factory in Miniature

Located just below the stomach is a small structure called the pancreas. Portions of the pancreas contain cells that are specialized to produce digestive enzymes. Although these cells have most of the organelles found in other cells, they contain enormous amounts of the organelles involved in protein synthesis. In fact, one cell may contain 100 times the amount of rough endoplasmic reticulum found in other cell types. Each cell is filled with ribosomes as well as rough ER. These cells also contain large Golgi apparatus filled with vacuoles that are loaded with soon-to-be-released protein. Cells of the pancreas are dominated by organelles needed for protein synthesis.

Do Your Cells Belong to You?

In 1976, John Moore was diagnosed as having hairy cell leukemia. With this rare form of cancer, a person has too many B lymphocytes that develop tiny whiskerlike projections. B lymphocytes are white blood cells responsible for making antibodies, which are substances that help the body fight off certain diseases.

At the recommendation of his doctor, Moore had his enlarged spleen removed by physicians at the University of California at Los Angeles (UCLA) Medical Center. Normally, the spleen, an organ located near the stomach, filters out worn out or damaged blood cells. But in a person suffering from hairy cell leukemia, the spleen becomes filled with cancerous cells and can no longer perform its function. In addition, the healthy spleen cells are destroyed. Removal of the spleen is not a cure, but it helps return the number of blood cells to normal.

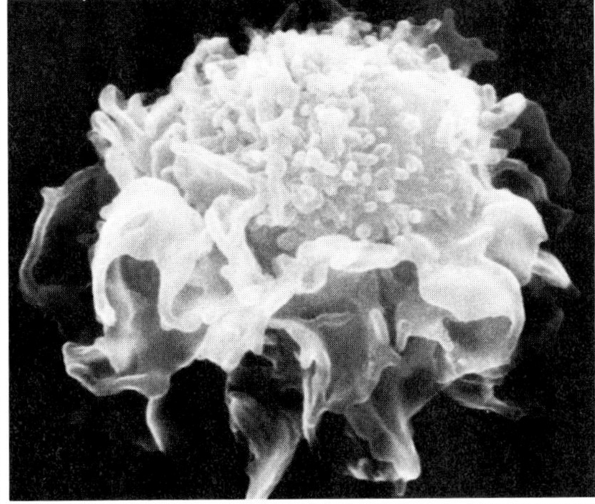

Whiskerlike projections on white blood cells are characteristic of a person who has hairy cell leukemia.

What Moore did not know until later, however, was that a portion of his spleen was saved and used by researchers to isolate and grow cells in culture—cells that produce a substance that may prove useful against cancer or AIDS. In 1984, UCLA obtained a patent for the cells and their products. One of these products was mass produced by a biotechnology company. The genetically engineered drug was then sold by a pharmaceutical firm. The development and sale of this new drug was proceeding well . . . that is, until Moore sued UCLA, his doctor, and others for patenting and profiting from parts of his body!

In response to the suit, UCLA and the doctor have claimed that Moore signed two consent forms. One form gave UCLA permission to remove Moore's spleen, a procedure that obviously saved his life. The other gave UCLA all rights to Moore's cells and any future product that might be developed from them. The doctor further stated that Moore gave up claims to his spleen tissue—tissue that was worthless, even dangerous, to him. It was through the application of scientific knowledge that this poisoned tissue was turned into something of value.

In 1988, Moore's case went to trial in California. The court ruled that a person has all legal rights to cells and tissues removed during surgery and later used in scientific research. For now, the ruling stands.

But this is a very complicated issue whose impact may be far reaching. Many researchers believe that this ruling will interfere with new research and raise the cost of its progress. They are also convinced that it will discourage people from donating tissues and organs because of fear that researchers may profit from them. At the heart of the issue is this question: Do people have the right to control the use of their cells even though it might delay or prevent a medical breakthrough?

ORGAN SYSTEMS

System	Function
Skeletal	Protection and support
Muscular	Support and movement
Skin	Protection
Digestive	Breakdown and absorption of food
Circulatory	Transport of oxygen, wastes, and digested food
Respiratory	Gas exchange
Excretory	Removal of liquid and solid wastes
Endocrine	Regulation
Nervous	Regulation, conduction, and coordination
Reproductive	Production of sex cells

Figure 5–24 *Which organ system breaks down food?*

A Light-Sensitive Cell

You are able to see because your eyes are sensitive to light. But only a few cell types in the eye are actually sensitive to light. These light-sensitive cells are composed of two very different parts. The lower part of the cell is packed with mitochondria, perhaps four or five times as many as in a typical cell. This is an indication that the cell uses a lot of energy. The upper part contains small flattened membranes piled upon each other like a large stack of pancakes.

The membranes, which are known as disks, contain a pigment called rhodopsin (roh-DAHP-sihn). Rhodopsin absorbs light and signals the rest of the cell that light has struck the disk. This action causes messages to be sent to other cells. These changes result in the sensation we call vision. The presence of many membranes ensures that even the smallest unit of light can be detected by this light-sensitive cell.

The Street Sweepers

The air we breathe is filled with dust, smoke, and even small bacteria. Why doesn't all this material collect in the lungs and clog its passageways? Lining these passageways are special cells that release a mixture of water, carbohydrates, and salts, called mucus. The particles of dust and dirt that are inhaled are trapped in this sticky mucus. Underneath this layer of mucus is another group of specialized cells that have cilia. As the cilia move, they create a sweeping action. This action keeps the most vital passageways in the body clean and open for business.

5–5 SECTION REVIEW

1. What is cell specialization?
2. What cell structures might the enzyme-producing cells in the pancreas contain? The cells in a muscle?

Section Objective

- Describe the four levels of organization in a multicellular organism.

5–6 Levels of Organization

In order to describe a multicellular organism such as the human, biologists have developed levels of organization. These levels make it easier to classify and describe the cells within an organism. **The levels of organization in a multicellular organism include cells, tissues, organs, and organ systems that make up the organism.**

Tissues

In multicellular organisms, cells—the first level of organization—are organized in specialized groups called **tissues**. A tissue is a group of similar cells that perform similar functions. Because they are organizations of cells, tissues are the second level of organization. The cells that produce digestive enzymes in the pancreas are one kind of tissue. So are the cells in the eye that respond to light and the cells that line your air passages. Most animals, which are multicellular organisms, have four main types of tissue. They include muscle, epithelial, nerve, and connective tissue.

Organs

Although hundreds or even thousands of cells may be involved in forming a tissue, many tasks within the body are too complicated to be carried out by just one type of tissue. In these cases, an **organ**, or a group of tissues that work together to perform a specific function, is needed. Organs make up the third level of organization. Many types of tissue may be used to form a particular organ. For example, each muscle in your body is an individual organ. However, within a muscle there is a lot more than muscle tissue. There is nerve tissue and connective tissue, a special tissue that connects different parts of the body. Each tissue performs an essential task to help the organ function successfully.

Organ Systems

In many cases, even a complex organ is not sufficient to complete a series of specialized tasks. As a result, an **organ system**, or a group of organs, works together to perform a certain function. Organ systems are the fourth level of organization. There are many organ systems in the body, including the muscular system, the skeletal system, the circulatory system, and the nervous system.

The organization of the cells of the body into tissues, organs, and organ systems makes possible a division of labor among those cells that makes multicellular life possible. Specialized cells such as nerve and muscle cells are able to exist precisely because other cells are specialized to obtain the food and oxygen that those cells need. This overall specialization and interdependence is one of the remarkable attributes of living things. Appreciating this is an important step in understanding the nature of living things.

5–6 SECTION REVIEW

1. Describe the four levels of organization within most animals.
2. How do an organ and a tissue differ?
3. Why is human blood classified as connective tissue?

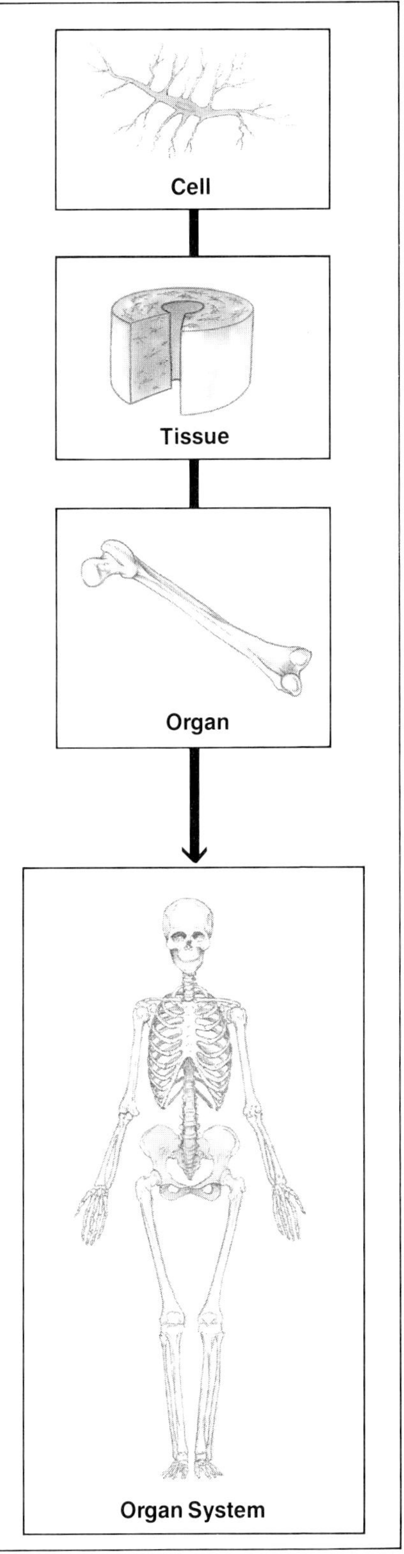

Figure 5–25 *This diagram shows four levels of organization in the human body.*

LABORATORY INVESTIGATION

OBSERVING OSMOSIS

PROBLEM

How can the process of osmosis be observed?

MATERIALS *(per group)*

glass-marking pencil	forceps
2 100-mL beakers	medicine dropper
50 mL water	2 glass slides
50 mL saturated sodium nitrate solution	teasing needle
scalpel	Lugol solution
small onion	2 coverslips
small potato	microscope

PROCEDURE

1. Using the glass-marking pencil, label one beaker "water" and the other "sodium nitrate." Add the water and sodium nitrate to the appropriately labeled beaker.
2. Using a scalpel, carefully cut the onion into quarters. **CAUTION:** *Be very careful when using a scalpel.* Each quarter will separate neatly into layers. Cut one layer into two pieces of equal size.
3. Again using the scalpel, carefully cut two slices from the potato. The slices should be about 2 to 3 mm in thickness. To determine the flexibility of the pieces of onion and potato, bend them back and forth a few times. Note their flexibility.
4. Place one piece of onion and one slice of potato in each beaker. Allow them to remain undisturbed in the beakers for 30 minutes.
5. After 30 minutes, remove the onion pieces and potato slices from the beakers with forceps. Note the degree of flexibility of each.
6. Return each onion piece and potato slice to its respective beaker.
7. Using a medicine dropper, place a drop of water in the center of a clean glass slide.
8. With the forceps, remove the onion piece from the beaker marked "sodium nitrate." Remove the thin membrane from the inner surface of the onion by bending the onion inward and lifting the membrane with the forceps. Then place the thin onion membrane in the drop of water on the glass slide.
9. Using the teasing needle, try to flatten the onion membrane as much as you can. Add a drop of Lugol solution to the onion membrane and water. Cover with a coverslip.
10. Observe the onion membrane under the low power of the microscope. Then observe the membrane under high power. Note the appearance of cytoplasm. Draw a labeled diagram of a few onion cells.
11. Repeat steps 7 through 10 using the piece of onion from the beaker marked "water."

OBSERVATIONS

1. What was the degree of flexibility of the onion and potato before they were placed in water and in the sodium nitrate solution?
2. What was the degree of flexibility of the onion and potato after 30 minutes in water? After 30 minutes in the sodium nitrate solution?
3. Describe the differences between the cells of the onion membrane that were placed in water and the cells that were placed in the sodium nitrate solution.

ANALYSIS AND CONCLUSIONS

1. What is the purpose of the Lugol solution?
2. Which beaker contained the higher concentration of water?
3. Relate the degrees of flexibility of the potato and the onion dry, in water, and in the sodium nitrate solution to the process of osmosis.
4. Relate the differences in degrees of flexibility of the onion to the appearance of the cells observed under the microscope.

STUDENT STUDY GUIDE

SUMMARIZING THE CONCEPTS

The key concepts in each section of this chapter are listed below to help you review the chapter content. Make sure you understand each concept and its relationship to other concepts and to the theme of this chapter.

5–1 The Cell Theory

- The cell theory states: All living things are composed of cells; cells are the basic units of structure and function in living things; all cells come from preexisting cells.

5–2 Cell Structure

- Most cells have a cell membrane, nucleus, and cytoplasm.
- Scientists divide cells into eukaryotic cells and prokaryotic cells.

5–3 Cytoplasmic Organelles

- Within the cytoplasm are organelles, or tiny structures that perform specialized functions. They include mitochondria, chloroplasts, ribosomes, endoplasmic reticulum, Golgi apparatus, lysosomes, vacuoles, plastids, and cytoskeleton.

5–4 Movement of Materials Through the Cell Membrane

- Diffusion is the process by which molecules move from areas of higher concentration to areas of lower concentration.
- Active transport is an energy-requiring process that enables material to move across a cell membrane against a concentration difference.

5–5 Cell Specialization

- Cell specialization is the process by which cells are uniquely suited to perform a particular function within the organism.

5–6 Levels of Organization

- In multicellular organisms, such as most animals, cells are organized into tissues, organs, and organ systems.

REVIEWING KEY TERMS

Vocabulary terms are important to your understanding of biology. The key terms listed below are those you should be especially familiar with. Review these terms and their meanings. Then use each term in a complete sentence. If you are not sure of a term's meaning, return to the appropriate section and review its definition.

5–1 The Cell Theory

cell
cell theory

5–2 Cell Structure

cell membrane
cell wall
nucleus
eukaryote
prokaryote
nuclear envelope
nucleolus
chromosome
cytoplasm

5–3 Cytoplasmic Organelles

organelle
mitochondrion
chloroplast
ribosome
endoplasmic reticulum
Golgi apparatus
lysosome
vacuole
plastid
cytoskeleton

5–4 Movement of Materials Through the Cell Membrane

diffusion
selectively permeable
osmosis
facilitated diffusion
active transport

5–5 Cell Specialization

cell specialization

5–6 Levels of Organization

tissue
organ
organ system

CHAPTER REVIEW

CONTENT REVIEW

Multiple Choice

Choose the letter of the answer that best completes each statement.

1. The basic unit of structure and function in living things is the
a. cell. c. organ.
b. tissue. d. organ system.

2. What is the outer boundary of an animal cell called?
a. cell wall c. cell membrane
b. nuclear envelope d. cytoplasm

3. The control center of the cell is the
a. lysosome. c. mitochondrion.
b. ribosome. d. nucleus.

4. Organisms whose cells do not have a nucleus are called
a. prokaryotes. c. organelles.
b. eukaryotes. d. plants.

5. What structure is the site of protein synthesis?
a. nucleus c. mitochondrion
b. lysosome d. ribosome

6. The process by which molecules of a substance move from areas of higher concentration of that substance to areas of lower concentration is
a. active transport. c. diffusion.
b. endocytosis. d. cell specialization.

7. Which is an example of active transport?
a. diffusion c. endocytosis
b. osmosis d. facilitated diffusion

8. A group of similar cells that perform a similar function is called a (an)
a. tissue. c. organ system.
b. organ. d. organism.

True or False

Determine whether each statement is true or false. If it is true, write "true." If it is false, change the underlined word or words to make the statement true.

1. <u>Van Leeuwenhoek</u> is given credit for developing the first microscope.

2. All cells have a <u>cell wall</u>.

3. <u>Eukaryotes</u> are organisms whose cells do not have a nucleus.

4. <u>Microtubules</u> are the main components of the cytoskeleton.

5. <u>Osmosis</u> is the diffusion of water.

6. Facilitated diffusion is a form of <u>active transport</u>.

7. <u>Cell specialization</u> is the process by which cells are suited to perform a particular function.

8. A group of tissues that work together is called an <u>organ system</u>.

Word Relationships

In each of the following sets of terms, three of the terms are related. One term does not belong. Determine the characteristic common to three of the terms and then identify the term that does not belong.

1. cytoplasm, cell membrane, cell wall, nuclear envelope
2. diffusion, osmosis, endocytosis, facilitated diffusion
3. tissue, ribosome, organ, organ system
4. mitochondrion, cytoplasm, ribosome, vacuole

CONCEPT MASTERY

Use your understanding of the concepts developed in the chapter to answer each of the following in a brief paragraph.

1. What were the contributions of van Leeuwenhoek, Hooke, Schleiden, Schwann, and Virchow to the development of the cell theory?
2. Why is it important for the cell membrane to be selectively permeable?
3. Describe the makeup of the nucleus.
4. How do materials enter and leave the nucleus?
5. Describe the structure of a mitochondrion. What is its function?
6. What are the functions of vacuoles? How do they differ in plant and animal cells?
7. How do plant and animal cells differ?
8. What is the difference between diffusion and osmosis?
9. What is osmotic pressure? Why is it important?
10. Explain the relationship between cells, tissues, organs, and organ systems.

CRITICAL AND CREATIVE THINKING

Discuss each of the following in a brief paragraph.

1. **Applying concepts** The beaker in the diagram has a selectively permeable membrane separating two solutions. Assume that the salt molecules are small enough to pass through the membrane but the starch molecules are too large to pass through. Will the water level on either side of the membrane change? Explain your answer.

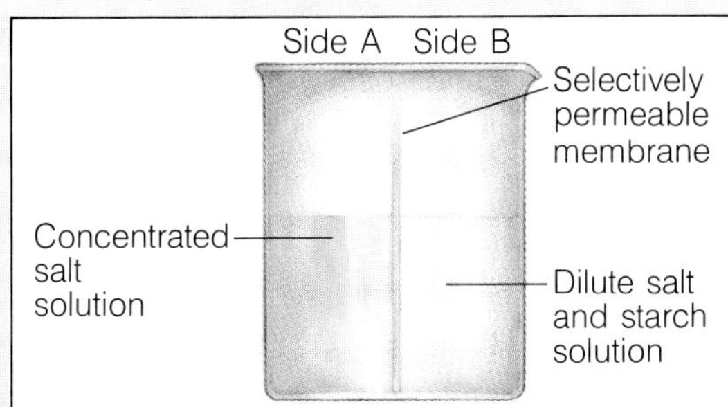

2. **Designing an experiment** You are given vegetable coloring and three beakers. The first beaker is filled with water at room temperature, the second beaker is filled with ice water, and the third with hot water. Design an experiment that will enable you to determine the effects of temperature on the rate of diffusion. Be sure to state your hypothesis and to include a control.
3. **Applying concepts** An animal cell contains about 10 to 20 Golgi apparatus, whereas a plant cell contains several hundred. Why do you think there is such a difference in the number of these organelles in each cell type?
4. **Using the writing process** Write a science fiction story entitled: "The Day Diffusion Stood Still."
5. **Using the writing process** One day, unicellular organisms got tired of being called simple organisms by the multicellular organisms. The unicellular organisms felt that they were rather complex individuals and should be recognized as such. In order to gain this recognition, they challenged the multicellular organisms to a debate. Pretend that you are a unicellular organism. What arguments would you use to defend your position?

CHAPTER 6

Cell Energy: Photosynthesis and Respiration

It may seem that little is happening in this peaceful sunny field. However, the trees, flowers, and grasses are actively involved in capturing energy from sunlight and transforming it into energy that can be used by all types of living things.

In contrast to the roar and fury of hurricanes and floods, a gentle sunrise over forest and field seems uneventful. But the movement of sunlight across a landscape is only the first event in the daily struggle of living things to obtain energy. The starting point for that struggle is the energy of sunlight and its conversion to chemical energy.

What kinds of organisms can trap the energy in sunlight? How is that energy changed into a form other organisms can utilize? In this chapter we shall examine these questions and, in so doing, discover one of the most important secrets of life: how organisms capture, store, and transform energy!

CHAPTER OUTLINE

6–1 Photosynthesis: Capturing and Converting Energy

Section Objectives

- Describe the experiments that contributed to the understanding of photosynthesis.
- Discuss the requirements for photosynthesis.

Energy is the ability to do work, and there is always work to be done, even at the level of the cell. In this chapter we will explore some of the ways in which living things capture, convert, store, and use energy. We will concentrate our attention on the way in which energy is used within the individual cell.

Photosynthesis

The study of energy and living things begins with photosynthesis. **In the process of photosynthesis, plants convert the energy of sunlight into the energy in the chemical bonds of carbohydrates—sugars and starches.** Put another way, plants use the energy of sunlight to produce carbohydrates in a process called **photosynthesis**.

An understanding of photosynthesis was first developed from studies of plant growth. For years gardeners had asked a perplexing question about plant growth: When a seedling with a mass of only a few grams grows into a tall tree with a mass of several tons, where does the tree's increase in mass come from? From the soil? From the water? From the air? In the seventeenth century, the Dutch physician Jan van Helmont devised an experiment to find out.

Figure 6–1 *The very culture of a human society may revolve around the way energy is used to heat homes, cook food, light buildings and streets, and provide for other human needs. In nature, as in human societies, some of the most important activities concern the processes in which energy is produced and distributed.*

Figure 6–2 *As a tiny seedling grows into a large tree, it uses water and air to make the chemicals needed for growth.*

Figure 6–3 *A burning candle soon uses up the oxygen in a glass jar and goes out. In the presence of light, a plant placed inside the jar releases oxygen. This allows the candle to be relighted. The candle continues to burn as long as enough oxygen is available.*

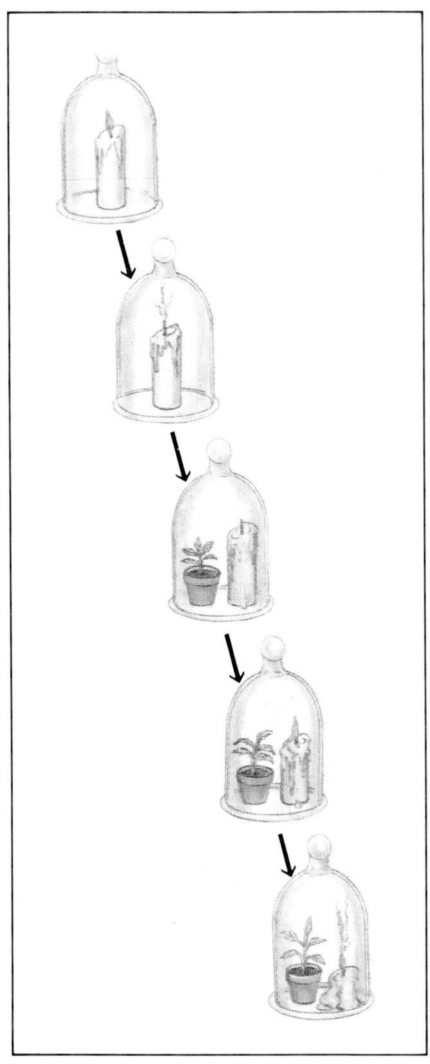

Van Helmont carefully found the mass of a pot of dry soil and a small seedling. Then he planted the seedling in the pot of soil. He took care of it and watered it regularly for five years. At the end of five years, the seedling, which by then was a small tree, had gained about 75 kilograms. However, the mass of the soil was almost unchanged. Van Helmont concluded that most of the mass must have come from water because that was the only thing that he had added to the pot.

Van Helmont's experiment accounts for the *hydrate*, or water, portion of the carbohydrate produced by photosynthesis. But where does the carbon of the *carbo* portion come from? Although Van Helmont did not realize it, carbon dioxide in the air made a major contribution to the mass of his tree. And it is the carbon in carbon dioxide that is used to make carbohydrates in photosynthesis. Even though Van Helmont had only part of the story, he had made a major contribution to science.

Almost a hundred years after Van Helmont's experiment, Joseph Priestley performed an experiment that would give another insight into the process of photosynthesis. Priestley took a candle, placed a glass jar over it, and watched as the flame gradually died out. Something in the air, Priestley reasoned, was necessary to keep a candle flame burning. When that substance was used up, the candle went out. Today we call this substance oxygen.

Priestley then found that if he placed a sprig of mint under the jar and allowed a few days to pass, the candle could be relighted and would remain lighted for a while. The mint plant had produced the substance required for burning. In other words, it released oxygen. Later, the Dutch scientist Jan Ingenhousz showed that the effect observed by Priestley occurred only when the plant was exposed to light. This means that light is necessary for plants to produce oxygen.

Requirements for Photosynthesis

The experiments performed by Van Helmont, Priestley, Ingenhousz, and other scientists reveal that in the presence of light, plants transform carbon dioxide and water into carbohydrates and release oxygen. This gives us the basic outline of the process of photosynthesis:

$$CO_2 + H_2O \xrightarrow{\text{light}} (CH_2O)_n + O_2$$

carbon dioxide + water $\xrightarrow{\text{light}}$ carbohydrate + oxygen

Because photosynthesis usually produces a particular carbohydrate—the sugar **glucose** ($C_6H_{12}O_6$)—we can rewrite and balance the equation for photosynthesis as follows:

$$6\ CO_2 + 6\ H_2O \xrightarrow{\text{light}} C_6H_{12}O_6 + 6\ O_2$$

carbon dioxide + water $\xrightarrow{\text{light}}$ glucose + oxygen

Do not be fooled by how simple this equation looks. In photosynthesis, a great deal happens between the beginning and the end of the equation. You do not get glucose and oxygen just by putting water and carbon dioxide together. Let us, then, examine some of the other requirements of photosynthesis.

SUNLIGHT Nearly all organisms on Earth depend on the sun for energy. Some organisms, such as green plants, can use the sun's energy directly. As a result, green plants are called **autotrophs** (AW-toh-trohfs). Autotrophs are organisms that are able to use a source of energy, such as sunlight, to produce food directly from simple inorganic molecules in the environment. Other organisms, such as animals, cannot use the sun's energy directly. These organisms, known as **heterotrophs**, (HEHT-er-oh-trohfs) obtain energy from the foods they eat. Heterotrophs may eat autotrophs, other heterotrophs, or both.

The sun bathes the Earth in a steady stream of light. What our eyes perceive as colorless "white" light is actually a mixture of different wavelengths of light. Many of these wavelengths are visible to our eyes and make up what is known as the visible spectrum. Our eyes perceive the different wavelengths of the visible spectrum as different colors.

Figure 6–4 *Plant pigments absorb some wavelengths of light and reflect others. Our eyes perceive the reflected wavelengths as different colors (left). Chlorophyll—the principal photosynthetic pigment of green plants—gives the chloroplasts in these plant cells their characteristic color (right).*

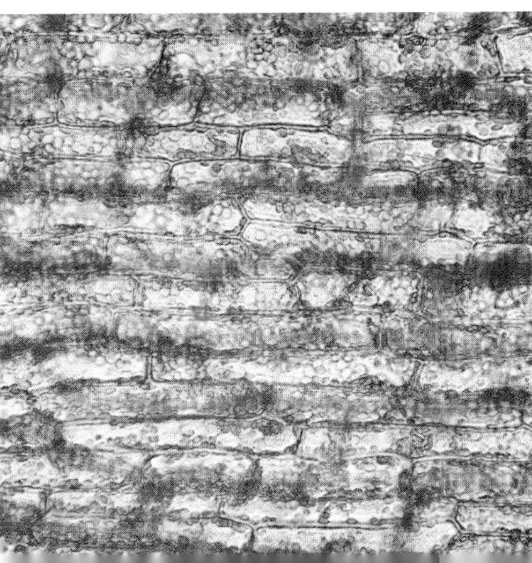

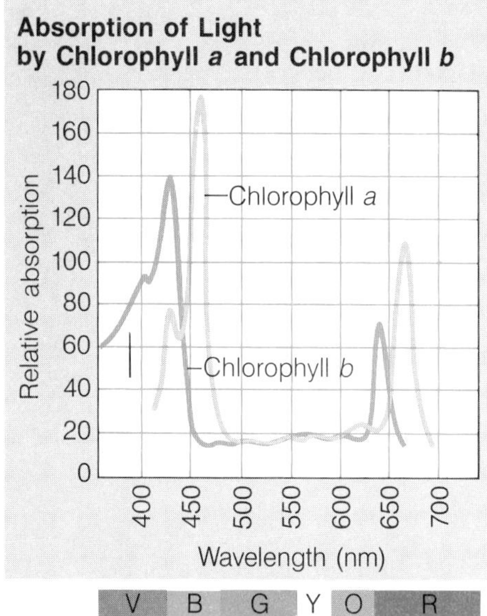

Figure 6–5 *Chlorophyll absorbs red and blue light quite well. Different forms of chlorophyll have their peak absorption at different wavelengths of light.*

PIGMENTS The process of photosynthesis begins when light is absorbed by **pigments** in the plant cell. Pigments are colored substances that absorb or reflect light. The principal pigment of green plants is known as **chlorophyll**. As you can see from the graph in Figure 6–5, chlorophyll absorbs red and blue light but does not absorb light in the middle region of the spectrum very well. Instead, it reflects these wavelengths.

ENERGY-STORING COMPOUNDS Because energy is involved in the formation of chemical bonds, the production of certain compounds can be used to store energy in chemical form. The most important energy-storing compound—one used by every living cell—is **adenosine triphosphate**, or **ATP**. As you can see in Figure 6–6, an ATP molecule consists of a nucleotide called adenine, a 5-carbon sugar called ribose, and three phosphate groups. Energy can be stored when a phosphate group, abbreviated as P, is bonded to adenosine monophosphate (AMP) to produce adenosine diphosphate (ADP). And still more energy can be stored when a third phosphate group is added to ADP to produce ATP. The bonds between the phosphate groups are the key to ATP's energy-storing qualities. Each of these two bonds is capable of storing chemical energy—energy that is released when the bonds are broken.

Some of this stored energy is released when the third phosphate group is split from ATP to produce ADP. Energy is also released when ADP is broken down to AMP.

$$\textbf{ATP} \rightarrow \textbf{ADP} + \textbf{P} + \textbf{energy}$$
$$\textbf{ADP} \rightarrow \textbf{AMP} + \textbf{P} + \textbf{energy}$$

Enzymes control the synthesis and breakdown of ATP within the cell. These enzymes enable ATP to be produced from

Figure 6–6 *Adenosine triphosphate, or ATP, is the most important energy-storing compound in living things.*

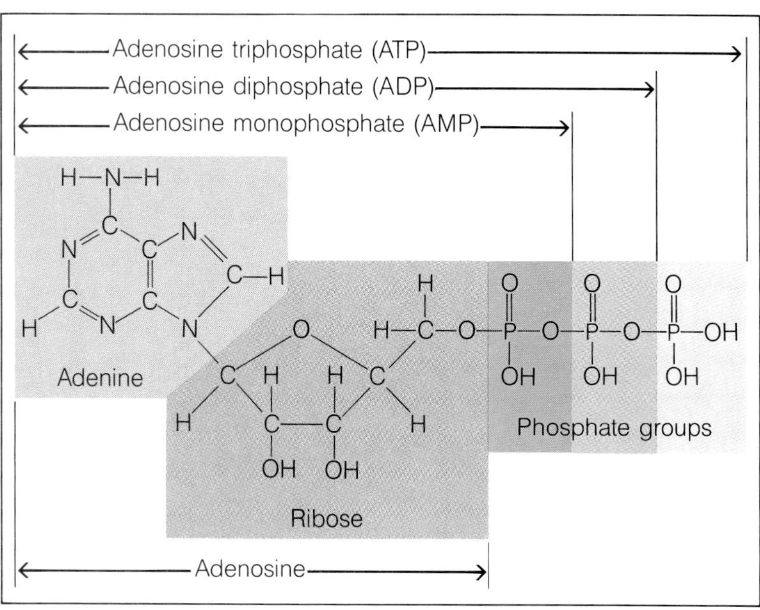

energy-releasing reactions and allow ATP to be used as a source of energy for reactions that require energy. ATP provides energy for a large number of cellular activities, including muscle contraction, protein synthesis, and active transport across cell membranes. During photosynthesis, the ATP produced by the first part of the process is used to provide energy for the second part.

6–1 SECTION REVIEW

1. Define photosynthesis.
2. What did Van Helmont's experiment prove about the source of material for plant growth? What did it not prove?
3. What is ATP?
4. Why is chlorophyll's efficiency in absorbing light energy important for photosynthesis?

PROBLEM SOLVING IN BIOLOGY

THE COLORS OF AUTUMN

In many parts of the country, the beautiful colors of autumn leaves provide inspiration to artists and poets as the countryside turns into a lovely blaze of red, orange, and yellow. What is the source of these colors? Do plants produce them in response to the changing of the seasons?

The pigments in plant cells, including chlorophyll, can be separated from one another by a technique known as paper chromatography. Study the results of the paper chromotography experiment shown on this page. The green chlorophyll spots, red-orange carotene spots, and yellow xanthophyll spots are labeled on samples taken from the leaves of a single maple tree in August, September, and October.

Using these three chromatographs as evidence, can you explain what seems to happen as the leaves change color as summer ends and autumn begins?

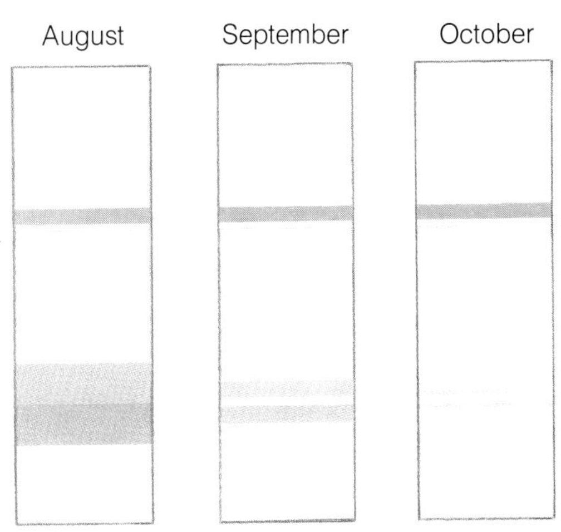

Paper chromatography is based on the fact that different substances (such as plant pigments) in a solvent will move through a piece of paper at different rates.

Section Objectives

- Discuss the light reactions of photosynthesis.
- Relate the dark reactions of photosynthesis to the light reactions.

6–2 Photosynthesis: The Light and Dark Reactions

The process of photosynthesis is divided into two parts: the **light reactions** and the **dark reactions**. As their name implies, the light reactions require light. **In the light reactions, the energy of sunlight is captured and used to make energy-storing compounds.** The dark reactions do not require light and thus are also called nonlight or light-independent reactions. However, the dark reactions can—and do—occur in the light. The dark reactions use the energy stored by the light reactions to make glucose.

Photosynthesis takes place in an organelle known as the chloroplast. Within the chloroplast are saclike **photosynthetic membranes** that contain chlorophyll. As you can see in Figure 6–8, the light reactions occur in the photosynthetic membranes, whereas the dark reactions occur outside the photosynthetic membranes.

The Light Reactions

The light reactions absorb the energy of sunlight and convert it to the energy that is stored in chemical bonds. This process occurs very rapidly. However, the light reactions can be divided into four basic processes: light absorption, electron transport, oxygen production, and ATP formation. These processes are closely linked and are dependent on one another. As you examine the light reactions in more detail, keep in mind that these processes occur nonstop in green plants as long as the sun shines.

Figure 6–7 The chloroplast is the site of photosynthesis. The light reactions take place in the saclike photosynthetic membranes. The dark reactions take place in the areas surrounding the photosynthetic membranes.

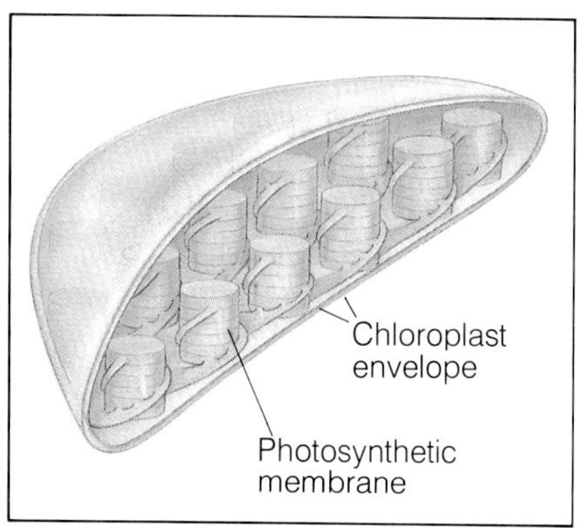

LIGHT ABSORPTION The photosynthetic membrane contains clusters of pigment molecules, or **photosystems**, that are able to capture the energy of sunlight. There are two photosystems in green plants: photosystem I and photosystem II. See Figure 6–8.

Each photosystem contains several hundred chlorophyll molecules, as well as a number of accessory pigments. These accessory pigments absorb light in the regions of the spectrum where chlorophyll does not and thus allow more of the available light energy to be used. The absorption of light causes electrons in a pigment molecule to be raised to a higher level, an "excited" state. This excitation energy is then passed from one pigment molecule to another until it reaches a special pair of chlorophyll molecules. Although all the photosystem pigments can absorb light, only the special pair of chlorophyll molecules can process the light energy. The special pair of chlorophyll molecules are surrounded by an apparatus that enables the excitation energy to be captured in chemical form.

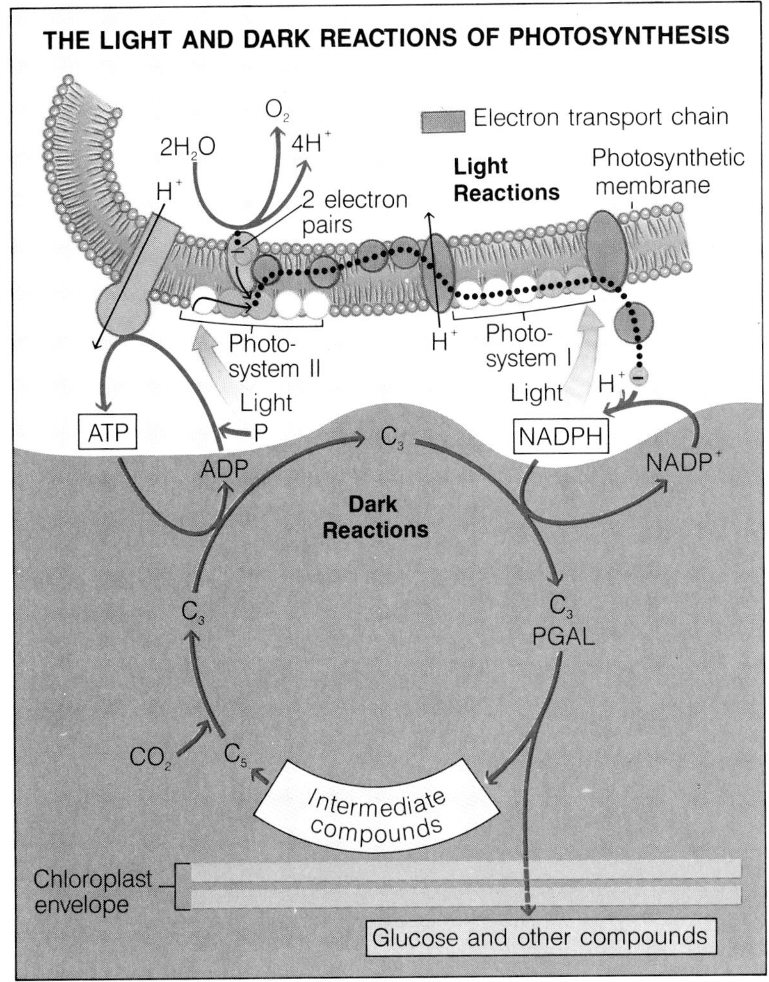

Figure 6–8 *Clusters of pigment molecules known as photosystems are embedded in the photosynthetic membrane. Photosystems capture the energy of sunlight, which is used to make energy-storing compounds. The energy in these compounds, in turn, is used to make biologically important compounds such as glucose.*

ELECTRON TRANSPORT The high-energy electrons produced by light travel from the special pair of chlorophyll molecules to an adjacent molecule called an electron carrier. This begins a process known as **electron transport**.

The high-energy electrons are transferred along a series of electron-carrier molecules in the photosynthetic membrane

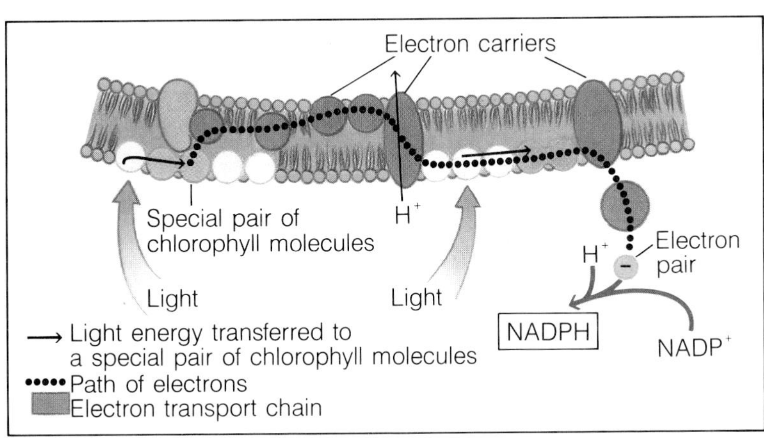

Figure 6–9 *The high-energy electrons produced by light are transferred from chlorophyll to the electron transport chain. The electrons are passed from one carrier in the chain to the next. At the end of the chain, they are used to make the energy-storing compound NADPH.*

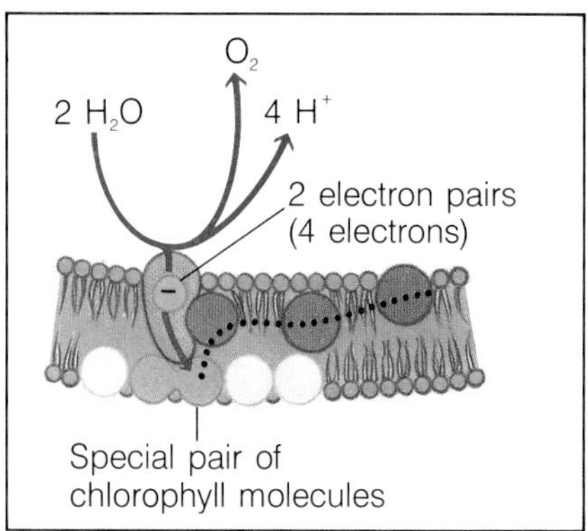

Figure 6–10 *The breakdown of water produces electrons that replace the electrons lost by the special pair of chlorophyll molecules. This process also results in the formation of hydrogen ions and oxygen gas.*

known as the electron transport chain. Electrons are passed from one carrier to another almost as pails of water are passed from one person to the next in a bucket brigade.

At the end of the chain is an enzyme that passes the high-energy electrons to an electron carrier called $NADP^+$, converting it to NADPH. Adding a pair of electrons to this electron carrier requires energy. This is the first way in which part of the energy of sunlight is trapped in chemical bonds. The electrons and energy stored in the bonds of NADPH will be used later on.

OXYGEN PRODUCTION As the light continues to shine, what happens to chlorophyll? Does it run out of electrons? No. The photosynthetic membrane contains a system that provides new electrons to chlorophyll to replace the ones that wound up in NADPH. These electrons are taken from water. Four electrons are removed from 2 water molecules (H_2O), leaving 4 hydrogen ions (H^+) and 2 oxygen atoms (O). The 2 oxygen atoms form a single molecule of oxygen gas (O_2) that leaves the chloroplast and is eventually released into the air.

ATP FORMATION The hydrogen ions left behind when water is "split" are released inside the photosynthetic membrane. In addition, as electrons are passed from chlorophyll to $NADP^+$, more hydrogen ions are pumped across the membrane. After a while, the inside of the membrane fills up with positively charged hydrogen ions. This makes the outside of the photosynthetic membrane negatively charged and the inside positively charged.

The difference in charges across the membrane is a source of energy. An enzyme in the photosynthetic membrane makes use of this energy to attach a phosphate molecule to ADP, forming ATP. This is the second way in which the energy of sunlight is trapped in chemical form.

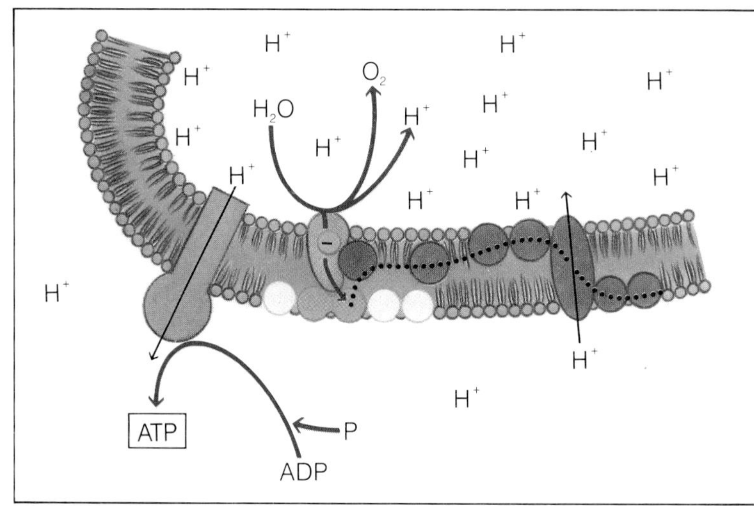

Figure 6–11 *The buildup of hydrogen ions (produced in the breakdown of water) inside the photosynthetic membrane produces a difference in charges across the membrane. This powers the formation of the energy-storing compound ATP.*

A SUMMARY OF THE LIGHT REACTIONS As we have seen, the light reactions use water, ADP, and $NADP^+$; they produce O_2 (which is of no help in photosynthesis but is of great use to us!) and the energy-storing molecules ATP and NADPH. The next stage of photosynthesis, the dark reactions, will convert these energy-storing molecules to a more convenient form.

The Dark Reactions

Do not be confused by the term dark reactions. The dark reactions generally take place in sunlight. However, light does not play a role in the dark reactions. If ATP and NADPH are supplied, the dark reactions can be carried out in a test tube, even in total darkness and without ever being exposed to light!

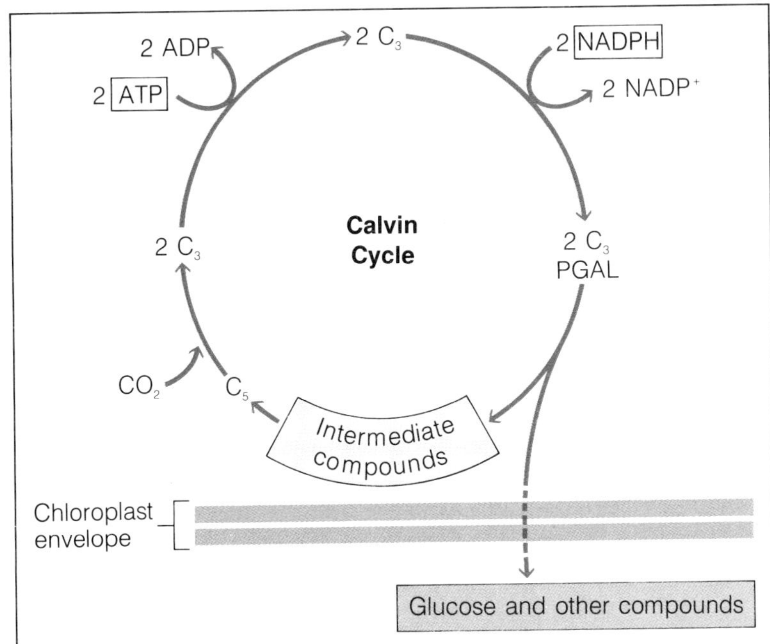

Figure 6–12 The dark reactions use carbon dioxide and the energy-storing compounds produced in the light reactions to form PGAL. PGAL is a chemical "building block" that can be used to make other organic compounds, such as the sugar glucose.

The series of chemical changes that make up the dark reactions is particularly critical to living things. In this part of photosynthesis, the simple inorganic molecule carbon dioxide is used to make a complex organic molecule. This molecule can be thought of as a building block that can be used to make other biologically important molecules, including glucose. The dark reactions form a cycle, or circular series of reactions. Because the chemistry of this remarkable cycle was worked out by the American scientist Melvin Calvin, the dark reactions are also known as the **Calvin cycle**.

Throughout this description of the Calvin cycle, you will find it helpful to refer to Figure 6–12. In the first reaction of the Calvin cycle, a 5-carbon sugar (C_5) combines with CO_2 to form two 3-carbon compounds (C_3). The first reaction of the Calvin cycle tends to be relatively slow. In order to compensate for this, the chloroplast is loaded with an enzyme that catalyzes this reaction. This enzyme is known as rubisco. There is far more rubisco in an active plant cell than any other protein molecule. Because there are many more plant cells than animal cells on Earth, we can make a remarkable statement about rubisco: It is the most abundant protein in the world!

In the next two reactions of the Calvin cycle, using the chemical energy available in ATP and NADPH, these 3-carbon compounds are converted to PGAL (**p**hospho**g**lycer**al**dehyde). Most PGAL molecules are recycled for the dark reactions, but 1

SCIENCE, TECHNOLOGY, AND SOCIETY BREAKTHROUGH

"If at First You Don't Succeed . . ."

In the dark reactions of photosynthesis, simple inorganic molecules are used to form organic molecules—food—that can be used by living things. The process of putting carbon into a form that can be used by living things is known as carbon fixation. Although carbon fixation in photosynthesis is crucial to living things, this process remained a mystery until the late 1940s.

Melvin Calvin worked out the chemistry of the dark reactions of photosynthesis.

It was obvious that the key to understanding the chemical steps of the dark reactions—and carbon fixation—was to find the very first molecule into which CO_2 was fixed, or used to make an organic molecule. But how do you trace the path of a molecule in a chemical reaction? And how can you tell that a particular molecule is really the one you want to observe?

Working at the University of California at Berkeley in 1946, Melvin Calvin and his associates decided to use newly discovered carbon-14, a radioactive isotope of carbon, in their experiments on carbon fixation. They reasoned that the molecule that fixed carbon dioxide would become radioactive when it joined with radioactive carbon dioxide, or carbon dioxide that contained carbon-14. However, when radioactive CO_2 was added to growing plants, within a few minutes nearly every type of carbon-containing molecule in the plant was radioactive. So it was back to the drawing board for the scientists.

Melvin Calvin and his associate John Bassham decided that if carbon was fixed quickly, they would have to act quickly. They put a suspension of green algae into a special flask, injected radioactive CO_2 into it, flashed a bright light at it, and opened a valve at the bottom of the flask. The algae cells dropped suddenly into a beaker of boiling alcohol, which killed the cells and stopped photosynthesis instantly. The molecules associated with carbon fixation, however, were preserved. This approach allowed Calvin and his associates to identify phosphoglyceric acid, a 3-carbon compound, as the product of the first reaction in carbon fixation.

The determination of these scientists to perform a difficult experiment produced the first (and most important) clue in working out the process of carbon fixation. Calvin and his associates continued their work, described the dark reactions, and made a major contribution to our understanding of photosynthesis.

out of every 6 is used to make glucose or other end products. How many times must the Calvin cycle go around to produce 1 molecule of glucose? (Hint: The formula for glucose is $C_6H_{12}O_6$)

Although we have emphasized the production of glucose in the Calvin cycle, the intermediate compounds of the cycle are also important because they can be used by the chloroplast in many ways. Some of the intermediates may be used to form sugars other than glucose; some of them may be used to make amino acids; and some can be converted to lipids. The dark reactions of photosynthesis provide the raw materials to produce almost everything the cell needs.

6-2 SECTION REVIEW

1. What are the products of the light reactions?
2. Where in the cell do the light reactions take place? The dark reactions?
3. Describe the Calvin cycle. Why are the light reactions important to the Calvin cycle?

6-3 Glycolysis and Respiration

Section Objectives

- Discuss the process of glycolysis.
- Describe respiration.
- Explain how breathing is related to respiration.

The ability of autotrophs to produce glucose and other food molecules reflects the fact that photosynthesis is able to trap some of the energy of sunlight in chemical bonds. In a way, the energy stored by photosynthesis is like money deposited in a savings account: It is available for future needs. But organisms—autotrophs and heterotrophs alike—must be capable of making "withdrawals" from that savings account; that is, they must be able to release energy by breaking down food molecules. In this section we will examine two processes used to release energy from glucose.

Glycolysis—Breaking Down Glucose

Glucose ($C_6H_{12}O_6$) is a simple 6-carbon sugar. If glucose is broken down completely in the presence of oxygen, carbon dioxide and water are produced:

$$\begin{array}{cccc} C_6H_{12}O_6 + & 6O_2 & \rightarrow\quad 6CO_2 & + 6H_2O \\ \text{glucose} + & \text{oxygen} & \rightarrow \text{carbon dioxide} & + \text{water} \end{array}$$

This reaction gives off 3811 **calories** per gram of glucose. A calorie is the amount of heat energy required to raise the temperature of 1 gram of water 1 degree Celsius. As you can see, glucose obviously contains a lot of energy. (Those of you who watch your calories should not be alarmed. The Calorie associated with food and diet books is actually a kilocalorie, which is equal to 1000 calories.)

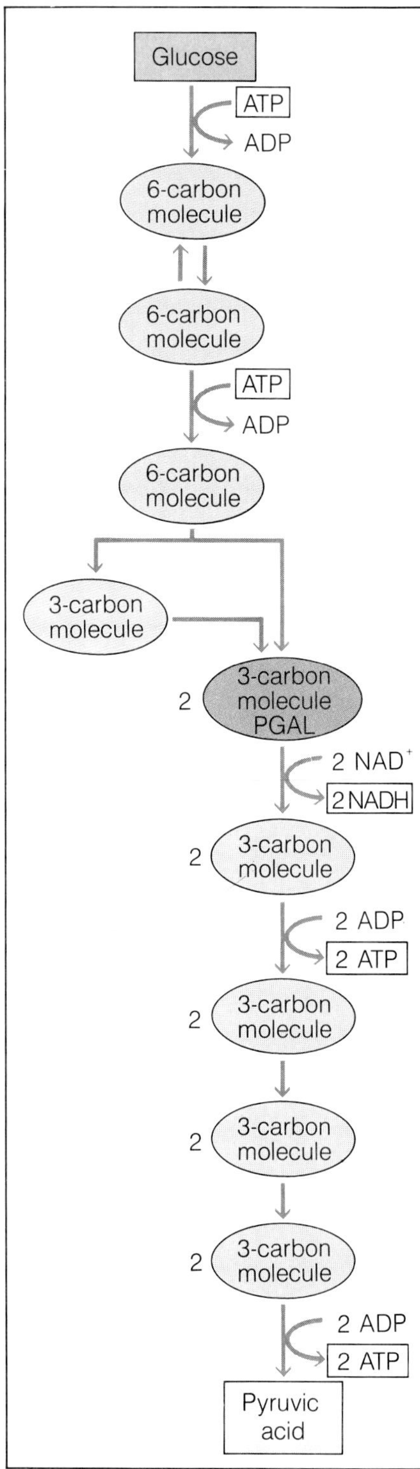

Figure 6–13 *In the process of glycolysis, glucose is broken down and transformed into other molecules. In addition, energy is released in the form of 2 molecules of ATP.*

A cell takes apart glucose slowly and captures the energy a little at a time. Remember, the energy stored in chemical bonds can be used when the bonds are broken. The first stage in this process is known as **glycolysis** (gligh-KAHL-ih-sihs), which means glucose-breaking. Glycolysis takes place in the cytoplasm of a cell. **In glycolysis, a series of enzymes catalyzes chemical reactions that change glucose, one step at a time, into different molecules.**

In the first step, a glucose molecule undergoes several chemical reactions that ultimately split the 6-carbon sugar into two 3-carbon PGAL molecules. See Figure 6–13. Two molecules of ATP are used up in the process. This means that the cell must use up a bit of its stored chemical energy to begin the breakdown of glucose.

Several more chemical steps then occur that transform the 2 PGAL molecules into 2 molecules of pyruvic acid, a 3-carbon compound. The energy from the 2 PGAL molecules is used to make 4 molecules of ADP and 2 molecules of NADH. NADH is an energy-storing compound similar to the NADPH that is formed in the light reactions of photosynthesis.

In the process of glycolysis, 4 molecules of ATP are synthesized from 4 molecules of ADP. Because 2 ATP molecules are used to start the process, we can do a little arithmetic and conclude that there is a net gain of 2 molecules of ATP during glycolysis.

The 2 ATP molecules produced in glycolysis represent no more than 2 percent of the total chemical energy in glucose. What happens to the rest? The answer depends on the presence of oxygen.

Respiration

If oxygen is available, a process known as **respiration** can take place. Because it requires oxygen, respiration is called an **aerobic** process. The word aerobic means with air—specifically, the part of the air called oxygen. **Respiration is the process that involves oxygen and breaks down food molecules to release energy.** Respiration uses the pyruvic acid formed in glycolysis. In breaking down pyruvic acid, respiration captures much of the remaining energy from glucose in the form of 34 additional molecules of ATP.

The term respiration may have a familiar ring. It is often used as a synonym for breathing. Because of this, some biologists use the term cellular respiration instead of respiration to refer to energy-releasing pathways within the cell. The double meaning of respiration points out a crucial connection between cell and organism: The energy-releasing respiratory pathways within the cells require oxygen, which animals take in by breathing—another type of respiration. Although plants do not breathe in the usual sense, they also need to take in oxygen for cellular respiration.

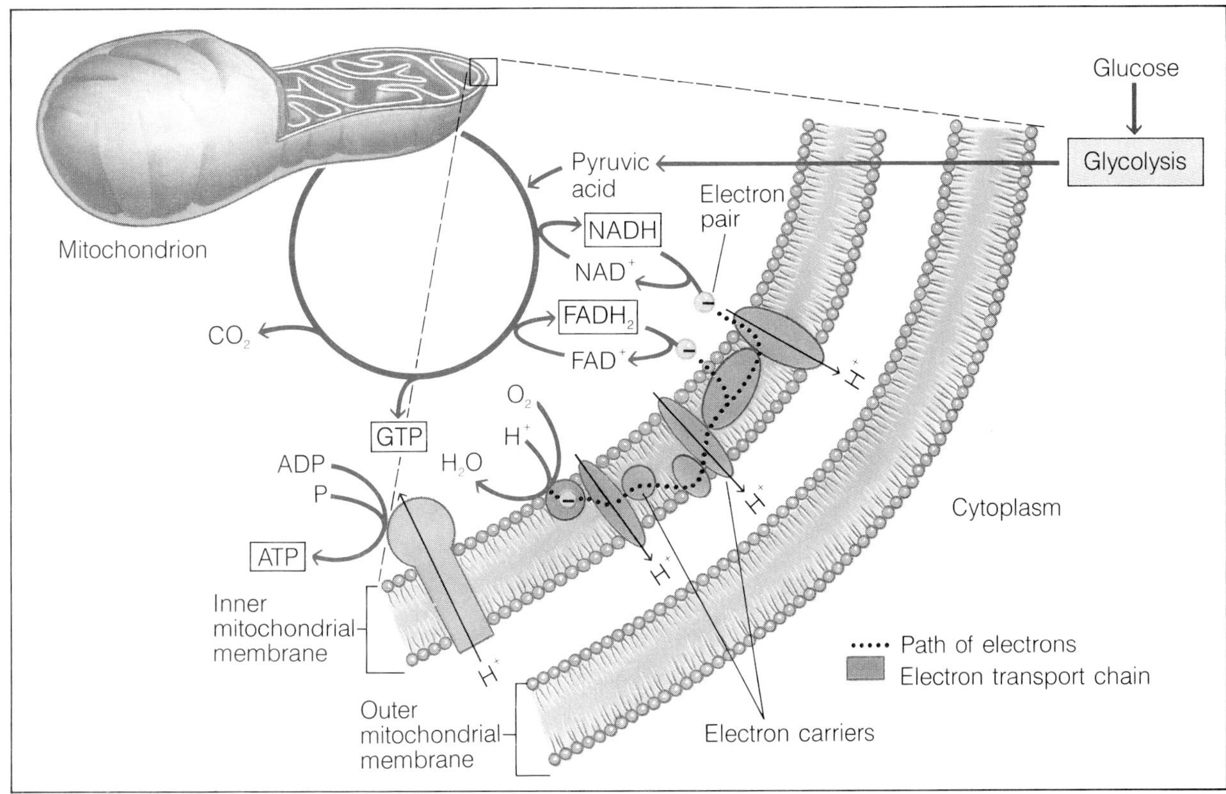

Figure 6–14 *Respiration, an aerobic process, takes place in the mitochondrion. The Krebs cycle takes place in the area enclosed by the inner mitochondrial membrane. Electron transport and ATP formation involve complex molecules embedded in the inner membrane.*

Respiration, like photosynthesis, is associated with a cell organelle. The chemical reactions of respiration take place in a cell's mitochondria. Recall from Chapter 5 that a mitochondrion consists of two membranes, an outer membrane and a folded inner membrane. The first set of reactions in respiration takes place in the area enclosed by the inner membrane. The second set of reactions takes place within the inner membrane itself. See Figure 6–14.

THE KREBS CYCLE The first set of reactions in respiration is the **Krebs cycle**, which is named for its discoverer, Hans Krebs. Unlike glycolysis, the Krebs cycle does not produce a final end product. Instead, it is a continuing series of reactions. See Figure 6–15.

The pyruvic acid produced during glycolysis travels from the cytoplasm to the mitochondrion. In the first reaction of respiration, pyruvic acid is broken down into carbon dioxide and a 2-carbon compound called acetic acid. Acetic acid then enters the Krebs cycle. Acetic acid reacts with a 4-carbon compound to produce citric acid, a 6-carbon compound. Because citric acid is the first compound formed in this series of reactions, the Krebs cycle is known as the citric acid cycle.

There are nine reactions and nine intermediates in the Krebs cycle. At two places in the cycle, CO_2 is released. At four places in the cycle, a pair of high-energy electrons are

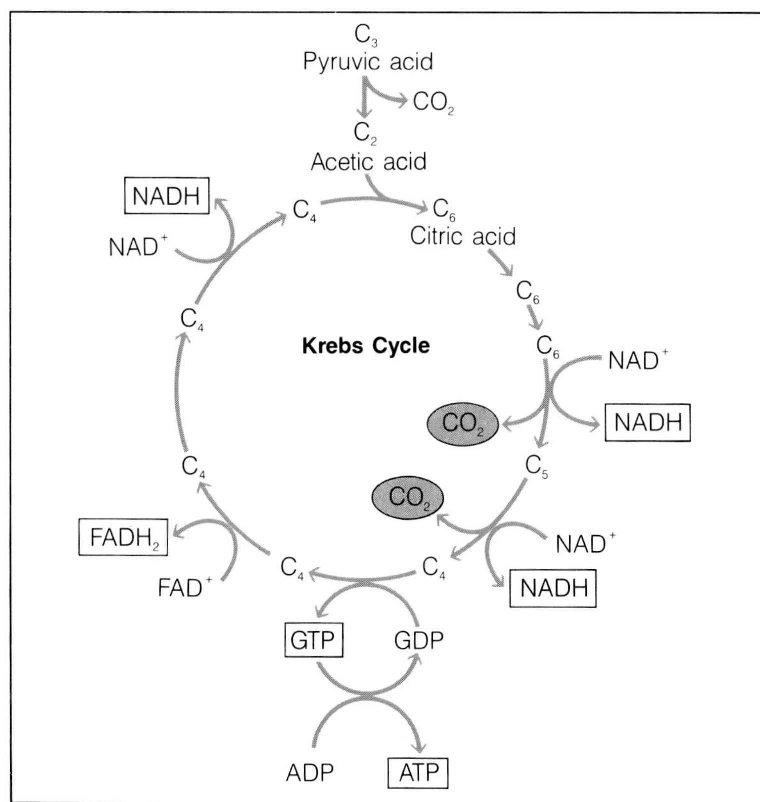

Figure 6–15 *The Krebs cycle, a continuing series of nine reactions involving nine intermediate compounds, produces carbon dioxide and energy-storing compounds.*

accepted by electron carriers, changing NAD^+ to NADH and FAD to $FADH_2$. See Figure 6–15. At one place in the cycle, a molecule of GDP (similar to ADP) is converted to GTP (similar to ATP). The GTP may then used to make ATP from ADP. We can summarize the events in the Krebs cycle as follows:

- **2 carbon atoms added (from the breakdown of pyruvic acid)**
- **2 carbon atoms removed (in 2 molecules of CO_2)**
- **3 molecules of NAD^+ converted to NADH**
- **1 molecule of FAD converted to $FADH_2$**
- **1 molecule of GDP converted to GTP**

Step by step, the carbon atoms in glucose wind up as carbon dioxide. The carbon dioxide produced by the Krebs cycle is a waste product that is released from the cell. But what does the cell do with the other products of the Krebs cycle: NADH and $FADH_2$? And where does oxygen fit into the process?

ELECTRON TRANSPORT IN THE MITOCHONDRION The high-energy electrons from NADH and $FADH_2$ are passed to a series of electron transport enzymes in the inner membrane of the mitochondrion. These enzymes form an electron transport chain along which electrons are passed. At the end of this chain is an enzyme that combines electrons from the electron transport chain, hydrogen ions (H^+) from the fluid inside the cell, and oxygen (O_2) to form water (H_2O). This is where oxygen comes in. Oxygen is the final electron acceptor in the process of respiration. Thus, oxygen is essential for obtaining energy from both NADH and $FADH_2$.

ATP FORMATION Recall that the photosynthetic electron transport chain was associated with the movement of hydrogen ions (H^+) across the photosynthetic membrane in the chloroplast. Electron transport in the mitochondrion causes a similar movement of hydrogen ions. As they accept electrons, some of the enzymes in the electron transport chain pump a hydrogen ion from the inside of the inner membrane to the outside. As in photosynthesis, the movement of hydrogen ions powers the formation of ATP. On average, the movement of a pair of electrons down the electron transport chain produces enough energy to form 3 ATP molecules from ADP.

Electron transport produces a difference in electric charge across the membrane. There are more hydrogen ions outside the inner membrane of the mitochondrion than inside it. Thus, the outside of the membrane is more positively charged than the inside. The difference in charge created by the imbalance of hydrogen ions supplies the energy to make ATP from ADP.

Like the photosynthetic membrane, the inner mitochondrial membrane has two special properties that make this process work: The electron transport chains in the membrane are arranged so that hydrogen ions are pumped in one direction across the membrane; and the membrane does not allow ions to "leak" back across (otherwise there would not be enough of a charge difference to provide energy for ATP synthesis).

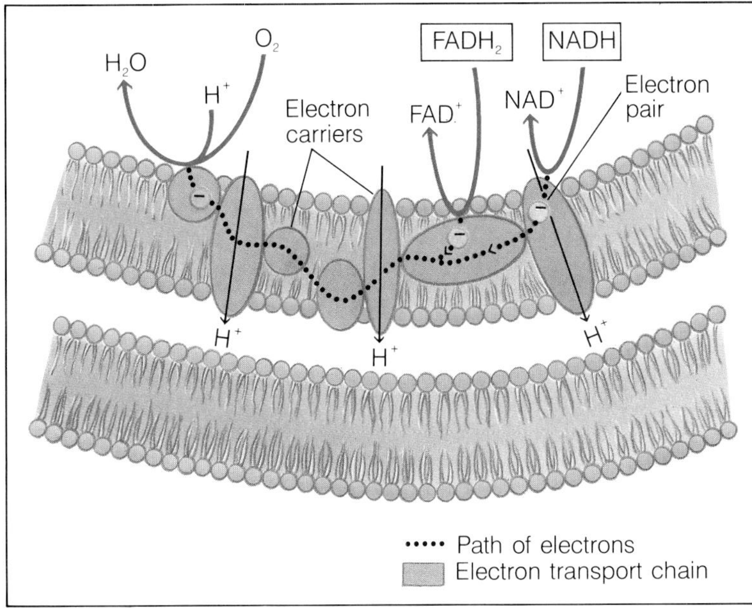

Figure 6–16 *The high-energy electrons in the energy-storing compounds NADH and $FADH_2$ are transferred to the molecules of the electron transport chain, which is located in the inner mitochondrial membrane. At the end of the chain, the electrons react with hydrogen ions and oxygen to form water.*

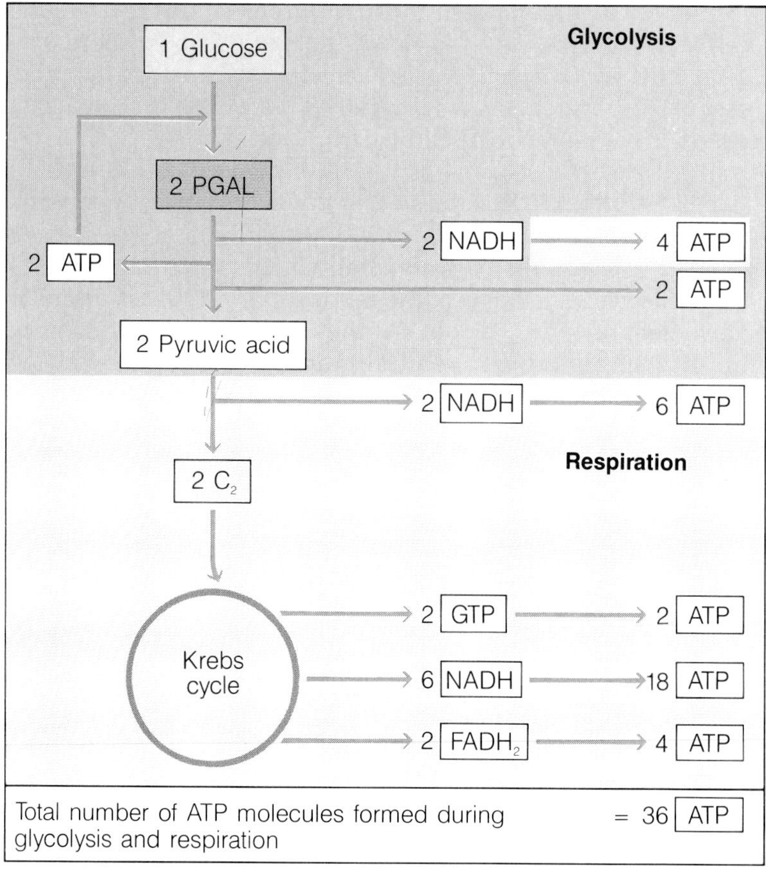

Figure 6–17 The complete breakdown of glucose through glycolysis and respiration results in the production of chemical energy in the form of 36 molecules of ATP.

THE TOTALS How much chemical energy is produced by the complete breakdown of glucose? Remember, glycolysis produces a net gain of 2 ATP molecules and passes high-energy electrons to 4 NADH molecules. The energy in these NADH molecules can be used to form 10 ATP molecules. In respiration, 6 more NADH, 2 GTP, and 2 $FADH_2$ molecules are produced in the Krebs cycle. The energy in the 2 GTP molecules can be used to form 2 ATP molecules. The electron transport chain uses the electrons in NADH and $FADH_2$ to produce 22 ATP molecules. See Figure 6–17. When the results of each of these biochemical pathways are considered, we find that a total of 36 molecules of ATP are produced from each glucose molecule. The energy in these 36 ATP molecules is about 37 percent of the total chemical energy available in glucose. That might not sound very impressive. However, the process of respiration is more efficient than the average automobile engine when it comes to converting fuel to usable energy.

Obtaining Energy from Food

Obviously very few of us eat a diet composed exclusively of glucose. But how is energy produced from foods other than glucose?

Complex carbohydrates are broken down into simple sugars that are then converted into glucose. At that point, the pathways we have discussed in this chapter can be used to produce energy. Most lipids and many proteins can be broken down into molecules that can enter glycolysis or the Krebs cycle at one of several places. Like a furnace that can burn wood, coal, or oil, the cell can generate chemical energy in the form of ATP from just about any source.

Breathing and Respiration

After all of this chemical detail, it is reasonable to point out why we have used the term respiration to refer to energy-releasing pathways. Remember that the final acceptor for all electrons produced in respiration is oxygen. Without oxygen, electron transport cannot operate, the Krebs cycle stops, and the synthesis of ATP in the mitochondrion stops. If we are starved for oxygen, our cells will attempt to make the ATP they require by glycolysis alone. But for most cells this is not sufficient.

With each breath we take, air flows into our lungs. Since ancient times, humans have realized that a constant supply of air into the lungs is necessary. But only in this century have we been able to understand why that air is necessary—oxygen has a critical role to play in the mitochondria of every cell!

Figure 6–18 *As this figure skater breathes, she takes in oxygen. The oxygen is used in the process of respiration, which provides energy in the form of ATP—energy that enables the skater to perform her feats on ice!*

Energy in Balance

Photosynthesis and respiration can be thought of as opposite processes. Earlier, we compared the chemical energy in glucose to money in a savings account. Photosynthesis is the process that "deposits" energy. Respiration "withdraws" energy. The equations for photosynthesis and for the complete breakdown of glucose (through glycolysis and respiration) are the reverse of each other. The products of photosynthesis are the reactants of glucose breakdown, and the products of glucose breakdown are the reactants of photosynthesis.

6–3 SECTION REVIEW

1. What is glycolysis?
2. List the products of the Krebs cycle. What happens to each of these products?
3. Why is breathing necessary for cellular respiration in animals?
4. None of the steps of the Krebs cycle involves oxygen. However, the Krebs cycle is considered to be an aerobic process. Explain why.

Section Objectives

- Relate fermentation to glycolysis.
- Compare lactic acid fermentation and alcoholic fermentation.

6–4 Fermentation

If oxygen is present, a cell can use the process of respiration to extract a great amount of energy from glucose. But what happens when no oxygen is available? Does this mean that we can no longer get energy from glucose?

As you may remember, glycolysis produces 2 ATP molecules per molecule of glucose and does not require oxygen.

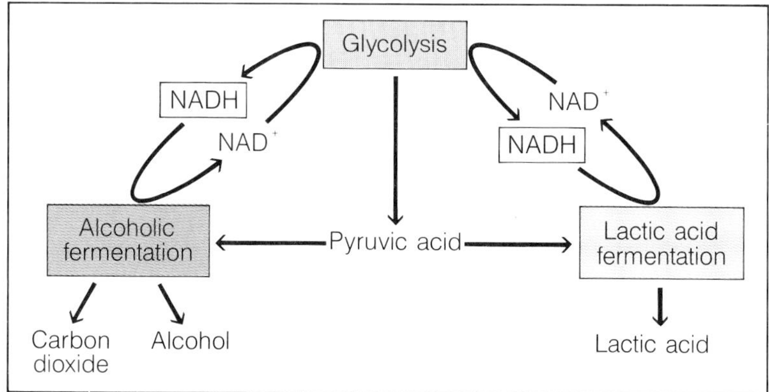

Figure 6–19 *The process of glycolysis produces energy and converts NAD+ to NADH. Fermentation is an anaerobic process that converts NADH back to NAD+, thus enabling cells to produce energy under anaerobic conditions.*

This enables cells to produce a limited amount of chemical energy in the form of ATP. Glycolysis also produces high-energy electrons that convert NAD^+ to NADH. In order for glycolysis to continue, NADH must be converted back to NAD^+.

This is where the process of **fermentation** comes in. Fermentation is **anaerobic**, which means that it does not require oxygen. In fermentation, NADH is converted to NAD^+ by adding the extra electrons in NADH to an organic molecule that acts as an electron acceptor. **Thus, fermentation enables cells to carry out energy production in the absence of oxygen.** The combination of glycolysis and fermentation produces 2 ATP molecules from a molecule of glucose.

In bacteria, many different organic molecules can serve as the final electron acceptor in fermentation. However, most eukaryotic cells use one of two fermentation pathways to change NADH to NAD^+. The two pathways are lactic acid fermentation and alcoholic fermentation.

Figure 6–20 *When the body cannot supply enough oxygen to muscles during vigorous exercise, muscle cells begin to produce energy by lactic acid fermentation. Even the best athletes are subject to the aches and pains that result from the buildup of lactic acid in the muscles.*

Lactic Acid Fermentation

In many cells, the pyruvic acid that accumulates as a result of glycolysis can be converted to lactic acid. Because this type of fermentation produces lactic acid, it is known as **lactic acid fermentation**. This process regenerates NAD^+ so that glycolysis can continue:

pyruvic acid + NADH → lactic acid + NAD^+

Lactic acid is produced in muscles during rapid exercise when the body cannot supply enough oxygen to the tissues to

produce all of the ATP that is required. The buildup of lactic acid causes a burning, painful sensation that every athlete is familiar with. When you exercise vigorously by running, swimming, or riding a bicycle as fast as you can, the large muscles of your arms and legs quickly run out of oxygen. Your muscle cells rapidly begin to produce ATP by fermentation. During this process, lactic acid is produced. This is why muscles may feel sore after only a few seconds of very rapid activity.

Figure 6–21 *When yeast cells (left) undergo alcoholic fermentation, they produce alcohol and carbon dioxide. The carbon dioxide produces the air spaces in bread and the bubbles in champagne.*

Alcoholic Fermentation

Another type of fermentation occurs in yeasts and a few other microorganisms. In this process, pyruvic acid (which is a 3-carbon compound) is broken down to produce a 2-carbon alcohol and carbon dioxide (CO_2). Because this type of fermentation produces alcohol, it is known as **alcoholic fermentation**. As in lactic acid fermentation, the process that alters pyruvic acid also changes NADH back into NAD^+:

$$\textbf{pyruvic acid} + \textbf{NADH} \rightarrow \textbf{alcohol} + \mathbf{CO_2} + \mathbf{NAD^+}$$

Alcoholic fermentation is of particular importance to bakers and brewers. The carbon dioxide produced by yeast during fermentation causes dough to rise and forms the air spaces you see in a slice of bread. The CO_2 released by fermentation is the source of bubbles in beer and sparkling wines. To brewers, alcohol is a welcome byproduct of fermentation. However, it is not desirable from a yeast cell's point of view. Alcohol is toxic. When the level of alcohol reaches about 12 percent, yeast cells die. Thus alcoholic beverages must be processed if higher concentrations of alcohol are desired.

6–4 SECTION REVIEW

1. What is fermentation? What are two types of fermentation?
2. How are respiration and fermentation similar? How are they different?
3. When oxygen is present, yeast cells undergo respiration. Explain why brewers must take special care to prevent air from entering fermentation tanks.

LABORATORY INVESTIGATION

OBSERVING THE RELATIONSHIP BETWEEN PHOTOSYNTHESIS AND RESPIRATION

PROBLEM

What is the relationship between the processes of photosynthesis and respiration?

MATERIALS *(per group)*

2 125-mL flasks
2 #5 rubber stoppers
100-mL graduated cylinder
bromthymol blue solution
2 *Elodea*
light source
drinking straw

PROCEDURE 

1. Using a graduated cylinder, measure out 100 mL of bromthymol blue solution for each of the two flasks.
   CAUTION: *Bromthymol blue is a dye and can stain your hands and clothing.*
2. Insert one end of a drinking straw into the bromthymol blue in one of the flasks. Gently blow through the straw. Keep blowing until there is a change in the appearance of the bromthymol blue solution. Repeat this procedure with the other flask.
3. Place a sprig of *Elodea* into each flask. Stopper the flasks.
4. Place one flask in the dark for 24 hours. Place the other flask on a sunny windowsill for the same amount of time. Artificial light may be used to supplement the sunlight.
5. After 24 hours, examine each flask. Note any change in the appearance of the bromthymol blue solution.

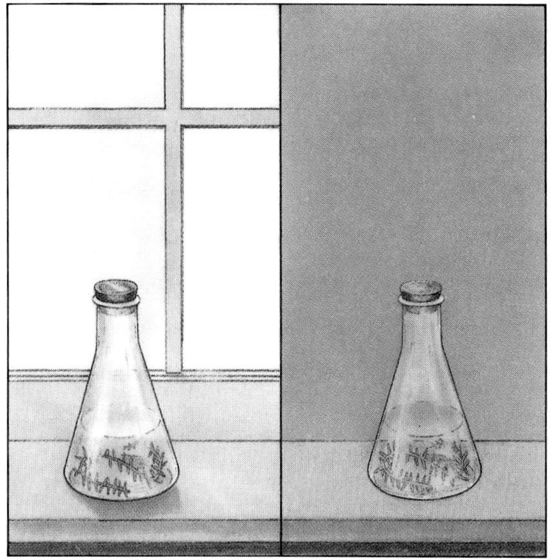

OBSERVATIONS

1. What was the color of the bromthymol blue solution before you exhaled into it? After you exhaled into it?
2. What was the color of the bromthymol blue solution in the flask that was placed in the dark for 24 hours? In the flask that was placed in the light for 24 hours?

ANALYSIS AND CONCLUSIONS

1. What substance was released into the bromthymol blue solution when you exhaled into it? How is this substance produced?
2. Explain why the color of the bromthymol blue solution changed after you exhaled into it.
3. Why was *Elodea* placed in both flasks?
4. Which flask is the control? Describe additional controls that you might use for this experiment.
5. Why are the results for the two flasks different?
6. How are photosynthesis and respiration related?

STUDENT STUDY GUIDE

SUMMARIZING THE CONCEPTS

The key concepts in each section of this chapter are listed below to help you review the chapter content. Make sure you understand each concept and its relationship to other concepts and to the theme of this chapter.

6–1 Photosynthesis: Capturing and Converting Energy

- In the process of photosynthesis, green plants capture the energy in sunlight and convert it into chemical energy. The balanced overall equation for photosynthesis is $6\ CO_2 + 6\ H_2O \xrightarrow{\text{light}} C_6H_{12}O_6 + 6\ O_2$.

6–2 Photosynthesis: The Light and Dark Reactions

- The light reactions can be broken down into four parts: light absorption, electron transport, oxygen production, and ATP synthesis.
- The dark reactions occur outside the photosynthetic membrane in the chloroplast. In the Calvin cycle, CO_2 is used to make PGAL, which can then be used to form glucose and other important molecules.

6–3 Glycolysis and Respiration

- Glycolysis is a series of chemical reactions that ultimately produces 2 molecules of ATP and 2 molecules of pyruvic acid.
- Respiration is an aerobic process that breaks down food molecules to release energy. This energy is stored in the form of ATP.

6–4 Fermentation

- Fermentation is an anaerobic process that regenerates NAD^+ for use in glycolysis. In fermentation, organic molecules take electrons from NADH, changing it back to NAD^+
- Photosynthesis stores energy; respiration releases energy. Products of photosynthesis are used in respiration. Products of respiration are raw materials for photosynthesis.

REVIEWING KEY TERMS

Vocabulary terms are important to your understanding of biology. The key terms listed below are those you should be especially familiar with. Review these terms and their meanings. Then use each term in a complete sentence. If you are not sure of a term's meaning, return to the appropriate section and review its definition.

6–1 Photosynthesis: Capturing and Converting Energy

photosynthesis
glucose
autotroph
heterotroph
pigment
chlorophyll
adenosine triphosphate (ATP)

6–2 Photosynthesis: The Light and Dark Reactions

light reactions
dark reactions
photosynthetic membrane
photosystem
electron transport
Calvin cycle

6–3 Glycolysis and Respiration

calorie
glycolysis
respiration
aerobic
Krebs cycle

6–4 Fermentation

fermentation
anaerobic
lactic acid fermentation
alcoholic fermentation

CHAPTER REVIEW

CONTENT REVIEW

Multiple Choice

Choose the letter of the answer that best completes each statement.

1. Which process is anaerobic?
   a. Krebs cycle
   b. mitochondrial electron transport
   c. glycolysis
   d. respiration
2. An experiment that showed that part of a growing plant's mass comes from water was performed by
   a. Priestley. c. Ingenhousz.
   b. Van Helmont. d. Calvin.
3. Autotrophs include
   a. ferns. c. yeasts.
   b. camels. d. birds.
4. Photosynthesis produces
   a. carbon dioxide. c. water.
   b. alcohol. d. glucose.
5. In respiration, the final electron acceptor is
   a. lactic acid. c. oxygen.
   b. alcohol. d. NAD^+.
6. Which of these is produced by the dark reactions?
   a. PGAL c. water
   b. oxygen d. ATP
7. A type of pigment found in green plants is
   a. NAD^+. c. ATP.
   b. NADPH. d. chlorophyll.
8. Which of these is not produced in the light reactions?
   a. NADPH c. ATP
   b. glucose d. oxygen

True or False

Determine whether each statement is true or false. If it is true, write "true." If it is false, change the underlined word or words to make the statement true.

1. In the dark reactions of photosynthesis, the energy in sunlight is captured and used to make ATP and NADPH.
2. Because they cannot make their own food, autotrophs rely on the food-making ability of green plants.
3. Photosystems are clusters of pigment molecules that are able to capture the energy of sunlight.
4. The light reactions occur outside the photosynthetic membrane.
5. ATP is formed when enzymes move hydrogen ions across a membrane to an area of greater concentration.
6. Glycolysis is an aerobic process that breaks down food molecules to produce energy.
7. When there is no oxygen present, yeast cells break down glucose to form lactic acid and carbon dioxide.
8. Approximately 36 molecules of ATP are formed during glycolysis.

Word Relationships

A. *In each of the following sets of terms, three of the terms are related. One term does not belong. Determine the characteristic common to three of the terms and then identify the term that does not belong.*

1. Calvin cycle, light absorption, electron transport, oxygen production
2. fermentation, respiration, glycolysis, photosynthesis
3. glucose, oxygen, water, energy

B. *An analogy is a relationship between two pairs of words or phrases generally written in the following manner: a:b::c:d. The symbol : is read "is to," and the symbol :: is read "as." For example, cat:animal::rose:plant is read "cat is to animal as rose is to plant."*

In the analogies that follow, a word or phrase is missing. Complete each analogy by providing the missing word or phrase.

4. food and oxygen:respiration::_______________:photosynthesis
5. oak tree:autotroph::human:_______________
6. PGAL:Calvin cycle::pyruvic acid:_______________
7. photosynthesis:chloroplast::respiration:_______________

CONCEPT MASTERY

Use your understanding of the concepts developed in the chapter to answer each of the following in a brief paragraph.

1. List the requirements for photosynthesis. Briefly describe how each is involved in the light reactions or the dark reactions.
2. Describe the process of ATP formation.
3. Name ten living things that you see every day. Identify each of these as an autotroph or a heterotroph.
4. What is the relationship between breathing and respiration?
5. How are photosynthesis and respiration related to each other?
6. Compare the reactants and products of two types of fermentation.

CRITICAL AND CREATIVE THINKING

Discuss each of the following in a brief paragraph.

1. **Making comparisons** Compare the chemical steps of the light and dark reactions of photosynthesis with those of glycolysis, the Krebs cycle, and the respiratory electron transport chain.
2. **Making an outline** Outline the process of photosynthesis.
3. **Applying concepts** Some desert animals such as the kangaroo rat never have to drink water. Explain how kangaroo rats can obtain the water they need to survive from the dry seeds they eat.
4. **Making inferences** Some scientists think that the dinosaurs may have become extinct because an asteroid struck the Earth and sent large amounts of dust into the upper atmosphere. The dust remained in the atmosphere a long time. Explain how this would have resulted in the dinosaurs dying off.
5. **Assessing concepts** Which is better: respiration or fermentation? Explain your answer.
6. **Using the writing process** You are a carbon atom. You have just returned to the air as carbon dioxide after being involved in the processes of photosynthesis and respiration. Describe what happened to you on your chemical journey. Where did you go? What other atoms (carbon and otherwise) did you find yourself bonded to? What molecules did you meet along the way, and what were they like?

CHAPTER 7

Nucleic Acids and Protein Synthesis

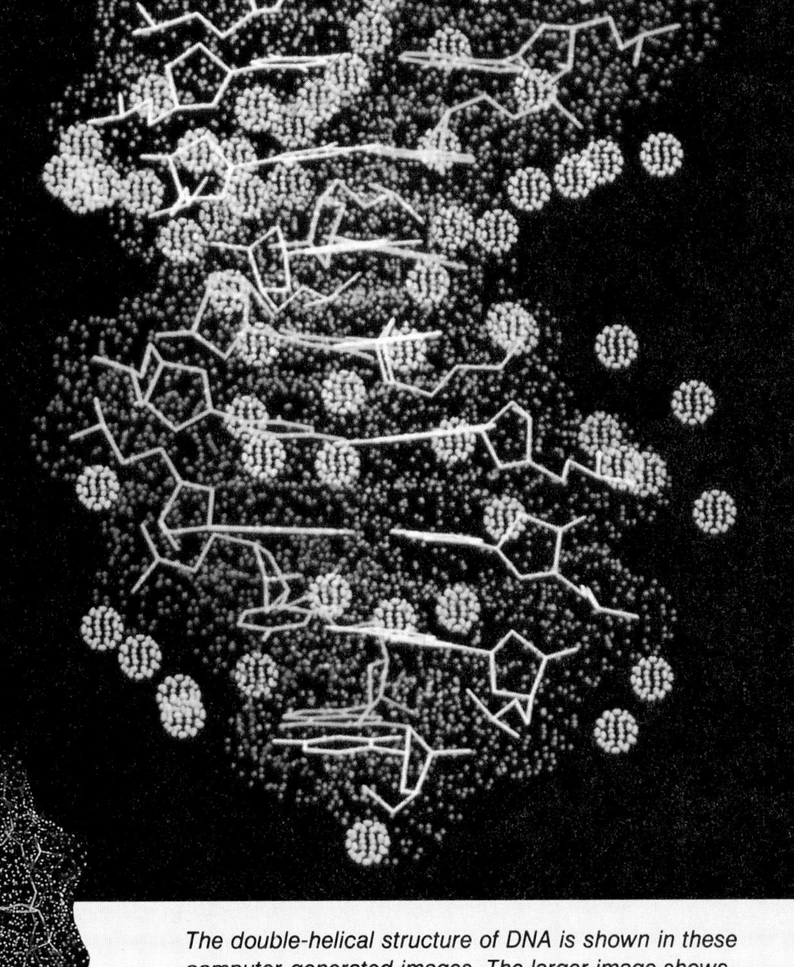

The double-helical structure of DNA is shown in these computer-generated images. The larger image shows a dark-blue structure and a purple structure coiling around each other. These structures represent the two linked strands of nucleotides in DNA. The smaller image shows DNA's double helix as it appears from above.

In the middle of the twentieth century, a great revolution began to take place in biology. Like many revolutions, its beginnings were modest. Its pioneers were a handful of investigators who sought to understand how information was transferred from one generation of life to the next. The discovery that nucleic acids carry and transfer that information has altered our view of living things. In this chapter we will begin to study the nucleic acids DNA and RNA, the genetic code they contain, and the way in which that code is put into action during protein synthesis.

CHAPTER OUTLINE

7–1 DNA

Section Objectives

- List the contributions of various scientists to the idea that DNA carries the genetic code.
- Describe the structure and function of DNA.
- Summarize the process of DNA replication.

By now it should be clear that living cells are able to do some remarkable things. We might go so far as to say that cells "know" a great deal about the business of life: how to produce ATP, how to build cilia and centrioles, how to produce enzymes and membranes. It is as though cells are preinstructed by a code, or programmed, about what to do and how to do it.

A program, or code, in living cells must be able to duplicate itself quickly and accurately and must also have a means of being decoded and put into effect. In this chapter we will begin to learn about the nature of the cellular program—what biologists know and don't know about the ways in which the program is constructed, duplicated, and carried out.

The Genetic Code

Biologists call the program of the cell the **genetic code.** The word genetic refers to anything that relates to heredity. The genetic code, therefore, is the way in which cells store the program that they seem to pass from one generation of an organism to the next generation.

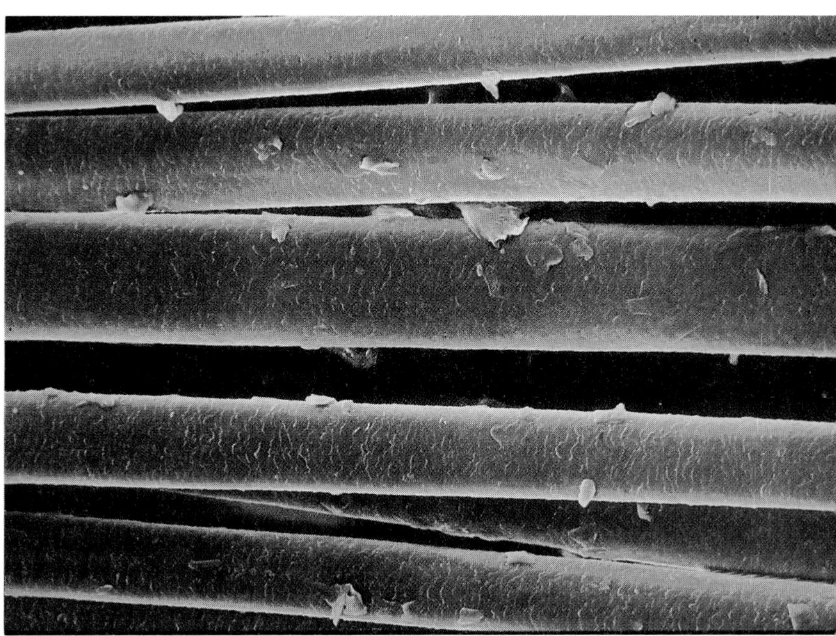

Figure 7–1 *The genetic code stores the program for making proteins, such as those that make up the strands of hair, and passes it on from generation to generation.*

Is there a molecule that carries the genetic code? As often happens in science, an opportunity to answer this question presented itself to someone who was actually interested in something else.

In 1928, the British scientist Frederick Griffith was studying the way in which certain types of bacteria cause the disease pneumonia. Griffith had in his laboratory two slightly different strains, or types, of pneumonia bacteria. Both strains grew very well in culture plates in his lab, but only one strain actually caused the disease. The disease-causing strain of bacteria grew into smooth colonies on culture plates, whereas the harmless strain produced colonies with rough edges. The differences in appearance made the two strains easy to distinguish.

When Griffith injected mice with the disease-causing strain of bacteria, the mice got pneumonia and died. When mice were injected with the harmless strain, they did not get pneumonia and they did not die. And when mice were injected with the disease-causing strain that had been killed by heat, these mice too survived. By performing this third experiment, Griffith proved to himself that the cause of pneumonia was not a chemical poison released by the disease-causing bacteria.

TRANSFORMATION Next Griffith did an experiment that produced an astonishing result. He injected mice with a mixture of live cells from the harmless strain and heat-killed cells from the disease-causing strain. To Griffith's surprise, the mice developed pneumonia!

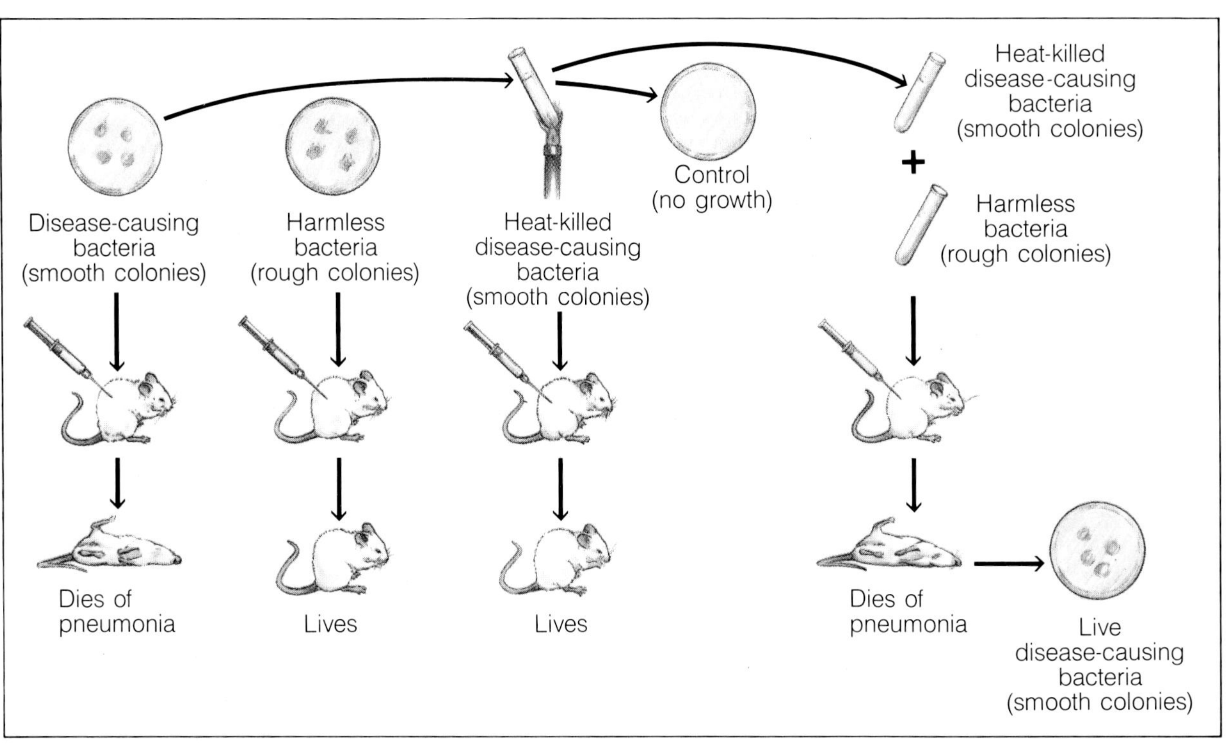

Figure 7–2 *The results of Griffith's experiments showed that "something" had been transferred from the heat-killed disease-causing bacteria to the live harmless bacteria, transforming them into live disease-causing bacteria. This something was later isolated and identified as DNA.*

Somehow Griffith's heat-killed strain had passed on its disease-causing ability to the live harmless strain. It was almost as if a farmer had scattered ground beef in a henhouse and then returned the next morning to discover that some of the eggs had begun to hatch into calves instead of baby chicks!

To confuse matters even more, Griffith recovered bacteria from the animals that had developed pneumonia. When these bacteria were grown on culture plates, they formed smooth colonies characteristic of the disease-causing strain. For all practical purposes, one strain of bacteria had been transformed into another. Griffith called this process **transformation.**

THE TRANSFORMING FACTOR Griffith theorized that when the live harmless bacteria and the heat-killed bacteria were mixed together, a factor was transferred from the heat-killed cells into the live cells. In 1944, a group of scientists at the Rockefeller Institute in New York City led by Oswald Avery, Maclyn McCarty, and Colin MacLeod decided to repeat Griffith's work and see if they could discover which molecules were Griffith's transforming factor, that is, which molecules were responsible for transformation.

Avery and his colleagues made an extract, or juice, from the heat-killed bacteria. When they treated the extract with enzymes that destroy lipids, proteins, and carbohydrates, they discovered that transformation still occurred. Obviously these molecules were not responsible for the transformation. If they were, transformation would not have occurred because the molecules would have been destroyed by the enzymes.

Avery and the other scientists repeated the experiment, this time using enzymes that would break down RNA (ribonucleic acid). The scientists found that again transformation took place. But when they performed the experiment again, now using enzymes that would break down **DNA** (deoxyribonucleic acid), transformation did not occur. DNA was the transforming factor! **DNA is the nucleic acid that stores and transmits the genetic information from one generation of an organism to the next.** In other words, DNA carries the genetic code.

BACTERIOPHAGES The work of Avery and his colleagues clearly demonstrated the role of DNA in the transfer of genetic information. Scientists, however, are notorious for being a skeptical group, and it sometimes takes many successful experiments to convince everyone.

One of the most important of these experiments was performed in 1952 by two American scientists, Alfred Hershey and Martha Chase. Hershey and Chase were interested in the kinds of viruses that infect bacteria. Such viruses are known as bacteriophages (bak-TIHR-ee-uh-fayj-uhz), which means bacteria eaters. Bacteriophages are composed of a DNA core and a protein coat. They attach themselves to the surface of a bacterium and then inject a material into the bacterium.

Figure 7–3 *This electron micrograph shows some T-2 bacteriophages attached to the bacterium* E. coli. *Once inside, the bacteriophages take over the bacterium's DNA and instruct it to make many copies of themselves (black ovals in the bacterium).*

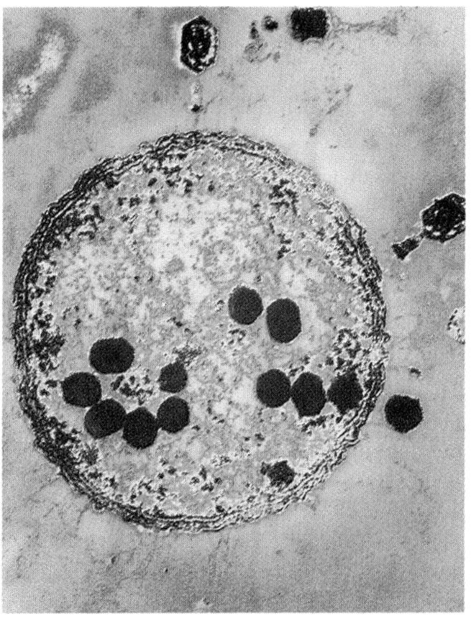

Once inside the bacterium, the injected material begins to reproduce, making many copies of the bacteriophage. Soon the bacterium bursts, and several hundred bacteriophages are released to infect other cells. Because the material injected into the bacterium produces new bacteriophages, it must contain the genetic code.

In their experiments, Hershey and Chase set out to learn whether the protein coat, the DNA, or both of these parts of the infecting virus was the material that entered the bacterium. First they prepared two batches of the virus. They added radioactive sulfur-35 to one batch and radioactive phosphorus-32 to the other batch. Sulfur-35 and phosphorus-32 are radioactive isotopes. You will recall from Chapter 3 that radioactive isotopes can be used as tracers to follow the pathway of certain materials.

By adding the radioactive isotopes to the viruses, Hershey and Chase were "labeling" the viruses' protein and DNA. The protein was labeled with sulfur-35, and the DNA was labeled with phosphorous-32. This was an excellent strategy because proteins contain little or no phosphorous, whereas DNA does not contain sulfur. If sulfur-35 was found in the bacteria, it would mean that the viruses' protein was injected into the bacteria. If phosphorous-32 was found in the bacteria, then it was the DNA that had been injected.

Figure 7–4 *As a result of their experiments, Hershey and Chase discovered that the DNA of a bacteriophage is injected into a bacterium, whereas the bacteriophage's protein coat remains outside the bacterium. New bacteriophages are produced inside the bacterium, indicating that DNA, not the protein, is the hereditary material of the bacteriophage.*

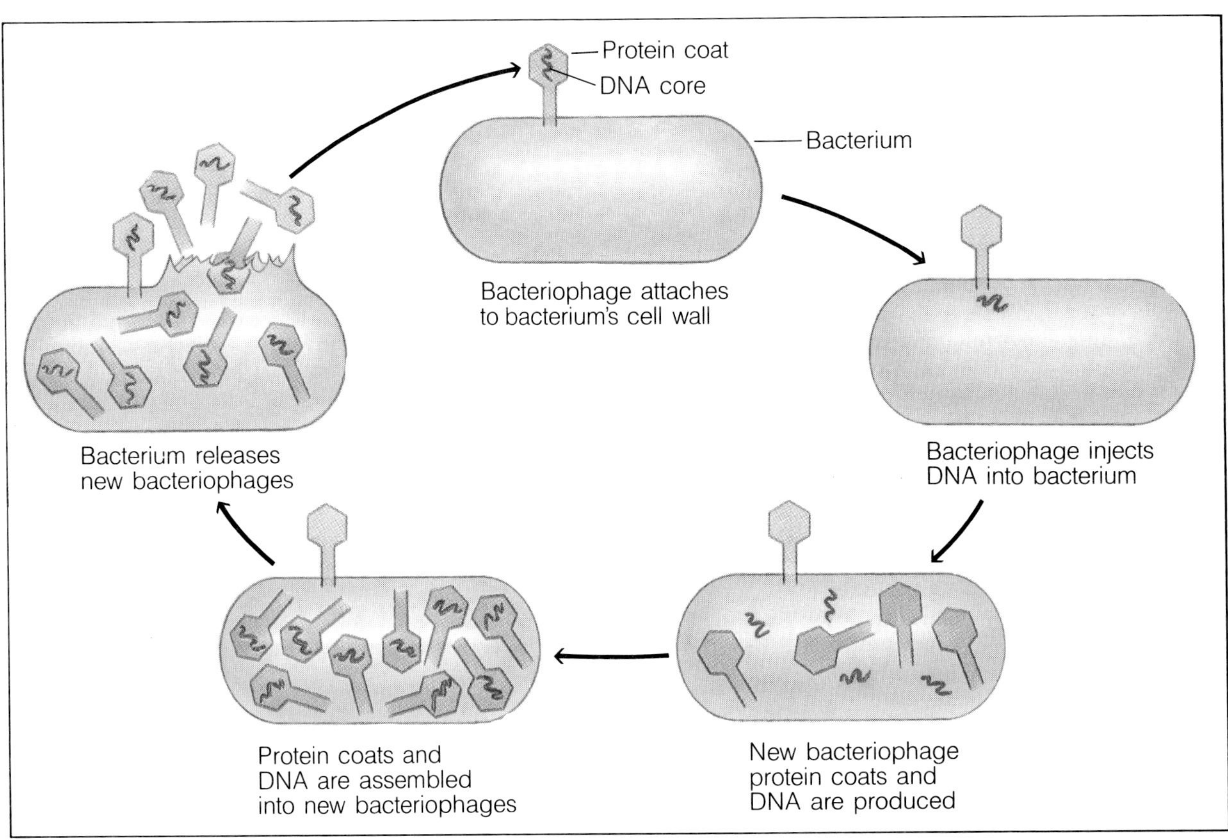

The two scientists mixed the radioactively labeled viruses with the bacteria. They waited a few minutes for the viruses to attach and inject the genetic material. Then they separated the viruses from the bacteria by placing the mixture in a mechanical blender and then centrifuging the mixture.

Hershey and Chase discovered that nearly all the radioactive sulfur remained within the viruses. By contrast, nearly all the radioactive phosphorous had entered the bacteria!

From these results, it was clear that the viruses' DNA enters the bacteria, and the protein coats remain outside the bacteria. This was convincing evidence that DNA contains the genetic information. When considered along with the earlier experiments on the transformation of pneumonia bacteria, the Hershey-Chase experiments showed conclusively that DNA was the molecule that carried the genetic code.

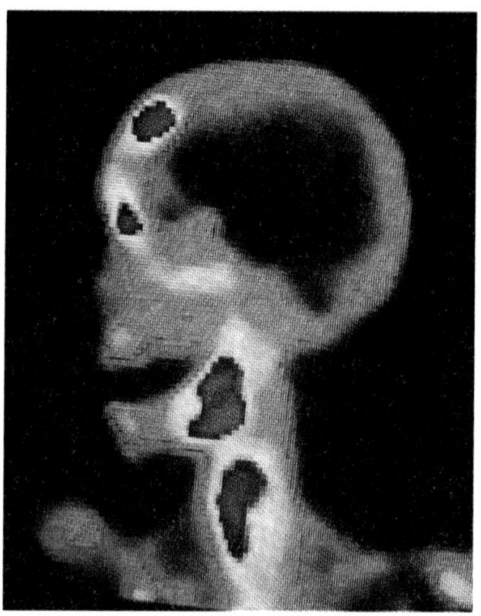

Figure 7–5 *Radioactive isotopes are used not only to follow the pathway of certain materials, but also to detect the presence of some types of cancer. This photograph shows how a radioactive isotope becomes more concentrated in a cancerous part of the body, in this case in bone, than in a healthy part of the body. The cancerous part appears in red.*

The Structure of DNA

Even if DNA was shown to be the crucial molecule for the passing on of genetic information, a question of overwhelming importance remained. How could a molecule such as DNA perform two significant tasks: store information and duplicate itself easily? Let's take a look at the structure of DNA to see if that explains how it accomplishes these tasks.

As you will recall from Chapter 4, DNA is a polymer formed from units called **nucleotides.** Each nucleotide is a molecule made up of three basic parts: a 5-carbon sugar called deoxyribose (dee-ahks-ee-RIGH-bohz), a phosphate group, and a nitrogenous, or nitrogen-containing, base.

DNA contains four nitrogenous bases. Two of the nitrogenous bases, **adenine** (AD-uh-neen) and **guanine** (GWAH-neen), belong to a group of compounds known as purines (PYOOR-eenz). The remaining two, **cytosine** (SIGHT-oh-seen) and **thymine** (THIGH-meen), are known as pyrimidines (pih-RIHM-uh-deenz).

Individual nucleotides are joined together to form a long chain. Notice in Figure 7–7 on page 142 that the sugars and phosphate groups form the backbone of the chain, and the nitrogenous bases stick out from the chain.

X-RAY EVIDENCE In the early 1950s, the British scientist Rosalind Franklin turned her attention to the DNA molecule. She purified a large amount of DNA and then stretched the DNA fibers in a thin glass tube so that most of the strands were parallel. Then she aimed a narrow X-ray beam on them and recorded the pattern on film. When X-rays pass through matter, they are scattered, or diffracted. This X-ray scattering produces a pattern that provides important clues to the structure of many molecules.

Franklin worked hard to prepare better and better samples until the X-ray patterns became clear. The result of her work is

Figure 7–6 *DNA is a polymer formed from units called nucleotides. A nucleotide is composed of three basic parts: a phosphate group, a 5-carbon sugar, and a nitrogenous base. What is DNA's 5-carbon sugar called?*

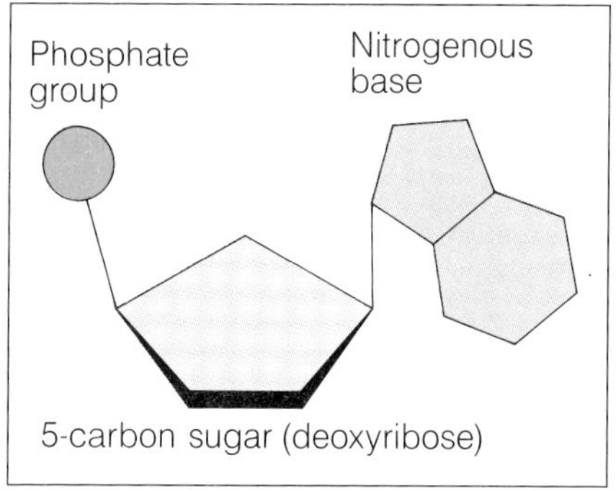

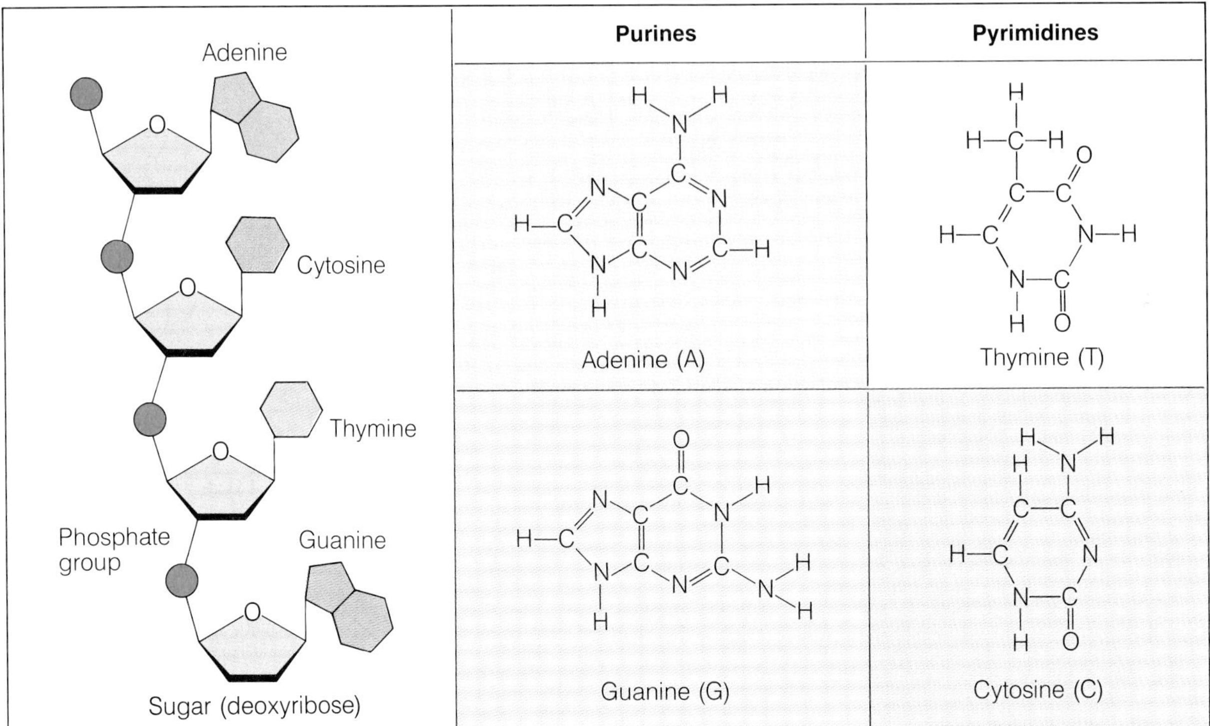

Figure 7–7 Individual nucleotides join together to form a DNA chain. Note that each nucleotide contains one nitrogenous base.

Figure 7–8 This X-ray diffraction photograph of DNA was taken by Rosalind Franklin in the early 1950s. The X-shaped pattern in the center indicates that the structure of DNA is helical.

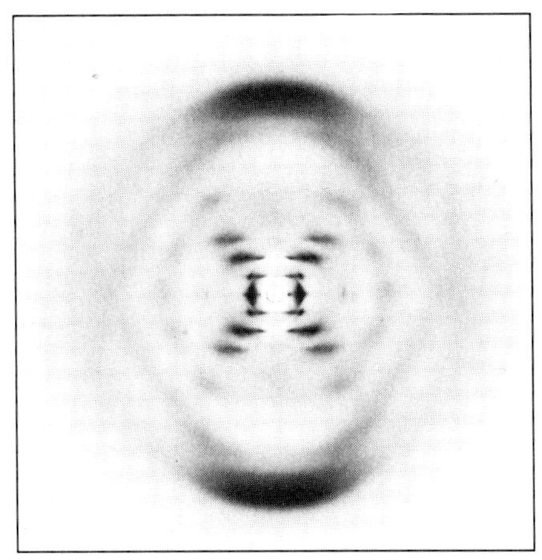

the X-ray pattern shown in Figure 7–8. This pattern does not prove anything immediately, but it does provide some very important clues about the structure of DNA. One important clue is that the fibers that make up DNA are twisted, like the strands of a rope. This is shown by the small X near the center of the pattern. The other important clue is that large groups of molecules in the fiber are spaced out at regular intervals along the length of the fiber.

Taken alone, neither of these facts was enough to determine the structure of DNA. The X-ray pattern was like a fingerprint or a scrap of cloth at the scene of a crime. Crucial evidence, perhaps, but it would only make sense when put into a larger picture by a clever detective—or an inventive scientist!

BUILDING A MODEL OF DNA At the same time that Franklin and her colleague, Maurice Wilkins, were doing their research, two young scientists working in Cambridge, England, were also trying to determine the structure of DNA. One of the scientists was Francis Crick, a British physicist. The other was James Watson, a 25-year-old American biochemist.

Watson and Crick had been trying to solve the mystery of DNA structure by building three-dimensional models of the atomic groups in DNA. They twisted and stretched the models in various ways to see if any of the structures that formed made any sense. Watson and Crick had some interesting ideas, but nothing to test them against.

Then, during a visit to London, Watson was able to observe Franklin's remarkable X-ray pattern of DNA. At once Watson and Crick realized that there was something important in that pattern. They immediately set out to use the clues that Franklin had provided. Within weeks, Watson and Crick had figured out the structure of DNA.

Figure 7–9 *This photograph of Watson and Crick with one of their first models of DNA was taken in 1953.*

THE DOUBLE HELIX Working with these clues, Watson and Crick began, quite literally, to play with their models of the DNA fiber. What they needed to do was to twist their model into a shape that would account for Franklin's X-ray pattern. Before long, they developed a shape that seemed to make sense. They called this shape a helix because it was similar to a spiral, or the way in which the threads are arranged in a screw. Using Franklin's idea that there were probably two strands of DNA, Watson and Crick imagined that the strands were twisted around each other, forming a double helix.

Watson and Crick's model explained one more characteristic about DNA's structure. The nitrogenous bases on each of the strands of DNA are positioned exactly opposite each other. This positioning allows weak hydrogen bonds to form between the nitrogenous bases adenine (A) and thymine (T), and between cytosine (C) and guanine (G).

Another interesting piece of information that helped Watson and Crick in working out their model of DNA's structure was provided by Erwin Chargaff, an American biochemist. Chargaff observed that in any sample of DNA, the number of adenine molecules was equal to the number of thymine molecules. The same was true for the number of cytosine and guanine molecules. Chargaff's observation enabled Watson and Crick to determine that adenine only bonds to thymine and cytosine only bonds to guanine. The two scientists further reasoned that the attraction of these bases for each other is very specific. The attraction between such bases is known as **base pairing.** Base pairing is the force that holds the two strands of the DNA double helix together. As you can see, Watson and Crick set out to solve one puzzle and found the answer to another puzzle too!

Figure 7–10 *This three-dimensional image of DNA magnified one million times was made through a scanning tunneling microscope (STM). This recently invented microscope can distinguish individual atoms. Previous images of DNA were made through electron microscopes that could magnify objects only 300,000 times.*

In 1953, after making careful drawings of their model of DNA, Watson and Crick submitted their findings to a scientific journal. Their model, although speculative in some areas, was almost immediately accepted by scientists the world over. Why? Because, as we will see, it contained a feature that explained a great mystery: how DNA could copy itself!

The importance of this work on DNA was acknowledged in 1962 by the awarding of the Nobel prize for medicine or physiology—the highest prize the international community can give for a scientific discovery—to its discoverers. Because Rosalind Franklin had died in 1958 and Nobel prizes are given only to living scientists, the prize was shared by Watson, Crick, and Franklin's associate, Maurice Wilkins.

The Replication of DNA

Because each of the two strands of the DNA double helix has all the information, by the mechanism of base pairing, to reconstruct the other half, the strands are said to be complementary. To illustrate this concept, we can use the analogy of a dollar bill that has been torn in half. Each half of the dollar bill tells us just what the other half must look like, even though the two halves are not identical.

Although there are four nitrogenous bases in DNA, the situation is really quite similar to that of the dollar bill. As you can see from Figure 7–11, even in a long and complicated DNA molecule, each half can specifically direct the sequence of the other half by complementary base pairing. This allows us to imagine a very simple scheme for copying the double helix, as shown in Figure 7–12. In effect, each strand of the double helix of DNA serves as a template, or pattern, against which a new strand is made.

Before a cell divides, it must duplicate its DNA. This ensures that each resulting cell will have a complete set of DNA molecules. This copying process is known as **replication.** DNA replication, or DNA synthesis, is carried out by a series of enzymes. These enzymes separate, or "unzip," the two strands of the double helix, insert the appropriate bases, and produce covalent sugar-phosphate links to extend the growing DNA chains. The enzymes even "proofread" the bases that have been inserted to ensure that they are paired correctly.

As proposed by Watson and Crick, DNA replication begins

Figure 7–11 The structure of the DNA double helix resembles a twisted ladder. The sugar-phosphate backbones form the sides of the ladder and the nitrogenous bases form the rungs of the ladder. What holds the nitrogenous bases together?

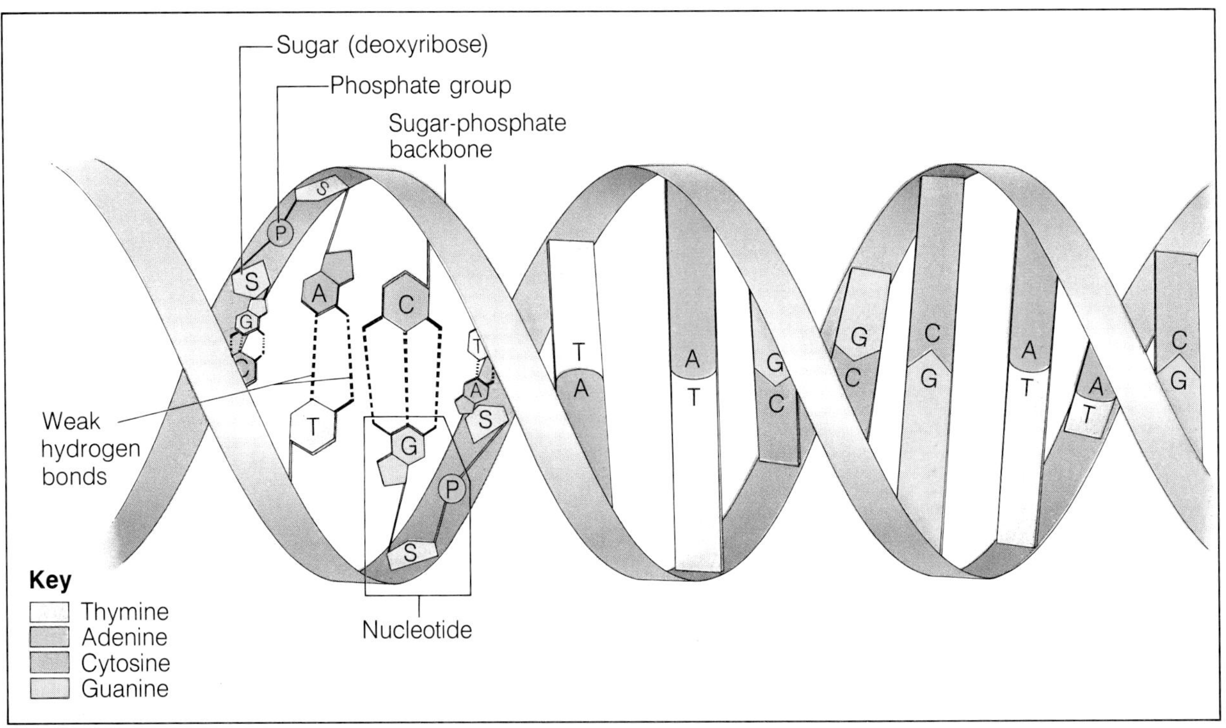

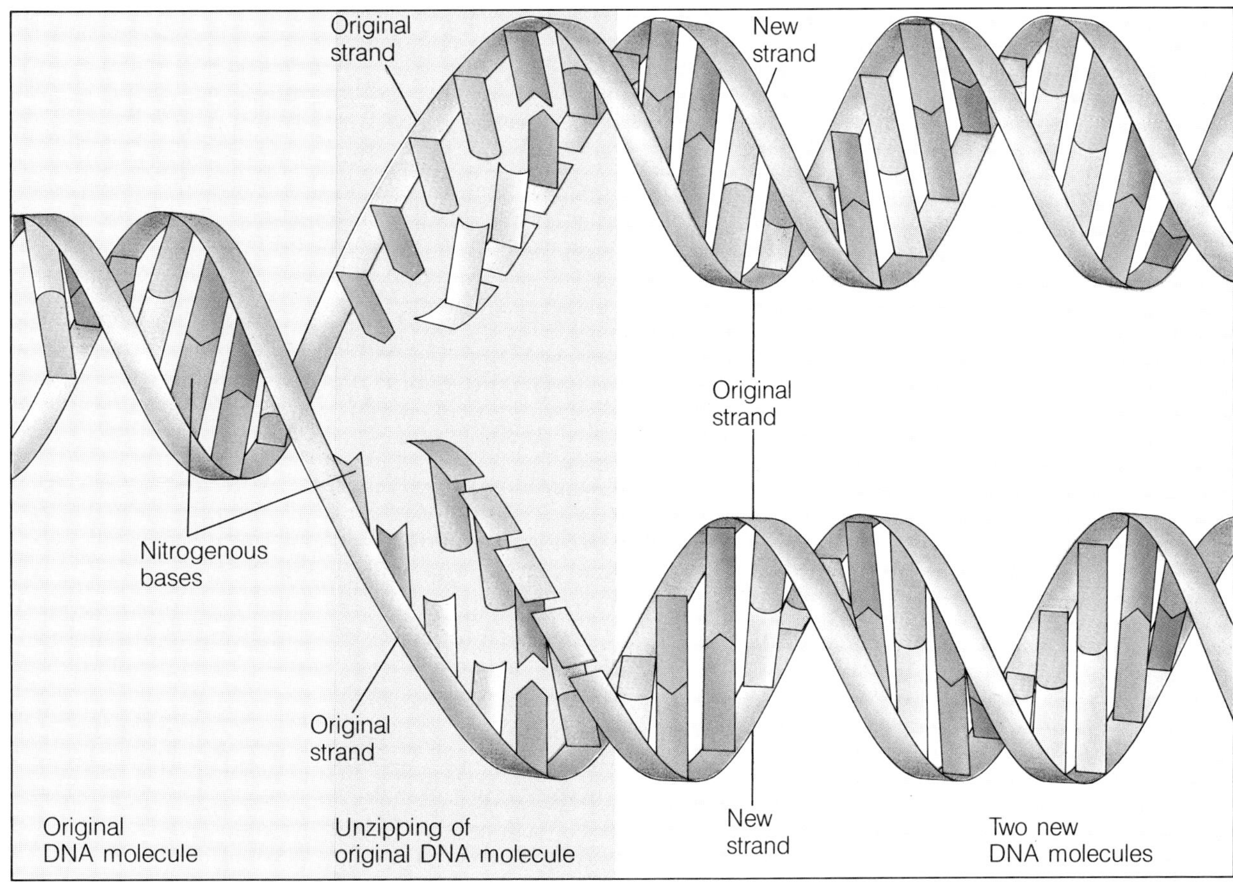

Figure 7–12 When DNA undergoes replication, each of the original strands unzips down the middle as the base pairs separate at the hydrogen bonds. Each of the original strands serves as the template along which a new complementary strand of DNA forms.

when a molecule of DNA "unzips." The unzipping occurs when the hydrogen bonds between the base pairs are broken and the two strands of the molecule unwind. Each of the separated strands serves as a template for the attachment of complementary bases. For example, a strand that has the bases T-A-C-G-T-T produces a strand with the complementary bases A-T-G-C-A-A. In this way, two DNA molecules identical to each other and to the original molecule are made.

7–1 SECTION REVIEW

1. Why was Griffith's work on transformation important in identifying DNA as the genetic material?
2. How did Hershey and Chase show that DNA was the molecule that carried the genetic code?
3. What is the function of DNA?
4. What are the parts of a DNA nucleotide?
5. Describe the shape of a DNA molecule.
6. Why is DNA replication necessary to life?

Section Objectives

- State the function of RNA.
- Compare the structures of RNA and DNA.
- Describe the process of transcription.

7–2 RNA

The double helix structure explains how DNA can be replicated, or copied. However, it does not explain how information is contained in the molecule or how that information is put to good use. As we will see, DNA contains a set of instructions that are coded in the sequence, or order, of nucleotides. The first step in decoding that message is to copy part of the sequence into **RNA** (ribonucleic acid). **RNA is the nucleic acid that acts as a messenger between DNA and the ribosomes and carries out the process by which proteins are made from amino acids.** As you will recall from Chapter 5, ribosomes are the organelles in which proteins are made.

The Structure of RNA

RNA, like DNA, consists of a long chain of macromolecules made up of nucleotides. Each nucleotide is made up of a 5-carbon sugar, a phosphate group, and a nitrogenous base. The alternating sugars and phosphate groups form the backbone of the RNA chain.

There are three major differences between RNA and DNA. The sugar in RNA is ribose, whereas the sugar in DNA is deoxyribose. Another difference between RNA and DNA is that RNA consists of a single strand of nucleotides, although it can form double-stranded sections by folding back on itself in loops. DNA, as you will recall, is double-stranded. Lastly, the nitrogenous bases found in DNA are adenine, thymine, cytosine, and guanine. RNA also contains adenine, cytosine, and guanine, but **uracil** (YOOR-uh-sihl) is present instead of thymine. Like DNA, RNA follows the base-pairing rules. Adenine bonds to uracil, and cytosine bonds to guanine.

Although a cell contains many different forms of RNA, there are three main types that are involved in expressing the genetic code. Each of the three main types of RNA will be discussed later in this section.

In its own way, an RNA molecule is a disposable copy of a segment of DNA. The ability to copy a DNA base sequence into RNA makes it possible for a specific place on the DNA molecule to produce hundreds or even thousands of RNA molecules with the same information as DNA.

Figure 7–13 *Like DNA, RNA consists of units called nucleotides. The nucleotides in RNA, however, contain the 5-carbon sugar ribose instead of deoxyribose and the nitrogenous base uracil instead of thymine.*

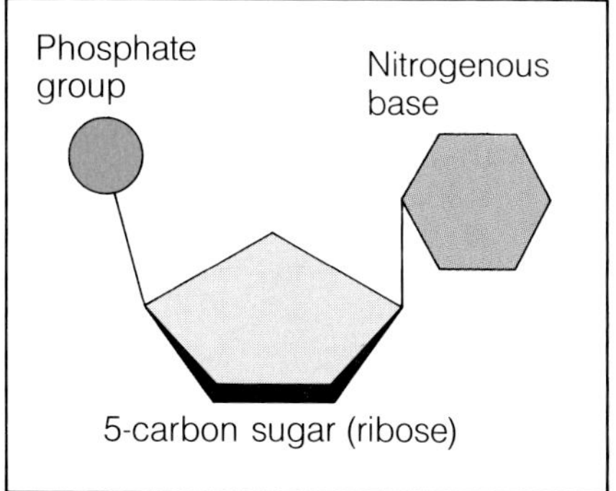

Transcription: RNA Synthesis

As you will recall, DNA replication is also known as DNA synthesis because the molecule being synthesized turns out to be the same as the molecule being copied. In RNA synthesis, the molecule being copied is just one of the two strands of a DNA molecule. Thus the molecule being synthesized is different from the molecule being copied. The term **transcription** is used to describe this process. **Transcription is the process by**

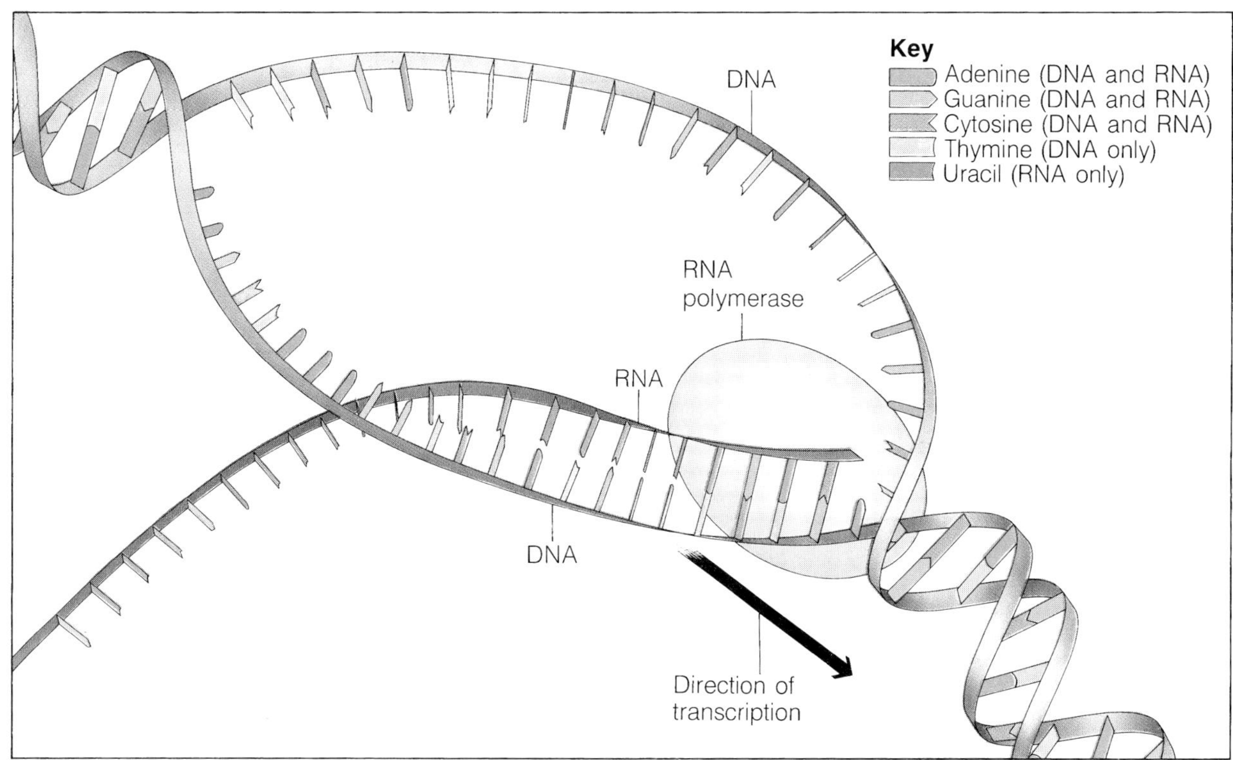

Figure 7–14 *During transcription, the enzyme RNA polymerase attaches to an area on the DNA molecule, causing it to open up. As the RNA polymerase moves along the DNA molecule, the two strands of DNA separate. Then RNA nucleotides link to the complementary bases on DNA. Which of RNA's nitrogenous bases pairs with adenine in DNA?*

which a molecule of DNA is copied into a complementary strand of RNA. In other words, transcription is the process of transferring information from DNA to RNA.

Why is it necessary for DNA to transfer its genetic information to RNA? Recall from Chapter 5 that DNA is found in the nucleus and ribosomes are located in the cytoplasm. Because DNA does not leave the nucleus, a messenger, or carrier, must bring the genetic information from the DNA in the nucleus out to the ribosomes in the cytoplasm. The molecule that performs this function is **messenger RNA** (mRNA), one of the three main types of RNA.

In order to more fully understand how transcription takes place, we must discuss the role that an enzyme known as RNA polymerase (PAHL-ih-mer-ayz) plays in this process. In Chapter 4 you learned that an enzyme is specific, that is, it works on only one substance. For this reason, part of its name is usually derived from the substance on which it works. Then the suffix *-ase* is added. Thus RNA polymerase works on the polymers RNA and DNA.

During transcription, RNA polymerase attaches to special places on the DNA molecule, separates the two strands of the double helix, and synthesizes a messenger RNA strand. The messenger RNA strand is complementary to one of the DNA strands. The base-pairing mechanism ensures that the messenger RNA will be a complementary copy of the DNA strand that serves as its template.

Special sequences in DNA serve as "start signals" and are recognized by RNA polymerase and other proteins associated with transcription. Other areas on the DNA molecule are recognized as termination sites where RNA polymerase releases the newly synthesized messenger RNA molecules.

7-2 SECTION REVIEW

1. What is the function of RNA?
2. What are three differences between RNA and DNA?
3. What is transcription?
4. Using the base-pairing rules, identify the bases on the messenger RNA strand that are transcribed from the following DNA strands: A-C-C-G-T-C-A-C; T-C-G-C-A-C-G-T.

Section Objectives

- List some of the functions of proteins in cells.
- Describe the process of translation.
- Explain the term codon.
- Identify the three main types of RNA.

7-3 Protein Synthesis

The information that DNA transfers to messenger RNA is in the form of a code. This code is determined by the way in which the four nitrogenous bases are arranged in DNA. To understand how the code works, we must answer two questions: What kind of information is contained in DNA, and how is that information decoded?

The nitrogenous bases in DNA contain information that directs protein synthesis. Why proteins and not other molecules? you might ask. The answer can be found in the diversity of things that proteins are capable of doing. Because most enzymes are proteins, proteins control biochemical pathways within the cell. Not only do proteins direct the synthesis of lipids, carbohydrates, and nucleotides, but they are also responsible for cell structure and cell movement. Like the manager of a factory, DNA does not work on the assembly line but can control what the cell factory makes by issuing orders to the organelles (workers). Together, DNA and its assistant, RNA, are directly responsible for making proteins. As you can see, DNA and RNA are like nucleic-acid executives who run the entire cell factory.

Figure 7–15 *If a single nucleotide coded for one amino acid, only four amino acids could be specified (top). If two nucleotides specified for one amino acid, there could be 16 amino acids (bottom)—still not enough to code for all 20 amino acids contained in proteins.*

Four Code Letters	
A	G
C	U

Sixteen Doublets from the Four Code Letters			
AA	AC	AG	AU
CA	CC	CG	CU
GA	GC	GG	GU
UA	UC	UG	UU

The Nature of the Genetic Code

As you will recall from Chapter 4, proteins are made by stringing amino acids together to form long chains called polypeptides. Each polypeptide contains a combination of any or all of the 20 different amino acids. How, then, can a particular order of nitrogenous bases in DNA and RNA be translated into a particular order of amino acids in a polypeptide?

As you know, DNA and RNA each contain different nitrogenous bases (DNA contains A, T, C, G; RNA contains A, U, C, G); hence, different nucleotides. For this reason, the genetic code must have a four-letter "alphabet." In order to code for the 20 different amino acids, more than one nucleotide must make up the code word for each amino acid. If code words were two nucleotides long, there would be 4^2, or 16, different code words. This is not enough for 20 amino acids. The four nucleotides arranged in triplets, or threes, however, produce 4^3, or 64, different code words. This is more than enough to produce a different code word for each amino acid. Therefore, the smallest size for a code word in DNA is three nucleotides.

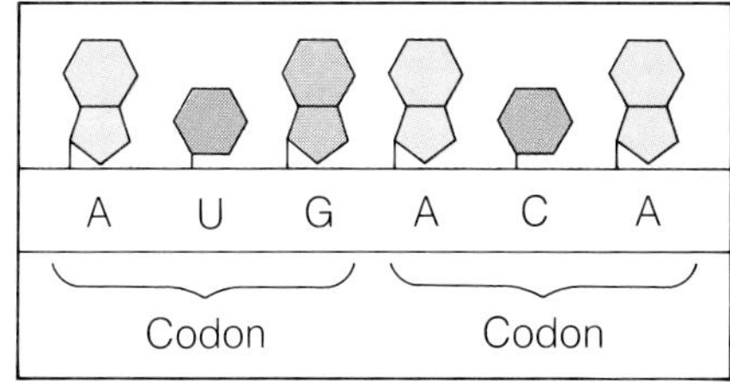

Figure 7–16 *Each combination of three nucleotides on messenger RNA is called a codon, or three-letter code word.*

The code words of the DNA nucleotides are copied onto a strand of messenger RNA. Each combination of three nucleotides on the messenger RNA is called a **codon** (KOH-dahn), or three-letter code word. **Each codon specifies a particular amino acid that is to be placed in the polypeptide chain.** See Figure 7–17. It is interesting to note that there is more than one codon for each amino acid. For example, the amino acid leucine (LOO-seen) has six different codons. There is also one codon, AUG, that can either specify the amino acid methionine (muh-THIGH-uh-neen) or serve as a starter for the synthesis of a protein. For this reason, AUG is called an "initiator" codon. Notice also that there are three "stop" codons. They do not code for an amino acid. Instead, these codons act like the period at the end of a sentence: They signify the end of a polypeptide.

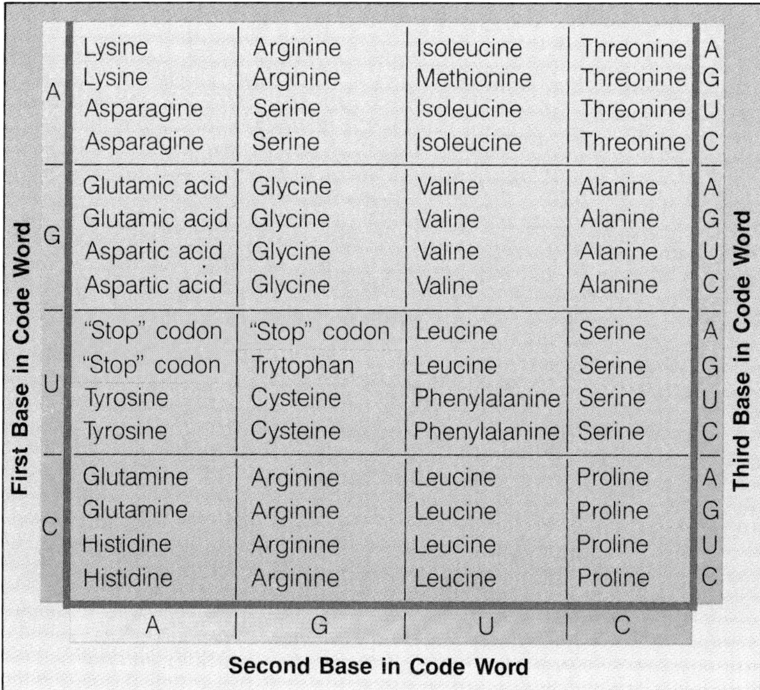

First Base in Code Word	A	G	U	C	Third Base in Code Word
A	Lysine	Arginine	Isoleucine	Threonine	A
A	Lysine	Arginine	Methionine	Threonine	G
A	Asparagine	Serine	Isoleucine	Threonine	U
A	Asparagine	Serine	Isoleucine	Threonine	C
G	Glutamic acid	Glycine	Valine	Alanine	A
G	Glutamic acid	Glycine	Valine	Alanine	G
G	Aspartic acid	Glycine	Valine	Alanine	U
G	Aspartic acid	Glycine	Valine	Alanine	C
U	"Stop" codon	"Stop" codon	Leucine	Serine	A
U	"Stop" codon	Trytophan	Leucine	Serine	G
U	Tyrosine	Cysteine	Phenylalanine	Serine	U
U	Tyrosine	Cysteine	Phenylalanine	Serine	C
C	Glutamine	Arginine	Leucine	Proline	A
C	Glutamine	Arginine	Leucine	Proline	G
C	Histidine	Arginine	Leucine	Proline	U
C	Histidine	Arginine	Leucine	Proline	C

Second Base in Code Word

Figure 7–17 *The genetic code consists of 64 codons along with their corresponding amino acids. These codons are found on messenger RNA. Of the 64 codons, 61 specify a particular amino acid. The other three are stop codons, which signify the end of a polypeptide chain. What are the three-letter code words for each of the stop codons?*

Translation

How does a messenger RNA molecule actually produce a polypeptide? The decoding of a messenger RNA message into a polypeptide chain (protein) is known as **translation.** Translation is an appropriate word for this process because it emphasizes that the message is being translated from the language of nucleic acids into a polypeptide. The messenger RNA molecule does not produce a polypeptide by itself. Instead, there is an elaborate mechanism that involves the two other main types of RNA—**transfer RNA** (tRNA) and **ribosomal RNA** (rRNA)—and the cytoplasmic organelle known as the ribosome.

Transfer RNA carries amino acids to the ribosomes, where the amino acids are joined together to form polypeptides. Transfer RNA is a single strand of RNA that loops back on itself. See Figure 7–18. There are different transfer RNA molecules for each of the 20 amino acids. Ribosomal RNA makes up the major part of the ribosomes.

THE ROLE OF TRANSFER RNA In order to translate the information from a single codon of messenger RNA, such as AUG, we would have to find out which amino acid is coded for by AUG. Look at Figure 7–17 on page 149. As you just read, the codon AUG codes for the amino acid methionine. Methionine is then brought to the polypeptide chain by transfer RNA.

Look at Figure 7–18. You will notice that there are three exposed bases on each transfer RNA molecule. These nucleotides will base pair with a codon on messenger RNA. Because the three nucleotides on transfer RNA are complementary to the three nucleotides on messenger RNA, the three transfer RNA nucleotides are called the **anticodon.**

Attached to each transfer RNA molecule is the amino acid specified by the codon to which it base pairs. By matching the transfer RNA anticodon to the messenger RNA codon, the correct amino acid is put into place. Each transfer RNA acts like a tiny beacon for its specific amino acid.

THE ROLE OF THE RIBOSOME Messenger RNA molecules do not automatically line up transfer RNA molecules and link their amino acids together any more than model airplane parts glue themselves together automatically. Instead, this process of protein synthesis takes place in organelles known as

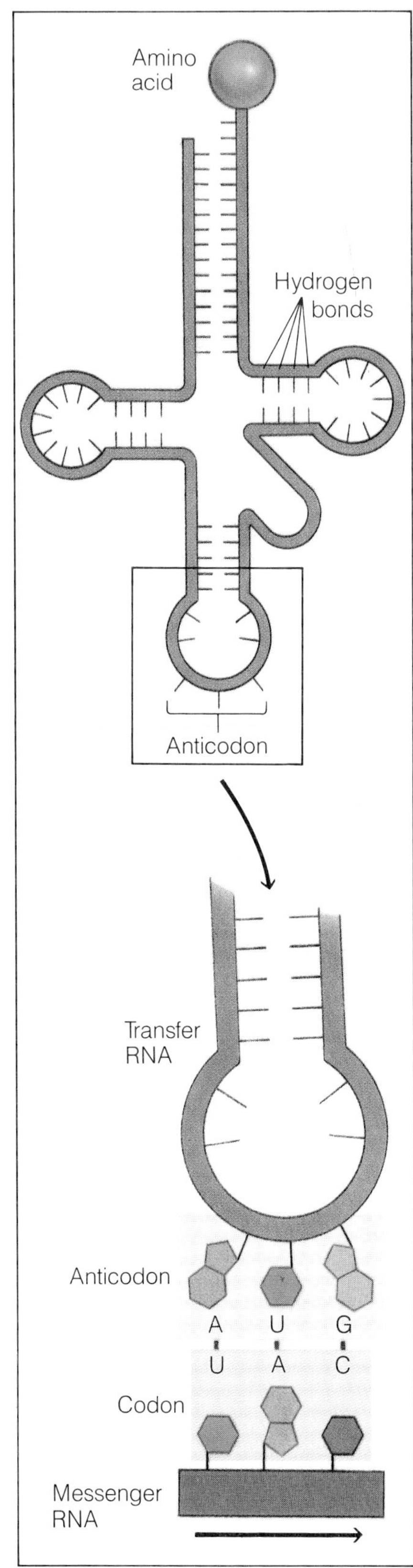

Figure 7–18 *Transfer RNA is a single strand of RNA that loops back on itself. Each transfer RNA molecule has two important sites of attachment. One site, called the anticodon, binds to the codon on the messenger RNA molecule. The other site attaches to a particular amino acid. During protein synthesis, the anticodon of a transfer RNA molecule base pairs with the appropriate messenger RNA codon.*

SCIENCE, TECHNOLOGY, AND SOCIETY **BREAKTHROUGH**

Seeing DNA in Action

In this chapter we have been talking about the roles of DNA and RNA in primarily eukaryotic cells, or cells that have a nucleus. However, there exist major groups of living organisms that do not have a nucleus. These organisms are called prokaryotes. Bacteria are examples of prokaryotes.

Because the DNA of a prokaryote is not tucked away in a separate compartment, there is nothing to stop protein synthesis from beginning as soon as the free end of a messenger RNA is available. This means that translation can begin at one end of a messenger RNA molecule before transcription is even completed. It is as if builders started to build one side of a house before the drawings for the other end were even completed!

Oscar Miller, a scientist at the University of Virginia, has pioneered a number of special techniques designed to allow DNA and RNA to be seen in the electron microscope in the act of translation and transcription. Miller's electron micrographs show how simultaneous transcription and translation actually take place. A strand of DNA is being made into messenger RNA at several places at once. Even before the RNA molecules have been completed, several ribosomes have attached themselves to the free ends of the RNA molecule and have begun to make polypeptides. The living cell, obviously, is in a big hurry!

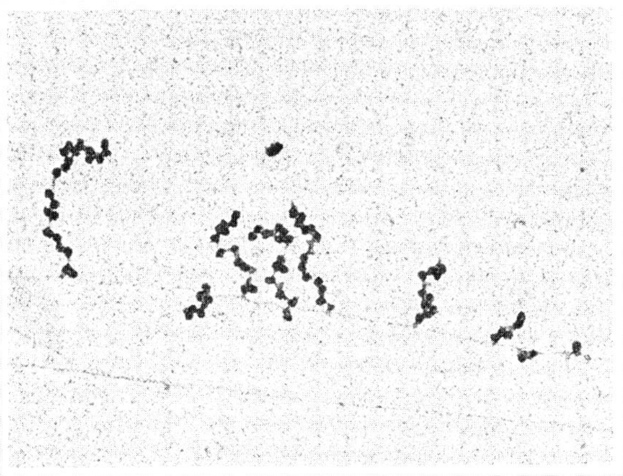

This electron micrograph of E. coli *genes shows transcription and translation occurring simultaneously.*

ribosomes. Ribosomes are made up of two subunits, a large one and a smaller one. Each subunit consists of ribosomal RNA and proteins (about 70 different types).

The first part of protein synthesis occurs when the two subunits of the ribosome bind to a molecule of messenger RNA. Then the initiator codon AUG binds to the first anticodon of transfer RNA, signaling the beginning of a polypeptide chain. Soon the anticodon of another transfer RNA binds to the next messenger RNA codon. This second transfer RNA carries the second amino acid that will be placed into the chain of the polypeptide.

As each anticodon and codon bind together, a peptide bond forms between the two amino acids. You will recall from

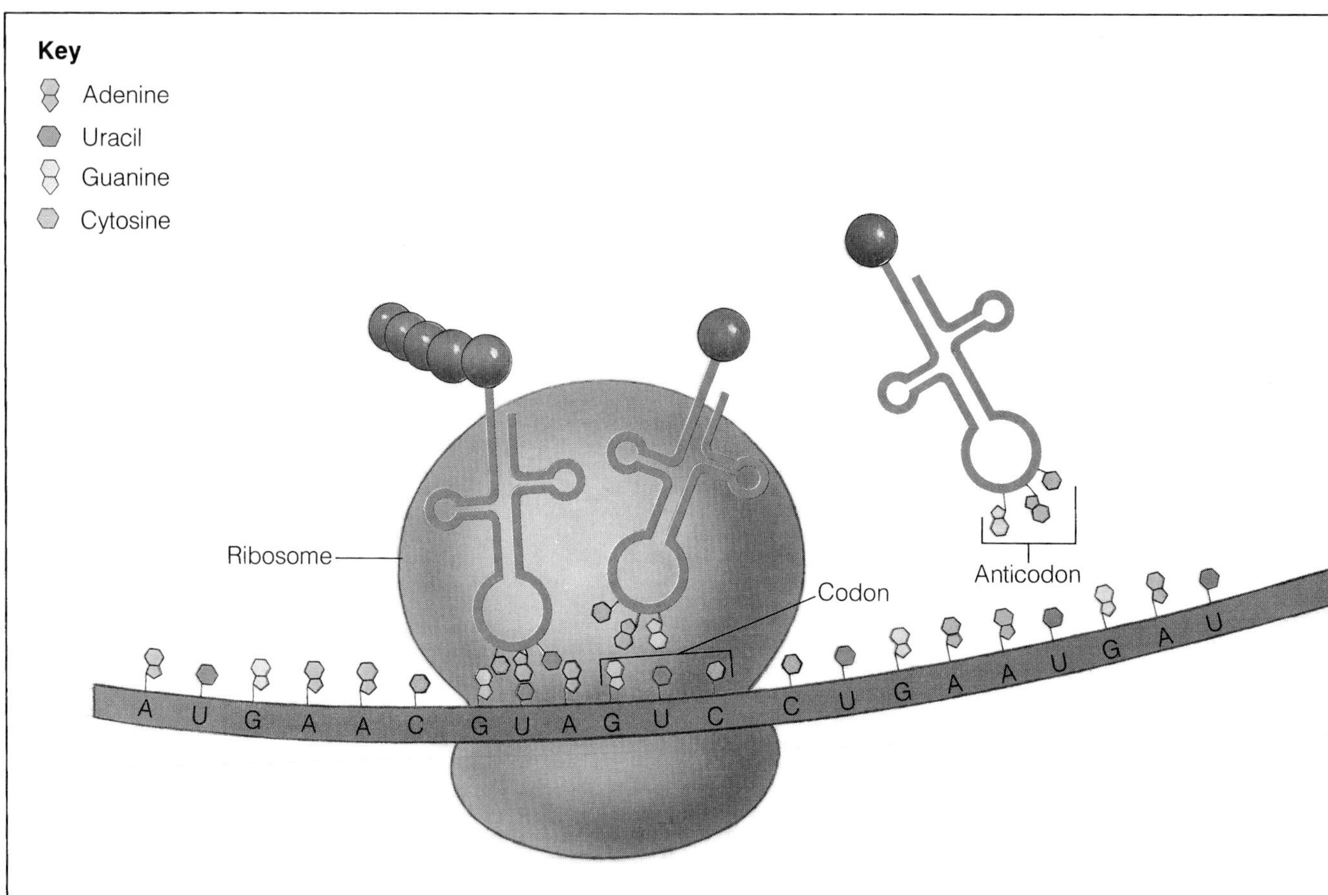

__Figure 7–19__ During translation, the language of the nucleic acids (DNA and RNA) is transferred to the language of the amino acids. In which cellular organelle does this process take place?

Chapter 4 that a peptide bond is the covalent bond that joins two amino acids together. The polypeptide chain continues to grow until the ribosome reaches a stop codon on the messenger RNA. A stop codon is a codon for which no transfer RNA molecules exist. When the stop codon reaches the ribosome, the ribosome releases the newly formed polypeptide and messenger RNA, completing the process of translation.

As you can now see, the ribosome, in its own way, is at the center of the whole business of making the genetic code work. In the nucleus, DNA directs the formation of three different kinds of RNA: transfer RNA, ribosomal RNA, and messenger RNA. They all leave the nucleus and then seem to go their separate ways. Despite these different paths, however, they all meet again in the ribosome where protein synthesis takes place. So the ribosome can be considered the place where a kind of "class reunion" of RNA molecules occurs. Here each type of RNA molecule plays a role in carrying out the instructions specified in the genetic code. And the genetic code stores the program for protein synthesis and passes it on from generation to generation.

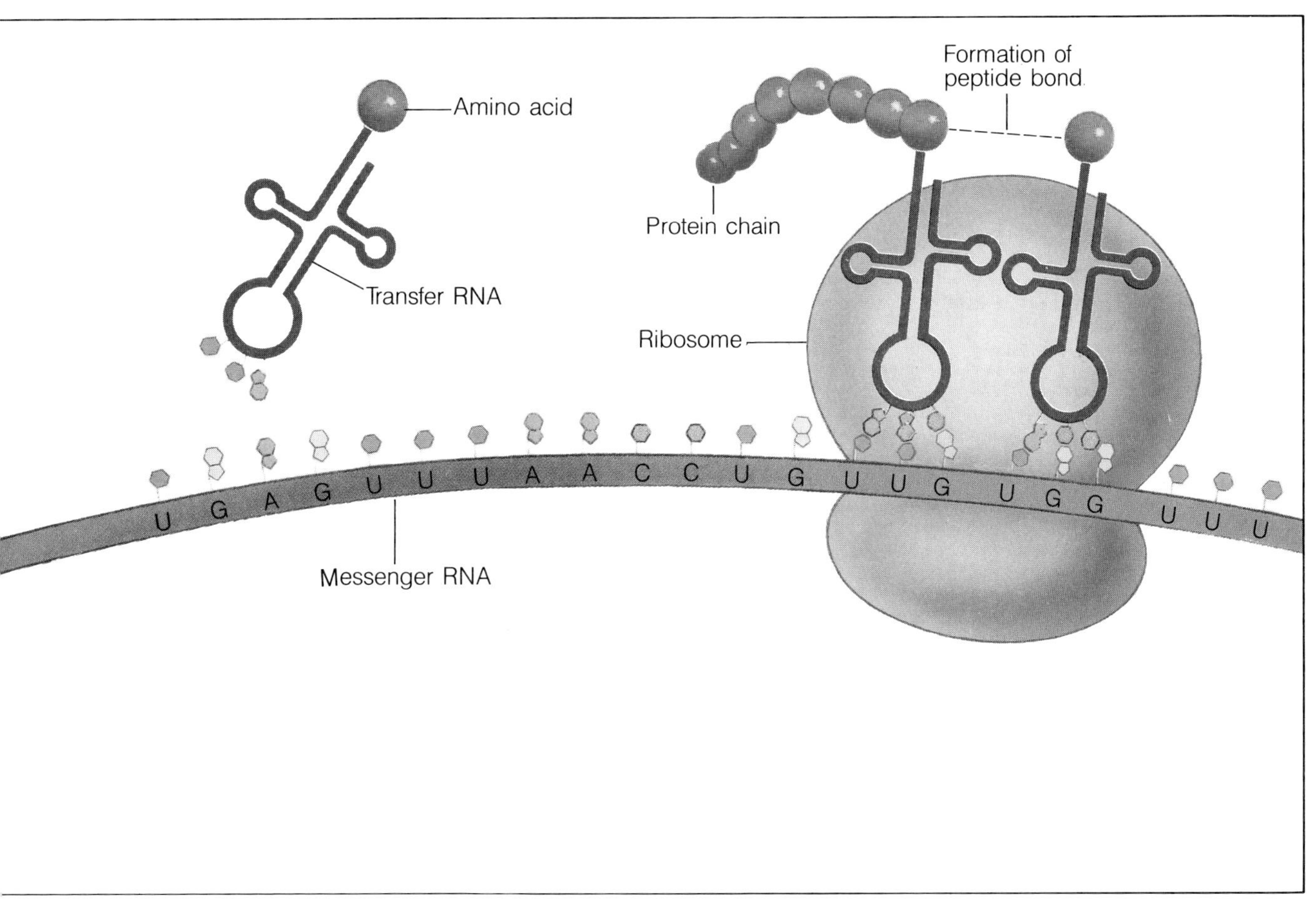

7–3 SECTION REVIEW

1. What is translation? Transcription?
2. UAG is a stop codon. What might happen if the uracil in this codon was changed to cytosine?
3. What is a codon? An anticodon?
4. Name and give the function of the three main types of RNA molecules.
5. Why is a ribosome essential for protein synthesis?
6. What is the role of transfer RNA in translation?
7. If a code on a DNA molecule is CTA for a specific amino acid, what is the messenger RNA codon? The transfer RNA anticodon?
8. A certain protein is made up of 100 amino acids. What is the smallest number of bases in the messenger RNA molecule that is needed to carry the code for the synthesis of this protein?

LABORATORY INVESTIGATION CONSTRUCTING A MODEL OF DNA REPLICATION

PROBLEM

How does DNA replicate?

MATERIALS *(per group)*

colored construction paper:

- white
- red
- dark blue
- light blue
- dark green
- light green

metric ruler
scissors
transparent tape

PROCEDURE

1. With the scissors, cut out the pieces of colored construction paper as indicated in the chart. **CAUTION:** *Be careful when using scissors.* Write the name of each part of your DNA model on the appropriate piece of construction paper.
2. To construct a model of a DNA nucleotide, tape a phosphate group, a sugar, and a guanine (G) together in the same manner as shown in Figure 7-6 on page 141. Then assemble eight additional nucleotide models with the following nitrogenous bases: T, T, A, C, A, A, T, C.

Part of DNA Model	Color	Size (cm x cm)	Number
Sugar	White	2 x 2	54
Phosphate group	Red	1 x 2	54
Adenine (A)	Dark blue	1 x 2	18
Thymine (T)	Light blue	1 x 2	18
Guanine (G)	Dark green	1 x 2	9
Cytosine (C)	Light green	1 x 2	9

3. Attach the nine nucleotide models together in the sequence given in step 2 (G, T, T, A, C, A, A, T, C) by taping the sugar on one nucleotide to the phosphate group on the next nucleotide. This will form the single strand of your DNA model.
4. Using the rules for base pairing, construct a second strand of the DNA model that is complementary to the first strand. Tape the nucleotides together as you did in step 3. Do not tape the two strands of DNA together.
5. Separate the two strands and use each to construct a new complementary strand.
6. Reassemble the original double strand of DNA. Tape this model of DNA together at its nitrogenous bases.
7. Again using the base-pairing rules, construct a complementary strand for each of the single strands of DNA you made in step 5. Tape these two new DNA models together at their nitrogenous bases. Compare the new double-stranded DNA models with your original DNA model.

OBSERVATIONS

1. What is the sequence of nitrogenous bases in the complementary strand of your original DNA model?
2. How many models of DNA did you construct from your original model of DNA? What is the base sequence for each of these new models?

ANALYSIS AND CONCLUSIONS

1. Why do you think complementary base pairing is necessary for replication?
2. Compare the base sequences of the original DNA model with the replicated models. Compare the base sequences of the replicated models.
3. If each triplet of nitrogenous bases on DNA codes for a specific amino acid, how many amino acids will your original DNA model code for?

STUDENT STUDY GUIDE

SUMMARIZING THE CONCEPTS

The key concepts in each section of this chapter are listed below to help you review the chapter content. Make sure you understand each concept and its relationship to other concepts and to the theme of this chapter.

7–1 DNA

- DNA is the nucleic acid that stores and transmits the genetic information from one generation of an organism to the next.
- DNA is a polymer that is made up of units called nucleotides. Each nucleotide is a molecule made up of three parts: a 5-carbon sugar called deoxyribose, a phosphate group, and a nitrogenous base.
- DNA has four nitrogenous bases: adenine, thymine, cytosine, and guanine. Adenine and guanine belong to a group of compounds called purines. Thymine and cytosine belong to a group of compounds called pyrimidines.
- During replication, the DNA molecule unzips, or separates, into two strands. Each of the separated strands serves as a template, or pattern, for the attachment of complementary nucleotides.

7–2 RNA

- There are three major differences between DNA and RNA: RNA contains the sugar ribose instead of deoxyribose; RNA is usually single-stranded instead of double-stranded; and RNA contains the nitrogenous base uracil instead of thymine.
- During transcription, the DNA code is transferred to messenger RNA, which carries the code out of the nucleus into the cytoplasm.

7–3 Protein Synthesis

- During translation, messenger RNA binds to the ribosomes on which ribosomal RNA is found. Amino acids in the cytoplasm are picked up by transfer RNA and are carried to messenger RNA. The anticodons in transfer RNA attach to the proper codons in messenger RNA. Thus the messenger RNA acts as the pattern for protein synthesis. In this way, amino acids are brought together in the correct sequence to form a protein molecule.

REVIEWING KEY TERMS

Vocabulary terms are important to your understanding of biology. The key terms listed below are those you should be especially familiar with. Review these terms and their meaning. Then use each term in a complete sentence. If you are not sure of a term's meaning, return to the appropriate section and review its definition.

7–1 DNA

genetic code
transformation
DNA
nucleotide
adenine
guanine
cytosine
thymine
base pairing
replication

7–2 RNA

RNA
uracil
transcription
messenger RNA

7–3 Protein Synthesis

codon
translation
transfer RNA
ribosomal RNA
anticodon

CHAPTER REVIEW

CONTENT REVIEW

Multiple Choice

Choose the letter of the answer that best completes each statement.

1. The process of changing one strain of bacteria into another is called
a. transformation. c. replication.
b. translation. d. transcription.

2. DNA is a
a. carbohydrate. c. nucleic acid.
b. lipid. d. sterol.

3. A nucleotide of DNA would contain
a. uracil, deoxyribose, and phosphate.
b. phosphate, deoxyribose, and thymine.
c. nitrogenous base, phosphate, and glucose.
d. adenine, ribose, and phosphate.

4. Watson and Crick described the DNA molecule as a
a. branching chain. c. single strand.
b. straight chain. d. double helix.

5. Between which types of compounds in a double-stranded DNA molecule must the bonds break before replication takes place?
a. phosphate–base c. adenine–thymine
b. sugar–phosphate d. sugar–base

6. To which organelles does messenger RNA attach?
a. chloroplasts c. mitochondria
b. ribosomes d. lysosomes

7. The coded information in a DNA molecule directly determines the formation of
a. polysaccharides. c. monosaccharides.
b. lipids. d. polypeptides.

8. If the code for an amino acid is ATG on the DNA molecule, this code on the transfer RNA molecule may be written as
a. ATG. c. AUG.
b. CTG. d. CTA.

True or False

Determine whether each statement is true or false. If it is true, write "true." If it is false, change the underlined word or words to make the statement true.

1. A molecular group consisting of a sugar molecule, a phosphate group, and a nitrogenous base is a <u>nucleic acid.</u>

2. In a DNA molecule, a base pair would be composed of adenine and <u>guanine.</u>

3. <u>Cytosine</u> and adenine are purines.

4. During the replication of DNA, bonds are broken between the <u>phosphate groups.</u>

5. RNA contains the nitrogenous base <u>uracil.</u>

6. There are <u>20</u> different amino acids in a cell.

7. The coded message carried by messenger RNA is translated into polypeptides at organelles called <u>chloroplasts.</u>

8. The decoding of a messenger RNA message into a polypeptide chain is known as <u>translation.</u>

Word Relationships

A. *In each of the following sets of terms, three of the terms are related. One term does not belong. Determine the characteristic common to three of the terms and then identify the term that does not belong.*

1. deoxyribose, phosphate, DNA, uracil
2. amino acid, polypeptide, protein, translation
3. ribose, RNA, thymine, adenine
4. A—T, C—G, A—U, C—T

B. *Replace the underlined definition with the correct vocabulary word.*

5. <u>The attraction between nitrogenous bases</u> is the force that holds the two strands of DNA together.

6. Each <u>combination of three nucleotides on messenger RNA</u> specifies a specific amino acid that is to be placed in the polypeptide chain.

7. <u>The RNA that carries amino acids to the ribosomes</u> is a single strand of RNA that loops back on itself.

8. As a ribosome moves along a strand of messenger RNA, each codon is paired with its <u>three nucleotides on transfer RNA that are complementary to the three nucleotides on messenger RNA</u>.

CONCEPT MASTERY

Use your understanding of the concepts developed in the chapter to answer each of the following in a brief paragraph.

1. Describe Griffith's experiments involving bacterial transformation.
2. How did the study of bacteriophages lead scientists to support the idea that DNA carries hereditary material?
3. What was the contribution made by Hershey and Chase to understanding the genetic code?
4. How did Franklin's work contribute to the discovery of the structure of DNA?
5. Describe the contribution of Watson and Crick.
6. Describe DNA replication. What is its importance?
7. List three differences between DNA and RNA.
8. How is messenger RNA formed during transcription?
9. What is the function of the ribosomes?
10. What is the relationship between an amino acid and a codon?

CRITICAL AND CREATIVE THINKING

Discuss each of the following in a brief paragraph.

1. **Identifying patterns** Oxytocin is a hormone that helps to regulate blood pressure and stimulates the uterus to contract during childbirth. Following is a DNA sequence that could code for a part of a molecule of oxytocin: ACA ATA TAG CTT TTG ACG GGG AAC CCC ATT. Write the sequence of messenger RNA codons that would result from the transcription of this portion of DNA.
2. **Relating facts** How many guanines are in a DNA molecule 1000 base pairs long if 20% of the molecule consists of thymines?
3. **Applying concepts** Write out the messenger RNA sequence that would be transcribed from the following strand of DNA: T–A–C–A–A–G–T–A–C–T–T–G–T–T–T–C–T–T. Then using Figure 7–17 on page 149, write the amino acid sequence that would be translated when the messenger RNA combines with a ribosome.
4. **Using the writing process** Write a short story that follows a protein molecule from its point of origin in a corn kernel, through its use as cattle food, to a position of importance as a protein in your body.

CHAPTER 8

Cell Growth and Division

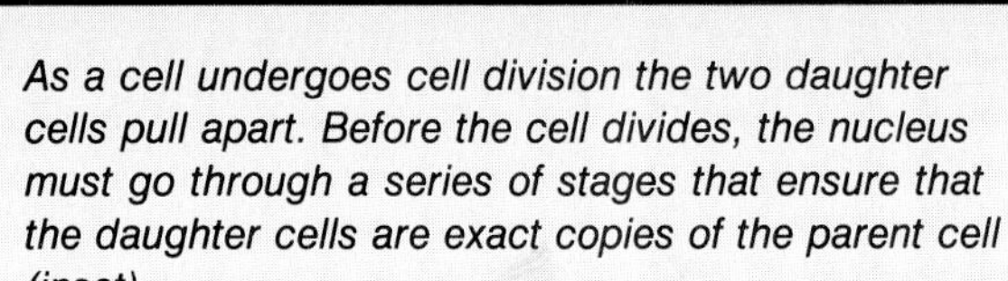
As a cell undergoes cell division the two daughter cells pull apart. Before the cell divides, the nucleus must go through a series of stages that ensure that the daughter cells are exact copies of the parent cell (inset).

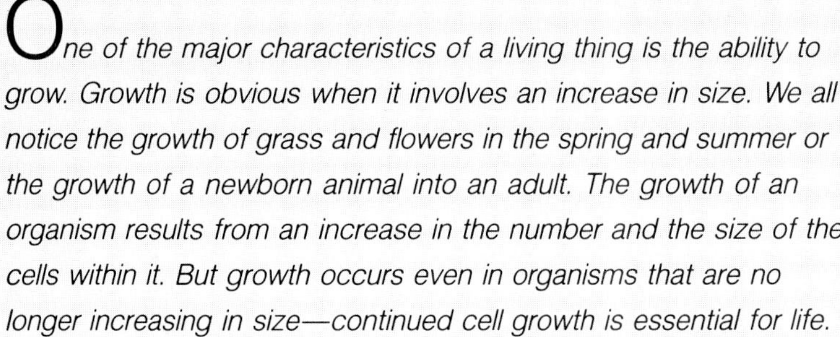
One of the major characteristics of a living thing is the ability to grow. Growth is obvious when it involves an increase in size. We all notice the growth of grass and flowers in the spring and summer or the growth of a newborn animal into an adult. The growth of an organism results from an increase in the number and the size of the cells within it. But growth occurs even in organisms that are no longer increasing in size—continued cell growth is essential for life.

How do cells grow? Is there a limit to the growth of a cell? In this chapter we will examine how cells grow in size and increase in number, and why growth is so essential to living things.

CHAPTER OUTLINE

8–1 Cell Growth

Section Objectives

- Describe cell growth.
- Define cell division.
- Relate cell growth to cell division.

As you already know, living things are made up of cells. And living things grow, or increase in size. Does a living thing grow because its cells get larger and larger or does it grow because it produces more and more cells? **In most cases, a living thing grows because it produces more and more cells.** The cells of a human adult are no larger than the cells of a human baby, but there are certainly more of them.

Does growth have to occur in this way? Or could an organism grow simply by allowing its cells to get larger and larger? Let's consider what would happen if this could occur.

Limits of Cell Growth

You will recall from Chapter 5 that it is through the cell membrane that food, oxygen, and water enter the cell and waste products leave the cell. How quickly this exchange takes place depends on the surface area of the cell, or the total area of the cell membrane. How quickly food and oxygen are used up and waste products are produced depends on the cell volume, or the amount of space within the cell.

If we were to take a typical cell and double its diameter, what would happen to the amount of membrane (surface area) compared to the amount of material inside the cell (cell volume)? Look at Figure 8–2 on page 160. Notice that as the cell

Figure 8–1 As living things grow they produce more cells. Although this adult white bengal tiger is larger than its cub, the sizes of its cells are the same as those of the cub's.

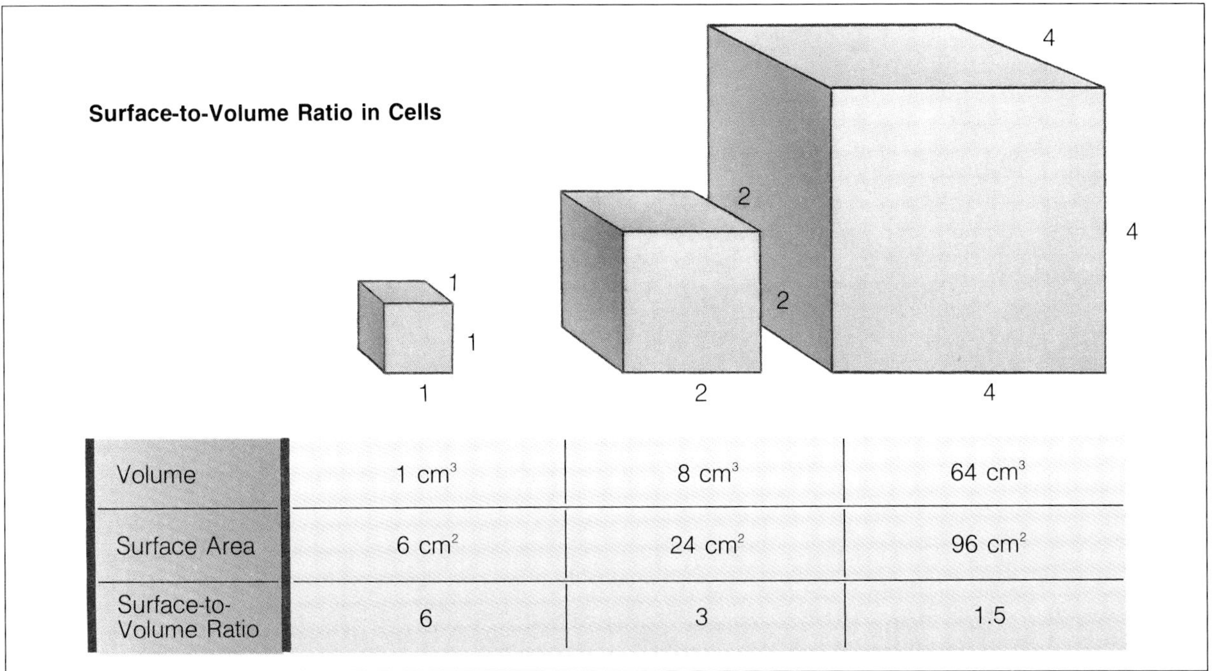

Volume	1 cm^3	8 cm^3	64 cm^3
Surface Area	6 cm^2	24 cm^2	96 cm^2
Surface-to-Volume Ratio	6	3	1.5

Figure 8–2 *If the length of each side of a cube-shaped cell doubles from 1 to 2 to 4, the volume increases more rapidly than does the surface area. As a result, the ratio of surface area to volume decreases and the cell with the largest volume has a more difficult time getting materials in and waste products out.*

increases in size, its volume increases at a faster rate than its surface area. For example, if the diameter of the cell increases 10 times, its surface area increases 100 times. Its volume, however, increases 1000 times!

The fact that surface area and volume do not increase at the same rate creates problems for the cell. The larger cell will have a more difficult time getting oxygen and nutrients in and waste products out.

To help you understand why the larger cell has a more difficult time than the smaller cell, let's compare the cells to a small and a large office building. Suppose the small office building that is serviced by a two-lane highway is replaced by a large office building. Now more people work in the office building. But the highway leading to the large building has not increased in size. It is the same two-lane highway that serviced the small office building. As a result, the people in the large building will have difficulty with traffic getting to the office in the morning and leaving the office in the evening.

A larger cell will experience similar problems—materials will have trouble entering and leaving the cell. This is one reason why cells do not grow much larger even if the organism of which they are a part does. There is another reason too.

As you will recall from Chapter 7, information for the cell's function and survival is stored in the sequence of nitrogenous bases in DNA. In eukaryotic cells, the DNA is stored in the nucleus of the cell. When the cell is small, copies of DNA that are stored in the nucleus are able to produce enough messenger RNA to make all the proteins the cell needs. But even though the cell increases in size, it does not make extra copies of DNA.

(There are a few exceptions that we will learn about later.) If a cell were to grow without limit, an "information crisis" would occur. Like a town that has tripled in size but has not added a single book to its library, the cell must now make greater demands on its available genetic library.

In many cases, the amount of messenger RNA that is produced in the cell increases—but within limits. After a time, the cell's DNA may no longer be able to make enough RNA to supply the increasing needs of the growing cell. The cell must slow down its growth, thus becoming less efficient. The cell undergoes a process called **cell division** to solve these problems. **Cell division is the process whereby the cell divides into two daughter cells.** We will discuss cell division in more detail later in the chapter.

Rates of Cell Growth

Cells can grow at astonishing rates. For example, the bacterium *Escherichia coli* (ehsh-uh-RIHK-ee-uh KOH-ligh), or *E. coli,* is a single-celled organism that can easily double its volume in about 30 minutes. It can then divide to form two new cells. If conditions are ideal, each of these cells can grow to form two new cells in the next 30 minutes.

Ideal conditions for this kind of growth can never be maintained for very long, however. A quick look at the consequences of rapid growth will explain why. In just one day, a single cell would grow into a 14-kilogram mass of bacteria. In three days, the mass of the cells would equal the mass of the Earth! Real conditions, or the circumstances that cells normally face, are very different.

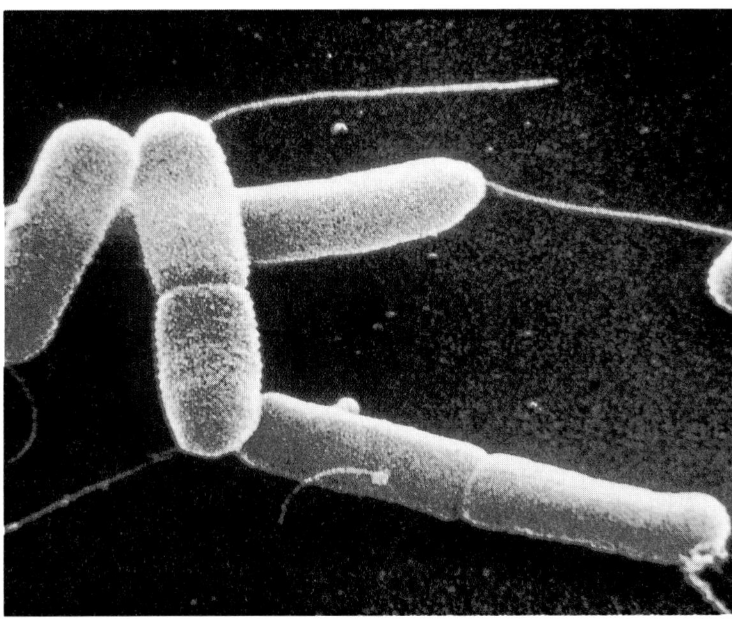

Figure 8–3 *Single-celled prokaryotic organisms reproduce by cell division. In this scanning electron micrograph of bacteria (*E. coli*), you can see two bacteria undergoing cell division.*

Figure 8–4 *The scientist in this photograph is growing pine tree cells on culture plates. As the cells divide they will form a continuous layer, one cell thick, across the surface of each culture plate. But when the cells come in contact with adjacent cells, they will stop growing and dividing.*

Controls on Cell Growth

One of the most striking aspects of cell behavior in a multicellular organism is how carefully cell growth and cell division are controlled. Cells in certain places in the body, such as the heart and the nervous system, rarely divide—if they divide at all. In contrast, the cells of the skin and digestive tract grow and divide rapidly throughout life, providing new cells to replace those that are worn out or broken down due to daily wear and tear.

We can observe the effects of controlled cell growth in the laboratory by placing some cells in a petri dish containing nutrient broth. The nutrient broth provides food for the cells. Most cells will grow until they form a thin layer covering the bottom of the dish. Then the cells will stop growing. Why do they stop growing? When cells come into contact with other cells, they respond by not growing. At present, scientists are trying to understand how this process works.

Controls on cell growth and cell division can be turned on and off. When an injury—such as a cut in the skin or a break in a bone—occurs, cells at the edges of the injury are stimulated to divide rapidly. This action produces new cells, starting the process of healing. When the healing process nears completion, the rate of cell division slows down, controls on growth seem to be reimposed, and everything returns to normal.

Uncontrolled Cell Growth

The consequences of uncontrolled cell growth in a multicellular organism are severe. Cancer, a disorder in which some

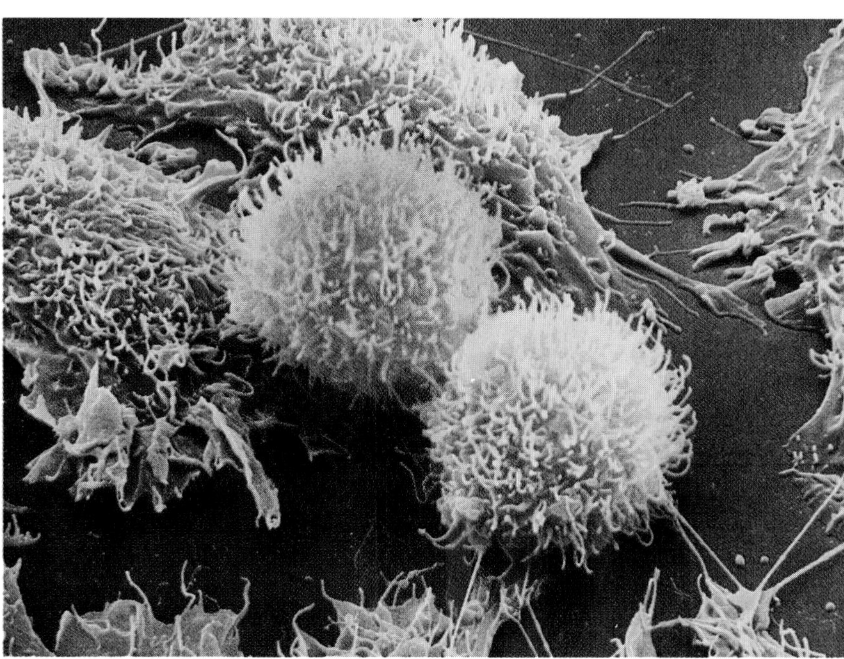

Figure 8–5 *Unlike normal cells, cancer cells do not stop growing and dividing even if they come in contact with other cells. Actually, cancer cells, such as those shown in this scanning electron micrograph, have lost their ability to control their own rate of growth.*

PROBLEM SOLVING IN BIOLOGY

SCIENTIFIC NOTATION

How many cells would you suspect there are in the human body? There are approximately 100,000,000,000,000 cells. And all these cells arise from a human egg cell that is only 0.0001 meter in diameter!

As you can see, there are numbers associated with biology that are so large that they are also difficult to write and understand. For this reason, scientific notation is used. Scientific notation is also known as exponential notation because it uses the exponential form of a number.

The exponential form of a number is made up of two parts: $M \times 10^n$
The first part, *M*, is a number between 1 and 10. The second part, *n*, is an exponent, or power, to which the base 10 is raised. An exponent indicates how many times the base is to be multiplied by itself.

Because the base is 10, what the exponent actually does is locate the decimal point in the number being represented. It does this by indicating how many places the decimal point in *M* must be moved. The decimal point is moved to the right if the exponent is positive and to the left if the exponent is negative. A negative exponent is a negative power of 10. It is shorthand for 1 divided by a power of 10.

To convert a large number to scientific notation, follow these steps.

1. Determine *M* by moving the decimal point in the number (100,000,000,000,000) to the left or the right so that only one digit is to the left of it.

   1 0 0, 0 0 0, 0 0 0, 0 0 0, 0 0 0.
   1.0 0, 0 0 0, 0 0 0, 0 0 0, 0 0 0

2. Determine *n* by counting the number of places the decimal point has been moved. If moved to the left, *n* is positive; if moved to the right, *n* is negative.

   1.0 0, 0 0 0, 0 0 0, 0 0 0, 0 0 0 **14 places to the left**

3. Then write the number 1 multiplied by the base 10 with its exponent.

   $$1 \times 10^{14} = 100{,}000{,}000{,}000{,}000$$

To convert a small number to scientific notation, follow these steps.

1. Determine *M* by moving the decimal point in the number (0.0001) to the left or the right so that only one digit is to the left of it.

   0.0 0 0 1
   0 0 0 0 1.

2. Determine *n* by counting the number of places the decimal point has been moved. If moved to the left, *n* is positive; if moved to the right, *n* is negative.

   0.0 0 0 1. **4 places to the right**

3. Then write the number 1 multiplied by the base 10 with its exponent.

   $$1 \times 10^{-4} = 0.0001$$

Complete the following exercises. Check your answers by using a calculator or computer, if one is available.

A. Expressing Numbers in Scientific Notation

1. The average length of a mitochondrion is 0.00000001 cm.
2. A rat contains approximately 10,000,000,000 cells.

B. Converting Scientific Notation into Numbers

1. The average diameter of a bacterium is 2×10^{-6} cm.
2. The resolving power of an electron microscope is 1×10^{6} times greater than that of the human eye.

cells have lost the ability to control their own rate of growth, is one such example. When cancer cells are placed in a culture of living tissue, they do not stop growing even though they come into contact with other cells. Cancer cells will continue to grow and divide until the supply of nutrients is exhausted.

Cancer is a serious disorder that claims many lives and affects all of us, directly or indirectly. To cell biologists, cancer provides valuable information concerning the importance of controls on cellular growth.

8–1 SECTION REVIEW

1. What is growth? What controls cell growth?
2. What is cell division?
3. A newly discovered strain of bacteria divides once every 60 minutes under ideal conditions. After 24 hours, a single bacterium produces cells that have a mass of 1 kilogram. From this information, calculate the average mass of a single bacterium.

Section Objectives

- Define mitosis and cytokinesis.
- Describe the cell cycle and the changes that take place during interphase.
- Discuss the events and the significance of mitosis.

8–2 Cell Division: Mitosis and Cytokinesis

In this section we will discuss how eukaryotic cells divide and form two cells. The division of eukaryotic cells occurs in two main stages. The first stage of cell division is called **mitosis** (migh-TOH-sihs). **Mitosis is the process by which the nucleus of the cell is divided into two nuclei, each with the same number and kinds of chromosomes as the parent cell.**

The second stage of cell division is known as **cytokinesis** (sight-oh-kih-NEE-sihs). **Cytokinesis is the process by which the cytoplasm divides, thus forming two distinct cells.**

Because the structure of a eukaryotic cell is complex, the process of cell division in this type of cell is complex too. The reason for this complexity may be found in the need to separate large amounts of DNA accurately and efficiently. With as many as 100 chromosomes to take care of, a mechanism must exist in the eukaryotic cell to make certain that each new cell gets one (and only one) copy of each chromosome. A mistake in the process could make it impossible for one or both daughter cells to remain alive.

Figure 8–6 When a cell is not dividing, the chromatin forms condensed and dispersed regions.

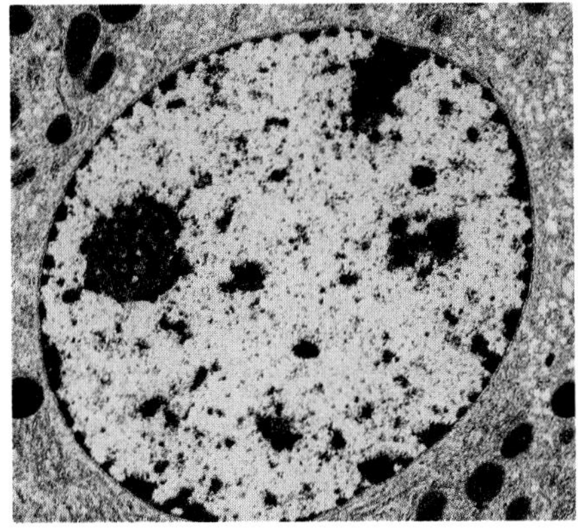

Chromosomes

You will recall from Chapter 5 that **chromosomes** are structures in the cell that contain the genetic information that is passed on from one generation of cells to the next. The word chromosome, meaning colored body, was derived from the fact that when a dye was added to the cell, the chromosomes picked up the color of the dye and were easily seen through the light microscope during cell division. Unfortunately, chromosomes are not visible in most cells except during mitosis.

Chromosomes contain the genetic information in the form of DNA. In prokaryotic cells, the chromosomes are made up of long circular molecules of DNA. In eukaryotic cells, the chromosomes are made up of distinct lengths of DNA. The cells of every organism contain a specific number of chromosomes. Human cells, for example, contain 46 chromosomes; goldfish cells contain 94 chromosomes. See Figure 8–7.

Organism	Chromosome Number
Ameba	50
Carrot	18
Cat	32
Chimpanzee	48
Dog	78
Earthworm	36
Goldfish	94
Human	46
Lettuce	18

Figure 8–7 *Which organism's chromosome number is closest to that of an ameba?*

COMPOSITION OF CHROMATIN Chromosomes are made up of a material called **chromatin** (KROH-muh-tihn). During the period of time between cell divisions, chromatin forms condensed and dispersed regions. See Figure 8–6. During the early stages of mitosis, the chromatin condenses and the chromosomes become visible.

Chromatin is composed of DNA and protein. Much of this protein is involved in the folding of DNA so that it can fit within the nucleus. This is an important job because the DNA double helix that makes up a chromosome is much longer than the chromosome itself. In fact, the total length of DNA in a typical human chromosome is about 10,000 times the length of the chromosome! How does all that DNA fit into the chromosome?

In 1973, the American scientists Don Olins, Ada Olins, and Christopher Woodcock discovered that the chromosomes' DNA was coiled around special proteins called histones. Together, the DNA and histone molecules formed beadlike structures

Figure 8–8 *Chromosomes contain highly coiled and supercoiled strands of DNA. Notice that a small part of the supercoil is made up of nucleosomes (inset).*

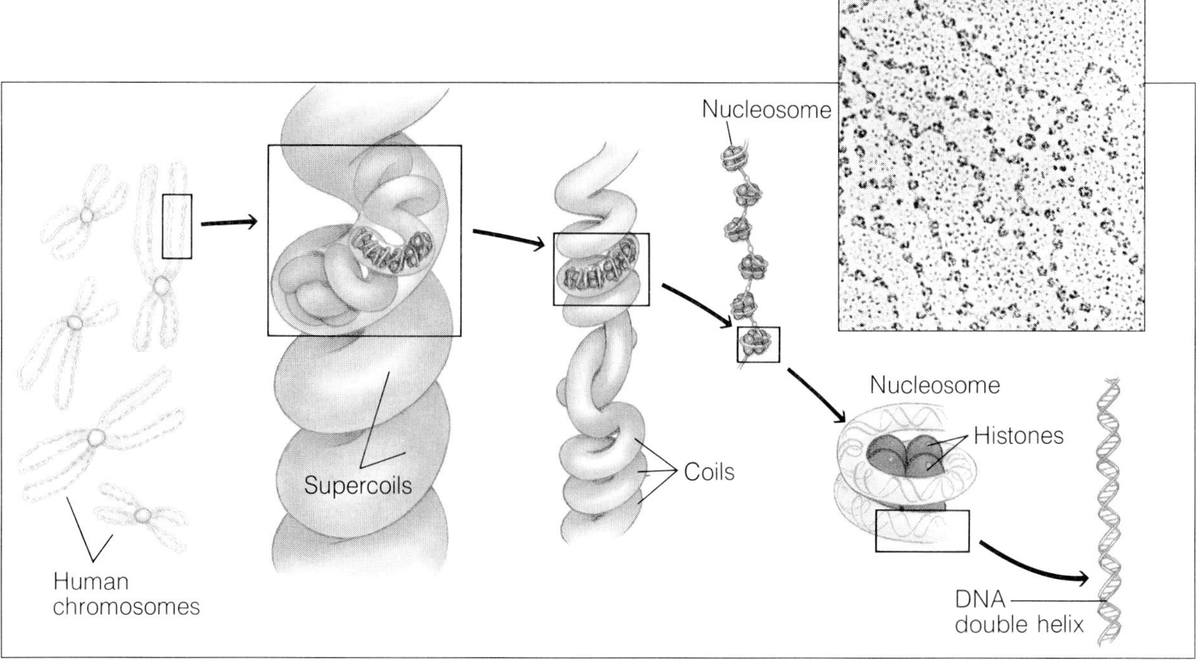

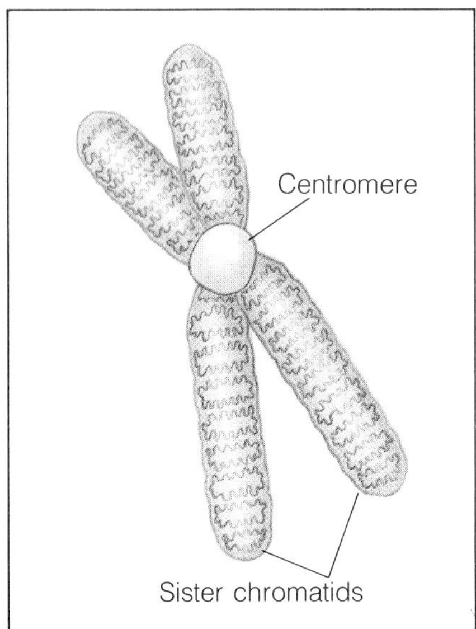

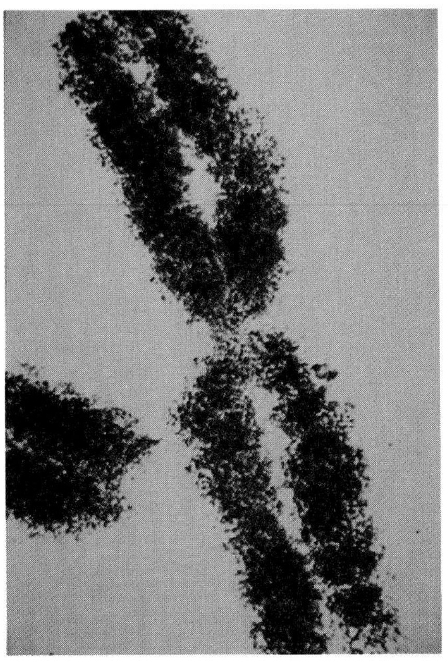

Figure 8–9 The diagram of a chromosome shows that it consists of two chromatids attached by means of a centromere. A human chromosome is shown as it appears through an electron microscope.

called nucleosomes (NOO-klee-oh-sohmz). The nucleosomes interact with one another to form a thick fiber, which is shortened by a system of loops and coils. The result is the tightly packed chromosomes that are seen through a light microscope in dividing cells. The tight packing of nucleosomes may be necessary in order to form a compact structure that can be separated during mitosis.

CHROMOSOME STRUCTURE After DNA replication, the chromosomes become visible by condensing. This is the beginning of mitosis. The chromosome contains two **chromatids** (KROH-muh-tihdz), or identical parts, which are often called sister chromatids. Each pair of chromatids is attached at an area called the **centromere** (SEHN-troh-mihr). Centromeres are usually located near the middle of the chromatids, although some centromeres lie near the ends of the chromatids. A human cell entering mitosis contains 46 chromosomes, each of which consists of two chromatids.

The Cell Cycle

At one time biologists described the life of a cell as one mitosis after another separated by an "in-between" period of growth called interphase. We now know more and can represent some of the events in the life of a cell by using a concept known as the **cell cycle**. The cell cycle is the period from the beginning of one mitosis to the beginning of the next. **During a cell cycle, a cell grows, prepares for division, and divides to form two daughter cells, each of which begins the cycle anew.**

The cell cycle includes mitosis, a period of active division, and interphase, a period of nondivision during which other processes take place. It also includes a process in which cytoplasm and its contents divide forming the two daughter cells. You will learn about this process, called cytokinesis, later in this section. Mitosis is represented as the M phase. During mitosis, the nucleus divides into two nuclei. Interphase is usually divided into three phases: G_1 (gap 1), S (DNA synthesis), and G_2 (gap 2). G_1 and G_2 were once thought to be gaps but are now known as periods of growth and activity.

The time required to complete a single turn of the cycle is the time required for a cell to reproduce itself. Not all cells move through the cell cycle at the same rate. In the human body, most muscle cells and nerve cells do not divide at all once they have developed. In contrast, the cells that line the organs of the digestive system grow and divide rapidly. In fact, these cells may pass through a complete cycle every six hours.

Interphase

Within the normal cell cycle, **interphase**, or the period between cell divisions, can be quite long, whereas the actual divi-

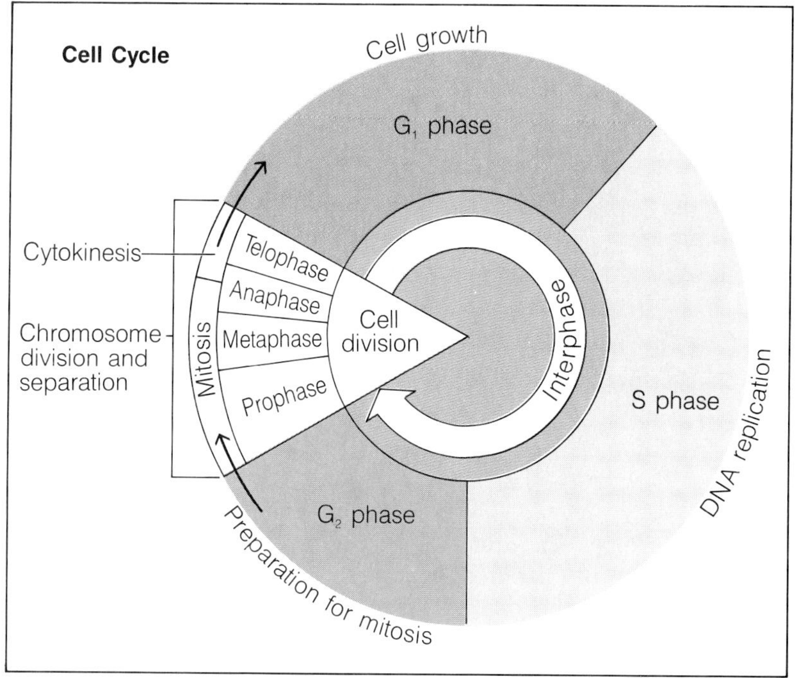

Figure 8–10 *The cell cycle includes mitosis, cytokinesis, and the three phases of interphase. What are the names of the three phases of interphase?*

sion of the cell takes place quickly. As you read, interphase is divided into three phases: G_1, S, and G_2. Each of these phases is characterized by specific events.

The G_1, or gap 1, phase is a period of activity in which cellular growth and development take place. G_1 is followed by the S, or DNA synthesis, phase. During this phase, DNA replication takes place. Several proteins, including those associated with the chromosomes, are synthesized during the S phase.

Finally, when the S phase is completed, the cell enters the G_2, or gap 2, phase. This phase is usually the shortest of the three phases of interphase. The G_2 phase involves the synthesis of organelles and materials required for cell division.

During interphase, the nucleus is active in synthesizing messenger RNA in order to direct cellular activities. Although the cell seems to be "quiet" during interphase, it is actually a period of intense activity. Proteins are made; DNA is copied; ATP is made and utilized. In multicellular organisms, cells that are specialized for jobs such as secretion, movement, and signaling do most of their work during interphase.

Prophase

Recall that mitosis, or the M phase of the cell cycle, is the process by which the cell's nucleus divides into two nuclei. Mitosis may last anywhere from a few minutes to several days, depending on the type of cell. **Mitosis is divided into four phases: prophase, metaphase, anaphase, and telophase.**

The first phase of mitosis, **prophase**, is the longest phase, frequently taking 50 to 60 percent of the total time required to

Figure 8–11 *Interphase is the part of the cell cycle that occurs before mitosis can take place. Notice that the chromatin in the nucleus appears as an indistinct mass of threadlike structures.*

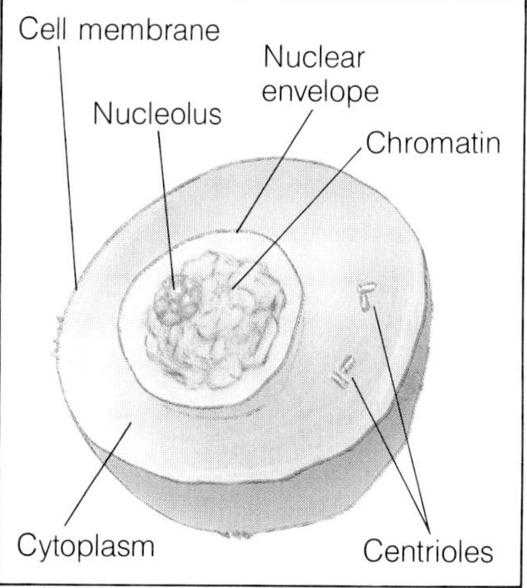

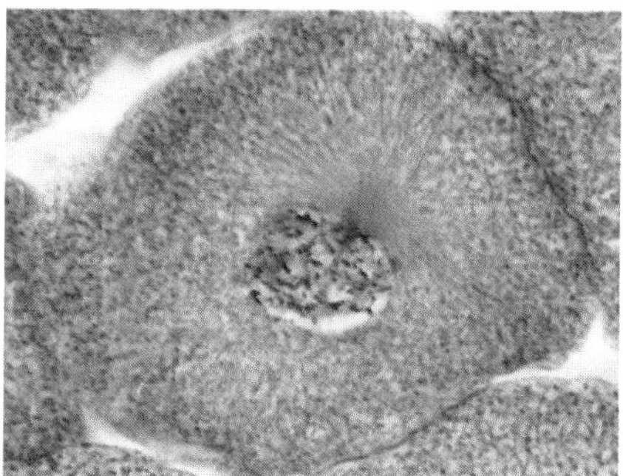

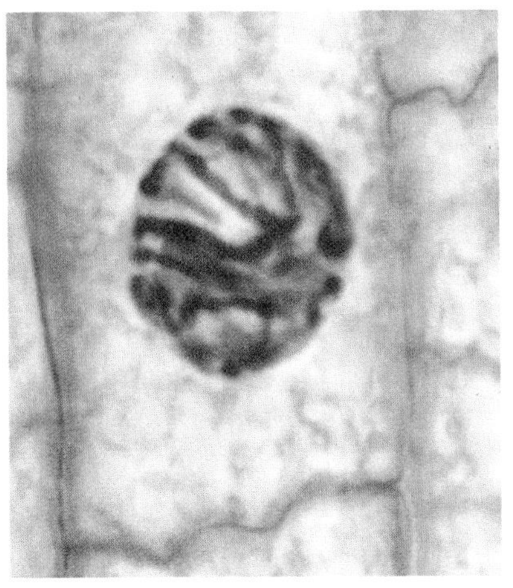

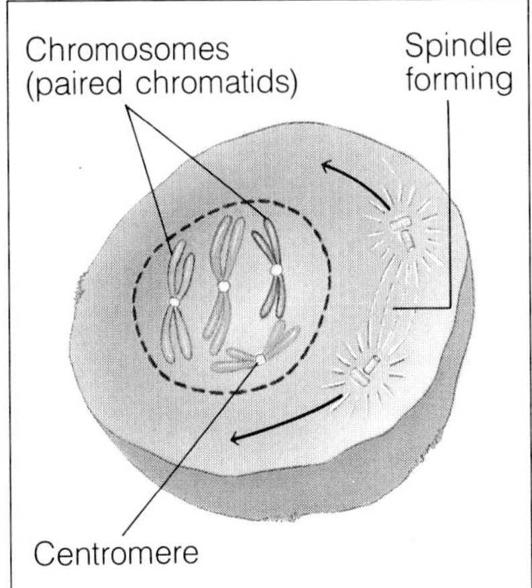

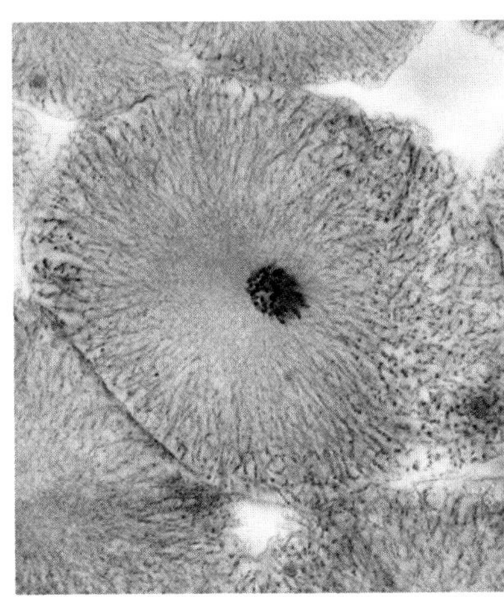

__Figure 8–12__ During prophase, the first stage of mitosis, the chromatin condenses into distinct chromosomes and the nucleolus disappears. The photomicrographs show prophase in a plant cell (left) and an animal cell (right).

complete mitosis. The first clue that prophase is beginning is the appearance of chromosomes. Chromosomes become visible as a result of the condensing and coiling of the yarnlike chromatin. Under a light microscope, each chromosome is seen as two identical chromatids lying side by side. Recall that the area where two chromatids are attached to each other is called the centromere.

During prophase, the **centrioles**, two tiny structures located in the cytoplasm near the nuclear envelope, separate from each other and take up positions on the opposite sides of the nucleus. Centrioles are structures that contain tubulin, a microtubule protein.

During prophase, the condensed chromosomes become attached to fibers in the **spindle** at a point near the centromere of each chromatid. The spindle, a meshlike structure that helps move the chromosomes apart, develops from the centrioles. Recall from Chapter 5 that plant cells do not contain centrioles. However, plant cells form a spindle that is almost identical in structure to that of animal cells. Like the centrioles, the fibers of the spindle are composed of microtubules.

Near the end of prophase, the coiling of the chromosomes becomes tighter. In addition, the nucleolus disappears and the nuclear envelope breaks down.

__Figure 8–13__ Notice the ringlike shape of a centriole in this electron micrograph. Centrioles are cellular structures that are found near the nuclear envelope of an animal cell and play a part in mitosis.

Metaphase

As prophase ends, **metaphase**, or the second phase of mitosis, begins. Metaphase is the shortest phase of mitosis. It often lasts only a few minutes.

During metaphase, the chromosomes line up across the center, or equator, of the cell. Microtubules connect the centromere of each chromosome to the poles of the spindle. Because of their starlike arrangement around the poles of the spindle, these microtubules are called asters, which is the Greek word for star. See Figure 8–14.

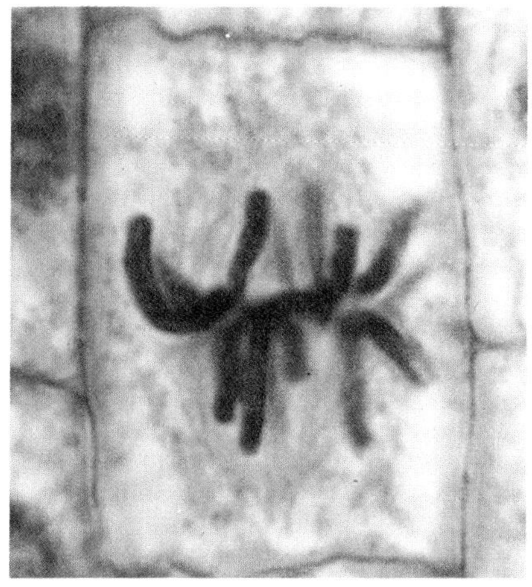

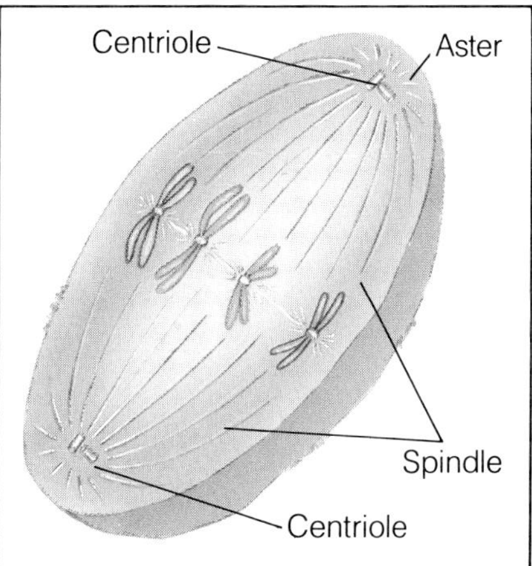

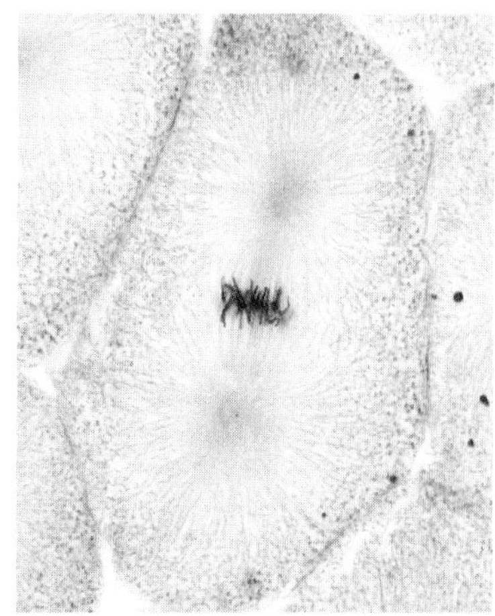

Figure 8–14 Notice how the chromatid pairs line up across the center of the plant cell (left) and the animal cell (right). This arrangement of chromatids marks metaphase, or the second phase of mitosis.

Anaphase

Anaphase, the third phase of mitosis, begins when the centromeres that join the sister chromatids split. This action causes the sister chromatids to separate, becoming individual chromosomes. As the two groups of chromosomes separate, the spindle itself grows longer. The chromosomes continue to move until they have separated into two groups near the poles of the spindle. See Figure 8–15. Anaphase ends when the movement of chromosomes stops.

For years, cell biologists have wondered what provides the force that separates the chromosomes during anaphase. Surprisingly, the answer is still not known. There is evidence that some proteins form bridges between the microtubules extending from opposite poles and use energy from ATP to push each microtubule toward its own pole. However, there is also a suggestion that the rapid assembly and breakdown of microtubules may cause chromosome movement. For the time being, this remains one of the cell's most intriguing riddles.

Figure 8–15 Anaphase, the third phase of mitosis, begins when the centromeres that link the sister chromatids split, allowing each chromatid to become an individual chromosome. Notice that centrioles are present in the animal cell (right) but not in the plant cell (left).

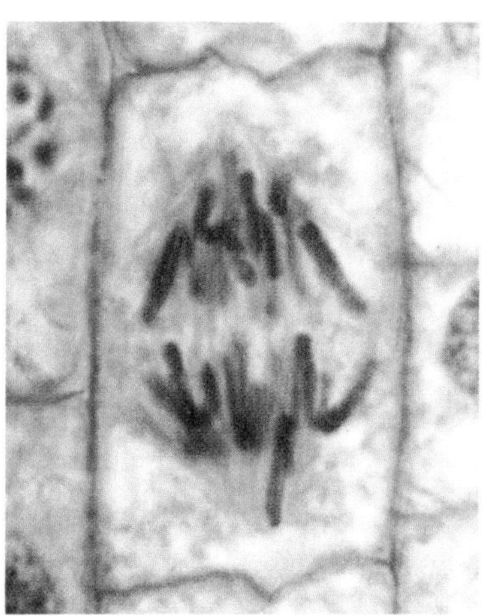

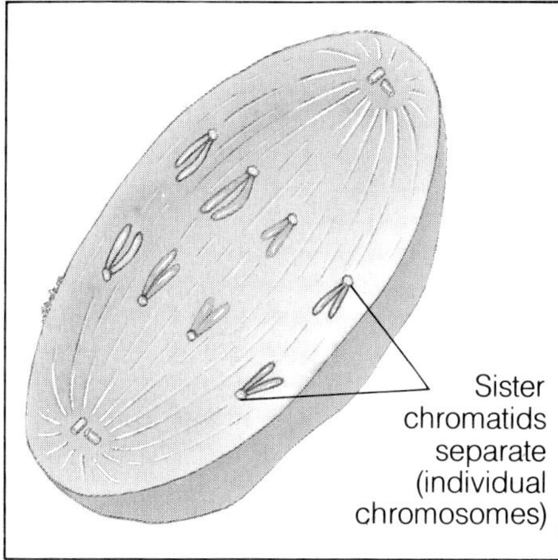

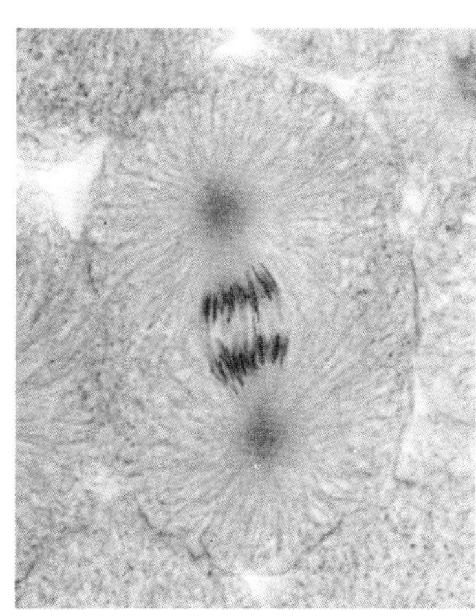

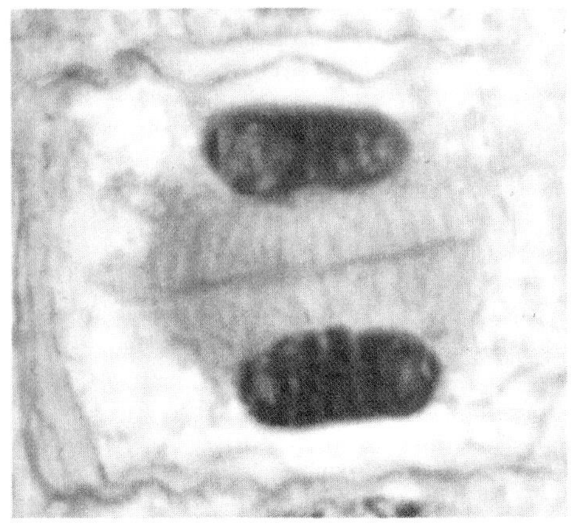

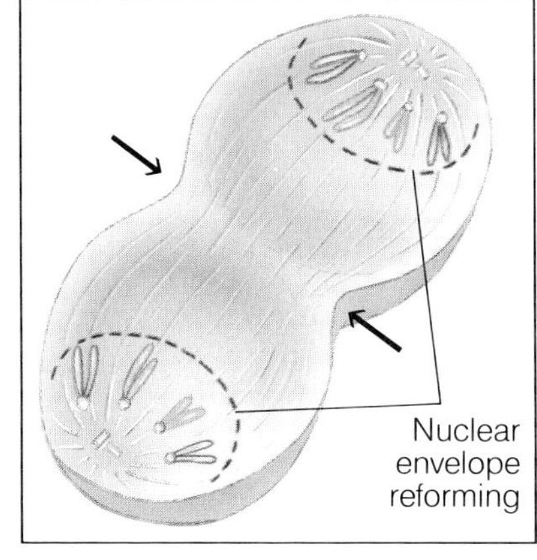

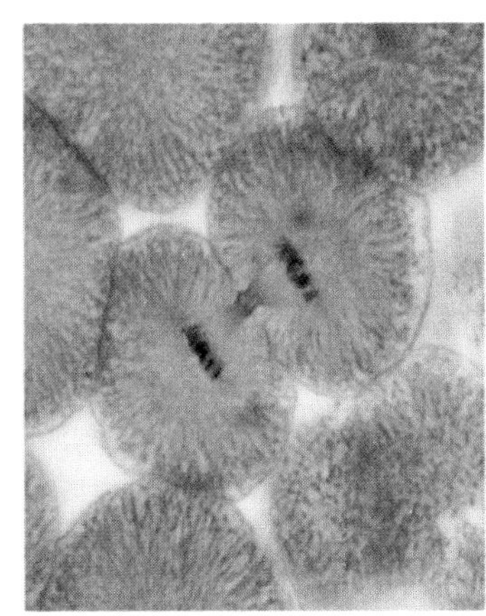

Figure 8–16 *In the final phase of mitosis, called telophase, two new daughter cells begin to form. Notice the two distinct groups of chromosomes in the plant cell (left) and in the animal cell (right).*

Telophase

Telophase is the final phase of mitosis. The chromosomes, which have been distinct and condensed all during mitosis, now begin to uncoil into a tangle of chromatin. This occurs in the two regions where the nuclei of the daughter cells will form. The nuclear envelope reforms around the chromatin, the spindle begins to break apart, and a nucleolus becomes visible in each daughter nucleus. Mitosis is now complete. However, the process of cell division is not.

Figure 8–17 *Cytokinesis is the division of the cytoplasm and its contents into two individual daughter cells. In plant cells, the cytoplasm is divided by a cell plate. The large dark structures in the electron micrograph are the chromosomes.*

Cytokinesis

As a result of mitosis, two nuclei—each with a duplicate set of chromosomes—are formed. Now it remains for the cytoplasm of the cell to divide. This is accomplished as cytokinesis quickly follows mitosis. Cytokinesis, you will recall, is the division of the cytoplasm into two individual cells.

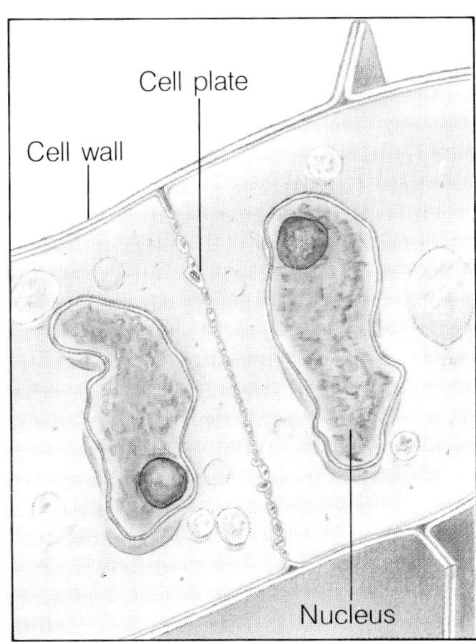

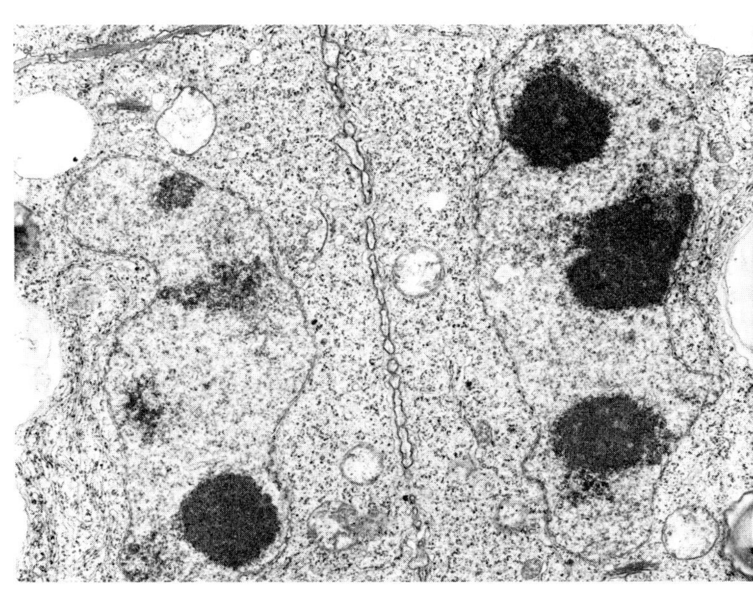

SCIENCE, TECHNOLOGY, AND SOCIETY BREAKTHROUGH

A Useful Poison

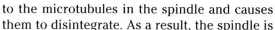

The meadow saffron, *Colchicum autumnale*, is a flowering plant that grows wild in the meadowlands of England, Ireland, and middle and southern Europe. Its lovely flowers, which range in color from lavender to white, bloom in the fall. But the meadow saffron's flowers are deceiving. Though beautiful, the colorful meadow saffron contains a poison known as colchicine (KAHL-chih-seen).

In the laboratory, however, colchicine is a very useful drug. Colchicine stops cell division, making it important in the study of chromosomes. When colchicine is added to a culture of growing cells, it attaches to the microtubules in the spindle and causes them to disintegrate. As a result, the spindle is destroyed and mitosis is stopped at metaphase. When the cells are examined under a light microscope, each chromosome is visible as a pair of chromatids that are joined at the centromere.

Laboratory technicians routinely use colchicine because it enables them to count and measure chromosomes. Cell biologists use the drug as a method of studying the assembly and disassembly of microtubules. Scientists were able to find an important use for a very poisonous drug.

Cytokinesis can take place in a number of ways. In most animal cells, the cell membrane moves inward until the cytoplasm is pinched into two nearly equal parts, each part containing its own nucleus and cytoplasmic organelles. In plants, a structure known as the cell plate forms midway between the divided nuclei. The cell plate gradually develops into a separating membrane. A cell wall begins to appear in the cell plate.

8–2 SECTION REVIEW

1. What is mitosis? Cytokinesis?
2. Describe the structure of a chromosome.
3. Name the three main stages of the cell cycle.
4. Briefly describe the three phases of interphase.
5. What are the four phases of mitosis?

LABORATORY INVESTIGATION

OBSERVING ONION ROOT TIPS

PROBLEM

What are the stages of the cell cycle in a plant cell?

MATERIALS *(per group)*

onion root tips	timer or clock with second hand
safety goggles	2 glass slides
metric ruler	2 medicine droppers
scalpel	toluidine blue
ethanol-acetic acid fixative	probe
3 50-mL beakers	paper towels
glass-marking pencil	coverslip
hydrochloric acid	pencil with eraser
forceps	microscope

PROCEDURE

1. Label the three 50-mL beakers with the glass-marking pencil as follows: fixative, hydrochloric acid, water. Put on your safety goggles and add 10 mL of each liquid to the appropriately labeled beaker. **CAUTION:** *Because acids can burn the skin, handle them with care.* Place the beaker containing the water aside for now.
2. Using the forceps, place the onion root tips in the hydrochloric acid for 4 minutes.
3. After 4 minutes, use the forceps to remove the root tips from the hydrochloric acid. Place them in the fixative for 4 minutes.
4. After 4 minutes, use the forceps to remove the root tips from the fixative and place them on a clean glass slide. Holding the root tips with the forceps, use the scalpel to cut off about 1 mm from each root tip. **CAUTION:** *Be careful when using a scalpel.* Discard the rest of the root tips.
5. Using the forceps, place one root tip on a clean glass slide and then place the glass slide on a paper towel.
6. With a medicine dropper, place a few drops of toluidine blue on the root tip. Allow the toluidine blue to remain on the root tip for 2 minutes. After 2 minutes, use a paper towel to absorb the excess liquid.
7. Using a clean medicine dropper, place two drops of water on the root tip. Cover it with a coverslip. Use the probe to lower the coverslip over the slide.
8. Place a paper towel over the slide and with the eraser end of the pencil gently press down on the area covered by the coverslip. This will squash the root tip. **CAUTION:** *Do not press so hard as to break the coverslip or the glass slide.*
9. With the microscope, examine the onion root tip under low power to find cells in various stages of the cell cycle. (**Note:** If you cannot clearly distinguish the stages of the cell cycle, repeat steps 5 through 9 using another root tip.)
10. After you have located the various stages of the cell cycle under low power, switch to high power. Draw and label a cell from each stage of the cell cycle. Be sure to identify each stage.

OBSERVATIONS

1. Describe what is happening in each stage of the cell cycle.
2. What stage occurs most frequently?
3. How is interphase different from the other stages?
4. What is the color of the chromosomes? Of other cell structures?

ANALYSIS AND CONCLUSIONS

1. What is the purpose of the toluidine blue?
2. In which area of the onion root tip do most of the cells appear to be undergoing mitosis?
3. How can you tell that mitosis is a continuous process?
4. Do some stages of the cell cycle occur more frequently than others? Identify the stage(s) and explain why.

STUDENT STUDY GUIDE

SUMMARIZING THE CONCEPTS

The key concepts in each section of this chapter are listed below to help you review the chapter content. Make sure you understand each concept and its relationship to other concepts and to the theme of this chapter.

8–1 Cell Growth

- Living things grow because they produce more and more cells.
- As a cell increases in size, its volume increases at a faster rate than its surface area.
- The amount of material entering and leaving a cell and the amount of DNA in the nucleus help to limit the size to which a cell can grow.
- Cell division is the process whereby the cell divides into two daughter cells.
- Cancer is a disorder in which some cells have lost the ability to control their rate of growth.

8–2 Cell Division: Mitosis and Cytokinesis

- Cell division in eukaryotic cells occurs in two main stages: mitosis and cytokinesis.
- Mitosis is the process by which the nucleus of the cell is divided into two nuclei, each with the same number and kinds of chromosomes as the parent cell.
- Cytokinesis is the process by which the cytoplasm divides, forming two distinct cells.
- Chromosomes are cellular structures that contain the genetic information that is passed on from one generation to the next. These structures are made up of chromatin, which is composed of DNA and protein.
- The two identical parts of a chromosome, called chromatids, are attached to each other at a centromere.
- During the cell cycle, a cell grows, prepares for division, and divides to form two daughter cells, which repeat the cycle.
- The cell cycle consists of three main stages: mitosis, interphase, and cytokinesis.
- Interphase, the period between cell divisions, is divided into three phases: G_1, S, and G_2.
- Mitosis has four phases: prophase, metaphase, anaphase, and telophase.
- Cytokinesis ends the process of cell division. In animal cells, the cell membrane moves inward until the cytoplasm is pinched in two, each half containing its own nucleus and cytoplasmic organelles. In plant cells, a cell plate forms midway between the divided nuclei, then a cell wall appears in the cell plate.

REVIEWING KEY TERMS

Vocabulary terms are important to your understanding of biology. The key terms listed below are those you should be especially familiar with. Review these terms and their meanings. Then use each term in a complete sentence. If you are not sure of a term's meaning, return to the appropriate section and review its definition.

8–1 Cell Growth

cell division

8–2 Cell Division: Mitosis and Cytokinesis

mitosis	chromatid	prophase	anaphase
cytokinesis	centromere	centriole	telophase
chromosome	cell cycle	spindle	
chromatin	interphase	metaphase	

CHAPTER REVIEW

CONTENT REVIEW

Multiple Choice

Choose the letter of the answer that best completes each statement.

1. Uncontrolled cell division is known as
a. cancer. c. cytokinesis.
b. mitosis. d. growth.

2. Chromatids are held together by a (an)
a. centriole. c. spindle.
b. centromere. d. aster.

3. Each chromosome strand is called a (an)
a. centriole. c. chromatid.
b. centromere. d. aster.

4. A cell has 12 chromosomes. How many chromosomes will each daughter cell have?
a. 24 c. 12
b. 6 d. 4

5. The phase of mitosis that is characterized by the lining up of chromosomes along the center of the cell is known as
a. prophase. c. anaphase.
b. metaphase. d. telophase.

6. During normal mitosis, which occurs first?
a. spindle formation
b. growth and development of daughter cells
c. chromosome duplication
d. cytoplasmic division of the cell

7. A cell that is undergoing mitosis is examined with a light microscope. The cell is most likely an animal cell if the
a. chromosome pairs separate from each other.
b. chromosomes twist about each other.
c. nucleoli disappear.
d. centrioles migrate.

8. A structure found during plant cell division that is not found during animal cell division is a
a. centromere. c. cell membrane.
b. cell plate. d. spindle.

True or False

Determine whether each statement is true or false. If it is true, write "true." If it is false, change the underlined word or words to make the statement true.

1. As a cell increases in size, its volume increases at a <u>faster</u> rate than its surface area.

2. As a result of mitosis, a cell having 10 chromosomes gives rise to two cells, each of which contains <u>20</u> chromosomes.

3. DNA replication occurs during <u>prophase</u>.

4. <u>Animal</u> cells contain centrioles.

5. <u>Interphase</u> is usually divided into three phases: G_1, S, and G_2.

6. <u>Anaphase</u> is the first phase of mitosis.

7. During <u>prophase</u>, the centrioles separate from each other and take up positions on the opposite sides of the nucleus.

8. In <u>animal</u> cells, a cell plate forms midway between the divided nuclei.

Word Relationships

A. *In each of the following sets of terms, three of the terms are related. One term does not belong. Determine the characteristic common to three of the terms and then identify the term that does not belong.*

1. anaphase, interphase, metaphase, telophase
2. chromatid, centromere, chromosome, centriole
3. spindle, aster, microtubule, chromosome
4. cell division, cytokinesis, mitosis, aster

B. *Replace the underlined definition with the correct vocabulary word.*

5. The structures in the cell that contain the genetic information are not visible in most cells except during mitosis.

6. The first phase of mitosis begins when the chromsomes become visible.

7. The meshlike structure that helps move the chromosomes apart develops from the centrioles.

8. In the final phase of mitosis, the chromosomes are found at opposite poles of the cell.

CONCEPT MASTERY

Use your understanding of the concepts developed in the chapter to answer each of the following in a brief paragraph.

1. How do living things grow? What are some factors that limit the growth of a cell?
2. Why do cells divide?
3. Distinguish between chromatin, chromosomes, chromatids, and centromeres.
4. List and describe the phases of the cell cycle.
5. What occurs during interphase? How are interphase and the cell cycle related?
6. Identify and describe the phases of mitosis.
7. Distinguish between cell division in an animal cell and cell division in a plant cell.
8. Why is cell division so complicated in eukaryotic organisms?
9. Compare spindles and asters.

CRITICAL AND CREATIVE THINKING

Discuss each of the following in a brief paragraph.

1. **Relating facts** The diagram below shows a phase of mitosis. Identify the phase of mitosis and indicate whether the cell is from a rose or a tiger. Give a reason for your answer.

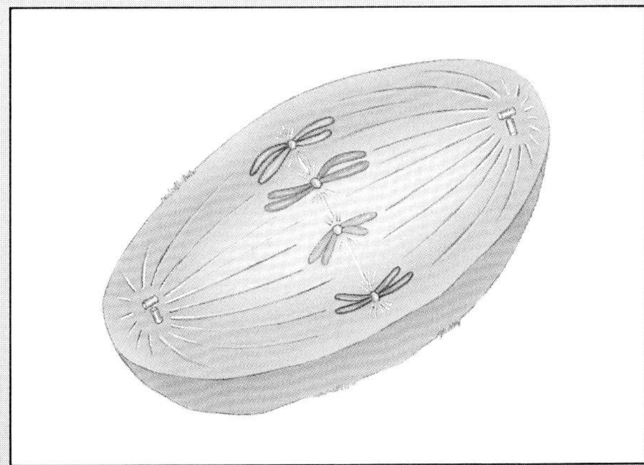

2. **Making calculations** A cell is 4μm long, 3μm wide, and 3μm high. Find the ratio of volume to surface area.
3. **Applying concepts** Is mitosis occurring in your body right now? If so, where? Explain your answer.
4. **Relating concepts** After muscle and nerve cells form in the body, they seldom undergo mitosis. Explain how this affects the human body.
5. **Relating cause and effect** What structure within the cell is most likely to play a major role in the development of generations of cancer cells? Explain your answer.
6. **Using the writing process** Suppose you were small enough to hitch a ride on a chromosome located in a cell that divides by mitosis. Describe what you would see happening during this process.

Electron Microscopist

Electron microscopes use beams of electrons to magnify objects. People who operate electron microscopes to view tiny cell structures are called electron microscopists. They produce photographs called micrographs that allow researchers to learn more about the normal activities of cells.

To become an electron microscopist, the requirements are a high school education and extensive training in the use of an electron microscope.

For information write to the National Society for Histotechnology, P.O. Box 36, Larnham, MD 20706.

Forensic Laboratory Technician

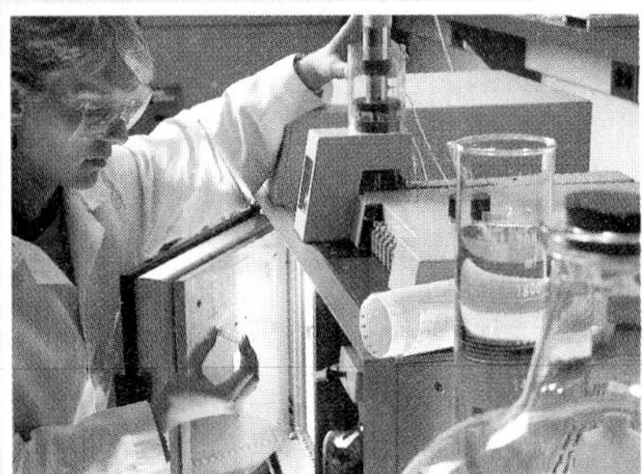

Forensic laboratory technicians use scientific principles and instruments to analyze evidence found at the scene of a crime. They find clues by examining a variety of biological materials that includes hair, blood, fingernails, bones, and tissues. They also study fingerprints, firearms, and bullets. Forensic technicians might be called upon to help reconstruct the scene of a crime or to testify in court.

Most forensic laboratory technicians have a Bachelor's degree with a good background in biology and chemistry.

To receive career information write to the American Academy of Forensic Sciences, 225 S. Academy Blvd., Colorado Springs, CO 80910.

Cell Biologist

Cell biologists examine the structure of cells in plants and animals. They study individual parts of different cells to learn how each part functions and how it is affected by chemical and physical factors. Using microscopes, stains, and other instruments, cell biologists can observe the growth and division of various cells.

Cell biologists usually have medical or Ph.D. degrees. They work in hospitals, universities, and research laboratories.

For information contact the American Society for Cell Biology, 9650 Rockville Pike, Bethesda, MD 20814.

HOW TO CHOOSE A TECHNICAL SCHOOL

Technicians are workers who are trained beyond high school in a specialized field of technology. A technical education mixes theory with practice and usually takes one to three years, depending on the field. Technicians receive either a certificate or an associate degree.

When choosing a technical school, seek reliable evaluations from past graduates and job placement statistics. Although many schools advertise, only the better schools are accredited by the government.

For information write to the National Association of Trade and Technical Schools, 2251 Wisconsin Ave., NW, Washington, DC 20007 and ask for a copy of the Handbook of Trade and Technical Careers and Training.

FROM THE AUTHORS

The first time I heard the term DNA mentioned was when I was in junior high. Although our textbook barely mentioned DNA, my science teacher had made a point of keeping up to date. He put up newspaper clippings about the double helix model; told us about the Nobel prize that was shared by Watson, Crick, and Wilkins; and even built a crude model of the molecule. He did his best to let us know that biology didn't stop when our textbook was written.

Way back then (when John F. Kennedy was in his last year in the White House) it was already clear that DNA was the future. The question was not whether DNA was important—it was clear that it was—but how the information in DNA was coded, expressed, and controlled. Three decades later, we know enough to answer many of the questions that seemed so puzzling to me in junior high. I could do better in Mr. Zong's mid-term exam today, but I think it's too late to improve my grade. One thing I can't improve on, however, is the sense he gave me of the future—the feeling that science was changing tomorrow.

Even as they change, things stay the same. It's tempting to think that we've solved all of the big questions, but it would be just as wrong to hold that attitude as it was in 1963. So look around, and pay attention to those newspaper clippings and science magazines in your classroom. No book contains the last word about biology. Tomorrow is up there on the wall.

Ken Miller

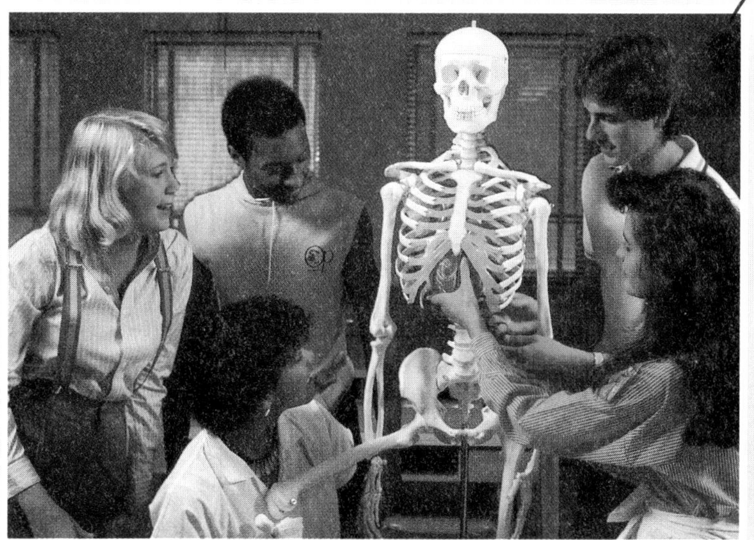

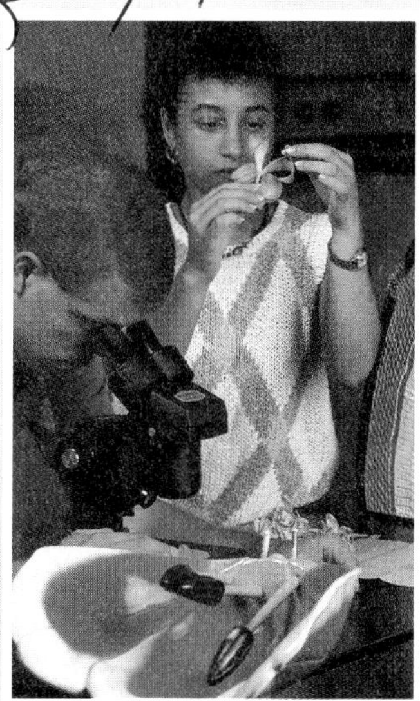

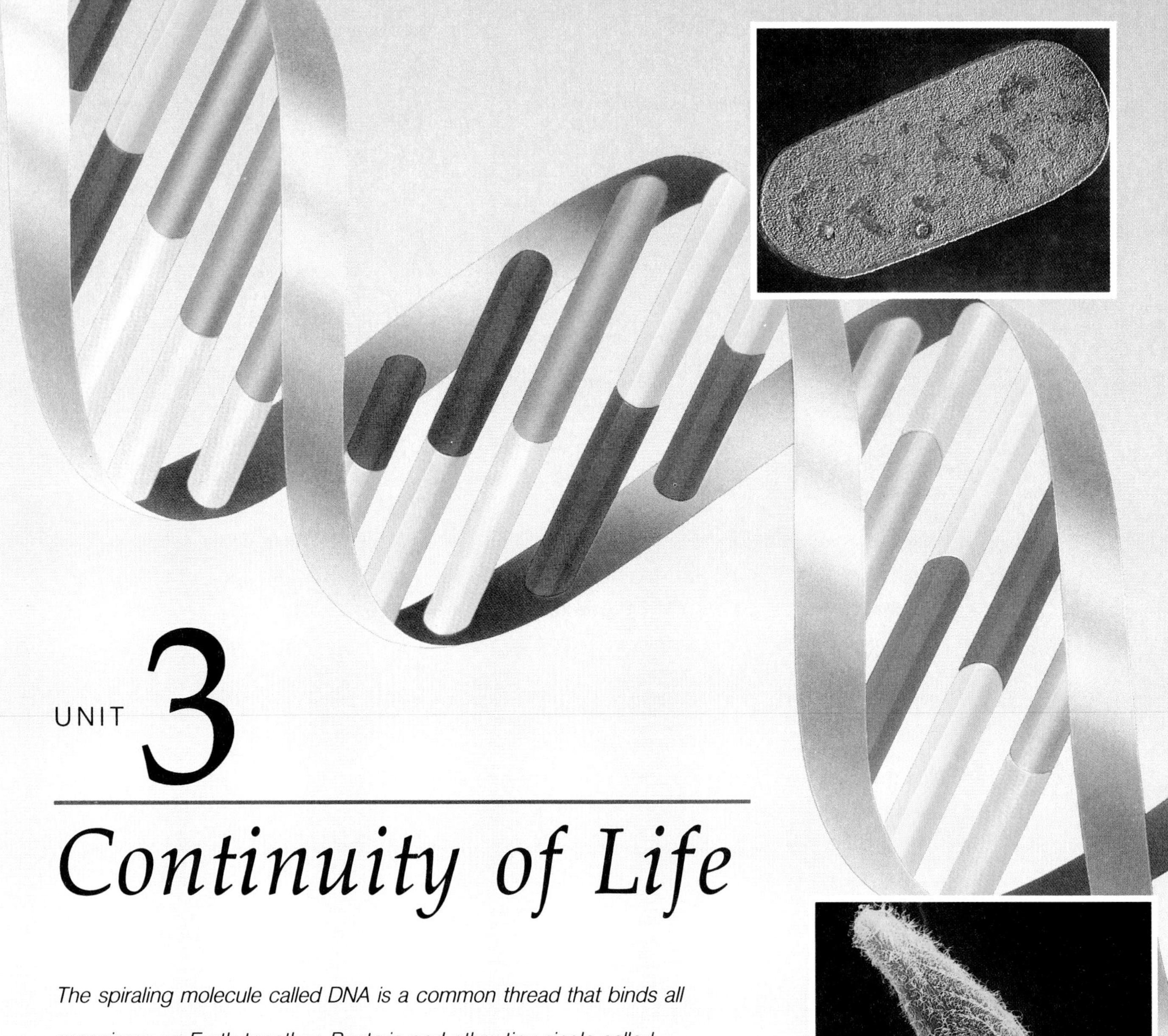

UNIT 3

Continuity of Life

The spiraling molecule called DNA is a common thread that binds all organisms on Earth together. Bacteria and other tiny single-celled organisms contain DNA, as do mushrooms, apple trees, snails, birds, and humans. In fact, all living things require DNA to grow, develop, and carry out the functions of life.

DNA is also necessary for life to continue from one generation to the next. Encoded in the pattern of chemicals within the molecule are all the instructions needed to transform a single fertilized egg cell into a complex, many-celled organism. Some of the most fascinating aspects of biology involve the transmittal of DNA from parents to offspring and the ways in which DNA controls the development of living things.

CHAPTERS

CHAPTER 9

Introduction to Genetics

There are few things as graceful and magnificent as a running horse. A good combination of many inherited traits—fine-boned legs, swiftness, and stamina, for example—helps thoroughbred race horses compete at Churchill Downs in the Kentucky Derby.

Inheritance is something that we are all familiar with; each of us has a biological inheritance. As a child you may have been told that you "inherited" your eyes from your grandfather, your hair from your grandmother, your intelligence from your mother, and your artistic talents from your father. Everyday experience shows us that offspring resemble their parents.

But why do we take after our parents and grandparents? Why do people expect great things from a newborn foal if his father won the Kentucky Derby? Why do the kittens born of a yellow tabby and a black cat have fur colored somewhere between yellow and black? In this chapter you will discover the answers to these questions as you explore the nature of biological inheritance.

CHAPTER OUTLINE

9–1 The Work of Gregor Mendel

Section Objectives

- Discuss Mendel's experiments.
- Describe dominance, segregation, and independent assortment.

Biological inheritance, or **heredity**, is the key to differences between species. Cats give birth to kittens, dogs produce puppies, and oak trees produce acorns from which, as the saying goes, mighty oaks may grow. Heredity, however, is much more than the way in which a few superficial characteristics are passed from one generation to another. Heredity is at the very center of what makes each species unique, as well as what makes us human. The branch of biology that studies heredity is called **genetics**.

Early Ideas About Heredity

Until the nineteenth century, the most common explanation for the resemblances between parent and offspring was the theory of blending inheritance. People reasoned that because both a male and a female were involved in producing offspring, each parent contributed factors that determined inheritance—factors that were blended in their offspring. The nature of these factors was unknown.

At first, the theory of blending inheritance seemed a reasonable explanation. It is common to see a little bit of both parents in a child. So it seemed fair to say that the characteristics of the mother and father have blended in making the new life. But in the last century biologists began to look at the details of heredity. When they did, they began to develop a very different

Figure 9–1 *Why don't the two baby guinea pigs look like each other? Why are they different from their mother? The science of genetics helps us answer questions such as these.*

view. The work of the Austrian monk Gregor Mendel was particularly important in changing people's views about how characteristics are passed from one generation to the next.

Gregor Mendel

Gregor Mendel was born in 1822 to peasant parents in what is now Czechoslovakia. He did very well in school and entered a monastery in the town of Brno at the age of 21. Four years later he was ordained a priest. The monastery was a center of scientific learning. In 1851, Mendel was sent to the University of Vienna to study science and mathematics. He returned two years later and spent the next fourteen years working in the monastery and teaching at the high school in Brno.

In addition to his teaching duties, Mendel had charge of the monastery garden. It was in this ordinary garden that he was to do the work that revolutionized biological science.

From his studies in biology, Mendel had gained an understanding of the sexual mechanisms of the pea plant. Pea flowers have both male and female parts. Normally, pollen from the male part of the pea flower fertilizes the female egg cells of the very same flower. Because the pollen produced by the plant fertilizes the egg cells of that very same plant, peas are said to produce seeds by **self-pollination**. Seeds produced by self-pollination inherit all of their characteristics from the single plant that bore them.

Mendel learned that self-pollination could be prevented. He carefully cut the male parts off all the flowers of one plant and the female parts off all the flowers of another plant. He then pollinated the two plants by dusting the pollen from one plant onto the flowers of the other plant. The fertilization of a plant's egg cells by the pollen of another plant is known as **cross-pollination**. Cross-pollination produces seeds that are the offspring of two different plants. With this technique, Mendel was able to cross plants with different characteristics.

Figure 9–2 *Mendel used the garden pea in his experiments on heredity. Garden peas usually reproduce by self-pollination because the male and female reproductive parts are tightly enclosed within the flower's petals (left) One method Mendel used to cross-pollinate his pea plants was to cut off the male parts of a flower (thus preventing self-pollination) and then dust the pollen from another plant onto that flower (right).*

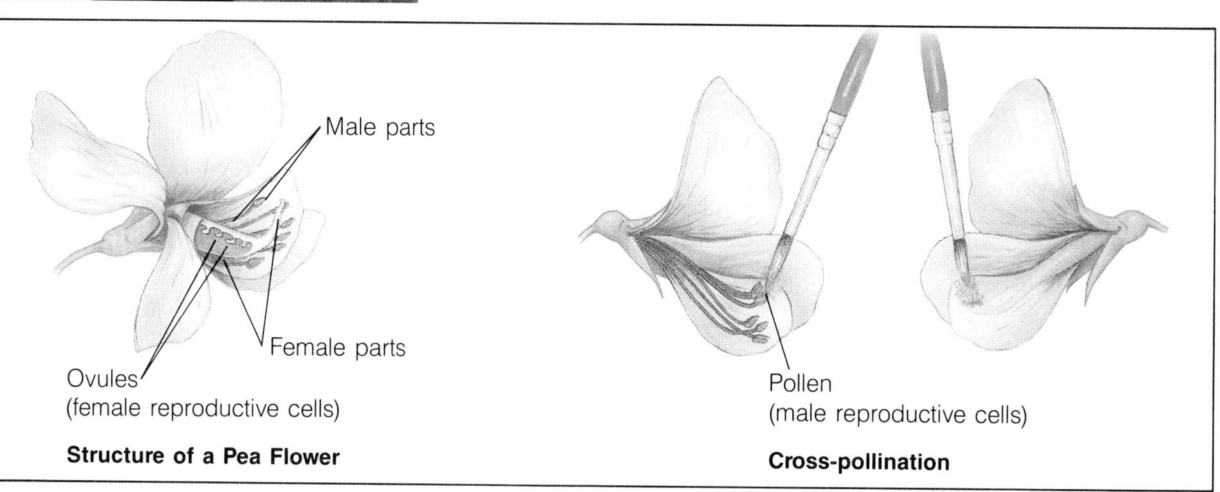

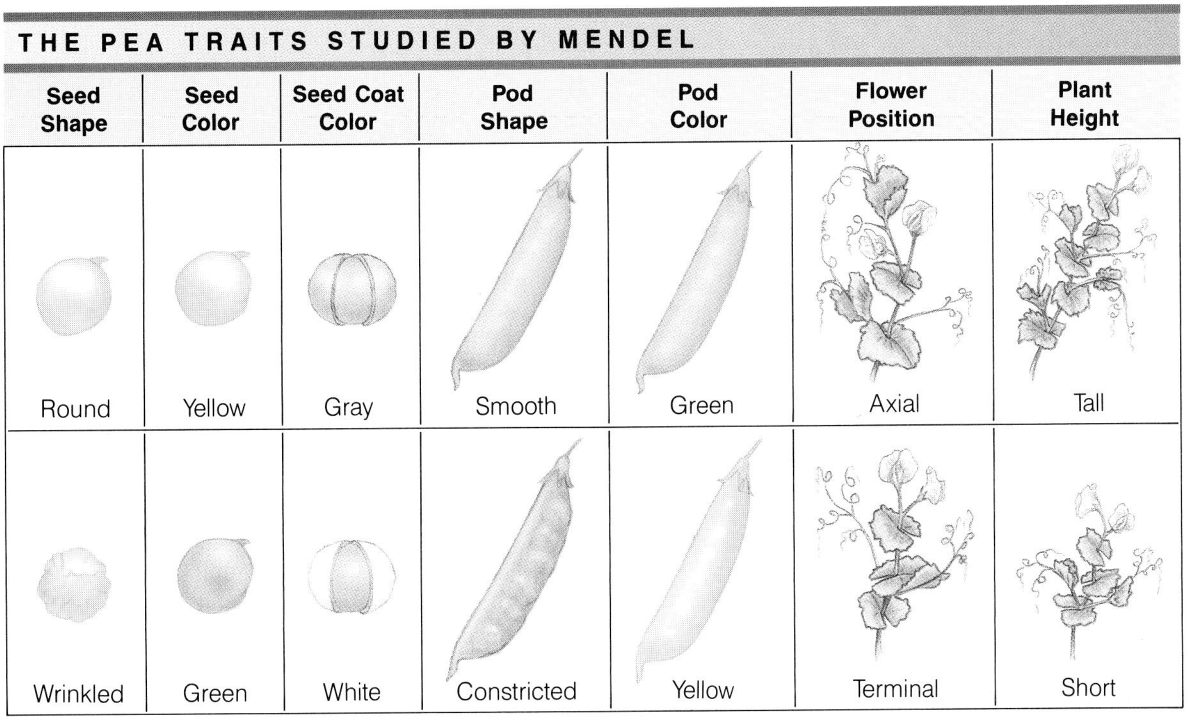

THE PEA TRAITS STUDIED BY MENDEL						
Seed Shape	**Seed Color**	**Seed Coat Color**	**Pod Shape**	**Pod Color**	**Flower Position**	**Plant Height**
Round	Yellow	Gray	Smooth	Green	Axial	Tall
Wrinkled	Green	White	Constricted	Yellow	Terminal	Short

Figure 9–3 *The seven pea traits studied by Mendel are seed shape, seed color, seed coat color, pod shape, pod color, flower position, and plant height. As you can see, each of these traits has two contrasting characters, or forms.*

One of the gifts that Mendel received when he took charge of the monastery garden was a stock of peas developed by earlier gardeners. These peas were **purebred**. This means that if they were allowed to self-pollinate, the purebred peas would produce offspring that were identical to themselves. One line of plants would produce only tall plants, another only short plants. One line would produce only green seeds, another only yellow seeds. These purebred plants were the basis of Mendel's experiments.

In many respects, the most important decision Mendel made was to study just a few isolated **traits**, or characteristics, that could easily be observed. In the case of the peas, one trait was the size of the plant, another the shape of the pod, another the color of the seed. Figure 9–3 shows the seven traits that Mendel studied. By deciding to restrict his observations to just a few such traits, Mendel made his job of measuring the effects of heredity much easier.

Genes and Dominance

What would you do if you were interested in heredity, had several kinds of purebred peas, and also knew how to cause cross-pollination? No, pea soup is not a good answer.

Mendel decided to see what would happen if he crossed pea plants with different characters for the same trait. A character is a form of a trait. For example, the flower-position trait has two characters: axial and terminal. Mendel crossed the tall

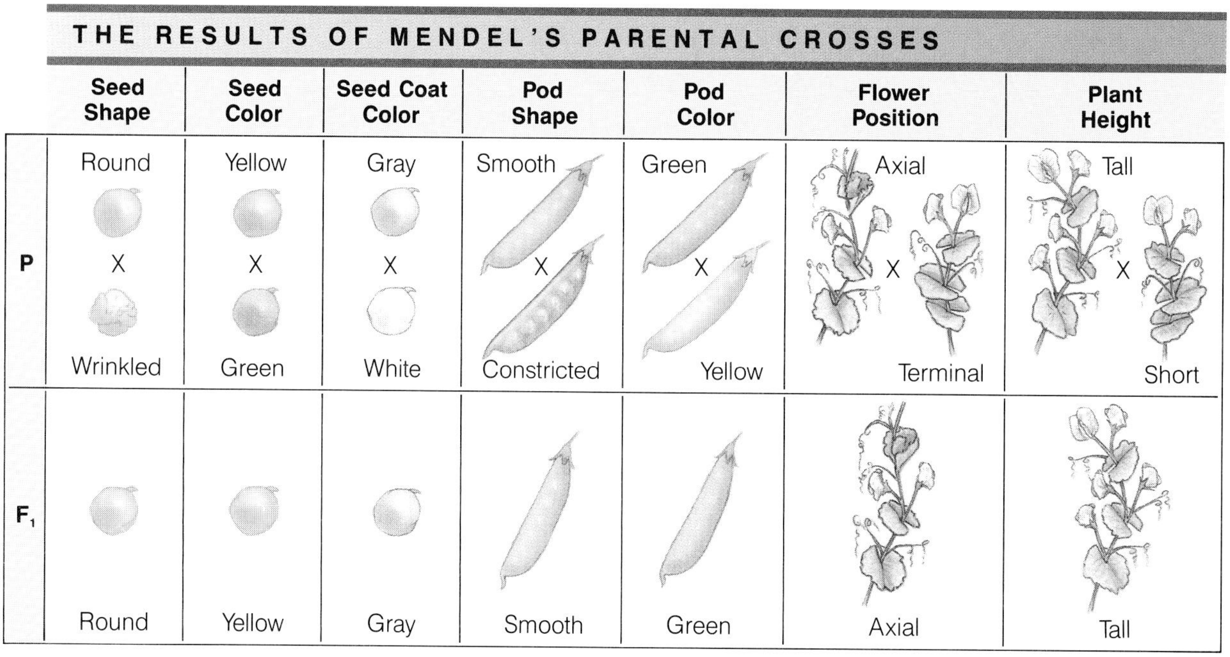

THE RESULTS OF MENDEL'S PARENTAL CROSSES

	Seed Shape	Seed Color	Seed Coat Color	Pod Shape	Pod Color	Flower Position	Plant Height
P	Round X Wrinkled	Yellow X Green	Gray X White	Smooth X Constricted	Green X Yellow	Axial X Terminal	Tall X Short
F_1	Round	Yellow	Gray	Smooth	Green	Axial	Tall

Figure 9–4 *When Mendel crossed plants with contrasting characters for the same trait, the resulting offspring had only one of the characters. From the results of these experiments, Mendel concluded that factors that do not blend control the inheritance of traits and that some of these factors are dominant, whereas others are recessive.*

plants with the short ones; the plants with yellow seeds with those with green seeds; and so on. From the crosses in his pea plants, Mendel obtained seeds that he then grew into plants. These plants were **hybrids**, or organisms produced by crossing parents with differing characters.

What were those hybrid plants like? Did the characters of the parent plants blend in the offspring? To Mendel's surprise, the plants were not half tall, nor were the seeds they produced half yellow. Instead, all of the offspring had the character of only one of the parents. The plants resulting from his crosses were all tall or produced only yellow seeds. The other character had apparently disappeared.

From this set of experiments, Mendel was able to draw two conclusions. The first is that individual factors, which do not blend with one another, control each trait of a living thing. Mendel used the word *Merkmal* to refer to these factors. *Merkmal* means character in German. Today the factors that control traits are called **genes**. Each of the traits Mendel studied was controlled by one gene that occurred in two contrasting forms. These contrasting forms produced the different characters of each trait. For example, the gene for plant height occurs in a tall form and a short form. The different forms of a gene are now called **alleles** (uh-LEELZ).

The second of Mendel's conclusions is often called the principle of **dominance**: Some factors (alleles) are **dominant**, whereas others are **recessive**. The effects of a dominant allele are seen even if it is present with a contrasting recessive allele. The effects of a recessive allele are not observed when the dominant allele is present. In Mendel's experiments, the tall and yellow alleles were dominant, whereas the short and green alleles were recessive. Although dominance is seen in the inheritance of many traits, it does not apply to all genes.

Segregation

Mendel was not content to stop his experimentation at this point. He wanted the answer to another question: What happened to the recessive characters? To answer this question, he allowed all seven kinds of hybrid plants to reproduce by self-pollination.

To keep the different groups of seeds and plants clear in his mind, Mendel gave them different names. He referred to the purebred parental plants as the P generation (P for parental). To the first generation of plants produced by cross-pollination, he gave the name F_1, which stood for first filial generation (from the Latin word *filius*, which means son). If the F_1 plants were crossed among themselves, he called the offspring F_2, for second filial generation, and so forth.

THE F_1 CROSS The results of the F_1 cross were remarkable. The recessive characters had not disappeared! Some of the F_2 plants produced by each of the F_1 crosses showed the recessive trait. This proved to Mendel that the alleles responsible for the recessive characters had not disappeared. But why did the recessive alleles disappear in the F_1 generation and reappear in the F_2? To answer this question, let's take a closer look at one of Mendel's crosses. Keep in mind that the concepts that apply to the crosses involving the trait of plant height also apply to the crosses for the other six traits.

EXPLAINING THE F_1 CROSS To begin with, Mendel assumed that the presence of the dominant tall allele had masked

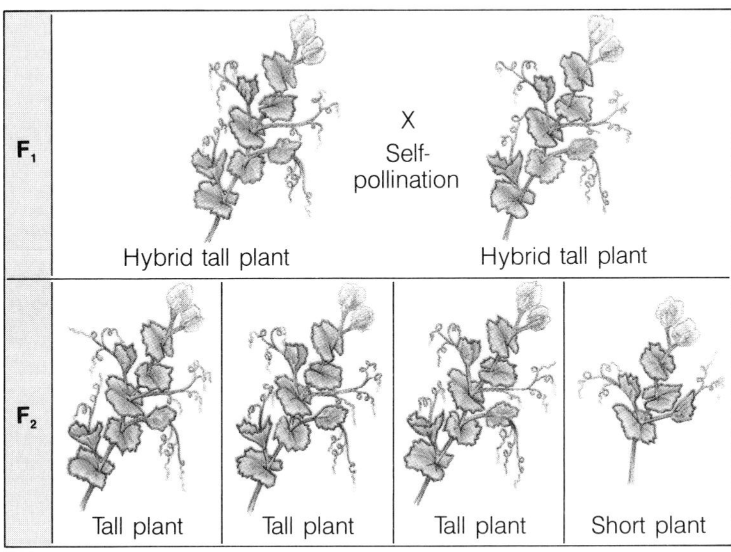

Figure 9–5 When the F_1 hybrid plants were allowed to reproduce by self-pollination, some of the resulting F_2 offspring had the recessive character.

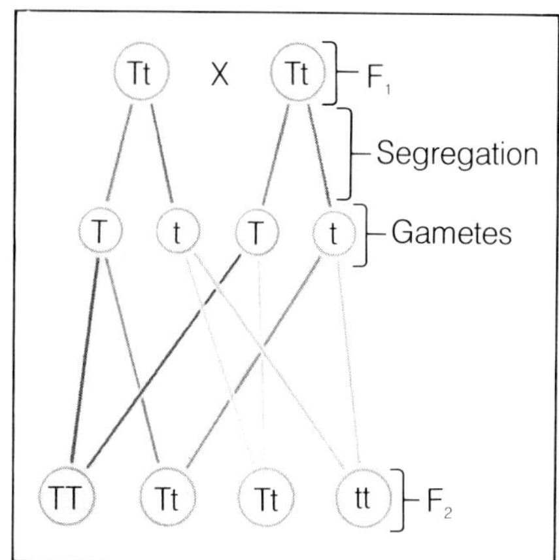

Figure 9–6 *Segregation of alleles occurs during gamete formation. The alleles are paired up again when gametes fuse during the process of fertilization.*

the recessive short allele in the F_1 generation. But the fact that the recessive allele was not masked in some of the F_2 plants indicated that the short allele had managed to get away from the tall allele. But how did this separation, or **segregation**, of alleles occur? Mendel suggested that during the formation of the reproductive cells (pollen and eggs), the tall and short alleles in the F_1 plants were segregated, or separated, from each other. Did that suggestion make sense?

Perhaps Mendel thought as follows: Let's assume that the F_1 plants have one tall factor from one parent and one short factor from the other parent. (Remember that Mendel did not know about genes and alleles.) Suppose such a plant forms flowers and the two factors are segregated from each other when reproductive cells are made. Each F_1 plant will produce two types of reproductive cells: one that has the tall factor and one that has the short factor. What should be the result when two F_1 plants are crossed?

If segregation occurs the way Mendel thought it did, then the possible gene combinations in the offspring that result from a cross can be determined by drawing a diagram known as a **Punnett square**. Biologists represent a particular gene by using a symbol. The dominant allele is represented by a capital letter. The recessive allele is represented by the corresponding lowercase letter. In this case, *T* represents the dominant tall allele and *t* represents the recessive short allele.

The Punnett square in Figure 9–7 shows the types of reproductive cells, or **gametes** (GAM-eets), produced by each F_1 parent along the top and left-hand side of the square. It also shows each possible gene combination for the F_2 offspring in the four boxes that make up the square.

You can see the probable results of the cross of two F_1 plants from the Punnett square: 1/4 of the F_2 plants have two tall alleles (*TT*); 2/4, or 1/2, of the F_2 plants have one tall allele and one short allele (*Tt*), and 1/4 of the F_2 plants have two short alleles (*tt*). Because tall is dominant over short, 3/4 of the F_2 plants should be tall and 1/4 of the F_2 plants should be short. These numbers are often expressed as ratios. For example, there are 3 tall plants for every 1 short plant in the F_2 generation. Thus the ratio of tall plants to short plants is 3:1. If, of course, Mendel's model of segregation is correct.

Figure 9–7 *This Punnett square shows a cross between two hybrid tall* (Tt) *pea plants.*

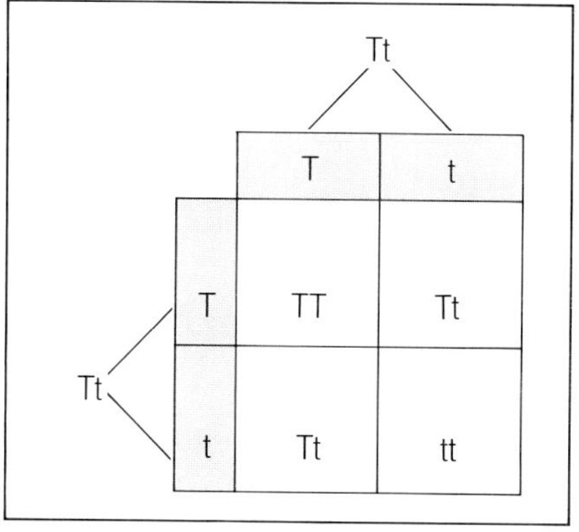

Did the data from Mendel's experiments fit his model? Yes. The predicted ratio—3 dominant to 1 recessive—showed up consistently, indicating that Mendel's assumptions about segregation had been correct. For each of his seven crosses, about 3/4 of the plants showed the dominant trait and about 1/4 showed the recessive trait. Segregation did indeed occur according to Mendel's model.

Look again at the Punnett square. You will see that three of the possible combinations result in tall plants. Because all these plants appear tall, we can say that they have the same **phenotype**, or physical characteristics. They do not, however, have the same **genotype**, or genetic makeup. The genotype of 1/3 of the tall plants is *TT*, whereas the genotype of 2/3 of the tall plants is *Tt*.

Organisms that have two identical alleles for a particular trait (*TT* or *tt* in our example) are said to be **homozygous** (hoh-moh-ZIGH-guhs) (*homo-* means same; *-zygous* refers to alleles). Organisms that have two different alleles for the same trait are **heterozygous** (heht-er-oh-ZIGH-guhs)(*hetero-* means different). In other words, homozygous organisms are purebred for a particular trait and heterozygous organisms are hybrid for a particular trait.

Figure 9–8 *Although these plants have different genotypes* (TT *and* Tt), *they have the same phenotype (tall).*

Independent Assortment

After establishing that genes segregate during the formation of gametes (reproductive cells), Mendel began to explore the question of whether they do so independently. In other words, does the gene that controls one trait have anything to do with the gene that controls a different trait? For example, does the gene that determines whether a seed is round or wrinkled in shape have anything to do with the gene for seed color? Must a round seed also be yellow? To answer these questions, Mendel first crossed purebred plants that produced round yellow seeds with purebred plants that produced wrinkled green seeds.

THE TWO-FACTOR CROSS: F_1 In this cross, the two kinds of plants would be symbolized like this:

Round yellow seeds *RRYY*

Wrinkled green seeds *rryy*

Because two traits are involved in this experiment, it is called a two-factor cross. As you examine this cross, keep in mind that you are looking at the kind of seeds the plant produces. (These seeds are not necessarily the same as the seeds from which the plants grew!)

The plant that bears round yellow seeds produces gametes that contain the alleles *R* and *Y*, or *RY* gametes. The plant that bears wrinkled green seeds produces *ry* gametes. An *RY* gamete and an *ry* gamete combine to form a fertilized egg with the genotype *RrYy*. Thus only one kind of plant will show up in the F_1 generation—plants that are heterozygous, or hybrid, for both traits. What is the phenotype of the F_1 plants? That is, what will the seeds produced by the F_1 plants look like? Because we know that round and yellow are dominant traits, we can conclude that the F_1 plants will produce seeds that are round and yellow. Remember that the concept of dominance tells us that the dominant traits will show up in a hybrid, whereas the recessive traits will seem to disappear.

Figure 9–9 *When an individual that is homozygous dominant for two traits is crossed with an individual that is recessive for the same two traits, all of the offspring are heterozygous dominant for those two traits.*

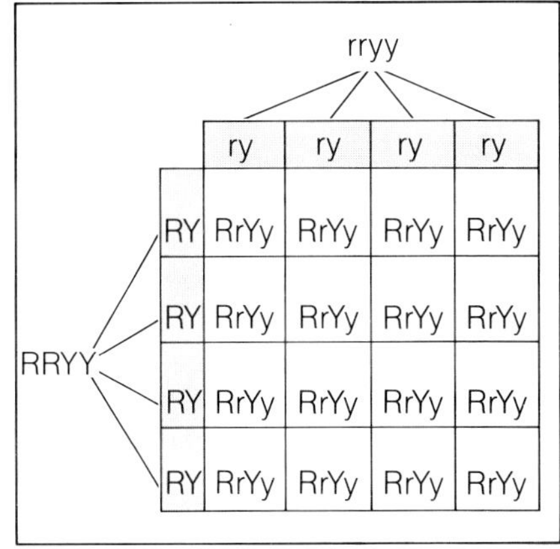

	ry	ry	ry	ry
RY	RrYy	RrYy	RrYy	RrYy
RY	RrYy	RrYy	RrYy	RrYy
RY	RrYy	RrYy	RrYy	RrYy
RY	RrYy	RrYy	RrYy	RrYy

This cross does not indicate whether genes assort, or segregate, independently. However, it provides the hybrid plants

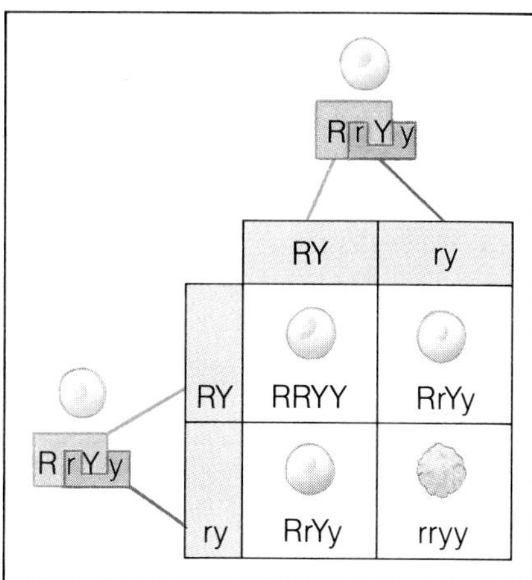

Figure 9–10 *If the genes for two traits are connected in some way, only two combinations of the traits are possible in the offspring.*

needed for the next cross—the cross of F_1 plants to produce the F_2 generation. The seeds from the F_2 plants will show whether the genes for seed shape and seed color have anything to do with one another. Now for the real experiment.

THE TWO-FACTOR CROSS: F_2 What will happen when F_1 plants are crossed with each other? If the genes for seed shape and color are connected in some way, then the dominant *R* and *Y* alleles (which came from one parent) and the recessive *r* and *y* alleles (which came from the other parent) will be segregated as matched sets into the gametes. Thus, the gametes could only contain one of two possible gene combinations: *RY* or *ry*. As you can see in Figure 9–10, all round seeds will be yellow and all wrinkled seeds will be green.

If the genes are not connected, then they should segregate independently, or undergo **independent assortment**. This produces four possible types of gametes: *RY*, *Ry*, *rY*, and *ry*. In addition, if the genes assort independently, some of the seeds produced by the F_2 plants will have new combinations of traits —they may be wrinkled and yellow, or round and green.

This two-factor cross is examined in the Punnett square in Figure 9–11. Now that we have four possible gamete types (and sixteen possible offspring) the square is especially useful. If the genes for seed shape and seed color are inherited independently, then the seeds produced by the offspring should be exactly as predicted by the Punnett square:

9/16	**yellow round seeds**	**(315)**
3/16	**yellow wrinkled seeds**	**(101)**
3/16	**green round seeds**	**(108)**
1/16	**green wrinkled seeds**	**(32)**

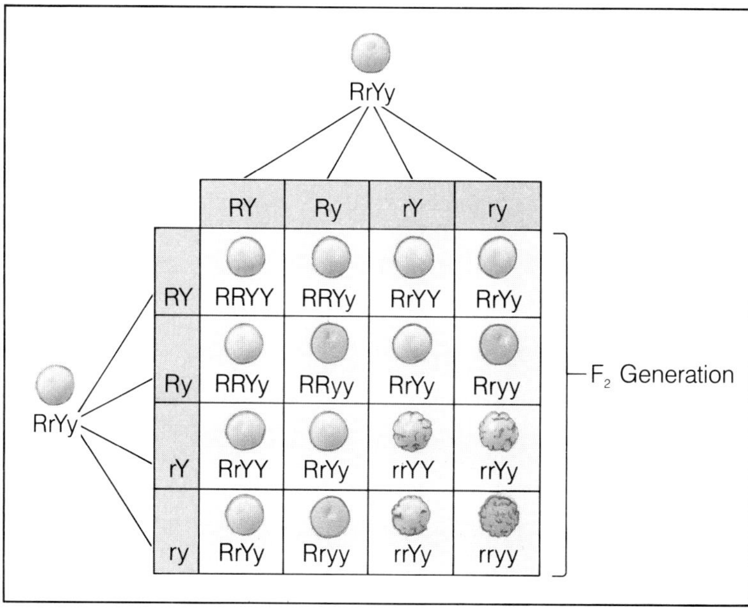

Figure 9–11 *If the genes for two traits are not linked, then they will undergo independent assortment. This results in new combinations of the traits. The phenotypic ratio of the offspring that results from crossing individuals that are hybrid for two traits is 9:3:3:1.*

Figure 9–12 *This young chameleon has obtained half of its genes—and a piggyback ride—from its parent.*

Mendel actually carried out this exact experiment, and his results, shown in parentheses, were very close to the 9:3:3:1 ratio that the Punnett square predicts. From these results, Mendel concluded that genes could segregate independently during the formation of gametes. In other words, genes could undergo independent assortment. As we shall see later, there is an important exception to independent assortment. Genes located on the same chromosome are linked and may not undergo independent assortment.

A Summary of Mendel's Work

Mendel's work on the genetics of peas can be summarized in four basic statements:

- **The factors that control heredity are individual units known as genes. In organisms that reproduce sexually, genes are inherited from each parent.**
- **In cases in which an organism possesses two forms of the gene for a single trait, some forms of the gene may be dominant and others may be recessive.**
- **The two forms of each gene are segregated during the formation of reproductive cells.**
- **The genes for different traits may assort independently of one other.**

9–1 SECTION REVIEW

1. What is dominance? Segregation?
2. What is independent assortment?
3. Define the terms genotype and phenotype. To which term does heterozygous refer?
4. Why were purebred peas important for Mendel's experiments?

Section Objectives

- Relate probability to genetics.
- Solve genetics problems using a Punnett square.

9–2 Applying Mendel's Principles

Mendel's careful record keeping and his knowledge of mathematics enabled him to see the patterns of heredity. His paper describing his experiments and conclusions was published in 1866 in the *Proceedings of the Brno Society of Natural Science*. Unfortunately, Mendel's ideas about heredity and his applications of mathematics and statistics to biology were far ahead of their time. Mendel's fellow scientists failed to understand and recognize the importance of his work. In fact, a prominent botanist encouraged Mendel to start working with a different kind of plant and to give up on the hybrid peas. Mendel's pioneering work in genetics remained unappreciated during his lifetime.

In the early 1900s, several scientists working independently rediscovered Mendel's paper. They realized that it correctly described the basic principles of genetics. More than twenty years after his death, Mendel's experiments and conclusions were recognized as important breakthroughs in biology.

Genetics and Probability

One of the most innovative things Mendel did was to apply the mathematical concept of **probability** to biology. **Probability is the likelihood that a particular event will occur.** Probability is determined by the following formula.

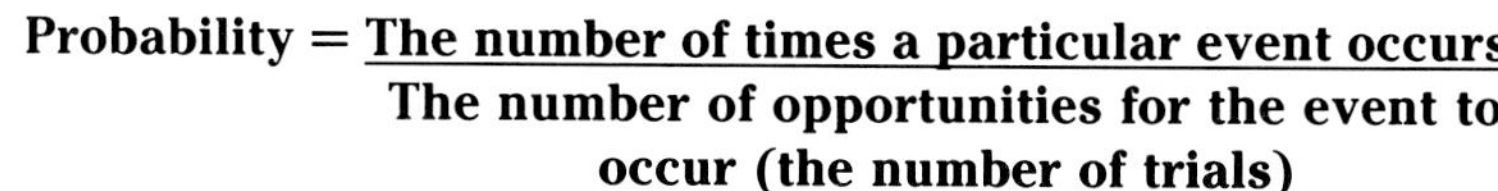

Probability = The number of times a particular event occurs / The number of opportunities for the event to occur (the number of trials)

Consider, for example, the flipping of a coin. When a coin is flipped, one of two possible events can occur: The coin can land heads up or it can land tails up. The probability of the coin coming up heads is 1/2, or 1:1. In other words, you will probably get heads (the particular event) one time out of every two times you flip the coin (the trials). And you will probably get tails one time out of every two times you flip the coin. Therefore, if you were to flip the coin 10 times, the most likely outcome would be 5 heads and 5 tails. However, there is a chance that you would wind up with a different outcome—perhaps 4 heads and 6 tails, or 10 heads and 0 tails.

These different outcomes reveal an important rule of probability: You only get the expected ratio for large numbers of trials. The larger the number of trials, the closer you get to the expected ratios. If you were to flip the coin hundreds of times, your final results would be much closer to 1:1. If you were to flip the coin thousands of times, your final results would be even closer to 1:1. With this in mind, why do you think Mendel worked with thousands of pea plants?

Figure 9–13 *The mathematical concept of probability allows us to calculate the likelihood that a particular event will occur. What is the probability that the next child in this family will be another girl?*

Suppose you flipped a coin and it came up heads ten times in a row. What are the chances of getting heads again on your next flip? Because of all the times the coin came up heads, you might think it is more likely that the coin will now come up tails rather than heads. But this is not the case. There is another important rule of probability: Previous events do not affect future outcomes. Each flip of the coin is a separate, independent event. For each flip of the coin, the probability of getting heads is always 1/2, or 1:1. It does not matter what happened on previous flips of the coin.

The rules of probability apply to genetics as well as to flipping a coin. Expected genetic ratios may not show up when only a few pea plants (or other organisms) are considered. The larger the number of organisms examined, the closer the numbers will get to the expected values. In addition, genetic ratios do not indicate what the outcome of a single event will be. Because previous events do not affect future outcomes, it cannot be assumed that a particular event will occur because it seems overdue. Despite such limitations, genetic ratios are still very useful because they make it possible to predict the most likely outcome for a large number of events.

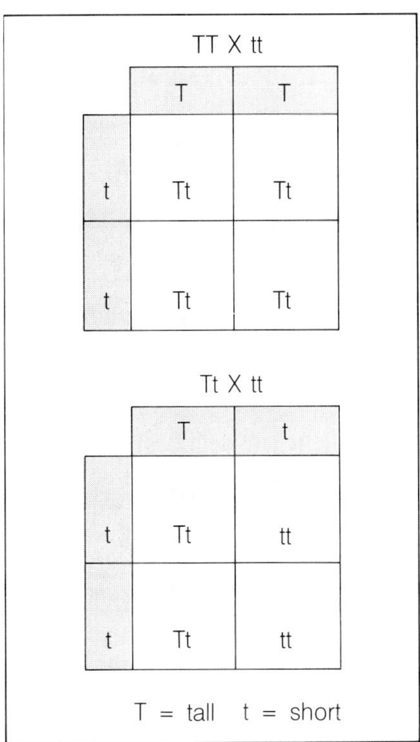

Figure 9–14 *A test cross is used to determine the genotype of an individual showing a dominant trait. If any of the offspring resulting from a test cross has the recessive phenotype, then the unknown parent is heterozygous.*

Using the Punnett Square

The Punnett square is a handy device for analyzing the results of an experimental cross, and it's a good idea to become familiar with its use. Practice using the Punnett square in the one-factor and two-factor genetics problems that follow.

ONE-FACTOR CROSS In pea plants, tall (T) is dominant over short (t). You have a tall plant. Design a cross to see if this plant is homozygous (TT) or heterozygous (Tt).
Solution:

Cross your tall plant with a short plant. The cross of an organism of unknown genotype and a homozygous recessive individual is called a **test cross**. Figure 9–14 shows how a test cross works.

As you can see in the Punnett squares, if any of the offspring resulting from a test cross shows the recessive phenotype, then the unknown parent must be heterozygous.

TWO-FACTOR CROSS In pea plants, green pods (G) are dominant over yellow pods (g), and smooth pods (N) are dominant over constricted pods (n). A plant heterozygous for both traits ($GgNn$) is crossed with a plant that has yellow constricted pods ($ggnn$). What are the probable genotypic and phenotypic ratios for this cross?
Solution:
Genotypic ratio = $4GgNn$:$4Ggnn$:$4ggNn$:$4ggnn$ = 4:4:4:4 = 1:1:1:1
Phenotypic ratio = 4 green smooth:4 green constricted:4 yellow smooth:4 yellow constricted = 4:4:4:4 = 1:1:1:1

Figure 9–15 *This Punnett square illustrates a cross between a pea plant that has the genotype* GgNn *and one that has the genotype* ggnn.

GgNn X ggnn

	GN	Gn	gN	gn
gn	GgNn	Ggnn	ggNn	ggnn
gn	GgNn	Ggnn	ggNn	ggnn
gn	GgNn	Ggnn	ggNn	ggnn
gn	GgNn	Ggnn	ggNn	ggnn

G = green g = yellow
N = smooth n = constricted

SCIENCE, TECHNOLOGY, AND SOCIETY

APPLICATION

Creating a New Breed of Cat

Siamese and Persian cats are two of the most popular kinds of purebred cats. They are also two of the most ancient breeds, with histories that go back several centuries. Siamese cats are slender, with light-colored bodies and dark markings on the face, legs, and tail. Persian cats are stocky and have long luxurious fur. A third breed of cat, the Himalayan, has the distinctive markings of the Siamese and the stocky build and long fur of the Persian. Unlike Siamese and Persian cats, Himalayans have been around for a relatively short time—less than 60 years. And unlike most breeds of cats, the Himalayan is an artificial breed.

The first Himalayan was born in 1935, the product of five years of genetics experiments at Harvard Medical School. The researchers were trying to determine how certain cat traits, such as long fur and Siamese markings, are inherited.

The scientists first crossed Siamese cats with gray, black, or striped Persian cats. The offspring of these crosses all had short hair and were gray, black, or striped in color. When two of the short-haired cats were mated, one of the female offspring had long black fur. This female, when mated to her male parent, produced a long-haired kitten with Siamese markings—the first Himalayan cat.

From their crosses, the scientists determined that short hair was dominant over long hair and that solid or striped colors were dominant over Siamese markings. Although the scientists had created a new type of cat, their role in the new Himalayan breed was over. After all, they had discovered what they had set out to find. Cat breeders in the United States and Britain took over where the scientists had left off. These breeders focused their attention, however, on the effects of other genes, such as those for general body type. By the early 1960s, more than 25 years after the birth of the first Himalayan, the breed was officially recognized by all of the major cat associations in the United States and Britain.

The Himalayan is an artificial breed of cat. It was created during the course of genetics experiments.

9–2 SECTION REVIEW

1. What is probability?
2. What is a test cross?
3. What kind of cross produces a 9:3:3:1 ratio of offspring?
4. A cross of F_1 plants heterozygous for height should produce a ratio of tall to short plants of 3:1. Three seeds from such a cross have been grown and they have produced three tall plants. What are the chances that a fourth seed will produce a short plant?

9–3 Meiosis

Section Objectives

- Describe the process of meiosis.
- Compare meiosis and mitosis.

The principles of genetics described by Mendel require that organisms inherit a single copy of each gene from each of their parents. These two copies are then segregated from each other during the formation of gametes. An obvious way to test Mendel's ideas would be to see if something similar to segregation takes place during the formation of gametes.

But how are gametes formed? In Chapter 8 you learned about mitosis, a process that involves the separation of chromosomes and the formation of new cells. Could gametes be formed by mitosis?

The answer to this question is no. If gametes were formed by mitosis in the common fruit fly, *Drosophila melanogaster*, each gamete would contain 8 chromosomes—as do the other cells of the fly. When sperm and egg fused in the process of fertilization, the first cell of the offspring would contain 16 (or 8 + 8) chromosomes. This is twice the number of chromosomes in the cells of the parents. If the number of chromosomes doubled in each generation, before long the cells would contain an unwieldy number of chromosomes.

Chromosome Number

The 8 chromosomes in a *Drosophila* cell can be divided into two sets: One set contains 4 chromosomes from the male parent and the other set contains 4 chromosomes from the female parent. Each chromosome in the male set has a corresponding chromosome in the female set. These corresponding chromosomes are said to be **homologous**. (The chromosomes themselves are called homologs.) A cell that contains both sets of homologous chromosomes (one set from each parent) is said to be **diploid**.

The diploid number is sometimes represented by the symbol 2N. Thus for *Drosophila* 2N=8. A diploid cell contains two complete sets of chromosomes and two complete sets of genes.

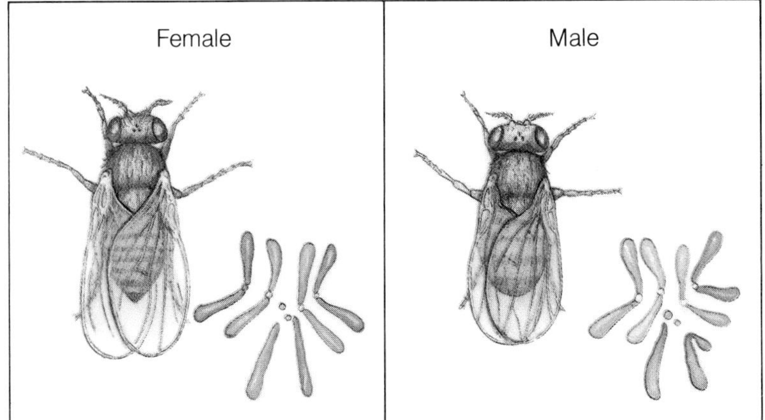

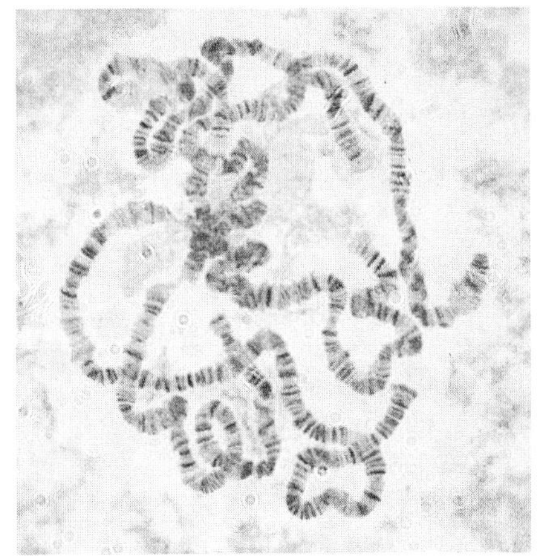

Figure 9–16 *Each body cell in a fruit fly contains 8 chromosomes—4 from the male parent and 4 from the female parent (left). This photograph shows the 4 pairs of giant chromosomes of the fruit fly* Drosophila *(right). These giant chromosomes consist of many chromatids attached in parallel.*

Figure 9–17 *In the process of meiosis, the number of chromosomes per cell is cut in half and homologous chromosomes are separated. Meiosis produces four haploid gamete cells that are genetically different from one another and from the original diploid parent cell.*

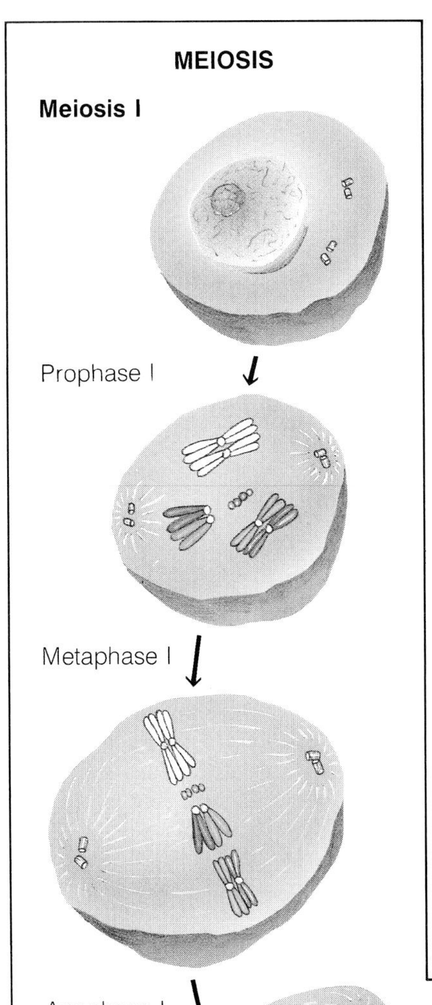

This agrees with Mendel's idea that all of an organism's cells (except the gametes) contain two alleles for a given trait. Mendel's model of segregation implies that gametes, unlike other cells, should contain only a single set of genes because alleles are separated during the process of gamete formation. This is exactly the case. The gametes of organisms that reproduce sexually contain a single set of chromosomes (and genes). Cells that contain a single set of chromosomes are said to be **haploid** and are represented by the symbol N. For *Drosophila*, N=4. In order for gametes to be produced, there must be a process that divides the diploid number of chromosomes in half.

The Phases of Meiosis

Haploid gametes are produced from diploid cells by the process of **meiosis** (migh-OH-sihs). Meiosis is a process of reduction division in which the number of chromosomes per cell is cut in half and the homologous chromosomes that exist in a diploid cell are separated.

In most organisms, meiosis takes place in two stages, known as the first and second meiotic divisions. Do not be confused because the phases of meiosis have the same names as the phases of mitosis. The phases of meiosis are actually very different from the phases of mitosis. We will examine meiosis in an organism with a diploid number of 8 (2N=8). Refer to Figure 9–17 as the process of meiosis is described.

MEIOSIS I In the first stage of meiosis, meiosis I, special cells in the reproductive organs undergo a round of DNA replication. The cells then enter a process of cell division that looks deceptively like mitosis. But it's not.

Recall that in mitosis the 8 chromosomes line up in the center of the cell. At this time, each chromosome contains 2 chromatids, which separate from each other as anaphase begins. But in prophase I of meiosis, each chromosome seeks out its corresponding homologous chromosome to form a special structure called a tetrad. The word tetrad comes from the Greek word *tetra*, which means four. And as you can see in

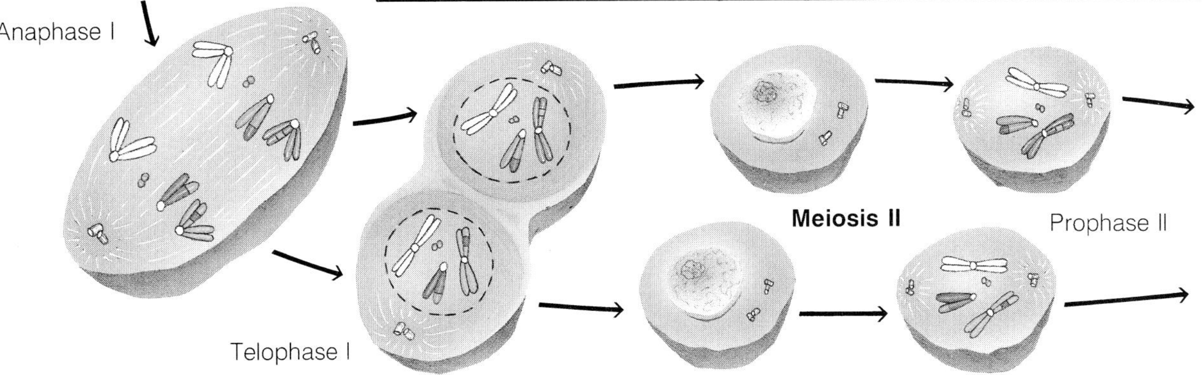

Figure 9–17, there are 4 chromatids in a tetrad. Tetrads, rather than individual chromosomes, line up in the center of the cell during metaphase I of meiosis.

As the homologous chromosomes pair up and form tetrads in meiosis I, they may exchange portions of their chromatids in a process called **crossing-over**. Crossing-over results in the exchange of genes between homologous chromosomes and produces new combinations of genes.

What happens next? The homologous chromosomes separate and two new cells are formed. Although each cell now has 8 chromatids (just as it would after normal mitosis) something is different. Look at Figure 9–17 closely. The two cells no longer have two complete sets of the 4 chromosomes. Instead, the maternal and paternal chromosomes have been shuffled like a deck of cards. The two cells produced by meiosis I have sets of chromosomes (and genes) that are different from each other. These sets are also different from the set in the cell that began the division.

MEIOSIS II The two cells produced by meiosis I now enter meiosis II. Unlike a cell undergoing a second mitotic division, neither cell goes through a round of DNA replication before entering the second meiotic division. Thus each of the cells' chromosomes contains 2 chromatids. During metaphase II of meiosis, 4 chromosomes line up in the center of each cell. In anaphase II, the paired chromatids separate. Each of the four daughter cells produced in meiosis II receives 4 chromatids. The four daughter cells contain the haploid number (N)—4 chromosomes each. The amount of genetic material has been reduced. In addition, the combinations of chromosomes in each gamete have been made at random.

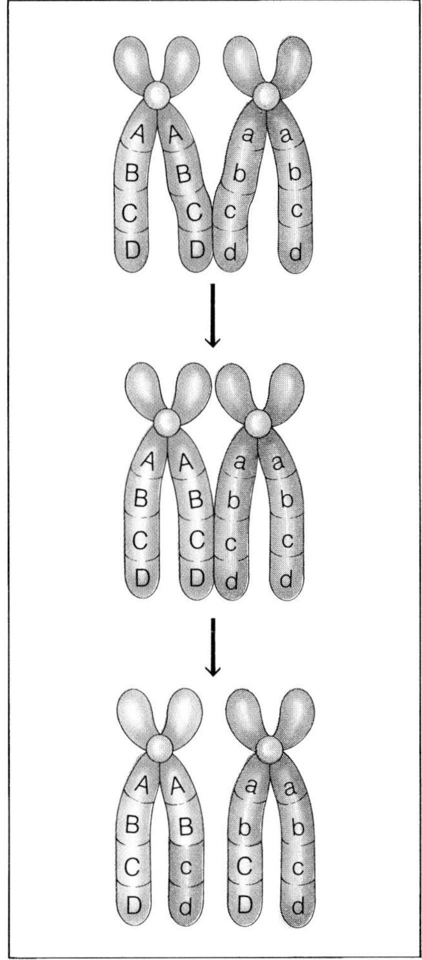

Figure 9–18 *During prophase I of meiosis, homologous chromosomes may exchange portions of their chromatids in a process called crossing-over.*

Meiosis and Genetics

As they pass through meiosis, the chromosomes do all the things that Mendel's ideas predicted structures that carry genes would do. Meiosis I results in segregation and independent assortment. During anaphase I of meiosis, the homologous chromosomes separate and are segregated to

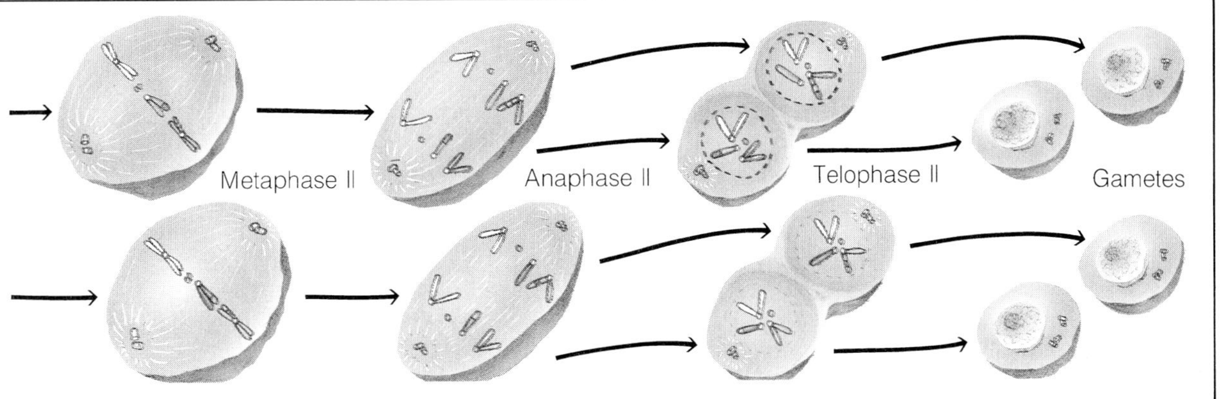

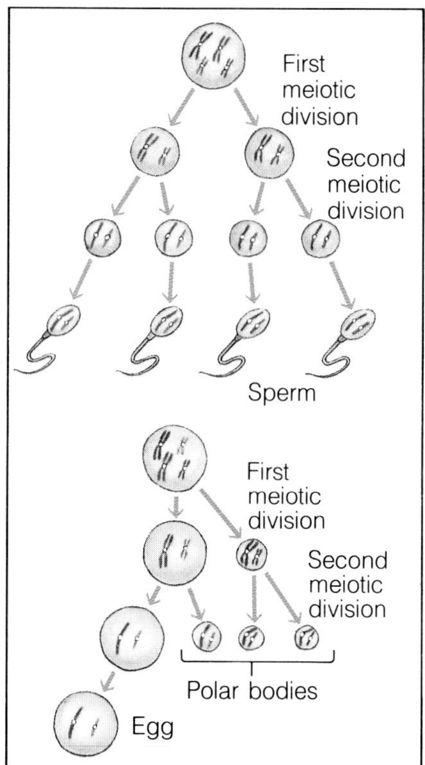

Figure 9–19 *In males, meiosis results in four gametes that are the same size as one another. In females, the four cells produced in meiosis are different sizes—three are small and one is large. The large cell is usually the only one of the four female cells that participates in reproduction.*

different cells. This also segregates the homologous forms of a gene, or alleles, that are located on these chromosomes. This agrees with Mendel's principles. The chromosomes themselves assort independently during meiosis I. The separation of chromosomes during the first meiotic division is completely random. Which cell receives the maternal copy of a chromosome and which cell receives the paternal copy is strictly a matter of chance.

Gamete Formation

In male animals, the haploid gametes produced by meiosis are called sperm. In higher plants, pollen grains contain haploid sperm cells. In female animals, generally only one of the cells produced by meiosis is used for reproduction. This female gamete is called an egg (animals) or ovule (higher plants). In female animals, the cell divisions at the end of meiosis I and meiosis II are uneven, so that the egg or ovule receives most of the cytoplasm. The other three cells produced in the female during meiosis are known as polar bodies and usually do not participate in reproduction.

Comparing Mitosis and Meiosis

In a way, it's too bad that the words mitosis and meiosis sound so similar and have the same names for their phases because the two processes are very different. Mitosis results in the production of two genetically identical cells. A diploid cell that divides by mitosis gives rise to two diploid daughter cells. The daughter cells have sets of chromosomes (and genes) identical to each other and to the original parent cell.

Meiosis, on the other hand, begins with a diploid cell but produces four haploid cells. These cells are genetically different from the diploid cell and from one another. This is because homologous chromosomes are separated during the first meiotic division and because crossing-over results in the production of new gene combinations on the chromosomes.

9–3 SECTION REVIEW

1. What is meiosis?
2. Define diploid and haploid.
3. In which meiotic division does segregation occur?
4. What are the principal differences between mitosis and meiosis?
5. In human cells, 2N=46. How many chromosomes would you expect to find in a sperm cell? In an egg cell? In a white blood cell? Explain your answers.

PROBLEM SOLVING IN BIOLOGY

SOLVING GENETICS PROBLEMS

One-Factor Crosses: Sample Problem

In pea plants, red flowers are dominant over white flowers. A heterozygous red flower is allowed to self-pollinate. What are the probable genotypic and phenotypic ratios in the offspring of this plant?

SOLUTION

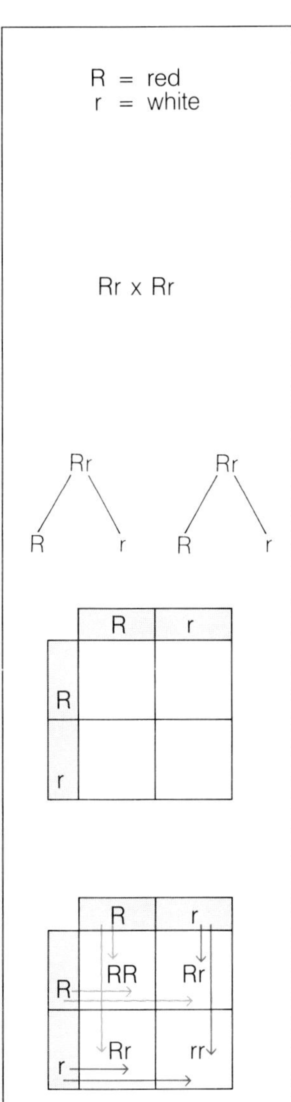

Step 1 **Choose a letter to represent the genes in the cross.**
Use a letter whose capital form does not look too similar to its lowercase form. This will make it easier for you to read your finished Punnett square. Except for that requirement, it is not important which letter you select. In this case, let's use *R* for the dominant red allele and *r* for the recessive white allele.

Step 2 **Write the genotypes of the parents.**
This step is often written as an abbreviation of the cross being studied. The X between the parents' genotypes is read "is crossed with." In this case, *Rr* X *Rr* is read "*Rr* is crossed with *Rr*." Although only one parent is involved in this problem, you must still write it as a cross in which you account for a male parent and a female parent.

Step 3 **Determine the possible gametes (reproductive cells) that the parents can produce.**
Remember that alleles are segregated during the formation of gametes. Each gamete has 1/2 the number of alleles in the parent.

Step 4 **Enter the possible gametes at the top and side of the Punnett square.**

Step 5 **Complete the Punnett square by writing the alleles from the gametes in the appropriate boxes.**
This step represents the process of fertilization. The allele from the gamete above the box and the allele from the gamete to the side of the box are combined inside each of the four boxes. If there is a combination of capital letter and lowercase letter in a box, write the capital letter first. The letters inside the boxes represent the probable genotypes of the offspring resulting from the cross. In this example, 1/4 of the offspring are genotype *RR*, 1/2 are *Rr*, and 1/4 are *rr*.

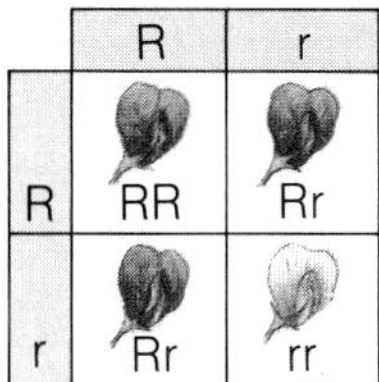

Step 6 **Determine the phenotypes of the offspring.**
Remember that phenotype refers to the physical appearance of an organism. The principle of dominance makes it possible to determine the phenotype that corresponds to each genotype inside the Punnett square. In this example, 3/4 of the offspring have red flowers and 1/4 of the offspring have white flowers.

Genotypic ratio = 1:2:1
Phenotypic ratio = 3:1

Step 7 **Using the results of Steps 5 and 6, answer the problem.**
Usually you will be asked to summarize the results of the cross by providing genotypic and phenotypic ratios. When writing such ratios, the numbers for the dominant genotype(s) or phenotype(s) come first. In this example, 1/4 of the offspring are genotype *RR*, 1/2 (or 2/4) are *Rr*, and 1/4 are *rr*. The genotypic ratio is therefore 1/4:2/4:1/4, or 1:2:1. Three fourths of the offspring have red flowers and 1/4 have white flowers. The phenotypic ratio is therefore 3/4:1/4, or 3:1.

Two-Factor Crosses: Sample Problem

In the fruit fly *Drosophila melanogaster*, wings (*A*) are dominant over a lack of wings (*a*) and red eyes (*E*) are dominant over sepia (brownish) eyes (*e*). A wingless fly that is heterozygous for eye color is crossed with a fly that is heterozygous for both eye color and presence of wings. What are the genotypic and phenotypic ratios for this cross? What fraction of the offspring from this cross will be wingless and have sepia eyes? What fraction will have the genotype *AaEe*?

SOLUTION

A = wings
a = wingless
E = red
e = sepia

Step 1 **Choose letters to represent the genes in the cross.**
In this particular problem, the letters to use are given to you. In the event that they are not, follow the same suggestions for choosing letters stated in Step 1 of the One-Factor Cross.

aaEe x AaEe

Step 2 **Write the genotypes of the parents.**

a a E e — aE ae aE ae

A a E e — AE Ae aE ae

Step 3 **Determine the possible gametes that the parents can produce.**

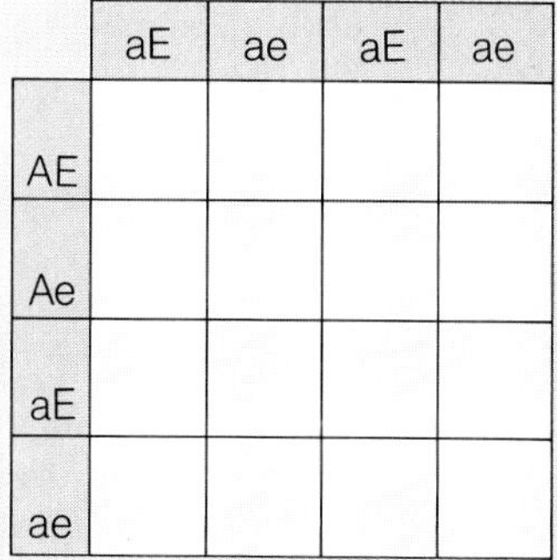

Step 4 **Enter the possible gametes at the top and side of the Punnett square.**

Step 5 **Complete the Punnett square by writing the alleles from the gametes in the appropriate boxes.**

The alleles from the gamete above the box and the alleles from the gamete to the side of the box are combined inside each of the boxes. Write the capital letter first for each pair of alleles. The letters inside each box represent the probable genotypes of the offspring resulting from the cross. In this example, 2/16 of the offspring are *AaEE*, 4/16 are *AaEe*, 2/16 are *Aaee*, 2/16 are *aaEE*, 4/16 are *aaEe*, 2/16 are *aaee*.

	aE	ae	aE	ae
AE	AaEE	AaEe	AaEE	AaEe
Ae	AaEe	Aaee	AaEe	Aaee
aE	aaEE	aaEe	aaEE	aaEe
ae	aaEe	aaee	aaEe	aaee

Step 6 **Determine the phenotypes of the offspring.**

In this example, 6/16 are winged and red-eyed, 2/16 are winged and sepia-eyed, 6/16 are wingless and red-eyed, 2/16 are wingless and sepia-eyed.

	aE	ae	aE	ae
AE	AaEE	AaEe	AaEE	AaEe
Ae	AaEe	Aaee	AaEe	Aaee
aE	aaEE	aaEe	aaEE	aaEe
ae	aaEe	aaee	aaEe	aaee

Step 7 **Using the results of Steps 5 and 6, answer the problem.**

Note that in this example, as in many of the genetics problems you will encounter, you are asked for more than just the ratios resulting from the cross. This is one reason why it is important to read genetics problems carefully. In this example, the genotypic ratio is 2/16:4/16:2/16:2/16:4/16:2/16 = 2:4:2:2:4:2 = 1:2:1:1:2:1. The phenotypic ratio is 6/16:2/16:6/16:2/16 = 6:2:6:2 = 3:1:3:1. And 4/16, or 1/4, of the offspring have the genotype *AaEe*.

One-Factor Crosses: Practice Problems

1. Pollen from a pea plant with white flowers is used to fertilize the ovules (female gametes) of a heterozygous plant. What are the possible phenotypes in the offspring from this cross?
2. You have a pea plant with red flowers. Design a cross to determine if this plant is homozygous or heterozygous. Use a Punnett square to show all possible crosses.

Two-Factor Crosses: Practice Problems

1. A purebred wingless red-eyed fruit fly is crossed with a purebred winged sepia-eyed fruit fly to produce F_1 flies. The F_1 flies are crossed to produce F_2 flies. What is the phenotypic ratio of the F_2 flies?
2. You have a winged red-eyed fruit fly. Design a cross to determine whether the fly is heterozygous for either or both traits. Use a Punnett square to show all possible crosses.

SIMULATING A ONE-FACTOR CROSS

PROBLEM

How is probability applied to genetics?

MATERIALS *(per student)*

2 labeled game markers
paper cup

PROCEDURE

1. On a separate sheet of paper, prepare a completed data table similar to the one below.
2. In pea plants, yellow seeds (*A*) are dominant over green seeds (*a*). Using a Punnett square, determine the probable color of the seeds produced by pea plants whose parents are heterozygous (*Aa*) for the seed-color trait. Record the expected genotypic and phenotypic ratios in the appropriate places in your data table.
3. Each labeled marker represents the alleles in the heterozygous plant. Tossing the labeled markers together represents the crossing of heterozygous plants.
4. Put the 2 labeled markers into the cup. Holding one hand over the mouth of the cup, shake the cup to toss the markers. Empty the cup onto your desk or laboratory table. Record the results of each of 10 tosses by making a tally mark in the appropriate box in your data table.
5. Toss the markers 100 times and record the results in your data table.
6. One student in the class will compile the data for 100 tosses by 10 students and report the results. Record this information.
7. Count the tally marks for each genotype in each series of tosses (10, 100, 1000). Record these totals in the appropriate box.
8. Determine the total number of seeds with the yellow phenotype for each series of tosses.
9. Using the data, calculate the genotypic and phenotypic ratios for each series of tosses. This is done by dividing each number in the ratio by the ratio's smallest number and rounding off to the nearest tenth's place. For example, suppose you obtained 23 *AA*, 51 *Aa*, and 26 *aa* for a series of 100 tosses. This gives you the ratio 1:2.2:1.1 (23/23 = 1, 51/23 = 2.2, 26/23 = 1.1)

OBSERVATIONS

1. Which genotype was obtained most often?
2. What were your expected genotypic and phenotypic ratios?
3. What were your genotypic and phenotypic ratios for a series of 10 tosses? 100 tosses? 1000 tosses?

ANALYSIS AND CONCLUSIONS

1. How do the experimental ratios compare with the expected ratios?
2. Which series of tosses produced the experimental ratios that were closest to the expected ratios? Explain your results.
3. How does probability apply to the results of your experiment? How does probability apply to the study of genetics?

Offspring Phenotype	Yellow				Green		Total Number of Yellow Seeds (*AA* + *Aa*)	Expected Genotypic Ratio	Expected Phenotypic Ratio	Experimental Genotypic Ratio	Experimental Phenotypic Ratio
Offspring Genotype	*AA*		*Aa*		*aa*						
	Tally	Total	Tally	Total	Tally	Total					
10 Tosses											
100 Tosses											
1000 Tosses											

STUDENT STUDY GUIDE

SUMMARIZING THE CONCEPTS

The key concepts in each section of this chapter are listed below to help you review the chapter content. Make sure you understand each concept and its relationship to other concepts and to the theme of this chapter.

9–1 The Work of Gregor Mendel

- Mendel's genetic experiments involved the mathematical analysis of the offspring resulting from crosses between pea plants.
- Genes are individual factors that control heredity.
- The different forms of a gene are called alleles. Some alleles are dominant; others are recessive.
- Because of dominance, the effects of the recessive gene are not observed when the dominant gene is present.
- Alleles for the same trait are separated during the process of segregation.
- The genes for different traits may undergo independent assortment.
- An organism's physical characteristics, which reflect its genetic makeup, are its phenotype. An organism's genetic makeup is its genotype.
- Organisms that have two identical alleles for a particular trait are said to be homozygous, or purebred, for that trait. Organisms that have two different alleles for the same trait are said to be heterozygous, or hybrid, for that trait.

9–2 Applying Mendel's Principles

- Probability is the likelihood that a particular event will occur. The rules of probability apply to genetics.
- Genetics problems can be solved by using a Punnett square.

9–3 Meiosis

- A cell that contains both sets of homologous chromosomes is said to be diploid (2N). A cell that contains a single set of chromosomes is said to be haploid (N).
- Meiosis is a form of cell division that results in the formation of haploid gametes. The cells formed in meiosis have different sets of chromosomes from one another and from the diploid mother cell.

REVIEWING KEY TERMS

Vocabulary terms are important to your understanding of biology. The key terms listed below are those you should be especially familiar with. Review these terms and their meanings. Then use each term in a complete sentence. If you are not sure of a term's meaning, return to the appropriate section and review its definition.

9–1 The Work of Gregor Mendel
heredity
genetics
self-pollination
cross-pollination
purebred
trait
hybrid
gene
allele
dominance
dominant
recessive
segregation
Punnett square
gamete
phenotype
genotype
homozygous
heterozygous
independent assortment

9–2 Applying Mendel's Principles
probability
test cross

9–3 Meiosis
homologous
diploid
haploid
meiosis
crossing-over

CHAPTER REVIEW

CONTENT REVIEW

Multiple Choice

Choose the letter of the answer that best completes each statement.

1. Alleles for the same trait are separated from each other during the process of
   a. mitosis. c. cross-pollination.
   b. meiosis II. d. segregation.
2. Organisms that have two identical genes for a particular trait are said to be
   a. haploid. c. heterozygous.
   b. homozygous. d. diploid.
3. Pea plants usually produce seeds through
   a. self-pollination. c. mitosis.
   b. cross-pollination. d. meiosis.
4. Because body cells contain two sets of chromosomes, they are
   a. homozygous. c. haploid.
   b. heterozygous. d. diploid.
5. An organism's physical appearance is its
   a. genotype. c. heredity.
   b. phenotype. d. homolog.
6. What is the exchange of genes between homologous chromosomes called?
   a. tetrad c. independent assortment
   b. segregation d. crossing-over
7. The phenotypic ratio in the offspring resulting from the cross $Tt \times Tt$ is
   a. 1:2:1. c. 1:1.
   b. 3:1. d. 9:3:3:1.
8. Some F_2 individuals show the recessive character because of
   a. dominance. c. crossing-over.
   b. segregation. d. independent assortment.

True or False

Determine whether each statement is true or false. If it is true, write "true." If it is false, change the underlined word or words to make the statement true.

1. The fertilization of a plant's ovules (egg cells) by the pollen of another plant is called <u>self-pollination</u>.
2. If allowed to self-pollinate, <u>hybrid</u> peas will produce offspring exactly like themselves.
3. Meiosis results in <u>haploid</u> cells.
4. The effects of a <u>recessive</u> allele are seen in a heterozygous organism.
5. The offspring produced by crossing F_1 plants are known as the <u>P generation</u>.
6. Reproductive cells are also called <u>gametes</u>.
7. Homologous chromosomes pair up during the first stage of <u>mitosis</u>.
8. Expected genetic ratios show up only when <u>small</u> numbers of offspring are considered.

Word Relationships

An analogy is a relationship between two pairs of words or phrases generally written in the following manner: a:b::c:d. The symbol : is read "is to," and the symbol :: is read "as." For example, cat:animal::rose:plant is read "cat is to animal as rose is to plant."

In the analogies that follow, a word or phrase is missing. Complete each analogy by providing the missing word or phrase.

1. mitosis:2N::meiosis: ______
2. allele:gene::green seeds:______
3. purebred:hybrid::homozygous:______
4. white fur:*ff*::phenotype:______
5. egg:ovule::sperm:______
6. *A*:dominant::*a*:______

CONCEPT MASTERY

Use your understanding of the concepts developed in the chapter to answer each of the following in a brief paragraph.

1. Why is Gregor Mendel sometimes called the "father of genetics"?
2. Describe the process of meiosis.
3. List the four basic principles of genetics that Mendel discovered in his experiments. Briefly describe each of these principles.
4. What is probability? How does probability relate to genetics?
5. How do the cellular events in meiosis account for Mendel's observations?

CRITICAL AND CREATIVE THINKING

Discuss each of the following in a brief paragraph.

1. **Applying concepts** In dogs, short hair is dominant over long hair. Two short-haired dogs are the parents of a litter of eight puppies. Six puppies have short hair and two have long hair. What are the genotypes of the parents?
2. **Applying concepts** Purebred tall plants with round seeds are crossed with purebred short plants with wrinkled seeds. Some of the offspring are then crossed with an unknown plant. The offspring from this second cross are 1/2 tall round and 1/2 tall wrinkled. What are the genotype and phenotype of the unknown plant?
3. **Making inferences** Explain why horse breeders will pay a lot of money to breed one of their horses to a horse that has won the Kentucky Derby.
4. **Making calculations** The probability of two independent events occurring simultaneously is the product of each of their probabilities. For example, if you flip two coins, the chance that both will come up heads is 1/4 (= 1/2 x 1/2). Suppose that you have ten Ping-Pong balls in a jar, each marked with a numeral from 0 to 9. If you mix them thoroughly and take out one, the chances are 1 in 10 (1/10) that you will get a particular numeral. Now suppose you have six such jars. What is your chance of drawing the number 531963?
5. **Making generalizations** In guinea pigs, a rough coat (*R*) is dominant over a smooth coat (*r*). A heterozygous guinea pig (*Rr*) and a homozygous recessive guinea pig (*rr*) have a total of nine offspring. Each has a smooth coat. Explain these results.

	R	r
r	Rr	rr
r	Rr	rr

6. **Designing an experiment** In sheep, white wool (*A*) is dominant over black wool (*a*). How would you determine the genotype of a white ram, or male sheep?
7. **Using the writing process** In the 1950s, a television series presented an imaginary voyage back in time. Each week a famous person in history was visited. The show was designed to provide insight into the work of the person being interviewed and the time in which he or she lived. You are in charge of producing such a program for today's television viewers. The first person you will visit is Gregor Mendel. Write a script for this program.

CHAPTER 10

Genes and Chromosomes

White tigers have inherited an altered gene for coat color. Because their cells cannot make orange pigment, white tigers are white where normal tigers are orange. Studies of the fruit fly *Drosophila* (inset) have given geneticists insight into how normal genes and altered genes regulate the inheritance of traits.

In the preceding chapters we set the stage for a detailed discussion of genes and their activities. We have seen that DNA is the genetic material. We know how the genetic code is written into DNA and how that code is translated into protein. We understand many of the things that proteins can do, and we appreciate their importance. We have recently learned how the science of genetics was developed, how the location of genes can be determined, how the chromosome is put together, and the rules that govern the passage of genetic information from one generation to the next. With all of these things behind us, we are like pilots with all of our ground training and study completed. Now we will begin to fly. We will see how the gene actually works!

CHAPTER OUTLINE

10–1 The Chromosome Theory of Heredity

Section Objectives

- Relate genes to chromosomes.
- Explain how gene linkage and crossing-over affect heredity.
- Describe the patterns of inheritance for sex-linked traits.

History records Gregor Mendel as the founder of the science of genetics. Yet Mendel's work was incomplete because he never asked an important question that was the logical outcome of his work: Where in the cell are the factors that control heredity? In other words, where are the genes?

We can hardly blame Mendel for this shortcoming. Even if he had been inclined to ask, he would not have been able to search for genes among the bewildering variety of structures and components within cells. Shortly after completing his genetic experiments, Mendel was promoted to abbot, or head of the monastery. His administrative duties kept him too busy to continue his experiments. Fortunately, other scientists who had the time had begun to study cell structures and the processes of cell division. Their observations would prove to have enormous impact on the study of heredity.

Genes and Chromosomes

By the time Mendel's work was rediscovered in 1900, cell biologists had discovered most of the major structures within cells. They had also recorded the sequences of events that

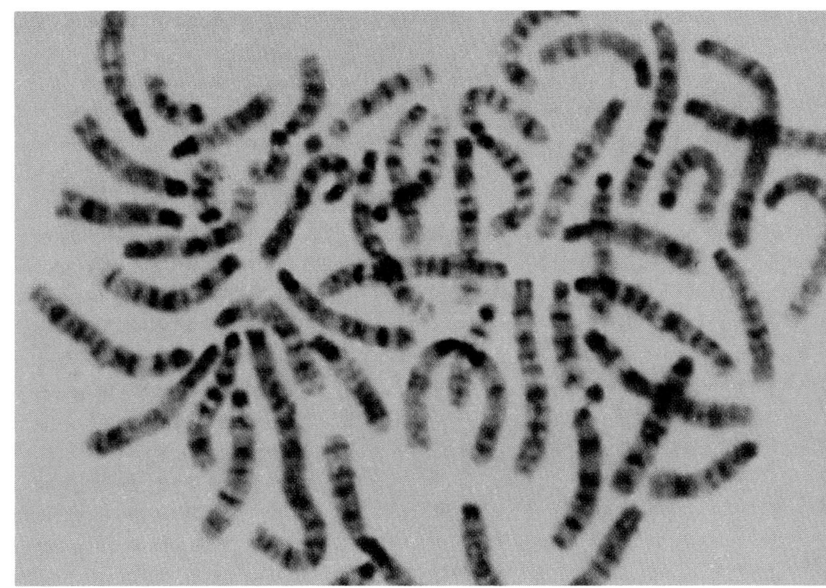

Figure 10–1 *These chromosomes are from a mouse cell. Chromosomes, which are located in the nucleus of a cell, are precisely separated during cell division—an indication that they contain something extremely critical to the cell.*

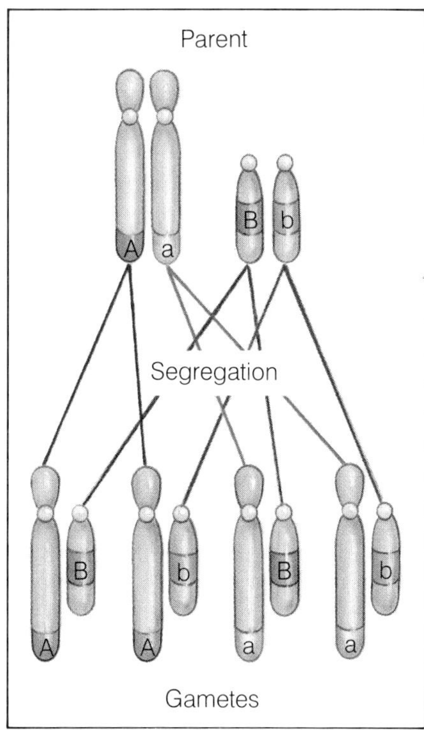

Figure 10–2 *According to Mendel's hypothesis, the two factors for each trait are segregated during gamete formation. Thus gametes have only one factor for each trait. This hypothesis is supported by the observations that homologous chromosomes are separated during meiosis and that gametes contain only one of the chromosomes of each homologous pair.*

occur during mitosis and meiosis. With this information, it seemed logical that the nucleus was the place for genes to be located. In addition to its large size and central location (which make it look important), the nucleus contains chromosomes—structures that behave in complex and interesting ways during cell divisions. The careful and precise mechanism by which chromosomes are separated during mitosis clearly suggests that they are structures vital to the cell. Could this be because they carry the cell's genes?

Further evidence that genes are located on chromosomes is the behavior of chromosomes during meiosis, the process by which reproductive cells are formed. In meiosis, diploid cells, which have 2 copies of each chromosome, divide to form haploid cells, which have 1 copy of each chromosome. This fits in with Mendel's hypothesis that an organism has 2 factors for each trait and that reproductive cells have only 1 factor for each trait. During the first part of meiosis, homologous chromosomes are separated from each other. This fits in with Mendel's hypothesis that the 2 factors for each trait are segregated, or separated, during the formation of gametes.

Walter Sutton, a young graduate student at Columbia University, arrived at the answer to the question of gene location in 1902. **The factors (genes) described by Mendel are located on chromosomes.** The tools with which Sutton made this discovery were a microscope—which he used to observe chromosomes during sperm formation in grasshoppers—and his own imagination, in which he compared the chromosomes to Mendel's factors. When the numbers and movements of chromosomes were analyzed, it was clear to Sutton that chromosomes behaved exactly as one would expect of the carriers of genetic information.

Sutton's **chromosome theory of heredity** states that genes are located on the chromosomes and each gene occupies a specific place on a chromosome. A gene may exist in several forms, or alleles, and each chromosome contains one allele for each gene.

Gene Linkage

The fact that genes are located on chromosomes is important. Genes on a chromosome are linked together. This means that they are inherited together. In other words, **linked genes** do not undergo independent assortment. Recall Mendel's experiment in which the genes for seed color and seed shape were shown to assort independently. Unlike linked genes, genes that are located on separate chromosomes do, in fact, assort independently during meiosis.

One of the earliest examples of linked genes was discovered in the first part of this century by the American geneticist Thomas Hunt Morgan. Morgan studied the tiny fruit fly, *Drosophila melanogaster,* which can produce a new generation every four weeks. This short generation time makes *Drosophila* an ideal organism to study because traits in succeeding generations can be observed relatively quickly.

THE EFFECTS OF GENE LINKAGE Morgan crossed purebred flies that had gray bodies and normal wings with purebred flies that had black bodies and small wings. Because gray (*G*) is dominant over black (*g*), and normal wings (*W*) are dominant over small wings (*w*), all of the F_1 flies should have been gray with normal wings (genotype *GgWw*). That is exactly what Morgan observed.

However, when the F_1 flies (*GgWw*) were crossed with black small-winged flies (*ggww*), Morgan did not observe the expected results. If the principle of independent assortment were true for the *GgWw* X *ggww* cross, Morgan would have observed 25 percent (1/4) gray normal-winged, 25 percent (1/4) black small-winged, 25 percent (1/4) gray small-winged, and 25 percent (1/4) black normal-winged. Instead, Morgan obtained very different results for the cross.

As you can see in Figure 10–4, Morgan's actual results differed significantly from those predicted. Most gray-bodied flies had normal wings, and most black-bodied flies had small wings. These results indicated that the gene for body color and the gene for wing size were somehow connected, or linked. Morgan concluded that the two genes were linked by a physical bond in such a way that they could not assort independently.

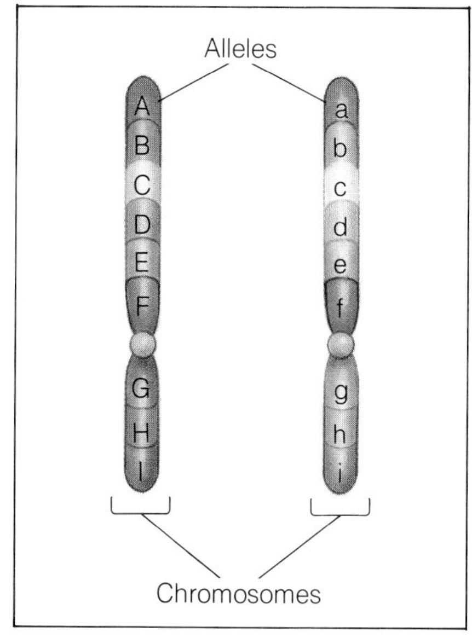

Figure 10–3 *According to Sutton's chromosome theory of heredity, genes are located on the chromosomes. Homologous chromosomes have alleles for the same traits. These alleles may be the same on both homologous chromosomes or they may be different.*

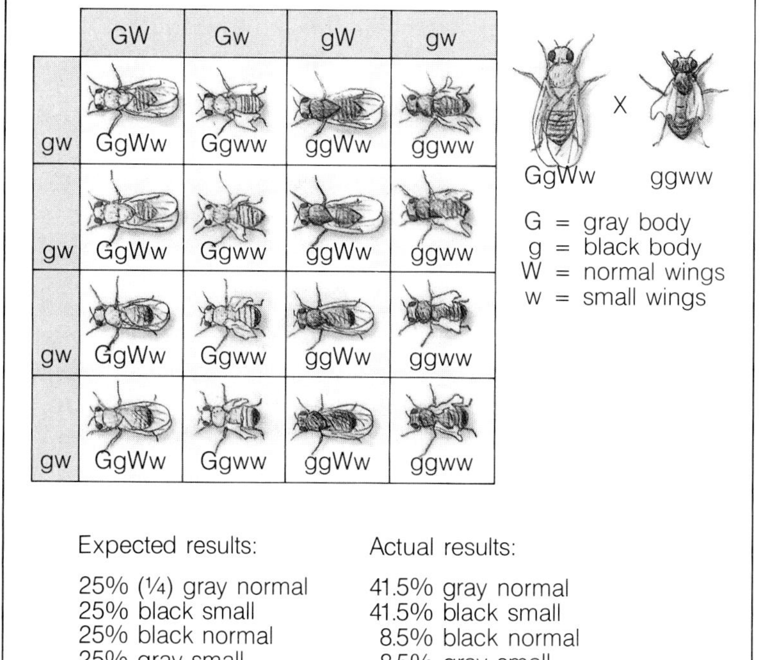

Figure 10–4 *If the principle of independent assortment were true for the genes for body color and wing size in the fruit fly* Drosophila, *the offspring of the cross* GgWw × ggww *would have a 1:1:1:1 phenotypic ratio. Because the actual results did not resemble the expected results, Morgan concluded that the genes for body color and wing size were linked.*

Figure 10–5 *A cobra has 38 chromosomes. How many linkage groups would this make?*

Figure 10–6 *During prophase I of meiosis, homologous chromosomes may exchange sections of their chromatids in a process called crossing-over.*

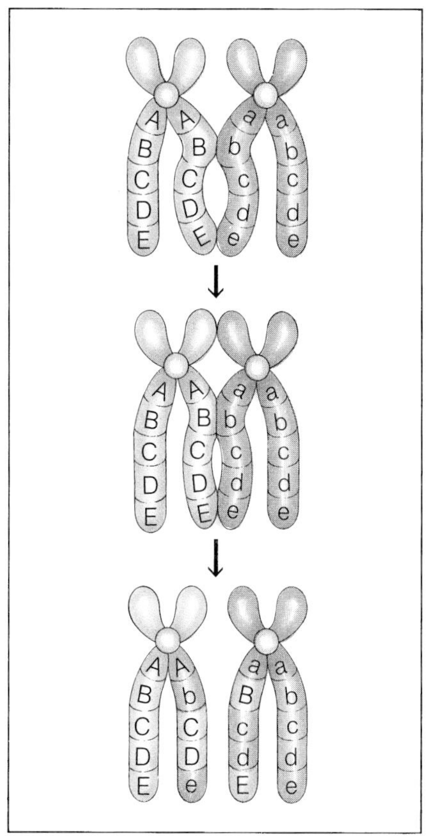

LINKAGE GROUPS As Morgan and his associates studied more and more genes, they found that the genes fell into distinct **linkage groups**, or "packages" of genes that always tended to be inherited together. The linkage groups themselves assorted independently, but all the genes on one group were inherited together. The linkage groups, of course, were chromosomes. Because homologous chromosomes contain the same genes, there is one linkage group for every homologous pair of chromosomes. *Drosophila* has four linkage groups. It also has four pairs of chromosomes. Corn has ten linkage groups and ten pairs of chromosomes.

Crossing-Over

Although the idea of linkage groups explains some of the results of the fruit fly crosses, it does not provide a complete explanation. Look at the results of the test cross between the *GgWw* and *ggww* flies again. Although 83 percent (41.5% + 41.5% = 83%) of the flies have gene combinations like their parents, 17 percent have new combinations. The 17 percent are, in the language of geneticists, **recombinants**—individuals with new combinations of genes.

If the genes for body color and wing size are linked, why aren't they linked all the time? Morgan and his associate, Alfred Sturtevant, proposed that the linkages could be broken some of the time. If two homologous chromosomes were positioned side by side, sections of the two chromosomes might cross, break, and reattach. As you can see in Figure 10–6, this process would rearrange the genes on the chromosome and produce new linkage groups. Morgan and Sturtevant called this hypothetical process crossing-over and suggested that it might be the reason for the recombinants in the offspring of the *Drosophila* test cross.

Crossing-over does indeed take place. It occurs during the first meiotic division, when homologous chromosomes are paired. Crossing-over produces new combinations of alleles on each chromosome and thus increases genetic variety.

Gene Mapping

Sturtevant further reasoned that crossing-over occurs at random along the linkage groups, and the distance between two genes determines how often crossing-over occurs between them. If two genes are close together, then crossing-over between them is rare. However, if two genes are far apart, then crossing-over between them is more common. Knowing the frequency with which crossing-over between two genes occurs makes it possible to map the positions of genes on a chromosome. This is precisely what Sturtevant tried to do with the genes in *Drosophila*'s linkage groups. And by 1915, just two years after he had begun, Sturtevant had mapped 85 genes in *Drosophila.*

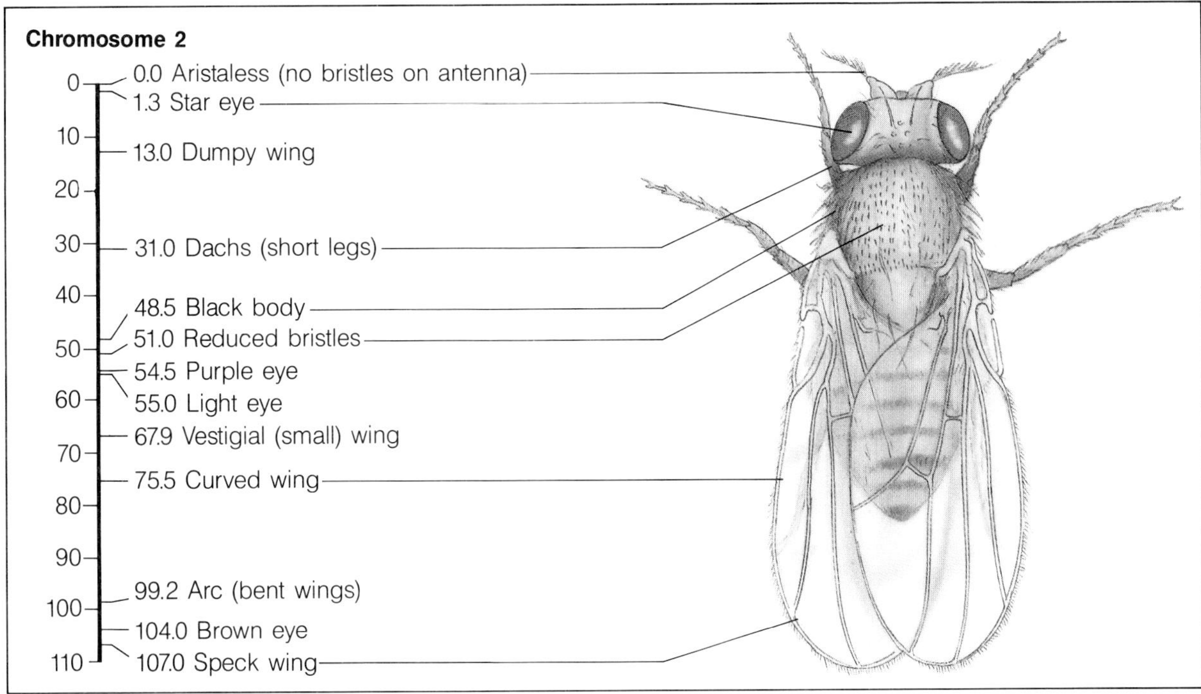

Figure 10–7 Knowing the frequency with which crossing-over occurs between genes makes it possible to map the positions of genes on chromosomes.

Morgan and Sturtevant were correct in their ideas about linkage groups, crossing-over, and the formation of gene maps. Today we have detailed maps of *Drosophila* that pinpoint the locations of more than 1500 different genes.

Sex Linkage

There is an exception to the rule that every chromosome has a corresponding homologous chromosome. This exception was discovered in 1905 by American biologist Nettie Stevens. She noticed that the cells of the female mealworm contain "20 large chromosomes, while those of the male contain 19 large ones and 1 small one." One of the pairs of chromosomes in the male mealworm is not, in the strictest sense of the term, homologous. The 2 chromosomes in the pair have very different shapes. Stevens found the same situation in *Drosophila.* The cells of the female *Drosophila* contain 8 chromosomes that can be arranged in 4 pairs of 2. The cells of the male, however, contain 3 sets of chromosomes that pair up nicely and 2 remaining chromosomes that do not match. One chromosome looks like a member of a pair of chromosomes found in the female, but the other looks completely different. It is small, shaped like a hook, and in no way similar to any of the other 7 chromosomes.

These seemingly mismatched chromosomes are the **sex chromosomes**. The other chromosomes, which are the same in both males and females, are called **autosomes**. The female *Drosophila* has two matching sex chromosomes—**X chromosomes**. The male has two dissimilar sex chromosomes—one X

Figure 10–8 A female fruit fly has 2 matching sex chromosomes—X chromosomes. A male fruit fly has sex chromosomes that do not match—1 X chromosome and 1 Y chromosome.

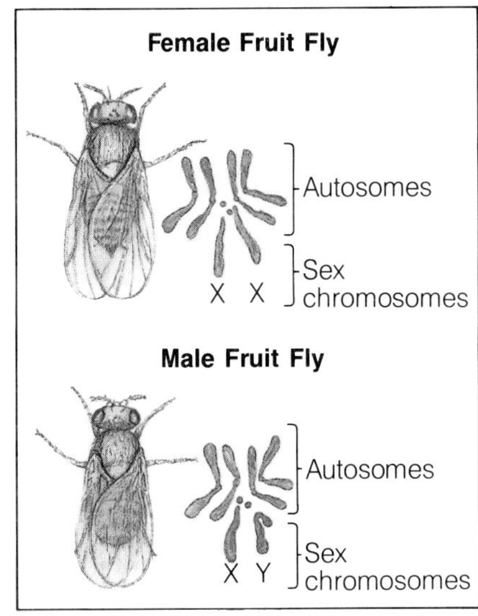

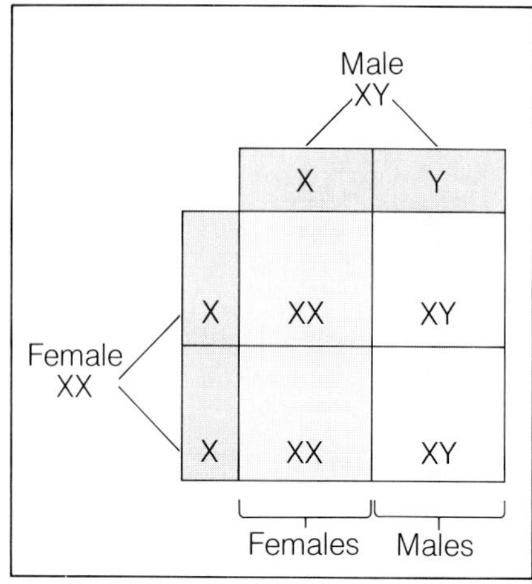

Figure 10–9 In animals such as fruit flies and humans, the sex chromosomes in the male's gametes usually determine the sex of the offspring.

Figure 10–10 Morgan discovered the first sex-linked gene in experiments with the fruit fly Drosophila. *The recessive allele, symbolized as* X^r, *causes white eyes in males—genotype* X^rY.

chromosome and one **Y chromosome**. It is the Y chromosome that is small and hook-shaped. If we consider just sex chromosomes, we can refer to the male as XY and the female as XX.

SEX DETERMINATION When female gametes are produced, meiosis separates one of the X chromosomes into each egg cell. In the male, meiosis separates the X and Y chromosomes so that 50 percent of the sperm cells carry a Y chromosome and 50 percent carry an X chromosome. When a Y sperm fertilizes an egg, a male fly (XY) is produced. When an X sperm fertilizes an egg, a female fly (XX) is produced. In a sense, the male is responsible for the sex of its offspring.

Many animals, including humans, follow the same system. We have 22 pairs of autosomes and 1 pair of sex chromosomes: XX in females and XY in males. Because about 50 percent of male sperm have the X chromosome and about 50 percent have the Y, the ratio of males to females is about 50:50, or 1:1.

GENES ON SEX CHROMOSOMES In addition to determining the sex of an individual, the sex chromosomes carry genes that affect other traits. A gene located on one of the sex chromosomes is said to be **sex-linked**. Morgan discovered the first sex-linked gene in his work with *Drosophila.*

Morgan crossed a group of white-eyed male flies with a group of red-eyed female flies. The allele for red eyes (*R*) is dominant over the allele for white eyes (*r*). Just as you might have expected, the hybrid flies of the F_1 generation all had red eyes. See Figure 10–10. Morgan allowed the F_1 flies to interbreed and produce a new generation of flies (the F_2 generation). Mendelian genetics predicts a 3 to 1 ratio of red-eyed flies to white-eyed flies, and that was exactly the ratio Morgan

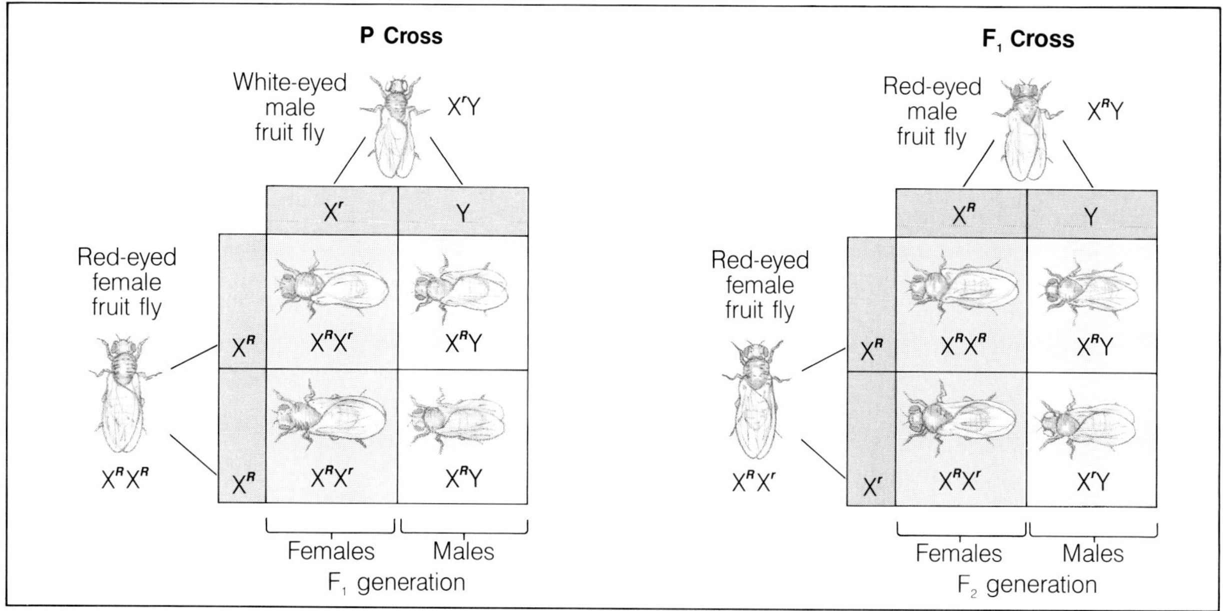

obtained. But Morgan noticed something strange about the F_2 flies. All of the white-eyed flies were male! There was not a single white-eyed female in the bunch.

Why should half of the males but none of the females have white eyes? Could it be that the gene for eye color was on one of the sex chromosomes?

Morgan realized that he could account for his results if the gene for eye color was on the X chromosome. Refer to the Punnett square in Figure 10–10 as you take a closer look at how the F_2 generation is formed.

The female flies produce two kinds of egg cells. One kind of egg cell has the *R* allele on its X chromosome (we can call those egg cells X^R); the other kind of egg cell has the *r* allele on its X chromosome (X^r). The male flies make two kinds of sperm cells: One kind of sperm cell has the X chromosome and the other kind of sperm cell has the Y chromosome. The X chromosome has the *R* allele (X^R) on it. The Y chromosome, however, has neither the *r* nor the *R* allele on it.

As you can see from the Punnett square, only one combination of chromosomes will produce a white-eyed fly—X^rY. And every fly with that combination of chromosomes is male.

Morgan tested his hypothesis that the gene for eye color was sex-linked in a famous experiment. He crossed the F_2 white-eyed males (X^rY) with F_1 (X^RX^r) females. The Punnett square in Figure 10–11 shows the probable results of the cross if, and only if, the gene for eye color is indeed on the X chromosome. According to the Punnett square, 1/2 of the offspring should have red eyes and 1/2 should have white eyes. In addition, the male offspring should be 1/2 red-eyed and 1/2 white-eyed. And the female offspring should also be 1/2 red-eyed and 1/2 white-eyed. Such results were exactly what Morgan obtained. He had confirmed his idea that the gene for eye color was sex-linked.

Sex-linked genes are not only found in *Drosophila*. They are important in humans as well. As you will see in Chapter 11, several important human genes are located on the X chromosome. Such genes include the genes for color vision and blood clotting. As with the eye color gene in *Drosophila*, the effects of recessive alleles tend to show up more frequently in males than in females.

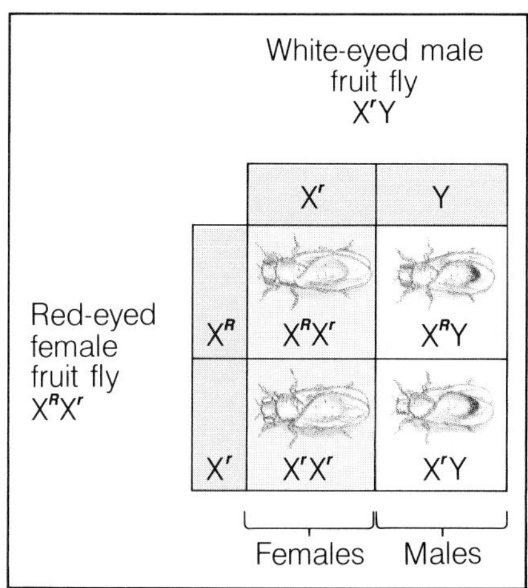

Figure 10–11 *The sex-linked* X^r *allele causes white eyes in females that have a "double dose" of the allele—genotype* X^rX^r. *White-eyed females inherit one* X^r *allele from their male parent (who must be* X^rY*) and one from their female parent (who must be either* X^RX^r *or* X^rX^r*).*

10–1 SECTION REVIEW

1. How are genes related to chromosomes?
2. How does crossing-over make genetic mapping possible?
3. What are sex chromosomes? Autosomes?
4. Why are the effects of recessive sex-linked alleles seen more often in males than in females?

10–2 Mutations

Section Objectives

- Describe different kinds of mutations.
- Explain how mutations can affect heredity.

As you will recall from Chapter 7, the processes involved in duplicating genetic information and transmitting it to the next generation are complex and precise. Although mistakes are rare, they do occur. These mistakes are called **mutations,** from a Latin word that means change. Not all mutations are harmful. Many mutations either have no effect or cause slight, harmless changes. And once in a while a mutation may be beneficial to an organism.

Mutations may occur in any cell. Mutations that affect the reproductive cells, or germ cells, are called germ mutations. The variant characters studied in genetics (such as white eyes in *Drosophila* or wrinkled seeds in pea plants) are the result of germ mutations. Mutations that affect the other cells of the body are called somatic (from the Greek word *soma,* which means body) mutations. Because they do not affect the reproductive cells, somatic mutations are not inheritable. Many cancers are caused by somatic mutations. Both somatic and germ mutations can occur at two levels—the level of chromosomes and the level of genes. **Chromosomal mutations involve segments of chromosomes, whole chromosomes, and even entire sets of chromosomes. Gene mutations involve individual genes.**

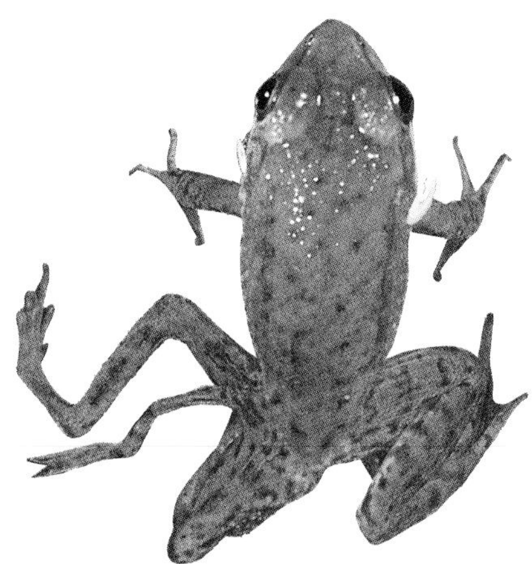

Figure 10–12 *Mutations in genes that regulate development resulted in extra hind legs on this frog.*

Chromosomal Mutations

Whenever a **chromosomal mutation** occurs, there is a change in the number or structure of chromosomes. There are four types of chromosomal mutations that involve a change in the structure of a chromosome: deletions, duplications, inversions, and translocations. A deletion involves the loss of part of a chromosome.

The opposite of a deletion is a duplication, in which a segment of a chromosome is repeated.

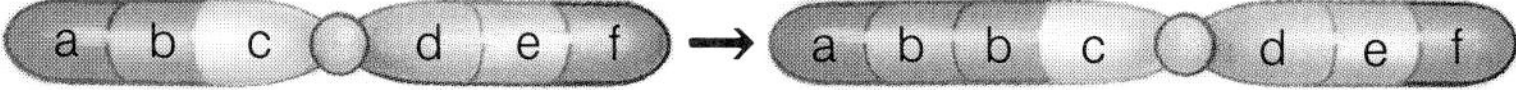

When part of a chromosome becomes oriented in the reverse of its usual direction, the result is an inversion.

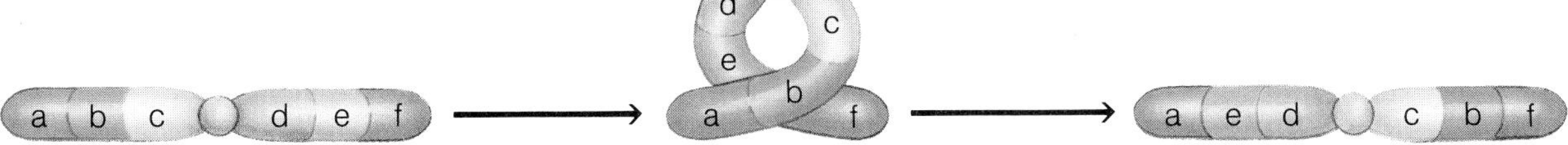

A translocation occurs when part of one chromosome breaks off and attaches to another, nonhomologous chromosome. In most cases, nonhomologous chromosomes exchange segments, so that two translocations occur at the same time.

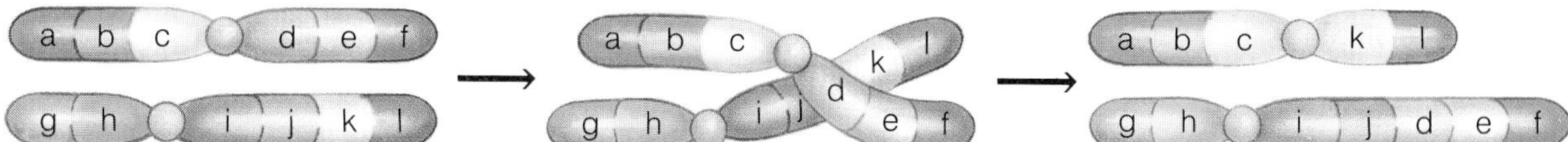

Chromosomal mutations that involve whole chromosomes or complete sets of chromosomes result from a process known as **nondisjunction**. Nondisjunction is the failure of homologous chromosomes to separate normally during meiosis. Nondisjunction literally means not coming apart.

When one chromosome is involved, nondisjunction results in an extra copy of a chromosome in one cell and a loss of that chromosome from the other. A number of human disorders that result from nondisjunction will be described in Chapter 11.

Nondisjunction can involve more than one chromosome. When all the homologous chromosomes fail to separate, the result may be a dramatic increase in chromosome number, producing triploid (3N) or tetraploid (4N) organisms. The condition in which an organism has extra sets of chromosomes is called **polyploidy**. Polyploidy is almost always fatal in animals. However, polyploid plants are often larger and hardier than normal plants.

Mutations in Genes

Mutations can occur in individual genes and can seriously affect gene function. Any chemical change that affects the DNA molecule has the potential to produce **gene mutations**. Some gene mutations result from a change involving many nucleotides within a gene; some involve only one nucleotide. The smallest changes, known as **point mutations**, affect no more than a single nucleotide.

Remembering how a DNA base sequence determines the amino acid sequence of a polypeptide, can you predict the possible effects of a point mutation in which one base is substituted for another? Because base substitutions usually affect only a single codon, only one amino acid is affected. In some cases, the sequence of amino acids that the gene codes for may not be changed at all, since different codons may code for the same amino acid. When the point mutation involves the insertion or deletion of a nucleotide, however, the situation may be much more serious. Remember that mRNA is read in groups of three bases. If a single base is inserted or deleted, the groupings are shifted for every codon following the point mutation. Such **frameshift mutations** can completely change the polypeptide product produced by a gene.

Figure 10–13 *A frameshift mutation, such as that caused by the addition of a single nucleotide, can greatly change the polypeptide product of a gene (top). This can make it as useless and nonsensical as a sentence in which the deletion of a letter and a frameshift has occurred (bottom).*

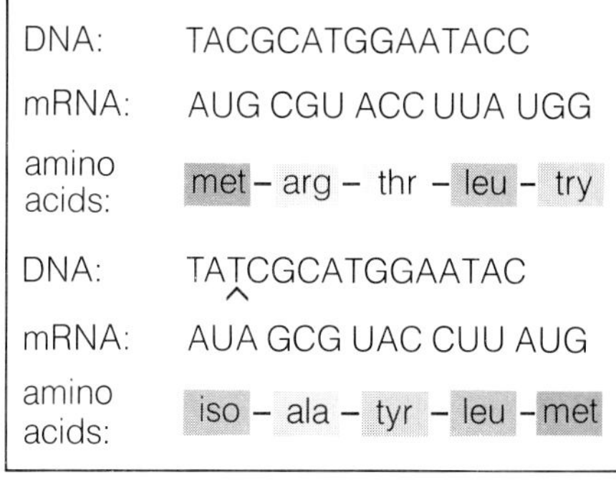

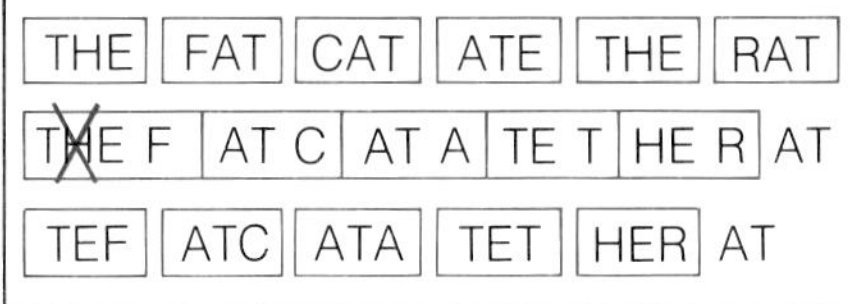

SCIENCE, TECHNOLOGY, AND SOCIETY **APPLICATION**

Manipulating Chromosome Numbers

From Mendel's work we have come to expect that organisms will be diploid (2N). In other words, they will have two sets of chromosomes—one set inherited from each parent. However, plants with the "wrong" number of sets of chromosomes do exist. And, interestingly enough, these plants are extremely useful in agricultural research.

For example, a plant with only one set of chromosomes shows the effects of all its genes, including potentially desirable recessive genes. A plant with only one set of chromosomes is obtained by taking cells formed in meiosis and growing them under special conditions. However, plants with only one set of chromosomes cannot reproduce sexually because meiosis cannot occur normally in their cells. If these plants show a desirable characteristic, they can be made into diploid plants by treating them with the drug colchicine. Colchicine prevents spindle formation during mitosis and thus causes the number of chromosomes in a cell to double. The diploid plants produced by treatment with colchicine are purebred for the desired traits and can reproduce normally.

By manipulating chromosome numbers with colchicine, it was possible to produce high-protein Triticale.

Colchicine can also be used to change the number of sets of chromosomes in a naturally occurring plant. For example, colchicine has been used to create strawberry and blueberry plants that are polyploid, or have more than two sets of chromosomes. Polyploid plants produce larger fruit than plants with the normal number of sets of chromosomes. The ability to change the number of sets of chromosomes makes it possible to cross plants that have different diploid numbers. The high-protein grain *Triticale* was created by crossing wheat (2N=42) and rye (2N=14). The plants grown from the hybrid seeds were sterile; they could not produce offspring. However, when the hybrid plants were treated with colchicine, the chromosome number was doubled and meiosis could occur normally. Thus the second-generation plants were fertile.

Manipulating chromosome numbers is useful in studying plant genetics. It is also a technique that allows researchers to create new and potentially better crops.

10–2 SECTION REVIEW

1. What is a somatic mutation? How does it differ from a germ mutation?
2. Compare a chromosomal mutation and a gene mutation.
3. How does nondisjunction result in chromosomal mutations?

10–3 Regulation of Gene Expression

Section Objectives

- Discuss gene interactions that influence gene expression.
- Explain how an operon is turned on and off.
- Describe introns and exons.

Like the individual cells of a large organism, individual genes do not function in isolation. The expression and activities of genes, like those of cells, are regulated and controlled, thereby enabling a complex genetic system to function smoothly. **As biologists have intensified their studies of gene activity, it has become clear that interactions between different genes and between genes and their environment are critically important.**

This section focuses on some of the ways in which genes are regulated by conditions within cells. However, genes are also influenced by environmental conditions such as temperature and light.

Gene Interactions

Dominance is the simplest example of how genes interact with each other. In Chapter 9, you learned that the effects of the dominant allele are seen even when the recessive allele is present. But what causes dominance?

Remember that a gene is a section of DNA, and DNA codes for a polypeptide, or string of amino acids. In many cases, the dominant allele codes for a polypeptide that works, whereas the recessive allele codes for a polypeptide that does not work. For example, suppose that the allele *B* codes for an enzyme that makes a black pigment in a mouse's fur and allele *b* codes for a defective enzyme that cannot make the pigment. A mouse that has the genotype *bb* will have white fur because it lacks the enzyme that makes the black pigment. But a mouse that has the genotype *BB* or *Bb* will have black fur because it possesses the enzyme that makes the black pigment. Although each cell in the *Bb* animal has just one copy of the functioning allele, that single copy can code for thousands of mRNA molecules. And each mRNA molecule can code for thousands of enzymes. This is the reason the *B* allele is dominant over the *b* allele.

INCOMPLETE DOMINANCE In 1760 the German scientist Josef Kölreuter reported on experiments in which he crossed white carnations (*rr*) with red carnations (*RR*). Kölreuter found that all of the offspring from his crosses had pink flowers (*Rr*). In other words, the hybrids had a phenotype that was intermediate between those of the parents. At first glance, it might appear as if the parents' genes had blended together. But when Kölreuter crossed his pink F_1 hybrids with each other to form an F_2 generation, the parents' phenotypes reappeared. In the F_2 generation, 1/4 of the plants had red flowers, 1/2 had pink flowers, and 1/4 had white flowers. (This 1:2:1 ratio should be familiar to you from Mendel's crosses.)

Figure 10–14 *For some organisms, such as these caterpillars, gene expression is regulated by chemicals in the food they eat. Each caterpillar of this species has the genetic ability to develop either the twiglike or the flowerlike form. However, caterpillars that eat gray-green oak twigs look like twigs (top). And caterpillars that eat fuzzy gold oak flowers look like flowers (bottom).*

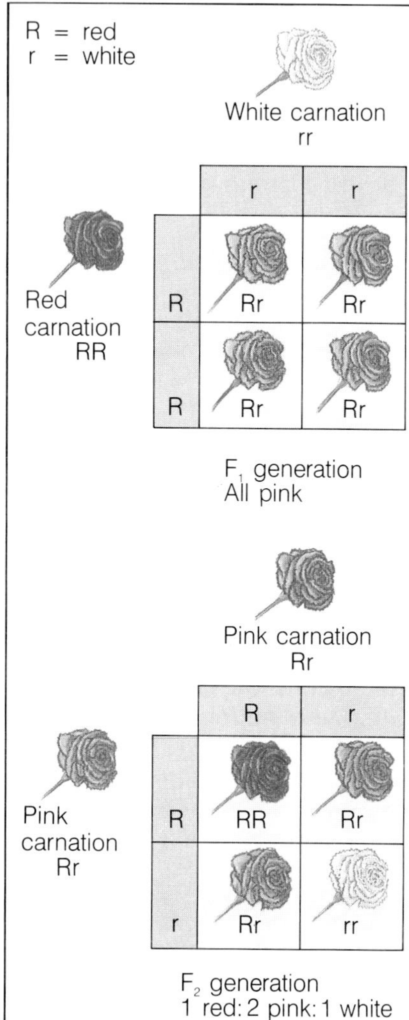

Figure 10–15 *Flower color in carnations is an example of incomplete dominance. The heterozygous phenotype, pink, is somewhere in between the homozygous phenotypes, red and white.*

In carnations, the *R* allele, which codes for an enzyme that makes red pigment, is incompletely dominant over the *r* allele, which codes for a defective enzyme that cannot make pigment. In **incomplete dominance** the active allele does not compensate for the inactive allele, and the heterozygous phenotype is somewhere in between the homozygous phenotypes.

CODOMINANCE Many genes display **codominance**, a condition in which both alleles of a gene are expressed. In other words, both alleles are active. (Remember that in incomplete dominance only one of the alleles is active.) Codominant alleles are written as capital letters with subscripts (for example, B_1 and B_2) or superscripts (for example, R and R').

Codominance is seen in many organisms. For example, red hair (H^R) is codominant with white hair (H^W) in cattle. Cattle that have the genotype H^RH^W are roan, or pinkish brown, in color because their coats are a mixture of red and white hairs. Much the same thing happens in certain varieties of chickens. Black feathers (F^B) are codominant with white feathers (F^W). Erminette chickens (F^BF^W) are speckled black and white.

POLYGENIC INHERITANCE It would be a great mistake to assume that all traits are produced by single genes. Many traits are produced by the interaction of many genes. Traits controlled by two or more genes are said to be **polygenic** (*poly-* means many). For example, at least three enzymes—each of which is produced by a different gene—are involved in making the reddish-brown pigment in the eyes of fruit flies. Different combinations of enzymes (which may be present in the normal form or altered or absent due to a mutation) produce different eye colors. More complicated traits, such as the shape of your nose or the color and markings on an animal's coat, are the result of interactions between large numbers of genes.

Gene Expression in Prokaryotes

In Chapter 7 you learned that individual genes on a chromosome serve as a template, or pattern, for the production of mRNA. In turn, mRNA serves as the instructions for the production of a protein (polypeptide). The genes of a single organism cannot all be activated at the same time. A cell that activated all of its genes at once would make a great many molecules that it did not need and would waste energy and raw materials in doing so. However, when the cell does need the product of a gene, it must be able to produce that product quickly and in adequate amounts.

When the product of a gene (a specific protein) is being actively produced by a cell, we say that the gene is being expressed. Within a single organism, some genes are rarely expressed, some are constantly expressed, and some are expressed for a time and then turned off. But how does a cell "know" when to make a protein and when not to make it? In other words, how does a cell "know" which genes to turn on and which to turn off?

THE OPERON The mechanisms by which genes are turned on and off are quite complex. In this section we will examine one way genes are regulated in prokaryotes (organisms without a nucleus). This particular mechanism was discovered by the French scientists François Jacob and Jacques Monod in 1961. They noticed that genes that work together are often clustered together on a small area of a prokaryote's chromosome. Jacob and Monod also determined that there are regions on a chromosome that lie near these gene clusters but that do not code for the production of proteins. These regions are, however, involved in the regulation and expression of nearby gene clusters. These regions and the gene cluster they regulate are called an **operon** because they operate together.

An operon consists of the following parts: a cluster of genes that work together; a region of the chromosome near the cluster of genes called the **operator**; and a region of the chromosome next to the operator called the **promoter**. As you can see in Figure 10–17, the operator and promoter regions overlap slightly.

Figure 10–16 In certain varieties of chickens, black and white feather colors are caused by codominant alleles. Thus the heterozygous phenotype, speckled black and white, is a result of the expression of both alleles.

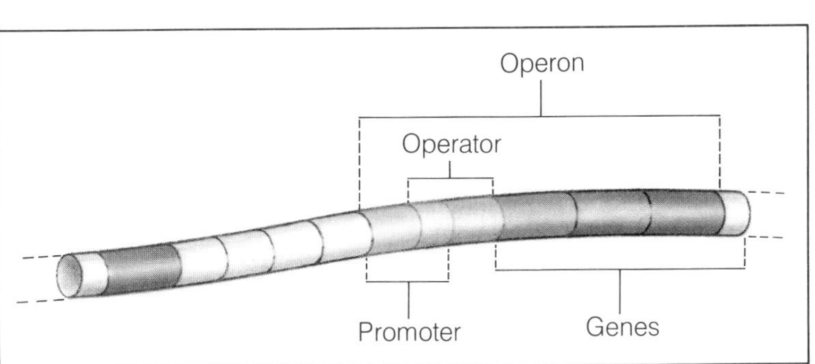

Figure 10–17 Some genes in prokaryotes are regulated by an operon. An operon consists of several sections of DNA that are operated together. The operon studied by Jacob and Monod, which breaks down the sugar lactose, consists of a promoter, an operator, and a cluster of genes that code for lactose-metabolizing enzymes.

The gene cluster in the operon that Jacob and Monod studied produces enzymes that break down lactose, a sugar that bacteria can use as a food source. Bacteria do not produce these lactose-breaking enzymes in large amounts unless lactose is present. In other words, the very presence of lactose induces the production of the enzymes necessary to break down lactose for use as food. In this operon system, lactose is called the **inducer** because it induces the production of enzymes.

In order to make the enzymes, RNA polymerase must move along the genes on the chromosome, producing mRNA in the process. Before the RNA polymerase can get to the desired genes, it must first attach to the promoter region near the genes. We might think of the promoter as a "Start Here!" instruction to RNA polymerase. Once the RNA polymerase attaches to the promoter, it can move along the chromosome, past the operator region, to the genes. When the RNA polymerase reaches the genes, it can produce mRNA, which "instructs" the ribosomes to make the enzymes. When this process is taking place, we say the genes are activated, or being expressed. The enzymes coded for by the genes can then perform their task in the cell—in this case, breaking down the inducer lactose.

Remember that Jacob and Monod observed that the enzymes coded for by the genes in the operon were not produced in the absence of the inducer (lactose). Does this mean that the cell has a way to turn the operon off? Indeed it does.

THE REPRESSOR The cell produces a special protein called a **repressor**. When the repressor nears the operator region of an operon, it attaches itself to the operator so that it sits between the promoter and the genes. The repressor's position blocks the access of RNA polymerase to the genes. Like the guard outside a locked factory, the repressor prevents the workers (RNA polymerase) from getting to their jobs (making mRNA). In other words, the repressor turns the genes of the operon off.

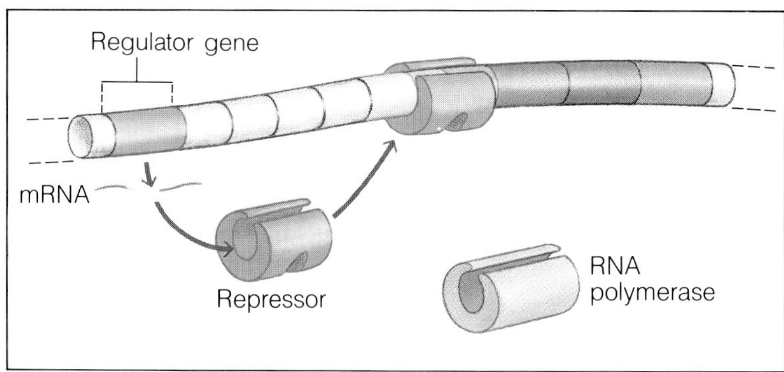

Figure 10–18 *The genes in this operon are turned off when a protein called the repressor binds to the operator and thus prevents the transcription of mRNA.*

You might wonder how the repressor "knows" which operon to attach to and thereby turn off. The actual mechanism is quite elegant and specific. Each repressor is shaped to fit a specific region of DNA on the chromosome. It can attach only to the specific operator on the operon it regulates. Thus each repressor turns off a specific operon.

GENE ACTIVATION You now know that a gene cluster is part of an operon that includes an operator and a promoter. And you also know that the genes are turned off when the repressor binds to the operator. But there is more to the story. How is the operon turned back on when it is needed?

When the inducer enters the cell, it binds to the repressor. And something quite remarkable happens: The repressor changes shape and can no longer bind to the operator. The repressor actually falls off the operator.

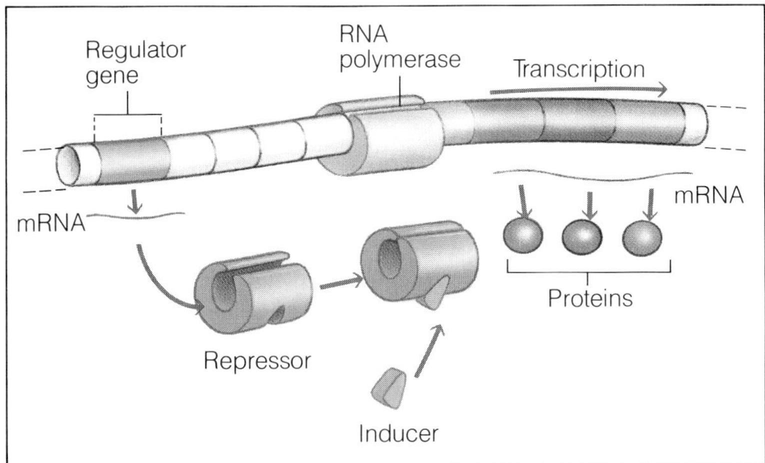

Figure 10–19 *The genes in this operon are turned on when lactose (the inducer) binds to the repressor and causes it to fall off the operator. This allows RNA polymerase to bind to the promoter, move across the operator, and transcribe mRNA from the cluster of genes. The operon system ensures that genes are activated only when their products are needed. In this case, the lactose-metabolizing enzymes are produced only when lactose is present.*

When the repressor falls off the operator, the RNA polymerase can bind to the promoter, move across to the genes, and produce messenger RNA. The mRNA codes for the enzymes that are used to break down the inducer. When the cell runs out of the inducer, the repressor can bind to the operator again, and the operon is turned off. The complete system is automatic and self-regulating. The presence of the inducer causes the cell to make the enzymes needed to use it. And when the inducer disappears, the enzymes are no longer made.

The repressor-operon system provides us with one model of how a group of genes can be regulated so that they are expressed only when they are needed. A number of other gene-regulation systems in prokaryotes have been identified. Some of these gene systems use repressors in a manner similar to that just described. Others use proteins that enhance the rate of transcription. In other systems, regulation occurs at the level of protein synthesis. Regardless of the actual system involved, the result is the same: Cells are able to turn their genes on and off, using the genes only when needed.

Gene Expression in Eukaryotes

The cells of eukaryotes contain a nucleus and membrane-enclosed organelles. Gene regulation in eukaryotes is more complex than in prokaryotes. Increased understanding of control systems in eukaryotes indicates that there are several systems of gene regulation. One system involves a substance called an inducer. Like the inducer in the operon system, inducers in eukaryotes induce, or cause, the activation of genes. In eukaryotes, inducers bind directly to DNA and either start or increase transcription of particular genes.

In 1976 Philip Sharp and Susan Berget discovered that mRNA produced during transcription may be altered before it is used to make protein (polypeptide) during translation. You may recall that during transcription, the base sequence in a

Figure 10–20 The sequence of bases on the mRNA for this egg-white protein does not exactly match that of its corresponding gene. The DNA sequences that are not complementary to the mRNA appear as loops called introns.

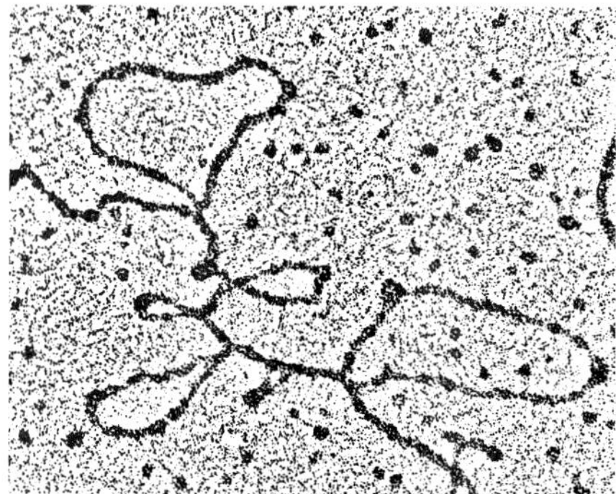

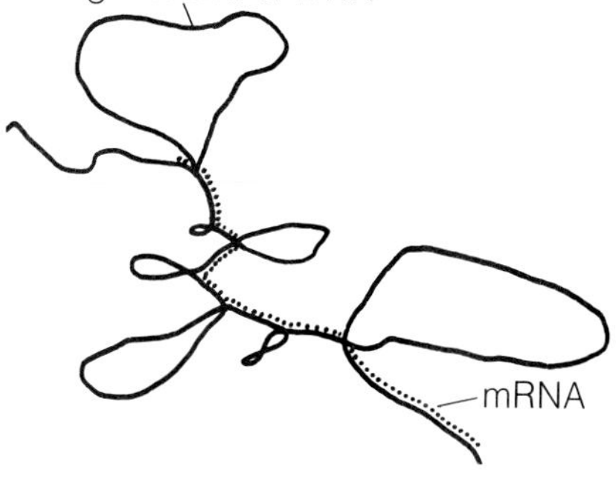

gene is transcribed into the complementary base sequence on mRNA. Most scientists assumed that a sequence of bases on mRNA was exactly complementary to a DNA sequence for a gene.

Sharp and Berget carefully compared the mRNA of a protein with a piece of DNA containing the gene for that protein. They expected to find an exact pairing between the bases on the gene and the bases on the mRNA that helps produce the protein. Instead, they discovered that the DNA fragment contained large sequences that were not complementary to the base sequence on the mRNA. What was going on?

Sharp and Berget quickly realized that the presence of DNA sequences that are not complementary to mRNA sequences implies that the gene is in "pieces." In other words, DNA sequences that code for protein (the gene pieces) are separated by DNA sequences that do not code for protein. Today we know that many eukaryotic genes contain sequences that are complementary to mRNA and sequences that are not. The sequences that are complementary code for protein. These "expressed" sequences are called **exons**. The segments that are not complementary do not code for protein. These "intervening" sequences are called **introns**.

When RNA polymerase moves along a gene, it transcribes the entire gene. This means that the RNA produced by transcription, or pre-mRNA, contains introns. Before the cell can produce protein, the pre-mRNA must be processed into functional mRNA. During this processing, the introns on the pre-mRNA are removed and the exons are spliced back together. In addition, a chemical "cap" and "tail" are attached to the RNA. At this point, the pre-mRNA can be called mRNA.

The conversion of pre-mRNA into mRNA has further significance because of the fact that the processing takes place entirely within the nucleus. This means that mRNA must complete its processing before it is allowed to leave the nucleus. There may be some kind of a molecular watchman at the gate of the nucleus that allows only processed molecules to leave. Such a system would regulate gene expression by preventing the protein products of a gene from being produced.

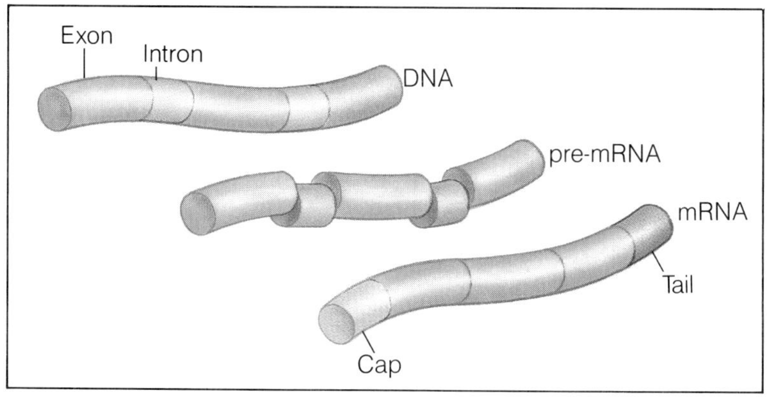

Figure 10–21 RNA polymerase transcribes an entire gene, introns and exons alike. Before the transcribed RNA, or pre-mRNA, can leave the nucleus and code for protein, the introns must be removed and a chemical "cap" and "tail" must be attached.

SCIENCE, TECHNOLOGY, AND SOCIETY **BREAKTHROUGH**

Jumping Genes

In the 1940s a young scientist named Barbara McClintock began to study certain genes in corn. She was particularly interested in why certain kernels of corn developed a spotty, or speckled, appearance. She knew that the color of each seed was genetically determined and that all of the cells in the coating of the seed had the same genetic makeup (genotype). Yet the speckled colors indicated that genes were being suddenly and unpredictably switched on and off in one cell or another. She could find only one reasonable explanation for this observation: There are special controlling elements that can be transposed or move from one place to another around the chromosome. These transposable elements, which are sometimes called jumping genes, can insert themselves into different parts of the chromosome and turn the genes near them on or off.

McClintock's theory of transposable elements was far ahead of its time, and found little support. But McClintock patiently continued her studies, providing experimental proof and documentation that she was right about these moving genes. Finally, in 1975, the techniques of molecular biology had advanced to the point where scientists could actually look for jumping genes. And scientists found jumping genes in bacteria, insects, mammals (including humans), and corn.

Jumping genes may play a role in gene regulation in some organisms, such as corn. They also are involved in the formation of certain proteins that show a great number of variations, such as antibodies—proteins that defend the body against disease-causing organisms. More jumping genes are discovered every day, and it will be a long time before scientists are able to explain all of their different functions.

McClintock has lived to see the importance of her discovery appreciated and is now the recipient of many honors, including the highest prize that can be awarded to a scientist, the Nobel prize (in 1983).

10–3 SECTION REVIEW

1. Compare incomplete dominance and codominance.
2. What is a polygenic trait?
3. Suppose the gene that codes for a repressor was deleted. What effect would this have on the operon?
4. "Mutations in introns are less likely to affect phenotype than mutations in exons." Defend or refute this statement.

LABORATORY INVESTIGATION

MAPPING CHROMOSOMES

PROBLEM

How can rates of crossing-over be used to map chromosomes?

MATERIALS *(per group)*

wooden stick from a frozen-dessert bar
metric ruler
pen
sheet of unlined paper

PROCEDURE

1. Using a pen and a ruler, draw a vertical line 15 cm long in the center of a clean sheet of unlined paper. Make a small horizontal mark at the bottom of the line. Measuring from the bottom of the line, add horizontal marks at 1 cm, 3 cm, 6 cm, 10 cm, and 15 cm.
2. Label each horizontal mark alphabetically (A through F), starting from the bottom.
3. The vertical line on the paper represents a chromosome that has six genes on it—A, B, C, D, E, and F. This chromosome's homologous chromosome is represented by the colored edge of the wooden stick.
4. Adjust the sheet of paper so that its bottom edge is about 15 cm from the edge of your lab table or desk. Move your chair back so that the front edge of your seat is about 30 cm from the edge of your lab table or desk.
5. Toss the wooden stick, underhand, toward the vertical line until the stick lands across the line. The landing of the stick across the line represents crossing-over.
6. When crossing-over occurs, look at the colored edge of the stick to determine which genes have been separated. Make a tally mark in the appropriate place in the data table for each gene that has become separated from gene A. For example, if the colored edge of the stick lands between D and E, make tally marks for genes E and F because they have been separated from gene A as a result of crossing-over.
7. Toss the stick and tally the results until crossing-over has occurred 100 times.
8. Count up the number of tally marks for each of the five genes. In the appropriate place in your data table, record the number of times each gene was separated from gene A.
9. Calculate the frequency of crossing-over by dividing the number of times each gene was separated from gene A by 100. Record the results of your calculations.
10. Calculate the location of each gene by multiplying the frequency of its crossing-over by 15 and rounding off to the nearest integer. Record the calculated gene locations.

OBSERVATIONS

Genes Separated from Gene A	Times Separated from Gene A		Frequency of Crossing-over	Gene Locations	
	Tally	Number		Calculated	Actual
B					1
C					3
D					6
E					10
F					15

1. Did every toss result in crossing-over?
2. Which genes became separated from gene A most frequently? Most infrequently?

ANALYSIS AND CONCLUSIONS

1. What is the relationship between the frequency of gene separation due to crossing-over and the distance between genes?
2. Are your calculated gene locations exactly the same as the actual gene locations? If so, discuss why the experiment went as expected. If not, discuss possible sources of error.
3. How can the frequencies of crossing-over be used to map chromosomes?

STUDENT STUDY GUIDE

SUMMARIZING THE CONCEPTS

The key concepts in each section of this chapter are listed below to help you review the chapter content. Make sure you understand each concept and its relationship to other concepts and to the theme of this chapter.

10–1 The Chromosome Theory of Heredity

- Genes are located on the chromosomes.
- Genes that are located on the same chromosome tend to be inherited together.
- Gene linkages may be broken by crossing-over. The farther apart genes are located on a chromosome, the more likely that they will be separated by a cross-over event.
- Sex-linked genes are located on the sex chromosomes.

10–2 Mutations

- Mutations are changes in the genetic material. There are two kinds of mutations. Chromosomal mutations involve segments of chromosomes, whole chromosomes, or entire sets of chromosomes. Gene mutations involve individual genes.

10–3 Regulation of Gene Expression

- Interactions between genes affect gene expression.
- Genes can be turned on when they are needed and turned off when they are not.
- Many genes contain sequences that are not expressed. These sequences are removed when the RNA transcribed from DNA is made into mRNA.

REVIEWING KEY TERMS

Vocabulary terms are important to your understanding of biology. The key terms listed below are those you should be especially familiar with. Review these terms and their meanings. Then use each term in a complete sentence. If you are not sure of a term's meaning, return to the appropriate section and review its definition.

10–1 The Chromosome Theory of Heredity

chromosome theory of heredity
linked genes
linkage group
recombinant
sex chromosome
autosome
X chromosome
Y chromosome
sex-linked

10–2 Mutations

mutation
chromosomal mutation
nondisjunction
polyploidy
gene mutation
point mutation
frameshift mutation

10–3 Regulation of Gene Expression

incomplete dominance
codominance
polygenic
operon
operator
promoter
inducer
repressor
exon
intron

CHAPTER REVIEW

CONTENT REVIEW

Multiple Choice

Choose the letter of the answer that best completes each statement.

1. An organism has an extra copy of a chromosome in all its cells. This is an example of
a. polyploidy.
b. a chromosomal mutation.
c. a gene mutation.
d. a somatic mutation.

2. Both alleles are expressed in
a. codominance. c. polyploidy.
b. nondisjunction. d. dominance.

3. The expressed allele does not make up for the inactive allele in
a. polyploidy.
b. translocation.
c. codominance.
d. incomplete dominance.

4. Which kind of mutation would result if an extra nucleotide were inserted into a gene?
a. germ c. chromosomal
b. frameshift d. deletion

5. Traits that are caused by the interaction of many genes are said to be
a. polyploid. c. polygenic.
b. linked. d. autosomal.

6. The gene product is not produced when the repressor binds to
a. the operator.
b. RNA polymerase.
c. lactose.
d. the enzyme gene.

7. A point mutation can best be classified as a
a. chromosomal mutation.
b. germ mutation.
c. deletion mutation.
d. gene mutation.

8. Gene linkages may be broken by
a. nondisjunction.
b. duplication.
c. crossing-over.
d. polyploidy.

True or False

Determine whether each statement is true or false. If it is true, write "true." If it is false, change the underlined word or words to make the statement true.

1. Crossing-over is more likely to occur between genes that are <u>close together</u>.

2. A <u>somatic</u> mutation affects sperm cells or egg cells and can be inherited.

3. The effects of recessive sex-linked alleles are seen more often in <u>males</u>.

4. Changes in DNA are called <u>mutations</u>.

5. Segments of nonhomologous chromosomes are exchanged in <u>crossing-over</u>.

6. Sex-linked genes are located on the <u>autosomes</u>.

7. <u>Polyploidy</u> is the condition of having extra sets of chromosomes.

8. A <u>point</u> mutation affects a single nucleotide.

Word Relationships

A. *In each of the following sets of terms, three of the terms are related. One term does not belong. Determine the characteristic common to three of the terms and then identify the term that does not belong.*

1. inversion, translocation, duplication, nondisjunction
2. operator, promoter, repressor, inducer
3. dominance, codominance, incomplete dominance, polygenic inheritance
4. gene mutation, point mutation, frameshift mutation, chromosomal mutation

B. *Give the vocabulary word whose meaning is opposite that of the following words.*

5. sex chromosome
6. crossing-over
7. somatic mutation
8. intron

CONCEPT MASTERY

Use your understanding of the concepts developed in the chapter to answer each of the following in a brief paragraph.

1. List and describe the four types of chromosomal mutations that result in a change in the structure of a chromosome.
2. Explain why the operon is turned on when the inducer is present and turned off in the absence of the inducer.
3. Describe two ways genes are regulated in eukaryotes.
4. What is a linkage group? What kind of evidence suggests that linkage groups are the same as chromosomes?

CRITICAL AND CREATIVE THINKING

Discuss each of the following in a brief paragraph.

1. **Making predictions** Would a mutation in an intron affect gene expression? Explain.
2. **Relating concepts** How are crossing-over and linkage related to gene mapping?
3. **Problem solving** Examine the data for the crosses in cats shown below. How are the black and yellow coat colors inherited? (*Hint:* Male cats are XY and female cats are XX.) Using a Punnett square, predict the results of a cross involving a black male and a tortoise-shell female.
4. **Applying concepts** Two of the genes that Mendel studied are located on the same chromosome. Despite this, they show independent assortment in test crosses. What can you conclude about their relative positions on the chromosome?
5. **Using the writing process** Pretend you are the sex-linked gene for colorblindness. Describe the effects you have on each generation as you are passed down through two generations.

Parents	Offspring
black male X yellow female	½ yellow males ½ tortoise-shell (black and yellow) females
yellow male X black female	½ black males ½ tortoise-shell females
yellow male X tortoise-shell female	¼ black males ¼ yellow males ¼ yellow females ¼ tortoise-shell females

CHAPTER 11

Human Heredity

In humans, as in all living things, traits such as sex and skin color are inherited.

Of all the organisms in the world, there is one that we find particularly fascinating. This organism is not, however, an ideal one for the study of genetics. Why? The reasons are many. It is composed of approximately 10^{14} (100 million million) cells. Its generation time (about 20 years) is much too long. It cannot be kept in the laboratory for study. It produces too few offspring for good statistics. It cannot be used in test crosses. And its genetic system contains nearly 100,000 genes. Despite these disadvantages, biologists have studied the genetics of this single organism, Homo sapiens, *for more than 80 years. The reason for so much scientific interest is clear: Of all the organisms on Earth, it is ourselves we long to know the best. In this chapter, you will discover how some human traits are inherited and how some inherited disorders can be cured or prevented.*

CHAPTER OUTLINE

11–1 "It Runs in the Family"

Section Objectives

- Explain how human traits are inherited.
- Distinguish between sex chromosomes and autosomes.
- Discuss the influence of the environment on gene expression.

How many times have you overheard two people discussing whether a newborn baby looks more like its mother or its father? People have always discussed such things. But when those of us who study biology engage in such discussions, we make an important assumption: Human children inherit characteristics from their parents as a result of gene interactions.

The principles of genetics that we have already discussed apply to humans. **Many human traits are inherited by the action of dominant and recessive genes, although other traits are determined through more complicated gene interactions.** Although the study of human genetics is difficult, it is one of the most important fields in biology. For we are interested in finding out as much as possible about ourselves, including the role that heredity plays in determining who and what we are and how some of the disorders and conditions that we inherit can be cured or prevented.

The Human Organism

The study of ourselves logically begins with a discussion of human chromosomes. Recall that a diploid cell has two sets of homologous chromosomes. A human diploid cell contains 46 chromosomes arranged in 23 pairs. These 46 chromosomes

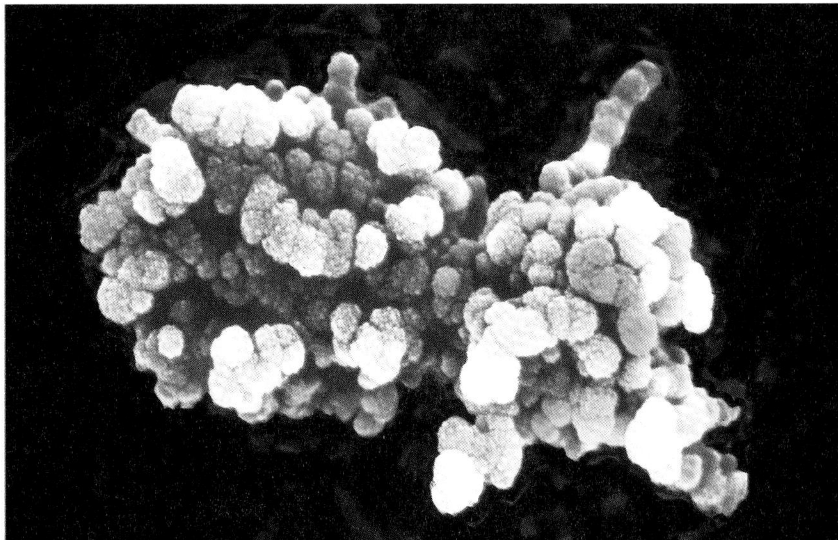

Figure 11–1 *Each human chromosome contains a specific set of genetic instructions that is passed on from parent to child. The human chromosome in this electron micrograph has been magnified approximately 20,000 times.*

contain 6 billion nucleotide pairs of DNA—6 billion individual characters of the genetic code. To get an idea of how long a complete human DNA sequence actually is, consider the following: In this textbook, there are approximately 3000 letters on each page. If a complete human DNA sequence were to be written in the same-size type as this textbook, it would comprise a book more than 1 million pages long!

As you will recall from Chapter 9, the principles of genetics described by Mendel require that organisms inherit a single copy of each gene from each parent. In humans, the **gametes**, or reproductive cells, contain a single copy of each gene. Gametes (sperm and eggs) are formed in the reproductive organs by the process of meiosis. Each egg cell and each sperm cell contain 23 chromosomes, or the haploid number of chromosomes. During fertilization, sperm and egg unite and a **zygote** (ZIGH-goht), or fertilized egg, is produced. The zygote contains 46 chromosomes (23 pairs), or the diploid number of chromosomes characteristic of the organism.

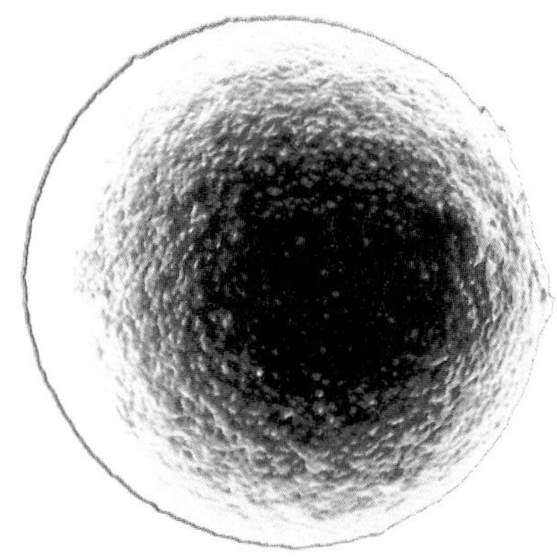

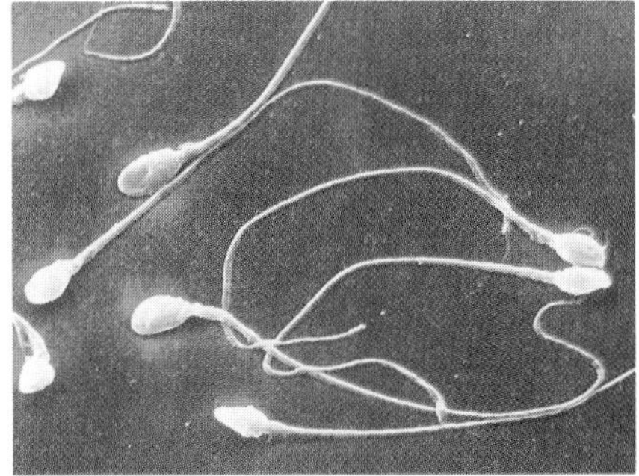

Figure 11–2 *In humans, the egg (top) and the sperm (bottom) contain 23 chromosomes each. During fertilization, these gametes unite to produce a zygote that contains 46 chromosomes.*

Of the 46 chromosomes found in a human diploid cell, two are the sex chromosomes, X and Y. The remaining 44 chromosomes are the autosomes. The inheritance of dominant and recessive human genes carried on any of the 44 autosomes follows Mendel's principles. Human genes carried on the sex chromosomes are sex-linked.

The simplest patterns of inheritance occur in traits that are influenced by a single gene. Fortunately, many such genes have now been described. Human genetics is advancing so rapidly that scarcely a week goes by without a new human gene being reported and mapped.

Human Traits

You will recall from Chapter 10 that the phenotype of an organism is only partly determined by its genotype. There are some traits that are strongly influenced by environmental, or nongenetic, factors. Environmental factors include nutrition and exercise. For example, recent studies show that improvements in infant and childhood nutrition in the twentieth century in the United States and Europe have greatly increased

Figure 11–3 *Notice the difference in the heights of these teenagers. Although the genes for height are inherited, the trait is strongly influenced by environmental factors, such as diet.*

SCIENCE, TECHNOLOGY, AND SOCIETY **BREAKTHROUGH**

How Do We Map Human Genes?

Preparing a human genetic map presents special challenges. As we saw in Chapter 10, crossing-over is the key to gene mapping in most organisms: Crossovers rarely occur between nearby genes but are common between distant genes. It is possible to map human genes in this way, but the need to gather crossover data from several generations has made human gene mapping slow and tedious. In the last few years, however, several breakthroughs have made it possible to map human genes much more rapidly.

One of the most exciting new techniques was developed by Jeanne Lawrence and Robert Singer at the University of Massachusetts Medical School. Their technique attaches a fluorescent label to pieces of DNA complementary to a particular gene. Once the labeled DNA fragments are mixed with a chromosome preparation, they attach to the DNA of the gene in question by a chemical bond known as a hydrogen bond. This action produces an intense fluorescent label at the place on the chromosome where the gene is located. The Lawrence-Singer technique is just one more tool in an increasingly powerful workshop for exploring the human genetic system.

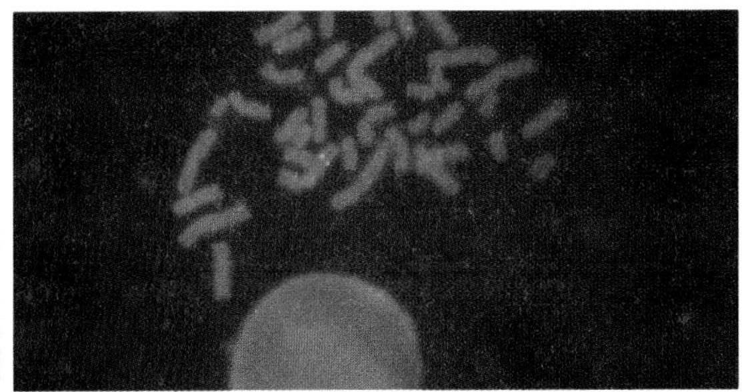

Two tiny yellow spots mark the location of the genes of the Epstein-Barr virus.

the average height of these populations over the nineteenth-century averages. Famine-stricken countries, however, were found to produce a generation with stunted growth.

Although it is important to consider the influence of the environment on the expression of some genes, it must be understood that environmental effects on gene expression are not inherited; genes are. Genes that are denied a proper environment in which to reach full expression in one generation can, in a proper environment, achieve full potential in a later generation.

11-1 SECTION REVIEW

1. How are human traits inherited?
2. What is a gamete? A zygote?
3. How many chromosomes are in a human diploid cell? A human haploid cell?
4. Distinguish between sex chromosomes and autosomes.
5. How does the environment influence gene expression?

Section Objectives

- Identify two human traits that are determined by multiple alleles.
- Explain how Huntington disease and sickle cell anemia are inherited.
- Distinguish between traits determined by multiple alleles and polygenic traits.

11–2 The Inheritance of Human Traits

At the writing of this textbook, more than 1000 human genes have been described and studied. Listing all of these genes would serve no purpose, but it is useful and interesting to examine a few cases in which particular genes affect us in very significant, and often dramatic, ways.

Human Blood Groups

Multiple alleles are three or more alleles of the same gene that code for a single trait. ABO and Rh blood groups are determined by multiple alleles. A number of other human traits are determined by **multiple alleles.**

ABO BLOOD GROUPS In 1900, the Austrian physician Karl Landsteiner discovered that human blood could be classified into four general groups, or types, known today as the Landsteiner blood groups. These four blood types are determined by the presence or absence of specific chemical substances in the blood.

Landsteiner observed that when he mixed together the red blood cells from different people, the red blood cells agglutinated, or clumped together. After doing extensive research, Landsteiner determined that the red blood cells contained two antigens, A and B. Antigens are molecules that can be recognized by the immune system.

The presence or absence of these antigens (A and B) produces four possible blood types: A, B, AB, and O. A person with type A blood has red blood cells that contain antigen A but not antigen B. A person with type B blood has red blood cells that contain antigen B but not antigen A. A person with type AB blood has both antigen A and antigen B. And a person with type O blood has neither antigen A nor antigen B.

Figure 11–4 *This photomicrograph shows the agglutination, or clumping, of human red blood cells that can occur when blood of two different types is mixed.*

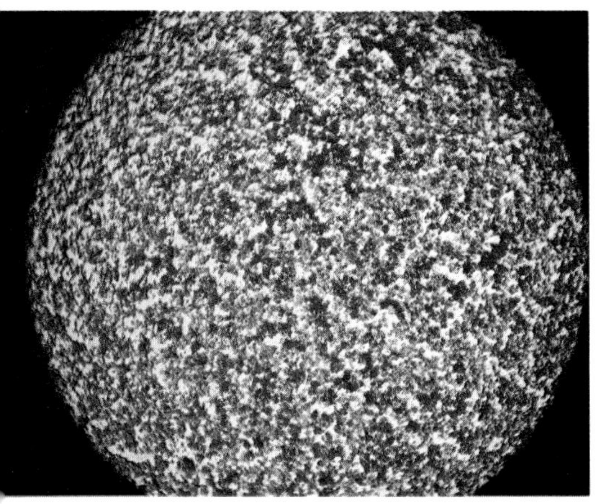

The ABO blood groups are of particular importance in blood transfusions. A transfusion of the wrong blood type can cause a violent, often fatal, reaction in the body as the immune system responds to the presence of an antigen not found on its own cells. For example, if type B blood is given to a person with type A or type O blood, a reaction will occur against the red blood cells containing the B antigen. Because people with type AB blood have both antigens on their red blood cells, they can receive blood from any of the four types.

The Landsteiner, or ABO, blood groups are determined by a single gene with three possible alleles: I^A, I^B, or i. Figure 11–5 illustrates the relationship of these alleles to the blood group phenotype. Because the I^A and I^B alleles are both expressed when they occur together, they are said to be codominant.

Rh BLOOD GROUPS In addition to the ABO antigens, there is another antigen on the red blood cells that determines the success or failure of transfusions. It is the Rh antigen (named after the rhesus monkey in which the antigen was first discovered by Landsteiner and Alexander Wiener). People who have the Rh antigen on their red blood cells are said to be Rh positive (Rh^+). People who do not have the Rh antigen on their red blood cells are said to be Rh negative (Rh^-). It is interesting to note that although the Rh blood groups are commonly referred to as either positive or negative, there are actually more than two alleles that determine these blood groups. In fact, there are eight common alleles and many that are rarer.

In blood banks, the ABO and Rh blood groups are often expressed together in symbols such as AB^- or O^+. The gene for the Rh antigen, however, displays simple dominance. Genotype Rh^+ Rh^+ and Rh^- Rh^+ produces the Rh positive phenotype. Only the double recessive genotype Rh^- Rh^- produces Rh negative blood.

Genotypes	Phenotypes
i i	O
I^A I^A, I^A i	A
I^B I^B, I^B i	B
I^A I^B	AB

Figure 11–5 *This chart illustrates the relationship between genotype and phenotype for each of the ABO blood groups. What are the possible genotypes of a person with phenotype B blood?*

Huntington Disease

Many of the tens of thousands of human genes are so essential to the normal functioning of cells and tissues that we do not notice them unless something goes wrong and a genetic disease results. **Huntington disease, which is produced by a single dominant allele (H), is an example of a genetic disease.** People who have this disease show no symptoms until they are in their thirties or forties, when the gradual damage to their nervous system begins. As you will recall from Chapter 10, the effects of a dominant allele are expressed even when the recessive allele is present. So people who have the dominant allele for Huntington disease have the disease and suffer painful progressive loss of muscle control and mental function until death occurs.

Until very recently, the only way people knew if they carried the gene for Huntington disease was the appearance of the disease later in their lives. Thus many Huntington disease sufferers had children who inherited the gene for this disease.

Figure 11–6 *This photograph shows a rhesus monkey, the type of monkey after which the Rh blood group was named.*

Sickle Cell Anemia

In 1904, Doctor James Herrick noticed an unusual ailment afflicting one of his young patients. His patient, a 20-year-old black college student, had been complaining of weakness and dizzy spells and had open sores on his legs. The Chicago physician examined the student's blood cells under a microscope and discovered that many of the red blood cells were bent and twisted into shapes that resembled sickles (farm tools used to cut grain). The normal shape of a red blood cell is that of a round, flattened disk. Doctor Herrick guessed correctly that these unusually shaped cells were the cause of his patient's

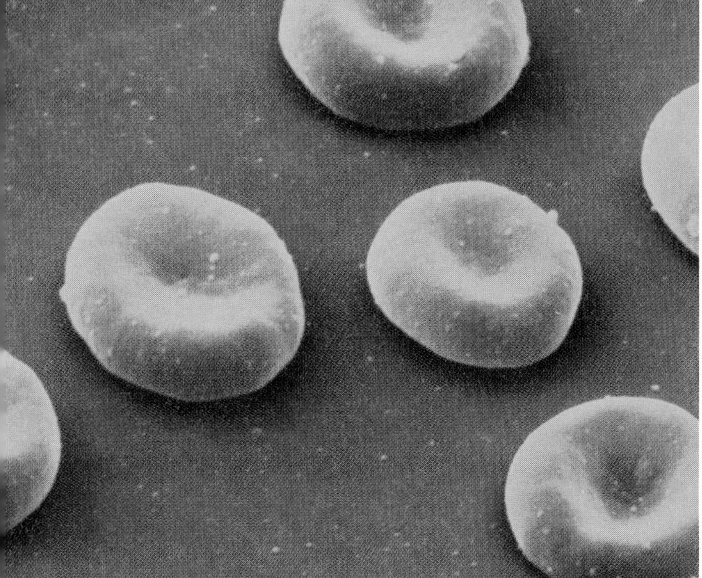

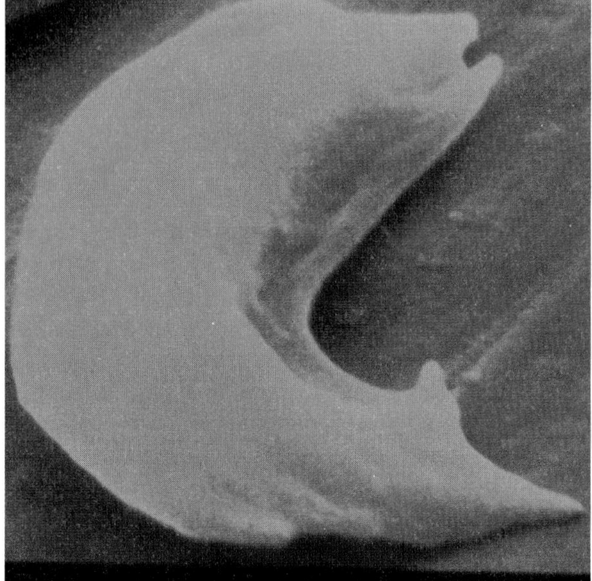

Figure 11–7 These scanning electron micrographs show human red blood cells that contain normal hemoglobin (left) and a red blood cell that contains the abnormal hemoglobin characteristic of sickle cell anemia (right). The red blood cells have been magnified approximately 10,000 times.

problems, and he gave the disease the name by which we know it today—sickle cell anemia.

THE CAUSE OF SICKLE CELL ANEMIA Sickle cell anemia is caused by a change in one of the polypeptides found in hemoglobin. Hemoglobin is the protein that carries oxygen in red blood cells.

When a person who has sickle cell anemia is deprived of oxygen (from heavy exercise, holding one's breath, or even nervousness or anxiety), the hemoglobin molecules join together and form fibers. These fibers cause the red blood cells to undergo the dramatic changes in shape that Doctor Herrick observed. The sickle-shaped red blood cells are more rigid and tend to become stuck in the capillaries, the narrowest blood vessels in the body. See Figure 11–8. As a result, the movement of blood through these vessels is stopped and damage to cells and tissues occurs. Serious injury or death may result.

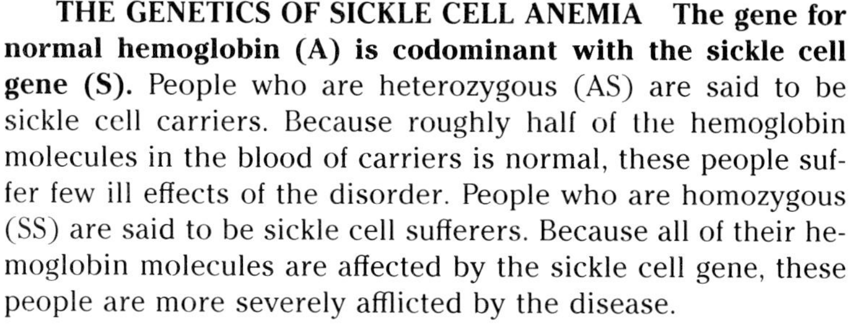

THE GENETICS OF SICKLE CELL ANEMIA **The gene for normal hemoglobin (A) is codominant with the sickle cell gene (S).** People who are heterozygous (AS) are said to be sickle cell carriers. Because roughly half of the hemoglobin molecules in the blood of carriers is normal, these people suffer few ill effects of the disorder. People who are homozygous (SS) are said to be sickle cell sufferers. Because all of their hemoglobin molecules are affected by the sickle cell gene, these people are more severely afflicted by the disease.

THE MOLECULAR BASIS OF SICKLE CELL ANEMIA The gene for sickle cell hemoglobin differs from the gene for normal hemoglobin by a single nucleotide. Why does this seemingly small difference cause so much trouble?

The substitution of one nucleotide in the gene results in the substitution of a different amino acid in the sickle cell

Figure 11–8 Capillaries, which are the narrowest blood vessels, are so small that they permit only one red blood cell at a time to pass through. What happens to sickle-shaped red blood cells as they move through the capillaries?

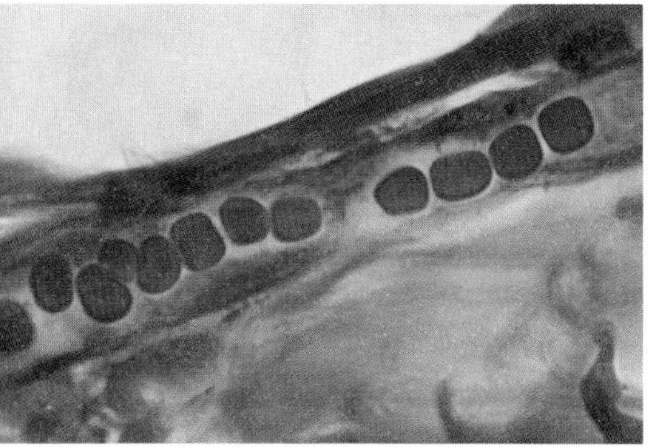

hemoglobin protein. This change makes hemoglobin less soluble in water. Most of the time the condition does not present a problem. But when the body is under even minor stress, the hemoglobin in a large proportion of red blood cells will come out of solution as crystals. This crystallization of hemoglobin causes the sickle-shaped cells to appear, accompanied by their medical consequences.

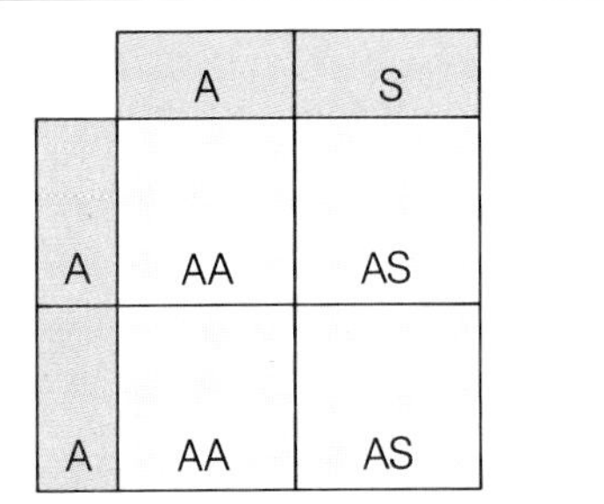

Figure 11–9 *This Punnett square shows the cross between a person who is heterozygous for sickle cell anemia and a person who is homozygous for normal hemoglobin. What are the possible genotypes of their offspring?*

THE DISTRIBUTION OF SICKLE CELL ANEMIA In the United States, people of African ancestry are the most common carriers of the sickle cell trait. In the rest of the world, sickle cell anemia is found in the tropical regions of Africa and Asia. Approximately 10 percent of Americans of African ancestry and as many as 40 percent of the population in some parts of Africa carry the trait. Why is sickle cell anemia so common in some regions and virtually unknown in others (such as Northern Europe and Asia)?

The answer to this question provides us with a surprising lesson in evolution. People who are heterozygous for sickle cell anemia (AS) are partially resistant to malaria, a serious disease that affects the red blood cells. The sickle cell hemoglobin offers this resistance because the malaria parasite, which lives within the red blood cell, can be killed when hemoglobin molecules crystallize out of solution. People who are homozygous for normal hemoglobin (AA), on the other hand, have no resistance to malaria.

The incidence of sickle cell anemia parallels the incidence of malaria throughout the tropical areas of the world. The sickle cell trait probably developed in many people throughout the world as a single mutation, or change in genetic material. That mutation conferred an advantage wherever malaria was common, and thus it was favored by natural selection. Sickle cell anemia has persisted wherever it has helped its carriers survive malaria.

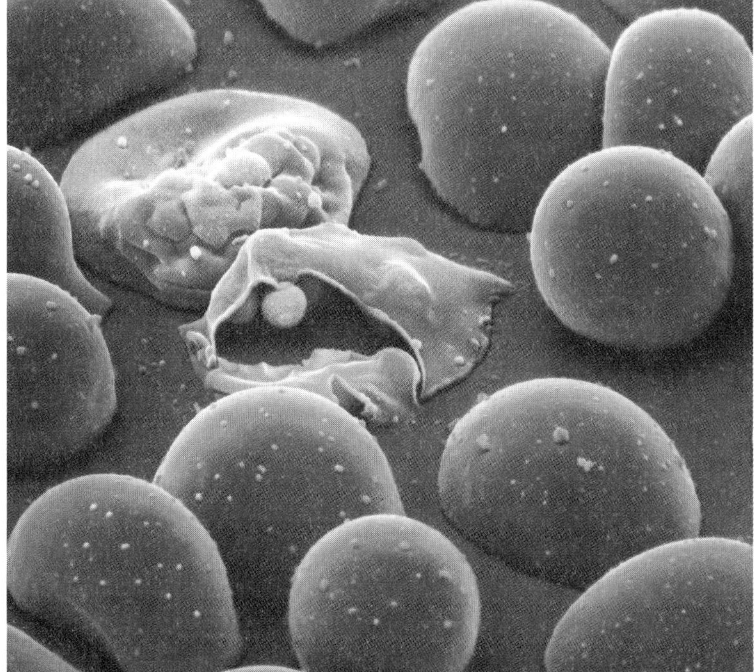

Figure 11–10 *Two of the red blood cells in this scanning electron micrograph have been invaded by the parasite that causes malaria. People who are heterozygous for sickle cell anemia are partially resistant to malaria.*

Figure 11–11 The color of human skin ranges from very light to very dark, depending upon the amount of melanin (dark pigment) present in the skin cells. Very dark-skinned people have alleles that code for production of melanin at all the gene positions for skin color. In very light-skinned people fewer of these positions are occupied by alleles that code for melanin production.

Polygenic Traits

Human traits that are controlled by a number of genes are called **polygenic** (pahl-uh-JEHN-ihk) **traits**. Examples of polygenic human traits include height, body weight, and skin color.

Unlike the simple skin pigmentation system of many animals, which allows a single gene to determine color, the human skin pigmentation system is rather complex. In humans, at least four different genes control skin color, and several of these genes may have multiple alleles. This means that the inheritance of skin color in our species can be somewhat unpredictable. And because skin color is a polygenic trait, children of the same mother and father may have quite different patterns of skin color—each pattern determined by which combination of genes they have inherited from their parents.

The color of human skin ranges from very dark to very light, depending upon the amount of melanin, a dark-colored pigment, present in skin cells. Very dark-skinned people have alleles that code for the production of melanin at all their gene positions for skin color. Light-skinned people, on the other hand, have alleles that code for the production of melanin at fewer gene positions for skin color. The range of human skin color, spread across the globe with no clear dividing line, is an illustration of what a wonderfully diverse species we are.

11–2 SECTION REVIEW

1. List several human traits determined by multiple alleles.
2. How is Huntington disease inherited?
3. What is sickle cell anemia?
4. What are polygenic traits? Give two examples of polygenic traits.
5. If a man with type O blood marries a woman with type AB blood, what are the possible genotypes of their offspring?

11–3 Sex-Linked Inheritance

Section Objectives

- Describe how sex is determined in humans.
- List two conditions of nondisjunction of sex chromosomes.
- Identify some human sex-linked traits.
- Compare sex-linked and sex-influenced traits.

As you will recall from Chapter 10, genes that are located on the sex chromosomes of an organism are inherited in a sex-linked pattern. As in many organisms, the sex in humans is determined by the X and Y chromosomes. In females, meiosis produces egg cells that contain one X chromosome and 22 autosomes. In males, meiosis produces sperm cells of which half contain one Y chromosome and 22 autosomes and the other half contain one X chromosome and 22 autosomes.

The sex of a person is determined by whether an egg cell is fertilized by an X-carrying sperm or a Y-carrying sperm. Males are normally 46XY, meaning that they have a total of 46 chromosomes, including an X chromosome and a Y chromosome. Females are normally 46XX.

Sex Determination

How do the X and Y chromosomes determine whether the sex of the zygote will be male or female? In *Drosophila* (fruit flies), which also have an XY system of sex determination, geneticists have found that sex is determined by the number of X chromosomes. A fruit fly that has a single X chromosome is male, regardless of whether it has a Y chromosome. A fruit fly that has two X chromosomes is female, regardless of whether a Y chromosome is present. This is not so in humans.

THE HUMAN XY SYSTEM Although meiosis is a precise mechanism that separates the two sex chromosomes of a diploid cell into single chromosomes of haploid gamete cells, errors sometimes do take place. The most common of these errors is nondisjunction. **Nondisjunction is the failure of chromosomes to separate properly during one of the stages of meiosis.** See Figure 11–12.

Nondisjunction can produce gametes that contain either two sex chromosomes or no sex chromosomes—a direct contrast to the normal condition of one sex chromosome. When one of these gametes joins with a normal gamete during fertilization, the result is a person with an abnormal number of sex chromosomes.

Figure 11–12 When homologous chromosomes fail to separate during meiosis, nondisjunction results.

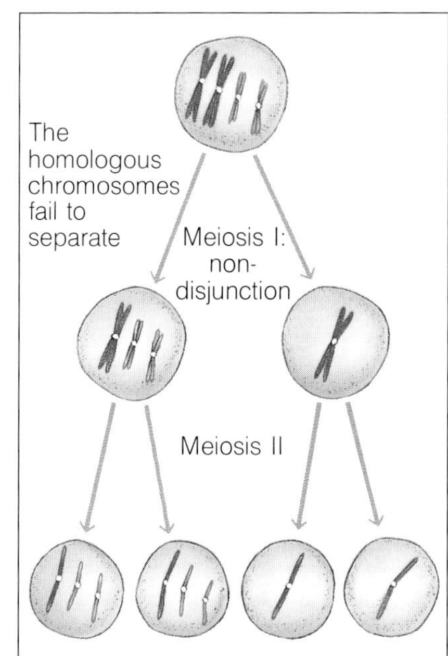

NONDISJUNCTION DISORDERS Roughly 1 birth in 1000 is affected by an abnormality involving nondisjunction of the sex chromosomes. The most common abnormalities are Turner syndrome and Klinefelter syndrome.

People who have Turner syndrome are female in appearance but their female sex organs do not develop at puberty and they are sterile, or unable to have children. Turner syndrome is abbreviated 45X or 45XO, where O denotes the absence of a second sex chromosome. People with Klinefelter syndrome are

SCIENCE, TECHNOLOGY, AND SOCIETY BREAKTHROUGH

Zeroing in on the Maleness Gene

Disorders such as Turner syndrome and Klinefelter syndrome make it clear that maleness is determined by a gene on the Y chromosome. But how would one go about finding that gene? The crucial first steps have now been taken by David Page, a young researcher at the Massachusetts Institute of Technology (MIT). As he studied human sex determination, Page learned that doctors had been treating a number of male patients whose genotypes were 46XX. In every case, these people were found to have portions of the Y chromosome attached to one of their X chromosomes. Page reasoned that these portions must contain the gene for male determination.

Each human has traits that result from the expression of inherited genes. Today, scientists are studying the genetic makeup of X and Y chromosomes to learn how maleness and femaleness are determined.

By analyzing the Y-chromosome portions, Page and his associates found that a single identical piece of the Y chromosome, about 100,000 DNA bases in length, was present in every one of the XX males. Investigators in many laboratories are now concentrating on the structure of this 100,000-base region. Surprisingly, a section of this region is almost identical to a normal fragment found on the X chromosome. No one is certain why the X and Y chromosomes should have a nearly identical fragment, but every new piece of information brings us that much closer to understanding one of the most fundamental of all human differences—maleness and femaleness.

male in appearance, and they, too, are sterile. The abbreviation for Klinefelter syndrome is 47XXY.

It is interesting to note that there have been no reported instances of babies being born without an X chromosome. Embryos without an X chromosome do not seem to develop properly because, as we will soon discover, the X chromosome contains a number of genes that are vital for normal development.

What can we learn from these abnormalities of the sex chromosomes? First, an X chromosome is absolutely essential for survival. Second, sex seems to be determined by the presence or absence of a Y chromosome and not by the number of X chromosomes. For example, there have been reported cases of people who have genotypes 48XXXY and 49XXXXY and are male in appearance.

After years of uncertainty, the reason for the genetic importance of the Y chromosome is finally becoming clear: The Y chromosome contains a gene that switches on the male pattern of growth during embryological development. If this gene is absent, the embryo follows a female pattern of growth.

Sex-Linked Genetic Disorders

Genes that are carried on either the X or the Y chromosome are said to be **sex-linked**. In humans, the small Y chromosome carries very few genes. The much larger X chromosome contains a number of genes that are vital to proper growth and development. And as you just read, it seems to be impossible for humans to develop without the genes of the X chromosome.

It is particularly easy to spot recessive defects in genes located on the X chromosome because the genes are expressed more commonly in males than in females. What is the reason for this? Recall that males have one X chromosome. Thus all X-linked genes are expressed in males, even if they are recessive. In order for a recessive gene to be expressed in females, there must be two copies of it, one on each of the two X chromosomes. If one of the X chromosomes contains a dominant gene, it will mask the expression of the recessive gene.

COLORBLINDNESS Colorblindness is a recessive disorder in which a person cannot distinguish between certain colors. **Most types of colorblindness are caused by sex-linked genes located on the X chromosome.** The genes for colorblindness render people unable to make some of the pigments in the eye necessary for color vision.

The most common type of colorblindness is red-green colorblindness. People afflicted with this trait have difficulty distinguishing the lighter shades of red and green. The frequency of this type of colorblindness varies among different populations. In most Caucasian populations, about 8 percent of the males are affected but only about 1 percent of the females are.

In humans, color vision depends on the varying sensitivity of three groups of specialized nerve cells (cones) in the retina of the eye. One group is sensitive to blue light, one to red light, and one to green light. Colors of any given shade excite a specific level of activity from each of the three groups of nerve cells. We will learn more about color vision in Chapter 37.

Because the gene for color vision is carried on the X chromosome, the dominant allele for normal color vision is represented as X^C and the recessive allele for red-green colorblindness is represented as X^c. Homozygous (X^CX^C) and heterozygous (X^CX^c) females have normal color vision. A female who is heterozygous for colorblindness is said to be a carrier because she carries the recessive allele but does not express it. Although she is not colorblind, she is capable of

Figure 11–13 *Colorblindness is an example of a sex-linked trait. In this cross, a female with normal color vision marries a colorblind male (P_1 generation). What are the phenotypes of the offspring in the F_2 generation?*

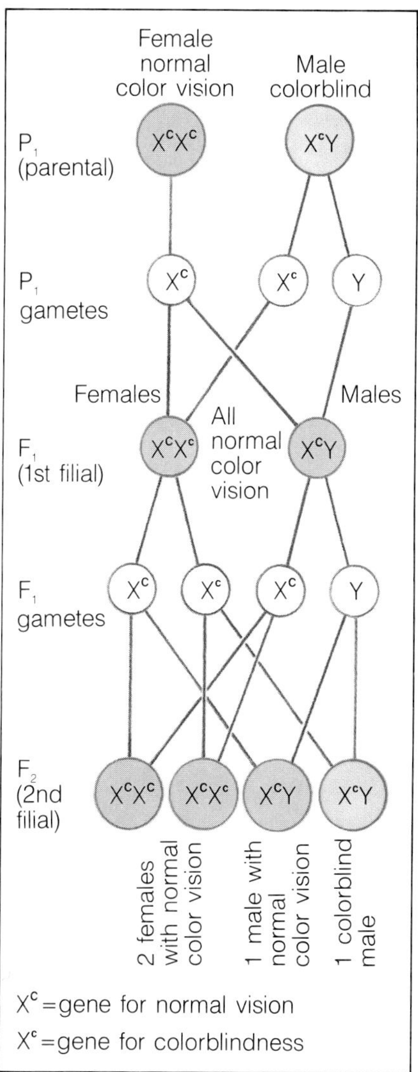

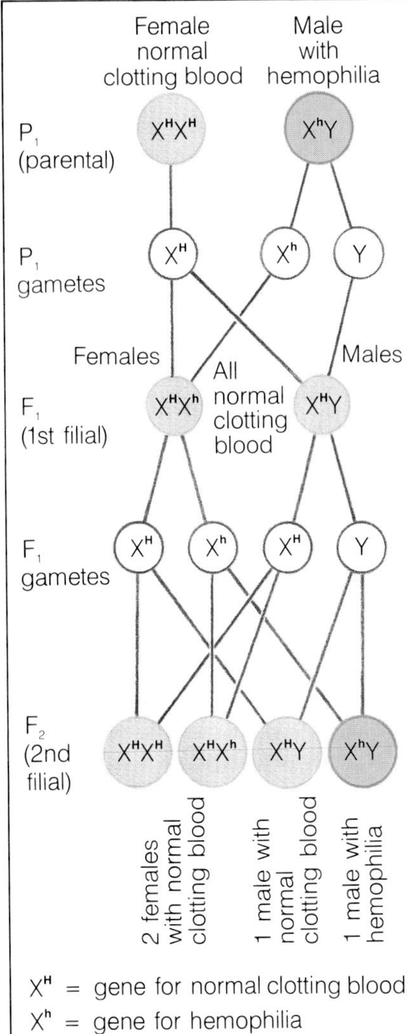

Figure 11–14 *Hemophilia is an example of a sex-linked trait that results in the blood not clotting normally. In this cross, a female with normal-clotting blood marries a male with hemophilia. What are the genotypes of their offspring?*

passing on the gene for colorblindness to her offspring. Only homozygous recessive females (X^cX^c) are colorblind. Because males have only one X chromosome, they are either colorblind (X^cY) or have normal color vision (X^CY).

HEMOPHILIA Another recessive gene on the X chromosome produces a disorder called hemophilia (hee-moh-FIHL-ee-uh), or "bleeder's disease." Hemophilia is a disorder in which the protein antihemophilic factor (AHF) necessary for normal blood clotting is missing. Not only is hemophilia a rarer disorder than colorblindness, affecting only about 1 male in 10,000 and only about 1 female in 100,000,000, it is also a more serious disorder.

People who have hemophilia can bleed to death from even the smallest cut. Internal bleeding (hemorrhaging) can occur from the slightest bump or bruise. In recent years, people who have hemophilia have been successfully treated by removing the AHF from donated blood and injecting it into their blood. Although this procedure is inconvenient and dangerous, since it makes people who have hemophilia susceptible to certain diseases carried in the blood, the use of AHF relieves the most serious effects of the disease.

MUSCULAR DYSTROPHY Muscular dystrophy (DIHS-truh-fee) is an inherited disease that results in the progressive wasting away of skeletal muscle. People who have this disease as young children seldom survive past early adulthood. The most common form of this disease, Duchenne muscular dystrophy, is caused by a gene carried on the X chromosome.

Sex-Influenced Traits

Many traits that may seem to be sex-linked, such as male pattern baldness, are actually caused by genes located on autosomes, not on sex chromosomes. Why then is baldness so much more common in men than it is in women? Male pattern

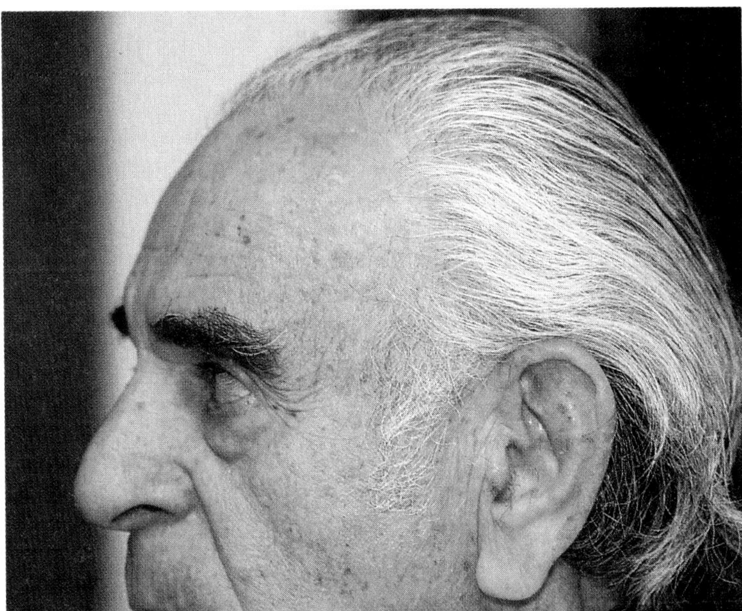

Figure 11–15 *Male pattern baldness is a sex-influenced trait. The expression of this trait is thought to be enhanced by the presence of male sex hormones.*

baldness is a **sex-influenced** trait. **A sex-influenced trait is a trait that is caused by a gene whose expression differs in males and females.**

Many genetic studies indicate that baldness is controlled by a single gene with two alleles, one for normal hair (B) and one for baldness (b). Men and women who have the genotype BB have normal hair, whereas those relatively rare people who have the genotype bb (two baldness alleles) tend to be bald, whether they are male or female. The difference between the sexes occurs in the heterozygous condition, Bb. Males who are heterozygous tend to be bald, whereas females do not. We are not certain how the sex of a person influences the expression of these genes, although it is possible that the male sex hormones may provide an answer.

11–3 SECTION REVIEW

1. How is sex determined in humans?
2. Describe two conditions that are caused by nondisjunction of the sex chromosomes.
3. What are some examples of sex-linked traits?
4. Distinguish between sex-linked and sex-influenced traits.

11–4 Diagnosis of Genetic Disorders

Section Objectives

- Describe how Down syndrome is inherited.
- Identify two methods of detecting genetic disorders during pregnancy.

Humans have been aware of genetic disorders throughout history. For centuries, religious and ethnic laws and customs have reflected a clear understanding on the part of people of the genetic nature of certain disorders. For years, physicians have longed for a way to detect and treat genetic disorders. Today, for some disorders detection is as simple as an examination of a person's chromosomes.

A Chromosomal Abnormality—Down Syndrome

You have just learned about several examples of chromosomal abnormalities. Failures of meiosis, including nondisjunction, cause abnormal combinations of chromosomes to be produced, including those responsible for Turner syndrome and Klinefelter syndrome. Nondisjunction affects autosomes, too.

An example of nondisjunction of autosomes is a condition known as Down syndrome (trisomy 21). In Down syndrome, there is an extra copy of chromosome 21. The presence of this

Figure 11–16 *Down syndrome results from the nondisjunction of chromosome 21. Although people with Down syndrome are physically challenged, they can live normal, active lives.*

extra chromosome can be detected in a careful examination of cells under the light microscope.

Down syndrome results in mental retardation that ranges from mild to severe. It is also characterized by an increased susceptibility to many diseases. In the United States, 1 baby in 800 is born with Down syndrome.

It is not clear why an extra copy of one chromosome should cause so much trouble, but scientists have recently discovered rare cases of Down syndrome in which only 46 chromosomes are present. In each of these cases, a small portion of chromosome 21 is attached to another chromosome. Scientists assume that this small portion must contain the genes that cause Down syndrome. A number of other genetic disorders are also produced by chromosomal abnormalities. Like Down syndrome, they too can be diagnosed by microscopic examination of chromosomes.

Prenatal Diagnosis

Down syndrome and other genetic disorders can now be diagnosed before birth by analyzing cells from the developing embryo. One technique, which is known as **amniocentesis** (am-nee-oh-sehn-TEE-sihs), requires the removal of a small amount of fluid from the sac surrounding the embryo. Cells from the fluid are carefully grown in the laboratory for a few days, treated with a chemical that prevents cell division, and then carefully broken and examined. A karyotype (KAR-ee-uh-tighp), which is a display of all the chromosomes in a cell nucleus, is then prepared to make certain that the chromosomes of the developing embryo are normal.

Chorionic villus biopsy (kor-ee-AHN-ihk VIHL-uhs BIGH-ahp-see), a new alternative to amniocentesis, is a method in which a sample of embryonic cells is removed directly from the membrane surrounding the embryo. Results are obtained more rapidly from this technique than from amniocentesis.

Both amniocentesis and chorionic villus biopsy make it possible to detect Down syndrome and other chromosomal abnormalities. Both techniques are also considered safe for the mother and the developing baby. Scientists are now developing procedures that can detect other genetic disorders. Some of these procedures test for biochemical abnormalities in the embryonic cells, whereas others test for the presence of certain DNA sequences that are characteristic of particular defective genes. The rapid advance of these techniques has made it possible to detect more than 100 genetic disorders from embryonic cells.

Ethical Considerations

Although it is impossible to doubt the effectiveness of prenatal (taking place before birth) diagnosis of genetic disorders, the rapid development of genetic screening techniques is forcing a new set of moral and ethical questions on society. As a society, how should we react to the news that a particular infant will be born with a serious or fatal genetic disorder? Do we favor a society in which such infants are not allowed to develop, or one in which every possible effort is made to preserve all human lives?

Biology has given us great gifts of knowledge and understanding, but it cannot tell us what is proper in such difficult cases. Answers to ethical questions do not come from the laboratory but from the great resources of the human spirit.

11–4 SECTION REVIEW

1. What is Down syndrome?
2. What is amniocentesis? Chorionic villus biopsy?
3. How is a karyotype useful in determining genetic disorders?

LABORATORY INVESTIGATION

OBSERVING HUMAN TRAITS

PROBLEM

What are some patterns of human heredity?

MATERIALS *(per student)*

sheet of paper pencil mirror

PROCEDURE 

1. Copy the data table onto the sheet of paper.
2. In the column labeled Trait, circle your phenotype for each trait listed. A description of the dominant allele for each trait follows.
   Tongue rolling (R) is the ability to roll the tongue up at the edges.
   Widow's peak (W) is a hairline that forms a V in the center of the forehead.
   Free earlobes (F) are those that hang below the point of attachment to the head.
   Dimples (D) are indentations on the cheeks.
   Freckles (F) are brownish spots on the skin.
3. Transfer the data from your data table onto the chalkboard, where your teacher has constructed a chart to collect class data.
4. After your classmates have recorded their data on the chalkboard, record the information in the appropriate place in your data table.
5. To determine the percentage of students demonstrating each trait, divide the number of students who have the trait by the total number of students in the class and then multiply this number by 100. Record the data in the appropriate place in your data table.

OBSERVATIONS

1. For each trait, which occurs more frequently: the dominant or recessive allele?
2. Which trait is the most common in your class? The least common?
3. What is the ratio of the percentages for each of the traits?

ANALYSIS AND CONCLUSIONS

1. Do dominant traits occur more often than recessive traits? Explain your answer.
2. What would happen to your results if you were to perform this investigation with five other classes and recorded their data?

Trait		Number of Students Demonstrating Dominant Phenotype	Number of Students Demonstrating Recessive Phenotype	Percentage Demonstrating Dominant Phenotype	Percentage Demonstrating Recessive Phenotype
Dominant	**Recessive**				
Tongue roller (R)	Nonroller (r)				
Widow's peak (W)	Straight hairline (w)				
Free earlobes (E)	Attached earlobes (e)				
Dimples (D)	No dimples (d)				
Freckles (F)	No freckles (f)				

STUDENT STUDY GUIDE

SUMMARIZING THE CONCEPTS

The key concepts in each section of this chapter are listed below to help you review the chapter content. Make sure you understand each concept and its relationship to other concepts and to the theme of this chapter.

11–1 "It Runs in the Family"

- Many human traits are inherited by the action of dominant and recessive genes, although other traits are determined through more complicated gene interactions.
- Each gamete (sperm cell or egg cell) contains 23 chromosomes.
- During fertilization, sperm and egg unite and a zygote is produced that contains 46 chromosomes.
- Of the 46 chromosomes found in the human diploid cell, 2 are the sex chromosomes (X and Y) and the remaining 44 are called autosomes.

11–2 The Inheritance of Human Traits

- Multiple alleles are three or more alleles of the same gene that code for a single trait. ABO and Rh blood groups are determined by multiple alleles.
- Sickle cell anemia is a disorder that causes the normally disk-shaped red blood cells to become sickle-shaped. The gene for normal hemoglobin is codominant with the sickle cell gene.
- Polygenic traits are traits that are controlled by a number of genes.

11–3 Sex-Linked Inheritance

- Nondisjunction is the failure of chromosomes to separate during one of the stages of meiosis.
- Genes that are carried on either the X or the Y chromosome are said to be sex-linked.
- A sex-influenced trait is a trait that is caused by a gene whose expression differs in males and females.

11–4 Diagnosis of Genetic Disorders

- Down syndrome is an example of a condition caused by the nondisjunction of autosomes.
- Many genetic disorders can now be diagnosed before birth because of such genetic screening techniques as amniocentesis and chorionic villus biopsy.

REVIEWING KEY TERMS

Vocabulary terms are important to your understanding of biology. The key terms listed below are those you should be especially familiar with. Review these terms and their meanings. Then use each term in a complete sentence. If you are not sure of a term's meaning, return to the appropriate section and review its definition.

11–1 "It Runs in the Family"
gamete
zygote

11–2 The Inheritance of Human Traits
multiple allele
polygenic trait

11–3 Sex-Linked Inheritance
sex-linked
sex-influenced

11–4 Diagnosis of Genetic Disorders
amniocentesis
chorionic villus biopsy

CHAPTER REVIEW

CONTENT REVIEW

Multiple Choice

Choose the letter of the answer that best completes each statement.

1. An example of a trait that is determined by multiple alleles is
a. Huntington disease.
b. ABO blood groups.
c. Down syndrome.
d. hemophilia.

2. Three brothers have blood types A, B, and O. What are the chances that the parents of these three will produce a fourth child whose blood type is AB?
a. 0 percent
c. 50 percent
b. 25 percent
d. 100 percent

3. A disorder that results from a change in an amino acid in the hemoglobin molecule is
a. sickle cell anemia.
b. hemophilia.
c. Down syndrome.
d. Turner syndrome.

4. Which is an example of a polygenic trait?
a. skin color
b. hemophilia
c. ABO blood groups
d. Huntington disease

5. Which parental pair could produce a colorblind female?
a. homozygous normal vision mother and colorblind father
b. colorblind mother and normal vision father
c. heterozygous normal vision mother and normal vision father
d. heterozygous normal vision mother and colorblind father

6. Which is an example of a sex-influenced trait?
a. Down syndrome
b. colorblindness
c. male pattern baldness
d. skin color

7. What is the total number of chromosomes in a diploid cell of a person with Down syndrome?
a. 22
c. 44
b. 23
d. 47

8. Which of the following techniques is directly associated with the diagnoses of certain genetic disorders by the examination of chromosomes?
a. blood typing
b. karyotyping
c. chemical screening
d. microsurgery

True or False

Determine whether each statement is true or false. If it is true, write "true." If it is false, change the underlined word or words to make the statement true.

1. During fertilization, sperm and egg unite and produce a <u>gamete</u>.

2. A person with <u>type A</u> blood has red blood cells that contain antigen <u>B</u>.

3. A genotype Rh^+Rh^- will <u>produce the Rh negative</u> phenotype.

4. People who are <u>heterozygous</u> for sickle cell anemia are <u>partially resistant</u> to malaria.

5. Based on the pattern of inheritance of sex-linked traits, if a male has hemophilia, he has <u>one gene</u> for this trait on the sex chromosomes in each of his diploid cells.

6. The dominant allele for normal color vision is represented as <u>X^C</u>.

7. In Down syndrome, there is an extra copy of chromosome <u>16</u>.

8. <u>Chorionic villus biopsy</u> is a genetic screening technique in which a small amount of fluid is removed from the sac surrounding the developing embryo.

CONCEPT MASTERY

Use your understanding of the concepts developed in the chapter to answer each of the following in a brief paragraph.

1. Why are humans not considered good organisms for genetic studies?
2. Explain why type O blood is sometimes referred to as the universal donor. Is this true in the case of O^+ blood?
3. What is the cause of sickle cell anemia?
4. Why is it easy to believe that the sickle cell trait may have arisen independently in several places throughout the world?
5. What is the evolutionary connection between the incidences of sickle cell anemia and the incidences of malaria?
6. Why are there more colorblind males than there are colorblind females?
7. What evidence suggests that an X chromosome is essential for normal development? Is the same true of the Y chromosome?
8. The genes for red-green colorblindness and hemophilia are located on the X chromosome. How might you determine whether these genes are closely linked?
9. How would you determine whether a human gene was sex-linked?

CRITICAL AND CREATIVE THINKING

Discuss each of the following in a brief paragraph.

1. **Applying concepts** Cystic fibrosis (CF) is caused by an autosomal recessive gene and is a fatal disorder that affects people of European ancestry. CF is characterized by a production of thick mucus that clogs the lungs and parts of the digestive system, making it difficult to breathe or eat. Suppose two people without a history of CF in their immediate families have a child with CF. They would like to have another child, but they are concerned about whether the second child will have CF. Can you help them predict the chances of having a second child with CF?
2. **Making diagrams** Polydactyly is a human characteristic in which a person has extra digits (fingers or toes) on his or her hands or feet. The trait for polydactyly is dominant over the trait for five digits on the hands and/or feet. Suppose a man who is heterozygous for this trait marries a woman with the normal number of digits. What are the possible genotypes and phenotypes of their offspring? Draw a Punnett square showing the possible results of this cross.
3. **Relating concepts** Nine of ten children in a family are right-handed. Right-handedness is a dominant trait. Assume that this trait is controlled by a pair of genes.
   a. What is the genotype of a left-handed child?
   b. What are the possible genotypes of the right-handed children?
   c. What are the possible genotypes of the parents?
   d. Could these parents have produced only right-handed children? Explain.
   e. If these parents had produced only one child, would this child have been left- or right-handed? Explain your answer.
4. **Making inferences** Discuss the impact of genetic screening techniques on society.
5. **Using the writing process** Your career ambition is to be a science reporter. You are sent by your school newspaper to interview a physician who works with human genetic disorders. Prepare a script of the questions you would like answered.

CHAPTER 12

Genetic Engineering

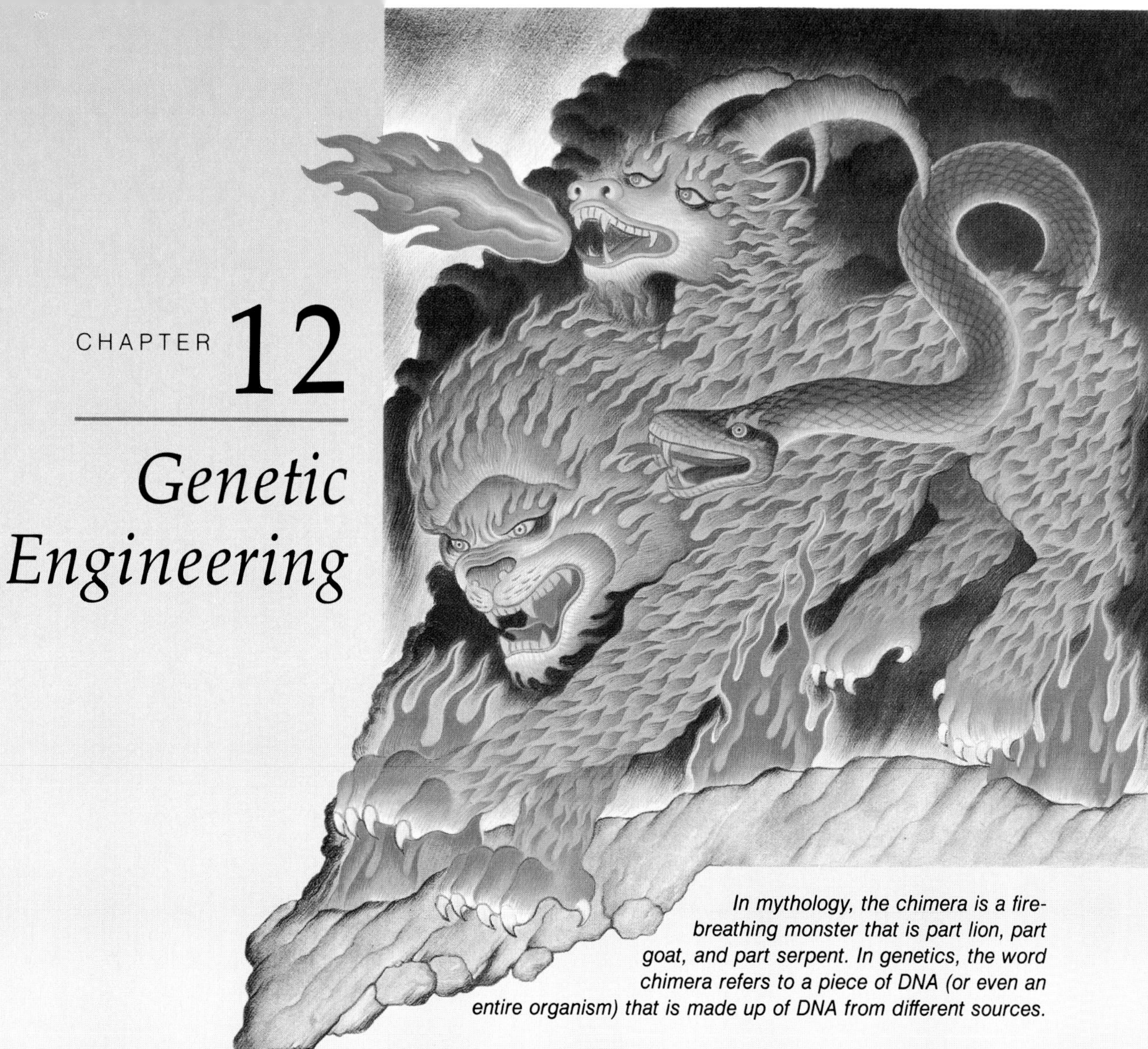

In mythology, the chimera is a fire-breathing monster that is part lion, part goat, and part serpent. In genetics, the word chimera refers to a piece of DNA (or even an entire organism) that is made up of DNA from different sources.

In Greek mythology, the chimera was a frightening beast with the head of a lion, the body of a goat, and the tail of a serpent. The idea of combining the characteristics of many animals into one, however, did not originate with the Greeks. The Sphinx of Egypt and the winged lions of Assyria are just two examples of composite monsters that predate the Greek myths. Although we do not take these stories seriously today, it is ironic to note that biology has progressed to the point where these old myths have been dusted off. Today the word chimera has a different meaning: It refers to fragments of DNA from two organisms that have been joined to make a single DNA molecule. Although these DNA chimeras have not yet merged the serpent, the goat, and the lion, they have carried human genes into mice, produced plants that glow in the dark, and made it possible to design new organisms to suit human needs.

CHAPTER OUTLINE

12–1 Modifying the Living World

Section Objectives

- Describe breeding strategies that have been used to modify living things.
- Explain how mutations in organisms can be useful to humans.

We humans are rarely, if ever, satisfied with the world around us. We are always trying to improve it. Humans are not content with merely altering the course of a river, building cities, or sailing the seas. For thousands of years we've been trying to do something equally remarkable: to make "better" living things.

Breeding Strategies

Farmers and ranchers throughout the world have long tried to improve the organisms with which they work. **By selecting the most productive plants or animals to produce the next generation, people have found that the productivity of a domesticated species can gradually be increased.** Such an increase in productivity results from using breeding strategies such as selective breeding and two special forms of selective breeding: inbreeding and hybridization.

SELECTIVE BREEDING The oldest and most obvious way of improving a species is by **selective breeding**, or selecting a few individuals to serve as parents for the next generation. By crossing only those individual plants or animals that have a

Figure 12–1 *The small horse is a full-grown miniature horse. Miniature horses, which are 86 centimeters high at the shoulder (or less), are the product of selective breeding. First produced in the mid-1700s, they were originally intended to pull ore carts in the low, narrow passages of mines. However, they were soon adopted as exotic pets by wealthy families.*

Figure 12–2 *Selective breeding has produced domestic animals such as pigs (top) that are very different from their wild ancestors (bottom).*

desired characteristic, the breeder can improve the yield of a crop plant, increase the milk production of cattle, or develop flowers of a particular color. Most present-day crop plants were first developed by selective breeding.

Luther Burbank of California (1849–1926) was perhaps the world's foremost selective breeder. Burbank produced more than 250 new varieties of fruit by selective breeding, but his work also extended to other plants, including the daisy and the famous Burbank Potato.

INBREEDING Once a breeder has successfully produced an organism with a useful set of characteristics, the next concern is to maintain a stock of similar organisms. The most direct method is **inbreeding**, or crossing individuals with similar characteristics so that those characteristics will appear in their offspring. Often the individuals crossed in inbreeding are closely related. The many varieties of purebred dogs—including German shepherds, toy poodles, and Great Danes—are maintained by inbreeding. Puppies are considered purebreds only if both their parents are registered members of the same breed.

Although inbreeding is useful in retaining a certain set of characteristics, it does have its risks. Because most of the members of an inbred line are genetically similar, the chances that recessive genetic defects will show up after repeated inbreeding become much greater. Problems in many dog breeds, including deformities in the joints and progressive blindness in German shepherds and golden retrievers, have resulted from repeated inbreeding.

HYBRIDIZATION One of the most useful of the breeder's techniques is **hybridization**, a cross between dissimilar individuals. Hybridization often involves crossing members of different (but related) species. Hybrids, the individuals produced by such crosses, are often hardier than either of the parents. This phenomenon is known as hybrid vigor. All breeds of corn that are grown commercially are hybrids, and every year corn breeders produce new hybrids that combine such basic characteristics as disease resistance, yield per acre, and nutritional value. Modern hybrid corn produces as much as ten times the crop per acre of older varieties of corn.

Mutations: Producing New Kinds of Organisms

As useful as selective breeding is, it is confined to characteristics that already exist in the population. But as you may recall from earlier chapters, mutations, which are inheritable changes in DNA, can sometimes produce organisms with new characteristics. If the new characteristics are desirable, breeders can use selective breeding to produce an entire population possessing these characteristics.

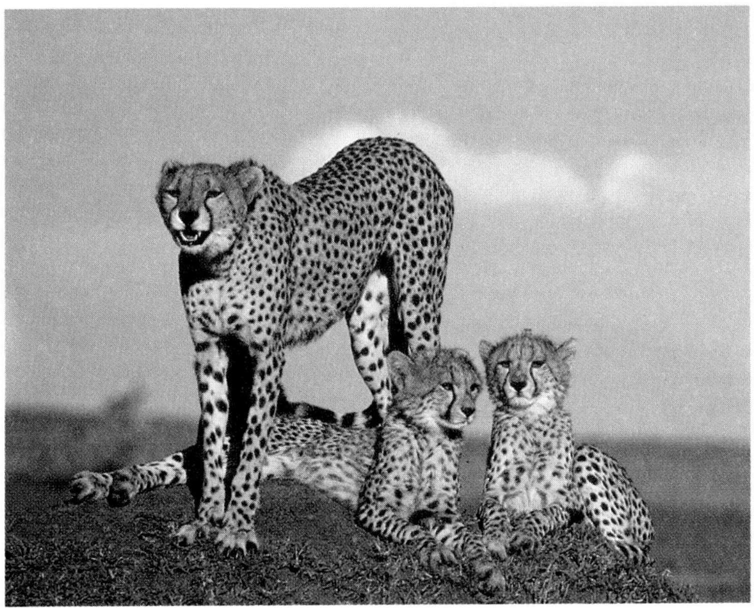

Figure 12–3 *Inbreeding has resulted in an increased susceptibility to diseases and deformities in cheetahs (bottom), dogs, and other organisms. Fortunately for this golden retriever puppy (top), which was bred by Ken Miller, its ancestors have been certified to be free of certain inherited defects. The puppy can be expected to lead a happy—and healthy—life.*

Figure 12–4 *Seedless oranges and hairless mice are the result of mutations.*

Of course, a breeder may not want to wait for a beneficial mutation to appear naturally. In such a case, a breeder may decide to artificially increase the chances of mutations occurring in a group of organisms. This can be done with agents or substances known as **mutagens**. Mutagens, which include radiation and chemicals, cause mutations. Many mutations are harmful; but with luck and perseverance, a few mutants (individuals with mutations) with desirable characteristics not found in the original population may be produced.

Mutagenesis, or using mutagens to increase the mutation rate, is particularly useful with bacteria. Their small size enables millions of organisms to undergo mutagenesis at the same time, thereby increasing the chances of producing a useful mutant. Using this technique, scientists have been able to develop hundreds of useful bacterial strains. It has even been possible to produce bacteria that can digest oil and are thus useful in cleaning up oil spills.

SCIENCE, TECHNOLOGY, AND SOCIETY

Uniformity or Diversity?

Why would any sensible person want to raise a breed of cows that produces less milk than other breeds? Or a breed of sheep that has coarser wool than other breeds?

At one time, the goals of livestock breeders were plain: to produce animals that yielded high-quality products, were highly productive, and completely predictable. Uniformity was particularly important. It is easier and less expensive to raise large numbers of animals if all the individuals have the same needs and growing times.

Although belted Galloway cattle are not as productive as modern breeds, they contain a wealth of potentially useful genes, such as those for the ability to thrive on poor-quality food.

However there is a problem associated with the improvements that result from uniformity in domestic animals. Modern breeds are homogeneous; that is, the genes of individuals are almost identical. Although genetic similarity is good in terms of raising livestock and producing animal products of uniformly high quality, it is potentially disastrous in the long run. Similar animals are similarly vulnerable to changes in their environment. For example, a single disease could wipe out an entire herd or flock of genetically similar animals. (In a group of genetically diverse animals, the same disease might kill only susceptible individuals. The resistant individuals could go on to produce resistant offspring.)

This is where the old-fashioned breeds come in. Although the productivity of old-fashioned breeds is lower than that of modern breeds, they have greater genetic diversity. They are vital to modern agriculture because they serve as banks of genes that may be useful in livestock at a future date.

So here's the dilemma for breeders: The breeding strategies for preserving genetic diversity are opposite those for producing commercially feasible livestock. To preserve genetic diversity, breeders must ensure that as many individuals as possible breed and pass on their genes to the next generation. Selective breeding—allowing only the best individuals to produce the next generation—automatically breeds out many genes. And these may be precisely the genes that are needed in the future.

12–1 SECTION REVIEW

1. What is selective breeding? Inbreeding? Hybridization?
2. What are some advantages of breeding strategies?
3. Why might breeders want to cause mutations in plants?
4. Many human societies have laws preventing close blood relatives from marrying. How are these restrictions related to the practice of inbreeding?

12–2 Genetic Engineering: Technology and Heredity

Section Objectives

- Describe how DNA is isolated, cut, spliced, and handled.
- Explain how DNA is used to transform cells and organisms.

Ultimately, the selection techniques that humans use to generate new breeds of plants and animals affect DNA, the molecule that carries genetic information. Hybridization, inbreeding, and mutagenesis are, after all, indirect techniques designed to alter the DNA of a particular organism.

In the last two decades molecular biologists have developed a powerful new set of techniques that affect DNA directly. For the first time biologists can engineer a set of genetic changes directly into an organism's DNA. Appropriately enough, this new form of manipulation is called **genetic engineering.**

The Techniques of Genetic Engineering

Genetic engineering could not have come about without the development of a technology to support the process. The Wright Brothers could not have built an airplane without the existence of a small gasoline engine and lightweight metal tubing. Such equipment was actually developed for the automobile and the bicycle; but once available, it was adapted to the needs of a flying machine. The story of genetic engineering is much the same.

Imagine for a moment the tools you would need to take a gene from one organism and place it into another. First, you would need a way to carefully cut the DNA containing the gene away from the genes surrounding it. Second, you would have to find a way to combine that gene with a piece of DNA from the recipient organism; that is, the organism that will receive the DNA. Third, you would have to insert the combined DNA into the new organism. Finally, it would be useful to have a way to read the sequences of nucleotide bases in the gene in order to analyze the genes that you are manipulating. Each of these tools is now available, making it possible to insert a gene from one organism into another.

Figure 12–5 These strands of artificial DNA were synthesized from DNA extracted from animal cells. The techniques of genetic engineering allow scientists to manipulate and change DNA directly.

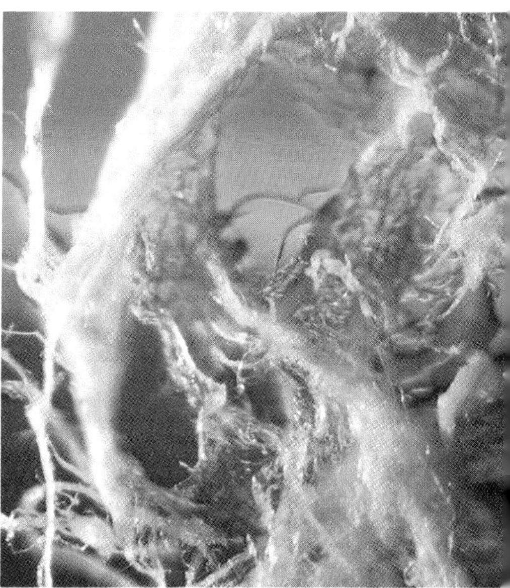

RESTRICTION ENZYMES Genes can be cut at specific DNA sequences by proteins known as **restriction enzymes.** More than 75 different kinds of restriction enzymes are known, and each one "recognizes" and cuts DNA at a particular sequence. The cutting sites of three typical restriction enzymes are shown in Figure 12–6 on page 252. Each one of the restriction enzymes shown "recognizes" a site of four to six nucleotide pairs and then makes a cut across both strands of DNA.

The accuracy of these enzymes is breathtaking. They will not cut any sequence other than the one they recognize, even if five out of six bases are identical to their recognition site. Restriction enzymes make it possible to cut DNA into fragments that can be isolated, separated, and analyzed.

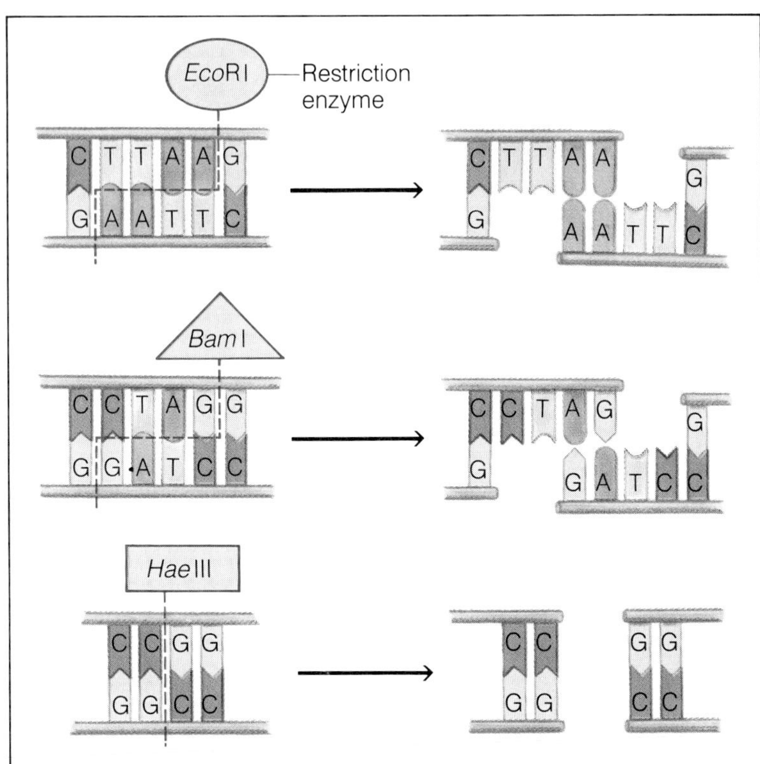

Figure 12–6 Different restriction enzymes "recognize" different sequences of bases on DNA molecules. Each restriction enzyme cuts DNA at the sites at which its recognition sequence occurs.

DNA RECOMBINATION DNA fragments cannot function all by themselves. They must become part of the genetic material of living cells before the gene they contain can be activated. In the second step of genetic engineering, DNA fragments are made into part of the recipient cell's genetic material. This is done by combining DNA fragments with DNA from the recipient cell.

For example, DNA fragments may be combined with bacterial DNA so that they can later be inserted into a bacterial cell. Bacteria often contain small circular DNA molecules known as **plasmids** in addition to their chromosomes. These plasmids can be removed from bacterial cells and cut with the same restriction enzyme used to produce the DNA fragments. The cuts made by the restriction enzyme produce matching "sticky ends" on the DNA fragments and the cut plasmids. These sticky ends are the sites at which a DNA fragment and a plasmid can be joined end to end, thereby forming a new plasmid that contains a piece of foreign DNA. See Figure 12–7.

Figure 12–7 Plasmids are small circular pieces of bacterial DNA.

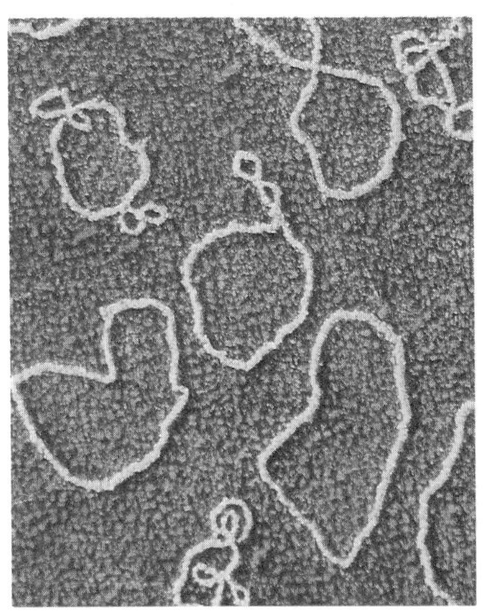

Like the mythical chimera (kigh-MIHR-ah), which you read about in the chapter opener, the combined DNA formed by fusing a DNA fragment and a plasmid consists of parts from different kinds of organisms. In genetic engineering, molecules of combined DNA are known as chimeras because they are produced by combining DNA from different species. Combined DNA is also known as **recombinant DNA**, since DNA from two sources has been recombined to produce it.

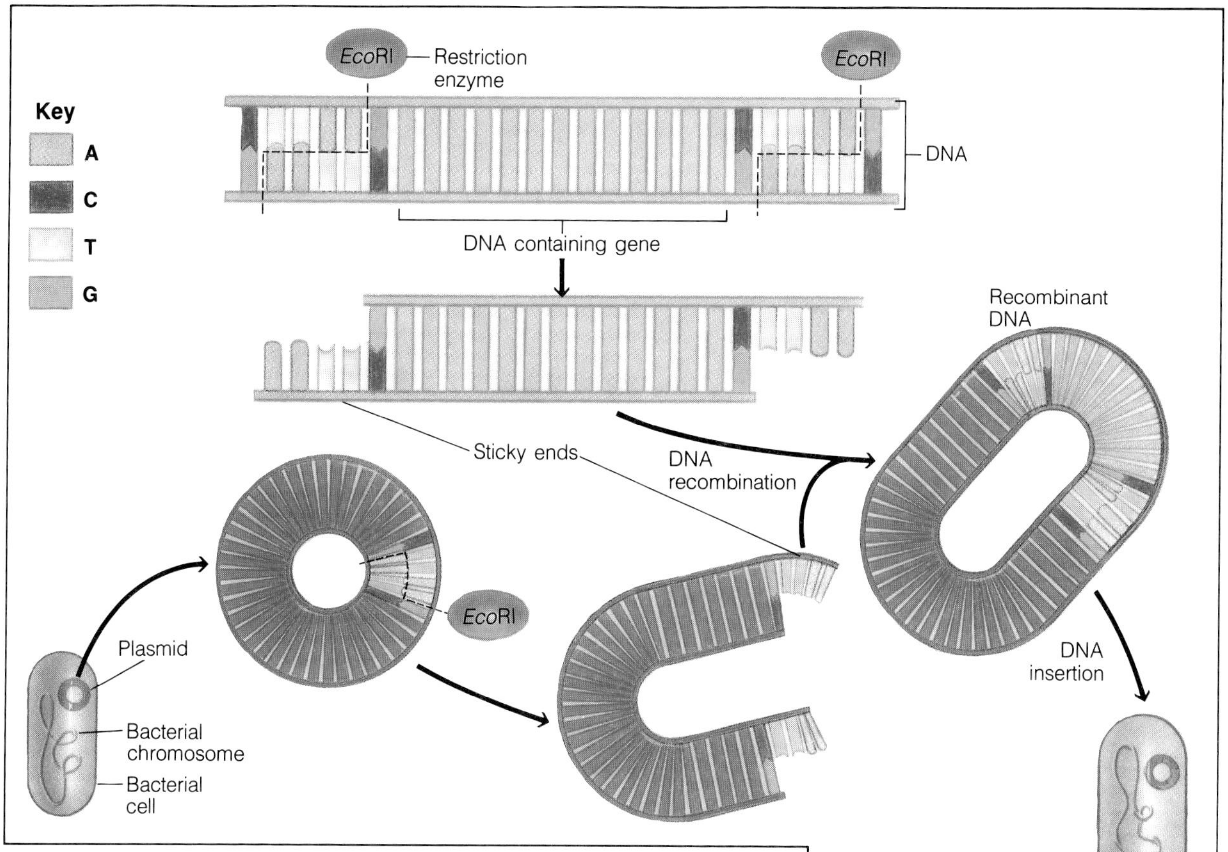

Key
A
C
T
G
EcoRI — Restriction enzyme
EcoRI
DNA
DNA containing gene
Recombinant DNA
Sticky ends
DNA recombination
EcoRI
Plasmid
Bacterial chromosome
Bacterial cell
DNA insertion

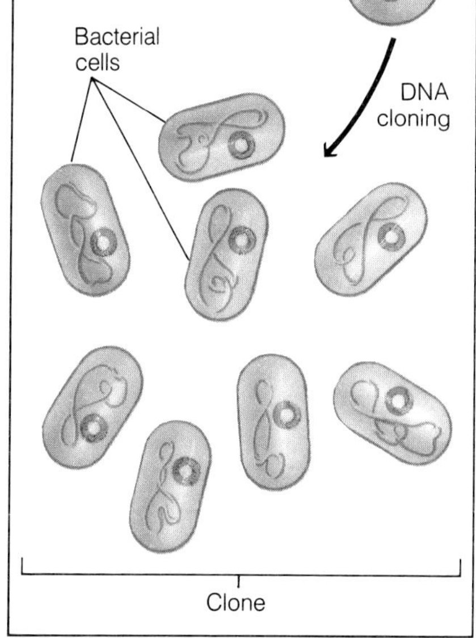

Figure 12–8 *In genetic engineering, foreign genes are inserted into plasmids. The altered plasmids are then used to carry the foreign genes into a bacterial cell.*

DNA INSERTION In the first two steps of genetic engineering, DNA fragments containing the desired gene are obtained and then inserted into DNA that has been removed from the recipient cell, thereby producing recombinant DNA. But how is this DNA put back into living cells?

It is easiest to insert DNA into bacterial cells. The recombinant DNA is mixed in with millions of bacteria suspended in a dense salt solution. After a few minutes, several bacteria will take up the DNA. These bacteria can then be isolated and grown into large colonies that contain the recombinant DNA. The technical term for a large number of cells grown from a single cell is **clone**, and so this technique is sometimes known as DNA cloning.

Using different techniques, recombinant DNA can be inserted into cells other than bacteria—for example, cells from yeasts, animals, and plants. These techniques include microinjection with a glass needle, fusion with plasmid-like DNA, and a new procedure in which DNA is attached to fine wirelike pellets that are then shot into cells with a microscopic gun.

DNA SEQUENCING Sequencing a piece of DNA, or reading the sequence of DNA bases along its length, can now be accomplished. Only one of the two strands of the DNA double helix is used in the process of DNA sequencing. However, many copies of this one strand are needed. These multiple copies can be produced through the process of DNA cloning.

DNA Sequencing

1. A radioactive label is attached to the "front" end of each strand of DNA.
2. The strands of DNA are divided among four test tubes. Each test tube undergoes a different chemical treatment. These treatments selectively break the chemical bonds between one of the DNA bases and the part of the DNA strand that follows that base. For example, the chemical added to test tube 1 breaks the DNA strand wherever adenine (A) occurs. Because only some of the bonds between adenine and the rest of the DNA strand are broken, the DNA is split into pieces of different lengths, some of which include the radioactive label.
3. The DNA pieces are carefully injected into a gel. A process called electrophoresis is used to separate these fragments. In electrophoresis, an electric field is used to separate substances by moving them through a gel. In this case, the pieces are separated according to their length because smaller pieces of DNA move faster than larger pieces. After a while, the DNA fragments appear as radioactive bands in the gel. The pattern of the bands reveals the order of the bases in the original strand of DNA. The DNA sequence can literally be read off the gel!

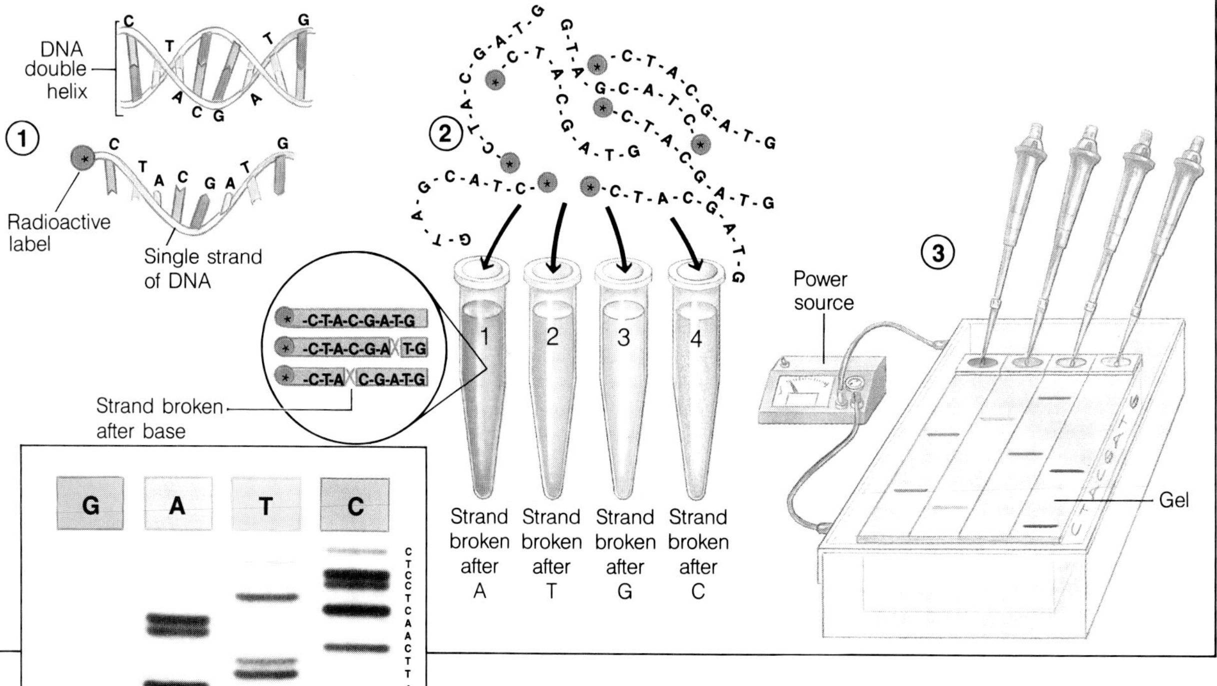

Figure 12–9 In DNA sequencing, DNA is treated to produce pieces that are then separated by electrophoresis. The bands on the gel that result from this process reveal the sequence of the bases in DNA (inset).

In DNA sequencing, a radioactive label (in the form of a radioactive phosphorus atom) is added to single-stranded DNA. The DNA is divided into four groups that undergo different chemical treatments. The chemical treatments break the DNA into pieces that when separated reveal the positions of the bases on the original strand. The DNA pieces are separated by an electrical field in a process called electrophoresis (ee-lehk-troh-fuh-REE-sihs). Refer to Figure 12–9 for a more detailed explanation of DNA sequencing.

Engineering New Organisms

Recombinant DNA technology has advanced rapidly in the past few years. Techniques now exist for cutting and splicing DNA molecules, for ensuring that the foreign gene becomes part of the chromosome of the recipient cell, and for controlling the gene once it has been inserted. Organisms that contain such foreign genes are said to be **transgenic**.

GENETIC ENGINEERING IN BACTERIA When a gene coding for a human protein is properly inserted into bacteria, the recombinant cells can be used to produce large amounts of the protein quickly and inexpensively. As recently as ten years ago, human growth hormone, a protein needed for normal growth and development, was rare and extremely costly. (It could only be obtained in small amounts from cadavers, or dead bodies used for scientific purposes.) Thus people who do not produce normal amounts of this hormone themselves could not always be guaranteed a supply. Genetically engineered bacteria that contain the human growth hormone gene now produce large quantities of this protein, making it plentiful enough to treat everyone who needs it. Other genetically engineered bacteria produce human insulin (another hormone) and interferon, a protein that blocks the growth of viruses and may be useful in cancer treatment.

Figure 12–10 *The hepatitis B vaccine being tested here for purity was produced by genetically engineered bacteria.*

GENETIC ENGINEERING IN PLANTS DNA can be injected into plant cells directly or attached to plasmids of certain species of bacteria that infect plant cells. Plant cell biologists have developed techniques that enable a complete transgenic plant to be grown from the cells containing recombinant DNA. The goals of genetic engineering in plants include the production of plants that manufacture natural insecticides and the production of plants that contain genes that enable them to produce their own nitrogen nutrients, thus eliminating the need for fertilizers. Australian researchers have successfully transferred into alfalfa the gene for an enzyme that aids in the synthesis of amino acids and thereby increases the protein content of the plants. These engineered plants will be a new source of protein-rich feed for Australian sheep.

Can genes from animals be made to work in plants? Steven Howell and his associates at the University of California at San Diego provided the answer to that question in 1986. They isolated the gene for luciferase, the enzyme that makes fireflies glow, and inserted it into tobacco cells. When whole plants were grown from the recombinant cells and the gene was activated, the plants glowed in the dark!

Figure 12–11 *Transgenic bacteria are used to make important chemicals such as human insulin (left). This transgenic tobacco plant contains firefly genes (right). When the firefly genes are activated, the plant glows!*

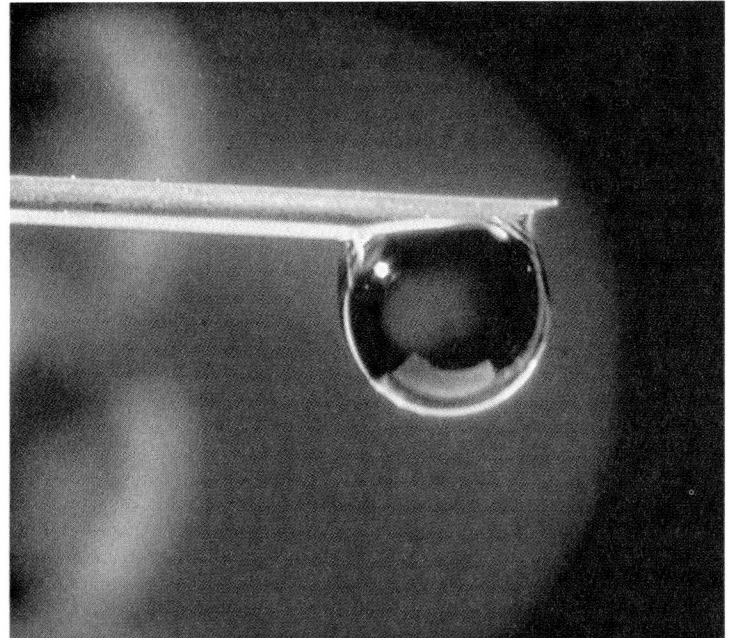

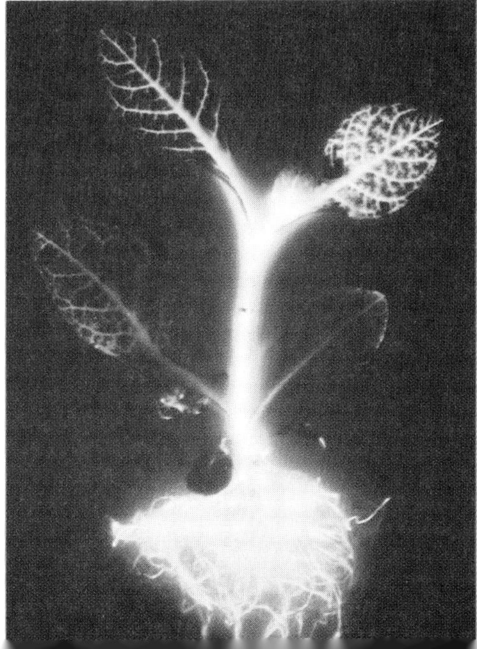

Figure 12–12 *This giant mouse, shown next to a normal mouse, is one of the first types of transgenic mammals. The giant mouse developed from a mouse egg that was injected with recombinant DNA containing the gene for rat growth hormone.*

GENETIC ENGINEERING IN ANIMALS Genetic engineering has successfully produced a variety of transgenic insects, roundworms, and vertebrates. In one experiment, a group of researchers introduced the growth hormone gene from rainbow trout into carp and produced a bigger, faster-growing fish. The genes of the AIDS virus have been introduced into mice to help develop a strain of mice that can be used for research on the AIDS disease. A number of research groups are now experimenting with transgenic farm animals in hopes of producing meat and milk more quickly.

12–2 SECTION REVIEW

1. What are restriction enzymes? How are they used in genetic engineering?
2. Define recombinant DNA, plasmid, and clone. How do these terms apply to genetic engineering?
3. What is a transgenic plant? How does it differ from a hybrid?
4. What are some of the advantages of genetically engineered proteins such as human growth hormone?

Section Objectives

- Describe some possible applications of analyzing and sequencing human DNA.
- Discuss ethical issues involving new genetic techniques.

12–3 The New Human Genetics

The rapid development of molecular biology has produced a number of other developments. For the first time it has become possible to think about curing genetic diseases. We have also begun to wonder about the practicality of decoding the entire human **genome**, which is all of the genes possessed by humans. And we have started to apply molecular biology to personal identification and the diagnosis of disease.

Analyzing Human DNA

As we saw in Chapter 11, researchers have already developed tests for genetic disorders, which compare human DNA to DNA sequences known to produce the disorders—Huntington disease and sickle cell anemia, for example. In the near future, DNA obtained from prenatal sampling may be tested for the presence of a great many other disorders, enabling physicians to treat some disorders before birth and to be prepared to treat others shortly after birth.

Researchers have also begun to look for genes that might predispose individuals to other medical problems, such as heart disease, diabetes, and cancer. If tests that identify individuals at risk can be developed, early medical attention would be able to prolong many lives.

DNA Fingerprinting

The great complexity of the human genome ensures that no individual is exactly like any other. In the last three years, medical researchers have used this biological fact to add a powerful new tool to criminal investigations. The tool is known as **DNA fingerprinting**. DNA fingerprinting takes advantage of the fact that large portions of the human genome are made up of repeated sequences of varying lengths that do not code for proteins. It has turned out that individuals may have completely different numbers of these repeated units between actual working genes. You may have 15 repeats between two genes; the person sitting next to you in class might have 6 repeats between the same two genes; and someone else may have 33.

Here's how DNA fingerprinting works: A small sample of human DNA is cut with a restriction enzyme. The resulting fragments are separated by size through the process of electrophoresis. Fragments that contain the repeats are then labeled

Figure 12–13 *DNA fingerprinting can be used to match up a suspect with blood, sperm, or other bits of DNA-containing material left at the scene of a crime.*

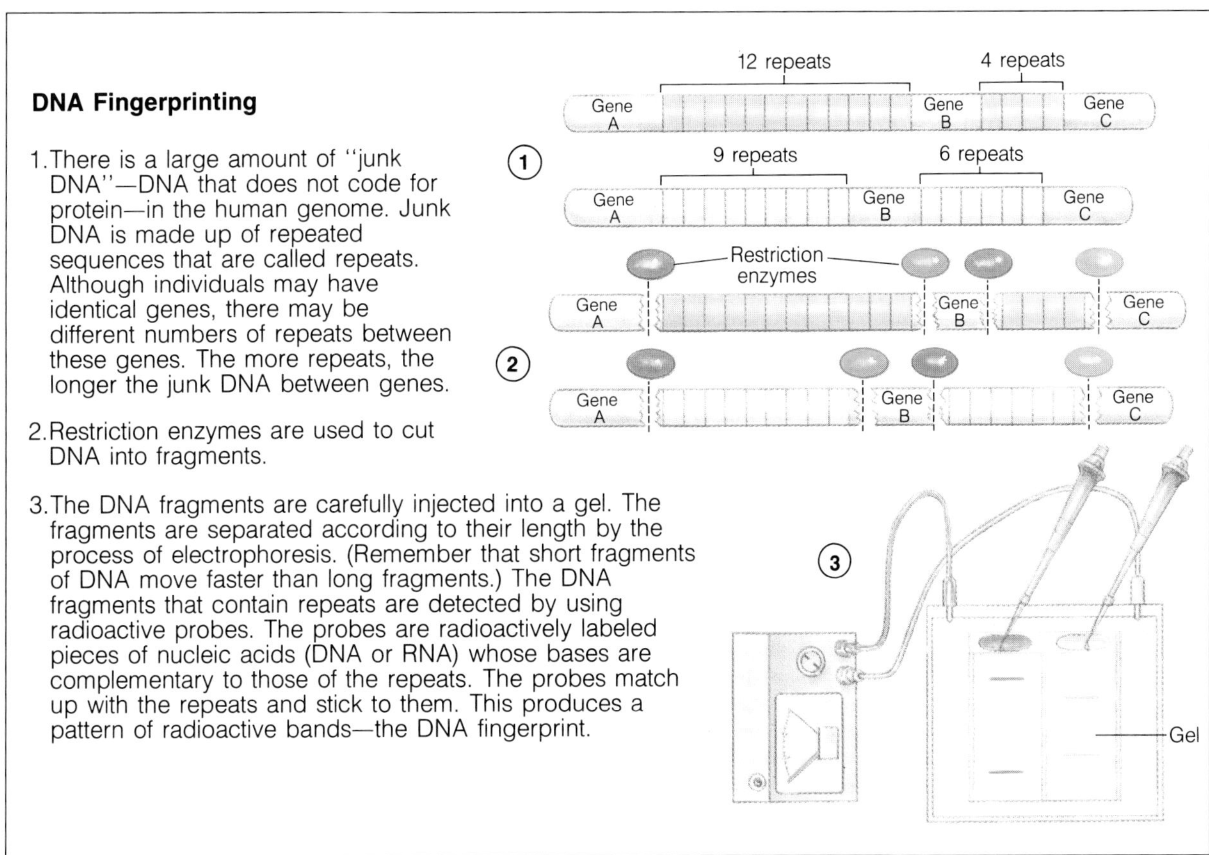

DNA Fingerprinting
1. There is a large amount of "junk DNA"—DNA that does not code for protein—in the human genome. Junk DNA is made up of repeated sequences that are called repeats. Although individuals may have identical genes, there may be different numbers of repeats between these genes. The more repeats, the longer the junk DNA between genes.
2. Restriction enzymes are used to cut DNA into fragments.
3. The DNA fragments are carefully injected into a gel. The fragments are separated according to their length by the process of electrophoresis. (Remember that short fragments of DNA move faster than long fragments.) The DNA fragments that contain repeats are detected by using radioactive probes. The probes are radioactively labeled pieces of nucleic acids (DNA or RNA) whose bases are complementary to those of the repeats. The probes match up with the repeats and stick to them. This produces a pattern of radioactive bands—the DNA fingerprint.
12 repeats
4 repeats
Gene A
Gene B
Gene C
1
9 repeats
6 repeats
Gene A
Gene B
Gene C
Restriction enzymes
Gene A
Gene B
Gene C
2
Gene A
Gene B
Gene C
3
Gel

with DNA "probe," which binds to the DNA sequence of the repeats. This produces a series of bands that by their position show the lengths of the fragments containing the repeats. If enough combinations of restriction enzymes and DNA probes are used, a pattern of bands is produced that can be distinguished from the pattern of any other individual in the world.

DNA samples can be obtained from blood, sperm, and even hair strands with small pieces of tissue at the base. It is clear that DNA fingerprinting will be useful in solving crimes. Several rape suspects have already been convicted in the United States and Great Britain because DNA fingerprinting showed that their DNA patterns matched blood or sperm samples recovered from their victims. And in at least one case, a wrongly accused person has been set free.

Sequencing the Human Genome

Because molecular techniques can help us read the DNA sequence, several prominent scientists have suggested that a large project to sequence the entire human genome should be undertaken. This would be no small task. Working with today's technology, a very productive scientist might be able to sequence about 1000 bases in a week—50,000 bases in a year (allowing for two weeks' vacation)! At that rate, it would take a single scientist more than 100,000 years to sequence the complete genome. However, many scientists are optimistic that automated sequencing methods can be developed so the process could be speeded up dramatically.

A crash program to sequence the human genome would be a vast project. The amount of information gathered would be so enormous that only complex computer systems would be able to manipulate all the data. Nonetheless, there is little doubt that sooner or later, crash program or not, the complete DNA sequence of the human genome will be determined. When that day comes, we will be closer than ever to achieving the poet Alexander Pope's directive: "Know then thyself . . . the glory, jest, and riddle of the world."

Genetic Engineering of Humans

Because humans are animals, too, there is no *technical* barrier to the insertion of foreign genes into human cells. Many transgenic mammals have been produced by injecting DNA into fertilized ova (eggs) and then transplanting the ova back into a female reproductive tract. This strategy could work with humans as well.

A review of a few of the genetic diseases found in our own species indicates that there is plenty of room for genetic engineering of human cells. Cystic fibrosis, Tay-Sachs disease, and a host of other genetic disorders might be treated by replacing defective genes. The genes for a polypeptide in human hemoglobin have already been inserted into bone marrow cells of mice, suggesting that it might be possible to treat human diseases like sickle cell anemia in the same way.

Ethical Issues

Despite these possibilities, there are problems, risks, and doubts that have persuaded many scientists that the time is not yet right to carry out these procedures on human beings. Of course it would be marvelous to be able to cure hemophilia or other genetic diseases. But could we be sure that experimentation on humans would involve only diseases? If human cells can be manipulated in this way, should we try to engineer taller people or change their eye color, hair texture, sex, blood type, ear shape? What will happen to the human species and to our conception of ourselves if we gain the opportunity to design our bodies? What will be the consequences if we develop the ability to "clone" ourselves by making identical genetic copies of our own cells? These are questions that science will rapidly force us to come to grips with.

If we acquire the ability to alter ourselves, we shall also acquire awesome responsibilities. How shall we decide which genes should be transplanted, altered, or redesigned? Who shall determine whether experiments with genetic engineering should be done? Scientists? A government agency? The local community?

As we said in Chapter 1, the purpose of science is to gain a better understanding of the nature of life. The more we understand life, the more we shall be able to manipulate it. As our power over nature increases, our society shall have to learn to use wisely the tools that science has given us. And we shall have to develop a thoughtful and ethical consensus of what should and should not be done with the human genome. Scientists alone should not be expected to assume all of the responsibility for these decisions. Society in its entirety should have to deal with these questions. To do anything less would be to lose control of our most precious gifts: our intellect and our humanity.

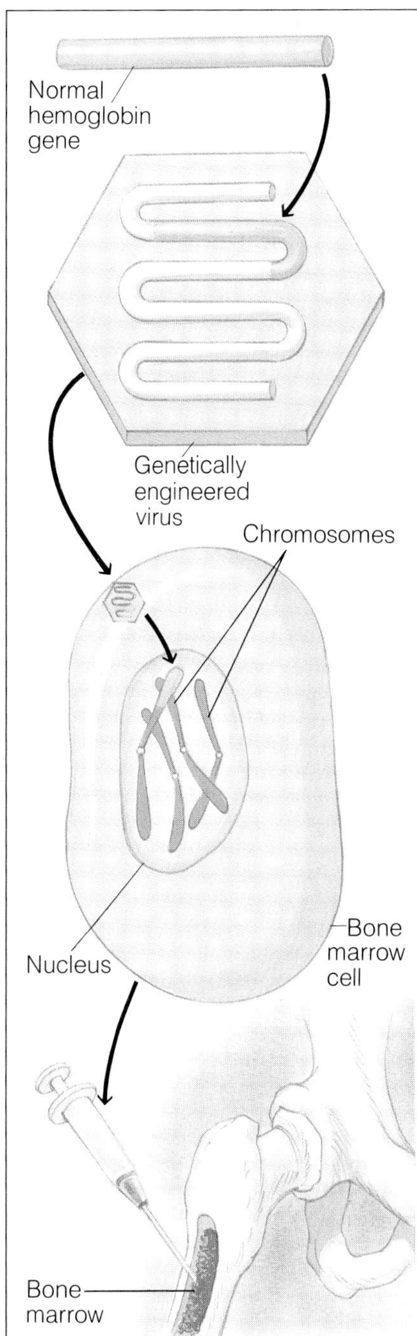

Figure 12–14 *Gene therapy may someday make it possible to "correct" cells that contain defective genes and thus cure genetic diseases.*

12–3 SECTION REVIEW

1. What are some potential benefits of genetic analysis?
2. What is DNA fingerprinting? How does it work?
3. What are some of the principal ethical issues involved in human genetic engineering?
4. If human bone marrow cells were removed, altered genetically, and reimplanted, would the change be passed on to a patient's children?

SIMULATING DNA FINGERPRINTS

PROBLEM

How can DNA be used for the identification of criminals?

MATERIALS *(per student)*

scissors	graph paper

PROCEDURE

1. The accompanying table describes the pattern of genes and repeats of a particular segment of DNA for five individuals. This information will be used to construct models of the DNA segment for each of the five individuals.

Individual	DNA Sequence
1	*G1 G2* **10R** *G3* **4R** *G4 G5* **7R** *G6* **6R** *G7*
2	*G1 G2* **1R** *G3* **15R** *G4 G5* **3R** *G6* **2R** *G7*
3	*G1 G2* **11R** *G3* **8R** *G4 G5* **5R** *G6* **3R** *G7*
4	*G1 G2* **6R** *G3* **2R** *G4 G5* **9R** *G6* **7R** *G7*
5	*G1 G2* **4R** *G3* **5R** *G4 G5* **12R** *G6* **4R** *G7*

Key: G = gene R = repeats

2. Cut a lengthwise strip of graph paper two boxes wide. Starting at the top, label the first box *G1* and the second box *G2*.
3. For each repeat, label a box *R*. For example, for individual 1, the ten boxes following G2 would be labeled *R*.
4. Continue labeling the boxes through to *G7*, remembering to put the proper number of *R*'s (repeats) in the correct locations. Write the number of the individual on the back of the strip.
5. Fold a clean sheet of graph paper into sixths lengthwise. Unfold the paper and number the boxes up the left-hand edge, starting at the bottom, from 1 through 25. This sheet will be used to record the DNA fingerprints of individuals 1 through 5 and of an unknown criminal. Label the first of the six columns *1* for individual 1; the second, *2* for individual 2; and so on. Label the sixth column *CRIMINAL*.
6. Select one of the five individuals to be a criminal. *Note: Do not tell your classmates which individual you have selected.* Make a duplicate strip of DNA for that individual following the procedure outlined in steps 3 through 5.
7. Cut the strip representing the criminal's DNA between genes 4 and 5. This represents the cutting of DNA by restriction enzymes.
8. Arrange the two pieces of the DNA strip in order of size, with the largest first. This represents the separation of DNA pieces through electrophoresis.
9. Count the number of boxes in the longest piece of DNA. Color in a box in the column of your data table marked *CRIMINAL* directly across from this number. Repeat this procedure using the shorter fragment. You should have two marks in the column. These represent the marks that DNA tagged with a radioactive probe would leave on a photographic plate—a DNA fingerprint.
10. Exchange the DNA fingerprint of your criminal with one of your classmates.
11. Prepare DNA fingerprints for individuals 1 through 5.

OBSERVATIONS

1. Did any of the five individuals have the same DNA fingerprints?
2. Which individual was the criminal?

ANALYSIS AND CONCLUSIONS

1. If the possible number of repeats between two genes varies between 1 and 20, what is the probability of having exactly 3 repeats?
2. Why is it unlikely that two individuals would have the same DNA fingerprint?
3. If blood or hair samples are recovered at the scene of a crime, how could they be used to make a positive identification of a criminal?

STUDENT STUDY GUIDE

SUMMARIZING THE CONCEPTS

The key concepts in each section of this chapter are listed below to help you review the chapter content. Make sure you understand each concept and its relationship to other concepts and to the theme of this chapter.

12–1 Modifying the Living World

- By using carefully selected individuals as parents for the next generation, people can improve and change domesticated plants and animals.
- Inbreeding involves crosses between similar individuals.
- Hybridization involves crossing dissimilar individuals.
- Random mutations, which can be caused artificially, can produce useful variations in organisms.

12–2 Genetic Engineering: Technology and Heredity

- Genetic engineering changes DNA through direct manipulation.
- Restriction enzymes are used to cut DNA. The cut DNA can be combined with other DNA molecules and inserted into organisms in various ways.
- There are techniques for reading the sequence of bases in DNA.
- Genetic engineering uses DNA to transform cells and organisms.

12–3 The New Human Genetics

- Human DNA can be analyzed to detect genetic diseases.
- DNA fingerprinting can be used to solve crimes and identify people.
- The technology exists to determine the sequence of the entire human genome.
- There are many ethical considerations that must be taken into account before new genetic techniques are applied to humans.

REVIEWING KEY TERMS

Vocabulary terms are important to your understanding of biology. The key terms listed below are those you should be especially familiar with. Review these terms and their meanings. Then use each term in a complete sentence. If you are not sure of a term's meaning, return to the appropriate section and review its definition.

12–1 Modifying the Living World

selective breeding
inbreeding
hybridization
mutagen

12–2 Genetic Engineering: Technology and Heredity

genetic engineering
restriction enzyme
plasmid
recombinant DNA
clone
transgenic

12–3 The New Human Genetics

genome
DNA fingerprinting

CHAPTER REVIEW

CONTENT REVIEW

Multiple Choice

Choose the letter of the answer that best completes each statement.

1. Crossing individuals that have similar characteristics and are often closely related is called
   a. hybridization. c. mutagenesis.
   b. inbreeding. d. genetic engineering.
2. A piece of DNA that is produced by combining DNA fragments from different sources is called
   a. hybrid DNA. c. plasmid DNA.
   b. cloned DNA. d. recombinant DNA.
3. A large number of cells grown from a single cell is called a
   a. clone. c. chimera.
   b. hybrid. d. plasmid.
4. A cross between dissimilar individuals is
   a. cloning. c. hybridization.
   b. mutagenesis. d. genetic engineering.
5. Organisms that contain foreign genes are
   a. mutagenized. c. hybridized.
   b. transgenic. d. inbred.
6. What is the name of the process of engineering changes directly into an organism's DNA?
   a. mutagenesis c. selective breeding
   b. hybridizing d. genetic engineering
7. Which technique takes advantage of repeated DNA sequences that do not code for protein?
   a. DNA fingerprinting
   b. DNA sequencing
   c. genetic engineering
   d. cloning
8. The process that uses electricity to separate DNA fragments according to their length is
   a. electrophoresis.
   b. DNA sequencing.
   c. genetic engineering.
   d. mutagenesis.

True or False

Determine whether each statement is true or false. If it is true, write "true." If it is false, change the underlined word or words to make the statement true.

1. Offspring resulting from a cross between <u>similar</u> individuals often show hybrid vigor.
2. A <u>plasmid</u> is a cell or organism whose DNA comes from different species.
3. Crossing similar individuals is called <u>selective breeding</u>.
4. Increasing the mutation rate is called <u>genetic engineering</u>.
5. <u>Transgenic</u> organisms contain foreign genes.
6. A <u>chimera</u> is a large number of cells grown from a single cell.
7. A circular piece of bacterial DNA is called a <u>clone</u>.
8. <u>DNA fingerprinting</u> produces a pattern of bands that is unique for each person.

Word Relationships

In each of the following sets of terms, three of the terms are related. One term does not belong. Determine the characteristic common to three of the terms and then identify the term that does not belong.

1. hybridization, genetic engineering, selective breeding, inbreeding
2. restriction enzymes, recombinant DNA, DNA cloning, mutagenesis
3. clone, chimera, transgenic, recombinant DNA

CONCEPT MASTERY

Use your understanding of the concepts developed in the chapter to answer each of the following in a brief paragraph.

1. Explain why inbreeding and hybridization are sometimes considered to be forms of selective breeding.
2. Describe the processes involved in creating bacteria that produce human proteins.
3. How is mutagenesis useful to humans?
4. The nuclei from certain cells in an adult frog can be placed into frog eggs from which the nuclei have been removed. This produces genetically identical frog embryos. Explain why these embryos are considered to be a clone.

CRITICAL AND CREATIVE THINKING

Discuss each of the following in a brief paragraph.

1. **Applying concepts** Suppose a plant breeder has thornless rose bushes that have pink flowers, thorny rose bushes that have sweet-smelling yellow flowers, and thorny rose bushes that have purple flowers. How might the plant breeder develop a purebred variety of thornless sweet-smelling purple roses?
2. **Problem solving** The following fragments are obtained when a gene that consists of 10 codons is cut by restriction enzymes. What is the sequence of bases in the gene? (*Hint:* Look for overlapping sequences on the fragments.)
3. **Making comparisons** Compare the advantages and disadvantages of breeding techniques and genetic engineering.
4. **Applying technology** Describe the processes involved in isolating, cloning, and sequencing a gene.
5. **Expressing an opinion** Should genetic engineering ever be done on humans? If so, under what circumstances? Explain your answer.
6. **Using the writing process** If you could create the "ideal organism" by combining the traits of two organisms, what two organisms would you select and why?

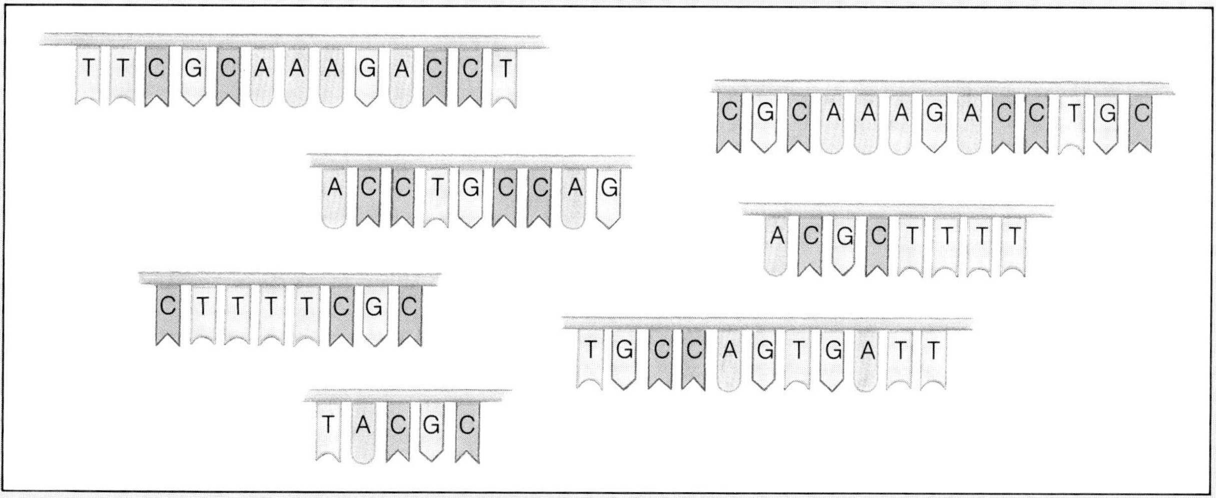

Holographic Technician

Holographic technicians work with laser beams to create three-dimensional images called holograms. The technicians operate the equipment, care for the mirrors and lenses, and develop the resulting film.

Holograms are used today in a variety of fields. They are particularly helpful in science and medicine, where computer-generated images allow researchers and doctors to view the structures of parts of living organisms.

A holographic technician must complete a high school education and have some additional training at a technical or junior college.

For information on this career write to the Museum of Holography, 11 Mercer St., New York, NY 10013.

Plant Breeder

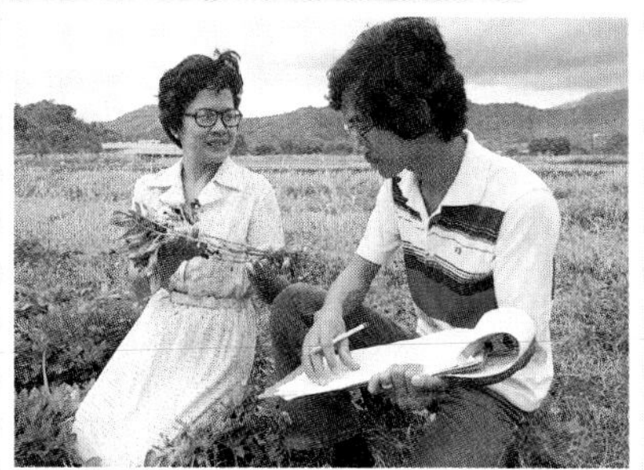

Plant breeders use a knowledge of genetics and biology to develop desirable traits in many kinds of plants. Traits that would be considered desirable include the ability to resist disease, to thrive in different soils and climates, and to produce large numbers of offspring. Plant breeders work in experimental nurseries, where they cross-breed various plants to observe and record the characteristics of the offspring.

A position as a plant breeder requires at least a Bachelor's degree in agronomy or horticulture.

For more information write to the American Society of Agronomy, 677 South Segoe Rd., Madison, WI 53711.

Molecular Geneticist

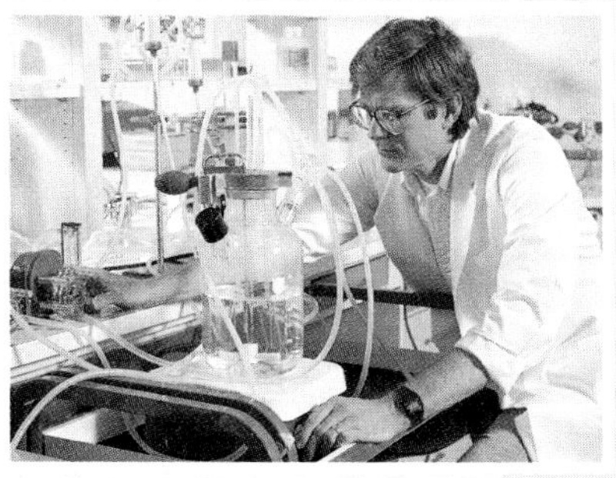

Molecular geneticists study patterns of heredity in various forms of life. They are concerned with how biological traits originate and are passed down from one generation to another. Some molecular geneticists specialize in studying diseases that are linked to genes and chromosomes.

To become a molecular geneticist, a person must earn a Bachelor's degree in chemistry or biology and a Ph.D. in genetics.

For more information write to the American Genetic Association, 818 18th St., NW, Washington, DC 20006.

HOW TO FIND THE RIGHT COLLEGE

When choosing a college, first consider what type of career or academic program interests you. Also decide what geographical location and student-body size would make you most comfortable. Other things to consider are financial constraints, availability of housing, and ease with which you can travel back and forth to school. Once you have a list of potential colleges, compare the courses they offer, their job placement records, and their extracurricular activities.

In addition to talking with counselors, you might want to read some college guides to learn about specific institutions. Two popular examples are Peterson's Guide to Four-Year Colleges *and* Barron's Profiles of American Colleges.

FROM THE AUTHORS

"You can choose your friends but not your relatives."

The first time that phrase made sense to me was when my baby cousin ruined a perfectly good trip to a restaurant by deciding that his meal would look better on the floor. Over the years my cousin turned out just fine, of course, and he even developed table manners. But for a few minutes I would rather have been related to a family of worms.

We don't choose our relatives, and we can't choose our genes. Each one of us has a biological inheritance that includes our blood type, our eye color, our appearance, and even our height. It's easy to feel trapped by that inheritance, limited by the biological traits that seem so important and so far beyond our abilities to change them. But don't make the mistake of being overwhelmed by your own genetics, especially in your studies. None of us reaches more than a fraction of the intellectual potential that we inherit. The limits on what we achieve in life stem less from our genes than from ourselves.

The biological capacities that we all inherit, regardless of our individual differences, are more than enough to give each of us the tools to achieve great things in whatever we set out to do. When you think about the men and women who have pioneered scientific research, dreamed up inventions, written great literature or music, what do you see? Great genes or great efforts? The answer, without a doubt, is the latter. What we inherit is the beginning of what we can be. It is not the end of it.

Ken Miller

UNIT 4

Diversity of Life

In the eerie stillness of the evening, the light of the setting sun forms blood-red puddles among the lifeless bones of a dinosaur. Something moves unexpectedly among the shadows of the giant ribs—small shapes appear and vanish like ghosts. With whiskers quivering, a tiny furry creature pokes its nose into the light and then scampers onto the dinosaur's skull. Reassured, other furry animals emerge from the shadows.

The small furry creatures chasing one another among the bones and squabbling over the last scraps of dinosaur meat may not seem impressive. However, their descendants include elephants, wolves, anteaters, horses, whales, and other mammals. Some of their descendants are even able to contemplate the diversity of life, theorize about the processes that formed many kinds of creatures from a single original kind, and imagine events that occurred millions of years ago.

CHAPTERS

CHAPTER 13

Evolution: Evidence of Change

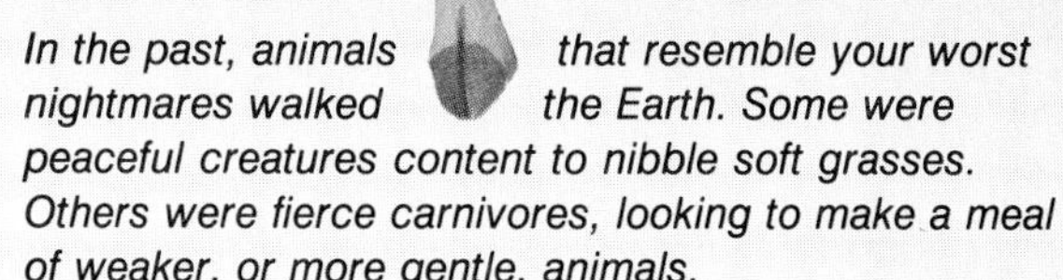

In the past, animals that resemble your worst nightmares walked the Earth. Some were peaceful creatures content to nibble soft grasses. Others were fierce carnivores, looking to make a meal of weaker, or more gentle, animals.

A grazing animal lifts its head; its three horns form a peculiar silhouette against the evening sky. Another type of grazer scratches itself with the forked horn on the end of its nose. Suddenly, a pack of sleek, bearlike predators bursts from the underbrush. The herds of grazers erupt into a flurry of moving hooves and horns. The predators pursue, single out their quarry, and close in. Their prey kicks and slashes with its triple horns, but to no avail. It is over in moments. The pack begins to feed.

Even though this scene is imaginary, the strange, remarkable animals were not. They lived some 7 million years ago in what is now Texas. How do we know of these ancient animals? Where did they come from? And why are they no longer alive? In this chapter you will learn about methods scientists use to reconstruct a picture of ancient life.

CHAPTER OUTLINE

13–1 Evolution and Life's Diversity

Section Objectives

- Relate Darwin's observations to his explanation of evolution.
- Explain how fitness is related to adaptation.

The idea that life on Earth has changed over time, or evolved, is very old. But just believing that change occurs is not enough to make evolution a science. In science, you will recall, observation, questioning, and constant testing of hypotheses must replace belief. Scientists have accumulated considerable evidence to show that organisms alive today have been produced by a long process of change over time. The process by which modern organisms have descended from ancient organisms is called **evolution**.

One man, Charles Darwin, contributed more to our understanding of the process of evolution than anyone else. For this reason, we will begin this chapter by looking at the natural phenomena that convinced Darwin that evolution occurred.

Darwin's Dilemma

Two days after Christmas in 1831, a young Englishman named Charles Robert Darwin (1809–1882) set sail on HMS *Beagle* for a cruise around the world. Although no one knew it then, this voyage would revolutionize scientific thought.

Darwin was well educated and had a strong interest in natural history. He also had keen powers of observation and an

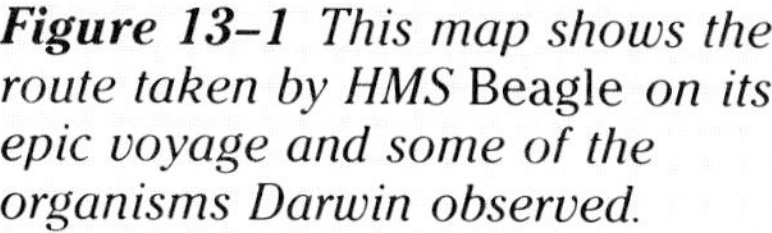

***Figure 13–1** This map shows the route taken by HMS* Beagle *on its epic voyage and some of the organisms Darwin observed.*

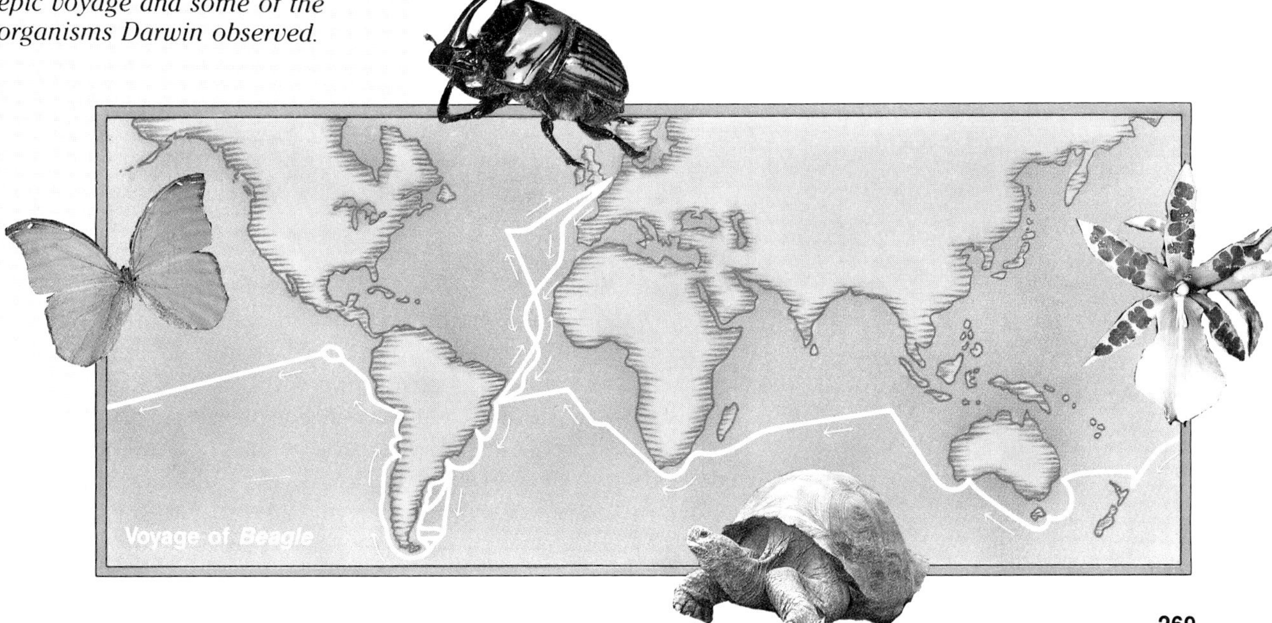

Figure 13–2 Roxie Laybourne is one of the world's experts on birds. These file drawers at the Smithsonian Institution are only a small part of the museum's collection of specimens. The specimens are used to compare birds collected in the wild with named species.

Figure 13–3 Reproductive behaviors can contribute to a species' survival. A female cuckoo laid her egg and abandoned it in this bird's nest. After the cuckoo hatched, it killed its foster brothers and sisters by pushing them out of the nest. Now alone and constantly hungry, it demands all the attention of its foster parents.

analytical mind. Over five years' time, the *Beagle* took Darwin to several continents and many remote islands. Darwin went ashore whenever the ship anchored. At each new place, he collected animal and plant specimens that he added to an ever-growing collection. At sea, between bouts of seasickness, Darwin examined his specimens and filled notebooks with his thoughts and observations. He also spent many hours reading the most current scientific books.

Throughout the voyage, Darwin witnessed countless wonders of nature for which his bright young mind demanded an explanation. Those same mysteries of life will spark your curiosity, too, if you stop to think about them.

The Diversity of Life

Our planet houses living organisms of every imaginable shape, size, and habit. This variety of living things is called the diversity of life. Only a tiny fraction of these organisms lived in Darwin's England—or in your hometown. But if you travel to or read about different countries, you will discover, as Darwin did, that the diversity of life is staggering.

When Darwin visited tropical South America, countless species of plants, mammals, birds, and insects passed before his eyes. In just one day in a Brazilian forest, Darwin collected 68 different species of beetles! This discovery amazed Darwin because he was not specifically looking for beetles. Darwin realized that the number of living species was enormous. Scientists now estimate that there are as many as 10 million species of organisms alive today.

Darwin soon realized that the diversity of life he observed was only one part of a much larger puzzle. For as he traveled, he found evidence that even more organisms had vanished from the Earth. Today, researchers estimate that of all the species that have at some time lived on Earth, more than 99.9 percent are now extinct! If that estimate is correct, several hundred million species have come and gone during Earth's long history. Where have all the marchers in this endless parade of life come from? Why have so many of them disappeared over time? These are two of the questions Darwin tried to answer.

Fitness: To Survive and Reproduce

Darwin was also impressed by the many different ways in which organisms survive and produce offspring. He noted that most animals and plants seem remarkably well designed to do the things they do. **The combination of physical traits and behaviors that helps organisms survive and reproduce in their environment Darwin called fitness.** How did all of these organisms develop the structures that give them their **fitness**? And why is there such an extraordinary variety of techniques for survival?

These are very difficult questions, so it is not surprising that Darwin wasn't able to provide answers overnight. It was not until 1859, nearly 30 years after he began his voyage on the *Beagle*, that Darwin published his explanations in a book called *The Origin of Species by Means of Natural Selection*. This book changed the way people think about the living world.

In *The Origin of Species*, Darwin maintained that modern organisms have been produced through evolution. Evolution is a long, slow process of change in species over time. Darwin argued that just as each new organism comes from preexisting organisms, each species has descended from other species over time. If you look back far enough in time, you will see that all species have shared, or common, ancestors. Since species have descended from common ancestors, Darwin called this principle **common descent.**

Darwin also argued that fitness arises through a process called **adaptation**. Successful adaptations enable organisms to become better suited to their environment, better able to survive and reproduce. Darwin also used the word adaptation to describe any inherited characteristic that increases an animal's or plant's fitness for survival. Thus, the long neck and legs of a giraffe are adaptations that permit giraffes to feed on the leaves of trees. With these adaptations, giraffes can eat leaves too high for most grazing animals to eat and thus are better able to survive and reproduce, passing their genes on to their young.

Figure 13–4 *The giraffe dines on leaves of trees out of the reach of even the tallest zebra's head. The sphinx moth uses a long feeding tube to reach the nectar in a flower. The vampire bat punctures the skin of another animal with its razor-sharp teeth and then greedily laps up blood from the wound.*

13–1 SECTION REVIEW

1. How did Darwin's voyage on the *Beagle* influence his thoughts about life on Earth?
2. Define diversity of life. How is the diversity of life related to evolution?
3. How is adaptation related to fitness?

Section Objectives

- Discuss how scientists determined that the Earth was much more than a few thousand years old.
- Distinguish between relative and absolute dating.
- Explain how radioactive elements in the Earth's rocks act as a natural clock.

13–2 The Age of the Earth

Darwin and other scientists have accumulated a vast amount of evidence that proves that evolution has occurred. Some of the evidence certifies that planet Earth is more than 4 billion years old. Other evidence makes it clear that both Earth and the life on it have changed dramatically over time. Still other evidence supports the principle of common descent and emphasizes the importance of adaptation to the environment. Much of the evidence is found in the rocks of the Earth itself. And it is this evidence that we will now examine.

Evidence in Stone

In the past, many people believed the Earth was relatively young—only a few thousand years old. They also believed that the Earth had remained unchanged over this time. Rocks and major geological features, they thought, had been produced suddenly by catastrophic events that humans rarely (if ever) witnessed and, even if they did, could not understand. But other people have offered a different explanation, an explanation based on evidence stored in the rocks of the Earth itself.

In the eighteenth and nineteenth centuries, scientists began to examine the Earth in great detail. And they offered the hypothesis that the Earth was indeed very old and had changed slowly over a long period of time by natural forces like weather. It was the work of these scientists that profoundly influenced Darwin's thoughts.

Figure 13–5 *These delicate stone arches were formed by the relentless forces of nature. Tiny particles of windborne sand constantly strike the rock face and wear it away.*

Evidence that supported the idea that the Earth was very old first came from geologist James Hutton in 1788. Hutton proposed that rocks, mountains, and valleys had been changed gradually by rain, heat, cold, the activity of volcanoes, and other natural forces. Because most of these processes operate slowly, Hutton argued, the Earth had to be much more than a few thousand years old.

In 1830, just before Darwin began his voyage, the geologist Charles Lyell carried these arguments further. Lyell agreed that the Earth had changed slowly and gradually over time. Lyell also argued that scientists must always explain past events in terms of events and processes they could observe themselves. That, Lyell insisted, was the only way the scientific method could work. Lyell's work, as you will discover in the next chapter, was an important influence on Darwin's thinking.

The evidence proved to Hutton and Lyell that the Earth was very old. Further evidence suggested to them that the land is constantly moving and shifting: Forces beneath the Earth's surface twist and bend some rock layers, bury others, and even push up some parts of the sea floor into mountain ranges. For these scientists, the Earth had indeed changed over the long period of its existence.

At the same time, other scientists found evidence that life on Earth had also changed over time. While examining the Earth's rocks, geologists—professional and amateur—began to make some startling discoveries. In the stones they examined they found **fossils**. Fossils are the preserved remains of ancient organisms. Some of these fossils resembled organisms still alive. Others did not. These fossils raised many questions that would remain unanswered for some time. Even though they could not explain the meaning of all the fossils they found, these early geologists made a great contribution. They created an interest in and a sense of wonder about the Earth and the life that lived upon it.

The Geologic Time Scale: A Clock in the Rocks

Earth's story is not complete without a "clock" to tell us when things happened. Both biologists and geologists date the

Figure 13–6 *This illustration represents changes that occurred in the evolution of the camel. Provided that the order of layers has not been disturbed, the "camels" in the lower layers are older than those in the layers above.*

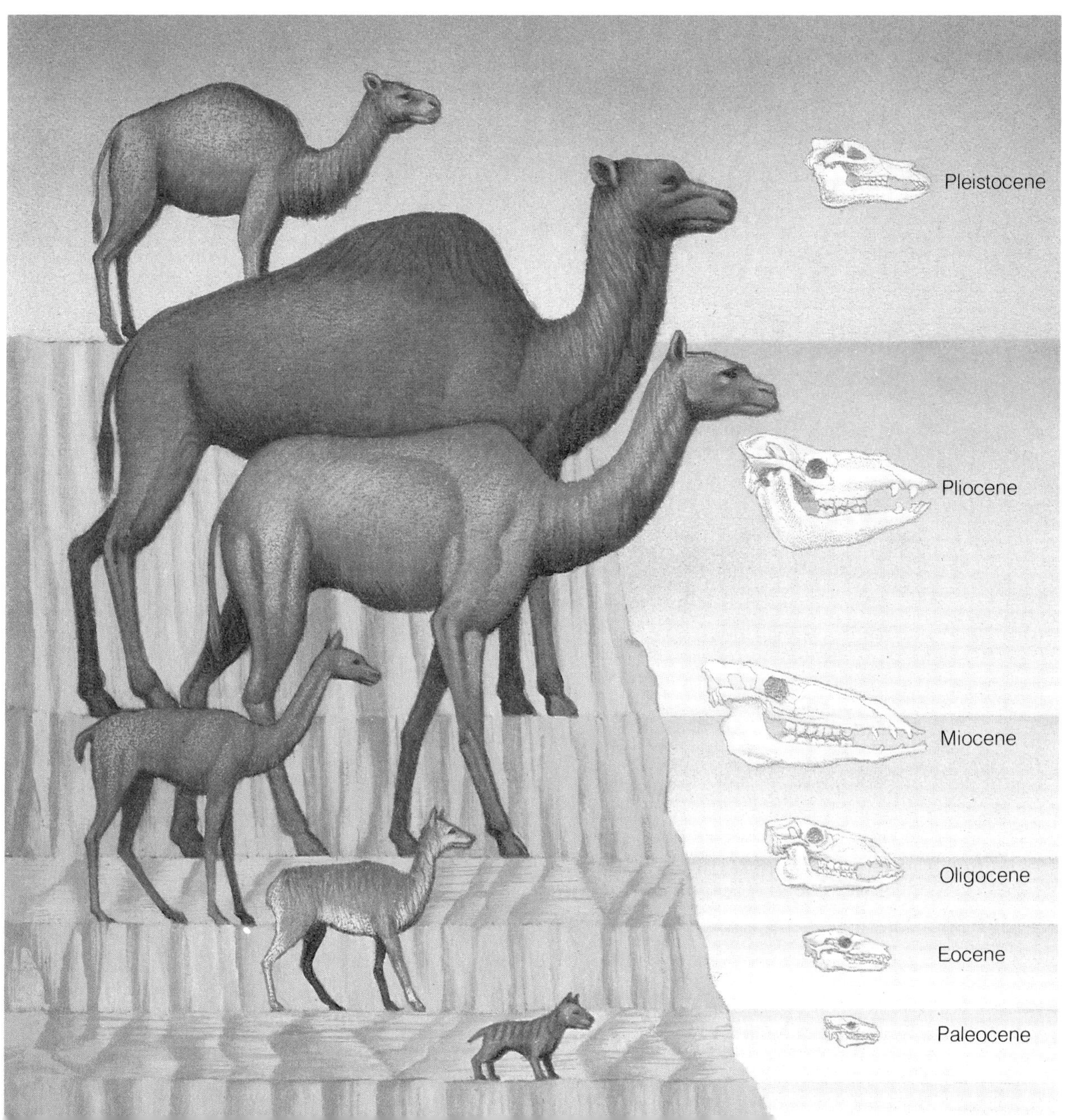

Earth's past with the help of a record in the rocks called the **geologic time scale**.

More than 100 years ago, researchers noticed that certain layers of rock often appeared in the same vertical order wherever they were found. It is the position of the layers relative to each other that determines their age. This knowledge helped geologists assemble a column of rocks in which each layer represented a different period of time. Geologists knew that the lower rock layers were deposited before the upper layers. Thus, lower layers are older than upper layers, provided that the layers have not been disturbed since they were formed. In addition, fossils found in lower layers are older than fossils found in the layers above them. **Relative dating** is a technique that is used by scientists to determine the age of fossils relative to other fossils in different layers of rock. However, because geologists did not know the amount of time it took for the different layers to form, they could not determine the actual age of the fossils.

Radioactive Dating

Near the middle of this century, our growing understanding of radioactivity provided scientists with a tool that could determine the actual age of rocks. Rocks are made up of many different elements. In certain rocks, some of these elements are radioactive. **Radioactive elements** decay, or break down, into nonradioactive elements at a very steady rate. Scientists measure this rate of radioactive decay in a unit called a **half-life**. A half-life is the length of time required for half the radioactive atoms in a sample to decay. This means that after one half-life, one half of the radioactive atoms in a sample have decayed. At the end of the next half-life, one half of the remaining radioactive atoms have decayed. In other words, one quarter of the original number of radioactive atoms remain after the second half-life reduces the remaining radioactive atoms by half.

Decay of a Radioactive Element with a Half-Life of 1 Million Years in a Fossil

Time	Amount of Radioactive Element	Amount of Decay Element
4 million years ago, when fossil formed	1 kg (1)	0 kg (0)
3 million years ago	0.5 kg (1/2)	0.5 kg (1/2)
2 million years ago	0.25 kg (1/4)	0.75 kg (3/4)
1 million years ago	0.125 kg (1/8)	0.875 kg (7/8)
Present	0.0625 kg (1/16)	0.9375 kg (15/16)

= Radioactive element = Decay element

Figure 13–7 *Scientists use the natural decay of radioactive elements to date certain fossils. It is the constancy of an element's half-life that makes radioactive dating accurate.*

SCIENCE, TECHNOLOGY, AND SOCIETY **APPLICATION**

Dating with Carbon-14

Archaeologists study buried artifacts to learn about past civilizations. Such artifacts can often be dated using techniques that measure radioactive decay.

Many collectors buy art and objects made by ancient people. In some cases, clever forgeries of ancient material have been made by individuals eager to cheat unsuspecting collectors or museums. But scientists have a way to date these artifacts and protect people from making expensive mistakes.

A common radioactive element, carbon-14, is often used to date fossils that are younger than about 60,000 years old. Carbon-14 has a half-life of about 5770 years. After about 60,000 years, or approximately ten half-lives, there is too little carbon-14 left to measure with accuracy.

Scientists use carbon-14 to date material that was once alive, such as a human bone, or to date an object that contains some once-living material.

For example, a pottery bowl or statue often contains a bit of straw that was used to hold the clay together when the bowl or statue was made. The straw contains enough carbon-14 to make radioactive dating possible.

Because it is present in the atmosphere, all living things take in carbon-14 while they are alive. The carbon-14 present in the body decays into nitrogen-14 at a fixed rate. In the case of the pottery bowl or statue, scientists can analyze the small amounts of once-living material, like straw, that are contained in the clay. They can then compute the ratio of carbon-14 to nitrogen-14 in the straw and determine how long ago the straw died. They assume, of course, that the straw was alive until shortly before it was used in the construction of the pottery.

Thus carbon-14 can be used to catch thieves and forgers of ancient art. Radioactive materials can make a pottery bowl or statue confess its true age.

Each radioactive element has a different half-life. For example, potassium-40 has a half-life of 1.3 billion years. During that time, one half of the potassium-40 atoms in a rock sample decay to argon-40. Uranium-238 has a half-life of 4.5 billion years. During that time, one half of the uranium-238 atoms in a rock sample decay into lead-206. Geologists can measure the amounts of uranium-238 and lead-206 present in a rock sample. By determining how much lead has been produced by decay since the rock was formed and by knowing the half-life of uranium, geologists can calculate the rock sample's age.

Half-Lives of Radioactive Elements	
Element	**Half-life**
Rubidium-87	50 billion years
Thorium-232	13.9 billion years
Uranium-238	4.5 billion years
Potassium-40	1.3 billion years
Uranium-235	713 million years
Carbon-14	5770 years

Figure 13–8 *As you can see from this chart, the half-life of a radioactive element is much longer than a human's whole life.*

Uranium-238 and potassium-40 are used to date rocks millions of years old. The different radioactive elements, each with its own half-life, thus provide a useful series of natural clocks that help date the rocks in which they are found.

Using radioactive dating, researchers can calculate the actual age of a rock sample. Because radioactive dating is so accurate, scientists call this method **absolute dating**. By using techniques of absolute dating, scientists have compiled an accurate history of the Earth. With a reliable radioactive clock, scientists have divided the Earth's history into units called **eras**. Eras are divided into **periods**, which in turn are divided into **epochs**. See Figure 13–9.

Through radioactive dating and the examination of rates of geological processes such as the breaking down of rocks by weather and other natural forces, scientists have determined that the Earth is about 4 1/2 billion years old.

13–2 SECTION REVIEW

1. Compare relative and absolute dating.
2. How might relative dating provide inaccurate data?

Figure 13-9 **GEOLOGIC HISTORY OF THE EARTH**

Era	Period	Epoch	End Date (millions of years ago)	Notes
Cenozoic	Quaternary	Recent		Humans are the dominant form of life; civilization begins and spreads
		Pleistocene	0.01	"The Ice Age"; modern humans present; mammoths and other animals become extinct
	Tertiary	Pliocene	2.5	Fossils of ancient humans near end of epoch; many birds, mammals, and sea life similar to modern types; climate cools
		Miocene	5	Many grazing animals; flowering plants and trees resemble modern types
		Oligocene	25	Fossils of primitive apes; elephants, camels, and horses develop; climate generally mild
		Eocene	38	Fossils of "dawn horse" (*Hyracotherium*); grasslands and forests present; many small mammals; larger mammals such as whales, rhinoceroses, and monkeys begin to develop

Era	Period	Epoch	End Date (millions of years ago)	Notes
Cenozoic	Tertiary	Paleocene	55	Beginning of "Age of Mammals."; flowering plants and small mammals abundant; many different climates exist
	Cretaceous		65	First flowering plants; placental mammals develop; dinosaurs die out, as do many marine animals, at end of period
Mesozoic	Jurassic		135	The Rocky Mountains rise; first birds; palms and cone-bearing trees dominant; largest dinosaurs thrive; primitive mammals develop
	Triassic		195	"Age of Reptiles" begins; first dinosaurs; first mammals; corals, insects, and fishes resemble modern types
	Permian		245	First cone-bearing plants; ferns, fishes, amphibians, and reptiles flourish; many marine invertebrates, including trilobites, die out
	Carboniferous		285	Ice covers large areas of the Earth; swamps cover lowlands; first mosses; great coal-forming forests form; seed ferns grow; first reptiles and winged insects appear
	Devonian		345	First forests grow in swampy areas; fishes flourish; first amphibians, sharks, and insects develop
Paleozoic	Silurian		400	"Age of Fishes" begins; coral reefs form; jawed fishes develop; first land plants appear; first air-breathing animals, including land arthropods
	Ordovician		430	First fishes (jawless) appear; invertebrates flourish in the sea
	Cambrian		500	"Age of Invertebrates" begins; trilobites, brachiopods, sponges, and other marine invertebrates are present
Precambrian			580	Earth's history begins; first life forms in the sea; first prokaryotes (bacteria) appear; as time passes, first eukaryotes appear

13–3 The Fossil Record

Section Objectives

- Describe how sedimentary rocks are formed.
- Explain how fossils provide evidence of evolution.
- Discuss why there may be problems in interpreting fossil evidence.

Since the early nineteenth century, biologists have learned about animals and plants that lived long ago by examining preserved traces of those organisms, or fossils. As you can see in Figure 13–10, there are many different kinds of fossils. A fossil can be as large and complete as an entire perfectly preserved animal or plant, or it might be as small and incomplete as a tiny fragment of a jawbone or leaf. There are fossil footprints, fossil eggs, and even fossilized animal droppings. Some of the fossils Darwin found in South America represented animals so strange that they resemble creatures from science fiction films more than they do any plant or animal alive today. How did these organisms leave their remains in stone? How do fossil remains help explain the history of life on Earth?

How Fossils Form

Fossils have been formed in a variety of ways, all of which depend a great deal on chance. In cold places, animals sometimes fell into crevasses in ice or became trapped in snow fields. Insects and other small animals were occasionally trapped in the sticky tree sap that eventually hardened into amber. Still other fossils were formed when animals became mired in peat bogs, certain kinds of quicksand, or tar pits. In all these cases, the material that surrounded the dead animal helped to protect it from decay and acted to preserve it as evidence of past life.

Most fossils are found in **sedimentary rock**. Sedimentary rocks are formed when exposure to rain, heat, and cold breaks down existing rocks into small particles of sand, silt, and clay.

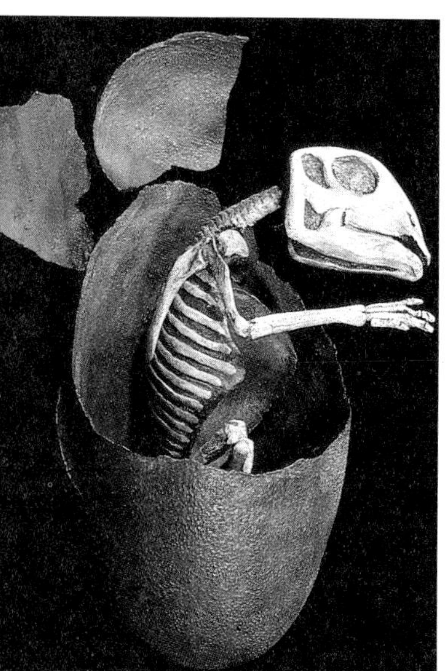

Figure 13–10 *This hatchling dinosaur did not live to become an adult, but its bones and even the delicate shell of its egg remain. The trilobite remains illustrate two kinds of fossils, a cast (center) and a mold (right).*

Figure 13–11 The Colorado River, flowing along the bottom of the Grand Canyon, has cut through layer upon layer of rock over millions of years, exposing fossils long buried in sedimentary rock.

Figure 13–12 Fossils are usually found in sedimentary rocks. Because lower sedimentary rock layers are older than upper rock layers, scientists can determine the sequence of changes in life forms on the Earth.

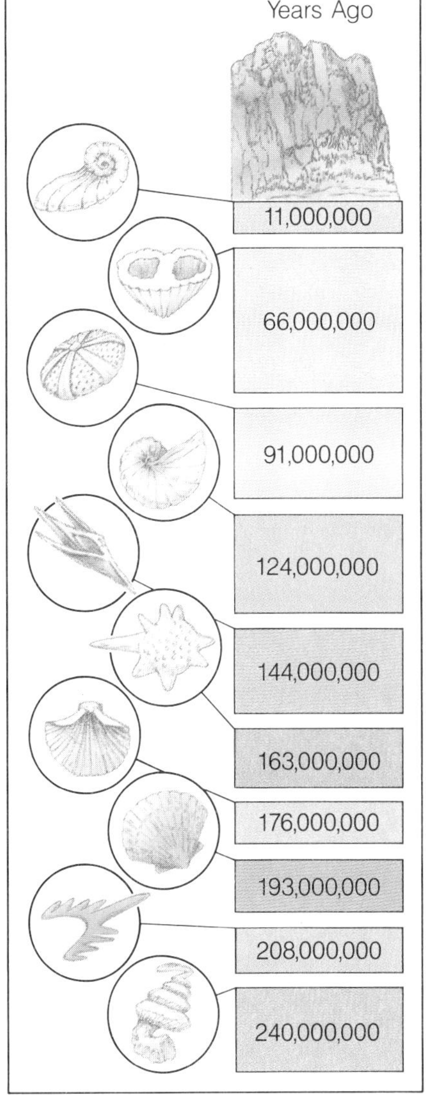

These particles are carried by streams and rivers into lakes or seas. Because the particles are heavier than water, they eventually settle to the bottom of the lake or sea. Here they build up in layer upon layer of sediments. Dead organisms, carried in the water, also eventually fall to the bottom. The organisms can become embedded in the sediment layers. As sediments pile up, pressure on the lower layers compresses the sediments and slowly turns them into rock, which thus preserves the remains of the dead organisms.

In some cases the small particles of rock that buried plant or animal remains preserved the organism's soft parts. In other cases, the hard parts of plants or animals were preserved when wood, shells, or bones were replaced with long-lasting mineral compounds. These fossils are petrified, or turned to rock.

Fossil Evidence: Problems in Assembling the Puzzle

You might think of fossils as pieces of a jigsaw puzzle. All the pieces, assembled correctly, would provide a complete picture of the history of life on Earth. But we do not have all the pieces, and we probably never will.

The chancy process by which organisms are fossilized means that the fossil record is not as complete as we would like it to be. For every organism that leaves a proper fossil, many die and vanish without leaving a trace. Because sedimentary rocks form only in certain bodies of water, organisms that live in mountains and deserts may never become part of the fossil record.

Finding fossils embedded in tons of rock is difficult, if not impossible. However, the natural forces that help make sedimentary rock may reveal hidden fossils. Rocks that contain fossils may be exposed by weather. Bit by bit, the upper, younger layers are worn away by wind and rain, and the older layers beneath are exposed. The Grand Canyon is an example of a place where many layers of rock have been exposed—in this case, by the moving water of the Colorado River. When a fossil is exposed, a fortunate (and observant) scientist may happen along at the right time and remove it for study.

The quality of fossil preservation also varies. Some fossils are preserved so perfectly that we can see the microscopic structure of tiny bones and feathers. Other fossils are not preserved as well and so raise fascinating questions about their meaning and importance. Often scientists must reconstruct an extinct species from a few fossil bits and pieces of bone, leaves, or stems. Fossil reconstruction requires a thorough knowledge of the anatomy of living animals and plants as well as a great amount of skill.

Dating fossils can also present difficulties. The long half-lives of some radioactive elements, such as uranium, make the elements useless for dating fossils younger than 100,000 years. In such cases, scientists must use radioactive elements with shorter half-lives to date the fossils. Carbon-14, with a half-life of 5770 years, is one radioactive element used to date "young" fossils. While they are alive, organisms take up radioactive carbon-14 from their environment along with nonradioactive carbon-12 and carbon-13. Carbon-14 decays to form nitrogen-14. By comparing the proportions of carbon-14 and nitrogen-14 within a fossil, researchers can date the relatively young bones of early humans. Because of its short half-life, however, carbon-14 is not useful in dating fossils more than about 60,000 years old.

What the Fossil Record Tells Us

Scientists who study fossils are called **paleontologists** (pay-lee-uhn-TAHL-uh-jihsts). Over the years, paleontologists

Figure 13–13 *Amber forms when sap flowing from a wound in the bark of a tree fossilizes. If the sticky sap traps an unsuspecting animal, as it did in the case of this tiny lizard, the animal's remains are preserved (left). Notice the minute details of the lizard's skin. Fossils can also provide evidence of the unseen world, such as these microfossils of bacteria preserved in gunflint chert (right). These tiny fossils have been magnified 24,000 times.*

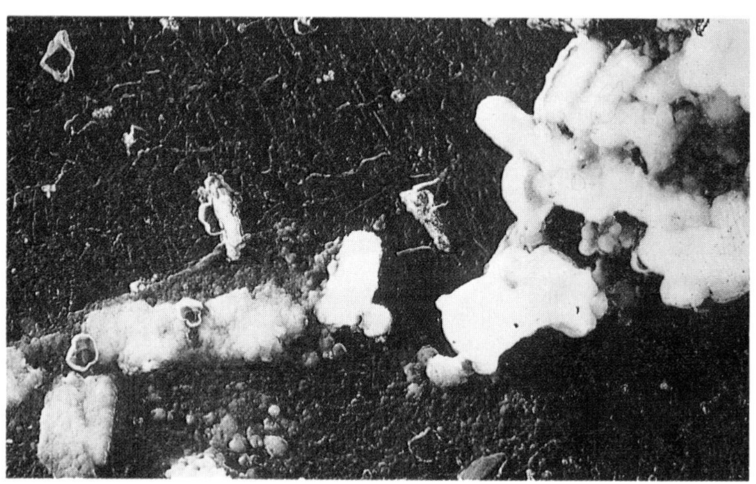

Figure 13–14 *Approximately 310 million years ago, places on Earth looked like this. At that time the dragonfly had a wingspan of about one meter. Compare this to a modern dragonfly that flits delicately above the surface of a pond.*

Figure 13–15 *The first horse was actually quite small, about the size of a small dog. This illustration shows the first horse, as well as several of the intermediate ancestors of today's horse.*

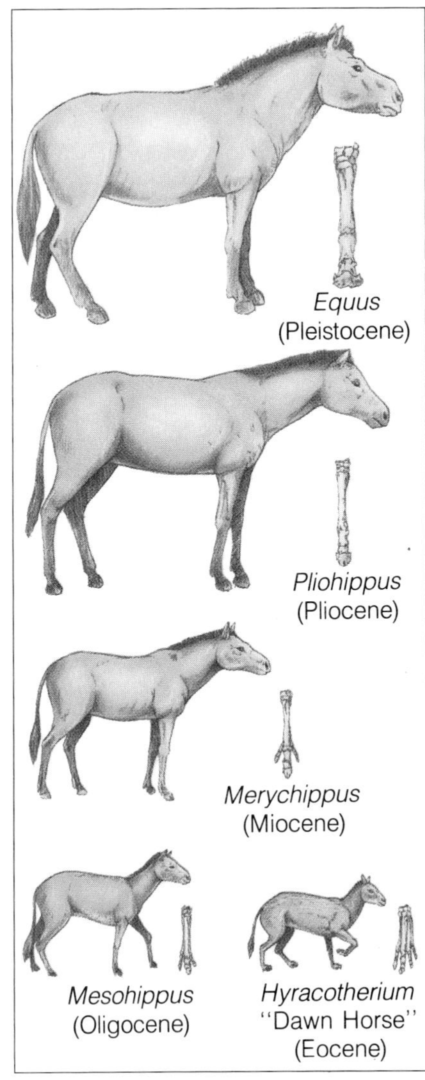

have collected millions of fossils to make up the **fossil record**. The fossil record represents the preserved collective history of the Earth's organisms. Although incomplete, the fossil record has long inspired scientists. As the naturalist Loren Eisley once wrote, " . . . every bone that one holds in one's hands is a fallen kingdom, a veritable ruined world, a unique object that will never return through time."

Our picture puzzle of ancient life has many missing pieces. But in spite of the missing pieces, paleontologists can offer a relatively clear picture of the evolution of many organisms. One example is the series of fossils that shows the development of the modern horse over 50 million years. You can see from Figure 13–15 that the "dawn horse" resembled a modern horse in only the most superficial ways. The evolutionary changes in the horse have been remarkable and quite dramatic.

The fossil record also tells of major changes that occurred in Earth's climate and geography. Fossil shark teeth have been found in Arizona, indicating that the deserts of the American Southwest were once covered by ancient seas. Giant fossil ferns found in Canada show that North America once had a much warmer, tropical climate. Every period, every epoch in Earth's history had a different climate and contained different kinds of organisms that were adapted to it.

But species do not last forever. As Earth's environments changed over time, many species died out. In the very spot where you now sit and read this book, giant dragonflies with wings that measured almost a meter across may have flitted over swamps filled with giant ferns. Dinosaurs appeared, thrived for a time, and eventually disappeared into Earth's fossil record. The huge fossil skeletons they left behind, when reconstructed, still have the power to amuse and amaze us. **The fossil record shows that change followed change on Earth.**

PROBLEM SOLVING IN BIOLOGY

RADIOACTIVE DATING

You are a famous paleontologist and an expert in radioactive-dating techniques. One day, two visitors to your laboratory present you with two different fossils. One fossil is a dinosaur footprint, the other a human jawbone. Both were found at the bottom of a deep valley cut by a stream through cliffs of sedimentary rock. Your guests are very excited. Because they found these fossils next to each other near the stream bed, they feel they have found conclusive evidence that humans and dinosaurs lived at the same time. You are asked to date the samples to confirm their claims.

You first test the human jawbone. You determine that it now contains 1/16 the amount of carbon-14 it contained when alive. How old is the jawbone?

You next examine the fossil footprint. You discover that the fresh mud that the dinosaur stepped in had just been covered with a thin layer of volcanic ash. You study the amount of potassium-40 and argon-40 in the ash. The ratio shows that 1/10 of one potassium-40 half-life has passed since the footprint was made. How old is the footprint?

Were your visitors' conclusions about these fossils' ages correct? If they were not, how could you explain the fact that they were found together at the bottom of the valley? Refer to Figures 13–7 and 13–8 and pages 274 and 276 for helpful information.

13–3 SECTION REVIEW

1. Describe how sedimentary rocks are formed.
2. What is a fossil? How are fossils formed?
3. How is radioactive dating used to determine the age of fossils?
4. What kind of changes are reflected in the fossil record?
5. Explain why the fossil record is incomplete.

13–4 Evidence from Living Organisms

Section Objectives

- Describe how similarities in embryos support the concept of common descent.
- Explain how homologous and vestigial structures indicate that evolution has occurred.
- Discuss how biochemical similarities are evidence of evolution.

Fossils of extinct organisms are not the only evidence that shows the ongoing process of evolution. All living organisms carry within their bodies traces of the history that links them to their ancestors.

Similarities in Early Development

In the late nineteenth century, scientists noticed that the **embryos** of many different animals looked so similar that it was difficult to tell them apart. Embryos are organisms at early stages of development. Today, no scientist would say that a human embryo is identical to a fish or a bird embryo. However, as you can see in Figure 13–16, all of these embryos are similar in appearance during early stages of development. But why are they so similar? And what do these similarities tell us?

Similarities in early development indicate that similar genes are at work. All genes in an organism are not active at the same time. But those that are active during the early development of fish, birds, humans, and related animals are the shared heritage from a common ancestor. The common ancestor of these different animals had a particular sequence of genes that controlled its early development. And this sequence of genes has been passed on to the species that descended from it.

As they grow and develop, the embryos gradually become more and more dissimilar. These differences in form are caused by genes that have changed during the course of evolution. Changes in form are produced by mutations, or changes in the genetic blueprint contained within an organism's DNA. Remember that this DNA blueprint is very complicated. Mutations that affect early stages of development are likely to be lethal, or deadly. An organism carrying such a mutation dies while it is an embryo, and its genes are not passed on. As a consequence, the portions of DNA that control the early stages of development remain relatively unchanged. Thus the embryos of different kinds of animals resemble each other.

Mutations that cause less drastic, as well as potentially useful, changes in structure are likely to occur at later stages of growth and development. Thus the later stages in the development of related organisms begin to show marked differences. An organism with this kind of mutation may survive to reproduce and pass the changes in its DNA to its offspring.

__Figure 13–16__ During certain embryological stages, vastly different organisms show similarities. During later stages of development, profound changes occur. Thus the adults bear little resemblance to one another.

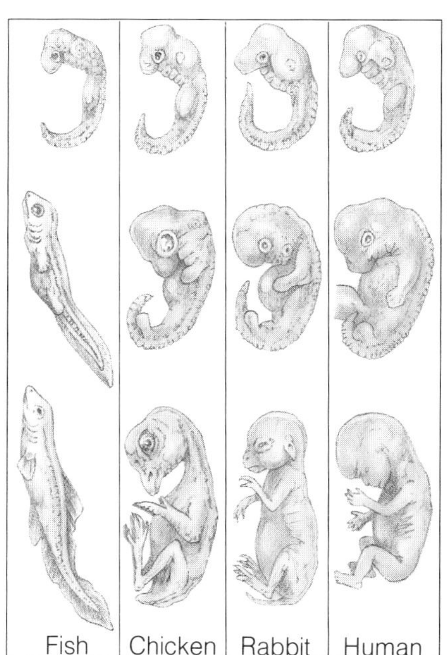

Similarities in Body Structure

In the embryos of many animals—humans, birds, horses, and whales, for example—the clumps of cells that develop into limbs look quite similar. But as the embryos mature, the limbs grow into arms, wings, legs, and flippers that differ greatly in form and function. These different forelimbs evolved in a series

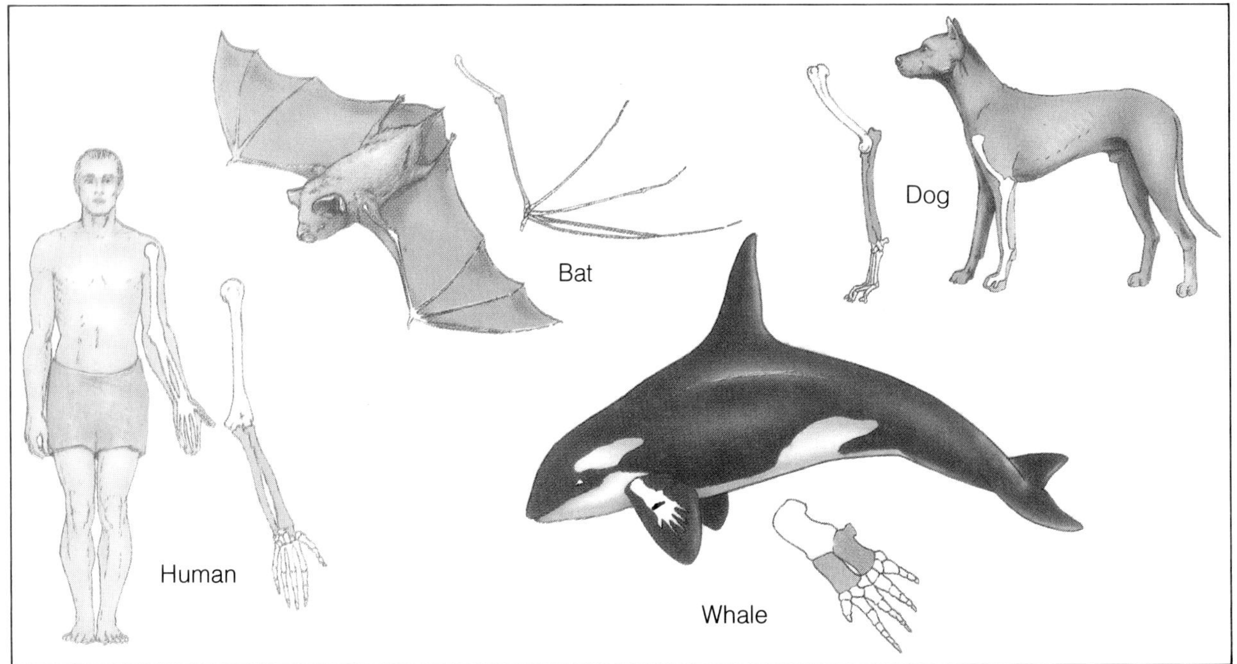

Figure 13–17 Superbly adapted to performing different tasks, the limbs of various organisms are remarkably similar in structure. Here you can see the homologous limbs of four mammals. How is the form of each limb adapted for different movements?

Figure 13–18 Albinism (lack of color) is the result of a gene mutation. In this photograph a normally colored penguin is "chatting" with an albino penguin. Perhaps it's scolding its pale companion for being out of uniform.

of evolutionary changes that altered the structure and appearance of the arm and leg bones of ancient animals. As you can see in Figure 13–17, the changes in the final structure of the limbs of different species are adaptations that enable each organism to survive in a different environment. Structures such as these that develop from the same body parts are called **homologous structures.**

Many animals have organs that look like miniature arms, legs, tails, or other structures. These organs are **vestigial organs.** Vestigial organs seem to serve no useful purpose at all. You may wonder why organs that are not needed are still present in an organism.

As you will see in the next chapter, evolutionary change occurs as species show new adaptations to their environment. The changes that occur may involve the modification of primitive limbs into wings or flippers. But evolution may also involve the loss or reduction of body structures that are no longer necessary. Structures that are not used may become smaller and smaller but may never disappear completely.

For example, we believe that snakes evolved from ancestors that had four legs. Today, species of pythons and boa constrictors still have useless tiny bones left over from those legs. See Figure 13–19. These tiny bones have no function. However, they act as reminders of the snake's early ancestors.

Humans, too, have vestigial organs. Examples of these are a set of tailbones at the base of the spine and, in most people, the muscles that move the ears. We also have an appendix that leads off the large intestine. This appendix does not seem to serve a useful purpose today. In fact, an appendix can cause medical problems and sometimes must be removed surgically.

Today, a large functioning appendix is found in some animals, such as the koala, that eat primarily plant materials. So it is probable that our appendix is left over from a time during which our ancestors needed this organ to digest their food.

Similarities in Chemical Compounds

All organisms—from bacteria to humans—share many biochemical details. All organisms use DNA and/or RNA to carry information from one generation to the next and to control growth and development. The DNA of all eukaryotic organisms always has the same basic structure and replicates in the same way. The RNAs of various species may act a little differently, but all RNAs are similar in structure from one species to the next. Remember, too, that ATP (adenosine triphosphate) is an energy carrier found in all living systems. A wide variety of complicated proteins, such as cytochrome *c*, are also shared by many organisms.

The more closely related two species are, the more closely their important chemical compounds resemble each other. In Chapter 15 we will discuss the importance of similar proteins in studying evolutionary relationships among species.

What Homologies Tell Us

Similarities in structure and biochemistry provide powerful evidence that all living things evolved from common ancestors. **The structural and biochemical similarities among living organisms are best explained by Darwin's conclusion: Living organisms evolved through gradual modification of earlier forms—descent from a common ancestor.** In a previous chapter you learned that life's chemical pathways are extremely complex. In a later chapter you will learn that tissues and organs are equally complex. If organisms had arisen independently of one another, there would be very little chance that they would have similar structures and biochemistries. The very complexity of life and its processes supports Darwin's conclusion.

Figure 13–19 *If you look closely, you can see the vestigial leg bones of this python, which serve no function—the snake can move quite well without them! Another example of a vestigial organ is the human appendix. In a Koala bear, however, the appendix is a functioning organ that helps the animal digest leaves.*

13–4 SECTION REVIEW

1. What are homologous structures?
2. What is a vestigial organ? Name a vestigial organ in a human.
3. How does evidence from embryology support the concept that all animals evolved from common ancestors?
4. How does biochemistry support the idea that all living things evolved from common ancestors?

LABORATORY INVESTIGATION

EXAMINING HOMOLOGOUS STRUCTURES

PROBLEM

How do homologous structures support the theory of common descent?

MATERIALS *(per group)*

preserved frog	dissecting pan
chicken wing	scalpel
human skeleton (model or chart)	scissors
	forceps

PROCEDURE

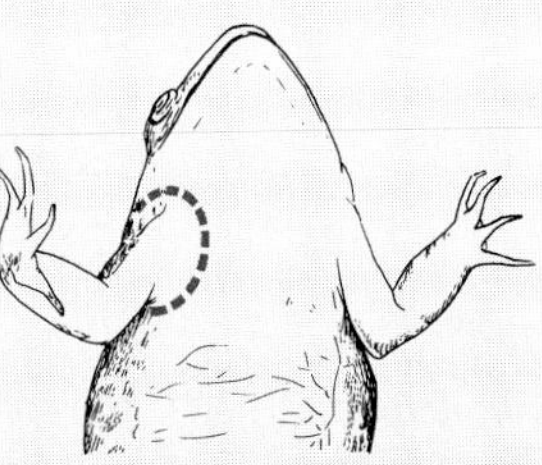

1. Put a preserved frog in a dissecting pan. Using your scissors, cut the skin around the base of the frog's arm where it joins the body. See the accompanying figure. Then grasp the cut edge of the skin with forceps and pull it down the arm until the skin is removed. The skin should come off the arm easily.
2. Pull the frog's arm up toward the head. Use your scissors to cut the muscles around the base of the arm. When you have completed your cut, the bones of the arm and shoulder should be visible. Pull back on the arm. The arm should come loose from the shoulder, but you may have to use your scissors to cut the connections that hold the arm in place.
3. With your scissors, cut the ends of the muscles away from the bone on the severed frog arm. Use your forceps to peel the muscles away from the bones. Remove as much of the muscles from the frog's arm as you can. Then, using a scalpel, gently and carefully scrape the bones clean. **CAUTION:** *Use care when using a scalpel. Always cut or scrape away from your body.*
4. Draw a diagram that shows the arrangement of the bones in a frog's arm.
5. Put a chicken wing in a dissecting pan. Use your scissors to cut the skin toward the wing-tip. The dotted line in the accompanying figure indicates where you should cut. Using the forceps, remove all the skin from the chicken wing.

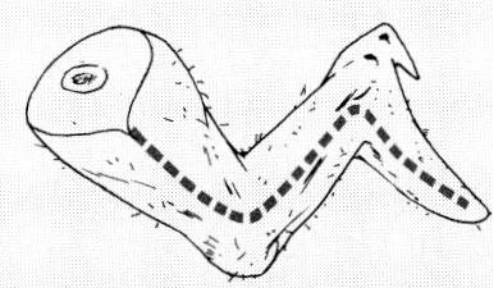

6. Carefully cut the muscles away from the bones using your scissors. With a scalpel, carefully scrape the bones clean. **CAUTION:** *Use care when using a scalpel. Always cut or scrape away from your body.*
7. Draw a diagram that shows the arrangement of the bones in a chicken wing.
8. Use the model or chart of the human skeleton to draw the arrangement of the bones in the human arm.

OBSERVATIONS

1. How many bones did you find in each of the limbs?
2. In what ways are the structures of the limbs similar?
3. In what ways are the shapes of the bones similar?

ANALYSIS AND CONCLUSIONS

1. List some functions of each of the three different limbs you have examined.
2. Even though the limbs of these organisms are very different in outward appearance and function, their internal structure is remarkably similar. How can you explain this observation?
3. From an evolutionary standpoint, what would it mean if these bones were very different in structure?

STUDENT STUDY GUIDE

SUMMARIZING THE CONCEPTS

The key concepts in each section of this chapter are listed below to help you review the chapter content. Make sure you understand each concept and its relationship to other concepts and to the theme of this chapter.

13–1 Evolution and Life's Diversity

- The observation of the diversity of living things on Earth contributed to the formation of Darwin's theory of evolution.
- Fitness is the combination of physical traits and behaviors, or adaptations, that help organisms survive.

13–2 The Age of the Earth

- Scientists use the decay of radioactive elements to date the Earth's rocks.
- The position of rock layers as well as the decay of radioactive elements have enabled scientists to set up a geological time scale.
- Dating techniques have shown that the Earth is about 4 1/2 billion years old.

13–3 The Fossil Record

- Fossils, the remains of ancient organisms, are preserved in sedimentary rock layers.
- Although the fossil record is not complete, fossil evidence shows that life on Earth has changed over time.

13–4 Evidence from Living Organisms

- Similarities in the structure and development of embryos provide evidence of descent from a common ancestor.
- Homologous structures and vestigial organs are additional evidence of descent from a common ancestor.
- The biochemistries of living organisms support the hypothesis that these organisms evolved from a common ancestor.

REVIEWING KEY TERMS

Vocabulary terms are important to your understanding of biology. The key terms listed below are those you should be especially familiar with. Review these terms and their meanings. Then use each term in a complete sentence. If you are not sure of a term's meaning, return to the appropriate section and review its definition.

13–1 Evolution and Life's Diversity

evolution
fitness
common descent
adaptation

13–2 The Age of the Earth

fossil
geologic time scale
relative dating
radioactive element
half-life
absolute dating
era
period
epoch

13–3 The Fossil Record

sedimentary rock
paleontologist
fossil record

13–4 Evidence from Living Organisms

embryo
homologous structure
vestigial organ

CHAPTER REVIEW

CONTENT REVIEW

Multiple Choice

Choose the letter of the answer that best completes each statement.

1. The length of time it takes for one half of a radioactive element to decay is a (an)
   a. era. c. year.
   b. half-life. d. epoch.
2. Another term for radioactive dating is
   a. relative dating.
   b. geologic time scale.
   c. calendar dating.
   d. absolute dating.
3. The ability of an organism to survive and reproduce is known as
   a. fitness. c. diversity.
   b. evolution. d. adaptation.
4. Fitness arises through a process called
   a. common descent. c. homologous change.
   b. half-life. d. adaptation.
5. Evidence for the age of the Earth is provided by all of the following except
   a. fossils.
   b. radioactive dating.
   c. the rate of sediment formation.
   d. vestigial organs.
6. Most fossils are found in
   a. sedimentary rock. c. ice.
   b. amber. d. tar pits.
7. A vestigial organ is
   a. always useful.
   b. useless.
   c. not evidence for evolution.
   d. sometimes useful.
8. Change in species over time is called
   a. fitness. c. diversity.
   b. evolution. d. relative dating.

True or False

Determine whether each statement is true or false. If it is true, write "true." If it is false, change the underlined word or words to make the statement true.

1. <u>Paleontologists</u> are scientists who study fossils.
2. The ability of an organism to survive and reproduce is known as <u>diversity</u>.
3. In the Earth's history, periods are divided into <u>eras</u>.
4. <u>Embryos</u> are early stages in an organism's development.
5. <u>Relative dating</u> is the same as radioactive dating.
6. Today, scientists have evidence that shows that the Earth is <u>1 million</u> years old.
7. The theory that organisms share a common ancestor is known as <u>common descent</u>.
8. A human's arm and a dog's leg are examples of <u>vestigial organs</u>.

Word Relationships

A. *In each of the following sets of terms, three of the terms are related. One term does not belong. Determine the characteristic common to three of the terms and then identify the term that does not belong.*

1. appendix, tailbones, ear muscles, heart
2. absolute dating, double dating, radioactive dating, relative dating
3. half-life, era, epoch, period
4. diversity, fitness, fossil, adaptation

B. *An analogy is a relationship between two pairs of words or phrases generally written in the following manner: a:b::c:d. The symbol : is read "is to," and the symbol :: is read "as." For example, cat:animal::rose:plant is read "cat is to animal as rose is to plant."*

In the analogies that follow, a word or phrase is missing. Complete each analogy by providing the missing word or phrase.

5. biologist:organism::paleontologist:_______________
6. era:periods::sedimentary rock:_______________
7. half-life:absolute dating::rock position:_______________
8. appendix:vestigial organ::bat wing and whale flipper:_______________

CONCEPT MASTERY

Use your understanding of the concepts developed in the chapter to answer each of the following in a brief paragraph.

1. Explain how radioactivity is used to date rock samples.
2. What is the geologic time scale? How was it developed?
3. What is a vestigial organ? Give an example of a vestigial organ in humans.
4. What does the phrase common descent mean?
5. What is a fossil?
6. How is sedimentary rock formed?

CRITICAL AND CREATIVE THINKING

Discuss each of the following in a brief paragraph.

1. Summarizing information Evolutionary biologists say that there is good reason for gaps in the fossil record. Can you explain why some extinct animals and plants were never fossilized?
2. Applying concepts A giraffe's long neck enables it to eat the leaves of trees. How does this adaptation help the giraffe survive?
3. Sequencing events How did the work of geologists help Darwin formulate his theory of evolution?
4. Applying technology Discuss the limitations of radioactive dating.
5. Making inferences How did the diversity of life that Darwin observed during the five-year voyage of the *Beagle* contribute to the development of his theory?
6. Using the writing process You have been given the opportunity to become the first person to travel back in time to the age when dinosaurs roamed the Earth. Describe your feelings as you observe these ancient creatures walk through the area you now call home.
7. Using the writing process This time you will travel forward in time several million years. Use your imagination to describe the kinds of organisms now living on Earth. (*Hint:* Remember that any organism you describe must be well adapted to the environment of Earth in the distant future.)

CHAPTER 14

Evolution: How Change Occurs

It was in this ship that Charles Darwin sailed around South America. By today's standards, it was a small ship, and time on board was spent in cramped quarters.

There is grandeur in this view of life, with its several powers, having been originally breathed into a few forms or one; and that, whilst this planet has gone cycling according to the fixed laws of gravity, from so simple a beginning endless forms most beautiful and most wonderful have been, and are being, evolved.

So wrote Charles Darwin in his conclusion to On the Origin of Species, *the book in which he attempted to explain what he among many had observed: that life on Earth has changed over time. But how does change occur? And how can one species evolve into another? It is this explanation in part that you will learn about in the pages that follow.*

14–1 Developing a Theory of Evolution

Section Objectives

- Discuss the importance of evolutionary theory.
- Identify the basic assumptions of Lamarck's theory of evolution.
- Explain some of the major ideas that helped shape Darwin's theory of evolution.

Evolutionary theory is the foundation on which the rest of biological science is built. In fact, the biologist Theodor Dobzhansky once wrote that nothing in biology makes sense except in the light of evolution. Much research in genetics, ecology, and medicine is based on evolutionary theory.

The fact that plants and animals have changed over time was obvious to Darwin and has been clear to scientists throughout the last century. Observing that evolution has occurred is relatively simple. Explaining how and why evolution occurs is more difficult.

Certain aspects of Darwin's original theory of evolution have been revised by biologists in the years since the publication of *On the Origin of Species*. But the revisions do not mean that evolutionary change itself is debatable or that evolutionary theory is merely a collection of vague hunches that are not supported by evidence. Evolutionary change is undeniable. **Evolutionary theory is a collection of carefully reasoned and tested hypotheses about how evolutionary change occurs.**

By way of comparison, consider that even today physicists do not completely understand gravity, although there is no doubt in anyone's mind that gravity exists. There are at least two competing modern theories that explain how gravity works. Both theories make important useful predictions of natural events. For example, there is no question that if you jump into the air, you will end up on the ground below. It makes no difference whether you understand—or even believe in—gravity. What goes up must come down. Just as definitely, life on Earth evolves, or changes over time. Explaining the fine points of evolutionary change will continue to be one of the great challenges of biology.

Figure 14–1 *Although the mouse and the pig do not look at all alike, an analysis of their DNA shows that these two animals are more closely related than appearances would indicate.*

An Early Explanation for Evolutionary Change

Jean Baptiste de Lamarck (1744–1829) was among the first scientists to recognize that living things changed over time. And long before Darwin, Lamarck also realized that organisms were somehow adapted to their environments. In explaining how adaptation occurred, however, Lamarck relied on three assumptions we now know to be incorrect.

A DESIRE TO CHANGE Lamarck thought that organisms change because they have an inborn urge to better themselves and become more fit for their environments. In Lamarck's view, for instance, the ancestors of birds acquired an urge to fly. Over many generations, birds' constant efforts to become airborne led to the development of wings. What a pity for the Wright Brothers that this element of Lamarck's theory proved not to be true!

USE AND DISUSE Lamarck also believed that change occurred because organisms could alter their shape by using their bodies in new ways. Organs could increase in size or change in shape depending on the needs of the organism. For example, by trying to use their front limbs for flying, birds could eventually transform those limbs into wings. In the opposite way, Lamarck believed that if an animal did not use a particular part of its body, that body part would decrease in size and might finally disappear.

Figure 14–2 *The ears of this adult Doberman pinscher have been clipped so that they stand up on her head. But the ears of her puppy still hang down by the side of its head. This is proof that traits acquired during a lifetime are not passed on to the next generation.*

PASSING ON ACQUIRED TRAITS Included in Lamarck's reasoning was the belief, shared by many biologists of that time, that acquired characteristics were inherited. He thought that if an animal acquired a body structure (such as long arms or feathers) during its lifetime, it could pass that change on to its offspring. By the same reasoning, structures that became smaller from disuse would eventually disappear.

Although later discoveries showed that Lamarck's explanation of evolution was incorrect, he is still credited with being one of the first people to devise a theory of evolution and adaptation. He is also credited with bringing the concept of evolution to the attention of scientists. Thus Lamarck paved the way for Darwin's theory of evolution.

Lamarck's ideas may seem strange to you now, yet his theory was consistent with knowledge of that time. It was not until a century after Lamarck proposed his theory that an improved understanding of genetics and the principles of heredity showed that the mechanisms he proposed would not work.

Lamarck, you see, knew nothing about genes. As you know now, only genes and changes in genes—not alterations in body structure—are passed from parents to offspring. There is no evidence that experience during its life can cause specific changes in an organism's genes. Years of proper exercise and diet, for example, can turn a weakling into a champion weight lifter. But that weight lifter's children cannot benefit genetically from the parent's pumping iron. If the children do not exercise and eat a proper diet, they will not develop large muscles, even if their parents were world champions!

Ideas That Shaped Darwin's Theory of Evolution

Personal experience on the *Beagle*'s voyage awakened Darwin's interest in explaining the diversity and fitness of life on Earth. But both during his trip and after his return, Darwin's thinking was also influenced by the books he read and by discussions with geologists, farmers, and others.

THE INFLUENCE OF GEOLOGY: LYELL'S IDEAS As you will remember from Chapter 13, the geologist Charles Lyell demonstrated that the Earth was very old and that it had changed over time. After reading Lyell's book *Principles of Geology,* Darwin became convinced that the Earth was much older than most people of his time believed. This was an important idea for Darwin. For in order to explain evolution—to even recognize that evolution had occurred—it was essential for Darwin to realize that the Earth was very old. The long periods of time it would have taken for millions of species to have evolved from a common ancestor could be accounted for only if the Earth was very old.

Figure 14–3 *Volcanoes can alter the Earth's face. This volcano, emerging from beneath the ocean, resulted in the formation of a new island. Within a short period of time, living organisms will discover this newly formed island and begin to exploit the opportunities that exist there. A volcanic eruption can produce a completely opposite effect, destroying an area of land and all its inhabitants.*

Figure 14–4 *The cabbage (top), Brussels sprouts (center), and cauliflower (bottom) are all varieties of the same plant family that have been "selected" over time to produce familiar food crops.*

Lyell's writing also caused Darwin to appreciate the geological phenomena he observed on his journey. In Chile, Darwin saw a spectacular volcanic eruption. Shortly thereafter, he observed that an earthquake had lifted a stretch of shoreline three meters higher than it had been before. With Lyell's writings fresh in his mind, Darwin came to realize that geological phenomena such as the ones he had observed could transform the face of the Earth over time. And if the Earth itself could change over time, so too could life on the Earth.

THE INFLUENCE OF FARMERS: ARTIFICIAL SELECTION While assembling his thoughts back in England, Darwin spoke extensively with plant and animal breeders. He learned that farmers altered and improved their crops and livestock through breeding programs. But how, Darwin wondered, did such programs work?

Farmers told Darwin that domesticated animals and plants vary a great deal. For example, in every corn field, some plants are larger than average; others are smaller than average. Certain cows produce a large amount of milk; other cows produce a small amount of milk. Here and there among a flock of white chickens, a gray or black chicken appears. The farmers convinced Darwin that many of these variations were often passed on to the animals' offspring. In other words, these were inheritable variations.

Darwin realized that farmers could not cause variation to occur. Variation either happened naturally or it did not. But once farmers encountered variation, they could use it to their advantage. They noted the variations they found and decided which organisms to use as breeding stock. Individuals with undesirable variations—scrawny bulls or cows that produced little milk, for example—were not allowed to mate. Superior animals—husky bulls or cows that produced much milk—would be mated as often as possible.

This process, which Darwin called **artificial selection**, allowed only the best organisms to produce offspring. Over the years, breeders have used artificial selection to produce plants and animals far superior to—and often dramatically different in

Figure 14–5 *Variation in a species is quite common in nature. These ladybug beetles show different markings.*

appearance from—their original stock. **In artificial selection, the intervention of humans allows only the best organisms to produce offspring.**

Darwin became convinced that a process similar to artificial selection must be at work in nature. This process would allow only those organisms best suited to their environment to survive and reproduce. But in nature there is no human intervention; so how, Darwin wondered, could such a process operate?

THE INFLUENCE OF MALTHUS: POPULATION CONTROLS An important influence on Darwin was the work of the economist Thomas Malthus (1766–1834). Malthus observed that babies were being born at a faster rate than people were dying. If the human population continued to increase in that way, Malthus reasoned, sooner or later there wouldn't be enough living space and food. The only conditions that would prevent the endless growth of human populations, Malthus observed, were famine, disease, and war. In time, these unpleasant observations were called the Malthusian Doctrine.

Darwin realized that the Malthusian Doctrine applied even more to animals and plants than to humans, for most other species produce far more offspring than we do. For example, every summer each mature maple tree produces thousands of seeds. Marine animals, such as the common mussel, produce millions of eggs each time they spawn. If all the offspring of just one of these maple trees or mussels survived, they would overcrowd the area where they lived. If each offspring then produced as many offspring as its parents and if all those offspring reproduced, there would soon be so many maple trees or mussels that they would cover the Earth or fill the oceans!

Obviously, the oceans are not filled with mussels and the continents are not covered with maple trees. Most baby mussels die during their first year of life. Most maple seeds never grow into mature trees. Thousands upon thousands of individuals of each species die and only a few survive. Even fewer successfully raise offspring. That much is clear. But what determines which individuals survive and reproduce?

Figure 14–6 *Some animals and plants produce enormous numbers of offspring. Eggs in this praying mantis egg case have begun to hatch (top). If all the young survived to reproduce, you can imagine how the number of mantises in the world would be affected. Each sunflower in this field is capable of producing hundreds of seeds (bottom). If each seed survived and reproduced, there would be uncountable numbers of sunflowers.*

14–1 SECTION REVIEW

1. What is the importance of evolutionary theory?
2. How did Lamarck explain evolution? What are the major problems with his explanation?
3. What is artificial selection? How did this concept influence Darwin's thinking?
4. Would Darwin have developed his theory of evolution if he had not read the works of Lyell and Malthus? Explain.

Section Objectives

- Describe the process of natural selection.
- Provide an example of natural selection in action.

14–2 Evolution by Natural Selection

Ultimately, Darwin recognized in nature a process that operates in a manner similar to the way artificial selection worked on farms and in fields. Darwin called this process **natural selection** and explained its action in terms of several important observations.

Darwin observed that wild animals and plants showed variations just as domesticated animals and plants did. His field notebooks were filled with records of height, weight, color, claw size, tail length, and other characteristics among members of the same species. Darwin did not understand the reasons for these variations, but he realized that many of them were inherited.

Darwin observed that high birthrates and a shortage of life's necessities forced organisms into a constant "struggle for existence," both against the environment and against each other. Plant stems grow tall in search of sunlight; plant roots grow deep into the soil in search of water and nutrients. Animals compete for food and space in which to build nests and raise young. But who among all the contenders wins the struggle for existence?

Figure 14–7 Life is a constant struggle for all organisms to survive. This smaller lizard has just come to the end of that struggle in the jaws of a gecko.

Darwin knew that each individual differs from all the other members of its species. Sometimes the differences are easy to observe; sometimes the differences are subtle. **Those individuals with characteristics best suited to their environment survive the struggle for existence. Other individuals lacking the characteristics best suited to their environment die or leave fewer offspring.** This principle Darwin called **survival of the fittest**.

Natural selection thus operates in a similar way to artificial selection, but over much longer periods of time. On farms, human breeders determine which plants and animals will reproduce. In nature, the struggle for existence permits only the fittest individuals to reproduce. The fact that the members of a species that are not the fittest do not survive and reproduce keeps the species from covering the Earth.

Peppered Moths: Natural Selection in Action

England's peppered moth provides an example of natural selection in action. It also offers us a chance to study the sorts of experiments that can be used to test evolutionary theory. The story is as follows. The peppered moth spends much of the daytime resting on the bark of oak trees. In the beginning of the nineteenth century, the trunks of most oak trees in England were light brown speckled with green. Most of the peppered moths of that time were mottled light brown too. There were always a few dark-colored moths around, but light-colored moths were always the most common.

Figure 14–8 Before the Industrial Revolution, soot was rare in the English countryside. A light-colored moth was difficult to see against the clean tree bark (top). After several years, during which the bark was darkened by the soot of burning coal, a light-colored moth stood out against the darkened tree bark (bottom). In each photograph, which moth would most likely be noticed by a hungry bird?

Then the Industrial Revolution began in England. Pollution (mostly soot from burning coal) stained London's tree trunks dark brown. At about the same time, biologists noticed that more and more moths with dark coloration were appearing. Why was the population changing color in this way?

The evolutionary hypothesis suggested by observation was straightforward. Birds are the major predators of peppered moths. It is much harder for birds to see, catch, and eat moths that blend in with the color of the tree bark than it is for them to spot moths whose color makes a strong contrast with the tree trunks. The moths that blend in with their background are said to be camouflaged.

As the tree trunks darkened, the rarer, dark-colored moths were better camouflaged and harder for birds to spot. Being harder to spot, the darker individuals were now better able to survive. The darker forms had greater fitness than the lighter forms. More of the darker moths survived and reproduced, passing on the genes for dark color to their offspring, and the moth population evolved darker coloration.

But a hypothesis that looks good is not enough. Scientific hypotheses must be tested by experiment whenever possible.

British ecologist H.B.D. Kettlewell devised just such a test for this hypothesis. Kettlewell learned how to capture both light- and dark-colored forms of the peppered moth and then managed to raise them in captivity. He also learned to mark living moths in such a way that birds could not see the marks.

Kettlewell then released equal numbers of light- and dark-colored moths in two types of areas. In one area, trees were normally colored. In the other area, they were blackened by soot. Later on, he recaptured, sorted, and counted all the marked moths he could. What type of results do you think Kettlewell needed to either prove or disprove the hypothesis?

Kettlewell found that in unpolluted areas, more of his light-colored moths had survived. In soot-blackened areas, more of his dark-colored moths had survived. Thus Kettlewell showed that in each environment the moths that were better camouflaged had the higher survival rate. It was logical to conclude that when soot darkened the tree trunks in an area, natural selection caused the dark-colored moths to become more common. Today Kettlewell's work is considered to be a classic demonstration of natural selection in action.

Figure 14–9 *Looking like something it's not can be helpful to an organism. It is difficult to spot the insect disguised as a thorn (top, left), the toad that resembles a fallen leaf (top, right), and the moth that looks like a plant leaf complete with diseased areas (bottom).*

14–2 SECTION REVIEW

1. What is natural selection? What observations led Darwin to develop this concept?
2. Define survival of the fittest. How are the concepts of natural selection and survival of the fittest related?
3. Explain how natural selection might produce a modern giraffe from short-necked ancestors.

14–3 Genetics and Evolutionary Theory

Section Objectives

- Explain how genes affect natural selection.
- Define evolution in genetic terms.
- Relate genes to fitness and adaptation.

In developing his theory of evolution, Darwin worked under a serious handicap. He had no idea how the inheritable traits so important to his theory were passed from one generation to the next. For although Mendel had formulated his genetic principles during Darwin's lifetime, his work remained unknown to most scientists until the early part of this century. The rediscovery of Mendel's work and the growth of our knowledge of genetics enable us to explain the mechanism of evolution more completely than Darwin could. Genetics and evolutionary theory are inseparable. Today we define fitness, adaptation, species, and the process of evolutionary change in genetic terms.

Genes: Units of Variation

Genes, the carriers of inheritable characteristics, are also the source of the random variation upon which natural selection operates. Mutations cause some variation. Much additional variation arises during meiosis as the parents' chromosomes are copied, shuffled like a deck of playing cards, and dealt out to the gametes.

It is important to remember that genetic variation does not occur because an animal needs or wants to evolve—an idea central to Lamarck's theory. Sometimes genetic variation occurs; sometimes it doesn't. There is no way for an organism to cause a particular change in its DNA. There is also no way for an organism to prevent variations that do occur.

Figure 14–10 *It is a zebra's genes that determine the exact pattern of the animal's stripes. Notice that there are slight variations in the stripes of each animal.*

Raw Material for Natural Selection

In the evolutionary struggle for existence, entire organisms, not individual genes, either survive and reproduce or do not. How then does natural selection operate? Natural selection can operate only on the phenotypic variation among individuals. As you learned in Chapter 9, an organism's phenotype includes all the physical and behavioral characteristics produced by the interaction of genotype and environment.

You can sample phenotypic variation by measuring the height of all the students in your class. Using mathematics, you can calculate an average height for this group. Many students will be just a little taller or shorter than average. However, a few very tall or very short individuals may be in your class. If you graph the number of individuals of each height, you will get a curve similar to the one shown in Figure 14–11 on page 300. This phenotypic variation is produced by a combination of genetic instructions and environmental influences, such as nutrition and exercise. If your classmates are not malnourished, most (though not all) of the variations in height you observe

Figure 14–11 *This photograph shows height distribution in a population of U.S. Army recruits. As you can see, most of the recruits fall in the range of average heights in the center of the curve. There are relatively few very tall or very short recruits.*

can be said to result from differences in genotype. Of course, you can also observe many other kinds of phenotypic variation among your classmates. For example, variations in skin, hair, and eye color, and variations in the shapes of noses, the curves of lips, and the amount of body hair can be observed.

In nature, organisms show as many variations as humans, although most humans are not aware of this. For example, to the casual observer, one zebra looks much like any other zebra. But when researchers study the characteristics of many individuals of a species, they find the same sort of distribution for each characteristic that you saw in human height. It is this sort of variation in organisms that provides the raw material for natural selection.

Evolution as Genetic Change

In order to describe the evolution of plants and animals, modern evolutionary biologists study groups of organisms called **populations**. A population is a collection of individuals of the same species in a given area whose members can breed with one another. For example, all the fishes of a certain species in a single pond could be considered one population. Individuals in another, separate pond would belong to a different population, even if that pond was close by.

Because all members of a population can interbreed, they and their offspring share a common group of genes, called a **gene pool**. Each gene pool contains a number of alleles—or forms of a certain gene at a given point on a chromosome—for each inheritable trait, including alleles for recessive traits. The number of times an allele occurs in a gene pool compared with the number of times other alleles for the same gene occur is called the **relative frequency** of the allele.

Sexual reproduction alone does not change the relative frequency of alleles in a population. To understand why, you can compare the combinations of alleles produced by sexual reproduction to the different hands you get when you shuffle and deal a deck of playing cards. Shuffling and reshuffling produce an enormous variety of different hands. But shuffling alone will not change the relative numbers of aces, kings, fours, or jokers in the deck.

With this in mind, we can define evolution in another way. **Evolution is any change in the relative frequencies of alleles in the gene pool of a population.** And, as you can see in Figure 14–13, when the relative frequencies of alleles in a population change, the curves that describe the distribution of traits controlled by those alleles also change. In the case of the peppered moths, as the alleles for dark color increased, more dark-colored moths appeared in the population. This is the visible result of evolutionary change.

Figure 14–12 All of the flamingoes in a given area make up a gene pool. Within that pool, it is possible for any one flamingo to breed with any other flamingo. It is individual choice that limits the number of potential mates a single flamingo may have.

Genes, Fitness, and Adaptation

Each time an organism reproduces, it passes copies of its genes to its offspring. Thus we can define evolutionary fitness as the success an organism has in passing on its genes to the next generation. And we can define an adaptation as any genetically controlled characteristic of an organism that increases its fitness.

Let's return to our discussion of human weight lifters for a moment. Muscles acquired as a result of exercise are not passed on to offspring. Thus they cannot be considered an evolutionary adaptation and cannot contribute to evolutionary fitness. A gene that somehow allowed an individual to develop stronger muscles by doing less work or by eating less food, on the other hand, might be a useful adaptation under certain circumstances. This gene could be passed on to offspring.

A Genetic Definition for Species

In the past, biologists defined a species as a group of organisms that looked alike. Species were defined according to precise physical descriptions, and differences among individuals were seen as imperfections or mistakes. This definition, however, did not recognize that variation in a population is the rule rather than the exception.

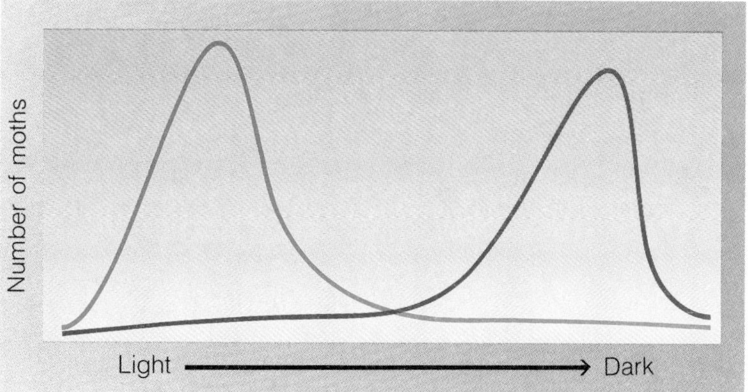

Figure 14–13 Sometimes the frequency of an allele changes in a population. The light-colored moths occurred with greater frequency before the Industrial Revolution. After the Industrial Revolution, the frequency of dark-colored moths became greater. How do you explain these changes?

Figure 14–14 *A species is a population of organisms that breed with one another and share a common gene pool. If this baby hippopotamus survives, it can pass on its genes to another generation.*

We now define a species as a group of similar-looking (though not identical) organisms that breed with one another and produce fertile offspring in the natural environment. This definition is important because it allows us to determine what it means to belong to the same or different species.

Because members of a species can breed with one another, they share a common gene pool. Because of that shared gene pool, a genetic change that occurs in one individual can spread through the population as that individual and its offspring mate with other individuals. If the genetic change increases fitness, that gene will eventually be found in many individuals in the population. Members of a species can thus evolve together and interact with their environment in similar ways.

14–3 SECTION REVIEW

1. What causes phenotypic variation? How is phenotypic variation related to natural selection?
2. Define evolution in genetic terms.
3. What are the genetic definitions of fitness and adaptation?
4. Scientists notice that the individuals in a certain plant species are growing taller with each successive generation. Explain what is happening to the gene pool of this population.

Evolution in Action

Evolution did not just happen millions of years ago. Evolutionary change occurs around us constantly. Scientists today have observed many examples of evolutionary change that have occurred in living organisms.

Many species of insects and microorganisms damage crops, spoil food, or make us ill. Farmers spray their crops with poisons that kill harmful insects. Doctors and veterinarians use antibiotics and other medicines to kill disease-causing bacteria and other microorganisms.

However, scientists have observed that many of the insect species are not killed by insecticides that killed others of that species several years ago. And some microorganisms are no longer eliminated by antibiotics. The resistance of certain pest species to chemicals that once controlled them are examples of evolutionary change.

How can this resistance be explained? The work of Darwin provides an answer. Remember, Darwin suggested that there is great variation among organisms. Suppose there were a few insects that were not killed by an insecticide that killed other members of their species. Suppose there existed a bacterium that was unaffected by an antibiotic proven to control other members of its species. The surviving organisms would be more fit. They could pass on their genes to their offspring.

Normally these resistant organisms are uncommon in a population. However, the use of insecticides and antibiotics changes the environment. These chemicals kill organisms that are not resistant. But at the same time, these chemicals increase the fitness to survive of resistant organisms. With less competition, these fit individuals survive and reproduce. And because they reproduce quickly, the genes that made them more fit are rapidly spread in a population. Soon many more resistant individuals are found in the population. And the chemicals that once controlled a pest population are no longer effective.

This example of evolution in action poses problems for human society. New chemical controls must constantly be developed. However, some physicians feel that we will run out of new and effective antibiotics before microorganisms run out of variations. To control crop pests, farmers now use chemicals that are potentially more dangerous—chemicals that may also threaten humans and the environment. So there is much work for future biologists.

Section Objectives

- Define niche.
- Relate the availability of niches to speciation.
- Describe the process of speciation.

14–4 The Development of New Species

We are now nearly ready to explain how new species evolve from old ones, a process biologists call **speciation**. But before we can explain how speciation occurs and how it can lead to diversity, we must first understand some basic concepts about the way species interact in their environment.

The Niche: How to Make a Living

Organisms, like members of a human community, need to survive and acquire the necessities of life. But like people crowded into a city, organisms would have difficulty surviving if they all tried to do the same kinds of work, eat the same kinds of food, and live in the same place. Isn't it hard to imagine, for example, an entire city of butchers or tailors? And certainly you wouldn't want the population of an entire city living in your house!

In human cities, thousands of people survive near one another. They have different jobs, they shop in different stores, and they live in different places. Animals and plants do much the same thing. The combination of an organism's "profession" and the place in which it lives is called its **niche** (NIHCH). If two species occupy the same niche in the same location at the same time, they will compete with each other for food and space. One of the species will not survive. **No two species can occupy the same niche in the same location for a long period of time.** Chances are, one of the species will be more efficient than the other. The more efficient species will survive, reproduce, and drive the less efficient species to extinction.

Figure 14–15 *Reproductive isolation can lead to the development of a new species. The fish on the left is a member of the same species as the fish on the right, although it is quite different in appearance. In time, if it is reproductively isolated, it may evolve into another species.*

If two species occupy different niches, however, they will not compete with each other as much. With less competition, there is less chance that one species will cause the other to become extinct. So in the evolutionary struggle for existence, any species (or a population within a species) that occupies an unoccupied niche will be better able to survive. We will soon see how this phenomenon can lead to the formation of entirely new species.

Figure 14–16 *Hundreds of years ago, the dodo was quite common on the island of Mauritius. This large bird, unable to fly, made its nest on the ground. In time, settlers arrived with dogs and other domestic animals. The helpless dodos were killed and their nests destroyed. The expression "dead as a dodo" is used today to refer to any organism that is now extinct.*

The Process of Speciation

Remember that biologists define a species as a group of organisms that can breed with one another and produce fertile offspring in a natural environment. This definition means that individuals in the same species share a common gene pool. Individuals in different species have different gene pools.

Scientists have learned that new species usually form only when populations are isolated, or separated. This separation of populations so that they do not interbreed to produce fertile offspring is called **reproductive isolation**. If two populations are not reproductively isolated, their gene pools will blend with each other. No new species will be formed. Reproductive isolation is the agent for the formation of new species.

Reproductive isolation may occur in a variety of ways. Geographic barriers such as rivers, mountains, and even roads may separate populations and prevent them from interbreeding. Differences in courtship behavior or fertile periods may result in organisms that breed only with individuals that are most similar to themselves.

Once reproductive isolation occurs, natural selection usually increases the differences between the separated populations. As the populations become better adapted to different

Figure 14–17 *The bower bird makes a nest, or bower, on the ground for his mate. In order to entice a suitable female, the male decorates his bower with bits of glass, colored stones, and shiny paper. This complicated behavior contributes to the bower bird's reproductive success.*

environments, their separate gene pools gradually become more dissimilar. Now the populations are separated not only by the physical or behavioral barriers that once separated them, but by vastly different genes. If the populations remain separated for a long time, their gene pools eventually become so different that their reproductive isolation becomes permanent. When this occurs, the groups of organisms are no longer separate populations. They have become separate species.

Darwin's Finches: An Example of Speciation

We can now use our understanding of evolution to explain the fascinating case of Darwin's finches, a group of 14 bird species on the Galapagos Islands. All these finch species evolved from a single ancestral species. Yet each of the 14 species exhibits body structures and behaviors that enable it to live in a different niche. For example, each species shows adaptations that allow it to feed differently. Some of the finch species eat small seeds, whereas others crack open much larger seeds or seeds with thicker shells. Some species pick ticks—small insectlike animals—off the islands' tortoises and iguanas. One finch species uses twigs or cactus spines to remove insects from inside dead wood. And some finches, often called vampire finches, drink the blood of large sea birds after pecking them at the base of their tail! How did so many strange and unusual finch species evolve on these islands? The evolution of the various species of finches on the Galapagos Islands shows how geographic and behavioral barriers and reproductive isolation eventually lead to the formation of new species.

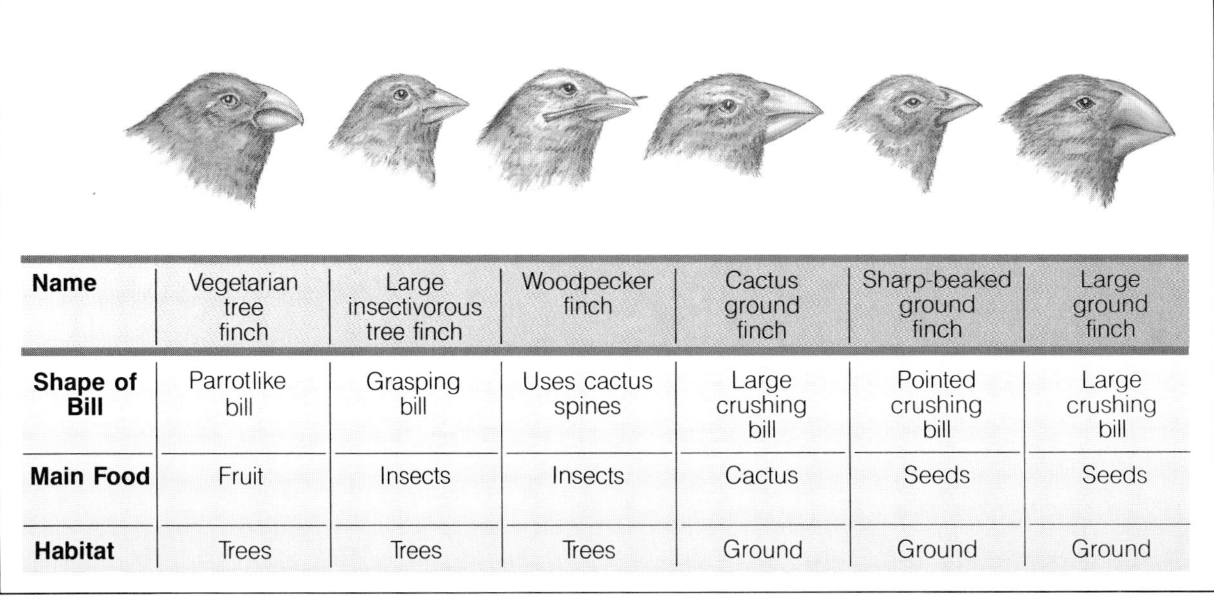

Name	Vegetarian tree finch	Large insectivorous tree finch	Woodpecker finch	Cactus ground finch	Sharp-beaked ground finch	Large ground finch
Shape of Bill	Parrotlike bill	Grasping bill	Uses cactus spines	Large crushing bill	Pointed crushing bill	Large crushing bill
Main Food	Fruit	Insects	Insects	Cactus	Seeds	Seeds
Habitat	Trees	Trees	Trees	Ground	Ground	Ground

Figure 14–18 *The many kinds of finches that Darwin observed on the Galapagos Islands evolved from a single species that emigrated from the South American mainland some kilometers away. How have the shapes of these birds' beaks contributed to their survival?*

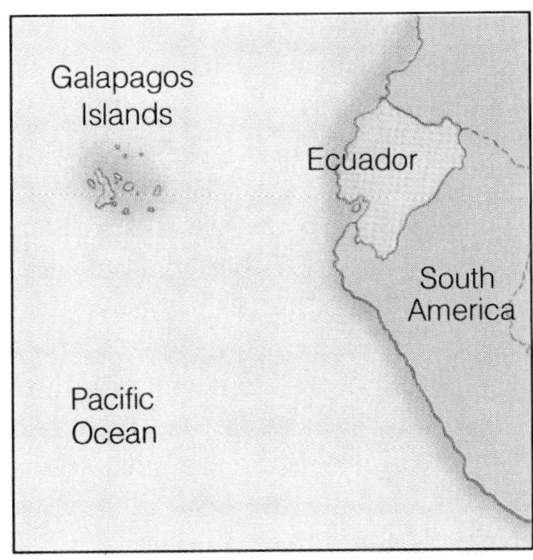

Figure 14–19 This map shows the location of the Galapagos Islands off the coast of Ecuador (left). Variation exists even among the giant tortoises that live on the Galapagos Islands. The shell of one type of tortoise is raised in the front (right), enabling it to lift its head farther off the ground than the tortoise with a shell rounded in the front (center). How does the shell shape contribute to the survival of each tortoise?

STEP 1: FOUNDING FATHERS AND MOTHERS Darwin's finches are descendants of a few ancestral finches that found their way to the Galapagos Islands from the South American mainland. Finches are small birds that do not usually fly far over open water. They may have gotten lost, or they may have been blown off course by a storm. In any case, once they arrived at one of the Galapagos Islands, which we can call Island A, they managed to survive and reproduce.

STEP 2: SEPARATION OF POPULATIONS Then, some birds from Island A crossed to another island in the Galapagos group. We will call this Island B. Remember, these birds do not like to fly over open water. So the populations on Islands A and B were essentially isolated from each other. Even though they were still members of the same species, the ocean between them prevented the blending of their gene pools.

STEP 3: CHANGES IN THE GENE POOL Over time, the populations on each island became adapted to the needs of their environments. For example, suppose the plants growing on Island A produced mainly small thin-shelled seeds, whereas the plants on Island B had larger thick-shelled seeds. Individual finches in the Island B population with larger, heavier beaks would be able to crack open and eat the seeds more easily. So birds with large beaks would be better able to survive on Island B. Over time, natural selection could have caused that population to evolve larger beaks.

STEP 4: REPRODUCTIVE ISOLATION Now imagine that a few birds from Island A cross to Island B. Will the birds from Island A be able to breed with the birds on Island B? Probably not. It happens that the finches prefer to mate with birds that have the same size beak they do. Thus differences in beak size, combined with mating behavior, act as a mechanism for reproductive isolation. The gene pools of the two bird groups do not mix. The two populations have become separate species.

STEP 5: SHARING THE SAME ISLAND The fate of the two species on Island B depends on the relationship between the birds and their environment. There are three possibilities: coexistence, extinction, or further evolution. If the two species occupy different niches, they can coexist, or live together without changing. But if the niches of the species are too similar, the species will compete with each other. If one species is much better at making a living than the other, it may cause its competitor to become extinct.

If, however, one species exhibits enough genetic variation, the competition it encounters may cause it to evolve further. A new species may result. For example, if the species' beak changes size again, it will be able to eat another kind of food for which it does not have to compete. Scientists believe that the 14 species of finches on the Galapagos Islands evolved from a single ancestor when speciation happened in this way again and again on different islands over time.

Speciation and Adaptive Radiation

The process we have just described on the Galapagos Islands, in which one species gives rise to many species, is called **adaptive radiation**. The process of adaptive radiation is also known as **divergent evolution**. In adaptive radiation, a number of different species diverge, or move away, from a common ancestral form, much as the spokes of a bicycle wheel radiate from the hub. During a period of adaptive radiation, organisms evolve a variety of characteristics that enable them to survive in different niches. Throughout the history of life on Earth, adaptive radiations have occurred many times and in many places. Adaptive radiation occurred on the Hawaiian Islands among a group of birds called Hawaiian honeycreepers. The dinosaurs experienced an adaptive radiation in their day, only to eventually become extinct. The mammals alive today were produced by another wave of adaptive radiation.

Evidence of past adaptive radiations can be observed in many organisms. The homologous structures discussed in the last chapter are evidence of past adaptive radiations in which the similar body parts of related organisms evolved to perform different tasks.

As you can see from Figure 14-20, adaptive radiations among different organisms often produce species that are similar in appearance and behavior. This phenomenon is known as **convergent evolution**. Convergent evolution has produced many of the **analogous structures** in organisms today. Analogous structures are similar in appearance and function, but they have different origins. Because they have different origins, analogous structures usually have very different internal structures. For example, the wings of butterflies, birds, and bats are analogous structures that allow the organisms to fly. However, a closer examination of these wings shows that a butterfly's wing is made of a thin nonliving membrane with an intricate network of supports. A bird's wing is made of skin, muscles, and arm bones. And a bat's wing is made of skin stretched between elongated finger bones.

Figure 14–20 *Adaptive radiation is the process by which many different species develop from a common ancestor. As you can see from this illustration, some of the descendants of the* Cotylosaur *do not resemble it in the least.*

Figure 14–21 The wings of a butterfly and the wings of a bat are analogous structures—similar in appearance and function. Although the wings of both the butterfly and the bat show adaptations for flight, they are made up of different tissues.

14–4 SECTION REVIEW

1. What is a niche? How do niches contribute to speciation?
2. How are speciation and reproductive isolation related?
3. What is adaptive radiation? Explain how Darwin's finches illustrate this process.
4. The first species to reach a newly formed volcanic island often undergoes an adaptive radiation. Explain this observation.

Section Objectives

- Discuss how gene pools can change in the absence of natural selection.
- Explain why some gene pools may change very little over time.
- Describe the theory of punctuated equilibria.

14–5 Evolutionary Theory Evolves

It should now be apparent to you that evolutionary theory has been modified over the years. With the contributions of scientists such as Lamarck and Darwin and a better understanding of heredity, scientists can now explain how variation occurs and define evolutionary concepts in terms of genetics. But even today, evolutionary theory continues to evolve as scientists formulate theories about the details of evolutionary change.

Genetic Drift

Natural selection is not always necessary for genetic change to occur. **With the aid of theories and genetic experiments, biologists have realized that gene pools can change —in other words, evolution can occur—in the absence of natural selection**. This does not mean that natural selection is not important. However, biologists now realize that chance plays an even larger part in evolutionary change than Darwin thought.

Geneticists have shown that an allele can become common in a population by chance. This kind of random change in the frequency of a gene is called **genetic drift**.

How does genetic drift work? One possibility is that an individual with a particular allele may produce more offspring than other members of its species—not because it is better adapted but just by chance. It is also possible for environmental events to wipe out many individuals who do not carry a particular allele. For example, the distribution of some alleles in the population of mountain goats in Washington State may have changed when Mount St. Helens erupted in 1980, killing many mountain goats in the area of the volcano. Thus, in very special circumstances, a new or previously rare allele may become common in a population after only a few generations. Genetic drift occurs most efficiently in small populations because chance events, such as a volcanic eruption, are less likely to affect all members of a very large population. Genetic drift could also have played a role in the evolution of Darwin's finches, since each new population was founded by relatively few birds.

Genetic drift implies that all characteristics of an organism do not have to contribute to its fitness. For example, consider the differences between the Indian rhinoceros (which has one horn) and the African rhinoceros (which has two). Both rhinoceros species use their horns to fight predators and to joust among themselves, so having a horn or two is useful. But it is not clear whether having two horns is better for survival than having one horn. If the two types of rhinoceros lived in the same area, the rhinoceros with one horn would probably have the same fitness as the rhinoceros with two horns. Thus the extra horn does not necessarily contribute to fitness. Most likely, the ancestral populations that gave rise to the two modern rhinoceros species developed slightly different horn systems just by chance. Natural selection provided a distinct advantage to individuals with horns; but the two populations developed different numbers of horns because of random genetic drift. Genetic drift probably led also to the evolution of one hump on African camels and two humps on Asian camels.

Figure 14–22 *The eruption of Mount St. Helens in 1980 drastically changed the environment. Trees were killed, as were many animals. Presently, plants are growing and some animals have returned to reclaim the altered landscape they called home.*

Figure 14–23 *The Indian rhinoceros (left) has a single horn; the African rhinoceros (right) has two. The number of horns may not contribute to survival, since one horn is as good as two in defending animals as grand as these.*

Figure 14–24 *This plant-eating dinosaur, which once munched plants in a quiet pond on ancient Earth, is today extinct. The environment on Earth changed, but, alas, the dinosaur did not.*

Unchanging Gene Pools

Modern evolutionary biologists recognize that although natural selection and genetic drift are both powerful forces of change, they do not cause genetic alterations in all species all the time under all conditions. And because sexual reproduction by itself does not change the frequency of alleles in a population, it is possible for the gene pool of a species to remain the same for a long time.

Every now and then there arises a species, particularly well adapted to an environment, that does not change over time. If no new species enter into competition with that species and if certain other conditions are met, that species may remain nearly unchanged for long periods of time. One example of such a species is the horseshoe crab, *Limulus*, whose living members are nearly identical to ancestors that lived hundreds of millions of years ago. Such organisms are often called living fossils. Though relatively rare among both plants and animals, living fossils are fascinating indications that under some conditions evolution can slow down.

Gradual and Rapid Evolutionary Change

Darwin, convinced by the work of Lyell of the slow and steady nature of geologic change, felt that biological change was also slow and steady. The theory that evolutionary change occurs slowly and gradually is known as **gradualism**. In many cases the fossil record shows that a particular group of organisms has indeed changed gradually over time.

But there is also evidence that many other species did not change very much from the time they appeared in the fossil record to the time they disappeared. In other words, much of the time these groups of animals and plants are in a state of **equilibrium** (ee-kwih-LIHB-ree-uhm), which means they do not change very much.

But every now and then, something happens to upset the equilibrium. At several points in the fossil record, changes in animals and plants occurred over relatively short periods of time. Some biologists argue that these rapid changes—rather than long, slow changes—are what create new species. Remember that when we say "short" and "rapid" we are talking about the geological time scale. Short periods of time for geologists can be hundreds of thousands, even millions, of years!

Rapid evolution after long periods of equilibrium can occur in several ways. It may occur when a small population of a species becomes isolated from the main part of the population. This small population can evolve more rapidly than the larger one because genetic changes can spread more quickly among fewer individuals. Or rapid evolution may occur when a small group of organisms migrates to a new environment, as happened with the Galapagos finches. The organisms then evolve rapidly to fill available niches.

Rapid evolution may also result from dramatic changes on the Earth. Every now and then, many species have vanished in a phenomenon known as a **mass extinction**. Some mass extinctions were caused by changes in global climates that altered many environments. The causes of other mass extinctions remain uncertain. But whatever their causes, the effects of mass extinctions are clear. When many species die, many niches are left unoccupied. The species that remain suddenly find lots of empty niches. Groups of animals with enough genetic variability can undergo adaptive radiations. These adaptive radiations can produce a large number of new species to fill those empty niches.

Scientists use the term **punctuated equilibria** to describe this pattern of long stable periods interrupted by brief periods of change. Punctuated equilibria theory, which has generated much debate, is still controversial among biologists today. It is clear, however, that evolution has often proceeded at different rates for different organisms at different times during the long history of life. But whatever the pace of change might have been, it is certain that organisms have evolved over time.

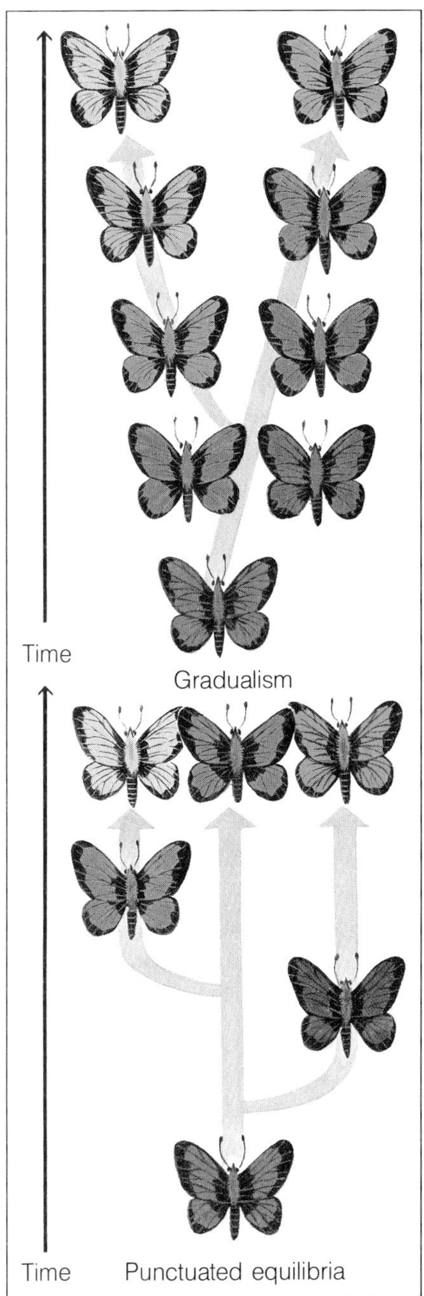

Figure 14–25 This illustration shows two possible ways in which a population of butterflies changes over time. The insects may change color gradually, with each succeeding generation showing only small color changes. Or the color of the population may remain fairly stable for long periods of time and then make great changes suddenly.

The Significance of Evolutionary Theory

Evolutionary theory is, in the minds of many biologists, the foundation on which all biological science is built. Only because all living organisms are related through common descent can we talk about universal characteristics of life. Only because the physiological properties of all multicellular organisms are so similar can we study other animals to learn how our own bodies operate. And only through application of evolutionary theory can we truly understand the way that organisms interact with each other and with their environments.

But the influence of evolutionary thought extends far beyond biology. Philosopher J. Collins has written that "there are no living sciences, human attitudes, or institutional powers that remain unaffected by the ideas . . . released by Darwin's work." We cannot even touch on these remote disciplines in this book, although we hope you will be inspired to read about them later in life. We will, however, use the remainder of this book to discuss the products of evolution: Earth's "most beautiful and wonderful" living organisms.

14–5 SECTION REVIEW

1. What is genetic drift? How does genetic drift affect a gene pool?
2. What three factors can cause an increase in the rate of evolution of a species?
3. Describe the theory of punctuated equilibria.

LABORATORY INVESTIGATION

SIMULATING NATURAL SELECTION

PROBLEM

What happens to harmful genes over time?

MATERIALS *(per group)*

small brown paper bag
400-mL beaker
250 g pinto beans
100 large lima beans
100 red kidney beans
stopwatch or clock with second hand

PROCEDURE 

1. After reading the investigation carefully, prepare a data table on a separate sheet of paper.
2. Examine and note the differences and similarities among the three types of beans.
3. Fill the beaker about three-fourths full with the pinto beans. Then pour the beans into the paper bag.
4. Add 50 lima beans and 50 kidney beans to the paper bag. The lima and kidney beans represent organisms. The pinto beans represent the environment in which the organisms are hiding.
5. Have one member of your group time you for 3 minutes. During the 3 minutes, remove one bean at a time from the paper bag. Without looking, try to remove as many lima and kidney beans as you can. Use the shapes of the beans to identify them.
6. Record the number of lima beans and kidney beans that you removed in the appropriate place in the data table.
7. To determine the number of lima beans and kidney beans that remain in the paper bag, subtract the number of lima beans removed from the starting number. Do the same for the kidney beans.
8. Add the numbers of remaining lima and kidney beans together. Record this information in the appropriate place in the data table.
9. To find the frequencies of lima beans and kidney beans that remain in the paper bag, divide the numbers of each of the remaining beans by the total number of remaining lima and kidney beans. Round these numbers off to the nearest hundredths place. Record this information in the appropriate place in the data table.
10. The frequencies of each of the beans that remain in the paper bag represent the distribution of genes in the population. To determine the starting number of lima beans and kidney beans that are present in the next generation, multiply the frequency of each bean by 100. Record the information in the appropriate place in the data table. Add lima beans and kidney beans to the bag to restore the same starting number for the next generation.
11. Repeat steps 5 through 9 until the information in the data table is complete for five generations.

OBSERVATIONS

1. What was the ratio of lima beans to kidney beans?
2. Based on your data, was one type of bean removed from the bag more frequently than the other? If so, which type?
3. What happened to the frequencies of the lima beans in the population over five generations? The frequencies of the kidney beans?
4. What happened to the total number of beans that remained over five generations?

ANALYSIS AND CONCLUSIONS

1. Which beans represent the beneficial genes in a population? The harmful genes? How do you know?
2. Explain why the frequency of remaining genes changes in each generation?
3. What do you think happens to harmful genes over time?

STUDENT STUDY GUIDE

SUMMARIZING THE CONCEPTS

The key concepts in each section of this chapter are listed below to help you review the chapter content. Make sure you understand each concept and its relationship to other concepts and to the theme of this chapter.

14–1 Developing a Theory of Evolution

- Lamarck was one of the first people to propose a theory of evolution and adaptation. He thought that organisms respond to the needs of their environment and pass on acquired characteristics to their offspring.

14–2 Evolution by Natural Selection

- In natural selection, only the organisms with the characteristics best suited for their environment survive and reproduce.

14–3 Genetics and Evolutionary Theory

- Gene mutations and gene recombinations provide the variations upon which natural selection acts.
- Evolution is a change in the relative frequencies of alleles in the gene pool of a population.

14–4 The Development of New Species

- A niche is the combination of an organism's "profession" and the place in which it lives. If two species occupy the same niche in the same location at the same time, they will compete with each other for food and space.
- Reproductive isolation is necessary for speciation.
- In adaptive radiation, one species gives rise to many new species.

14–5 Evolutionary Theory Evolves

- Genetic drift—a random change in the frequency of a gene—occurs most efficiently in small populations.
- The theory of punctuated equilibria states that there are long periods of stability punctuated by brief periods of rapid change.

REVIEWING KEY TERMS

Vocabulary terms are important to your understanding of biology. The key terms listed below are those you should be especially familiar with. Review these terms and their meanings. Then use each term in a complete sentence. If you are not sure of a term's meaning, return to the appropriate section and review its definition.

14–1 Developing a Theory of Evolution

artificial selection

14–2 Evolution by Natural Selection

natural selection
survival of the fittest

14–3 Genetics and Evolutionary Theory

population
gene pool
relative frequency

14–4 The Development of New Species

speciation
niche
reproductive isolation
adaptive radiation
divergent evolution
convergent evolution
analogous structure

14–5 Evolutionary Theory Evolves

genetic drift
gradualism
equilibrium
mass extinction
punctuated equilibria

CHAPTER REVIEW

CONTENT REVIEW

Multiple Choice

Choose the letter of the answer that best completes each statement.

1. Darwin was familiar with the works of all of the following except
a. Mendel. c. Lamarck.
b. Lyell. d. Malthus.

2. Which of the following is needed for new species to form?
a. a niche
b. homologous structures
c. analogous structures
d. reproductive isolation

3. Farmers change the gene pool of a population by
a. adaptive radiation.
b. natural selection.
c. artificial selection.
d. convergent evolution.

4. The source of random variation on which natural selection operates are changes in
a. a niche.
b. genes.
c. relative frequency.
d. the survival of the fittest.

5. An example of analogous structures are a
a. whale's flipper and a bat's wing.
b. bird's wing and a butterfly's wing.
c. hawk's wing and a robin's wing.
d. dog's leg and a horse's leg.

6. Which of the following ideas proposed by Lamarck was later found to be incorrect?
a. Acquired characteristics can be inherited.
b. Analogous structures can be inherited.
c. Living things change over time.
d. The Earth is very young.

7. Malthus thought that all of the following would prevent the endless growth of the human population except
a. famine. c. disease.
b. war. d. evolution.

8. Natural selection is also known as
a. adaptive radiation.
b. convergent evolution.
c. survival of the fittest.
d. divergent evolution.

True or False

Determine whether each statement is true or false. If it is true, write "true." If it is false, change the underlined word or words to make the statement true.

1. The theory of gradualism states that the fossil record shows long periods of stability and short periods of rapid evolution.

2. Lamarck and Wallace both developed a theory of evolution by natural selection.

3. Members of a population share a common group of genes, called a gene pool.

4. Speciation is any change in the relative frequencies of alleles in the gene pool of a population.

5. The combination of an organism's "profession" and the place in which it lives is called its niche.

6. Divergent evolution has produced many of the analogous structures in organisms today.

7. Random change in the frequency of a gene is called relative frequency.

8. More dark-colored peppered moths were found when soot darkened the color of tree trunks. This is an example of artificial selection.

Word Relationships

Give the vocabulary word whose meaning is opposite that of the following words.

1. gradualism
2. convergent evolution
3. natural selection
4. interbreeding

CONCEPT MASTERY

Use your understanding of the concepts developed in the chapter to answer each of the following in a brief paragraph.

1. Explain how the work of Lamarck, Lyell, and Malthus influenced Darwin's thinking.
2. What are two errors in Lamarck's theory of evolution?
3. What is punctuated equilibria?
4. How can farmers change a population of chickens?
5. Why is reproductive isolation needed for a new species to form?
6. How do genes provide the raw material for natural selection?
7. What is survival of the fittest?
8. Two organisms cannot occupy the same niche at the same time. Explain why this is so.

CRITICAL AND CREATIVE THINKING

Discuss each of the following in a brief paragraph.

1. **Applying concepts** How does punctuated equilibria try to explain gaps in the fossil record?
2. **Making predictions** Domesticated turkeys cannot fly. This is an advantage to a farmer who raises thousands of birds. What would happen to these birds if they escaped from the farm into the woods? Explain your answer.
3. **Evaluating theories** Is protecting endangered species defying natural selection? Explain.
4. **Relating cause and effect** The giant panda occupies a very small niche by eating only one kind of food: bamboo. How can being adapted to such a small niche actually endanger this species' survival?
5. **Applying concepts** How might having a small gene pool cause a species to become extinct?
6. **Using the writing process** A friend of yours invents a time machine through which you both embark on a trip far into the future. When you arrive at your destination, you discover that Earth is much warmer and the sunlight more intense. You see many plants and animals that are unlike any you have ever seen before. Write a short story that describes the new life forms that are able to survive under these different conditions. You may wish to accompany your story with one or more drawings depicting these unusual plants and animals.

CHAPTER 15

Classification Systems

The lemur is a primate that lives only on Madagascar, an island off the coast of Africa. The iguana, a reptile, lives on one of the Galapagos Islands off the coast of South America. Both of these animals—so different in appearance—are part of the great diversity of life on planet Earth.

From the numerous observations you make in your daily life, you are probably aware that a great many different kinds of organisms share planet Earth. In the last two chapters of this textbook, you glimpsed but a small part of this great diversity of life. The next twenty chapters will provide you with a broad overview of the many kinds of life that share your planet. But these chapters will touch on only a small fraction of Earth's species. Only a small fraction in twenty chapters might make you wonder how many species there are all together and how scientists can possibly keep them organized. The explanation of just how scientists do this is what this chapter is all about.

CHAPTER OUTLINE

15–1 Why Classify?

Section Objectives

- Discuss the usefulness of classification systems.
- List the characteristics of a good biological classification system.

Scientists have identified more than 2 1/2 million species of organisms on Earth so far, and their job is not even close to completion! Some biologists estimate that there may be another million species living in tropical rain forests and an unspecified number living in the depths of Earth's as yet unexplored waters.

No one, not even the world's greatest experts, can think about 2 1/2 million species at one time. The only way we can possibly study and understand this great diversity of living organisms is to divide them up into small, manageable groups. But what kinds of groups should we divide Earth's life into? **To help us work with the diversity of life we need a system of biological classification that names and orders living organisms in a logical manner.**

All accepted biological classification systems have two important characteristics. First, they assign a single universally accepted name to each organism. In this way, an American scientist, for example, can write to colleagues in Egypt, India, or Peru and be certain that everyone knows exactly what organism is being discussed. Second, good biological classification systems place organisms into groups that have real biological

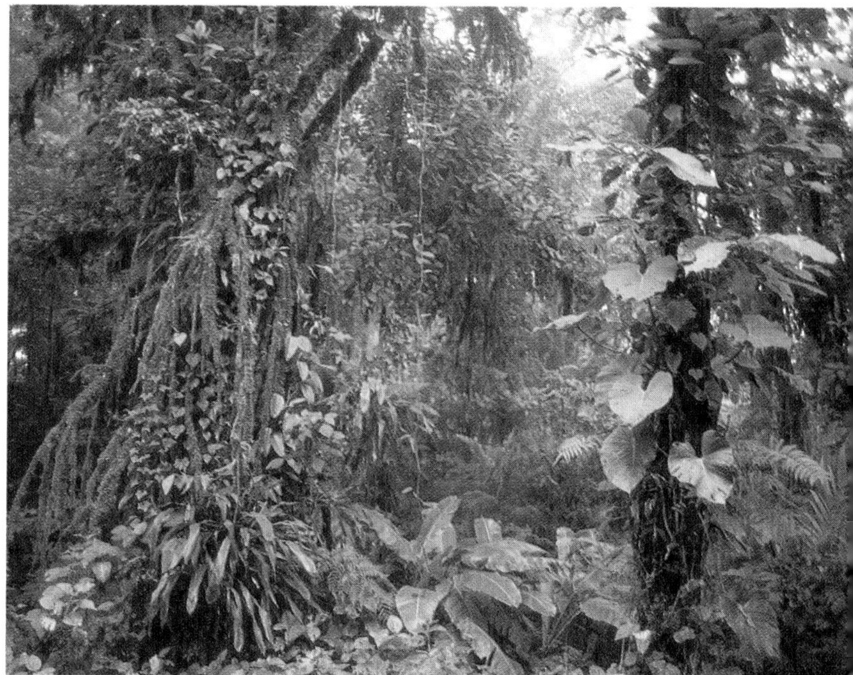

Figure 15–1 *There are so many different species of organisms in the tropical rain forests that these areas have been called the "nurseries of the globe." Because many rain forest organisms have never been collected, studied, and classified, scientists view with alarm the destruction of these areas.*

Figure 15–2 *These three organisms are worms. Although they share certain characteristics, they differ from one another in major ways. Classifying and naming these organisms permit scientists all over the world to know which particular worm is being discussed in any type of scientific communication.*

meaning. Thus researchers can expect members of a group to share important characteristics. Any useful classification system requires a set of universally accepted rules for grouping organisms.

15–1 SECTION REVIEW

1. Why are classification systems useful?
2. What are two characteristics of a good classification system?
3. What advantage is there for two scientists on opposite sides of the world to use a single name for a particular organism?
4. Give an example of a system you use to classify objects or people around you.

Section Objectives

- Describe the importance of the classification system developed by Carolus Linnaeus.
- Identify the different taxa that make up the classification system developed by Linnaeus.

15–2 Biological Classification

By the eighteenth century, European scientists, responding to the need for a universally recognized naming system, no longer used common names in local languages to describe organisms. Instead, they used names based on Latin or ancient Greek words because these languages were understood by scientists everywhere.

These early scientific names described the physical characteristics of a species in great detail and were often twenty words long! For example, the English translation of the name of a particular tree might have been "Oak with deeply divided leaves that have no hairs on their undersides and no teeth around their edges."

This cumbersome system of naming organisms had another major drawback. It was difficult to standardize names of organisms because different scientists sometimes chose to describe different characteristics of the same species. Thus the same organism might have had different names.

The Naming System of Carolus Linnaeus

Some order was made out of all this confusion by the work of Carolus Linnaeus. Linnaeus, a Swedish botanist, developed a system for naming plants and animals that is still in use today. This system is known as **binomial nomenclature** (bigh-NOH-mee-uhl NOH-muhn-klay-cher).

In his system of binomial nomenclature, Linnaeus gave each organism a two-part scientific name. For example, the tree we call the red maple is called *Acer rubrum.* The first part of the name, *Acer,* is the genus name (JEE-nuhs; plural: genera, JEHN-er-uh). A genus name refers to the relatively small group of organisms to which a particular type of organism belongs. All maple trees carry the genus name *Acer,* the Latin word for maple. The second part of the name, *rubrum,* is the species name. The species name is usually a Latin description of some important characteristic of the organism. Red maples are called *Acer rubrum* because *rubrum* is the Latin word for red. Another kind of maple, which has no English common name, has a leaf that resembles a human hand. That maple is called *Acer palmatum. Palmatum* comes from the Latin word for hand.

Notice that when we use the Latin name for an organism, we always capitalize the genus name but not the species name. We also print the entire name in italics. This rule helps us recognize scientific names as we read.

Today this system of two Latin names is used by scientists everywhere. Even in a scientific book written in Chinese, you will see the names of any organisms described in the text given in this form. An international committee makes certain that once a scientific name has been chosen, it is used consistently. That committee, as well as other scientists, also makes sure that there is a carefully selected specimen of each species on file for reference. By maintaining a library of organisms in zoology and botany museums, scientists can compare the specimen they are examining with a named preserved specimen. If the specimens match, the scientist knows that the species being examined has already been described and named. If the specimen does not match anything on file, the scientist may have found a new species—in which case he or she has the privilege of naming it.

Figure 15–3 *Using a classification system based on physical descriptions would have mistakenly suggested that these three oak leaves—the red oak (top and bottom) and the white oak (center)— represented three species.*

The Classification System of Linnaeus

After naming organisms, Linnaeus grouped them together according to the body structures they shared. He did this by examining the structural characteristics of organisms and deciding which structures were the most important for classifying the organisms. Organisms that shared important characteristics were classified in the same group. The groups to which Linnaeus assigned organisms are called taxa (singular: taxon), and the science of naming organisms and assigning them to these groups is called **taxonomy.**

Figure 15–4 *This herbarium sheet will become part of a major botanical garden's collection. The collection is used by scientists to compare unfamiliar plants with known plants in order to identify them.*

Figure 15–5 *This illustration shows the classification groups that contain a grizzly bear. As you can see, the species name of this bear provides a pretty accurate description of its personality.*

The smallest **taxon** is the **species**, which we have previously defined as a population of organisms that share similar characteristics and that can breed with one another. If two species share many features but are clearly separate biological units, they are classified as different species within the same **genus**. Genus is the next largest taxon within the Linnaean system of classification. All the various species included in the same genus have many common characteristics. The common house cat, for example, is named *Felis domesticus*. The genus *Felis* to which the house cat belongs contains other species, such as the familiar mountain lion, *Felis concolor*. All members of the genus *Felis* share many characteristics. For example, they all have similar teeth, feet, and claws.

There are other catlike animals, however, that differ enough from those in genus *Felis* that they are placed in different genera. Lions *(Panthera leo)* and tigers *(Panthera tigris)* belong to the genus *Panthera*. And cheetahs *(Acinonyx jubatus)*, although similar to lions and tigers, belong to a different genus —the genus *Acinonyx*. Groups of genera such as these, which share many common characteristics, are gathered into larger units called **families**. A family is a larger taxon than a genus. All genera of catlike animals belong in the family Felidae.

Several families of similar organisms make up the next largest taxon—an **order**. Cats (family Felidae) are placed in the same order as dogs (family Canidae). The order to which these two families, as well as several others, belong is called Carnivora. All members of the order Carnivora are carnivores, or meat-eaters.

Orders are grouped into **classes**. All members of the order Carnivora are warmblooded, have body hair, and produce milk for their young. For these reasons, they are placed together with humans (order Primates) and other similar animals in the class Mammalia.

In turn, several classes are placed in a **phylum** (FIGH-luhm), which includes a large number of very different organisms. These organisms, nevertheless, share some important basic characteristics. For example, mammals are placed in the phylum Chordata along with birds, fishes, and reptiles because all of them share certain similar characteristics.

In the classification system that was designed by Linnaeus, all phyla belonged in one of two giant taxa called **kingdoms**. Animals formed the kingdom Animalia, and plants formed the kingdom Plantae. The system developed by Linnaeus looks like this:

Kingdom
  Phylum
    Class
      Order
        Family
          Genus
            Species

Figure 15–6 These animals are all cats—some cute and cuddly, others not. Scientists group cats that roar in the genus Panthera *and cats that purr in the genus* Felis. *The cheetah is a special case, however. It belongs to the separate genus* Acinonyx, *because unlike other cats, it cannot retract its claws.*

15–2 SECTION REVIEW

1. Why is the system of binomial nomenclature a good way to name organisms?
2. What is the smallest taxon? What is the largest taxon? Which of these taxons is the most specific?
3. Two groups of organisms are in different genera but they are included in the same family. What does this information tell you about the two groups?

15–3 Taxonomy Today

Section Objectives

- Discuss how taxa show evolutionary relationships between different organisms.
- Explain how modern scientific techniques contribute to the classification of organisms.

Taxonomy, particularly the grouping of organisms into higher taxa, is not as simple as it might seem. Ideas about the arrangement of organisms into families, orders, phyla, and kingdoms have changed dramatically since the time of Linnaeus. How and why has taxonomy changed so much?

Remember that despite the importance of taxonomy to biologists, the only taxon that has a clear biological identity is the species. Members of a species share a common gene pool because they breed with one another. So members of a species form a very real biological unit. We might even say that organisms themselves determine which individuals belong to their species and which do not.

The taxa above the level of species, however, do not have a clear biological identity. This is because taxonomists, or scientists who classify organisms, draw the lines between one genus and another and between one family and another. Of course, taxonomists try to create taxa that group organisms according to biologically important characteristics. But different scientists have different ideas about which characteristics are biologically most important. As a result, organisms have sometimes been "moved" from one taxon to another.

Figure 15–7 The mountain gorilla (right) and the lowland gorilla (left) belong to different species. As their names indicate, they live in different areas. Although they are both gorillas, they represent two species because they do not breed with each other. They do not share a common gene pool.

Taxonomy and Evolutionary Relationships

Today, evolutionary theory teaches that living species have evolved from earlier species. This unifying biological principle thus provides both a purpose and a guiding philosophy to modern classification systems. For this reason, taxonomists attempt to group organisms in ways that show their evolutionary relationships. Taxonomists do this by identifying and studying homologous structures in adult organisms, in developing embryos, and in well-preserved fossils. **Species shown to be closely related are classified together. Other species that may look alike but possess analogous structures only are classified in different groups.**

Deciding which structures are most important is not always easy though, and researchers often disagree on how to classify certain organisms. In writing this textbook, we have adopted one of the classification systems most widely accepted among biologists.

Figure 15–8 Long thought to be extinct, the coelacanth was discovered in the Chalumna River in Africa. This photograph is one of the few taken of a living coelacanth. Coelacanths are believed to be relatives of the early fish that developed into four-legged land mammals.

Biochemical Taxonomy

All organisms share many important organic molecules that are almost—but not exactly—identical from species to species. For example, mammals, birds, amphibians, reptiles, and fishes have hemoglobin in their blood, but each species has a slightly different variety of hemoglobin. All green plants have chlorophyll molecules, which are used in the process of photosynthesis. But some groups of green plants have chlorophyll molecules that differ in structure from other groups.

Biochemists can use similarities and differences among the compounds of life to classify organisms—just as anatomists use similarities and differences between homologous structures. The more similar the proteins of two species are, the more closely related these species are likely to be. Biochemists also study molecules of DNA and RNA, which vary in number, appearance, and amino acid sequence among different organisms.

Virtually every organism has its own form of cytochrome *c*, a complicated protein molecule found in the electron transport chain. Figure 15–9 illustrates differences among cytochrome *c* of various organisms. These differences are the result of mutations that occurred after the ancestors of the various species split apart. If two species diverged millions of years ago, there has been lots of time for mutations to alter the structure of cytochrome *c* molecules in each species. Note, for example, the large difference between human cytochrome *c* and cytochrome *c* of *Neurospora*, a bread mold. This tells us that these two species are not closely related at all. The similarity between cytochrome *c* of chickens and that of penguins, on the other hand, shows that these two species are closely related.

The study of DNA sequences in mammals has yielded some surprising results. For example, scientists have found that humans and chimpanzees have DNA that differ in fewer than 1 percent of their nucleotide sequences.

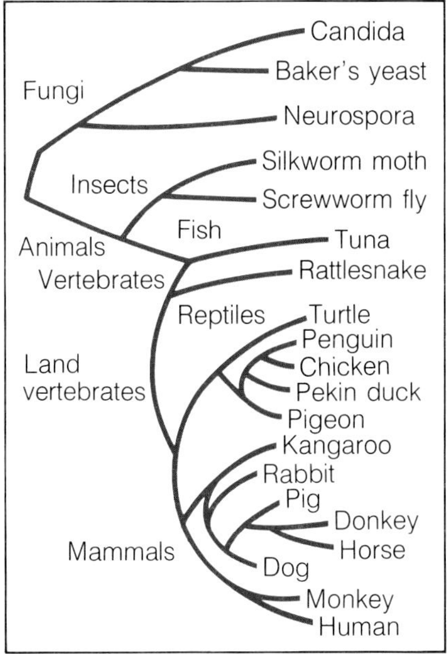

Figure 15–9 *Cytochrome* c *can be used to show relationships between organisms. Organisms on branches near one another are more closely related.*

15–3 SECTION REVIEW

1. Which taxon has a clear biological identity? Explain your answer.
2. Why did evolutionary theory prove important in taxonomy?
3. How can a study of biochemistry help taxonomists?

15–4 The Five-Kingdom System

Section Objectives

- Explain why the five-kingdom system more accurately represents evolutionary trends.
- Discuss characteristics of organisms placed in each of the five kingdoms.

Linnaeus created his taxa in the eighteenth century, basing his system on the knowledge available at that time. As biologists gathered more and more information over the years, it became clear that Linnaeus's two kingdoms were not sufficient to logically include all organisms.

For example, microorganisms, which were discovered only after the development of microscopes, look and act significantly different from plants and animals. Some of these microorganisms lack nuclei, mitochondria, and chloroplasts. As you may remember, organisms that lack a nucleus are known as prokaryotes. Scientists now consider these prokaryotes to be fundamentally different from other living things, so they have placed them in a separate kingdom: Monera. Most scientists also feel that many single-celled eukaryotes are different enough from multicelled eukaryotes that they belong in yet another kingdom: Protista. Finally, molds and yeasts, once included in the plant kingdom, are now considered different enough from green plants to be in their own kingdom: Fungi.

As a result of discoveries of new life forms and changing ideas about those characteristics of greatest importance in classifying organisms, the most generally accepted classification system now contains five kingdoms. **The five kingdoms are Monera, Protista, Fungi, Plantae, and Animalia.**

Figure 15–10 *These five kingdoms have been used as a basis for classification in this textbook.*

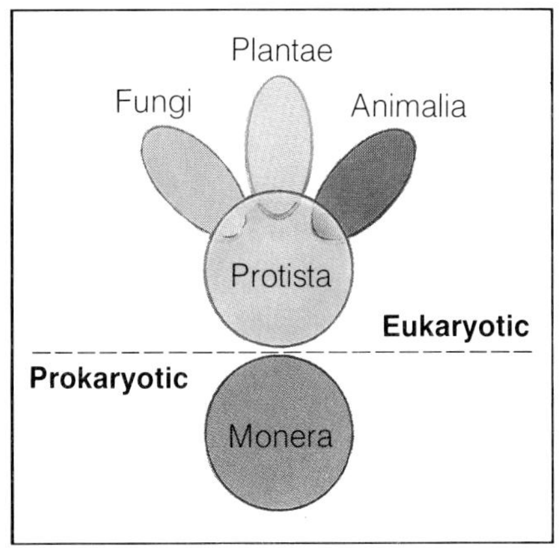

So Little Time, So Many Names

Will we have time to identify and classify all of the organisms with whom we share this planet? Probably not. For even with the modern methods used to classify organisms, time is running out. Throughout the world, species are becoming extinct. It has been estimated that 15 to 20 percent of the species on Earth will become extinct in the next 30 to 40 years. In one part of the world—the tropical rain forests—the rate of extinction has become critical. Scientists are concerned that organisms there are being destroyed faster than they can be classified. Tropical rain forests are home to more species than all other parts of the world combined. But only about 15 percent of these species have been identified.

Increasing economic pressures are threatening huge areas of tropical rain forests, and with these areas the future of life on Earth. In many parts of the world tropical rain forests are being destroyed so that farm crops can be grown and farm animals can be raised. Areas of tropical rain forests are usually cleared by burning the vegetation to the ground. Many other species—such as insects, birds, and small mammals—are destroyed as the flames level the plant life. If the rate of destruction of tropical rain forests continues, many species of organisms will become extinct before their value can be calculated and appreciated.

There is one especially sad footnote to the destruction of tropical rain forests. The soil there is very poor and can support farming for only a few years. When the soil, depleted of nutrients, can no longer support the growth of farm crops, it is abandoned. New areas must then be burned. Thus more and more land, and the life on it, is destroyed for very limited benefits.

The destruction of rain forests is a serious issue. Biologists argue that we must do everything possible to save the organisms that live in these rain forests, many of which exist nowhere else on Earth. But people who live in these areas argue that they cannot preserve the rain forest without sacrificing their own survival. As in most issues, both sides have a valid point.

In many areas, a shortage of space to grow crops forces people to cut down and burn rain forests. The soil in these areas contains few nutrients, and so more areas must be cut down and burned to continue the production of food crops.

You should keep in mind that not all scientists agree on this grouping. More research may someday show that other classification systems make more sense. But right now most scientists view this five-kingdom classification system as a useful tool for studying organisms, which is what taxonomy is all about. In order to understand why the five kingdoms are arranged as they are, it helps to think of them as representing a simple evolutionary tree. Following are brief descriptions of the five classification kingdoms.

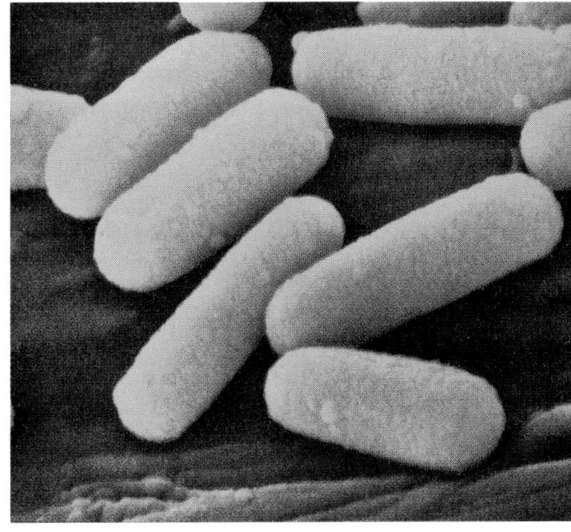

Figure 15–11 These rod-shaped bacteria, photographed on the head of a pin, are placed in the kingdom Monera. The bacteria have been magnified more than 4000 times to make them visible.

Monera

All prokaryotes are placed in the kingdom **Monera.** You will learn in the next chapter about the strong biochemical and fossil evidence that indicates that prokaryotes were the earliest life forms on Earth. Like prokaryotes alive today, the ancient prokaryotes lacked nuclei, mitochondria, and chloroplasts, and reproduced by splitting apart in a process called binary fission.

Monerans are therefore placed at the base of our evolutionary tree. This does not mean that other organisms evolved from living prokaryotes. Rather, it means that other organisms probably evolved from extinct organisms that were very similar to modern prokaryotes.

Protista

Unlike prokaryotes (Monerans), all eukaryotes possess membrane-enclosed organelles. All eukaryotes have a nucleus and mitochondria; some eukaryotes have chloroplasts. In the five-kingdom classification system, all single-celled eukaryotic organisms are placed in the kingdom **Protista**.

The kingdom Protista is further divided into three groups: animallike protists, plantlike protists, and funguslike protists. Ancestors of animallike protists may have evolved into animals. Ancestors of plantlike protists may have evolved into land plants. And ancestors of funguslike protists may have evolved into the living fungi.

Recall, however, that taxonomic groups are set up by biologists, not by the organisms that make up the groups. In the next several chapters you will see that the division between the protists and the three multicellular kingdoms is not clear-cut at all. Many species straddle the line between single-celled and multicellular plants, animals, and fungi. These organisms are important examples of in-between steps in evolution that link the modern groups of organisms together.

Figure 15–12 The fragile appearance of this paramecium belies its strong constitution. Parameciums, which are placed in the kingdom Protista, are widely distributed in many bodies of water throughout the world. Can you see why the paramecium is called the "slipper organism"? Its shape looks much like the impression made by a slipper on wet sand.

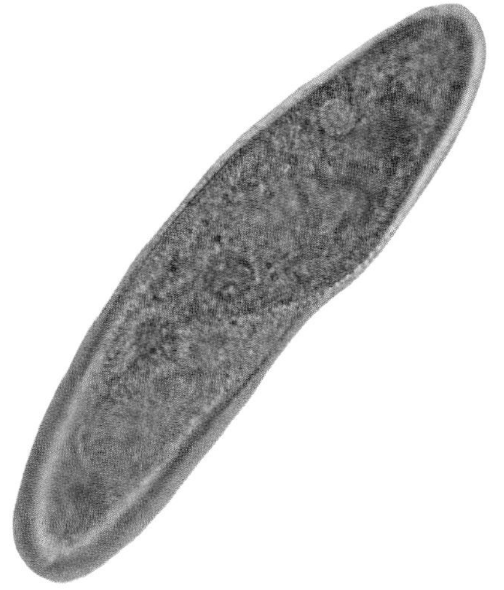

Fungi

Members of the kingdom **Fungi** build cell walls that do not contain cellulose. Fungi are heterotrophic. Heterotrophs do not carry on photosynthesis. And although fungi have many nuclei,

Figure 15–13 *The fly agaric (left), a beautiful and colorful member of the kingdom Fungi, is poisonous. The small maple tree in the foreground and the moss plants growing on the tree (right) are both members of the kingdom Plantae.*

they do not always have separate cells divided by complete cell walls. For these reasons, the fungi are not included with the plants and are placed in their own kingdom.

Plantae

Members of the kingdom **Plantae** are multicellular, have cell walls that contain cellulose, and are autotrophic. Autotrophic plants are able to carry on photosynthesis using chlorophyll. The plant kingdom includes all the plants you have come to know by now, such as the flowering plants, mosses, and ferns. In our classification system, the plant kingdom also includes multicellular algae.

Figure 15–14 *Both of these organisms are placed in the kingdom Animalia. The orange sponge (left) grows attached to the ocean bottom, unable to move from place to place. Unlike the sponge, the huge elephant (right) is able to move about.*

Animalia

Members of the kingdom **Animalia** are multicellular, heterotrophic, and have cell membranes without cell walls. As you will see in later chapters, there is incredible diversity within the animal kingdom.

PROBLEM SOLVING IN BIOLOGY

CLASSIFYING COMMON OBJECTS

Imagine that you are setting up a hardware store and have just received an assortment of items used to fasten things together. To help your customers find the items they need, you must devise a sensible way to group and arrange these objects on your shelves. In grouping the fasteners, you will proceed in much the same way that scientists do in classifying organisms.

In order to make sensible groupings, you should first examine the similarities among these objects as well as the differences. You must determine how these similarities and differences relate to the objects' functions. Finally, you must decide which functions are most important to your customers.

Even a quick glance reveals several possible ways to group your hardware. You may feel that the most important feature of these objects is the tool used to drive them. Some of the fasteners can be driven with a screwdriver; others with a hammer. The shape of the fasteners' head will indicate how they are driven. Thus you could group the fasteners by the shape of their head.

You may feel, however, that a more important feature of the fasteners is whether they are meant to be used to fasten wood or metal. Or perhaps what the fasteners are made of is the most important feature to you. Or whether they have threads.

Notice that there is no single correct way to classify these fasteners. Each classification scheme serves a different purpose for you and your customers.

With this in mind, choose one approach to begin this exercise and create a classification system for these objects. Your smallest taxon should contain only items that are very similar to one another. Your largest taxon might include all the objects used as fasteners. If partway through this exercise you feel your system is not the best one, save your work and begin developing another strategy. Compare your results with those of your classmates, noting similarities and differences in the various schemes.

What information about the objects and about the classification process have you learned from this exercise? Do you now understand why taxonomists often disagree about the classification of organisms? Do you now have a greater appreciation for why classification is useful?

15–4 SECTION REVIEW

1. Why did the five-kingdom system of classification become widely used?
2. Why are the fungi placed in a separate kingdom?
3. A single-celled organism could be placed in the Monera or the Protista kingdom. What factor would be the most significant for determining into which kingdom this organism should be placed?

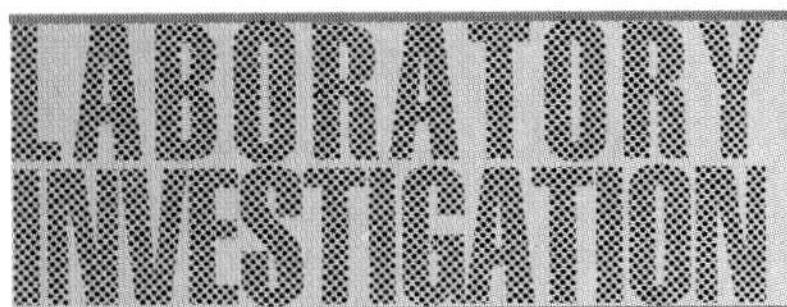

PREPARING A COLLECTION OF ORGANISMS

PROBLEM

How do you prepare a collection of organisms that represents each of the five kingdoms?

MATERIALS *(per group)*

microscope	bread
medicine dropper	sour milk, sauerkraut, or yogurt
glass slides	pond water
coverslips	small plastic food bags
forceps	transparent tape
baby food jars with lids	labels
70% ethanol	mosses and other plants
petri dishes and covers	worms and insects
nutrient agar	

PROCEDURE 

1. List characteristics of organisms in each of the five kingdoms of the classification system used in this textbook. You may refer to material already presented in this chapter. After you examine each organism in this investigation, decide which kingdom it belongs to. Be prepared to defend your decisions.
2. Use a medicine dropper to put a drop of liquid from sauerkraut, yogurt, or sour milk on a glass slide. Cover the drop with a coverslip. Examine your specimen under the high-power objective of the microscope. Draw what you observe. Label the drawing with the kingdom of the organism.
3. Use a medicine dropper to place a drop of pond water on a glass slide. Place a coverslip over the drop. Use the microscope to examine the pond water. Draw the organisms you observe. Label the drawing with the kingdom of the organism.
4. Moisten a piece of bread and place it in an open petri dish. Leave the dish on a windowsill for several days. After that time, use a forceps to remove some of the "fuzzy" material that has grown on the bread. Place this material on a glass slide. Add a drop of tap water and cover the drop with a coverslip. Examine this slide with the low-power objective. Draw what you observe. Remove another sample from the bread and place this sample in a jar. Fill the jar with ethanol. Cover the jar tightly and label it with the name of the kingdom to which the organism belongs.
5. Examine several small plants, leaves, or flowers. Put each sample in a separate baby food jar. Fill the jar with ethanol. Cover tightly. Label each jar and display.
6. Look for worms, grubs, and pill bugs in the soil. Find some insects on plants in areas near your home or school. Place each specimen in a baby food jar. Fill the jar with ethanol and cover tightly. Label each jar and display.

OBSERVATIONS

1. For organisms in which kingdoms did you require a microscope for observation?
2. What similarities and differences do you observe among organisms from different kingdoms?
3. For which kingdom was it easiest to find a variety of organisms? Most difficult?

ANALYSIS AND CONCLUSIONS

1. Why are photographs or drawings necessary for making a display of protists and monerans?
2. What difficulties did you encounter in classifying organisms?

STUDENT STUDY GUIDE

SUMMARIZING THE CONCEPTS

The key concepts in each section of this chapter are listed below to help you review the chapter content. Make sure you understand each concept and its relationship to other concepts and to the theme of this chapter.

15–1 Why Classify?

- A classification system allows us to name and order living organisms in a logical manner.
- A good classification system provides a universally accepted name to each organism.

15–2 Biological Classification

- Because they assigned a long, complicated series of names to an organism, early classification systems were very difficult to learn and cumbersome to use.
- Carolus Linnaeus gave each organism he classified a simple two-part scientific name.

15–3 Taxonomy Today

- Taxonomy is the science that names organisms and assigns the organisms to groups known as taxa.
- Taxa show evolutionary relationships among organisms.
- Today, biochemists use similarities and differences among chemical compounds to classify organisms. Molecules of DNA and RNA are often used to demonstrate evolutionary relationships among different kinds of organisms.

15–4 The Five-Kingdom System

- Because living things are so diverse and complex, Linnaeus's two-kingdom classification system is considered inadequate today in accurately representing relationships between all living things.
- A five-kingdom classification system has been developed and is widely used. This classification system shows relationships between different groups of organisms. This five-kingdom system more accurately groups organisms based on evolutionary trends.
- The Monera, Protista, Fungi, Plantae, and Animalia are five kingdoms that are used to group organisms.

REVIEWING KEY TERMS

Vocabulary terms are important to your understanding of biology. The key terms listed below are those you should be especially familiar with. Review these terms and their meanings. Then use each term in a complete sentence. If you are not sure of a term's meaning, return to the appropriate section and review its definition.

15–2 Biological Classification

binomial nomenclature
taxonomy
taxon
species
genus
family
order
class
phylum
kingdom

15–4 The Five-Kingdom System

Monera
Protista
Fungi
Plantae
Animalia

CHAPTER REVIEW

CONTENT REVIEW

Multiple Choice

Choose the letter of the answer that best completes each statement.

1. The largest taxon is a
a. kingdom. c. family.
b. species. d. phylum.

2. A good classification system does all of the following except
a. show relationships.
b. show evolutionary trends.
c. create confusion.
d. use one name for an organism.

3. The two-name system for classifying organisms was developed by
a. Charles Darwin. c. a Swedish king.
b. Thomas Edison. d. Carolus Linnaeus.

4. *Acer rubrum* and *Acer palmatum* are both names of different kinds of maple trees. What is the genus name for all maple trees?
a. *Acer*
b. *rubrum*
c. *palmatum*
d. Cannot be determined from the information given.

5. The science of naming organisms and placing them in groups is called
a. biology. c. ornithology.
b. taxonomy. d. ecology.

6. Each of the following is the name of a taxon except
a. group. c. family.
b. genus. d. kingdom.

7. The only taxon that has a clear biological identity is the
a. kingdom. c. genus.
b. phylum. d. species.

8. The kingdom that includes all prokaryotes is the
a. Monera. c. Protista.
b. Fungi. d. Plantae.

True or False

Determine whether each statement is true or false. If it is true, write "true." If it is false, change the underlined word or words to make the statement true.

1. All members of the kingdom Protista are <u>prokaryotes</u>.

2. <u>Linnaeus</u> developed the two-name system for naming organisms.

3. Fungi are <u>photosynthetic</u>, heterotrophic organisms.

4. All members of the plant kingdom are <u>unicellular</u>.

5. A good classification system uses <u>standardized</u> names.

6. *Acer rubrum* is the scientific name for the red maple. *Acer* is the <u>species</u> name for this organism.

7. The largest taxa is the <u>species</u>.

8. Several families of similar organisms make up <u>an order</u>.

Word Relationships

A. *In each of the following sets of terms, three of the terms are related. One term does not belong. Determine the characteristic common to three of the terms and then identify the term that does not belong.*

1. family, phylum, group, species
2. plants, animals, fungi, prokaryotes
3. biochemistry, cytochrome *c*, DNA and RNA, height
4. Monera, Protista, Fungi, Carnivora

B. *An analogy is a relationship between two pairs of words or phrases generally written in the following manner: a:b::c:d. The symbol : is read "is to," and the symbol :: is read "as." For example, cat:animal::rose:plant is read "cat is to animal as rose is to plant."*

In the analogies that follow, a word or phrase is missing. Complete each analogy by providing the missing word or phrase.

5. genus:species::family:________________
6. Darwin:evolution::Linnaeus:________________
7. orders:classes::phyla:________________
8. biochemistry:cytochrome *c*::homologous organ:________________

CONCEPT MASTERY

Use your understanding of the concepts developed in the chapter to answer each of the following in a brief paragraph.

1. Why were some of the early classification systems difficult to use?
2. What are three characteristics of a good classification system?
3. List the taxa in the classification system in current use from the smallest to the largest.
4. How does a workable classification system promote scientific understanding?
5. Suppose an organism had three common names in different parts of the United States. How might these names lead to confusion?

CRITICAL AND CREATIVE THINKING

Discuss each of the following in a brief paragraph.

1. **Making comparisons** In what ways was the classification system developed by Linnaeus an advantage over previous classification systems?
2. **Applying technology** How has the development of new technologies changed the ways we classify organisms?
3. **Applying concepts** Suppose you discovered a new single-celled organism. This organism had a nucleus, mitochondria, and a giant chloroplast. In what kingdom would you place this organism? What are your reasons?
4. **Making inferences** It has been said that organisms decide which individuals belong to their species and which do not. What does this statement mean?
5. **Assessing concepts** Libraries use the Dewey Decimal System to group books by similarities. How do the major groupings in this system help you locate research materials more quickly?
6. **Using the writing process** It has been estimated that there are more unknown organisms in the tropical rain forests than there are known organisms in the world. Scientists are concerned that these rain forests might be destroyed before the organisms in them can be classified. Write an editorial for a television news program protesting the destruction of rain forests. Offer reasons why rain forests should be protected.

Museum Curator's Assistant

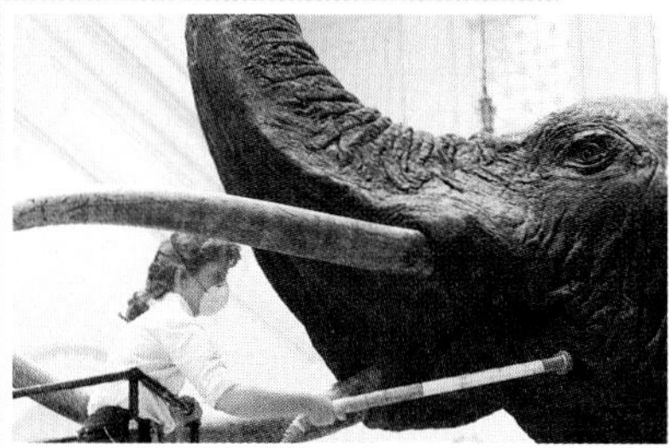

Museum curator's assistants help prepare museum collections by cleaning, sorting, labeling, and numbering animal and plant specimens under the supervision of the museum curator. They also help to design exhibits by arranging specimens in glass cases or by constructing entire fossil skeletons.

Museum curator's assistants must be organized, pay attention to detail, and develop a solid knowledge of the collection with which they wish to work.

To receive information write to the American Association of Museums, 1055 Thomas Jefferson St., NW, Washington, DC 20007.

Taxonomist

Taxonomists identify and name organisms so that they can be organized into groups. Taxonomists must understand the relationships among various organisms. The work of taxonomists helps biologists identify the characteristics of an organism by knowing the group to which it belongs.

Taxonomists need a Bachelor's degree with a strong background in the biological sciences.

For additional information contact the Society of Systematic Zoology, Smithsonian Institution (NHB), Washington, DC 20560.

Archaeologist

Archaeologists are involved in gathering and analyzing remains of earlier cultures. They use special techniques to find materials such as pottery, clothing, tools, and weapons from houses and cities that existed long ago. With this information, they are often able to determine the customs, languages, traditions, and religious beliefs of earlier societies.

Archaeologists need a Ph.D. degree to qualify for positions in colleges, museums, and government agencies.

For information write to the Society for American Archaeology, 1511 K St., NW, Ste. 716, Washington, DC 20005.

HOW TO USE THE WANT ADS

Help-wanted ads are a good place to begin a job search. They list positions that are available and provide some idea of which fields are hiring people, what salaries are being offered, and what qualifications are necessary.

Want ads can be found in a variety of publications. Newspapers usually have a section listing job openings under the title of the position. Trade magazines, which are periodicals related to a specific field, also list job openings.

As you look through the want ads, be sure to check all the categories that apply to you. Answer ads that give specific information about the position and the company that placed the ad. Respond promptly with a neatly typed letter and make sure you include all the information requested in the ad.

FROM THE AUTHORS

The shelves in my office are crammed with books about every living thing you can imagine. There are books about plants, animals, viruses, and people. There are books about how our brains work, how fishes swim, and how termites build their nests. The studies on which these books are based were performed by thousands of researchers. Yet none of them could have been written without the work of Charles Darwin. Darwin, by finding order in the chaos of the living world, helped create modern biology. Evolutionary theory unites all living things into one enormous family—from the tallest redwoods to the tiniest bacteria to each and every human on Earth. And, most importantly, the evolutionary history of life makes it clear that all living things—all of us—share a common destiny on this planet. If you remember nothing else from this course ten years from now, remember this, and your year will have been well spent.

Joe Levine

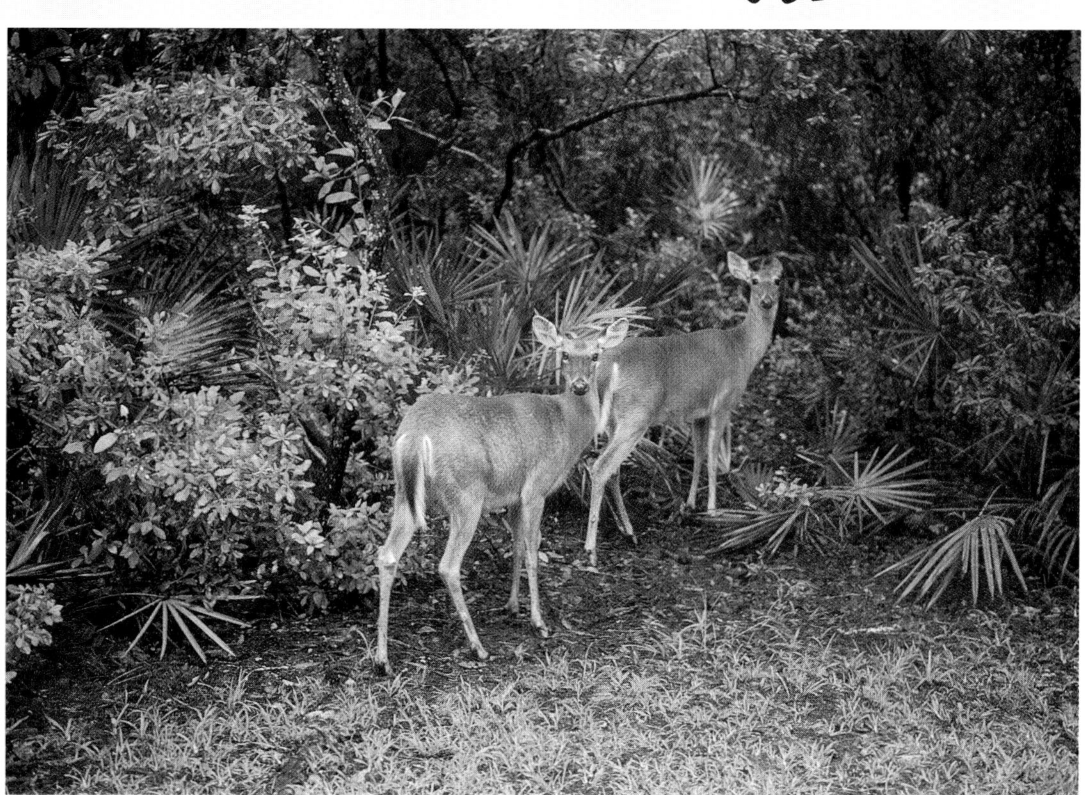

UNIT 5

Life on Earth: Monerans, Protists, and Fungi

> I discovered in a tiny drop of water, incredibly many very little animalcules and these of diverse sorts and sizes.

So reported Anton van Leeuwenhoek in 1675 after examining a sample of water from a well. Van Leeuwenhoek was certainly among the first to examine the secret world of microscopic organisms that share our planet.

Today, the world of the very small is huge—visible to prying eyes through wonderful microscopes that reveal the tiniest organisms and the smallest details of their cells.

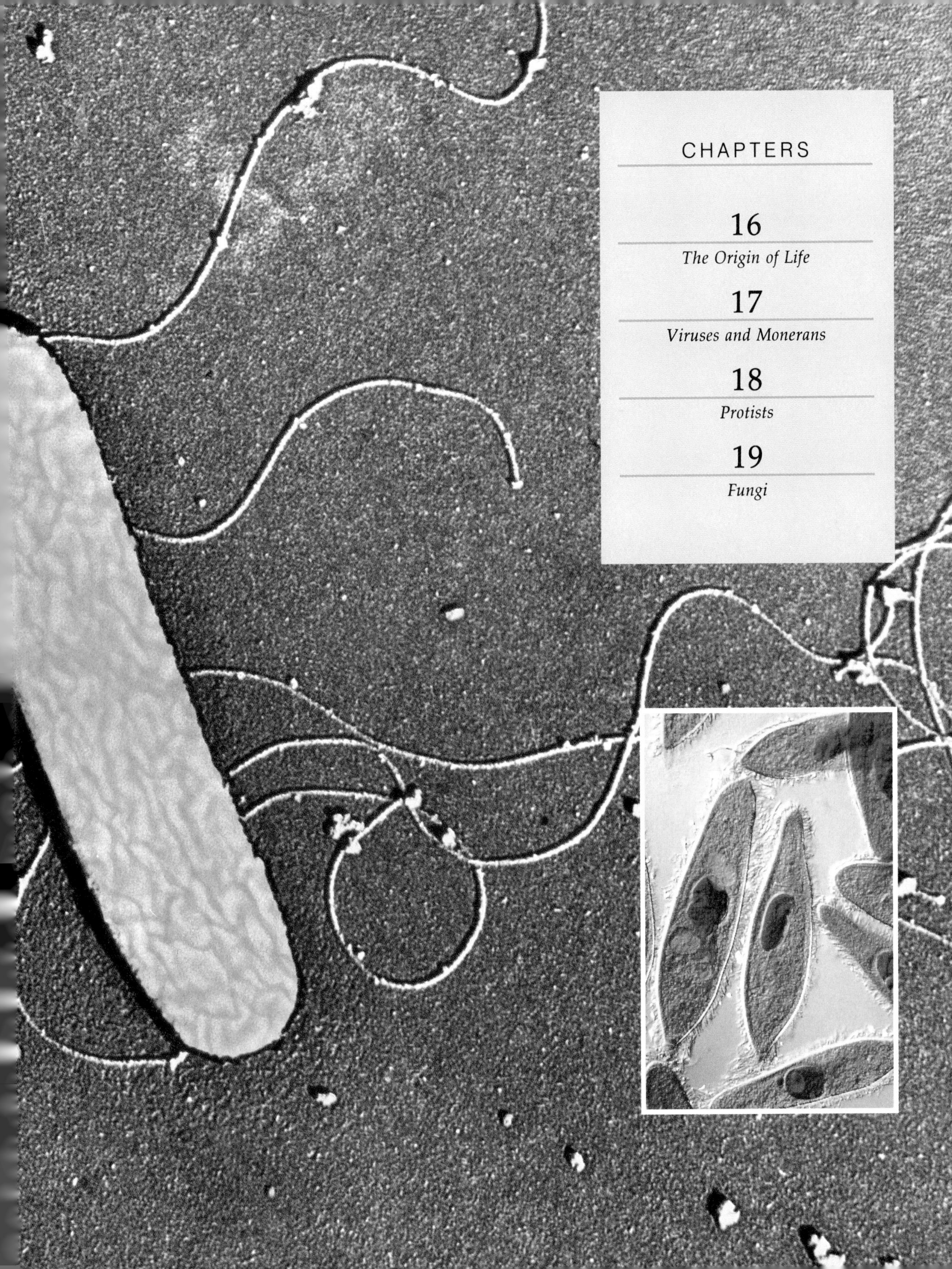

CHAPTERS

CHAPTER 16

The Origin of Life

Tests performed by the Viking spacecraft on Martian soil indicated that there is no life on Mars today. Astronauts who walked on the moon confirmed what scientists already knew: There is no life on our lunar neighbor.

We shall not cease from exploration.
And the end of all our exploring
Will be to arrive where we started
And know the place for the first time.
T.S. Eliot, *Four Quartets*

In this work by T.S. Eliot, the author suggests that to truly understand ourselves and the world about us, we must return to our roots and discover where we came from and how we came to be. Although the author is not speaking about biology, his words have meaning to scientists, as well as students of literature.

This chapter deals with the origin of life on planet Earth. Here you will discover that there are many current hypotheses regarding the formation of life. But you will also learn that, as in much of science, there are many unanswered questions as well.

CHAPTER OUTLINE

16–1 Spontaneous Generation

Section Objectives

- Define spontaneous generation.
- Describe the experiments of Redi, Spallanzani, and Pasteur.

Scientists have always wondered how life on Earth began. For many centuries, they believed that life simply "arose" from nonliving matter. They believed, in fact, that life arose from nonlife all the time. Mice, for example, arose from piles of grain. Bees were "produced" in the carcasses of cattle. Those who disputed this idea were ridiculed. The English naturalist Ross expressed a common feeling when he wrote, "To question that beetles and wasps were generated in cow dung is to question reason, sense, and experience." **The hypothesis that life arises regularly from nonlife is called spontaneous generation.**

Spontaneous Generation: True or False?

Lazzaro Spallanzani was born in Italy in 1729—three years before the birth of George Washington. As he grew up, he developed an interest in the natural world and began to consider one of the burning questions that people argued about in his school: **spontaneous generation.** Those who believed in spontaneous generation often supported their argument with the example of rotting meat. As meat spoiled, it was said to give rise to maggots, which eventually changed into flies. The rotting of

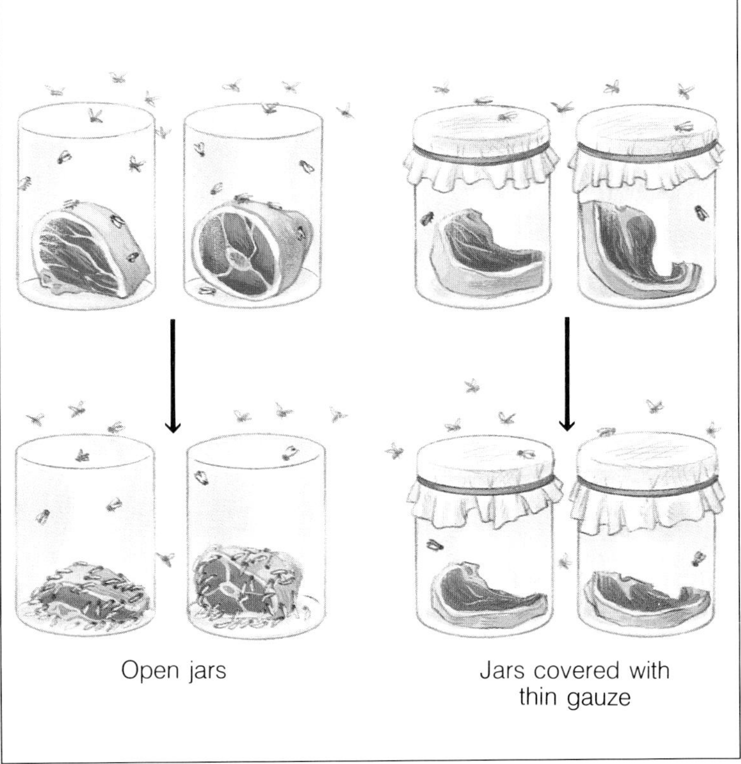

Figure 16–1 Redi's experiments helped disprove spontaneous generation. No maggots were found on the meat in jars that were covered with netting or were tightly sealed. Maggots appeared only when adult flies were able to enter the jars and deposit their eggs.

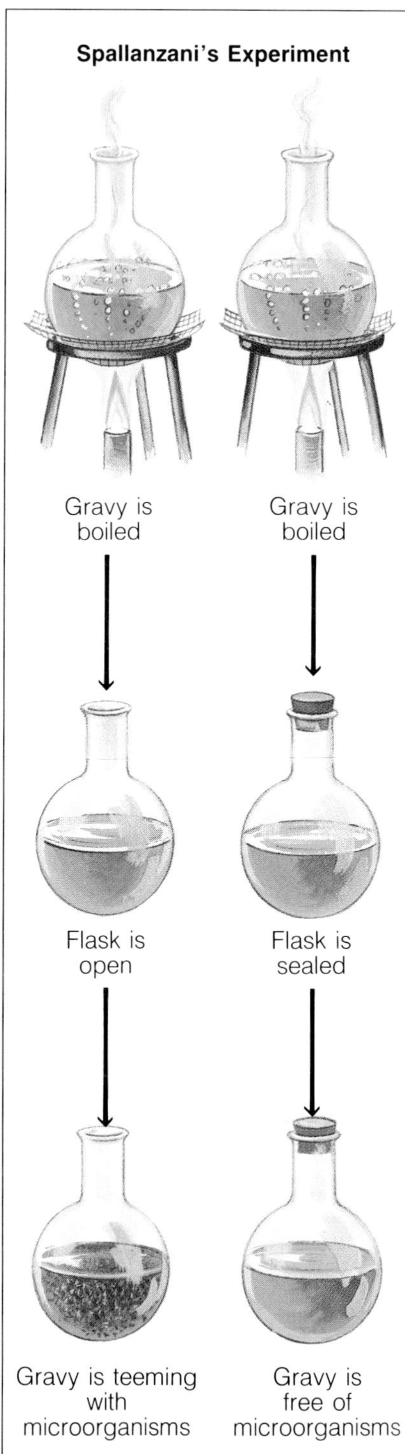

Figure 16–2 *Spallanzani's experiment showed that microorganisms do not grow in nutrient broth that has been boiled and placed in sealed flasks.*

meat in the warm Italian climate was a common experience before refrigeration. Everyone seemed to agree that the maggots were produced from the meat.

Spallanzani was already skeptical of the idea that life could arise from nonlife when he came upon a small book written by another Italian scientist, Francesco Redi. In his book, Redi hypothesized that the maggots actually arose not from the meat itself but from eggs. He believed that flies laid their eggs, which were too small to be seen with the unaided eye, directly on the meat. The eggs then developed into maggots, which later became adult flies. Redi described the simple experiment he had performed to test his spontaneous generation hypothesis. See Figure 16–1 on page 339.

Redi placed pieces of meat in several jars. Half of the jars he left open to the air so that flies could land on the meat. The other jars were covered with a thin gauze. Although these jars were open to the air, the gauze prevented flies from landing on the meat. After a few days, the meat in all the jars had spoiled. But maggots were found only on the meat in the uncovered jars. Redi concluded that the maggots did not arise spontaneously; rather, the maggots developed from the eggs laid by the flies.

Redi's conclusions were attacked by another eighteenth-century scientist, the Englishman John Needham. Needham claimed that spontaneous generation could occur under the right conditions and cited his own experiment as proof. He sealed some gravy in a bottle. Then he heated the bottle, killing (he claimed) all living things in the gravy. After several days, he examined the contents of the bottle under a microscope and found it swarming with microscopic organisms. "These little animals," he argued, "can only have come from the juice of the gravy."

The work of both Redi and Needham was well known to Spallanzani, and it is to his role in spontaneous generation that we will now return. Spallanzani believed that Needham was wrong and that all the organisms had not been completely killed when the gravy was heated. He could have written Needham with his objections. Instead, he chose to perform an experiment to prove his hypothesis. See Figure 16–2.

Spallanzani prepared some gravy identical to that used by Needham. He placed half of the gravy into one jar and half into another jar. He then boiled the gravy in both jars thoroughly. Spallanzani sealed one of the jars tightly and left the other jar open to the air.

After a few days, Spallanzani noticed that the gravy in the open jar was teeming with microscopic organisms. The gravy in the sealed jar contained no living things. Spallanzani concluded that the microorganisms did not develop from the gravy—from nonlife—but entered the jar from the air. If this was not the case, he argued, then both jars should contain microorganisms.

Pasteur and Spontaneous Generation

Despite the work of Redi and Spallanzani, many people still believed in spontaneous generation. They argued that air was necessary for spontaneous generation and because Spallanzani had kept air out of the sealed jar, spontaneous generation could not have occurred in that part of his experiment. It was not until 1864, and the elegant experiment of French scientist Louis Pasteur, that the hypothesis of spontaneous generation was finally disproved.

Pasteur placed nutrient broth, a substance similar to Needham's gravy, in a flask that had a long, curved neck. Although the end of the neck was open to the air, the curve in the neck served to trap dust and other airborne particles. Pasteur boiled the flask thoroughly to kill any microorganisms it might contain. But he did not seal the open end of the flask. Pasteur waited an entire year. In all that time, no microorganisms could be found in the flask. See Figure 16–4.

Pasteur took his experiment even further. He broke off the neck of the flask, allowing air, dust, and other particles to enter the broth. In just one day the flask was clouded from the growth of microorganisms. Pasteur had clearly shown that the microorganisms had entered the flask along with dust particles from the air. Pasteur, like Redi and Spallanzani before him, had shown that life comes only from life.

Figure 16–3 *According to the spontaneous generation hypothesis, living things, such as a wasp, could arise from inorganic matter.*

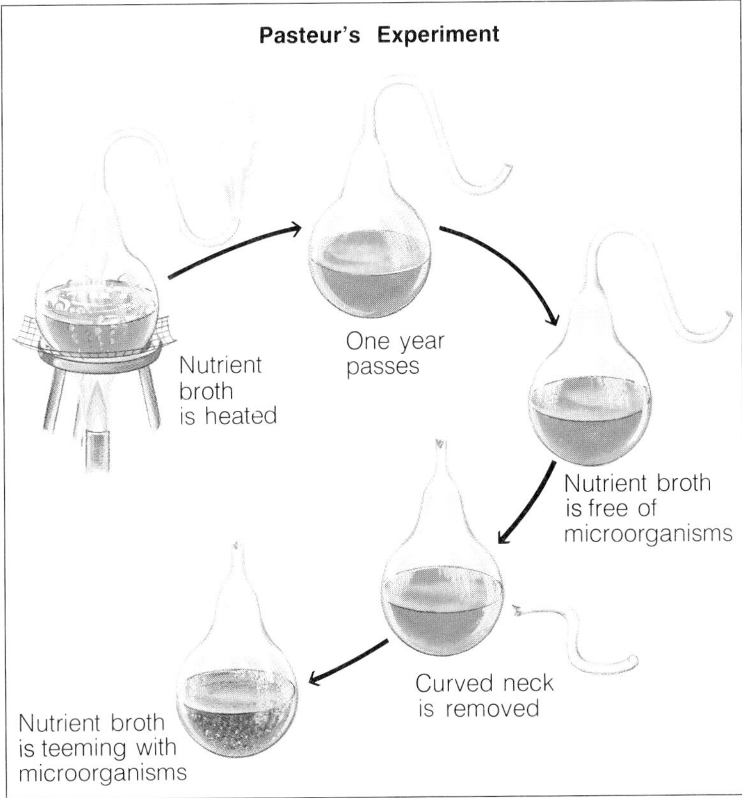

Figure 16–4 *Louis Pasteur put an end to the spontaneous generation hypothesis. He showed that microorganisms did not arise in a boiled nutrient broth, even if the broth was exposed to the air, as long as dust particles and other airborne matter were not allowed to enter the broth.*

16–1 SECTION REVIEW

1. Define spontaneous generation.
2. What evidence did Spallanzani give to refute Needham's experiment?
3. In Redi's first experiment he used only open jars and sealed jars. What arguments might scientists have come up with that caused Redi to redo his experiment with open jars and jars covered with gauze?
4. How did Pasteur's use of a flask with a long, curved neck finally disprove spontaneous generation?

16–2 The First Signs of Life

Section Objectives

- Describe conditions on ancient Earth.
- Define microfossil.
- Discuss various hypotheses on the evolution of cells.

If life can come only from life, how did life on Earth first arise? For that matter, does life exist (or has it ever existed) on Mars? Or Venus? By studying the beginnings of life, we examine our own origins.

Our planet was born approximately 4.6 billion years ago as a great cloud of gas and dust condensed into a sphere. As gravity pulled this matter tightly together, heat from great pressure and radioactivity melted first the planet's interior and then most of its mass. As far as we can tell, Earth cooled enough to allow the first solid rocks to form on its surface about 4 billion years ago. For millions of years afterward, violent planet-wide volcanic activity shook the crust. At the same time, an intense meteor shower bombarded Earth with missiles from space.

Figure 16–5 *You can see from this illustration depicting primitive Earth that most living things would not easily survive, even if the atmosphere were similar to the atmosphere you breathe today.*

What was Earth like 4 billion years ago? Had you been able to visit, you wouldn't have recognized the place. In fact, you wouldn't have been able to survive, even for an instant! For the first atmosphere that covered our planet was lost to space before the Earth cooled. And there was no liquid water at all.

Where did our atmosphere come from? We know from studying volcanoes that eruptions pour out carbon dioxide, nitrogen, and other gases. We also know that meteorites carry water (in the form of ice) and many carbon-containing compounds. So it is reasonable to propose that between 4 billion and 3.8 billion years ago, a combination of volcanic activity and a constant stream of meteorites released the gases that created Earth's early atmosphere.

What was that early atmosphere like? **The Earth's first atmosphere most likely contained water vapor (H_2O), carbon monoxide (CO) and carbon dioxide (CO_2), nitrogen (N_2), hydrogen sulfide (H_2S), and hydrogen cyanide (HCN).** Notice that this atmosphere contained no free oxygen gas and thus could not support life as we know it. Geological evidence supports this hypothesis because rocks from this time contain almost no rust or other compounds that require free oxygen to form.

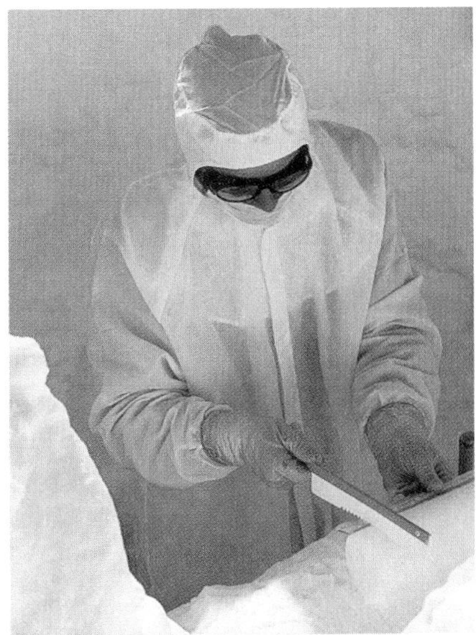

Figure 16–6 *Scientists collect ice samples from Earth's polar regions. Dust trapped in the ice helps scientists study changes in Earth's early atmosphere.*

Where did the oceans of ancient Earth come from? Oceans could not exist at first because Earth's surface was extremely hot. Any rain that fell upon it would immediately boil away. But, about 3.8 billion years ago, Earth's surface cooled enough for water to remain a liquid on the ground. Thunderstorms drenched the planet for many thousands of years, and oceans began to fill. We know this because the earliest sedimentary rocks, which are laid down in water, have been dated to this time period.

No one can say with certainty exactly when life first formed on ancient Earth. But paleontologists working near Lake Superior have found microscopic fossils, called **microfossils**, that have been dated as far back as 3.5 billion years. **Microfossils provide outlines of ancient cells that have been preserved in enough detail to identify them as prokaryotes, similar to bacteria alive today**. See Figure 16–7.

Figure 16–7 *You can see 2-billion-year old microfossil bacteria in this thin slice of rock.*

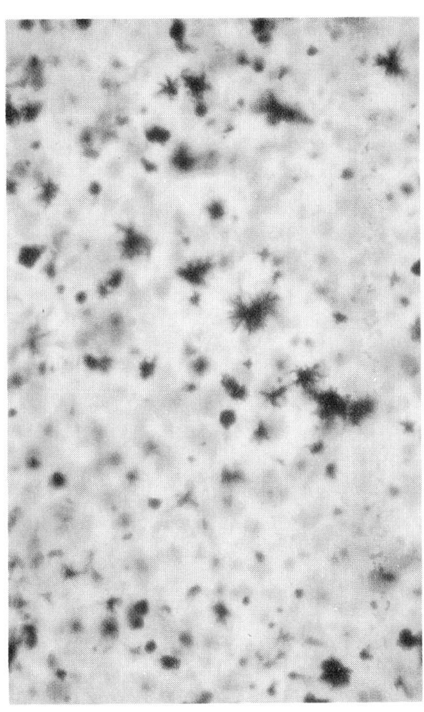

Somehow these earliest life forms appeared within half a billion years after the formation of Earth's first rocks. How might that have happened?

Starting from Scratch: The Molecules of Life

Experiments first performed in 1953 by American scientists Stanley Miller and Harold Urey provide a fascinating glimpse of events leading to the appearance of Earth's first life forms. Miller recreated what he thought might have been Earth's earliest atmosphere by mixing methane, ammonia, water, and hydrogen in a flask. He then exposed the flask to ultraviolet light

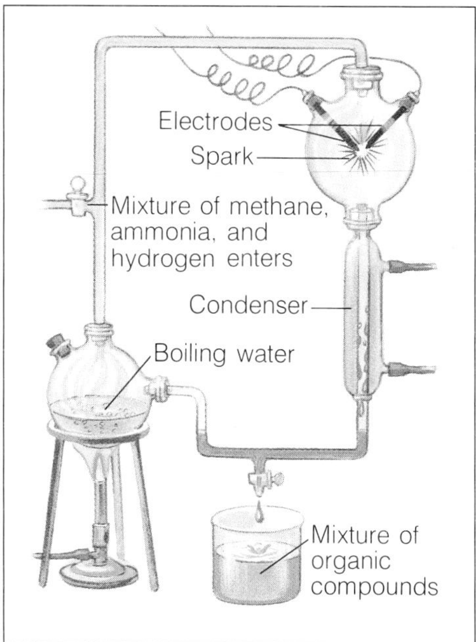

Figure 16–8 *An experiment performed by Stanley Miller (top) and Harold Urey first demonstrated how organic matter may have formed in Earth's primitive atmosphere. By recreating the early atmosphere (ammonia, water, hydrogen, and methane) and passing an electric spark (lightning) through the mixture, Miller and Urey proved that organic matter such as amino acids could have formed spontaneously (bottom).*

electric sparks to simulate sunlight and lightning on primitive Earth. See Figure 16–8.

In just a few days, an organic "soup" of complex molecules formed. Analyzing this soup, Miller found urea, acetic acid, lactic acid, and several amino acids. Other researchers have since repeated Miller's experiments using slightly different mixtures of gases that reflect more current views of the early atmosphere. All these experiments produced important organic molecules, including ATP and the nitrogenous base adenine, in the absence of oxygen. Thus, over the course of millions of years, at least some of the basic building blocks of life could have been produced in great quantities on early Earth.

In another exciting development, astronomers have discovered that the synthesis of life's building blocks is not limited to Earth alone. Meteors, comets, and even the dust scattered across the universe are filled with organic molecules, ice, and other elements essential to life. No one knows how these compounds are produced in the bitter cold of outer space. But more than 75 molecules, ranging from hydrogen gas (H_2) to a variety of amino acids, have been found in space.

A large meteorite that crashed to Earth in Australia in 1969 even contained lipids and all five nitrogenous bases that form the structures of DNA and RNA. Thus, meteors that bombarded the young Earth could have showered the planet with a rain of organic molecules that mixed with those already forming.

The Formation of Complex Molecules

A collection of organic molecules such as amino acids is certainly not life. What, then, happened next? Experiments by Russian scientist Alexander Oparin and American scientist Sidney Fox have shown that the organic soup that formed in the oceans of Earth would not necessarily have remained as simple chemical mixtures. In the absence of oxygen, for example, amino acids tend to link together spontaneously to form short chains. And as you will remember, chains of amino acids are called polypeptides (proteins). Other compounds can link together to form simple carbohydrates, alcohols, and lipids.

Even more fascinating is the fact that collections of molecules such as these tend to gather into tiny round droplets. Some of these droplets grow all by themselves, and others even reproduce. See Figure 16–9. Still others can break down glucose. At this stage, we would still not say that these droplets are alive. But we might call them "proto-life" because they have begun to perform tasks necessary for life.

From Proto-life to Cells

The next step in our story is the most difficult to understand completely. From the jumbled mixture of molecules in the organic soup that formed in Earth's oceans, the highly organized structures of RNA and DNA must somehow have

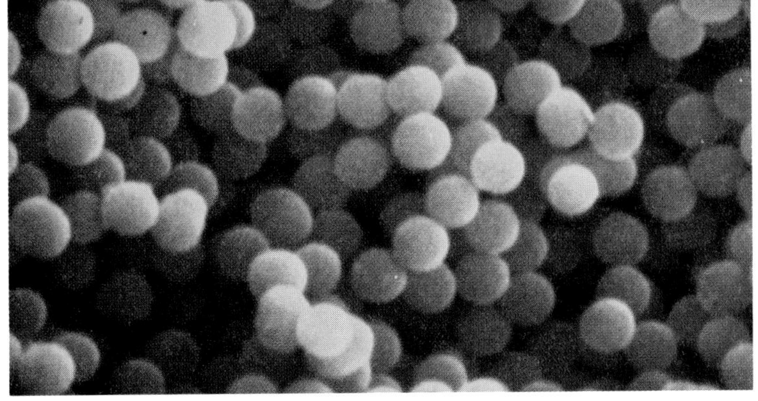

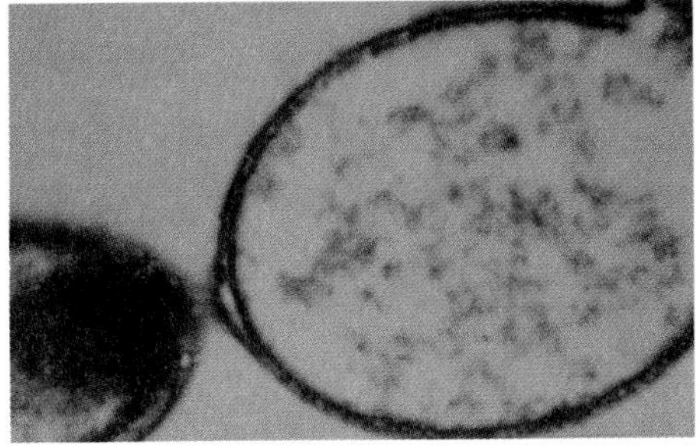

Figure 16–9 *These droplets (left), magnified 3000 times, were created in the laboratory of Sidney Fox. Although the droplets are not alive, they can perform some of the basic life functions, including breaking down glucose. Some droplets can actually reproduce by dividing into two separate droplets (right).*

evolved. Scientists do not know how these vital information-carriers formed, but there are several interesting hypotheses.

Some biologists believe that the first true cells arose in a shallow pool containing an organic soup. Experiments show that when such a soup is dried, lipids spontaneously form spheres, or droplets, around small DNA molecules. Given enough time, a form of DNA capable of replicating itself could have arisen within such proto-cells.

An alternative hypothesis is offered by G. Cairns-Smith and J. Bernal. They noted that various attractive forces can concentrate amino acids and nucleic acids (DNA and RNA) onto the regular, repeating structures that make up clay crystals. Held together in such a manner, these organic molecules might have combined to form lengths of both DNA and proteins.

Building on this second hypothesis, several scientists propose that the first cells formed near a volcanic vent far beneath the ocean, not in a shallow pool. In such places, molten rock heats water to very high temperatures. When this water gushes out of the vent into the ocean, it is filled with energy-rich sulfur compounds. See Figure 16–10. Thus these vents offer a set of conditions favorable for the chemical reactions leading to life: an assortment of necessary chemicals, strong currents to mix those compounds together, a source of naturally formed chemical energy, and deposits of clay.

Researchers who duplicate these conditions in the laboratory observe the spontaneous synthesis of both amino acids and stretches of RNA. As you will see in the next chapter, the oldest living prokaryotes—a group of bacteria that survive by obtaining energy from sulfur compounds—still live near these hot vents today. This is one piece of evidence supporting this interesting, but as yet unproven, hypothesis.

Figure 16–10 *One hypothesis about the origin of life suggests that living things evolved around hot sea vents, which spew out high-energy sulfur compounds. Today, bacteria that can use the sulfur compounds as a source of energy live in areas near deep-sea vents.*

The First True Cells

Although the origin of the first true cells is uncertain, we can identify several of their characteristics with certainty. They were prokaryotes that resembled types of bacteria alive today. They were heterotrophs that obtained their food and energy from the organic molecules in the soup that surrounded them. And they must have been **anaerobes**. Anaerobes are organisms that can live without oxygen. Why can we be certain these first cells were anaerobes?

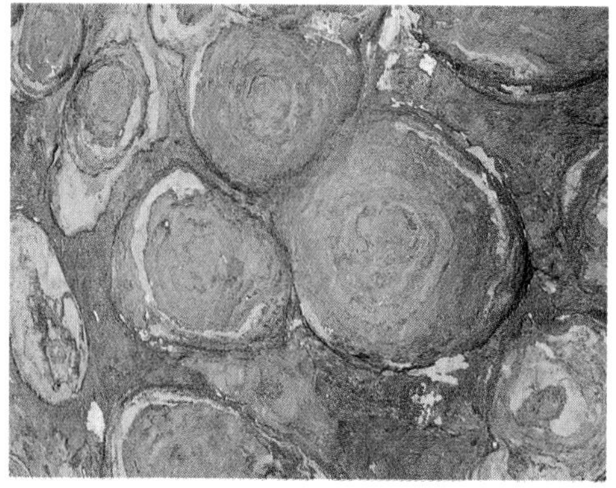

Figure 16–11 *The first autotrophs grew in layered mats called stromatolites. Fossils of such stromatolites can be found in rock layers throughout the world (top). However, Shark Bay, Australia, is one of the few places on Earth where living stromatolites still exist (bottom).*

The Evolution of Photosynthesis

The first heterotrophic cells could have survived without difficulty for a long time because there were plenty of organic molecules for them to "eat." But as time went on, the complex molecules in the organic soup would have begun to run out. In order for life to continue, some organisms would have had to develop a way to make complex molecules from simpler ones. In addition, the intense pressure of natural selection would have favored organisms that could harness an outside source of energy for their own purposes. The stage was set for the appearance of the first autotrophs.

At some point an ancient form of photosynthesis evolved. Photosynthesis in early cells, however, was very different from the photosynthesis that occurs in modern plants, which you read about in Chapter 6. The first true cells probably used hydrogen sulfide (H_2S) the way modern photosynthetic organisms use water (H_20).

These first autotrophs were enormously successful, spread rapidly, and were commonplace on Earth about 3.4 billion years ago. They grew in layered, matlike formations called stromatolites (the prefix *stroma-* means layer). Today, living stromatolites can be found only in special habitats such as Shark Bay, Australia. See Figure 16–11. However, fossils of stromatolites have been found in many parts of the world.

Life from Nonlife

In Section 16–1 you read about some experiments that disproved the hypothesis of spontaneous generation. "Hey, what's going on?" you might exclaim. If we just said that life did arise from nonlife billions of years ago, why couldn't it happen again? The answer is simple: Today's Earth is a very different planet from the one that existed billions of years ago. On primitive Earth, there were no bacteria to break down organic compounds. Nor was there any oxygen to react with the organic compounds. As a result, organic compounds could accumulate over millions of years, forming that original organic soup. Today, however, such compounds cannot remain intact in the natural world for a long enough period of time to give life another start.

16–2 SECTION REVIEW

1. List five gases in Earth's first atmosphere.
2. What is a microfossil?
3. Name two sources for Earth's first organic molecules.
4. Why did photosynthesis (or something like it) have to evolve if life was to continue past its earliest stages?

16–3 The Road to Modern Organisms

Section Objectives

- Relate oxygen production in photosynthesis to the evolution of aerobic metabolism.
- Describe the importance of membrane-bound organelles and sexual reproduction to the evolution of life on Earth.

Once life evolved on Earth, things would never be the same. For over millions of years, life has changed the Earth in ways that have affected our planet dramatically. The first great change occurred roughly 2.2 billion years ago when a more modern form of photosynthesis evolved. By substituting H_2O for H_2S in their metabolic pathways, photosynthetic organisms released a deadly new gas into the atmosphere. That gas was oxygen—a waste product of photosynthesis!

Because you rely on oxygen to survive, you might be surprised to learn that it can be deadly. However, oxygen is a very reactive gas that destroys organic compounds. So imagine the catastrophe that struck Earth's earliest life forms. Over a period of 500 million years, a waste product (oxygen) produced by some organisms transformed Earth from a totally anaerobic planet into a planet whose atmosphere is nearly 1/5 oxygen.

Because oxygen was deadly to anaerobes, such organisms were forever banished from the planet's surface. Today, organisms that cannot tolerate oxygen survive only deep in mud or in other places where the atmosphere does not reach. The very first case of living organisms producing a kind of pollution that made the entire Earth uninhabitable for many forms of life had occurred. Let us hope that we as a species do not make decisions that have similar results!

One effect of oxygen in the atmosphere, however, was beneficial to those organisms that survived. The first atmosphere had allowed ultraviolet radiation from the sun to strike the Earth's surface. Ultraviolet radiation is damaging, even toxic, to many life forms. But as oxygen gas (O_2) from photosynthesis reached the upper atmosphere, some of it was broken apart by ultraviolet radiation into individual oxygen atoms (O). These atoms quickly recombined with oxygen molecules to form the gas ozone (O_3). In time, an ozone layer formed in the Earth's atmosphere. This ozone layer absorbs much of the ultraviolet radiation from the sun, shielding living things from the dangerous rays. In Unit 10 of this textbook, you will read how the burning of fossil fuels and the release of certain compounds into our atmosphere is slowly but surely destroying the ozone layer so very important to life on our planet.

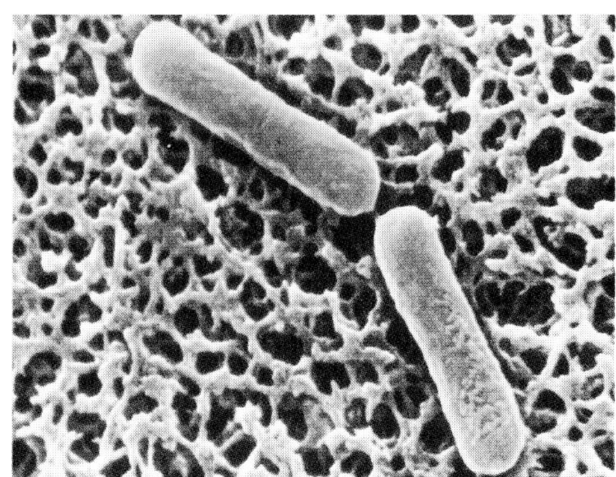

Figure 16–12 Once Earth's atmosphere contained oxygen, anaerobic bacteria such as these were banished to places where the atmosphere could not reach.

The Evolution of Aerobic Metabolism

The addition of oxygen to the atmosphere began a new chapter in the history of life on Earth. That chapter started with the evolution of organisms that not only survive in oxygen but utilize it in their metabolic pathways. Metabolism is the sum total of all the chemical reactions that occur in a living thing. These new aerobic pathways allowed organisms to obtain 18 times more energy from every sugar molecule than anaerobic pathways did. As you may recall from Chapter 6, these new aerobic pathways are part of the process of obtaining energy called cellular respiration.

The Evolution of Eukaryotic Cells

Between 1.4 and 1.6 billion years ago, the first eukaryotic cells evolved, fully adapted to an aerobic world. Eukaryotes have a nucleus that contains DNA. The outer membrane of the nucleus is called the nuclear envelope. Eukaryotic cells also carry other membrane-bound organelles such as mitochondria and chloroplasts.

The Evolution of Sexual Reproduction

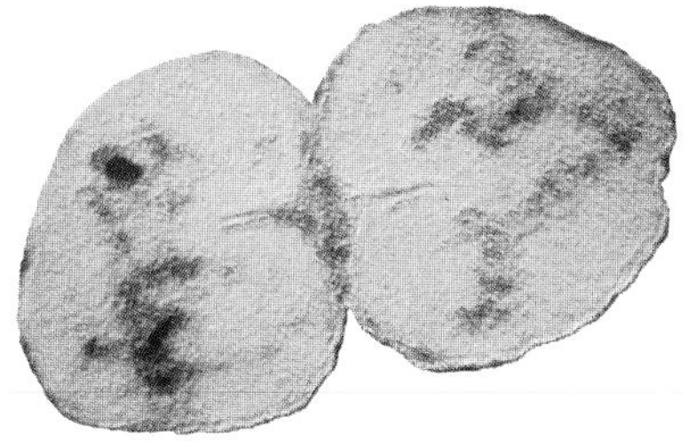

Figure 16–13 *In asexual reproduction, such as the division of a bacterium into two new bacteria, each new cell is an exact copy of the original cell (top). In sexual reproduction, however, offspring contain genes from each parent, and genetic variation is increased. How boring it would be if we all contained the exact same genes and looked exactly alike (bottom).*

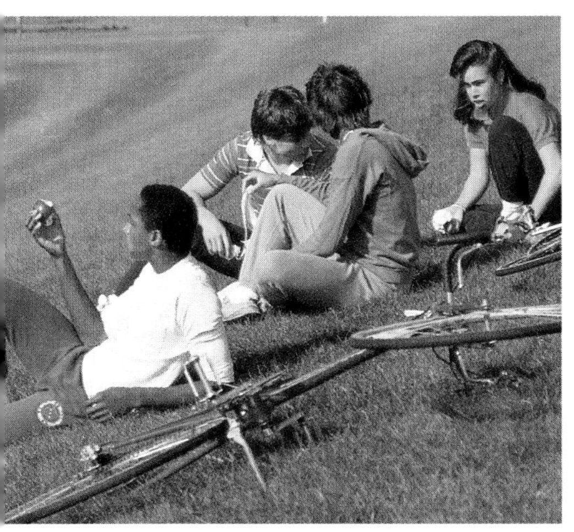

Among the most important steps in the evolution of eukaryotic life was the emergence of sexual reproduction. The advent of sexual reproduction catapulted the process of evolution forward at far greater speeds than ever before. But why did sexual reproduction speed up the evolutionary process? Isn't it just another form of reproduction?

Most prokaryotes reproduce asexually. Often they simply duplicate their genetic material and divide into two new cells. (This process, called binary fission, will be discussed in detail in the next chapter.) Although this is an efficient and effective form of reproduction, it yields daughter cells that are exact duplicates of the original parent cell. As such, this type of reproduction restricts genetic variation to mistakes or mutations in DNA. As you read in Chapter 14, genetic variation is crucial to the process of adaptive radiation and the evolution of new species.

Sexual reproduction, on the other hand, shuffles and reshuffles genes in each generation, much like a person shuffling a deck of cards. The offspring of sexually reproducing organisms, therefore, never resemble their parents (or each other) exactly. This increase in genetic variation greatly increases the chances of evolutionary change in a species due to natural selection.

The evolution of sexual reproduction, along with the development of the membrane-bound organelles mitochondria and chloroplasts, were of enormous importance to the history and development of life on Earth. If not for these developments, multicellular organisms may not have evolved.

The Evolution of Multicellular Life

A few hundred million years after the evolution of sexual reproduction, evolving life forms crossed another great threshold: the development of multicellular organisms from single-celled organisms. In the blink of an evolutionary eye, these first multicellular organisms experienced a great adaptive radiation. Earth's parade of life was well on its way.

SCIENCE, TECHNOLOGY, AND SOCIETY **BREAKTHROUGH**

The Symbiotic Theory of Eukaryotic Origins

For many years biologists have wondered how eukaryotic cells evolved from prokaryotic cells. Eukaryotic cells contain membrane-bound organelles and a nucleus surrounded by a nuclear envelope, or membrane.

Of particular interest to scientists are the organelles called mitochondria and chloroplasts. Why? Although these organelles usually act like ordinary parts of a cell, they contain their own DNA. That DNA is different from the DNA found within the nucleus of the cell. These organelles also reproduce on their own when the cell divides.

Some years ago biologists noted that mitochondria and chloroplasts strongly resemble living prokaryotes. Mitochondria resemble certain aerobic bacteria, whereas chloroplasts resemble certain photosynthetic bacteria. One American scientist, Lynn Margulis, has championed an intriguing hypothesis about the evolution of eukaryotic cells.

Margulis feels that eukaryotic cells evolved when ancient aerobic prokaryotes similar to modern chloroplasts and mitochondria took up residence within other prokaryotic cells. Over time, a long-lasting symbiosis developed. Symbiosis refers to any relationship in which two organisms live closely together. This ancient symbiosis was particularly helpful to both organisms. The organisms, which evolved into mitochondria and chloroplasts, now lived within the nutrient-rich cytoplasm of their host cell. The host cell containing mitochondria-type prokaryotes could now produce energy faster and more efficiently because it could utilize oxygen in its metabolic pathways. If the host cell contained chloroplast-type prokaryotes, it could now use the energy from the sun to produce food. In time, of course, mitochondria and chloroplasts came to function more and more as part of the cell structure in eukaryotes.

It was not easy, at first, for scientists to accept the idea that eukaryotic cells developed as communities. But both structural and chemical evidence strongly supports the theory proposed by Margulis. The symbiotic theory of eukaryotic origins is now accepted by most biologists. However, there are still many unanswered questions in the search for eukaryotic origins. We still do not know, for example, how the earliest eukaryotes developed the nuclear envelope that surrounds their DNA.

16–3 SECTION REVIEW

1. What compound replaced H_2S in the photosynthetic process?
2. What is the importance of the Earth's ozone layer?
3. How did the development of sexual reproduction speed up the evolutionary process?

LABORATORY INVESTIGATION

INVESTIGATING SPONTANEOUS GENERATION

PROBLEM

Does spontaneous generation occur on Earth today?

MATERIALS *(per group)*

600-mL beaker	hot plate
3 125-mL flasks	safety goggles
#5 rubber stopper	beaker tongs
#5 one-hole rubber stopper with S-tube	heat-resistant gloves
	dried grass
	Bunsen burner

PROCEDURE 

1. Place two handfuls of dried grass in the 600-mL beaker. Pour water into the beaker until the water level is about 1 cm below the top of the beaker.
2. Put on the safety goggles. Carefully place the beaker on the hot plate. Set the hot plate to its highest level. **CAUTION:** *Do not touch the top of the hot plate.*
3. Allow the water to boil for about 30 minutes. **CAUTION:** *If the water level drops below the midpoint of the beaker, have your teacher replenish the water with some more boiling water.*
4. After the water has boiled for 30 minutes, turn off the hot plate. Light the Bunsen burner. Pass the front of the tongs through the flame of the burner several times. Turn off the burner. Now use the tongs to remove all of the grass from the water in the beaker. Discard the grass.
5. At this point, ask your teacher for three sterile flasks, a rubber stopper without a hole, and a rubber stopper with an S-tube in the hole.
6. Put on the heat-resistant gloves. Pick up the hot beaker and pour 100 mL of the hot grass solution into each flask. Do not allow any grass to fall into the flasks.
7. As quickly as possible, place the rubber stoppers into two of the flasks. Do not stopper the third flask. Set the flasks aside and observe each flask twice a week for three weeks.
8. On a separate sheet of paper, prepare a data table similar to the one shown. Record your observations in the data table. If you observe thin threadlike structures, you are probably seeing the growth of mold. If the solution in the flask becomes clouded, you are probably seeing evidence of bacterial growth.

OBSERVATIONS

1. Describe what you saw in each flask after three weeks.
2. How long did it take before you saw living things in any of the flasks?

ANALYSIS AND CONCLUSIONS

1. What purpose did the grass serve in this investigation?
2. Why was it necessary to boil the water containing the grass before adding the grass/water solution to the flasks?
3. Why was it necessary to use sterile flasks and stoppers?
4. If living things appeared in any of the flasks, where did the living things come from?
5. Do the results of this investigation provide evidence for or against spontaneous generation?

Week	Observation	Appearance of Liquid in Each Flask		
		Stopper	No Stopper	Stopper with S-tube
1	1			
	2			

STUDENT STUDY GUIDE

SUMMARIZING THE CONCEPTS

The key concepts in each section of this chapter are listed below to help you review the chapter content. Make sure you understand each concept and its relationship to other concepts and to the theme of this chapter.

16–1 Spontaneous Generation

- The hypothesis that life arises from nonlife is called spontaneous generation.
- Louis Pasteur, a French scientist, put an end to the spontaneous generation controversy when he showed that a nutrient broth that had been thoroughly heated did not have any signs of microorganisms even when left open to the air. Pasteur had allowed air but not dust or other particles to reach the broth. When he did allow dust and other particles to enter the broth, microorganisms soon appeared. Pasteur had proved that the microorganisms in the broth did not develop spontaneously.

16–2 The First Signs of Life

- The atmosphere on ancient Earth was very different from our modern atmosphere. It contained water vapor, carbon monoxide, carbon dioxide, nitrogen, hydrogen sulfide, and hydrogen cyanide. The atmosphere did not contain free oxygen gas.
- Microfossils indicate that the first life forms were prokaryotes, similar to modern bacteria.
- Many organic compounds, including amino acids and ATP, could have formed when ultraviolet rays and lightning reacted with the gases in the early atmosphere. Laboratory experiments have recreated the formation of these compounds on early Earth. The organic compounds formed an organic "soup" containing the basic building blocks of life.
- The first true cells were prokaryotic heterotrophic anaerobes.
- In time, some cells developed the ability to harness energy from the sun in a primitive form of photosynthesis.

16–3 The Road to Modern Organisms

- Once organisms that used water and produced oxygen as a waste product during photosynthesis developed, the atmosphere slowly accumulated oxygen gas.
- Once oxygen was plentiful, aerobic metabolism utilizing cellular respiration evolved. Aerobic metabolism provided more energy than earlier forms of anaerobic metabolism.
- Around 1.4 billion years ago, eukaryotic cells containing membrane-bound organelles evolved.

REVIEWING KEY TERMS

Vocabulary terms are important to your understanding of biology. The key terms listed below are those you should be especially familiar with. Review these terms and their meanings. Then use each term in a complete sentence. If you are not sure of a term's meaning, return to the appropriate section and review its definition.

16–1 Spontaneous Generation

spontaneous generation

16–2 The First Signs of Life

microfossil
anaerobe

CHAPTER REVIEW

CONTENT REVIEW

Multiple Choice

Choose the letter of the answer that best completes each statement.

1. The hypothesis that mice can arise from spoiled grain is called
   a. evolution.
   b. microfossil.
   c. spontaneous generation.
   d. metabolism.
2. One scientist who believed in spontaneous generation was
   a. Redi. c. Pasteur.
   b. Needham. d. Spallanzani.
3. Earth's early atmosphere did not contain free
   a. nitrogen. c. carbon dioxide.
   b. oxygen. d. hydrogen cyanide.
4. Microfossils indicate that the first living cells were not
   a. prokaryotes. c. eukaryotes.
   b. heterotrophic. d. anaerobes.
5. Modern photosynthetic organisms have replaced H_2S with
   a. HCN. c. H_2O.
   b. CO_2. d. O_2.
6. In the atmosphere, oxygen forms a layer of O_3, or ozone, that protects organisms from
   a. sunlight.
   b. infrared radiation.
   c. ultraviolet radiation.
   d. hydrogen cyanide.
7. Cells with membrane-bound organelles are called
   a. prokaryotes. c. chloroplasts.
   b. mitochondria. d. eukaryotes.
8. Sexual reproduction can speed up evolution because it provides more
   a. chromosomes. c. identical cells.
   b. genetic variation. d. organelles.

True or False

Determine whether each statement is true or false. If it is true, write "true." If it is false, change the underlined word or words to make the statement true.

1. The hypothesis that nonlife arises from life is called spontaneous generation.
2. Redi showed that the flies that developed on raw meat did not arise spontaneously.
3. Earth formed around 4.6 billion years ago.
4. In the presence of oxygen, amino acids spontaneously link to form short chains.
5. The first true cells were prokaryotes.
6. The first heterotrophs were similar to modern-day stromatolites.
7. The ozone layer protects living things from ultraviolet radiation from the sun.
8. Genetic variation increases when organisms reproduce asexually.

Word Relationships

A. *In each of the following sets of terms, three of the terms are related. One term does not belong. Determine the characteristic common to the three terms and then identify the term that does not belong.*

1. early atmosphere, hydrogen sulfide, oxygen, nitrogen
2. organelle, amino acid, lipid, carbohydrate
3. RNA, DNA, amino acid, nucleic acid
4. aerobic, first true cells, heterotrophic, anaerobic
5. eukaryote, asexual, prokaryote, single-celled

B. *Replace the underlined definition with the correct vocabulary word.*

6. Pasteur helped disprove the life arises from nonlife hypothesis.
7. Microscopic fossils provide outlines of ancient cells in rocks.
8. The first true cells were organisms that can live without oxygen.

CONCEPT MASTERY

Use your understanding of the concepts developed in the chapter to answer each of the following in a brief paragraph.

1. Explain why scientists believe the first true cells were anaerobic heterotrophic prokaryotes.
2. Discuss the experiments of Redi, Needham, Spallanzani, and Pasteur as they relate to spontaneous generation.
3. Which is more likely to result in increased variety among organisms, sexual reproduction or asexual reproduction? Why?
4. In one early experiment, Pasteur used flasks that had curved necks. He tipped some of the flasks so that the nutrient broth ran into the flasks. Pasteur later observed microorganisms in these flasks. Explain this observation.
5. Discuss how scientists believe the Earth's early atmosphere and oceans formed.
6. Describe the symbiosis theory of eukaryotic development.

CRITICAL AND CREATIVE THINKING

Discuss each of the following in a brief paragraph.

1. **Sequencing events** Draw a time line that begins with the formation of the Earth and ends with the development of multicellular life. Make sure every significant event discussed in the chapter is included.
2. **Applying facts** Describe the ways in which the evolution of photosynthesis changed not only living things but the environment of Earth as well.
3. **Making predictions** Predict how modern life on Earth would have evolved if organisms did not begin using H_2O instead of H_2S in photosynthesis.
4. **Relating cause and effect** When people believed in spontaneous generation, a scientist developed this recipe for producing mice: Place a few wheat grains and a dirty shirt in an open pot; wait 3 weeks. Suggest a reason why this recipe may have worked. How could you prove that the mice were not due to spontaneous generation?
5. **Drawing conclusions** Although scientists have recreated some of the events that led to the formation of complex organic compounds, they do not believe that similar events could occur in the natural world today. Explain why not.
6. **Making inferences** Suppose autotrophic organisms had not evolved. What would life on Earth be like today?
7. **Using the writing process** You are asked to develop a television program for young children that explains the origin of life on Earth. Write a script for this show. You might like to videotape your presentation.
8. **Using the writing process** Did you ever wonder what it would have been like to be the first cell on Earth? Pretend you are that first cell. Keep a written diary of your first week on Earth.

CHAPTER 17

Viruses and Monerans

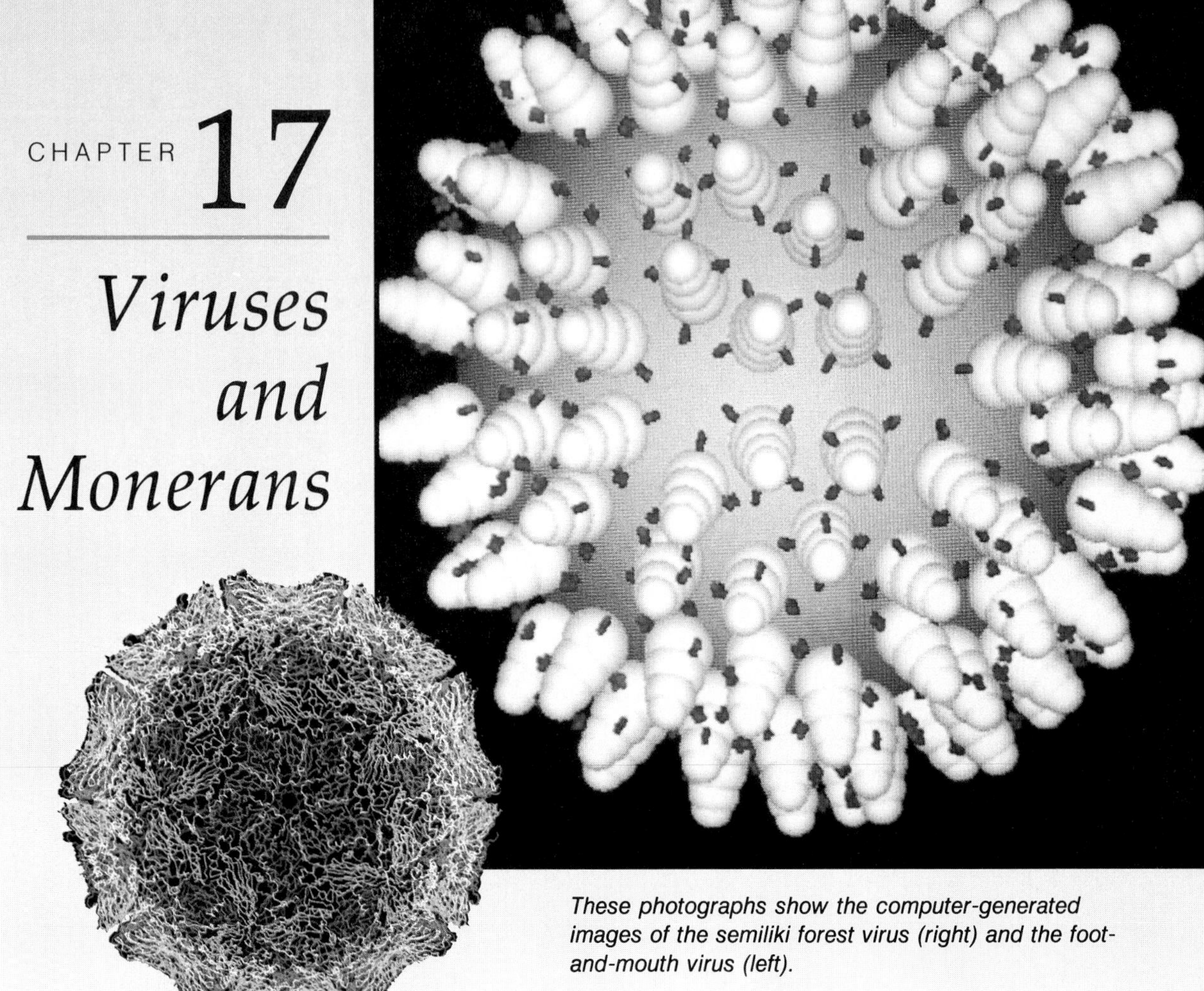

These photographs show the computer-generated images of the semiliki forest virus (right) and the foot-and-mouth virus (left).

We are accustomed to thinking of ourselves as complex organisms—and that view is correct. By comparison, there must be simpler organisms—and that view too is correct. According to this standard, the simplest organisms should be the single-celled bacteria. Even simpler than bacteria must be viruses, which cannot live outside a living cell.

As useful as this reasoning is, it has two flaws. First, no species should be thought of as simple. Even the tiniest bacterium has a complexity of organization that is almost beyond description. Second, every species has been shaped by millions of years of natural selection. The result is a world filled with spectacular examples of life's ability to adapt to and master challenges. What are viruses and bacteria? How are they classified? How do they adapt to their surroundings? Read on to find out.

CHAPTER OUTLINE

17–1 Viruses

Section Objectives

- Describe the structure of viruses.
- Discuss two methods by which viruses infect living cells.

Imagine for a moment that you have been presented with a great challenge. A disease has begun to destroy certain crops. The leaves of diseased plants are covered with large bleached spots that form a pattern farmers call a mosaic. As the disease progresses, the leaves turn yellow, wither, and fall off, killing the plants.

To determine what is causing the disease, you take some leaves from a diseased plant and crush them until a juice is extracted. Then you place a few drops of the juice on the surfaces of leaves of healthy plants. A few days later, you discover that wherever you have placed the juice on the healthy leaves, a mosaic pattern has appeared. You reason that the cause of the disease must be in the juice of the infected plant.

You then search for a microorganism that might be responsible for the disease, but none can be found in the juice. In fact, even when the juice is passed through a filter with pores so fine that not even cells can pass through, the juice still causes the disease. When you look at a small amount of the filtered juice under the light microscope, you see no evidence of cells. The juice, which is capable of transferring the disease from one plant to another, must contain disease-causing particles so

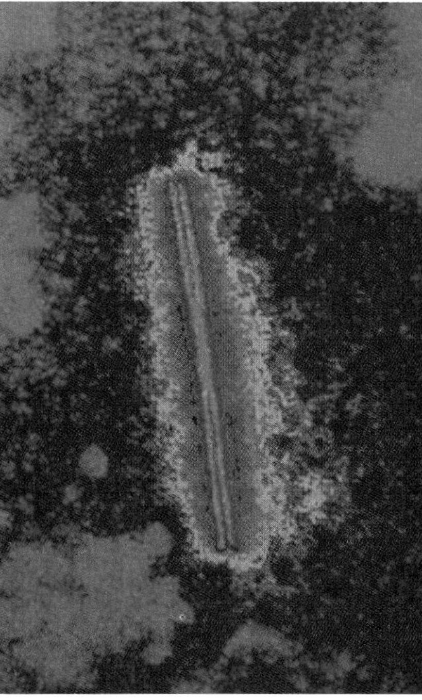

Figure 17–1 *The tobacco mosaic virus causes the leaves of tobacco plants to develop large bleached spots that form a pattern called a mosaic (left). The color-enhanced micrograph shows a tobacco mosaic virus that has been magnified approximately 41,800 times.*

small that they are not visible under the light microscope. Although you cannot see the disease-causing particles, you decide to give them the name viruses, from the Latin word meaning poison.

With a few exceptions, most of these events actually took place. About 100 years ago in what is now the Soviet Union, an epidemic of tobacco mosaic disease occurred that seriously threatened the tobacco crop. The disease-causing nature of the juice from infected leaves was discovered by the Russian biologist Dimitri Iwanowski. A few years later, the Dutch scientist Martinus Beijerinck named these disease-causing particles **viruses**.

Figure 17–2 *A bacteriophage is a virus that infects bacteria. Compare the structures shown in the diagram of the bacteriophage to those in an actual bacteriophage.*

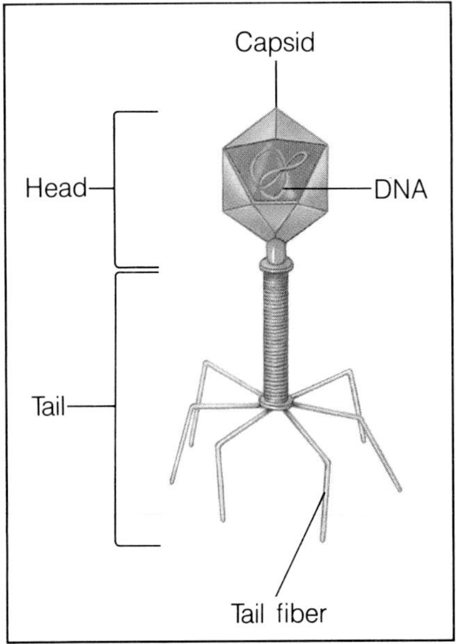

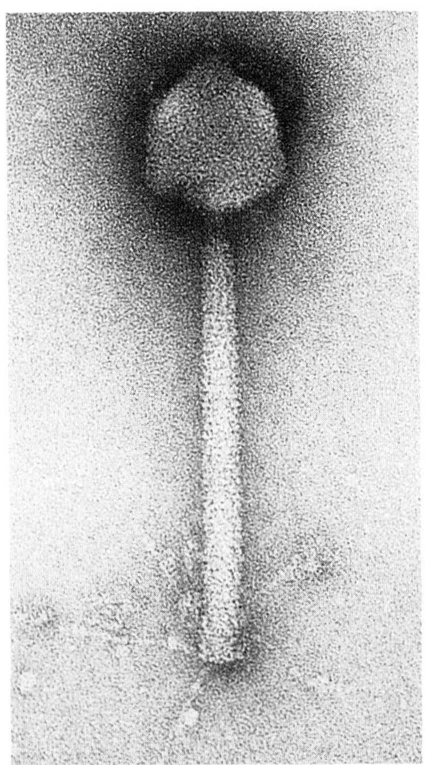

What Is a Virus?

You have just read how scientists hypothesized the existence of viruses, which they thought were cells even smaller than one-celled bacteria. This idea persisted until 1935 when the nature of a virus was discovered by the American biochemist Wendell Stanley. He had set out to chemically isolate the particle responsible for the tobacco mosaic disease. Stanley identified the particle as the tobacco mosaic virus (TMV).

Since Stanley's discovery, many viruses have been identified, largely through the use of the electron microscope, which was invented in the 1930s. We now appreciate the fact that viruses have distinct structures that are complex and fascinating. **A virus is a noncellular particle made up of genetic material and protein that can invade living cells.**

STRUCTURE OF A VIRUS A typical virus is composed of a core of nucleic acid surrounded by a protein coat called a capsid. The capsid protects the nucleic acid core. Depending on the virus, the core is either DNA or RNA but never both. The core may contain several genes to several hundred genes.

A more complex structure occurs in certain viruses known as **bacteriophages**. You may recall from Chapter 7 that bacteriophages are viruses that invade bacteria. A bacteriophage has a head region, composed of a capsid (protein coat), a nucleic acid core, and a tail. Bacteriophages are interesting to study because their hosts (bacteria) multiply quickly. The most commonly studied bacteriophages are those of the T group. They are named T1, T2, T3, T4, and so on.

The bacteriophage known as T4 has a core of DNA contained within a protein coat. A number of other proteins (about 30 in all) form the other parts of the virus, including the tail fibers. The tail fibers are the structures by which the virus attaches itself to a bacterium.

Viruses come in a variety of shapes. Some, such as the tobacco mosaic virus, are rod-shaped. Others, such as the bacteriophages, are tadpole-shaped. Still others are many-sided, helical, or cubelike. Figure 17–3 shows some of these shapes.

Viruses vary in size from approximately 20 to 400 nanometers. A nanometer is one billionth of a meter. The tobacco mosaic virus is about 300 nanometers long, whereas the virus that causes polio is about 20 nanometers in diameter.

SPECIFICITY OF A VIRUS Usually, specific viruses will infect specific organisms. For example, a plant virus cannot infect an animal. There are some viruses that will infect only humans. Others, such as the virus that causes rabies, infect all mammals and some birds. Still others infect only coldblooded animals (animals with body temperatures that change with the surrounding air). There are even some viruses that will infect species of animals that are closely related. For example, viruses that infect mice may infect rats. So you can see that viruses are capable of infecting virtually every kind of organism, including mammals, birds, insects, and plants.

Life Cycle of a Lytic Virus

In order to reproduce, viruses must invade, or infect, a living host cell. However, not all viruses invade living cells in exactly the same way. When T4 bacteriophages invade living cells, they cause the cells to lyse, or burst. Thus T4 viruses are known as lytic (LIHT-ihk) viruses.

INFECTION A virus is activated by chance contact with the right kind of host cell. In the case of T4, molecules on its tail fibers attach to the surface of a bacterium. The virus then injects its DNA into the cell. In most cases, the complete virus particle itself never enters the cell.

GROWTH Soon after entering the host cell, the DNA of the virus goes into action. In most cases, the host cell cannot tell the difference between its own DNA and the DNA of the virus. Consequently, the very same enzyme RNA polymerase that makes messenger RNA from the cell's own DNA begins to make messenger RNA from the genes of the virus. This viral messenger RNA now acts like a molecular wrecking crew, shutting down and taking over the infected host cell. Some of these viral genes turn off the synthesis of molecules that are important to the infected cell. One viral gene actually produces an enzyme that destroys the host cell's own DNA but does not harm the viral DNA!

REPLICATION As the virus takes over, it uses the materials of the host cell to make thousands of copies of its own protein coat and DNA. Soon the host cell becomes filled with hundreds of viral DNA molecules. When *Escherichia coli*, or *E. coli*, the bacterium found in the human intestine, is infected by a T4 bacteriophage, this sequence of infection, growth, and replication can happen in as brief a time as 25 minutes!

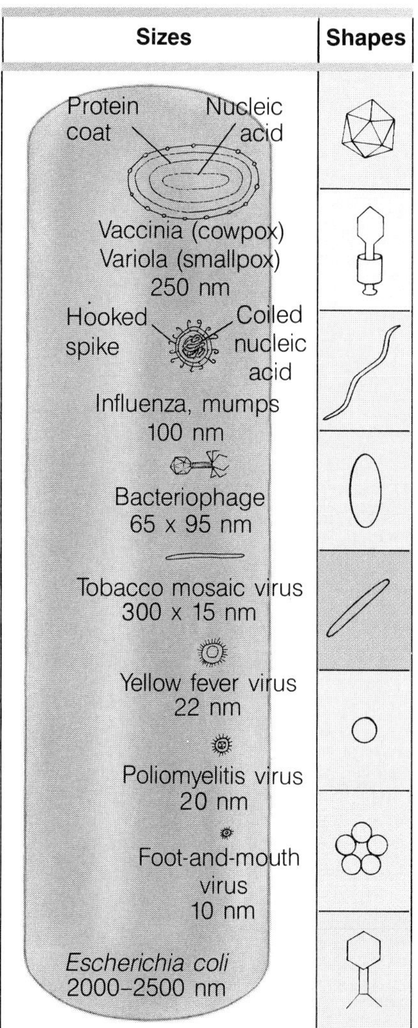

Figure 17–3 *Viruses come in a variety of sizes and shapes. Notice the size of the bacterium* E. coli *as compared to the sizes of the viruses.*

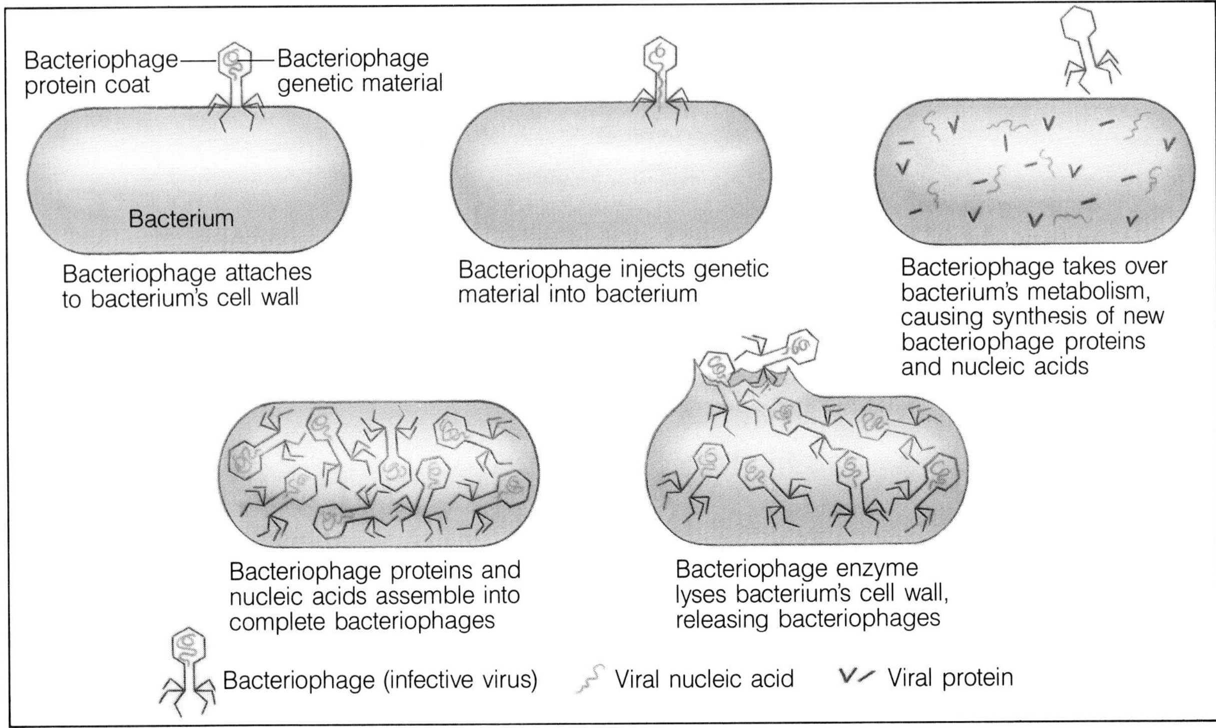
Bacteriophage protein coat
Bacteriophage genetic material
Bacterium
Bacteriophage attaches to bacterium's cell wall
Bacteriophage injects genetic material into bacterium
Bacteriophage takes over bacterium's metabolism, causing synthesis of new bacteriophage proteins and nucleic acids
Bacteriophage proteins and nucleic acids assemble into complete bacteriophages
Bacteriophage enzyme lyses bacterium's cell wall, releasing bacteriophages
Bacteriophage (infective virus)
Viral nucleic acid
Viral protein

Figure 17–4 *In the life cycle of a lytic virus, the virus invades a bacterium, reproduces, and is scattered when the bacterium lyses, or breaks.*

During the final stage of reproduction, the DNA molecules serve as the starting points around which new virus particles are assembled. Before long, the infected cell lyses (bursts) and releases hundreds of virus particles that may now infect other cells. Because the host cell is lysed and destroyed, this process is called a **lytic infection**. Lytic infections are one way in which viruses can infect host cells.

The life cycle of a lytic virus such as T4 consists of repeated acts of infection, growth, and cell lysis. We may imagine the virus as a desperado moving into a town in the Old West. First, the desperado eliminates the town's existing authority (host cell DNA). Then the desperado demands to be outfitted with new weapons, horses, and riding equipment by terrorizing the local merchants and businesspeople (using the machinery of the host cell to make proteins). Finally, the desperado recruits more outlaws and forms a gang that leaves the town and attacks new communities (the host cell bursts, releasing hundreds of virus particles).

Figure 17–5 *This electron micrograph shows bacteriophages attacking the bacterium* E. coli. *How do viruses attach themselves to the bacterium?*

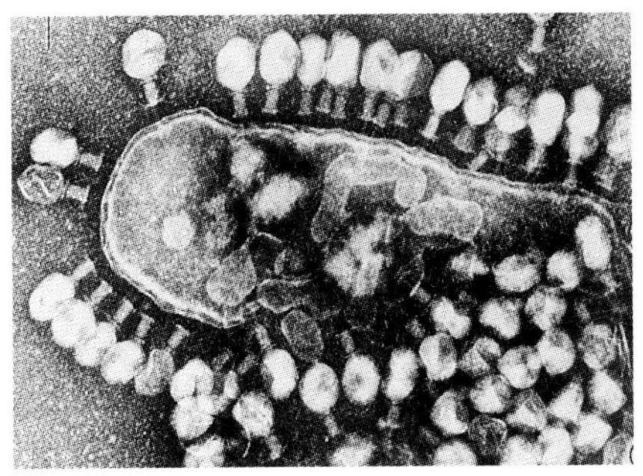

Lysogenic Infection

Another way in which a virus infects a cell is known as a **lysogenic** (ligh-soh-JEHN-ihk) **infection**. In a lysogenic infection, the virus does not reproduce and lyse its host cell—at least not right away! Instead, the DNA of the virus enters the cell and is inserted into the DNA of the host cell. Once inserted into the host cell's DNA, the viral DNA is known as a **prophage**.

The prophage may remain part of the DNA of the host cell for many generations. An example of a lysogenic virus is the bacteriophage *lambda*, which infects *E. coli.*

PROPHAGE ACTIVITY The presence of the prophage can block the entry of other viruses into the cell and may even add useful DNA to the host cell's DNA. For example, a lambda virus can insert the DNA necessary for the synthesis of important amino acids into the DNA of *E. coli.* As long as the lambda virus remains in the prophage state, *E. coli* can use the viral genes to make these amino acids.

A virus may not stay in the prophage form indefinitely. Eventually, the DNA of the prophage will become active, remove itself from the DNA of the host cell, and direct the synthesis of new virus particles. A series of genes in the prophage itself maintains the lysogenic state. Factors such as sudden changes in temperature and availability of nutrients can turn on these genes and activate the virus.

RETROVIRUSES One important class of viruses are the **retroviruses**. Retroviruses contain RNA as their genetic information. When retroviruses infect a cell, they produce a DNA copy of their RNA genes. This DNA, much like a prophage, is inserted into the DNA of the host cell. Retroviruses received their name from the fact that their genetic information is copied backward—that is, from RNA to DNA instead of from DNA to RNA. The prefix *retro-* means backward. Retroviruses are responsible for some types of cancer in animals and humans. One type of retrovirus produces a disease called AIDS.

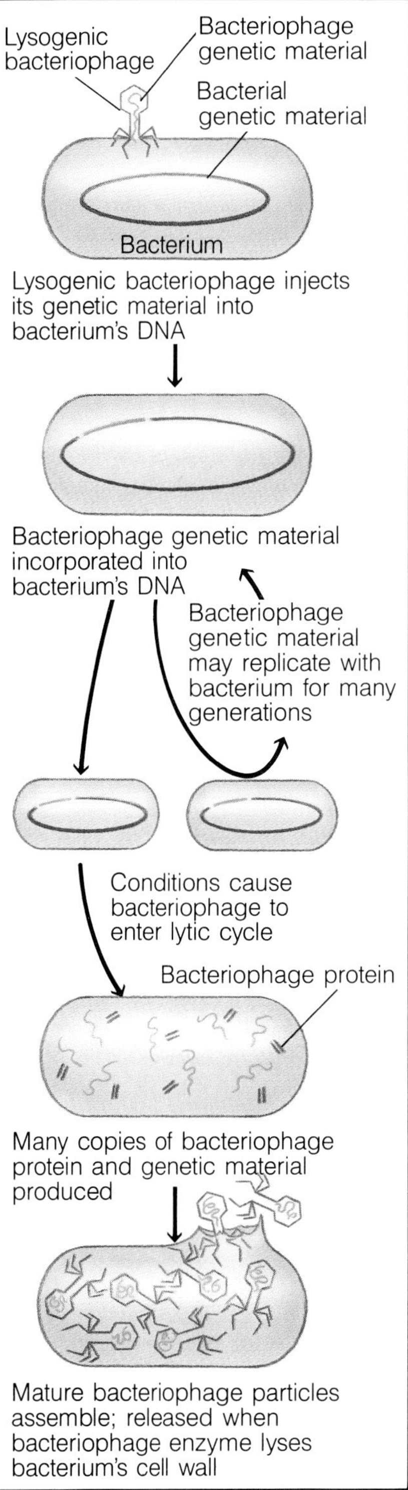

Figure 17–6 *In a lysogenic infection, the DNA of the bacteriophage enters the host cell and is inserted into its DNA.*

Viruses and Living Cells

As you have just learned, viruses must infect living cells in order to carry out their functions of growth and reproduction. They also depend upon their hosts for respiration, nutrition, and all of the other functions that occur in living things. Thus viruses are **parasites**. A parasite is an organism that depends entirely upon another living organism for its existence in such a way that it harms that organism.

Are viruses alive? If we require that living things be made up of cells and be able to live independently, then viruses are not alive. However, when they are able to infect living cells, viruses can grow, reproduce, regulate gene expression, and even evolve. Viruses have so many of the characteristics of living things that it seems only fair to consider them as part of the system of life on Earth.

Because it is possible to study the genes that viruses bring into cells when they infect them, viruses have been extremely valuable in genetic research. Many of the major breakthroughs in genetics and molecular biology have been made by studying the regulation and expression of viral genes.

Origin of Viruses

Although viruses are smaller and simpler than the smallest cells, they could not have been much like the first living things. Viruses are completely dependent upon living cells for growth and reproduction, and they cannot live outside their host cells. Thus it seems more likely that viruses developed after living cells. In fact, the first viruses may have evolved from the genetic material of living cells and have continued to evolve, along with the cells they infect, over billions of years.

17–1 SECTION REVIEW

1. What is a virus?
2. List and describe the parts of a bacteriophage.
3. Describe two methods of viral infection.
4. How can a virus be helpful before it is harmful?

Section Objectives

- Describe the four major phyla of monerans.
- Compare autotrophic and heterotrophic monerans.
- Describe growth and reproduction in monerans.
- Identify the role of monerans in the environment.

17–2 Monerans—Prokaryotic Cells

Imagine living all your life as the only family on your street. Then, on a morning like any other, you open the front door and there are houses all around you, cars and bicycles on the street, neighbors tending their gardens, children walking to school. Where did they come from? What if the answer turned out to be that they were always there—you just couldn't see them? In fact, they lived on your street for years and years before your house was even built. How would your view of the world change? What would it be like to go, almost overnight, from being the only family on the block to just one family in a crowded community? A bit of a shock?

Because of Robert Hooke and Anton van Leeuwenhoek, the human species had just such a shock. The invention of the light microscope opened our eyes to what the world around us is really like. And it opened our eyes almost overnight. Suddenly we saw that the block is very crowded!

Microscopic life covers nearly every square centimeter of planet Earth. What form does that microscopic life take? As you learned in Chapter 5, there are cells of every size and shape imaginable, even in a drop of pond water. The smallest and most common of these cells are the **prokaryotes**. Prokaryotes are cells that do not have a nucleus.

Where do we find prokaryotes? Everywhere! Prokaryotes exist in almost every place on Earth. They grow in numbers so great that they form colonies you can see with the unaided eye.

Figure 17–7 *With a nutrient-rich culture medium on which to grow, these bacteria have produced thousands of colonies.*

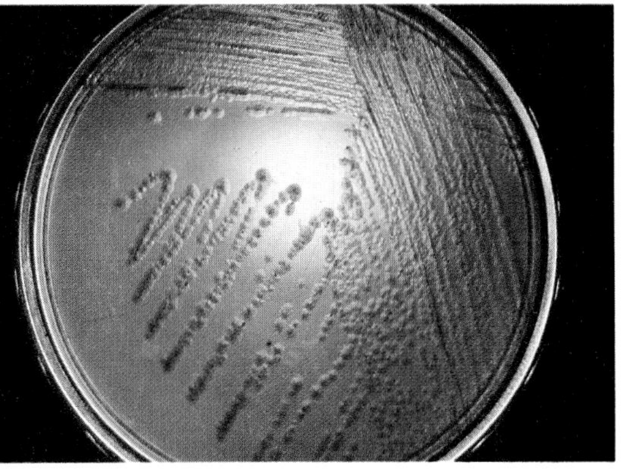

Classification of Monerans

All prokaryotes are placed in the kingdom Monera. The monerans are the first large group of organisms that we shall consider as we examine each of the five kingdoms of living things. In this textbook we have divided the kingdom Monera into four phyla. These phyla are Eubacteria (yoo-bak-TIHR-ee-uh), Cyanobacteria (sigh-uh-noh-bak-TIHR-ee-uh), Archaebacteria (ahr-kee-bak-TIHR-ee-uh), and Prochlorobacteria (proh-klor-oh-bak-TIHR-ee-uh). Although there are important differences among these four groups of organisms, each group shares enough similarities with the others to allow them to be called **bacteria**, or one-celled prokaryotes.

Bacteria range in size from 1 to 10 micrometers (one micrometer is equal to one thousandth of a millimeter). Bacteria are much smaller than eukaryotic cells, or cells with a nucleus, which generally range from 10 to 100 micrometers in diameter. The reason for the difference in size is that bacteria and other monerans do not contain the complex range of membrane-enclosed organelles that are found in most eukaryotic cells.

EUBACTERIA The phylum Eubacteria ("true" bacteria) is the largest of all the moneran phyla. Members of this phylum have always been referred to as bacteria. Eubacteria are generally surrounded by a cell wall composed of complex carbohydrates. The cell wall protects the bacterium from injury. Within the cell wall is a cell membrane that surrounds the cytoplasm. Some eubacteria are surrounded by two cell membranes. In some organisms, long whiplike flagella protrude from the membrane through the cell wall. Flagella are used for movement.

Within the phylum Eubacteria is a wide variety of organisms that have many different lifestyles. Some species live in

Figure 17–8 *A bacterium such as* E. coli *(right) has the basic structure typical of most bacteria: cell wall, cell membrane, region of genetic material, cytoplasm, and flagellum.*

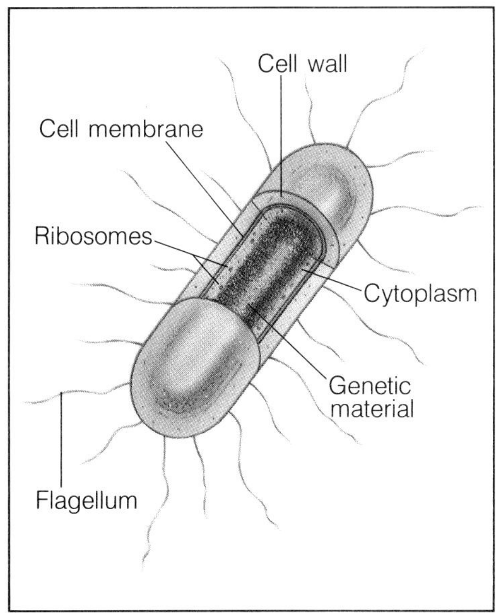

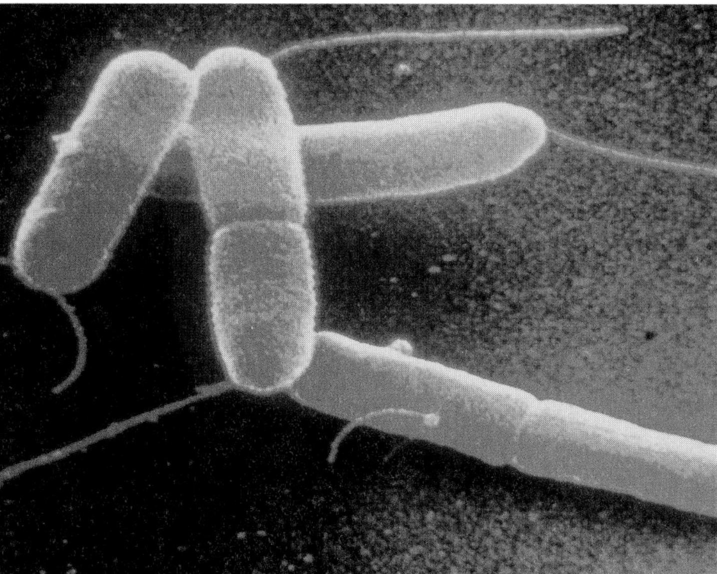

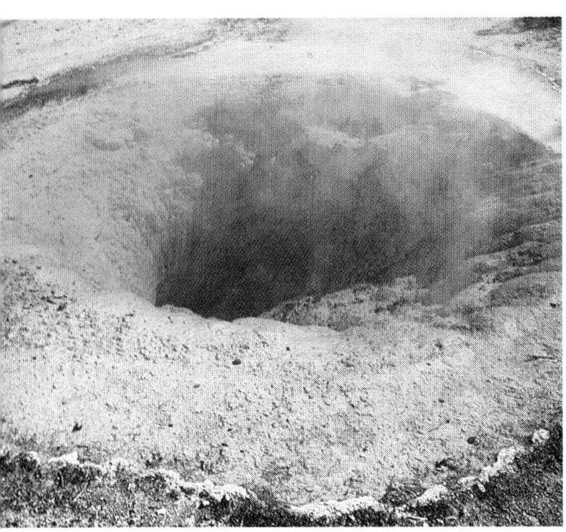

Figure 17–9 *Bacteria can survive in many environments that support no other forms of life, such as in a near-boiling hot spring called Morning Glory Pool in Yellowstone National Park, Wyoming.*

the soil. Others infect larger organisms and produce disease. Still others are photosynthetic. Photosynthetic bacteria are those bacteria capable of making their own food by using light energy. Later in this chapter we will examine some of the important roles that eubacteria play in the natural environment and some of the ways in which they affect us.

CYANOBACTERIA The bacteria that belong to the phylum Cyanobacteria are photosynthetic. Cyanobacteria are also known as blue-green bacteria. At one time, cyanobacteria were called blue-green algae, but today we use the word algae only for eukaryotes. In fact, only a few of the blue-green bacteria are a blue-green color. Those monerans that are blue-green in color contain a blue pigment called phycocyanin. They also contain chlorophyll *a*, which you will recall from Chapter 6 is green. The presence of these two pigments gives the name blue-green to the entire group of cyanobacteria. The presence of other pigments, however, may change the color of these monerans to yellow, brown, or even red.

Cyanobacteria contain membranes that carry out the light reactions of photosynthesis. These membranes contain the photosynthetic pigments and are quite different from and simpler than the chloroplasts (organelles that trap light energy and convert it to chemical energy) in plant cells.

Cyanobacteria are found throughout the world—in fresh and salt water and on land. A few species can survive in extremely hot water, such as that in hot springs. Others can survive in the Arctic, where they can even grow on snow. In fact, cyanobacteria are often the very first species to recolonize the site of a natural disaster, such as a volcanic eruption.

ARCHAEBACTERIA AND PROCHLOROBACTERIA Recent studies of monerans have led to the establishment of two new phyla that include organisms that differ from eubacteria and cyanobacteria. One phylum, Archaebacteria, includes organisms that live in extremely harsh environments. For example, one group of archaebacteria lives in oxygen-free environments such as thick mud and the digestive tracts of animals. These archaebacteria are called **methanogens** because they produce methane gas. Other archaebacteria live in extremely salty environments, such as the Great Salt Lake in Utah, or in extremely hot environments, such as hot springs where temperatures approach the boiling point of water.

The prochlorobacteria are a newly discovered group of photosynthetic organisms that contain chlorophyll *a* and *b* as their principal pigments. The presence of these pigments makes prochlorobacteria more similar to chloroplasts of green plants than to cyanobacteria. For this reason, prochlorobacteria are sometimes called Prochlorophyta *(-phyta* means plants) to emphasize this similarity. To date, only two species of prochlorobacteria have been discovered.

Identifying Monerans

Identifying living organisms can be a simple task. If we were given an unknown plant or animal, we would search through the photographs and diagrams in a reference book until we found one that resembled our unknown specimen. Such a method works for organisms that we can identify by appearance. But what about bacteria? How can they be identified?

CELL SHAPE One way in which bacteria can be identified is by their shape. **Bacteria have three basic shapes: rod, sphere, and spiral.** Rod-shaped bacteria are called **bacilli**

SCIENCE, TECHNOLOGY, AND SOCIETY 

A Separate Kingdom?

One of the more unusual groups of organisms in the kingdom Monera are the methanogens, which are methane-producing bacteria. Methanogens obtain their energy by producing methane gas (CH_4) from carbon dioxide gas (CO_2) and hydrogen gas (H_2). These monerans live in places where there is little available oxygen, such as beneath the surfaces of muddy marshes, in sewage, and even in human intestines.

Recently, a rather startling suggestion was made by Carl Woese of the University of Illinois. After carefully comparing hundreds of organisms, Woese proposed that the methanogens be placed in a new kingdom called Archaebacteria. The ribosomes and ribosomal RNA of Archaebacteria are so different from other living things, Woese argued, that they must be placed in a separate living kingdom.

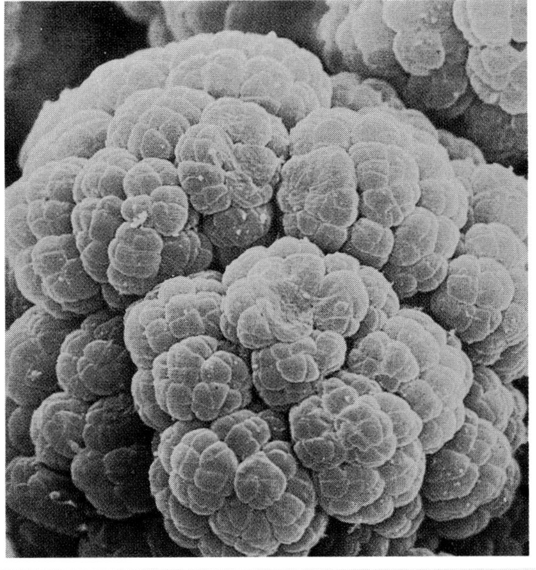

The methanogen Methanosarcina mazei

Is Woese right? He may well be. But one thing is certain: His findings and suggestions have touched off a debate among biologists as to how living things should be classified. This debate has prompted dozens of scientists from all over the world to test Woese's ideas and to devise new experiments and new ways of comparing living organisms. This flurry of activity can lead to a better understanding of living organisms.

Getting back to the issue at hand: Are methanogens deserving of their own kingdom? We will have to wait and see. Who knows, in a few years we may find ourselves with a new addition to the present scheme of classification.

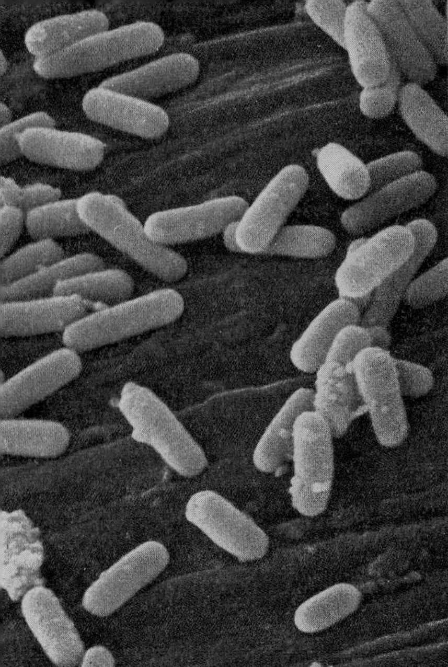
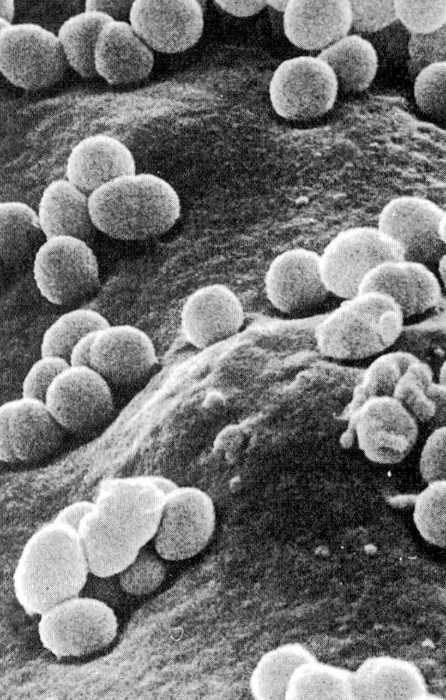
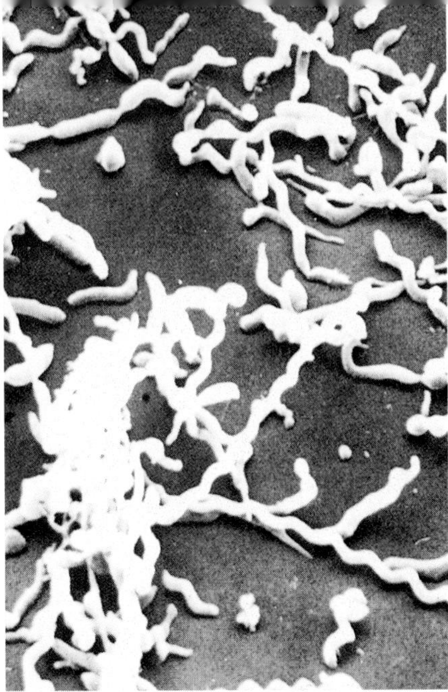

Figure 17–10 *Bacteria have three basic shapes. Rod-shaped bacteria are called bacilli (left), spherical bacteria are called cocci (center), and spiral-shaped bacteria are called spirilla (right).*

(buh-SIHL-igh; singular: bacillus). Spherical bacteria are called **cocci** (KAHK-sigh; singular: coccus). And spiral-shaped bacteria are called **spirilla** (spigh-RIHL-uh; singular: spirillum). See Figure 17–10.

Individual bacterial cells can also arrange themselves in a number of different ways. For example, cocci cells sometimes grow in colonies containing two cells. These two-celled colonies are called diplococci. Other cocci cells grow into long chains called streptococci. Still other cocci cells form large clumps and clusters called staphylococci. Using this information, we can now identify some bacterial cells by looking at them under the microscope.

Unfortunately, many bacteria look the same under the microscope. So we need to find another characteristic by which to distinguish one type from another. Fortunately, there are three other characteristics of bacteria that improve our ability to identify them: their cell walls, the kind of movement they are capable of, and how they obtain energy.

Figure 17–11 *When spherical bacteria grow into long chains, they are called streptococcus.*

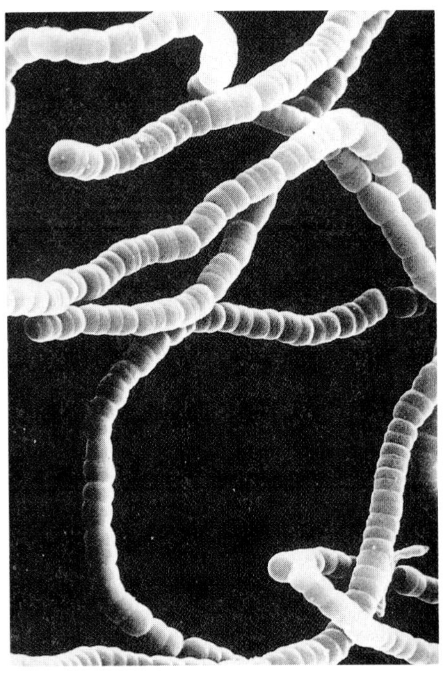

CELL WALL The chemical nature of bacterial cell walls can be studied by means of a method called Gram staining—which is named after its inventor, the Danish physician Hans Christian Gram. Gram's stain consists of two dyes—crystal violet (purple) and safranine (red).

When Gram added his stain to bacteria, he noticed that the bacteria took up either the purple dye or the red dye. The bacterial cells with only one thick layer of carbohydrate and protein molecules outside the cell membrane took up the crystal violet. They appeared purple under the light microscope. These bacteria are called Gram-positive bacteria. The bacterial cells with a second, outer layer of lipid and carbohydrate molecules took up the safranine. They appeared red under the microscope. These bacteria are called Gram-negative bacteria.

BACTERIAL MOVEMENT We can also identify bacteria by studying how they move. Some bacteria are propelled by means of one or more flagella. Others lash, snake, or spiral forward. Still others glide slowly along a layer of slimelike material that they secrete themselves. And there are some bacteria that do not move at all.

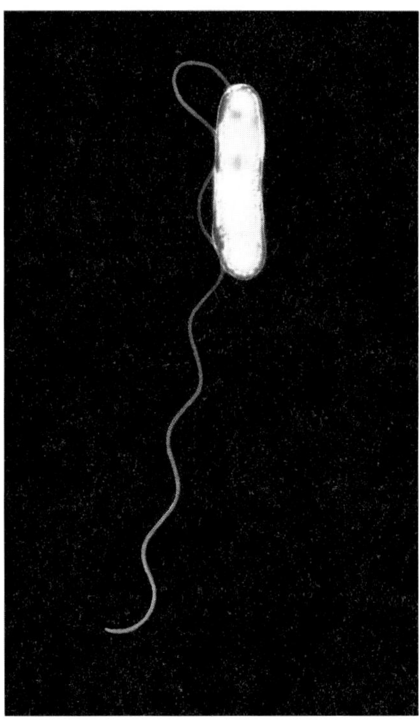

Figure 17–12 *Many types of bacteria, such as the bacterium that causes Legionnaires' disease, move by means of a whiplike flagellum.*

How Monerans Obtain Energy

Although the structure of monerans is rather simple, their lifestyles are remarkably complex. No characteristic of monerans illustrates this point better than the ways in which they obtain energy.

AUTOTROPHS Monerans that trap the energy of sunlight in a manner similar to green plants are called **phototrophic autotrophs.** Examples of phototrophic autotrophs include the cyanobacteria and some photosynthetic eubacteria.

Monerans that live in harsh environments and obtain energy from inorganic molecules are called **chemotrophic autotrophs.** The inorganic molecules that are used by chemotrophic autotrophs include hydrogen sulfide, nitrites, sulfur, and iron. *Nitrosomonas* is an example of a chemotrophic autotroph that uses ammonia and oxygen to produce energy.

HETEROTROPHS Many bacteria obtain energy by taking in organic molecules and then breaking them down and absorbing them. These bacteria are called **chemotrophic heterotrophs**. Most bacteria, as well as most animals, are chemotrophic heterotrophs.

Because we are chemotrophic heterotrophs ourselves, many bacteria compete with us for food sources. For example, *Salmonella* is a bacteria that grows in foods such as raw meat, poultry, and eggs. If these foods are not properly cooked, *Salmonella* will get to your dinner table before you do! Once there, these bacteria will not only "eat" some of the food ahead of time, but they will release poisons into the food. Food poisoning can result. The symptoms of food poisoning range from an upset stomach to serious illness.

There is another group of heterotrophic bacteria that has a most unusual means of obtaining energy. These bacteria are photosynthetic—they are able to use sunlight for energy. But they also need organic compounds for nutrition. These bacteria are called **phototrophic heterotrophs**. There is nothing quite like these organisms in the rest of the living world.

Bacterial Respiration

Like all organisms, bacteria need a constant supply of energy to perform all their life activities. This energy is supplied by the processes of respiration and fermentation. Respiration

PROBLEM SOLVING IN BIOLOGY

FOOD POISONING

Every year, thousands of cases of bacterial food poisoning are reported. In each case, a medical detective is assigned to find out how the person got food poisoning. Once the cause of the food poisoning has been determined, the medical detective can move to correct the conditions that led to the food poisoning.

Two types of bacteria that cause food poisoning are salmonella and staphylococci. A medical detective knows that these bacteria produce very different symptoms. So in order to determine which bacteria is the culprit, the detective will ask a series of important questions. The first thing the detective will want to know is exactly what the patient ate in the 24 hours prior to becoming ill and where the food was eaten. Other important information that the detective will gather includes how long after eating the patient became ill and whether the patient developed a fever. The detective will also want to know if the patient developed chills. Armed with answers to these questions, the detective can determine what caused the food poisoning and which meal contained the tainted food. But how?

The medical detective knows many details about these two types of bacterial food poisoning. For example, staphylococci produce a toxin, or poison, that is secreted into the food source as the bacteria multiply. Once a person eats the tainted food, the toxin will be carried throughout his or her body by the bloodstream. Within a few hours after the food has been ingested, the toxin will usually cause symptoms that include diarrhea, vomiting, nausea, and abdominal cramps. Fortunately, recovery is usually complete 24 to 48 hours after the onset of the symptoms.

Like staphylococci, salmonella produce a toxin. This toxin, however, is contained in the bacteria's cell walls and is released only when the bacteria lyse, or burst. Because of this difference, the symptoms produced by salmonella are somewhat unlike those produced by staphylococci. For example, it takes longer for a person to feel the effects of salmonella, often 12 hours or more. Salmonella infections almost always cause diarrhea. And they also generally result in a fever, chills, frequent vomiting, and abdominal pain. It may also take a patient quite a bit longer to recover from a case of salmonella food poisoning.

Now it's time for you to play medical detective.

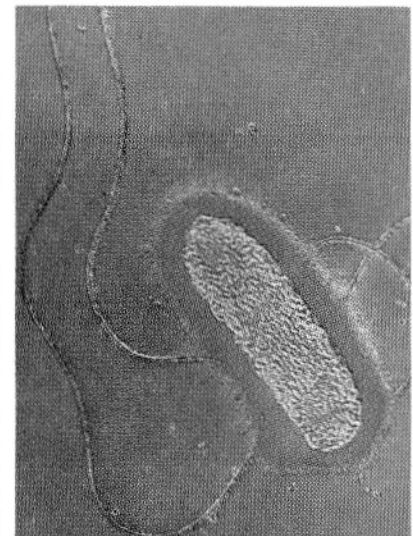

Salmonella bacterium magnified 12,600 times

Case Study 1 A patient with food poisoning reports that he ate his last meal at about 6 P.M. Although he felt fine the next morning, the patient became very sick at work. Due to severe abdominal pain and vomiting, the patient returned home. The patient also had a fever, chills, and severe diarrhea. He still felt sick the next day and did not fully recover for several days.

Case Study 2 You interview a patient who is suffering from food poisoning. However, this patient shows signs of recovery and feels well enough to go back to work. You discover that the last time the patient ate was about 6 P.M. the night before. While watching television later that evening, the patient became ill and had extremely severe abdominal cramps. The patient had a mild case of diarrhea that has subsided. There was no fever.

Analysis Analyze each case study to determine whether the food poisoning was caused by salmonella or staphylococci. Support your diagnoses based on the data provided.

is the process that involves oxygen and breaks down food molecules to release energy. Fermentation, on the other hand, enables cells to carry out energy production without oxygen.

Organisms that require a constant supply of oxygen in order to live are called **obligate aerobes**. We, and many species of bacteria, are obligate aerobes. Some bacteria, however, do not require oxygen, and in fact may be poisoned by it! These bacteria are called **obligate anaerobes**. Obligate anaerobes must live in the absence of oxygen.

An example of an obligate anaerobe is the bacterium *Clostridium botulinum*, which is often found in soil. Because *Clostridium* is unable to grow in the presence of oxygen, it normally causes very few problems. However, if these bacteria find their way into a place that is free of air (air contains oxygen) and filled with food material, they will grow very quickly. As they grow, the bacteria produce **toxins**, or poisons, that cause botulism. Botulism is a rare form of food poisoning that interferes with nerve activity and can cause paralysis and, if the breathing muscles are paralyzed, death. A perfect place for these bacteria to grow is in the space inside a can of food. Most commercially prepared canned foods are safe because the bacteria and their toxins have been destroyed by heating the foods for a long time before the cans are sealed. However, botulism is always a danger when food is canned at home. Thus experienced canners thoroughly heat food before sealing it in jars.

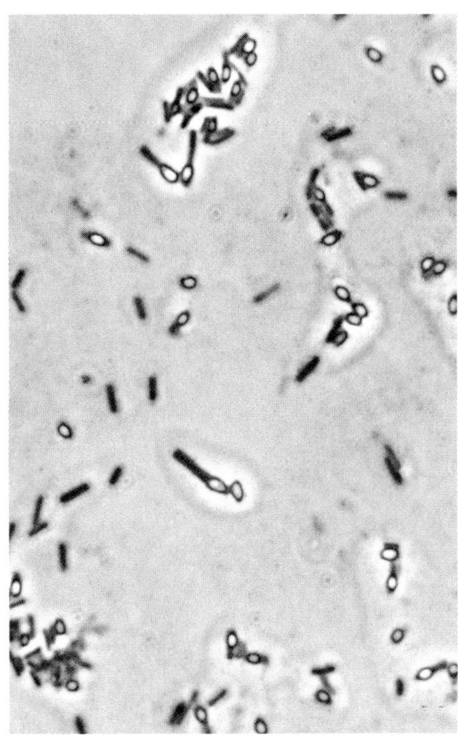

Figure 17–13 *Botulism, a kind of food poisoning, is caused by the bacterium* Clostridium botulinum. *The small round structures on some of the bacteria are endospores.*

A third group of bacteria are those that can survive with or without oxygen. They are known as **facultative anaerobes**. Facultative anaerobes do not require oxygen, but neither are they poisoned by its presence. What does such diversity imply? It means that bacteria can live in virtually every place on the surface of planet Earth. And indeed they do! Bacteria are found in freshwater lakes and ponds, at the bottom of the ocean, at the tops of the highest mountains, in the most sterile hospital rooms, and even in our own digestive systems!

Bacterial Growth and Reproduction

When conditions are favorable, bacteria can grow and reproduce at astonishing rates. Some types of bacteria can reproduce as often as every 20 minutes! If unlimited space and food were available to a single bacterium and if all of its offspring divided every 20 minutes, then in just 48 hours (2 days) they would reach a mass approximately 4000 times the mass of the Earth! Fortunately for us, this does not happen. In nature, the growth of bacteria is held in check by the availability of food and the production of waste products. However, bacteria do reproduce, and they do so in a number of ways.

BINARY FISSION When a bacterium has grown so that it has nearly doubled in size, it replicates its DNA and divides in half, producing two identical daughter cells. This type of

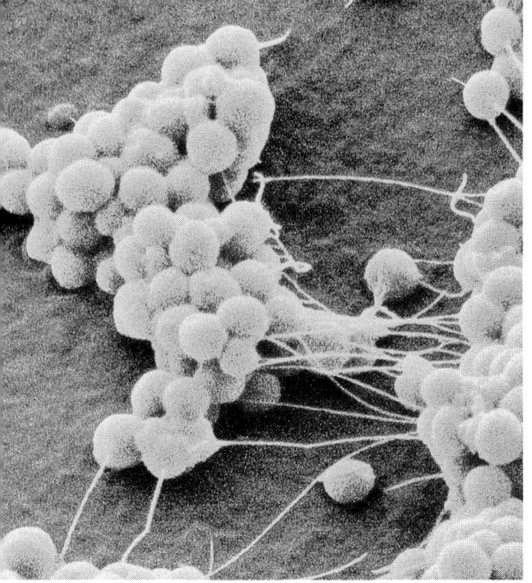
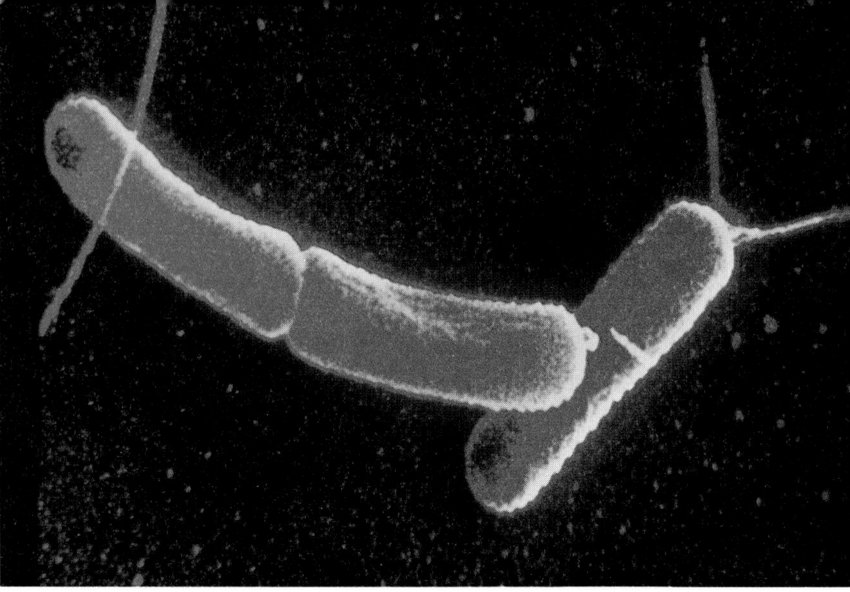
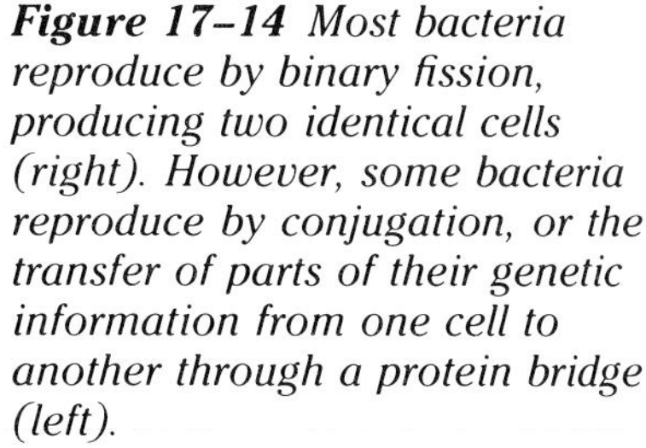

Figure 17–14 *Most bacteria reproduce by binary fission, producing two identical cells (right). However, some bacteria reproduce by conjugation, or the transfer of parts of their genetic information from one cell to another through a protein bridge (left).*

reproduction is known as **binary fission**. Because binary fission does not involve the exchange or recombination of genetic information, it is an asexual form of reproduction. The bacterium *E. coli* undergoes binary fission. See Figure 17–14.

CONJUGATION Although many bacteria reproduce only through asexual binary fission, others take part in some form of sexual reproduction. Sexual reproduction involves the exchange of genetic information. One form of sexual reproduction that occurs in some bacteria is known as **conjugation**. See Figure 17–14.

During conjugation, a long bridge of protein forms between and connects two bacterial cells. Part of the genetic information from one cell, called the donor, is transferred to the other cell, called the recipient, through this bridge. When the process of conjugation is complete, the recipient cell has a different set of genes from those it had before conjugation occurred. The new combinations of genes that result from conjugation increase the genetic diversity in that population of bacteria. Genetic diversity helps to ensure that even if the environment changes, a few bacteria may have the right combinations of genes to survive.

SPORE FORMATION When growth conditions become unfavorable, many bacteria form structures called spores. One type of spore, called an **endospore**, is formed when a bacterium produces a thick internal wall that encloses its DNA and a portion of its cytoplasm.

The endospore can remain dormant for months or even years, waiting for more favorable growth conditions. When conditions improve, the endospore will open and the bacterium will begin to grow again. Strictly speaking, spore formation in bacteria is not a form of reproduction because it does not result in the formation of new bacterial cells. However, the ability to form spores makes it possible for some bacteria to survive harsh conditions that would otherwise kill them.

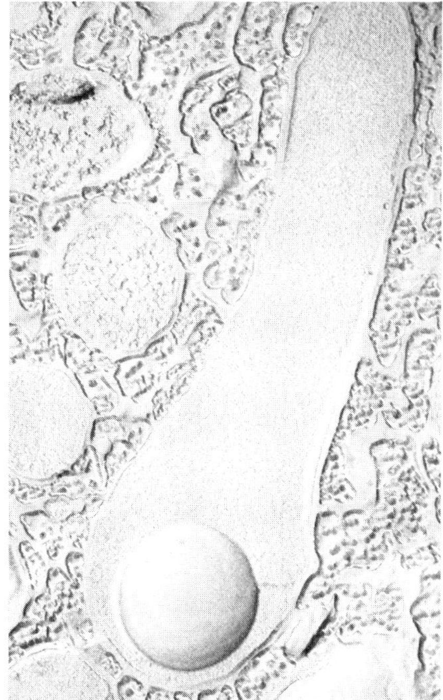

Figure 17–15 *The round circle at the bottom of this electron micrograph of a bacterium is an endospore. Endospores enable bacteria to survive unfavorable conditions, such as high temperature.*

Importance of Monerans

Many of the remarkable properties of monerans provide us with products upon which we depend every day. For example, bacteria are used in the production of a wide variety of foods and beverages, such as cheese, yogurt, buttermilk, and sour cream. Some bacteria are used to make pickles and sauerkraut, and some make vinegar from wine.

Bacteria are also used in industry. One type of bacteria can digest petroleum, which makes them helpful in cleaning up small oil spills. Some bacteria remove waste products and poisons from water. Others can even help to mine minerals from the ground. Still others have been useful in synthesizing drugs and chemicals through techniques of genetic engineering.

Many kinds of bacteria develop a close relationship with other organisms in which the bacteria or the other organism or both benefit. Such a relationship is called **symbiosis** (sihm-bigh-OH-sihs). The symbiotic relationships that bacteria develop with other organisms are particularly important. Monerans form symbiotic relationships with organisms from all of the other four kingdoms.

Our intestines are inhabited by large numbers of bacteria, including *E. coli.* Indeed, the species name *coli* was derived from the fact that these bacteria were discovered in the human colon, or large intestine. In the intestines, the bacteria are provided with a warm safe home, plenty of food, and free transportation. We, in turn, get help in digesting our food. These bacteria also make a number of vitamins that we cannot produce on our own. So both we and the bacteria benefit from this symbiotic relationship.

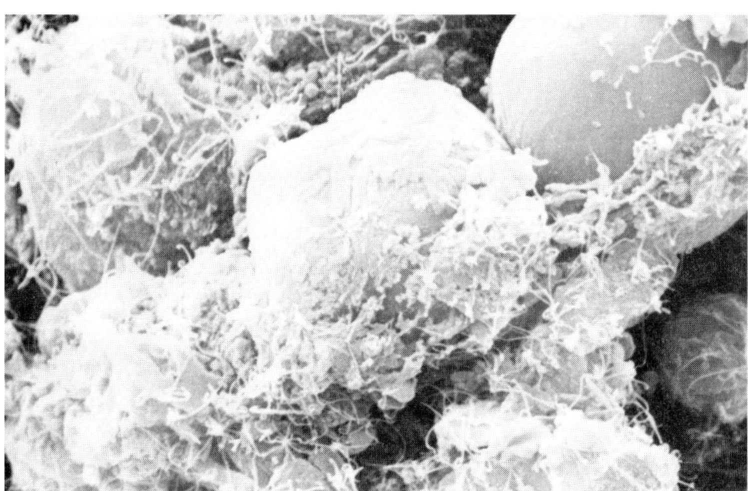

Figure 17–16 *The large round structures in this electron micrograph are cells that form the intestinal wall of the human large intestine, or colon. The smaller rod-shaped cells are the bacteria* E. coli, *which inhabit the large intestine.*

Animals such as cattle are also dependent upon the symbiotic relationship they have with the bacteria in their intestines. You see, no vertebrate (animal with a backbone) can produce the enzymes necessary to break down cellulose, the principal carbohydrate in grass and hay. Bacteria living in the digestive systems of such animals can make these enzymes, thus allowing the animals to digest their food properly.

Bacteria in the Environment

Sometimes we are bold enough to consider ourselves the principal actors on the stage of life. We tend to place other organisms in supporting roles, like the minor actors in a play. But no drama can begin without the dozens of workers who are never seen on stage. The bacteria are like these unseen stagehands. We seldom think about them, but they are absolutely vital to maintaining the kind of living world we see about us.

NUTRIENT FLOW Every living thing depends on a supply of raw materials for growth. If these materials were lost forever when an organism died, then life could not continue. Before long, plants would drain the soil of the minerals they need, plant growth would stop, and the animals that depend on plants for food would starve.

Bacteria recycle and decompose, or break down, dead material. When a tree dies and falls to the forest floor, it begins to undergo many changes. Over the course of a few summers, the bark peels off and the wood begins to weaken because it becomes infested with insects. Then the tree crumbles into the soil. Over time, the whole substance of the tree disappears. What happens to all of the material that made up the tree?

From the moment the tree dies, armies of bacteria attack and digest the dead wood, breaking it down into simpler substances. These bacteria are called **saprophytes** (SAP-ruh-fights). Saprophytes are organisms that use the complex molecules of a once-living organism as their source of energy and nutrition. Gradually, the material of the tree is recycled, enriching the soil in which it grew. Although bacteria play a major role in this process, some eukaryotic organisms, such as insects and fungi, have a supporting role.

Figure 17–17 *Most bacteria are heterotrophs, or organisms that obtain food from the organic compounds of other organisms. Many of these heterotrophs live as saprophytes, decomposing dead organisms such as this tree.*

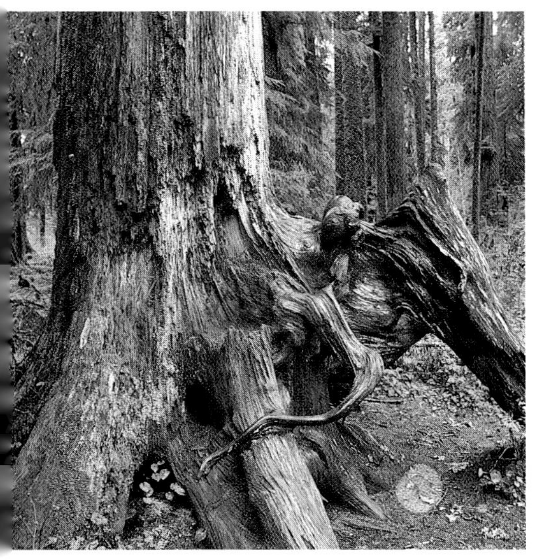

SEWAGE DECOMPOSITION Humans take advantage of the ability of bacteria to decompose material in the treatment of sewage. One of the critical steps in sewage treatment is carried out by a diverse mixture of bacteria that is added directly to the waste water. Waste water contains human waste, discarded food, organic garbage, and even chemical waste. Bacteria grow rapidly in this mixture. As they grow, they break down the complex compounds in the sewage into simpler compounds. This process produces purified water, nitrogen gas and carbon dioxide gas, and leftover products that can be used as crop fertilizers.

SCIENCE, TECHNOLOGY, AND SOCIETY APPLICATION

The Littlest Miners

Copper is one of the most important minerals in the Earth—our modern civilization needs large amounts of it. Most, however, is low-grade copper ore, which means that the ore has a low percentage of copper in it. This is especially true of the copper ore deposits located in the United States. A way must be found to get the small amount of copper out of the ore in a pure enough form to make it worth mining. Does such a job require big, strong, burly miners? Not at all! The best miners for the job are bacteria, and the process is called bioleaching.

A copper leaching dump in Bingham Canyon, Utah, where low-grade ore is extracted using the bacterium Thiobacillus ferrooxidans

The process of bioleaching begins by stacking large piles of low-grade copper ore out in the open. Then water that has been made acidic is sprayed on the surfaces of the piles. The acidified water helps a bacterium called *Thiobacillus ferrooxidans* to grow. *Thiobacillus,* which occurs naturally in the copper ore, helps to break down sulfate-containing minerals, releasing sulfuric acid and ferric iron. The sulfuric acid and ferric iron react with copper-containing minerals in the ore to produce copper sulfate, which is water soluble. The copper sulfate dissolves in the water, forming copper ions. The dissolved copper sulfate is washed out of the pile and leaks through the bottom of the heap, where it is collected in basins. The copper ions are then separated from the copper sulfate solution to produce metallic copper.

Thiobacillus does what human miners cannot—it extracts copper from low-grade copper ore. Presently, about 10 percent of the copper produced in the United States is mined by using bacteria. A few mining companies have begun to apply the same biotechnological process to extract gold from sulfur-containing gold ore, giving the term gold bug a whole new meaning!

NITROGEN FIXATION All organisms on our planet are totally dependent on monerans for nitrogen. All green plants need nitrogen to make amino acids, which are the building blocks of proteins. And because animals eat plants, plant proteins are ultimately the source of proteins for animals.

Although our atmosphere is made up of approximately 80 percent nitrogen gas (N_2), plants are not able to use the nitrogen gas. Neither can most other organisms. Living organisms generally require that nitrogen be "fixed" chemically in the form of ammonia (NH_3) and related nitrogen compounds. Chemists can make synthetic nitrogen-containing fertilizers by mixing nitrogen gas and hydrogen gas, heating the mixture to 500°C, and then squeezing it to 300 times the normal atmospheric pressure. The process is expensive, time-consuming, and sometimes dangerous.

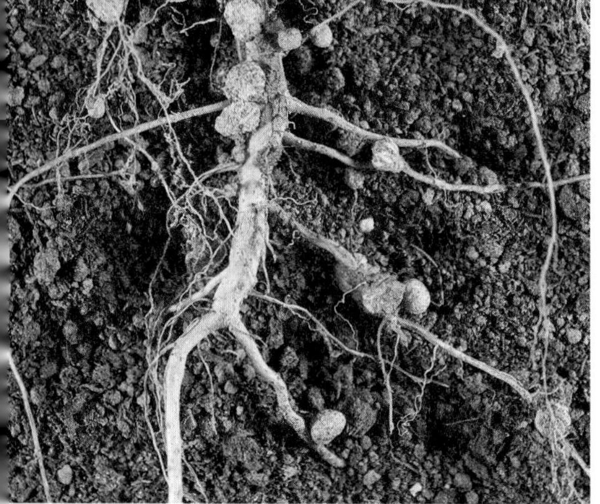

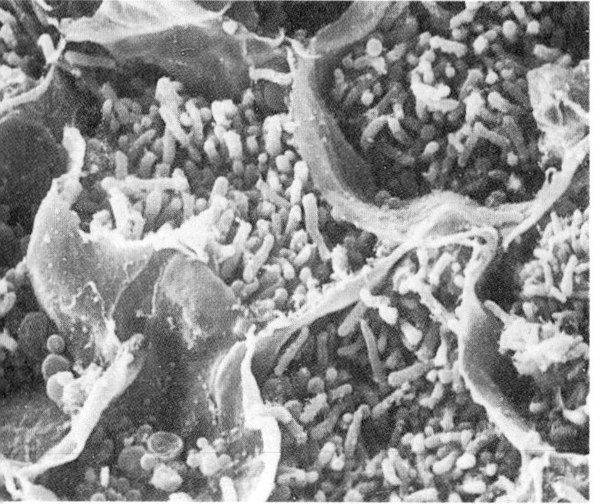

Figure 17–18 The knoblike structures growing on the roots of this soybean plant are called nodules (top). Within these nodules are the nitrogen-fixing bacteria Rhizobium, *which have a characteristic rod-shaped appearance (bottom).*

In contrast to this difficult process, many cyanobacteria and other bacteria can take nitrogen from the air and convert it to a form that plants can use. This conversion process is known as **nitrogen fixation**. Monerans are the only organisms capable of performing nitrogen fixation.

Many plants have symbiotic relationships with nitrogen-fixing bacteria. The soybean, which hosts the bacterium *Rhizobium*, is among the best known. *Rhizobium* grows in nodules, or knobs, that form on the roots of the soybean plant. The soybean plant provides a home and a source of nutrients for the nitrogen-fixing *Rhizobium*; the bacterium fixes nitrogen directly from the air into ammonia for the plant. All plants benefit from the nitrogen-fixing ability of monerans, but soybeans are a step ahead. With a little help from their "friends," soybeans have their own fertilizer factories built right into their roots.

As you have learned, eukaryotes are dependent upon monerans to fix nitrogen and release it into the environment. And it is because of the nitrogen-fixing ability of these organisms that more than 170 million metric tons of nitrogen are released into the environment every year.

17–2 SECTION REVIEW

1. Describe the four major phyla of the kingdom Monera.
2. Compare the three basic shapes of bacteria.
3. Distinguish between autotrophic and heterotrophic monerans. Between obligate aerobes, obligate anaerobes, and facultative anaerobes.
4. Describe binary fission and conjugation.
5. List some ways in which bacteria are important.
6. Suppose monerans lost the ability to fix nitrogen. How would this affect other organisms?

Section Objectives

- List some diseases caused by viruses and bacteria.
- Describe two methods of controlling the growth of bacteria.

17–3 Diseases Caused by Viruses and Monerans

Contrary to popular belief, only a small number of viruses and monerans are capable of producing disease in humans. Despite their small numbers, these **pathogens**, or disease-producing agents, are responsible for much human suffering.

From the point of view of a microorganism, however, disease is nothing more than a conflict of lifestyles. All viruses infect living cells, and disease results when the infection causes harm to the host. All bacteria require nutrients and energy, and disease results only when bacteria interfere with the host in obtaining them.

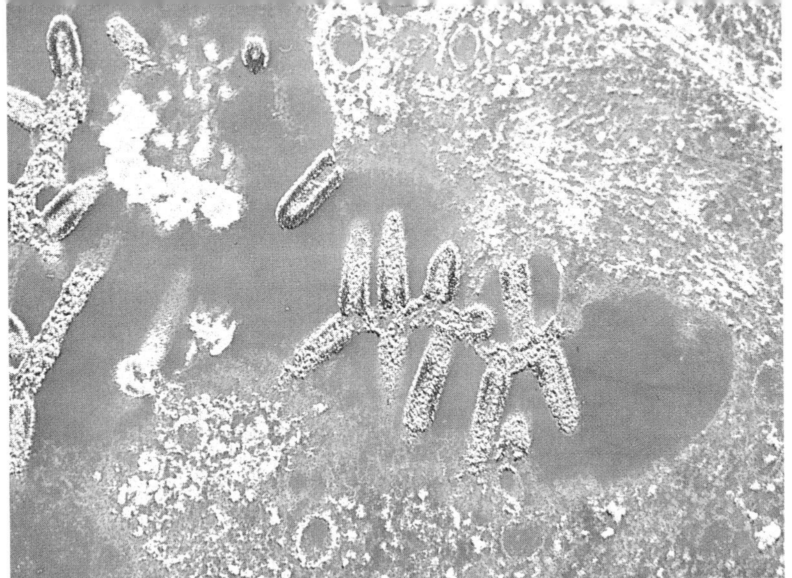

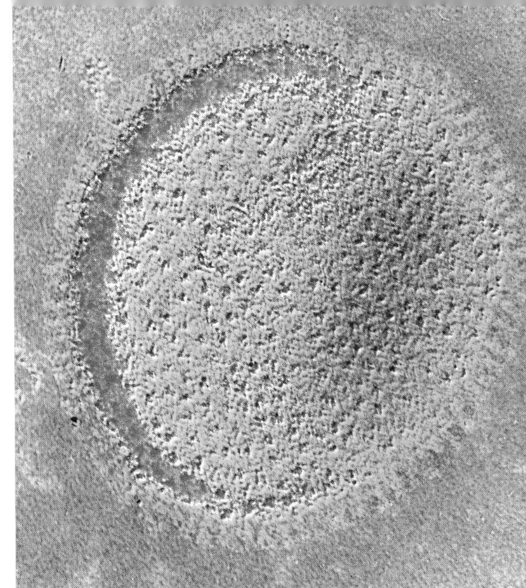

Figure 17–19 Viruses are the cause of many human diseases. Here you see the virus responsible for influenza (right) and the one that causes rabies (left).

Viruses and Disease

Viruses are the cause of such human diseases as smallpox, polio, measles, AIDS, mumps, influenza, yellow fever, rabies, and the common cold. In most viral infections, viruses attack cells of the body in the same way that the T4 bacteriophage attacks *E. coli.* As the virus reproduces, it destroys the cells that it infects, causing the symptoms of the disease.

Although we tend to think that some viral diseases are curable, the only successful protection against most of them lies in preventing their infection. In order to do this, the body's own immune system must be stimulated to prevent the infection. A vaccine is a substance that contains the weakened or killed disease-causing virus. When injected into the body, the vaccine provides an immunity to the disease. Diseases such as smallpox and polio have all but been eliminated because vaccines were developed to stop their spread. As powerful as they are, however, vaccines can only provide protection if they are used before an infection begins. Once a viral infection starts, there is often little that medical science can do to stop the progress of the disease. However, sometimes the symptoms of the infection can be treated.

INTERFERONS One possible approach in the treatment of viral diseases is the use of substances called interferons. Interferons are small proteins that are produced by the body's cells when the cells are infected by viruses. When interferons are released from virus-infected cells, they seem to make it more difficult for the viruses to infect other cells. The word interferon is derived from the fact that these proteins interfere with the growth of the virus. The specific way in which these proteins work is not yet entirely understood. Until recently, interferons cost millions of dollars a milliliter to isolate and purify. But new techniques using genetically engineered bacteria have made the production of interferons less expensive and more plentiful.

Figure 17–20 These flasks contain interferons, which were produced by genetically engineered bacteria. Interferons, proteins made by virus-infected cells, inhibit the growth of viruses.

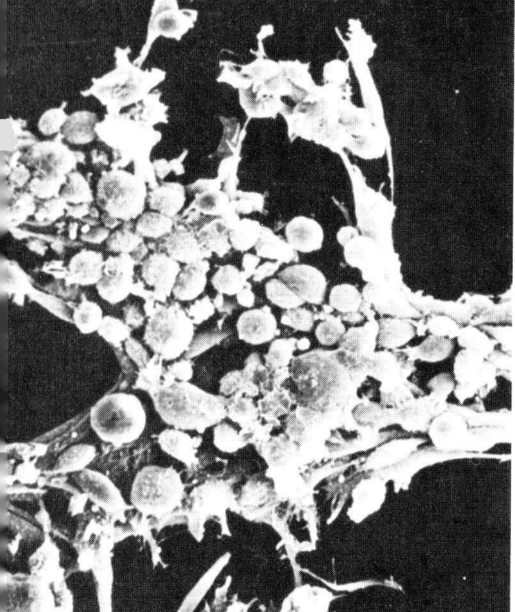

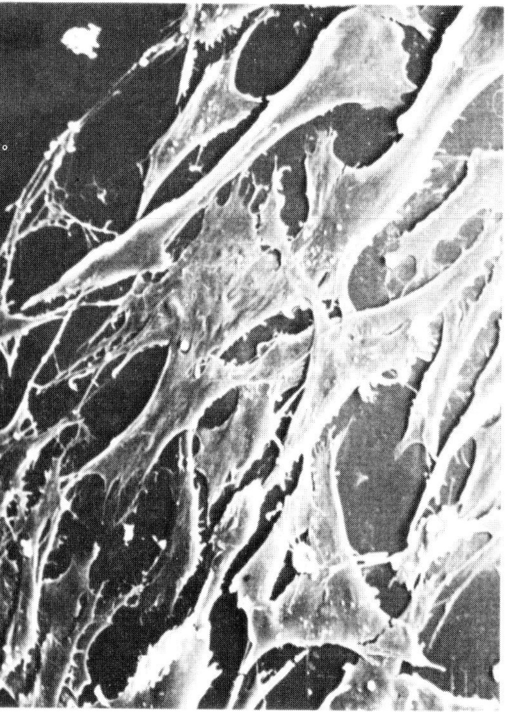

Figure 17–21 These cells of chicken connective tissue clearly show the effects of invasion by a virus. Notice that the normal cells are flat (bottom), whereas those infected with Rous sarcoma virus are round (top).

CANCER Certain viruses cause cancer in animals. These cancer-causing viruses are known as oncogenic (*onco-genic* means tumor-making) viruses. One example is the Rous sarcoma virus (RSV), discovered by the American physician Peyton Rous. RSV causes cancer in chickens and other domestic fowl. As we shall see in Chapter 44, this virus adds certain genes to the infected cell that seem to turn it into a cancer cell. Although it is clear that not all cancers are caused by viruses (cancer is generally not spread by a person-to-person infective process), a few cancers are. This has caused scientists to study cancer-causing viruses closely.

Bacteria and Disease

Of all the bacteria in the world, there are only a few that produce disease. The lifestyles of these few disease-causing organisms have, unfortunately, made us think of disease whenever we think of the word bacteria.

The French chemist Louis Pasteur was the first person to show convincingly that bacteria cause disease. Pasteur established what has become known as the germ theory of disease when he showed that bacteria were responsible for a number of human and animal diseases.

Some of the diseases caused by pathogenic bacteria include diphtheria, tuberculosis, typhoid fever, tetanus, Hansen disease, syphilis, cholera, and bubonic plague. Bacteria cause these diseases in one of two general ways. They may damage the cells and tissues of the infected organism directly by breaking down its living cells to use for food. Or they may release toxins (poisons) that travel throughout the body, interfering with the normal activity of the host.

Many bacteria can be grown in a culture dish without depending on a host organism. One class of bacteria known as Rickettsiae (rih-KEHT-see-ee) are a curious exception to this rule. In order for Rickettsiae to grow, they must be inside a living cell. In this respect, Rickettsiae are similar to viruses. Rickettsiae seem to possess "leaky" cell walls and membranes that allow them to live directly inside a living cell and absorb nutrients from the cell's cytoplasm. Rickettsiae cause Rocky Mountain spotted fever, typhus, and Legionnaires' disease.

Although we shall discuss the medical measures that are used to fight disease in Chapter 45, it is worth pointing out that many of these diseases can be prevented by stimulating the body's immune system through the use of vaccines. If an infection does occur, however, there are many more effective measures to fight the infection if it is bacterial than if it is viral. These measures include a number of drugs and natural compounds, known as **antibiotics**, that can attack and destroy bacteria. One of the major reasons for the dramatic increase in life expectancy in the last two centuries is an increased understanding of how to prevent and cure bacterial infections.

Controlling Bacteria

Although most bacteria are harmless and many are beneficial, the risks of bacterial infection are great enough to warrant efforts to control bacterial growth.

STERILIZATION The growth of potentially dangerous bacteria can be controlled by sterilization. This process destroys living bacteria by subjecting them either to great heat or to chemical action. Heating is the simplest way to control bacterial growth. Bacteria cannot survive high temperatures for a long time, so most can be killed in boiling water.

An entire hospital, of course, cannot be dropped into boiling water. But it can be sterilized, one room at a time, by using disinfectants. A disinfectant is a chemical solution that kills bacteria. Disinfectants are also used in the home to clean bathrooms, kitchens, and other rooms where bacteria may grow and spoil food or cause disease.

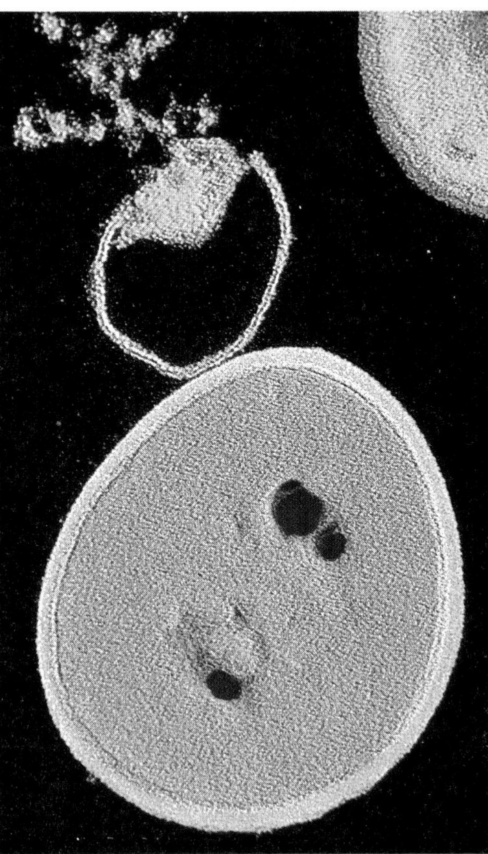

Figure 17–22 The addition of an antibiotic, or a substance that destroys bacteria, has caused the bacterium Staphylococcus aureus *to burst.*

FOOD PROCESSING As you have learned, bacteria are everywhere, including in our food. If we are not careful, the bacteria will begin to "eat" our food before we do. In doing so, the bacteria will cause the food to spoil. One method to stop food from spoiling is to refrigerate those foods in which bacteria might grow. Bacteria, like most organisms, grow slowly at low temperatures. For this reason, food that is stored at a lower temperature will keep longer because the bacteria will take much longer to grow and cause damage. In addition, many kinds of food are sterilized by boiling, frying, or steaming them. Each of these cooking techniques raises the temperature of the food to a point where all the bacteria are killed.

If the food is to be preserved for a long time by canning, the sterilized food must be immediately placed into sterile glass jars or metal cans and sealed. Food that has been properly canned will last almost indefinitely. Finally, a number of chemical treatments will inhibit the growth of bacteria in food. These include treating food with everyday chemicals such as salt, vinegar, or sugar. Salted meat, pickled vegetables, and jam are examples of chemically preserved foods.

17–3 SECTION REVIEW

1. What are some diseases caused by viruses? By bacteria?
2. How can viral and bacterial diseases be prevented? How can they be treated?
3. Describe several methods of controlling bacterial growth.
4. Why is it important to cook food thoroughly before canning?

LABORATORY INVESTIGATION

EXAMINING BACTERIA

PROBLEM

What are some of the characteristics of bacteria?

MATERIALS *(per group)*

100-mL beaker
10 lima beans
2 medicine droppers
2 glass slides
2 coverslips
microscope
methylene blue
flat toothpick

PROCEDURE

1. Fill the beaker halfway with water. Put the lima beans in the beaker and then put the beaker and its contents in a warm place where they will remain undisturbed overnight.
2. After 24 hours, examine the beaker to make sure that the beans are covered with water. If necessary, add more water to cover the beans. Again put the beaker of beans in a warm place overnight.
3. After 48 hours, the water in the beaker should appear cloudy because of the presence of a large number of bacteria. Using a medicine dropper, remove a drop of water from the beaker and place it in the center of a clean glass slide.
4. Cover the drop of water with a coverslip. Examine the drop of water under the low-power objective of the microscope.
5. Examine the drop of water under the high-power objective. **CAUTION:** *When switching to the high-power objective, you should always look at the objective from the side of your microscope so that the objective does not hit or damage the slide.* Notice the shapes and methods of movement of the bacteria.
6. With the second medicine dropper, place a drop of methylene blue in the center of a clean glass slide.
7. Using the broad end of a flat toothpick, gently scrape the inside of your cheek. The scraping should contain some of your cheek cells. Using the same end of the toothpick, mix the scraping from your cheek with the drop of methylene blue.
8. Add a drop of water from the beaker containing the beans to the mixture of cheek scraping and methylene blue. Cover this mixture with a clean coverslip.
9. Locate a cheek cell under the low-power objective of the microscope. Then switch to the high-power objective and use the fine adjustment to locate some bacteria near a cheek cell.
10. Observe the sizes of the bacteria, the cheek cell, and the nucleus of the cheek cell.

OBSERVATIONS

1. Describe the colors and shapes of the bacteria.
2. Are the bacteria arranged singly, in pairs, in chains, or in clusters?
3. Are the bacteria capable of movement? If so, describe the ways in which they move.
4. Compare the size of the bacteria to the sizes of the cheek cell and the nucleus of the cheek cell.

ANALYSIS AND CONCLUSIONS

1. What was the source of the bacteria? How were they able to grow in the beaker containing water and lima beans?
2. Explain why methylene blue was added to the scraping from the cheek.
3. Bacteria are prokaryotic cells, whereas cheek cells are eukaryotic cells. Explain this statement.

STUDENT STUDY GUIDE

SUMMARIZING THE CONCEPTS

The key concepts in each section of this chapter are listed below to help you review the chapter content. Make sure you understand each concept and its relationship to other concepts and to the theme of this chapter.

17–1 Viruses

- A virus is a noncellular particle made up of genetic material and protein.
- Viruses cannot carry out any life processes unless they are within a living host cell.
- Infection and destruction of the host cell by a virus is called a lytic infection.
- In a lysogenic infection, the virus does not reproduce at once and lyse the host cell.

17–2 Monerans—Prokaryotic Cells

- Bacteria are prokaryotes, or cells that do not have a nucleus.
- Rod-shaped bacteria are called bacilli; spherical bacteria are called cocci; and spiral-shaped bacteria are called spirilla.
- Obligate aerobes need oxygen to live. Obligate anaerobes must live in the absence of oxygen. Facultative anaerobes can survive with or without oxygen.
- Some bacteria reproduce by binary fission or conjugation.
- Many bacteria form a symbiotic relationship with other organisms. Some are saprophytes.
- Many bacteria can take nitrogen from the air and convert it into a form that plants can use to make proteins.

17–3 Diseases Caused by Viruses and Monerans

- Although vaccines are the only successful protection against some viral diseases, interferons are being considered as another possible treatment. Antibiotics are substances that can attack and destroy bacteria.

REVIEWING KEY TERMS

Vocabulary terms are important to your understanding of biology. The key terms listed below are those you should be especially familiar with. Review these terms and their meanings. Then use each term in a complete sentence. If you are not sure of a term's meaning, return to the appropriate section and review its definition.

17–1 Viruses

virus
bacteriophage
lytic infection
lysogenic infection
prophage
retrovirus
parasite

17–2 Monerans—Prokaryotic Cells

prokaryote
bacterium
methanogen
bacillus
coccus
spirillum
phototrophic autotroph
chemotrophic autotroph
chemotrophic heterotroph
phototrophic heterotroph
obligate aerobe
obligate anaerobe
toxin
facultative anaerobe
binary fission
conjugation
endospore
symbiosis
saprophyte
nitrogen fixation

17–3 Diseases Caused by Viruses and Monerans

pathogen
antibiotic

CHAPTER REVIEW

CONTENT REVIEW

Multiple Choice

Choose the letter of the answer that best completes each statement.

1. Viruses contain
   a. cell walls. c. nuclei.
   b. cell membranes. d. protein coats.
2. Viruses that invade cells and cause them to burst are said to be
   a. parasitic. c. saprophytic.
   b. lysogenic. d. lytic.
3. Methanogens are members of the phylum
   a. Cyanobacteria. c. Prochlorobacteria.
   b. Archaebacteria. d. Eubacteria.
4. A rod-shaped bacterium is known as a
   a. spirillum. c. coccus.
   b. bacillus. d. virus.
5. Organisms that need a constant supply of oxygen in order to live are called
   a. obligate anaerobes.
   b. facultative anaerobes.
   c. chemotrophic autotrophs.
   d. obligate aerobes.
6. A structure that forms when a bacterium produces a thick internal wall that encloses its DNA and part of its cytoplasm is called a (an)
   a. endospore. c. prophage.
   b. capsid. d. spirillum.
7. Organisms that use the complex molecules of once-living organisms for energy and nutrition are called
   a. parasites. c. saprophytes.
   b. viruses. d. eukaryotes.
8. An example of a disease caused by a bacterium is
   a. influenza. c. AIDS.
   b. measles. d. syphilis.

True or False

Determine whether each statement is true or false. If it is true, write "true." If it is false, change the underlined word or words to make the statement true.

1. In a <u>lysogenic</u> infection, the virus does not reproduce and lyse its host cell immediately.
2. A virus is composed of a <u>nucleus</u> surrounded by a protein coat.
3. Bacteria are <u>eukaryotes</u>.
4. <u>Spirilla</u> are spherical bacteria.
5. Bacteria that can live with or without oxygen are known as <u>obligate</u> anaerobes.
6. Monerans that trap the energy of sunlight in a manner similar to green plants are called <u>chemotrophic</u> autotrophs.
7. In bacteria, <u>spore formation</u> involves the transferring of genetic material from one cell to another cell.
8. <u>Methanogens</u> are disease-causing agents.

Word Relationships

A. *In each of the following sets of terms, three of the terms are related. One term does not belong. Determine the characteristic common to three of the terms and then identify the term that does not belong.*

1. obligate anaerobe, facultative anaerobe, phototrophic autotroph, obligate aerobe
2. *E. coli*, T4, *Rhizobium*, *Salmonella*
3. prophage, bacillus, spirillum, coccus
4. measles, polio, rabies, tetanus

B. *An analogy is a relationship between two pairs of words or phrases generally written in the following manner: a:b::c:d. The symbol : is read "is to," and the symbol :: is read "as." For example, cat:animal::rose:plant is read "cat is to animal as rose is to plant."*

In the analogies that follow, a word or phrase is missing. Complete each analogy by providing the missing word or phrase.

5. eukaryote:human::prokaryote:________________
6. rod-shaped:bacillus::spherical:________________
7. oxygen:obligate aerobe::no oxygen:________________
8. eubacteria:true bacteria::cyanobacteria:________________

CONCEPT MASTERY

Use your understanding of the concepts developed in the chapter to answer each of the following in a brief paragraph.

1. Why are viruses considered parasites?
2. What is the relationship between cell wall structure and whether a bacterium is Gram positive or Gram negative?
3. What is the difference between bacterial autotrophs and heterotrophs?
4. Describe a symbiotic relationship between bacteria and another organism.
5. What are some ways in which bacteria are important to the environment?
6. Compare the different methods of bacterial reproduction.

CRITICAL AND CREATIVE THINKING

Discuss each of the following in a brief paragraph.

1. **Interpreting graphs** Describe the growth of the bacteria shown in the graph. Explain why growth levels off in stage 3.

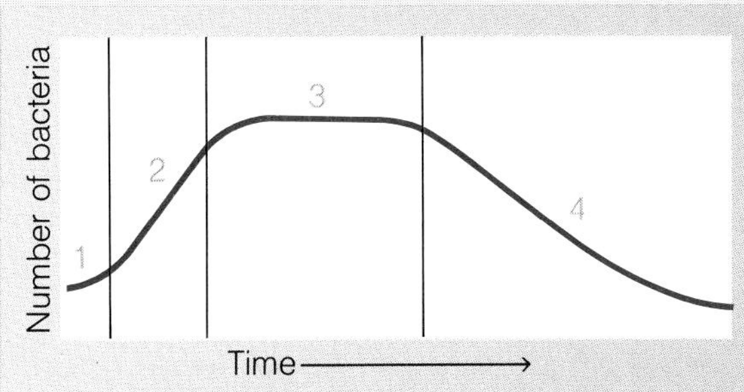

2. **Relating concepts** Bacteria can be grown in the laboratory on synthetic media. Can viruses be grown in this way? Can viruses be grown on cultures of bacteria?
3. **Using the writing process** As you know, many diseases are caused by microorganisms. Imagine that you have the ability to develop a chemical capable of wiping out all viruses and monerans on Earth. Write an advertising campaign for your new chemical in which you describe its benefits and dangers.
4. **Using the writing process** In *The War of the Worlds*, a wonderful book written by H. G. Wells, Earth is invaded by aliens. No weapons can kill the invaders, and the Earth seems doomed. The Earth is saved, however, when the invaders die from diseases they contract here. Using a similar premise, write a story about people from Earth voyaging to another planet some time in the future.

CHAPTER 18

Protists

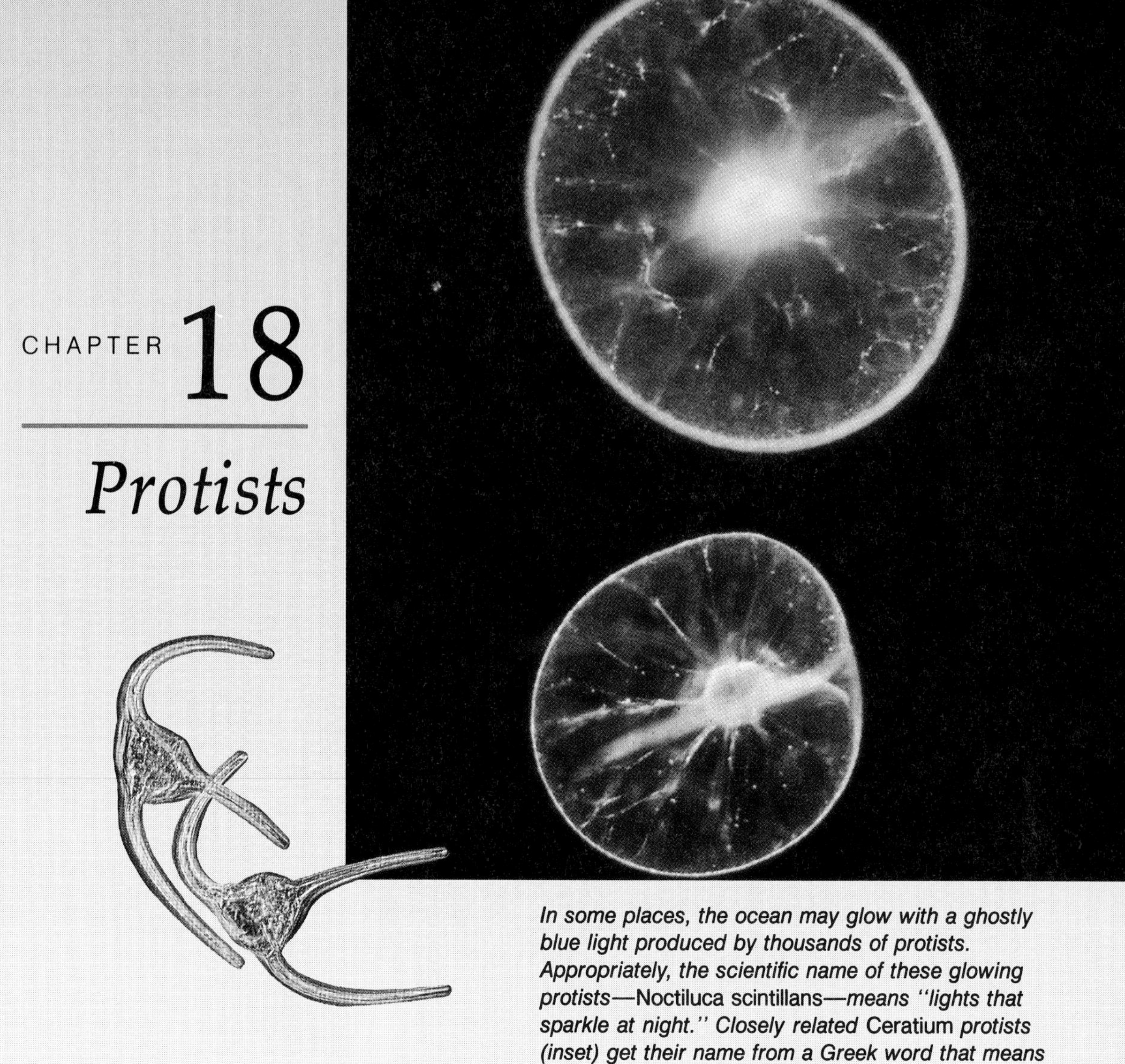

*In some places, the ocean may glow with a ghostly blue light produced by thousands of protists. Appropriately, the scientific name of these glowing protists—*Noctiluca scintillans*—means "lights that sparkle at night." Closely related* Ceratium *protists (inset) get their name from a Greek word that means horn or antler.*

On a moonless night, a fishing boat motors toward a New England harbor. The dark water sparkles in its wake, glittering in a thousand places and leaving a ghostly glowing tail as it makes its way to port. Half a world away, the sun is high over a village in equatorial Africa. Although it is harvest time and many members of his family are in the fields working, a young man shudders in his bed, delirious from the burning fever of malaria. These two scenes, as different as they are, have one fundamental biological fact in common: The glowing ocean and the ravages of malaria are both produced by protists—organisms that belong to the kingdom Protista, the first kingdom of eukaryotic organisms.

CHAPTER OUTLINE

18–1 The Kingdom Protista

Section Objectives

- Describe the major characteristics of protists.
- Discuss the Endosymbiont Hypothesis.

The first kingdom of eukaryotic organisms (organisms whose cells contain nuclei and membrane-enclosed organelles) that we will consider is the kingdom **Protista**. The name is appropriate, for it is derived from a Greek word that means first. The term **protist** refers to any member of the kingdom Protista. **Protists are defined as being unicellular, or single-celled, eukaryotic organisms.** However, as you will discover later in this chapter, a few types of protists stretch the concept of unicellular. Many protists are solitary, which means that they live as individual cells. However, other protists are colonial, which means that they live in groups of individuals of the same species that are attached to one another.

As you learned in Chapter 16, the oldest fossils of monerans (single-celled organisms that lack a nucleus and membrane-enclosed organelles) are more than 3.5 billion years old. Compared with the kingdom Monera, the kingdom Protista is relatively young—the oldest fossils of protists are only about 1.5 billion years old. This indicates that the evolution of the first eukaryote may have taken nearly 2 billion years.

Classification of Protists

The kingdom Protista is an extremely diverse group that includes more than 115,000 species. In the past, many of these species were extremely difficult to classify because they had characteristics in common with more than one of the three kingdoms of multicellular organisms: Animalia (animals), Plantae (plants), and Fungi. The kingdom Protista was created

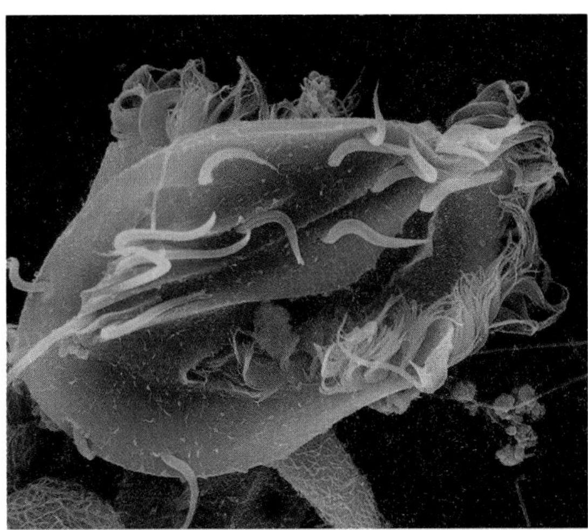

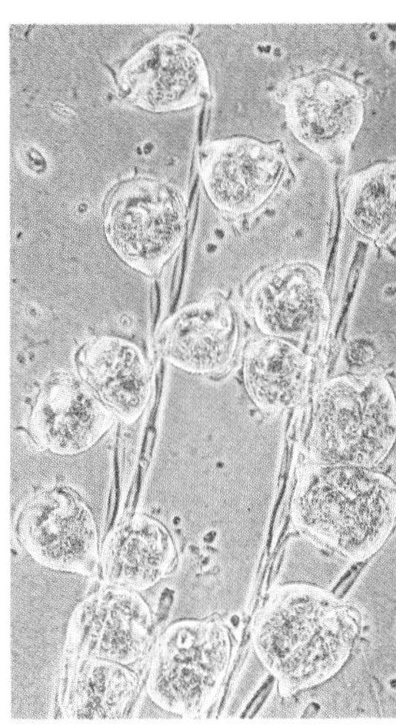

__Figure 18–1__ This solitary protist zips through the water by means of swimming bristles formed of fused cilia (left). These colonial protists also have cilia. However, they lead a less active existence because they are attached to one another and to a base such as a stone or a water plant.

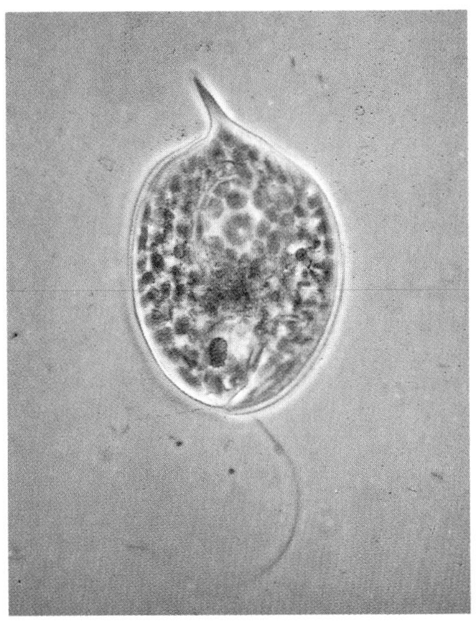

Figure 18–2 Protists often share characteristics with more than one multicellular kingdom. Some are photosynthetic like plants and can move like animals (bottom). Others are similar to fungi in life cycle and appearance but move like animals and have cells that are more like those of animals than those of fungi (top).

primarily to solve the problem of classifying these difficult organisms and only partly because the protists may share an evolutionary ancestry. In fact, the American biologist Lynn Margulis wrote that the kingdom Protista "is defined by exclusion: its members are neither animals . . . , plants . . . , fungi . . . , nor prokaryotes."

Scientists do not agree on how organisms in the kingdom Protista should be classified. They do not even agree on which organisms should be considered protists! However, most would agree that there is much we can learn from protists. In this chapter we will examine the major kinds of protists and see what roles they play in the living world.

Evolution of Protists

Where did the first protists come from? Did prokaryotic cells gradually evolve nuclei? For many years, most biologists considered this a reasonable explanation. In recent years, however, biologist Lynn Margulis has revived an alternative explanation—one that many biologists now find persuasive. She suggests that the first protist cell was formed by a symbiosis among several prokaryotes. (Symbiosis literally means living together and is defined as the living together in close association of dissimilar organisms.)

Margulis noted that a number of organelles in eukaryotic cells are very similar in structure to prokaryotes. For example, mitochondria and chloroplasts closely resemble bacteria and blue-green bacteria, respectively. The flagella and cilia of many eukaryotic cells are similar to a group of bacteria known as the spirochetes. The similarities between organelles and prokaryotes, Margulis reasoned, are not merely coincidental—organelles are descended from symbiotic prokaryotes.

According to Margulis's **Endosymbiont Hypothesis**, these prokaryotes lived within another moneran as endosymbionts (symbiotic organisms that live within another organism, which is called the host organism). The endosymbionts and their

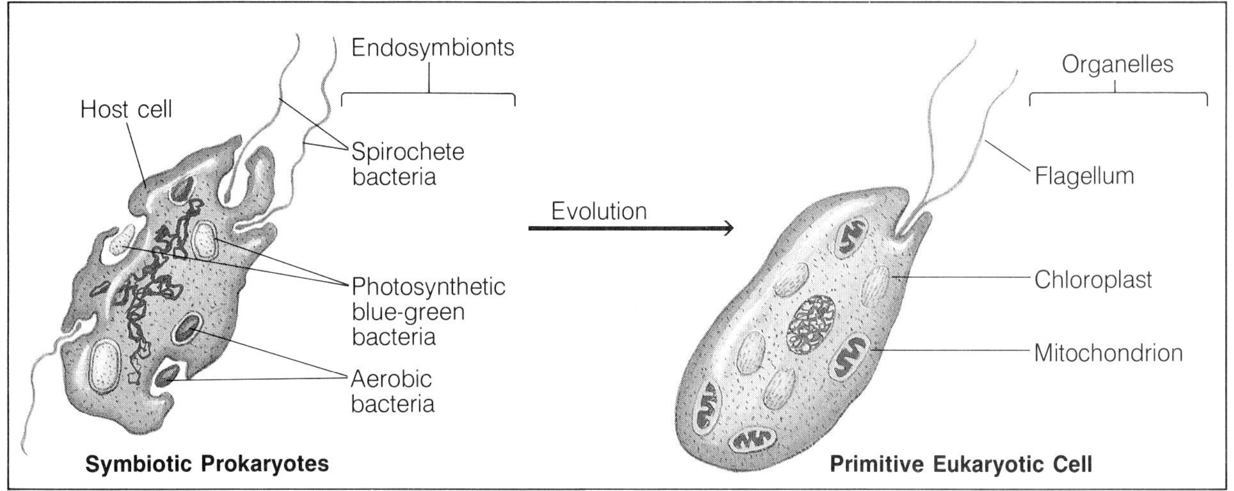

Figure 18–3 *According to the Endosymbiont Hypothesis, the organelles in eukaryotic cells evolved from symbiotic prokaryotes that lived inside a host cell.*

host cell formed an effective team—each member benefited from the relationship. But eventually the endosymbionts lost their independence, were unable to live without one another or outside the host cell, and gave rise to the organelles that we observe today in eukaryotic cells.

We will never be sure that Margulis's Endosymbiont Hypothesis is correct. But it does provide a model for how the first eukaryotic cell—the first protist—may have developed. Is there something in nature that supports this model? Are there cells alive today that suggest this is a reasonable idea?

The answer to each of these questions is yes. The protist *Cyanophora paradoxa* was first thought to be a kind of alga. However, it was soon learned that the "chloroplasts" within it were not chloroplasts at all. They were blue-green bacteria that could be removed from the cell in which they lived as endosymbionts. They could be grown outside the rest of the cell! The relationship between *Cyanophora paradoxa* and its blue-green bacteria may be similar to the relationships that produced the first protists. Thus when we examine a present-day eukaryotic cell, we may actually be dealing with the descendants of more than one organism!

18–1 SECTION REVIEW

1. What are protists? When did protists first appear on Earth?
2. What evidence has led scientists to believe that symbiosis played an important role in the evolution of protists?
3. How might the Endosymbiont Hypothesis explain the double membranes that surround organelles such as the nucleus, chloroplast, and mitochondrion?

Section Objectives

- Name and describe the four phyla of animallike protists.
- Discuss how animallike protists fit into the world.

18–2 Animallike Protists

At one time, many of the protists were called protozoa, which means first animals. Protozoa were classified separately from more plantlike protists. But biologists have found that the similarities between some animallike protists and the plantlike protists are so great that it no longer makes sense to place each in a separate kingdom. Four phyla within the kingdom Protista, however, are known as the animallike protists. These are the first protists that we shall examine.

Figure 18–4 Ciliates include trumpet-shaped Stentor *(top) and egg-shaped* Didinium *(bottom). As you can see,* Didinium *is a carnivore that feeds on other ciliates such as* Paramecium.

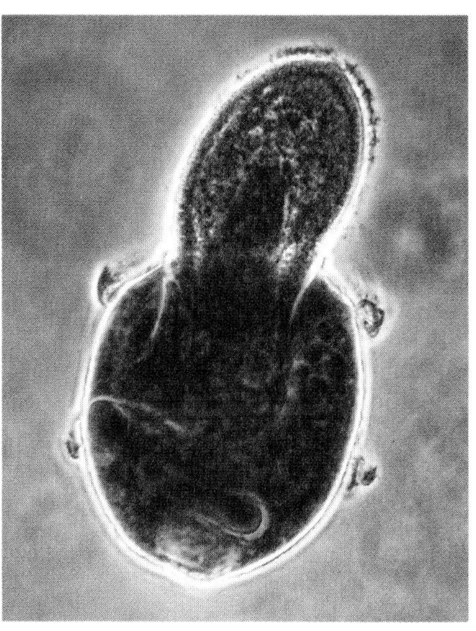

Ciliophora: Cilia-bearing Protists

Members of the phylum **Ciliophora** (sihl-ee-AHF-uh-rah) are either solitary or colonial organisms. These organisms are often known as **ciliates** (SIHL-ee-ihts) because they have **cilia** (singular: cilium). (Ciliophora literally means cilia-bearing.) Cilia are short hairlike projections that produce movement. The internal structure of cilia consists of microtubulelike structures. The beating of cilia, like the pull of hundreds of oars in an ancient ship, propels the cell rapidly through water. Ciliates are found in both fresh and salt water—many may live in a lake or stream near your home.

More than 7000 species of ciliates are known. Most ciliates are free-living, which means that they do not exist as parasites or symbionts. A well-studied example of the ciliates is found in the genus *Paramecium.*

A **paramecium** is a large organism (as unicellular organisms go)—as much as 350 micrometers in length. In the electron microscope, the cell membrane and cilia can be observed closely. A paramecium's cell membrane and associated underlying structures make up a complex living outer layer called the **pellicle** (PEHL-ih-kuhl). The pellicle is folded in a repeating pattern that gives the surface of the cell a quiltlike appearance. Embedded in the pellicle are a series of tiny flask-shaped structures known as **trichocysts** (TRIHK-oh-sihsts). Trichocysts are used for defense. When a paramecium is confronted by serious danger, the trichocysts discharge. The spiny projections produced in this way can injure a nearby cell as well as cover a paramecium with protective bristles.

Like almost all ciliates, a paramecium possesses two different kinds of nuclei. Each cell normally has a **macronucleus** and a smaller **micronucleus**. We will examine the roles that these two kinds of nuclei play when we consider the process of reproduction in ciliates.

A paramecium obtains food by using its cilia to force water into the **gullet**, an indentation in one side of the cell. Particles that include bits of food such as bacteria are trapped in the gullet and then forced into cavities called **food vacuoles** that form at the base of the gullet. The food vacuoles break off into the cytoplasm and eventually fuse with lysosomes, which are

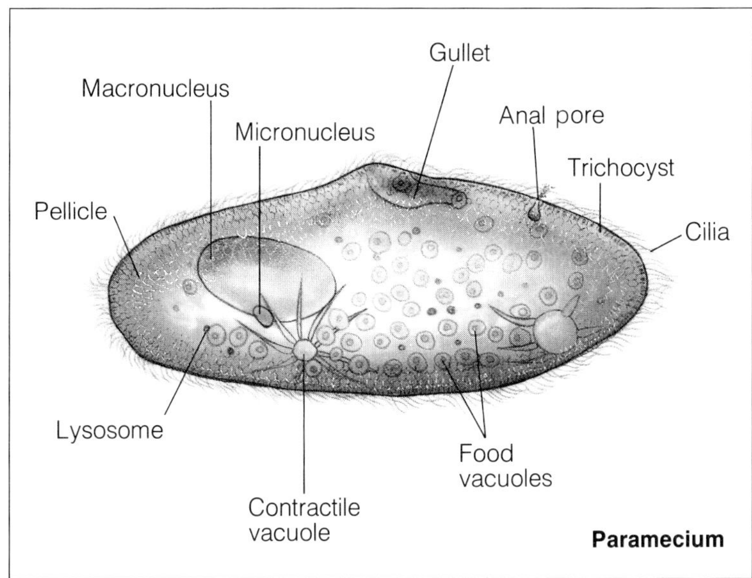

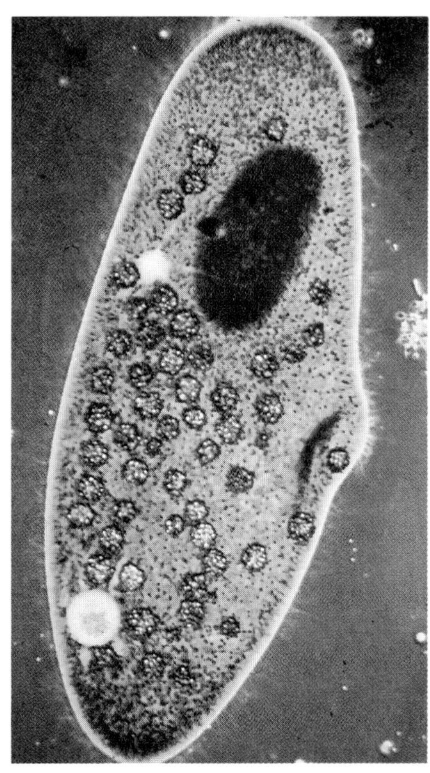

Figure 18–5 *The essential life functions of a paramecium are divided among many organelles (left), several of which can be seen in this live paramecium (right). The small green circles are food vacuoles that contain bits of algae.*

organelles that contain digestive enzymes. Thus the material in the food vacuoles is digested and the organism obtains the nourishment it requires. Waste materials are emptied into the environment when the food vacuole fuses with a region of the cell membrane called the **anal pore**.

Excess water (which moves into a cell in fresh water because of osmosis) is collected in other vacuoles. These vacuoles empty into canals that are arranged in a star-shaped pattern around structures known as **contractile vacuoles**. When a contractile vacuole is filled with water, it "contracts" quickly and pumps water out of the cell.

Under most conditions, a paramecium reproduces asexually by means of a form of mitotic cell division called binary fission. During this process, a single paramecium elongates, its gullet splits into two, and the cell divides in half crosswise. Binary fission results in two cells that are genetically identical.

Under certain circumstances, including starvation and temperature stress, paramecia will engage in a form of sexual reproduction known as conjugation. Refer to Figure 18-7 on page 386 as you read about the process of conjugation. In the first stages of conjugation, two paramecia attach themselves to each other. Their macronuclei disintegrate, and their diploid (2N) micronuclei undergo meiosis. When meiosis is complete, each paramecium contains 4 haploid (N) micronuclei. In the next stages of conjugation, 3 of the 4 micronuclei disintegrate. The 1 remaining micronucleus then divides to form 2 genetically identical haploid micronuclei. The paramecia exchange one set

Figure 18–6 *A paramecium can discharge its trichocysts to produce a shield of protective bristles.*

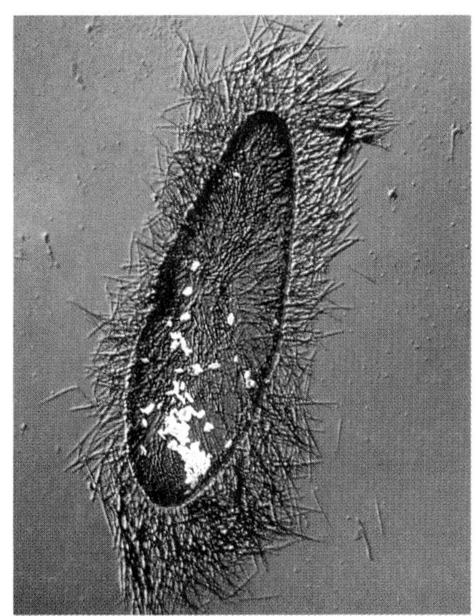

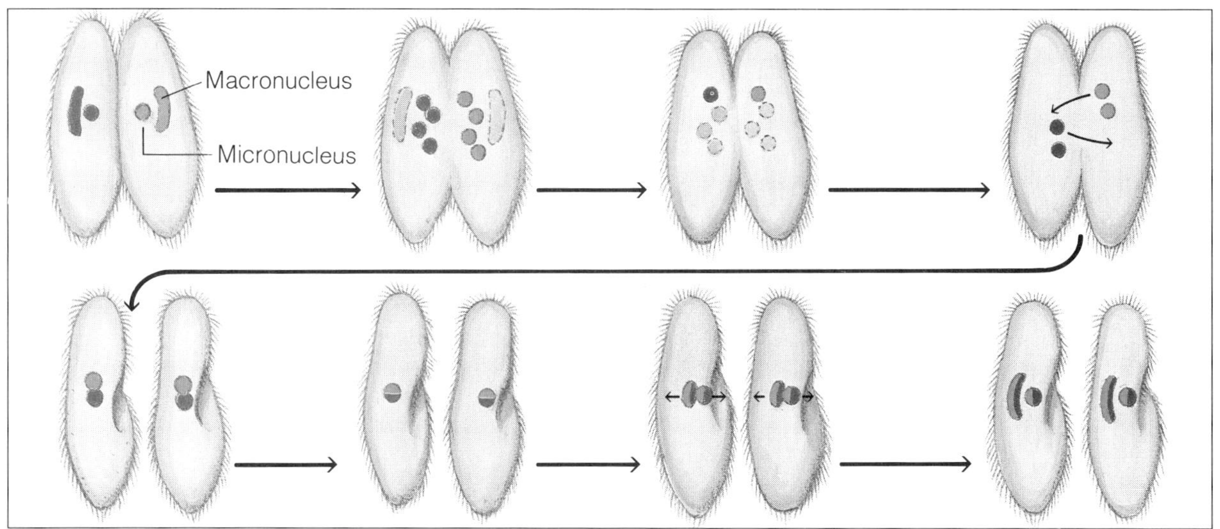

Figure 18–7 *In the process of conjugation, two paramecia join together and share genetic information. Conjugation produces new combinations of genes—combinations that may give paramecia a better chance of survival.*

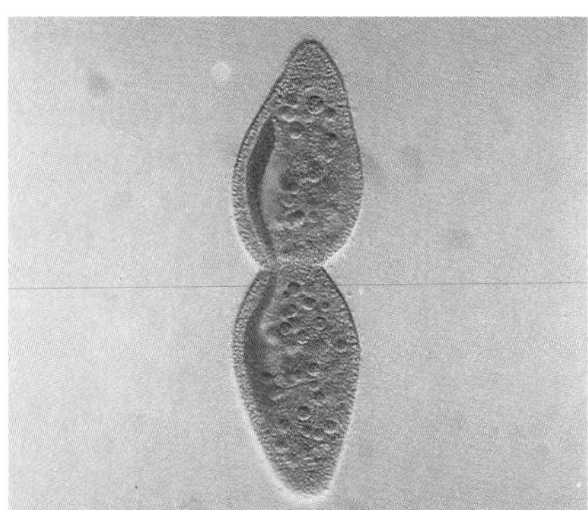

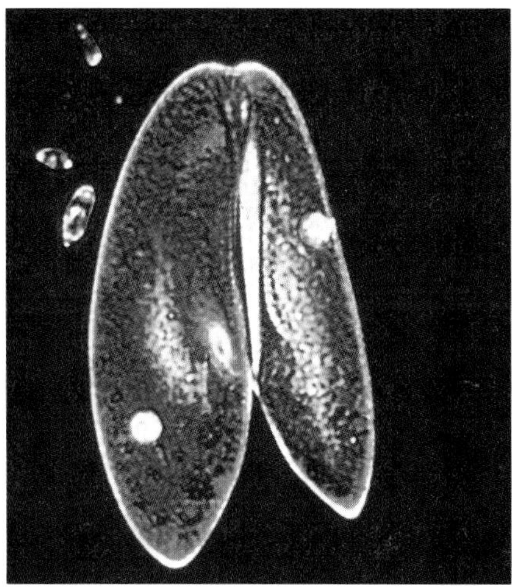

Figure 18–8 *Paramecia usually reproduce asexually through binary fission (top). Under certain circumstances, paramecia will undergo a form of sexual reproduction called conjugation (bottom).*

of micronuclei, so that each cell has 1 micronucleus obtained from the other cell and 1 micronucleus of its own. In the final stage of conjugation, the paramecia separate from each other. The 2 haploid micronuclei in each paramecium fuse to form a new diploid micronucleus. From the new micronucleus, a new macronucleus is formed. The two paramecia that participated in conjugation are now genetically identical.

Strictly speaking, conjugation is not reproduction. No new cells are produced—2 cells enter conjugation and 2 leave it. Nonetheless, it is still a sexual process. New combinations of genetic information are produced. Within a large population, the process of conjugation helps to create genetic diversity and ensures the ultimate survival of the species.

Zoomastigina: Animallike Protists with Flagella

The phylum **Zoomastigina** (zoh-oh-mas-tuh-GIGH-nuh) consists of animallike protists that move through the water by means of **flagella**. Flagella are long, whiplike projections that have an internal structure identical to that of cilia. The number of flagella varies from one zoomastiginan to the next, ranging from one to four or more. Because they have flagella, zoomastiginans are called **flagellates**. The term flagellate is also used for plantlike protists and unicellular algae that have flagella. Because of this, zoomastiginans are sometimes called zooflagellates, which means animal flagellates.

Zoomastiginans are generally able to absorb food through their cell membranes, which are not enclosed in shells or cell

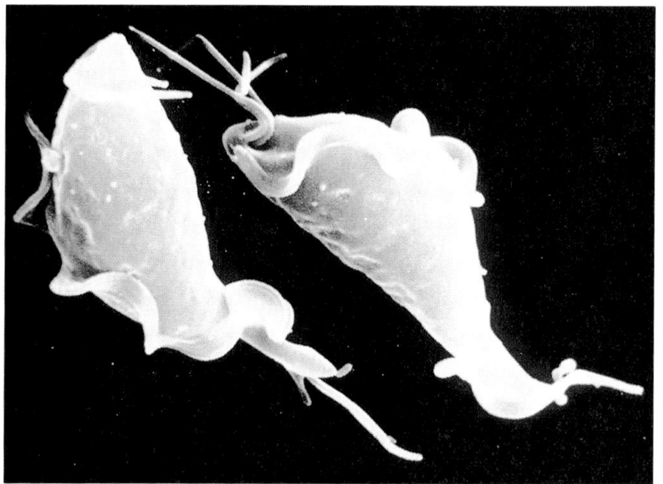

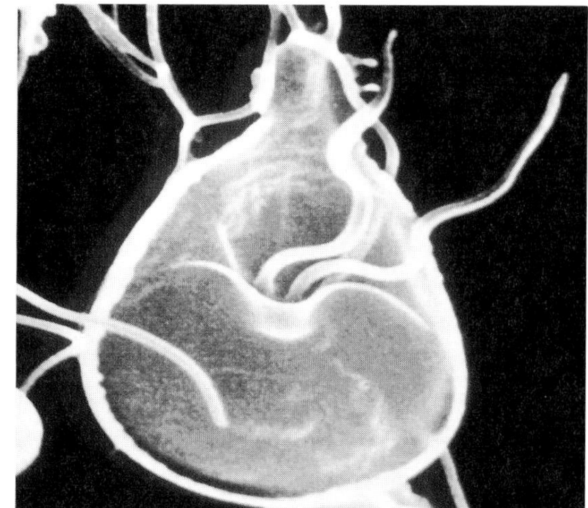

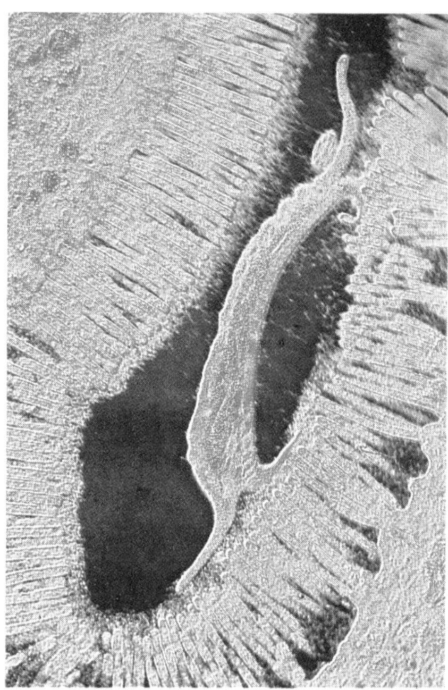

Figure 18–9 *Many zoomastiginans are parasites.* Giardia *(top, right and bottom) attaches to the lining of the small intestine in humans, causing much irritation and digestive disturbance.* Trichomonas *(top, left) causes intestinal and venereal diseases in humans. It is also responsible for a number of diseases in livestock and poultry.*

walls. Some zoomastiginans have found special environments in which they are able to find enough food to absorb. Others live within the bodies of other organisms, taking advantage of the food that the larger organism provides.

Zoomastiginans can reproduce asexually by binary fission, although most also have a sexual life cycle as well. During sexual reproduction, gamete cells are produced by meiosis. Sometimes meiosis is triggered by a change in the food supply or in the amount of oxygen in the water. In some species, meiosis occurs only at certain times of the year. The gametes formed by meiosis fuse together, forming an organism with a new combination of genetic information.

Some zoomastiginans are found in lakes and ponds. Others exist as parasites or symbionts of other organisms. You will learn about the relationships of these zoomastiginans to other organisms shortly, when we consider how the animallike protists fit into the world.

Sporozoa: Spore-producing Parasitic Protists

The members of the phylum **Sporozoa** (spohr-oh-ZOH-uh) are nonmotile, which means that they do not move. All sporozoans are parasitic; that is, they live in a host organism and cause it harm. Sporozoans are parasites on a wide variety of other organisms, including worms, insects, fish, birds, and humans. Many sporozoans have complex life cycles that involve more than one host. Sporozoans reproduce by means of spores, which are cells or groups of cells enclosed in a protective membrane. Under the right conditions, spores are able to attach themselves to a host cell, penetrate it, and then live within it as parasites. A typical sporozoan is *Plasmodium,* which causes the human disease malaria.

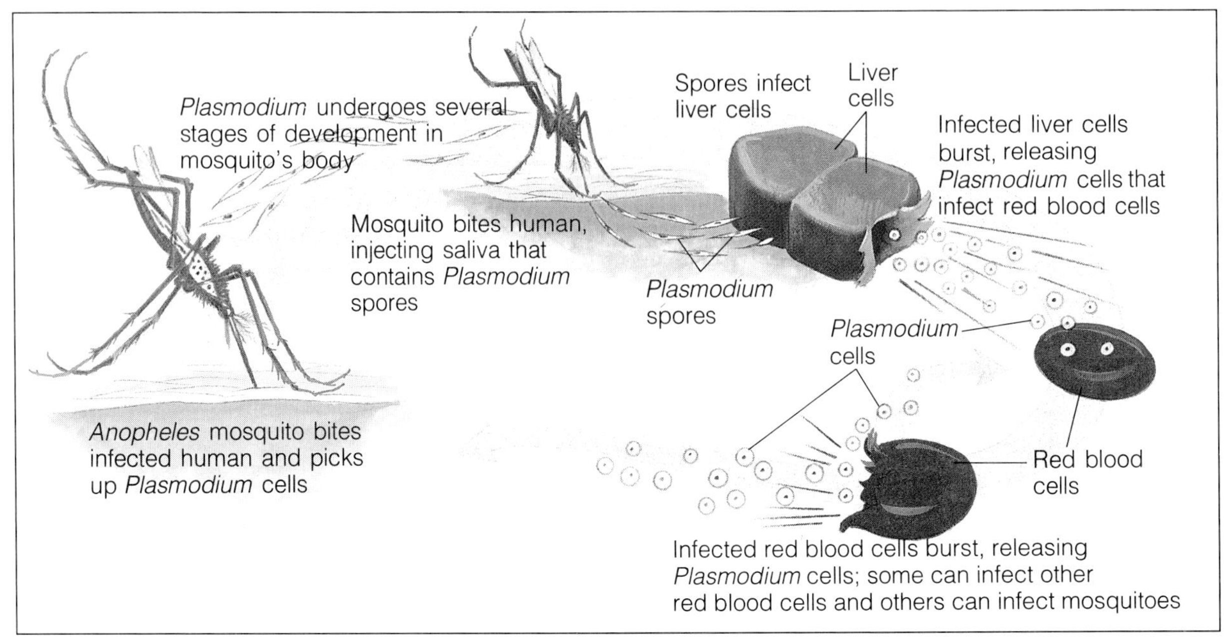

Figure 18–10 Plasmodium *causes the human disease malaria.*

Malaria is carried by the *Anopheles* (uh-NAHF-uh-leez) mosquito. When an infected mosquito bites a human, some of its saliva, which contains spores of the parasite, is injected into the bloodstream. Once inside the body, *Plasmodium* infects liver cells and then red blood cells. *Plasmodium* grows rapidly within the infected cells and eventually causes these cells to burst at intervals of 48 or 72 hours. When millions of parasite-filled red blood cells burst, they dump large amounts of toxins into the bloodstream. The toxins produce chills and fever—the symptoms of malaria.

Figure 18–11 *Malaria is transmitted to a human through the bite of an infected mosquito.*

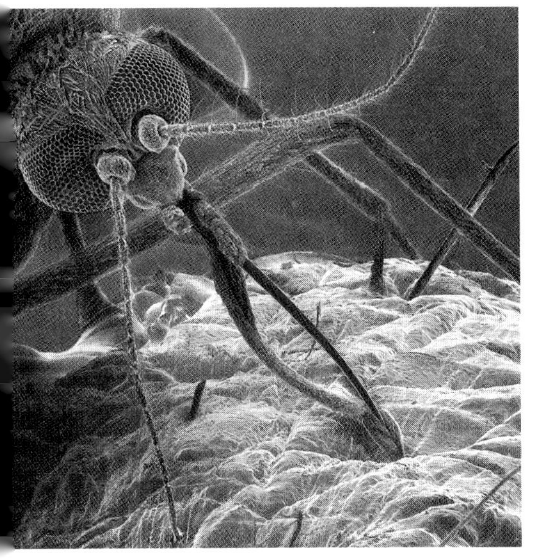

The disease is transmitted back to the mosquito if a mosquito bites a human infected with malaria. The blood that the mosquito swallows contains *Plasmodium.* In the insect's digestive system, *Plasmodium* grows rapidly and penetrates the insect's entire body, including the salivary glands. After a time, the infected insect contains active *Plasmodium* spores in its saliva and is able to pass the infection on to another human. Malaria is a serious disease that weakens an infected individual and may lead to death. In areas of the world where *Anopheles* mosquitoes flourish, malaria is a serious problem. Every year, more than 250 million people suffer from malaria, and more than 2 million people die from it. Although drugs such as chloroquinine are effective against some forms of the disease, many strains of malaria-causing *Plasmodium* sporozoans are resistant to these drugs. To date, the most effective way to control malaria is to destroy breeding areas for *Anopheles* mosquitoes. This interrupts the life cycle of *Plasmodium* and thus prevents the spread of malaria.

Sarcodina: Protists with False Feet

The phylum **Sarcodina** (sahr-kuh-DIGH-nuh) contains protists that use temporary projections of cytoplasm to move and feed. Such a projection is called a **pseudopod** (SOO-doh-pahd), which literally means false foot. Pseudopods are usually thought of as being rounded and broad. However, some sarcodines have thin, strandlike pseudopods and others have weblike pseudopods. The name Sarcodina comes from the word sarcode, which was coined in the nineteenth century to describe the homogeneous "jelly" from which these cells were thought to be composed.

One major family of Sarcodina is the **amebas**. Amebas are flexible, active cells without cell walls, flagella, cilia, and even a definite shape. Amebas move by means of thick pseudopods, which they extend out of the central mass of the cell. The cytoplasm of the cell streams into the pseudopod, and the rest of the cell follows. This motion is known as ameboid movement.

An ameba is capable of capturing and eating particles of food and even other cells. It does so by first surrounding its meal with streaming cytoplasm and then taking it inside the cell to form a food vacuole. Once inside the cell, the material is digested rapidly and the nutrients are passed along to the rest of the cell. Amebas reproduce by means of binary fission—one large ameba divides by mitosis to produce two smaller, but genetically identical, amebas.

Amebas are not the only members of the phylum Sarcodina. The phylum also includes three groups known as heliozoans, radiolarians, and foraminifers (for-uh-MIHN-ih-ferz). Most of these protists are beautiful organisms that produce external shells to help support their unusual shapes. Although some heliozoans and radiolarians do not have shells, many produce delicate shells of silica (SiO_2), a glasslike substance.

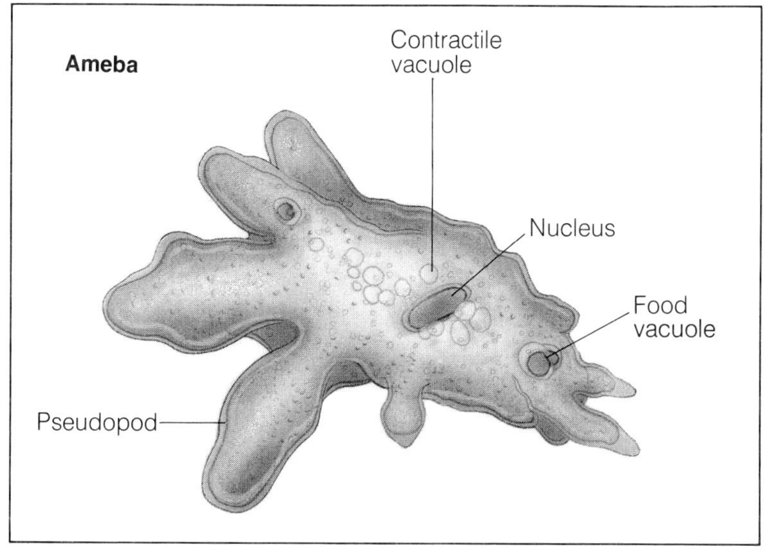

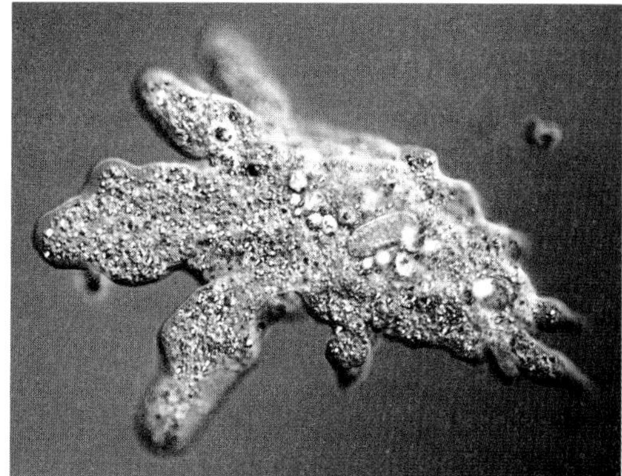

Figure 18–12 *Although a live ameba may at first appear to be a featureless blob (right), careful study reveals its internal structure is well-organized.*

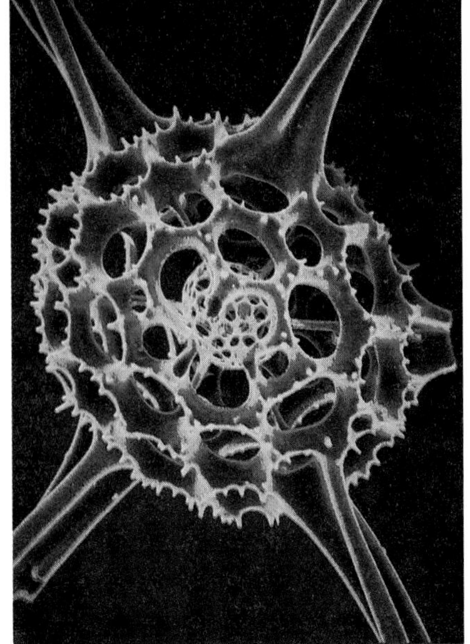

Figure 18–13 Radiolarians have delicate shells of silica.

Foraminifers secrete shells of calcium carbonate ($CaCO_3$). These protists are abundant in the warmer regions of the oceans. As foraminifers die, the calcium carbonate from their shells accumulates on the ocean bottom. In some regions, thick deposits of foraminifer skeletons have formed on the ocean floor. The white chalk cliffs of Dover, England, are huge deposits of foraminifer skeletons that were raised above sea level by geological processes.

Most species of foraminifers are known not from living specimens but from fossils of their skeletons. Because they have continued to change and evolve over millions of years, the species of foraminifers found in sedimentary rocks are useful measures of the ages of such rocks. By examining foraminifer fossils from rock samples, geologists can determine the age of the samples. This makes it possible to date certain other fossils and also to predict where oil may be found. Because the richest oil deposits were formed at certain times in the Earth's history, foraminifer fossils are valuable clues to the presence of oil in rocks.

Summary of the Animallike Protists

- **Members of the phylum Ciliophora, such as *Paramecium*, are known as ciliates. Almost all ciliates use cilia for movement.**
- **Members of the phylum Zoomastigina are known as flagellates because they use flagella for movement.**
- **Members of the phylum Sporozoa, such as *Plasmodium*, reproduce by means of spores. Sporozoans are nonmotile and parasitic.**
- **The phylum Sarcodina includes amebas and foraminifers. Sarcodines use pseudopods for feeding and movement.**

Figure 18–14 A live foraminifer, which resembles a clump of tinsel, captures food with its threadlike pseudopods (left). Foraminifers produce shells of calcium carbonate (right).

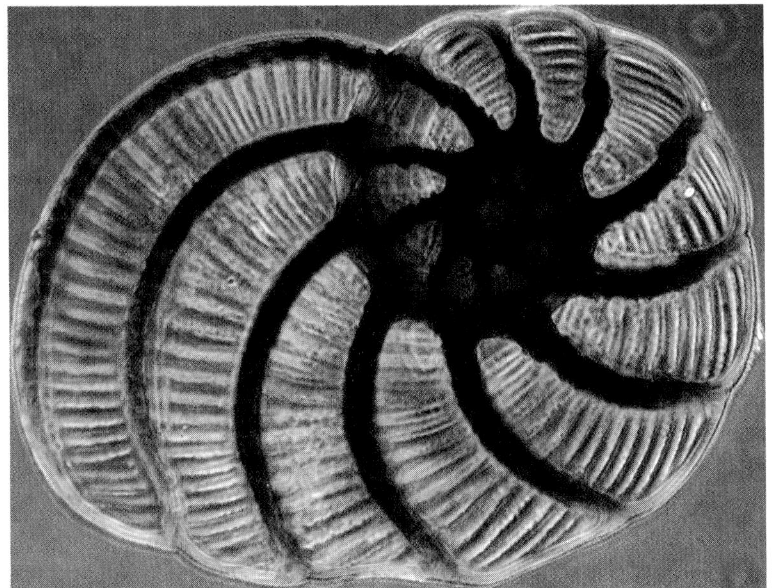

PROBLEM SOLVING IN BIOLOGY

INTERPRETING GRAPHIC DATA ABOUT A FORAMINIFER

Globigerinoides sacculifer is a foraminifer that lives near the surface of the ocean. The shell of *G. sacculifer* consists of several bubble-like chambers that are covered with long iridescent spines. Numerous perforations in the chambers of its shell permit *G. sacculifer* to extend many threadlike pseudopods among its spines. These pseudopods are used to capture microscopic animals and protists. In the laboratory, *G. sacculifer* is fed day-old brine shrimp.

Study these graphs, which show the results of experiments involving the growth of *G. sacculifer*'s shell under different conditions. Answer the questions that follow.

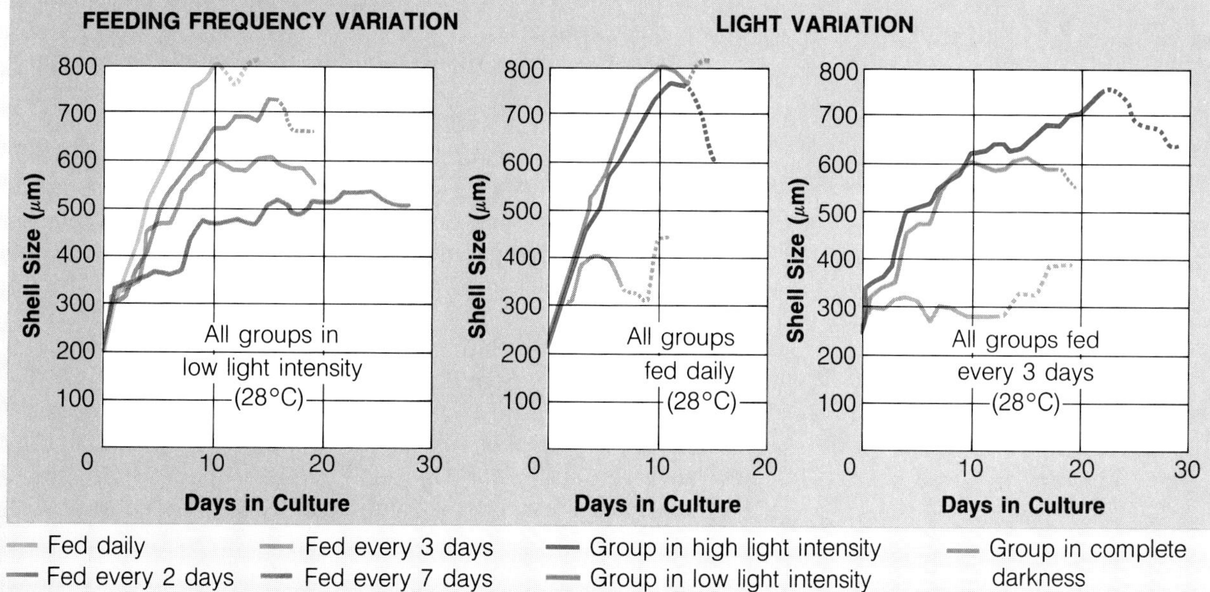

Fed daily
Fed every 2 days
Fed every 3 days
Fed every 7 days
Group in high light intensity
Group in low light intensity
Group in complete darkness

The shell of Globigernoides sacculifer *grows at different rates under different conditions. It stops growing when the protist dies or undergoes gamete formation. (In gamete formation, the body of the foraminifer divides into many tiny cells that leave through the pores of the shell.)*

1. What variables were tested in these experiments?
2. According to these graphs, what is the maximum shell size in *G. sacculifer*?
3. Explain why the data represented by the dotted lines are less significant than the data shown by the rest of the curve.
4. *G. sacculifer* has symbiotic dinoflagellates that live in its cytoplasm. How might this fact explain why the groups of foraminifers raised in complete darkness died or underwent premature gamete formation?
5. How does light intensity affect final shell size?
6. How does feeding frequency affect final shell size?
7. What is the dominant factor in shell growth in *G. sacculifer*? Explain your answer.

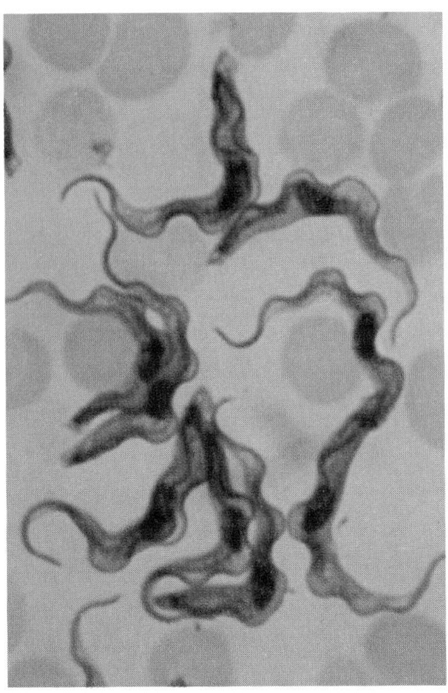

Figure 18–16 *Trypanosomes are parasites that live in the blood of vertebrates and cause a number of diseases, such as African sleeping sickness and Chagas disease.*

How Animallike Protists Fit into the World

The animallike protists are found throughout the world. They are some of the most common organisms in the oceans, and they are also abundant in fresh water, on land, and in the bodies of larger organisms.

HARMFUL RELATIONSHIPS Unfortunately for us and for other organisms, there are a great many parasitic protists. Parasitic protists affect plants, all types of animals (including humans), and even other protists. You have already read about one important protist parasite and pathogen (something that causes disease)—the genus of sporozoans called *Plasmodium*, which causes malaria.

Zoomastiginans, which belong to the genus *Trypanosoma*, are another example of pathogenic protists. Trypanosomes (trih-PAN-oh-sohmz) live in the blood of vertebrates such as humans and other mammals and cause a number of diseases. Although these diseases have different common names, any disease caused by trypanosomes is called trypanosomiasis, which means trypanosome infection. One form of trypanosomiasis that affects humans is commonly known as African sleeping sickness.

The trypanosomes that cause African sleeping sickness are passed from one person to another by an insect known as the tsetse (TSEET-see) fly. These trypanosomes destroy blood cells and infect other tissues in the body. The symptoms of infection include fever, chills, and skin rash. As the trypanosomes attack the nervous system, infected individuals become weak and lose consciousness, passing into a deep and often fatal sleep from which the disease gets its name.

Some trypanosome species infect domestic livestock. In areas infested with the tsetse fly, which include vast regions of central Africa, the raising of cattle is virtually impossible. The control of the tsetse fly and the protist pathogens that it spreads is a major goal of scientists in Africa and around the world. The only trypanosome native to the Western Hemisphere is *T. cruzi*, which causes Chagas disease. This disease can result in heart failure because the trypanosomes invade and weaken muscle, especially heart muscle. Some historians believe that Charles Darwin contracted this disease during his visit to South America and that it was this parasite that made him ill much of his life.

A third kind of pathogenic protist is similar in appearance to the harmless amebas that you may find in a nearby pond or examine under a microscope. In certain regions of the world, many people are infected with species of *Entamoeba*, which cause a disease known as amebic dysentery. The parasitic amebas that cause this disease live in the intestines, where they absorb food from the host. They also attack the wall of the intestine itself, destroying parts of it in the process and causing severe bleeding. These amebas are passed out of the body in feces. In places where sanitation is poor, the amebas may then find their way into supplies of food and water. In some areas of the world, amebic dysentery is a major health problem, weakening the human population and contributing to the spread of other diseases.

HELPFUL RELATIONSHIPS Although many animallike protists are responsible for disease, there are many that are beneficial to other organisms. An interesting example of a beneficial protist is *Trichonympha*, a zoomastiginan that lives within the digestive systems of the termite and the wood roach. Termites eat wood, the major component of which is the carbohydrate cellulose. But termites do not have enzymes to break apart the chemical bonds that hold the simple sugars in cellulose together. Neither do we, incidentally, so it does us little good to munch on a woodchip. How, then, does a termite digest cellulose? It doesn't. *Trichonympha* does.

Young termites ingest some of the feces of an adult termite, thereby swallowing several thousand *Trichonympha*, which then take up residence in the termites' digestive system. Experiments have shown that insects deprived of these protists cannot live more than a few days. *Trichonympha* and other organisms living in the termites' gut manufacture cellulase, the enzyme that the termites need to break the chemical bonds in cellulose. Without these symbionts, termites and wood roaches would be no more able to digest wood than we are.

Figure 18–17 *Particles of wood appear as irregular grains inside the body of* Trichonympha, *a wood-digesting protist (left).* Trichonympha *lives in the digestive system of insects such as termites (right), making it possible for them to obtain nutrients from the wood they eat.*

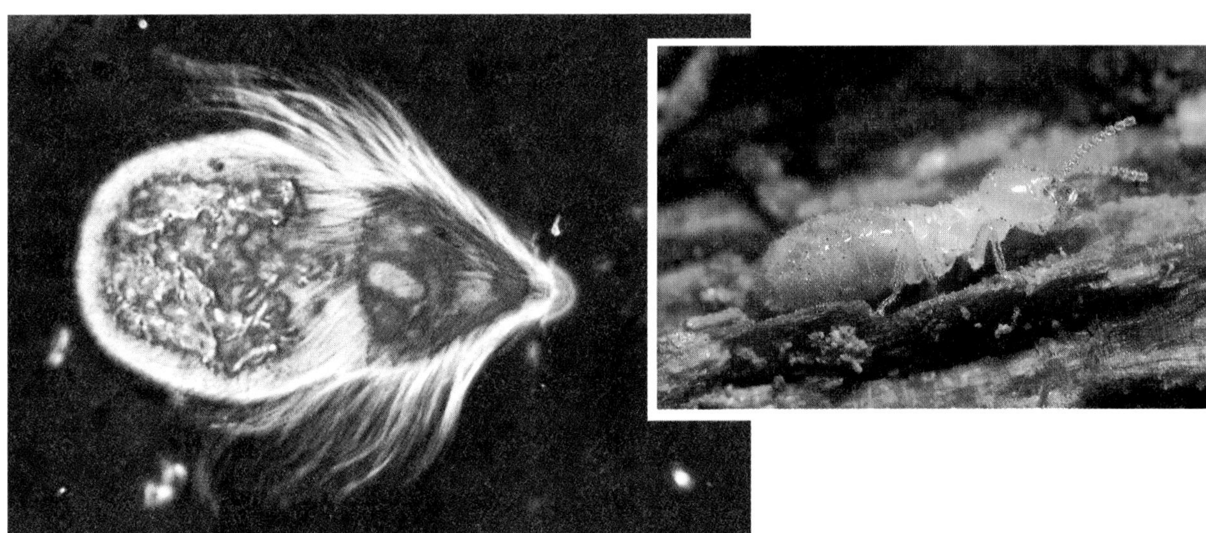

The animallike protists play another major role in the living world. Enormous numbers of protists living in the seas are food for tiny multicellular animals that in turn serve as food for larger animals. A similar role is played by protists in freshwater lakes, streams, and ponds. Without such tiny organisms, the larger fish would have no food supply. The animallike protists thus perform an essential function for all other living things.

18–2 SECTION REVIEW

1. List the four phyla of animallike protists. Give an example of each.
2. Compare the forms of locomotion used by the four phyla of animallike protists.
3. Describe the process of conjugation. Is conjugation a form of reproduction? Explain your answer.
4. In what ways are animallike protists helpful to other living things?

Section Objectives

- Name and describe the five phyla of plantlike protists.
- Discuss how plantlike protists fit into the world.

18–3 Plantlike Protists

In addition to the four phyla of animallike protists, we recognize five phyla of plantlike protists. Like other protists, these organisms are unicellular and most of them are motile. We call them plantlike because most contain the pigment chlorophyll and carry out photosynthesis. Like zoomastiginans, many plantlike protists are called flagellates because they have flagella. These organisms are known as phytoflagellates, which means plant flagellates, to distinguish them from zoomastiginans (zooflagellates).

Three of the phyla of plantlike protists—Euglenophyta, Pyrrophyta, and Chrysophyta—are considered to be types of algae. These simple plantlike organisms, found in water or damp places, lack true roots, stems, and leaves. As a result, these three phyla are sometimes classified as plants. The unusual slime molds, which are placed in phyla Acrasiomycota and Myxomycota, are not photosynthetic and have many funguslike characteristics. They are sometimes known as funguslike protists, or are even classified as fungi.

Euglenophyta: Flagellates with Chloroplasts

The members of the phylum **Euglenophyta** (yoo-glee-nuh-FIGHT-uh) are closely related to zoomastiginans. In some classification schemes, euglenophytes and zoomastiginans are actually considered to be in the same phylum. The main reason for grouping them together is that except for the fact that euglenophytes possess chloroplasts, the two phyla of protists closely resemble each other.

The most famous members of the phylum Euglenophyta belong to the genus from which the entire phylum takes its name: *Euglena*. As you can see in Figure 18–18, a **euglena** is a long cell that has a pouch that contains two flagella at its front end. The longer of these two flagella extends far out of the euglena's pouch and is used to propel the cell forward through the water. A euglena is an excellent swimmer and can move very quickly in this manner. However, when a euglena is forced against a surface—for example, when it is squeezed down on a glass laboratory slide—it is able to move in a different manner. The euglena changes shape rapidly and crawls along the surface by a process called euglenoid movement. Thus a euglena is able to move along in a distinctly animallike fashion.

A red eyespot at the front end of the cell (the end with the flagella) helps a euglena find the brightest areas of its immediate environment. Finding sunlight is important to a euglena because it is filled with between 10 and 20 oval chloroplasts. A euglena is a full-fledged phototrophic autotroph, or an organism that makes its own food from light and simple raw materials, and thus is able to carry out the light and dark reactions of photosynthesis.

When sunlight is not available, a euglena can also live as a heterotroph, or an organism that eats food made by other organisms. If dissolved nutrients are available in the water, a euglena can absorb them and get along in darkness with no ill effects. In nature this gives euglenas the ability to live as saprophytes, or organisms that absorb the nutrients available in decayed organic material.

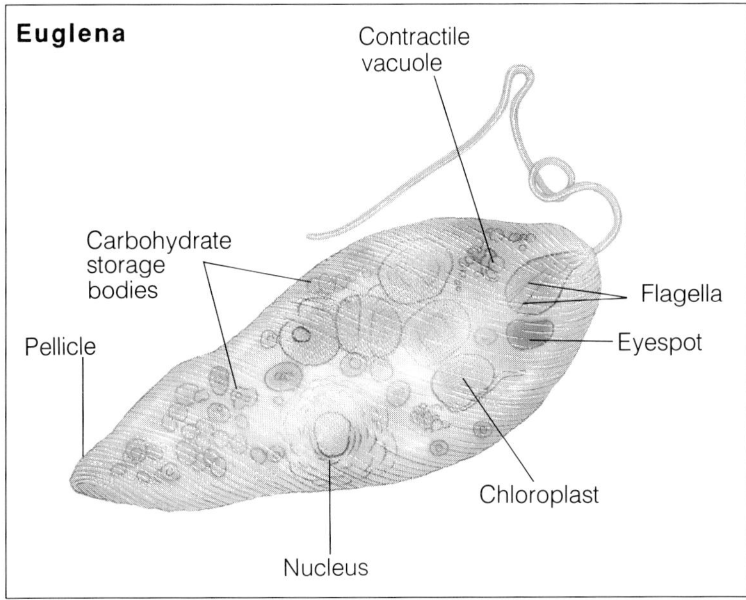

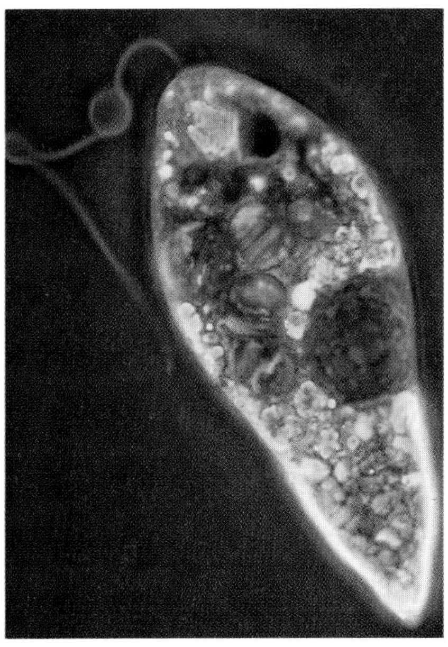

Figure 18–18 *A euglena's organelles include a large prominent nucleus, whiplike flagella, green chloroplasts, and grainy yellow food-storage structures.*

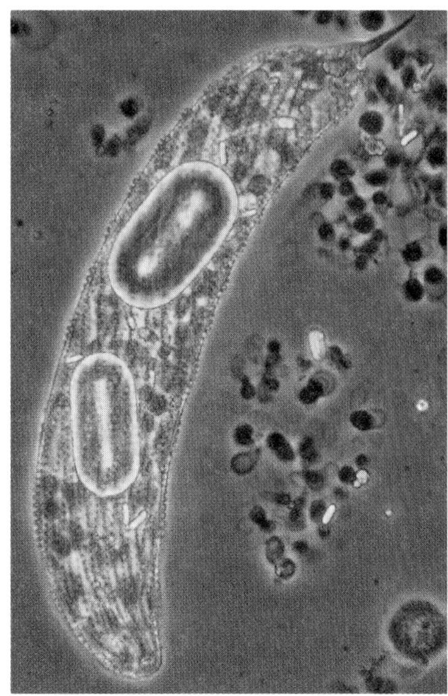

Figure 18–19 *A euglena is a photosynthetic protist that swims by means of flagella. The ridges that spiral around the body of the euglena are part of its pellicle.*

The pellicle (the cell membrane and associated structures) of *Euglena* is of special interest to many biologists because of its unusual structure. The pellicle consists of a series of ribbonlike ridges that spiral around the surface of the organism. See Figure 18–19. Underneath each ridge is a small sac and a set of microtubules. The microtubules and the sacs probably are important in maintaining the shape of the cell when it is swimming and in generating the force for euglenoid movement.

A euglena reproduces asexually by binary fission. In this process, a single euglena divides in two, beginning at the end with the flagella and finally separating at the base. Just prior to cell division, the cell doubles the number of ridges in its pellicle by producing tiny new ridges between the old ones. Because of their adaptability—there are few organisms able to exist as both autotrophs and heterotrophs—euglenas are able to live in many different places and are quite common.

Pyrrophyta: Fire Protists

The members of phylum **Pyrrophyta** (pigh-roh-FIGHT-uh) are a group of organisms known as the **dinoflagellates**. Most dinoflagellates are photosynthetic, although a few have lost their chloroplasts and exist as heterotrophs. The cells usually swim by means of two flagella. In most dinoflagellates, one flagellum wraps around the organism like a belt, whereas the other trails behind like a tail. Many dinoflagellates are surrounded by thick plates that give them a strange armored appearance. Dinoflagellates reproduce asexually by binary fission.

The dinoflagellates have two interesting properties that set them apart from most other protists and, indeed, most other organisms. First, a great many dinoflagellate species are luminescent. When agitated by sudden movement in the water, they give off light. Many areas of the ocean are so filled with dinoflagellates that the movement of an oar or the wake of a boat will cause the dark water to shimmer with a ghostly blue light. This is a remarkable sight, and one that gives the phylum its name (Pyrrophyta means fire plants).

The second interesting property of dinoflagellates has to do with their genetic material. Like other organisms, dinoflagellates store genetic information in the form of DNA. In the case of all other eukaryotic cells, however, that DNA is tightly bound with special proteins known as histones. Dinoflagellates do not have histones. In fact, they are the only eukaryotes that do not. The reason for this difference, as well as an explanation of how the roles of the histone proteins are carried out without them in dinoflagellates, remains a mystery.

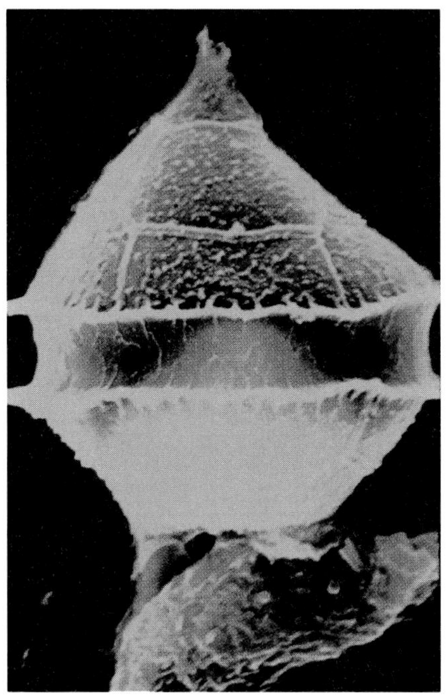

Figure 18–20 *Dinoflagellates are plantlike protists. They often have thick protective shells that give them bizarre shapes.*

easily distinguishable from soil amebas. These ameboid, or amebalike, cells reproduce very rapidly. When the food supply is exhausted, groups of ameboid cells gather together to produce a large mass of cells that begins to function as a single organism. This unusual behavior forces scientists to stretch the definition of protists. Protists are defined as being unicellular —but here is a group of protists acting like a primitive multicellular organism!

These solid masses of cells may migrate for several centimeters. They then form a reproductive structure called a fruiting body that produces spores by mitosis. These spores give rise to ameboid cells that repeat the cycle.

Cellular slime molds are an interesting system for biologists who study how cells communicate. The formation of an intricate structure such as the fruiting body from what was previously a mass of independent cells is a most intriguing process. It has kept biologists busy for decades, and its secrets are still not fully understood.

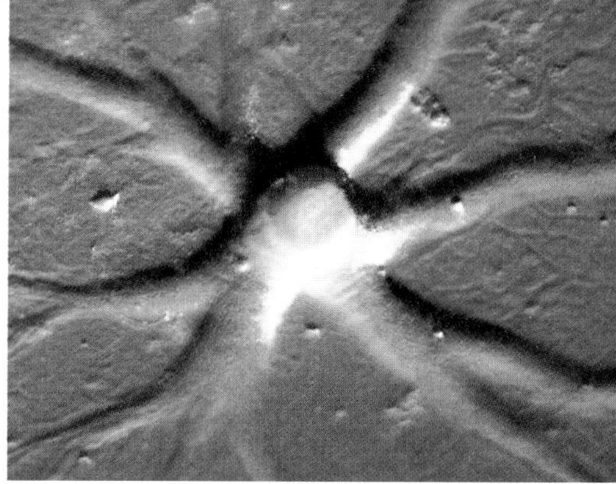

Figure 18–22 *When the food supply runs out, cellular slime mold cells come together. The collection of cells that results from this process looks and acts much like a simple multicellular organism.*

MYXOMYCOTA: ACELLULAR SLIME MOLDS Acellular slime molds belong to the phylum **Myxomycota** (mihks-uh-migh-KOH-tuh). Like a cellular slime mold, an acellular slime mold begins its life cycle as an amebalike cell. However, acellular slime molds produce structures known as **plasmodia** (singular: plasmodium) that contain thousands of nuclei enclosed in a single cell membrane. In contrast to the cellular slime molds, the large plasmodium of an acellular slime mold is a single multinucleate cell. A plasmodium may grow as large as several centimeters in diameter.

Eventually small structures known as fruiting bodies spring up from the plasmodium. The fruiting bodies produce haploid spores by meiosis. These spores scatter to the ground where they germinate into flagellated cells. These flagellated cells fuse to produce diploid ameboid cells that repeat the cycle.

Figure 18–23 *At one point in its life cycle, an acellular slime mold forms a structure called a plasmodium, which contains many nuclei and creeps about like a giant ameba (left). Later, reproductive structures called fruiting bodies are produced by the plasmodium (right).*

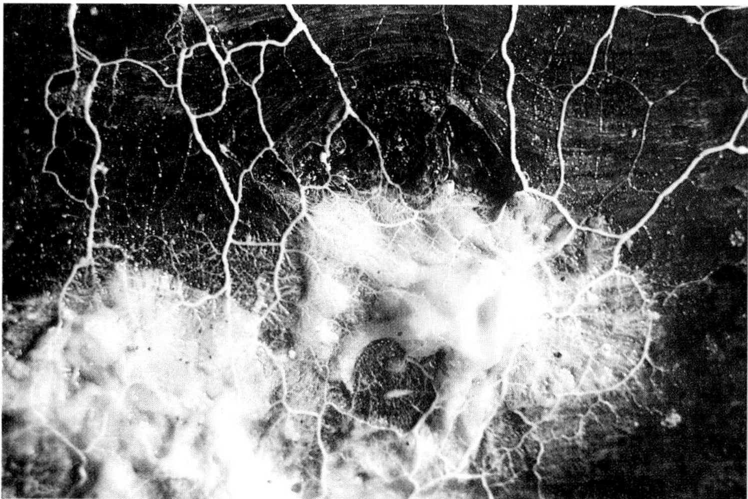

Summary of the Plantlike Protists

- **Members of the phylum Euglenophyta are very similar to zoomastiginans. Euglenophytes, such as *Euglena,* are photosynthetic flagellates.**
- **Members of the phylum Pyrrophyta are called dinoflagellates. Most dinoflagellates are photosynthetic, and some are luminescent.**
- **The phylum Chrysophyta is a diverse group of protists that have gold-colored chloroplasts. Most of the species of chrysophytes are diatoms, photosynthetic protists that lack flagella and live in beautiful glasslike "boxes."**
- **Slime molds are unusual organisms that are difficult to classify. Cellular slime molds belong to the phylum Acrasiomycota. Acellular slime molds belong to the phylum Myxomycota.**

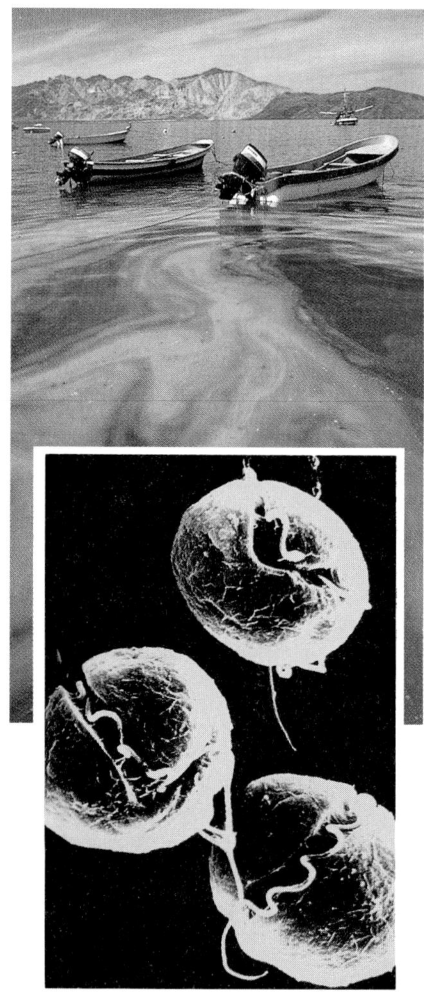

Figure 18–24 *Red tide (top) is produced by blooms of the dinoflagellate* Gonyaulax *(bottom).* Gonyaulax *contains a toxin that can become concentrated in the tissues of shellfish such as clams and oysters, making them unfit to eat. This toxin can also kill fish and other marine animals.*

How the Plantlike Protists Fit into the World

Like the animallike protists, plantlike protists are found throughout the world in bodies of fresh water, in the ocean, and on land. Unlike animallike protists, most plantlike protists are autotrophs rather than heterotrophs. Although plantlike protists can be harmful to other organisms, few plantlike protists are truly parasitic.

HARMFUL RELATIONSHIPS In lakes and ponds, euglenophytes are among the most common organisms. In areas into which large amounts of sewage are discharged, euglenophytes may thrive. Because they are able to absorb organic material directly and use it for food, they grow rapidly in such regions and their presence may actually turn the water of a lake or slow-moving stream a murky green. They play a vital role in helping to recycle sewage and other waste materials. But when the amount of waste dumped into a body of water is excessive, the euglenophytes and other green organisms may grow into enormous masses of cells known as **blooms**. While not harmful in themselves, these blooms quickly run out of nutrients and the cells begin to die in great numbers, compounding the problem of disposing of waste matter.

Great blooms of the dinoflagellate *Gonyaulax polyhedron* have occurred in recent years on the east coast of the United States, although scientists are not sure of the reasons. This species contains a toxin that can cause paralysis and even death if ingested in large amounts. Fortunately for all but the most allergic people, it simply is not possible to swallow enough of the "red tide" of *Gonyaulax* while swimming to be affected by the toxin. Thus the blooms of dinoflagellates are not harmful to most swimmers. However, shellfish such as clams and oysters filter enormous amounts of sea water in order to trap organisms like *Gonyaulax* for food and thus become filled with the toxin. Eating shellfish from areas infected with red tide can cause serious illness. In addition, the toxin can kill fish and weaken or even kill dolphins.

HELPFUL RELATIONSHIPS The plantlike protists form some spectacular symbiotic relationships with other organisms. Many types of coral contain intercellular dinoflagellates. These dinoflagellates allow the tiny animals that form the coral to use the products of photosynthesis, allowing coral to grow in areas where nutrients are few. In turn, the dinoflagellates can use many of the waste products of the coral organisms before they are diluted by diffusion through sea water.

Other dinoflagellates make their homes with other organisms. In the giant clam *Tridacna gigas*, a special tissue called the mantle contains large numbers of symbiotic photosynthetic protists. These dinoflagellates are held in a position from which they are able to gather as much sunlight as possible and increase the nutrient benefit to the organism.

Figure 18–25 *Symbiotic photosynthetic protists live inside the tissues of animals such as sea anemones (top) and giant clams (bottom).*

Plantlike protists play a major ecological role: They make up a considerable part of the **phytoplankton**. The term phytoplankton is applied to any small photosynthetic organism found in great numbers near the surface of the ocean. Thus it can apply to any photosynthetic organism, regardless of kingdom or phylum.

The importance of the phytoplankton for other forms of life cannot be underestimated. More than 70 percent of the photosynthesis that occurs on Earth goes on near the surface of the oceans. The result of this photosynthesis is that the rest of the organisms on our planet are provided with enormous amounts of oxygen and food. The phytoplankton provide a direct source of nourishment for organisms as diverse as shrimp and whales. And even land animals such as humans obtain nourishment indirectly from the phytoplankton. When you eat a tuna fish sandwich, you are eating fish that fed on smaller fish that fed on still smaller animals that fed on phytoplankton!

Figure 18–26 *Phytoplankton provide enormous amounts of food and oxygen for other organisms on Earth.*

18–3 SECTION REVIEW

1. List the five phyla of plantlike protists. Give an example of an organism in each phylum.
2. What are slime molds? Why is it appropriate for the slime molds to be considered protists?
3. Why is red tide particularly damaging to the shellfish industry?
4. "Life on Earth depends on plantlike protists." Defend or refute this statement.

LABORATORY INVESTIGATION

EXAMINING PROTISTS

PROBLEM

What characteristics of protists can be observed with a microscope?

MATERIALS *(per group)*

pond water	cotton
coverslips	microscope
microscope slides	protist identification guide
medicine dropper	

PROCEDURE 

1. Using the medicine dropper, put a drop of pond water in the center of a clean glass microscope slide.
2. Pull apart a small piece of cotton and put a few threads in the drop of pond water. **Note:** *Only a few threads are necessary.*
3. Cover the drop of pond water with a coverslip. With your microscope set on low power, look for signs of life in the water.
4. When you find microorganisms, switch to medium power and focus with the fine adjustment. Observe what happens when one of the microorganisms bumps into the thread.
5. Try to get a microorganism in the center of the field of view. Switch to high power and focus with the fine adjustment. **Note:** *Use only the fine adjustment to focus when using the high-power objective. When using the high-power objective, do not focus downward (do not bring the objective closer to the slide) while looking through the microscope.*
6. Draw the protist on a separate sheet of paper. Next to your drawing, write down your observations of the protist's appearance and behavior. Note its shape and color and the organelles that are visible. Try to determine how it moves—a "fluttery" edge on the protist, for example, is a sure sign of cilia.
7. Repeat steps 5 and 6 with as many different protists as you can find.
8. Using a protist identification guide, try to identify the protists in your drawings.

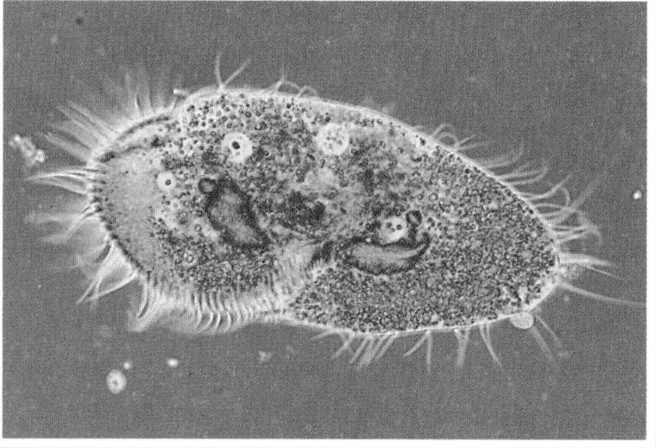

OBSERVATIONS

1. What types of movement did you observe in the protists?
2. What organelles did you observe in the protists?
3. Describe what protists do when they bump into an obstacle such as a thread.
4. What characteristics did the protists have in common?
5. How were the protists different from one another?

ANALYSIS AND CONCLUSIONS

1. What important characteristics of protists are difficult or impossible to observe with a light microscope?
2. Why was the cotton put into the drop of pond water? Predict what you might have observed if there were no cotton in the pond water.
3. Was it easy to identify the protists you observed? Explain.
4. Suggest what might be done to make it easier to observe and identify protists.

STUDENT STUDY GUIDE

SUMMARIZING THE CONCEPTS

The key concepts in each section of this chapter are listed below to help you review the chapter content. Make sure you understand each concept and its relationship to other concepts and to the theme of this chapter.

18–1 The Kingdom Protista

- Protists, or members of the kingdom Protista, are unicellular eukaryotic organisms.
- The Endosymbiont Hypothesis states that the first eukaryotic cell was formed by a symbiosis among several prokaryotes.

18–2 Animallike Protists

- Ciliates possess cilia.
- Zoomastiginans possess flagella.
- Sporozoans are nonmotile parasitic protists.
- Sarcodines use pseudopods for locomotion and feeding.
- Some animallike protists are symbionts of other organisms. A few species are pathogens. Animallike protists are a source of food for small organisms that in turn are food for larger organisms.

18–3 Plantlike Protists

- Euglenophytes are photosynthetic flagellates that are similar in form to zoomastiginans.
- Pyrrophytes are also known as dinoflagellates. Some dinoflagellates are luminescent.
- Most of the species in the phylum Chrysophyta are diatoms.
- Slime molds are also known as funguslike protists. Unlike most plantlike protists, slime molds are not photosynthetic.
- Cellular slime molds form a mass of cells that function like a single organism at one point in their life cycle.
- Acellular slime molds form plasmodia at one point in their life cycle.
- Photosynthetic plantlike protists form an important part of the phytoplankton, which supplies much of the earth's oxygen.

REVIEWING KEY TERMS

Vocabulary terms are important to your understanding of biology. The key terms listed below are those you should be especially familiar with. Review these terms and their meanings. Then use each term in a complete sentence. If you are not sure of a term's meaning, return to the appropriate section and review its definition.

18–1 The Kingdom Protista

Protista
protist
Endosymbiont Hypothesis

18–2 Animallike Protists

Ciliophora
ciliate
cilium
paramecium
pellicle
trichocyst
macronucleus
micronucleus
gullet
food vacuole
anal pore
contractile vacuole
Zoomastigina
flagellum
flagellate
Sporozoa
Sarcodina
pseudopod
ameba

18–3 Plantlike Protists

Euglenophyta
euglena
Pyrrophyta
dinoflagellate
Chrysophyta
diatom
slime mold
Acrasiomycota
Myxomycota
plasmodium
bloom
phytoplankton

CHAPTER REVIEW

CONTENT REVIEW

Multiple Choice

Choose the letter of the answer that best completes each statement.

1. All protists are
   a. solitary. c. motile.
   b. colonial. d. eukaryotic.
2. Which organism causes malaria?
   a. *Paramecium* c. *Plasmodium*
   b. *Trypanosoma* d. *Euglena*
3. Short hairlike projections that produce movement in certain protists are
   a. cilia. c. flagella.
   b. pseudopods. d. microtubules.
4. Diatoms belong to the phylum
   a. Ciliophora. c. Pyrrophyta.
   b. Chrysophyta. d. Myxomycota.
5. Which of the following organisms are not placed in the phylum Sarcodina?
   a. amebas c. heliozoans
   b. radiolarians d. flagellates
6. A euglena moves by means of
   a. pseudopods. c. spores.
   b. cilia. d. flagella.
7. Which organism is not associated with a disease in humans?
   a. *Trichonympha* c. *Trypanosoma*
   b. *Entamoeba* d. *Plasmodium*
8. A paramecium excretes excess water through the
   a. gullet. c. contractile vacuole.
   b. trichocysts. d. micronucleus.

True or False

Determine whether each statement is true or false. If it is true, write "true." If it is false, change the underlined word or words to make the statement true.

1. Red tides are caused by <u>dinoflagellates</u>.
2. <u>Cellular slime molds</u> produce plasmodia.
3. <u>Animallike protists</u> make up a considerable part of the phytoplankton.
4. During conjugation, paramecia exchange <u>macronuclei</u>.
5. <u>Sporozoans</u> use pseudopods to move.
6. In some protists, the cell membrane and associated structures make up the <u>flagellum</u>.
7. A paramecium uses flask-shaped structures called <u>contractile vacuoles</u> for defense.
8. Some species in the phylum <u>Pyrrophyta</u> are luminescent.

Word Relationships

A. *In each of the following sets of terms, three of the terms are related. One term does not belong. Determine the characteristic common to three of the terms and then identify the term that does not belong.*

1. dinoflagellate, diatom, ameba, euglena
2. macronucleus, micronucleus, flagella, cilia
3. red tide, malaria, African sleeping sickness, amebic dysentery
4. sporozoan, foraminifer, radiolarian, heliozoan

B. *Replace the underlined definition with the correct vocabulary word.*

5. Flexible, active cells without cell walls, flagella, cilia, and even a definite shape engulf prey by using pseudopods.
6. Slime molds are heterotrophic organisms that feed on dead or decaying organic material.
7. The oldest fossils of members of the kingdom that consists of unicellular eukaryotic organisms are about 1.5 billion years old.
8. Diatoms, chrysophytes, and euglenophytes are an important part of the small photosynthetic organisms that are found in great numbers near the surface of the ocean.

CONCEPT MASTERY

Use your understanding of the concepts developed in the chapter to answer each of the following in a brief paragraph.

1. What is the significance of the Endosymbiont Hypothesis?
2. Are the categories animallike, plantlike, or funguslike useful in classifying protists? Explain your answer.
3. Why are diatom shells often used in toothpaste and reflective paint?
4. Explain why protists are difficult to classify.
5. Make a table that contains the following information about each protist phylum: Name of Phylum; Animallike or Plantlike; Representative Members; Means of Locomotion; Relationships with Other Organisms.

CRITICAL AND CREATIVE THINKING

Discuss each of the following in a brief paragraph.

1. **Developing a hypothesis** A scientist observes that termites that are fed a certain antibiotic die of starvation after a few days. The scientist also notices that certain protists that live inside the termite's gut are affected by the antibiotic in a peculiar way: Although the protists continue to thrive, they lose a certain kind of structure in their cytoplasm. Develop a hypothesis to explain these observations.

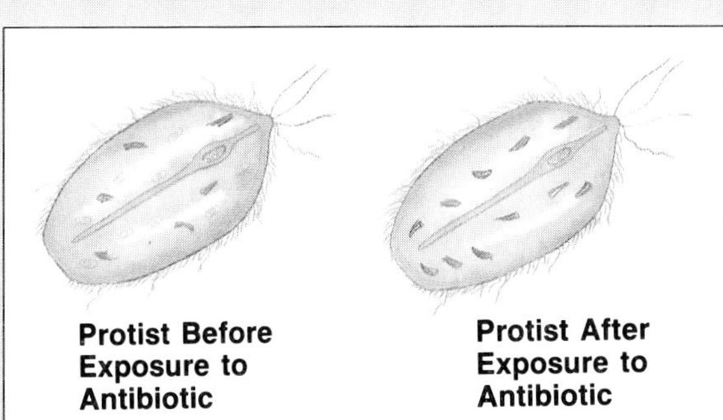

2. **Relating cause and effect** How might water pollution result in a red tide?
3. **Making predictions** Growing "holes" in the Earth's ozone layer may increase the amount of radiation that reaches the surface of the ocean. If this radiation were to affect the growth of phytoplankton, what long-term consequences might this have on the Earth's atmosphere?
4. **Using the writing process** Imagine that you could shrink down to microscopic size and fit inside a paramecium. Describe the adventures you and the paramecium have in a small pond one summer day.

CHAPTER 19

Fungi

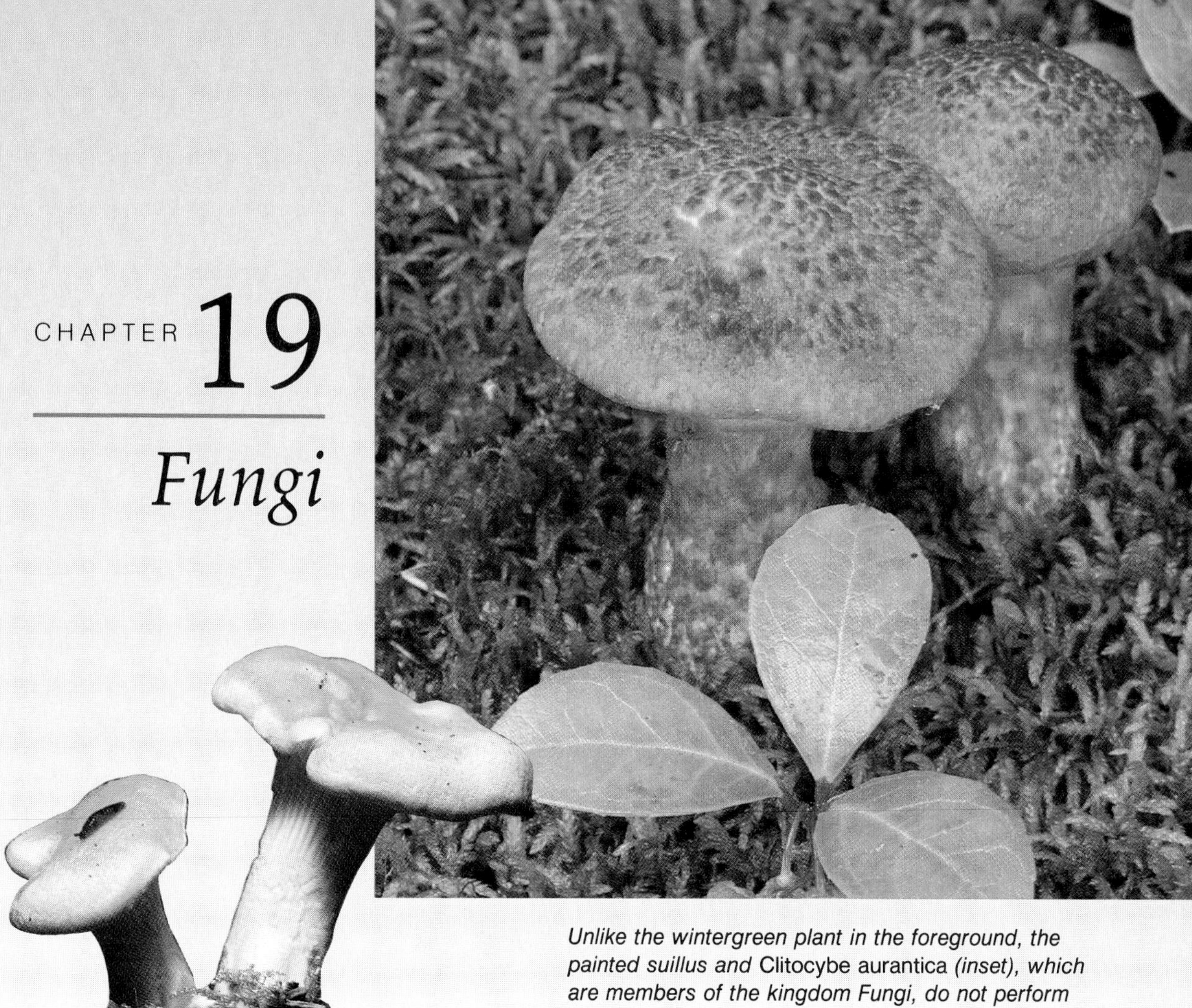

Unlike the wintergreen plant in the foreground, the painted suillus and Clitocybe aurantica *(inset), which are members of the kingdom Fungi, do not perform photosynthesis.*

Imagine forms of life that are found nearly everywhere on Earth yet seem poorly suited for the type of lifestyle that exists on our planet. These organisms usually cannot move from place to place. They do not perform photosynthesis, nor do they get their food by capturing other organisms. Instead, these organisms grow on their food source, digest the food outside their bodies, and then absorb it.

Despite their apparent limitations, these organisms are so common that it is virtually impossible to obtain a sample of soil that does not contain them. These unique life forms are fungi, and their world, as different as it may seem from ours, affects us every day. In this chapter, you will examine some of the characteristics of fungi and discover just what role they play in our environment.

CHAPTER OUTLINE

19–1 The Fungi

Section Objectives

- Describe the structure of a typical fungus.
- Explain how fungi obtain food.
- Identify the five phyla of fungi.
- Summarize the methods of reproduction in fungi.

For many of us, the most common encounters with **fungi** (FUHN-jigh; singular: fungus) are unwanted ones: molds spoil our fruits and breads, mildew weakens our fabrics, and athlete's foot attacks our skin. In tropical areas, more than 50 percent of the food that is produced is spoiled by fungi before it can be eaten. And in temperate regions, trees such as the elm die of a fungal disease known as Dutch elm disease.

For reasons such as these, when we think of fungi, we think of death and decay. Fungi, however, are among the most interesting organisms in the living world. Not only do they help shape the natural environment, they also provide us with food —and in so doing, they display some remarkable and exotic lifestyles.

Characteristics of Fungi

Fungi are eukaryotic heterotrophs. You will recall from Chapter 17 that heterotrophs depend on other organisms for food. Many fungi are saprophytes, or organisms that obtain food from decaying organic matter. Others are parasites, which are organisms that live directly on the body of a plant or animal host and in so doing harm that organism. Still other fungi are symbionts, or organisms that live in close association with an organism of another species.

Figure 19–1 *All fungi are heterotrophs, or organisms that obtain food from organic compounds of other organisms. Many of these heterotrophs, such as the bracket fungi shown here, live as saprophytes, decomposing dead matter such as this tree.*

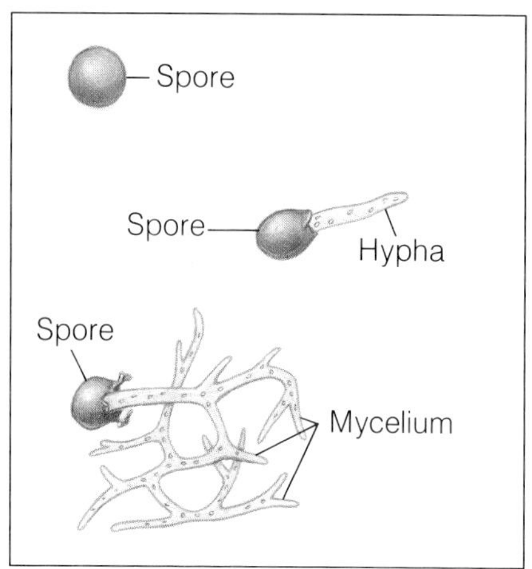

Figure 19–2 *A fungus develops from a spore that grows into a threadlike hypha. The hypha grows rapidly and branches until it resembles a tangled mass of threads called a mycelium.*

Fungi do not ingest their food. Instead, they absorb it through their cell walls and cell membranes. Fungi release digestive enzymes into their environment. The enzymes break down leaves, fruit, or other organic material into simple molecules, which then diffuse across the cell walls and cell membranes. This method of obtaining food makes fungi very important in nature: They produce powerful digestive enzymes that speed the breakdown of dead organisms, helping to recycle nutrients and essential chemicals. Together with the bacteria, fungi are the major **decomposers,** or organisms of decay.

Except for yeasts, which are unicellular, the body of a typical fungus is made up of many tiny filaments tangled together into a thick mass called a **mycelium** (migh-SEE-lee-uhm). The individual filaments are called **hyphae** (HIGH-fee; singular: hypha). In many fungi, the hyphae are divided by cross walls into cells containing one or more nuclei. See Figure 19–3. The cell walls of most hyphae are made up of chitin, a complex carbohydrate that is also found in the external skeleton of insects. The cell walls of other hyphae contain cellulose, the complex carbohydrate that makes up the cell walls in plants. The mycelium, or tangled mass of hyphae, is well suited to absorbing food because it permits a larger surface area to come in contact with the food source.

Most fungi reproduce both asexually and sexually. Asexual reproduction occurs either by the production of spores or by the fragmentation of the hyphae (each fragment becomes a new fungus). In some fungi, spores are produced in structures called **sporangia** (spoh-RAN-jee-uh; singular: sporangium). Sporangia are found at the tops of specialized hyphae called **sporangiophores.**

Figure 19–3 *Some hyphae are divided by cross walls that contain one or more nuclei. Other hyphae are coenocytic, meaning they lack cross walls.*

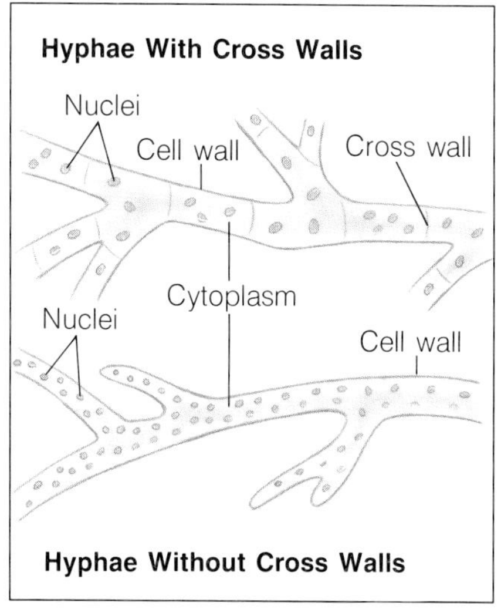

In many fungi, sexual reproduction involves two different mating types. One mating type is referred to as + (plus) and the other is referred to as – (minus). When the hyphae of opposite mating types meet, each hypha forms a **gametangium** (gam-uh-TAN-jee-uhm), or gamete-forming structure. Then the two gametangia fuse, and some of the nuclei pair and join to form zygote nuclei.

During the greater part of their life cycle, the nuclei of most fungi are haploid (N). Diploid (2N) nuclei form during sexual reproduction. Shortly after the nuclei fuse, meiosis (reduction division) occurs and produces haploid nuclei that dominate the remainder of the life cycle of fungi.

Fungi are classified according to their methods of reproduction and their basic structure. At one time fungi were classified either in the kingdom Plantae or in the kingdom Protista. Today, fungi are placed in their own kingdom, the Fungi.

We have divided the kingdom Fungi into five phyla: Oomycota, Zygomycota, Ascomycota, Basidiomycota, and Deuteromycota. Notice that the name of each phylum ends in *-mycota.* This suffix is derived from the Greek word for mushroom, which is *mykes. Mykes* is also the root for mycelium.

Oomycota—Protistlike Fungi

Because the fungi in the phylum Oomycota (oh-uh-migh-KOHT-uh) are so closely related to the plantlike protists, many scientists include them as one of the phyla within the kingdom Protista. Members of this phylum, called oomycetes, commonly form a white fuzz on aquarium fish or on organic matter sitting in water. Despite the phylum's common name of water molds, a few oomycetes are able to grow on land, but only under damp, humid conditions. Although these fungi are not common on land, they do cause a number of serious diseases among crop plants, including potato blight. We will consider these diseases when we examine how fungi fit into the environment.

The cell walls of oomycetes are made of cellulose. It is through these thin cell walls that the water molds absorb food. Oomycetes are the only fungi that produce motile spores. These spores swim through water and raindrops to new sources of food. The hyphae of oomycetes lack cross walls. As a result, the hyphae are multinucleate (have many nuclei).

The life cycle of a water mold is shown in Figure 19–4. Notice the two types of reproduction that can occur: asexual and sexual. In asexual reproduction, portions of the hyphae develop into sporangia (spore cases). Each sporangium produces flagellated spores that swim away from the sporangium in search of food. When food is found, the spores develop into hyphae, which grow into new organisms.

Figure 19–4 *The water mold, an oomycete, reproduces both asexually and sexually. During asexual reproduction, flagellated spores are produced by the diploid (2N) mycelium. These spores grow into new mycelia. During sexual reproduction, the male gamete fuses with the female gamete.*

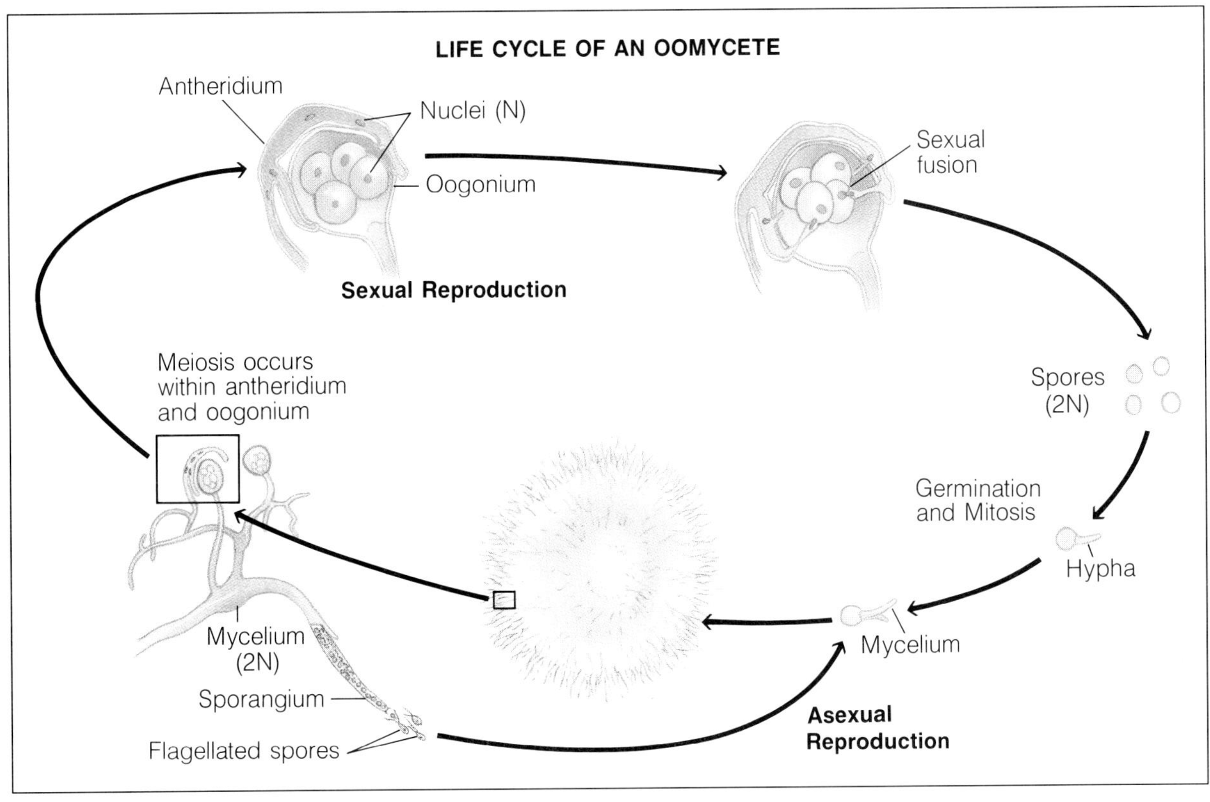

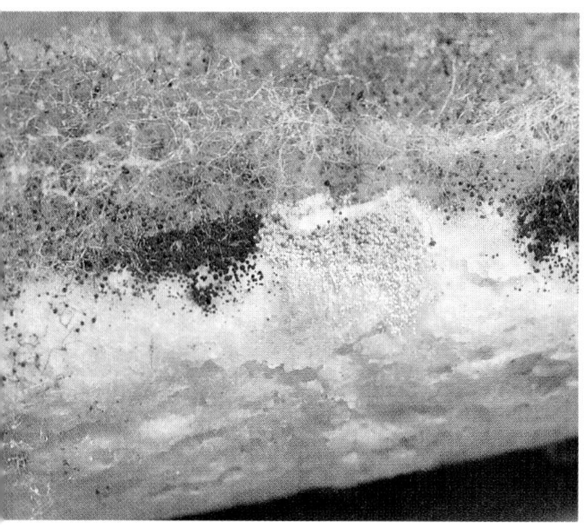

Figure 19–5 The black bread mold Rhizopus stolonifer, *a zygomycete, is commonly found growing on bread. The round black-colored structures at the top of the threadlike hyphae are the sporangia, or spore cases.*

Sexual reproduction takes place in specialized structures that are formed by the hyphae. One of these structures, called the antheridium (an-thuh-RIHD-ee-uhm), produces sperm cells (male gametes). The other structure, called the oogonium, produces egg cells (female gametes). Fertilization occurs within the oogonium and, like spores, the zygotes that form develop into new organisms.

Zygomycota—Common Molds

Fungi that belong to the phylum Zygomycota (zigh-go-migh-KOHT-uh) are called zygomycetes and are terrestrial organisms. During sexual reproduction, they form a thick-walled zygote known as a **zygospore.** The hyphae of zygomycetes lack cross walls although there are cross walls present that isolate the reproductive structures from the rest of the hypha. We have all had some experiences—most often unpleasant ones—with members of this phylum. These common molds are the molds that grow on meat, cheese, and bread.

An example of a zygomycete is the black bread mold *Rhizopus stolonifer.* You can grow this mold yourself by exposing a slice of freshly baked bread (not the processed kind) to some airborne dust. Then keep the bread from drying out by putting it in a covered container and placing it in a warm spot.

Figure 19–6 Sexual reproduction in black bread mold occurs when two hyphae from different mating types fuse, forming gametangia. The gametangia develop into a zygospore, which grows into new hyphae that form sporangia. Asexual reproduction occurs when the spores are discharged from the sporangia.

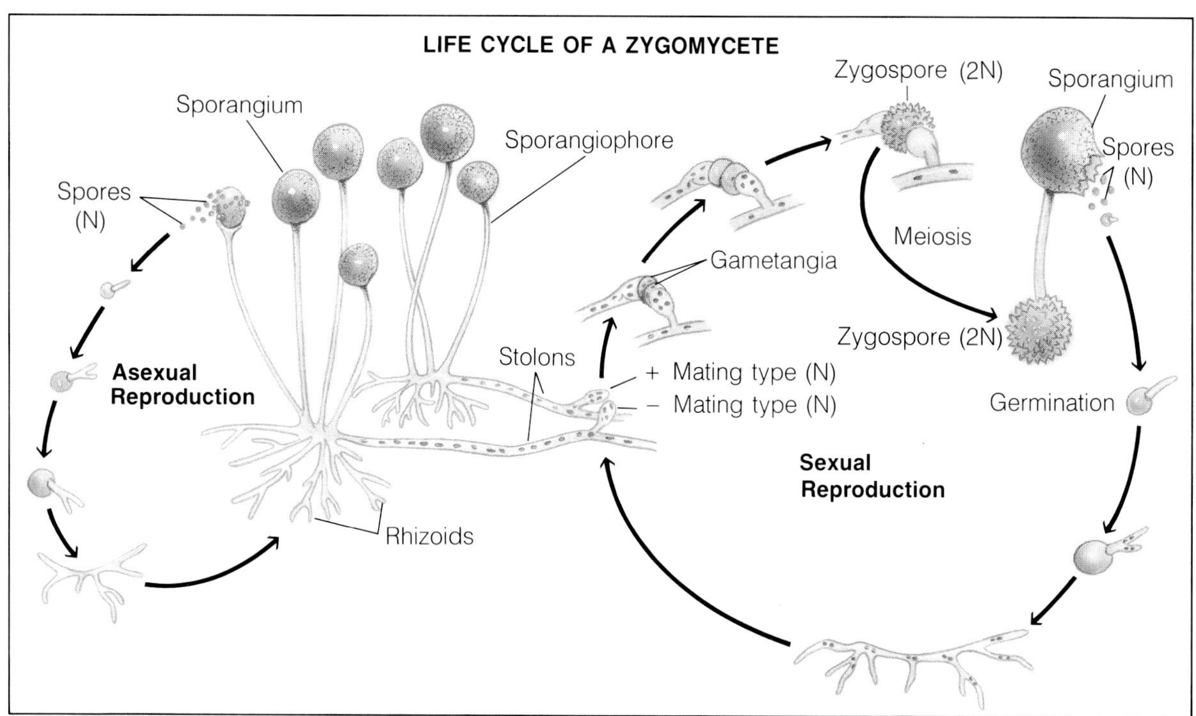

If you were to examine the fuzz with a magnifying glass, you would see tangles of delicate hyphae, or mycelia. Actually, you would be seeing more than one kind of hypha. The rootlike hyphae that penetrate the surface of the slice of bread are called **rhizoids.** Rhizoids anchor the fungus to the bread (much like roots anchor a plant), release digestive enzymes, and absorb digested organic material. The stemlike hyphae that run along the surface of the bread are called **stolons.** And the hyphae that push up into the air are the sporangiophores, which form sporangia at their tips.

During asexual reproduction, sporangia produce spores. A single sporangium may contain as many as 40,000 spores. When fully developed, the sporangium opens, scattering the spores to the wind. Under proper conditions of warmth and moisture, the spores germinate, producing new masses of hyphae.

Sexual reproduction occurs in bread molds and other zygomycetes when two hyphae from different mating types come together, forming gametangia (gamete-producing structures). Haploid gametes are produced in the gametangia. Gametes of one mating type fuse with gametes of the opposite mating type, forming diploid (2N) nuclei. A thick wall develops around the nuclei, producing a zygospore. The tough, resistant zygospore may remain dormant for months. Eventually, when conditions become favorable, the zygospore germinates, undergoes meiosis, and develops into a hypha. The hypha then forms a sporangium and releases spores. Each spore can develop into a new mycelium.

In zygomycetes, as in other organisms, the main function of a sexual reproductive process is to produce new combinations of genetic information. The sexual reproductive process is an effective way to maintain genetic diversity in a species.

Figure 19–7 Ascomycetes are the largest phylum of fungi, containing 30,000 species. Among the ascomycetes are the common morel (bottom) and a type of cup fungus (top).

Ascomycota—Sac Fungi

The phylum Ascomycota (as-kuh-migh-KOHT-uh) is the largest phylum of the kingdom Fungi. There are more than 30,000 species of ascomycetes, as members of this phylum are called. The nuclei in the hyphae of ascomycetes are separated by cross walls so that individual cells do exist within the organism. In the cross walls, however, there are tiny openings through which the cytoplasm and the nuclei can move. Some ascomycetes, such as the morels, are large enough to be visible when they grow above the ground. Others, such as yeasts, are microscopic.

The life cycle of an ascomycete usually includes both asexual and sexual reproduction. Asexual spores are formed at the tip of specialized hyphae called **conidiophores** (koh-NIHD-ee-uh-forz). Because these spores are very fine, they are called **conidia** (koh-NIHD-ee-uh; singular: conidium) from the Greek word *konis*, which means dust.

Sexual reproduction in ascomycetes involves the formation of an **ascus,** or tiny sac. The ascomycetes are named for this reproductive structure. In most ascomycetes, sexual reproduction occurs between two different mating types (+ and −), which produce gametangia. The gametangia grow together to allow the haploid (N) nuclei to fuse. The cell that results from this fusion begins to develop into a structure that forms the ascus. See Figure 19–8. At first the cell has two nuclei, indicating that the nuclei of the two mating types do not fuse right away. When fusion does eventually occur, a diploid (2N) zygote is formed. The fusion is quickly followed by meiosis, producing 4 haploid cells. In most ascomycetes, meiosis is followed by a round (or two) of mitosis, so that 8 or 16 cells are found within the ascus. The cells produced within the ascus are known as **ascospores.** Like conidia, ascospores are capable of growing into new organisms.

The fruiting bodies of ascomycetes can be spectacular. A fruiting body is the part of the fungus that you see above the ground. It contains the spore-producing structures. The morel is an edible ascomycete in which the fruiting body bearing the asci has become the largest visible part of the organism.

The yeasts, which are unicellular, are one of the most interesting groups of ascomycetes. Most of their reproduction is asexual and takes place by mitosis and by budding. Budding is the formation of a smaller cell from a larger one.

Under the right circumstances, yeasts also reproduce sexually. They form asci that contain ascospores. Most scientists

Figure 19–8 *As in most fungi, the life cycle of ascomycetes includes both asexual and sexual reproduction. During asexual reproduction, spores called conidia are formed at the tip of conidiophores, or special hyphae. During sexual reproduction, an ascus, or tiny sac that contains ascospores, forms.*

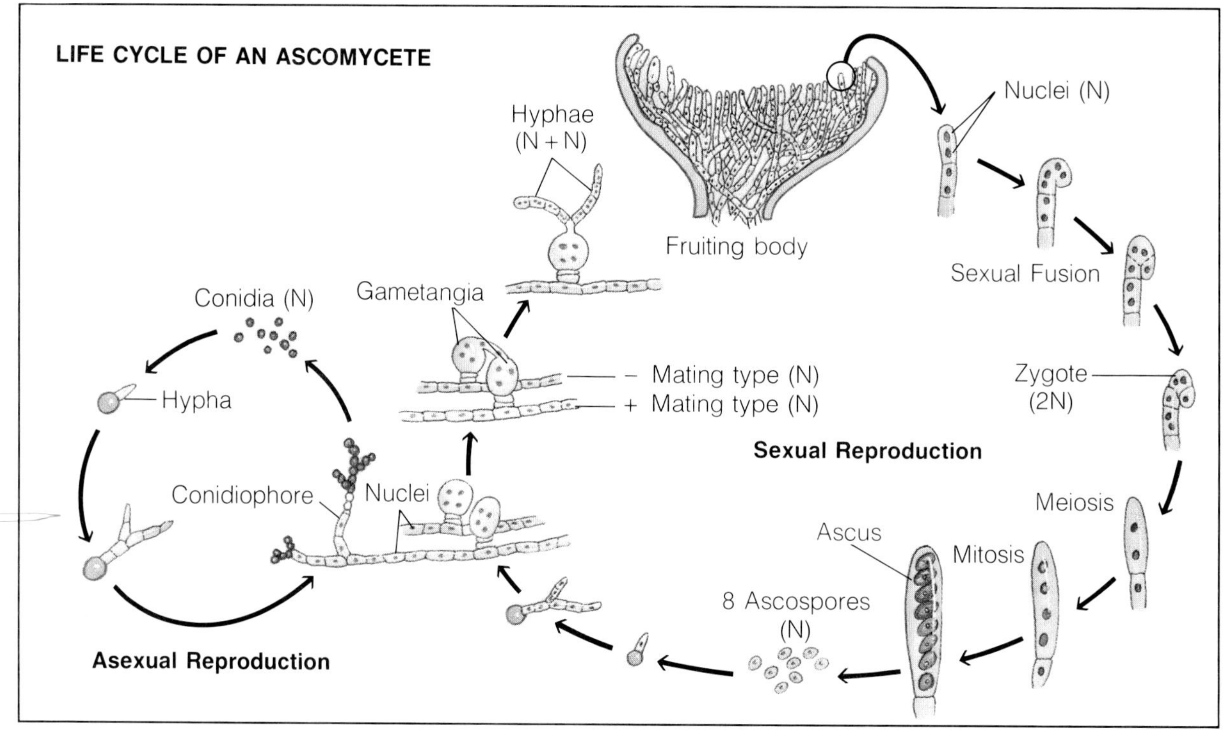

believe that yeast evolved from more complicated (and more typical) ascomycetes that lost the ability to form hyphae and became unicellular.

You probably think of yeast as the dry granules used to make bread, cakes, and rolls. The dry granules actually contain ascospores, which become active in a moist environment. By adding a small amount of the yeast granules to a mixture of water and sugar and waiting less than an hour, you would be able to observe under a microscope mitosis in the rapidly growing yeast cells.

Basidiomycota—Club Fungi

Most of the organisms that we call mushrooms belong to the phylum Basidiomycota (buh-sihd-ee-uh-migh-KOHT-uh) and are known as basidiomycetes. The phylum gets its name from a specialized reproductive structure that resembles a club. This spore-producing structure is called a **basidium** (buh-SIHD-ee-uhm; plural: basidia). In mushrooms, basidia are found in the cap.

Basidiomycetes undergo what is probably the most elaborate life cycle of all the fungi. A **basidiospore** germinates to produce haploid primary mycelia. The haploid primary mycelia of different mating types fuse. A secondary mycelia containing two nuclei—one nucleus from each mating type—is formed. (The nuclei themselves do not fuse at this stage.)

Figure 19–9 *All basidiomycetes, or club fungi, are composed of masses of hyphae. The coral fungus (top, left), shaggy mane fungus (right), and jelly fungus (bottom, left) illustrate the many different shapes that masses of hyphae can form.*

Figure 19–10 This photograph shows the underside of a parasol mushroom. Notice the gills and the stalk. The ringlike structure on the stalk is called the annulus.

The secondary mycelia may grow in the soil for many years, reaching an enormous size. When the right combination of moisture and nutrients is achieved, the formation of a fruiting body (spore-producing structure) begins. The "mushroom" that you see above the ground is actually a fruiting body, which consists of a base, a stemlike stalk, and an umbrella-shaped cap. The mycelia are found below the ground.

The mushroom (fruiting body) begins as a mass of growing hyphae that forms a button, or thick bulge, at the soil's surface. The bulge expands with astounding speed and force, producing fully developed mushrooms overnight. This rapid growth occurs because the cytoplasm from thousands of hyphae in the soil quickly streams into the growing mushroom, enlarging it and producing a great amount of force.

When the mushroom cap opens, it exposes hundreds of tiny gills on its underside. Each gill is lined with basidia. Within a few days, the two nuclei in each basidium fuse to form a true diploid (2N) zygote cell. The diploid cells quickly undergo meiosis, forming clusters of haploid basidiospores. The basidiospores form at the edge of each basidium and, within a few hours, are ready to be scattered. Mushrooms are truly amazing reproductive structures—a single mushroom can produce as many as one billion spores!

In addition to common mushrooms, this phylum includes shelf (bracket) fungi, which grow near the surfaces of dead or decaying trees. The visible bracketlike structure that forms is actually a reproductive structure, and it too is an amazing producer of spores. Puffballs, toadstools, jelly fungi, and plant parasites known as rusts are other examples of basidiomycetes.

Figure 19–11 The most familiar basidiomycetes are the mushrooms. The mushroom cap, which contains basidia, is made up of masses of tightly packed hyphae. Basidia are the club-shaped structures that produce the basidiospores.

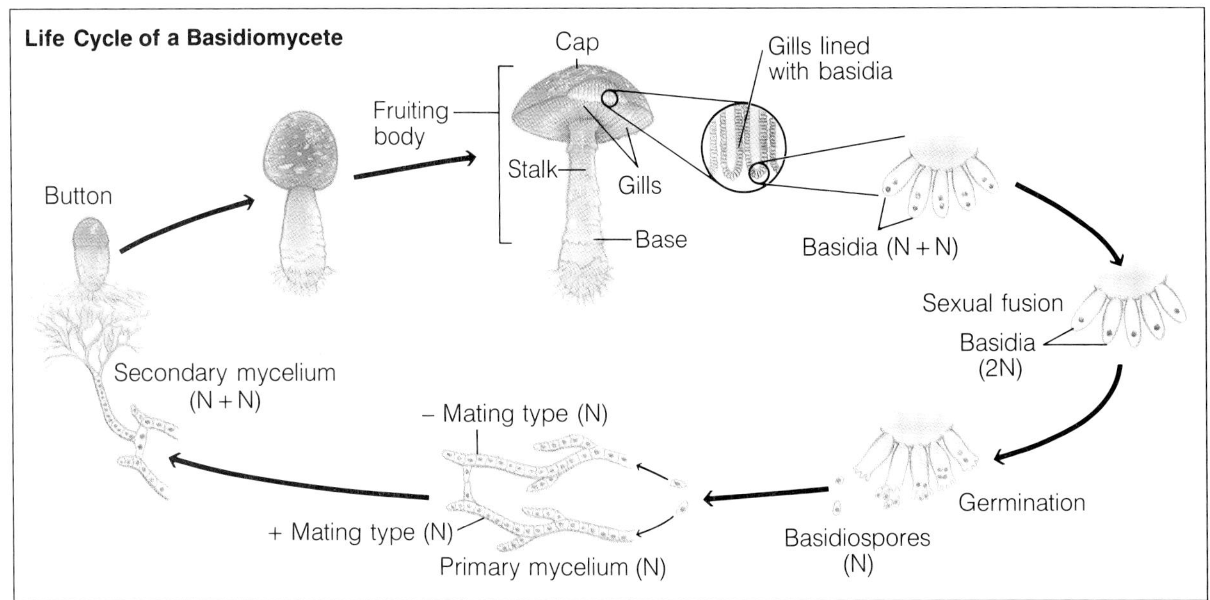

Deuteromycota—Imperfect Fungi

The phylum Deuteromycota (doo-ter-uh-migh-KOHT-uh) includes fungi that cannot be placed in any of the other phyla because their sexual reproduction has never been observed. The word imperfect is a botanical term referring to a lack of sexual reproduction; hence, the name imperfect fungi.

A great majority of the deuteromycetes (as they are also known) closely resemble ascomycetes. Others are similar to basidiomycetes. And a few are much like zygomycetes. An example of a deuteromycete that is similar to ascomycetes is *Penicillium*. *Penicillium* is a mold that frequently grows on fruit and is the source of the antibiotic penicillin. *Penicillium* forms large mycelia on the surfaces of its food source. And like ascomycetes, *Penicillium* reproduces asexually by means of conidia. Biologists believe that *Penicillium* may have developed from a type of ascomycete that lost the ability to carry out the sexual phase of its life cycle.

The deuteromycetes include some of the most infamous members of the kingdom Fungi: those that are responsible for ringworm, athlete's foot, and other skin infections that affect humans. Other deuteromycetes cause several plant diseases, including black spot of roses and early tomato blight.

Figure 19–12 Aspergillus niger, *a deuteromycete, contains spore-bearing structures called conidiophores (inset), which form at the tips of hyphae.*

Figure 19–13 *Five phyla of fungi*

Phylum	Examples	Characteristics	Reproduction	
			Asexual	**Sexual**
Oomycota (protistlike fungi)	Water molds, downy mildew, potato blight fungus	Cell walls with cellulose; coenocytic diploid hyphae	Flagellated oospores in sporangia	Fusion of gametes in gametangia resulting in oospores
Zygomycota (common molds)	*Rhizopus* (black bread mold), *Pilobolus* (a dung fungus)	Cell walls with chitin; coenocytic hyphae	Unflagellated spores in sporangiophores	Fusion of gametes in gametangia resulting in zygospores
Ascomycota (sac fungi)	Yeasts, morels, truffles, *Neurospora* (red bread mold)	Hyphae divided by perforated cross walls; short stage in which cells have two nuclei	Conidia on conidiophores	Fusion of hyphae resulting in ascospores in ascus
Basidiomycota (club fungi)	Mushrooms, puffballs, bracket fungi, rusts, jelly fungi, toadstools	Hyphae divided by perforated cross walls; long stage in which cells have two nuclei	None or conidia on conidiophores	Fusion of cells on tips of hyphae resulting in basidiospores on a basidium
Deuteromycota (imperfect fungi)	*Penicillium*, *Aspergillus*, ringworm and athlete's foot fungus, black spot on roses fungus, tomato blight fungus, cucumber scab fungus	Some resemble ascomycetes; others similar to basidiomycetes; few like zygomycetes	Conidia on conidiophores	None known

SCIENCE, TECHNOLOGY, AND SOCIETY **BREAKTHROUGH**

Cyclosporine

When disease or injury destroys one of a patient's vital organs, physicians often try to transplant the organ from a donor into the patient. This procedure, however, poses a serious and often life-threatening problem. In most transplants, the recipient's immune system recognizes the transplanted organ tissue as foreign and attacks it, causing the rejection of the organ. It was not until 1972 that a substance was discovered that would suppress the immune system's response to a foreign organ.

While working in Switzerland, Jean Borel, a Swiss immunologist, isolated a new strain of deuteromycetes, called *Tolypocladium inflatum,* from soil samples that were obtained in Wisconsin and Norway. This strain produced a substance, later named cyclosporine, that was capable of suppressing the immune system's response to transplanted organs. In other words, the substance was remarkably effective in preventing transplant rejection.

Cyclosporine has revolutionized the field of medical transplantation. Before it became available in 1979, fewer than half of all kidney transplants were successful. With the advent of cyclosporine, the percentage of survival has risen to 90 percent.

Cyclosporine is indeed a wonder drug—but it is not perfect. It causes severe side effects and is not successful in all cases. However, the discovery of cyclosporine has opened up a new frontier in medicine, and we cannot help but wonder how many other pleasant surprises the fungi have in store for us in the future.

Synthetic crystals of cyclosporine (right) and fungus Tolypocladium inflatum *that produces cyclosporine (left)*

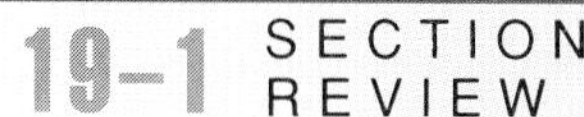

19–1 SECTION REVIEW

1. Describe the structure of a typical fungus.
2. How do fungi obtain food?
3. What are the five phyla of fungi? Describe the characteristics of each.
4. What are some methods by which fungi reproduce?
5. Sensitive tests show that tissue from several mushrooms gathered near the base of a tree are genetically identical. How might you explain this finding?

19–2 Fungi in Nature

Section Objectives

- Describe some methods of spore dispersal.
- Discuss the symbiotic relationships of fungi.
- Summarize the beneficial and harmful effects of fungi.

As you have learned, fungi live by feeding on living organisms or on the remains of dead ones. Although this may paint a grim picture of fungi—linking them with death and decay—they are actually some of the most beautiful organisms on Earth. In this section we will take a very human-centered view of the kingdom Fungi as we examine what effects these organisms have on us and the rest of the living world.

Ecological Significance

The principal role fungi play in the environment is to decompose and recycle living material. Imagine a world in which fungi do not exist: The ground would be littered with leaves, fallen wood, and the bodies of dead animals. What impact would this have on organisms living in this world?

First, you may recall that the material of which a living organism is composed is rich in chemical energy. Because this energy exists, we can make a crackling fire out of wood or a good snack out of an apple. If such material does not undergo decay, the energy it contains will be lost. Second, many organisms, particularly green plants, require small amounts of trace elements and nutrients in order to survive. During their development, green plants remove these materials from the soil. If the materials are not eventually returned, the soil will soon be depleted and the destruction of plants, as well as animals whose lives depend on the plants, will result.

Figure 19–14 *Together with bacteria, fungi—such as this mushroom—are the major decomposers and recyclers of living material on Earth.*

WHERE ARE FUNGI FOUND? There are remarkably few places on Earth where one species of fungus or another does not make its home. Even more amazing is the fact that fungal spores are found in almost every environment. Indeed, this is why molds seem to spring up in any location that has the right combination of moisture and food.

In many places, large mycelia occupy a nearly permanent place in the environment and last for many years. A mushroom develops from a mycelium located just below the ground. As the mycelium grows, new mushrooms pop up from the mycelium wherever nutrients are available. This is why strands of mushrooms are often part of the same organism.

As time goes by, the available nutrients near the center of the mycelium become depleted, causing new mushrooms to sprout only at the edges of the mycelium. This produces a ring of mushrooms called a fairy ring. People once thought fairies dancing in circles during warm nights produced these rings, so they called them fairy rings. Over many years, fairy rings can become enormous, forming rings 10 to 20 meters in diameter.

SPORE DISPERSAL Many fungi, including most common mushrooms, produce dry, almost weightless, spores that are

Figure 19–15 The giant puffball contains as many as 7 trillion spores. In the common puffball, the dispersal of spores can be triggered by the slightest touch, even by a raindrop.

easily scattered by the wind. On a clear day, a few liters of fresh air may contain hundreds of spores from many species of fungi. Some of these species have remarkable ways of getting their spores into places where they are likely to grow.

For fungi, spore placement is crucial. A single spore has a slim chance of finding the proper combination of temperature, moisture, and food so that it can germinate. Even under the best of circumstances, the odds of a spore producing a mature organism can be more than one in a billion. So you can see why anything that might help reduce those odds is considered a selective advantage to that species.

The puffballs (basidiomycetes) go to extremes to produce their spores. A mature puffball is virtually a warehouse of spores. The simple action of a raindrop falling on a puffball can release thousands of spores in a small cloud of dust.

Other species of fungi trick animals into dispersing their spores for them. The stinkhorns (*Phallus*) go so far as to mimic rotting meat. The surface of a stinkhorn is covered with a fluid that has the odor of rotting flesh. Flies are drawn to the stinkhorn. Then they land on the stinkhorn to taste the sticky fluid. Once ingested, the spore-containing fluid will pass unharmed out of the flies' digestive systems, depositing spores over great distances.

Symbiotic Relationships

Many fungi associate with members of other species in symbiotic relationships. In some of these relationships, such as early tomato blight, fungi are harmful. But in other cases, fungi form relationships in which both partners benefit. Such is the situation with the **lichens** (LIGH-kuhnz) and **mycorrhizae** (migh-koh-RIGH-zee).

Lichens are symbiotic partnerships between a fungus and a photosynthetic organism. The fungus in the relationship is usually an ascomycete, although it can be a basidiomycete. The photosynthetic organism is either a cyanobacterium (blue-green bacterium) or a green alga.

Figure 19–16 Fungi have remarkable ways of dispersing their spores. The lacy stinkhorn attracts flies by producing a spore-containing fluid that has the odor of rotting flesh. The spores pass unharmed through the flies' digestive system and are deposited over great distances. Pilobolus *(inset) fires its sporangia at an initial speed of 50 kilometers per hour—as far as 1 meter.*

Because they are extremely resistant to drought and cold, lichens grow in places where few other organisms can survive —on dry, bare rock in deserts and on the tops of mountains. Lichens are able to survive in these harsh environments because of the relationship between the two partner organisms. The alga carries out photosynthesis, providing the fungus with a source of organic nutrients. The fungus, in turn, provides the alga with water and minerals that it has collected from the surfaces on which it grows.

Lichens are often the first organisms to enter barren environments, gradually breaking down the rocks upon which they grow. In this way, lichens help in the early stages of soil formation and eventually form an environment that is hospitable to other organisms.

Another symbiotic relationship, called mycorrhizae, forms between fungi and green plants (mycorrhiza means fungus root in Greek). The tiny hyphae of the fungi aid plants in absorbing water, minerals, and nutrients. They do this by producing a network that covers the roots of the plants and increases the effective surface area of the root system. The plants, in turn, provide the fungi with the products of photosynthesis.

An example of mycorrhizae involves orchids, which are considered by many as the most beautiful of the flowering plants. The seeds of orchids germinate in nature only in the presence of a certain species of fungi. These fungi penetrate the seed, providing it with moisture and food during the early stages of the orchid's growth.

The symbiotic relationships between green plants and fungi have existed for millions of years. Some of the earliest fossils of land plants contain evidence of fungi. This suggests that fungi may have played a crucial role in the colonization of the land by green plants.

Figure 19–17 *Lichens generally grow in three forms. Crustose lichens are flat (top), foliose lichens resemble leaves (center), and fruticose lichens grow upright (bottom).*

Fungi and Human Life

Two of the oldest discoveries of civilization are the techniques for making bread and alcohol. Interestingly enough, both techniques rely on a cooperative effort between humans and fungi and provide an important example of the many ways in which humans have made use of this living kingdom.

Because of the role yeasts play in baking and brewing, one might argue that they are the most important fungi to humans. The common yeasts used for baking and brewing are members of the genus *Saccharomyces* (sak-uh-roh-MIGH-seez). To grow these yeasts, a rich nutrient mixture containing very little oxygen is prepared. In brewing, it is a vat of grape juice or barley malt. In baking, it is a mound of thick dough. The yeasts within the mixture quickly begin the process of alcoholic fermentation in order to obtain enough energy to survive. The byproducts of alcoholic fermentation are carbon dioxide and alcohol. The carbon dioxide gas makes bread rise (by producing bubbles

Figure 19–18 In France, pigs are used in the search for truffles. Truffles (left) are considered by many people to be a rare and delicious treat.

within the dough) and beverages bubble. The alcohol is used in alcoholic beverages or as a fuel.

As you may recall from Chapter 12, yeasts are now used for genetic engineering. Because they are eukaryotes, yeasts often process the protein products of genes cloned from other eukaryotes more efficiently than bacteria (prokaryotes) do. It is not impossible to imagine that sometime in the near future, genetically engineered yeasts may be used to produce a wide variety of biologically important compounds.

Some types of fungi have long been considered a delicacy by humans. One example are the mushrooms (basidiomycetes). There are approximately 10,000 different species of mushrooms found throughout the world. Many of these mushrooms are cultivated and prepared by people and then sold in supermarkets and specialty food shops. These species of mushrooms are easy to grow, taste good when properly cooked, and do not pose a danger to anyone who eats them.

Wild mushrooms are a different story: Although some are edible, many are poisonous. You may have heard someone say that only toadstools are poisonous, whereas mushrooms are safe to eat. Unfortunately, this is not true. For toadstools are mushrooms. Furthermore, poisonous mushrooms do not belong to just one order or family of basidiomycetes.

Because many species of poisonous mushrooms look almost identical to edible mushrooms, it is best not to pick or eat any mushrooms found in the wild. Instead, mushroom gathering should be left to experts who can positively identify each mushroom they collect. The result of eating a poisonous mushroom is severe illness and sometimes death.

History records that the Roman Emperor Claudius was given a plate of mushrooms, known as deathcaps (*Amanita phalloides*), by his palace guards in a plot to remove him from the throne. He ate heartily. Although the deathcaps were delicious, the meal served its purpose and the throne was empty the next day.

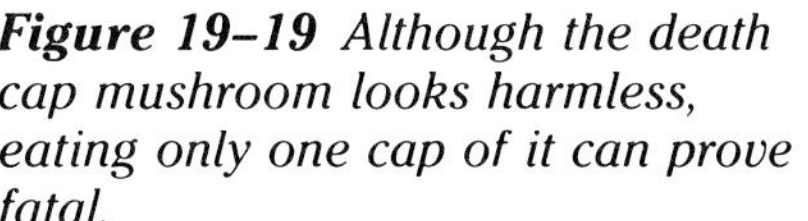

Figure 19–19 Although the death cap mushroom looks harmless, eating only one cap of it can prove fatal.

Diseases Caused by Fungi

Not all fungi are suited to human needs. Some species of fungi cause tremendous losses of food and crops every year, and some cause disease in humans.

POTATO BLIGHT In their own way, the plant diseases caused by fungi have influenced history. In 1845, the potato crops of Ireland and Europe were devastated by a fungus that destroyed the foliage of the plant and infected the potatoes themselves. The culprit was the oomycete *Phytophthora infestans,* which causes the disease known as late potato blight.

Potatoes that are infected with the blight may appear normal at harvest time. But within a few weeks, the fungus makes its way into the potato, reducing it to a spongy sac of spores and dust. During the years that followed the potato blight infection, more than one million people in Ireland died of starvation as the result of the destruction of their main food source. Many others left Ireland and emigrated to the United States rather than face a similar fate.

WHEAT RUST Another fungal disease, called rust, affects wheat, one of the most important crops grown in North America. During the early part of this century, farmers in the Midwest watched helplessly as their plants developed tiny rustlike spots on their leaves. These spots gradually expanded and killed the plants before they could be used to produce grain. A similar incident occurred in the 1930s, when great plagues of rust disease added to the economic misery of the Great Depression. During this time, farmers not only lost their crops but their farms as well.

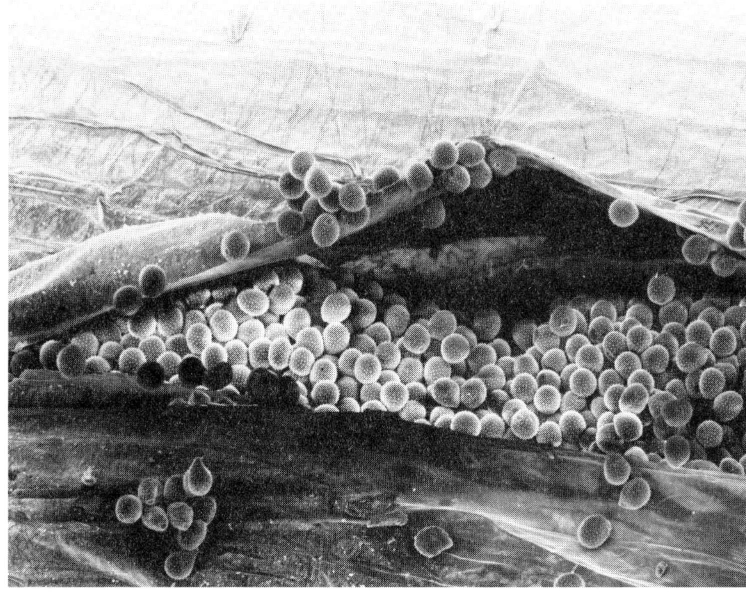

Figure 19–20 *This electron micrograph shows a cluster of spores of the wheat rust fungus bursting through the plant's epidermis, or outer covering.*

Rusts are caused by a type of basidiomycete that needs two different plants in order to complete its life cycle. Spores produced by the rust in the barberry plant are carried by the wind into wheat fields. There the spores germinate and infect wheat plants. The patches of rust produce a second type of spore that infects other plants, allowing the disease to spread through a field of wheat at an alarming rate.

Later in the year, often after the wheat crop has been ruined, new kinds of spores are produced by the rust. These black-colored spores are tough enough to survive through the winter. In the spring, they go through a sexual phase and produce spores that infect the barberry plant. Once on the barberry leaves, the rust produces the spores that infect the wheat plant, and the cycle continues. Fortunately, the life cycle of the rust can be broken and the disease brought under control by destroying the barberry plant.

OTHER PLANT DISEASES Fungi that attack crop plants cause other diseases such as corn smut, which destroys the corn kernels, and mildews, which infect a wide variety of fruits. It is estimated that fungal diseases are responsible for the loss of approximately 15 percent of the crops grown in temperate regions of the world. In tropical areas, where high humidity favors fungal growth, the loss of crops is sometimes as high as 50 percent. As you can see, these organisms are in direct competition with us for our own food supply.

HUMAN DISEASES Although most fungal diseases are associated with plants rather than animals, there are several fungi that cause disease in humans. These pathogenic (disease-causing) organisms are deuteromycetes (imperfect fungi). One type can infect the areas between the toes, causing athlete's foot. The fungus forms a mycelium directly within the outer layers of skin. This produces a red, inflamed sore from which the spores can easily spread from person to person.

When the same fungus infects the skin of the scalp, it produces a red scaling sore known as ringworm. Contrary to popular belief, ringworm is not caused by a worm; it is caused by a fungus. Ringworm can be passed from person to person by the exchange of hats, combs, and athletic headgear. The fungi that cause athlete's foot and ringworm can be destroyed by the application of fungicides, or chemicals that kill fungi.

Another type of fungal disease that infects humans is caused by the yeast *Candida albicans.* This fungus grows in moist regions of the body, such as the mouth and the urinary tract. Usually its growth is kept in check by competition from bacteria and by the body's immune system. This normal balance can be upset by many factors, including the use of antibiotics, which kill bacteria, or by damage to the immune system. When this happens, *Candida* may produce thrush, a serious and painful mouth infection, or infections of the urinary tract.

Figure 19–21 *This ant has been killed by a fungus called* Cordyceps lloydii. *Once the fungus's tiny spore enters the insect's body, it begins to multiply. Within days, the fungus digests all but the ant's outer covering. The umbrellalike structures growing out of the ant's body are the fungus's fruiting bodies.*

ANIMAL DISEASES As serious as human fungal diseases can be, few approach the deadliness of *Cordyceps lloydii.* This fungus infects ants in forests near the basin of the Amazon River in Venezuela. Microscopic spores become lodged in the ant, where they germinate and produce enzymes that slowly penetrate the insect's tough exoskeleton (external skeleton). Once the spores have gained entry, they multiply in the insect's blood, digesting all its cells and tissues until the insect dies. To complete the process of digestion, hyphae develop, cloaking the decaying exoskeleton in a web of fungal material. Reproductive structures, which will produce more spores that will spread the infection, then emerge from the ant's remains.

19–2 SECTION REVIEW

1. What is the major role of fungi in the environment?
2. What are some methods by which fungi disperse their spores?
3. Describe the role of fungi in two important symbiotic relationships.
4. Why can lichens survive in harsh environments?
5. What are some beneficial effects of fungi? Some harmful effects?
6. Why are fungi a more serious problem in tropical regions of the world than they are in temperate regions?

LABORATORY INVESTIGATION

COMPARING A MOLD AND A MUSHROOM

PROBLEM

What are some similarities and some differences between a mold and a mushroom?

MATERIALS *(per group)*

bread	microscope
petri dish	iodine solution
2 medicine droppers	paper towel
2 glass slides	mushroom
dissecting needle	forceps
2 coverslips	

PROCEDURE 

1. Moisten a piece of bread with tap water. Place the moistened bread in the bottom of the petri dish.
2. Allow the petri dish to remain uncovered for 30 minutes. After 30 minutes, put the cover on the petri dish.
3. Place the petri dish in a warm, dark place where it will remain undisturbed for 1 to 2 weeks. Examine the bread daily for mold.
4. After the bread becomes moldy, use a medicine dropper to place a drop of water in the center of a glass slide.
5. With the dissecting needle, separate a small piece of the mold from the bread. **CAUTION:** *Be careful when using a dissecting needle.* Add the mold to the water on the glass slide and cover with a coverslip.
6. Locate some hyphae (threadlike filaments) with the low-power objective of the microscope. Then switch to the high-power objective and use the fine adjustment to locate some hyphae. Notice their color.
7. With the other medicine dropper, place a drop of iodine solution at one edge of the coverslip. Hold a piece of paper towel at the opposite edge of the coverslip to draw the iodine solution across the coverslip.
8. Examine the hyphae again under the low and high powers of the microscope. Observe the shape and arrangement of the hyphae. Notice the sporangia, or bulb-shaped structures, at the ends of some of the hyphae. Make a labeled diagram of the structures of the mold.
9. Place a drop of water in the center of the second glass slide.
10. Break the stalk off the mushroom slightly below the place where the stalk meets the cap. Insert the dissecting needle just under the surface of the stalk and carefully remove a small flap of the stalk.
11. With the forceps, peel off a thin layer of mushroom that runs parallel to the stalk. This layer contains the secondary mycelia (mass of hyphae).
12. Place the thin layer of mycelia in the water on the glass slide. Flatten the layer before covering it with a coverslip.
13. Repeat steps 6 through 8 using the mass of hyphae of the mushroom.

OBSERVATIONS

1. How many different kinds of mold do you see growing on the bread?
2. What is the color of the hyphae in the bread mold? In the mushroom stalk?
3. Describe the shape and arrangement of the structures of the mold and the mushroom.

ANALYSIS AND CONCLUSIONS

1. Explain why the bread was exposed to the air.
2. Why was the bread allowed to remain undisturbed in a warm, dark place for several weeks?
3. What was the purpose of examining the unstained mold and mushroom structures under the microscope?
4. How are a mold and a mushroom similar? How are they different?

STUDENT STUDY GUIDE

SUMMARIZING THE CONCEPTS

The key concepts in each section of this chapter are listed below to help you review the chapter content. Make sure you understand each concept and its relationship to other concepts and to the theme of this chapter.

19–1 The Fungi

- Fungi are eukaryotic heterotrophs that are placed in the kingdom Fungi. They may be saprophytes, parasites, or symbionts.
- Together with bacteria, fungi are the major decomposers, or organisms of decay.
- Hyphae secrete digestive enzymes that break down food into simpler molecules and absorb them into their cells.
- The body of a fungus consists of tiny filaments tangled together into a thick mass called a mycelium. The individual filaments are called hyphae.
- Most fungi reproduce asexually and sexually.
- The kingdom Fungi is divided into five phyla: Oomycota, Zygomycota, Ascomycota, Basidiomycota, and Deuteromycota.
- Oomycetes reproduce asexually by producing flagellated spores in structures called sporangia, or spore cases. Sexual reproduction results in the formation of male and female gametes. The nuclei of these gametes fuse, forming a diploid cell.
- Zygomycetes, ascomycetes, basidiomycetes, and deuteromycetes reproduce asexually by spores, which develop in sporangia. With the exception of deuteromycetes, these fungi reproduce sexually when two mating types come into contact, producing cells in the gametangia. The sexual part of the life cycle of deuteromycetes has never been observed.
- Ascomycetes produce spores sexually in an ascus, or tiny sac. Basidiomycetes produce spores in club-shaped basidia.

19–2 Fungi in Nature

- The principal role that fungi have in the environment is to decompose and recycle living material.
- Lichens are symbiotic partnerships between a fungus and a photosynthetic organism. The fungus is usually an ascomycete, and the photosyntheic organism is either a cyanobacterium or a green alga.
- Some fungi cause tremendous losses of food and crops, and some cause disease in humans and other animals.

REVIEWING KEY TERMS

Vocabulary terms are important to your understanding of biology. The key terms listed below are those you should be especially familiar with. Review these terms and their meanings. Then use each term in a complete sentence. If you are not sure of a term's meaning, return to the appropriate section and review its definition.

19–1 The Fungi

fungus
decomposer
mycelium
hypha
sporangium
sporangiophore
gametangium
zygospore
rhizoid
stolon
conidiophore
conidium
ascus
ascospore
basidium
basidiospore

19–2 Fungi in Nature

lichen
mycorrhiza

CHAPTER REVIEW

CONTENT REVIEW

Multiple Choice

Choose the letter of the answer that best completes each statement.

1. Fungi consist of tiny filaments called
   a. asci. c. basidia.
   b. hyphae. d. sporangia.
2. Fungi obtain nutrients by
   a. photosynthesis.
   b. external digestion of food.
   c. ingestion of small organisms.
   d. absorption through cilia.
3. What are the small rootlike hyphae in bread mold called?
   a. rhizoids c. basidia
   b. mycelia d. caps
4. Yeasts are
   a. ascomycetes. c. zygomycetes.
   b. basidiomycetes. d. deuteromycetes.
5. Basidiomycetes are also known as
   a. sac fungi. c. water molds.
   b. imperfect fungi. d. club fungi.
6. Lichens are symbiotic partnerships between a
   a. fungus and a plant.
   b. green alga and a cyanobacterium.
   c. fungus and a cyanobacterium.
   d. green alga and a plant.
7. Which fungal disease destroyed Ireland's main source of food in 1845?
   a. wheat rust
   b. potato blight
   c. corn smut
   d. cucumber scab
8. Athlete's foot is caused by a (an)
   a. oomycete. c. deuteromycete.
   b. basidiomycete. d. ascomycete.

True or False

Determine whether each statement is true or false. If it is true, write "true." If it is false, change the underlined word or words to make the statement true.

1. Fungi are <u>autotrophs</u>.
2. Fungi reproduce by <u>binary fission</u>.
3. During asexual reproduction, zygomycetes form thick-walled zygotes called <u>basidiospores</u>.
4. In the bread mold, the hyphae that run along the surface of the bread are called <u>stolons</u>.
5. Mushrooms belong to the phylum <u>Oomycota</u>.
6. Sexual reproduction has never been observed in <u>deuteromycetes</u>.
7. A <u>morel</u> is a symbiotic partnership between a fungus and a photosynthetic organism.
8. <u>Yeasts</u> are used in the baking and brewing industries.

Word Relationships

A. *In each of the following sets of terms, three of the terms are related. One term does not belong. Determine the characteristic common to three of the terms and then identify the term that does not belong.*

1. oomycetes, ascomycetes, basidiomycetes, zygomycetes
2. zygomycetes, ascomycetes, basidiomycetes, deuteromycetes
3. athlete's foot, rust, thrush, ringworm
4. stolon, rhizoid, sporangiophore, zygospore
5. mushroom, morel, truffle, yeast

B. *An analogy is a relationship between two pairs of words or phrases generally written in the following manner: a:b::c:d. The symbol : is read "is to," and the symbol :: is read "as." For example, cat:animal::rose:plant is read "cat is to animal as rose is to plant."*

In the analogies that follow, a word or phrase is missing. Complete each analogy by providing the missing word or phrase.

6. ascus:sac fungus::basidium: ________________

7. water mold:oomycete::club fungus: ________________

8. fungus and green alga:lichen::fungus and green plant: ________________

CONCEPT MASTERY

Use your understanding of the concepts developed in the chapter to answer each of the following in a brief paragraph.

1. Discuss the general characteristics of fungi.
2. How do oomycetes differ from the other members of the kingdom Fungi? How do deuteromycetes differ?
3. Discuss reproduction in the bread mold *Rhizopus stolonifer.*
4. Explain the basis for the classification of fungi.
5. Why are yeasts useful in genetic research?
6. What is the ecological importance of lichens and mycorrhizae?
7. Why is the absence of oxygen important for fermentation by yeast?
8. Describe the life cycle of wheat rust.

CRITICAL AND CREATIVE THINKING

Discuss each of the following in a brief paragraph.

1. **Identifying relationships** Heavily polluted fresh water contains few fungi. How might this affect life in a lake?
2. **Applying concepts** Explain why there are more fungi in a forest than in a field.
3. **Making predictions** What would be the effect on humans of a fungicide capable of killing all types of fungi?
4. **Classifying fungi** Develop your own system of classification for the fungi. Draw a diagram to represent your system.
5. **Relating concepts** While on a walk in the forest, you come upon some fungi, similar to those shown in the photograph, growing from the trunk of a fallen tree. You examine the underside of one of the fungi with a magnifying glass and notice some club-shaped structures. To which phylum do these fungi belong? Explain your answer.

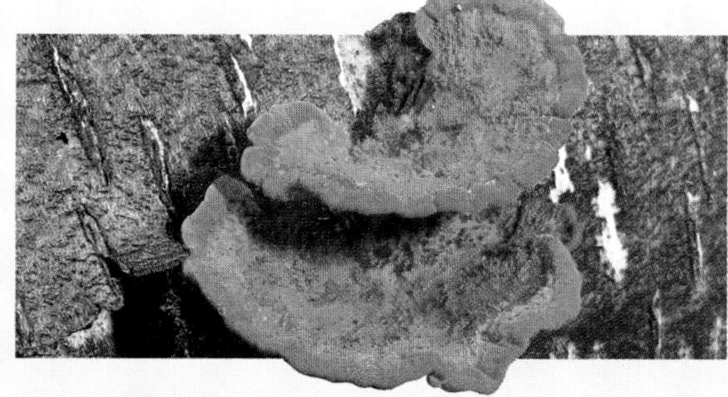

6. **Using the writing process** A debate is raging in your classroom. Some people argue that because fungi cause human disease and damage crops, they should be eradicated from Earth. Their case seems compelling. But you are responsible for defending the opposing viewpoint. Let the fungi be, you maintain. Write the script for the argument you would present in the debate.

Biological Technician

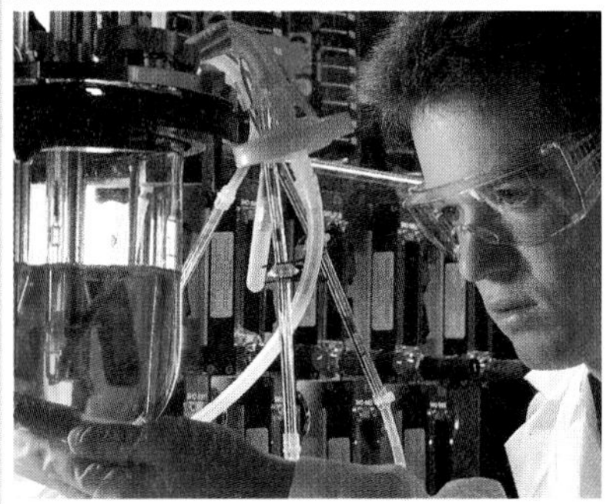

Biological technicians assist biologists by performing laboratory experiments on biological substances and living organisms. Biological technicians use a variety of laboratory techniques and equipment that includes microscopes, chemical scales, and centrifuges. The data they gather enable biologists to develop new substances—such as medications, food additives, and insecticides—and to reach conclusions about how organisms function.

Biological technicians require at least a high school education, but further training in biology is recommended.

For more information write to the American Chemical Society, 1155 16th St., NW, Washington, DC 20036.

Microbiologist

Microbiologists study the growth, structure, and development of microscopic organisms such as bacteria, viruses, molds, and algae. They work in laboratories with electron microscopes, computers, and other complex equipment.

Many microbiologists specialize in studying specific types of organisms. Some study only those microbes that cause disease, others study those that cause pollution, and still others study those that harm animals.

Microbiologists must have at least a Bachelor's degree in biology or microbiology. Many continue their education to earn advanced degrees.

For information contact the American Society for Microbiology, 1913 I St., NW, Washington, DC 20006.

Virologist

Virologists isolate and study viruses in order to learn how they cause disease. With this information, virologists develop and test ways to fight or control different viruses.

Virologists also determine which viruses can be useful to us. For example, certain viruses have been identified that kill insects harmful to crops without hurting the plant.

Virologists perform research for the government, hospitals, pharmaceutical companies, and universities. They are required to have an advanced degree in virology, usually a Ph.D.

For more information write to the American Public Health Association, 1015 15th St., NW, Washington, DC 20005.

HOW TO FIND A SUMMER JOB

Various summer jobs are available to high school students. Your local newspaper probably lists summer job openings specifically meant for students in a separate section of the classified ads.

Local and state governments often provide summer work programs for students. Contact your local government to find out if such programs are available in your area. Many companies and local businesses also hire students to work part time or full time during the summer. Your school or community library may have a list of such employers. It is important to begin looking for a summer job before you are actually ready to begin working.

FROM THE AUTHORS

I remember thinking that it was the easiest question on the exam. I had to write a short essay comparing the animallike and plantlike protists. Our teacher then asked us to comment on whether the distinctions between "plantlike" and "animallike" organisms were valid. I wrote a terrific answer. Honest, I did. A **B** for sure . . . maybe an **A**, I thought. But next week the exam came back with a big **0** at the top of the question. No comments, nothing marked wrong. Just a zero and two innocent words underlined in a simple sentence:

> In many of these simple organisms, the distinction between plant and animal is not valid.

After class I approached my teacher. I got all my courage together and asked about the grade. He didn't answer. Instead he motioned me back to the small prep room behind the classroom where he kept a few microscopes and specimens. He put a drop of water under the microscope, telling me that he had gotten it from the pond, which was a short walk from the high school. He made me look. I could recognize a couple of the organisms from our labs in class, but most of them were a complete mystery. There were clusters of green cells in groups of two and three. There were little ciliated cells that swam around like bullets. There were a couple of massive slow-moving amebas. There were marvelous flower-shaped cells with cups in the center and long stalks busily filtering everything in sight in search of food.

"Can you explain to me how those little cells know that they've bumped into something and then reverse direction," he asked. "No," I said. "How about those cone-shaped cells? Are those green clusters yellow or green algae? Is the red spot in the little cell an eyespot or a vacuole? How does an eyespot work?" I admitted that I knew the answers to none of his questions. "Fine," he said. "Then you will never call these organisms 'simple' again, Mr. Miller?" "No, sir," I said, as I rushed out. And since that day, I never have.

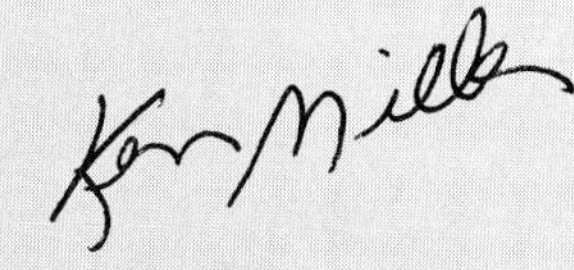

UNIT 6

Life on Earth: Plants

A stroller on a summer's walk can't help but notice the wonderful green color of planet Earth. This color comes in large part from plants. Plants provide beauty for the eye—and much, much more.

Plants constantly replenish our supply of oxygen, which they give off during photosynthesis. During the same process, they make nutrients and, in turn, become food sources for other living things. Plants also give off water, which cools the temperature of the air.

Plants cover much of the surface of the Earth, existing in a multitude of forms and surviving in a variety of environments. It is plants that make it possible for other forms of life to share this planet.

CHAPTERS

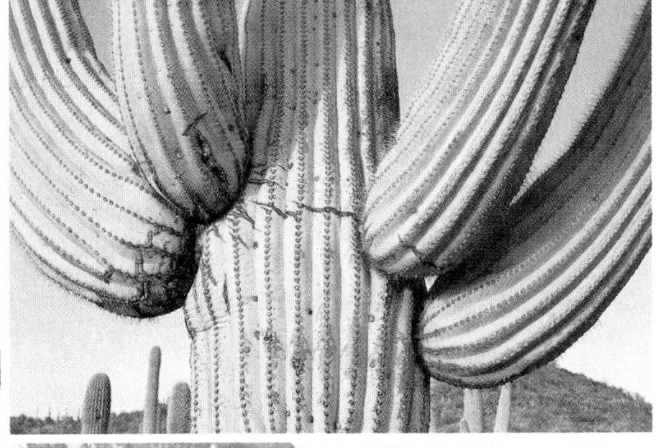

CHAPTER 20

Multicellular Algae

Sea otters, among the most appealing species of animals, make their home in the kelp forests off the coast of California. They wrap themselves in strands of algae to keep from floating away on the ocean waves.

Along the coasts of Washington, Oregon, and northern California, pine and redwood forests crown rocky cliffs that dive steeply into the pounding surf. Beneath the ocean waves, invisible to the casual observer, another type of forest thrives—a forest of giant greenish-brown kelp. Kelp are huge seaweeds that grow as long or longer than the tallest forest trees. Growing with amazing speed, kelp offer both home and food to a wide variety of fish, shellfish, and sea otters.

The kelp forest is but one scene from the little-known world of life beneath the sea, a world fed and sheltered by algae. What are algae? Where do they live? In this chapter we shall examine this extraordinary group of plants and explore the many ways in which algae are adapted to life on Earth.

CHAPTER OUTLINE

20–1 Characteristics of Algae

Section Objectives

- Discuss the characteristics of algae.
- Describe the adaptations of algae to life in a water environment.

Algae are photosynthetic organisms that live in streams, ponds, lakes, swamps, and all the oceans of the world. Algae also live on damp tree trunks and rocks and in moist soil. The stringy green filaments you may have seen in a local pond are algae. So are the giant brown seaweeds that wash up on a beach after a storm. And if you keep tropical fish, you may have noticed algae covering the walls of the tank.

From these examples, you may already have determined one important characteristic of algae: Algae must live in or near a source of water. **Unlike land plants, most algae lack an internal system of tubes to move water and materials from one part of the plant to another.** The water in which algae live bathes their cells with carbon dioxide, oxygen, and nutrients, and carries away wastes produced by the cells.

Algae can be unicellular or multicellular and, therefore, vary considerably in size. Most algae are multicellular. Some species of multicellular algae, such as the giant kelp, can grow to more than 60 meters in length. Most unicellular algae are microscopic, resembling plantlike protists.

Figure 20–1 *Giant kelp are often washed up on shore when storms tear the plants loose from the holdfasts that anchor them to the bottom. These giant algae can be as long as a football field.*

Figure 20–2 *Different kinds of algae, along with many kinds of small animals, live in tide pools. With each crashing wave, water brings food for the animals and plants. Wastes produced by the organisms are carried away as the ocean water seeps from the tide pool.*

The cells of all algae have a cell wall. Algae never develop the specialized root, stem, and leaf structures found in land plants. All algae contain chlorophyll *a,* one of several forms of chlorophyll. Some species of algae contain another form of chlorophyll in addition to chlorophyll *a.* Many species of algae have a complicated reproductive cycle in which stages of sexual reproduction alternate with stages of asexual reproduction.

There is some disagreement among scientists about the classification of algae. Because some species of algae are unicellular, some scientists place all algae in the kingdom Protista. But because many species of algae are multicellular, other scientists place all algae in the kingdom Plantae.

In this textbook we have chosen to use the following classification: The single-celled Chrysophytes (diatoms), Euglenophytes (euglenas), and Pyrrophytes (dinoflagellates) are placed in the kingdom Protista. (You read about these types of algae in Chapter 18.) But because of their chemistry and reproductive cycles, multicellular algae are placed in the kingdom Plantae. This chapter deals primarily with these multicellular species of algae. However, as you will notice in reading the chapter, certain single-celled algae have been included. These algae are more plantlike than protistlike and thus are grouped together with the multicellular algae they most resemble. You should also notice in reading this chapter that although some botanists call the major plant groups divisions, we call them phyla—as we do the major groups of all other organisms.

Adaptations of Algae to Life Under Water

Most algae live under water and show different adaptations from those of land plants. For example, underwater plants do not need protection from drying out. Thus many kinds of algae have very thin (often only two cells thick) leaflike structures that lack a waterproof covering. These thin structures can exchange oxygen, carbon dioxide, and nutrients directly with the water around them. As you already learned, algae have no specialized tissues to carry such materials throughout their body.

Because algae are supported by water, they do not need stemlike structures to keep them from falling over, such as land plants do. And, as you will soon learn, sexual reproduction can be more easily accomplished in water because reproductive cells can swim through water and the fragile young plants do not dry out.

Chlorophyll and Accessory Pigments

Life under water poses one major problem for plants: a lack of light for photosynthesis. As you will remember, light is necessary for the food-making process, and it is chlorophyll that traps the energy of sunlight. However, water absorbs much of this energy as sunlight passes through it. In particular, seawater absorbs large amounts of energy corresponding to the red and violet wavelengths of sunlight. And it is exactly these two wavelengths that chlorophyll *a* uses best. Because seawater absorbs most of the red and violet wavelengths, light becomes much dimmer and bluer in color as the depth of water increases. The dim blue light that penetrates into deep water contains very little light energy that chlorophyll *a* can use.

In adapting to the challenge of life with little light, various groups of algae have evolved different forms of chlorophyll. Each form of chlorophyll—chlorophyll *a,* chlorophyll *b,* chlorophyll *c,* and chlorophyll *d*— absorbs different wavelengths of light. As you have read, all algae contain chlorophyll *a.* Some species contain chlorophyll *a* in combination with *b, c,* or *d.* The result of this evolution of different forms of chlorophyll is that more of the energy of sunlight available to algae can be used.

Algae have also evolved compounds that absorb different wavelengths of light than chlorophyll absorbs. These light-absorbing compounds are called **accessory pigments.** Accessory pigments pass the energy they absorb on to the algae's photosynthetic machinery. For example, some accessory pigments make blue light more useful for photosynthesis. So, algae that contain these accessory pigments can live in deeper water than plants that contain only chlorophyll. Because accessory pigments also reflect different wavelengths of light than chlorophyll, they give algae a wide range of colors.

Figure 20–3 *The color of this beautiful plumelike red alga results from combinations of accessory pigments and chlorophyll. If you look closely, you can see tiny hooks on the alga. The alga uses the hooks to attach itself onto stationary algae, thus ensuring that it will remain in one place.*

20–1 SECTION REVIEW

1. What are two characteristics of algae?
2. In which kingdom are multicellular algae placed?
3. Why are some unicellular algae classified with multicellular algae?
4. How are algae adapted to life in water?

20–2 Groups of Algae

Section Objectives

- Identify the characteristics of three algae groups.
- Recognize differences between colonial and multicellular algae.

The colors provided by chlorophyll and accessory pigments, as well as the form in which food is stored, are characteristics used to classify algae into different groups. **There are three groups of multicellular algae: green algae, brown algae, and red algae.**

Green algae are members of phylum Chlorophyta (kluh-RAH-fuh-tuh). All green algae contain chlorophylls *a* and *b.* It is these chlorophylls that give the algae their green color. All green algae store food in the form of starch.

Figure 20–4 As you can see, the colors of algae are quite varied. The red algae (left), brown algae (right), and green algae (center) illustrate how different combinations of pigments can result in dramatically different colors.

Brown algae are members of phylum Phaeophyta (fee-AH-fuh-tuh). Brown algae contain chlorophylls *a* and *c*, as well as a brown accessory pigment called fucoxanthin (fyoo-koh-ZAN-thihn). The combination of fucoxanthin and chlorophyll *c* gives these plants their yellow-brown color. Brown algae store food in the form of special starches and oils.

Red algae are members of phylum Rhodophyta (roh-DAH-fuh-tuh). All red algae contain chlorophyll *a*. Some species of red algae also contain chlorophyll *d*. All red algae contain reddish accessory pigments called phycobilins (figh-koh-BIHL-ihnz). Phycobilins are very efficient at absorbing the energy of blue light and making it available for photosynthesis. Thus red algae can live deeper in the ocean than other kinds of algae. Depending on the amount of phycobilins they carry, red algae can be pink, red, purple, or even black. Red algae store food in the form of a special kind of starch.

Figure 20–5 The green alga Ulva *is called sea lettuce because the blades of this plant are flat and resemble salad greens.*

Chlorophyta—The Green Algae

Green algae are found primarily in moist areas on land and in fresh water. Some species of green algae live in the oceans. Green algae have evolved many forms in adapting to these widely different environments. Green algae may live as single cells. Some species of single-celled green algae form a **colony,** which is a group of cells that are joined together and show few specialized structures, or structures that perform a particular function. Other green algae are multicellular and have well-developed specialized structures. All species of green algae have reproductive cycles that include both sexual and asexual reproduction.

The multicellular green algae have cellulose in their cell walls, contain chlorophylls *a* and *b*, and store food in the form of starch, just like land plants. One stage in the life cycle of mosses—small land plants you will learn about in the next chapter—looks remarkably like a tangled mass of green algae strands. All these characteristics lead scientists to believe that the ancestors of modern land plants looked a lot like certain species of living green algae. Unfortunately, algae rarely form fossils, so there is no single specific fossil that scientists can call an ancestor of both living algae and mosses. However, scientists believe that mosses and green algae shared such a common algaelike ancestor millions of years ago.

CHLAMYDOMONAS—A SINGLE-CELLED GREEN ALGAE *Chlamydomonas* (clam-uh-DAH-muh-nuhs), which is a single-celled green alga, grows in ponds, ditches, and wet soil. *Chlamydomonas* is a small egg-shaped cell with two flagella. A light-sensitive area called the eyespot cannot actually see but can sense whether the organism is in bright light or darkness.

Chlamydomonas has a large cup-shaped chloroplast. At the base of the chloroplast is a small pyrenoid (pigh-REE-noid), an organelle that synthesizes and stores starch. *Chlamydomonas* lacks the large vacuoles found in the cells of land plants. Instead it has two small contractile vacuoles. Unlike land plants, *Chlamydomonas* has a cell wall that does not contain cellulose.

As you can see, *Chlamydomonas* has characteristics of both the algae grouped in the Protist kingdom and land plants. This combination of characteristics has led botanists to believe that *Chlamydomonas* is a good example of one step in the evolution of multicellular plants from unicellular protists.

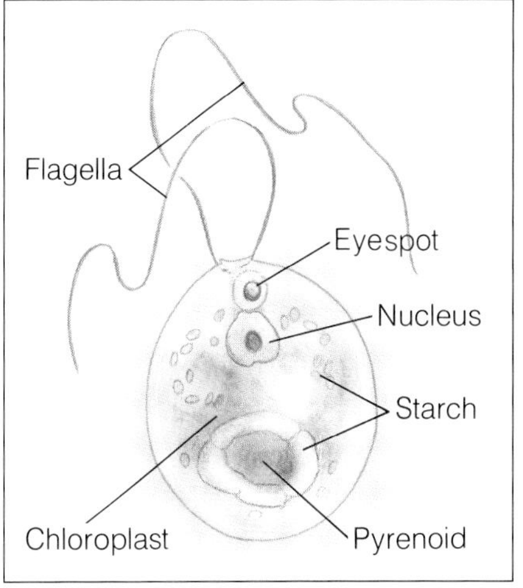

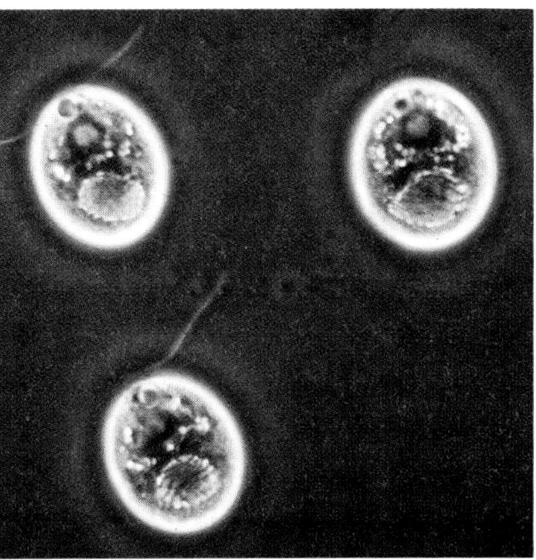

Figure 20–6 *The single-celled alga* Chlamydomonas *is a favorite subject of laboratory study. This alga is able to move about when it beats its two flagella back and forth in the water. It also has an eyespot that is sensitive to light.*

COLONIAL GREEN ALGAE Several species of green algae provide an idea of how multicellular plants may have evolved. From single-celled species such as *Chlamydomonas*, species such as *Gonium* (GOH-nee-uhm) may have evolved. *Gonium* is a colonial alga composed of between 4 and 32 cells. In a colony, many identical cells live together although each cell still functions independently. The cells do not form specialized tissues. If the colony is broken apart, each cell can live and grow into a new colony.

Other species of green algae form larger colonies. The beautiful genus *Volvox* (VAHL-vahks) is one example. *Volvox* can form colonies consisting of as few as 500 or as many as 50,000 cells. Observation of *Volvox* provides two interesting details of the way this organism functions.

First, the cells in a *Volvox* colony are connected to one another by strands of cytoplasm. Thus the cells that make up this colony can communicate. Communication is necessary for the *Volvox* colony to swim: When the cells on one side of the colony "pull" with their flagella, the cells on the other side of the colony have to "push."

Second, although most cells in a *Volvox* colony are identical, a few cells are specialized for reproduction. These cells, which produce gametes, are the first step in the development

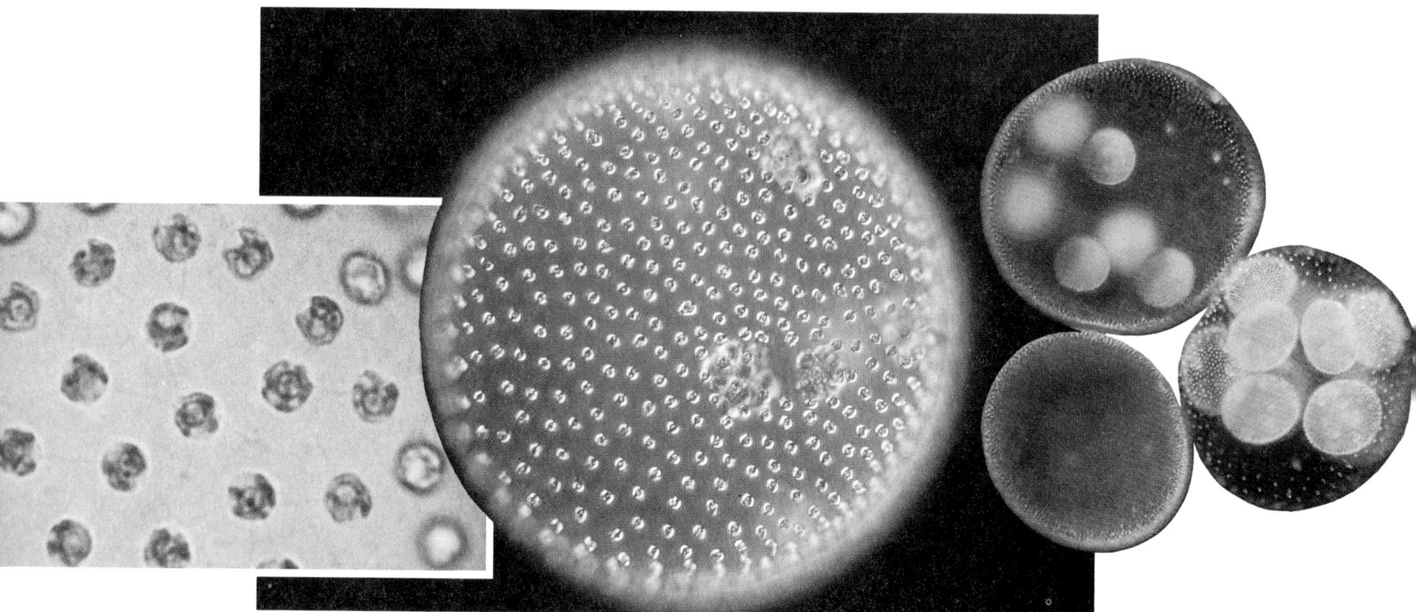

Figure 20–7 Beautiful globes of the green alga Volvox *can often be seen in bodies of fresh water (center). Each cell of this colonial alga is connected to other cells by strands of cytoplasm (left). New colonies often develop within a colony. Eventually the old colony ruptures, freeing the smaller colonies developing within (right).*

of specialized tissues that become more common in plants adapted to life on land. Because it shows some cell specialization, *Volvox* straddles the fence between colonial and multicellular life.

Figure 20–8 Long strands of the green alga Oedogonium *often grow in ponds. This alga can reproduce sexually by producing gametes. New algae can also form when pieces of the strands break off and develop into new plants.*

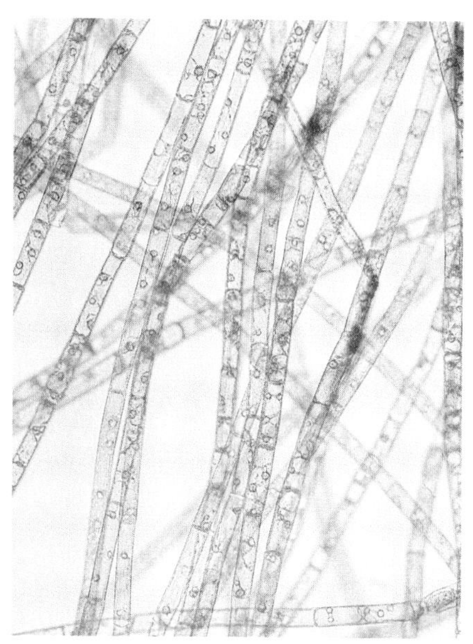

SPIROGYRA AND OEDOGONIUM—THREADLIKE GREEN ALGAE Many green algae form long threadlike colonies called **filaments,** the cells of which are shaped like soda cans stacked end on end. *Spirogyra* (spigh-roh-JIGH-ruh) and *Oedogonium* (ee-duh-GOH-nee-uhm) are two common examples of freshwater filamentous green algae. Filamentous algae can grow and reproduce asexually. For example, if the algae filaments are broken, the cells of each piece can continue to divide and grow. Many filamentous green algae can also reproduce sexually. *Oedogonium,* like *Volvox,* forms two different specialized reproductive cells, or gametes. Each *Oedogonium* filament is attached to the bottom of a lake or pond by another kind of specialized cell called a **holdfast cell.**

ULVA—A MULTICELLULAR GREEN ALGA *Ulva* (UHL-vuh), or "sea lettuce," is a bright-green multicellular marine alga that is commonly found along rocky seacoasts. Although *Ulva* plants are only two cells thick, they are tough enough to survive the pounding of waves on the shores where they live. A group of specialized cells at the base of the plant form holdfasts that attach *Ulva* to the rocks.

Phaeophyta—The Brown Algae

Brown algae are important marine plants that are found in cool shallow coastal waters of temperate or arctic areas. The brown algae have very complicated structures, although they are not as highly developed as land plants. Most of what are commonly called sea weeds are species of brown algae. The largest alga in the world is a form of giant kelp that can grow more than 60 meters long. Another brown alga called *Sargassum* (sahr-GAS-suhm) forms huge floating mats many kilometers long in an area of the Atlantic Ocean near Bermuda known as the Sargasso Sea. Bunches of *Sargassum* often drift on currents to beaches in the Caribbean and southern United States.

One common brown alga is *Fucus* (FYOO-kuhs), or rockweed, which lives along the rocky coast of the eastern United States. Each *Fucus* plant has a holdfast that glues the plant to the bottom. The body of the plant consists of flattened stemlike structures called stipes, leaflike structures called blades, and gas-filled swellings called bladders. Many species of brown algae have bladders, which keep the plants floating upright in the water.

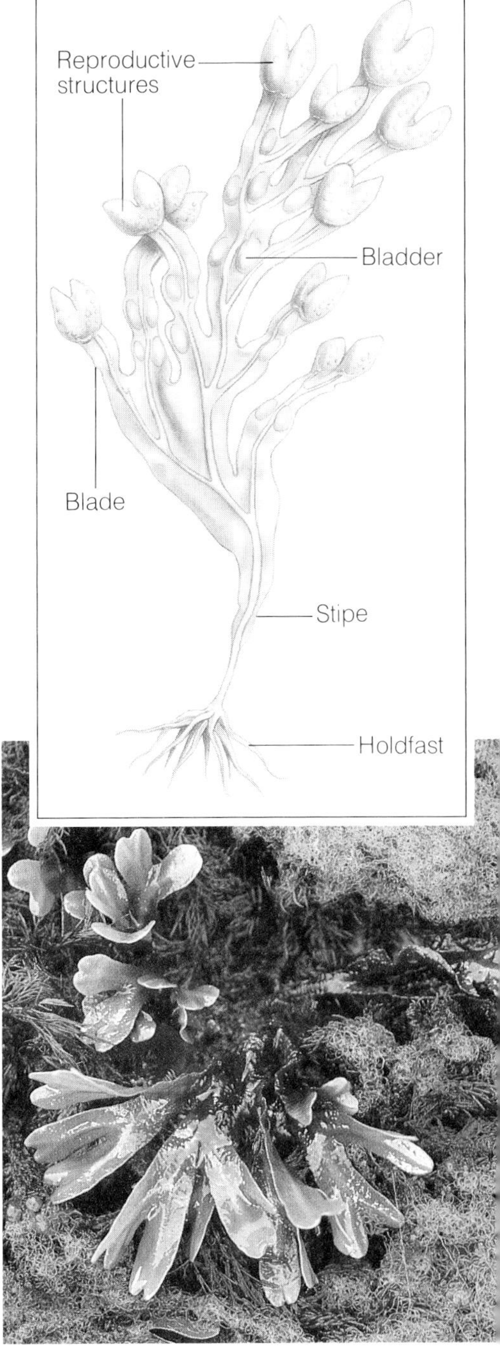

Figure 20–9 Because the brown alga Fucus *commonly grows attached to rocks along the shoreline, it is called rockweed.*

Rhodophyta—The Red Algae

The *Rhodophyta* are another important group of marine algae that can be found in waters from the far north to the tropics. These algae can grow anywhere from the ocean's surface to depths of up to 170 meters. *Rhodophyta* can exist at such extreme depths because they have special pigments that enable them to trap whatever energy is contained in the small amount of light that penetrates there. Most species of red algae are multicellular, and all species have complicated life cycles.

One common red alga is *Chondrus crispus,* or Irish moss. It grows in tide pools and on rocky coastlines. Some red algae, known as the coralline algae, play an important role in the formation of coral reefs. In Japan, the red alga *Porphyra* (por-FIHR-uh) is grown on special marine farms. Dried *Porphyra*—called *nori* in Japanese—is used to wrap portions of rice to make sushi rolls.

20–2 SECTION REVIEW

1. What important factors are used to group algae?
2. What is one important difference between *Chlamydomonas* and *Volvox*?
3. Red algae often live in deep water. What important adaptation do red algae show that enables them to do this?

Section Objectives

- Define alternation of generations.
- Discuss various ways groups of algae reproduce.

20–3 Reproduction in Algae

The life cycles of most algae include both a diploid and a haploid generation. Diploid cells have the normal number of chromosomes for a particular species, whereas haploid cells have half the normal number of chromosomes. The switching back and forth between the production of diploid and haploid cells is called **alternation of generations.** In addition to alternating generations, most species of algae also shift back and forth between sexual reproduction that involves the production of gametes and asexual reproduction that involves haploid cells called **zoospores** (ZOH-oh-sporz).

Complex life cycles that involve alternation of generations are characteristic of all members of the plant kingdom. These life cycles are much more complicated than the simple kinds of sexual reproduction that occur in familiar animals such as birds and mammals.

Figure 20–10 As you can see from this diagram of the life cycle of Chlamydomonas, *this green alga reproduces asexually by producing zoospores and sexually by producing zygospores.*

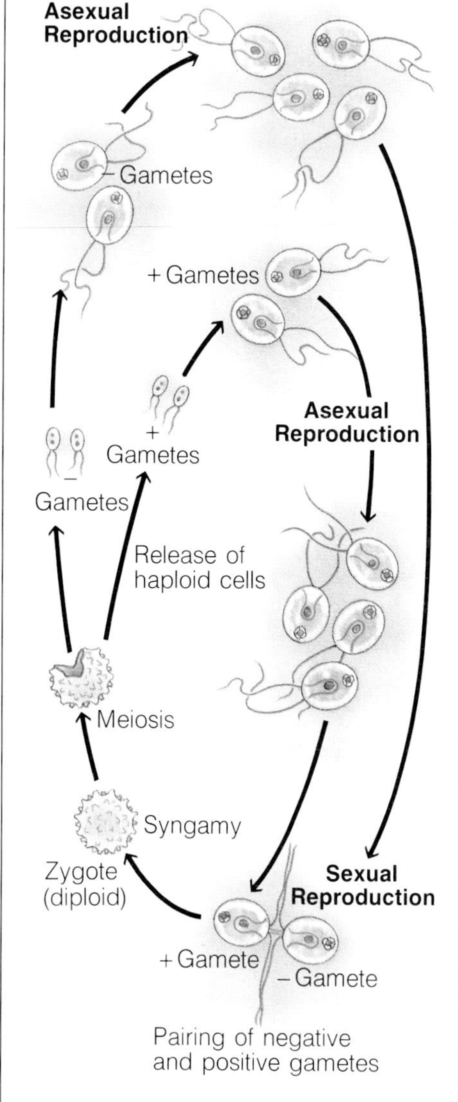

Reproduction in *Chlamydomonas*

The single-celled *Chlamydomonas* spends most of its life in the haploid stage. As long as its living conditions are suitable, this haploid cell reproduces asexually by mitosis. Each time the cell divides, it produces identical haploid zoospores. Smaller than the parent cell, the zoospores soon mature and are able to reproduce asexually. This sequence may be repeated over and over again.

If conditions become unfavorable, *Chlamydomonas* can switch to a stage that reproduces sexually. See Figure 20–10. The haploid cells continue to undergo mitosis, but instead of releasing zoospores, the cells release gametes. Different parent cells produce gametes of two different types, which we call (+) and (–). To our eyes, these gametes appear to be identical. The condition in which the gametes of an organism appear identical is called **isogamy** (igh-SAHG-uh-mee). *Iso* means equal; *gamy* refers to cells that are involved in sexual reproduction. So isogamy means identical reproductive cells.

During sexual reproduction, the gametes gather in large groups. Then (+) and (–) gametes form pairs that soon move away from the group. The paired gametes join flagella and spin around in the water. Both members of the pair then shed their cell walls and fuse, forming a diploid zygote. The fusing of gametes is called **syngamy** (SIHNG-guh-mee).

The zygote sinks to the bottom of the pond or ditch and grows a thick protective wall. Within this protective wall *Chlamydomonas* can survive freezing or drying conditions that would ordinarily kill it. When conditions once again become favorable, the zygote begins to grow. It divides by meiosis to produce four flagellated haploid cells. These haploid cells can swim away, mature, and reproduce asexually.

Reproduction in *Ulva*

The life cycle of *Ulva* involves an alternation of generations in which both the diploid and the haploid stages are multicellular plants. See Figure 20–11. The diploid plant is called the **sporophyte,** or "spore producer," because it produces spores. The haploid plant is called the **gametophyte** (guh-MEET-uh-fight) because it produces gametes.

Ulva actually has two different types of gametophytes. Each type produces a different kind of gamete, one of which is larger than the other. The production of two different kinds of gametes is called **heterogamy.**

When the two different gametes fuse, the resulting diploid zygote does not enter a resting stage. Instead, it begins to grow into a multicellular diploid sporophyte. Specialized cells within the sporophyte reproduce asexually by undergoing meiosis and releasing haploid zoospores. These zoospores then divide by mitosis to grow into the two different types of multicellular gametophytes. The two different types of gametophytes produce their gametes and the cycle continues. The only tricky part of the *Ulva* life cycle, at least for humans, is that all three multicellular plants—the two gametophytes and the sporophyte—look exactly the same to the unaided eye!

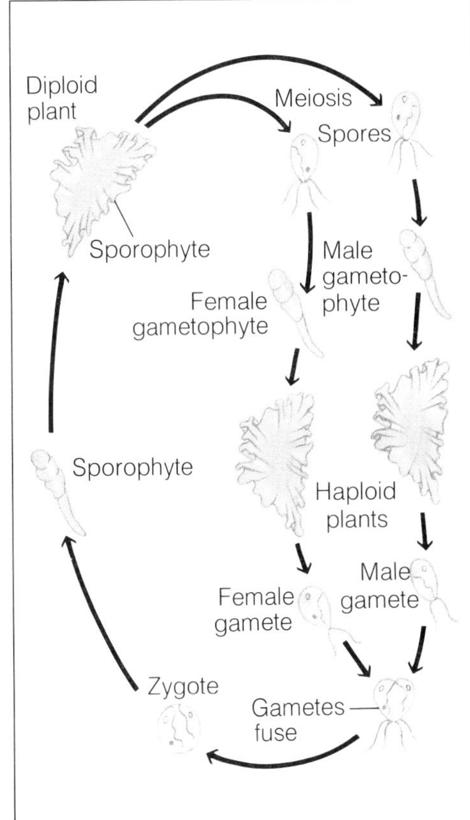

Figure 20–11 Both generations of the green alga Ulva *are multicellular plants.*

Reproduction in *Fucus*

The brown alga *Fucus* demonstrates both alternation of generations and heterogamy. Here, the two gametes are radically different from each another. The female gamete, or **egg,** is large and cannot swim. The male gamete, or **sperm,** is small, has a flagella, and can swim. Differences between male and female gametes develop further in plants adapted to land.

Fucus resembles land plants in that the multicellular haploid gametophyte is missing. The diploid sporophyte plant is the only multicellular part of the life cycle. There are two different types of specialized reproductive areas on the tips of the *Fucus* blades. One area produces eggs; the other area produces sperm. Both eggs and sperm are released into the water. If some of the sperm manage to swim to the drifting eggs, fertilization occurs and a zygote is formed. The zygote sinks, and with some luck, lands on a rock to which it will attach itself and grow by mitotic division into a new diploid sporophyte.

Figure 20–12 Reproductive structures form on the tips of the blades of the brown alga Fucus. *Most species of brown algae reproduce sexually.*

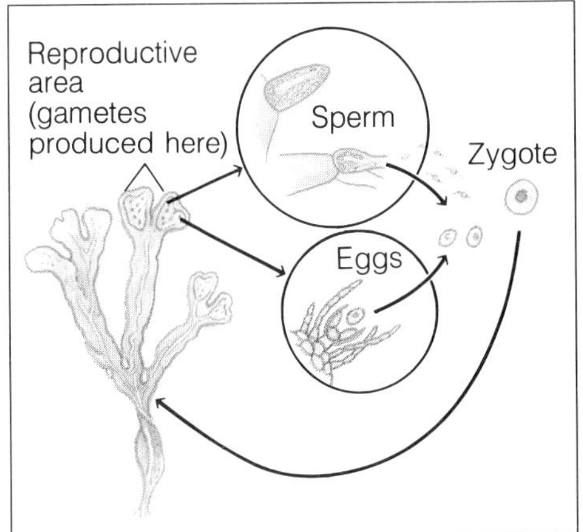

20–3 SECTION REVIEW

1. What is alternation of generations?
2. What is an advantage of asexual reproduction?
3. What is an advantage of sexual reproduction?
4. How is alternation of generations an effective way of ensuring that fit individuals survive?

Section Objectives

- Discuss the importance of algae to life on Earth.
- List several commercial applications of algae.

20–4 Where Algae Fit into the World

Single-celled algae, together with blue-green bacteria and some green flagellates, are food for most of the life in the oceans. Because they are such an important source of food, algae have been called the grasses of the seas. Algae also provide homes for many species of animals. The huge brown kelp forests along the coasts of the United States are home not only to sea otters but to many animal species.

Life as we know it would never have evolved without algae, for they produce much of Earth's free oxygen through photosynthesis. Scientists calculate that between 50 and 75 percent of all the photosynthesis that occurs on Earth is performed by algae. This fact alone makes algae one of the most important groups of organisms on the entire planet.

Over the years, people have learned to use algae—and the chemicals produced by algae—in many different ways. Many species of algae are rich in vitamin C and iron. Other chemicals in algae are used to treat stomach ulcers, lung ailments, high blood pressure, arthritis, and other health problems.

Algae are also used in the manufacture of many food products. Algae are used to make ice cream smooth and candy bars last longer. Algae are used in pickle relishes, salad dressings, chip dips, pancake syrups, egg nogs, and canned chow mein. In Japan and other parts of Asia, algae farms produce crops of red and brown algae that are eaten by millions of people. Algae are eaten as a vegetable and used as flavorings in soups, meat dishes, and candy. Toothpastes, adhesives, hand lotions, and finger paints all contain algae.

Modern industry has even more uses for algae. Chemicals from algae are used to make plastics, waxes, transistors, deodorants, paints, lubricants, and even artificial wood. Algae products are found in poultry feed, cake batters, pie fillers, bakery jellies, and doughnut glazes. Algae even have an important use in scientific laboratories. The compound agar-agar, derived from certain seaweeds, thickens the nutrient mixtures scientists use to grow bacteria and other microorganisms. As you can see, our lives would be very different without algae.

Figure 20–13 *Although polar bears are carnivores, they will eat algae. People eat algae, too. Algae are often used to thicken frozen dairy desserts—much to the delight of these two youngsters.*

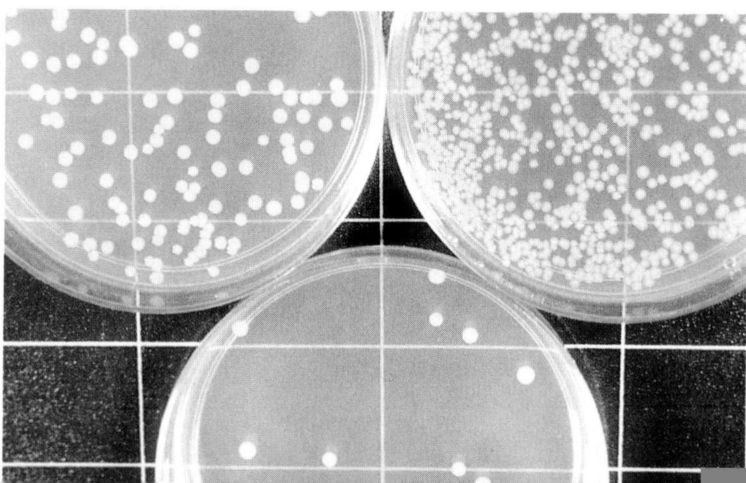

Figure 20–14 *One important product of algae is agar, a substance used to thicken growth media. Colonies of bacteria are growing on agar in the petri dishes shown here.*

SCIENCE, TECHNOLOGY, AND SOCIETY **APPLICATION**

Algae: A Natural Sewage Treatment Plant

Researchers are studying ways to use algae to clean sewage produced by cities and towns. Sewage, or waste water, contains the liquid and solid wastes each of us produces every day. Since there is no way to avoid producing sewage, we must learn to dispose of it without harming the environment. Untreated sewage released into streams and ponds has several unpleasant consequences. One is that algae in the streams and ponds begin to grow rapidly. Algae may grow so rapidly, in fact, that they cover the surface of the water. This increased growth is called an algal bloom. An algal bloom may harm other forms of life that live in the water.

Why does sewage cause algal blooms? Human wastes—like the wastes of all animals—contain substances that plants use as nutrients for growth. As algae grow, they remove these nutrients from sewage. In other words, sewage acts as fertilizer for algae.

Some researchers think they have found a way to put this characteristic of algae to use in treating sewage. Their plan works as follows: First the sewage is diluted. Then the sewage is trickled through large tanks of algae. As the algae grow, they remove nutrients contained in the sewage. Eventually, treated water can be released carefully into the environment. Because it contains a smaller concentration of harmful wastes, this water does not threaten the environment as much as untreated sewage does. If researchers can grow the right kinds of algae, not only will they be able to treat sewage, but they may also be able to produce plants for use in industry.

As they grow, algae take in chemicals and other substances from water. Various species of algae are being used in pilot programs to design new methods of treating sewage.

20–4 SECTION REVIEW

1. How have algae changed the atmosphere on Earth?
2. How would life on Earth be different if all algae suddenly became extinct?
3. What two foods contain algae products?
4. How have algae contributed to our understanding of human disease?

LABORATORY INVESTIGATION

STUDYING FILAMENTOUS GREEN ALGAE

PROBLEM

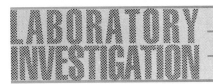

What are the characteristics of *Spirogyra?*

MATERIALS *(per group)*

microscope
prepared slide of *Spirogyra*

PROCEDURE 

1. Using a microscope, examine a prepared slide of *Spirogyra* under the low-power objective. Notice the general shape of *Spirogyra.* On a separate sheet of paper, draw a diagram of a filament of *Spirogyra.* Indicate the appearance of individual cells. Note the arrangement of the chloroplasts.
2. Move your slide until you locate two parallel filaments that are attached to each other by small "bridges," or tubes. This attachment is a form of sexual reproduction called conjugation. Switch to the medium-power objective and focus. Draw the portion of the filaments that shows the conjugation tubes. If possible, locate a portion of the filaments where material is passing from one cell to another through the tubes. Draw these cells.
3. Switch to the high-power objective. Use the fine adjustment to focus on a nucleus in one of the cells. Draw a diagram of a single cell and its nucleus. Label the nucleus.
4. Leaving the high-power objective in place, move the slide to focus on a portion of a chloroplast. Draw a diagram of a chloroplast.

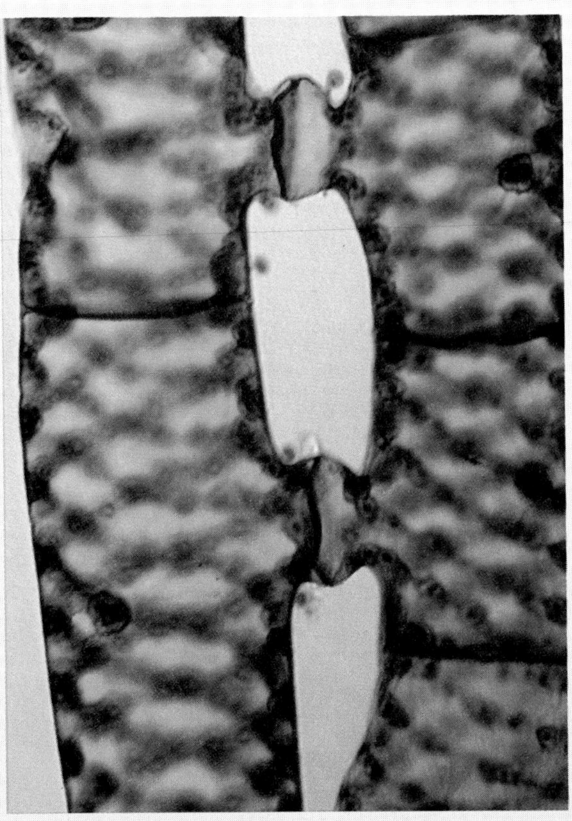

OBSERVATIONS

1. Are there different kinds of cells in *Spirogyra?*
2. What is the shape of *Spirogyra?*
3. Based on your observations, describe what happens during conjugation in *Spirogyra?*
4. How is the nucleus held in place?
5. What is the shape of the chloroplasts?

ANALYSIS AND CONCLUSIONS

1. Are *Spirogyra* multicellular or colonial algae? Explain your answer.
2. What is the function of the conjugation tubes?
3. How are *Spirogyra* adapted to life in water? Would these plants survive on land? Explain your answer.

STUDENT STUDY GUIDE

SUMMARIZING THE CONCEPTS

The key concepts in each section of this chapter are listed below to help you review the chapter content. Make sure you understand each concept and its relationship to other concepts and to the theme of this chapter.

20–1 Characteristics of Algae

- Algae must live in or near a source of water.
- Algae vary in size, shape, and color. Some species of algae are unicellular, other species form colonies, and still other species are multicellular.
- Algae show many different adaptations to life in water. Unlike land plants, most algae lack a system of internal tubes to move water and nutrients from one part of the plant to another. Since algae live in water, they do not need protection from drying out or stemlike structures to keep them upright.
- Algae contain accessory pigments in addition to different forms of chlorophyll. These pigments give algae their color. Scientists group algae on the basis of the chlorophylls and pigments they contain, as well as the form in which they store food.

20–2 Groups of Algae

- There are three groups of multicellular algae: green algae, red algae, and brown algae. Each group receives its color from combinations of special pigments and chlorophyll.
- The three different groups of algae store the food they make as special starches and/or oils.

20–3 Reproduction in Algae

- Algae have complex life cycles that involve alternation of generations.
- Many algae produce special cells during reproduction that enable the algae to survive harsh environmental conditions. These cells can resume growth when environmental conditions improve.

20–4 Where Algae Fit into the World

- Algae produce much of the Earth's free oxygen during photosynthesis. Without this oxygen, life on Earth as we know it would never have evolved.
- Algae provide food for animals and people. Algae are also used in the manufacture of many foods and industrial products.

REVIEWING KEY TERMS

Vocabulary terms are important to your understanding of biology. The key terms listed below are those you should be especially familiar with. Review these terms and their meanings. Then use each term in a complete sentence. If you are not sure of a term's meaning, return to the appropriate section and review its definition.

20–1 Characteristics of Algae

accessory pigment

20–2 Groups of Algae

colony
filament
holdfast cell

20–3 Reproduction in Algae

alternation of generations
zoospore
isogamy
syngamy
sporophyte
gametophyte
heterogamy
egg
sperm

CHAPTER REVIEW

CONTENT REVIEW

Multiple Choice

Choose the letter of the answer that best completes each statement.

1. Unlike most plants, algae lack
   a. chloroplasts.
   b. accessory pigments.
   c. a nucleus.
   d. an internal system of tubes.
2. Which of the following algae are able to live in deep ocean water?
   a. red algae
   b. green algae
   c. *Volvox*
   d. *Spirogyra*
3. Algae take in nutrients through their
   a. holdfast.
   b. stipe.
   c. blade.
   d. cell membrane.
4. Some single-celled algae are included in the kingdom
   a. Monera.
   b. Protista.
   c. Animalia.
   d. Fungi.
5. Red algae have a special pigment that enables them to absorb energy from
   a. red light.
   b. yellow light.
   c. violet light.
   d. blue light.
6. Green algae live in each of the following environments except
   a. dry land.
   b. a pond.
   c. moist areas on land.
   d. a lake.
7. Filaments of some forms of green algae are attached to the bottom of a lake or pond by a (an)
   a. stipe.
   b. holdfast cell.
   c. air bladder.
   d. egg.
8. The largest algae in the world are the
   a. red algae.
   b. filamentous algae.
   c. green algae.
   d. brown algae.

True or False

Determine whether each statement is true or false. If it is true, write "true." If it is false, change the underlined word or words to make the statement true.

1. Alternation of generations is a characteristic of all plants.
2. Chlorophyll can make blue light more useful for photosynthesis.
3. Fucus are single-celled green algae.
4. Kelp are the largest algae in the world and can grow longer than 60 meters.
5. Filamentous algae can reproduce sexually when they break apart.
6. A colony is a group of cells that are joined together and that show few specialized structures.
7. Special light-absorbing pigments found in some kinds of algae are called gametes.
8. Most algae get necessary gases and nutrients from the air.

Word Relationships

In each of the following sets of terms, three of the terms are related. One term does not belong. Determine the characteristic common to three of the terms and then identify the term that does not belong.

1. eggs, sperm, spores, stipes
2. red, brown, green, yellow
3. *Chlamydomonas, Volvox, Spirogyra, Fucus*
4. ponds, lakes, rivers, oceans

CONCEPT MASTERY

Use your understanding of the concepts developed in the chapter to answer each of the following in a brief paragraph.

1. Explain the importance of algae to life.
2. Describe two characteristics that help scientists classify algae.
3. How are some kinds of red algae adapted to life in deep ocean water?
4. What is the main difference between a colony and a multicellular organism?
5. What is alternation of generations?
6. Why do some scientists place all algae in the kingdom Protista?
7. How are algae different from land plants?
8. Accessory pigments do more than provide color for algae. What important function do accessory pigments perform?

CRITICAL AND CREATIVE THINKING

Discuss each of the following in a brief paragraph.

1. **Applying concepts** How does having a method of both asexual reproduction and sexual reproduction contribute to an organism's survival?
2. **Making predictions** Suppose all species of algae on Earth died out. What effects would this have on other organisms?
3. **Relating cause and effect** Suppose you were able to design a new species of algae that could live in deep water. What important characteristics would you include? Why?
4. **Applying technology** You have been chosen to work on a new space probe that will carry humans deep into space. A friend suggests that it would be important to have a population of algae on this trip. How could these algae help human space travelers on a long voyage in space?
5. **Analyzing concepts** You know that all life comes from life. Your friend observes that a pond in the area has dried up and appears to lack life. Later, this pond fills with water again. Algae begin to grow. Your friend is puzzled. How could you explain the growth of algae in this pond?
6. **Relating concepts** Some scientists think that a form of algae was an ancestor of certain land plants. What are some changes that would have to occur in order to make algae able to survive on land?
7. **Using the writing process** The huge kelp forests along the west coast of the United States are home to the sea otter. There are relatively few of these animals alive in the wild. The otters are fond of eating abalone and other shellfish. Because of their eating preferences, they often come into conflict with local people who earn a living by capturing and selling the shellfish. These local people want to eradicate the kelp. They feel that the sea otters will move away if the kelp is destroyed. You are the lawyer hired by the government to protect the kelp and the otters. The local newspaper wants you to write an article detailing your position. Here is your chance to influence people. Write an article for the paper. Save the otters!

CHAPTER 21

Mosses and Ferns

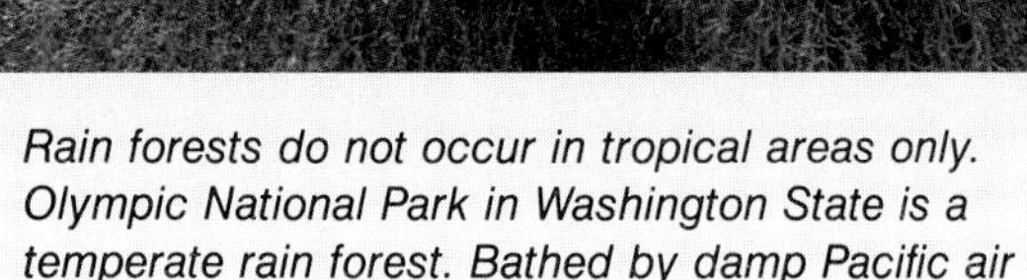

Rain forests do not occur in tropical areas only. Olympic National Park in Washington State is a temperate rain forest. Bathed by damp Pacific air currents, ferns and tiny mosses (inset) grow well.

Life began in the sea, and for millions of years living things remained in the sea. Yet, slowly, life emerged onto land. On empty ancient continents, new opportunities existed. But new challenges to survive and reproduce awaited as well.

The first land plants were the first multicellular organisms to meet these challenges. To these plants we owe a great debt: Had they not colonized the land, animals would not have been able to follow. In this chapter you will glimpse the struggle of early plants to survive on land—a struggle whose evidence is visible in the form of living plants that remain suspended in a life halfway between water and land.

CHAPTER OUTLINE

21–1 Plants Invade the Land

Section Objective

- Describe some of the adaptations plants need to survive on land.

Because the first multicellular organisms evolved in water, their entire lives were designed around an aquatic environment. All the processes that ensured survival—from photosynthesis to sexual reproduction—took place in water.

But over time, some organisms adapted to life in drier environments. In the following pages you will learn about some living plants and some extinct plants that represent stages in this process of adaptation. These plants illustrate steps in the evolution of structures to acquire, transport, and conserve water. They also demonstrate how land plants evolved reproductive cycles that enable them to survive in terrestrial environments, or land environments.

The First Land Plants

The fossil record does not provide much information about the very earliest stages of the evolution of land plants. Remember that it is the hard parts of organisms, such as shells and bones, that form the best fossils. Because the first land plants were soft-bodied, they have left few fossils. But we do have enough evidence about early plant life on land to say several things with certainty.

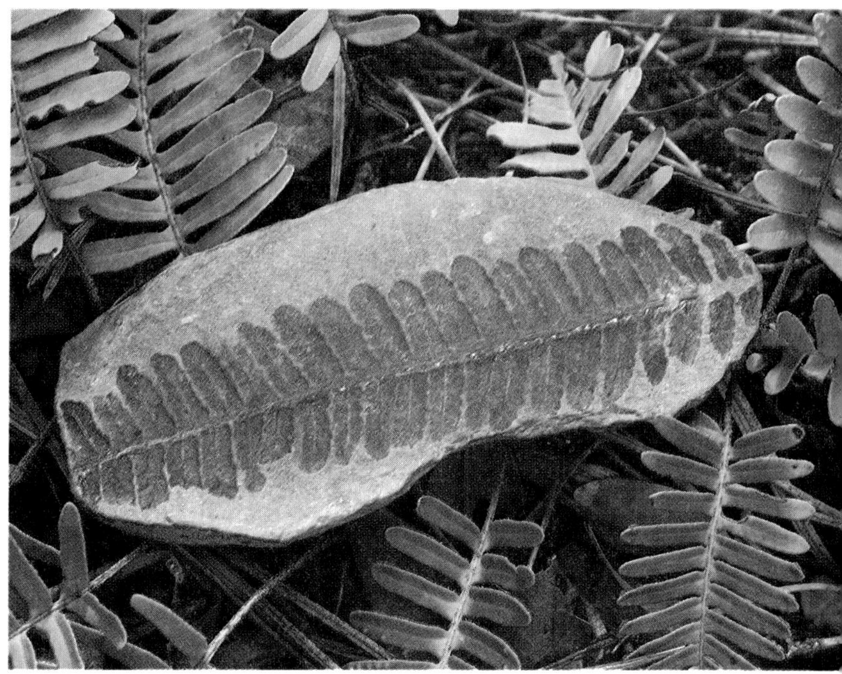

Figure 21–1 *Dating from the Carboniferous Period, this fossil fern looks very much like its still-growing relatives. As you can see, these plants have changed little over time.*

Figure 21–2 *Ferns can grow in water as well as on land. This fern,* Marsilia, *resembles a floating four-leaf clover.*

The adaptation of plants to life on land was a long, slow process. Algae that could live out of water at least part of the time evolved 500 to 600 million years ago. From these plant pioneers, at least two separate groups of algaelike land plants evolved between 450 and 500 million years ago.

One group developed into the phylum Bryophyta (brigh-oh-FIGHT-uh), which includes mosses, liverworts, and hornworts. The other group evolved into the phylum Tracheophyta (tray-kee-oh-FIGHT-uh), which includes the ferns and the rest of the higher plants. Both the bryophytes and the tracheophytes faced the same set of problems in adapting to terrestrial environments, but each group evolved its own set of solutions.

Demands of Life on Land

The adaptations that enabled aquatic organisms to survive in dry environments were not simple. To understand how important these adaptations were, let us examine some of the requirements of life on land.

- All cells need a constant supply of water. For this reason, land plants must obtain water and deliver it to all of their cells, even those cells that grow above ground in dry air. Once plants provide water to their tissues, they must protect that water against loss by evaporation to the atmosphere.
- The parts of the plant that make food for the plant must be exposed to as much sunlight as possible. Aquatic plants that float on the surface of the water have no problem obtaining

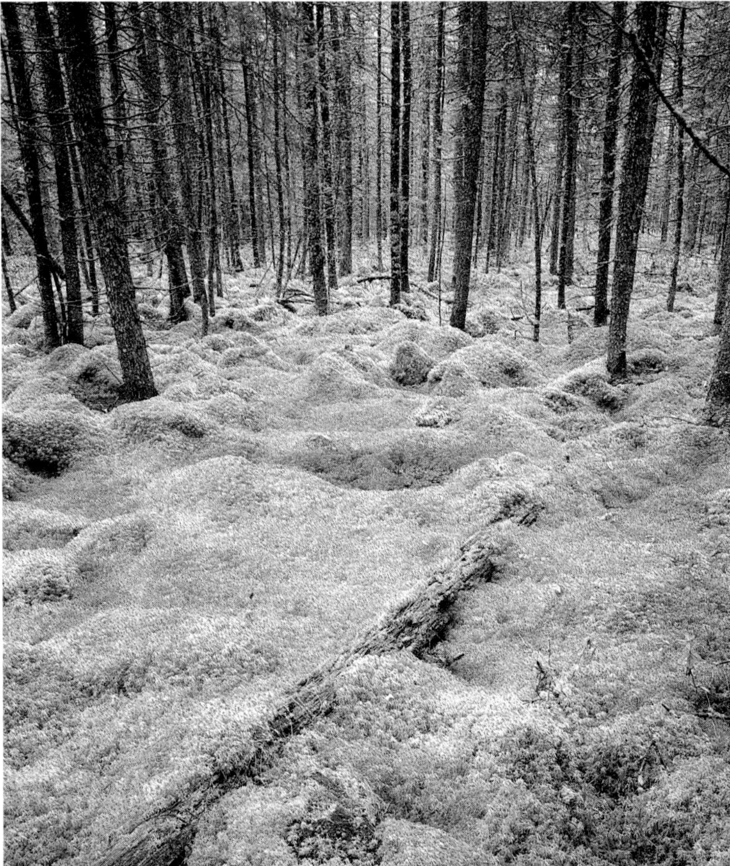

Figure 21–3 *Mosses grow well in the shade of trees, as this carpet of mosses on the floor of a pine forest illustrates. You can be certain that the ground beneath the pines remains relatively damp, for mosses grow best under damp conditions.*

sunlight because there is little water above them to interfere with the absorption of the sun's energy. Land plants, however, need rigid supports to hold their leaves up to the sun in ways that expose the leaves to sunlight.

- Land plants take up water and nutrients in roots but make food in leaves. To supply all cells with the necessities of life, land plants must transport water and nutrients upward and the products of photosynthesis downward.
- Land plants must exchange water and carbon dioxide with the environment without losing too much water in the process.
- Fully terrestrial plants must be able to reproduce in environments that lack standing water in which the sperm can swim. In many terrestrial situations, the zygotes and young embryos of land plants are in danger of drying out.

The bryophytes have partially solved these problems. Bryophytes no longer need to be constantly submerged in water, but they do need to remain wet most of the time. The simplest tracheophytes—the ferns—have evolved further toward complete independence from water. But as you will see, ferns still have not solved all the problems posed by a terrestrial life.

21–1 SECTION REVIEW

1. What are two of the problems faced by plants that live on land?
2. What are the names of the two main phyla of land plants? Give examples of each.
3. Your friend finds a small plant growing in the desert. He identifies the plant as a moss. Explain why this plant is probably not a moss.

21–2 The Mosses, Liverworts, and Hornworts

Section Objectives

- Identify the characteristics of the three main groups of bryophytes.
- Describe some adaptations shown by bryophytes that enable them to survive on land.
- Identify patterns of reproduction in bryophytes.

The phylum Bryophyta includes the mosses, liverworts, and hornworts. **Bryophytes, like the algae from which they evolved, have life cycles that involve an alternation of generations between a haploid gametophyte and a diploid sporophyte. Also like the algae, bryophytes need water for reproduction to occur**. Thus bryophytes can thrive only in wet areas, or in areas where rainfall is plentiful at least part of the year. Bryophytes grow most abundantly in swamps, marshes, near streams, and in rain forests in tropical areas and along the western coast of the United States.

Figure 21–4 *The tiny brown structures on the tip of these moss plants (left) are the sporophyte plants. When the spores are ripe, they are shed from the brown capsules like pepper from a shaker. Looking much like fallen leaves, these liverworts (right) have raised what appear like little green umbrellas. These structures produce gametes.*

Bryophytes vary in appearance. Some look like miniature evergreen trees; others, like the softest green carpet; still others, like leaves of a higher plant lying on the ground. Regardless of variations in appearance, almost all bryophytes are less than a few centimeters tall.

The moss plants you might observe on a walk through the woods are actually clumps of haploid moss gametophytes growing close together. Each moss plant has a thin upright shoot that looks like a stem with tiny leaves. Because the plant does not have tubes that conduct water and other substances, however, these are not true leaves and stems. From the base of the shoot grow a number of thin branches called **rhizoids** that penetrate into the ground and act like roots to securely anchor the plant.

The odd little plants called liverworts are bryophytes too. These plants are scarcer than mosses and need to live in places that remain wet constantly. Liverwort gametophytes look like flat green leaves growing along the ground. When these plants mature, the gametophytes produce structures that look like tiny green umbrellas. These "umbrellas" carry the structures that produce eggs and sperm.

The gametophytes of hornworts look very much like the gametophytes of liverworts. The hornwort sporophyte, however, differs from the liverwort sporophyte. Instead of looking like a tiny umbrella, the hornwort sporophyte looks like a tiny horn, which is why this plant received its common name.

Physical Characteristics of Bryophytes

Bryophytes are well-adapted to life in wet habitats, where they often grow much better than do the higher plants that you will learn about in the next chapter. But outside of wet habitats, bryophytes do not usually grow well because they lack several critical adaptations to life in dry places.

Bryophytes lack the water-conducting tubes that are found in higher plants. In bryophytes, water passes from cell to cell by osmosis and by means of surface tension around the stems. These methods of transporting water work well over short distances only. This is one reason bryophytes never grow tall.

Bryophytes lack a protective surface covering to keep water from evaporating from their cells. Because their "leaves" are only one cell thick, the plants lose the water they contain very quickly if the surrounding air is dry.

Bryophytes lack true roots. True roots contain water-conducting tubes that enable a plant to absorb and transport water efficiently. Instead of roots, bryophytes have rhizoids that anchor them in the ground. Rhizoids, however, do not play a major role in the absorption and transport of water and minerals.

Bryophytes have sperm cells that must swim through water to fertilize the eggs. The sperm cells use their flagella to propel themselves. For this reason, bryophytes must live in areas that are wet for at least part of the year. Some bryophytes can survive dry periods, but to do so they must stop growing.

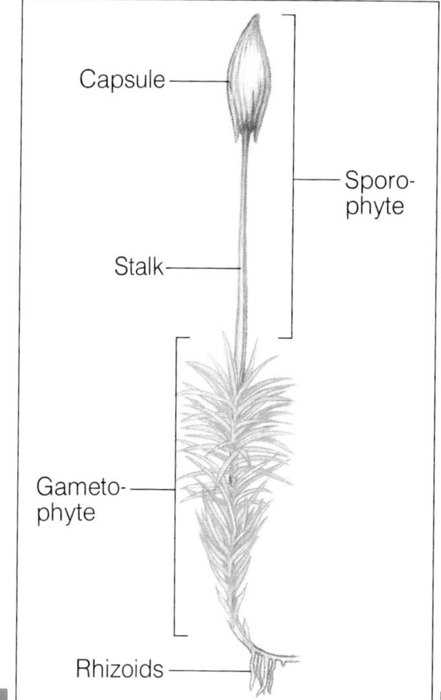

Figure 21–5 *This illustration (top) shows the parts of a typical moss plant. How many of these parts can you locate in the photograph?*

Alternation of Generations in Mosses

The life cycle of the moss *Mnium*, a typical bryophyte, is shown in Figure 21–6 on page 454. At the tips of the gametophytes are reproductive structures similar to those of several species of algae. One structure, the **antheridium** (an-ther-IHD-ee-uhm), produces tiny flagellated sperm cells. Another structure, the **archegonium** (ahr-kuh-GOH-nee-uhm), produces eggs. Unlike the reproductive structures of algae, the reproductive structures of mosses are designed to protect the gametes from drying out. Thus the eggs of mosses have a better chance of surviving during dry conditions.

Some species of mosses have both male and female reproductive organs on one gametophyte; other species have male and female reproductive structures on separate gametophytes. Mosses can reproduce sexually only when standing water is present. Sperm can swim to the archegonium only when the gametophytes are covered with rainwater or dew. When a sperm swims to an egg, syngamy (the fusing of gametes) occurs and a diploid zygote is produced.

When the zygote germinates, or begins to grow, it produces a diploid sporophyte. As it grows, the sporophyte is supplied with water and nutrients by the gametophyte. Moss sporophytes cannot live independent of the gametophyte from which they grow. This is one way in which bryophytes differ from all other land plants. The mature sporophyte is composed of a "foot" that remains stuck in the gametophyte—a long stalk—and a capsule that looks like a salt shaker. Inside the capsule,

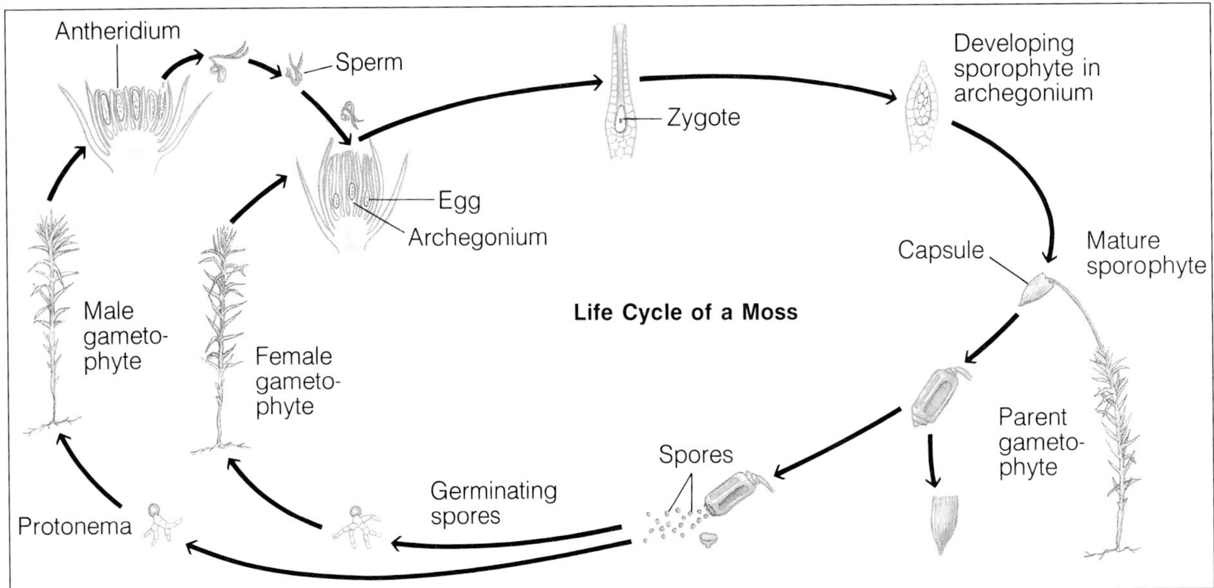

Figure 21–6 *Moss plants are usually short and grow close to the ground. These tiny plants need a supply of standing water in order for sperm to swim to and fertilize an egg.*

haploid spores are produced by meiosis. When the capsule ripens, special pores—and in some cases the whole top of the capsule—open. The spores are shaken out, to be carried off by wind and water.

If a spore lands in a moist place, it germinates and grows into a mass of tangled green filaments called a **protonema**. Moss protonemas look remarkably like filamentous green algae. (This resemblance is evidence that mosses evolved from either ancient green algae or from an ancestor common to both mosses and algae.) As the protonema grows, it forms rhizoids that grow into the ground and shoots that grow into the air. These shoots develop into the familiar moss gametophytes, and the cycle continues.

We can summarize the life cycle of mosses as follows:

1. The haploid gametophyte is the dominant, obvious stage. It is in fact the stage commonly thought of as a moss plant.
2. Standing water is needed for sperm to swim to and fertilize eggs.
3. The diploid sporophyte is small and can grow only with nourishment provided by the gametophyte.

21–2 SECTION REVIEW

1. List the characteristics of the three main groups of bryophytes.
2. What are two adaptations that enable bryophytes to survive on land?
3. What is an archegonium? An antheridium? Why are these structures important in the life cycle of a moss?

21–3 The Ferns and the First Vascular Plants

Section Objectives

- Recognize the importance of vascular tissue to land plants.
- Identify characteristics of club mosses and horsetails.
- Discuss ways in which ferns resemble other land plants.
- Describe alternation of generations in ferns.

Remember that although bryophytes live on land, they depend upon an abundant supply of water to survive. **The members of the phylum Tracheophyta are "true" land plants because they have evolved ways of freeing themselves from dependence on wet environments.**

Among the most important adaptations of tracheophytes are specialized tissues called **vascular tissues**. Vascular tissues transport water and the products of photosynthesis throughout the plant. There are two types of vascular tissue: **xylem** and **phloem**. Xylem tissue is associated with the movement of water from the roots to all parts of the plant. Phloem tissue is responsible for the transport of nutrients and the products of photosynthesis.

One important type of cell present in vascular tissue is the **tracheid**. Tracheid cells carry water from roots in the soil to leaves in the air. Thus they are the most important type of cells in xylem tissue. Tracheid cells have thick, strong cell walls that strengthen stems and help plants stand up against the pull of gravity. All plants in the phylum Tracheophyta have tracheids; in fact, the phylum is named after this type of cell.

The other kind of vascular tissue, phloem tissue, carries important nutrients and the products of photosynthesis from place to place within a plant. Both xylem and phloem tissue will be discussed in more detail in Chapters 22 and 23.

With the development of vascular tissue, tracheophytes have evolved true roots and true leaves. True roots have vascular tissues gathered in a central area of the root that is called the **vascular cylinder**. True leaves are photosynthetic organs

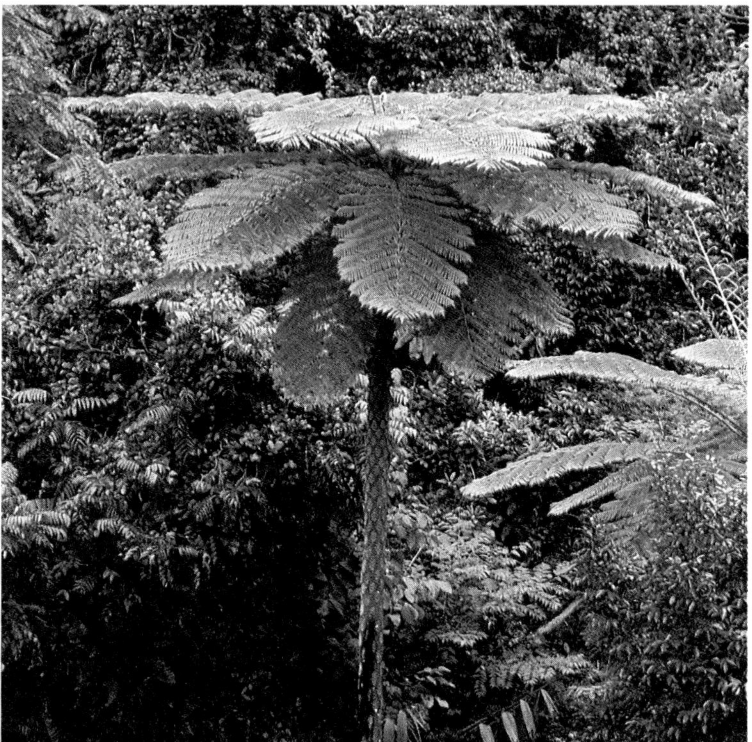

Figure 21–7 *Ferns are able to grow much taller than mosses because they have an internal system of water-conducting tubes. This tree fern is growing in a rain forest in New Caledonia. Although tree ferns were once widespread, today they are limited to the tropical areas on Earth.*

Figure 21–8 *The* Psilotum *plant is commonly called the wisk fern. Scientists believe that the first true land plants resembled this organism.*

that contain one or more bundles of vascular tissue gathered into **veins**. The leaves of tracheophytes usually have a waxy covering called a **cuticle** that helps prevent water loss by evaporation. These structures will also be discussed in more detail in Chapters 22 and 23. But it is important that you have an understanding of these terms as we begin a discussion of early vascular plants.

The First Vascular Plants

Fossils of psilophytes, the first vascular plants, were first found early in this century. These small creeping plants had primitive xylem and phloem tissues, but they lacked true roots and true leaves. Although most botanists think the psilophytes are extinct, some believe that two species of living plants (classified as ferns) are actually living psilophytes. At present, neither group of botanists can prove conclusively that they are correct. But both groups wonder why no psilophyte fossils more recent than the Devonian Period (400 million years ago) have been found.

Club Mosses and Horsetails

The club mosses (lycophytes) and horsetails (sphenophytes) alive today are the only living descendants of large and ancient groups of land plants. The first of these primitive tracheophytes appeared more than 400 million years ago. Over the next 100 to 200 million years, many more species evolved. Some ancient lycophytes and sphenophytes grew into huge trees—up to 40 meters tall. The Earth's very first forests were made up of vast numbers of these plants. At one point in the Earth's history, the entire area of what is now Pennsylvania was covered with a dense tropical jungle of these plants. It is the fossilized remains of these primitive tracheophytes that were transformed into Pennsylvania's huge beds of coal.

Over time, however, the climate of the Earth changed. (Pennsylvania does not have a tropical climate today!) For some reason, these primitive plants could not compete with new types of plants that evolved with the changing climate. Forests of lycophytes and sphenophytes were replaced by forests of entirely new plants. The few species of lycophytes and sphenophytes alive today are relatively small plants that live in moist woodlands and near stream beds and marshes.

Lycopodium (ligh-koh-POH-dee-uhm), the common club moss, looks like a miniature pine tree about 9 centimeters tall. Another common name for *Lycopodium* is "ground pine." *Lycopodium* has small scalelike leaves that cling to the stems.

The only living genus of sphenophytes is *Equisetum* (ehk-wih-SEET-uhm), a plant that grows about 1 meter tall. *Equisetum* is commonly called horsetail or scouring rush because its stems contain crystals of silica, which are quite abrasive. During Colonial times, horsetails were commonly used to scrape,

Figure 21–9 *This* Lycopodium *plant (left), which resembles a small evergreen tree, is better known by its common name ground pine. It is often used as a holiday decoration. Horsetails (right) incorporate silica, the main component of sand, in their stems. Silica gives the stems a rough texture, which is why these plants were once used as a scouring material for cleaning pots and pans.*

or scour, pots and pans. If you should some day set up camp near some *Equisetum*, you will know you can use this plant to clean your pots and pans. Like the lycophytes, horsetails have true leaves, stems, and roots. The leaves of horsetails are arranged in whorls at joints along the stems.

Physical Characteristics of Ferns

Ferns probably evolved about 400 million years ago, at about the same time as the lycophytes and sphenophytes. Ferns were an important part of the lycophyte forests that covered the ancient Earth. Ferns, however, have been more successful at competing with other plants that have appeared during the Earth's long history. Today more than 11,000 species of ferns are still alive!

In many respects, ferns are well-developed tracheophytes. They have true vascular tissues, strong roots, creeping or underground stems called **rhizomes**, and large leaves called **fronds**. Ferns that commonly grow in the United States range in height from a few centimeters to about one meter.

Ferns are most abundant in wet, or at least seasonally wet, habitats around the world. Ferns grow throughout the United States, but they grow best in the rain forests of the Pacific Northwest, and in wet tropical areas. In tropical forests, some species of ferns grow as large as small trees.

Figure 21–10 *The leaves of ferns are covered by a waxy coating that prevents water loss. The waxy coating also causes drops of water to bead up on the leaf surface, much like wax on a car causes water to form beads.*

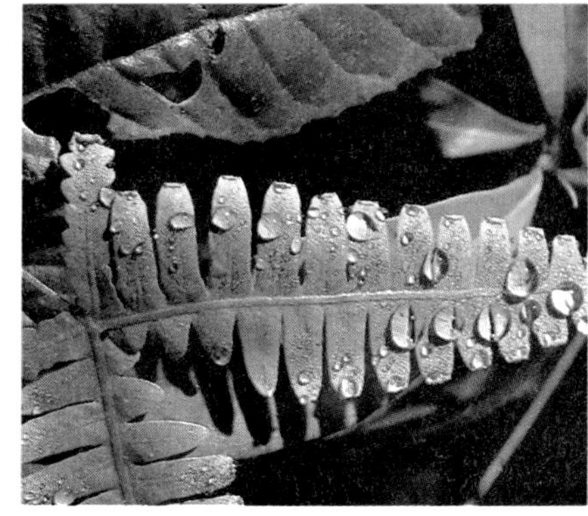

Alternation of Generations in Ferns

Like the life cycles of all other plants, those of ferns involve alternation of generations. The plants that are recognizable as ferns are the diploid sporophytes. Because of their well-developed vascular tissues, these sporophytes can grow in drier places than can bryophyte sporophytes. But sexual reproduction in ferns still depends upon the presence of standing water for sperm to swim to eggs.

Figure 21–11 *Clusters of sporangia form on the underside of fern leaves. As you can see, sporangia can form many varied, beautiful patterns.*

Fern sporophytes produce haploid spores on the underside of their fronds. Spores are produced in tiny containers called **sporangia**. Sporangia do not occur individually but are grouped into large clusters called **sori** (singular: sorus).

When spores are ripe, they are released from the sporangia and may be carried by wind and water over long distances. If environmental conditions are right for the spores to germinate, they develop into haploid gametophytes. The gametophyte first grows a set of rootlike rhizoids. Then it flattens out into a thin heart-shaped green structure called a **prothallium** (proh-THAL-ee-uhm). Antheridia and archegonia, which produce gametes, are found on the underside of the prothallium. If there is a moist woods near your home where you have seen ferns growing, take a close look at the ground near the base of the plants. See if you can spot the tiny prothallia among the mature plants.

When the antheridia are mature, sperm are released. Fertilization can take place when the ground and the prothallia are covered with a thin film of water. As in bryophytes, fern sperm have to swim to the archegonia to fertilize the eggs.

The diploid zygote produced by fertilization immediately begins to grow into a new sporophyte plant. The developing sporophyte quickly puts out its first fronds and then its creeping stems, or rhizomes. As the sporophyte grows, the gametophyte withers away. Fern sporophytes often live for many years. In some species, the fronds produced in the spring die in

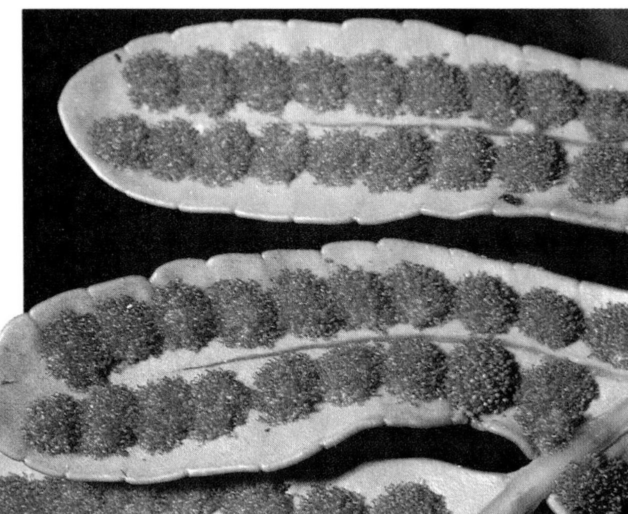

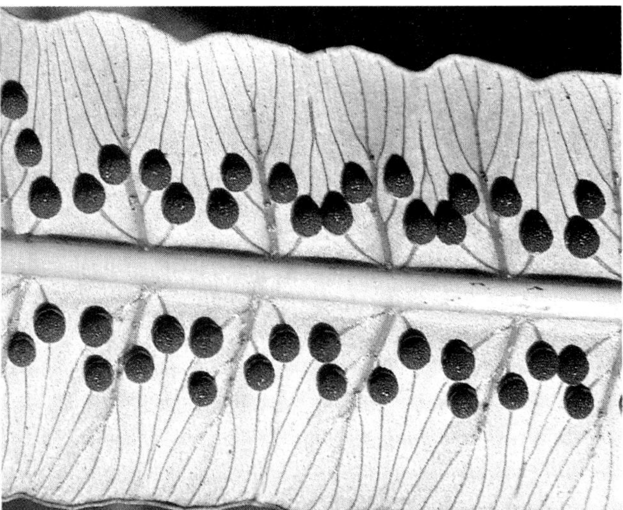

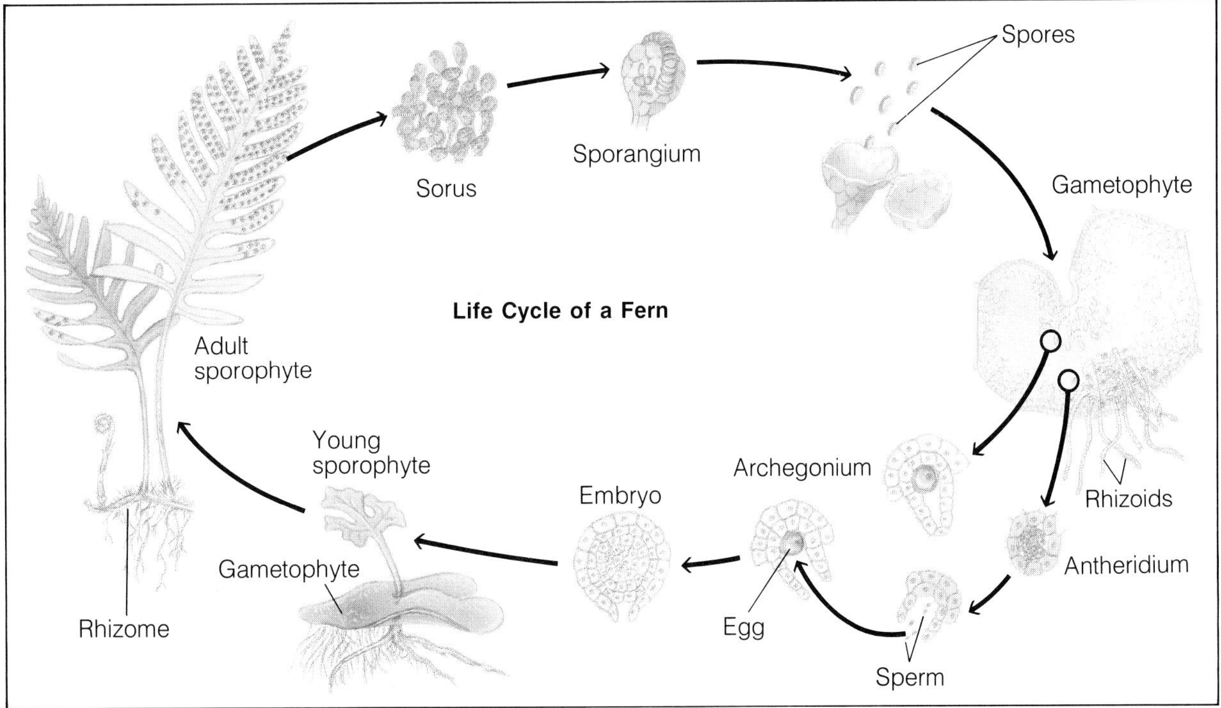

the fall, but the rhizomes live through the winter and sprout again the following spring.

We can summarize the life cycle of ferns as follows:

1. Ferns employ alternation of generations, but in ferns the diploid sporophyte is the dominant, obvious stage. The gametophyte is tiny and lives for only a short time.
2. The sporophyte is a well-developed land plant with true vascular tissues. The gametophyte lacks vascular tissues, is very tiny and delicate, and can grow only in moist areas.
3. Sexual reproduction in ferns still requires water because sperm from the antheridia must swim to the archegonia to fertilize eggs.

It should be obvious to you that ferns still need abundant water to reproduce sexually. In the next chapter you will see how the evolution of the seed has freed the higher tracheophytes from this dependence on water.

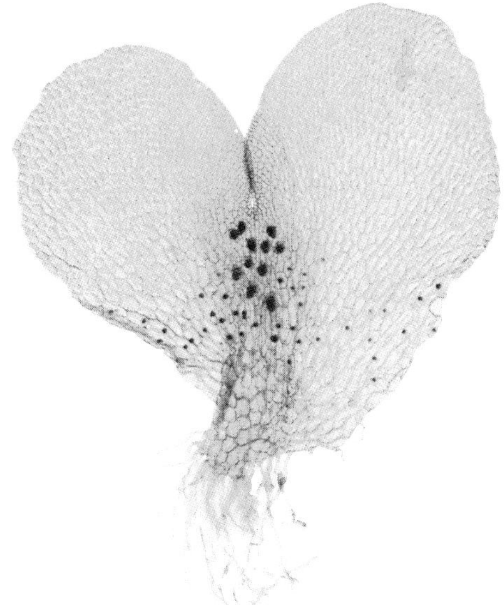

Figure 21–12 *In the life cycle of a typical fern, the heart-shaped gametophyte plant (bottom) is small and requires dampness for the sperm it produces to fertilize an egg. The young sporophyte grows from the gametophyte plant. In ferns, the sporophyte plant is large and obvious.*

21–3 SECTION REVIEW

1. What is vascular tissue?
2. What adaptations do ferns show that help them survive on land?
3. What generation in ferns is most obvious? What substance is needed by ferns to reproduce sexually?
4. Even though ferns survive under many of the same environmental conditions as mosses, ferns are able to grow much larger than mosses. Why is this so?

Section Objectives

- Describe ways in which certain characteristics of mosses make these plants useful to people.
- List ways in which ferns are used by people.

21–4 Where Mosses and Ferns Fit into the World

Mosses and ferns are well-adapted to certain types of environments. Mosses are quite common in areas that remain damp for much of the year. Ferns, which can thrive with only little light, are often found living in the shadows of forest trees, where direct sunlight hardly penetrates the forest's leafy umbrella. But wherever conditions are right, mosses and ferns grow abundantly.

Both mosses and ferns are important plants to gardeners. Several kinds of mosses are grown in gardens for decorative purposes. For example, mosses are often used to carpet the ground in Japanese-style gardens.

Mosses are frequently added to garden soil. Dried sphagnum moss absorbs many times its own weight in water and thus acts as a sort of natural sponge. Over time sphagnum moss decomposes into peat moss. Gardeners add peat moss to the soil because it improves the soil's ability to retain water. In addition, peat moss has a low pH, so when added to the soil it increases the soil's acidity. Some plants, such as azaleas, will grow well only if planted in acid soil. Sphagnum peat moss is also used to add organic material to sandy soil.

SCIENCE, TECHNOLOGY, AND SOCIETY APPLICATION

Ferns as Fertilizer

Rice farmers in Southeast Asia have learned to make good use of the floating water fern *Azolla.* In nature, *Azolla* does not grow alone but rather in association with *Anabaena,* a blue-green bacteria. Colonies of *Anabaena* live within tiny cavities in the flat *Azolla* fronds, where they grow much more rapidly than they do when they live in water.

Like several other Monerans, Anabaena can take nitrogen out of the air and "fix" it into a form that other plants can use. Rice farmers plant the fern and its accompanying bacteria along with rice in their paddies. The nitrogen that the blue-green bacteria fix makes the use of expensive chemical fertilizers unnecessary. In fact, the nitrogen fixed by *Azolla* can increase the rice paddy yield by 150 percent. *Azolla* is so important to the people of Southeast Asia that a temple in Vietnam has been dedicated to this useful plant.

The water fern Azolla *is often grown in rice paddies. This plant is able to convert nitrogen in the air into fertilizer that can be used by rice plants.*

Figure 21–13 *Maidenhair ferns are one of the more beautiful ferns (left). The leaves are produced on thin stems that quiver in even the most gentle breeze. Maidenhair ferns are frequently grown in gardens or as a houseplant. Mosses often carpet the floor of Japanese gardens (right). Although moss plants appear quite similar to one another at first glance, different species vary in color and shape.*

Many different varieties of ferns are planted and cultivated by gardeners for their ornamental value. Although they do not produce flowers, fern fronds can be quite beautiful.

At one time, mosses were ground up and used by Native Americans to treat burns and bruises. Aside from its many uses in gardening, sphagnum moss is also used to add flavor to Scotch whisky. The moss is burned by brewers. The smoke produced by the burning moss gives Scotch whisky its characteristic "smoky" flavor.

Certain species of moss form peat. Peat forms after mosses die and are subjected to enormous pressure for long periods of time. Peat is actually a kind of coal that is cut from the ground and burned as a fuel.

A few types of ferns are eaten by humans. In the early spring, fern fronds emerge from the ground. When they are just beginning to grow, the fronds look very much like the top part of a violin. For this reason, the fern fronds are called fiddleheads. If picked when they are young and cooked when they are fresh, fiddlehead greens are considered a delicacy. Unless you are certain which ferns are edible, it is best to purchase fiddleheads in a supermarket or at a vegetable stand.

Figure 21–14 *These unfurling fern fronds resemble the top of a violin and are thus called fiddleheads. At this stage they are quite tender and can be eaten. However, you should not eat wild plants.*

21–4 SECTION REVIEW

1. In what kinds of areas would you expect to find mosses growing in nature?
2. What characteristics of mosses make them useful?
3. What are two ways in which ferns are used by people?

LABORATORY INVESTIGATION

COMPARING MOSSES AND FERNS

PROBLEM

Are ferns better adapted to live on land than mosses?

MATERIALS *(per group)*

2 microscope slides	metric ruler
2 coverslips	scissors
medicine dropper	fern plant
microscope	moss plant

PROCEDURE 

1. Examine a fern frond carefully. Notice whether the top surface of the frond is shiny or dull. Notice whether the bottom surface of the frond is shiny or dull. Draw a diagram of the frond on a separate piece of paper.
2. Bend the fern frond gently back and forth. Notice whether the frond bends easily.
3. Use a ruler to measure the length and width of the frond. Record your observations.
4. Remove a few moss plants from the clump of moss provided by your teacher. Bend one plant gently back and forth. Notice whether the moss bends easily.
5. Use a ruler to measure the length and width of a moss plant.

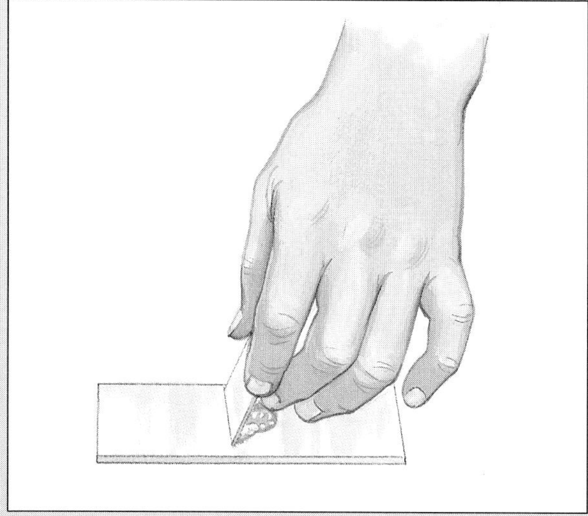

6. Cut a small piece (about 5 mm long) from the tip of one of the leaflets of the fern frond. Place it face down on a clean microscope slide. Use the medicine dropper to place a drop of water on top of the piece of fern. Cover the fern with a coverslip.
7. Examine the fern leaflet under the low-power objective of your microscope. Focus on the midline of the leaflet. Notice whether there are veins in the leaflet. Draw a diagram of what you observe.
8. Remove a single moss plant from the clump of moss. Place the plant in the center of another clean microscope slide. Use a medicine dropper to place a drop of water on top of the moss plant. Cover the moss with a coverslip.
9. Examine the moss "leaflet" under the low-power objective of your microscope. Draw a diagram of what you observe.

OBSERVATIONS

1. What are the dimensions of the fern frond? Of the moss plant? Which plant grows larger?
2. Which surface of the fern frond is shinier?
3. Which is firmer, the fern frond or the moss plant?
4. Which plant has veins in its leaves?

ANALYSIS AND CONCLUSIONS

1. Why is the fern able to grow larger than the moss?
2. How can you explain the firmness of the fern frond?
3. What do you think makes the surface of the fern frond shiny? How is this an adaptation to life on land?
4. Which of the plants shows adaptations that make it better able to survive on land? Explain.

STUDENT STUDY GUIDE

SUMMARIZING THE CONCEPTS

The key concepts in each section of this chapter are listed below to help you review the chapter content. Make sure you understand each concept and its relationship to other concepts and to the theme of this chapter.

21-1 Plants Invade the Land

- At least two separate groups of algaelike land plants evolved between 450 and 500 million years ago. One group developed into the Bryophyta; the other group developed into the Tracheophyta.
- Land plants have certain adaptations that enable them to live in a dry environment. These adaptations prevent water loss from the plant; expose the plant to the sunlight; take up water and nutrients from the soil; and move water and nutrients, along with the products of photosynthesis, throughout the plant. Special adaptations have evolved to permit plants to reproduce in land environments.

21-2 The Mosses, Liverworts, and Hornworts

- Like the algaelike organisms from which they evolved, mosses, liverworts, and hornworts have a complex life cycle that involves an alternation of generations between a haploid gametophyte and a diploid sporophyte.
- Bryophytes lack the water-conducting tubes that are found in higher plants. Without these tubes, bryophytes can never grow tall.

21-3 The Ferns and the First Vascular Plants

- The ferns were among the first land plants to develop vascular tissue: xylem and phloem. Vascular tissue is a system of tubes that move water and other materials throughout the plant. A well-developed vascular system enables ferns to grow tall. Some ferns may even grow as tall as a small tree.
- Ferns have true roots, stems, and leaves. They also have a thick waxy covering called a cuticle. The cuticle helps prevent water loss from the cells.

21-4 Where Mosses and Ferns Fit into the World

- Because mosses and ferns are well-adapted to life in certain environments, they are grown in many gardens.

REVIEWING KEY TERMS

Vocabulary terms are important to your understanding of biology. The key terms listed below are those you should be especially familiar with. Review these terms and their meanings. Then use each term in a complete sentence. If you are not sure of a term's meaning, return to the appropriate section and review its definition.

21-2 The Mosses, Liverworts, and Hornworts

rhizoid
antheridium
archegonium
protonema

21-3 The Ferns and the First Vascular Plants

vascular tissue
xylem
phloem
tracheid
vascular cylinder
vein
cuticle
rhizome
frond
sporangium
sorus
prothallium

CHAPTER REVIEW

CONTENT REVIEW

Multiple Choice

Choose the letter of the answer that best completes each statement.

1. All of the following plants are bryophytes except
   a. ferns. c. liverworts.
   b. mosses. d. hornworts.
2. Fern leaves are called
   a. sori. c. rhizomes.
   b. fronds. d. spores.
3. The most obvious stage of a moss is the
   a. sporophyte. c. protonema.
   b. parent. d. gametophyte.
4. Mosses are used for all of the following except
   a. food. c. soil additive.
   b. garden plants. d. fuel.
5. Mosses do not grow in
   a. swamps. c. deserts.
   b. marshes. d. rain forests.
6. Each of the following can be found on a fern sporophyte except a
   a. sorus. c. prothallium.
   b. frond. d. rhizome.
7. The moss sporophyte lives
   a. a solitary life.
   b. attached to the gametophyte.
   c. attached to a spore.
   d. attached to a leaf.
8. The waxy covering on the leaves of a tracheophyte is called the
   a. cuticle. c. xylem.
   b. sori. d. phloem.

True or False

Determine whether each statement is true or false. If it is true, write "true." If it is false, change the underlined word or words to make the statement true.

1. Mosses are <u>tracheophytes</u>.
2. Moss <u>sporophytes</u> are the most obvious stage of the moss life cycle.
3. Fern <u>gametophytes</u> are small heart-shaped structures.
4. Fern leaves are called <u>sori</u>.
5. <u>Sexual reproduction</u> in ferns depends on the presence of water.
6. <u>Xylem</u> tissue conducts water in a plant stem.
7. There are <u>many</u> fossils of early land plants.
8. In mosses, the archegonium produces <u>sperm</u>.

Word Relationships

A. *In each of the following sets of terms, three of the terms are related. One term does not belong. Determine the characteristic common to three of the terms and then identify the term that does not belong.*

1. sori, sporangium, spore, sperm
2. xylem, phloem, tracheids, cuticle
3. sperm, egg, zygote, spore
4. antheridium, archegonium, gametophyte, sporophyte
5. rhizoid, frond, rhizome, vascular cylinder

B. *Give the vocabulary word whose meaning is opposite that of the following words.*

6. archegonium **7.** gametophyte **8.** gametes

CONCEPT MASTERY

Use your understanding of the concepts developed in the chapter to answer each of the following in a brief paragraph.

1. Why is water needed for reproduction to occur in mosses?
2. Describe the appearance of the moss sporophyte.
3. Briefly describe sexual reproduction in a fern.
4. What are two uses of mosses and ferns?
5. Mosses must live in areas that remain damp for much of the time. Ferns can live in drier environments. What adaptations do ferns show that enable them to survive in areas that would not support moss plants?
6. Briefly summarize the life cycle of a typical moss plant.

CRITICAL AND CREATIVE THINKING

Discuss each of the following in a brief paragraph.

1. **Applying concepts** Moss plants are small. Ferns can grow as tall as a small tree. Explain why this is so.
2. **Relating concepts** Suppose you wanted to grow a garden of mosses in your backyard. What kinds of conditions would you have to provide to make these plants grow well?
3. **Applying concepts** What stage in a fern's life cycle would require more water to survive? Why?
4. **Identifying patterns** This photograph shows the structure of a tracheophyte. What structure is it? To what kind of plant does this structure belong? Is this a part of a sporophyte or a gametophyte plant?
5. **Making predictions** A friend of yours lives in a desert area of New Mexico. She wants to grow a garden of mosses. Is this a good idea? What will probably happen to her garden?
6. **Using the writing process** Imagine that you are a moss plant living in the Olympic Forest in Washington State. Every day, moist fogs roll in from the Pacific Ocean. One day the prevailing winds that blow from the west abruptly change direction. Now the winds blow from the east. Write a brief autobiography that describes your life before the winds changed direction, explaining the transformation that would occur in you and your forest home as a result.

CHAPTER 22

Plants with Seeds

This bee is busy gathering nectar from flowers. Pollen produced by the flowers sticks to the bee's body. An oak tree produces more than enough acorns to satisfy hungry squirrels and more than enough to produce new oaks.

Try to imagine what life would be like without plants. It's a rather difficult image to conjure up, especially because without plants there would be no animals. Almost every animal on the face of the Earth ultimately depends on food produced by plants. And just as importantly, plants shape environments in which animals live.

Humans and other land animals are able to benefit from plants only because members of one certain plant group have evolved in ways that allow them to live in a variety of different places. Most mosses and ferns cannot survive in many habitats because they need an almost constant supply of water. But seed plants—which include nearly all the plants you encounter—have, as a result of many evolutionary changes, been freed from dependence on water. It is this evolutionary story that you will uncover in this chapter.

CHAPTER OUTLINE

22–1 Seed Plants—The Spermopsida

Section Objectives

- Describe several adaptations of seed plants to life on land.
- Identify the functions of roots, stems, and leaves.
- Explain why reproduction in seed plants is not dependent upon water.

Compared to life in water, life on land offers several benefits to plants. Life on land provides abundant sunlight for photosynthesis. On land there is continuous free movement of gaseous carbon dioxide and oxygen, which plants use during photosynthesis and respiration.

But life on land also presents significant problems to plants. Water and nutrients are available to most land plants only from the soil. On land, dry air draws water from exposed plant tissues by the process of evaporation. On land, photosynthetic tissues must be held upright to capture sunlight. And unlike the reproductive cycles of mosses and ferns, the reproductive cycles of most land plants must work without standing water.

Seed Plants—Designed for Life on Land

Seed plants, members of the subphylum Spermopsida, exhibit numerous adaptations that allow them to survive the difficulties of life on land. Note that seed plants did not evolve

Figure 22–1 *Fields of sunflowers follow the daily movement of the sun. Here thousands of plants grow in conditions that are quite favorable. But plants often grow in less hospitable places, such as a tiny crack in the surface of a road.*

Figure 22–2 Roots, such as these of a corn plant, anchor the plant in the soil (top). The stem of the white pine is strong enough to support the plant for many meters above the ground (bottom, left). The leaves of most plants are green, the color of chlorophyll. However, leaves such as those of the brilliantly colored croton often show other colors besides green (bottom, right).

these adaptations because they "wanted" to or because the processes of evolution somehow "knew" that such adaptations would be useful on dry land. Rather, in every generation of plants, the types of genetic variations we discussed in earlier chapters produced individuals with different characteristics. Over time, those individuals with characteristics best suited to their environments survived and produced offspring.

In this way, over hundreds of millions of years, the ancestors of seed plants evolved a variety of new adaptations that enabled them to survive in many places in which mosses and ferns could not. These ancient plants evolved well-developed vascular tissues that conduct water and nutrients between roots and leaves. They evolved roots, stems, leaves, and structures that enable them to live everywhere—from frigid mountains to scorching deserts. And, seed plants, as their name implies, evolved seeds—the key adaptation in a new form of sexual reproduction that does not require standing water. Let us briefly examine these adaptations one at a time.

Roots, Stems, and Leaves

Just like the cells in your body, the cells in a plant are organized into different tissues and organs. The three main organs in a plant are roots, stems, and leaves. Each organ shows adaptations that make the plant better able to survive.

ROOTS Roots perform several important functions. They absorb water and dissolved nutrients from moist soil. They anchor plants in the ground. Roots also hold plants upright and prevent them from being knocked over by wind and rain. Roots are able to do all these jobs because as they grow, they develop complex branching networks that penetrate the soil and grow between soil particles.

STEMS Stems hold a plant's leaves up to the sun. Although plenty of sunlight reaches the Earth, plants compete

with one another for this solar energy. Many plants have tall stems and branches that reach above other plants around them. To support such tall plants, stems must be very sturdy.

LEAVES Leaves are the organs in which plants capture the sun's energy—a process vital to photosynthesis. Leaves evolved because plants that had broad, flat surfaces over which to spread their chlorophyll were able to capture more solar energy than plants that did not have such surfaces. So over time, in most habitats, plants with leaves had higher fitness—and produced more offspring—than plants without leaves. But those broad, flat leaves also exposed a great deal of tissue to the dryness of the air. These tissues must be protected against water loss to dry air. That's why most leaves are covered with a waxy coating called the cuticle. Because water cannot pass through the cuticle, this coating slows down the rate of evaporation of water from leaf tissues. Adjustable openings in the cuticle help conserve water while allowing oxygen and carbon dioxide to enter and leave the leaf as needed.

Figure 22–3 *Growing tall can be an advantage to a plant's survival. Tall plants receive more of the sun's light and are less likely to be shaded by other plants. Vascular tissues transport water from the roots to leaves at the tallest part of a plant.*

Vascular Tissue

As plants evolved longer and longer stems, the distance between their leaves and roots increased. The leaves of a tall tree might be 100 meters above the ground. Thus tall plants face an important challenge: Water must be lifted from roots to leaves, and compounds produced in leaves must be sent down to roots. Over time, the evolutionary forces of variation, chance, and natural selection produced a well-developed vascular system. This remarkable two-way plumbing system consists of two kinds of specialized tissue: xylem and phloem.

XYLEM Xylem is the vascular tissue primarily responsible for carrying water and dissolved nutrients from the roots to stems and leaves. Because xylem cells often have thick cell walls, they also provide strength to the woody parts of large plants such as trees. Oddly enough, most xylem cells grow to maturity and die before they function as water carriers.

PHLOEM Phloem tissue carries the products of photosynthesis and certain other substances from one part of the plant to another. Whereas xylem cells conduct water in only one direction (upward), phloem cells can carry their contents either upward or downward. Unlike xylem cells, functioning phloem cells are alive and filled with cytoplasm.

Reproduction Free from Water

Like other plants, seed plants have alternation of generations. However, the life cycles of seed plants are well-adapted to the rigors of life on land. All of the seed plants you see

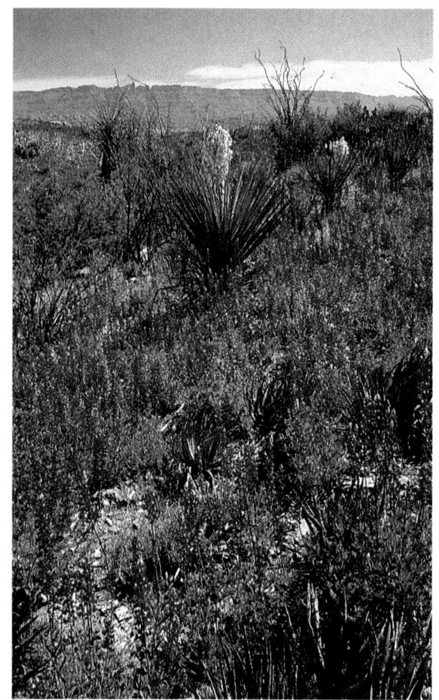

Figure 22–4 Texas bluebonnets are a wildflower that grows in huge numbers. Flowers are a plant's reproductive structures.

Figure 22–5 Seeds are a promise and a plant's insurance. A seed contains the promise of a plant to come and the insurance that a species will have a chance to survive.

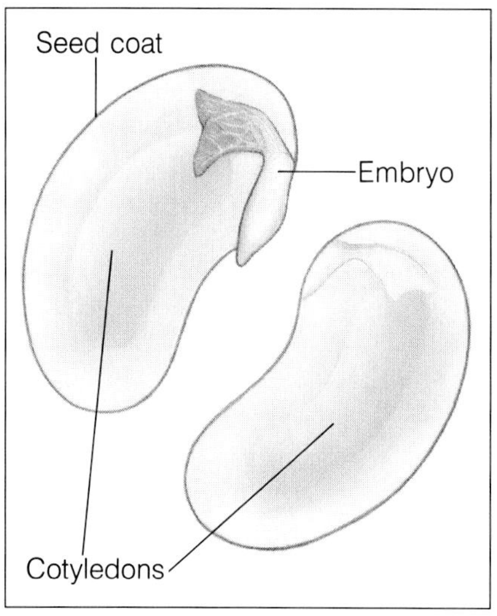

around you are members of the sporophyte generation. By comparison, the gametophytes of seed plants are tiny, consisting of only a few cells. This size difference can be seen as the final result of an evolutionary trend in plants in which the gametophyte becomes smaller as the sporophyte becomes larger.

FLOWERS AND CONES The tiny gametophytes of seed plants grow and mature within the parts of the sporophyte we call flowers and cones. Flowers and cones are special reproductive structures of seed plants, which we shall discuss later. Because they develop within the sporophyte plant, neither the gametophytes nor the gametes need standing water to function. Thus the special reproductive structures of seed plants (flowers and cones) can be considered important adaptations that have contributed to the success of these plants.

POLLINATION The entire male gametophyte of seed plants is contained in a tiny structure called a **pollen grain**. Sperm produced by this gametophyte do not swim through water to fertilize the eggs. Instead, the entire pollen grain is carried to the female gametophyte by wind, insects, birds, small animals, and sometimes even by bats. The carrying of pollen to the female gametophyte is called **pollination**. Pollination is an important process that we shall discuss shortly.

SEEDS Seeds are structures that protect the zygotes of seed plants. After fertilization, the zygote grows into a tiny plant called an **embryo**. The embryo, still within the seed, stops growing while it is still quite small. When the embryo begins to grow again later, it uses a supply of stored food inside the seed. A **seed coat** surrounds the embryo and protects it and the food supply from drying out. Inside the seed coat, the embryo can remain dormant for weeks, months, or even years. Seeds can survive long periods of bitter cold, extreme heat, or drought—beginning to grow only when conditions are once again right. Thus the formation of seeds allows seed plants to survive and increase their number in habitats where mosses and ferns cannot.

22–1 SECTION REVIEW

1. What are three adaptations of seed plants that enable them to live on land?
2. What are the functions of roots, stems, and leaves?
3. How are xylem and phloem tissues similar? How are they different?
4. What is a seed? Why are seeds important to plant life on land?

22–2 Evolution of Seed Plants

Section Objectives

- Describe the evolution of seed plants.
- List several characteristics of gymnosperms and angiosperms.
- Compare monocots and dicots.

The history of plant evolution is marked by several great adaptive radiations. **Each time a group of plants evolved a useful new adaptation (such as vascular tissue or seeds), that group of plants gave rise to many new species.** Because of the new adaptation, some new species were able to survive in previously empty niches. For other new species, the new adaptation made them better suited to their environments than existing species that did not possess the new adaptation. Over time, the better adapted species survived and the older species became extinct.

It is important to remember that Earth's environments did not remain constant through time. Over a period of millions of years, landmasses moved and mountain ranges rose. In some cases, plant species produced by an adaptive radiation continued to evolve in ways that enabled them to survive as their environment changed. Such species survived for long periods. In other cases, plant species could not survive changing environments. These species became extinct.

Mosses and ferns, for example, underwent major adaptive radiations during the Devonian and Carboniferous periods, 300 to 400 million years ago. During these periods, land environments were much wetter than they are today. Tree ferns, tree lycopods, and other spore-bearers grew into lush forests that covered much of the Earth.

But over a period of millions of years, continents became much drier, making it harder for spore-bearing plants to survive and reproduce. For that reason, many moss and fern species became extinct. They were replaced by seed plants whose adaptations equipped them to deal with drier conditions. To help you understand how seed plants became successful, we shall now trace the evolution of these fascinating organisms.

Figure 22–6 *Seed ferns are part of the fossil record. They represent a link between ferns that do not form seeds and seed plants that do. This ancient plant had leaves that resemble the leaves of modern ferns.*

Seed Ferns

The first seed-bearing plants, which appeared during the Devonian Period, resembled ferns. But these plants were different from ordinary ferns in one very important respect: They reproduced by using seeds instead of spores. Fossils of these so-called seed ferns document several evolutionary stages in the development of seed plants. Although seed ferns were quite successful for a time, they were rapidly replaced by other plant species. Today, no seed ferns survive.

Gymnosperms

The most ancient surviving seed plants belong to three classes: the Cycadae, Ginkgoae, and Coniferae. In plants of these classes, a number of leaves have evolved into specialized male and female reproductive structures called **scales**. Scales

Figure 22–7 *Confusingly named the sago palm, this cycad is not a palm at all (left). Cycads grow primarily in warm and temperate areas. Cycads produce reproductive structures that look like giant pine cones (right).*

are grouped into larger structures called male and female cones. Male cones produce male gametophytes called pollen. Female cones produce female gametophytes called eggs. Later, the female cones hold seeds that develop on their scales. Each seed is protected by a seed coat, but the seed is not covered by the cone. Because their seeds sit "naked" on the scales, Cycads, Ginkgoes, and Conifers are called naked seed plants, or **gymnosperms** (*gymno-* means naked; *-sperm* means seed).

CYCADS Cycads are beautiful palmlike plants that first appear in the fossil record during the Triassic Period, 225 million years ago. Huge forests of cycads thrived when dinosaurs roamed the Earth. Many biologists think that some species of dinosaurs ate the young leaves and seeds of cycads. Today, only nine genera of cycads, including the confusingly named sago palm, remain. Cycads can be found growing naturally in tropical and subtropical places such as Mexico, the West Indies, Florida, and parts of Asia, Africa, and Australia.

GINKGOES Ginkgoes were common when dinosaurs were alive, but today only a single species, *Ginkgo biloba*, remains. The living ginkgo species looks almost exactly like its fossil ancestors, so it is truly a living fossil. In fact, *Ginkgo biloba* may be the oldest seed plant species alive today. This single species may have survived only because the Chinese have grown it in their gardens for thousands of years.

Conifers: Cone Bearers

Conifers, commonly called evergreens, are the most abundant gymnosperms today. They are also the most familiar and important. Pines, spruce, fir, cedars, sequoias, redwoods, and yews are all conifers. Some conifers, such as the dawn redwood, date back 400 million years to the Devonian Period—well before the time of the cycads. But although other classes of gymnosperms are largely extinct, conifers still cover vast

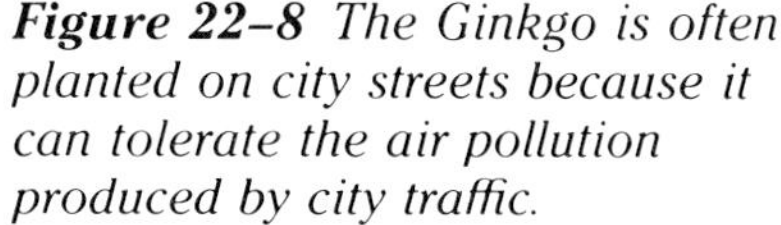

Figure 22–8 *The Ginkgo is often planted on city streets because it can tolerate the air pollution produced by city traffic.*

areas of North America, China, Europe, and Australia. Conifers grow on mountains, in sandy soil, and in cool moist areas along the northeast and northwest coasts of North America. Some conifers live more than 4000 years and can grow more than 100 meters tall.

ADAPTATIONS The leaves of conifers are long and thin, and are often called needles. Although the name evergreen is commonly used for these plants, it is not really accurate because needles do not remain on conifers forever. A few species of conifers, like larches and bald cypresses, lose their needles every fall. The needles of other conifer species remain on the plant for between 2 and 14 years. These conifers seem as if they are "evergreen" because older needles drop off gradually all year long and the trees are never completely bare.

REPRODUCTION Like other gymnosperms, most conifers produce two kinds of cones. The scales that form these cones carry structures called sporangia that produce male and female gametophytes. Both male and female gametophytes are very small. Male cones, called **pollen cones**, produce male gametophytes in the form of pollen grains. Female cones, called seed cones, house the female gametophytes that produce ovules. Some species of conifers produce male and female cones on the same plant, whereas other species have separate male and female plants.

Each spring, pollen cones release millions of dustlike pollen grains that are carried by the wind. Many of these pollen grains fall to the ground or land in water and are wasted. But some pollen grains drift onto seed cones (female cones), where they may be caught by a sticky secretion. When a pollen grain lands near a female gametophyte, it produces sperm cells by mitosis. These sperm cells burst out of the pollen grain and fertilize ovules. After fertilization, zygotes grow into seeds on the surfaces of the scales that make up the seed cones. It may take months or even years for seeds on the female cones to mature. In time, and if they land on good soil, the mature seeds may develop into new conifers.

Figure 22–9 *Pine cones may be either male or female. Male cones (top) produce windborne pollen that is carried to female cones (bottom). Female cones nurture and protect the developing seeds, which often take two years to mature.*

Angiosperms: Flowering Plants

Angiosperms are the flowering plants. All angiosperms reproduce sexually through their **flowers** in a process that involves pollination. Unlike the seeds of gymnosperms, the seeds of angiosperms are not carried naked on the flower parts. Instead, angiosperm seeds are contained within a protective wall that develops into a structure called a **fruit**. The scientific term fruit refers not only to the plant structures normally called fruits but also to many structures often called vegetables. Thus, by definition, apples, oranges, beans, pea pods, pumpkins, tomatoes, and eggplants are all fruits.

***Figure 22–10** These pear flowers are a form of floral advertising that attracts bees and other insects. The insects pollinate the flowers. Six weeks after pollination has occurred, the developing pears are still quite small. In time they will ripen.*

Today, angiosperms are the most widespread of all land plants. More than a quarter of a million species of angiosperms live everywhere from frigid mountains to blazing deserts, from humid rain forests to temperate backyards near your home. Some angiosperms even live under water. Different species of angiosperms have evolved specialized tissues that allow them to survive extreme heat and cold, as well as long periods of drought.

Angiosperms can be separated into two subclasses: the Monocotyledonae (mahn-oh-kaht-'l-EED-'n-ee), called monocots for short, and the Dicotyledonae (digh-kaht-'l-EED-'n-ee), called dicots for short. The **monocots** include corn, wheat, lilies, daffodils, orchids, and palms. The **dicots** include plants such as roses, clover, tomatoes, oaks, and daisies.

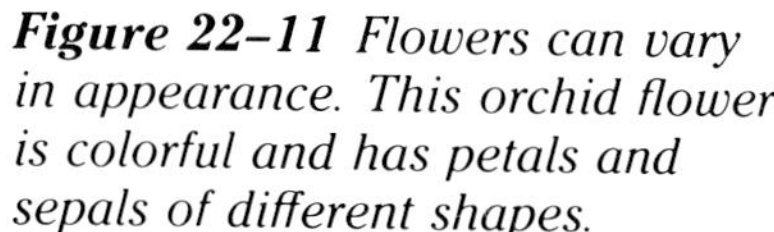

***Figure 22–11** Flowers can vary in appearance. This orchid flower is colorful and has petals and sepals of different shapes.*

There are several differences between monocots and dicots. The simplest difference has to do with the number of leaves the embryo plant has when it first begins to grow, or germinate. The leaves of the embryo are called **cotyledons**, or seed leaves. Monocotyledons have one seed leaf (*mono-* means one). Dicotyledons start off with two seed leaves (*di-* means two). In some species, cotyledons are filled with food for the germinating plant. In other species, the cotyledons are the first leaves to carry on photosynthesis for the germinating plant.

Figure 22–12 shows several characteristics of monocots and dicots. These differences are summarized below:

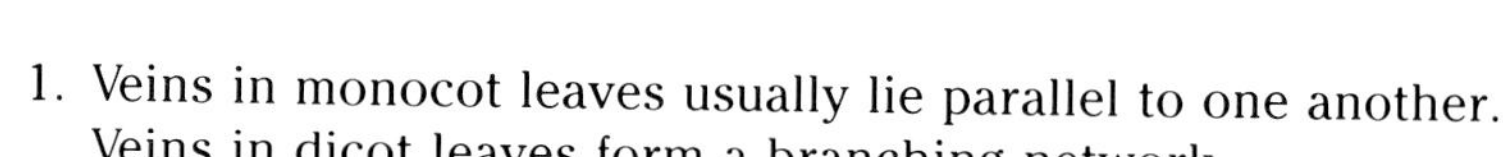

1. Veins in monocot leaves usually lie parallel to one another. Veins in dicot leaves form a branching network.
2. In monocot flowers, petals and other flower parts are usually found in threes or multiples of three (3, 6, 9, and so on). In dicot flowers, petals and other flower parts occur in fours or fives or in multiples of four (4, 8, 12) or five (5, 10, 15).
3. In monocot stems, xylem and phloem tissues are gathered into **vascular bundles** that are scattered throughout the stem. In dicot stems, these vascular bundles are arranged in a ring near the outside of the stem.

	Monocots	Dicots
Leaves	Veins in leaves of most monocots are parallel to each other.	Veins in leaves form a branching network.
Flower	Flower parts in threes or multiples of three.	Flower parts in fours or fives or multiples of four or five.
Vascular bundles in stem	Vascular bundles are scattered in a cross section of a stem.	Vascular bundles are arranged in a ring in a cross section of a stem.
Vascular bundles in root	Bundles of xylem and phloem alternate with one another in a circle.	A single mass of xylem forms an "X" in the center of the root; phloem bundles are located between the arms of the "X."
Stem thickness	Stems of most monocots do not grow thicker from year to year.	Stems can grow thicker from year to year.

Figure 22–12 *Flowering plants are placed into two main subclasses, Monocotyledonae and Dicotyledonae. This chart identifies the differences between these two classes. Which class contains plants whose leaves have veins that are parallel to one another?*

4. In monocot roots, bundles of xylem and phloem alternate with each other in a circular arrangement, like the spokes of a bicycle wheel. In dicot roots, a single mass of xylem tissue forms an X in the center of the root, and bundles of phloem tissue are positioned between the arms of the "X."
5. Most monocots have stems and roots that do not grow thicker from year to year. For this reason there are very few treelike monocots. Palms are one of the few treelike monocots. Some dicot stems and roots can grow thicker from year to year. Most of the flowering trees you see are dicots.

Figure 22–13 *This tiny bean seed has pushed its stem above the soil surface and into the light. Just below the leaves at the top of the plant, the two bean-shaped cotyledons remain attached to the stem. Later, when the plant is large enough to make its own food, the cotyledons will shrivel and fall off.*

22–2 SECTION REVIEW

1. What is a seed fern? Why is it important in the evolution of seed plants?
2. Compare gymnosperms and angiosperms.
3. Which generation is more obvious in seed plants? How do the relative sizes of these generations follow a trend in the evolution of plant reproduction?
4. Suppose you found a plant whose leaves have parallel veins and whose flowers have six petals. Is this plant a monocot or a dicot? What is your reasoning?

Section Objectives

- Describe the process of pollination in seed plants.
- Explain plant-animal coevolution.
- Discuss the importance of seed dispersal to the success of the seed plants.

22–3 Coevolution of Flowering Plants and Animals

Watching bees travel from flower to flower is such a common experience that most of us probably do not think about it. We take for granted the fact that flowers are brightly colored and beautifully perfumed. Rarely do we wonder why fruits are tasty and nutritious as well as colorful. But how and why did insects begin exhibiting flower-visiting behavior? When did animals begin to eat fruits and seeds? And why have plant flowers and fruits evolved into their present forms?

The process by which two organisms evolve structures and behaviors in response to changes in each other over time is called **coevolution**. Some of the most fascinating examples of coevolution involve relationships between angiosperm flowers and fruits and a wide variety of animal species.

To understand plant-animal coevolution, we must look once again at the evolutionary history of plants. The first flowering plants probably evolved during the early Cretaceous Period, about 125 million years ago. At that time, gymnosperms and other plants formed huge forests. Dinosaurs were the dominant land animals. During the Cretaceous Period, the first birds and mammals began to appear in the fossil record. Flying insects, particularly beetles of several types, became common. Thus the first flowering plants evolved at about the same time as the earliest mammals, a short time after the earliest birds, and a good while after the earliest insects.

Then, toward the end of the Cretaceous Period, the Earth's climate changed dramatically. Dinosaurs and many gymno-

Figure 22–14 *Many different animals pollinate plants. Bees, such as this honeybee covered with pollen, are perhaps the most common (right). Bees are responsible for the pollination of many of the plant varieties that produce the fruits we eat. Bananas, like this one growing in Southeast Asia, are often pollinated by bats, not by bees (left).*

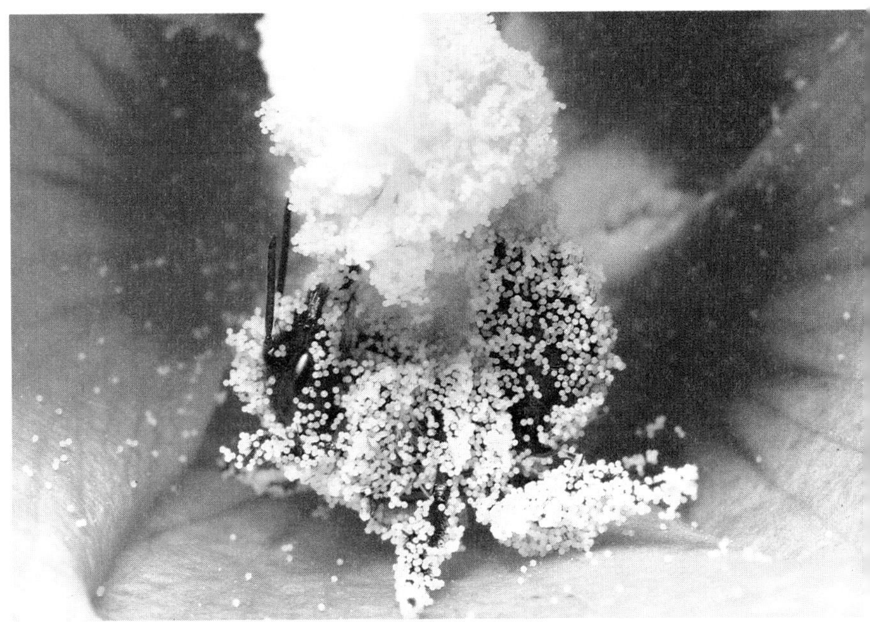

sperms became extinct. This mass extinction opened up many niches for other organisms. New adaptive radiations of both animals and plants occurred. New species of birds and mammals evolved and filled niches vacated by the dinosaurs. New species of angiosperms replaced disappearing gymnosperms. And many new species of insects—including moths, bees, and butterflies—evolved.

The coincidence of angiosperm evolution with the evolution of modern insects, birds, and mammals is very important. Flowers and fruits are specialized reproductive structures that could evolve only in the presence of insects, birds, and mammals. Let us now see how and why this is so.

Flower Pollination

Pollination is essential to the reproduction of flowering plants. Over millions of years, a variety of ways to ensure that pollination will occur has evolved. For example, some plants are pollinated by the wind. Wind-pollinated plants include willow trees, ragweed, and grasses such as corn and wheat. The tiny pollen grains of these plants fall off their flowers without difficulty, making it easy for them to be carried by the wind to other flowers. Wind-pollinated plants usually have small, plain simple flowers with little or no fragrance.

But most angiosperms are not pollinated by the wind. Most flowering plants are pollinated by insects, birds, or mammals that carry pollen from one flower to another. In return, the plants provide the pollinators with food. The food may take the form of pollen or a liquid called nectar, which may contain up to 25 percent glucose, or a combination of pollen and nectar.

Figure 22–15 *Hummingbirds are able to flap their wings so fast that they hover in place. This hummingbird is drinking nectar from a flower. Because hummingbirds are able to see red and orange quite well, they are attracted to these flower colors.*

It is easy to imagine how pollinators such as bees first learned to visit certain flowers. When a bee finds food on a particular flower, it remembers clearly the color, shape, and odor of that flower. So if a bee finds edible pollen on a flower of a particular type, it will search for more flowers of that same type. While feeding on different flowers, a bee may accidentally pick up extra pollen that it then carries to the next flower it visits. Because the bees remember the color and odor of flowers so well, it is probable that pollen picked up from one flower will be deposited on another flower of the same species.

This kind of interaction between animals and plants increases the evolutionary fitness of both organisms. Insects benefit by learning to identify dependable sources of food. Plants benefit because this kind of **vector pollination**, or pollination by the actions of animals, is a very efficient way of getting the male gametophyte to the female gametophyte. Vector pollination is much more efficient than wind pollination, which wastes enormous amounts of pollen.

Of course, flowers that depend upon specific animals to pollinate them could only have evolved after those animals evolved. When angiosperms first appeared, this sort of relationship began accidentally. But over time the coevolutionary relationship strengthened because it proved beneficial to the survival of both plants and animals. Coevolutionary relationships can be very specific. The following examples of flower-pollinator pairs illustrate this fact.

__Figure 22–16__ These flowers appear quite different to a human's eyes than they do to a bee's eyes. Under ultraviolet light, the white flowers glow with a strange purple hue, a color that is easily seen by foraging bees.

One common pollinator is the honeybee. To attract bees to their flowers, many plants have brightly colored flower petals that bees can see well. Because bees can see ultraviolet, blue, and yellow light the best, these are the colors of most bee-pollinated flowers. We cannot see ultraviolet light under ordinary circumstances. But special film can make this color visible to our eyes. In Figure 22–16 you can see a picture of a flower taken in ultraviolet light. The petals of some flowers even have markings that point to the center of the flower. These markings are like a secret sign for bees alone to see! The markings direct the bee to the center of the flower—the source of nectar. On its way to the food, the bee might pollinate the flower, thus ensuring the survival of the plant species. Flowers that are pollinated by bees usually have some kind of landing platform because bees gather nectar only when they are standing, not when they are flying.

Flowers that have coevolved with animals other than bees show different methods of attracting pollinators. For example, some flowers are pollinated by night-flying moths that cannot see color but have an excellent sense of smell. The petals of these flowers are often plain and white, but the flowers themselves are very fragrant—especially at night. (We use many of these floral fragrances—jasmine, for example—in perfumes.) Moth-pollinated flowers usually do not have landing platforms because unlike bees, moths feed while hovering in midair. The nectar of moth-pollinated flowers is usually contained deep within the flower, where only the long tongue of a moth can reach it.

Several species of flowers are pollinated by flies that lay their eggs in the bodies of dead and decaying animals. You certainly would not want to grow these flowers in your house because they smell like rotting meat! The smell produced by the flowers attracts the flies that are looking for a place to lay their eggs. The flowers of these plants even heat up when they are ready to be pollinated, thus intensifying the smell they produce to lure additional flies that may act as vector pollinators.

Some flowers are pollinated by birds. Birds have a very poor sense of smell but a good sense of sight. Birds can easily see the colors orange and red. Not surprisingly, bird-pollinated flowers, such as the beautiful bird-of-paradise flower, are a reddish-orange color. These flowers usually have no fragrance.

Figure 22–17 *The stapelia flower, also called the carrion flower, smells like a piece of rotting meat. Although not attractive to us, the smell proves alluring to a fly looking for a place to lay her eggs.*

Seed Dispersal

Just as flowers have different methods that ensure pollination, angiosperm fruits have adaptations that help scatter seeds away from the parent plant. The process of distributing seeds away from parent plants is **seed dispersal**. Seed dispersal is very important to plants. Why? If the seeds of a plant are not dispersed but instead fall to the ground beneath the parent plant, the seedlings will compete with one another and with the parent plant for sunlight, water, and nutrients. This competition will reduce the chances of survival for the growing seeds. Seed dispersal also enables plants to colonize new environments. Although adult plants cannot move around, their seeds can be carried to new environments.

Figure 22–18 *The seeds of the milkweed (left) and the dandelion (right) are carried by the wind.*

SCIENCE, TECHNOLOGY, AND SOCIETY **BREAKTHROUGH**

Designer Genes Create Better Plants

At one agricultural laboratory, a single tomato plant in a cage full of hungry caterpillars remains untouched while its neighbor is stripped bare of leaves. The cells of the protected tomato are able to manufacture an insecticide because of genes transplanted from a bacterium. At another laboratory, a newly developed potato manufactures a chemical that repels both potato beetles and leaf hoppers, two notorious insect pests. The new potato plant produces an insect repellant previously made only by a few varieties of wild potato from South America.

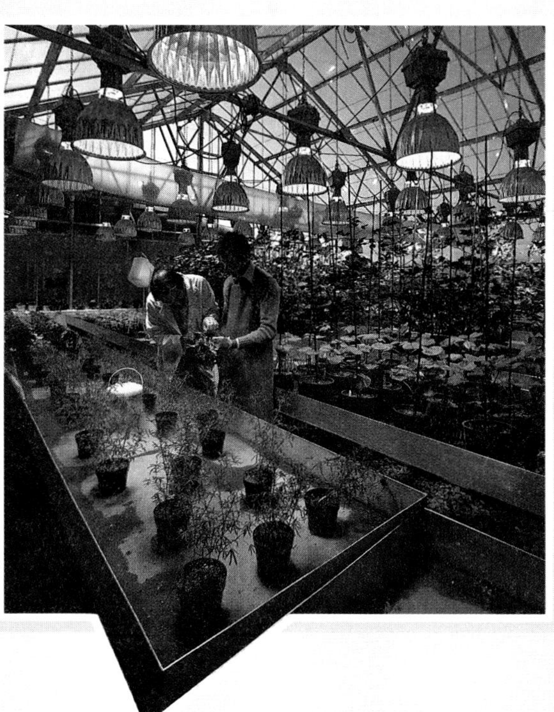

These are just two of the new and improved plant varieties being produced by the application of biotechnology to agriculture. Using a variety of techniques (including techniques of genetic engineering you read about in Chapter 12) researchers are now designing and producing new plants that exhibit traits breeders could once only dream about.

With genes transplanted from other organisms, such as bacteria, plants may be able to manufacture their own insecticides. These insecticides do not harm the environment because they remain within the plant that produced them. Gene manipulation may result in the production of plants that produce seeds or fruits with higher protein content or with protein more nutritionally complete for humans. Still other plants may soon manufacture drugs for human use or have resistance to fungal and bacterial infections. Although most of these techniques of plant development are still experimental, researchers hope to be able to produce plants for market in the near future. A great agricultural revolution has begun!

Several different methods of seed dispersal have been observed in angiosperms. The seeds and fruits of some angiosperms, like those of dandelions, are carried by the wind. In other angiosperms, pressure builds inside the fruit and finally forces seeds out of the ripe fruit like bullets from a gun. The common garden plant Impatiens has fruits that spring open when touched, scattering the seeds over substantial distances.

Many fruits have coevolved with animal species that help disperse the fruits' seeds. For example, some fruits have sharp barbs that catch in fur or feathers, allowing the seeds inside to hitch rides on mammals or birds. As they move from place to place, such animals may enter a new environment. If the seeds fall off the animals and land on a spot that provides good growing conditions, they will develop into new plants. In this way, plants are carried to new environments.

Some fruits have attractive colors, pleasant tastes, and contain a variety of nutritious compounds. These fruits and the seeds inside them are eaten by mammals and birds. The fleshy, nourishing, and tasty pulp of the fruit is digested by the animal, but the seeds, which are protected by tough seed coats, are not. These seeds pass through the digestive tract of the animal without being damaged. While inside the animal, seeds may be carried over great distances. Eventually the seeds are deposited, along with a convenient dose of natural fertilizer, in a new location where they can grow.

Have you ever wondered why so many unripe fruits are green and have a bitter taste? Think about the function of fruits in relation to the evolutionary fitness of plants. Inside the unripened fruits the seeds are still maturing. If the fruits are eaten too soon, the immature seeds will not be able to grow. The plant's fitness for survival would decrease. But plants manufacture bitter-tasting compounds that they pump into fruits as the fruits develop. These bitter-tasting compounds discourage animals from eating fruits that are not ripe. The green color of unripe fruits makes it more likely that animals will not notice the fruits hidden among the green leaves of plants. When the seeds are mature, plants either remove the bitter-tasting compounds from the fruits or chemically break down the compounds completely. Plants then pump sugars into the fruits. At the same time, the fruits change color. The brightly colored fruits are more easily noticed by birds and other animals. The distribution of seeds in fruits is yet another example of plant-animal coevolution.

Figure 22–19 *The tiny seeds of the cocklebur have many hooks (top). The hooks catch onto the fur of animals and are carried to new environments. When the seeds are ripe, raspberries turn a bright red and can easily be seen by birds and other animals (bottom). After the fruits are eaten, the indigestible seeds pass through the animal and are deposited, along with other solid wastes, in a new environment.*

22–3 SECTION REVIEW

1. What is a pollinator? Why is the role of a pollinator important to seed plants?
2. Explain how plant–animal coevolution has led to the development of relationships between vector pollinators and flowers.
3. What is seed dispersal? Why is it important?
4. Explain how fruits are dispersed by animals. How does fruit dispersal contribute to seed dispersal?

LABORATORY INVESTIGATION

COMPARING RIPE AND UNRIPE FRUITS

PROBLEM

Why do fruits get ripe?

MATERIALS *(per group)*

unripe banana	hot plate
ripe banana	ruler
balance	scalpel
400-mL beaker	4 test tubes
Benedict's solution	test tube holder
sugar (dextrose) solution	test tube rack
	hand lens
2 100-mL graduated cylinders	glass-marking pencil

PROCEDURE

1. Fill a 400-mL beaker halfway with water. Place the beaker on a hot plate. Turn the hot plate on high.
2. Use a glass-marking pencil to label four test tubes. Label the first test tube *C,* for control; the second *S,* for sugar; the third, *R,* for ripe banana; and the fourth, *U,* for unripe banana.
3. Use a graduated cylinder to put 5 mL of water into the test tubes labeled *C, R,* and *U.* Place 5 mL of a sugar (dextrose) solution into the test tube labeled *S.*
4. With a clean graduated cylinder, add 5 mL of Benedict's solution to each of the test tubes.
5. Observe the color and appearance of the unripe banana. Peel it. Use a scalpel to cut a slice, or cross section, 5 mm thick. **CAUTION:** *Always cut away from yourself and others.*
6. Cut the slice of banana in half along its diameter. Then make a cut parallel to the diameter, about 5 mm from the cut edge, as shown in the accompanying illustration.
7. Measure the mass of the cut piece. It should have a mass of about 1 g. Put this piece of banana into the test tube marked *U.*
8. Repeat steps 5 to 7 with the ripe banana. Make sure the mass of the piece of ripe banana is the same as the mass of the unripe banana. Place this piece in the test tube marked *R.*

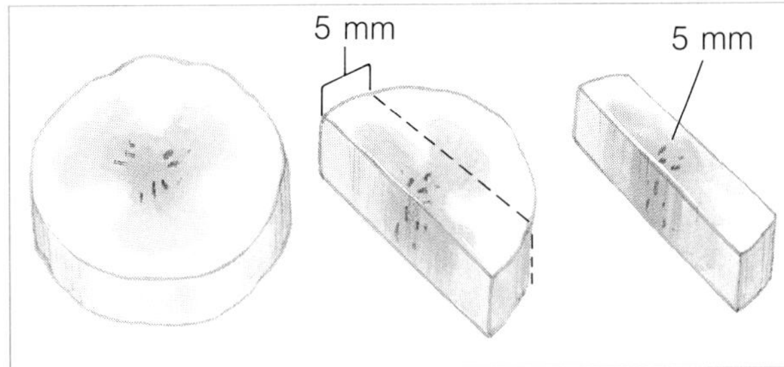

9. Place the test tubes in the beaker of boiling water on the hot plate. **CAUTION:** *Use the test tube holder. Place the tubes carefully.*
10. Observe the four test tubes. When the test tube that contains the sugar solution changes color, observe the color of the other test tubes.
11. Use the test tube holder to remove the test tubes from the beaker. Place the test tubes in the test tube rack. Turn off the hot plate and allow the beaker to cool.
12. Make several more slices of the ripe banana. Use a hand lens to examine the region near the center of each slice.

OBSERVATIONS

1. What did the peel of the unripe banana look like? The ripe banana?
2. In which test tubes did the greatest change occur?
3. Describe the structures you observed in the center of the banana slices.

ANALYSIS AND CONCLUSIONS

1. What do the results of the tests with Benedict's solution show?
2. What are the structures in the center of a banana?
3. How do animals help disperse banana seeds?
4. What changes occur when a banana ripens?
5. Why would an animal be more likely to find and eat ripe bananas than unripe bananas?

SUMMARIZING THE CONCEPTS

The key concepts in each section of this chapter are listed below to help you review the chapter content. Make sure you understand each concept and its relationship to other concepts and to the theme of this chapter.

22–1 Seed Plants—The Spermopsida

- Seed plants have roots, stems, and leaves that show adaptations that enable them to perform different functions.
- Seed plants are able to reproduce without the need for standing water. Seed plants produce seeds that are able to survive periods of time that are unfavorable for growth.

22–2 Evolution of Seed Plants

- The gymnosperms are the most ancient group of surviving seed plants. The name gymnosperm means naked seed.
- The most common gymnosperms are the conifers. Conifer means cone-bearing. Most conifers produce cones, which are special reproductive organs.
- All flowering plants belong to the angiosperms. Flowers are the angiosperms' reproductive organs.
- There are two main subclasses of angiosperms: monocots and dicots. Monocots have one seed leaf; dicots have two. The veins in monocot leaves are parallel to one another. The veins of dicots form a branching network in the leaves. The flower parts of monocots occur in threes or multiples of three. The flower parts of dicots occur in fours or fives or multiples of four or five. The vascular bundles in monocots form a ring around the stem. The vascular bundles of dicots are scattered around the stem.

22–3 Coevolution of Flowering Plants and Animals

- Some flowering plants are pollinated by the wind. These plants shed vast amounts of pollen into the air.
- The process by which two organisms evolve structures and behaviors in relation to or complementary to one another is called coevolution.
- Many animals are pollinators of flowers, or agents that transfer pollen from one flower to another.

REVIEWING KEY TERMS

Vocabulary terms are important to your understanding of biology. The key terms listed below are those you should be especially familiar with. Review these terms and their meanings. Then use each term in a complete sentence. If you are not sure of a term's meaning, return to the appropriate section and review its definition.

22–1 Seed Plants—The Spermopsida

pollen grain
pollination
embryo
seed coat

22–2 Evolution of Seed Plants

scale
gymnosperm
pollen cone
angiosperm
flower
fruit
monocot
dicot
cotyledon
vascular bundle

22–3 Coevolution of Flowering Plants and Animals

coevolution
vector pollination
seed dispersal

CHAPTER REVIEW

CONTENT REVIEW

Multiple Choice

Choose the letter of the answer that best completes each statement.

1. Flowering plants are in the class
   a. cotyledonae. c. angiospermae.
   b. gymnospermae. d. coniferae.
2. A red flower is most probably pollinated by a (an)
   a. bat. c. insect.
   b. gust of wind. d. bird.
3. Each of the following is an adaptation of plants to a life on land except
   a. tall stems. c. xylem and phloem.
   b. a waxy cuticle. d. seeds.
4. The entire male gametophyte of a seed plant is contained within the
   a. embryo. c. pollen grain.
   b. fruit. d. xylem.
5. The first seed-bearing plants were the
   a. ferns. c. conifers.
   b. mosses. d. seed ferns.
6. You examine a flower and find six petals. This flower is most likely from a
   a. monocot. c. dicot.
   b. conifer. d. fern.
7. Each of the following is a fruit except a
   a. potato. c. squash.
   b. tomato. d. strawberry.
8. Inside a seed coat, an embryo
   a. continues to grow.
   b. is kept warm.
   c. is protected from drying out.
   d. awaits fertilization.

True or False

Determine whether each statement is true or false. If it is true, write "true." If it is false, change the underlined word or words to make the statement true.

1. <u>Codevelopment</u> is the process by which two organisms evolve structures and behaviors complementary to each other.
2. <u>Leaves</u> are the organs in which most plants make food.
3. <u>Stems</u> absorb water and dissolved nutrients from the soil.
4. <u>Phloem</u> carries water up a plant stem.
5. A flower that smells like rotten meat most likely attracts <u>birds</u> for pollination.
6. The process of distributing seeds away from the parent plant is called <u>seed dispersal</u>.
7. A plant whose leaf veins form a branching network is most probably a <u>dicot</u>.
8. Bees gather nectar while <u>flying</u>.

Word Relationships

A. *An analogy is a relationship between two pairs of words or phrases generally written in the following manner: a:b::c:d. The symbol : is read "is to," and the symbol :: is read "as." For example, cat:animal::rose:plant is read "cat is to animal as rose is to plant."*

In the analogies that follow, a word or phrase is missing. Complete each analogy by providing the missing word or phrase.

1. gymnosperm:cones::angiosperm:____________
2. fruit:seeds::cones:____________
3. xylem:water::phloem:____________
4. ferns:spores::conifers:____________

B. *In each of the following sets of terms, three of the terms are related. One term does not belong. Determine the characteristic common to three of the terms and then identify the term that does not belong.*

5. net veins, parallel veins, one cotyledon, nine petals
6. bee, bird, bat, wind
7. strawberry, blueberry, apple, potato

CONCEPT MASTERY

Use your understanding of the concepts developed in the chapter to answer each of the following in a brief paragraph.

1. What is seed dispersal? How does it contribute to the survival of a plant species?
2. What is a cotyledon?
3. How do seed plants help humans survive?
4. Why do botanists consider a tomato and a squash fruits?
5. How do roots and vascular tissues contribute to a redwood tree's great size?
6. How are seed plants better able to survive drier conditions than mosses and ferns?
7. What is a conifer? How does a conifer differ from an angiosperm?
8. What is wind pollination? How does wind pollination differ from vector pollination?
9. Why is it important that seeds provide food for the embryo plant?

CRITICAL AND CREATIVE THINKING

Discuss each of the following in a brief paragraph.

1. **Applying concepts** In nature, flowers have a limited range of colors. In a garden, however, flowers can have many more colors. Apply your knowledge of pollination and artificial selection to explain why.
2. **Making predictions** In a time in the future, a terrible fatal disease is found to affect all monocots. Predict the effect of this disease on the human population.
3. **Relating cause and effect** Scientists invent a new insecticide that can kill all the insects in the world. What important harmful effect would this have on plants?
4. **Interpreting diagrams** Examine the plant in this photograph. How many cotyledons would the seeds of this plant have? Explain your reasoning.

5. **Applying concepts** A farmer decides not to plant her fields one year. Later in the year heavier than normal rains fall on the field. Now the farmer wishes she had planted her crops. Why do you think she changed her mind?
6. **Applying concepts** Making a cut through the bark of a tree in a complete circle around the trunk often results in the death of the tree. Using your knowledge of vascular tissue, explain why this might happen.
7. **Relating facts** The seeds of a gymnosperm are probably not likely to be dispersed by animals, whereas the seeds of angiosperms are likely to be dispersed by animals. Explain why this is so.
8. **Using the writing process** Suppose all gymnosperms died out tomorrow. Write a story that details ways in which your life would be changed.

CHAPTER 23

Roots, Stems, and Leaves

Growing through a crack in the top of a mountain, this pine tree demonstrates the ability of plants to grow under adverse conditions. The sunflower, too, growing in the ever-moving desert sands, shows the same tenacity.

On a mountain ridge, the twisted roots of an ancient pine tree cling to solid rock in subzero temperatures. In a desert, a sagebrush plant survives in the blazing sun for months without rain. On a dune by the seashore, a clump of beach grass flowers in poor, salty sand. And in the Everglades, mangrove trees live with their roots submerged in rich, organic mud.

These plants have adaptations that enable them to live under difficult conditions. How do these plants obtain the water and nutrients they need to survive in their harsh surroundings? For that matter, how does any plant extract what it needs from soil and air? The answers to these questions will become clear in this chapter.

CHAPTER OUTLINE

23–1 Soil: A Storehouse for Water and Nutrients

Section Objectives

- Discuss the importance of soil for plant growth.
- Describe the composition of soil.
- List the nutrients essential for plant growth.

Seed plants are autotrophs; they make the organic molecules they need from raw materials such as water, carbon dioxide, and several inorganic nutrients. Where do they get these raw materials? Carbon dioxide is removed from the air by the leaves. Water and inorganic nutrients are taken in from the soil by plant roots. Soil is a "bank" of nutrients plants use to grow.

Types of Soil

An understanding of soil will help explain how plants function. What exactly is soil? **Soil is a complex mixture of sand, silt, clay, and bits of decaying animal and plant tissue.** Soil in different places and at different depths contains varying amounts of these ingredients. The ingredients define the soil and determine, to a large extent, the kinds of plants that can grow in it.

Sandy soil is composed mostly of sand grains. Because sand grains are large and irregularly shaped, there are large empty spaces between them. That's why water poured on sand drains through it so quickly.

Clay soil is composed mostly of very fine clay particles that have extremely small spaces between them. Horticulturists—professional growers of plants—use the word heavy to describe soil that contains large amounts of clay particles. Water poured on clay soil sinks in slowly.

Figure 23–1 *Wildflowers grow well in the dappled forest shade. The soil beneath the trees contains decaying leaves and other organic materials that are used by plants as natural fertilizer.*

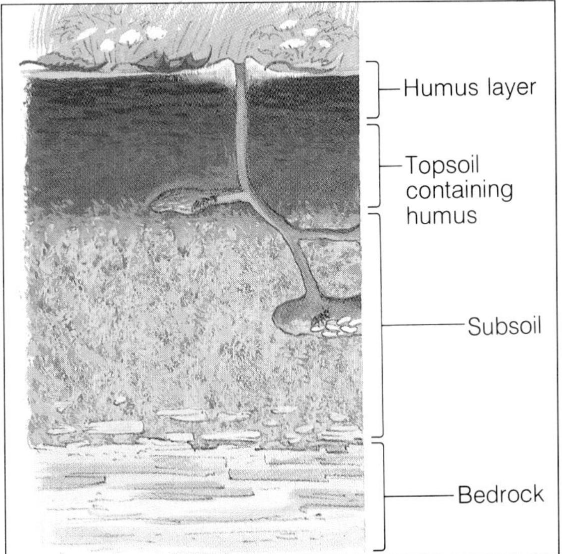

Figure 23–2 Soil is composed of layers of materials such as humus, sand, clay, minerals, and rocks. The topmost layer is usually richest in organic material. Together the layers make up the soil profile.

Loamy soil contains decaying organic matter formed from plant and animal tissue, in addition to particles of sand and clay. Particles of organic matter are usually larger than sand or clay particles. Organic matter helps increase the soil's ability to hold air and water. Nitrogen, phosphorus, and other nutrients that can be used by plants are released from the soil as the organic matter is broken down by fungi and bacteria.

Soil Profiles

If you cut a trench in the ground, you will see that the soil is arranged in layers, with each layer corresponding to a different kind of soil. The particular order of layers is called a soil profile. See Figure 23–2. Most organic matter is on top, where it forms the humus layer. The humus layer in forest soil can be several centimeters thick. In grasslands, however, the humus layer may be much thinner.

Under the humus layer is the topsoil, which is a mixture of humus, sand, clay, and minerals. The thickness of topsoil varies with the location. Topsoil in the fertile plains of the Midwest is often a meter thick, whereas in northeastern forests it may be only a few centimeters deep. Plant roots grow best in the humus and topsoil layers.

Beneath the topsoil is the subsoil, a mixture of rocks and inorganic soil particles often tightly packed together. Subsoil offers little room for air, water, and plant roots. Beneath the subsoil is bedrock, a layer of rock that usually cannot be penetrated by plant roots.

Almost half the total volume of good garden soil actually consists of open spaces between soil particles. These open spaces are important for several reasons. They are home to beneficial bacteria, fungi, and protozoa that help plants grow.

The tiny pockets of water and air are essential to the good health of plant roots and soil microorganisms. Air pockets allow roots to breathe. Water pockets are vital because nutrients are available to plants only when they are dissolved in water. Finally, roots do not actually grow "in" soil. Roots really grow into and through the spaces between soil particles. If there are not enough spaces, roots cannot grow properly.

Essential Nutrients

To grow, flower, and produce seeds, plants require a variety of inorganic nutrients in addition to carbon dioxide and water. These inorganic nutrients are located in the soil. And it is from the soil's bank of nutrients that plants withdraw their needs. The most important of these nutrients are nitrogen, phosphorus, potassium, calcium, magnesium, and various trace elements.

Nitrogen is essential for proper leaf growth and color. A lack of nitrogen will stunt plant growth and cause the foliage to turn a sickly yellow color.

Phosphorus is used to make DNA in all cells and is important in the development of roots, stems, flowers, and seeds. Too little phosphorus causes poor flowering and stunted growth.

Potassium (sometimes called potash) plays a critical role in the making of proteins and carbohydrates by plants. Potassium also plays a role in the development of roots, stems, and flowers, and helps plants resist cold and disease. The first sign of a potassium deficiency is usually stunted roots, which soon result in stunted leaves.

Calcium is used in cell metabolism and is necessary for cell growth and division and cell wall strength.

Magnesium is a critical part of the chlorophyll molecule. A lack of magnesium will prevent the manufacture of chlorophyll and may eventually kill the plant.

Trace elements, which plants require in small quantities, include sulfur, iron, zinc, molybdenum, boron, copper, manganese, and chlorine. To maintain proper plant growth, trace elements are needed in very small amounts. In fact, large amounts of trace elements in the soil can be poisonous.

Figure 23–3 *Plants need minerals from the soil in order to grow well. The rhododendron in the top photograph shows the effects of iron deficiency. The rhododendron in the bottom photograph received a good supply of needed minerals. What differences can you observe between the two plants?*

23–1 SECTION REVIEW

1. What is soil? Why is soil important for plant growth?
2. Why are the spaces between soil particles important?
3. What are some of the essential nutrients found in soil? Why is each important for plants?
4. Which type of soil is best for plant growth? Explain your answer.

SCIENCE, TECHNOLOGY, AND SOCIETY **APPLICATION**

Small Friends

In our daily struggle to live a healthy life, we tend to view all microorganisms as harmful. Microorganisms are the cause of many human and plant diseases. That is a fact. However, many of the microorganisms we rightly view with alarm have relatives that make important contributions to human and plant life. The benefits of microorganisms to humans are discussed elsewhere in this textbook. Here you will read about the benefits to plants.

You know that plants need to take in vital minerals and other inorganic compounds from the soil. These compounds are so important that farmers often spend millions of dollars to add them, in the form of fertilizers, to their soils. However, some plants carry their own "fertilizer factories" right on their roots. The factories are actually hard-working bacteria. The bacteria, many from the genus *Rhizobium*, are able to take nitrogen from the air and convert it into a form that plants can use. (You may remember that nitrogen makes up most of the air we breathe.) In this way the bacteria "fertilize" the plants on which they live. Farmers have found that these bacteria commonly grow on legumes such as peas and beans. Unlike most crop plants, which deplete, or use up, the minerals in the soil, legumes actually improve the soil in which they grow.

Other plants grow well only when they have a fungus infecting their roots. This may seem strange, but the fungus is able to improve the plant's ability to absorb important minerals from the soil. The association of plant roots and fungi is called mycorrhizae. This word comes from two Greek words that mean fungus and root. Pines, orchids, blueberries, and rhododendrons are but a few of the plants that form mycorrhizae. In fact, these plants do not grow well without the fungi!

These are only two of the benefits accrued to plants from microorganisms. Scientists are currently working to improve plant growth by exploiting these unseen relationships. In the future they may be able to harness these tiny microscopic farmers that live in soil.

Bacteria that live in these nodules on the root of a pea plant are able to change atmospheric nitrogen into a form that can be used by plants.

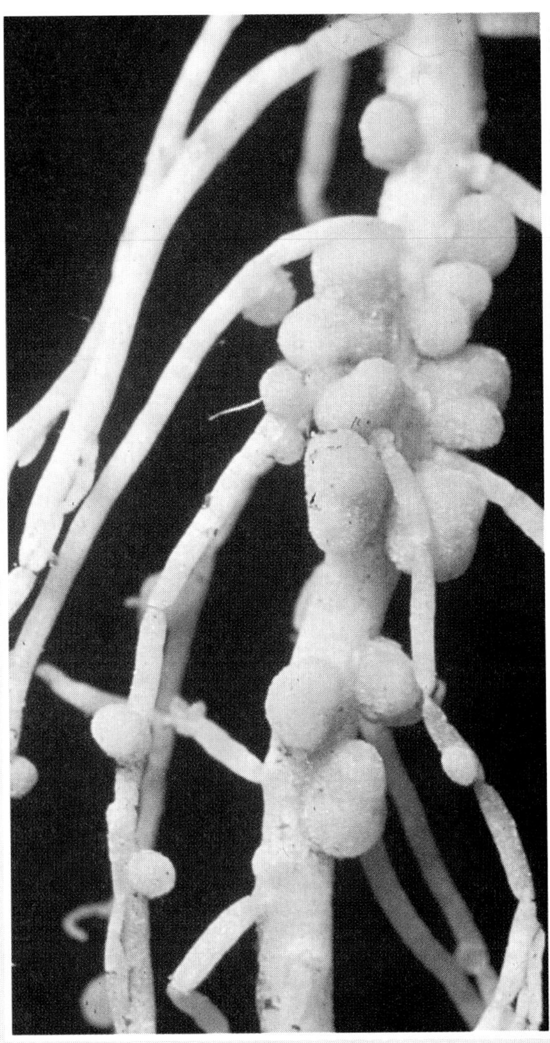

23–2 Specialized Tissues in Plants

Section Objectives

- Describe the importance of meristematic tissue in plants.
- Explain the important functions of different kinds of plant tissues.

Seed plants have several different kinds of tissue, each of which is specialized to perform different tasks. This specialization allows each tissue to perform efficiently. Later in this chapter when we examine the structure of roots, stems, and leaves, you will see how the tissues in plants are exquisitely adapted to perform different functions.

Meristematic Tissue

Mature plant cells can grow in length, and they can also expand to store water or food. But most mature plant cells do not divide to form new cells. Yet plants do grow—which means new cells must be formed.

Meristematic (mer-uh-stuh-MAT-ihk) **tissue** is the only plant tissue that produces new cells by mitosis. Meristematic cells divide rapidly and have thin cell walls. At first, all cells produced in meristematic tissue look alike. As meristematic cells mature, however, they differentiate into tissues of various kinds.

Meristematic tissue is found in several places. At the end, or tip, of each growing stem and root is an **apical meristem.** Apical meristems enable stems and roots to grow in length. In fact, plants have what is known as an open type of growth. They continue to grow from their tips as long as they live. For example, trees increase their height above ground and the length of their roots below ground for the duration of their lives. This is in contrast to humans and animals, who reach a certain size and then cease to grow (in height, not necessarily in width).

Two other kinds of meristematic tissue—**cork cambium** and **vascular cambium**—allow stems and roots to branch as well as to grow thicker. Cork cambium produces the outer covering of stems. Vascular cambium produces vascular tissues and increases the thickness of stems over time. Another kind of cambium, the **pericycle,** is found in roots. The pericycle enables roots to grow thicker and makes it possible for roots to branch.

__Figure 23–4__ Plants are made up of relatively few kinds of tissue. New cells are formed in meristematic tissue found at the tips of both the stem and the roots.

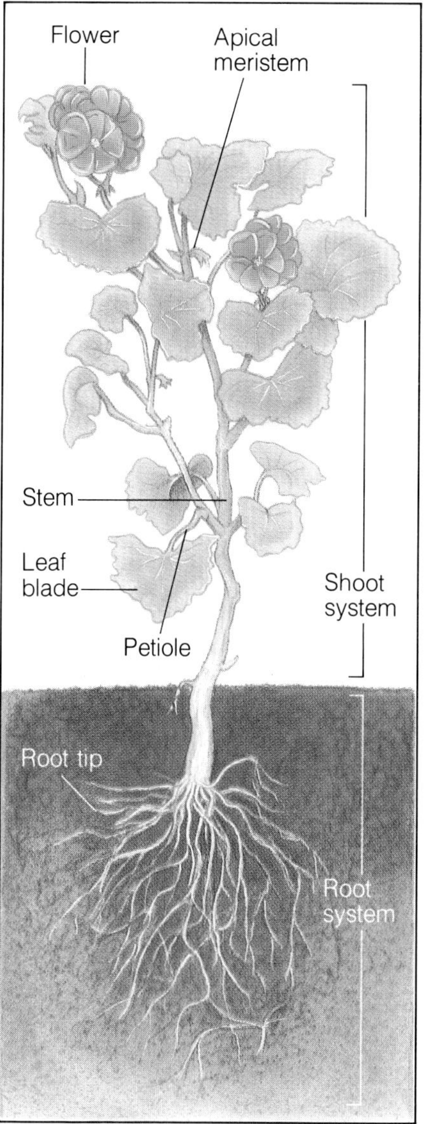

Surface Tissue

Epidermal (the prefix *epi-* means on or on the outside of; *dermal* means of the skin) tissues form the outer, or surface, layers of leaves, stems, and roots. Some epidermal tissues, like the cork tissue in tree bark, protect plants from water loss. The epidermal tissue of roots, on the other hand, helps in the absorption of water.

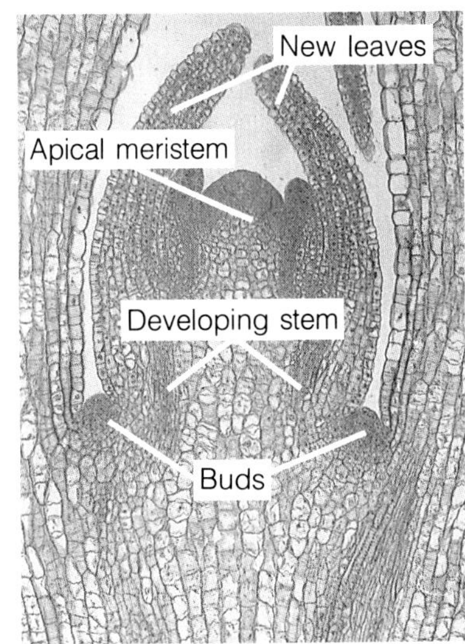

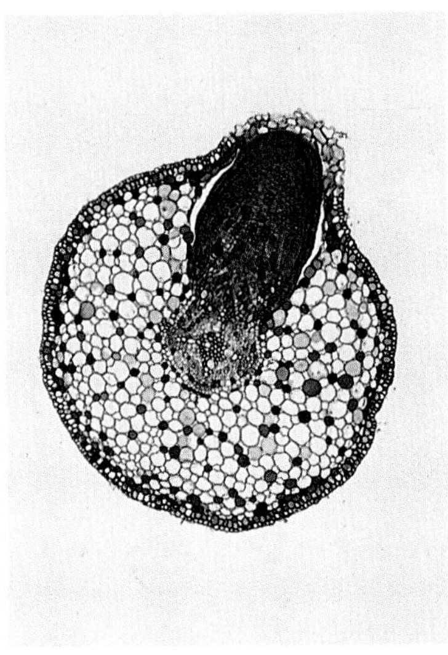

Figure 23–5 *The growing tip of a flax plant in this photomicrograph shows newly dividing cells in the dome-shaped cluster of cells near the top of the stem (left). Over the cluster of cells, forming an arch that resembles two arms held overhead, are two young leaves. Actively dividing cells are also found in roots, as this photomicrograph of a branch root being formed in the root of a willow tree shows (right).*

Parenchyma

Parenchyma (puh-REHNG-kih-muh) tissue is composed of thin-walled cells found in leaves, stems, and roots. These cells often have large central vacuoles surrounded by a thin layer of cytoplasm. Most of the plant roots we eat—such as potatoes and radishes—are composed primarily of parenchyma cells. Certain parenchyma cells in leaves and stems contain chlorophyll. It is in these cells that most photosynthesis takes place. Some parenchyma cells use vacuoles to store the products of photosynthesis.

Sclerenchyma

Sclerenchyma (sklih-REHNG-kih-muh) cells have tough, thick cell walls that strengthen and support plant tissues. Some sclerenchyma cells are star-shaped and are scattered throughout parenchyma tissue. Other sclerenchyma cells grow into long, narrow fibers. Linen, a fine cloth, is made from the sclerenchyma fibers of the flax plant.

Vascular Tissue

Xylem tissue conducts water. All seed plants have a type of xylem cell called a **tracheid**. Tracheids are long, narrow cells with walls that are impermeable to water. These walls, however, are pierced by openings that connect neighboring cells to one another. When tracheids mature, they die, and their cytoplasm disintegrates. This leaves a network of hollow connected cells through which water can pass. See Figure 23–6.

Angiosperms have yet another kind of xylem cell called a **vessel element**. Vessel elements are much wider than tracheids, but like tracheids, they mature and die before they

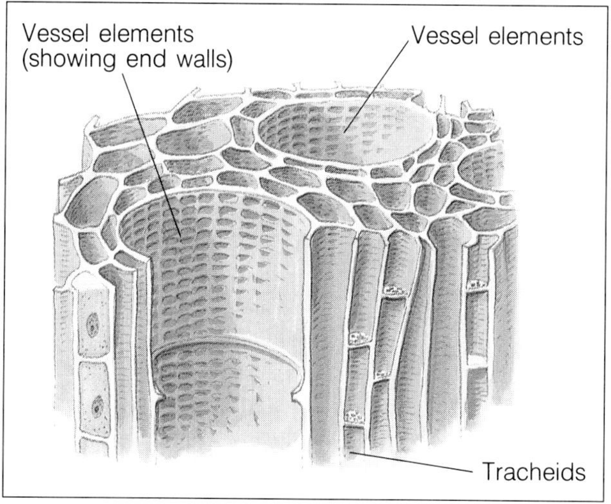

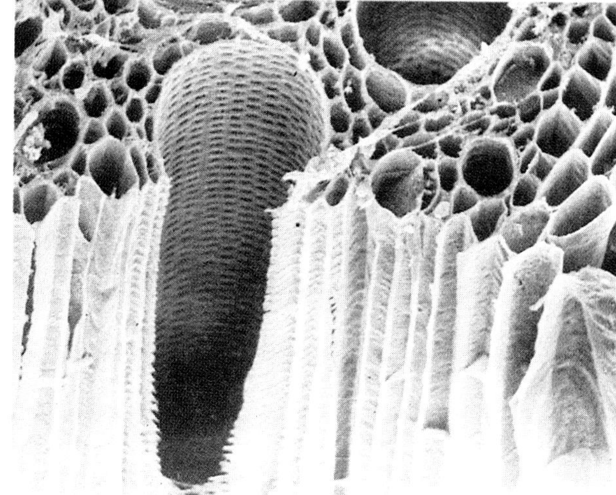

Figure 23–6 In vascular plants, xylem tissue conducts water from roots to the rest of the plant. The photomicrograph shows the hollow dead cells that make up xylem tissue.

conduct water. Vessel elements are arranged end to end on top of one another like a stack of tin cans. The cell walls at both ends are lost when the cells die. At that time, the stacked vessel elements become continuous tubes through which water can move freely.

Phloem tissue conducts a variety of plant products. The main phloem cells are the **sieve tube elements**. These cells are arranged end to end, like the vessel elements, to form sieve tubes. The end walls of sieve tube elements have many small holes in them. Materials can move from one adjacent cell to another through these holes. As sieve tube elements mature, they lose their nuclei and most of the other organelles in their cytoplasm. The remaining organelles hug the inside of the cell wall. The rest of the cytoplasm can be moved from cell to cell to carry substances around in the plant.

Companion cells are phloem cells that surround sieve tube elements. Companion cells keep their nuclei and other organelles throughout their lifetime. Companion cells are believed to control the activity of the sieve tube elements.

Figure 23–7 Phloem tissue conducts a variety of materials, mostly carbohydrates, throughout a plant.

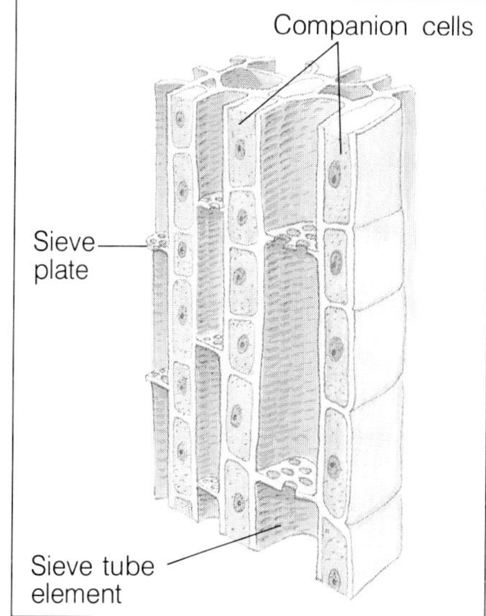

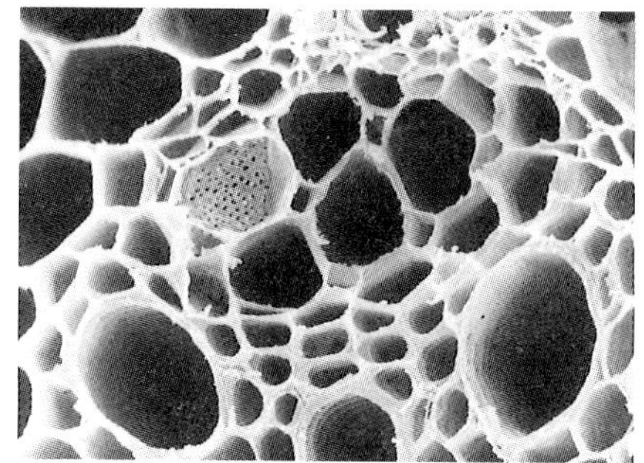

23–2 SECTION REVIEW

1. What is meristematic tissue? Why is it important?
2. What is the function of parenchyma tissue? Sclerenchyma tissue?
3. What is the function of vascular tissue? What are the two types of vascular tissue?
4. What is the most important type of phloem cell? Why?

Section Objectives

- Describe the structure and function of plant roots.
- Relate the structure of plant roots to the movement of water and minerals.

23–3 Roots

As soon as a seedling begins to grow, it puts out its first root: the primary root. Other roots, called secondary roots, branch out from this primary root. See Figure 23–8. When the root first begins to grow, it resembles all other plant roots. Later in its development, the pattern of growth changes.

Taproots and Fibrous Roots

In some plants the primary root grows longer and thicker, whereas secondary roots remain small. This type of primary root is called a **taproot**. Taproots of oak and hickory trees grow so long that they can reach water far below the earth's surface. Carrots, dandelions, beets, and radishes have short, thick taproots that store sugars or starches. Taproots make it extremely difficult to remove certain plants from a lawn. For example, if you pull on the green leaves of a dandelion, it breaks off above the root. The taproot that remains in the ground can grow new leaves. Sometimes even a small piece of a taproot can produce a new plant.

In plants in which taproots do not form, secondary roots grow and branch. In these plants no single root grows larger than the rest. Such plants, of which grasses are an example, are said to have **fibrous roots**. The fibrous root system of a single rye plant—a plant in the grass family—can have as many as 14 million secondary roots. If these roots were laid end to end in a single line, they would have a total length of over 600 kilometers—much longer than the distance from New York City to Washington, D.C.! The extensive root systems produced by some plants are extremely important in holding topsoil so that it does not get washed away by rains.

Root Tissues

The tissues of mature roots can be divided into three groups: epidermis, cortex, and vascular cylinder. The arrangement of these tissues differs between monocots and dicots, as you can see in Figure 23–9.

Each of these tissues performs important functions that are directly related to its structure. The **epidermis** is a thin layer of cells that take in water and nutrients. The **cortex** transports water and nutrients inward through the root and may store

Figure 23–8 *Roots of plants vary greatly in appearance. The long taproot of a dandelion (top) makes it extremely difficult to eradicate this plant from a lawn. If even the smallest piece of the brittle taproot is left in the soil, the dandelion will grow anew. The fibrous root system of an onion (bottom) is different from the taproot of a dandelion. Onions can be pulled from the ground with ease.*

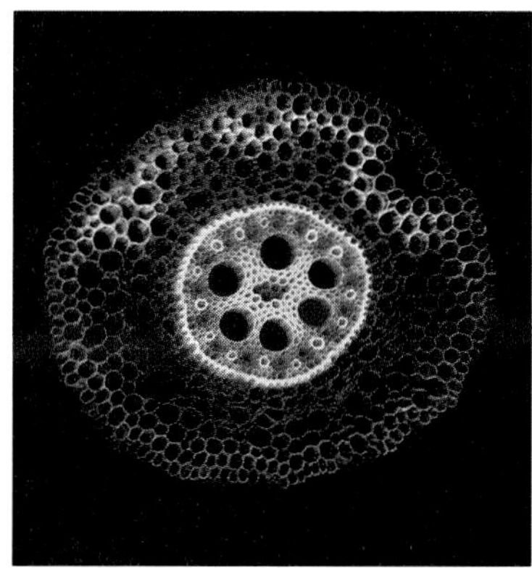

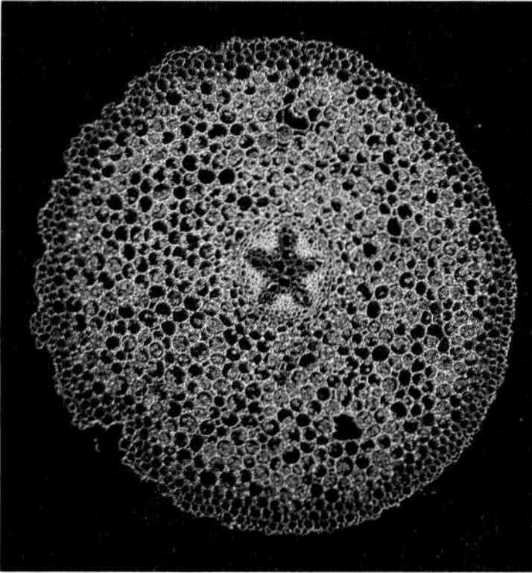

Figure 23–9 *Cross sections of the root of a corn plant (left) and the root of a buttercup (right) are shown in these photomicrographs. Most dicot roots have a central column of xylem cells with radiating arms. Which plant is the dicot?*

sugars or starches. The **vascular cylinder** contains xylem and phloem. We will discuss these tissues and their functions, in order, from the outside of the root to its center.

The Epidermis: Uptake of Water and Nutrients

The outermost layer of cells, the epidermis, absorbs water and nutrients from the soil. Epidermal cells grow slender projections called root hairs. Although individual root hairs are very small, there are an enormous number of them on a typical plant. The rye plant you just read about can have more than 14 billion root hairs!

Root hairs penetrate the spaces between soil particles. It is through the delicate tissues of the root hairs that water and nutrients enter plant roots. Although each individual root hair has a small surface area, the combined surface area of the huge numbers of root hairs is tremendous. That single rye plant's 14 billion root hairs provide the plant with a root surface area of more than 400 square meters! Root hairs thus enable roots to make close contact with a large area of soil.

NUTRIENT ABSORPTION Root hairs absorb dissolved nutrients from soil spaces through the process of active transport. Recall from Chapter 5 that active transport is a process in which a cell expends energy to move something from one side of a membrane to the other. In roots, active transport is necessary because nutrient ions are present in soil water in lower concentrations than they are in epidermal cells. In fact, these ions would tend to move out of root hairs by diffusion if active transport did not pull them inside.

As you may remember, active transport requires ATP (as a source of energy) and oxygen. Thus roots need a constant supply of oxygen to survive. Normally, roots obtain oxygen from the air in soil spaces. But if soil spaces are filled with water, the roots of most land plants cannot obtain the oxygen they need. This is one reason why floods destroy farm crops so quickly. It is also the reason why you can kill your houseplants by overwatering them. Later in this chapter we will see how aquatic and swamp plants have evolved solutions to the problem of having their roots constantly in water.

WATER ABSORPTION Despite the importance of water to living cells, there is no active transport mechanism that can grab water molecules on one side of a cell membrane and drag them to the other side. Yet a single corn plant takes in more than 200 liters of water in a growing season that lasts little more than three months! How can plants move so much water into their roots?

To move water across membranes, plants use the power of osmosis. Recall that water will move across a membrane by osmosis from an area of high concentration of water molecules to an area of low concentration of water molecules. The cytoplasm of root epidermal cells is filled with amino acids, sugars, and other dissolved compounds. There are relatively few water molecules in root epidermal cells. The water in soil spaces usually contains only a small amount of dissolved minerals and many molecules of water. Thus the concentration of water molecules is higher in the soil spaces and lower in the root epidermal cells. Because of this difference in water concentration and because the thin cell walls of root hairs are permeable to water, water moves by osmosis from the soil spaces into the cytoplasm of root epidermal cells. See Figure 23–10.

Note that this process will not work if soil water carries a high concentration of dissolved minerals. In fact, if the concentration of water in the soil spaces is too low, water may even move out of root hairs and back into the soil. This situation is called root burn. Root burn can occur in nature if soil is saturated with salty water. Root burn can affect house, garden, and farm plants if too much fertilizer is added to the soil.

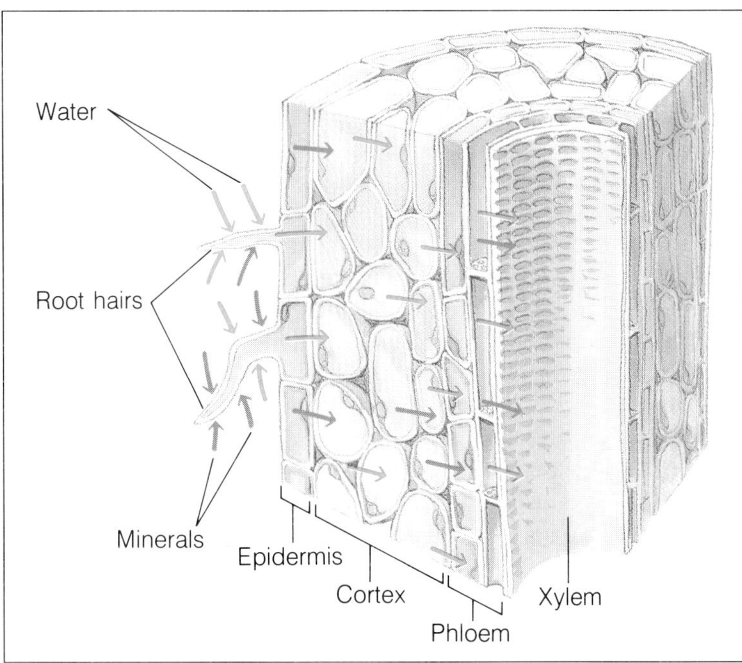

Figure 23–10 *It is through the tiny hairs on plant roots that most molecules of water and minerals enter a plant. Water moves from the outside of the roots into the xylem, where it is then transported throughout the plant.*

The Cortex: Transport of Water and Nutrients

The parenchyma cells of the root cortex perform the next step in the movement of water in plants. The cell walls and cell membranes of root parenchyma cells are permeable to water. Thus water moves easily through and around these cells. Root cortex cells also have active transport mechanisms in their membranes. Active transport in these root cortex cells keeps water and nutrients moving deeper toward the center of the root.

How does this process work? First, active transport moves dissolved nutrients through the cortex toward the center of the root. As the concentration of nutrient ions in the center of the root increases, the relative concentration of water molecules in the cells in that region decreases.

Next, water in the outer cortex moves by osmosis to "follow" the nutrient ions and to "equalize" the water concentration in all cortex cells. Thus, both water and nutrients move toward the center of the root.

Figure 23–11 *Cells in the endodermis are surrounded by Casparian strips. These strips are waterproof and thus prevent water molecules from seeping back between the cells.*

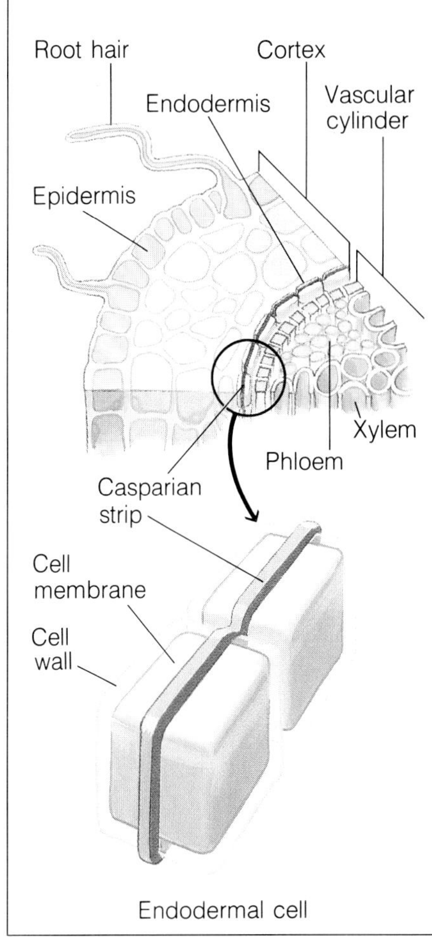

The Endodermis: One-Way Passage

At the inner boundary of the cortex is a single layer of cells called the endodermis (*endo-* means inside; *dermis* means skin). The endodermis, which looks like a circle in cross section, encloses the vascular cylinder and stretches up and down the entire length of the root. The endodermis is composed of many individual cells, each shaped like a brick. Each of these cells is surrounded on four sides by a waterproof strip called the **Casparian strip**. To imagine how the Casparian strip looks, imagine a brick with a thick, sticky rubber band stretched around four sides. See Figure 23–11. Now imagine many such bricks placed edge to edge to build a cylinder. The rubber bands around the individual cells touch each other and stick together like mortar between the bricks in a brick wall.

The Casparian strips of the endodermal cells are not permeable to water. Thus water and nutrients cannot move around endodermal cells—only through them. This is the key to understanding how the root works. Endodermal cells use active transport to pump dissolved nutrients into the vascular cylinder. As dissolved nutrients build up inside the vascular cylinder, water moves through the endodermal cells by osmosis to equalize the relative concentration of water molecules in the tissues.

But neither water nor dissolved nutrients can cross the Casparian strips that seal the spaces between endodermal cells. So both substances are trapped in the vascular cylinder. Dissolved nutrients cannot go back through the endodermal cells because those cells use active transport to force the

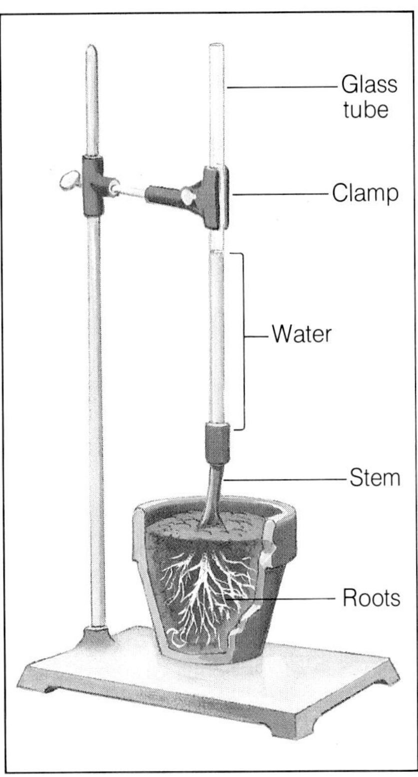

Figure 23–12 *Pressure exerted by roots can move water a distance up the tube. However, root pressure alone cannot force water to the top of a tall plant.*

nutrients inside. Water cannot move back through the endodermal cells because to do so would mean moving from an area of low concentration of water molecules to an area of high concentration of water molecules. Thus there is a one-way passage of materials into the vascular cylinder in plant roots.

Root Pressure: Pushing Water and Nutrients Upward

As more nutrients are pumped into the vascular cylinder, more molecules of water follow. Because neither nutrients nor water can move back into the cortex, pressure known as root pressure builds up inside the vascular cylinder. This increased root pressure forces water into the xylem. As you will soon see, root pressure is part of the driving force behind the movement of water from roots to leaves.

As root pressure in the vascular cylinder forces water into the xylem, and as more and more water moves from the cortex into the vascular cylinder, the water in the xylem is forced upward through the root into the stem. In short plants such as grasses and strawberries, root pressure alone can push water through stems from roots to leaves. In tall plants such as trees, however, root pressure alone cannot accomplish this process.

You can see root pressure in action if you cut the stem of certain plants close to the ground and place a glass tube over the stump. A liquid called sap will continue to come out of the stump and rise up the glass tube for some distance.

How do we know that active transport by root cells creates root pressure? If we poison the root or cut off its supply of oxygen, the movement of sap stops. Because once the endodermal cells in the root stop pumping dissolved nutrients into the vascular cylinder, water stops moving in by osmosis.

23–3 SECTION REVIEW

1. What is the difference between a taproot and a fibrous root?
2. Why is it difficult to remove dandelions from a lawn by pulling them out by the leaves?
3. Why do roots need a constant supply of oxygen?
4. What is the importance of root hairs in the absorption of water and nutrients?
5. Why is it important that the root epidermis permits only a one-way passage of materials?

23–4 Stems

Section Objectives

- List two important functions of plant stems.
- Describe the four basic types of stem tissue.

Stems vary greatly in size and shape from one plant species to another. Some stems are tiny; others are a hundred meters tall. Some grow entirely underground; others reach far into the air. **Regardless of size and shape, all stems have two important functions: They hold leaves up in the sunlight and they conduct various substances between roots and leaves.** Some stems may also store water and nutrients.

Stems have four basic types of tissue: parenchyma tissue (pith), vascular tissue (xylem and phloem), cambium tissue (vascular cambium and cork cambium), and cork tissue (outer bark). Looking at cross sections of monocot and dicot stems, such as those in Figure 23–13, you can see that some of these tissues are arranged differently in stems than they are in roots.

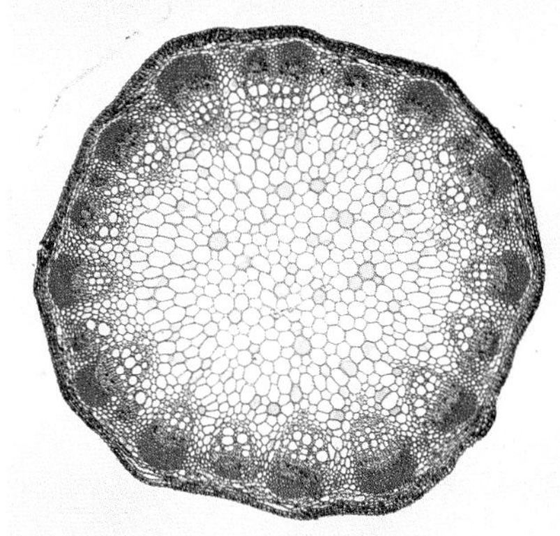

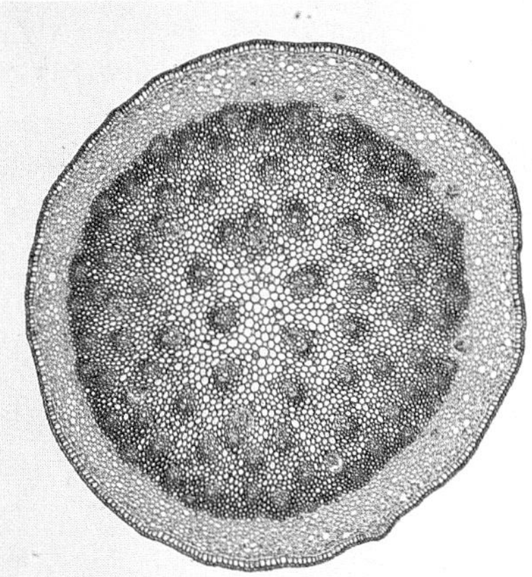

Figure 23–13 *The arrangement of vascular tissue in the stem of a dicot differs from that in the stem of a monocot. In a dicot, vascular tissue is arranged in a ring. In a monocot, it is scattered in bundles throughout the stem. Is the sunflower (top) a monocot or a dicot?*

Parenchyma

In monocot stems, parenchyma, or pith, is distributed throughout the stem and is often used for storage. In dicot stems, a core of pith is laid down in the center of the stem, where it is surrounded by layers of xylem.

Vascular Tissue in Woody Stems

Vascular tissue in stems conducts water, nutrients, and various plant products up and down the plant. To accomplish this, xylem and phloem tissues form continuous tubes from the roots through the stems to the leaves. Stem xylem is connected to root xylem, and stem phloem is connected to root phloem.

In young dicot stems, bundles of xylem, vascular cambium, and phloem are arranged in a ring. The xylem faces the interior of the stem, whereas the phloem faces the exterior. In woody dicots, such as trees, new xylem and phloem cells are produced as the plant grows. Other tissue joins the xylem and phloem bundles into two complete rings. The xylem ring is closest to the center of the stem, and the phloem ring surrounds the xylem.

It is actually xylem tissue that makes up the rings of trees. By counting the number of rings in a cross section of a tree, you can estimate the age of the tree. The size of the rings can provide information about weather conditions in the area over time. Thick rings indicate that weather conditions were favorable for tree growth; thin rings indicate that weather conditions were not. For example, in a year with abundant rainfall, a tree might make thick rings. In a year when rainfall was scarce, the rings might be thin. As woody stems grow thicker from year to year, the older xylem near the center of the stem becomes what is known as heartwood. Heartwood no longer conducts

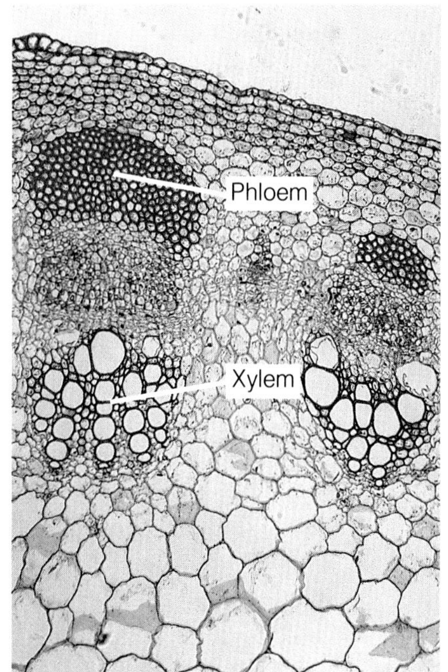
Phloem
Xylem

__Figure 23–14__ A small portion of the vascular bundles in a dicot stem can be seen in this photomicrograph. The much larger xylem cells are found at the edge of the vascular bundle and point toward the center of the stem. The smaller phloem cells face the outside of the stem.

__Figure 23–15__ Trees can increase their diameter as they grow. In which layer does the division of cells account for this increase?

water. The outer rings of living cells, known as sapwood, transport liquids.

Phloem tissue forms the inner part of what is called bark. Phloem carries sugars and other products of photosynthesis from the leaves to other plant parts that do not make their own food. For this reason, if the phloem in tree bark is removed in a ring around the trunk, the roots of the tree will starve and the tree will die.

Rings of xylem and phloem are separated by a thin layer of tissue called the vascular cambium. The vascular cambium makes more xylem and phloem cells, enabling the stem to grow thicker. You will learn more about this process in Chapter 24.

Cork Cambium and Cork

Outside the phloem tissue in woody dicots is the cork cambium, which produces cork tissue—the outer bark of trees. Cork cells have thick walls and usually contain fats, oils, or waxes. These waterproof substances help prevent the loss of water from the stem. The outermost cork cells are usually dead. As the stem increases in size, this dead bark often cracks and flakes off in strips or patches, depending on the tree species.

Stems Modified for Food Storage and Dormancy

In addition to support and the transport of materials from roots to leaves, stems also perform other functions. Plants often store food in their stems during their growth period. Plants need to store food to enable them to survive **dormancy**. During dormancy, a plant's growth slows or stops. Dormancy occurs during cold winters or long dry periods that may last for months or even years. When conditions once again support

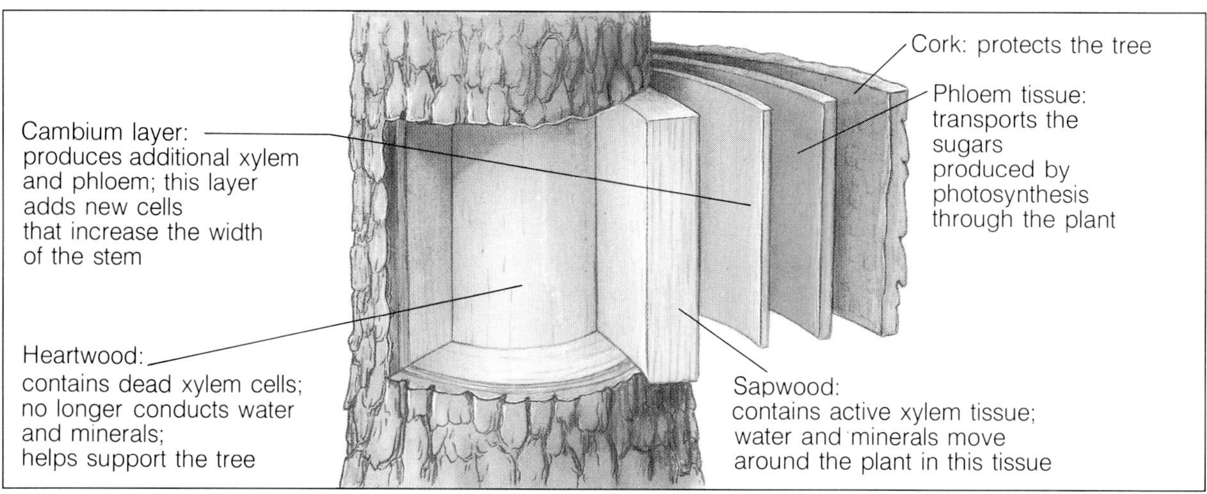
Cork: protects the tree
Phloem tissue: transports the sugars produced by photosynthesis through the plant
Cambium layer: produces additional xylem and phloem; this layer adds new cells that increase the width of the stem
Heartwood: contains dead xylem cells; no longer conducts water and minerals; helps support the tree
Sapwood: contains active xylem tissue; water and minerals move around the plant in this tissue

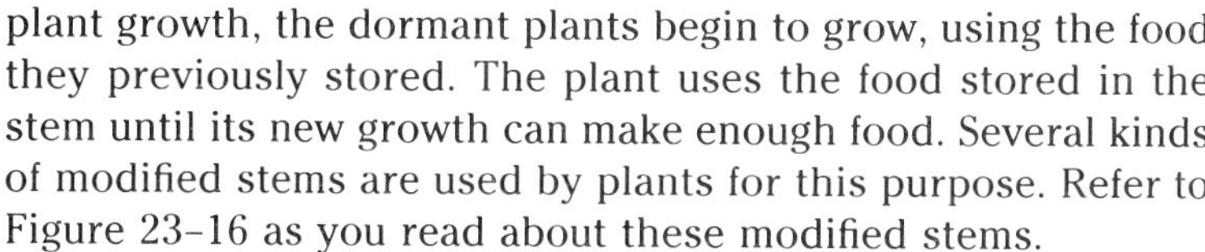

plant growth, the dormant plants begin to grow, using the food they previously stored. The plant uses the food stored in the stem until its new growth can make enough food. Several kinds of modified stems are used by plants for this purpose. Refer to Figure 23–16 as you read about these modified stems.

Rhizomes are thick, fleshy, creeping stems that grow either along or just beneath the surface of the ground. Along the length of rhizomes are buds from which leaves and stems can grow. When the frosts of winter kill the above-ground parts of plants, the rhizomes survive to grow again the following spring. Garden plants such as irises, canna lilies, and many species of grasses survive cold winters and grow year after year because of rhizomes.

Tubers are modified underground stems that are swollen with stored food, usually in the form of starch. Many tubers, such as potatoes, hardly look like stems at all. But tubers have one or more prominent "eyes," which are actually lateral buds. From these buds grow new above-ground stems and leaves.

Bulbs, such as those of tulips and daffodils, have underground stems too. The stem at the center of the bulb is small. Most of the food stored in the bulb is located in the layers of short, thick leaves that wrap around and protect the stem.

Figure 23–16 *The rhizome of the iris is a thick creeping stem (top, left). Tubers—underground stems that store food—are characteristic of the potato (bottom, left). Bulbs, like the daffodil, are also underground stems, although the stem is small, cannot be seen, and is found in the center of the bulb (top, right). Corms, such as this gladiolus (bottom, right), are similar to a bulb in structure but they have thinner leaves.*

Corms are similar to bulbs, but they have much thinner leaves. Most of the stored food in corms is located in the stem itself. Thin, scalelike leaves surround the stem and serve mainly to protect it. Crocuses and gladioli are common garden plants that produce corms.

23-4 SECTION REVIEW

1. What are the functions of plant stems?
2. How does vascular tissue contribute to the strength of plant stems?
3. What are tree rings? What important information do tree rings provide?
4. How do rhizomes and corms contribute to a plant's survival?

23–5 Leaves

Section Objectives

- Describe the three specialized leaf tissues.
- Explain how gas exchange and water conservation are balanced in a leaf.

The leaves of green plants are the world's oldest solar energy collectors. Leaves are also the world's most important manufacturers of food. Sugars, starches, and oils manufactured by plants are sources of virtually all food for all land animals. Even animals that do not eat plants must eat other animals that do.

Leaf Structure

To collect sunlight, most leaves have large thin, flattened sections called blades. The blade is attached to the stem by a thin structure called the **petiole**.

Leaf blades occur in an incredible variety of shapes and sizes, depending on the environment to which they are adapted. Simple leaves have only one blade and one petiole. Compound leaves have several blades, or leaflets, that are joined together and to the stem by several petioles. These leaflets can be joined together in several ways. The leaflets of some compound leaves spread out like the fingers of a hand. The leaflets of others grow in pairs along a long central petiole. In still another pattern, leaflets are arranged on petioles that, in turn, are arranged along a long central petiole.

Figure 23–17 *Leaves are arranged differently in different plants. The oak leaf is solitary and held to a stem by a single petiole (top). Both the strawberry and the poison ivy have three leaflets attached to a single petiole (bottom).*

Leaves contain several specialized tissues. Like roots and stems, leaves have an outer covering of epidermal cells, inner layers of parenchyma cells, and vascular tissues.

Epidermis: Controlling Water Loss

All leaves are covered on the top and bottom by a layer of tough cube-shaped epidermal cells that do not contain chloroplasts. The epidermal layer of many leaves is also covered by a waterproof waxy coating called the cuticle. The cuticle and epidermal cells together form a waterproof barrier that protects delicate tissues inside the leaf by slowing down the loss of water through evaporation.

But no leaf could survive completely sealed off from the atmosphere that surrounds it. Plants need to "breathe" just as we do. Leaves must take in carbon dioxide and give off oxygen during photosynthesis. And in order to use the food they make, leaves must take in oxygen and give off carbon dioxide (just as animals do). Plants need to exchange enormous amounts of gases with the surrounding atmosphere. But in order for a gas to enter the cells of a leaf, it must be dissolved in a thin film of water. So all leaf cells that need to exchange gases with the air must be kept wet.

But you know what happens to a wet surface exposed to the air—the water evaporates and the surface dries out! To keep the surface wet, more water must constantly be added to it. The more exposed the tissue is to the air, the faster the water will evaporate and the more quickly it will need to be replaced.

If all the moist tissues of leaves were exposed to the air, leaves would lose water much faster than roots could replace it. The plant would wilt and die. This is exactly the problem that mosses have. Without cuticles and vascular tissues, mosses must grow in wet soil and have their green parts in moist air all the time or they will dry out.

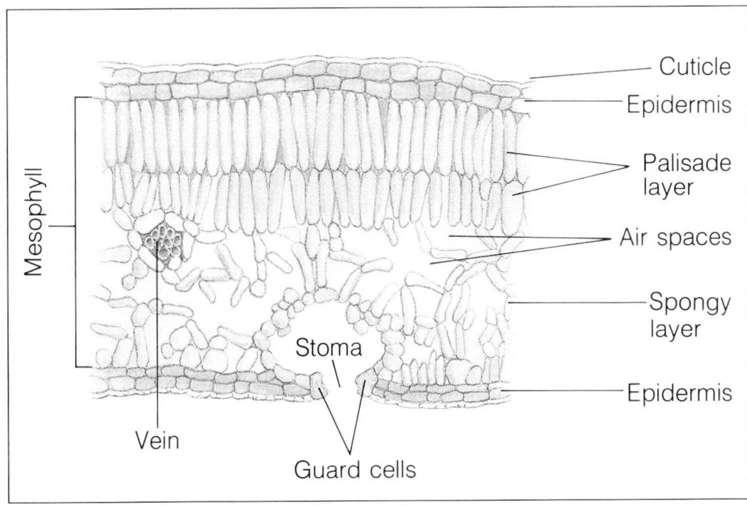

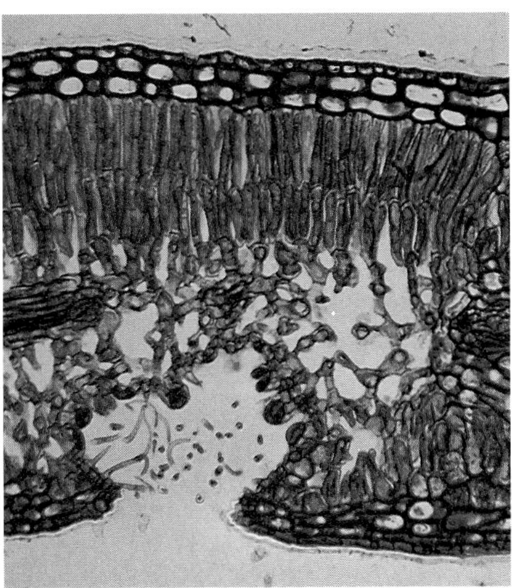

Figure 23–18 *Some of the most important manufacturing sites on Earth are found in the leaves of plants. The cells in plant leaves are able to use light energy to make carbohydrates. What is the opening at the bottom of a plant leaf called?*

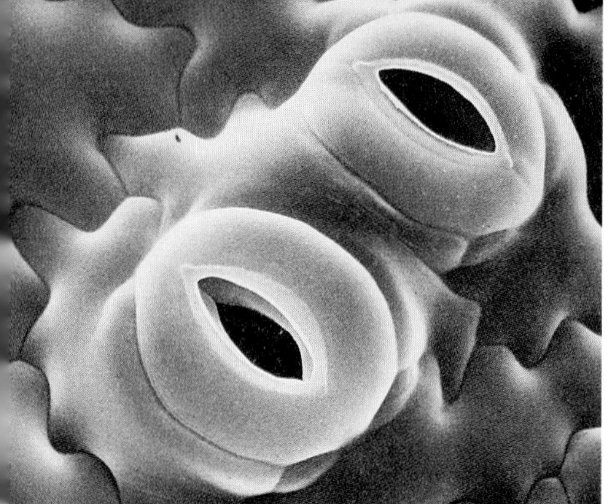

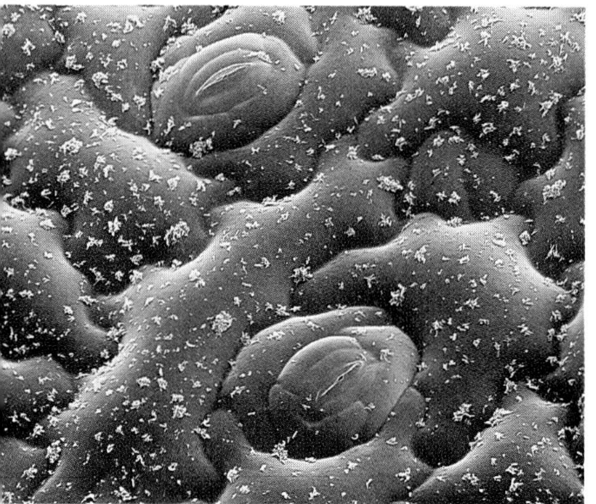

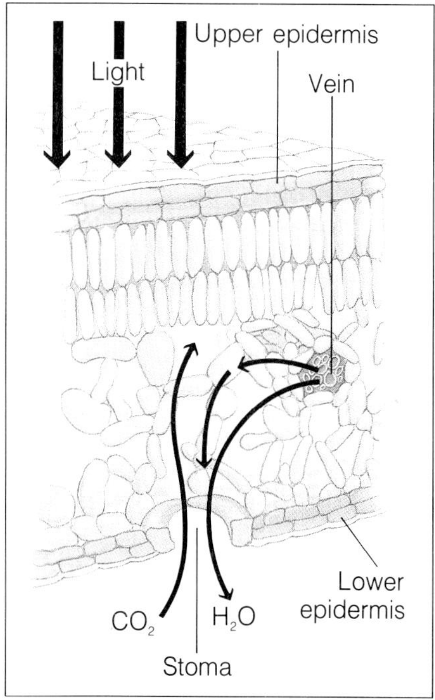

Figure 23–19 *Stomata open (top) and close (center) to let gases in and out of the leaves. On a hot day, are the stomata more likely to be open or closed?*

Seed plants solve this problem by striking a balance between their need for gas exchange and their need to conserve water. Plants control the loss of water from their leaves by allowing air in and out of their waterproof covering only through small openings called **stomata** (singular: stoma). Stomata open to allow the leaf to "breathe" and close when the leaf does not need much air exchange. Stomata also close when the plant loses too much water and begins to wilt. Most of the stomata of terrestrial plants are located on the undersides of their leaves, but there are some stomata along green stems too.

Stomata are formed by two specialized epidermal cells called **guard cells**. The stomata open and close in response to changes in water pressure within the guard cells. When water pressure within the guard cells is high, the thin outer walls of the cells are forced into a curved shape. This pulls the thick inner walls of the guard cells away from each other, opening the stoma. When water pressure within the guard cells decreases, the springiness of the inner walls pulls them together. The stoma closes.

Because water is lost through the same stomata that let in carbon dioxide, guard cells have a difficult job. On hot, dry days, open stomata will allow large amounts of water to leave the leaf. But if the stomata are closed all the time, the inside of the leaf will run out of carbon dioxide, and photosynthesis will slow down or stop. Each type of plant has guard cells that balance water loss against the need for carbon dioxide.

Vascular Tissue: The Veins of a Leaf

The vascular system of leaves is directly connected to the vascular tissues of stems. In leaves, xylem and phloem tissues are gathered together into bundles that run out of the stem and into the petiole. As the bundles enter the leaf blade, they are surrounded by parenchyma and sclerenchyma cells. All these tissues together form the veins of a leaf. In most monocot leaves, veins run parallel to one another. In dicot leaves, they may run in different patterns.

Mesophyll Tissue: The Food Factory of the Leaf

Most leaf tissue is composed of specialized cells called leaf **mesophyll**. Mesophyll cells contain many chloroplasts and perform most of the plant's photosynthesis. Just under the upper epidermal covering of the leaf is a layer of tall, column-shaped mesophyll cells called the **palisade layer**. Under the palisade layer is a thick layer called the **spongy mesophyll**. The spongy mesophyll gets its name from the fact that it really does look like a sponge. Cells of the spongy mesophyll are arranged in a network with a great many air spaces between them. These air spaces connect with the stomata and allow carbon dioxide and oxygen to diffuse into and out of the leaf.

The surfaces of spongy mesophyll cells are kept moist so that gases can enter and leave the cells easily. The water necessary to do this is supplied by the branching network of leaf veins that runs through the mesophyll. The opening and closing of stomata regulate the amount of contact the air in the spongy mesophyll spaces has with the drier air outside. Although the stomata cut down on the loss of moisture through evaporation, a substantial amount of water is still lost to the outside through evaporation.

23–5 SECTION REVIEW

1. Compare simple leaves and compound leaves. How are these shapes related to solar energy collecting?
2. What is the function of the epidermis and cuticle layers? What is the function of the openings in these layers?
3. Describe the structure and function of mesophyll tissue.
4. Describe how vascular plants control gas exchange and water loss.

23–6 Transport in Plants

Section Objectives

- Explain how water is moved through a plant.
- Describe the importance and mechanism of phloem transport.

You now know how the tissues of a typical plant are put together—from the root tips all the way up to the leaves. Remember that water and dissolved nutrients from the soil are absorbed through root hairs by active transport. The pressure created by water entering the tissues of a root can push water upward in a plant stem, but only for a short distance. How then does water reach the topmost needles of a redwood tree 90 meters above the ground?

Water Movement in Xylem

Xylem tissue forms a continuous set of tubes that stretch from roots through stems and out into the spongy mesophyll of leaves. **Root pressure forces water into the xylem, but root pressure alone cannot account for the movement of water and dissolved materials in plants.** Obviously, other powerful forces must also be at work.

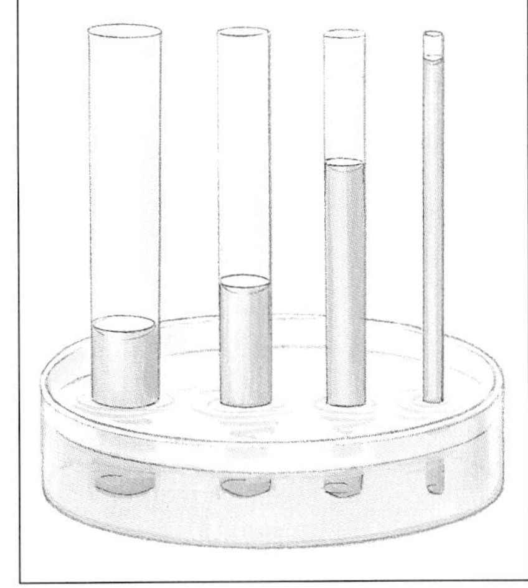

Figure 23–20 *Capillarity—the ability of water molecules to stick to one another and to the walls of a tube—accounts in part for the movement of water up xylem tissue.*

ADHESION, COHESION, AND CAPILLARITY If water is not pushed up, could it perhaps be pulled up? It is indeed. Two characteristics of water make this pulling action possible.

Water molecules are attracted to one another by a force called cohesion. Water molecules are also attracted to other molecules by a force called adhesion. The combination of cohesion and adhesion explains the phenomenon known as capillarity, which is the movement of water upward in a small solid tube. Capillarity can be observed when water climbs up a small glass tube placed in a beaker. Although gravity pulls the water in the tube down, the force of adhesion between the water molecules and the walls of the glass tube pulls the water up. At the same time, the water molecules cling to one another by cohesion, pulling molecule after molecule up inside the tube. The smaller the diameter of the tube, the higher the water will climb. Although capillarity accounts for the movement of water in tiny xylem vessels in short plants, it is much too weak a force to move water up the xylem tubes in a redwood. Another force must be at work.

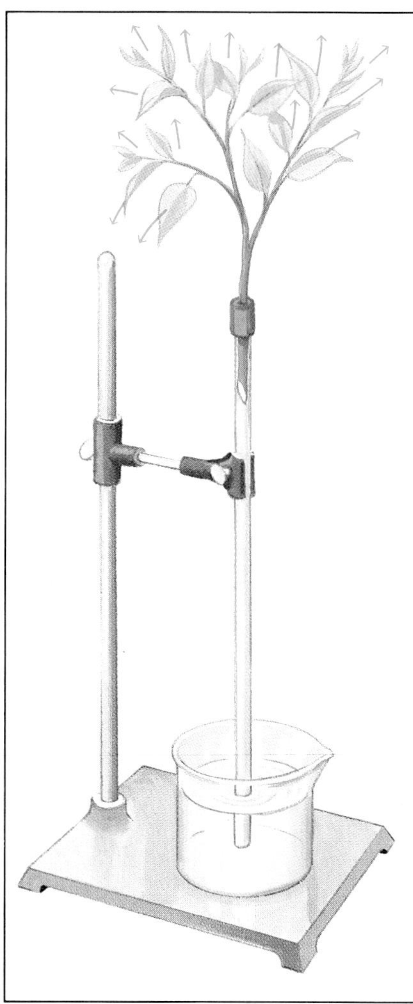

Figure 23–21 *This apparatus shows that transpiration—the movement of water molecules out of leaves—can pull water up a thin tube. The faster water evaporates, the faster it is pulled up in the tube.*

TRANSPIRATION PULL The final pull necessary to get water up into leaves is provided by the power of evaporation itself. This idea may sound strange, but evaporation is a powerful process. Except in rare cases when the atmosphere is totally saturated with water vapor, water will always evaporate from a wet surface. Therefore, water will almost always evaporate from leaves into the air. The evaporation of water from plant leaves is called **transpiration**.

Remember all those wet cells in the spongy mesophyll layer of leaves? As water evaporates from those cells, their water content drops. When this happens, water from nearby mesophyll cells moves by osmosis into the spongy mesophyll. This in turn causes the water content of these other mesophyll cells to drop below the water content of the cells that surround the veins. Once again water moves by osmosis to replace water lost by evaporation—this time from the cells surrounding the veins into the mesophyll.

As the cells surrounding the veins lose their water, water moves by osmosis out of the xylem into these cells. Finally, as water is removed from xylem vessels in the leaves, adhesion and cohesion pull other water molecules up the tubes from the roots through the stems. Because this entire process is driven by transpiration, it is called **transpiration pull**.

Transpiration pull is a very powerful force. A good-sized tree can move more than 1800 liters of water from the ground into the atmosphere in a single day. The hotter and drier the air, and the windier the day, the greater the amount of water lost by transpiration and the greater the amount of water drawn up from the roots.

Transport of Materials in Phloem

Phloem transports most organic molecules in plants. During the day, phloem transports products of photosynthesis out of the leaves and down into the stems and roots, where they are either stored or used.

But this is not the only job phloem does. For example, many plants pump sugars into their fruits. Such action often requires moving sugars out of leaves or roots into stems and then through stems to the fruits. All this movement of sugars occurs in the phloem. In addition, many plants living in cold climates pump food down into their roots for winter storage. This stored food must be moved back up into the trunk and branches before the plant begins to grow again in the spring—another job done in the phloem. It is this rich, sugary sap moving through the phloem that is tapped from maple trees in late winter and early spring to make maple syrup.

Botanists at one time thought that the function of phloem tissue was limited to the transport of organic compounds only. But phloem also transports inorganic ions. And this transport is not always away from the leaves. For example, phosphorus is needed in large amounts by young, actively growing leaf tissues. Xylem moves phosphorus from the roots up through the stems into the growing tips of the plant. But when growth in those tissues slows down, phloem helps recycle extra phosphorus. Phloem transport moves phosphorus out of the growing leaves and back down into the main stem of the plant. From there it can be carried up into the growing tip when it is needed.

Figure 23–22 *Tree sap often has industrial uses. After being collected, the sap of a pine tree is made into turpentine, a chemical often used as a solvent for paint.*

How Phloem Transport Works

The exact mechanism by which phloem transport works is not completely understood. We know that the process requires energy. We also know that material moves through phloem cells much faster than it possibly could if it was powered by diffusion alone. For these reasons, it is clear that some kind of active transport is involved.

In order to explain one hypothesis, it is necessary to use the following terminology: When plants move sugars from their leaves to their roots, the leaf mesophyll tissue is called the source of the sugars and the parenchyma tissue of the root is called the sink. Active transport moves sugars into the phloem at the source. Similar active transport moves sugars out of the phloem into storage tissue at the sink.

When sugars are pumped into the phloem at the source, phloem tissue contains more dissolved minerals and less water than the surrounding tissue. Thus water moves into the phloem by osmosis. Pressure increases in the phloem at the source. When sugars are pumped out of the phloem at the sink, water also moves out. The movement of water out of the phloem at the sink causes a drop in pressure at the sink. Because pressure builds up at the source and drops at the sink, the contents of the sieve tube elements are forced down from source to sink.

If the plant needs to move sugars from the roots to the leaves, it simply reverses the pumping action at these two locations. The root tissue thus becomes the source, and the leaf

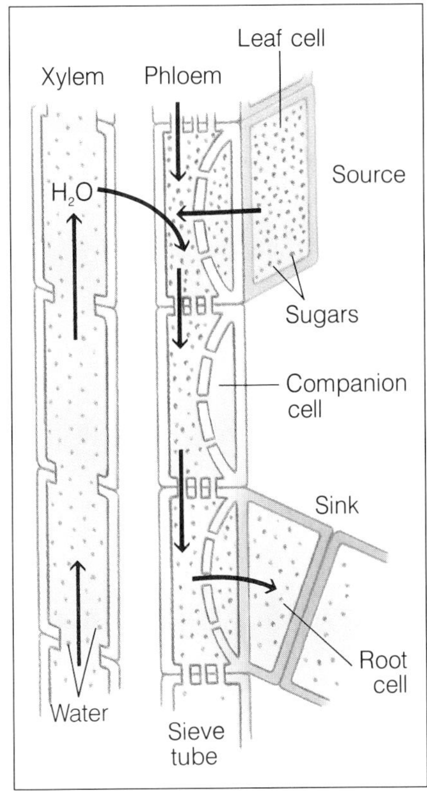

Figure 23–23 *This illustration shows a current hypothesis that explains the movement of sugar molecules in phloem tissue. As you can see, materials move from the source, where they are available in great supply, to the sink, where they are scarce.*

becomes the sink. The phloem then carries sugars upward. Any dissolved compounds can be moved through the phloem in either direction by changing the location of the source and the sink. This hypothesis about phloem function is called the pressure flow hypothesis.

23-6 SECTION REVIEW

1. What role do cohesion and adhesion of water molecules play in the movement of water in xylem tissue?
2. Describe the process of transpiration pull.
3. How does the pressure flow hypothesis explain how phloem functions?

Section Objective

- List some adaptations shown by plants that enable them to survive in many different environments.

23-7 Adaptations of Plants to Different Environments

Flowering plants grow in a variety of places: in deserts, in ponds, on mountaintops, in salt water, in arctic regions, and in the tropics. **Angiosperms can survive in these areas because through natural selection the basic designs of their roots, stems, and leaves have evolved to fulfill the particular needs of each location.** In this section we will see how roots, stems, and leaves have been modified through evolutionary change to serve different functions. In many cases, different families of plants show similar adaptations to similar environmental conditions.

Desert Plants

Desert plants must survive where strong sun and daytime heat combine with sandy soil and infrequent rainfall. Instead of staying near the surface, rainwater sinks rapidly through desert soils. The hot, dry air quickly removes moisture from any wet surface, making life difficult for plants.

Figure 23–24 *Unlike the stomata of most plants, those of water lilies are clustered on the top of their leaves. How is this an adaptation for life in water?*

Two families of desert plants are cactuses (family Cactaceae), which evolved in the Americas, and the crown-of-thorns family (family Euphorbiaceae), which evolved in Africa. Figure 23–25 shows examples of these families of desert plants. Both families have either a root system that spreads out for long distances just under the soil surface or a root system that reaches deep down into the soil. In each of these root systems, the roots have many root hairs that quickly pick up water after a rainstorm, before the water sinks too far down in the soil.

Most water loss in plants occurs through transpiration from the leaves. Both families of desert plants either have leaves that are very small or have no leaves at all. In cactuses, leaves have been reduced to thin, sharp spines. In euphorbias, leaves either are tiny or can be dropped if the weather gets too dry. Both plant families have thick green stems, where photosynthesis occurs. These stems are also adapted to store water. The stems of cactuses, in particular, swell during rainy periods, as the plants greedily store water, and shrivel during dry spells, when the plants are forced to use up their water reserves.

Seeds of many desert plants can remain dormant for years, germinating only when sufficient moisture guarantees them a chance for survival. Other desert plants have bulbs, tubers, or rhizomes that can remain dormant for several years if necessary. When rain does come, the plants grow with amazing speed. They mature, flower, and set seed in a matter of weeks or even days—before the water disappears.

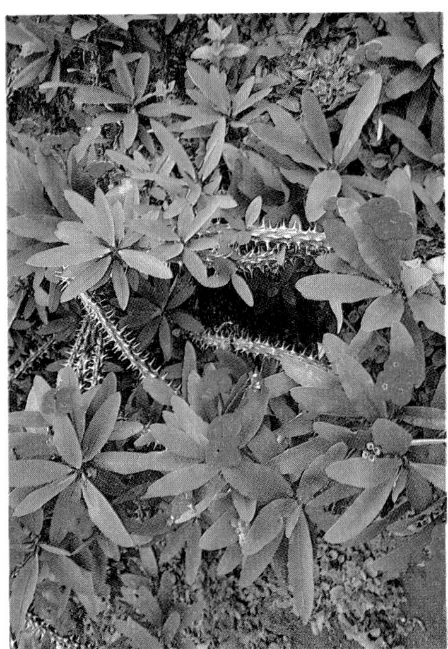

Figure 23–25 Plants that live in dry environments show adaptations to conserve water. The cactus leaves have been reduced to spines (top). The euphorbia has leaves that drop off in dry seasons (bottom).

Plants Adapted to Life in Water

Some plants, such as waterlilies, have the opposite problem of desert plants. Their roots and stems grow in water or in mud that is saturated with water and nearly devoid of oxygen. To supply oxygen to their roots, these plants have large open spaces in the long petioles that reach from their leaves down to the roots at the bottom. These open spaces are filled with air through which oxygen can diffuse to the roots.

Many other plants show similar adaptations. Several species of mangrove trees grow in shallow water along tropical seacoasts. Stately baldcypress trees thrive in freshwater

Figure 23–26 Mangrove roots, which look like a series of stilts, support the plant. In time, a mangrove plant grows to cover a huge area.

swamps in the southern United States. The roots of these trees, like those of waterlilies, must survive in mud that has little or no oxygen. Mangroves survive by growing special roots called air roots. Air roots have large air spaces in them, just like waterlily stems. These spaces conduct air down to the buried roots so the root tissues can respire normally. Baldcypress trees grow structures called knees, which protrude above the water. The knees bring oxygen-rich air down to the roots.

Salt-Tolerant Plants

In addition to getting air to their roots, mangroves have another problem. As you have seen, when plant roots take in dissolved minerals, a difference in the concentration of water molecules is created between the root cells and the surrounding soil. This concentration difference causes water to enter the root cells by osmosis. For plants growing in salt water, this means taking in much more salt than the plant can use. The roots of plants such as mangroves can tolerate salt concentrations that would quickly burn the root hairs off most plants. And the leaves of these plants have special cells that actively pump salt out of the plant tissues and onto the leaf surfaces, where it is washed off by rain.

Figure 23–27 *The stem of the morning glory twines around and around its support. Twining stems enable plants to grow "taller" by climbing up the stems of other naturally tall plants so that they can capture more of the sun's energy.*

Climbing Plants

In environments such as tropical rain forests, the struggle for sunlight is fierce. Here any plant that can quickly climb up the trunk of another plant to escape the darkness of the forest floor has a considerable advantage over its neighbors. Vines are plants that have evolved specialized root, stem, and leaf structures that enable them to climb on rocks or other plants.

The stems of many climbing plants do not grow straight up. Rather, the growing tips point sideways. See Figure 23–27. As the tip of a shoot grows, it spins around in a circle. In this way, the plant "looks" for something to climb on. When the tip encounters an object, it quickly wraps around it.

Some climbing plants have long, twisting leaf tips or petioles that wrap tightly around small objects. Other plants have extra growths called tendrils that emerge near the base of the leaf petioles and wrap tightly around any object they encounter.

Still other vines, such as the strangler fig, grow aerial roots along the entire length of their stem. These roots attach to rocks or trees and help anchor the climber in place. Sometimes these aerial roots can be so numerous and so large that they end up strangling the host plant.

Plants That Eat Animals

Some plants live in very wet places called bogs, where there is little or no nitrogen present in the watery soil. Because conditions are too wet and too acid in bogs, bacteria of decay

cannot survive. Without these bacteria, neither plant nor animal material is broken down into the nutrients plants can use.

A number of plants have overcome this difficulty by evolving specialized leaves that trap and digest insects. The best known of these carnivorous plants is the Venus' flytrap. This plant has bright-red leaf blades that are hinged at the middle. Insects are attracted to the leaf by the bright color. If an insect touches the trigger hairs on the leaf, the leaf folds up suddenly —trapping the animal inside. During a period of several days, the leaf secretes enzymes that digest the insect and release nitrogen for the plant to use.

There are several other kinds of carnivorous plants. Pitcher plants drown their prey in brightly colored pitchers that hold rainwater and digestive enzymes. Sundews trap insects on leaf hairs tipped with sticky secretions. There are even underwater carnivorous plants, such as bladderworts, that prey upon tiny water insects. See Figure 23–28.

Figure 23–28 *Some plants show special adaptations to catch and digest insects. The pitcher plant (top, left) and the sundew (bottom) are land plants that trap insects. The bladderwort (top, right) is a water plant able to catch its own food.*

23–7 SECTION REVIEW

1. What are two adaptations shown by desert plants to their environment?
2. Why do climbing plants survive better in tropical rain forests than do some nonclimbing plants?
3. Describe the adaptations of a mangrove tree to a saltwater environment.
4. How is insect eating an adaptation that contributes to the survival of the Venus' flytrap?

LABORATORY INVESTIGATION

EXPLORING THE STRUCTURE OF LEAVES

PROBLEM

How are leaves suited to their function?

MATERIALS *(per group)*

- 4 clean microscope slides
- 3 coverslips
- microscope
- forceps
- 2 clean medicine droppers
- scalpel
- scissors
- iodine solution
- leaves: *Elodea* and yew *(Taxus)*

PROCEDURE

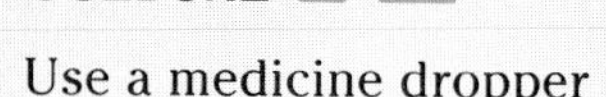

1. Use a medicine dropper to put a drop of water in the center of a slide.
2. Pull a small leaf from the tip of a sprig of *Elodea* in the drop of water on the slide. Cover the leaf with a coverslip.
3. Place the slide on your microscope. Focus the low-power objective on the *Elodea* leaf. Observe the leaf. Switch to the high-power objective. Focus with the fine adjustment. Look for pigmented structures in the cells. Note their shape and color. Remove the slide.
4. Place another slide on a flat surface. Put a yew leaf on the slide. Cut the tip off the leaf by pressing straight down with a scalpel about 1 mm from the end of the leaf. **CAUTION:** *The scalpel is very sharp. Always cut away from yourself and others.* Discard the tip of the leaf. Shave off 6 thin slices, or cross sections, from the cut end of the leaf. See the accompanying illustration. Make the slices as thin as possible by pressing the scalpel straight down as close to the cut end of the leaf as allowable.

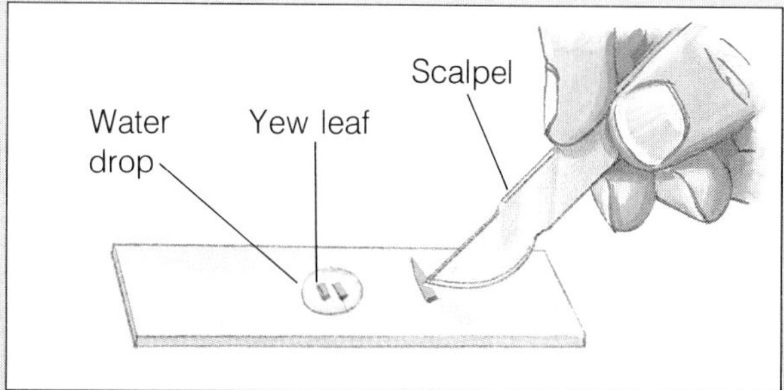

5. Use a medicine dropper to put a drop of water in the center of another slide. Slide the leaf cross sections over to the drop of water. Position the cross sections so that they lie next to each other. Cover the leaf cross sections with a coverslip.
6. Place the slide on a microscope. Focus the low-power objective on the thinnest cross section on the slide. Switch to the medium-power objective.
7. Draw a diagram of the leaf cross section. Locate the following structures and label them on your drawing: epidermis; palisade layer; spongy layer; vein. Remove the slide.

OBSERVATIONS

1. What is the shape and color of the pigmented structures in the *Elodea* leaf?
2. Describe the appearance of the yew leaf cross sections. What is the shape and color of the cells?

ANALYSIS AND CONCLUSIONS

1. What are the pigmented structures in the *Elodea* leaf? What is the function of these structures?
2. What is the function of each labeled structure in the yew leaf?
3. Which parts of the leaf help in food production? In delivering water?
4. How do the shape, structures, and positions of the structures you observed contribute to the functioning of a leaf?

STUDENT STUDY GUIDE

SUMMARIZING THE CONCEPTS

The key concepts in each section of this chapter are listed below to help you review the chapter content. Make sure you understand each concept and its relationship to other concepts and to the theme of this chapter.

23–1 Soil: A Storehouse for Water and Nutrients

- Plants take in the water and inorganic materials they need from the soil.

23–2 Specialized Tissues in Plants

- Vascular tissue, xylem and phloem, is the plant's circulatory system.

23–3 Roots

- Roots anchor a plant in the ground and enable the plant to take in water and nutrients.

23–4 Stems

- Stems hold leaves up to sunlight and conduct water and other substances from roots to leaves.

23–5 Leaves

- Leaves are solar energy collectors as well as the food-making center in most plants.

23–6 Transport in Plants

- Root pressure and transpiration pull are the forces that move water in xylem tubes.
- Scientists offer the pressure flow hypothesis to explain phloem transport. In this hypothesis, materials move from a source, an area of high concentration of materials, to a sink, an area of low concentration of materials.

23–7 Adaptations of Plants to Different Environments

- Flowering plants show a great many adaptations to different environments.

REVIEWING KEY TERMS

Vocabulary terms are important to your understanding of biology. The key terms listed below are those you should be especially familiar with. Review these terms and their meanings. Then use each term in a complete sentence. If you are not sure of a term's meaning, return to the appropriate section and review its definition.

23–2 Specialized Tissues in Plants

meristematic tissue
apical meristem
cork cambium
vascular cambium
pericycle
parenchyma
sclerenchyma
tracheid
vessel element
sieve tube element
companion cell

23–3 Roots

taproot
fibrous root
epidermis
cortex
vascular cylinder
Casparian strip

23–4 Stems

dormancy
rhizome
tuber
bulb
corm

23–5 Leaves

petiole
stoma
guard cell
mesophyll
palisade layer
spongy mesophyll

23–6 Transport in Plants

transpiration
transpiration pull

CONTENT REVIEW

Multiple Choice

Choose the letter of the answer that best completes each statement.

1. In order to grow well, roots need
   a. minerals. c. carbon dioxide.
   b. oxygen. d. water.
2. Openings that permit gases to enter and leave the leaf are called
   a. stomata. c. palisade cells.
   b. cuticles. d. chloroplasts.
3. A nutrient that plants use for proper leaf growth and color is
   a. zinc. c. calcium.
   b. potassium. d. nitrogen.
4. The type of plant tissue that divides by mitosis is
   a. meristematic. c. phloem.
   b. xylem. d. surface.
5. The inner part of bark is made of
   a. xylem. c. phloem.
   b. parenchyma. d. cuticle.
6. A meristematic tissue that increases the thickness of plant stems over time is
   a. vascular cambium. c. pericycle.
   b. apical meristem. d. epidermal meristem.
7. Thin-walled cells that store the products of photosynthesis are
   a. tracheids. c. sclerenchyma cells.
   b. companion cells. d. parenchyma cells.
8. A primary root that grows longer and thicker is
   a. a fibrous root. c. easy to remove.
   b. a taproot. d. not found in plants.

True or False

Determine whether each statement is true or false. If it is true, write "true." If it is false, change the underlined word or words to make the statement true.

1. Carbon dioxide enters a plant through the roots.
2. Plants lose water through the leaves by perspiration.
3. Trees grow taller because cells in the apical meristem are able to divide.
4. The waterproof covering on the outside of the leaf is the cambium.
5. Xylem tissue conducts the products of photosynthesis up through a plant's stem.
6. There is a one-way passage of materials into the vascular cylinder in plant roots.
7. The rings of a tree are made up of phloem tissue.
8. Tubers are underground roots.

Word Relationships

An analogy is a relationship between two pairs of words or phrases generally written in the following manner: a:b::c:d. The symbol : is read "is to," and the symbol :: is read "as." For example, cat:animal::rose:plant is read "cat is to animal as rose is to plant."

In the analogies that follow, a word or phrase is missing. Complete each analogy by providing the missing word or phrase.

1. xylem:water::phloem: ________________
2. parenchyma:storage::sclerenchyma: ________________
3. root hairs:roots::mesophyll: ________________
4. water:osmosis::nutrients: ________________

CONCEPT MASTERY

Use your understanding of the concepts developed in the chapter to answer each of the following in a brief paragraph.

1. Plants are said to have an open growth pattern. What does this mean?
2. If you were weeding a lawn, would you be more successful at removing weeds with a taproot or weeds with fibrous roots? Explain your answer.
3. What are three adaptations shown by plants that are able to survive in a desert?
4. Leaves are able to trap solar energy. How does their shape enable them to perform this job efficiently?
5. How are root hairs important to plants?
6. What are stomata? How do they work?
7. Why is it important for tissues in the spongy mesophyll of the leaf to remain constantly moist?

CRITICAL AND CREATIVE THINKING

Discuss each of the following in a brief paragraph.

1. **Applying concepts** Certain Native Americans used bark cut from birch trees to make canoes. Removing the bark did not kill the trees. What precautions did they take when they removed the bark?
2. **Relating concepts** The leaves of cactuses have been modified into thorns. What two functions does this modification have?
3. **Drawing conclusions** Suppose you were going away on vacation and you couldn't find anyone to water your houseplants. You knew that plants lose water through the stomata in their leaves, so you decided to cover the leaves with petroleum jelly to prevent water loss. When you returned home, you found your plants had died. What is the most logical explanation for this?
4. **Designing an experiment** Your friend says it's necessary to fertilize plants every time they are watered. His plants grow well. You decide to test his claim. Design an experiment to test your friend's hypothesis.
5. **Relating cause and effect** A corn farmer decides to save money by not fertilizing the fields. The crop grows well the first year but diminishes each succeeding year. How would you explain this situation?
6. **Relating cause and effect** In Japan, the art of growing miniature trees is highly valued. By cutting the roots and tips of the branches, the tree remains small. The trunk of the tree, however, continues to increase in diameter. How do you explain the ever-increasing diameter of the trunk?
7. **Applying concepts** During the nineteenth century, people often raised ferns and other delicate plants that normally require a great deal of water in enclosed glass containers called Wardian cases. Plants in Wardian cases did not have to be watered for years. What is the most logical explanation for this phenomenon?
8. **Applying concepts** In cold northern climates many trees lose their leaves in autumn. How is this an adaptation that helps the trees survive the cold of winter?
9. **Using the writing process** Many people find insectivorous plants interesting. Most of these plants are collected from the wild. Some scientists are concerned that too many of these plants are being collected. Write a letter to your congressional representative proposing a law to protect these plants.

CHAPTER 24

Plant Growth and Development

An oak forest is home for many different animals. Some eat the acorns produced by oaks, others make their home in tree trunks, and still others find safety in the lush oak foliage.

You have probably heard the old saying, "Mighty oaks from tiny acorns grow." But have you ever thought about the amazing changes that take place during the long life of such a tree? A tiny embryo oak plant sits within an acorn for months, maybe even years. Then one spring, it sprouts. Its roots grow deep into the soil in search of water and nutrients. Its leaves reach toward the sun—toward the light energy that powers the life of the plant. In autumn, growth slows. The oak's leaves turn color and fall to the ground. The entire plant undergoes the changes necessary to survive the approaching cold winter weather.

Many years later, the tree matures. Suddenly it produces hundreds, perhaps even thousands, of flowers. Some of the flowers produce seeds that mature into acorns. When the acorns ripen, they fall to the ground, where they may be buried or eaten by squirrels. With luck, the process of growth begins again.

CHAPTER OUTLINE

24–1 Patterns of Growth

Section Objectives

- Compare annual, biennial, and perennial plants.
- Compare the growth of monocot and dicot stems.
- Explain how roots increase in length.

Plants grow in different ways. If you have ever grown plants from seeds, you may be aware that some plants mature and produce flowers in the same year they are sown. Other plants take longer. **Plants are classified into three main groups—annuals, biennials, and perennials—depending on how long it takes them to produce flowers and how long they live.**

Annuals, Biennials, and Perennials

Some plants grow from seed to maturity, flower, produce seeds, and die all in the course of one growing season. These plants are called **annuals** (from the Latin word *annus*, which means year). Many common plants—such as marigolds, corn, and peas—are annuals.

Biennials (*bi* is the Latin word for two) are plants that usually live for two years. During the first growing season, biennials grow roots, stems, and leaves. The leaves and stems die back to the ground in winter, but the below-ground roots remain alive. The following season, new leaves and stems grow from the roots. In this second season, however, the plant produces flowers. Once the flowers produce seeds, the plant dies. Common biennial plants include some species of foxglove, sugar beets, carrots, and turnips.

Perennials are plants that live for more than two years. Peonies, popular perennial garden plants, often outlive the person who planted them. Other perennials, such as dawn redwoods, have trunks and branches that live and grow larger for hundreds, even thousands, of years. Trees and shrubs are

Figure 24–1 *The zinnia (left) is one of the many plants that live for only one growing season. Plants such as the foxglove (right) take two growing seasons to complete their life cycle.*

Figure 24–2 The chrysanthemum (left) and the peony (right) are perennials, which means they are able to grow for many years. Cold winter temperatures cause the top parts of the plants to die down to the ground. The roots, locked in the frozen soil, remain alive and will begin to grow again with the warmth of spring.

perennials because they live for indefinite periods of time. Trees and shrubs whose stems contain woody tissue are called woody plants.

Plants whose stems have little or no woody tissue are called **herbaceous** (her-BAY-shuhs) plants. In cold climates, herbaceous plants die back to their roots every year. For example, perennials such as chrysanthemums and tulips grow new leaves and stems every spring. In tropical climates, the above-ground parts of both woody and herbaceous plants can grow throughout the year.

Growth of Stems

As you may recall from Chapter 23, stems grow longer at their tip as cells in the apical meristem divide. These newly formed cells then grow larger in an area behind the meristem called the **zone of elongation**. Farther back from the zone of elongation is the **zone of maturation**. Here cells differentiate into the various cells that make up a plant stem. In herbaceous plants, almost the entire stem is composed of tissue produced by the apical meristem. Tissue produced by the apical meristem is called **primary tissue**.

It should be clear to you that if a perennial plant is to grow larger year after year, its stems must increase in thickness as well as in length. Yet, as you may remember, only meristematic tissue can produce new cells for growth. In perennial plant stems, new tissue is added by special meristematic tissues called the vascular cambium and cork cambium. The addition

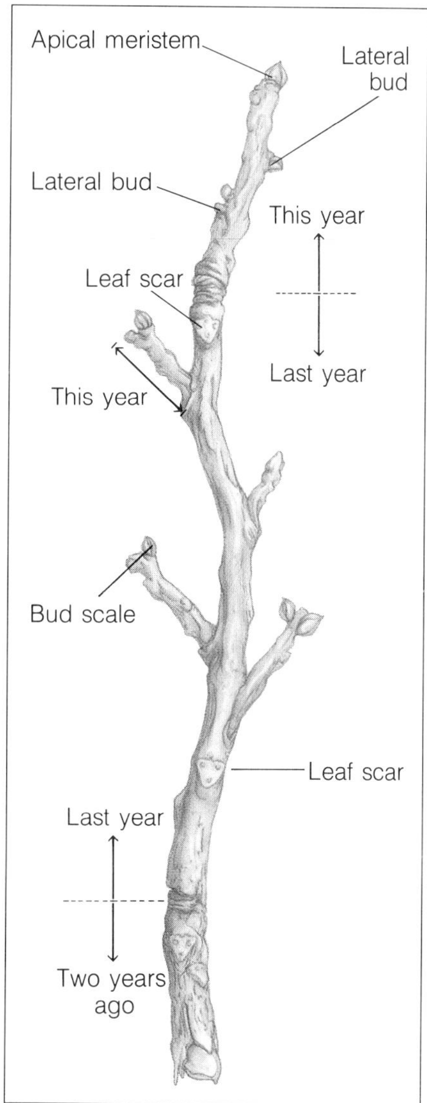

Figure 24–3 A twig taken from a tree in winter shows how the apical meristem—the place where plant cells divide—is protected from the cold by thick bud scales. Twigs from different plant species have different markings, which can be used by botanists to identify the species—even without the benefit of leaves.

of new tissue in these cambium layers increases the thickness of the stem, which is needed to support a larger plant.

Growth in Dicot Stems

In woody dicot stems, a layer of vascular cambium located between the xylem and phloem tissues remains alive through the plant's first winter. In the following spring, this vascular cambium becomes active as its cells begin to divide. Xylem cells are formed on the surface of the vascular cambium that faces the center of the stem. Phloem cells are formed on the surface that faces the outside of the stem. These new layers of vascular tissue are called **secondary xylem** and **secondary phloem**. Both secondary layers spread sideways from each vascular bundle in the cambium layer, soon uniting the circle of vascular bundles into a solid ring. The xylem tissue is on the inside of the ring, and the phloem tissue is on the outside. The vascular cambium remains between the xylem and phloem.

XYLEM GROWTH The new ring of xylem tissue formed during every growing season plus the older xylem become the wood of trees. Although the cells of the older xylem layers are dead, they still conduct water for several years. Xylem is called **sapwood** as long as it conducts water. After some time, however, the oldest xylem cells become clogged with tars and resins and are no longer able to conduct water. This xylem tissue, which no longer conducts water but gives strength and support to the tree, is called **heartwood**.

You have probably seen tree rings, or **annual rings**, in the wood of trees. Tree rings are formed because the vascular cambium makes large xylem cells during the spring and smaller xylem cells during late summer and fall. The large cells of spring wood look lighter than the smaller cells of summer wood. Thus the tree accumulates set after set of alternating light and dark rings, one set for every year the tree is alive.

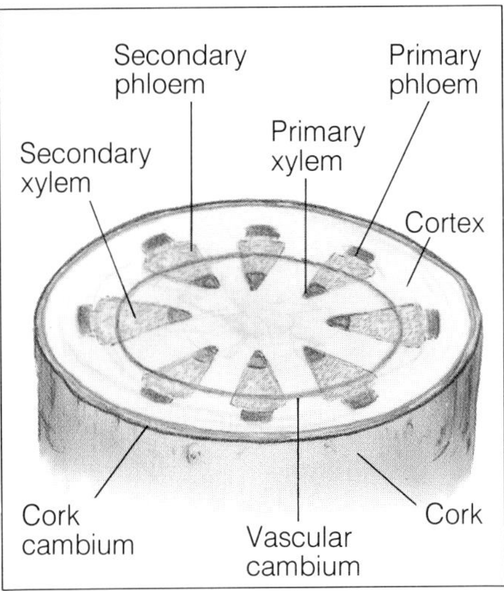

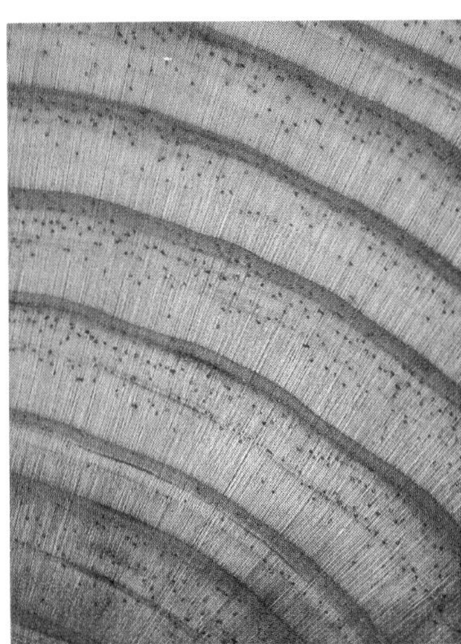

Figure 24–4 *Each tree ring represents a season's growth. During a single growing season, secondary xylem and phloem are produced by the vascular cambium. Note the variations in the sizes of the rings.*

Figure 24–5 Beavers are known for their sharp teeth, which have produced the results you see here. The bark and the delicate underlying phloem tissue of the tree have been gnawed away. The tree has been girdled and will eventually die.

PHLOEM GROWTH The vascular cambium makes new phloem cells at the same time it makes new xylem cells. These secondary phloem cells are added to the inner surface of the previous year's phloem. The phloem layer, however, never becomes as thick as the xylem layer. One reason for this is that the cambium makes only one new phloem cell for every six or eight xylem cells. Another reason is that phloem cells have thinner walls than xylem cells and are crushed as the stem grows thicker.

Phloem tissue forms the inner half of tree bark. Here it carries sugars and other products of photosynthesis from leaves to those plant parts that do not make their own food. For this reason, a tree will die if the phloem in tree bark is damaged or removed in a ring around the trunk.

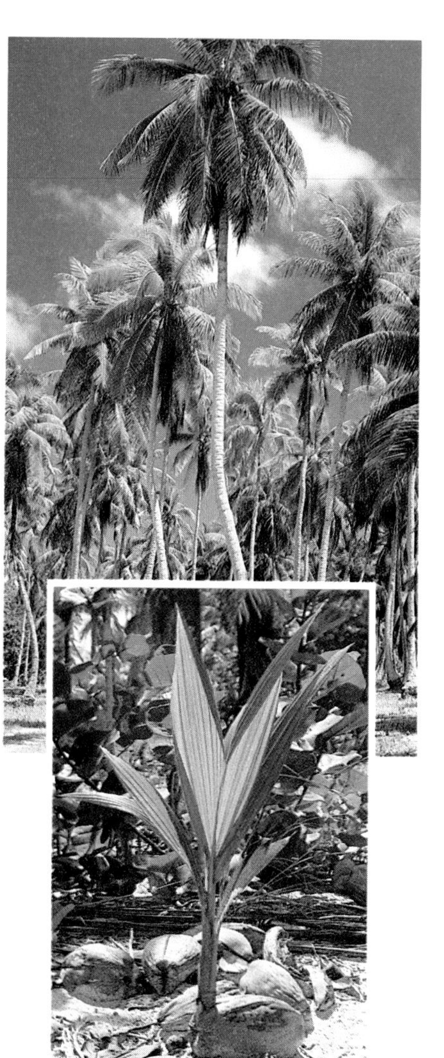

Growth in Monocot Stems

Recall that in monocots (corn and lilies, for example) xylem and phloem tissues are arranged in vascular bundles scattered throughout the stem. In most monocots, these bundles lack a vascular cambium, so no new xylem and phloem cells can be produced. This means that once the apical meristem of a monocot produces a stem, that stem cannot grow thicker. Few monocots grow more than several meters tall.

But there are a few tall monocots. Palms are one example. The few monocot trees remain short for several years. During this time, they produce leaf after leaf, without growing very tall. While they are producing leaves, however, the apical meristem as well as the stem below it grow wider. Finally, the meristem produces a stem strong enough to serve as a trunk. At that point, the monocot tree starts to grow taller. Unlike dicot stems, the stem of a palm does not increase greatly in width once the tree begins to grow tall.

Growth of Roots

Roots, like stems, grow in length as their apical meristem produces new cells near the root tip. The fragile new cells are covered by a tough **root cap** that protects the root as it forces its way through the soil. As the root grows, the root cap secretes a slippery substance that lubricates the progress of the root through the soil. Because cells at the very tip of the root cap are constantly being scraped away, new root cap cells are continually added by the meristem.

Figure 24–6 Palms are one of the few monocot trees. Palms remain short for a time, as their apical meristem increases in width (inset). However, the tiny palm will eventually grow tall.

Figure 24–7 *Only the cells in the root tip divide. In the area just behind the root tip, the newly divided cells increase in length, pushing the root tip farther into the soil. The root cap, located just ahead of the root tip, protects the dividing cells as they are pushed forward.*

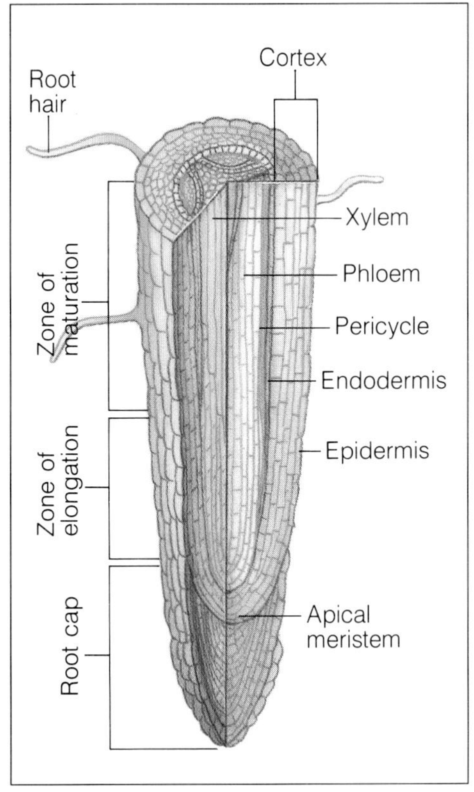

Most of the actual increase in root length occurs in the zone of elongation immediately behind the meristem. There, the small cells produced by the meristem grow longer. In the zone of maturation, these cells take on the structures and functions of mature root cells.

24–1 SECTION REVIEW

1. How does an annual plant differ from a perennial plant?
2. Why don't most monocot stems grow thicker?
3. How do stems and roots grow in length?
4. The tallest humans stop growing eventually, yet a tall tree increases its height year after year. Why are plants able to continue to grow taller as long as they live?

24–2 Control of Growth and Development

Section Objectives

- Describe the effects and importance of hormones on plant growth.
- Identify several plant tropisms.
- Compare long-day, short-day, and day-neutral plants.

Plants grow in response to important environmental factors such as light, moisture, temperature, and gravity. But just how do roots "know" to grow down and stems "know" to grow up toward light? The answers to these questions involve the actions of special chemicals that direct, or control, the growth of a plant.

Hormones and the Control of Plant Growth

In plants, as in animals, the division, growth, maturation, and differentiation of cells is controlled by a diverse group of chemical substances called hormones. A **hormone** is a substance produced in one part of an organism that affects another part of the organism. Plant hormones are manufactured primarily in apical meristems, in young leaves, and in growing seeds and developing fruits. Plant hormones control a plant's branching pattern, the rate at which its stems elongate, and its responses to environmental conditions.

How does a stem respond if a plant is knocked over? How do roots grow when they come up against a rock in the soil? How does a plant adjust its growth rate when winter or a dry season approaches? How do plants flower at the proper season? All these phenomena are controlled by hormones.

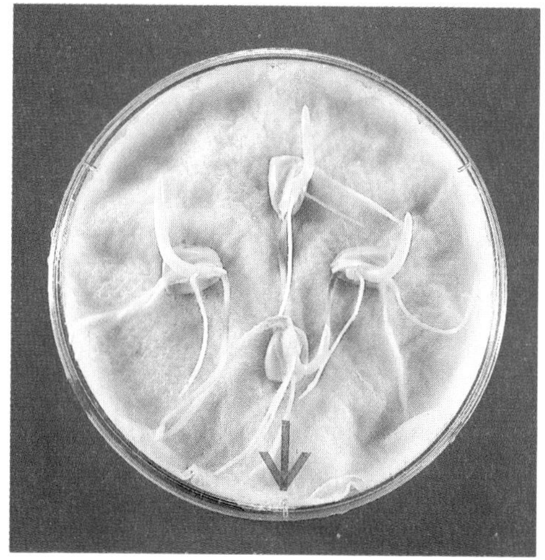

Figure 24–8 The roots of the corn seeds in this petri dish are growing in the same direction even though the seeds have been planted upside down (top). Stems grow toward the light (bottom). Why is it important that roots and stems grow the way they do?

The Nature of Hormone Action

The part of the organism affected by a hormone is known as the target tissue or **target organ**. The effects of a given hormone on a target tissue or target organ can vary a great deal for several reasons.

One reason is that the same concentration of a particular hormone can have two different effects on two different target tissues. For example, the identical concentration of a hormone can stimulate growth in stem tissues but inhibit growth in root tissues. Another reason is that different concentrations of a particular hormone can produce different effects on the same target organ. For example, low concentrations of a hormone can cause meristematic cells to divide, but high concentrations of that same hormone can prevent division. This phenomenon will help explain branching in plants. And a third reason is that two or more hormones can interact in a variety of ways. For example, the effect of one particular hormone may depend on whether or not another particular hormone is present. Systems of interacting hormones are important in regulating reproduction in plants.

The Role of Auxin

One well-known plant hormone is indoleacetic acid, commonly called **auxin**. Auxin can produce different effects on different plant tissues. High concentrations of auxin stimulate elongation of stem cells and inhibit elongation of root cells. Let us see how auxin directs the growth of stems and roots.

AUXIN AND STEM GROWTH Auxin produced in the apical meristem of a stem causes the stem to grow toward light and away from the pull of gravity. This effect was first noticed by Charles Darwin and his son Francis in experiments they performed in the 1880s. The Darwins observed that light caused "some influence" (they did not know what the influence was) to be transmitted from the tip of a growing stem down to the zone of cell elongation. This mysterious influence, the Darwins felt, caused the stem to bend and grow toward the source of light.

Other experiments performed between 1910 and 1920 by the Danish scientist P. Boysen-Jensen and the Hungarian researcher A. Paal showed that the "influence" the Darwins had observed was a chemical manufactured in the apical meristem. This chemical, the hormone we call auxin, is produced in the apical meristem and moves down the stem.

Today we understand that high concentrations of auxin stimulate young stem cells to elongate. If the source of light is directly overhead, and if the stem is growing vertically, the concentration of auxin will be the same on all sides of the stem. All the cells in the zone of elongation will grow at the same rate and the stem will grow straight up.

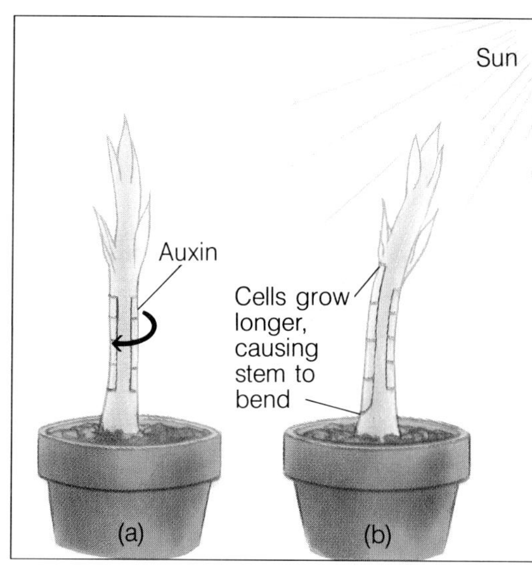

Figure 24–9 *Plants will bend toward a source of light. This fact is explained by the stimulating effect of plant hormones on cell growth. How do plant hormones cause a plant stem to bend?*

If the source of light is to one side of the stem, however, auxin will move away from the light to the shaded part of the stem. The higher concentration of auxin in the shaded side of the stem will stimulate cells in that side to elongate more than cells in the lighted side. This will cause the stem to bend toward the light.

If a plant is knocked on its side, auxin will accumulate in the lower side of the stem, or the side along the ground, because this side is darker than the upper side. It is the shaded side of the stem. The auxin-stimulated cells in the lower side will elongate more than the cells in the upper side. The stem will curve up, even in the absence of light.

AUXIN AND ROOT GROWTH Auxin produced in the apical meristem of roots causes the roots to grow away from light and toward the pull of gravity. If a growing root is exposed to light, auxin will concentrate in the shaded side of the root, just as it did in the shaded side of the stem. But high concentrations of auxin inhibit the elongation of root cells. Thus cells in the side of the root where auxin concentration is high will not elongate. Cells in the lighted side of the root will elongate normally, causing the root to bend away from the light.

If a growing root is directed sideways by an obstacle in the soil such as a rock, auxin will accumulate in the lower side of the root. Once again, high concentrations of auxin inhibit root cell elongation. The uninhibited root cells will elongate more than the auxin-inhibited root cells, and the root will bend downward.

AUXIN AND BRANCHING In addition to controlling cell elongation, auxin can also cause cell division in meristematic regions to stop or start. As a stem grows in length, cells in its apical meristem periodically produce other meristematic areas. These meristematic areas, called **lateral buds**, are on the sides of the stem. See Figure 24–11 on page 524. If these lateral buds begin to grow, they give rise to side branches that grow from the main stem.

If you grow plants at home or in the classroom, you know that most lateral buds do not start growing right away. Instead, they begin to grow only after the main growing tip of the plant has grown a distance above them. However, you can force these lateral buds into growth at any time by "pinching," or removing, the apical meristem. Why should this be the case?

Again, the action of auxin provides an explanation for the growth of lateral buds. Scientists have learned that high concentrations of auxin inhibit the growth of lateral buds, whereas low concentrations of auxin stimulate growth. Thus the high

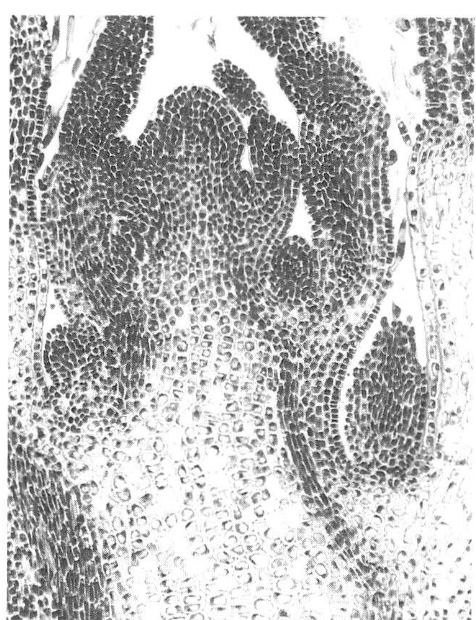

Figure 24–10 *A cross section through the tip of a plant stem can be seen in this photomicrograph. Lateral buds can be seen just behind the apical meristem. These lateral buds will remain dormant as long as the tip of the plant remains intact nearby.*

Apical meristem

Apical meristem removed

Lateral buds

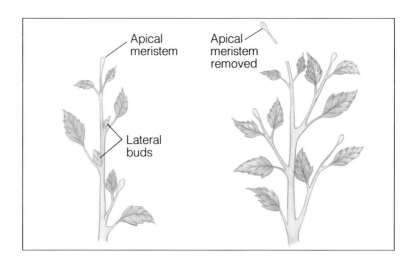

Figure 24–11 *The dormant lateral buds are kept from growing because of the production of hormones by the apical meristem. If the apical meristem is removed, however, the lateral buds will begin to grow. Pinching the apical meristem is one way a plant can be made to grow more bushy.*

concentration of auxin produced by the apical meristem inhibits the growth of lateral buds near the tip of the shoot. This inhibition is called apical dominance. When the apical meristem grows away from the lateral buds, or when it is removed, the auxin concentration in the lateral buds drops. Apical dominance ends, and the lateral buds begin to grow.

Cytokinins

Growing roots manufacture hormones called **cytokinins**. These hormones move upward in plants. Some cytokinins are also produced in developing fruits and seeds. Cytokinins stimulate cell division and cause dormant seeds to sprout. Several of the effects produced by cytokinins are the opposite of the effects produced by auxins. For example, whereas auxins stimulate cell elongation, cytokinins inhibit elongation and cause cells to grow thicker. Whereas auxins inhibit the growth of lateral buds, cytokinins stimulate lateral bud growth. Cytokinins have different effects on different tissues.

In growing plants, therefore, the relative concentrations of auxin, cytokinin, and other hormones determine how the plant will grow. You will learn in later chapters that the interactions of hormones are common in animals as well as in plants.

Figure 24–12 *The effects produced by the growth hormone gibberellin are dramatic. The short seedlings have not been treated with the hormone; the tall seedlings have.*

Gibberellin

In the 1920s, Japanese biologists studying certain rice plants made an important discovery. The rice plants they were observing seemed to be afflicted by a "disease" that made them grow unusually tall and spindly. Eventually the rice plants grew so tall that they could no longer be supported by their stems, and so they fell over. The scientists found that the plants' extraordinary growth was caused by a substance produced by the fungus *Gibberella fujikuroi*. They named the growth-producing substance **gibberellin** (jihb-er-EHL-ihn) after the fungus that produced it. Later, researchers learned that there are several different gibberellins. They also learned that gibberellins are hormones manufactured by all higher plants.

Tropisms

The responses of plants to environmental stimuli are called **tropisms** (TROH-pihz-uhmz) from the Greek word that means turning. If a plant grows toward a stimulus, it is said to have a positive tropism. If it grows away from a stimulus, it is said to have a negative tropism. There are several different kinds of tropisms. A plant's response to light is called **phototropism**. A response to gravity is called **gravitropism**. A response to touch is called **thigmotropism**.

For example, as soon as the primary root emerges from a germinating seed, it grows down and away from light. The root thus shows negative phototropism (away from the stimulus, light) and positive gravitropism (toward the stimulus, gravity). The stem, on the other hand, immediately starts growing toward the surface of the soil and toward light. The stem has a positive phototropism (toward the stimulus, light) and a negative gravitropism (away from the stimulus, gravity). From the very beginning of a plant's life, these positive and negative tropisms direct the plant's growth. And as you learned, these relatively simple responses of plants are controlled by hormones.

Winter Dormancy

Auxin and other hormones work together to control the growth, dormancy, and death of leaves in deciduous plants. During the growing season, auxin is produced in the leaves. At summer's end, days become shorter and nights become longer. The change in the length of light and dark periods causes a change in the chemistry of a protein called phytochrome. This change in phytochrome causes several things to happen to the plant's production of hormones. Auxin production drops, but the production of the hormones abscisic (ab-SIHS-ihk) acid and ethylene gas increases.

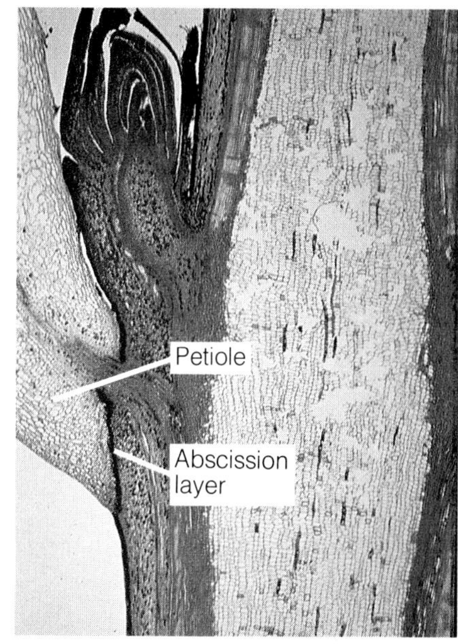

Figure 24–13 *In the fall, when winter's chill approaches, a tree prepares to shed its leaves. Here you can see the formation of the abscission layer at the base of a leaf petiole. When the abscission layer is complete, even the most gentle breeze will cause the cells to tear and the leaf to fall to the ground.*

These changes in hormone production have several effects. One is that the cells that join leaf petioles to their stems become weak, forming a band called the **abscission layer**. Another effect is that chlorophyll synthesis in leaves slows down and stops. The chlorophyll that remains in the leaves is slowly broken down by the plant or destroyed by sunlight. When this happens, brightly colored accessory pigments (such as those you learned about in the chapter on algae) become visible. During the summer, the green color of chlorophyll hides these pigments. But when the chlorophyll is no longer present in the leaves, these once-hidden pigments appear, providing the beautiful colors we associate with autumn foliage.

A third effect of changes in hormone production is that cell division in apical meristems changes. Instead of producing leaves, the meristems produce thick, waxy **bud scales**. These bud scales wrap around the apical meristems, protecting the terminal buds. Enclosed in its coat of scales, a terminal bud can survive the coldest winter days. At the onset of winter, xylem and phloem tissues pump themselves full of ions and organic compounds. These molecules act like antifreeze in a car, preventing the tree's sap from freezing.

During this time, the abscission layers at the bases of the leaves continue to develop. Eventually only a network of fragile vascular bundles holds the leaves on the stems. Sooner or later, a gust of wind or a rainstorm breaks the delicate abscission layers apart and the leaves fall. Where the leaves were once attached to the stems, only leaf scars remain as evidence of a season of growth.

SCIENCE, TECHNOLOGY, AND SOCIETY **APPLICATION**

Flowering by the Clock

For many people, flowers have special meanings. Flowers are often given as gifts, as tokens of affection, and to wish friends well. But the life of a grower of gift plants and flowers is not an easy one. In addition to the problem of insects and diseases that may harm the crop, there is the question of timing. A plant produced for Valentine's Day would be of little use if it flowered even a day late. Poinsettia plants grown for winter holiday decoration would be worthless if they flowered in June. Fortunately, you can buy roses on February 14 and poinsettias on December 25. Like clockwork, these flowers and plants are ready when they can be sold most profitably. How does this happen?

Growers of plants take advantage of day length to produce their plants at the proper times. For example, the poinsettia is a plant that flowers in nature during the winter. It is, as you might suspect, a short-day plant because it flowers naturally at the time of the year when nights are longest. In order to coax poinsettias into flowering at the "correct" time of the year, horticulturists cover the plants with thick cloths called blackout cloths during late-fall afternoons. The cloths prevent light from reaching the plants and interrupting the flowering cycle. In effect, the plants are tricked into believing that the days are short.

By covering some plants and adding additional light to others, horticulturists can almost guarantee that they will have plants and flowers available at suitable times. By taking advantage of the natural cycles of plant growth and flowering, consumers can be assured that they will have plants and flowers when they want them.

Long after the sun has ceased to shine, the plants in this greenhouse receive supplemental lighting to encourage, or in some cases delay, flowering.

Day Length and Flowering

"To everything there is a season," a popular song tells us, and nowhere is this more evident than in the regular cycles of growth in plants. Year after year, some plants flower in the spring, others in summer, and still others in the fall. How do plants time their flowering so precisely?

You know that there are fewer hours of daylight in winter than there are in summer. In the Northern Hemisphere, the shortest day occurs on or about December 21 and the longest day occurs on or about June 21. This means that from mid-winter through spring, days increase in length.

In the early 1920s, W. W. Garner and H. A. Allard, of the United States Department of Agriculture, learned that tobacco plants time their flowering according to the number of hours of light and darkness they receive. It soon became clear that many other plants also respond to periods of light and darkness. This response is called **photoperiodicity**.

At first, researchers assumed that plants respond primarily to the number of hours of light they receive. Plants such as chrysanthemums and poinsettias, which flower when days are short, were called short-day plants. Petunias, clover, and hollyhocks, which flower when days are long, were called long-day plants. The flowering of some plants, such as corn and tomatoes, did not seem to be affected by day length to any great extent. These plants were called day-neutral plants.

Today we know that the important factor in photoperiodicity is the length of the night or darkness period, not the length of the day or light period. Short-day plants actually flower because the nights are long. Long-day plants flower because the nights are short.

How do changes in the length of night cause plants to flower? As you learned earlier, changes in the length of light and darkness periods cause changes in compounds called phytochromes. In a manner that is still not understood, these changes in phytochrome chemistry stimulate plants to flower.

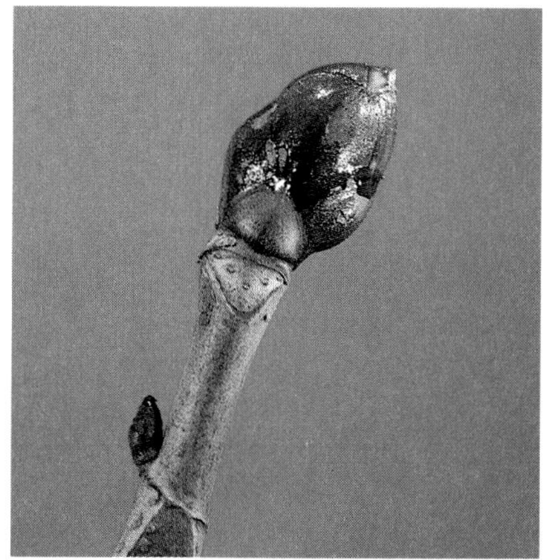

Figure 24–14 *During the winter, tight, thick bud scales encase the apical meristem on a twig (top). Most deciduous plants that grow in cold winter areas need a period of below-zero temperatures before their buds will begin to grow. However, when warm spring days encourage new growth, the bud scales open to reveal the new year's leaves and flowers (bottom).*

24–2 SECTION REVIEW

1. What are hormones? What is their role in plant growth and development? Where are most plant hormones produced?
2. How do different auxin concentrations affect cell elongation in stems? In roots? How do these effects explain phototropism and gravitropism in roots and stems?
3. What is the role of auxin in branching?
4. What environmental cue do plants use to time their flowering? How is this cue related to short-day plants and long-day plants?

LABORATORY INVESTIGATION

UNDERSTANDING PLANT TROPISMS

PROBLEM

How do roots find water and how do leaves find light?

MATERIALS *(per group)*

aluminum foil	2 index cards
2 150-mL beakers	medicine dropper
transparent tape	milk carton
15 corn seeds	petri dish
cotton	scissors
filter paper	potting soil

PROCEDURE 

1. Place some water in a beaker. Add 15 corn seeds. Soak the seeds for 2 days.
2. Select 4 swollen corn seeds and place them in the bottom of a petri dish. Arrange the seeds in a straight line across the center of the dish, with each seed at right angles to the adjacent seed. See the accompanying illustration.

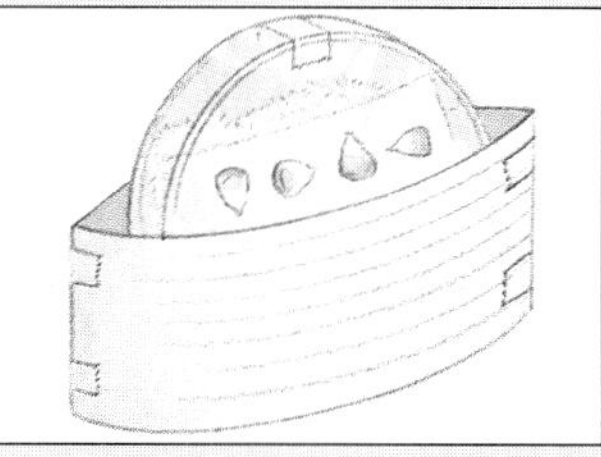

3. Put a piece of wet filter paper over the seeds. Cover the filter paper with enough wet cotton so that when the petri dish is closed, the seeds are held tightly in place. Cover the petri dish and tape it closed.
4. Make a stand for the petri dish from two index cards, as shown in the accompanying illustration. Fold the index cards in half. Then bend the cards so that the folds form right angles. Tape the cards together back to back. Slip the petri dish between the cards.
5. Fill the other 150-mL beaker with potting soil. Select 6 swollen corn seeds. Plant the seeds just below the surface of the soil, as far away from each other as possible. Moisten the soil.
6. Place the petri dish and the beaker in a dark place until the seeds have sprouted. This will take 2 or 3 days. Keep the soil evenly moist.
7. Examine the seeds in the petri dish after they have sprouted. Observe the directions in which the roots and leaves grow.
8. Make 3 small caps by wrapping small pieces of aluminum foil around the tip of a pen or pencil. Gently place these caps on half of the corn seedlings in the beaker.
9. Use scissors to cut the top off the large milk carton. Turn the milk carton upside down. Cut a small window on one side of the carton. Cut the window so that its base will be at the same level as the top of the beaker.
10. Place the beaker in a brightly lighted spot. Cover it with the milk carton. Position the carton so that light can reach the seedlings.
11. Leave the corn seedlings in bright light for about 4 days. During this time, water the plants with a medicine dropper if necessary.

OBSERVATIONS

1. In which direction are the leaves of the corn seeds in the petri dish growing? The roots?
2. In which direction are the leaves of the covered corn plants in the beaker growing?
3. In which direction are the leaves of the uncovered plants in the beaker growing?

ANALYSIS AND CONCLUSIONS

1. Why were the seeds in the petri dish grown in the dark?
2. What was the main influence on the direction of growth of the leaves and the roots of the corn plants in the petri dish?
3. How did the aluminum caps influence the direction of leaf growth in the corn plants?
4. What influenced the direction of growth of the leaves of the corn plants in the beaker?

STUDENT STUDY GUIDE

SUMMARIZING THE CONCEPTS

The key concepts in each section of this chapter are listed below to help you review the chapter content. Make sure you understand each concept and its relationship to other concepts and to the theme of this chapter.

24–1 Patterns of Growth

- There are three main groups of plants: annuals, biennials, and perennials.
- Stems increase in length as cells in their tip divide. These cells elongate in the zone of elongation behind the stem tip. The same cells differentiate in the zone of maturation, which occurs farther back from the tip.
- Roots increase in length as cells in the apical meristem in the root tips divide. These newly formed root cells elongate in a zone of elongation immediately behind the root tip. And they differentiate in a zone of maturation that is found farther from the tip.

24–2 Control of Growth and Development

- Hormones—special chemicals made by plants—direct the growth of plants.
- Auxin is an important plant hormone. High concentrations of auxin stimulate stem cells to grow longer. The same high concentrations of auxin can inhibit the elongation of root cells. Auxin also controls plant branching, since auxin inhibits the growth of lateral buds.
- Cytokinins are hormones produced in plant roots and developing fruits and seeds. These hormones stimulate cell division and cause seeds to sprout.
- Gibberellins are hormones produced by all plants.
- A tropism is the response of a plant to an environmental stimulus. A positive tropism is a response toward the stimulus. A negative tropism is a response away from the stimulus.
- During cold winters, many plants are dormant. Dormancy in plants is coordinated by the actions of several hormones. Dormancy is a reaction to environmental conditions that do not favor active plant growth.

REVIEWING KEY TERMS

Vocabulary terms are important to your understanding of biology. The key terms listed below are those you should be especially familiar with. Review these terms and their meanings. Then use each term in a complete sentence. If you are not sure of a term's meaning, return to the appropriate section and review its definition.

24–1 Patterns of Growth

annual
biennial
perennial
herbaceous
zone of elongation
zone of maturation
primary tissue
secondary xylem
secondary phloem
sapwood
heartwood
annual ring
root cap

24–2 Control of Growth and Development

hormone
target organ
auxin
lateral bud
cytokinin
gibberellin
tropism
phototropism
gravitropism
thigmotropism
abscission layer
bud scale
photoperiodicity

CHAPTER REVIEW

CONTENT REVIEW

Multiple Choice

Choose the letter of the answer that best completes each statement.

1. The response of plants to periods of light and dark is called
   a. gravitropism. c. thigmotropism.
   b. photoperiodicity. d. gibberella.
2. A plant that grows, matures, makes seeds, and dies within one year is a (an)
   a. biennial. c. annual.
   b. tree. d. perennial.
3. A part of a plant that shows positive phototropism and negative gravitropism is a
   a. leaf. b. root. c. flower. d. stem.
4. One way to coax a plant to branch is to
   a. fertilize it.
   b. trim the roots.
   c. remove the growing tip.
   d. keep the plant in the dark.
5. A plant that is laid on its side will
   a. die.
   b. grow very slowly.
   c. flower.
   d. bend its stem upward.
6. A chemical that directs the growth of a plant is called a (an)
   a. apical meristem. c. sapwood.
   b. hormone. d. heartwood.
7. An example of a monocot tree is a
   a. pine. c. palm.
   b. lily. d. maple.
8. A band of weak cells that forms where a leaf petiole joins a stem is called a (an)
   a. chlorophyll layer. c. abscission layer.
   b. meristem. d. cambium layer.

True or False

Determine whether each statement is true or false. If it is true, write "true." If it is false, change the underlined word or words to make the statement true.

1. The hormone that makes cells in the apical meristem divide is called <u>acetic acid</u>.
2. Brightly colored accessory pigments appear in the autumn when <u>chlorophyll</u> in the leaves breaks down.
3. Cells increase in length in the <u>zone of maturation</u>.
4. <u>Bud scales</u> protect the apical meristem from cold temperatures.
5. The response of plants to the length of day and night is called <u>phototropism</u>.
6. In autumn, the layer of weak cells that forms between the leaf petiole and the stem is called the <u>abscission layer</u>.
7. A <u>hormone</u> is a substance made in one part of an organism that affects another part.
8. The trunks of most trees increase in width as cells in the <u>apical meristem</u> divide.

Word Relationships

In each of the following sets of terms, three of the terms are related. One term does not belong. Determine the characteristic common to three of the terms and then identify the term that does not belong.

1. xylem, auxin, gibberellin, cytokinin
2. marigold, corn, dawn redwood, peas
3. breakdown of chlorophyll, formation of abscission layer, increase in the number of water molecules in xylem and phloem, formation of bud scales
4. summer, long days, short nights, long nights

CONCEPT MASTERY

Use your understanding of the concepts developed in the chapter to answer each of the following in a brief paragraph.

1. What is a tropism? Give an example of both a positive tropism and a negative tropism for a stem. For a root.
2. What is a herbaceous plant? Give an example of one.
3. How does auxin make a plant grow toward a light source?
4. What is photoperiodicity? How does it affect flowering plants?
5. What is a biennial? How does a biennial plant differ from a perennial plant?
6. What happens in the zone of maturation in a plant stem?
7. What is primary plant tissue?

CRITICAL AND CREATIVE THINKING

Discuss each of the following in a brief paragraph.

1. **Designing an experiment** One of your classmates suggests that all root cells have the ability to increase their length. Another classmate suggests that the cells in a root increase in length only in the zone of elongation just behind the root tip. Design an experiment to show which hypothesis is correct.
2. **Applying concepts** The sweet bay in the photograph was grown as a "standard." As you can see, a standard plant is grown to resemble a small tree. Next to it is a "normal" sweet bay plant. Use your knowledge of plant growth to determine the techniques used in growing a standard sweet bay.

3. **Applying concepts** People grow houseplants on windowsills. Many books advise giving houseplants a quarter turn every week. Why is this good advice to follow if you want to grow attractive plants?
4. **Relating cause and effect** Some dormant plants need an extended period of cold before their buds begin to grow. Some dormant plants even have to undergo two periods of freezing temperatures before their buds start growing again. Why is an extended period of cold or two freezing periods necessary for growth to resume?
5. **Making inferences** The black walnut tree grows in the northeastern part of the United States. Scientists have observed that few plants grow near the trunk of a black walnut. Offer an explanation for this observation.
6. **Using the writing process** Plants use the energy of light to make food. The flowering of some plants is affected by the length of day and night. Suppose light affected people in similar ways. Write a story about a person whose growth was affected by light.

CHAPTER 25

Reproduction in Seed Plants

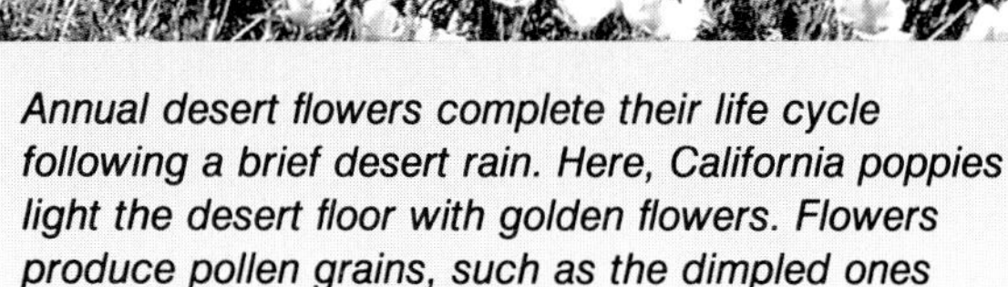

Annual desert flowers complete their life cycle following a brief desert rain. Here, California poppies light the desert floor with golden flowers. Flowers produce pollen grains, such as the dimpled ones belonging to a rose (inset).

You have probably seen many different kinds of pine cones during your lifetime. Cones smaller than a golf ball or larger than your hand are produced by various species of gymnosperms. You have also probably noticed many different kinds of flowers. Flowers vary from the familiar beauty of a fragrant rose to the bizarre shapes and exotic colors of tropical gingers and bananas. But have you ever stopped to think about why plants produce these structures? Do you know what benefits cones and flowers offer plants? In this chapter you will gain an understanding of why plants invest the time and energy to produce cones and flowers.

CHAPTER OUTLINE

25-1 Cones and Flowers as Reproductive Organs

Section Objectives

- Explain reproduction in gymnosperms.
- Describe the structure of a flower.
- Discuss reproduction in flowering plants.

The cones of gymnosperms and the flowers of angiosperms are plant structures that are specialized for the purpose of sexual reproduction. It is in the cones and flowers that the vital process that ensures the continuation of the species takes place. Thus, cones and flowers are as important to the survival of plant species as roots, stems, and leaves are to the survival of individual plants.

As you may recall, all plants have life cycles in which a diploid sporophyte generation alternates with a haploid gametophyte generation. Gametophyte plants produce male and female gametes. When male gametes and female gametes join, they form a zygote. The zygote develops into the next sporophyte generation. In seed plants, the sporophyte generation is large and obvious. The gametophyte generation is small and often hidden within the cones or flowers.

As you read about the process of reproduction in seed plants, keep this important concept in mind: The development of cones and flowers and the production of seeds have enabled seed plants to reproduce without being dependent upon standing water. In this way, seed plants differ dramatically from mosses and ferns. The methods of reproduction evolved by seed plants help them survive the dry conditions of life on land better than mosses and ferns.

Figure 25–1 *Female pine cones bear the seeds produced by pine plants. As you can see, pine cones vary greatly from the long, thin cones produced by the Eastern white pine to the short, squat cones produced by the Virginia pine.*

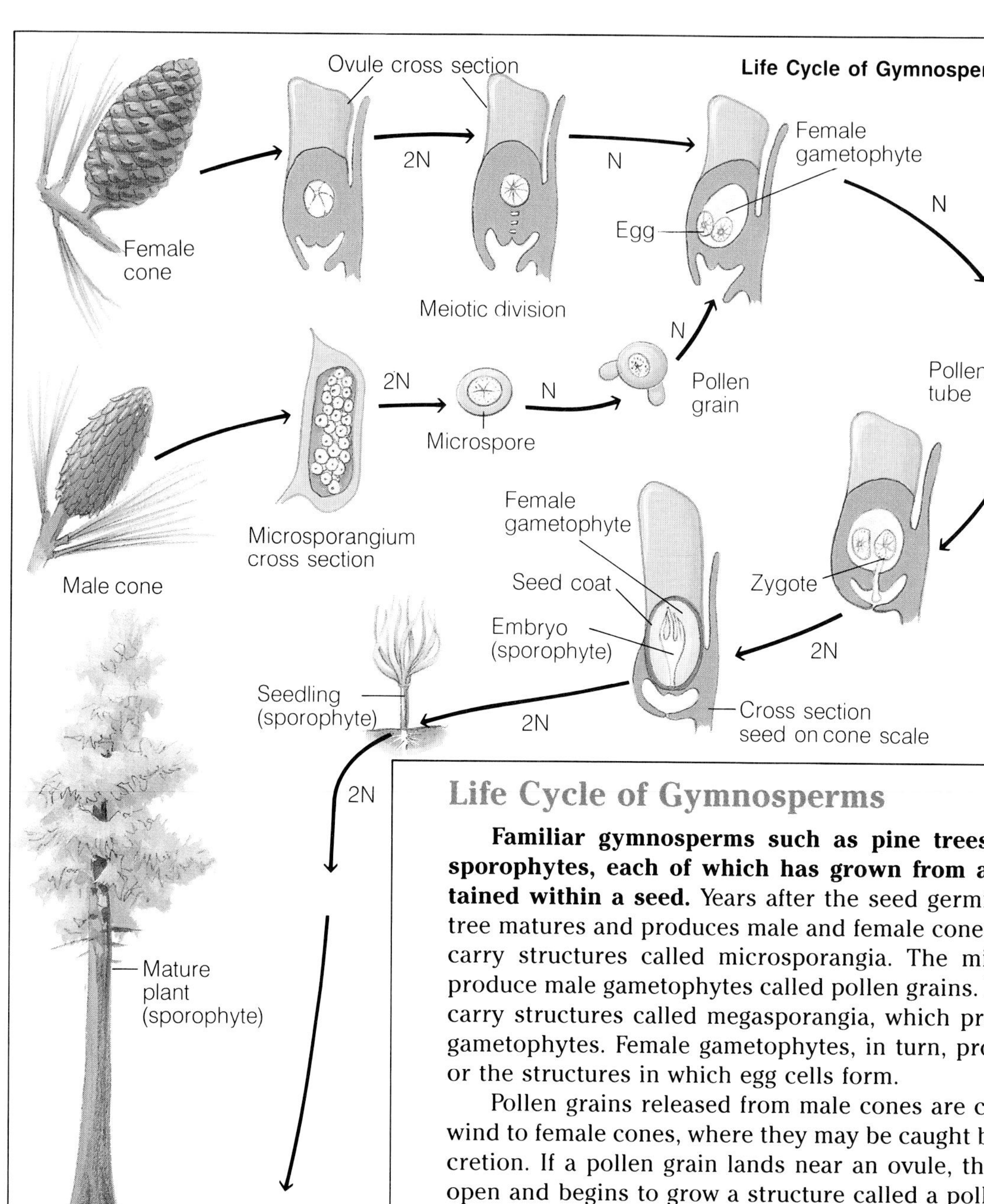

Figure 25–2 A pine tree produces both male and female cones. Male cones produce pollen; female cones produce ovules. If an ovule is fertilized, it becomes a zygote that is nourished by the female cone. In time the zygote develops into a seed.

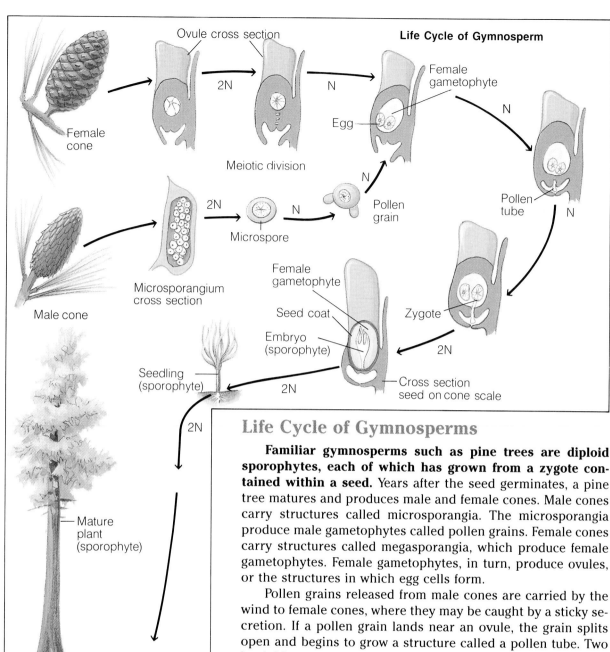

Life Cycle of Gymnosperms

Familiar gymnosperms such as pine trees are diploid sporophytes, each of which has grown from a zygote contained within a seed. Years after the seed germinates, a pine tree matures and produces male and female cones. Male cones carry structures called microsporangia. The microsporangia produce male gametophytes called pollen grains. Female cones carry structures called megasporangia, which produce female gametophytes. Female gametophytes, in turn, produce ovules, or the structures in which egg cells form.

Pollen grains released from male cones are carried by the wind to female cones, where they may be caught by a sticky secretion. If a pollen grain lands near an ovule, the grain splits open and begins to grow a structure called a pollen tube. Two haploid sperm are located within the pollen tube. Inside an ovule is an unfertilized egg. The pollen tube grows into the ovule, and eventually the two sperm break out of the tube. One sperm fertilizes the egg; the other sperm disintegrates. The zygote that is formed grows into an embryo encased within what later develops into a seed. The seed is rather a neat package, for contained within it is an embryo plant as well as a supply of food for the embryo when it begins to grow.

Life Cycle of Angiosperms

Angiosperms, or flowering plants, are the dominant forms of plant life on Earth today. During the long process of evolution, many kinds of angiosperms have developed. Today, angiosperms grow in most land environments and in many watery ones. The complicated life cycle of angiosperms must receive most of the credit for the tremendous evolutionary success of these plants. Angiosperms have evolved a life cycle that liberates the reproductive stages of these plants from standing water. Thus, angiosperms were able to spread over the face of the land, colonizing most of planet Earth.

You may not think of a flower as anything but a decorative object, but flowers are visible evidence of the angiosperms' success. Each flower represents proof of a plant's survival and offers assurance that a plant species will produce more of its own kind.

Figure 25–3 *The flower and the structures associated with the flower contain the reproductive organs of a plant.*

Structure of a Flower

The following description is of a typical flower. This flower produces both male and female gametes. Many plants, however, produce flowers that differ somewhat from this general plan. In some plants, the male and female gametes are produced in separate flowers on the same plant. Corn, for example, produces male gametophytes in flowers at the top of the plant and female gametophytes in flowers located along the stem below the male flowers. Other plants, such as willows, produce male and female gametes on separate plants. Many other variations occur in the structure of flowers. As you read about the parts of a typical flower, use Figure 25–4 to locate them. You will thus be familiar with the names and functions of the various flower parts, even if a flower you examine differs somewhat from the generalized description.

Flowers are actually miniature stems that produce four kinds of specialized leaves: sepals, petals, stamens, and carpels. These specialized leaves are arranged in circles and have been modified during the course of evolution to serve different purposes related to reproduction. The outermost circle of flower parts consists of several **sepals**. In many flowers, sepals are green and actually resemble leaves. Sepals enclose the flower bud before it opens and protect the flower while it is developing. All the sepals in a flower together form the **calyx**.

Petals make up the second circle of flower parts. Petals, which are often brightly colored, are found just inside the sepals. All of the petals in a flower form the **corolla**. In some plant species, both petals and sepals are similarly colored. Brightly colored flower parts act as a kind of "flower advertisement," attracting insects and other pollinators to the flower. Because they produce no gametophytes, the sepals and petals of a flower are called sterile leaves.

Fertile leaves are located inside the petals. The fertile leaves contain the structures that produce male and female gametophytes. The first circle of these fertile leaves consists of **stamens.** Each stamen has a long, thin **filament** that supports an **anther**. Inside the anther are microsporangia in which the

Figure 25–4 *This illustration shows the parts of a typical flower. Keep in mind that individual flowers may not have all the parts shown here. What parts make up the female reproductive organ? The male reproductive organ?*

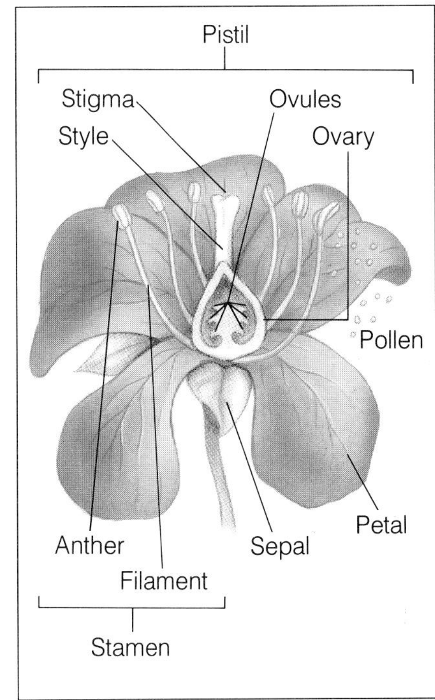

Figure 25–5 *The stamens in this lily flower are not quite ready to release their pollen (top). At this stage, the stamens are smooth. Later, when pollen is ripe and ready to be released, it covers the outside of each stamen (bottom).*

male gametophytes, the microspores, are produced. In most species of angiosperm, each flower has several stamens.

Carpels comprise the centermost circle of flower parts. Carpels are produced from fertile leaves that have rolled up. This rolling places megasporangia—the structures in which female gametophytes are produced—inside the female leaves, rather than on the outer surface of cones, as they are in gymnosperms. A single flower may contain one or more carpels. When multiple carpels are present in a flower, they may be either separate or fused. One or more carpels form the **pistil**. The pistil consists of a base called the **ovary**, a stalk called the **style**, and the **stigma**, located at the top of the style. In some plants the style is short; in other plants it can be quite long. For example, the style of a corn plant (actually, the long thread often called a corn silk) can be more than 30 centimeters long. The stigma is the surface upon which pollen is deposited by wind or animal pollinators. In many plants the stigma is sticky or contains many small projections that help catch pollen.

The Female Gametophyte

Located inside each ovary is one or more megasporangia called **ovules**. A single diploid (2N) cell called the megaspore mother cell grows inside each ovule. Each megaspore mother cell produces a female gametophyte in a series of steps. First, the megaspore mother cell undergoes meiosis, producing four haploid (N) cells, three of which die. Next, the remaining haploid cell divides mitotically to produce eight nuclei. These eight nuclei and the membrane that surrounds them are called the **embryo sac**. The embryo sac is the entire female gametophyte. Note that this gametophyte is much smaller and simpler than the female gametophytes of mosses and ferns.

Inside the embryo sac, the eight nuclei move around. Eventually two nuclei locate themselves in the center of the sac, and three nuclei clump together at each end. The nuclei in the center are called the **polar nuclei**. Finally, one of the three nuclei in the group closest to the opening in the ovule enlarges to become the **egg nucleus**. The two other nuclei flank the egg nucleus. The three nuclei cells at the opposite end of the embryo sac die. The female gametophyte now contains a female gamete (egg nucleus) ready to be fertilized.

The Male Gametophyte

The male gametophyte is even smaller than the female gametophyte. Inside the anthers, microsporangia called **pollen chambers** produce many diploid (2N) microspore mother cells. Each microspore mother cell divides by meiosis to produce four haploid (N) microspores. Each microspore ultimately becomes a single pollen grain. The wall of each pollen grain thickens to protect the pollen grain's contents from dryness and physical damage when it is released from the anther.

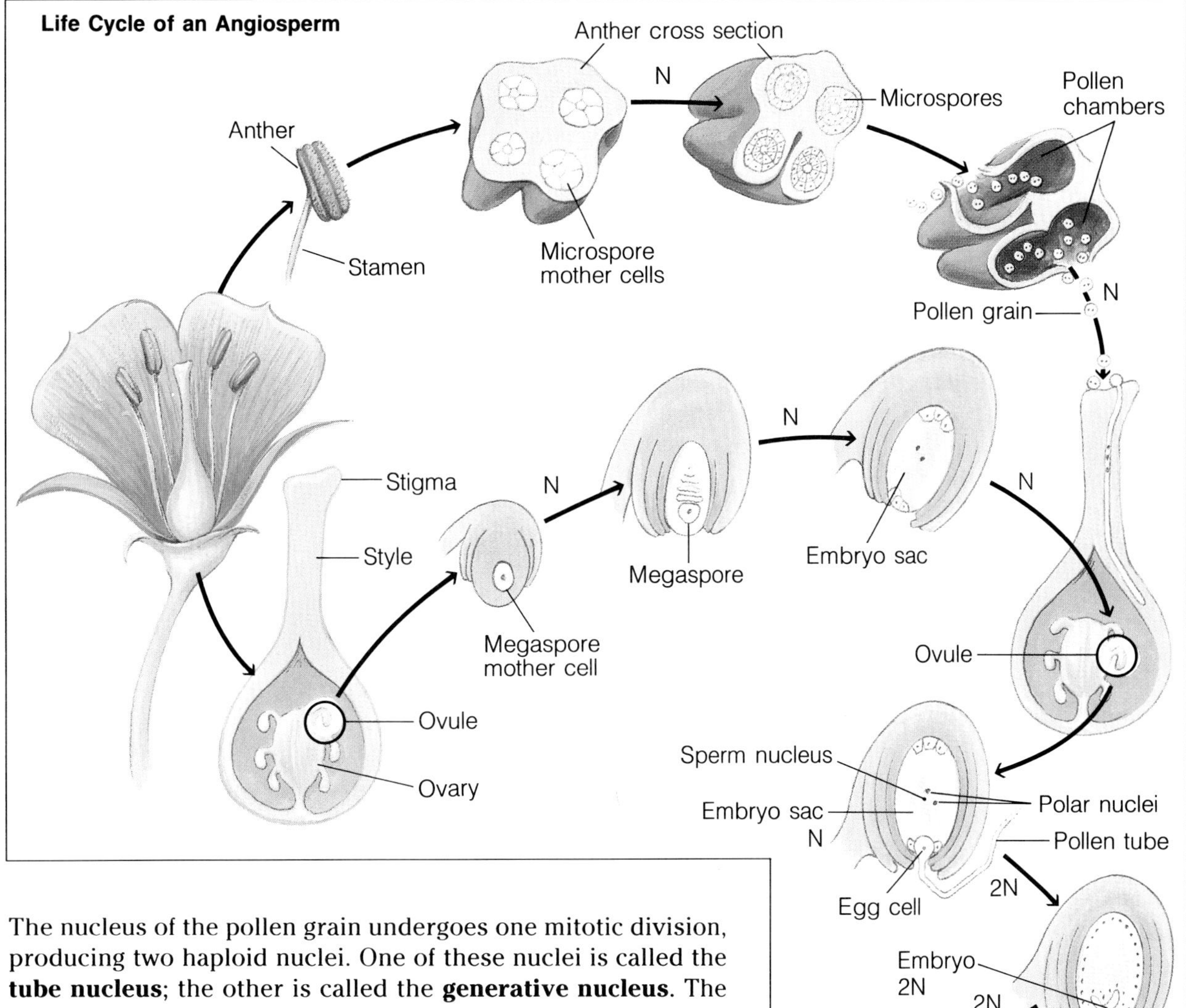

The nucleus of the pollen grain undergoes one mitotic division, producing two haploid nuclei. One of these nuclei is called the **tube nucleus**; the other is called the **generative nucleus**. The tube nucleus disintegrates. The generative nucleus divides to form two sperm cells. The pollen grain, which is the entire male gametophyte, usually stops growing until it is deposited on a stigma.

Eventually the anther dries out, its pollen chambers split open, and mature pollen grains are released. This process can easily be observed in a lily flower. When a lily flower first opens, its anthers are large and smooth. After a few days (depending on environmental conditions such as temperature) the pollen in the chambers ripens. The chambers split, shrink, and turn inside out, exposing the dustlike mature pollen.

__Figure 25–6__ Species of flowering plants have evolved complicated lifestyles to ensure their survival. The developing seeds of a flowering plant are protected and nourished inside the ovary located at the base of a flower.

Pollination

At this point in the reproduction process pollen must be transferred from an anther to a stigma. The transfer of pollen from anther to stigma is called **pollination**. There are two types of pollination that occur in different plant species.

Some plants, such as the peas Mendel worked with, allow pollen to fall from the anther to the stigma of the same flower. This process is called **self-pollination**. Most plants, however, do not self-pollinate. The majority of flowering plants have evolved complicated methods of reproduction that ensure that seeds will form only when pollen from one flower is transferred to the stigma of a flower on another plant. The transfer of pollen from one flower to a flower on another plant is called **cross-pollination**. In Chapter 22 you read about a few of the many relationships that exist between flowers and pollinators.

Why is self-pollination uncommon in many plant species? Recall that sexual reproduction allows the exchange of genetic material between individuals. This exchange increases variation in offspring. Usually, the more variation there is in a population, the more likely it is that at least some individuals will survive to reproduce.

Figure 25–7 *Some fruits like the apple and banana are familiar to you. Some, like the spikey Durian, are not. Bright colors and sweet tastes attract animals that eat the fruits and help distribute the ripe seeds.*

Fertilization

Once a pollen grain has landed on the stigma of an appropriate flower, it begins to grow a **pollen tube**. The generative nucleus within the pollen grain divides and forms two **sperm nuclei**. The pollen tube now contains a tube nucleus and two sperm nuclei. Following a chemical trail, the pollen tube grows down the style. Eventually the pollen tube reaches the ovary and enters the ovule through a small hole.

When the pollen tube reaches the female gametophyte (embryo sac), the sperm nuclei enter. Both nuclei participate in a process called **double fertilization**. Double fertilization occurs only in angiosperms. During this process, one sperm nucleus fuses with the egg nucleus to form the zygote. The other sperm nucleus fuses with the two polar nuclei. These three nuclei form the triploid (3N) **endosperm**. It is the endosperm that provides food for the embryo, which is produced when the zygote begins to grow. It is interesting to note that many animals eat the endosperm because it is so rich in important nutrients. Indeed, most of the food supply of humans is the endosperm of grasses. Three important examples are corn, wheat, and rice.

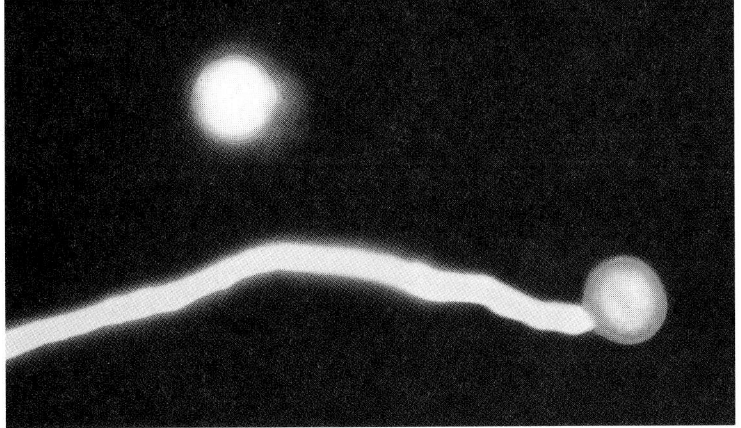

Figure 25–8 *A pollen grain begins to grow when it lands on a suitable pistil. Here you can see a growing pollen tube produced by a pollen grain from a tomato plant.*

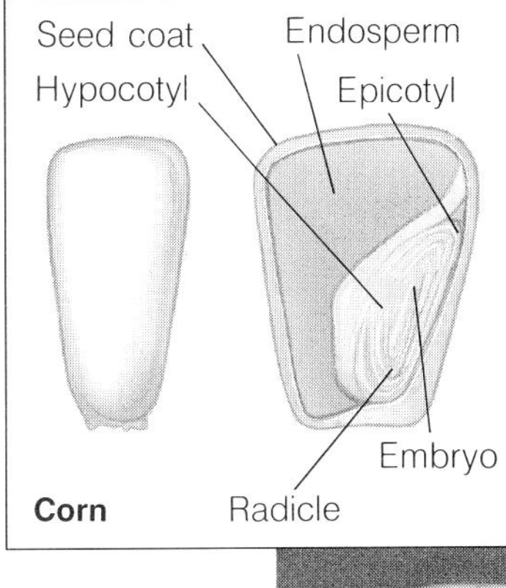

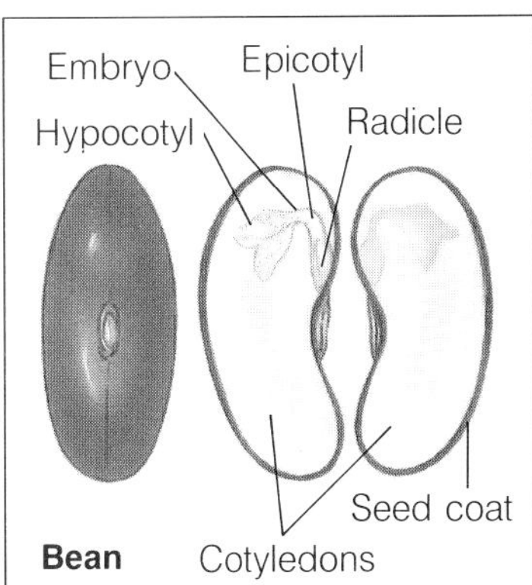

Figure 25–9 *Corn is a monocot; a bean is a dicot. In what ways are corn seeds different from bean seeds? In what ways are they similar?*

Fertilization causes rapid changes to occur in the ovule, ovary, and other structures of the flower. Parts of the ovule toughen to form a seed coat. The seed coat protects the delicate embryo and its tiny food supply. The ovary wall thickens and joins with other parts of the flower stem to become the **fruit** that holds the seeds. A fertilized flower produces hormones that induce the plant to pour energy into the developing fruits and seeds. If a flower is not fertilized, these hormones are not produced. The flower withers and falls away.

Formation of Seeds

The development of seeds was a major factor in the success of angiosperms on land. Seeds provide nourishment and protection for delicate embryos. Although different plants produce seeds with different structures, most of the essential parts of all seeds are alike.

Angiosperm seeds have either one or two seed leaves called **cotyledons**. Cotyledons contain stored food that is used when a seed germinates, or begins to grow. Monocots, such as corn, have one cotyledon. Dicots, such as beans, have two.

The various parts of the embryo are named according to their point of attachment to the cotyledon or cotyledons. The length of the stem above the cotyledon(s) is called the **epicotyl** (*epi-* means above or on top of). The epicotyl develops into the plant's stem. At the tip of the epicotyl is the tissue that will become the apical meristem. The length of the stem below the cotyledon(s) is called the **hypocotyl** (*hypo-* means below). At the very base of the hypocotyl is a region called the **radicle**, which contains the apical meristem of the root. The radicle will become the primary root of the plant.

In many plants the food stored in the endosperm is almost completely used up by the time the seed is mature. In these seeds the food used by the embryo during germination is stored in large cotyledons. The two halves of a bean, for example, are actually two cotyledons. The small embryo plant can be observed if these two bean-shaped cotyledons are split open. In other plants, such as corn and coconuts, much endosperm remains in the mature seed. In fact, the bulk of the space in these seeds is taken up by endosperm. In a coconut, the "milk" is liquid endosperm and the "meat" is solid endosperm. In seeds that retain a great deal of endosperm, the cotyledons look more like typical leaves produced by the plant.

Seed coats can be either thin and fragile or thick and woody. Thick seed coats protect seeds from dryness, salt water, and other adverse environmental conditions. As you learned in Chapter 22, many seeds are eaten by animals when the attractive fruits that contain them are eaten. Tough seed coats protect these seeds from the animal's teeth as well as from the strong chemicals present in its digestive system. These seeds often germinate after they are eliminated by the animal along with digestive wastes. In fact, the digestive wastes provide a bit of natural fertilizer that the plant can use as it begins to grow. Passing through an animal's digestive system provides an additional benefit to the seeds. The seeds usually pass out of the animal some distance away from where the fruit was eaten. This lessens competition for available food and water between the adult plant and its seeds. The animal also distributes seeds in other areas that may provide a suitable environment for the seeds' survival.

25–1 SECTION REVIEW

1. What is the function of the male cone in gymnosperms? The female cone?
2. Give the location and function of the following flower parts: sepals, petals, stigma, anther, ovary.
3. What is pollination? What are two types?
4. Describe the parts of a typical seed.
5. How does the formation of seeds contribute to the survival of a plant species?

Section Objectives

- Explain the germination of seeds.
- Discuss dormancy in seeds.

25–2 Seed Development

One of the rites of spring for many people is planting a garden. During cold winter days, often when the soil is frozen beneath one's feet, avid gardeners begin to thumb through seed catalogues. The written descriptions and the colorful photographs that accompany them are a gardener's dream. Based on the promises offered by prose and pictures, gardeners eagerly order seeds. Rarely are they disappointed. Within a period of time—a period that always seems much too long—tiny plants begin to appear above the surface of the ground.

Germination

When seeds germinate, they absorb water. The absorbed water causes the endosperm and cotyledons to swell, cracking open the seed coat. Through the cracked seed coat, the radicle emerges and grows into the primary root.

In most monocots the single cotyledon remains within the seed. The growing shoot emerges protected by a sheath. In some dicots the hypocotyl starts growing soon after the primary root starts growing. The hypocotyl forms an arch that pushes up through the soil. The cells in the hypocotyl are much tougher than the cells in the fragile apical meristem, and thus they can scrape against rocks and sand grains without being badly damaged. Once the arch breaks out of the soil and into the sunlight, the hypocotyl straightens and the cotyledons and epicotyl are pulled into the sunlight.

In other dicots the cotyledons remain in the soil. In these plants the epicotyl grows out of the ground, carrying the apical meristem with it. The epicotyl grows in an arch that protects the delicate shoot tip until it breaks through the surface of the soil. See Figure 25-10.

Figure 25-10 *Beneath the ground, this bean seed absorbed a great deal of water from the soil—an important reason to water seeds well when you plant them. Eventually the seed pushed its way above the ground. Now the tiny leaves of the bean plant, using the energy of sunlight, can make their own food.*

Seed Dormancy

Some seeds germinate so rapidly that they are practically instant plants. Bean seeds are a good example. With proper amounts of water and warmth, a newly planted mature bean seed rapidly develops into a bean plant. But many seeds will not grow when they first mature. Instead, these seeds enter a period of **dormancy**, a period during which the embryo is alive but not growing. The length of dormancy varies in different plant species. A number of environmental factors can cause a seed to end dormancy and germinate.

Seed dormancy serves several purposes for plants. The seeds of a coconut palm have a long dormant period. During

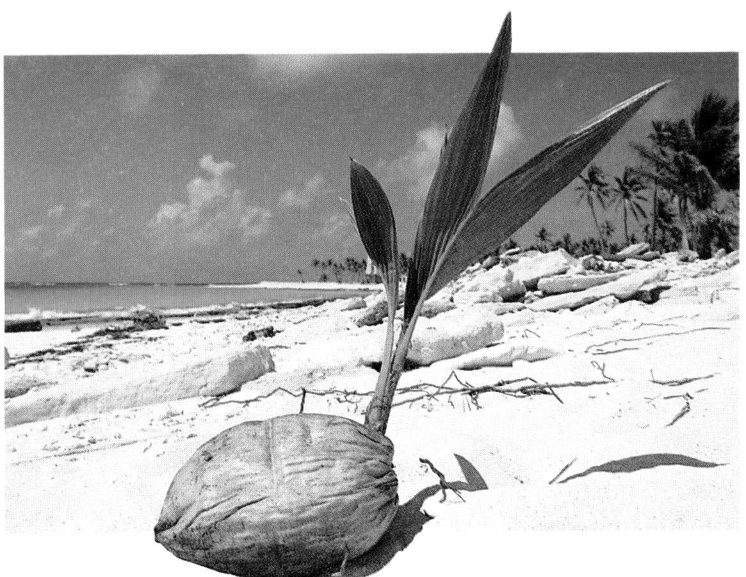

Figure 25-11 *This coconut was carried on ocean currents far from its parent tree. During its voyage, the seed remained dormant. Now, after being swept by waves onto a warm beach, it begins to grow.*

dormancy coconuts can float across the sea for weeks or even months until they wash ashore on a beach far from the parent plant. Thus coconuts can be dispersed by water and waves to new areas where, if conditions are suitable, the coconuts may survive and grow. Another important purpose of dormancy is to allow seeds to wait to germinate until environmental conditions support plant growth. For example, it is best if seeds of many temperate plants do not germinate during the hot summer or the cold winter. During these periods, extremes of temperature would make it impossible for fragile seedlings to survive. Thus these seeds remain dormant during the winter and germinate in the spring, when conditions are best for growth. The long period of cold temperatures during which the seeds are dormant is required before growth can begin.

Other environmental conditions can end seed dormancy. Some plants, particularly several species of pine, would not survive if they began growing on the dark forest floor shaded by mature pines. But when a forest fire kills mature trees, some of these seeds not only survive but are stimulated by the heat to grow! These seeds then germinate in a light-filled environment cleared of competition by the fire.

25–2 SECTION REVIEW

1. What happens when a seed germinates?
2. Why do some seeds remain dormant before they germinate?
3. Why is it advantageous for some seeds to undergo a period of cold temperatures before they germinate?
4. How does seed dormancy allow you to order packets of seeds through the mail?

Section Objectives

- Define vegetative reproduction.
- Describe how plants are reproduced by cuttings, layering, and grafting.

25–3 Vegetative Reproduction

Flowering plants, both wild and cultivated, reproduce sexually when they produce flowers and seeds. Sexual reproduction contributes to the genetic diversity of the species. Many kinds of flowering plants also reproduce asexually through vegetative reproduction. **Vegetative reproduction enables a plant that is well adapted to a particular environment to produce many offspring genetically identical to itself.**

Vegetative Reproduction in Nature

It is not uncommon for many angiosperms to produce new plants by reproducing asexually. Strawberries, for example, send out long trailing stems called stolons that produce roots when they touch the ground. Bamboo plants grow long underground stems that can send up new shoots in several places. In fact, bamboo forests that cover huge areas are often the descendants of one bamboo plant that has, over a long time period, reproduced in this way.

Several species of angiosperms produce tiny plants on their leaves or along their stems. If the parent plant is knocked over, these plantlets can grow into new plants. They can also grow into new plants if they drop off the parent plant. Plants that reproduce in this way include *Tolmeia*, the "piggyback plant" often grown as a houseplant, and the kalanchoe, shown in Figure 25–12. New plants can also grow from the leaves of a parent plant if the leaves fall to the ground under conditions that allow them to root. The African violet and certain species of begonia often grow from leaves.

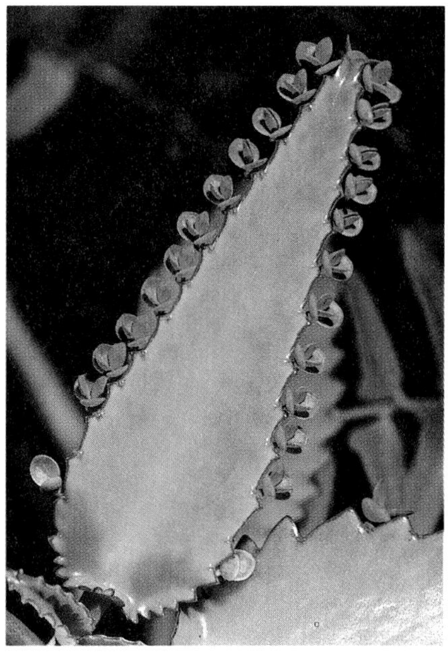

Figure 25–12 *Although it is a flowering plant and can produce seeds, this kalanchoe also produces small plants along the edges of its leaves.*

Artificial Vegetative Reproduction

Sometimes the characteristics of a particular plant are so attractive or beneficial that horticulturists want to make many exact copies of the plant. But the growers also want to avoid the variation that would result if the plant was reproduced sexually by seeds. In addition, new varieties of some plants, such as grapefruits and navel oranges, do not produce seeds. In either of these cases, horticulturists must reproduce these plants asexually by vegetative reproduction.

CUTTINGS One of the simplest ways to reproduce plants vegetatively is by cuttings. A grower "cuts" a length of stem that includes a number of lateral buds from the plant. That stem is then partially buried in soil or in a special rooting mixture. Some common plants, such as coleus, root so easily that no other treatment is necessary. The cuttings of many woody plants, however, do not develop roots easily. To help cuttings of these plants form roots, growers use mixtures of plant hormones called rooting powders. These powders contain auxins and other compounds that stimulate root growth.

Figure 25–13 *Some plants can be reproduced when a piece of stem, called a cutting, is placed in water. This begonia cutting is already growing tiny roots at the base of the stem.*

LAYERING Layering is used with plants that take a long time to root as cuttings. The stem is cut partway through and the cut area is dusted with rooting powder. Then the stem is either wrapped in moistened moss or bent to the ground and buried. In this way, the treated stem receives water and nutrients from the parent plant while it develops its own roots. When rooting is completed, the rooted stem is separated from the parent plant and allowed to grow on its own. Several common houseplants, such as rubber plants, are often reproduced by layering.

GRAFTING AND BUDDING Grafting and budding are used to reproduce seedless plants and varieties of woody

Figure 25–14 *Plants can be grafted onto other plants. First, a small branch is inserted into the stem of the other plant (top). In making a graft, it is important that the cambium layers of the two pieces align properly (center). Then the two pieces are wrapped to hold them in position until they begin to grow together (bottom).*

plants that do not produce strong root systems. In both grafting and budding, new plants are grown on plants that have strong root systems. To do this, a piece of stem or a lateral bud is cut from the parent plant and attached to another plant. The cut piece is called the **scion**, and the plant to which it is attached is called the **stock**. When stems are used as scions, the process is called grafting. When buds are used as scions, the process is called bud grafting or budding.

Grafting usually works best when plants are dormant because the wounds created can heal before new growth starts. In all cases, grafts are successful only if the vascular cambiums of scion and stock are firmly connected to each other.

SCIENCE, TECHNOLOGY, AND SOCIETY

APPLICATION

Cloning Plants

It is possible to produce large numbers of identical plants rapidly through a process called cloning. In the first step of the cloning process, a branch containing meristematic tissue is sterilized. Then, under sterile conditions, a portion of the meristem is removed and placed into a culture medium that contains essential plant nutrients. The growth of the meristematic tissue can be controlled by the careful addition of selected plant hormones to the culture medium.

In the next step, the tissue is encouraged to produce a mass of meristematic cells. These meristematic cells can be split apart by shaking or cutting. Each mass of cells will continue to grow as long as conditions are suitable.

Eventually auxins and cytokinins are added to induce the mass of meristematic cells to begin to develop other plant tissues. Soon, tiny plantlets begin to form. These plantlets are grown in a nutrient medium for a time and then carefully planted in soil. In this manner, thousands upon thousands of genetically identical plants can be produced. Plants cloned in this way are used both in agriculture and in research laboratories.

Plants are cloned in sterile test tubes. Here, small clumps of cells have been removed from (left to right) a sundew, Venus' flytrap, fern, African violet, and kalanchoe. The clumps of cells have been placed into individual test tubes. Each clump of cells will produce plants genetically identical to the plants from which they were removed.

25–3 SECTION REVIEW

1. Describe two ways plants reproduce vegetatively in nature.
2. What is a cutting? How do gardeners use cuttings to increase the number of their plants?
3. Compare grafting and budding.
4. You want to reproduce one of your houseplants to give to your friend. This plant, however, does not make roots easily. How could you reproduce this plant?

LABORATORY INVESTIGATION

COMPARING DIFFERENT TYPES OF FLOWERS

PROBLEM

What kinds of adaptations for reproduction do different kinds of flowers show?

MATERIALS *(per group)*

tulip blossom	3 glass slides
daisy blossom	2 coverslips
scalpel	medicine dropper
scissors	hand lens
forceps	microscope

PROCEDURE 

1. Examine a tulip blossom. Count the number of petals. Look inside the blossom. The structure in the center of the flower is the pistil. Find the stamens and count them.
2. On a separate sheet of paper, draw the tulip flower. Label the parts.
3. Peel the petals off the tulip blossom. Carefully remove the stamens. Tap one of the stamens on a clean glass slide. Notice what happens.
4. Put the remainder of the flower down on a clean glass slide. Using a scalpel, cut across the ovary at the base of the pistil about one fourth of the way up from the bottom. **CAUTION:** *The scalpel is very sharp, so use care. Always cut away from you.* Discard the top part of the pistil.
5. With the cut portion of the pistil still on the glass slide, shave off several thin cross sections by pressing straight down with the scalpel as close as you can to the cut edge of the pistil. Lay the cross sections flat on the slide. With the medicine dropper, place a drop of water over each cross section. Cover the cross sections with a coverslip.
6. Examine the cross sections of the pistil under the low-power lens of the microscope.
7. Examine a daisy blossom. Try to locate the same structures you found in the tulip. The yellow central portion of a daisy is called a disk. Petallike structures surround the disk.
8. A daisy is a composite flower, which means it is made up of many tiny separate flowers. Each of the petallike structures is a single-ray flower. Each ray flower has a cup-shaped bottom with a tiny pistil poking up from it.
9. Look closely at the disk of the daisy. It, too, is composed of many separate flowers. Rub your thumb over the center of the disk to remove a few disk flowers. Examine a single disk flower with a hand lens. Use a forceps to remove the pistil. Use the scissors to cut straight down through the disk flower to open up the flower.
10. Put the open disk flower on a clean glass slide. Place a drop of water over the flower. Cover the flower with a coverslip.
11. Examine the slide under the low-power lens of the microscope. Draw your observations.

OBSERVATIONS

1. How many petals and stamens does a tulip have?
2. What happens when you tap a tulip stamen on a clean glass slide?
3. What did you observe inside the pistil of a tulip flower?
4. Describe the appearance of a daisy flower and the individual flowers that compose it.

ANALYSIS AND CONCLUSIONS

1. Based on your observations, is the tulip a monocot or a dicot? Explain your answer.
2. What is the function of a flower? What structures in a flower carry out this function?
3. Despite their differences in form, how are a tulip and a daisy suited to their function?

STUDENT STUDY GUIDE

SUMMARIZING THE CONCEPTS

The key concepts in each section of this chapter are listed below to help you review the chapter content. Make sure you understand each concept and its relationship to other concepts and to the theme of this chapter.

25–1 Cones and Flowers as Reproductive Organs

- The sporophyte generation in seed plants is most obvious; the gametophyte generation is small and often hidden.
- Gymnosperms make seeds in special structures called cones. Male cones produce pollen; female cones produce ovules. It is within the female cones that seeds develop.
- The parts of a flower have different forms and functions. The anthers produce pollen. The pistil consists of an ovary and the style.
- Seeds are an important reason for the survival of gymnosperms and angiosperms in land environments. They enable plants to be dispersed into different environments and to survive environmental conditions that would be difficult for adult plants.

25–2 Seed Development

- In flowers, sexual reproduction exchanges genetic material and increases variability in offspring. Asexual reproduction increases the number of plants, but the newly formed plants are genetically identical.

25–3 Vegetative Reproduction

- Many plants reproduce asexually. Horticulturists often produce new plants using asexual methods of reproduction.

REVIEWING KEY TERMS

Vocabulary terms are important to your understanding of biology. The key terms listed below are those you should be especially familiar with. Review these terms and their meanings. Then use each term in a complete sentence. If you are not sure of a term's meaning, return to the appropriate section and review its definition.

25–1 Cones and Flowers as Reproductive Organs

sepal
calyx
petal
corolla
stamen
filament
anther
carpel
pistil
ovary
style
stigma
ovule
embryo sac
polar nuclei
egg nucleus
pollen chamber
tube nucleus
generative nucleus
pollination
self-pollination
cross-pollination
pollen tube
sperm nuclei
double fertilization
endosperm
fruit
cotyledon
epicotyl
hypocotyl
radicle

25–2 Seed Development

dormancy

25–3 Vegetative Reproduction

scion
stock

CHAPTER REVIEW

CONTENT REVIEW

Multiple Choice

Choose the letter of the answer that best completes each statement.

1. The part of the flower that receives pollen is the
a. stigma. c. style.
b. ovary. d. scion.

2. The seed leaves in angiosperms are also called
a. roots. c. stigmas.
b. cotyledons. d. epicotyls.

3. The thickened part of the ovary wall that holds the seeds is called the
a. petal. c. anther.
b. fruit. d. cone.

4. The parts of a flower that are most involved with attracting pollinators are the
a. pistils. c. anthers.
b. seeds. d. petals.

5. The part of the embryo that develops into a root is the
a. radicle. c. epicotyl.
b. hypocotyl. d. endosperm.

6. One way to reproduce plants asexually is by
a. planting seeds. c. cross-pollination.
b. making cuttings. d. self-pollination.

7. In gymnosperms, seeds are produced in
a. flowers. c. pollen.
b. male cones. d. female cones.

8. The part of a seed that protects the seed from dryness, salt water, and other adverse environmental conditions is called the
a. seed coat. c. endosperm.
b. radicle. d. sepal.

True or False

Determine whether each statement is true or false. If it is true, write "true." If it is false, change the underlined word or words to make the statement true.

1. Gymnosperms produce seeds in flowers.
2. Cuttings are a way to reproduce plants sexually.
3. The sporophyte generation in seed plants is large and obvious.
4. Pollen is produced in the stigma.
5. The petals protect the developing flower.
6. All of a flower's parts are made up of modified leaves.
7. A corn silk is a long style.
8. The plant to which a graft is attached is called a stigma.

Word Relationships

An analogy is a relationship between two pairs of words or phrases generally written in the following manner: a:b::c:d. The symbol : is read "is to," and the symbol :: is read "as." For example, cat:animal::rose:plant is read "cat is to animal as rose is to plant."

In the analogies that follow, a word or phrase is missing. Complete each analogy by providing the missing word or phrase.

1. anther:pollen::pistil: ______________
2. asexual reproduction:graft::sexual reproduction: ______________
3. stamens:calyx::petals: ______________
4. radicle:root::epicotyl: ______________

CONCEPT MASTERY

Use your understanding of the concepts developed in the chapter to answer each of the following in a brief paragraph.

1. Describe one way a plant can be reproduced asexually.
2. Give the functions of the following plant parts: petals, pistil, stigma, sepals, anther.
3. Plants need light to make food. How do seeds planted beneath the ground grow?
4. How does cross-pollination help plants survive in many different environments?
5. What is a pollen tube? How is a pollen tube important in the formation of seeds?
6. In what two ways do seeds help a plant species survive?
7. What is double fertilization?
8. What is a fruit? Which of the following are fruits: apple, tomato, potato, string bean?

CRITICAL AND CREATIVE THINKING

Discuss each of the following in a brief paragraph.

1. **Applying concepts** Suppose you find a plant growing on a mountain. You find that this plant can only reproduce vegetatively. What disadvantage does this method of reproduction have to the plant?
2. **Relating concepts** You observe that all the flowers on a garden plant lack anthers. On another plant of the same species, you observe that all the flowers have anthers. What conclusion can you make about the plants' method of sexual reproduction? Does this method offer any advantages?
3. **Designing an experiment** A friend suggests that seeds do not need cotyledons to grow. You argue that cotyledons are important to seeds. Design an experiment that shows the effect on seed growth of removing cotyledons.
4. **Interpreting photographs** Identify the parts of the flower that are shown in this photograph. Give the function of each part.

5. **Applying concepts** Gardeners must freeze and thaw the seeds of some plants before the seeds will germinate. Why is this done? What does freezing and thawing do for a plant?
6. **Applying concepts** Many plants have small flowers, often green in color, that are hard to see. Ragweed, a common wild plant, is an example. These plants are often pollinated by wind, not by animals. How does the color and shape of the plants' flowers explain its method of pollination?
7. **Making comparisons** Compare sexual reproduction in gymnosperms with sexual reproduction in angiosperms.
8. **Using the writing process** Some cities give unused land to community groups to use as a garden. People plant seeds and produce food crops and flowers in the small plots of ground allocated to them. Write a proposal to your city or town government supporting this use of unused city land. Detail the benefits to the community.

Farmer

Farmers produce most of the food we eat every day. Farmers often use complex equipment and breeding techniques to develop better crops and livestock and improve the efficiency of agricultural production.

There are no specific educational requirements to become a farmer, but a successful farmer should have a knowledge of soil preparation and cultivation, disease control, and machinery maintenance.

For information on farming write to the United States Department of Agriculture, Washington, DC 20250.

Landscape Architect

Landscape architects plan and design outdoor areas such as those around houses, schools, and offices. They analyze the physical features of the land and attempt to make the best use of those features without endangering the natural environment.

Landscape architects combine the skills of scientists, engineers, and architects as they study the land and draw detailed plans for its use.

Landscape architects must have a Bachelor's degree in landscape architecture. A license is also required in some states.

For more information on this career write to the American Society of Landscape Architects, 4401 Connecticut Ave., NW, Washington, DC 20008.

Plant Pathologist

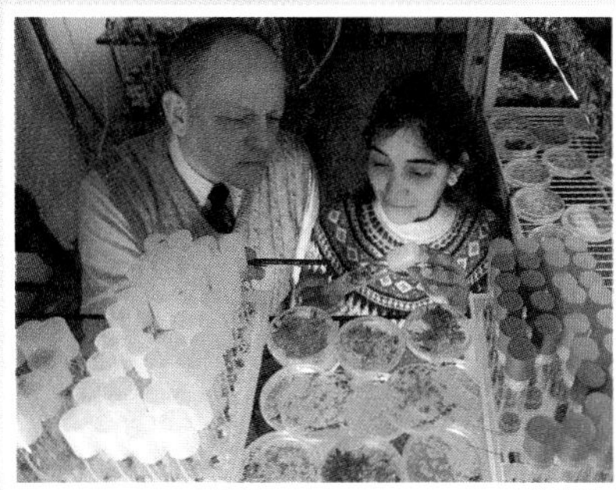

Plant pathologists research diseases in plants. They attempt to identify the symptoms of different diseases, determine their causes, and develop ways to control these diseases. Plant pathologists also try to predict disease outbreaks by studying how different soils, climates, and geographical locations affect the spread of plant diseases.

Plant pathologists must complete degree programs beyond the college level.

For more information write to the American Society of Plant Physiologists, 15501 Monona Dr., Rockville, MD 20855.

HOW TO SELECT COMPANIES TO CONTACT

When searching for a job, you will probably want to send your résumé to a large number of companies. Unless you have specific employers in mind, you may find it rather confusing to choose those companies. However, there are publications in your school or community library that will be of help to you. These publications list major employers—either alphabetically, by industry, or by geographical location. They also give a brief description of the company and list the major positions or careers that are available at that company. Two such publications are The National Job Bank *and* Dun's Employment Opportunity Directory.

FROM THE AUTHORS

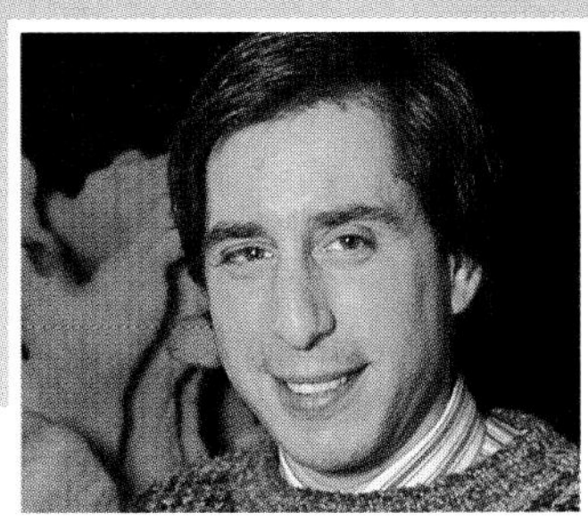

I have finished this unit during March, a special time of year for those of us who like plants. On my windowsills, houseplants that did nothing all winter are flowering. Around the house, seeds I planted weeks ago are germinating. Some sprouted quickly and are crowding each other, ready for transplanting into larger pots. Others, which sprouted from seeds as fine as dust, are almost too small to see without a magnifying glass. Still others, which need a cold period to sprout, are ready to move from my refrigerator to the grow-lights in my office. All of them bring alive for me the wonder of plant adaptations to life in different environments. And as I look from the green on my windowsills to the gray winter outside, I think of how dull and dreary the world would be without plants.

Joe Levine

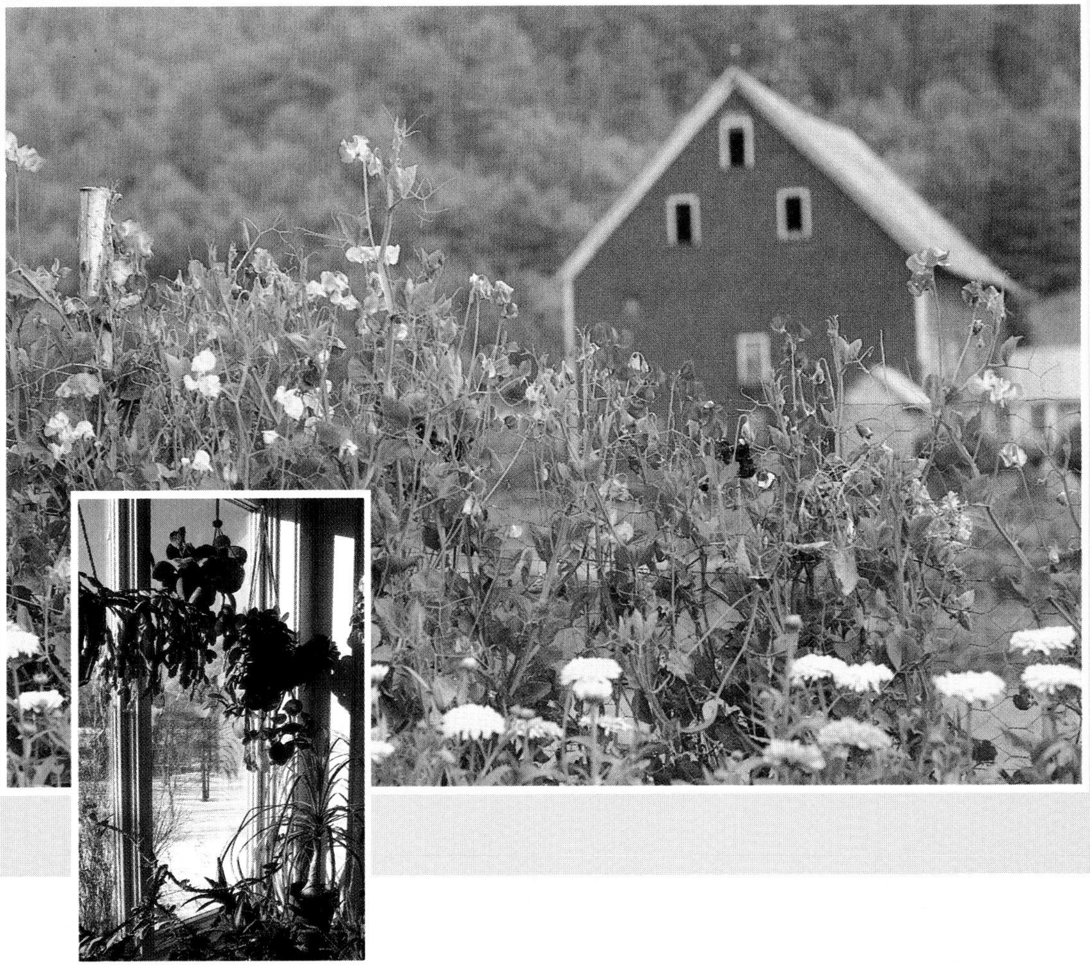

UNIT 7

Life on Earth: Invertebrate Animals

Smaller than the head of a pin, a tardigrade (inset) waddles on its eight stubby legs and clawed feet. Although commonly known as water bears, most tardigrades live on the moist surfaces of mosses and lichens and not in bodies of water. When conditions become adverse, tardigrades pull in their legs, lose nearly all the water in their body, and enter a dormant state. In this state—which can last up to seven years—tardigrades are able to survive conditions that would kill almost all other living things! A few drops of water are all that is needed to revive the shriveled, apparently lifeless tardigrade once conditions again become favorable.

Tardigrades are just one example of invertebrates, or animals without backbones. Invertebrates range in size from creatures even smaller than tardigrades to marine worms several centimeters long, such as the one shown here, to squids many meters long. They vary in form, color, and habits as much as they do in size. In their incredible diversity, invertebrates provide an endless source of amusement, horror, beauty, and wonder.

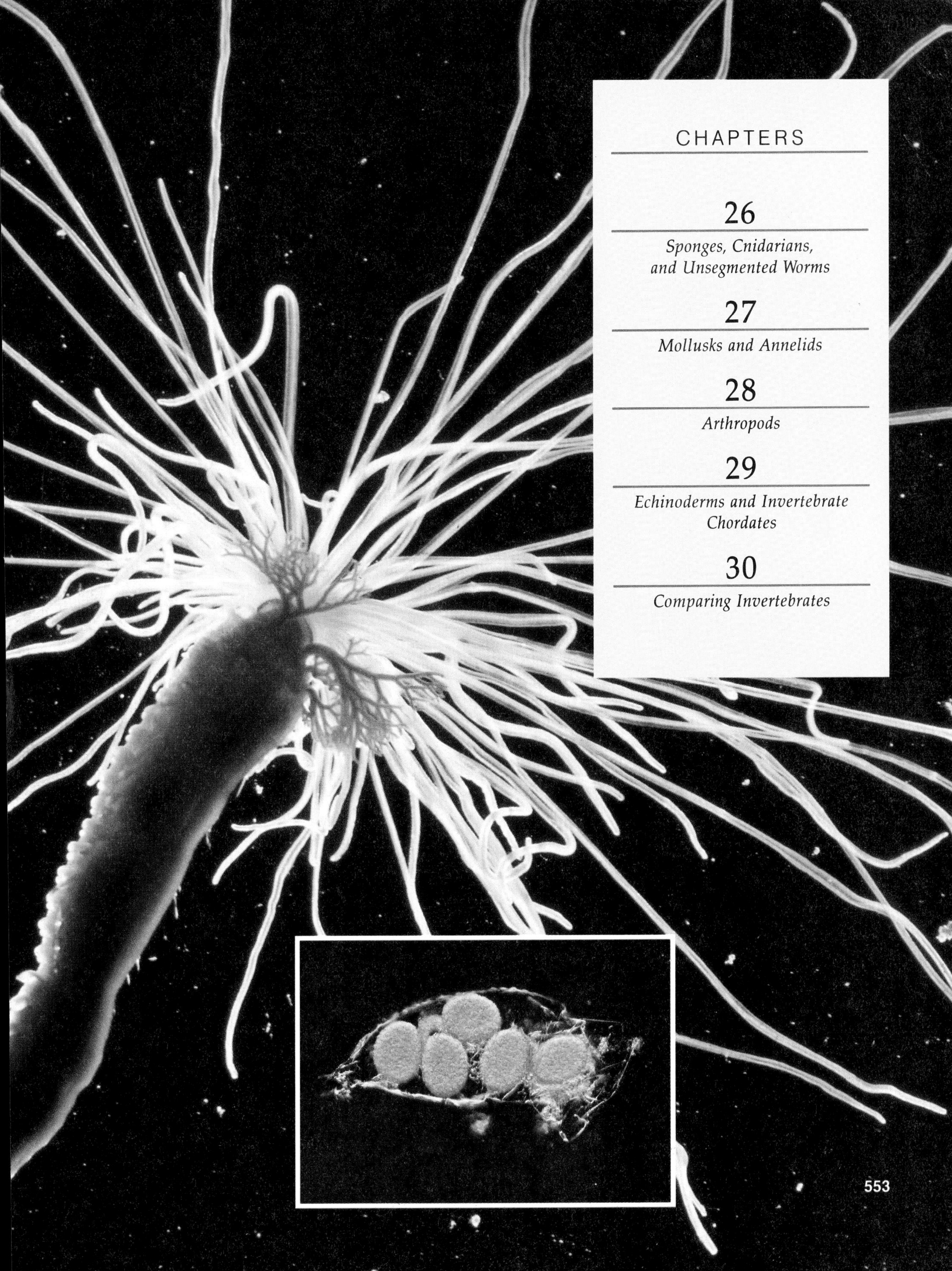

CHAPTERS

CHAPTER 26

Sponges, Cnidarians, and Unsegmented Worms

Sponges, such as the yellow tube sponge and red bath sponge shown here, are the simplest type of animals. Although flatworms (inset) are the simplest animals that have bilateral symmetry, they are much more complex than sponges.

The world around us swarms with an incredible variety of animals, as you probably realize. What you may not be aware of, however, is that most animal species are not the birds and mammals that are most familiar to us. The vast majority are much smaller and far stranger in appearance. Some are as strange as anything you've ever seen in a science fiction movie. Many of them are also much more important than birds or mammals in the grand scheme of life on Earth. What are these animals? What do they look like and where are they found? How do they perform the essential functions common to all living things? How do they fit into the world? In this chapter we shall begin our exploration of the world of animals by first considering those animals without backbones—the invertebrates.

CHAPTER OUTLINE

26–1 Introduction to the Animal Kingdom

Section Objectives

- List the essential functions of animal life.
- Describe some trends in animal evolution.

Of all the kingdoms of organisms, the animal kingdom is the most diverse in form. Some animals have forms that are comfortingly familiar. Others resemble creatures from a nightmare or a horror movie. Some animals are so small that they can live inside our bodies. Others are many meters long and live in the depths of the sea. Animals can be black, white, beautifully colored, or nearly transparent. Animals walk, swim, crawl, burrow, and fly all around us. In every case, each animal performs the essential functions of life in its own special way.

You will soon become acquainted with several major divisions in the animal kingdom. One division that we refer to often is that between **vertebrates** and **invertebrates**. Vertebrates, such as humans, have a backbone, or vertebral column. Invertebrates, the subjects of this unit, have no backbone.

What Is an Animal?

As different as they are, all animals share certain basic characteristics. Animals are heterotrophs, which means that they do not make their own food. Instead, they obtain the nutrients and energy they need by feeding on organic compounds that have been made by other organisms. Animals are multicellular, which means that their bodies are composed of more than one cell. And animal cells are eukaryotic—they contain a nucleus and membrane-enclosed organelles. Unlike plant cells or fungus cells, animal cells do not have cell walls. **We can thus define an animal as a multicellular eukaryotic heterotroph whose cells lack cell walls.**

Figure 26–1 *A yak is a vertebrate (left). Its thick, shaggy coat helps it survive the cold winters in central Asia and Tibet, where it makes its home. A hickory horned devil is an invertebrate (right). Despite its frightening appearance, this caterpillar is quite harmless.*

Figure 26–2 Animals get the nutrients and energy they need by eating organic compounds that have been made by other organisms. The squirrel is munching on a hazelnut, and the crayfish is nibbling on a worm.

Cell Specialization and Division of Labor

The bodies of animals contain many types of specialized cells. Each specialized cell has a shape, physical structure, and chemical composition that make it uniquely suited to perform a particular function within a multicellular organism. For this reason, groups of specialized cells carry out different tasks for the organism—a phenomenon known as **division of labor**.

You may wonder what advantage there is in dividing up different tasks among specialized cells. After all, monerans and protists do just fine as single cells! But large numbers of cells growing together simply cannot function the way single cells do. Recall from Chapter 8 that cells require a certain amount of surface area to take in food and oxygen and remove wastes. Cells that grow together have little, if any, of their surface exposed to the environment. They would soon be starved for food and oxygen and smothered in carbon dioxide and other wastes if there were no efficient systems to carry out essential functions such as feeding, respiration, and elimination of wastes. In multicellular organisms, efficient systems require specialization. Specialized cells can perform their tasks more efficiently than unspecialized cells.

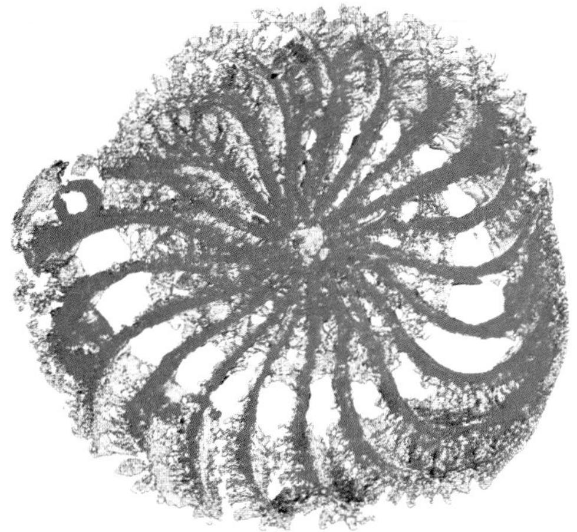

Figure 26–3 Unicellular organisms, such as this foraminifer, do not have division of labor. They perform all life functions with only their single cell.

What Animals Must Do to Survive

In order to survive, animals must be able to perform a number of essential functions. For each animal group we study in the next several chapters, we shall examine these functions and describe the cells, tissues, organs, and organ systems that perform them. To help you make a checklist of those functions, we shall briefly describe them here.

FEEDING Animals have evolved a variety of ways to feed. **Herbivores**, or animals that eat plants, may feed on roots, stems, leaves, flowers, or fruits. Some herbivores even feed on the nutrient-rich fluids in plant vascular tissues. **Carnivores**, or

organisms that eat animals, may also feed on any part of their prey—fat, muscle, bone marrow, or even blood. **Parasites** live and feed either inside or attached to outer surfaces of other organisms, thereby doing harm to their hosts. Many aquatic animals, called **filter feeders**, strain tiny floating plants and animals from the water around them. And many animals feed not on living organisms but on tiny bits of decaying plants and animals called detritus (dee-TRIGHT-uhs). **Detritus feeders** are easy to overlook, but they are vitally important members of the living world.

Figure 26–4 *Animals have many different modes of feeding. The puffin (left), which is holding a meal of sand eels in its beak, is a carnivore. The white structures on the back of the caterpillar (right) are cocoons of parasites that have devoured the insides of their host. Sea cucumbers (bottom, right) are detritus feeders.*

RESPIRATION As you learned in Chapter 6, living cells consume oxygen and give off carbon dioxide in the process of cellular respiration. Thus entire animals must respire, or breathe, in order to take in and give off these gases. Small animals that live in water or in moist soil may respire through their skin. For large active animals, however, respiration through the skin is not efficient enough. The respiratory systems these animals have evolved take many different forms in adaptations suited to different habitats.

INTERNAL TRANSPORT Some aquatic animals, such as small worms, can function without an internal transport system. But once an animal reaches a certain size, it must somehow carry oxygen, nutrients, and waste products to and from cells deep within its body. Thus many multicellular animals have evolved a circulatory system in which a pumping organ called a heart forces a fluid called blood through a series of blood vessels. You will see in the next several chapters that circulatory systems can be simple or quite complex.

EXCRETION Cellular metabolism produces chemical wastes such as ammonia that are harmful and must be eliminated. Small aquatic animals depend on diffusion to carry wastes from their tissues into the surrounding water, which then carries the wastes away. But larger animals, both in water

Figure 26–5 Sense organs, such as eyes, help animals gather information about the environment. The ghost crab uses its stalked eyes to peek from its hiding place under the sand and see if the coast is clear (top). Six of the wolf spider's eight eyes can be seen from the front (bottom). The other two are on the side of its head.

and on land, must work to remove poisonous metabolic wastes. As we study animals from worms to mammals, we shall follow the development of the excretory systems that store and dispose of these wastes.

RESPONSE Animals must keep watch on their surroundings to find food, spot predators, and identify others of their own kind. To do this, animals use specialized cells called nerve cells, which hook up together to form a nervous system. Sense organs, such as eyes and ears, gather information from the environment by responding to light, sound, temperature, and other stimuli. The brain, which is the nervous system's control center, processes the information and regulates how the animal responds. The complexity of the nervous system varies greatly in animals.

MOVEMENT Some animals are sessile, which means that they live their entire adult lives attached to one spot. But many animals are motile, which means that they move around. To move, most animals use tissues called muscles that generate force by contracting. In the most successful groups of animals, muscles work together with a skeleton, or the system of solid support in the body. Insects and their relatives wear their skeletons on the outside of their bodies. These are called exoskeletons (*exo-* means outside). Reptiles, birds, and mammals have their skeletons inside their bodies. These are called endoskeletons (*endo-* means inside). We call the combination of an animal's muscles and skeleton its musculo-skeletal system.

REPRODUCTION Animals must reproduce or their species will not survive. Because reproduction is so important, and because animals use many different methods to reproduce, we

Figure 26–6 The sea urchin larva (inset) looks and acts nothing like the adult (right). What kind of development do sea urchins undergo?

shall spend a lot of time studying reproduction. Some animals, such as jellyfish, switch back and forth between sexual and asexual reproduction. (Note that this is not the same as alternation of generations in plants, during which diploid (2N) and haploid (N) generations alternate. The sexual and asexual generations in animals are both diploid.) Many animals that reproduce sexually bear their young alive. Others lay eggs. The eggs of some species hatch into baby animals that look just like miniature adults. As they grow, these baby animals increase in size but do not change in overall form. This type of development is called direct development. In other species, eggs hatch into **larvae** (singular: larva), which are immature stages that look and act nothing like the adults. As larvae grow, they undergo a process called **metamorphosis** in which they change shape dramatically. This type of development is called indirect development.

Trends in Animal Evolution

As we explore the invertebrate phyla, keep in mind that these phyla share an evolutionary heritage. In Chapter 30, the relationships between the different phyla of invertebrates will be represented in an evolutionary tree of the animal kingdom. This evolutionary tree will show our best understanding of the way in which animal phyla are related to one another. For now, focus on tracing a few important evolutionary trends and patterns as you move from one animal phylum to the next.

The levels of organization become higher as animals become more complex in form. The essential functions of less complex animals are carried out on the cell or tissue level of organization. As you move on to more complex animals, you will observe a steady increase in the number of specialized tissues. You will also see those tissues joining together to form more and more specialized organs and organ systems.

Some of the simplest animals have radial symmetry; most complex animals have bilateral symmetry. Some of the simplest animals, such as sea anemones, have body parts that repeat around an imaginary line drawn through the center of their body. These animals exhibit **radial symmetry**. See Figure 26–7. Animals with radial symmetry never have any kind of real "head." Many of them are sessile, although some drift or move about in a more or less random pattern. Complex invertebrates and all vertebrates have body parts (at least outside body parts such as arms and legs) that repeat on either side of an imaginary line drawn down the middle of their body. One side of the body is the mirror image of the other. These animals are said to have **bilateral symmetry**. Animals with bilateral symmetry have specialized front and back ends as well as upper and lower sides. The **anterior** is the front end and the **posterior** is the back end. The **dorsal** is the upper side and the **ventral** is the lower side.

Figure 26–7 *Starfish have radial symmetry, which means that their body parts repeat around an imaginary line drawn through the center of the body.*

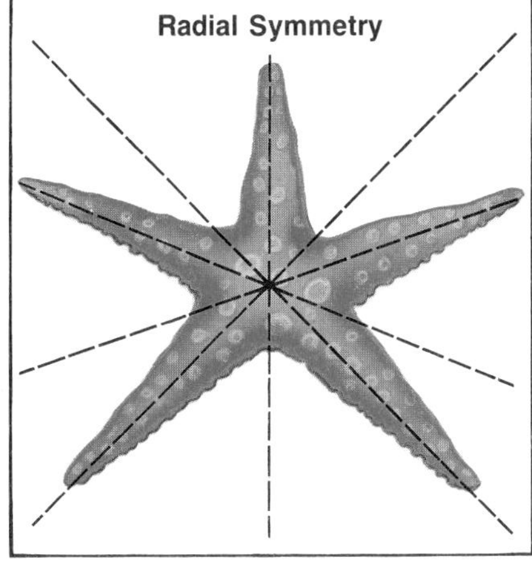

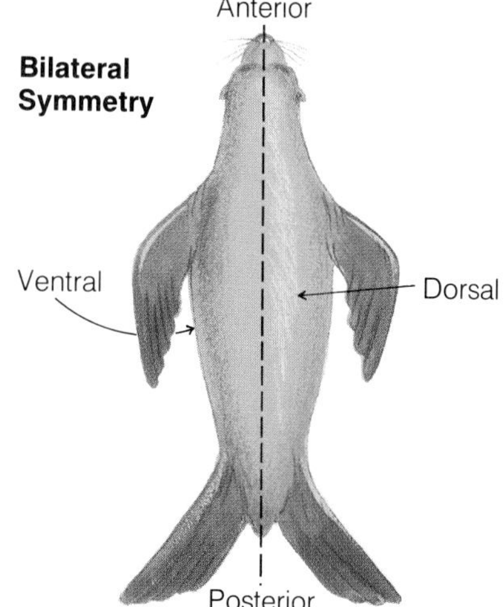

Figure 26–8 *Most of the more complex animals have bilateral symmetry, which means that the body parts repeat on either side of an imaginary line drawn down the center of the body.*

More complex animals tend to have a concentration of sense organs and nerve cells in their anterior (head) end. Because animals with bilateral symmetry usually move with their anterior end forward, this end encounters new parts of the environment first. As you might imagine, natural selection favors animals that can sense the nature of the environment into which they are moving before their entire body is exposed to the new environment. It is not wise to back up into a potentially dangerous situation! Thus sense organs tend to gather at the anterior end. As the sense organs collect up front, so do the nerve cells that process information and "decide" what the animal should do. Eventually, the anterior end is different enough from the posterior end that we call it a head. This gathering of sense organs and nerve cells into the head region is called **cephalization** (*cephalo-* means head).

Cephalization becomes more pronounced as animals become more complex. Nerve cells in the head gather into clusters that process the information gathered by the nervous system and control responses to stimuli. Small clusters of nerve cells are called **ganglia** (singular: ganglion). In the most complex animals, large numbers of nerve cells gather together to form larger structures called brains.

26–1 SECTION REVIEW

1. What is an animal? Why is it important to study animals?
2. List seven essential functions in animals. Define these functions in your own words.
3. Compare two different kinds of symmetry found in the animal kingdom.
4. Describe three basic trends in animal evolution.
5. Why are specialized cells necessary in multicellular animals?

Section Objectives

- Describe the structure of a sponge.
- Discuss how sponges perform essential functions.

26–2 Sponges

Sponges are among the most ancient of all animals that are alive today. The first sponges date back to the beginning of the Cambrian Period (about 580 million years ago), when the first traces of multicellular animals appeared in the fossil record. Most sponges live in the sea, although a few live in freshwater lakes and streams. Sponges inhabit almost all areas of the sea—from the polar regions to the tropics and from the low-tide line down into water several hundred meters deep. Sponges belong to the phylum **Porifera** (por-IHF-er-ah). This name, which literally means pore-bearers, is appropriate because sponges have tiny openings all over their body.

Sponges were once thought to be plants, which is easy to understand in light of the fact that adult sponges are sessile

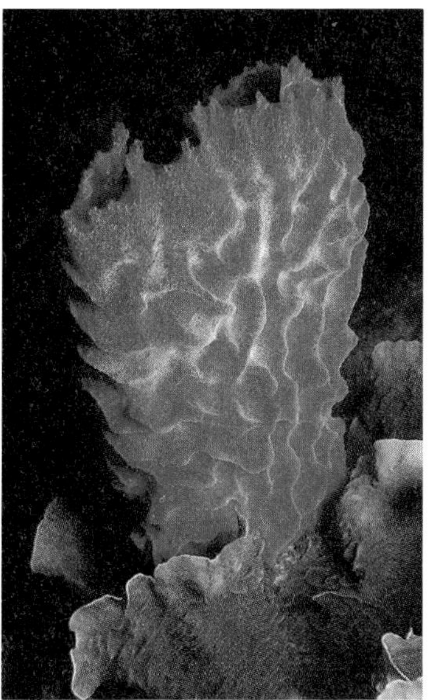

Figure 26–9 Sponges come in a wide variety of shapes, colors, and sizes. Some, such as this basket sponge (center), are larger than humans!

and show little detectable movement. As far as modern biologists are concerned, sponges are clearly multicellular animals —sponges are heterotrophic, have no cell walls, and contain several specialized cell types that live together. But sponges are very different from all other animals. **Sponges have nothing that even vaguely resembles a mouth or gut, and they have no specialized tissues or organ systems. For these reasons, most biologists believe that sponges evolved from single-celled ancestors separately from other multicellular animals.** The evolutionary line that gave rise to sponges was a dead end that produced no other groups of animals.

Form and Function in Sponges

The body plan of a typical sponge is simple. Refer to Figure 26–10 as you read about the structure of a sponge. The body of a sponge forms a wall around a central cavity. In this wall are thousands of openings, or pores. A steady current of water moves through these pores into the central cavity. This current is powered by the flagella of cells called **collar cells.** The water that gathers in the central cavity exits through a large hole called the **osculum** (AHS-kyoo-luhm). The current of water that flows through the body of a sponge delivers food and oxygen to the cells and carries away cellular waste products. The water also transports gametes or larvae out of the sponge's body.

Many sponges manufacture thin, spiny **spicules** that form the skeleton of the sponge. A special kind of cell called an **amebocyte** (ah-MEE-boh-sight) builds the spicules from either chalklike calcium carbonate ($CaCO_3$) or glasslike silica (SiO_2). These spicules interlock to form beautiful and delicate skeletons, such as the Venus' flower basket shown in Figure 26–11 on page 562. The softer but stronger sponge skeletons that we know as natural bath sponges consist of fibers of a protein called **spongin.** Some sponges have skeletons that are made up of both spongin and spicules.

Figure 26–10 The essential life functions of sponges are performed at the level of cells or tissues. There are no true organs in sponges. Each different type of cell in a sponge—epidermal cells, pore cells, collar cells, and amebocytes—performs specific functions.

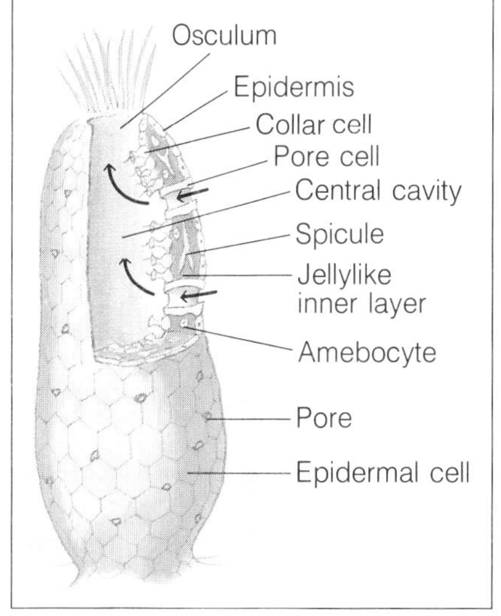

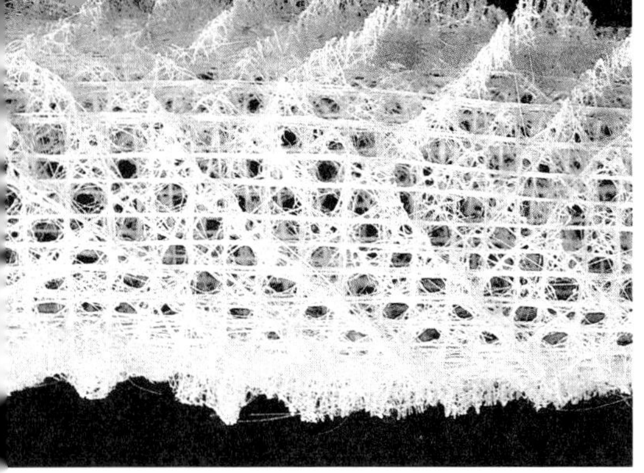

Figure 26–11 The lacy skeleton of a glass sponge consists of thousands of spicules of silica.

Sponges are filter feeders that sift microscopic particles of food from the water that passes through them. As the water moves through the sponge, tiny food particles stick to the collar cells. The trapped particles are then engulfed by the collar cells (endocytosis), where they may be digested. If the collar cells do not digest the food, they pass it on to the amebocytes. When the amebocytes are finished digesting the food particles, they wander around, delivering digested food to other parts of the sponge. Note that all digestion in sponges is intracellular; that is, it takes place inside cells.

The water flowing through a sponge simultaneously serves as its respiratory, excretory, and internal transport system. As water passes through the body wall, sponge cells remove oxygen from it and give off carbon dioxide into it. Metabolic wastes produced by cellular respiration (such as ammonia) are also released into the water, which carries them away. The amount of water that is pumped through a sponge is amazing. A sponge 10 centimeters in height and 1 centimeter in diameter was found to pump 22.5 liters of water per day through its body.

The water that flows through the body of the sponge also plays a role in sexual reproduction. Although eggs are kept inside the body wall of the sponge, sperm are released into the water flowing through the sponge and are thus carried out into the open water. If those sperm are taken in by another sponge, they are picked up by amebocytes and carried to that sponge's eggs, where fertilization occurs. The zygote (fertilized egg) that results develops into a larva that swims and can be carried by currents for a long distance before it settles down and grows into a new sponge.

Figure 26–12 In some sponges, the eggs are fertilized inside the body wall of the parent sponge (bottom). In others, the eggs are squirted into the surrounding water, where they may be fertilized (top).

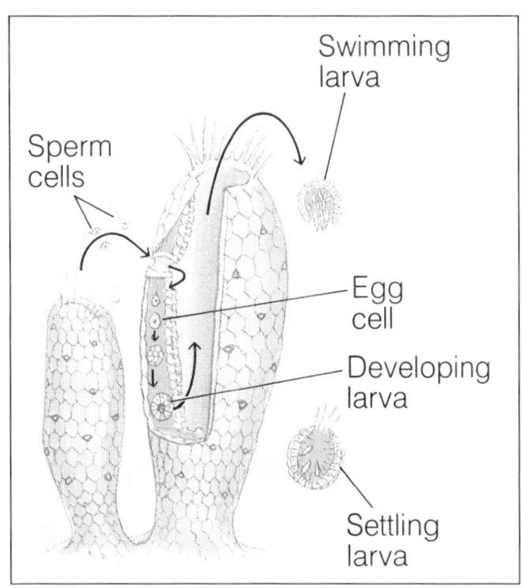

Sponges reproduce asexually as well as sexually. Faced with cold winters, some freshwater sponges produce structures called **gemmules** (JEHM-yoolz). Gemmules are sphere-shaped collections of amebocytes surrounded by a tough layer of spicules. Gemmules can survive long periods of freezing temperatures and drought, which would kill adult sponges. When conditions again become favorable, gemmules grow into new sponges. Sponges can also reproduce asexually by **budding**. In this process, part of a sponge simply falls off the parent and grows into a new sponge.

Budding is one indication of the sponges' remarkable powers of regeneration (the ability to regrow a lost or damaged part). In fact, if you were to grind up a sponge, separate its cells by passing them through a filter, and place the cells in a container of water, the cells would clump together and grow into several new sponges! It is not surprising, therefore, that sponges can easily repair torn body parts.

How Sponges Fit into the World

Sponges are often the most common forms of life in dark places such as the walls of underwater caves and on dock pilings. Many other marine animals—certain kinds of worms, shrimp, snails, and starfish, for example—live on, in, and under sponges. Sponges are also involved in symbiotic relationships with organisms that are not animals. Certain sponges contain symbiotic bacteria, blue-green bacteria, or plantlike protists. The photosynthetic symbionts provide food and oxygen to the sponge and remove wastes. Although sponges produce spicules and protective chemicals that discourage most animals from feeding on them, sponges are important parts of the diets of certain snails, starfish, and fishes.

The family of sponges known as the boring sponges are particularly important in "cleaning up" the ocean floor. Special amebocytes in these sponges release chemicals that allow the sponges to bore, or drill, tunnels through old shells and pieces of coral. These tunnels weaken the shells and coral and thus help break them down.

Since the time of the Greeks and Romans, humans have used the dried and cleaned bodies of some sponges in bathing. Most sponges you see in supermarkets today are artificial, but natural bath sponges are still available. Recently, scientists have found uses for parts of the sponge other than its skeleton. In a series of exciting new developments, scientists are learning to use several chemicals manufactured by sponges.

Figure 26–13 *Since ancient times, the soft skeletons of certain types of sponges have been used by humans for bathing.*

Because sponges cannot move, they must protect themselves from their enemies in other ways. Bacteria, algal spores, and many tiny organisms are constantly looking for surfaces on which to settle. To protect themselves from being overgrown by these organisms, sponges manufacture numerous compounds that are toxic to such organisms. These chemicals also discourage many animals from chewing on sponges. Researchers have found that many of these chemicals are powerful antibiotics that can be used to fight bacteria and fungi that cause disease. Other sponge chemicals act against viruses almost as well as antibiotics fight bacteria. One compound taken from a Caribbean sponge may be useful against leukemia and herpes viruses. Another may help fight certain forms of arthritis. Still other sponge chemicals may be effective against the bacteria that cause strep throat and those that become resistant to penicillin. Although most of these drugs are still in the experimental stage, scientists hope that they will soon be ready for human use.

26–2 SECTION REVIEW

1. How do sponges respire, catch their food, and eliminate their waste products?
2. How are sponges proving useful to medical science?
3. Why are sponges thought to be an evolutionary dead end?

Section Objectives

- Describe the structure of a cnidarian.
- Discuss how cnidarians perform essential functions.
- Name and give examples of the three classes of cnidarians.

26–3 Cnidarians

The phylum **Cnidaria** (nigh-DAIR-ee-ah) includes many animals with brilliant colors and unusual shapes. Delicate jellyfish float in ocean currents. Brightly colored sea anemones cling to rocks, looking more like underwater flowers than animals. These beautiful and fascinating animals are found all over the world, but most species live only in the sea.

What Is a Cnidarian?

Cnidarians are soft-bodied animals with stinging tentacles arranged in circles around their mouth. Some cnidarians live as single individuals. Others live as groups of dozens or even thousands of individuals connected into a colony. All cnidarians exhibit radial symmetry and have specialized cells and tissues. Many cnidarians have life cycles that include two different-looking stages, the sessile flowerlike **polyp** (PAH-lihp) and the motile bell-shaped **medusa** (meh-DOO-sah).

The body plans of a typical cnidarian polyp and a medusa are shown in Figure 26–15. As you can see, both polyps and medusae have a body wall that surrounds an internal space called the **gastrovascular cavity**. It is in the gastrovascular cavity that digestion takes place. The body wall consists of three layers: epidermis, mesoglea, and gastroderm. The epidermis is a layer of cells that covers the outer surface of the cnidarian's body. The gastroderm is a layer of cells that covers the inner surface, lining the gastrovascular cavity. Between these two cell layers is the mesoglea (mehz-oh-GLEE-ah). The mesoglea ranges from a thin noncellular membrane to a thick jellylike material that may contain wandering amebocytes. In general, the mesoglea is a thin layer in polyps and a thick layer in medusae.

Figure 26–14 *Some cnidarians, such as sea nettles (top, left) and sea anemones (left), are solitary. Others, such as gorgonian coral polyps (right), are colonial.*

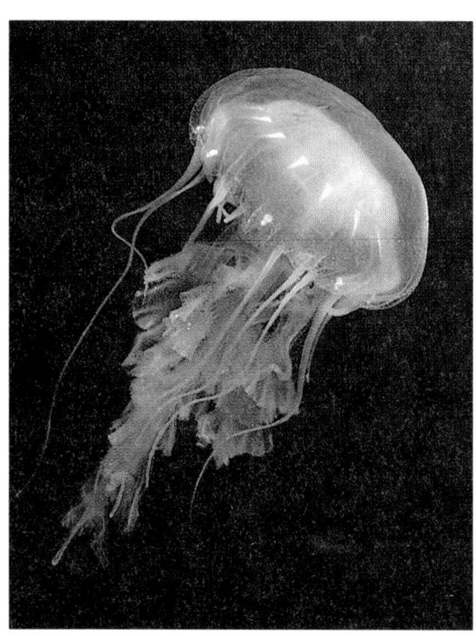

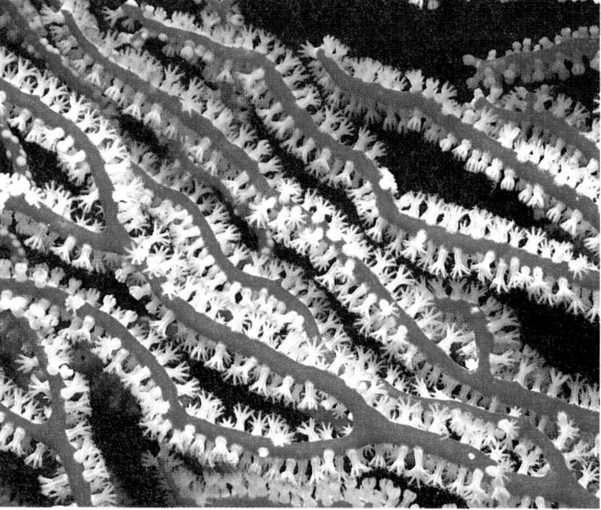

Form and Function in Cnidarians

Almost all cnidarians capture and eat small animals by using stinging structures called **nematocysts** (neh-MAT-oh-sihsts), which are located on their tentacles. Each nematocyst is a poison-filled sac containing a tightly coiled "spring-loaded" dart. When another animal touches a nematocyst, the dart uncoils as if it had exploded and buries itself in the skin of the animal. The dart carries with it enough poison to paralyze or kill the prey. Once the prey is rendered helpless, the cnidarian's tentacles push the food through the mouth and into the gastrovascular cavity. There the food is gradually broken up into tiny pieces. These food fragments are taken up by special cells in the gastroderm that digest them further. The nutrients are then transported throughout the body by diffusion. Any materials that cannot be digested are passed back out through the mouth, which is the only opening in the gastrovascular cavity, several hours later.

Although most cnidarians are considered carnivores, many do not actually "eat" much, thanks to an extraordinary symbiosis, which we talked about in Chapter 18. In many cnidarians, tiny photosynthetic protists grow right inside the living cells of the gastroderm. This relationship between autotrophic protist and heterotrophic animal works very efficiently. The photosynthetic protists use the carbon dioxide and other metabolic wastes produced by the cnidarian's cells to manufacture oxygen and organic compounds such as carbohydrates and proteins. The protists use some of the oxygen and organic compounds themselves and release the rest into the tissues of their cnidarian hosts. Many cnidarians depend on this symbiosis to such an extent that they can live only in bright sunlight! These cnidarians will slowly starve if kept in a darkened laboratory tank, even if they are fed pieces of shrimp and fish.

Because most cnidarians are only a few cell layers thick, they have not had to evolve many complicated body systems in order to survive. Some colonial cnidarians and some jellyfish have long, tube-shaped, branching gastrovascular cavities that help carry partially digested food through their bodies. Because these animals live in clean constantly flowing water, they can respire and eliminate waste products by diffusion directly through their body walls. There is no organized internal transport network or excretory system in cnidarians.

Cnidarians also lack a centralized nervous system and anything that could be called a brain. They have simple nervous systems called nerve nets. The nerve net is concentrated around the mouth, but it does spread throughout the body.

Information about the environment is transmitted to the rest of a cnidarian's nervous system by specialized sensory cells. Both polyps and medusae have sensory cells in the epidermis that detect chemicals from food and the touch of foreign objects. In medusae, some groups of sensory cells are organized into simple organs. These organs, which are called

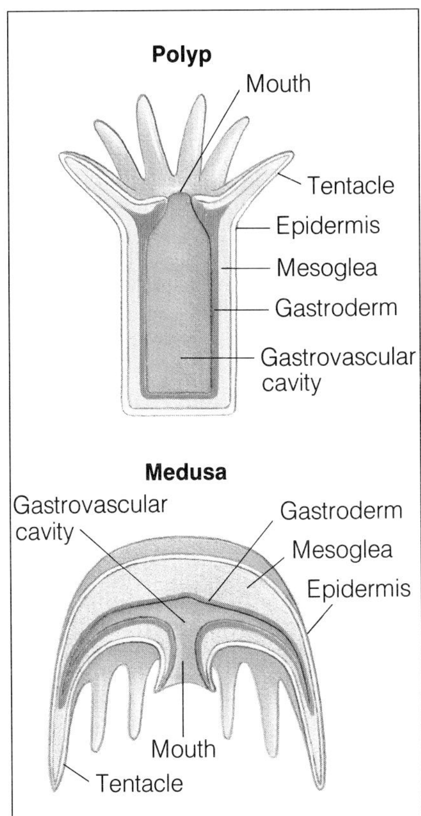

Figure 26–15 *Two basic body forms are seen in cnidarians: the flowerlike polyp and the bell-shaped medusa.*

Figure 26–16 *The body wall of a cnidarian consists of three layers: epidermis, mesoglea, and gastroderm.*

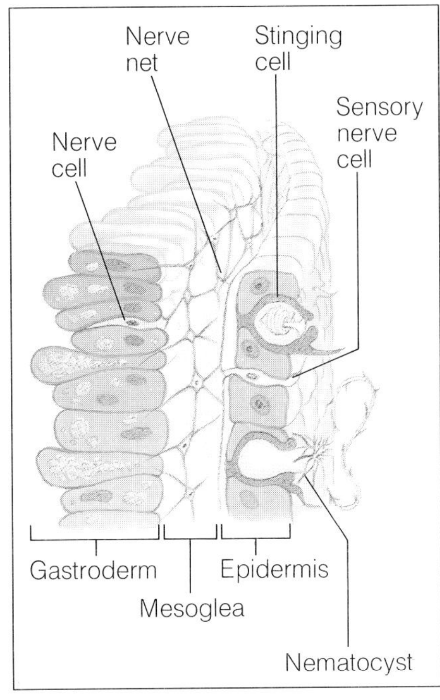

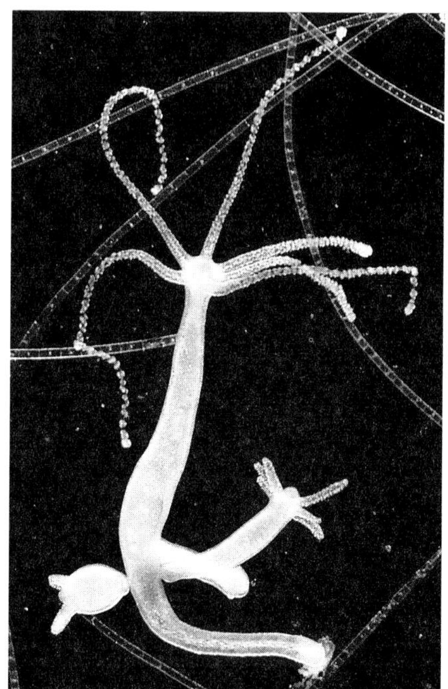

Figure 26–17 The buds at the base of this hydra's body will develop into new individuals that are genetically identical to their parent.

statocysts and ocelli, are arranged around the rim of a medusa's bell. Statocysts are involved with balance—they help an organism determine which way is up. Ocelli (oh-SEHL-igh; singular: ocellus), or eyespots, detect the presence of light.

Cnidarians lack the muscle cells that most other animals use to move about. But many of the epidermal cells in cnidarians can change shape when stimulated by the nervous system. Thus these cells serve the same function as muscles. Cnidarian polyps can expand, shrink, and move their tentacles by relaxing or contracting these epidermal cells. In medusae, contractions of the special epidermal cells change the bell-shaped body, causing it to "close" like a folding umbrella. The "closing" of the body pushes water out of the bell. This moves a medusa forward by jet propulsion.

Most cnidarians can reproduce both sexually and asexually. As you can see in Figure 26–17, polyps can produce new polyps asexually by budding. Budding begins with a swelling on the side of an existing individual. This swelling eventually grows into a complete polyp. Many polyps also reproduce asexually by budding off tiny medusae. When the medusae mature, they reproduce sexually by releasing gametes into the water. Depending on the species, fertilization occurs either in open water or inside an egg-carrying medusa. The zygote (fertilized egg) grows into a ciliated larva that swims around for some time. Later, the larva settles down, attaches to a hard surface, and changes into a polyp that begins the cycle again.

Figure 26–18 In this colonial hydrozoan, the polyps with tentacles are used in feeding and defense. The round buds found inside the reproductive polyps will eventually develop into medusae.

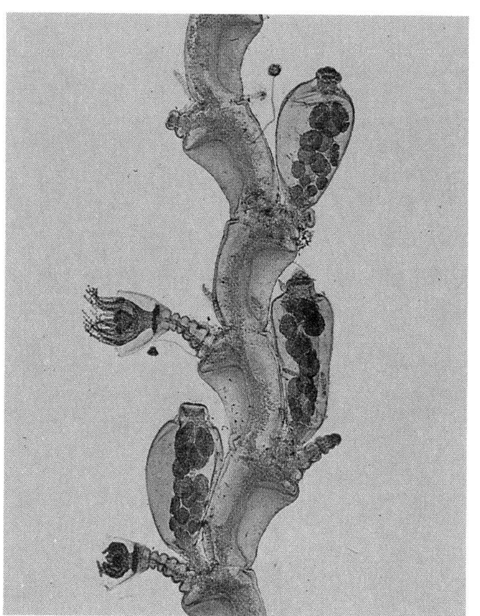

Hydras and Their Relatives

The class Hydrozoa (high-droh-ZOH-ah) is made up of cnidarians that spend most of their lives as polyps, although they usually have a short medusa stage. As you can see in Figure 26–18, most hydrozoan polyps grow in branching sessile colonies. Hydrozoan colonies range in length from a few centimeters to more than a meter. In each of these colonies, specialized polyps perform particular functions, such as feeding, reproduction, or defense. Reproductive polyps produce free-swimming medusae by budding. These medusae are usually less than 2 centimeters in diameter. Soon after they form, the medusae produce both eggs and sperm and then die.

The most common freshwater hydrozoans are the hydras. Hydras are not typical hydrozoans because they live as solitary polyps and lack the medusa stage in their life cycle. Unlike most other polyps, hydras can move around with a curious somersaulting movement. Hydras can reproduce either asexually by budding or sexually by producing eggs and sperm in their body walls. In most species of hydras, the sexes are separate. In other words, individuals are either male or female. However, a few species are hermaphroditic. A **hermaphrodite** is an individual that has both male and female reproductive organs and thus produces both sperm and eggs.

Figure 26–19 *Many cnidarians, such as the jellyfish* Aurelia, *have life cycles that include both medusa and polyp stages.*

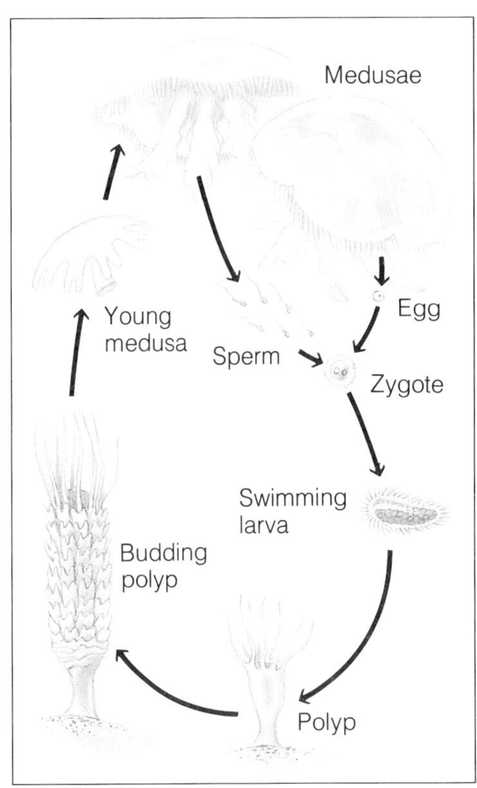

One unusual hydrozoan is the Portuguese man-of-war. These animals form floating colonies that contain several specialized kinds of polyps. In each Portuguese man-of-war, one polyp forms a balloonlike float that keeps the colony on the surface. This float may be up to 30 centimeters long. Some of the polyps in the colony produce long stinging tentacles that hang several meters below the float and paralyze and capture prey. Some polyps digest the food held by the tentacles, and still others do nothing but make eggs and sperm. Portuguese man-of-war nematocysts are strong enough to sting humans very badly, so swimmers and beach-goers must take care when these animals are spotted near shore.

Jellyfish

The class Scyphozoa (sigh-foh-ZOH-ah) contains the true jellyfish. Jellyfish go through the same life-cycle stages as hydrozoans. However, in scyphozoans the medusa is large and long-lived, and the polyp is restricted to a tiny larval stage.

Some jellyfish, such as the lion's mane, which is found in the north Atlantic, often grow up to 2 meters in diameter. The largest jellyfish ever found was more than 3.6 meters in diameter and had tentacles more than 30 meters long. The nematocysts of most jellyfish are harmless to humans, but a few can cause painful stings. One tiny Australian jellyfish has a toxin powerful enough to cause death in 3 to 20 minutes!

Sea Anemones and Corals

The class Anthozoa (an-thoh-ZOH-ah) contains sea anemones and corals, which are among the most beautiful and ecologically important invertebrates. Anthozoans have only the polyp stage in their life cycles. Adult polyps reproduce sexually by producing eggs and sperm that are released into the water. The zygote grows into a ciliated larva that settles to the ocean bottom and becomes a new polyp. Many anthozoans also reproduce asexually by budding.

Sea anemones are solitary polyps that live in the sea from the low-tide line to great depths. Although sea anemones can catch food with the nematocysts on their tentacles, many shallow-water species depend heavily on their photosynthetic symbionts. Some sea anemones can grow up to a meter in diameter.

Figure 26–20 *Sea fans (top) and sea pens (bottom) are two types of exotic colonial anthozoans. The purple-and-white feather stars clinging to the sea fan are relatives of starfish.*

Figure 26–21 Sea anemones (bottom, left) are solitary polyps. The polyps of stony corals, such as tube coral (left) and staghorn coral (right), are similar in structure to sea anemones. Unlike sea anemones, stony corals produce hard skeletons of calcium carbonate. Most stony corals are colonial.

Corals grow in shallow tropical waters around the world. Coral polyps are very similar in form to sea anemones. However, corals produce skeletons of calcium carbonate ($CaCo_3$), or limestone. Although a few corals are solitary, most are colonial. As a coral colony grows, new polyps are produced by budding, and more and more limestone is laid down. Coral colonies grow very slowly, but they may live for hundreds, or even thousands, of years. Together, countless coral colonies produce huge structures called coral reefs. Some of these reefs are enormous and contain more rock and living tissue than even the largest human cities. The Great Barrier Reef off the coast of Australia is more than 2000 kilometers long and some 80 kilometers wide.

How Cnidarians Fit into the World

Cnidarians form a number of interesting symbiotic relationships with other animals. Certain fish, shrimp, and other small animals live among the tentacles of large sea anemones. The sea anemone protects and provides scraps of food for these symbionts, which are unaffected by the sea anemone's nematocysts. In turn, the symbionts are thought to help clean the sea anemone and protect it from certain predators.

Corals and the reefs they form are extremely important in the ecology of tropical oceans. Because coral reefs are built from many separate coral colonies attached together, they contain tunnels, caves, and deep channels. In these recesses live some of the most beautiful and fascinating animals in the world.

Corals are important to humans in many ways. Coral reefs provide a home for food fishes and other edible animals, as well as for organisms that produce valuable shells, pearls, and other products. Reefs also protect the land from much of the action of waves. When coral reefs are destroyed or severely

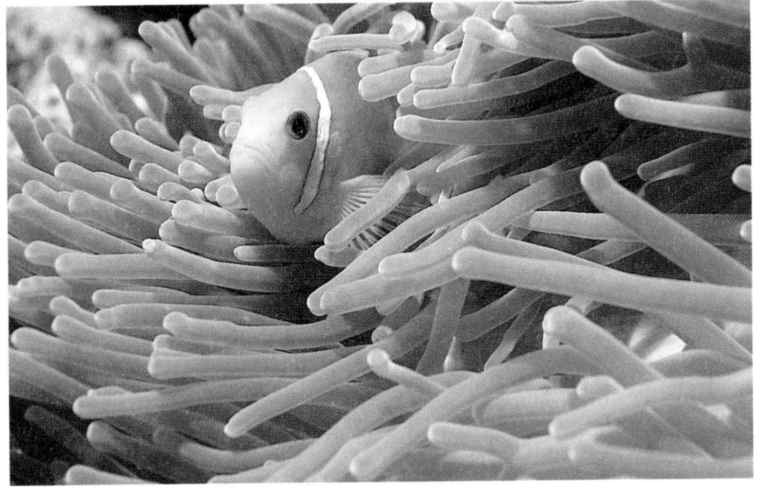

Figure 26–22 Although large sea anemones often eat fish, this clownfish is perfectly safe because it is "immune" to sea anemone stings. In addition, the clownfish and sea anemone are engaged in a symbiotic relationship that is thought to benefit both organisms.

damaged, large amounts of shoreline may be washed away. Fossil reefs offer important clues to geologists about the locations of oil deposits. Large blocks of coral have been used to build houses and to filter drinking water. Humans have long used certain corals to make jewelry and decorations.

Some cnidarians are used in medical research. Corals, like sponges, produce chemicals to protect themselves from being infected, overgrown, or settled upon by other organisms. Some of these chemicals may provide us with anti-cancer drugs, and others may help us learn more about cancer itself. The nerve toxins produced in cnidarian nematocysts are another powerful research tool. Whenever a compound poisons a biological system, studies of how the poison operates reveal a lot about how the system works. Cnidarians such as the sea wasp jellyfish produce several strong nerve poisons that have already helped scientists better understand nerve-cell function.

26–3 SECTION REVIEW

1. What is a cnidarian? What kind of symmetry do cnidarians have?
2. List the three classes of cnidarians. Give an example of each class.
3. Describe the life cycle of a typical cnidarian.
4. Discuss symbiotic relationships and other interactions between cnidarians and other living things.
5. A medusa usually has specialized sense organs. It may also have nerves that are organized into rings that encircle its body and structures that control body contractions. Explain why a medusa needs a more complex nervous system than a polyp. (*Hint:* How does the lifestyle of a medusa differ from that of a polyp?)

Section Objectives

- Discuss how unsegmented worms perform essential functions.
- Name and give examples of the three classes of flatworms.
- Describe some diseases caused by parasitic roundworms.

26–4 Unsegmented Worms

When most people think of worms, they think of earthworms—long, squiggly creatures that spend their time making tunnels in the ground. But there are many animals called worms that look nothing like earthworms. Many live in fresh water, a large number live in the ocean, and lots of them are important to humans. The two phyla of wormlike animals that we shall examine in this section are much simpler in structure than earthworms. They are known as **unsegmented worms** because their bodies are not divided into special segments. The phylum **Platyhelminthes** (pla-tee-hehl-MIHN-theez) consists of simple animals called **flatworms**. The phylum **Nematoda** (nee-mah-TOHD-ah) consists of long, thin worms called **roundworms.**

Flatworms

The members of the phylum Platyhelminthes are the simplest animals with bilateral symmetry. Most members of this phylum exhibit enough cephalization, or development of the anterior end, to have what we call a head. Because flatworms really are flat, the name of the phylum is quite appropriate (*platy-* means flat and *helminth* means worm). Many flatworms are no more than a few millimeters thick, although they may be up to 20 meters long. Flatworms have more developed organ systems than either sponges or cnidarians.

Figure 26–23 *Members of the phylum Platyhelminthes, such as this spotted marine flatworm, are the simplest animals with bilateral symmetry.*

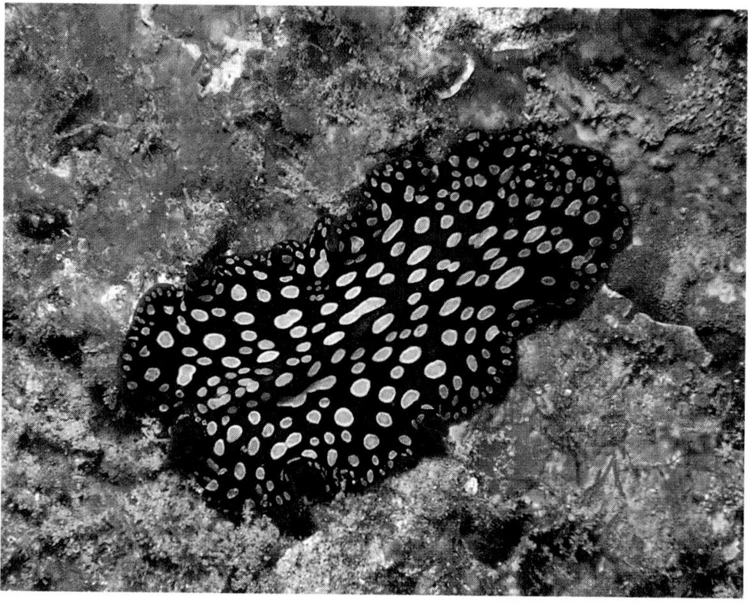

Form and Function in Flatworms

Flatworms feed in either of two very different ways. Some are aquatic and free-living, which means that they wander around in streams, lakes, and oceans. These worms may be carnivores that feed on tiny aquatic animals, or they may be scavengers that feed on recently dead animals. (You can probably catch flatworms in a local stream by leaving a piece of liver in the water overnight.) Free-living flatworms have a gastrovascular cavity with one opening at the end of a muscular tube called a **pharynx** (FAR-ihnks). See Figure 26–24. They use the pharynx to suck food into the gastrovascular cavity. The gastrovascular cavity forms an intestine with many branches along the entire length of the worm. In the intestines, enzymes help break down the food into small particles. These particles are taken inside the cells of the intestinal wall, where digestion is completed. Because the intestine branches into nearly all parts of the body, completely digested food can diffuse to other body tissues. Like cnidarians, flatworms expel undigested materials through the mouth.

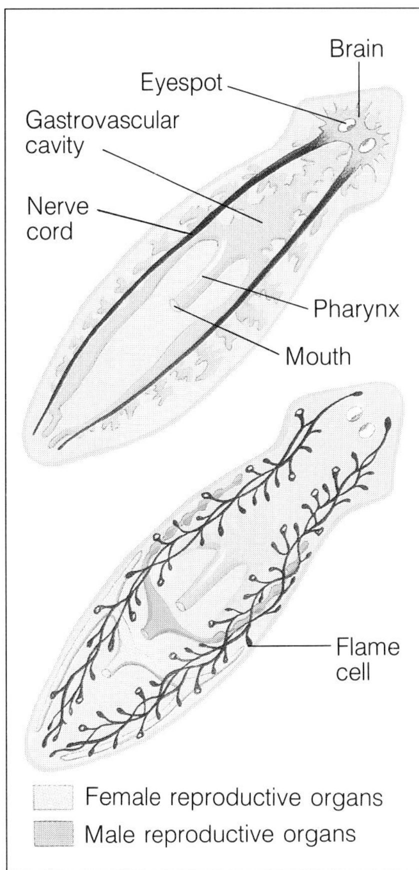

Figure 26–24 *Flatworms, such as planarians, perform their essential life functions at the level of organ systems.*

Many other flatworms are parasites that feed on blood, tissue fluids, or pieces of cells inside the body of their host. Some of these animals have a pharynx that pumps food into a pair of dead-end intestinal sacs where the food is digested. But in many parasitic flatworms, the digestive tract is simpler than in free-living forms. Tapeworms, which live within the intestines of their host, do not have any digestive tract at all. They have hooks and/or suckers with which they latch onto the intestinal wall of the host. From this position, they can simply absorb the food that passes by—food that has already been broken down by the host's digestive enzymes.

Flatworms lack any kind of specialized circulatory or respiratory system. Because they are so flat, they can depend on diffusion to transport oxygen and nutrients to their tissues. And they can get rid of carbon dioxide and most other metabolic wastes by allowing them to diffuse out through their body walls. Freshwater flatworms such as planarians have structures called flame cells that help them get rid of extra water. Many flame cells join together to form a network that empties through tiny pores in the animal's skin.

Free-living flatworms have nervous systems that are much more developed than those of cnidarians and sponges. They have a definite head in which a simple brain is located. This brain is the control center of a simple nervous system that stretches throughout the body. One or more long nerve cords run from the brain down the length of the body on either side. Shorter nerve cords run across the body. Many flatworms have one or more pairs of light-sensitive organs called ocelli, or eyespots. These eyespots do not see objects as our eyes do; they

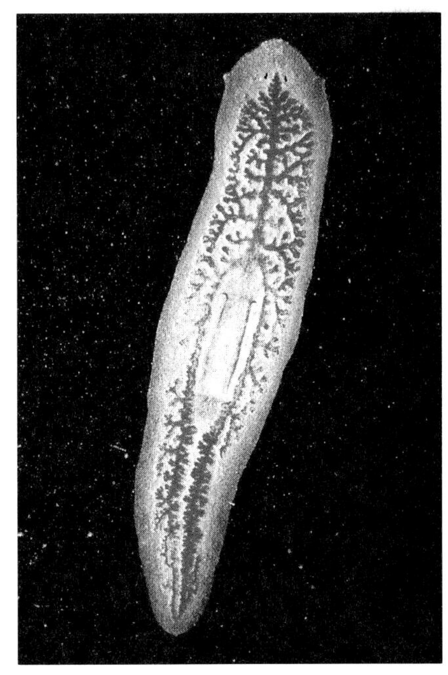

Figure 26–25 *The branching gastrovascular cavity and the pharynx can be clearly seen in this planarian.*

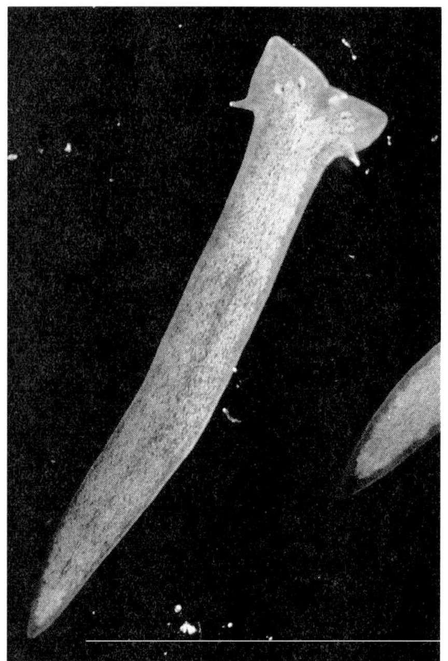

Figure 26–26 *An injury divided the head of this planarian in half, and the two halves regenerated their lost parts. Eventually, the two-headed planarian will split lengthwise to form two new planarians.*

simply detect whether the animal is in light or in darkness. Most flatworms have cells that are sensitive to chemicals found in food, and other cells that tell the worm which way the water around them is flowing. These cells are usually scattered all over the body. The nervous system of free-living flatworms allows them to gather information from their environment—information that they use to locate food and to find dark hiding places beneath stones and logs during the day.

Parasitic flatworms often do not have much of a nervous system. As you can imagine, there is not much need for a nervous system in an organism that mainly hangs onto an intestinal wall and absorbs food! In fact, in tapeworms the nervous system has completely disappeared as the worms have adapted to their parasitic lifestyle.

Free-living flatworms usually use two means of locomotion at once. Cilia on their epidermal cells help them glide through the water and over the bottom. Muscle cells controlled by the nervous system allow them to twist and turn so that they are able to react to environmental conditions rapidly.

Reproduction in free-living flatworms can be either sexual or asexual. Most free-living flatworms are hermaphrodites, which means that they have both male and female organs. During sexual reproduction, the worms join in pairs. One worm delivers sperm to the other worm while receiving sperm from its partner at the same time. The eggs, which are laid in small clusters, hatch within a few weeks. Asexual reproduction by fission is also common among free-living flatworms. Most of these worms have incredible abilities of regeneration. In one form of asexual reproduction, a worm will simply "fall to pieces" and each piece will grow into a new worm! Parasitic flatworms do not reproduce asexually. They often have complicated life cycles, as you will see shortly.

Figure 26–27 *Like planarians, marine flatworms belong to the class Turbellaria.*

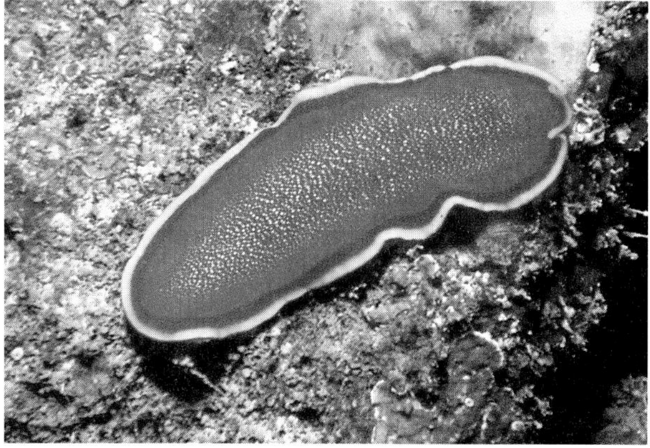

PLANARIANS The free-living flatworms belong to the class Turbellaria. The most familiar members of this class are planarians, the "cross-eyed" freshwater worms. Turbellarians vary greatly in color, form, and size. See Figure 26–27. Although most turbellarians are less than 1 centimeter in length, some giant land planarians, which are found in moist tropical areas, can attain lengths of more than 6 meters!

FLUKES The members of the class Trematoda are parasitic flatworms known as flukes. Some flukes are external parasites that live on the skin, mouth, gills, or other outside parts of a host. Most flukes, including the ones that affect humans, are internal parasites that infect the blood and organs. These flukes have complicated life cycles that involve at least two different host animals. Although many flukes are less than a centimeter long, the damage they cause to their host during their life cycle sounds like the script for a horror movie! Refer to Figure 26–28 as you read about the life cycle of a blood fluke. Keep in mind that the pattern of multiple hosts is typical of most parasitic flukes and, indeed, of many parasites in general.

Blood flukes are found primarily in Southeast Asia, North Africa, and other tropical areas. As you might expect, blood flukes live in the blood—specifically, the blood within the tiny blood vessels of the intestines. Humans are the primary hosts of blood flukes that belong to the genus *Schistosoma.* (The primary host of a parasite is the host organism in which adult parasites are found and in which sexual reproduction of the parasite occurs.)

Most flukes are hermaphrodites and undergo sexual reproduction in a manner similar to that of free-living flatworms. (However, the sexes are separate in *Schistosoma.*) Flukes produce many more eggs than free-living flatworms—about 10,000 to 100,000 times as many! Blood flukes lay so many eggs that the tiny blood vessels of the host's intestine break open. The broken blood vessels leak both blood and eggs into the intestine. The eggs are not digested by the host and thus become

Figure 26–28 *The blood fluke* Schistosoma mansoni *causes a serious human disease. The life cycle of the schistosome involves two hosts—humans and snails.*

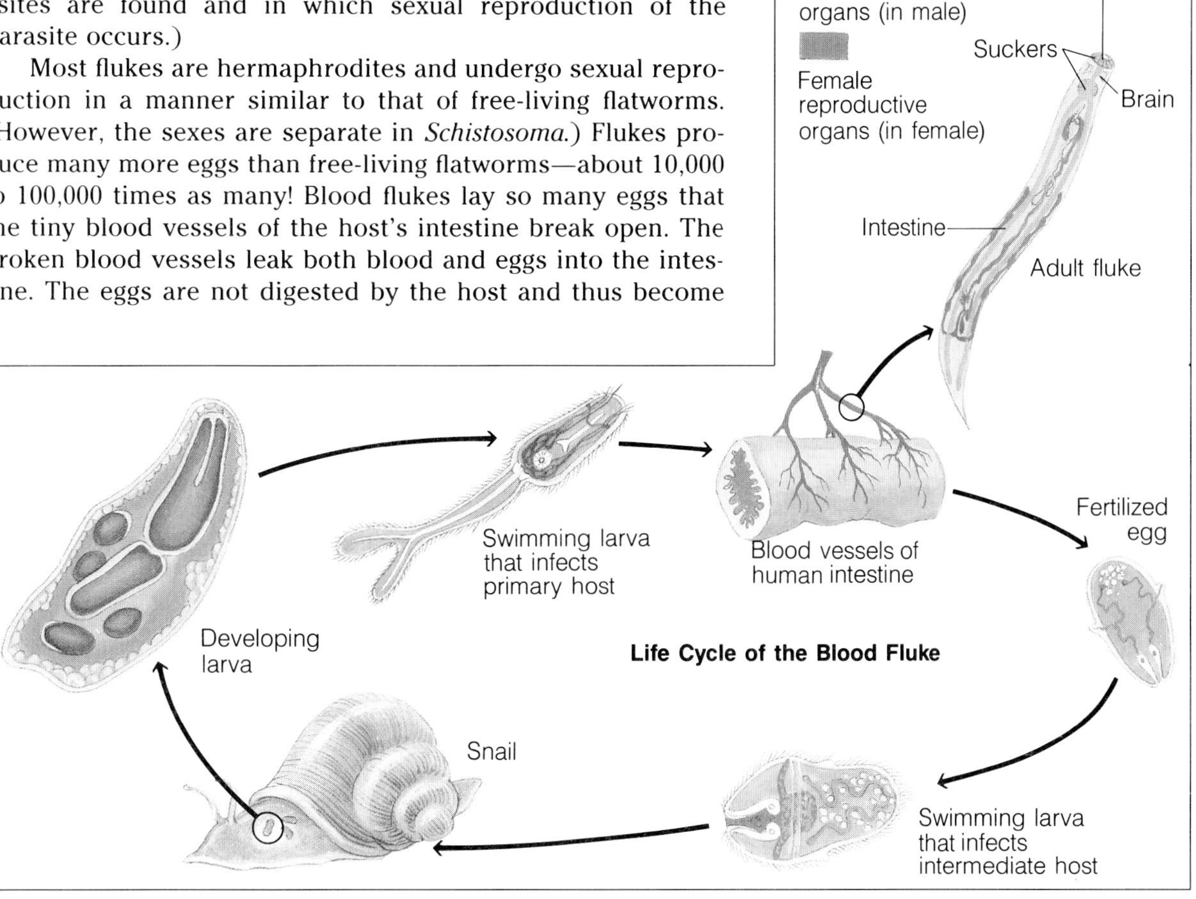

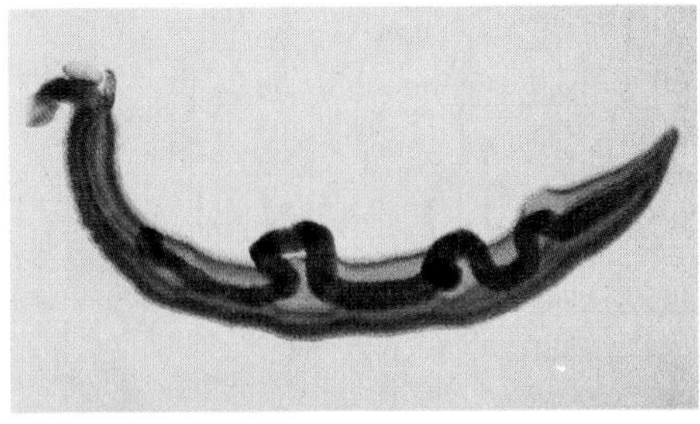

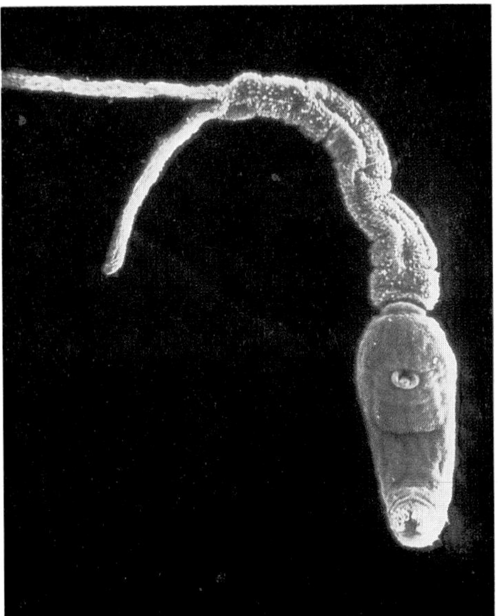

Figure 26–29 *In* Schistosoma mansoni, *the adult male is about 6 to 10 millimeters long and has a groove running the length of its body. The female, which is longer and thinner than the male, lives within this groove (top). If the schistosome larva shown here encounters a human, it will burrow through the skin, enter the bloodstream, and develop into an adult (bottom).*

part of the feces. In developed countries, where there are toilets and proper sewage systems, these eggs are usually destroyed in the sewage treatment process. But in many undeveloped parts of the world, human wastes are simply tossed into streams or even used as fertilizer.

Once the fluke eggs get into the water, they hatch into swimming larvae. When these larvae find a snail of the correct species, they burrow inside it and digest its tissues. The snail is an intermediate host for the fluke. Although sexual reproduction does not occur in an intermediate host, this host is still an essential part of the parasite's life cycle. In the intermediate host (in this case, a snail), the flukes reproduce asexually. The resulting new worms break out of the snail and swim around in the water. If they find a human, the worms bore through the skin and eat their way to the blood vessels. In the blood, they get carried around through the heart and lungs to the intestine, where they live as adults.

People infected with blood flukes get terribly sick. They become weak and often die—either as a direct result of the fluke infection or because they cannot recover from other diseases in their weakened condition. Blood flukes cause some of the most serious health problems in the world today. But because the species dangerous to humans live only in the tropics, most people in the United States know nothing about them—even though hundreds of millions of people suffer from blood flukes.

There are only one or two kinds of blood flukes in lakes and streams of the United States. These flukes normally have fishes or water birds as their primary hosts. If these worms find human swimmers, they try to burrow through the skin. This causes what is known as "swimmers itch." But because they are not adapted as human parasites, the worms cannot live in human bodies. The itch goes away after a time and the body repairs the damage.

TAPEWORMS Members of the class Cestoda are long, flat parasitic worms that live a very simple life. They have a head called a scolex (SKOH-leks) on which there are several suckers and a ring of hooks. These structures attach to the intestinal walls of humans and other animals. Inside the intestine, these worms are surrounded with food that their primary host has already digested for them. The worms absorb this food through their body walls. Adult human tapeworms can be up to 18 meters long! Tapeworms almost never kill their hosts, but they do use up a lot of food. For this reason, hosts may lose weight and become weak.

Behind the scolex of the tapeworm is a narrow neck region that is constantly dividing to form the many proglottids (proh-GLAH-tihds), or sections, that make up most of the body of the tapeworm. As you can see in Figure 26–30, the youngest and smallest proglottids are at the anterior (head) end of the tapeworm, and the largest and most mature proglottids are at the posterior (tail) end. Proglottids contain little more than male

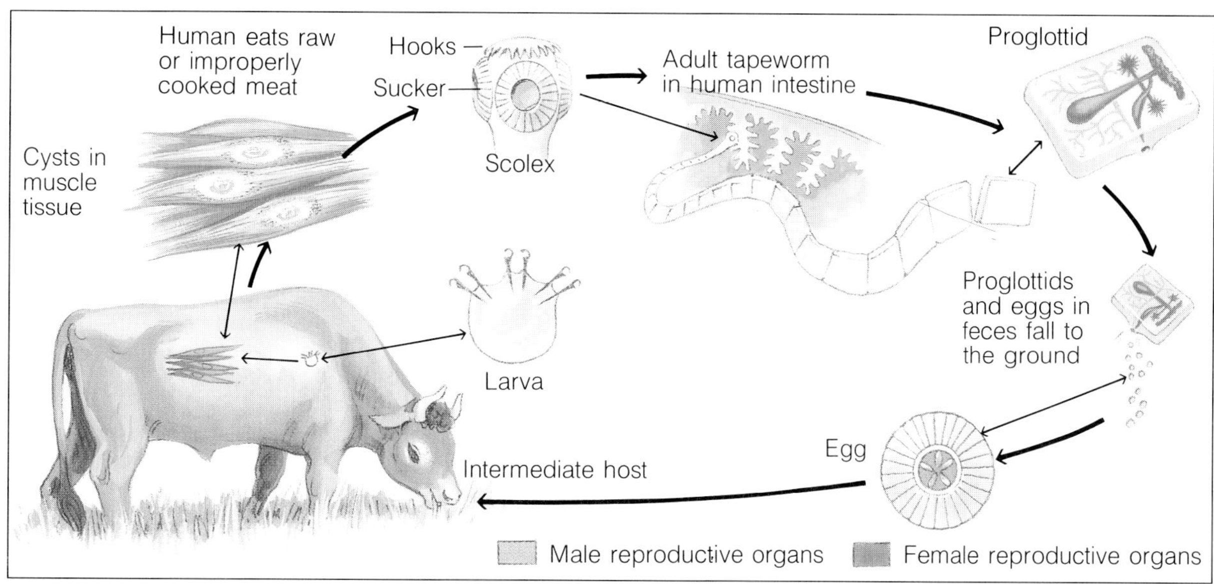

Figure 26–30 Cattle are secondary hosts to beef tapeworms; humans and other beef-eating animals are primary hosts.

and female reproductive organs. Sperm produced by the testes, or male reproductive organs, can fertilize eggs in the proglottids of other tapeworms or of the same individual. Fertilized tapeworm eggs are released when mature proglottids break off the posterior end of the tapeworm and burst open. A mature proglottid may rupture either in the host's intestine or after it has been passed out of the host's body with the feces. A single proglottid may contain over 100,000 eggs, and a single worm can produce more than half a billion eggs each year!

If food or water contaminated with tapeworm eggs is consumed by cows, pigs, fishes, or other intermediate hosts, the eggs enter the intermediate host and there hatch into larvae. These larvae grow for a time and then burrow into the muscle tissue of the intermediate host and form a dormant protective stage called a cyst. If a human eats raw or incompletely cooked meat containing these cysts, the larvae become active within the human host. Once inside the intestine of the new host, they latch onto the intestinal wall and grow into adult worms.

Figure 26–31 The scolex, or head, of a tapeworm has suckers and other structures that enable it to attach to the inside of its host's intestine.

Roundworms

Members of the phylum Nematoda, which are known as roundworms, are among the simplest animals to have a digestive system with two openings—a mouth and an anus. Food enters through the mouth, and undigested food leaves through the anus. Roundworms, which range in size from microscopic to a meter in length, may be the most numerous of all multicellular animals. It is difficult to imagine just how many roundworms there are around us all the time. A single rotting apple can contain as many as 90,000 roundworms! And a small bucketful of garden soil or pond water may house more than a million roundworms.

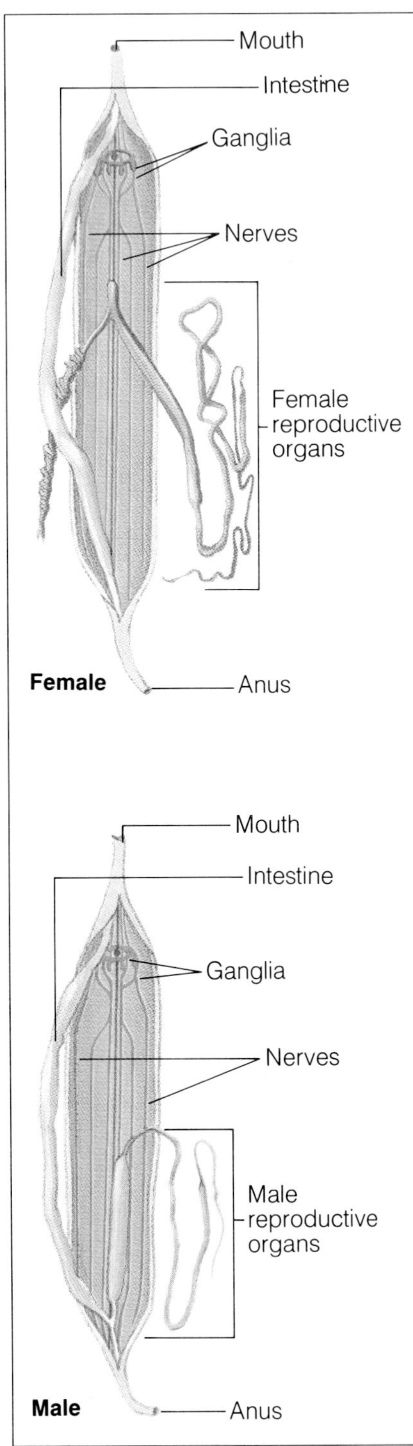

Figure 26–32 *The internal organs of male and female ascarids are shown here. Ascarids, like other roundworms, have a digestive tract with two openings—a mouth and an anus.*

Form and Function in Roundworms

Most roundworms are free-living. Free-living roundworms are found in virtually all parts of the Earth—in soil, salt flats, and aquatic sediments; in polar regions and in the tropics; in fresh water, oceans, and hot springs. There are, however, many species of parasitic roundworms. Parasitic roundworms affect almost every kind of plant and animal.

All roundworms have a long tube-shaped digestive tract with openings at both ends. This system is very efficient because food can enter through the mouth and continue straight through the digestive tract. Any material in the food that cannot be digested leaves through an opening called the anus.

Free-living roundworms are often carnivores that catch and eat other small animals. Some soil-dwelling and aquatic forms eat small algae, fungi, or pieces of decaying organic matter. Some actually live on the organic matter itself. Others digest the bacteria and fungi that break down dead animals and plants. Many roundworms that live in the soil attach to the root hairs of green plants and suck out the plant juices. These parasitic worms cause tremendous damage to many crops all over the world. Roundworms are particularly fond of tomato plants. For this reason, many tomato plants have been specially bred to be resistant to roundworms. Other roundworms live inside plant tissues, where they cause considerable damage.

Like flatworms, roundworms breathe and excrete their metabolic wastes through their body walls. They have no internal transport system and thus depend on diffusion to carry nutrients and wastes through their body.

Roundworms have simple nervous systems. They have several ganglia, or groups of nerve cells, in the head region, but they lack anything that can really be called a brain. Although roundworms have several types of sense organs, these are simple structures that detect chemicals given off by prey or hosts. Several nerves extend from the ganglia in the head and run the length of the body. These nerves transmit sensory information and control movement. The muscles of roundworms run in strips down the length of their body walls. Aquatic roundworms contract these muscles to move like snakes through the water. Soil-dwelling roundworms simply push their way through the soil by thrashing around.

Roundworms reproduce sexually. Most species of roundworms have separate males and females, but a few species are hermaphroditic. Fertilization takes place inside the body of the female. Roundworms that are parasites on animals often have complex life cycles. Two or three hosts may be involved in the life cycle of some roundworms. In other roundworms, such as *Ascaris*, the stages of the life cycle take place in different organs of one host.

Ascaris is a parasitic roundworm that lives in humans. Species that are closely related to *Ascaris* affect horses, cattle, pigs, chickens, dogs, cats, and many other animals. *Ascaris* and its relatives, which are collectively known as ascarids, have life cycles that are similar to one another. One of the reasons puppies are wormed while they are young is to rid them of the ascarid that affects dogs.

Adult ascarid worms live in the intestines, where they produce many eggs that leave the host's body in the feces. If food or water contaminated with these feces is eaten by another host, the eggs hatch in the small intestine of the new host. The young worms burrow into the walls of the intestines and enter surrounding blood vessels. Carried around in the blood, the tiny worms end up in the lungs. Here they break out into the air passages and climb up into the throat, where they are swallowed. Carried back into the intestines, they mature and the cycle repeats itself.

How Unsegmented Worms Fit into the World

Unsegmented worms do not exert much positive influence on the daily lives of humans, and thus they are easy to ignore. Most unsegmented worms lead inoffensive lives. They eat small organisms and are eaten by larger organisms; some help aerate the soil with their burrows. However, unsegmented worms are generally known by the parasitic rather than the free-living members of their phylum. We have already talked about parasitic flatworms. In this section we shall focus our attention on parasitic roundworms, which are responsible for some of the most painful and horrific diseases known. Parasitic roundworms include hookworms, trichinosis-causing worms, filarial worms, eye worms, and a host of others too numerous to be mentioned here.

Hookworms are serious human intestinal parasites that are often found in the southern United States and are common in tropical countries. As many as one fourth of the people in the world today are infected with hookworm! Hookworm eggs hatch outside the body of the host and develop in the soil. If they find an unprotected foot, they use sharp teeth and hooks to burrow into the skin and enter the bloodstream. Like *Ascaris*, these worms travel through the blood to the lungs and then

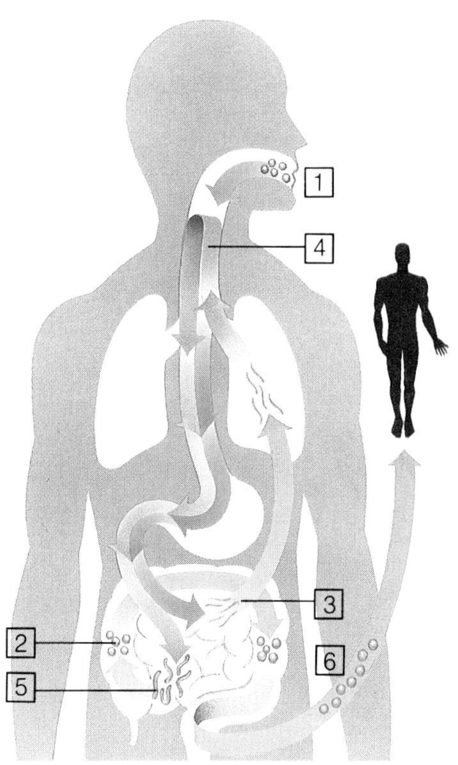

1	Eggs in food or water are ingested by host
2	Eggs hatch in small intestine
3	Larvae enter blood vessels and are carried to the lungs
4	Larvae travel to throat and are swallowed
5	Adult ascarid worms live in the small intestine
6	Eggs leave host in feces

Figure 26–33 *The stages of the life cycle of the human ascarid,* Ascaris lumbricoides, *take place in several different host organs.*

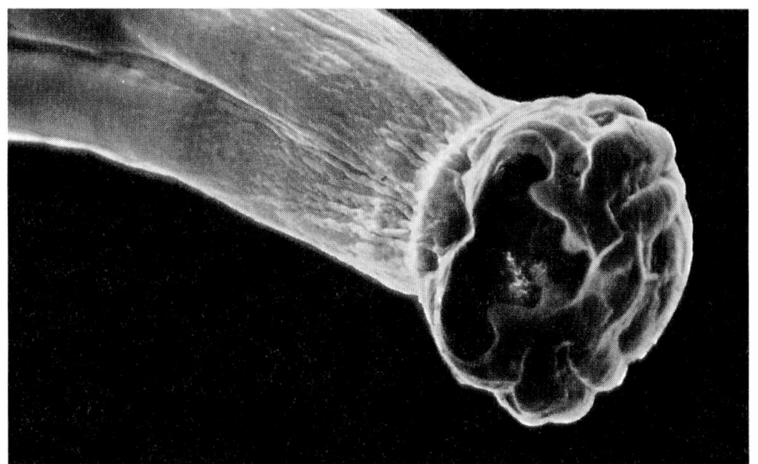

Figure 26–34 *Hookworms use the sharp teeth and hooks on their anterior end to burrow through a host's skin.*

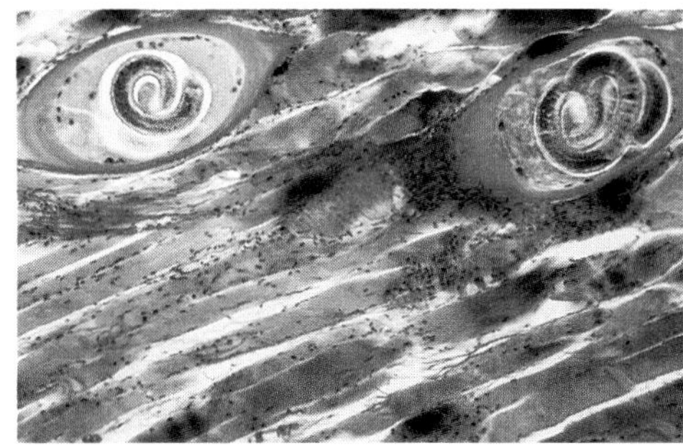

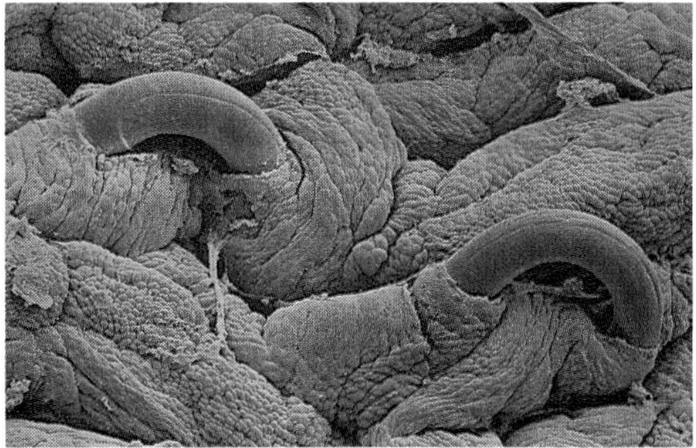

Figure 26–35 Trichinella *worms, which cause the disease trichinosis, form cysts in the muscle tissue of their host (top). These threadworms, tunneling through the tissues of a sheep's intestine, are parasitic roundworms (bottom).*

down the throat to the intestines. There, the adult worms dig into the intestinal wall and suck the blood of the host. These worms can devour enough blood to cause weakness and poor growth.

Trichinosis (trihk-ih-NOH-sihs) is a terrible disease caused by the roundworm *Trichinella*.. Adult worms, which are hard to see without a microscope, live and mate in the intestines of the host. Females carrying fertilized eggs burrow into the intestinal wall, where each releases up to 1500 larvae. These larvae travel through the bloodstream, from which they eventually exit through small blood vessels, and then burrow into organs and tissues. This causes terrible pain for the host. The larvae then form cysts in the host's muscle tissue and become inactive.

The only way these encysted worms can complete their life cycle is if infected muscle tissue is eaten. This means that hosts for *Trichinella* must be carnivorous—animals that do not eat infected meat do not get trichinosis. Two very common hosts for *Trichinella* are rats and pigs. (Rats eat any meat they can find, and may even eat each other. Pigs regularly catch and eat rats and other small animals.) Humans get trichinosis almost exclusively by eating raw or incompletely cooked pork.

Filarial worms, which are found primarily in tropical regions of Asia, are threadlike worms that live in the blood and lymph vessels of birds and mammals such as humans. They are transmitted from one primary host to another through biting insects, especially mosquitoes. In severe infections, large numbers of filarial worms may block the passage of fluids within the lymph vessels. This causes elephantiasis, a condition in which an affected part of the body swells enormously. Fortunately, extreme cases of elephantiasis are now rare.

Eye worms are closely related to the filarial worms that cause elephantiasis. They are found in Africa and affect both humans and baboons. Eye worms live in and burrow through the tissues just below the skin of their host. In their travels, the worms occasionally move across the surface of the eye—hence the name eye worm.

26–4 SECTION REVIEW

1. What is a flatworm? Name and give examples of the three classes of flatworms.
2. How do the body structures of parasitic flatworms differ from those of free-living forms?
3. What is a roundworm? What are the major differences in structure between roundworms and flatworms?
4. How do unsegmented worms perform essential functions?
5. Explain why you should cook meat and fish thoroughly in areas that have parasitic worms.

SCIENCE, TECHNOLOGY, AND SOCIETY **BREAKTHROUGH**

River Blindness: A Lifelong Battle Almost Won

The sight is a familiar one in many parts of West Africa: A child leads an adult along the banks of a river. The adult, like many others in the village, is blind—a victim of the disease onchocerciasis, or river blindness. It has been called river blindness because the tiny black flies that spread the disease breed in fast-moving water. River blindness affects an estimated 18 million people living in Africa and the Middle East, more than 300,000 of whom have been blinded.

River blindness is caused by a parasitic roundworm that enters the body when a black fly, which has picked up the roundworm by biting an infected human, bites another victim. The roundworm larvae deposited by the black fly quickly grow into threadlike adult worms, which can live under the skin for as long as 12 years. It is not the adult worms that cause this dreadful disease but their offspring—millions of microworms that swarm through the skin and eyes.

Blindness is not the only effect of this disease. As the microworms migrate under the skin, intolerable itching results. Over time, the skin begins to decay and often loses its pigment.

The scourge of river blindness has economic implications as well. When the rate of blindness in a village becomes significant, fearful young people abandon their homes. Farm production in fertile river valleys is curtailed because there are limited laborers to grow and harvest the crops.

Since 1974, when an ambitious effort to reduce the numbers of black flies was undertakin, the World Health Organization (WHO) has been battling this disease with limited success. Spraying with an ecologically safe insecticide has halted the transmission of river blindness in certain areas to some extent. But complications have developed. Some insects have become resistant to the available insecticides. And several areas once cleared of the black flies have been reinvaded as the insects prove to be more mobile than expected.

What is giving WHO and victims of river blindness cause to rejoice is the arrival of ivermectin. Developed in the 1970s as a weapon against worm parasites in livestock, ivermectin has been shown in a series of human trials to be an effective weapon against river blindness. Although ivermectin does not kill the parasitic roundworm, it does destroy the microworm offspring. And it also appears to inhibit, for a time, the production of more offspring.

Though not a total cure, ivermectin's advantages are obvious. Taken in pill form as infrequently as once a year, it protects those already infected from the worst symptoms. By temporarily ridding a victim's skin of microworms, ivermectin slows the transmission of the disease by preventing the flies that bite the victim from picking up the parasitic roundworm. And ivermectin is so safe that it can be dispensed in mass campaigns in isolated villages rarely visited by doctors.

With ivermectin now easily available, those affected by river blindness in one way or another can look to the future with hope. Although the drug cannot restore the sight of victims of the disease, it can spare hundreds of thousands of children from this scourge.

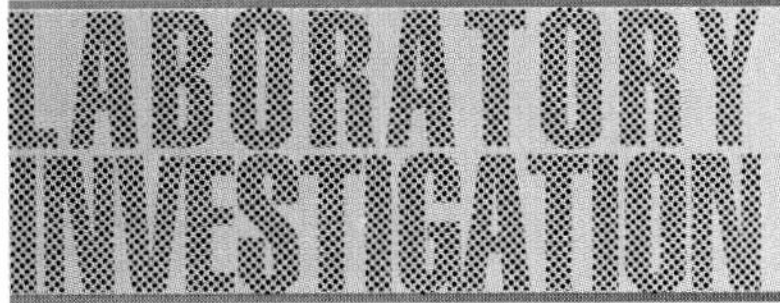

COLLECTING AND STUDYING ROUNDWORMS

PROBLEM

How do roundworms move?

MATERIALS *(per group)*

2 150-mL beakers	paper towel
cheesecloth	ring stand
coverslip	10-cm rubber tubing
depression slide	rubber band or twist tie
funnel	scissors
pinch clamp	soil
ring clamp	vital methylene blue
2 medicine droppers	microscope

PROCEDURE 

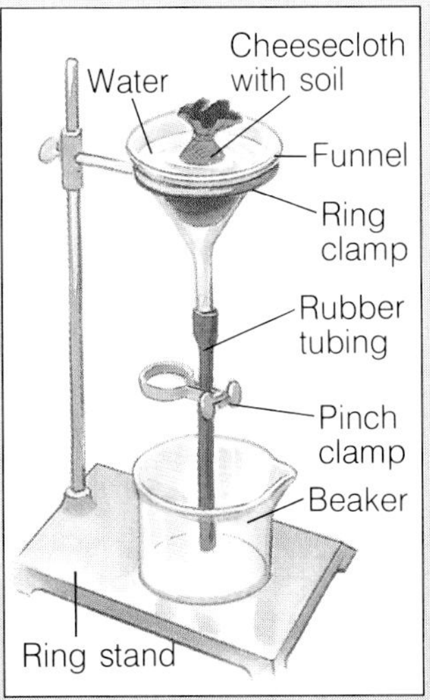

1. Assemble the apparatus for collecting roundworms as shown in the accompanying diagram.
2. Using scissors, cut a piece of cheesecloth with dimensions of approximately 30 cm by 15 cm. Fold the cheesecloth over to make a square.
3. Put a handful of soil in the center of the cheesecloth and pull the corners together to make a small bag. Tie the bag closed with a rubber band or twist tie.
4. Using a beaker, pour some water into the funnel to make sure the pinch clamp does not leak. Once you are certain the pinch clamp works properly, place the bag of soil in the funnel. Fill the funnel the rest of the way with water, making sure that the bag is submerged.
5. Leave the apparatus undisturbed for about 24 hours.
6. Open the pinch clamp briefly, allowing only a small amount of water to empty into the beaker below.
7. Using a dropper, put a few drops of water from the beaker in the center of a clean depression slide. Cover the water with a coverslip.
8. With the microscope set on low power, locate some roundworms on the slide. Observe how the roundworms move.
9. Using a clean dropper, put a drop of vital methylene blue at one edge of the coverslip. Hold a piece of paper towel at the opposite edge of the coverslip to draw the vital methylene blue underneath.
10. Locate a stained roundworm. Switch to high power and focus on the stained roundworm using the fine adjustment.
11. On a separate sheet of paper, draw a diagram of the roundworm you observed under high magnification.

OBSERVATIONS

1. Describe the appearance of a roundworm.
2. Describe how roundworms move.

ANALYSIS AND CONCLUSIONS

1. Based on the way the roundworms move, what can you infer about the arrangement of muscles in roundworms?
2. Are roundworm movements more effective in soil than they are in the water on the slide? Explain.
3. Explain how the apparatus used in this investigation helps in the collection of roundworms. (*Hint:* Do soil roundworms seem capable of swimming against gravity?)
4. Based on your answer to question 3, would you expect to find more or fewer roundworms in subsequent samples of water from the funnel? Explain.

STUDENT STUDY GUIDE

SUMMARIZING THE CONCEPTS

The key concepts in each section of this chapter are listed below to help you review the chapter content. Make sure you understand each concept and its relationship to other concepts and to the theme of this chapter.

26–1 Introduction to the Animal Kingdom

- Animals are multicellular eukaryotic heterotrophs whose cells lack cell walls. Invertebrates are animals that lack a backbone.
- Essential functions for life include feeding, respiration, internal transport, elimination of waste products, response to environmental conditions, movement, and reproduction.
- Evolutionary trends in animals include performing essential functions at higher levels of organization, moving from radial to bilateral symmetry, and increasing cephalization.

26–2 Sponges

- Sponges belong to the phylum Porifera. Sponges are simple organisms that lack tissues and organs.

26–3 Cnidarians

- Cnidarians are aquatic animals that exhibit radial symmetry and stinging structures called nematocysts on their tentacles. Many cnidarians have two body forms in their life cycles—a flowerlike polyp and a bell-shaped medusa.

26–4 Unsegmented Worms

- Unsegmented worms include phylum Platyhelminthes and phylum Nematoda.
- Flatworms are the simplest animals with bilateral symmetry.
- Roundworms have a digestive tract with two openings. Parasitic roundworms cause a variety of diseases in humans and other animals.

REVIEWING KEY TERMS

Vocabulary terms are important to your understanding of biology. The key terms listed below are those you should be especially familiar with. Review these terms and their meanings. Then use each term in a complete sentence. If you are not sure of a term's meaning, return to the appropriate section and review its definition.

26–1 Introduction to the Animal Kingdom

vertebrate
invertebrate
division of labor
herbivore
carnivore
parasite
filter feeder
detritus feeder
larva
metamorphosis
radial symmetry
bilateral symmetry
anterior
posterior
dorsal
ventral
cephalization
ganglion

26–2 Sponges

Porifera
collar cell
osculum
spicule
amebocyte
spongin
gemmule
budding

26–3 Cnidarians

Cnidaria
polyp
medusa
gastrovascular cavity
nematocyst
hermaphrodite

26–4 Unsegmented Worms

unsegmented worm
Platyhelminthes
flatworm
Nematoda
roundworm
pharynx

CHAPTER REVIEW

CONTENT REVIEW

Multiple Choice

Choose the letter of the answer that best completes each statement.

1. All animals are
   a. unicellular. c. radially symmetric.
   b. sessile. d. heterotrophic.
2. A hydra is best described as a
   a. herbivore. c. parasite.
   b. carnivore. d. filter feeder.
3. In which animal would you expect to observe cephalization?
   a. jellyfish c. roundworm
   b. sponge d. sea anemone
4. Which animal is free-living?
   a. *Hydra* c. *Schistosoma*
   b. *Trichinella* d. *Ascaris*
5. Animals in the phylum Cnidaria include
   a. flukes. c. medusae.
   b. roundworms. d. sponges.
6. Which animal is most likely to possess ocelli, statocysts, and a nerve net?
   a. sponge c. coral
   b. jellyfish d. flatworm
7. Which animal lacks a digestive system and digestive organs?
   a. jellyfish c. planarian
   b. hookworm d. tapeworm
8. An immature animal that looks and acts nothing like the adult of that species is called a
   a. gemmule. c. bud.
   b. larva. d. proglottid.

True or False

Determine whether each statement is true or false. If it is true, write "true." If it is false, change the underlined word or words to make the statement true.

1. Invertebrates have a backbone.
2. Organisms that eat animals are called herbivores.
3. Flukes and tapeworms are best described as detritus feeders.
4. Trichinosis is usually caused by eating flukes in raw fish.
5. Planarians have bilateral symmetry.
6. Sea anemones are polyps that have skeletons of calcium carbonate (limestone).
7. Adult parasites undergo sexual reproduction in their intermediate host.
8. Jellyfish are placed in the class Anthozoa.

Word Relationships

In each of the following sets of terms, three of the terms are related. One term does not belong. Determine the characteristic common to three of the terms and then identify the term that does not belong.

1. spicule, ganglia, osculum, collar cell
2. nematocyst, epidermis, gastroderm, mesoglea
3. tapeworm, hookworm, ascarid, planarian
4. Porifera, Cestoda, Cnidaria, Nematoda
5. dorsal, ventral, anterior, sessile
6. Anthozoa, Protozoa, Scyphozoa, Hydrozoa
7. multicellular, heterotroph, eukaryotic, cell walls

CONCEPT MASTERY

Use your understanding of the concepts developed in the chapter to answer each of the following in a brief paragraph.

1. Draw a human, a sea anemone, and a dog. Label each drawing using as many of the following terms as are appropriate: radial symmetry, bilateral symmetry, anterior, posterior, dorsal, ventral, sessile, motile.
2. Suppose you placed a harmless purple-colored mixture of red dye and blue dye in the water beside a vase-shaped sponge. After a while, you noticed blue dye coming out of the top of the sponge. Describe how the blue dye got from the outside environment into the sponge. Propose an explanation for what happened to the red dye. How might you determine if your explanation about the red dye is correct?
3. Explain how flukes and tapeworms display the following parasitic adaptations: (a) organs for attachment to the host, (b) reduced sense organs, (c) modifications in food-getting, (d) increased reproductive capabilities and well-developed reproductive organs, (e) larvae that allow the transfer from one host to another.
4. At one time, diet pills containing tapeworm eggs were sold. Why would such pills work? Why are such pills dangerous?
5. State three basic trends in animal evolution in your own words.

CRITICAL AND CREATIVE THINKING

Discuss each of the following in a brief paragraph.

1. **Interpreting diagrams** Refer to the diagram of the life cycle of a typical liver fluke to explain the following: To help prevent liver fluke infections, experts often recommend that ponds, irrigation ditches, and other bodies of water be treated with snail-killing pesticides. Why does killing snails prevent liver fluke infections in humans?

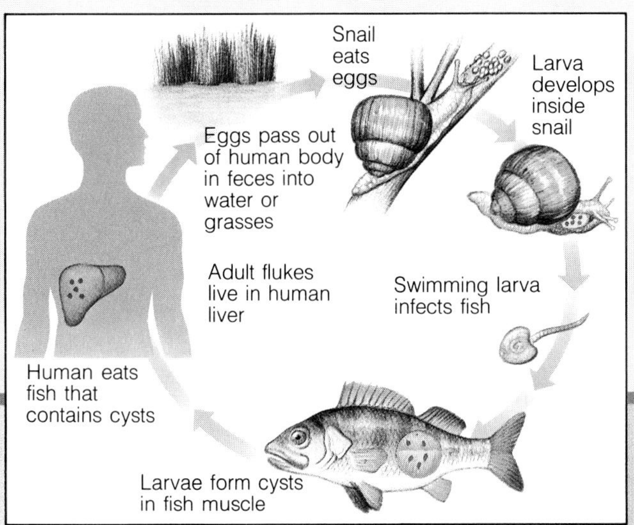
Snail eats eggs
Larva develops inside snail
Eggs pass out of human body in feces into water or grasses
Adult flukes live in human liver
Swimming larva infects fish
Human eats fish that contains cysts
Larvae form cysts in fish muscle

2. **Relating concepts** Flukes that are internal parasites are often facultative anaerobes. This means that although they can use cellular respiration to obtain energy from food, they usually use anaerobic processes (glycolysis and fermentation) instead. Explain how this metabolic switch hitting might be an adaptation of flukes to a parasitic lifestyle.
3. **Developing a hypothesis** You observe that a hydra that lives in fresh water often squirts water out of its mouth. Because this water does not contain particles, you assume that the hydra's behavior is not involved with the removal of solid wastes. How can you explain this behavior?
4. **Using the writing process** Write a humorous dialogue in which a person tries to explain to a tapeworm that there is no such thing as a free lunch.

CHAPTER 27

Mollusks and Annelids

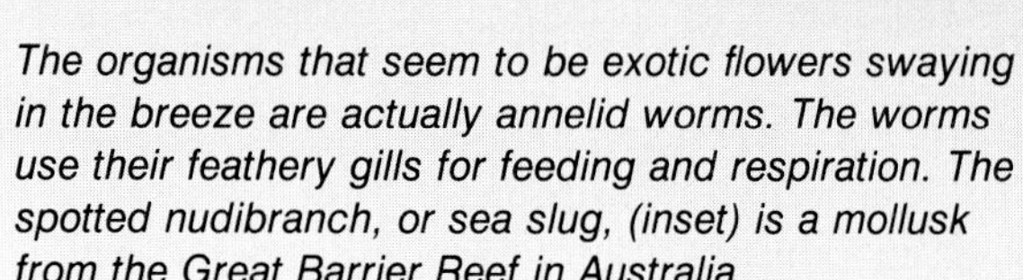

The organisms that seem to be exotic flowers swaying in the breeze are actually annelid worms. The worms use their feathery gills for feeding and respiration. The spotted nudibranch, or sea slug, (inset) is a mollusk from the Great Barrier Reef in Australia.

Have you ever eaten fried clams, broiled scallops, or calamari in tomato sauce? Have you ever gone fishing with live worms as bait? If you have, you are already familiar with some of the more common members of the two phyla that we shall study in this chapter: mollusks and annelids (segmented worms). Both of these phyla are ancient, very large, and remarkably diverse. Both provide many examples of how evolution can mold a single basic animal body plan into many different shapes. And both remind us that animals with ancient and simple body plans can be very well adapted to their environments.

What are mollusks and annelids? How are they related to one another? How are they adapted to their environments? What relationships do they have with other living things? You will find the answers to these questions in the pages that follow.

CHAPTER OUTLINE

27–1 Mollusks

Section Objectives

- Explain how mollusks perform their essential life functions.
- Describe and give examples of the three major classes of mollusks.
- Discuss how mollusks affect humans and other living things.

Members of the phylum Mollusca are known as **mollusks**. Mollusks evolved in the sea more than 600 million years ago and have experienced a long and successful adaptive radiation. Today there are more than 100,000 mollusk species, which are divided into seven classes. Mollusks live everywhere—from deep ocean trenches to mountain brooks to the tops of trees. They range in size from snails as small as a grain of sand to giant squids that may grow more than 20 meters long. And as you can see in Figure 27–1, mollusks come in a wide range of forms and colors.

What Is a Mollusk?

Why are animals that look and act so differently grouped in the same phylum? One reason mollusks are classified together is that they share similar developmental patterns. (As you may recall from Chapter 15, many animals are classified on the basis of shared features during early development.) Most mollusks have a special kind of larva called a trochophore (TROH-koh-for). See Figure 27–2 on page 586. Trochophore larvae swim in open water and feed on tiny floating plants.

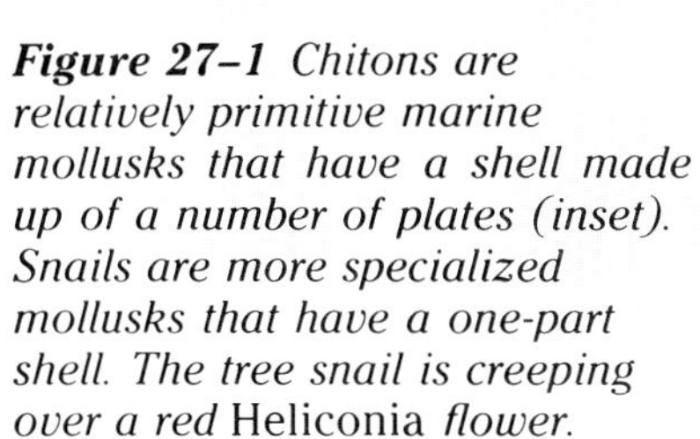

Figure 27–1 *Chitons are relatively primitive marine mollusks that have a shell made up of a number of plates (inset). Snails are more specialized mollusks that have a one-part shell. The tree snail is creeping over a red* Heliconia *flower.*

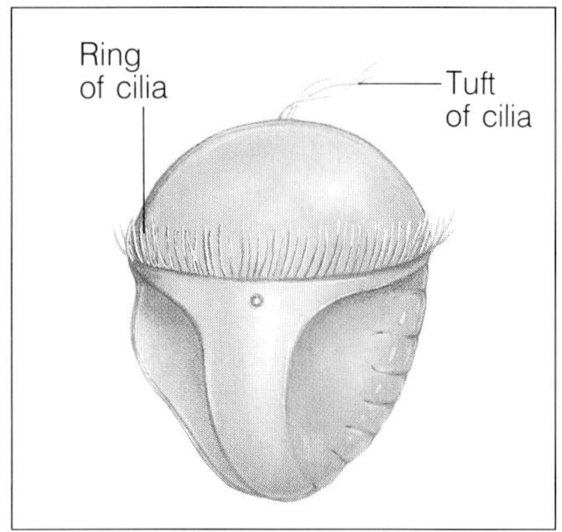

Figure 27–2 *The trochophore larva of a chiton, like other trochophore larvae, has a tuft of cilia making up the "handle" on its top-shaped body and a band of cilia encircling its body.*

Trochophore larvae are also seen in segmented worms, which belong to the phylum Annelida. Biologists believe that this indicates that mollusks and annelids evolved from a common ancestor that existed during the Precambrian Period (more than 580 million years ago) and had a trochophore larva. Because the phyla Mollusca and Annelida are closely related to each other, we shall discuss them both in this chapter.

Another reason mollusks are placed in a single phylum is that their different forms are the results of variations on the same basic body plan. **Mollusks are defined as soft-bodied animals that have an internal or external shell.** Their name is derived from the Latin word *molluscus*, meaning soft. Although a few present-day mollusks lack shells, they are thought to have evolved from shelled ancestors.

Form and Function in Mollusks

As you can see in Figure 27–3, the body plan of almost all mollusks consists of four basic parts: **foot**, **mantle**, **shell**, and **visceral mass**. The soft muscular foot usually contains the mouth and other structures associated with feeding. The foot takes many different shapes in mollusks: Flat surfaces adapted to crawling, spade-shaped structures for burrowing, and tentacles for capturing prey are a few examples. The mantle is a thin, delicate tissue layer that covers most of a mollusk's body, much like a cloak. The shell, which is found in almost all mollusks, is made by glands in the mantle that secrete calcium carbonate ($CaCO_3$). Just beneath the mantle in most mollusks is the visceral mass, which contains the internal organs.

Figure 27–3 *The basic body parts of mollusks are the foot, mantle, shell, and visceral mass. Note that the form and function of the foot and shell vary greatly among mollusks.*

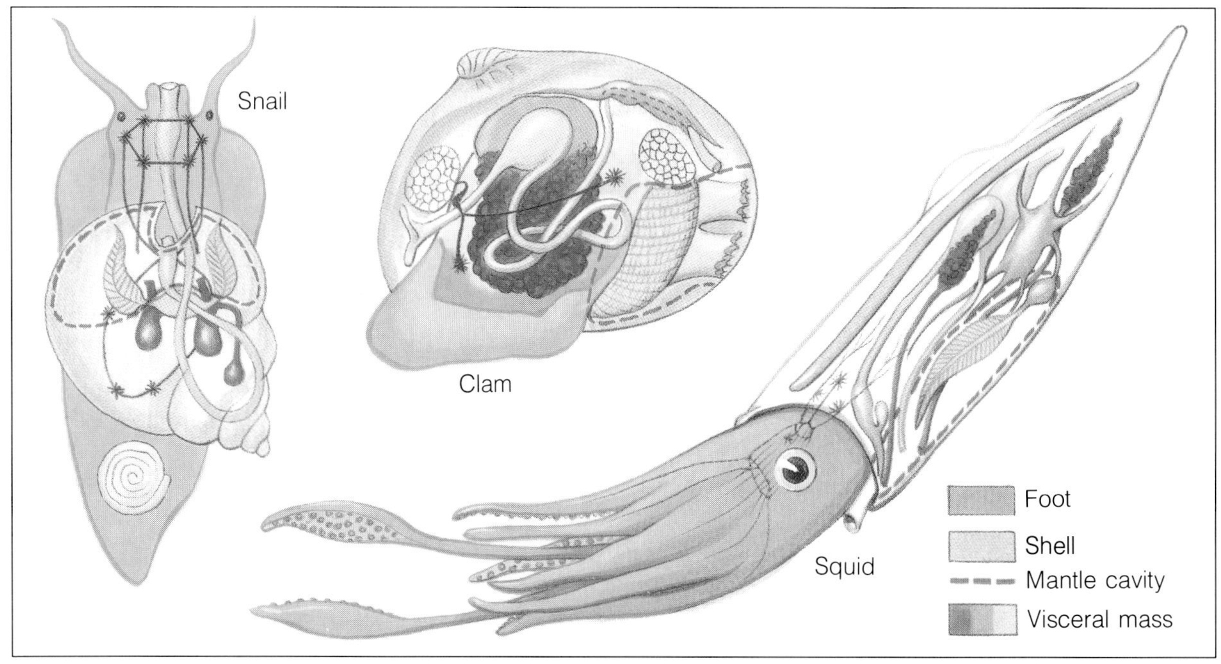

These basic body parts have taken on different forms as mollusks evolved adaptations to different habitats. The type of foot and the kind of shell that mollusks have are used to group them into classes. Later in this chapter we shall examine the three major classes of mollusks.

FEEDING Mollusks have evolved many types of feeding mechanisms and feed on many kinds of food. In fact it would be simpler to list the few things these animals do not eat than it would be to describe everything they can feed on! Every mode of feeding is seen in the phylum Mollusca. Most mollusks are herbivores, carnivores, or filter feeders, but a few species are detritus feeders and others are parasites.

Many mollusks—snails and slugs, for example—feed with a tongue-shaped structure called a **radula** (RAJ-oo-lah). The radula is a layer of flexible skin that carries hundreds of tiny teeth, which make it look and feel like sandpaper. Inside the radula is a stiff supporting rod of cartilage. When the mollusk feeds, it places the tip of the radula on the food and pulls the sandpapery skin back and forth over the cartilage. Mollusks that are herbivores use their radula to scrape algae off rocks and twigs in the water or to eat the buds, roots, and flowers of land plants. Mollusks that are carnivores use their radula to drill through the shells of other animals. Once they have made a hole through the shell, these carnivores extend their mouth and radula into the shell and tear up and swallow the prey's soft tissue. In the carnivorous snails called cone shells, the tiny rasping teeth of the radula have evolved into long hollow darts that are attached to poison glands. A cone shell uses these darts to stab and poison prey such as small fish.

Although they may have a radula, carnivorous mollusks such as octopi and certain sea slugs typically use sharp jaws to eat their prey. Like cone shells, some octopi produce poison to subdue their prey. Although cone shells and octopi generally feed on fish and other small animals, the poisons produced by some species are strong enough to hurt or even kill humans.

Mollusks such as clams, oysters, and scallops are filter feeders. They use their feathery **gills** to sift food from the water. As these animals pass water over their gills, phytoplankton (tiny photosynthetic organisms) in the water become trapped in a layer of sticky mucus. Cilia on the gills move the mixture of mucus and food into the mouth.

__Figure 27–4__ Many mollusks scrape bits of food into their mouth by pulling the tooth-covered skin of the radula back and forth over a supporting rod of cartilage. The scanning electron micrograph shows the teeth on the radula of a land snail.

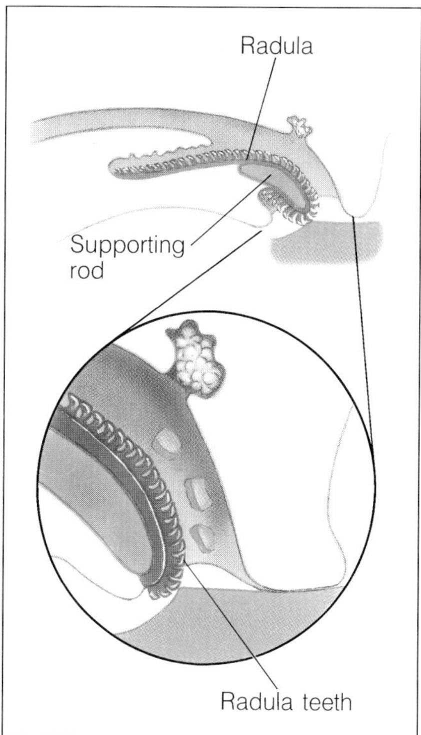

RESPIRATION Gills serve as organs of respiration as well as filters for food. In fact, in most species gills are used only for breathing. Aquatic mollusks such as snails, clams, and octopi breathe by using gills located inside their mantle cavities. But land snails and slugs breathe by using a specially adapted mantle cavity that is lined with many blood vessels. The mantle is wrinkled or folded to fit a larger surface within the limited

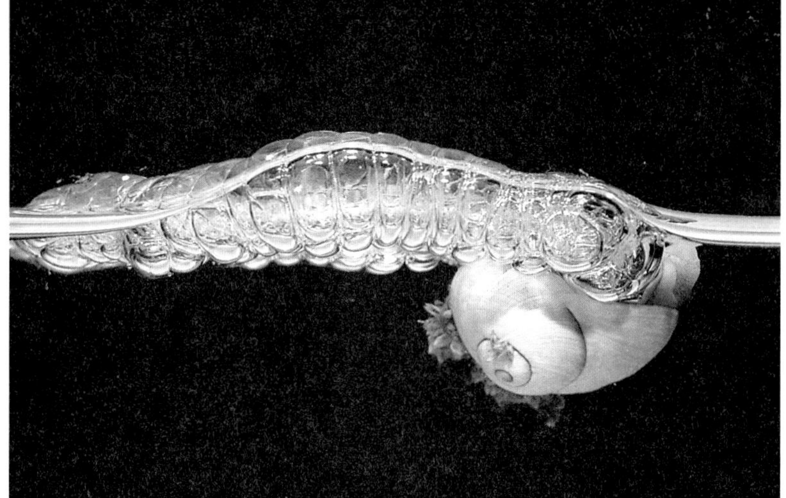

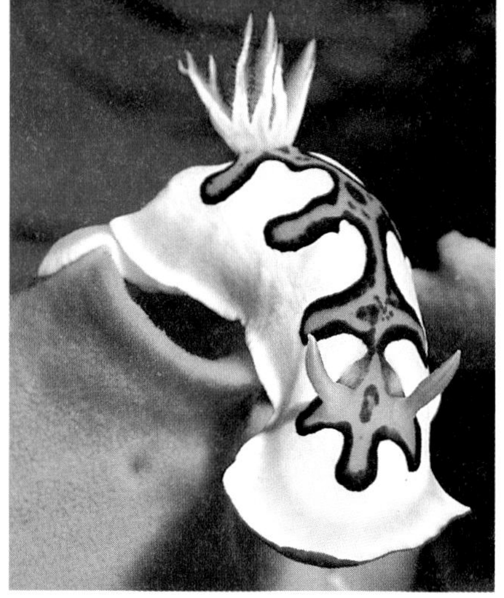

Figure 27–5 *The nudibranch (right) breathes through its skin and tuft of gills.* Janthina *(left), which uses a raft of air bubbles to float at the ocean surface, breathes with gills inside its shell. Many land snails (bottom) use their mantle cavity as a lung.*

space of the cavity. This surface is constantly kept moist so that oxygen can enter the cells. Because the mantle loses water in dry air, most land snails and slugs must live in moist places. They prefer to move around at night, during rainstorms, and at other times when the air is humid.

INTERNAL TRANSPORT Oxygen that is taken in by the respiratory system and nutrients that are the products of digestion are carried by the blood to all parts of a mollusk's body. The blood is pumped by a simple heart through what is called an **open circulatory system**. "Open" does not mean that blood can spill to the outside of the animal! It means that blood does not always travel inside blood vessels. Instead, blood works its way through body tissues in open spaces called sinuses. These sinuses lead to vessels that pass first through the gills, where oxygen and carbon dioxide are exchanged, and then back to the heart. Open circulatory systems work well for slow-moving or sessile (attached to one spot) mollusks like snails and clams. But the flow of blood through sinuses is not efficient enough for fast-moving octopi and squids. Those animals have **closed circulatory systems**, in which blood always moves inside blood vessels.

EXCRETION Like other animals, mollusks must eliminate waste products. Undigested food becomes solid waste that leaves through the anus in the form of feces. Cellular metabolism produces nitrogen-containing waste in the form of ammonia. Because ammonia is poisonous, it must be removed from body fluids. Mollusks get rid of ammonia by using simple tube-shaped organs called **nephridia** (neh-FRIHD-ee-ah; singular: nephridium). Nephridia remove ammonia from the blood and release it to the outside.

RESPONSE Mollusks vary greatly in the complexities of their nervous systems and their abilities to respond to environmental conditions. Clams and other two-shelled mollusks, many of which lead basically inactive lives burrowing in mud or sand, have simple nervous systems. They have several small ganglia near the mouth, a few nerve cords, and simple sense organs such as chemical and touch receptors, statocysts (simple organs for balance), and ocelli (eyespots). Octopi and other tentacled mollusks, on the other hand, are active and intelligent predators that have the most highly developed nervous systems of all members of their phylum. Because of their well-developed brain, these animals can remember things for long periods of time, and they may even be more intelligent than some vertebrates. The numerous complex sense organs these mollusks possess help them distinguish shapes by sight and texture by touch. Octopi can be trained to perform different tasks in order to obtain a reward or avoid punishment. Because of these abilities, octopi are often studied by psychologists interested in the way animals learn.

Figure 27–6 *Like most mollusks, coquina clams (inset) have an open circulatory system. Cephalopod mollusks, such as cuttlefish, have a closed circulatory system.*

REPRODUCTION As with almost all other essential functions, mollusks accomplish the function of reproduction in different ways. In most mollusks, the sexes are separate and fertilization is external. These mollusks—which include many snails, almost all two-shelled mollusks, and most of the species in the four minor classes of mollusks—release eggs and sperm into open water in enormous numbers. Eggs and sperm find each other by chance, and free-swimming larvae develop from the resulting fertilized eggs. In tentacled mollusks and certain snails, fertilization takes place inside the body of the female. Fertilization is also internal in some hermaphrodites (organisms that have both male and female reproductive organs). For example, many hermaphroditic snails get together in pairs and fertilize each other's eggs at the same time. Some other hermaphroditic mollusks, such as certain oysters, switch from one sex to the other. Sometimes they are male (and thus produce sperm) and sometimes female (and thus produce eggs)!

Figure 27–7 *A scallop gathers information about its environment with tiny round eyespots and sensory tentacles.*

Snails, Slugs, and Their Relatives

Members of the class Gastropoda are called **gastropods** (GAS-troh-pahdz). The name gastropod literally means stomach foot. This name is quite appropriate because most gastropods move by means of a broad, muscular foot located on their ventral (stomach) side. Gastropods include the familiar pond snails and land slugs as well as more exotic mollusks such as abalones, sea butterflies, sea hares, and nudibranchs.

Many gastropods have a one-piece shell that protects their soft bodies. This shell may be simple and shieldlike, as in limpets, or coiled, as in snails. When threatened, many snails can pull up completely into their coiled shells. Some snails are additionally protected by a hard disk on their foot that forms a solid "door" at the mouth of their shell when they withdraw.

Some gastropods have small shells or, as is the case with slugs, lack shells completely. This would seem to make them easy prey for hungry predators. However, these gastropods are not entirely helpless. Most land slugs are protected by their behavior—they spend the daylight hours hiding under rocks and logs, hidden from birds and other animals that might eat them. Some sea hares have a special ink-producing gland that they use when threatened to squirt ink into the surrounding water. This confuses predators and allows the sea hare to escape under its "smoke screen." Some gastropods, such as sea butterflies, escape predators by swimming rapidly. Many nudibranchs, or sea slugs, have chemicals in their bodies that taste bad or are poisonous. When a predator nibbles on one of these bad-tasting morsels, it gets sick. In addition, some nudibranchs use nematocysts from the cnidarians they eat to sting predators. The bad-tasting, poisonous, stinging, or otherwise booby-trapped nudibranchs are usually brightly colored. The bright colors warn predators to stay away. If a predator ignores the warning colors and eats a nudibranch, the consequences usually guarantee that the predator will remember the bright

Figure 27–8 *The ringed top snail (bottom, left) is found in the oceans of the Pacific Northwest. Despite their lack of a protective shell, the marine nudibranch (bottom, right) and terrestrial banana slug (top) are not likely to be eaten by predators—their bright colors and patterns indicate that these gastropods are poisonous.*

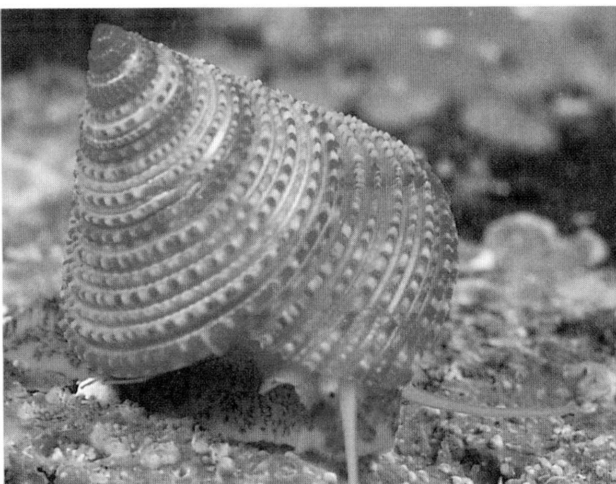

colors of the nudibranch and avoid it in the future! (While this does not help the first nudibranch, it does protect others of its kind.) Thus shell-less gastropods do have means of protection.

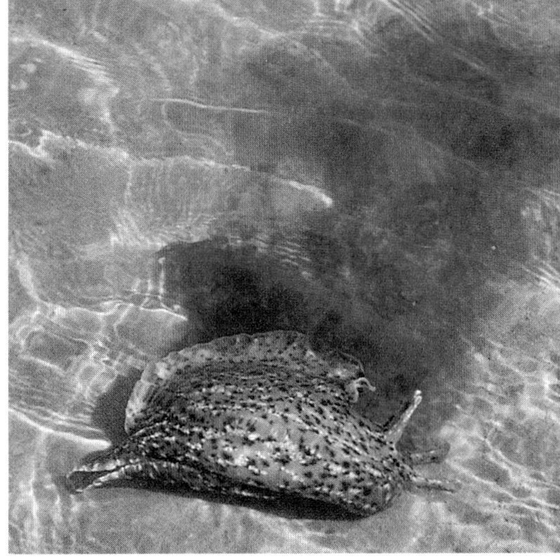

Figure 27–9 *When threatened, a sea hare releases purple ink into the water. This confuses predators and allows the sea hare to make its escape.*

Two-Shelled Mollusks

Members of the class Bivalvia (*bi-* means two; *valve* means shell) have two shells that are hinged together at the back and held together by one or two powerful muscles. Common **bivalves** include clams, oysters, and scallops. Bivalves may be tiny or as large as the giant clam *Tridacna*, which has been known to grow as large as 1.9 meters in length.

Although bivalve larvae are free-swimming, they soon settle down to a relatively quiet life on the bottom of a body of water. Some bivalves, such as clams, burrow in mud or sand. Others, such as mussels, secrete sticky threads to attach themselves to rocks. Although most adult bivalves are sessile, some, such as scallops, can move around rapidly by flapping their shells when threatened.

The mantles of bivalves, like those of most other mollusks, contain glands that manufacture the shells. These mantle glands also keep the shell's inside surfaces smooth and comfortable by secreting layers of mother-of-pearl. If a foreign object—a sand grain or small pebble, for example—gets caught between mantle and shell, the mantle glands cover it with this secretion. After many years these objects become completely coated and are called pearls.

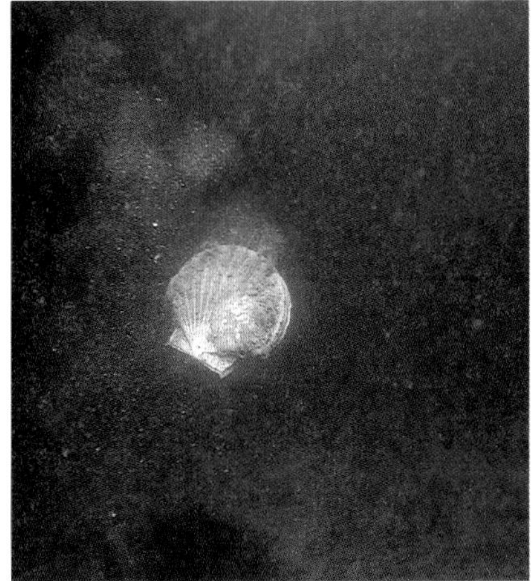

Figure 27–10 *The internal structures of a clam, a typical bivalve, are shown in the diagram on the left. Another bivalve, the scallop, can swim by rapidly opening and closing its shell (top). Pearls—objects coated by smooth, shiny secretions of a bivalve's mantle—may be beautiful and valuable gems or they may be fascinating curios, like the pearl fish (bottom).*

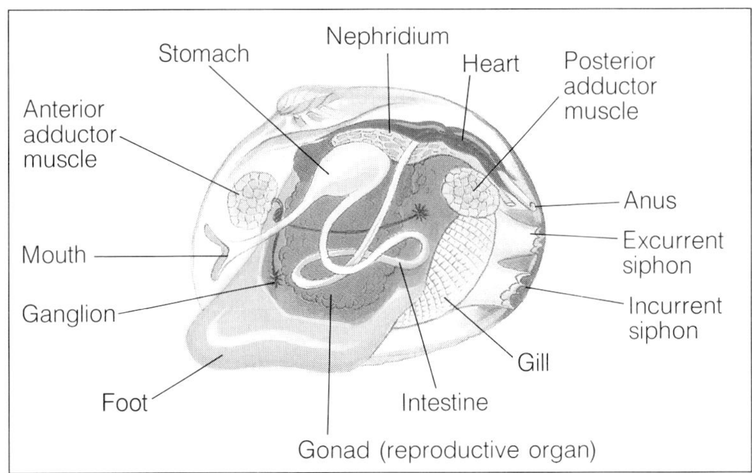

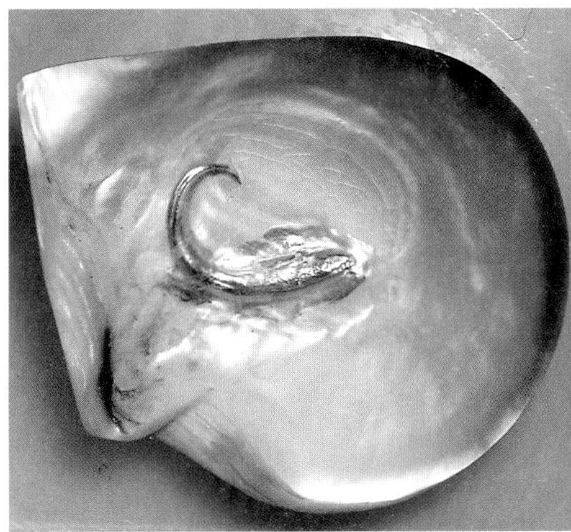

Tentacled Mollusks

Cephalopods (SEHF-uh-loh-pahdz)—members of the class Cephalopoda—are among the most active and interesting mollusks. This class includes octopi, squids, cuttlefish, and nautiluses. Cephalopoda means head-foot (*cephalo-* means head; *-pod* means foot). This name refers to the fact that a cephalopod's head is attached to its foot, which is divided into tentacles, or arms. Cephalopods range in size from tiny cuttlefish less than 2 centimeters long to giant squids, which are thought to grow to more than 20 meters long.

Most cephalopods have eight flexible tentacles equipped with a number of round sucking disks that are used to grab and hold fish and other prey. In addition to these tentacles, cuttlefish and squids also have two long, slender arms with suckers on the end. Nautiluses have many more tentacles (38 to 90) than other cephalopods. Their tentacles lack suckers but are made sticky by a mucuslike covering.

Although fossil evidence indicates that their ancestors had large external cone-shaped or coiled shells, most modern cephalopods have small internal shells or no shells at all. The only present-day cephalopods with shells are the few species of nautiluses. These cephalopods look much like fossil cephalopods from the beginning of the Cambrian Period, more than 500 million years ago. Cuttlefish have small shells that are found inside their bodies. The shells of some cuttlefish are thin and coiled, whereas others (which serve as the cuttlebone on which pet birds condition their beaks) are flat, platelike, and do not resemble shells at all. In both nautiluses and cuttlefish, gases in the shell help the cephalopod remain upright and allow it to float in the water. A squid's internal shell has evolved into a thin, flexible supporting rod known as a pen. Octopi have lost their shells completely.

Although most cephalopods lack a protective shell, they do have other means of protection. Most cephalopods can move quickly, either by swimming or crawling. They can also move by using a form of jet propulsion. The cephalopods draw water into their mantle cavities and then force that water out through the tubelike siphon. By pointing the siphon in different directions, they can shoot out a jet of water that propels them backward, away from danger. In addition, many cephalopods can release large amounts of dark-colored, foul-tasting ink when they are frightened. After squirting out a large cloud of ink, they make a hasty retreat. Perhaps most fascinating of all, octopi can quickly change color to match the colors of their surroundings. The match is often close enough that the octopi are nearly invisible.

Figure 27–11 *The luminescent squid (top), chambered nautilus (center), and extremely venomous blue-ringed octopus (bottom) are examples of cephalopods.*

How Mollusks Fit into the World

Mollusks play many different roles in living systems. For example, they feed on plants, prey on animals, and "clean up" their surroundings by eating detritus. Some of them are hosts to symbiotic algae or to parasites; others are themselves parasites. In addition, mollusks are an important source of food for many organisms, including humans.

Modern-day scientists have found some new uses for mollusks. Because filter-feeding bivalves concentrate dangerous pollutants and microorganisms in their tissues, careful checks of bivalves can warn biologists and public health officials of health problems long before scientists can detect these dangers in the open water. Besides acting as environmental monitors, mollusks also serve as subjects in biological research. Some current investigations are based on the observation that snails and other mollusks never seem to develop any form of cancer. If scientists can determine what protects the cells of these animals from cancer, they will gain valuable insights into how to fight cancer in humans.

Although mollusks are beneficial in many ways, they do have some negative relationships with humans. For example, land slugs and snails are plant eaters that can do much damage to gardens and crops. The bivalves called shipworms, which use their shells to drill their way slowly through pieces of wood in the water, are sometimes described as the termites of the sea. They settle on wood in large numbers and can reduce a good-sized log to a pile of wet sawdust over the course of a few years. Shipworms cause millions of dollars worth of damage to wooden boats and docks every year. Another problem with mollusks is associated with their use as food. Clams and oysters, which are among the few marine animals that are farmed in the sea, are filter feeders and thus gather and concentrate particles floating in the water—including bacteria, viruses, and the toxic protists that cause red tides. Eating bivalves that contain high concentrations of pathogens (things that cause disease), toxins, or pollutants can result in sickness or even death.

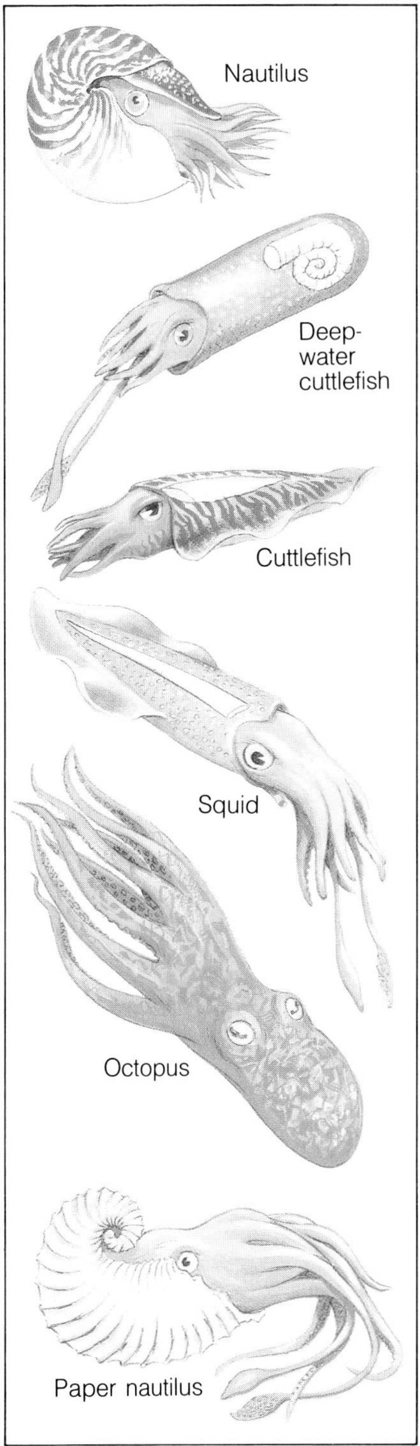

Figure 27–12 *One trend in cephalopod evolution has been a reduction in the size of the shell. Most modern species have a small shell or no shell at all. The "shell" of the paper nautilus is actually an egg case.*

27–1 SECTION REVIEW

1. What are mollusks? List the three major classes of mollusks and give an example of each.
2. Describe some of the ways mollusks affect humans.
3. What are some different ways mollusks use a radula?
4. How do mollusks protect themselves?
5. How is a cephalopod adapted to a fast-moving, predatory existence? (*Hint:* Compare the organ systems of a typical cephalopod with those of a bivalve or gastropod.)

Section Objectives

- Describe how annelids perform their essential life functions.
- List and give examples of three classes of annelids.

27–2 Annelids

If you have ever dug in a garden, you have probably met the most common terrestrial, or land-dwelling, segmented worm. But this species is only one of approximately 9000 species of segmented worms that live in soil, in fresh water, and in the sea. Segmented worms, or annelids, live everywhere in the world except Antarctica and Madagascar (a large island located off the southeastern coast of Africa). But because most segmented worms live in the sea, and many others spend their lives underground, only a few species are familiar to us.

What Is an Annelid?

Members of the phylum Annelida are known as **annelids**, or segmented worms. **An annelid is a round, wormlike animal that has a long, segmented body.** The name Annelida is derived from the Latin word *annellus*, which means little ring, and refers to the ringlike appearance of the body segments.

Annelids range in size from tiny aquatic worms less than half a millimeter long to giant earthworms more than 3 meters long. Although they also vary greatly in color, patterning, number of bristles, and other superficial features, most annelids are quite wormlike in appearance.

Form and Function in Annelids

The many segments of an annelid's body are separated by internal walls called septa (singular: septum). Most of the body segments are virtually identical to one another. However, some segments are modified to perform special functions. For example, the first few segments may carry one or more pairs of eyes, several pairs of antennae, and other sense organs.

Figure 27–13 *Many polychaete annelids, such as the sandworm* Neresis, *use hooklike jaws to capture prey or nibble on algae.*

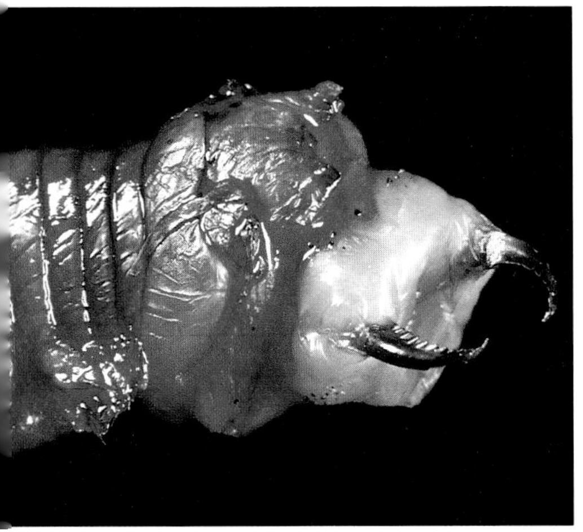

FEEDING The digestive tract, or gut, is a long tube within the body cavity of the worm that extends from the mouth to the anus (in the tip of the "tail"). Food enters through the mouth and travels through the gut, where it is digested. Like mollusks, annelids have evolved structures and behaviors that allow them to use a wide variety of foods.

One feeding organ that has evolved many different forms in different groups of annelids is the pharynx, or the muscular front end of the digestive tube. Many annelids can extend the pharynx through the mouth. In carnivorous annelids, this type of pharynx usually has two or more sharp jaws attached to it. When a suitable animal approaches, the worm lunges forward, rapidly extends the pharynx, and grabs the prey with its jaws. Jaws are also present in herbivores, which use them to tear off bits of algae. In some detritus feeders, the pharynx is covered with sticky mucus. When these worms extend the pharynx and press it against the sea-floor sediments, food particles stick to

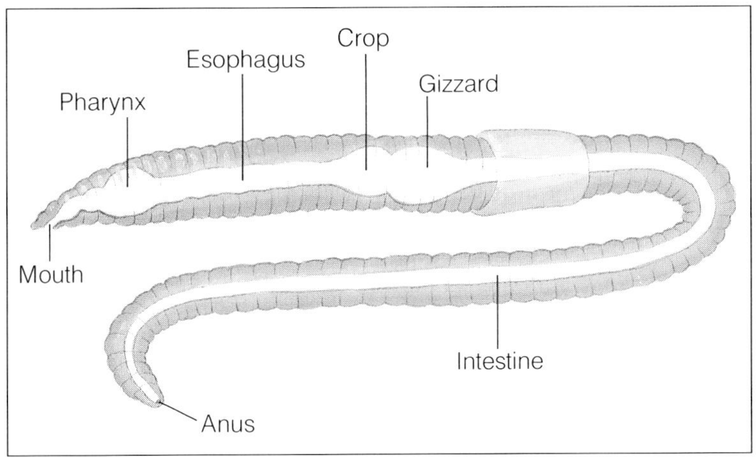

Figure 27–14 *The digestive system of an earthworm is shown here. The pharynx pumps a mixture of food and soil into a tube called the esophagus. The food then moves through the crop, where it can be stored, and through the gizzard, where it is ground into smaller pieces. The food is digested in the intestine. Undigested materials pass through the intestine and are eliminated through the anus.*

it. When the pharynx returns to its normal position, it carries these food particles back into the gut. In other detritus feeders, such as earthworms, the pharynx acts like a pump. It sucks a mixture of soil and detritus through the mouth and forces it down into the gut. In parasites, such as leeches, the pharynx is used to suck blood and tissue fluids from the host.

Annelids have a number of other structures that are used in feeding. For example, some annelids filter-feed by fanning water through their tubelike burrows and catching passing food particles in a mucus bag. In other filter-feeding annelids, such as the plume worm shown in Figure 27–15, the first segment forms featherlike structures that sift detritus and plankton from the surrounding water. These feeding structures are also used as gills for respiration.

RESPIRATION Aquatic annelids often breathe through gills. In some of these annelids, such as feather-duster worms, the large brightly colored feathery gills protrude from the opening of the worm's burrow or tube. In other annelids, small

Figure 27–15 *The spaghetti worm (left) uses long tentacles to pluck bits of detritus from the ocean floor. In plume worms (right), a brush-shaped structure on the head is used in filter feeding and in respiration.*

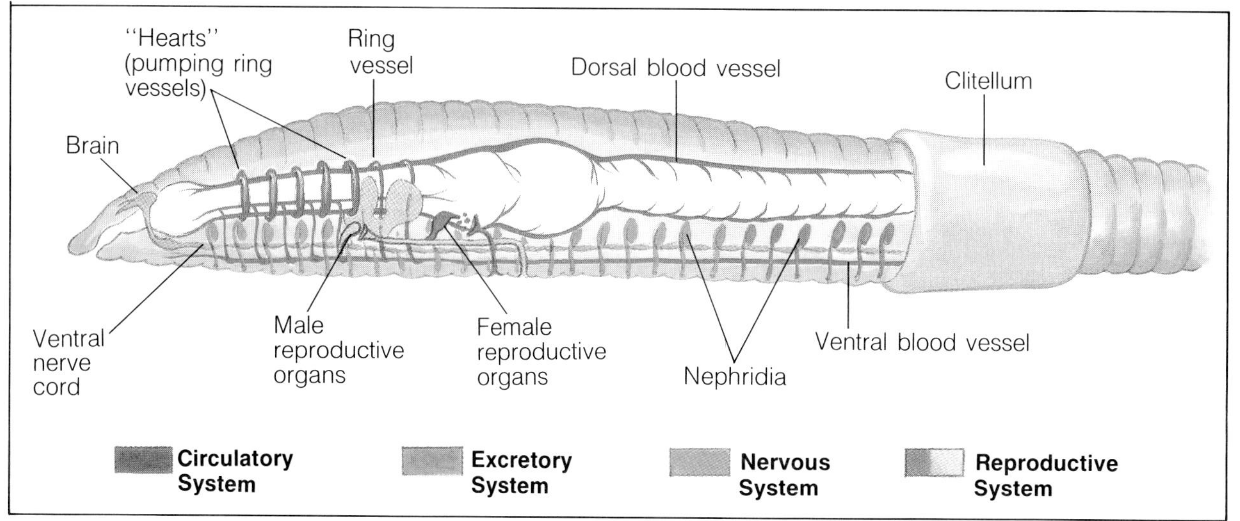

Figure 27–16 *The circulatory, excretory, nervous, and reproductive systems of an earthworm are shown here. How many "hearts" does an earthworm have?*

delicate gills are located on the sides of the body. The tube-dwelling annelids with this type of gill breathe by fanning water through their tubes. Many annelids take in oxygen and give off carbon dioxide through their skin. Because the skin must stay moist to make gas exchange possible, the worms die if the skin dries out. To help guard against this, terrestrial annelids, such as earthworms, secrete a thin protective coating called a cuticle to hold moisture around them.

INTERNAL TRANSPORT Annelids typically have closed circulatory systems organized around two blood vessels that run the length of their bodies. Blood moves toward the head of the worm in the dorsal (top side) vessel and toward the back of the worm in the ventral (bottom side) vessel. In each body segment is a pair of smaller vessels called ring vessels that connect the dorsal and ventral vessels and supply blood to the internal organs. In annelids such as earthworms, several of the ring vessels near the anterior (front) end of the worm are larger than the other ring vessels and have muscle tissue in their walls. These vessels are often called hearts because they contract rhythmically and help pump blood through the system. In other annelids, blood is moved through the body by muscle contractions when the worm moves.

EXCRETION Like other animals, annelids produce two kinds of wastes. Solid wastes pass out through the anus at the end of the gut. Wastes resulting from cellular metabolism are eliminated by nephridia (simple tube-shaped excretory organs). A pair of nephridia in each body segment removes waste products from the body fluids and carries them to the outside.

RESPONSE Many annelids are active animals with well-developed nervous systems. The brain sits on top of the gut at the front end of the body. Two large nerves pass around the gut and connect the brain with a pair of ganglia below. From these ganglia, a ventral nerve cord runs the entire length of the worm. Nerves from each segment of the worm enter and leave the nerve cord at a pair of small ganglia. These nerves help carry messages from sense organs and coordinate the movements of muscles.

Sense organs are best developed in the free-living marine species of annelids. Many of these annelids have sensory tentacles, statocysts, chemical receptors, and two or more pairs of eyes. Although the eyes are usually simple light detectors, in a few species the eyes can actually perceive objects. Most tube-dwelling species have light-sensitive cells either on their gills or near their mouths. These cells allow the animals to detect the shadows of predators passing overhead. When a shadow is detected, the worm pulls back into the shelter of its tube with amazing speed. In addition to specialized sense organs, these free-living marine worms also have various types of isolated sensory cells scattered along their epidermis. These cells respond to light, chemicals, and vibration.

Figure 27–17 *Sense organs are best developed in free-swimming annelids such as the paddleworm, which has a pair of beady eyes and a number of sensory tentacles on its head.*

Many other annelids have much simpler sensory systems. For example, earthworms have no specialized sense organs. They rely on simple sensory cells in the skin that are similar to those found in the skin of marine annelids.

Most free-living annelids do not have body structures that protect them from predators. Many depend on rapidly burrowing or swimming away from danger. Some, like earthworms, grab onto the walls of their burrows to make it harder to pull them out. Others, such as the marine fanworms, secrete protective tubes of calcium carbonate into which they withdraw if frightened. But some annelids do fight back. Several carnivorous annelids use their sharp jaws to attack animals that try to eat them. And the marine fireworms have tufts of poisonous bristles that easily break off and penetrate skin, causing painful sores and a burning sensation.

MOVEMENT Annelids have two major groups of muscles in their body walls. One group, called longitudinal muscles, runs from the front of the worm to the rear. When these muscles contract, they make the worm shorter. Another group of muscles runs in circles around the body of the worm. When these muscles contract, they make the worm skinnier. Marine annelids can swim by using these muscles to wriggle through the water. Burrowing annelids use their muscles to force their way through heavy sediment—not an easy thing for a soft-bodied animal to do!

REPRODUCTION Although a few annelids are able to reproduce asexually by budding, most annelids reproduce sexually. Some species have separate sexes and external

Figure 27–18 *Although they look very different from each other, both the fanworm (left) and the fireworm (right) are polychaetes. The fanworm is a filter feeder that retreats into its tube when threatened. The fireworm defends itself with poisonous bristles that break off and penetrate skin at the slightest touch. The pain caused by these bristles gives the fireworm its name.*

fertilization. This means that females and males release eggs and sperm, respectively, into the open water where fertilization takes place. Of course, the chances of fertilization taking place are enhanced if many worms in an area release their eggs and sperm at the same time. This is exactly what happens in some species. In the South Pacific, islanders eagerly await the autumn spawning season of the annelids called palolo worms. At a particular phase of the moon, hundreds of thousands of male and female palolo worms swarm at the surface of the water to release their eggs and sperm. Just before sunrise, the sea is literally covered with these worms. The islanders, who consider these worms a great delicacy, join sea birds and fishes that gather to feast on the spawning worms.

Some annelids, such as earthworms and leeches, are hermaphrodites that undergo internal fertilization. Although an individual worm produces both sperm and eggs, it rarely fertilizes its own eggs. Instead, worms pair up, attach themselves to each other, and exchange sperm. Each worm stores the sperm it has received in special sacs. When eggs are ready for fertilization, a band of thickened, specialized segments called the clitellum (cligh-TEHL-um) secretes a mucus ring into which eggs and sperm are released. The ring then slips off the worm's body and forms a cocoon that shelters the eggs.

Sandworms, Bloodworms, and Their Relatives

The class Polychaeta (*poly-* means many; *chaeta* refers to bristles) contains many common and important marine worms. **Polychaetes** (PAHL-ee-keets) are characterized by paired paddlelike appendages on their body segments. These appendages are tipped with the bristles that give this class its name. In the sea mouse, shown in Figure 27–19, the bristles are so long that they extend over the back of the worm and look like hair or fur.

Polychaetes live in cracks and crevices in coral reefs, in sand, mud, and piles of rocks, and even out in the open water. Some burrow through or crawl over sediments. Others live almost entirely in tubes they build for themselves. Some polychaetes are dull in color and rather uninteresting; some are brightly colored, iridescent, or even luminescent.

Figure 27–19 *The long bristles of the sea mouse look like iridescent fur.*

Earthworms and Their Relatives

The class Oligochaeta contains earthworms and related species. Two **oligochaetes** (AHL-ih-goh-keets) that you might be familiar with are earthworms and tubifex worms. Earthworms are long pink worms that often show up on the surfaces of lawns and sidewalks after it rains, are dug up in gardens, or are sold as fishing bait. Tubifex worms are red threadlike aquatic worms that are sold as tropical-fish food in pet stores. Most oligochaetes live in soil or fresh water, although some species live in the ocean. As the name of the class indicates (*oligo-* means few), oligochates have fewer bristles than polychaetes. These bristles, which can be felt as a roughness on the ventral (bottom) side of an earthworm, help anchor it in its burrow.

Although earthworms spend most of their lives hidden under ground, an observant person may find evidence of their presence above ground in the form of squiggles of mud known as castings. Recall that an earthworm (which swallows just about anything it can get into its mouth) uses its pharynx to suck a mixture of detritus and soil particles into its mouth. As the mixture of food and soil passes through the intestine, part of it is digested. Sand grains, clay particles, and indigestible organic matter pass out through the anus in large quantities, producing castings. Some tropical earthworms produce enormous castings—as large as 18 centimeters long and 2 centimeters in diameter!

Figure 27–20 *Earthworms are hermaphrodites that undergo internal fertilization. The sperm from one worm fertilizes the eggs of its partner, and vice versa.*

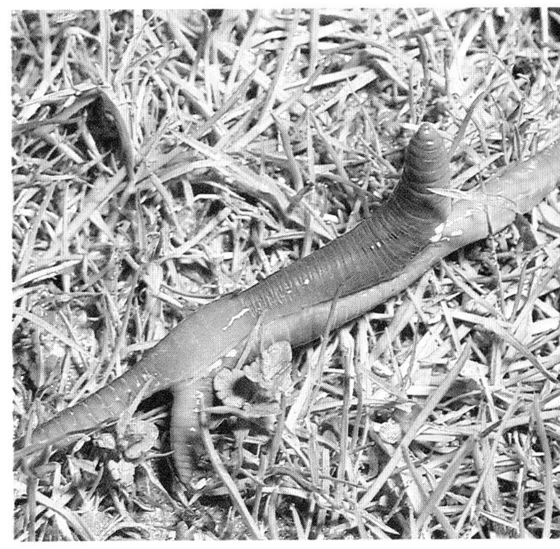

Leeches

The class Hirudinea contains the **leeches**, most of which live in moist tropical countries. Leeches are typically no more than 6 centimeters long, but there are some tropical species that are as long as 30 centimeters. Most leeches are freshwater organisms that exist as external parasites, drinking the blood and body fluids of their host. However, there are some marine and terrestrial leeches. And roughly one fourth of all leeches are carnivores rather than parasites. Carnivorous leeches, which feed on soft-bodied invertebrates such as snails, worms, and insect larva, either swallow their prey whole or suck all the soft parts from its body.

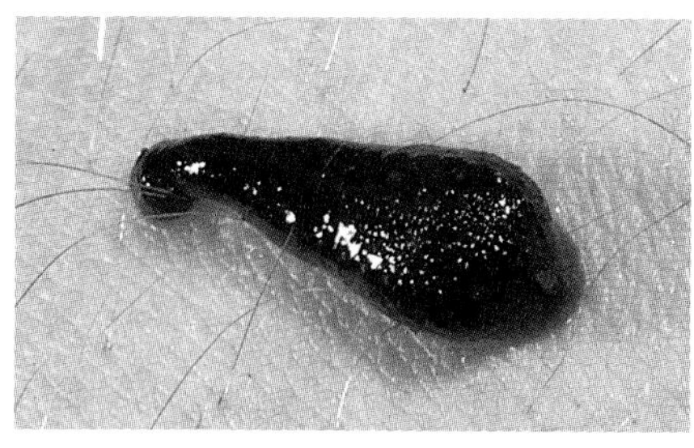

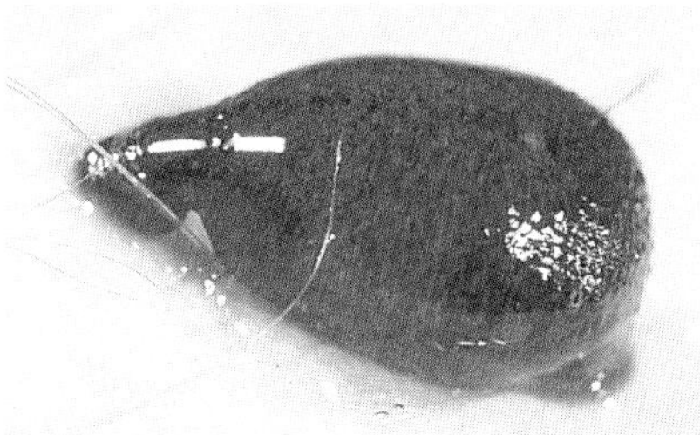

Figure 27–21 *A leech attaches to its host with suckers on its anterior and posterior ends (top). As it feeds, the body of the leech swells to accommodate as much as ten times its mass in blood (bottom).*

All leeches have powerful suckers at both ends of their bodies. These suckers—especially the anterior one, which usually surrounds the mouth—are used to attach a leech to its host. The posterior sucker is also used to anchor a leech to rocks, leaves, and other objects as it waits for a host to come by. Leeches penetrate the skin of their host in one of two ways. Some leeches use a muscular proboscis (proh-BAHS-ihs), or tubular organ, that they force into the tissue of their host. Others slice into the skin of their hosts with a razor-sharp pair of jaws. Once the wound has been made, the leech uses its muscular pharynx to suck blood from the area. Both types of leeches release a special secretion from their salivary glands to prevent the blood from clotting as they drink it. Some leeches also produce a substance that anesthetizes the wound—thus keeping the host from knowing it has been bitten!

During feeding, a leech can swallow as much as 10 times its weight in blood. Such a huge meal can take the leech up to 200 days to digest, with the help of symbiotic bacteria that live in its gut. A leech can live for a year before it must feed again.

How Annelids Fit into the World

Annelids are important in many habitats. Small polychaetes and their larvae are members of the ocean plankton, where they are food for many fishes, crabs, and lobsters. Bottom-dwelling polychaetes are important items in the diets of food fishes such as flounder.

Oligochaetes, particularly earthworms, perform an essential task in conditioning soil, as Charles Darwin noted in a lengthy and detailed study. By constantly burrowing through the ground, earthworms help aerate the soil. And by grinding and partially digesting the incredible amount of soil and detritus that passes through their guts, earthworms speed the return of nitrogen and other important nutrients from dead organisms to forms that can be used by plants. Without the continual efforts of these annelids, the structure and fertility of farm soils would degenerate quickly, lowering crop yields.

27–2 SECTION REVIEW

1. What is an annelid? List and give examples of three classes of annelids.
2. Discuss three different adaptations for feeding in annelids.
3. Describe the structure of the digestive tract in an earthworm.
4. How do polychaetes (free-living marine annelids) protect themselves from predators?

SCIENCE, TECHNOLOGY, AND SOCIETY APPLICATION

Leeches: Modern Applications of Ancient Medicine

There are few medical techniques as ancient as leeching, or applying leeches to a patient. The earliest known reference to leeching was written by a Greek physician more than 2200 years ago. And experts believe that leeching is much older than that!

Many people once believed that diseases could be cured by using leeches to remove blood from the patient. However when people began to better understand the nature of disease, leeches ceased to be popular medical tools. After all, it seemed senseless to remove blood from a patient when it was clear that microorganisms—not "bad blood"—caused disease. But interestingly enough, leeches are once again in the medical spotlight.

One modern medical problem faced by surgeons is that blood tends to collect in body parts reattached by microsurgery. Here is where leeches come in handy. They are used to remove the excess blood until the blood vessels in the reattached part have healed.

The chemicals in leech saliva make it possible to use leeches for a variety of other medical purposes. These chemicals prevent blood from clotting, dissolve existing blood clots, expand blood vessels (to keep blood flowing), loosen the connections between cells (to help disperse the other chemicals), and anesthetize the area of the bite. Researchers are currently developing medicines based on chemicals extracted from leech saliva. These new medicines may soon be used to clear blocked blood vessels and to treat a variety of circulatory-system diseases.

Leeches also produce chemicals that harm bacteria—chemicals that they may inject into the host as they feed. Symbiotic bacteria inside the leech's gut produce an antibiotic that keeps stored blood fresh by killing bacteria. And the chemical in leech saliva that loosens or dissolves connections between host cells may also dissolve the protective coating on bacteria, thus making them vulnerable to an attack by the immune system.

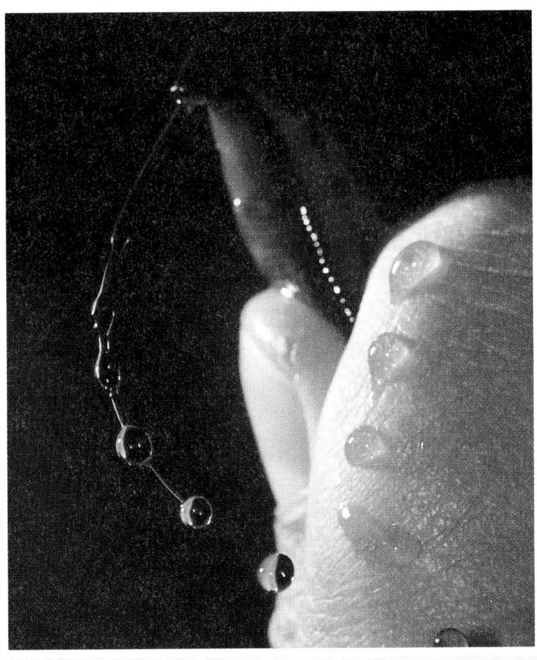

The leech shown here is being "milked" for its saliva. Researchers are currently developing medicines based on the chemicals found in leech saliva.

As medical researchers discover new uses for leeches, they are reminded that the ancient practice of leeching may not have been quite as senseless as it seemed. They are also reminded of the role evolution plays in shaping and refining the relationships between organisms (such as leeches and vertebrates). Of course, the leeches themselves didn't decide to perform a useful function for humans. But recall that parasites must evolve along with their hosts. Under pressure from natural selection, leeches have evolved adaptations that enable them to feed effectively on vertebrate hosts, including humans. Although leeches appeared on Earth long before humans, the chemicals they produce still affect us. Why? Due to common descent, our body chemistry is similar to that of other vertebrates—including the leech's original vertebrate host.

LABORATORY INVESTIGATION

OBSERVING EARTHWORM RESPONSES

PROBLEM

How do live earthworms respond to moisture and light?

MATERIALS *(per group)*

2 live earthworms in a storage container
tray
paper towels
piece of cardboard
desk lamp
medicine dropper

PROCEDURE

1. Open the storage container and examine the earthworms. Record your observations of their physical characteristics. Fill the medicine dropper with water and use it to give your earthworms a "bath." **Note:** *Make sure you keep your earthworms moist by giving them frequent baths. If an earthworm's skin dries out, it dies.*
2. Fold a dry paper towel and place it on one side of your tray, as shown in the accompanying figure. Fold a dampened paper towel and place it on the other side of the tray.
3. Place the earthworms in the center of the tray, between the dry paper towel and the moist paper towel. Cover the tray with the piece of cardboard.
4. After 5 minutes, remove the cardboard and observe the location of the earthworms. Record your observations.
5. Return the earthworms to their storage container. Using the dropper, moisten the earthworms with water.
6. Cover the entire bottom of the tray with a damp paper towel.
7. Place the earthworms in the center of the tray.
8. Cover one half of the tray with the piece of cardboard. Position the lamp above the open side of the tray.
9. After 5 minutes, observe the location of the earthworms. Record your observations.
10. Return the earthworms to their storage container. Using the dropper, moisten the earthworms with water. Cover the container.

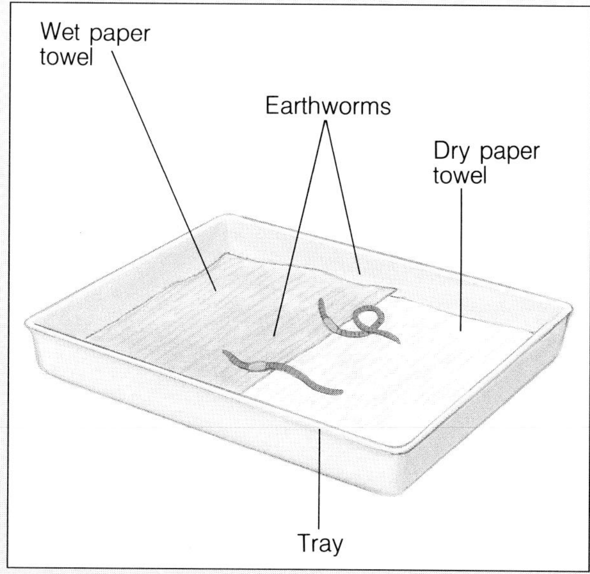

OBSERVATIONS

1. Which kind of surface did the earthworms prefer—moist or dry?
2. Do earthworms prefer light or darkness?
3. Describe the earthworms' color, texture, external features, and other physical characteristics.

ANALYSIS AND CONCLUSIONS

1. How does an earthworm's response to moisture help it survive?
2. Does an earthworm's response to light have any protective value? Explain.
3. How is an earthworm's body adapted for movement into and through soil?
4. Would you expect to find earthworms in hard soil? Explain.

STUDENT STUDY GUIDE

SUMMARIZING THE CONCEPTS

The key concepts in each section of this chapter are listed below to help you review the chapter content. Make sure you understand each concept and its relationship to other concepts and to the theme of this chapter.

27–1 Mollusks

- Mollusks are soft-bodied animals such as snails, clams, and squids that usually have an internal or external shell. The body plan of mollusks consists of four basic parts: foot, mantle, shell, and visceral mass.
- Most gastropods move by means of a broad, muscular ventral foot. Many gastropods have a one-piece shell.
- Bivalves have a hinged two-part shell. Although larvae are motile, most adult bivalves are sessile.
- Cephalopods have a well-developed nervous system, relatively advanced sense organs, and a closed circulatory system. A cephalopod's foot is divided into eight or more tentacles.
- Mollusks play many roles in the natural world. Many products that are important or valuable to humans are made by mollusks.

27–2 Annelids

- Annelids, which are also known as segmented worms, are round, wormlike animals with long, segmented bodies. An annelid's segments are very similar to one another and are separated by internal partitions.
- Polychaetes have a pair of paddlelike appendages on each segment. Most polychaetes are free-living marine worms.
- Oligochaetes have few bristles and lack appendages. Many are burrowing worms. Most live in fresh water or in soil.
- Leeches are typically blood-sucking external parasites that live in fresh water.
- Annelids interact in many different ways with other parts of the living world. Burrowing annelids such as earthworms are important in aerating soil.

REVIEWING KEY TERMS

Vocabulary terms are important to your understanding of biology. The key terms listed below are those you should be especially familiar with. Review these terms and their meanings. Then use each term in a complete sentence. If you are not sure of a term's meaning, return to the appropriate section and review its definition.

27–1 Mollusks

mollusk
foot
mantle
shell
visceral mass
radula
gill
open circulatory system
closed circulatory system
nephridium
gastropod
bivalve
cephalopod

27–2 Annelids

annelid
polychaete
oligochaete
leech

CHAPTER REVIEW

CONTENT REVIEW

Multiple Choice

Choose the letter of the answer that best completes each statement.

1. Which characteristic do many mollusks and annelids have in common?
   a. segmented body
   b. one- or two-part shell
   c. open circulatory system
   d. trochophore larvae
2. One major class of mollusks is
   a. Cephalopoda. c. Oligochaeta.
   b. Hirudinea. d. Polychaeta.
3. A mollusk that swims by flapping its broad, muscular foot is probably a
   a. bivalve. c. cephalopod.
   b. gastropod. d. polychaete.
4. Which organ is used for both respiration and filter feeding in some animals?
   a. nephridium c. gill
   b. radula d. ganglion
5. A bristly marine worm that has paired appendages on each segment belongs to Class
   a. Annelida. c. Oligochaeta.
   b. Polychaeta. d. Cephalopoda.
6. An oligochaete probably
   a. is a parasite.
   b. has paired appendages.
   c. has septa.
   d. has a mantle, foot, and visceral mass.
7. A scraping organ used for feeding is a
   a. nephridium. c. mantle.
   b. pharynx. d. radula.
8. In earthworms, the clitellum
   a. is involved in asexual reproduction.
   b. secretes a cocoon for the eggs.
   c. often has a pair of jaws.
   d. grinds food particles into smaller pieces.

True or False

Determine whether each statement is true or false. If it is true, write "true." If it is false, change the underlined word or words to make the statement true.

1. A <u>pharynx</u> is an organ used in excretion.
2. Softbodied animals that typically have a shell are known as <u>oligochaetes</u>.
3. Segmented worms belong to phylum <u>Hirudinea</u>.
4. Pearls and the shells of mollusks are formed by secretions from the <u>radula</u>.
5. Many <u>leeches</u> are blood-sucking parasites.
6. <u>Cephalopods</u> are characterized by a one-part shell and a broad, muscular foot.
7. <u>Gastropods</u> are usually sessile as adults.
8. Hermaphrodites usually undergo <u>external</u> fertilization.

Word Relationships

A. *An analogy is a relationship between two pairs of words or phrases generally written in the following manner: a:b::c:d. The symbol : is read "is to," and the symbol :: is read "as." For example, cat:animal::rose:plant is read "cat is to animal as rose is to plant."*

In the analogies that follow, a word or phrase is missing. Complete each analogy by providing the missing word or phrase.

1. one-part shell:gastropod::two-part shell:________________
2. cocoon:clitellum::shell:________________
3. shell:nematocyst and chemicals::snail:________________
4. light detection:balance::ocelli:________________

B. *Replace the underlined definition with the correct vocabulary word.*

5. Octopi have a circulatory system in which the blood is always contained in blood vessels.
6. Earthworms are members of the segmented worms phylum.
7. The part of a mollusk that contains the mouth and is often used in locomotion in cephalopods is divided into tentacles.

CONCEPT MASTERY

Use your understanding of the concepts developed in the chapter to answer each of the following in a brief paragraph.

1. How are mollusks adapted to different modes of feeding?
2. Compare the ways in which polychaetes and oligochaetes perform their essential functions.
3. How are clams adapted for burrowing in mud and sand?
4. How do mollusks fit into the world?
5. Explain why a person might purchase earthworms to put in a garden.

CRITICAL AND CREATIVE THINKING

Discuss each of the following in a brief paragraph.

1. **Assessing concepts** Although a number of animals are hermaphrodites, they rarely fertilize their own eggs. Explain why cross-fertilization is usually better than self-fertilization. Under what circumstances might self-fertilization be better than cross-fertilization?

Although many nudibranchs are simultaneously male and female, they do not fertilize their own eggs.

2. **Making inferences** Some oligochaetes can survive in areas that have little oxygen and can even tolerate a complete lack of oxygen for short periods of time. Some of these oligochaetes die when exposed to normal oxygen levels for a long period of time. What is probably the natural habitat of these oligochaetes? Explain.
3. **Developing a hypothesis** Female octopi die after brooding their eggs (tending and protecting eggs until they hatch). However, if certain glands near the brooding octopus's eyes are surgically removed, the octopus stops brooding, resumes feeding, and has a life span longer than the normal three to four years. Develop a hypothesis to explain this phenomenon. How might you go about testing your hypothesis?
4. **Using the writing process** Suppose that the topic of a debate is, "Resolved: It is better to be a free-swimming polychaete than a sessile one." Take either the affirmative or the negative stance and prepare a persuasive argument for your position.

CHAPTER 28

Arthropods

Arthropods display a wide range of forms and habits. The butterfly is a terrestrial herbivore. The crab (inset) is a marine carnivore.

Beneath the frigid sea off Alaska, a giant king crab scuttles along the ocean floor on legs nearly a meter long. In the lukewarm waters of a Louisiana bayou, two crayfish battle for control of a burrow beneath a cypress tree. And in the heart of a Florida swamp, 43 different species of mosquitoes swarm in such numbers that the buzzing of their wings fills the hot, humid air.

All these animals, and more than a million other species, belong to the phylum Arthropoda—the largest, most diverse, and arguably the most successful of all the animal phyla. Arthropods live in virtually every habitable environment on Earth—from ice fields in the polar regions to brine pools on the equator. Some arthropods are among the most destructive animals on Earth. Others are beneficial, and even essential, to the survival of other organisms.

What are arthropods? What common characteristics do they possess? How do they carry out their life functions? You will discover the answers to these questions in the pages that follow.

CHAPTER OUTLINE

28–1 Introduction to Arthropods

Section Objectives

- Describe the four subphlya of arthropods.
- Explain how arthropods perform their essential life functions.
- Discuss metamorphosis in arthropods.

To describe even a fraction of the living **arthropods** would take several books. More than a million arthropod species have been described, and scientists are certain there are many more in the tropics that have not as yet been found! As you will soon learn, members of this phylum vary enormously in size, shape, and habits.

Diversity and Evolution in Arthropods

You already know about many common arthropods. In fact, you have probably even eaten a number of them! Today most biologists divide arthropods into four subphyla:

- *Trilobita* This is thought to be the oldest subphylum of arthropods. **Trilobites** (TRIGH-loh-bights) were dwellers in ancient seas. They are now all extinct.
- *Chelicerata* **Chelicerates** (keh-LIHS-er-ayts) include spiders, ticks, mites, scorpions, and horseshoe crabs.
- *Crustacea* **Crustaceans** (kruhs-TAY-shuhnz) include such familiar (and edible) organisms as crabs and shrimp.
- *Uniramia* **Uniramians** (yoo-nih-RAY-mee-ahnz) include most arthropods: centipedes, millipedes, and all insects—including bees, moths, grasshoppers, flies, and beetles.

Why are there so many different kinds of arthropods? One reason is that they have been evolving on Earth for a long time. The first arthropods appeared in the sea more than 600 million years ago. Since that time, these animals have experienced several adaptive radiations. Some arthropods have remained in

Figure 28–1 *Members of the three living subphyla of arthropods are shown here. The scorpion, which is a chelicerate, is feeding on a hawk moth, which is a uniramian (left). The white-booted shrimp is a crustacean (right).*

Figure 28–2 *The velvet worm belongs to a phylum that has characteristics of both annelids and arthropods. The existence of these in-between animals supports the idea that modern annelids and uniramian arthropods are descended from a common ancestor.*

the water, where they have colonized all parts of the sea and most freshwater habitats. Others were among the very first members of the animal kingdom to colonize the land. The descendants of those pioneers were on hand when the first flowering plants appeared millions of years later.

The roots of the arthropod family tree are cloaked in mystery because the ancestors of the arthropods were soft-bodied animals that left few fossils. But by studying both living and fossil invertebrates, researchers have accumulated many clues to arthropod evolutionary history. Insects, centipedes, and millipedes seem to have evolved from ancestors that were closely related to the ancestors of modern annelid worms. Living evidence for this line of descent can be found in the form of small wormlike animals that live today in the moist tropics only. See Figure 28–2. Other arthropods, including crustaceans, spiders, and the extinct trilobites, evolved from more ancient and more distantly related ancestors.

The body form of the earliest arthropods is thought to be similar to that of the trilobites. A typical trilobite's body had a thick, tough outer covering and was composed of many segments, each of which bore a pair of appendages. Each appendage was divided to form two branches, one a walking leg and one a featherlike gill. See Figure 28–3.

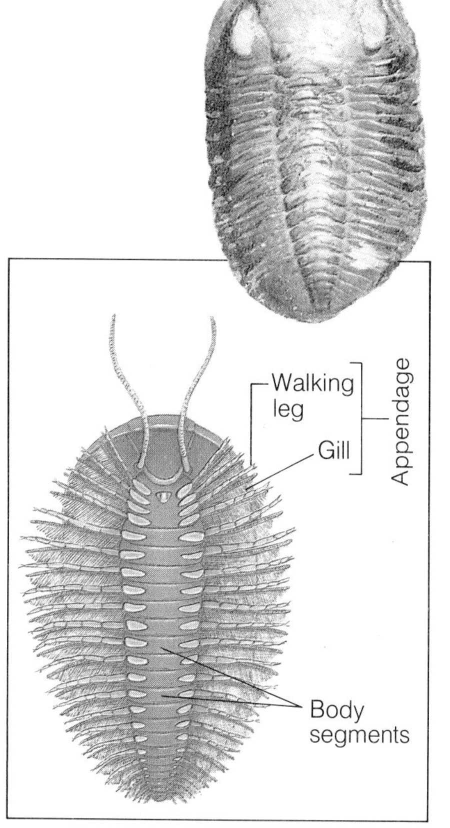

Figure 28–3 *The dorsal side of a fossil trilobite clearly shows the three lengthwise body lobes that give the animal its name (inset). An artist's rendering of the ventral side of a trilobite as it might have appeared when the animal was alive reveals numerous similarly shaped appendages.*

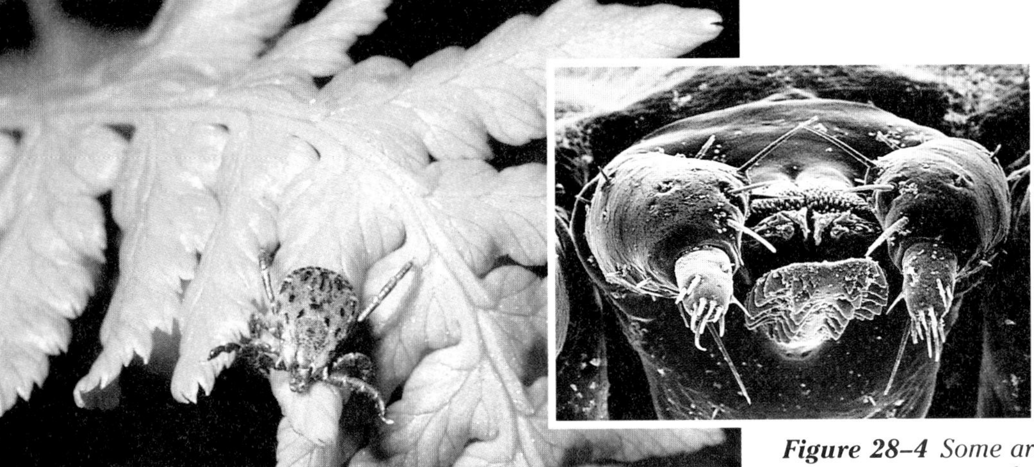

Figure 28–4 Some arthropods, such as the spiny lobster (center) and the tick (top), have extremely hard, tough exoskeletons. The mouthparts of a tick (inset) are adapted for biting and hanging onto a host. Other arthropods, such as the emperor gum moth caterpillar (bottom), have flexible, leathery exoskeletons.

Most living arthropods exhibit two evolutionary trends away from the trilobite form. First, many have far fewer body segments. The many segments found in their embryos fuse into larger segments during development. Second, arthropod appendages have become increasingly specialized for feeding, locomotion, and other functions.

Form and Function in Arthropods

Although living arthropods are quite different from one another, all arthropods exhibit several key features. **The three most important arthropod features are a tough exoskeleton, a series of jointed appendages, and a segmented body.** Other characteristics of arthropods include a brain located in the dorsal part of the head, a ventral nerve cord, and an open circulatory system powered by a single heart.

THE ARTHROPOD BODY PLAN The **exoskeleton** (*exo-* means outside) is a system of external supporting structures that are made primarily of the protein **chitin** (KIGH-tihn). Some exoskeletons, such as those of most insects, are leathery and flexible. Others, such as those of ticks, crabs, and lobsters, are extremely hard. These tough exoskeletons provide excellent protection from physical damage. The exoskeletons of many terrestrial arthropods are waterproof. This adaptation restricts the loss of water from the body and makes it possible for arthropods to live in extremely dry environments such as deserts. The exoskeleton also helps arthropods move efficiently and adapt to their environment in many other ways.

Although the exoskeleton protects an arthropod's body like a suit of armor, it has the disadvantages you might expect from such a covering. Because an exoskeleton is a solid coating, not a living tissue, it cannot grow as the animal grows. (You will learn how arthropods deal with this problem shortly.) And movement can occur only at the joints of the "armor."

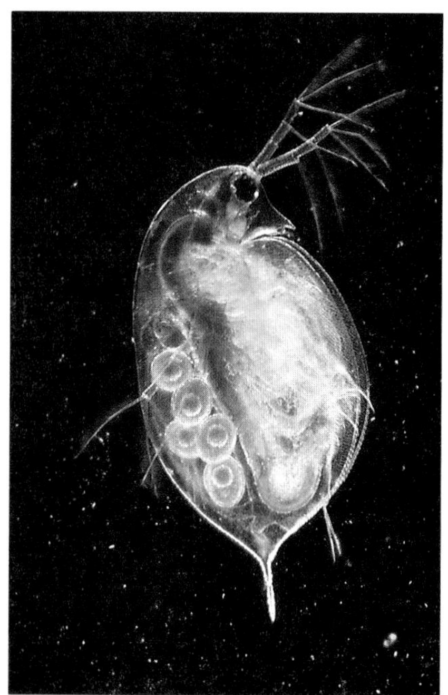

Figure 28–5 The waterflea is a tiny freshwater crustacean that lacks external segmentation and uses its antennae to propel it through the water. The round structures on the waterflea's back are its eggs.

All arthropods have jointed appendages (*arthro-* means joint; *-pod*, which literally means foot, refers to the appendages) that enable them to move. In primitive arthropods, such as trilobites, every body segment carries a single pair of appendages. But in species in which body segments are fused together, some appendages have been lost. Over millions of years, the remaining appendages have evolved into marvelously versatile adaptations to different environments. Arthropod appendages include antennae, claws, walking legs, wings, flippers, and other specialized structures.

All arthropods have segmented bodies. Some, such as millipedes and centipedes, have long, wormlike bodies with many visible segments. Others, such as insects, spiders, and crabs, have lost some segments in the course of evolution or had the segments fuse together to form a few large body parts.

FEEDING The appendages of arthropods have evolved in ways that enable these animals to eat almost any food you can imagine. Every mode of feeding is seen in arthropods—herbivores, carnivores, parasites, filter feeders, and detritus feeders. Although some herbivores, such as locusts, eat just about anything green, other herbivores are more selective. Some herbivores are specialized to eat specific parts of plants. Others feed exclusively on a particular kind of plant. Some carnivores, such as spiders, praying mantises, centipedes, and king crabs, catch and eat other animals. Other carnivores, such as many crabs and crayfish, feed primarily on animals that are already dead. External parasites—such as ticks, fleas, and lice—drink the blood and body fluids or nibble on the skin of other animals, including humans. Some internal parasites passively absorb nutrients through the body wall, whereas others eat away at the host from inside. Many marine arthropods are filter feeders that use comblike bristles on their mouthparts or legs to filter tiny plants and animals from the water.

Figure 28–6 The praying mantis (left) is a carnivore. The lubber grasshopper (right) is a herbivore.

RESPIRATION Arthropods have evolved three basic types of respiratory structures—gills, book gills and book lungs, and tracheal tubes. Although most arthropods have only one of these types of respiratory structures, a few species have both book lungs and tracheal tubes. And some species completely lack specialized respiratory organs.

Many aquatic arthropods, such as crabs and shrimp, have gills that look like a row of feathers located just under cover of their exoskeleton. These gills are formed from part of the same appendages that form mouthparts and legs. Movement of the mouthparts and other appendages keeps a steady stream of water moving over the gills.

Book gills (which are found in horseshoe crabs) and book lungs (which are found in spiders and their relatives) are unique to these arthropods. In both these structures, several sheets of tissue are layered like pages in a book. The many tissue layers increase the surface area for gas exchange. A horseshoe crab's book gills are carried beneath its body, whereas a spider's book lungs are contained inside a sac within the body. An opening called the spiracle (SPIHR-ah-kuhl) connects the sac containing the book lungs with the fresh air outside.

Most terrestrial arthropods—insects, some spiders, and millipedes, for example—have another respiratory device found in no other animals. From spiracles, long branching tracheal tubes reach deep into the animals' tissues. The network of tracheal tubes supplies oxygen by diffusion to all body tissues. As the arthropods walk, fly, or crawl, the movements of their body muscles cause the tracheae to shrink and expand, pumping fresh air in and out of the spiracles. Tracheal tubes work well only in small animals; large animals require a more efficient way to deliver oxygen and remove carbon dioxide.

Figure 28–7 *Although a fiddler crab spends much time on land, it uses gills for respiration. The male crab's large claw is used to attract females and to fight with other males.*

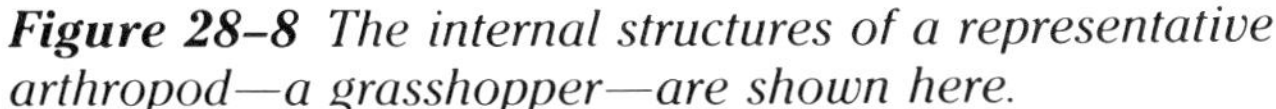

Figure 28–8 *The internal structures of a representative arthropod—a grasshopper—are shown here.*

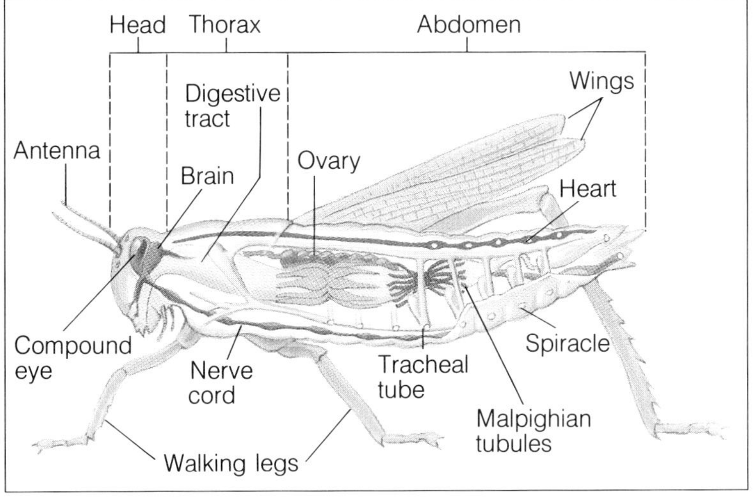

Figure 28–9 *The diamond beetle (left) uses Malpighian tubules to get rid of nitrogen-containing wastes, whereas the hermit crab (right) uses its green glands and gills.*

INTERNAL TRANSPORT In arthropods, a well-developed heart pumps blood through an open circulatory system. In spiders and some insects, the heart is long and narrow and stretches along the abdomen. In lobsters and crayfish, the heart is smaller and lies about halfway down the body. When the heart contracts, it pumps blood through arteries that branch into smaller vessels and enter the tissues. There the blood leaves the vessels and moves through spaces in the tissue called sinuses. Eventually, the blood collects in a large cavity surrounding the heart, from which it re-enters the heart through small openings and is pumped around again.

EXCRETION In arthropods, as in many other animals, undigested food becomes solid waste that leaves through the anus. The nitrogen-containing wastes that result from cellular metabolism are removed in different ways in different arthropods. Most terrestrial arthropods, such as insects and spiders, dispose of nitrogen-containing wastes by using a set of Malpighian tubules (mal-PIHG-ee-an TOO-byools). Malpighian tubules, like other arthropod organs, are bathed in blood inside the body sinuses. The tubules remove wastes from this blood, concentrate them, and then add them to undigested food before it leaves via the anus. Terrestrial arthropods may have small excretory glands at the bases of their legs in addition to, or instead of, Malpighian tubules. In aquatic arthropods, cellular wastes diffuse from the body into the surrounding water at unarmored places such as the gills. Many aquatic arthropods, such as lobsters, also eliminate nitrogen-containing wastes through a pair of green glands located near the base of the antennae. These wastes are emptied to the outside through a pair of openings on the head.

RESPONSE Most arthropods have well-developed nervous systems. All have a brain that consists of a pair of ganglia in the head. These ganglia serve as central switchboards for incoming information and outgoing instructions to muscles. From the brain, a pair of nerves runs around the esophagus and connects the brain to a nerve cord that runs along the ventral part of the body. Along this nerve cord are several more ganglia, usually one for each original body segment. These ganglia serve as local command centers to coordinate the movement of legs and wings. (That's why many insects can still walk or flap their wings after their heads are cut off!) Where many body segments have fused together, as in insects, there are several ganglia for each major body part.

Arthropods have simple sense organs such as statocysts and chemical receptors. Most arthropods also have sophisticated sense organs such as compound eyes for gathering information from their environment. Compound eyes may have more than 2000 separate lenses and can detect color and motion very well. In fact, insects can see certain things better than we can. (That's one reason it is so hard to swat flies and mosquitoes!) For example, the blades of a quickly moving fan—just a blur to our eyes—are clearly visible to a fly. And many insects can see ultraviolet light, which is invisible to humans.

Both crustaceans and insects have a well-developed sense of taste, although their taste receptors are located in strange places. The chemical receptors associated with the senses of taste and smell are located on the mouthparts, as might be expected, but also on the antennae and legs! Flies, for example, know immediately whether a drop of water they step in contains salt or sugar. Crustaceans and insects have sensory hairs that detect movement in the air or water (another reason insects are hard to swat or catch). As an object moves toward them, they can feel the movement of the displaced air or water and respond appropriately. Many insects have well-developed ears that hear sounds above the human range. Insect ears are often in odd places. The eardrums in grasshoppers, for example, are behind their legs.

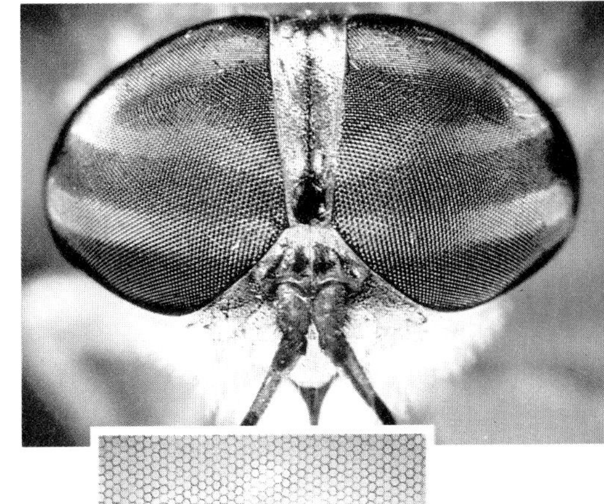

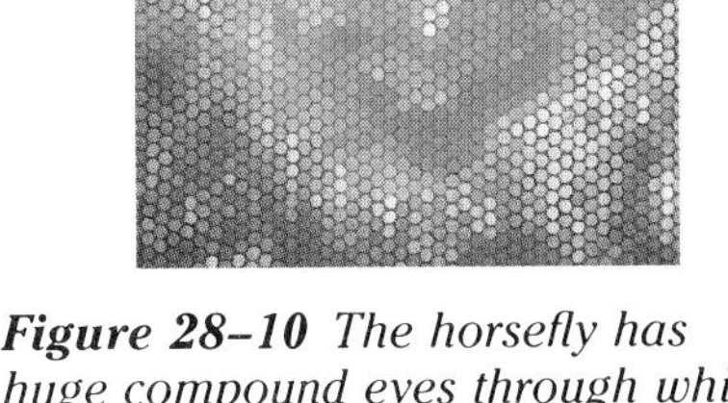

Figure 28–10 *The horsefly has huge compound eyes through which it sees poppy flowers much as they appear here (inset).*

Figure 28–11 *A harlequin beetle (left) uses its long antennae as "feelers." The red hourglass on the abdomen of the black widow spider (right) warns of the spider's venomous bite.*

Figure 28–12 *Can you find the grasshopper in the photograph? The stick grasshopper's shape is a form of camouflage (left). The markings and behavior of this caterpillar trick insect-eating birds into thinking it is a bird-eating viper (center). The harmless hoverfly mimics a stinging honeybee (right).*

An arthropod's well-developed sense organs help it detect and escape predators. The combination of these sense organs and a tough exoskeleton is enough to protect many arthropods. But some arthropods have additional means of protection. Scorpions, bees, and some ants have venomous stings, and many spiders and centipedes have venomous bites. Lobsters and crabs can attack potential enemies with powerful claws. And many insects and millipedes fight back using nasty chemicals. Some arthropods trick predators by creating a diversion. For example, some crabs can drop a claw or leg. This body part keeps on moving to distract predators while the rest of the animal scurries away. The crab then grows back the lost limb. Other arthropods use visual trickery to fool predators. Some hide through camouflage—matching the color and texture of their surroundings so closely that they seem to disappear. Others imitate the warning coloration of poisonous or dangerous species—a phenomenon called mimicry.

Figure 28–13 *Muscles attached to the inside of an exoskeleton bend and straighten the joints.*

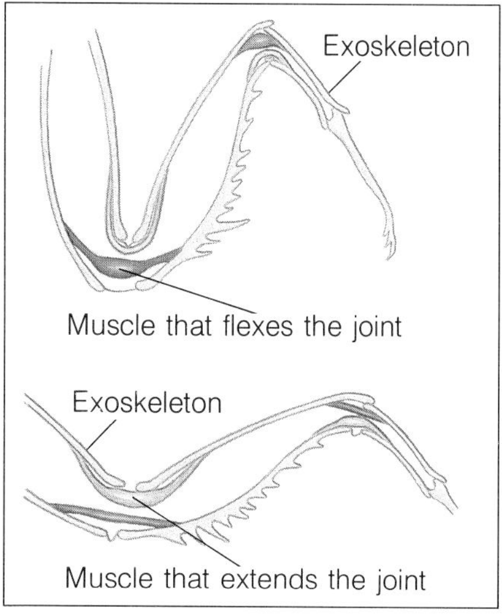

MOVEMENT Arthropods have well-developed muscle systems that are coordinated by the nervous system. Muscles generate force by contracting, then transfer that force to the exoskeleton. At each body joint, some muscles are positioned to flex the joint and other muscles to extend it. See Figure 28–13. The pull of muscles against the exoskeleton allows arthropods to beat their wings against the air to fly, push their legs against the ground to walk, or beat their flippers against the water to swim.

REPRODUCTION Reproduction in most arthropods is simple. Males and females produce sperm and eggs, respectively, and fertilization usually takes place inside the body of the female. In spiders and some crustaceans, the male deposits a small packet of sperm that the female picks up. In most insects and crustaceans, however, the male uses a special reproductive organ to deposit sperm inside the female.

Growth and Development in Arthropods

Exoskeletons, as useful as they are, present a problem in terms of growth. As a growing student, you can understand that problem. Imagine that you had a skin-tight suit of clothes tailored for you last year. Could you fit into it now? Probably not. You need larger clothes as you grow. Similarly, arthropods must replace their exoskeletons with larger ones in order to allow their bodies to increase in size as they mature. The problem is not a simple one, however, because the exoskeleton not only covers all appendages and sense organs, but also lines the gut as far down as the stomach. In order to grow, all arthropods must **molt**, or shed, their exoskeletons. This complicated process is controlled by several important hormones, the most important of which is called molting hormone.

When molting time is near, the epidermis (the layer of cells that covers the outside of the body) digests the inner part of the exoskeleton and absorbs much of the chitin in order to recycle the chemicals in it. After it secretes a new exoskeleton inside the old one, an arthropod pulls completely out of its old exoskeleton. Arthropods often eat what is left of the old exoskeleton. The animal then expands to its new, larger size, and the new exoskeleton (which is still soft) stretches to cover it. The animal must then wait for the new exoskeleton to harden, a process that can take from a few hours to a few days. During this time, the new shell stays soft and the animal is quite vulnerable. Thus arthropods hide from predators during molting.

Most arthropods molt several times between hatching and adulthood. In most cases the process of growth and development involves **metamorphosis**, or a dramatic change in form.

Some arthropods, such as grasshoppers, mites, and crustaceans, hatch from eggs into young animals that look much like the adults. However, these young animals lack functioning sexual organs and often lack other adult structures such as wings. As the young grow, they keep molting and getting larger until they reach adult size. Along the way, they gradually acquire the characteristics of adults. In insects, this kind of gradual change during development is called incomplete metamorphosis.

Figure 28–14 *The adult cicada is emerging from the molted exoskeleton of an immature stage. Arthropods molt in order to increase in size and also to change from one body form to another in the process of metamorphosis.*

Figure 28–15 *The grasshopper undergoes incomplete metamorphosis, whereas the monarch butterfly undergoes complete metamorphosis.*

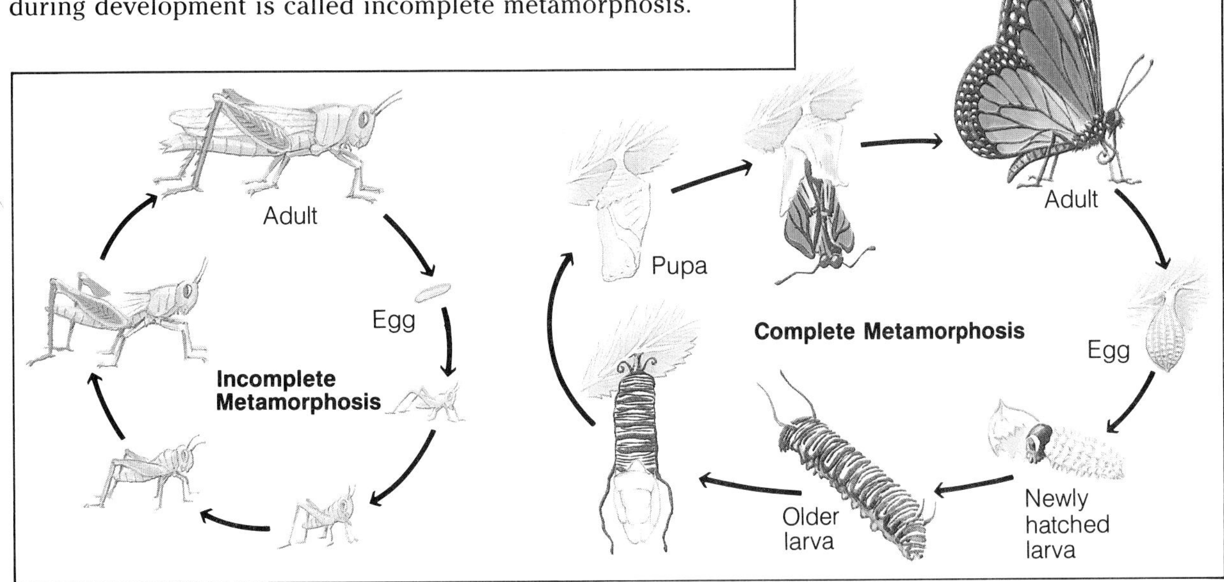

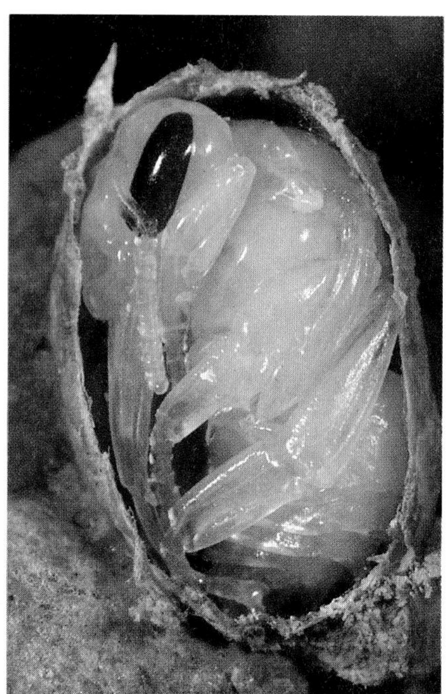

Figure 28–16 *Insect pupae are often surrounded by a protective covering. The bumblebee pupa in this photograph is surrounded by a wax case. Many caterpillars spin cocoons of silk.*

Many insects, such as bees, moths, and beetles, undergo a four-stage process of development called complete metamorphosis. Refer to Figure 28–15 on page 615 as you read about the process of complete metamorphosis. The eggs of insects that undergo complete metamorphosis hatch into larvae that look nothing like their parents. As these larvae grow, they molt repeatedly, growing larger each time but changing little in appearance. When a larva reaches a certain age, it sheds its larval skin one last time and becomes a **pupa** (PYOO-pah; plural: pupae). During the pupal stage, the insect's body is totally rearranged—adult structures grow from tiny buds and larval structures are broken down to supply the raw materials for the adult structures. When metamorphosis is complete, the animal emerges as a fully grown adult with both internal and external body parts that are completely different from what it had before. Not only does this adult look like a totally different animal, it acts differently too.

Metamorphosis is controlled by a complicated interaction of several hormones, including molting hormone. In insects that undergo complete metamorphosis, the levels of juvenile hormone help regulate the stages of development. High levels of juvenile hormone keep an insect in its larval form each time it molts. As the insect matures, however, its production of juvenile hormone decreases. At some point, the level of juvenile hormone drops below a certain critical point. The next time the insect molts, it becomes a pupa. And when no juvenile hormone is produced, the insect undergoes a pupa-to-adult molt.

Because the balance of juvenile hormone, molting hormone, and other hormones is critical in arthropod development, it is possible to combat insects by tampering with their hormone levels. Certain plants defend themselves against herbivorous insects by producing chemicals that prevent molting, cause insects to develop at the wrong rate, or keep insects from becoming functional adults. In recent years, researchers have developed chemicals that act in a similar manner. These chemicals may eventually enable people to control crop-eating insects without using dangerous poisons.

28–1 SECTION REVIEW

1. Name the four subphyla of arthropods. Which subphyla is thought to be the oldest?
2. Compare complete and incomplete metamorphosis.
3. Describe the different types of organs that are used in arthropod respiration.
4. Terrestrial arthropods often have valves that can open and close the spiracles. How are these valves an adaptation to life on land? (*Hint:* What is the function of the stomata on leaves?)

28–2 Spiders and Their Relatives

Section Objectives

- Discuss the distinguishing characteristics of chelicerates.
- Describe and give examples of members of the two main groups of animals in the subphylum Chelicerata.
- Explain how arachnids obtain food.

Spiders and their relatives—horseshoe crabs, ticks, and scorpions, for example—belong to the subphylum Chelicerata. **Chelicerates are arthropods that are characterized by a two-part body and mouthparts called chelicerae.** These arthropods also lack the sensory "feelers" that are found on the heads of most other arthropods.

All chelicerates have a body that is divided into two parts: the cephalothorax (sehf-ah-loh-THOR-aks) and the abdomen. The anterior end of the cephalothorax contains the brain, eyes, mouth and mouthparts, and esophagus. The posterior end of the cephalothorax carries the front part of the digestive system and several pairs of walking legs. The abdomen contains most of the internal organs. See Figure 28–17.

All chelicerates have two pairs of appendages attached near the mouth that are adapted as mouthparts. The first pair of mouthparts are called chelicerae (keh-LIHS-er-ee; singular: chelicera). The second pair of mouthparts, which are longer than the chelicerae, are called pedipalps (PEHD-ih-palps). Both sets of mouthparts are adapted to serve different purposes in feeding in different species.

Horseshoe Crabs

Among the oldest chelicerates are the horseshoe crabs. This name is somewhat misleading because these animals are not true crabs (which are crustaceans). Horseshoe crabs appeared in the Ordovician Period (more than 430 million years ago) and have not changed much since then—they are true "living fossils." Horseshoe crabs are heavily armor-plated,

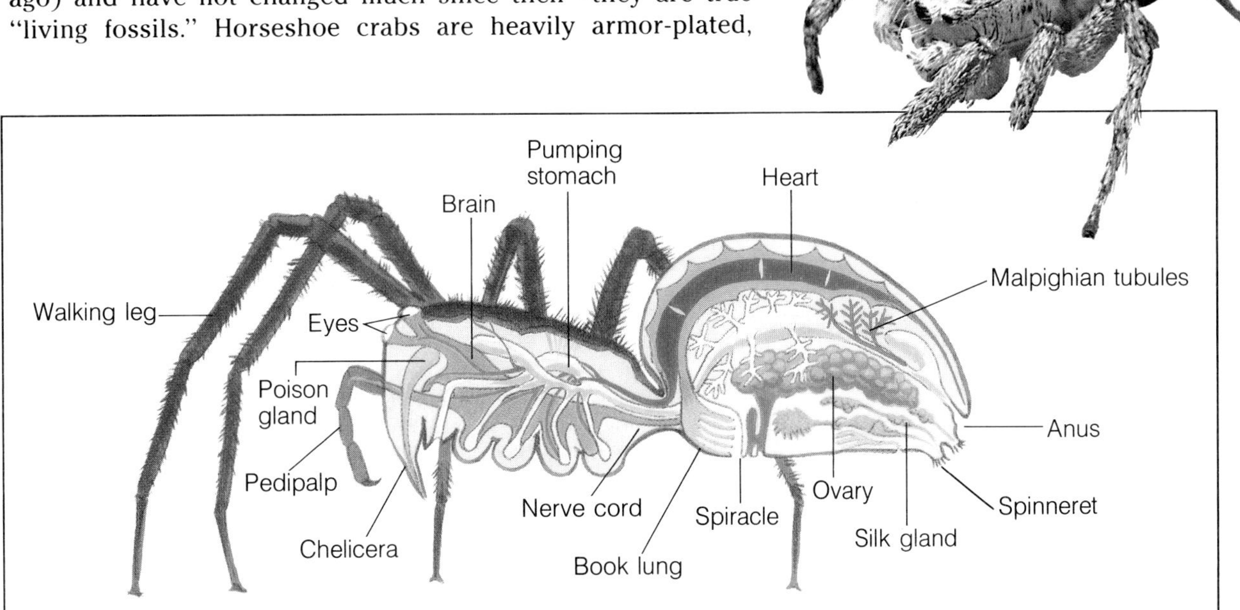

Figure 28–17 *The internal structures of a typical spider are shown in this diagram. A jumping spider (inset) captures prey by pouncing on it, rather than by catching it in a web.*

Figure 28–18 *A horseshoe crab's tiny pincerlike chelicerae and five pairs of walking legs are visible when the animal is turned on its back. The platelike structures on the abdomen cover and protect the book gill's "pages." The long tail is not seen here because the horseshoe crab has pushed it into the sand to right itself.*

have five pairs of walking legs, and long spikelike tails. They can grow up to 60 centimeters long—about the size (and shape) of a frying pan. When they first hatch, however, horseshoe crabs are only about 1 centimeter long. These newly hatched horseshoe crabs are called trilobite larvae because they look much like their extinct distant relatives.

Arachnids

The most familiar chelicerates are the **arachnids**, which include spiders, scorpions, ticks, and mites. All adult arachnids have four pairs of walking legs on their cephalothorax. Many arachnids are carnivores that have pedipalps adapted for capturing and holding prey and chelicerae adapted for biting and sucking out their soft parts.

SPIDERS Spiders are predators that usually feed on insects. However, a few large tropical spiders are capable of catching and eating small vertebrates, such as hummingbirds. Spiders capture their prey in a variety of ways. Some spiders ensnare their prey in webs. Others stalk and then pounce on the prey. And some lie in wait beneath the lid of a camouflaged underground burrow, leaping out to grab unlucky insects that venture too near.

Once a spider captures its prey, it uses its hollow fanglike chelicerae to inject paralyzing venom into it. When the prey is paralyzed, the spider's mouth introduces enzymes into the wounds made by the chelicerae. These enzymes break down the prey's tissues, enabling the spider to suck up the liquefied tissues with its esophagus and a specialized pumping stomach. The pumping stomach then forces the liquid food through the rest of the spider's digestive system.

Whether or not they spin webs, all spiders produce a strong, flexible protein called silk. Silk, which is produced in special glands located in the abdomen, is five times stronger

Figure 28–19 *The wolf spider (left) ambushes prey from its silk-lined burrow. Large tarantulas (right) are capable of catching and devouring small vertebrates, such as lizards.*

than steel. It is strong enough, in fact, to withstand the equivalent of the impact of a jet fighter every time a spider's web traps a fly. Spiders spin silk into webs, cocoons for eggs, wrappings for prey, and other structures by forcing liquid silk through organs called spinnerets. As the liquid silk is pulled out of the spinnerets, it hardens into a single strand. Interestingly, the complicated behavior of web-spinning seems to be "preprogrammed" into a spider's brain. The spiders of web-spinning species can build their intricate webs almost as soon as they hatch—without having to learn how.

Figure 28–20 *Some spiders build webs to capture prey.*

MITES AND TICKS Mites and ticks are small arachnids, many of which are parasites on humans, on farm animals, and on important agricultural plants. Most species are smaller than 1 millimeter, but some ticks can be as large as 3 centimeters. In many mites and ticks, the chelicerae are needlelike structures that are used to pierce the skin of their hosts. These chelicerae may also have large teeth to help the parasite keep a firm hold on the host. The pedipalps are often equipped with claws for digging in and holding on. Some species, such as spider mites, damage houseplants and are major agricultural pests on crops such as cotton. Others—including chiggers, mange, and scabies mites—cause painful itching rashes in humans, dogs, and other mammals. A whole host of ticks parasitize humans and the animals we raise. Tick bites are not just annoying—they can be dangerous. In the United States, ticks can spread Rocky Mountain spotted fever and Lyme disease.

SCORPIONS Scorpions are widespread in warm areas around the world, including the southwestern United States. All scorpions are carnivores that prey on other invertebrates, usually insects. The pedipalps of scorpions are enormously enlarged into a pair of claws. The abdomen, which is long and segmented, terminates in a venomous barb used to sting prey. Usually, a scorpion grabs prey with its pedipalps, then whips

Figure 28–21 *Red velvet mites are similar in form to other members of their class (right). However, they are unusual in that they are not parasites and are relatively large (about 1 centimeter long). The loser of a fight between two scorpions will be stung and eaten by the winner (left). Biologists can locate scorpions at night by shining ultraviolet (UV) light on the desert floor. Under UV light, scorpions glow brightly with a white, yellow, or orange light.*

its abdomen over its head to sting the prey, thus killing or paralyzing it. The scorpion then chews its meal with its chelicerae. Because scorpions like to crawl into moist, dark places, people in areas with scorpions should check inside their shoes before putting them on in the morning. Most North American scorpions have venom powerful enough to cause about as much pain as a wasp sting. However, the venom of one genus of scorpions that lives in Mexico, New Mexico, and Arizona has killed small children who were stung accidentally.

28–2 SECTION REVIEW

1. What are chelicerates? Name and give examples of the two main groups of chelicerates.
2. What is silk? How do spiders use silk?
3. How are chelicerae modified for feeding in spiders? In ticks?

28–3 Crustaceans

Section Objectives

- Discuss the distinguishing characteristics of crustaceans.
- Describe the anatomy of a typical crustacean.

The subphylum Crustacea contains over 35,000 species. Crustaceans are primarily aquatic, although there are some terrestrial species. Crustaceans range in size from microscopic water fleas less than 0.25 millimeter long to Japanese spider crabs that are thought to grow up to 6 meters across and lobsters that have a mass of more than 20 kilograms. And crustaceans vary in form as much as they vary in size!

Although crustaceans adapted to different conditions are quite dissimilar in form, all crustaceans share a number of structural similarities. **In general, crustaceans are characterized by a hard exoskeleton, two pairs of antennae, and mouthparts called mandibles.** As we examine a little of the enormous diversity of form and function in crustaceans, we will focus on a representative species, the crayfish. Refer to Figure 28–23 as you read about structure and function in crustaceans.

Figure 28–22 The pill bug is a terrestrial crustacean. When threatened, a pill bug curls into a ball to protect its soft underside.

The main crustacean body parts are the head, thorax, and abdomen. In crayfish, as in many other crustaceans, the head and thorax have fused into a cephalothorax that is covered by a tough shell called the carapace. Unlike most other arthropods, many large crustaceans have calcium carbonate (limestone) in the exoskeleton. This is what makes the shells of crustaceans such as crabs and lobsters hard and stony.

In crustaceans, the first two pairs of appendages are "feelers" called antennae, which bear many sensory hairs. Antennae serve primarily as sense organs in crayfish, but in some other crustaceans they are used in filter feeding. Still other crustaceans, such as water fleas, use their antennae as oars to push them through the water.

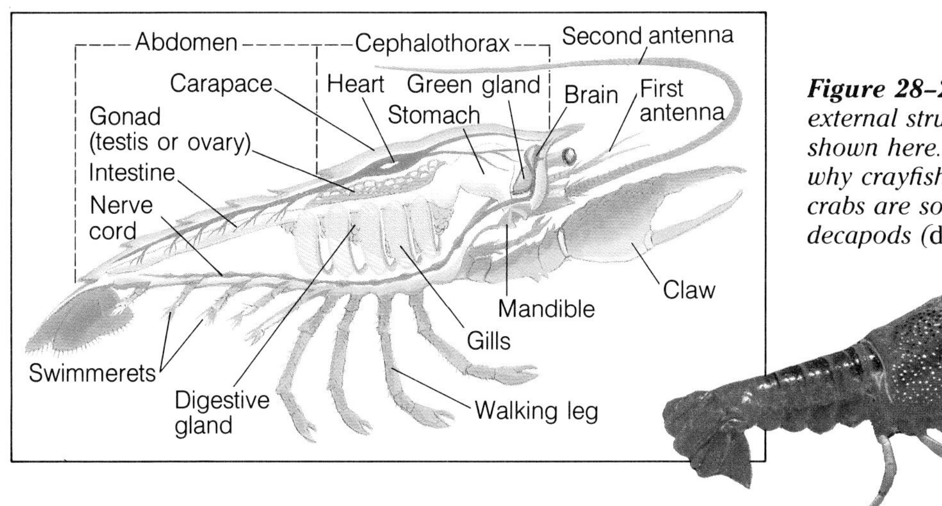

Figure 28–23 *The internal and external structures of a crayfish are shown here. Can you now explain why crayfish, shrimp, lobsters, and crabs are sometimes known as decapods (*deca-* means ten)?*

The third pair of appendages are mouthparts that are called **mandibles**. In many species of crustaceans, including crayfish, mandibles are short heavy structures designed for biting and grinding food. In other species, mandibles are bristly structures used in filter feeding, probelike structures used for finding and picking up detritus, or needlelike structures used to suck blood from a host.

The appendages on the thorax and abdomen vary greatly from one group of crustaceans to another. Some, such as barnacles, have delicate, feathery appendages for filter feeding; others have legs for walking or paddles for swimming. Appendages may be modified for internal fertilization, carrying eggs, spearing prey, burrowing, or many other functions.

As you can see in Figure 28–23, the appendages on a crayfish's thorax and abdomen are adapted for several different functions. A pair of large claws, which are used to catch prey and pick up, crush, and cut food, are located on the thorax. Four pairs of walking legs are also attached to the thorax. Flipperlike appendages called swimmerets, which are used for swimming, are located on the abdomen. A large pair of paddlelike appendages are found on the second-to-last abdominal segment. The paddlelike appendages and the final abdominal segment together form a large, flat tail. When the muscles of the abdomen contract, the crayfish's tail snaps forward. This provides a powerful swimming stroke that can rapidly pull the animal backward.

Figure 28–24 *The abdomen of a crab is tucked beneath its cephalothorax. A female crab uses its abdomen and the swimmerets attached to it to carry its eggs.*

28–3 SECTION REVIEW

1. What is a cephalothorax?
2. Describe the types of appendages on crayfish and give their functions.
3. Suppose you want to catch a crayfish with a net. Should you try to scoop up the crayfish head first or tail first? Explain your answer.

Section Objectives

- Describe and give examples of three classes in the subphylum Uniramia.
- Discuss the anatomy of a typical insect.
- Explain how insects communicate.

28–4 Insects and Their Relatives

The subphylum Uniramia contains more species than all other groups of animals alive today. It includes centipedes, millipedes, and insects. Uniramians are characterized by one pair of antennae and appendages that do not branch (*uni-* means one; *ramus* means branch). (Recall that the appendages in crustaceans and trilobites have two branches—usually a gill and a leg.) These arthropods, which display a multitude of forms and habits, are thought to have evolved on land about 400 million years ago. They inhabit almost every terrestrial habitat on Earth. In addition, some species live in fresh water and a few other species live in marine environments.

Centipedes and Millipedes

Centipedes and millipedes are many-legged animals. Compared to crustaceans and insects, these two classes of arthropods are quite small in number—there are approximately 3000 species of centipedes and 7500 species of millipedes. **Centipedes and millipedes are characterized by a long, wormlike body composed of many leg-bearing segments.** Because they lack closable spiracles and a waterproof coating on their exoskeleton, their bodies lose water easily. Thus they tend to live beneath rocks, in soil, or in other relatively moist areas.

Figure 28–25 *A centipede (top) is a carnivore that has one pair of legs per body segment. A millipede (bottom) is a herbivore that has two pairs of legs per body segment.*

CENTIPEDES Centipedes are carnivores that have, in addition to other mouthparts, a pair of poison claws in their head region. These poison claws are used to catch and stun or kill prey. Centipedes eat other arthropods, earthworms, toads, small snakes, and even mice. The North American centipedes that may be familiar to you are usually red-brown in color and about 3 to 6 centimeters long. Some tropical species are brightly colored and quite large—up to 26 centimeters long. Despite their name, which means 100 legs (*centi-* means hundred; *-pede* refers to legs), centipedes may have from 15 to 170 pairs of legs, depending on the species. Each segment that makes up the body of the centipede bears one pair of legs, except for the first segment (which bears the poison claws) and the last three segments (which are legless).

MILLIPEDES Although millipedes do not have a thousand legs (*milli-* means thousand), they do seem to have twice as many as centipedes. Each millipede body segment is formed from the fusion of two segments in the embryo and thus bears two pairs of legs. Millipedes are timid creatures that live in damp places under rocks and in decaying logs. They feed on dead and decaying plant material. When disturbed, many millipedes roll up into a ball to protect their softer undersides. Some can also defend themselves by secreting unpleasant or toxic chemicals.

Insects

We know of more than 900,000 insects, and new ones are discovered in the tropics all the time. Insects are extremely varied in body shape and habits. However, all members of this class share basic structural similarities. **Insects are characterized by a body that is divided into three parts—head, thorax, and abdomen—and that has three pairs of legs attached to the thorax.** In addition, a typical insect has one pair of antennae and one pair of compound eyes on the head, two pairs of wings on the thorax, and uses a system of tracheal tubes for respiration.

Insects get their name from the Latin word *insectum*, meaning notched, which refers to the division of their body into three main parts: head, thorax, and abdomen. In many insects, such as ants, the three body parts are clearly separated from each other by narrow connections. In other insects, such as grasshoppers, the divisions between the three body parts are not as sharply defined.

The essential life functions in insects are carried out in basically the same ways as they are in other arthropods. However, insects show a variety of interesting adaptations in feeding, movement, and behavior that deserve a closer look.

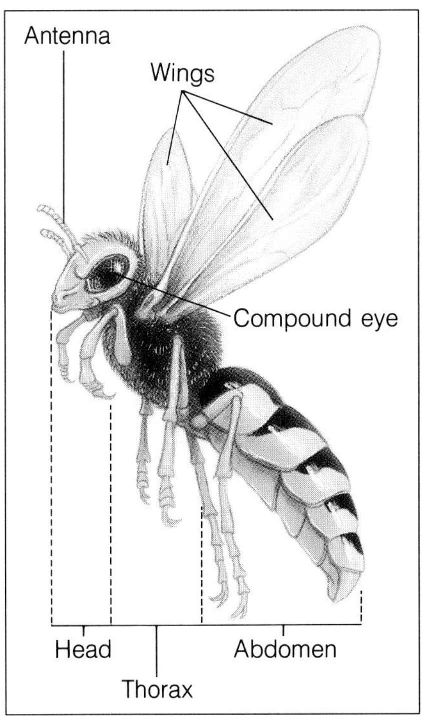

Figure 28–26 *An insect is characterized by a three-part body, six legs, two pairs of wings, one pair of antennae, and one pair of compound eyes.*

FEEDING Insects have three pairs of appendages that are used as mouthparts, including a pair of mandibles. Mouthparts can take on an enormous variety of shapes in species adapted to feed on different foods. For example, a grasshopper's mouthparts are designed to cut and chew plant tissues into a fine pulp. A female mosquito's mouthparts form a sharp tube that is used to pierce skin and suck blood. A butterfly's mouthparts

Figure 28–27 *Although insect mouthparts are adapted for many different eating habits, they all evolved from the same basic structures.*

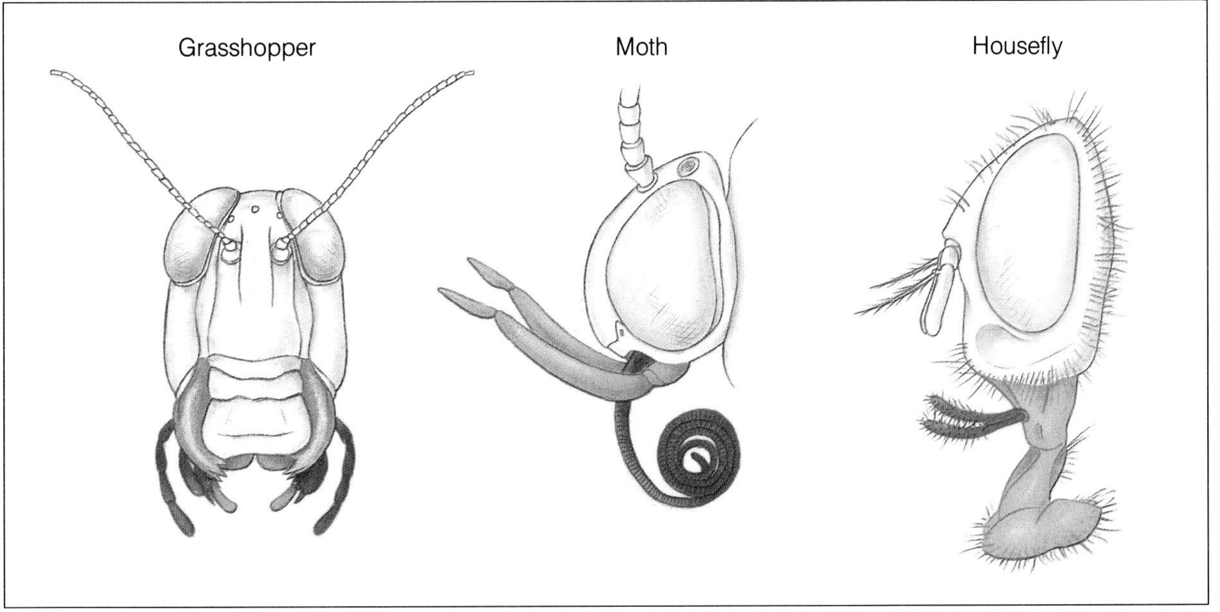

are fused together to form a long tube that is used for sipping nectar. A bee has mouthparts that are used for chewing and gathering nectar. And a fly has a spongy mouthpart that is used to soak up food.

Insect adaptations for feeding are not restricted to the shapes of the mouthparts. Many insects produce saliva that contains digestive enzymes and helps break down food. The saliva of female mosquitoes, which is injected when the mosquito bites, contains chemicals that prevent blood from clotting. (Unfortunately for humans and other animals, mosquito saliva also contains chemicals that cause the body's familiar itching reaction. It may contain pathogens as well.) Honeybees have a number of adaptations for gathering, processing, and storing food. The legs and bodies of worker bees are covered with hairs that collect pollen. Chemicals in bee saliva help change nectar into a more digestible form—honey. And glands on the abdomen secrete wax, which is used to build storage chambers for food and other structures within a beehive.

MOVEMENT As you have just read, insects have three pairs of walking legs. These legs are often equipped with spines and hooks for holding onto things and for defense. In addition to being used for walking, the legs may be adapted for functions such as jumping (as in grasshoppers and fleas) or capturing and holding prey (as in praying mantises).

Along with birds and bats, insects are the only living organisms that are capable of unassisted flight. The flying ability of insects varies greatly. Butterflies fly quite slowly and have limited maneuverability. But certain flies, bees, and moths can hover, change direction rapidly, and dart off at speeds up to 53 kilometers an hour. In flying insects, most of the space in the thorax is taken up by the large muscles that operate the wings. The enormous amount of energy required by these muscles during flight is supplied by oversized mitochondria (which are about half the size of a human red blood cell). The wing muscles in many insects also have a special blood supply that helps retain heat produced by muscle activity. For example, bees can maintain a wing muscle temperature of up to 35 degrees Celsius. This means that bees can keep their flying muscles warmer than the outside temperature and operate efficiently even when it is cold outside.

Figure 28–28 *Insects, along with birds and bats, are the only living organisms capable of unassisted flight. The hard brown wing covers on the may bug are modified forewings; in may bugs and other beetles, only the hindwings are used for flight.*

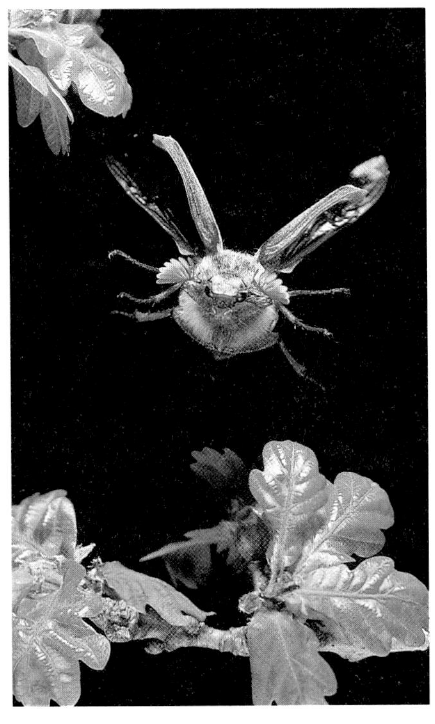

INSECT SOCIETIES Many animals and protists form colonies, which are collections of individuals of the same species that live together. Several types of insects are unique among invertebrates in that they form a special type of colony known as a society. In a society, separate individuals are dependent on one another for survival. Insects that live in societies, such as many species of termites, wasps, bees, and ants, are called social insects. These insects have developed complicated societies that may be composed of from half a dozen to more than

Figure 28–29 *Leaf-cutter ant workers carry pieces of leaves and flower petals to their underground nest. Certain chambers in the nest are "farms" in which the ants grow edible fungi on the bits of vegetation.*

7 million individuals. Within such societies there is division of labor: Different individuals perform the tasks necessary for the survival of the entire group. There are several castes, or types of individuals, within insect societies. Each caste has a body that is specialized for its functions and is therefore distinctly different from that of another caste. The basic castes are reproductive females, reproductive males, and workers.

The reproductive females, which are called queens, lay eggs that hatch into new individuals for the society. Most insect societies have only one queen, who is typically the largest individual in the colony. Termite queens, for example, may be 14 centimeters long (more than 10 times longer than a worker) and 3.5 centimeters wide. Most of a termite queen's body consists of a grotesquely swollen abdomen that contains enlarged reproductive organs. A termite queen can produce more than 30,000 eggs a day!

The reproductive males function only to fertilize the queen's eggs. In some insect societies, such as those of termites, a single reproductive male stays with the queen as a permanent member of the colony. In other societies, such as those of bees, the queen receives all the sperm she needs for her eggs after a single mating with one or more reproductive males. The successful males die after mating, and the unsuccessful males are ejected from the colony and soon perish.

The workers perform all the colony's tasks except for reproduction: They care for the queen, eggs, and young; they gather, store, and even grow food; they build, maintain, and defend the colony's home; and they perform all other necessary jobs. In societies of ants, bees, and wasps, the workers are all females; in those of termites, there are both male and female workers. Bee and wasp workers are capable of performing all of their societies' tasks for workers. Ant and termite workers are specialized and are able to carry out only their specific tasks, such as defending the colony or storing food.

Figure 28–30 *Mature termite queens are approximately the size and shape of a hot dog. The large termite next to the queen is a reproductive male. The smaller brown termites with the large heads are called soldiers. The tiny white termites are workers.*

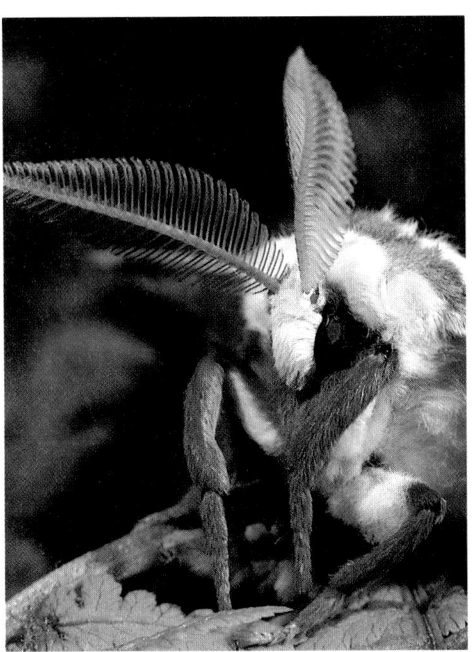

Figure 28–31 *A male luna moth's feathery antennae can detect pheromones released by a female several kilometers away.*

INSECT COMMUNICATION All insects use sound, visual, chemical, and other types of signals for communication. Much of the communication done by nonsocial insects involves finding a mate. To attract females, male crickets chirp by rubbing their forewings together, and male cicadas buzz by vibrating special membranes on the abdomen. Male fireflies turn a light-producing organ in their abdomens on and off, producing a distinct series of flashes. When female fireflies (which are wingless and are known as glowworms) see the correct signal, they flash back a signal of their own and the males fly to them. This is not always a good thing from the male firefly's point of view—the carnivorous females of one genus of fireflies can mimic the signal of another genus and lure males to their death. Many female moths release chemicals that attract distant males to them. These chemicals are a type of **pheromone**, which is a specific chemical messenger that affects the behavior and/or development of other individuals of the same species.

Communication in social insects is generally more complex than in nonsocial insects. A sophisticated system of communication is necessary to organize a society. Each species of social insect has its own "language" of visual, touch, sound, and chemical signals that convey information among members of the colony.

Pheromones are particularly important in insect societies. Certain pheromones function as rapid short-term messages that signal alarm, the death of a member of the colony, or the presence of food. For example, when a worker ant finds food, she heads back to the nest, dragging her abdomen along the ground. As she does so, she leaves behind a trail of a special kind of pheromone. Her nestmates can detect her trail by using sensory hairs on their antennae and follow it back to the food. Other pheromones act as long-term controls over the colony. For example, a queen honeybee produces a pheromone, called queen substance, that prevents the development of rival queens. Queen substance makes worker bees unable to lay eggs. It also causes them to raise female larvae as workers, not as queens. However, when the amount of queen substance in the hive is low, worker bees feed a few female larvae a special diet. This causes the larvae to develop into queens.

Honeybees communicate with sound and movement as well as with pheromones. Worker bees are able to convey information about the type, quality, direction, and distance of a food source by "dancing." The language of the bee's dance was decoded by Austrian biologist Karl von Frisch. Von Frisch discovered that bees have two basic dances: a round dance and a waggle dance.

In the round dance, the bee that has found food circles first one way and then the other, over and over again. This dance tells the other bees that there is a source of food within 50 meters of the hive. The frequency with which the dancing bee

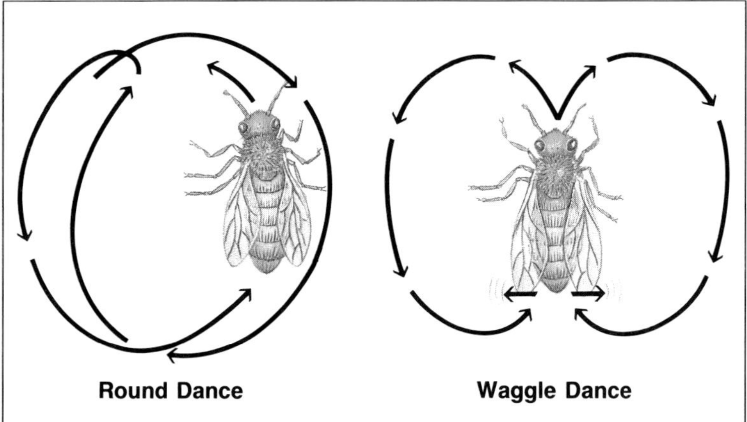

Figure 28–32 Bees communicate information about food sources by using a language of movement. The round dance tells members of the hive that a source of food is nearby. The waggle dance gives information about a more distant food source.

changes direction indicates the quality of the food source—the more frequent the changes in direction, the greater the energy value of the food. By smelling the dancer with the chemical receptors on their antennae, the other bees can determine what kind of flowers she has found.

In the waggle dance, the bee that has found food runs forward in a straight line while waggling her abdomen, circles around one way, runs in a straight line again, and circles around the other way. See Figure 28–32. The waggle dance tells the other bees that the food is more than 50 meters away. Most of the information about the food source is conveyed by the part of the waggle dance called the straight run. The longer the bee takes to perform the straight run and the more she waggles, the farther away the food. The direction of the straight run indicates in which direction the food is to be found. For example, if the dancer runs straight up the vertical honeycomb, the food source is in the same direction as the sun.

28–4 SECTION REVIEW

1. Compare the body plans and feeding habits of millipedes and centipedes.
2. What is an insect? Describe the basic body plan of an insect.
3. Give three specific examples of why and how insects communicate.
4. Explain how the mouthparts of bees, mosquitoes, and butterflies are adapted to different food sources.
5. How does the waggle dance of honeybees convey information about the location of a food source?
6. If all worker bees are females, why is the queen the only egg-layer in the colony?

Controlling Agricultural Pests

Until recently, farmers relied on chemical sprays to control agricultural pests such as herbivorous insects and mites. Although chemical pesticides were initially praised as an example of how modern technology can improve human life, it soon became clear that they created more problems than they solved. They were dangerous and even deadly to humans, livestock, and wildlife—including the natural enemies of pests. They were expensive. And they were eventually ineffective—the pests evolved resistance to them. In 1938, there were only 7 pests that were resistant to chemicals; by 1985, there were 447.

Clearly, it was necessary to find another approach to controlling agricultural pests. Researchers began to focus their attention on nature's control of pest populations, as well as on traditional agricultural techniques.

In nature, pests rarely get out of control because they are killed by natural enemies: predatory spiders, ladybugs, and birds; parasitic wasps; and disease-causing bacteria, for example. In addition, plants have evolved defenses that naturally control the numbers of pests. For example, hairy or sticky stems trap pests. And certain chemicals produced by plants disrupt pest development or are poisonous.

Certain ancient agricultural practices are today proving successful in controlling the numbers of pests. Many of these practices encourage animals that prey on pests to live in farmers' fields. Other traditional practices prevent pests from becoming well-established in an area by leaving fields unplanted every few growing seasons and thus starving the pests.

Today, agricultural experts favor the use of naturally occurring chemicals, predators, and certain farming practices to control pests. Although these forms of control are safer and less expensive than chemical pesticides, they do have some drawbacks. They are not as convenient as spraying chemicals; indeed, many are quite labor-intensive. If the infestation of pests is severe, they are not as effective as artificial pesticides. Natural controls take time to work and thus cannot save crops immediately. There is always the possibility that an organism chosen to kill pests may get out of control and become a pest itself. Although natural chemicals are less harmful to the environment than artificial chemicals, they can still become ineffective as pests evolve resistance to them. Even chemicals to which pests cannot become resistant, such as those that mimic the action of juvenile hormone, have their disadvantages. Although they prevent insects from reproducing, such chemicals are not useful in the short term because they cause the pest to live for an extended period of time in its most destructive (larval) stage.

The question of how agricultural pests should be controlled still remains a stubborn one, and the answers are not as clear as they might once have seemed. However, it is obvious that people will need to consider the advantages and disadvantages of pest-control methods carefully as long as there are crops to grow and pests to destroy them.

Adult ladybugs and their larvae feed on crop-eating pests. In the long run, the use of natural pest controls is safer and more efficient and effective than the use of artificial chemical pesticides.

28–5 How Arthropods Fit into the World

Section Objectives

- Describe how arthropods interact with other organisms in nature.
- Discuss how arthropods affect humans.

As you might expect from such a large, diverse group of animals, arthropods play many roles in the natural world. They are a direct source of food for many carnivorous organisms—from protists such as radiolarians to plants such as Venus' flytraps to animals such as sea anemones, fishes, frogs, turtles, birds, whales, and humans. And they are also an indirect source of food for many other organisms.

The interactions of arthropods with other organisms are not limited to eating or being eaten. Two thirds of the world's flowering plants depend on insects to pollinate them. Some plants live even more intimately with arthropods. The bull's horn acacia tree has hollow swellings at the base of some of its thorns that house symbiotic ants and special structures that feed the ants. The ants protect the acacia by eating herbivorous insects and by driving away larger herbivores with their painful bites and stings. Animals are also involved in symbiotic relationships with arthropods. It is amazing to see a large fish allow a bite-sized cleaner shrimp to crawl on its body and even into its mouth. But by allowing the cleaner shrimp to go unharmed, the fish is cleaned of annoying parasites and bits of dead tissue, and the cleaner shrimp gets a meal.

Figure 28–33 *The damselfly has been trapped by a carnivorous sundew plant. Although sundews and other carnivorous plants are photosynthetic, they need to "eat" insects and other small animals to obtain the nitrogen compounds they need to survive.*

Figure 28–34 *The cleaner shrimp and fish such as the queen angelfish, shown here, engage in a symbiotic relationship that benefits both organisms. The cleaner shrimp gets a meal by eating parasites on the fish and the fish gets rid of annoying pests. A number of fishes can sometimes be observed congregating around a shrimp's cleaning station, waiting for their turn to be cleaned!*

Figure 28–35 Millions of microscopic dust mites live in human homes. The mites feed on the tiny flakes of dead skin that are constantly being shed from the bodies of humans.

Humans encounter arthropods almost everywhere. The pores of our skin are home to thousands of harmless microscopic mites that feed on dead skin and oil. And no matter how neat and clean we are, our homes, even our beds, contain millions of microscopic dust mites. For the most part, these tiny harmless mites are of little consequence. But many of the more visible arthropods are of significance because they are either useful to us or a great nuisance.

Arthropods contribute enormously to the richness of human life. Agriculture would be impossible without the bees, butterflies, wasps, moths, and flies that pollinate crops. Bees manufacture honey, and silkworms produce silk. In Southeast Asia and Japan, whole shrimp and shrimp paste are important sources of protein and major ingredients in cooking. In the United States, shrimp, crab, crayfish, and lobster are considered delicacies. In Africa and Asia, many people eat insects such as grasshoppers and termites. (These insects, which are quite nutritious, are said to taste rather good.) And many insects and spiders are predators or parasites that prey upon harmful species.

There are many useful chemicals that may be obtained from arthropods—far too many to list here. An extract of horseshoe-crab blood, for example, is used to test the purity of medications. Chitin extracted from crustacean shells is used to dress wounds and to make thread for surgical stitches. The chemical that makes fireflies glow is used in medical tests and as a marker in genetic engineering.

Many new applications of arthropod chemicals are currently being investigated. For example, chitin could be sprayed onto fruit and frozen food to prevent spoilage and to preserve flavor. The adhesive that barnacles use to attach themselves to rocks, which sets quickly and hardens under water into a permanent bond, could be useful in applications ranging from dentistry to underwater construction and repair. Chemicals in spider venom are being tested for potential applications as pesticides. And scientists are currently trying to produce genetically engineered spider silk that could be used in making products as diverse as aircraft, helmets, bulletproof vests, and surgical thread.

Not all arthropods are beneficial to humans, however. Insects (such as locusts and "medflies") and arachnids (such as mites and ticks) cause billions of dollars in damage each year to livestock and crops around the world. Mosquitoes inflict

Figure 28–36 Some species of grasshoppers exist in two distinctly different forms: a dull-colored solitary grasshopper or a brightly colored gregarious locust (shown here). Locusts travel in immense swarms that may contain as many as 50 thousand million individuals. A swarm can devastate huge areas of crops. One swarm destroyed 167,000 tons of growing grain—enough to feed 1 million people for a year.

PROBLEM SOLVING IN BIOLOGY

IDENTIFYING ARTHROPODS

Having heard that you are now an expert on arthropods, some of your friends bring you the creatures pictured below and ask you to identify them. Can you place each in the correct arthropod group? Be as specific as possible. (*Hint:* Check the following important features: number of body segments, walking legs, and pairs of antennae; presence of wings; presence of claws. Compare the animals with the descriptions and photos in the text.)

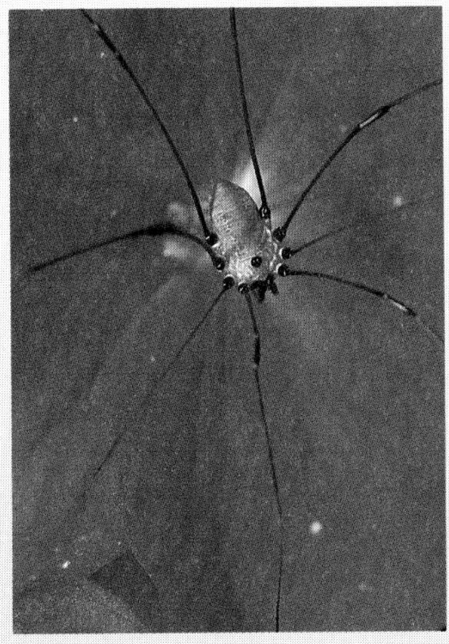

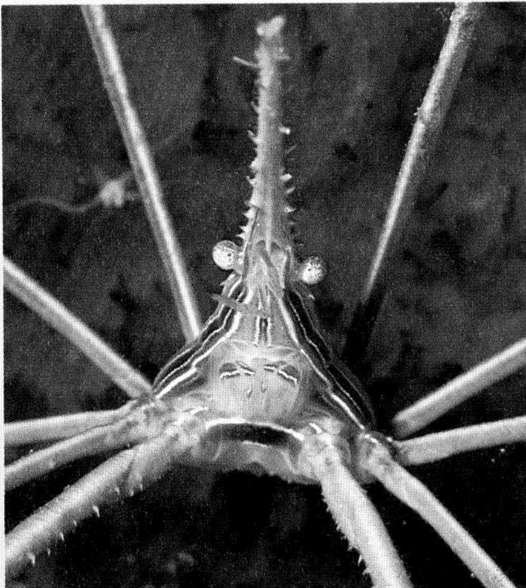

annoying bites, and some species carry malaria and yellow fever. Biting flies carry diseases such as sleeping sickness and river blindness, and fleas can carry bubonic plague. Termites cause extensive damage to wooden structures. Locusts have destroyed crops from the time humans first began to farm. Boll weevils are notorious for the trouble they cause cotton farmers in the South. For many years, farmers all over the world have spent billions of dollars on poisonous chemicals to save their crops from these pests.

28–5 SECTION REVIEW

1. Why are certain insects essential to agriculture?
2. How are arthropods beneficial to other living things? Give specific examples.
3. Name three dangerous or destructive arthropods and explain how they cause problems for humans.

LABORATORY INVESTIGATION

OBSERVING INSECT METAMORPHOSIS

PROBLEM

What changes occur as some insects grow and develop?

MATERIALS *(per group)*

600-mL beaker	hand lens
cheesecloth	25 mealworms
corn flakes	probe
dissecting tray	rubber band

PROCEDURE 

1. Fill a 600-mL beaker halfway with corn flakes.
2. Put 25 mealworms into the beaker of corn flakes. Observe their behavior.
3. Using a probe, slide one of the mealworms into a dissecting tray. The mealworm is the larval stage of the *Tenebrio* beetle. Carefully examine the larva with a hand lens, noting the location and number of appendages. Draw a diagram of the larva.
4. Put the mealworm back into the beaker of corn flakes. Cover the beaker with a piece of cheesecloth and secure the cheesecloth in place with a rubber band.
5. Check the beaker every other day for a few months by moving the probe carefully through the corn flakes. Be careful not to injure the larvae. Look for any changes in the larvae with respect to size or shape. Do you find any lifeless shells that look like the exoskeletons of the larvae?
6. If you find a short, thick motionless football-shaped object among the corn flakes, carefully slide it into the dissecting tray with a probe. This is the pupal stage of the *Tenebrio* beetle. Carefully examine the pupa with a hand lens, noting the location and number of appendages. Draw a diagram of the pupa.
7. Put the pupa back into the beaker. Continue making observations until you find adult beetles.
8. Do not remove the beetles from the corn flakes, as they may fly. Instead, try to keep a beetle uncovered in the beaker and examine it with a hand lens. Note the location and number of appendages. Draw a diagram of the adult.

OBSERVATIONS

1. What did the mealworms do when you placed them in the corn flakes?
2. How many legs does each of the stages have? What other appendages does each of the stages have?
3. What happened to the sizes of the larvae over time?
4. Compare the larval, pupal, and adult stages in terms of appearance and behavior.

ANALYSIS AND CONCLUSIONS

1. What did the mealworms use for food during growth and development?
2. What evidence did you find of molting? Why is molting necessary?
3. What changes occur as *Tenebrio* beetles grow and develop?

STUDENT STUDY GUIDE

SUMMARIZING THE CONCEPTS

The key concepts in each section of this chapter are listed below to help you review the chapter content. Make sure you understand each concept and its relationship to other concepts and to the theme of this chapter.

28–1 Introduction to Arthropods

- Arthropods are characterized by an exoskeleton of chitin, jointed appendages, and a segmented body.
- In order to grow, arthropods must periodically shed their exoskeletons in a process called molting.
- The process of growth and development in arthropods often involves metamorphosis.

28–2 Spiders and Their Relatives

- Chelicerates have a body that consists of two parts—cephalothorax and abdomen. Chelicerates have chelicerae and lack antennae.
- Arachnids, such as spiders, scorpions, and mites, are typically carnivores that have four pairs of walking legs.

28–3 Crustaceans

- Crustaceans, such as crabs and crayfish, are characterized by a stony exoskeleton, two pairs of antennae, and mandibles.

28–4 Insects and Their Relatives

- Uniramians include centipedes, millipedes, and insects.
- Centipedes are carnivores that have poison claws and possess one pair of legs per body segment. Millipedes are herbivores that have two pairs of legs per body segment.
- Insects have a body that is divided into three parts: head, thorax, and abdomen. They have three pairs of legs attached to the thorax.
- Members of insect societies are specialized for performing different functions.
- Insects communicate. Some forms of communication rely on pheromones.

28–5 How Arthropods Fit into the World

- Arthropods play many roles in the natural world.
- Some arthropods are of little significance to humans; others are important because they are useful or a great nuisance.

REVIEWING KEY TERMS

Vocabulary terms are important to your understanding of biology. The key terms listed below are those you should be especially familiar with. Review these terms and their meanings. Then use each term in a complete sentence. If you are not sure of a term's meaning, return to the appropriate section and review its definition.

28–1 Introduction to Arthropods

arthropod
trilobite
chelicerate
crustacean
uniramian
exoskeleton
chitin
molt
metamorphosis
pupa

28–2 Spiders and Their Relatives

arachnid

28–3 Crustaceans

mandible

28–4 Insects and Their Relatives

pheromone

CHAPTER REVIEW

CONTENT REVIEW

Multiple Choice

Choose the letter of the answer that best completes each statement.

1. Which of these is an arachnid?
   a. scorpion c. grasshopper
   b. horseshoe crab d. lobster
2. A free-living arthropod is certain to have
   a. antennae. c. jointed appendages.
   b. chelicerae. d. gills.
3. Insects are characterized by
   a. a stony exoskeleton containing calcium carbonate.
   b. chelicerae and pedipalps.
   c. three pairs of legs on the thorax.
   d. many body segments, each of which bears two pairs of legs.
4. In crustaceans, nitrogenous wastes are excreted with the help of
   a. green glands c. Malpighian tubules.
   b. spiracles d. pheromones.
5. A wormlike immature animal undergoes a resting stage during which it changes into an adult that has four wings and six legs. This animal is a (an)
   a. crustacean. c. chelicerate.
   b. insect. d. trilobite.
6. Most spiders breathe using
   a. mandibles. c. Malpighian tubules.
   b. tracheal tubes. d. book lungs.
7. Which is most likely to be a herbivore?
   a. spider c. tick
   b. centipede d. millipede
8. Trilobites
   a. are primarily terrestrial.
   b. are extinct.
   c. have highly specialized appendages.
   d. communicate by "dancing."

True or False

Determine whether each statement is true or false. If it is true, write "true." If it is false, change the underlined word or words to make the statement true.

1. If the level of juvenile hormone in an insect's body is high, the insect is in the <u>pupal</u> stage.
2. Arthropods have a <u>closed</u> circulatory system.
3. <u>Centipedes</u> are herbivores that have two pairs of legs on each segment.
4. A spider uses fanglike <u>pedipalps</u> to inject venom into its prey.
5. All the members of the class <u>Uniramia</u> are now extinct.
6. Horseshoe crabs are classified as <u>crustaceans</u>.
7. Arthropods are characterized by an exoskeleton composed of <u>calcium carbonate</u>.
8. Arthropods must periodically <u>molt</u>, or shed, their exoskeletons.

Word Relationships

In each of the following sets of terms, three of the terms are related. One term does not belong. Determine the characteristic common to three of the terms and then identify the term that does not belong.

1. tracheal tube, book lung, spiracle, pupa
2. green gland, gill, Malpighian tubule, chitin
3. mandible, chelicera, pedipalp, walking leg
4. chelicerate, uniramian, crustacean, insect

CONCEPT MASTERY

Use your understanding of the concepts developed in the chapter to answer each of the following in a brief paragraph.

1. Beetles undergo complete metamorphosis and dragonflies undergo incomplete metamorphosis. Describe the major events of the life cycles of beetles and dragonflies. Be sure to include a comparison of their life cycles.
2. In some classification schemes, arthropods are divided into two subphyla—Chelicerata and Mandibulata—based on the type of mouthparts they possess (chelicera and mandibles, respectively). Which groups of arthropods belong to the subphylum Mandibulata according to this classification scheme? Explain why many experts do not favor this method of grouping arthropods.
3. Using a crayfish as your representative organism, discuss the distinguishing characteristics of arthropods.
4. Certain chemicals bind with juvenile hormone and make it inactive. Describe how exposure to such chemicals would affect the development of a moth.

CRITICAL AND CREATIVE THINKING

Discuss each of the following in a brief paragraph.

1. **Applying concepts** Explain why you will never see spiders three stories tall or ants big enough to eat New York (except in the movies).
2. **Relating concepts** Blue crabs usually have hard, stony shells. However, some blue crabs have thin, papery shells. These crabs are called soft-shell crabs and are a popular food for some people, who eat them whole—shell and all! Explain why some crabs are soft-shelled.
3. **Relating cause and effect** People who squash an annoying hornet are often unpleasantly surprised to find themselves suddenly under attack by dozens of hornets. Explain this phenomenon.
4. **Making inferences** Instead of spraying a field with chemicals, a plane disperses tens of thousands of tiny wasps over the growing plants. What is the most likely reason for such an action?
5. **Applying concepts** At the park one day, you observe a bee flying around an open can of soda. Soon after, you notice that there are a lot of bees buzzing around this can. However, there are no bees on other open cans of soda a few meters away.
   a. Explain how the bees probably found the first can of soda.
   b. Explain why the bees do not seem interested in the other cans of soda.
6. **Assessing concepts** Which do you think is a better arrangement for an insect society: having workers that can each perform all necessary tasks or having workers that are specialized for specific tasks? Explain your answer.
7. **Using the writing process** Certain crabs have a peculiar symbiotic relationship with coral: They cause branches of coral to grow around them to form a protective prison. The imprisoned crab obtains food and oxygen from the currents of water that flow through its coral cage. Write a short story or play in which one of these imprisoned crabs converses with a more typical crustacean.

CHAPTER 29

Echinoderms and Invertebrate Chordates

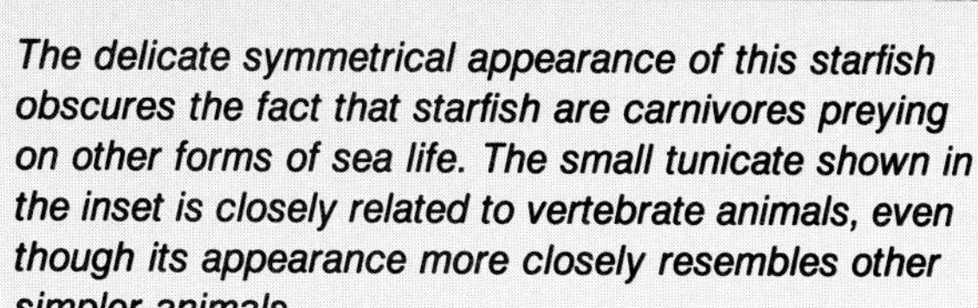

The delicate symmetrical appearance of this starfish obscures the fact that starfish are carnivores preying on other forms of sea life. The small tunicate shown in the inset is closely related to vertebrate animals, even though its appearance more closely resembles other simpler animals.

When most people see a starfish, they immediately think of the ocean—an appropriate reaction, considering that starfish and their relatives live only in the sea. Surprisingly, not all of the members of this phylum resemble stars. Some look like graceful long-stemmed flowers; others, like a peculiar cross between a polka-dotted pickle and a stalk of cauliflower. Some are as round and prickly as a pincushion. Others are flat bristly disks with holes and notches around their edges. Still others resemble armored feather dusters, pentagon-shaped cookies, or the curlicues and flourishes beneath an old-fashioned signature.

What other animals belong to this phylum? How are they all adapted to the ocean world? Why do scientists consider them to be closely related to the vertebrates? You will discover the answers to these questions in the pages that follow.

CHAPTER OUTLINE

29–1 Echinoderms

Section Objectives

- Relate the structure of echinoderms to essential life functions.
- Describe the characteristics of the classes of echinoderms.

Nearly everyone who has visited the seashore has seen starfish, sea urchins, sand dollars, or their remains washed up on the beach. These animals are members of the phylum Echinodermata (*echino-* means spiny; *dermis* means skin), a phylum that has a long and fascinating history stretching back to the beginning of the Cambrian Period, more than 580 million years ago.

What Is an Echinoderm?

As their name indicates, **echinoderms** (ee-KIGH-noh-dermz) are spiny-skinned animals. **In addition to having a spiny skin, echinoderms are characterized by five-part radial symmetry, an internal skeleton, a water vascular system, and suction-cuplike structures called tube feet.** The internal skeleton, or endoskeleton, is made up of hardened plates of calcium carbonate, which are often bumpy or spiny.

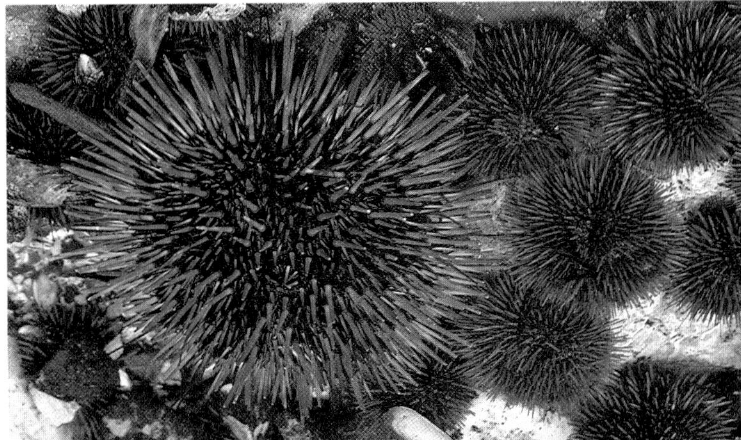

Figure 29–1 *Echinoderm means spiny skin, which as you can see from this sea urchin (bottom) is an appropriate name. The sea cucumber (top) is also an echinoderm. Although its skin is smooth, it shows another characteristic of echinoderms—five-part symmetry.*

The **water vascular system**, which you will learn more about shortly, consists of an internal network of fluid-filled canals connected to external appendages called **tube feet**. The water vascular system is involved with many essential life functions in echinoderms, including feeding, respiration, internal transport, elimination of waste products, and movement.

Some echinoderms, such as starfish and sand dollars, live in shallow water and are thus familiar to beach-goers. Other echinoderms live only on coral reefs or on the floor of the deep ocean. Although echinoderms possess certain characteristics found in no other animals, living or extinct, they share several important features with members of our own phylum (Chordata). For example, certain stages in the development of echinoderm larvae are remarkably similar to stages seen in some members of the phylum Chordata. In addition, echinoderms have an internal skeleton (as do vertebrates) rather than an external skeleton (as do other invertebrates). For these reasons, biologists believe that among invertebrates, echinoderms are most closely related to humans!

Echinoderm species vary greatly in appearance. Starfish exhibit a fragile beauty and perfection in shape that stirs wonder in most observers. Some sea cucumber species fascinate because their ugliness has a certain repulsive appeal. Regardless of appearance, however, echinoderms have adaptations that make them successful survivors in the world of the sea. As you read this section, keep in mind that echinoderms are survivors of history. Their success is confirmed by the fact that some echinoderms alive today look much like their ancient ancestors who lived in the seas millions and millions of years ago.

Figure 29–2 *Starfish, or sea star, species vary greatly. This bat star lives in the ocean off the coast of southern California. Lacking the thin arms of other starfish, this species resembles a pentagon.*

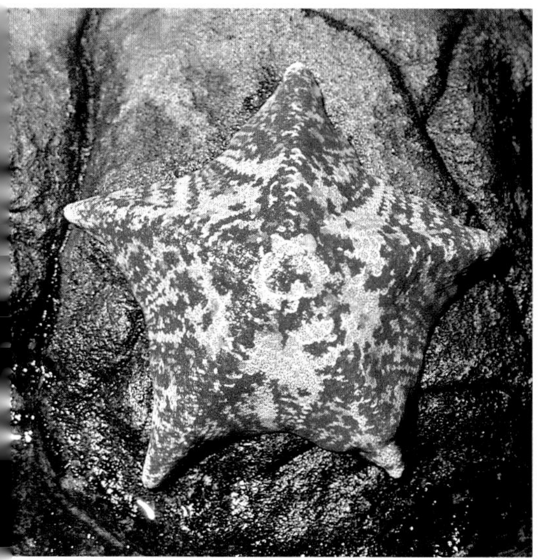

Form and Function in Echinoderms

Adult echinoderms have a body plan with five parts organized symmetrically around a center. As a result of this body plan, adult echinoderms typically have neither an anterior nor a posterior end and no brain. However, most echinoderms are two-sided. The side where the mouth is located is called the oral surface, and the opposite side is called the aboral surface.

All echinoderms have a unique system of internal tubes called a water vascular system. The water vascular system opens to the outside through a sievelike structure called the madreporite (ma-druh-POR-ight). In starfish, the madreporite connects to a tube called the ring canal that forms a circle around the animal's digestive system. From the ring canal, five radial canals extend into each body segment. Attached to each radial canal are hundreds of movable tube feet. The entire water vascular system operates like a series of living hydraulic pumps that can propel water in or out of the tube feet. When water is pushed into a tube foot, the tube foot expands. When water is pulled out, the cup on the end of the tube foot shrinks,

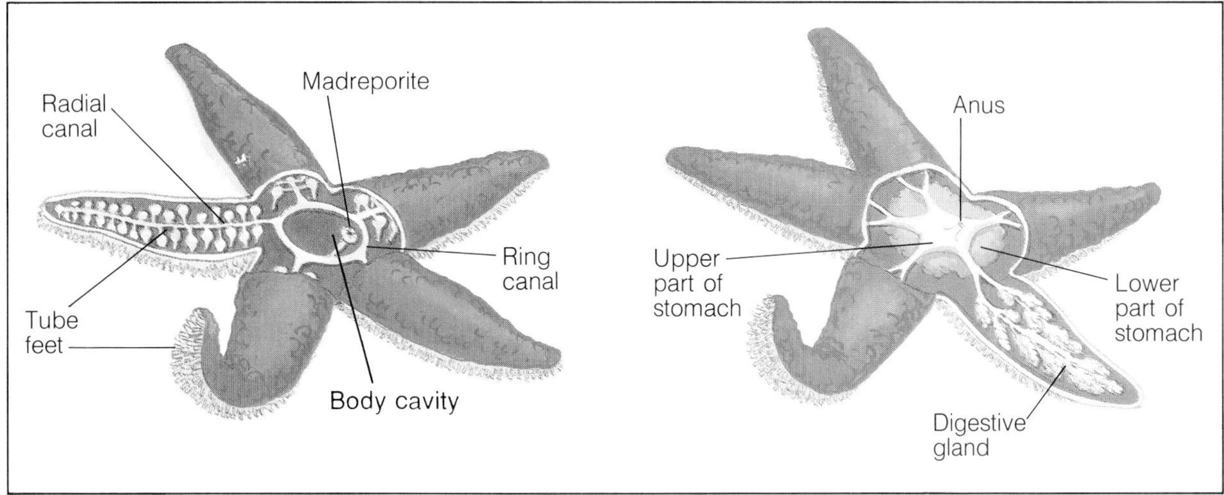

__Figure 29–3__ The pressure exerted by the water vascular system of the starfish (left) moves the animal along the ocean bottom. The digestive system of a starfish (right) breaks down food, which is then transported throughout the animal's body in the digestive glands and in the fluid within the body cavity.

creating a partial vacuum that holds onto whatever the foot is touching. In this way, the tube feet act like living suction cups. A single tube foot alone cannot accomplish much, but hundreds acting together create enormous force. All echinoderms "walk" with their tube feet, and some use their tube feet for feeding.

FEEDING Echinoderms have several methods of feeding. Carnivores, such as many species of starfish, use their tube feet to pry open the shells of bivalve mollusks such as clams and scallops. Once the bivalve's shell is opened, the starfish flips its stomach out of its mouth, pours out enzymes, and digests its prey in the prey's own shell. When the starfish has finished dining, it moves its stomach back into its mouth, leaving behind an empty shell as the only evidence of its deed. Starfish also eat snails, corals, and even other echinoderms. Herbivores, such as sea urchins, scrape algae from rocks by using their five-part jaw. Filter feeders, such as sea lilies, basket stars, and some brittle stars, use tube feet on flexible arms to capture plankton that float by on ocean currents. Detritus feeders, such as sea cucumbers, move much like a bulldozer across the ocean floor, taking in a mixture of sand and detritus. Then, like an earthworm, they digest the organic material and pass the sand grains out in their feces.

RESPIRATION Echinoderms, like other animals, need to exchange carbon dioxide for oxygen. In most species the thin-walled tissue of the tube feet forms the main respiratory surface. In some species small outgrowths called skin gills also function in gas exchange.

INTERNAL TRANSPORT The functions of transporting oxygen, food, and wastes—which are performed by the circulatory system in many animals—are shared by different systems

Figure 29–4 *Tube feet, located on the underside of a starfish's arms, are used to perform many life functions (left). Starfish use their tube feet to open clams (right). Once the starfish has opened the clam shell, it flips its stomach out of its mouth and begins to digest the clam right in the shell. No wonder starfish are not welcome in clam beds!*

in echinoderms. Because respiration (gas exchange) and the removal of metabolic wastes occur through skin gills and tube feet located all over the body, a system to deliver oxygen and carry away carbon dioxide and other wastes is not essential. The distribution of nutrients is performed primarily by the digestive glands and the fluid within the body cavity.

EXCRETION In almost all echinoderms, solid wastes are released through the anus in the form of feces. (The exceptions are brittle stars, which lack an anus and thus release undigested materials through the mouth.) Echinoderms, like many other marine invertebrates, excrete nitrogen-containing cellular wastes primarily in the form of ammonia. Wastes seem to be excreted in many of the same places around the body in which gas exchange takes place—the tube feet and the skin gills.

RESPONSE As you might expect in animals that have no head, echinoderms have primitive nervous systems. Most echinoderms have a nerve ring that surrounds the mouth and radial nerves that connect the ring with the body sections. Scattered sensory cells that are sensitive to chemicals released by potential food are also characteristic of most species. Starfish additionally have up to 200 light-sensitive cells clustered in eyespots at the tip of each arm. Although these structures have lenses, they do little more than tell the animal whether it is light or dark. Some echinoderms also possess statocysts (simple organs for balance that tell an organism whether it is right side up).

Although you might think that the tough, spiny skins of echinoderms protect them from predators, spines actually offer protection for only a few species—the crown-of-thorns starfish, for example. Many predators have learned ways around the spiny defenses of echinoderms. For example, basket stars, feather stars, and spiny sea urchins are very slow moving. Clever fishes (and you will meet some clever fishes in Chapter 31) have learned to turn these animals over and attack them through their unprotected underside. For this reason, many echinoderms hide under rocks and in crevices by day, coming out to feed at night, when most predators are asleep.

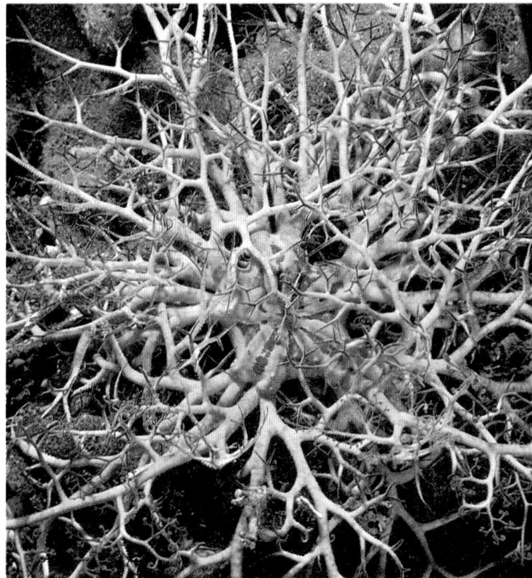

Figure 29–5 The basket star spreads its branching arms to filter particles of food from the water. When disturbed, the basket star curls up these arms and exposes the armored surface for protection.

MOVEMENT Most echinoderms use tube feet and thin layers of muscle fibers attached to the plates of the endoskeleton to move. An echinoderm's mobility is determined in part by the structure of its endoskeleton. In sand dollars and sea urchins, the plates are fused together to form a rigid box that encloses the animal's internal organs. These animals usually have movable spines attached to their endoskeleton, which they use along with their tube feet to creep from one place to another or to burrow in the sand. In starfish, brittle stars, and feather stars, the skeletal plates move around a series of flexible joints, enabling these echinoderms to use their arms for locomotion. Feather stars can swim for short distances by flapping their arms like wings, but starfish and brittle stars are only able to crawl. In sea cucumbers, the plates are reduced to tiny vestiges inside a soft, muscular body wall. The loss of the plates makes the body of sea cucumbers very flexible. Some species are able to crawl along the ocean floor like large, fat worms by contracting the muscles of the body wall.

REPRODUCTION Most echinoderms are either male or female, although some are hermaphrodites. In starfish, the sperm or eggs are produced in testes or ovaries, respectively, which fill the arms during the reproductive season. The animals shed their sperm and eggs into the water. Individual starfish detect gametes of their own species in the water, and they respond to that stimulus by releasing their own gametes. Fertilization takes place in open water, and larvae swim around for some time as members of the huge community of plankton that swarm in the ocean. Eventually the larvae, which have bilateral symmetry, swim to the ocean bottom, where they mature and metamorphose into adults that have radial symmetry.

Many starfish have incredible abilities to repair themselves when damaged. In fact, if a starfish is pulled into pieces, each piece can grow into a new animal as long as it contains a portion of the central part of the body. This ability of a starfish to regenerate itself has caused a great deal of trouble to people who earn their living fishing for bivalves (two-shelled mollusks). In the past, angry shellfishermen who were aware that starfish ate bivalves would tear the animals into two or three pieces and toss them overboard. Imagine their surprise when they noticed even more starfish in their bivalve beds. Today, shellfishermen know that starfish have the ability to regenerate and that every piece of torn starfish they throw back could develop into a completely new organism.

Figure 29–6 Unlike adults, which mostly crawl along the ocean bottom, echinoderm larvae are free-swimming. These larvae resemble closely the free-swimming larvae of invertebrate chordates.

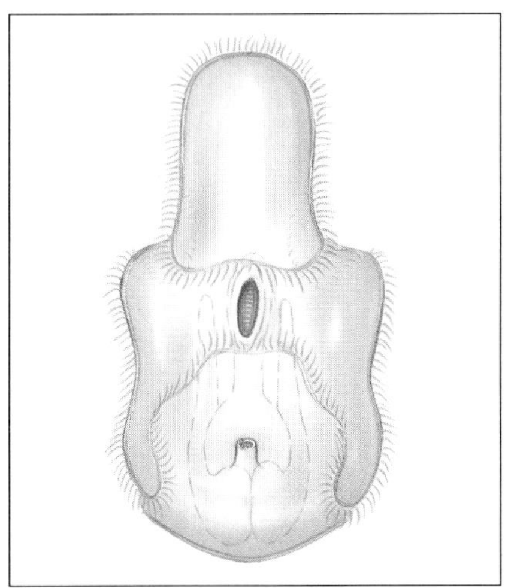

The Echinoderm Classes

The almost 6000 species of living echinoderms are found in almost every ocean in the world. However, no echinoderms have ever entered fresh water, and they cannot survive for long on land. Although they share certain characteristics, echinoderm species are remarkably diverse in appearance. The following descriptions of echinoderm classes will provide a brief introduction to these animals.

STARFISH This class contains the common starfish, which are also known as sea stars. Starfish occur in many colors, and you may be surprised to learn that many species have more than five arms. Starfish creep slowly along the ocean bottom. Most are carnivorous, preying upon the bivalves they encounter as they move. Some species of starfish are important predators in rocky areas along the coast.

BRITTLE STARS These animals live in tropical seas, especially on coral reefs. They look much like a common starfish, but they have longer, more flexible arms and are thus able to move much more rapidly. In addition to using speed for protection, brittle stars protect themselves by shedding one or more of their arms when attacked. The detached parts keep wriggling violently, distracting predators, while the rest of the animal escapes. Brittle stars are filter and detritus feeders that hide by day and wander around in search of food only under the cover of night.

Figure 29–7 *The brittle star gets its name from the fact that it can shed its arms when it is threatened (left). This distracts predators so that the brittle star can escape. In time, it will regrow the missing arm. Some starfish, such as the sun star, have more than five arms (right).*

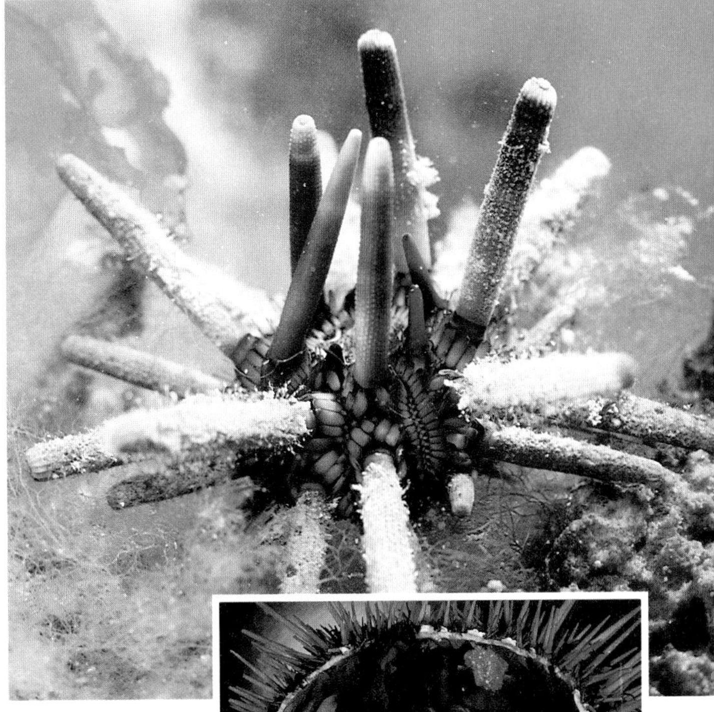

Figure 29–8 The slate urchin (top, right) has thick, strong spines that were once harvested for use as implements for writing on slateboards—thus, its name. Sea urchins have a lanternlike set of bony plates inside their body that power their jaws (inset). The sand dollar (top, left) gets its name from its flattened, coin-shaped appearance.

SEA URCHINS AND SAND DOLLARS This class includes disk-shaped sand dollars, oval heart urchins, and round sea urchins. Many of these animals, which are found in marine environments all over the world, are grazers that eat large quantities of algae. Others are detritus feeders. Heart urchins and sand dollars live hidden in burrows that they dig in sand or mud. Most sea urchins wedge themselves in crevices in rock during the day and come out only at night. However, many sea urchins have formidable defenses in the form of long, sharp spines. One type of sea urchin even has small blue poison sacs covering the tips of each spine, ensuring that wounds it inflicts will be painful!

SEA CUCUMBERS As their name implies, these echinoderms look like warty moving pickles with a mouth at one end and an anus at the other. Most sea cucumbers are detritus feeders. Although these animals are not numerous in shallow water, herds containing hundreds of thousands of them often cover areas of the sea floor at great depths. A few species of sea cucumbers expel sticky substances that attach to a predator. The predator, in all probability an attacking crustacean, is immobilized as it is glued into a helpless ball.

SEA LILIES AND FEATHER STARS These filter feeders, which have 50 or more long, feathery arms, comprise the most ancient class of echinoderms. Although sea lilies and feather stars are not common today, a rich fossil record indicates that

Figure 29–9 *Acting much like a living vacuum cleaner, this sea cucumber (top) moves along the ocean bottom swallowing organic material along with sand. Sea lilies (center) and feather stars (bottom) feed by filtering floating organic material from the water. The names reflect the delicate beauty of these animals.*

they were once widely distributed. Sea lilies are sessile animals that are attached to the ocean bottom by a long, stemlike stalk. Modern sea lilies live at depths of 100 meters or more. Many feather stars live on coral reefs, where they perch on top of rocks at night and use their tube feet to catch floating plankton.

How Echinoderms Fit into the World

Echinoderms are numerous in most marine habitats. In many areas, starfish are important carnivores that control the populations of other animals. Sometimes their numbers rise or fall suddenly, causing major changes in the numbers of other forms of marine life. For example, several years ago the coral-eating crown-of-thorns starfish suddenly appeared in great numbers over wide areas of the Pacific Ocean. Within a short span of time, these starfish caused extensive damage to many coral reefs. The extent of their damage surprised and alarmed marine biologists, many of whom took drastic action to kill the starfish by injecting them with poisonous chemicals. We still do not know what caused this population explosion in the crown-of-thorns starfish or what will be its long-term effects on coral reefs.

In many coastal areas, sea urchins are important because they control the distribution of algae. However, if present in large numbers, they can threaten to literally "eat out of house and home" the other dwellers that share this habitat.

In various parts of the world, some echinoderms—for example, sea urchin eggs and sea cucumbers—are considered delicacies by some people. Many more echinoderms, however, are useful as research subjects and as possible sources of medicine. Several chemicals extracted from starfish and sea cucumbers are currently being studied as potential anti-cancer and anti-viral drugs. Sea urchins have been the subject of pioneering studies in embryology. These animals are easy to study because they produce large eggs that are fertilized externally and develop in plain sea water. Sea urchin embryos also make excellent subjects for testing the effects of drugs on cell division and development.

29–1 SECTION REVIEW

1. What is an echinoderm? Name five kinds of echinoderms.
2. How do tube feet help echinoderms carry out their essential life functions?
3. How do starfish move? How do starfish open clams and other bivalves?
4. Why is tearing a starfish apart and throwing it back into the water not a good way to limit a starfish population?

29–2 Invertebrate Chordates

Section Objectives

- Name and discuss the three distinguishing characteristics of chordates.
- Describe the two subphyla of invertebrate chordates.

The phylum Chordata, to which fishes, frogs, birds, snakes, dogs, cows, and humans belong, will be the subject of many of the chapters to come. Most of the **chordates** (KOR-dayts) are vertebrates, which means that they have backbones, so they are placed in the subphylum Vertebrata. But there are also some invertebrate chordates. The invertebrate chordates are divided into two subphyla—tunicates and lancelets. Because they show possible links between vertebrates and the rest of the animal kingdom, the invertebrate chordates are of great evolutionary interest.

What Is a Chordate?

Members of the phylum Chordata are called chordates. **Chordates are animals that are characterized by a notochord, a hollow dorsal nerve cord, and pharyngeal (throat) slits.** Some chordates possess these distinguishing characteristics as adults; others, only as embryos. However, all chordates display these three characteristics at some stage of their life.

The first chordate characteristic, the **notochord**, is a long, flexible supporting rod that runs through at least part of the body, usually along the dorsal surface just beneath the nerve cord. Most chordates have a notochord only during the early part of embryonic life. In most vertebrates, the notochord is quickly replaced by the backbone.

The second chordate characteristic, the **hollow dorsal nerve cord**, runs along the dorsal surface just above the notochord. Remember that in most invertebrates, nerve cords run along ventral surfaces. In most chordates, the front end of this nerve cord develops into a large brain. Nerves leave this cord at regular intervals along the length of the animal and connect to internal organs, muscles, and sense organs.

The third chordate characteristic, **pharyngeal slits**, are paired structures in the pharyngeal (fuh-RIHN-jee-uhl), or throat, region of the body. (Remember that pharynx is another word for throat.) In aquatic chordates such as lancelets and fishes, the pharyngeal slits are gill slits that connect the pharyngeal cavity with the outside. The location of gills is very important. Many invertebrates have gills of some sort in various places, but only chordates have pharyngeal gills. In terrestrial chordates that use lungs for respiration, pharyngeal slits are present for only a brief time during the development of the embryo. These slits soon close up as the embryo develops. In chordates such as humans, pouches form in the pharyngeal region but never open up to form slits. For this reason, some scientists regard pharyngeal pouches, not slits, as the "true" chordate characteristic.

Figure 29–10 *Although it seems like a simple animal, the tunicate is a chordate. It is, therefore, a relative of ours—although a very distant one.*

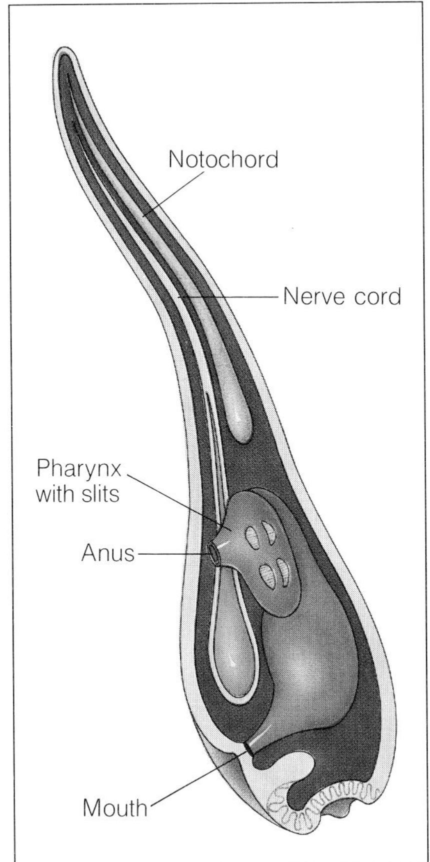

TUNICATES Tunicates are small marine chordates that eat plankton they filter from the water. They get their name

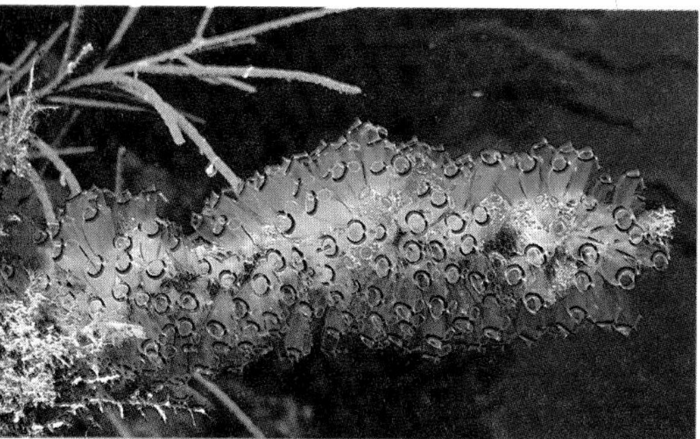

Figure 29–11 Sea squirts are tunicates. As adults, these organisms are sessile, living firmly attached to one place. However, the larvae of these animals, like the larvae of echinoderms, are free-swimming.

from a special body covering called the tunic. Only the tadpole-shaped larvae of tunicates have a notochord and a dorsal nerve chord. When most tunicate larvae mature, they undergo metamorphosis and become sessile adults that grow into colonies attached to a solid surface. Both larval tunicates and adults filter feed and breathe at the same time through a pharyngeal basket pierced by gill slits.

LANCELETS The small fishlike creatures called lancelets live in the sandy bottom of shallow tropical oceans. Unlike tunicates, adult lancelets have a definite head. They have a mouth that opens into a long pharyngeal region with up to a hundred pairs of gill slits. Lancelets feed by passing water through their pharynx, where food particles are caught in a sticky mucus. This mucus is swallowed into a digestive tract that starts at one end of the pharynx and continues straight through the animal to the anus, near the tail.

Lancelets have a simple, primitive heart that pumps blood through vessels in a closed circulatory system. Additionally, lancelets show evidence of segmentation in the arrangement of their nerves and muscles. A lancelet's muscles are organized into V-shaped units that are paired on either side of the body. Each muscle unit receives a branch from the main nerve cord. A similar segmented nerve and muscle organization is found in all living vertebrates. Unlike most vertebrates, lancelets have no jaw. Their mouth is composed entirely of soft tissues. Lancelets also lack appendages and can move only by bending their bodies back and forth.

How Invertebrate Chordates Fit into the World

In some ways, studying invertebrate chordates is like using a time machine to study the ancestors of our own subphylum. It is important to remember that living vertebrates did not evolve from living lancelets or tunicates. Both these subphyla have evolved over time. However, similarities in structure and embryological development indicate that vertebrates and invertebrate chordates evolved from common ancestors many millions of years ago.

Figure 29–12 Lancelets are small fishlike creatures that often live with their body half buried in sand. They filter food particles from the water.

29–2 SECTION REVIEW

1. What characteristics are found in a chordate?
2. What characteristics of tunicates and lancelets make them seem like close relatives of vertebrates?
3. Which characteristics of tunicates and lancelets are unlike vertebrate characteristics?

SCIENCE, TECHNOLOGY, AND SOCIETY **APPLICATION**

The Secret Life of Salps

Sometimes a remarkably simple change in the techniques biologists use to study the world causes us to alter our ideas about the way the living world works. For example, the invention of the microscope opened up the world of "unseen life." Recently, new methods have contributed to our understanding of the once mysterious open-water tunicates known as salps.

Salps are free-swimming animals that live in the open sea. Biologists have known about their existence for many years, but they knew little about their importance. This lack of information was due to the fact that research vessels had no way of collecting and identifying salps. These beautiful animals are so fragile that they literally fall to pieces if they are handled roughly. And that was exactly what happened in the collecting nets marine biologists used to gather plankton. Any salps that entered the net were squeezed into a clear, featureless mush.

Once scuba-diving scientists became sufficiently experienced (and sufficiently brave) to hop off their boats in the middle of the ocean, however, our knowledge of salps increased dramatically. It became clear that salps are everywhere. Giant herds of salps drift just beneath the surface. Certain species form huge snakelike colonies that stretch for many meters.

By collecting salps carefully, researchers have learned how they live. In many places, salps form important links in the ecology of the open sea. Salps eat certain plankton and are themselves food for other plankton, sea turtles, and certain fishes. This new knowledge has come to light because of a simple change in research techniques. Although these vital creatures have been nearly ignored for decades, marine biologists can now study them closely and discover how they fit into the web of life.

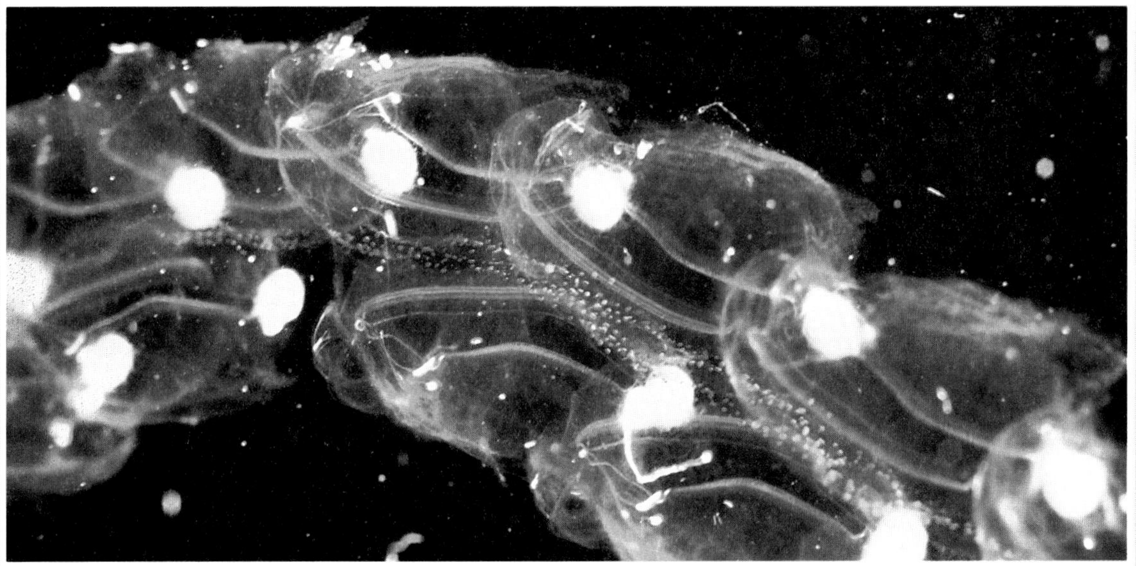

Salps are free-swimming invertebrate chordates found in the open ocean.

IDENTIFYING ECHINODERMS

PROBLEM

How can echinoderms be identified?

MATERIALS *(per group)*

assorted echinoderms
(pictures or preserved specimens)

PROCEDURE

1. On a separate piece of paper, draw a data table similar to the one shown here.
2. Your teacher will provide either pictures or preserved echinoderm specimens. Each specimen will be numbered.
3. Use the key to identify each numbered specimen. Start at step 1 and read descriptions A and B. Only one of the descriptions correctly applies to the specimen you are examining. At the end of a description is the identity of the specimen or directions to proceed to another step. Continue to follow the directions step by step until you identify the specimen.
4. After you identify the specimen, write its name next to its identification number in the data table. Then proceed to the next numbered specimen.

Specimen Identification Number	Identity of Specimen (from Identification Key)
1	
2	
3	
4	

OBSERVATIONS

1. What feature did all of the echinoderms you examined have in common?
2. How did the echinoderms you examined differ?
3. Did any echinoderms with visible differences have the same identity?

ANALYSIS AND CONCLUSIONS

1. How is the use of an identification key similar to the process of classification?
2. Why is it possible for two organisms that look different to have the same identity based on the key used in this investigation?

Identification Key

1	A.	Has obvious radial symmetry	Go to 2
	B.	Appears to have bilateral symmetry	Sea Cucumber
2	A.	Has arms or branches	Go to 3
	B.	Spherical, oval, or disk shaped	Go to 5
3	A.	Arms in multiples of five	Go to 4
	B.	Arms are branched and feathery	Go to 7
4	A.	Arms are long, slender, and flexible	Brittle Star
	B.	Arms are thick and less flexible	Starfish
5	A.	Spherical; covered with spines	Sea Urchin
	B.	Not spherical	Go to 6
6	A.	Oval	Heart Urchin
	B.	Flattened disk	Sand Dollar
7	A.	Has a long stalk	Sea Lily
	B.	Stalk short or absent	Feather Star

SUMMARIZING THE CONCEPTS

The key concepts in each section of this chapter are listed below to help you review the chapter content. Make sure you understand each concept and its relationship to other concepts and to the theme of this chapter.

29–1 Echinoderms

- Echinoderms are spiny-skinned animals with five-part radial symmetry, an internal skeleton, a water vascular system, and suction-cuplike structures called tube feet.
- Echinoderms are marine animals; no echinoderms live in fresh water or on land. Certain stages in the development of echinoderm larvae are similar to stages seen in members of the phylum Chordata.
- All echinoderms have a water vascular system that opens to the outside through a sievelike structure called the madreporite.
- In a starfish, the madreporite connects to a tube that leads to the ring canal, a part of the water vascular system, which forms a circle around the starfish's digestive system. Nutrients are moved around the animal in the digestive glands and the body cavity.
- Starfish reproduce externally by pouring eggs and sperm into the ocean water. The larvae that result from a fertilized egg float as part of the plankton.
- In spite of their fragile appearance, echinoderms are important predators in many environments.

29–2 Invertebrate Chordates

- Most chordates are vertebrates, which means they have backbones. However, a few chordate species are invertebrates. There are two subphyla of invertebrate chordates —tunicates and lancelets.
- At some stage of their life, all chordates possess these distinguishing characteristics: a notochord, a hollow dorsal nerve cord, and pharyngeal (throat) slits.
- Tunicates are small chordates that live in the ocean. Tunicate larvae resemble tadpoles and can move around in the water.
- Lancelets are small fishlike creatures that live in sandy ocean bottoms. Adult lancelets have a definite head.
- Invertebrate chordates are important because they indicate that vertebrate and invertebrate chordates evolved from common ancestors many millions of years ago.

REVIEWING KEY TERMS

Vocabulary terms are important to your understanding of biology. The key terms listed below are those you should be especially familiar with. Review these terms and their meanings. Then use each term in a complete sentence. If you are not sure of a term's meaning, return to the appropriate section and review its definition.

29–1 Echinoderms

echinoderm
water vascular system
tube feet

29–2 Invertebrate Chordates

chordate
notochord
hollow dorsal nerve cord
pharyngeal slit

CHAPTER REVIEW

CONTENT REVIEW

Multiple Choice

Choose the letter of the answer that best completes each statement.

1. A kind of echinoderm that is eaten by some people is a
   a. sea urchin. c. starfish.
   b. sea lily. d. lancelet.
2. To open a clam, a starfish uses its
   a. tube feet. c. madreporite.
   b. brain. d. stomach.
3. Echinoderms have
   a. a backbone.
   b. a long history on Earth.
   c. lungs.
   d. smooth skin.
4. Echinoderms show
   a. bilateral symmetry.
   b. top and bottom symmetry.
   c. radial symmetry.
   d. no symmetry.
5. Digested nutrients are moved around the body of a starfish in its
   a. skin gills. c. bony plates.
   b. digestive glands. d. water vascular system.
6. Tunicates and lancelets are examples of
   a. vertebrates. c. echinoderms.
   b. fish. d. chordates.
7. The side of an echinoderm where the mouth is located is called the
   a. aboral surface. c. oral surface.
   b. tunicate. d. vascular surface.
8. Invertebrate chordates lack a
   a. larva. c. nerve cord.
   b. notochord. d. backbone.

True or False

Determine whether each statement is true or false. If it is true, write "true." If it is false, change the underlined word or words to make the statement true.

1. All echinoderms have bilateral symmetry.
2. In echinoderms, tube feet and skin gills are used in respiration and excretion.
3. Lancelets have a primitive heart.
4. Echinoderms have nerves attached to plates in their endoskeleton.
5. A sea cucumber is a herbivore.
6. Tube feet are able to create suction when air is pumped out of them.
7. Some echinoderms have madreporites that tell them whether they are right side up.
8. If a piece of a starfish contains a portion of the central part of the body, the piece is able to regenerate.

Word Relationships

A. *An analogy is a relationship between two pairs of words or phrases generally written in the following manner: a:b::c:d. The symbol : is read "is to," and the symbol :: is read "as." For example, cat:animal::rose:plant is read "cat is to animal as rose is to plant."*

In the analogies that follow, a word or phrase is missing. Complete each analogy by providing the missing word or phrase.

1. starfish:echinoderm::tunicate:____________
2. sea cucumber:detritus feeder::feather star:____________
3. eyespots:light::statocysts:____________
4. madreporite:aboral surface::mouth:____________

B. *In each of the following sets of terms, three of the terms are related. One term does not belong. Determine the characteristic common to three of the terms and then identify the term that does not belong.*

5. starfish, sea lily, lancelet, sea urchin
6. ring canal, radial canal, tube feet, skin
7. notochord, hollow dorsal nerve cord, pharyngeal slits, vertebrae
8. tube feet, brain, water vascular system, madreporite

CONCEPT MASTERY

Use your understanding of the concepts developed in the chapter to answer each of the following in a brief paragraph.

1. What is radial symmetry? Name an animal that shows this kind of symmetry.
2. Briefly explain how a starfish eats a clam.
3. How does the water vascular system of a starfish help this animal to move?
4. What structures on a starfish tell this animal about its environment?
5. How do starfish reproduce?
6. How does a sea cucumber feed?
7. What characteristics does a lancelet share with vertebrate chordates?
8. Why is it not a good idea to break up a starfish and throw the pieces back into the water, especially if you fish for oysters?

CRITICAL AND CREATIVE THINKING

Discuss each of the following in a brief paragraph.

1. Making predictions Suppose that you are living alone on a small tropical island in the Pacific Ocean. This island is protected by a coral reef that surrounds it. One day while you are skin diving, you notice several crown-of-thorns starfish eating some of the coral animals that are part of your reef. Predict what might happen if the crown-of-thorns starfish increase in number.
2. Making comparisons Compare the form and function of a starfish and a sea cucumber. Describe the animals' adaptations for movement and feeding.
3. Applying concepts Explain why many fertilized starfish eggs never develop into adult starfish.
4. Designing an experiment Your friend tells you that starfish can regenerate themselves from even a small portion of an arm. You challenge this assumption. Design an experiment to prove who is correct.
5. Using the writing process Suppose that humans had the ability to regenerate themselves. For example, an arm might be able to grow a whole new body. Write a science fiction story that describes how this process might work for a person who was severely injured in an automobile accident.

CHAPTER 30

Comparing Invertebrates

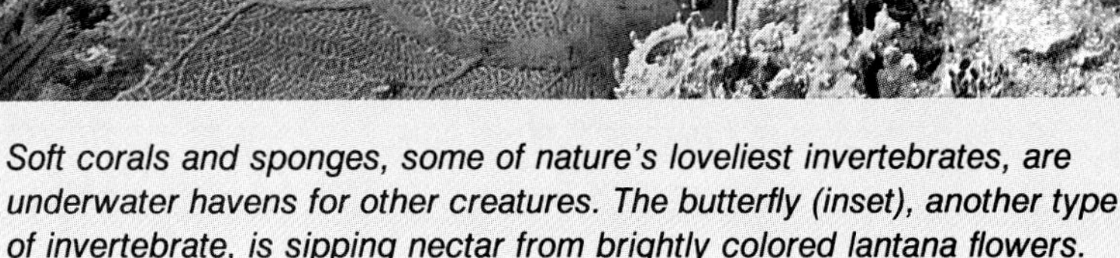

Soft corals and sponges, some of nature's loveliest invertebrates, are underwater havens for other creatures. The butterfly (inset), another type of invertebrate, is sipping nectar from brightly colored lantana flowers.

Beneath the shimmering surface of the ocean, a profusion of animals lives unseen by landbound eyes. Long, fingerlike sponges sway with the movement of waves far above. Tiny coral polyps shrink into themselves as a spotted flatworm swims by. Microscopic roundworms swarm in the miniature world between sand grains on the ocean floor. An octopus lurks in a crevice beneath the coral, its body slowly pulsing as it pumps water over its gills. A polychaete worm extends its feathery gills from the opening of its burrow and begins to strain tiny crustaceans and other bits of food from the water. Nearby, a spiny sea urchin slowly nibbles a path through the algae next to a colony of purple tunicates.

All of these wonderfully diverse animals are invertebrates. How did invertebrates evolve? How are different kinds of invertebrates related to one another? And what evidence do scientists examine to determine the nature of these relationships? You will discover the answers to these questions as you read the pages that follow.

CHAPTER OUTLINE

30–1 Evolution of the Invertebrates

Section Objectives

- Explain how evolutionary relationships are shown on a phylogenetic tree.
- Compare the development of protostomes and deuterostomes.
- Compare acoelomate, pseudocoelomate, and coelomate animals.

The evolutionary relationships between different groups of organisms can be shown in the form of a diagram called a **phylogenetic** (figh-loh-juh-NEHT-ihk) **tree**. *Phylo-* literally means tribe and refers to taxonomic groups; *-geny* means origin and development. Thus, as its name indicates, a phylogenetic tree shows our best understanding of which phyla originate from a common ancestor and approximately when evolutionary lines diverged. See Figure 30–3 on page 654. The base of the tree represents the common ancestor of all the groups shown on the tree. Branches that originate close to the bottom of the tree represent groups that evolved long ago; branches that originate near the top of the tree represent groups that evolved relatively recently. The tips of the branches represent living groups. Some phylogenetic trees show "dead" branches that do not reach the outside of the tree. Dead branches represent extinct evolutionary lines. There are no living groups from these lines.

How do scientists decide where animals belong on a phylogenetic tree? Recall from Chapter 13 that evidence for evolutionary relationships is found in the fossil record, in the body structure and chemical compounds of living organisms, and in the early development of organisms. Scientists examine many characteristics in each of these categories, looking for similarities and differences that indicate how closely organisms are related to one another.

Figure 30–1 *The tropical katydid, here munching on a leaf, is one of the more endearing terrestrial invertebrates.*

Figure 30–2 *The bubblelike sea squirts, clustered like berries on a branch of red coral, are deuterostomes.*

As you can see in Figure 30–3, there are several major branches on the phylogenetic tree—including **protostomes** and **deuterostomes**; **acoelomates**, **pseudocoelomates**, and **coelomates**. These branches represent basic evolutionary lines in animals with bilateral symmetry. **The division of animals into deuterostomes and protostomes is based on events in early development. The division of animals into acoelomates, pseudocoelomates, and coelomates is based on the structure of the body cavity.**

Early Development

Protostomes include flatworms, roundworms, annelids, mollusks, arthropods, and the members of most of the minor invertebrate phyla. Deuterostomes include echinoderms, several small phyla of strange-looking marine animals we have not discussed, and all members of our own phylum, Chordata. To understand the reasons for dividing animals into protostomes and deuterostomes, we must examine the earliest stages in the development of animals.

Figure 30–3 *The phylogenetic tree shows our best understanding of the evolutionary relationships between different groups of organisms. Which three groups of invertebrates appear to be most closely related to vertebrates?*

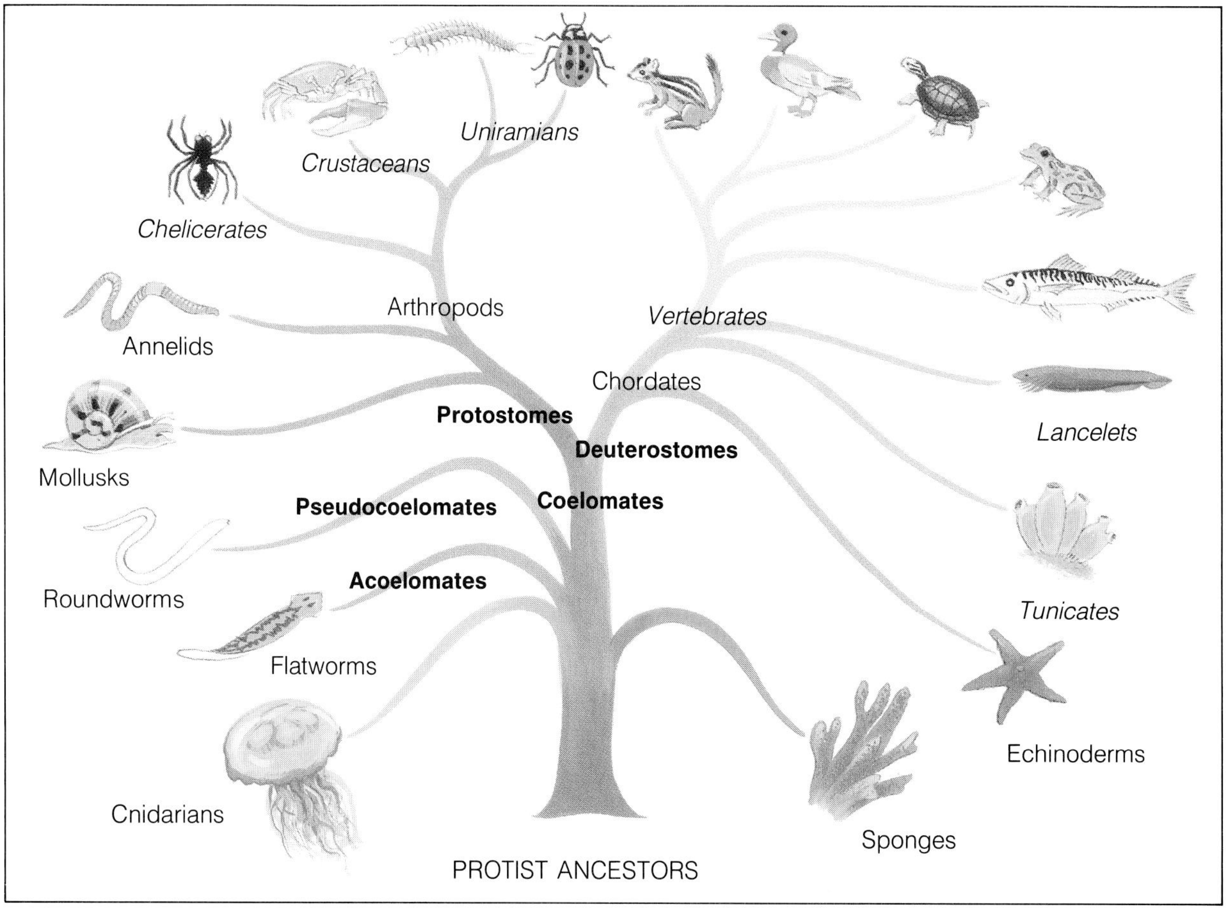

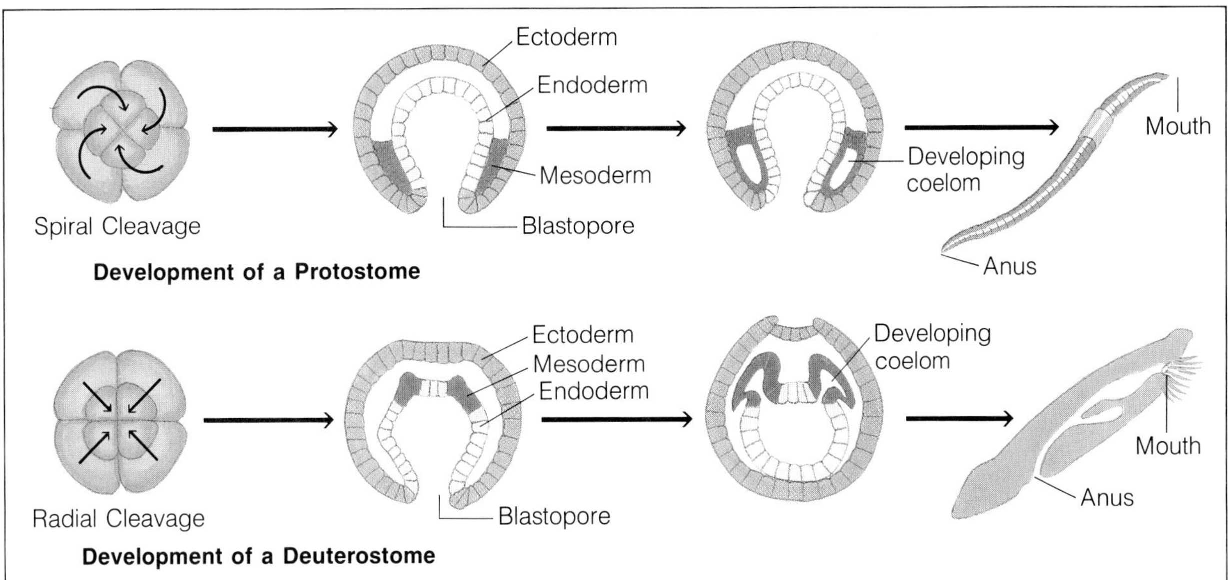

Figure 30–4 *In protostomes, the blastopore becomes the mouth. In deuterostomes, the blastopore becomes the anus.*

Soon after an egg has been fertilized, it begins a series of divisions. These divisions lead first to a two-cell stage and then to a four-cell stage. When the embryo grows from four cells to eight cells, the new cells can be arranged in different ways. In spiral cleavage, which occurs in almost all protostomes, the four new cells sit in between the four older cells. In radial cleavage, which occurs in almost all deuterostomes, the four new cells sit directly on top of the four older cells. It is important for you to note that neither of these patterns is "better" than the other. Radial and spiral cleavage are just two different patterns of growth that have evolved in the animal kingdom.

In both protostomes and deuterostomes, the cells of the embryo continue to divide until they form a hollow ball. Then the ball becomes flattened on one side and folds in on itself. This change in shape is similar to what you would get if you pushed your fist slowly into a partially inflated balloon. The layer of cells on the outside of the ball is called the ectoderm (*ecto-* means outside; *-derm* means skin). The layer of cells that has folded inside the ball is called the endoderm (*endo-* means inside). Both the ectoderm and the endoderm eventually develop into several different kinds of tissue.

The round central cavity enclosed by the endoderm will become the digestive tract of the developing embryo. The opening of this cavity to the outside is called the blastopore. And it is the fate of the blastopore that determines whether an animal is a protostome or a deuterostome. If the blastopore becomes the mouth, the animal is a protostome (*proto-* means first; *stoma* means mouth). If the blastopore becomes the anus and an opening that appears later becomes the mouth, the animal is a deuterostome (*deutero-* means second).

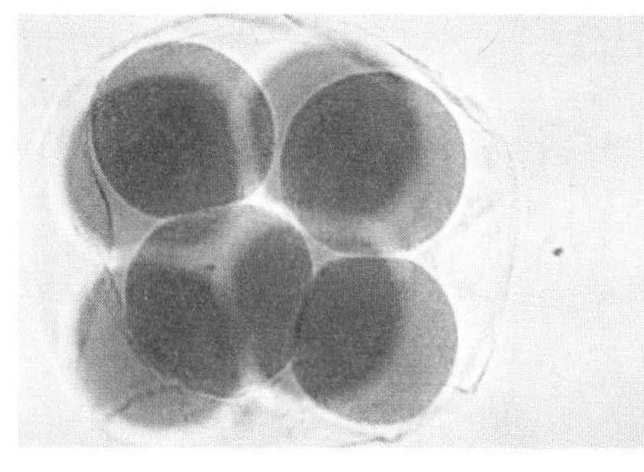

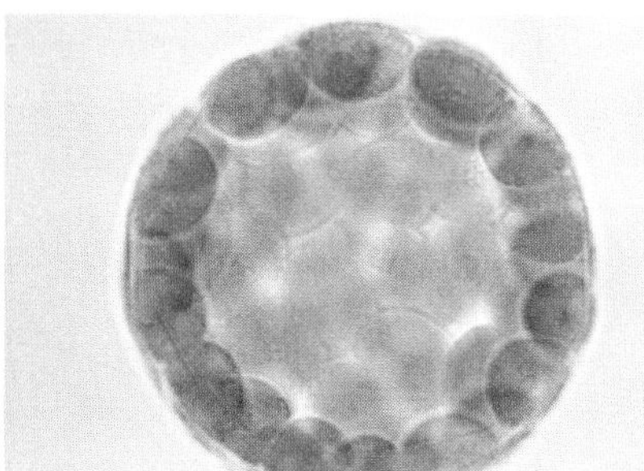

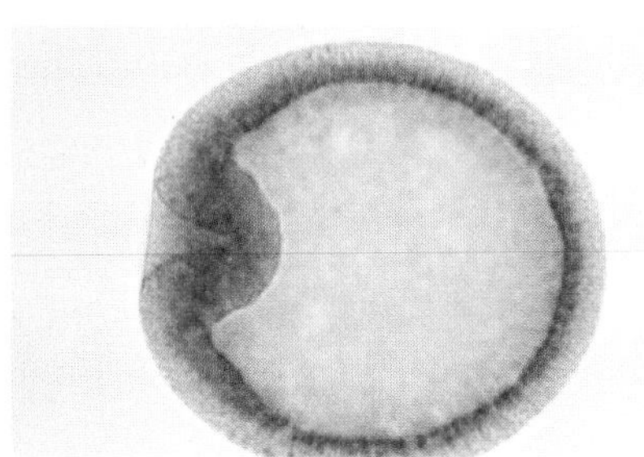

Figure 30–5 *As the embryos of animals develop, a single fertilized egg cell divides to form two cells, then four cells, then eight cells, and so on. The starfish embryo at the top is in the eight-cell stage. Later in development the cells form a hollow ball, as in the starfish embryo in the center. In the embryos of most animals, the hollow ball eventually begins to indent, as in the starfish embryo at the bottom.*

There is a third cell layer in embryos, called the mesoderm (*meso-* means middle), which is located between the endoderm and the ectoderm. In most protostomes, the bulk of the mesoderm is produced by a few cells in the area where the ectoderm meets the endoderm. In deuterostomes other than vertebrates, the mesoderm is typically produced from pouches of endoderm. See Figure 30–4 on page 655. Many important tissues, including muscles, develop from the mesoderm. And as you will learn shortly, the mesoderm is also important in defining the nature of an animal's body cavity—a characteristic that provides the basis for another division of the animal kingdom into major evolutionary lines.

Body Cavities

One of the most significant features of animal body plans is the presence or absence of a fluid-filled body cavity located between the digestive tract and the body wall. Body cavities are important for several reasons. They provide a space in which internal organs can be suspended so that they are not pressed on by muscles and twisted out of shape by body movements. Thus body systems can work in a more efficient and controlled manner. Body cavities also allow room for internal organs to develop and expand—for example, when ovaries fill with eggs. In addition, body cavities contain fluids that may be involved with internal transport, or the carrying of food, wastes, and other materials from one part of the body to another.

Some phyla, such as flatworms, have no body cavity at all. The body is basically a solid mass of mesoderm sandwiched between an inner layer of endoderm and an outer layer of ectoderm. Animals in these phyla are called acoelomates (ay-SEE-loh-mayts) (*a-* means without; *coelom* refers to the body cavity).

Figure 30–6 *The marine flatworm (left) has no body cavity—it is an acoelomate. The bubble-blowing ghost crab (right) has a body cavity that is completely lined with mesoderm—it is a coelomate.*

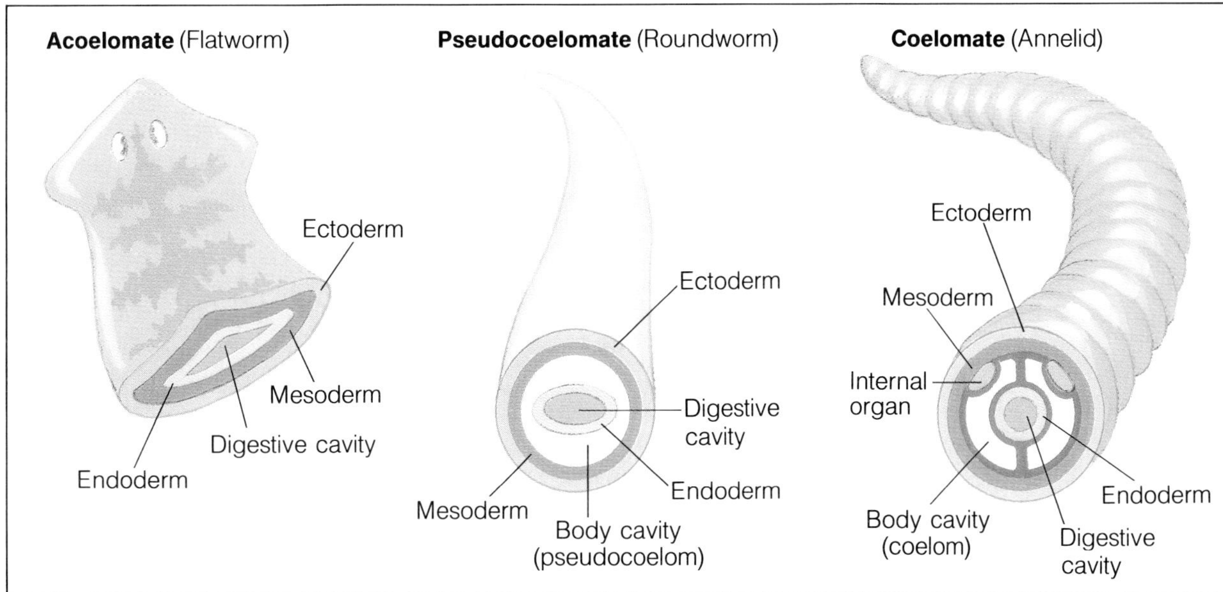

Figure 30–7 The basic body cavities and three body layers of an acoelomate, pseudocoelomate, and coelomate are shown here. Note that a pseudocoelom is only partially lined with mesoderm, whereas a coelom is completely lined.

Other phyla, such as roundworms, have a body cavity that is partially (but not completely) lined with mesoderm. Animals with this kind of body cavity are called pseudocoelomates (soo-doh-SEE-loh-mayts) (*pseudo-* means false.)

Still other phyla have a true **coelom** (SEE-lohm), or body cavity that is completely lined with mesoderm. Animals with this kind of body cavity are called coelomates and are considered to be more advanced than acoelomates and pseudocoelomates. The complete mesoderm lining of the coelom makes it possible for the digestive tract to develop specialized regions and organs, allows for the formation of blood vessels (which are formed from mesoderm), and makes it easier for complex organ systems to develop.

30–1 SECTION REVIEW

1. What is a phylogenetic tree?
2. What are the two main branches of the animal kingdom's evolutionary tree? On which branch do humans belong?
3. How do the names protostome and deuterostome relate to the differences in the development of animal embryos?
4. Compare acoelomate, pseudocoelomate, and coelomate animals.
5. Explain why the specialization of internal organs in coelomates is much greater than that in pseudocoelomates.

Section Objectives

- Discuss the ways in which different invertebrate phyla carry out their essential life functions.
- Describe the evolution of various body systems in invertebrates.

30–2 Form and Function in Invertebrates

In many ways, each animal phylum represents an experiment in the design of body structures to perform the tasks necessary for survival. Of course, there has never been any kind of plan to these experiments because evolution works without either plan or purpose. Nevertheless, the appearance of each phylum in the fossil record represents the random evolutionary development of a basic body plan that is different in some way from other body plans. The rest of the history of each phylum is the story of further evolutionary changes in that plan.

We can learn a great deal about the nature of life by comparing body systems among invertebrate groups and by tracing the patterns of change as we move from one phylum to another. As we do so, it is important to keep this concept in mind: **Evolution is random and undirected.** A common misconception is that evolution has proceeded from one group of organisms toward a goal of perfection. This is definitely not true. Organisms are not better or worse than one another—they are simply different. And the ways in which organisms carry out their essential life functions are neither more nor less perfect than one another—they are merely different methods of accomplishing the tasks necessary for survival.

The body systems that perform the vital functions of life have taken many different forms in different phyla. Some systems are complex; others are simple. Some are efficient; others are not. It is important to remember, however, that more complicated and efficient systems are not necessarily "better" in any absolute sense than simpler systems. The fact that these systems are found in living animals is testimony to their success in performing the functions they have evolved to perform.

__Figure 30–8__ Three main kinds of skeletal systems are characteristic of most animals. In animals that have endoskeletons or exoskeletons, muscles pull against hard supporting structures to produce movement. In animals that have hydrostatic skeletons, muscles push against a fluid-filled body cavity when they contract.

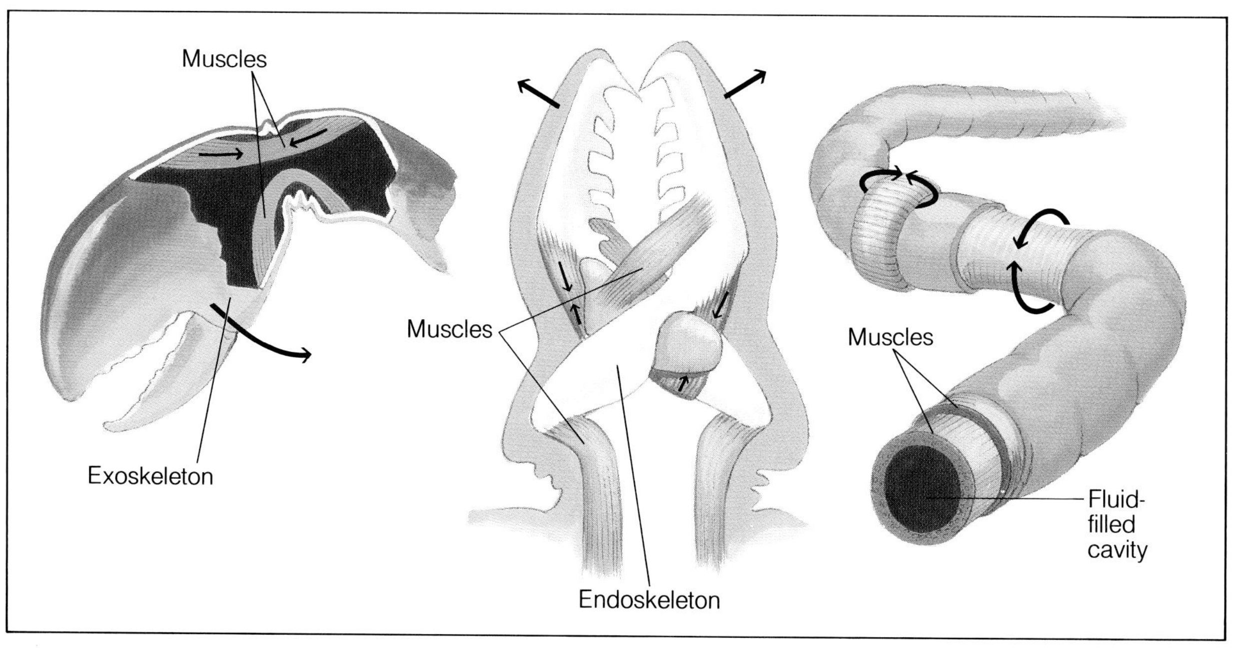

Movement

Almost all animals use specialized tissues called muscles to move. (There are a few exceptions: Sponges do not move at all; animals such as small flatworms use cilia to get from one place to another; and the contractile cells in cnidarians are not true muscles.) Without muscles, animals could not swim, fly, burrow, or run. In fact, most animals could not breathe, pump blood, or perform other life functions without muscles. Muscles work only by contracting. When muscles are stimulated, they generate force by getting shorter. When they are not stimulated, they relax.

In most animals, muscles work together with some sort of skeletal system that provides firm support. There are three main kinds of skeletal systems: **hydrostatic skeletons**, exoskeletons, and **endoskeletons**.

Figure 30–9 *The thick, armorlike exoskeleton of this crustacean serves in movement and in protection.*

Hydrostatic skeletons, unlike endoskeletons and exoskeletons, do not contain hard structures, such as bones or chitin plates, for muscles to pull against. Instead, the muscles surround and are supported by a water-filled body cavity. When the muscles contract, they push against the water in the body cavity. Cnidarians, some flatworms, roundworms, some mollusks, and annelids are animals that have hydrostatic skeletons.

The term exoskeleton usually refers to the hard nonliving coating that encloses an arthropod's internal organs and muscles. However, the shells of mollusks can also be considered exoskeletons. Muscles attached to the inside of an arthropod's exoskeleton are used to bend and straighten the joints. Muscles attached to the shell in mollusks make it possible for snails to withdraw into their shell and for bivalves to close their two-part shell.

Endoskeletons are frameworks located inside the body of animals. Sponges, echinoderms, and vertebrates have endoskeletons. Animals with endoskeletons typically have muscles that attach to the outside surface of the endoskeleton. (The only exceptions to this rule are sponges, which lack muscles and cannot move.)

Feeding

There are many sources of food in nature. And as you have learned, many different modes of feeding and kinds of digestive systems have evolved in invertebrates that enable them to utilize these resources.

As you move through the invertebrate phyla from simpler animals such as sponges to more complex animals such as arthropods, you can observe three major evolutionary trends. First, simpler animals such as sponges, cnidarians, and flatworms break down their food primarily through **intracellular digestion**. More complex animals use **extracellular digestion**.

SCIENCE, TECHNOLOGY, AND SOCIETY **APPLICATION**

The Twisting Tentacle: No Bones About It

Until recently, squid tentacles, elephant trunks, and human tongues posed an unanswerable question to biologists. These animal body parts have neither exoskeletons nor endoskeletons. They also lack the fluid-filled cavities associated with hydrostatic skeletons. Without some sort of support to work against, the muscles in these body parts should not be able to work at all. And yet they work extremely well! Squid tentacles, for example, can shoot forward to catch prey in a mere 30 milliseconds. How do these body parts work?

Scientists have recently identified the mechanical principles that permit an octopus's tentacles to move.

Researchers have discovered that the muscles in squid tentacles (and similar structures) pull against one another to produce movement. Like all cells, muscle cells are made up primarily of water. Thus each muscle cell can act like a fluid-filled cavity in a hydrostatic skeleton, providing support and giving other muscle cells something to work against. The arrangement of muscles in squid tentacles gives the animal extremely precise control over movement. For example, a tentacle can bend or twist at any point along its length. In contrast, a human limb or an insect limb can bend only where there are joints.

These new lessons about muscle function have already found applications in industry. Engineers have designed robot arms based on the same principles as squid tentacles. These robot arms are more efficient than those modeled after human arms. They are also less prone to damage and more adaptable to working in narrow, awkward spaces.

As you may recall, the collar cells in sponges take in microscopic food particles by endocytosis and then pass them to wandering cells called amebocytes. The food is digested inside food vacuoles within the amebocytes, and the nutrients from the food are then passed on to the other cells of the sponge by diffusion from the amebocytes. This is an example of intracellular (*intra-* means inside) digestion because food is digested, or broken down, inside the cells. In extracellular (*extra-* means outside) digestion, food is broken down outside the cells—specifically, in a digestive tract. Extracellular digestion is an adaptation that enables animals to eat and digest pieces of food that are much larger than the animals' cells. In the majority of cnidarians and flatworms, most of the process of digestion is intracellular—it occurs inside the cells that line the gastrovascular cavity. However, food particles are partially broken down in the gastrovascular cavity. Mollusks, annelids, arthropods, echinoderms, and chordates typically rely on extracellular digestion.

Second, cnidarians and some flatworms have a simple digestive system that has a single opening through which food enters and through which solid wastes are expelled. More advanced digestive systems, such as those found in roundworms, mollusks, annelids, arthropods, echinoderms, and chordates, have two openings—a mouth at one end and an anus at the other. Animals with a two-opening digestive tract are said to have a tube-within-a-tube body plan. The inner tube is the digestive tract and the outer tube is the body wall. Between these two tubes is the body cavity.

Third, the digestive tract tends to acquire more and more specialized regions. Simpler animals, such as flatworms, have a gastrovascular cavity in which one part does not differ very much from another part. The tube-within-a-tube body plan in more complex animals, such as mollusks and arthropods, allows for specialization because food passes through in one direction. As the food travels from the mouth to the anus, it is processed by each specialized region in turn.

The digestive system is not the only system to become more specialized as you move from simpler animals to more complex animals. As you may recall from Chapter 26, this evolutionary trend is seen in most of the other systems responsible for performing essential life functions. Keep this concept in mind as you read about these other invertebrate systems.

Figure 30–10 *The jellyfish (top) has a digestive system with only one opening. The plume worm (bottom) has a digestive system with two openings—a mouth and an anus.*

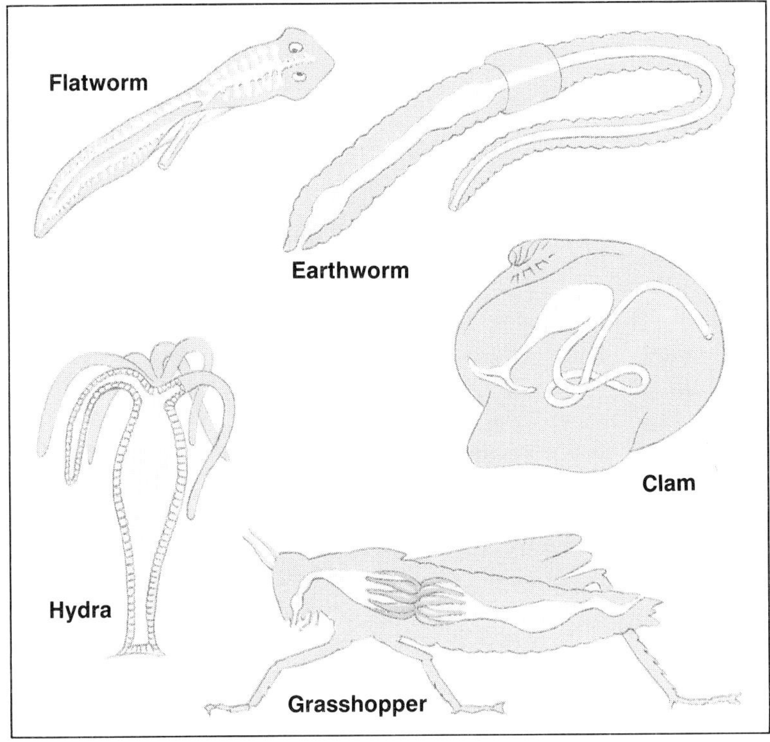

Figure 30–11 *As animals become more complex, extracellular digestion and two-opening digestive systems become more common than intracellular digestion and one-opening systems. In addition, the regions of the digestive tract become more specialized.*

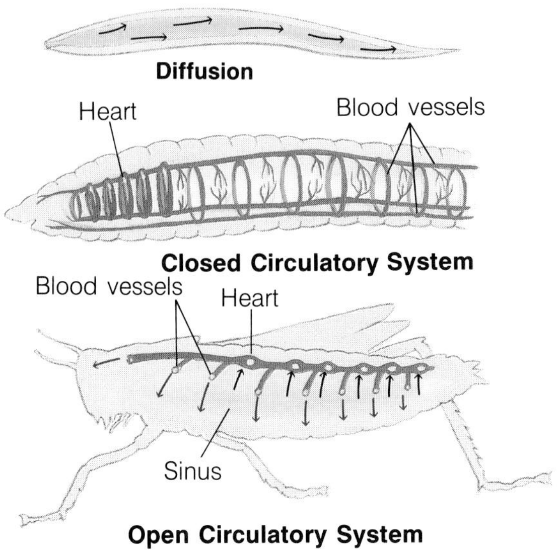

Diffusion

Heart

Blood vessels

Closed Circulatory System

Blood vessels

Heart

Sinus

Open Circulatory System

Figure 30–12 *The body cavity of a roundworm can be thought of as an extremely simple circulatory system. As the roundworm moves, fluid sloshes around the body cavity and dissolved materials are transported from one body region to another. A grasshopper has an open circulatory system, whereas an earthworm has a closed circulatory system.*

Internal Transport

All cells of multicellular animals must be supplied with oxygen and nutrients and must dispose of metabolic wastes. The smallest and thinnest multicellular animals manage to fulfill their internal transport needs through diffusion between their body surface and the environment. Although echinoderms are relatively large, they rely on this diffusion as well as diffusion between their body tissues and the fluid within their body cavity for their transport needs. Most complex multicellular animals, however, have a collection of pumps and tubes called a circulatory system. Typically, the pumps (hearts) force a fluid (blood) that carries food, oxygen, carbon dioxide, and other important substances through tubes (blood vessels) that extend throughout the body. There are two basic types of circulatory systems: open circulatory systems and closed circulatory systems. Open circulatory systems, which are found in arthropods and most mollusks, do not keep blood contained within blood vessels. At some point, the blood comes in direct contact with the tissues, collects in body sinuses, and then makes its way back to the heart. Closed circulatory systems, which are found in annelids and chordates, keep the blood completely contained within a network of blood vessels that stretches throughout the body. Materials diffuse from the blood to the tissues (and vice versa) through the walls of the blood vessels. Thus the blood normally does not come in direct contact with the tissues. In large active animals, a closed circulatory system offers greater control over blood flow and allows more efficient direction of blood to various parts of the body.

Respiration

In order to supply oxygen to and remove carbon dioxide from their tissues, animals must exchange these gases with the environment. Remember that diffusion of gases into and out of an animal's body requires a thin moist membrane. Thus two features are common to all respiratory systems. First, they almost always have structures that maximize the amount of surface area in contact with air or water. The more membrane exposed to the environment, the greater the amount of gas exchange that can occur. Second, they have some way of keeping the gas exchange surfaces moist so that diffusion can occur.

Aquatic animals have no problem in this regard—their watery environment keeps their respiratory surfaces moist. But terrestrial animals have a problem: Air contains little water and thus dries out the respiratory surfaces. To make matters worse, respiratory surfaces in terrestrial animals have a large surface area, so more membrane can dry out and more water can be lost from the body by diffusion. To prevent excessive water loss, the respiratory surfaces of terrestrial animals are kept moist with a coating of either water or mucus. In addition, the respiratory surfaces are often contained within the body (which is mostly water). Air is moistened as it travels through the body to the respiratory surface, reducing its drying effects.

Some animals that live in water or in very moist soil, such as cnidarians and flatworms, respire through their skin. Dry skin is more than just a cosmetic problem for these animals—it is death by suffocation! For most active animals larger than worms, however, respiration through the skin is not sufficient. Aquatic organisms—mollusks, crustaceans, some insects, and many annelids, for example—have gills that help them exchange gases with the water around them.

Terrestrial invertebrates have evolved several organs for breathing air. These include the highly modified mantle cavities of land snails, the book lungs of spiders, and the tracheal tubes of insects. See Figure 30–14.

Figure 30–13 *The gills of a plume worm are made up of threadlike projections that help maximize the surface area available for respiration.*

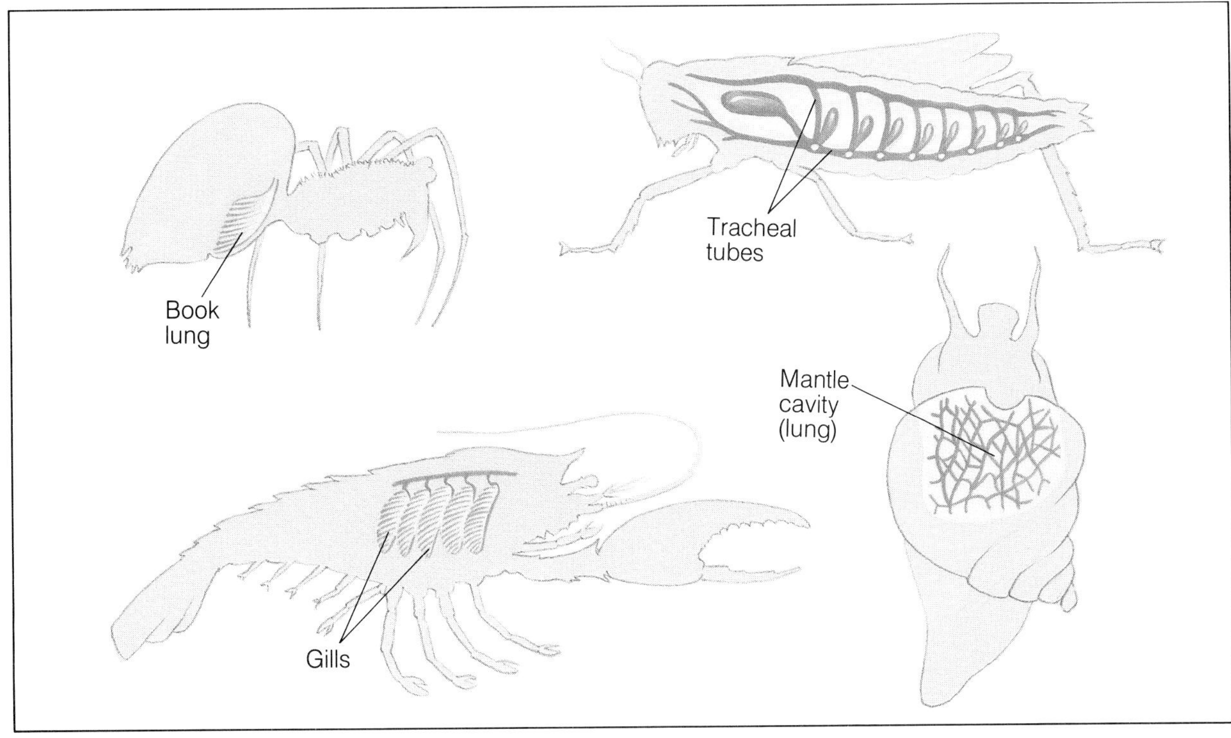

Figure 30–14 *Invertebrates use a variety of structures for respiration. A crayfish has gills. A spider has book lungs. Many land snails have a mantle cavity that acts as a lung. A grasshopper has tracheal tubes.*

Excretion

Multicellular animals, whether they live in water or on land, must control the amount of water in their tissues. Freshwater animals, for example, constantly take in water through the process of osmosis. In order not to blow up like water balloons, they must get rid of that extra water. Terrestrial and many marine animals, on the other hand, must protect their body tissues against water loss to the environment. At the same time, all animals—aquatic and terrestrial—must get rid of toxic nitrogenous (nitrogen-containing) wastes produced as a result of normal cellular metabolism. Excretory systems in invertebrates have evolved in ways that enable these animals to both regulate the amount of water in the body and get rid of nitrogenous wastes.

In all animals, the breakdown of amino acids during cellular metabolism produces ammonia (NH_3). Most aquatic invertebrates leave their nitrogenous wastes in this form, despite the fact that ammonia is highly toxic. They are able to do this because ammonia is also highly soluble; it dissolves readily in water. Many aquatic animals simply allow ammonia to diffuse through their body tissues and out into the surrounding water, which immediately dilutes it and carries it away.

Terrestrial animals, however, have a double problem: They must conserve body water and get rid of nitrogenous wastes at the same time. In order to do this, many invertebrates convert ammonia into a compound called urea. Urea is soluble in water and is much less toxic than ammonia. For this reason, urea can be concentrated by the excretory system. The waste product produced by the excretory system, which is called urine, is expelled from the body. Thus terrestrial animals can get rid of more wastes in less water than their aquatic counterparts.

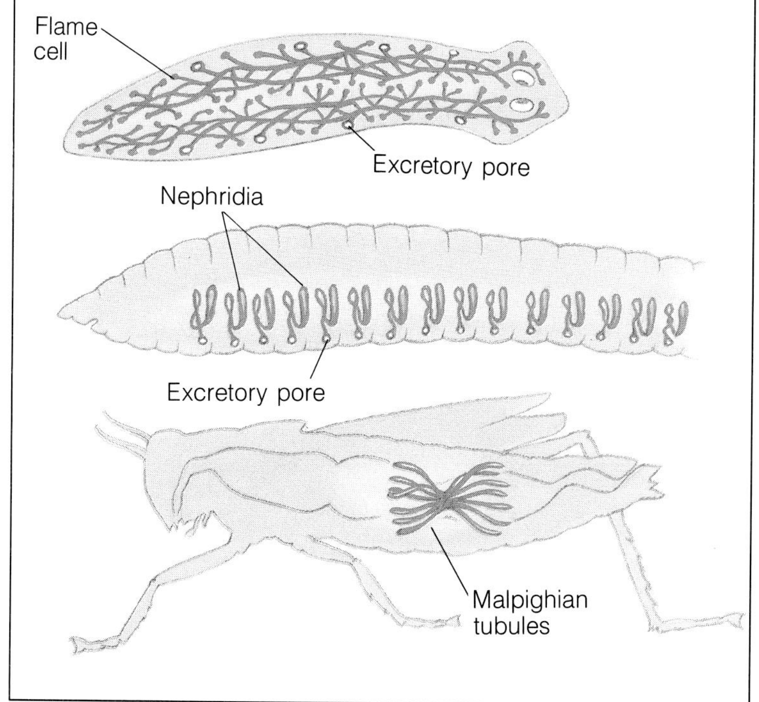

Figure 30–15 *Flame cells help remove excess water from a planarian's body. In many arthropods, Malpighian tubules filter nitrogenous wastes from the blood, concentrate the wastes in the form of uric acid, and dump the uric acid into the intestine. In some animals—earthworms, for example—nephridia remove nitrogenous wastes and concentrate them in the form of urea.*

Some land animals, including insects, convert nitrogenous wastes to uric acid, a compound that is less toxic than ammonia but is also much less soluble in water. When a solution of uric acid is concentrated in the excretory system, uric acid forms solid crystals. The excretory system can then return most of the water to the body tissues and get rid of the uric acid in the form of a thick paste.

What sorts of excretory systems are found in invertebrates? Simpler animals—sponges, cnidarians, and roundworms, for example—tend to depend on diffusion through body surfaces to get rid of nitrogenous wastes in the form of ammonia. In freshwater flatworms, such as planarians, flame cells help get rid of excess water, but ammonia still leaves primarily through the body surfaces. Insects and some arachnids have Malpighian tubules, which absorb fluid from the blood in the body sinuses. Nitrogenous wastes are concentrated in the tubules and are added to the undigested wastes in the intestine as a paste of uric acid crystals. Annelids, mollusks, and chordates have tubelike excretory structures called nephridia. Nephridia take in body fluids, remove nitrogenous wastes, and return most of the water and important compounds from those fluids to the body. They then concentrate waste products in urine, which is discharged from the body.

As urine becomes more concentrated, more wastes can be eliminated in the same amount of water. Advanced kinds of excretory systems, such as Malpighian tubules and the nephridia in more complex animals, are better at producing concentrated urine than simpler kinds of excretory systems. Thus animals with more advanced excretory systems can live in drier habitats because such systems allow for water conservation.

Response

Nervous systems gather information from the environment, process information, and allow animals to respond to it. The simplest nervous systems, which are found in cnidarians and some of the more primitive flatworms, are called nerve nets. Nerve nets consist of individual nerve cells that form a netlike arrangement throughout the animal's body.

As you can see in Figure 30–17 on page 666, invertebrates show three obvious trends in the evolution of the nervous system: centralization, cephalization, and specialization. Refer to Figure 30–17 as you read about these evolutionary trends.

The cells that make up a hydra's nerve net are quite spread out, although they are concentrated in the tentacles and around the mouth. In animals such as jellyfish and flatworms, the nerve cells are more concentrated, or centralized. They form nerve cords or nerve rings in certain areas. These structures transmit signals more quickly and efficiently than nerve nets and help coordinate responses.

Most animals that have bilateral symmetry also have a concentration of nerve tissue in the anterior end of the body. As

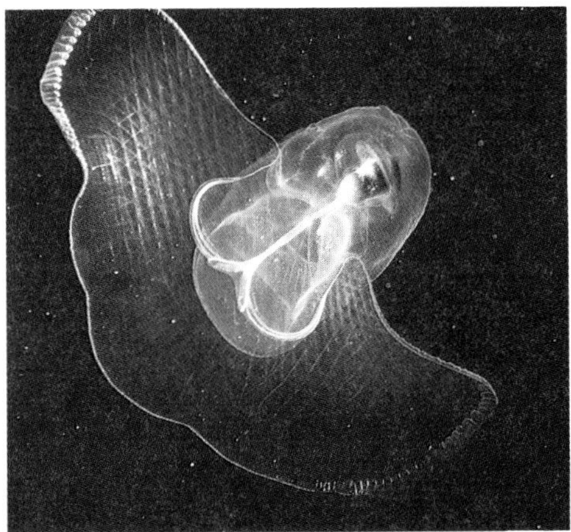

Figure 30–16 *Nervous systems enable invertebrates to respond to danger. The gooseneck barnacle, a sessile crustacean, jerks its feathery legs back to safety and snaps its shell shut (top). The sea butterfly, a gastropod mollusk, escapes a threat by "flying" rapidly through the water using its winglike foot (bottom).*

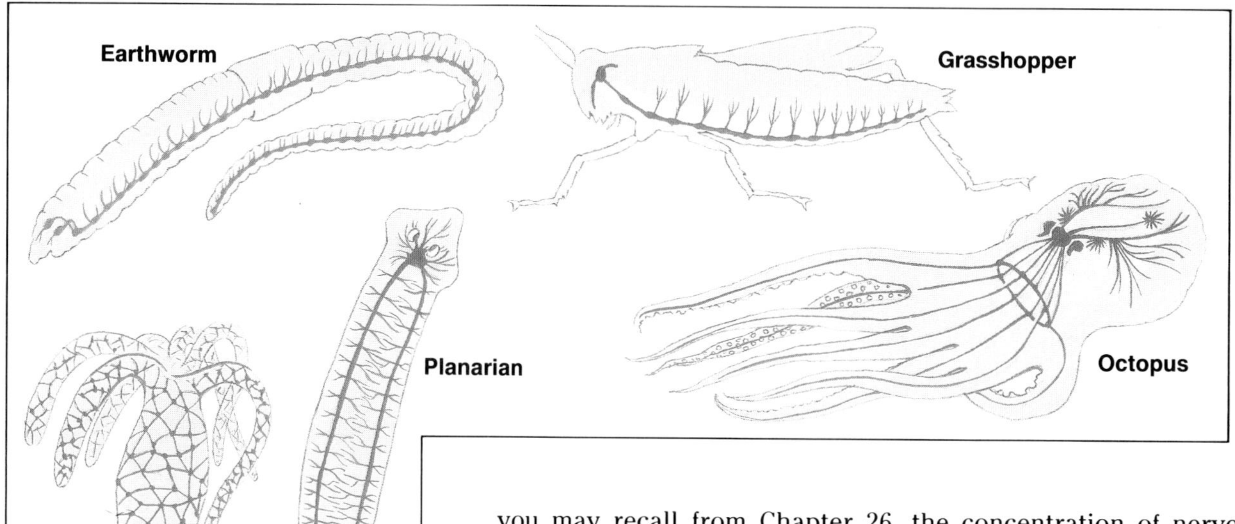

Figure 30–17 *The nervous system in a hydra is relatively diffuse. In a planarian, the nervous system is concentrated in some areas, forming nerve cords and ganglia. More advanced animals tend to have a brain, specialized sense organs, and a highly developed nervous system.*

you may recall from Chapter 26, the concentration of nerve cells and sense organs in the head region is known as cephalization. Cephalization tends to increase as animals become more complex. In simpler animals, such as flatworms, there are a few small clumps of nerve tissue, or ganglia, in the head. In more advanced animals—cephalopod mollusks and arthropods, for example—the ganglia are organized into a brain that controls and coordinates the nervous system.

In general, the more complex the animal, the more highly specialized its sense organs. For example, planarians have simple ocelli, or eyespots, that do little more than detect the presence of light. More complex animals, such as insects, have eyes that can detect motion and color and can form images. Complex animals may have a variety of specialized sense organs that detect light, sound, chemicals, movement, and sometimes even electricity to help them discover what is happening around them.

Reproduction and Development

Many simple invertebrates reproduce asexually through fragmentation or budding. In fragmentation, which occurs in several kinds of worms and cnidarians, an organism breaks into pieces. Each piece then regenerates into an entire individual. In budding, which occurs in sponges and cnidarians, new individuals are produced from outgrowths of the parent's body wall. A number of more complex animals, such as certain insects, also reproduce asexually. However, these animals do not undergo fragmentation or budding. Instead, their offspring develop from unfertilized eggs.

Asexual reproduction allows animals to produce offspring rapidly from a single individual. This enables species to quickly take advantage of new opportunities in the environment. The obvious disadvantage of asexual reproduction is that the offspring are genetically identical to the parent. And, as you may recall, a lack of genetic diversity makes populations less able to deal with changes in the environment.

Sexual reproduction maintains genetic diversity in a population. Although sexual reproduction does not create new

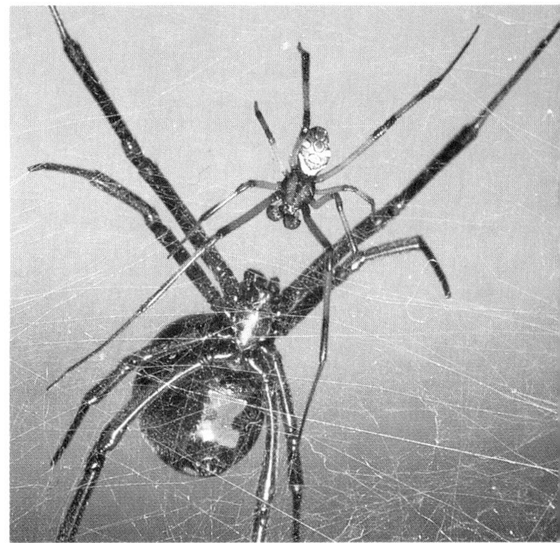

Figure 30–18 Some invertebrates undergo asexual reproduction. Others, such as butterflies (right) and spiders (bottom), undergo sexual reproduction. A few species of invertebrates, such as certain aphids (left), undergo both asexual and sexual reproduction. Note the rather obvious differences in appearance of the male and female spiders.

genes, it does result in new combinations of genes. Such combinations may improve an individual's chances of surviving and coping with change. Most of the more complex animals reproduce sexually. The majority of these animals have separate sexes—individuals are either males (sperm producers) or females (egg producers). But many animals, including certain mollusks and echinoderms, are hermaphrodites that produce both sperm and eggs at the same time. Hermaphrodites have some advantages over animals with separate sexes. One advantage is that anytime two sexually mature individuals meet each other, they can mate. (In species with separate sexes, of course, the individuals must be of different sexes or they cannot produce offspring together.) Another advantage is that one mating results in two batches of offspring (one per mated individual), rather than just one.

FERTILIZATION There are two basic ways in which sperm cells and egg cells are brought together in sexual reproduction: **external fertilization** and **internal fertilization**. External fertilization is generally associated with less complex animals, although there are examples of both external and internal fertilization in most animal phyla. In invertebrates that have external fertilization—jellyfish, clams, and sea urchins, for example—the eggs are fertilized outside the body. Adults release sperm and eggs into the surrounding water, and sperm swim to the eggs to fertilize them. Although this system is simple, it does have disadvantages. Clearly, as we saw earlier with plants, it can work only under water or in very wet places. It is also both risky and wasteful of sperm and eggs because many sperm cells never find an egg to fertilize and many eggs are never fertilized. To increase the chances of the eggs being fertilized, animals that use external fertilization release huge numbers of eggs and sperm when they spawn.

Internal fertilization is associated with more complex animals. In internal fertilization, the egg is fertilized inside the female's body. Usually, the males use specialized organs to deposit sperm inside the female's reproductive tract. Most land animals use internal fertilization.

Figure 30–19 *Some invertebrates care for their eggs and young. Its warning colors readily apparent, the harlequin bug stands guard over its eggs (top). The female wolf spider carries its numerous offspring on its back to keep them out of danger (bottom).*

PARENTAL CARE Many invertebrates do not take care of their fertilized eggs or young. The eggs are ignored as soon as they are laid. In many invertebrates, the fertilized eggs and resulting young live in the water and drift wherever currents may take them. Most of the young are eaten or are exposed to adverse environmental conditions and die. Perhaps this seems wasteful to you. But for animals in which the adults are cemented permanently in one spot, such as corals and barnacles, floating eggs and free-swimming larvae offer the only chance for the next generation to find a new spot in which to settle and spend the rest of their lives. Although each egg has only a tiny chance of surviving to adulthood, a few manage to make it. In other invertebrates, the females lay their eggs in a spot where they are hidden from predators or where food will be available for emerging young. These young have better chances of surviving than young that emerge in inhospitable places or in locations where no food is nearby.

Some invertebrates take care of their offspring. For example, queen bees lay their eggs in special compartments in a well-provisioned and protected hive. The small octopus called the paper nautilus builds a special shell to carry and protect her eggs. Some scorpions carry eggs and young around on their back. Some of the ways in which invertebrates care for their offspring may seem horrifying to humans. For example, the eggs of some species of mites hatch within the female's body. The larvae immediately begin to devour their mother from the inside! Within two days—while still inside their mother's nearly empty exoskeleton—the young mites mature, mate, and eat their way to the outside. The males die within a few hours. The females seek out prey in the form of insect eggs and begin to feed—even as their own offspring start chewing on their internal organs.

30–2 SECTION REVIEW

1. Name and describe the three main types of skeletal systems found in the animal kingdom.
2. Describe how the digestive system evolves as animals become more complex.
3. Compare internal transport in echinoderms, arthropods, and chordates.
4. Compare asexual and sexual reproduction. What are their advantages? Disadvantages?
5. Discuss three evolutionary trends in the development of the nervous system.
6. What are the three forms of nitrogenous wastes excreted by animals? How is the type of waste an animal excretes related to its environment?

PROBLEM SOLVING IN BIOLOGY

WHAT IS IT?—ANALYZING FUNCTION THROUGH FORM

Imagine yourself a world famous invertebrate biologist who is often called upon to describe the habits of newly discovered organisms by comparing their structures to other animals you know. One day specimens belonging to the same species are brought into your laboratory, and you are asked to describe the animal's habits as best you can.

Some of the specimens are larvae that closely resemble one another, although none looks like the adult specimens. These larvae have a tough dark-brown exoskeleton, six legs with tips flattened like canoe paddles, and gills supplied with many tracheal tubes. Larval mouthparts look like a collection of butcher knives—sharp and menacing.

Adult specimens have two pairs of wings and six legs. Their brightly colored exoskeleton is covered with a thick, waxy coating. They have well-developed tracheal tubes spread throughout their body. Two of their mouthparts are relatively sharp, but the rest are blunt and clearly adapted for grinding and pulverizing food. You can tell from samples at the end of the gut that these animals excrete their nitrogenous wastes in the form of uric acid.

Practice your expertise in identifying unknown animals by answering the following questions about this imaginary creature.

1. To what phylum and class does this species probably belong?
2. Describe the probable life cycle of this animal. What sorts of specimens of this species would help you confirm your hypothesis about how this organism develops?
3. Where do you think the larvae live? Explain your answer.
4. What type of food do the larvae probably eat? Explain your reasoning.
5. What sorts of food do the adults probably eat? What evidence leads you to this conclusion?
6. Could the adults of this species survive in dry habitats? Why or why not?

What can you infer from your examination of this mysterious (and fictitious) creature?

LABORATORY INVESTIGATION

COMPARING DEVELOPMENT IN ECHINODERMS AND MOLLUSKS

PROBLEM

How do patterns of development compare in echinoderms and mollusks?

MATERIALS *(per group)*

prepared slides showing the early development of a starfish and a clam
microscope

PROCEDURE 

1. Using the low-power objective of the microscope, examine a slide showing starfish development. Locate a single cell alone. This is an egg cell. Switch to the high-power objective and focus with the fine adjustment. Draw a diagram of the egg cell and label it.
2. After fertilization, the egg cell begins to divide. Switching back to low power, locate an embryo in the 2-cell stage of development. Examine it in detail under high power and draw a labeled diagram of it.
3. Repeat step 2 for each of the following stages of development: 4-cell, 8-cell, 16-cell, and 32-cell. In the 8-, 16-, and 32-celled stages, note whether the cells are directly above or behind one another or whether the cells appear to be between one another.
4. Notice the size of the individual cells and the size of the entire embryo as the number of cells in the embryo increases.

5. Eventually, the embryo develops into a solid ball-shaped cluster of cells in which individual cells can be seen. This cluster is called a morula. Locate a morula under low power. Then switch to high power to examine it. Draw a diagram of a morula and label it.
6. As cleavage (cell division) continues, the embryo becomes a hollow ball called a blastula. A blastula looks like a sphere with a dark circle of cells near the edge. Locate a blastula under low power. Then switch to high power. Draw a diagram of the blastula and label it.
7. As development continues, the sphere-shaped embryo indents on the bottom. This indented stage is called a gastrula. Locate a gastrula under low power. Then switch to high power. Draw a diagram of the gastrula and label it.
8. Repeat this procedure using the slide showing clam development. Note any similarities and differences between starfish development and clam development.

OBSERVATIONS

1. What similarities did you observe between echinoderm (starfish) development and mollusk (clam) development?
2. What differences did you observe between echinoderm cleavage and mollusk cleavage?
3. What happened to the size of the embryo as the number of cells increased?
4. What happened to the size of the individual cells as the number of cells in the embryo increased?

ANALYSIS AND CONCLUSIONS

1. Which organism undergoes spiral cleavage?
2. Which organism undergoes radial cleavage?
3. How do patterns of development compare in echinoderms and mollusks?

SUMMARIZING THE CONCEPTS

The key concepts in each section of this chapter are listed below to help you review the chapter content. Make sure you understand each concept and its relationship to other concepts and to the theme of this chapter.

30–1 Evolution of the Invertebrates

- A phylogenetic tree shows the evolutionary relationships between different organisms.
- In protostomes, the blastopore becomes the mouth, cleavage typically is spiral, and the mesoderm usually arises from a few cells near the blastopore. In deuterostomes, the blastopore becomes the anus, cleavage typically is radial, and the mesoderm characteristically arises from pouches of endoderm.
- Acoelomates lack a body cavity. Pseudocoelomates have a body cavity that is partially lined with mesoderm. Coelomates have a body cavity that is completely lined with mesoderm, which is called a coelom.

30–2 Form and Function in Invertebrates

- There are three main types of skeletal systems: hydrostatic skeletons, exoskeletons, and endoskeletons.
- Simpler animals tend to use intracellular digestion. More complex animals tend to use extracellular digestion, in which food is broken down in a digestive tract.
- Simpler digestive systems have just one opening through which food is taken in and wastes are expelled. More complex digestive systems have two openings—a mouth and an anus.
- In an open circulatory system, blood comes in direct contact with body tissues. In a closed circulatory system, the blood is always contained within blood vessels.
- Respiratory systems require a thin moist membrane and a large surface area for effective gas exchange.
- Excretory systems regulate the amount of water in the body and dispose of nitrogenous wastes.
- Three trends in the evolution of the nervous system are centralization, cephalization, and specialization.
- Asexual reproduction makes it possible for one individual to rapidly produce many genetically identical offspring. Sexual reproduction creates new combinations of genes.
- Fertilization may be internal or external.

REVIEWING KEY TERMS

Vocabulary terms are important to your understanding of biology. The key terms listed below are those you should be especially familiar with. Review these terms and their meanings. Then use each term in a complete sentence. If you are not sure of a term's meaning, return to the appropriate section and review its definition.

30–1 Evolution of the Invertebrates

phylogenetic tree
protostome
deuterostome
acoelomate
pseudocoelomate
coelomate
coelom

30–2 Form and Function in Invertebrates

hydrostatic skeleton
endoskeleton
intracellular digestion
extracellular digestion
external fertilization
internal fertilization

CHAPTER REVIEW

CONTENT REVIEW

Multiple Choice

Choose the letter of the answer that best completes each statement.

1. Which of the following statements about a protostome is true?
   a. It is an acoelomate.
   b. It has radial cleavage.
   c. Its blastopore becomes its mouth.
   d. Its mesoderm arises from pouches of endoderm.
2. Roundworms, which have body cavities that are partially lined with mesoderm, are
   a. deuterostomes. c. acoelomates.
   b. coelomates. d. pseudocoelomates.
3. An animal that lives in an extremely dry climate probably
   a. has a very efficient excretory system.
   b. tends to gain water through osmosis.
   c. has a hydrostatic skeleton.
   d. excretes ammonia.
4. The nitrogenous waste that is least soluble in water is
   a. urine. c. uric acid.
   b. ammonia. d. urea.
5. Which animal has the greatest amount of cephalization?
   a. starfish c. jellyfish
   b. flatworm d. octopus
6. Sea urchins produce huge numbers of sperm cells or egg cells. These animals probably
   a. are hermaphrodites.
   b. have internal fertilization.
   c. have external fertilization.
   d. care for their young.
7. An animal with a tube-within-a-tube body plan always has a
   a. coelom.
   b. digestive tract with two openings.
   c. hydrostatic skeleton.
   d. highly specialized digestive tract.
8. Which animal has the most complex circulatory system?
   a. clam c. flatworm
   b. sea anemone d. squid

True or False

Determine whether each statement is true or false. If it is true, write "true." If it is false, change the underlined word or words to make the statement true.

1. A body cavity that is completely lined with mesoderm is called a <u>blastopore</u>.
2. Most <u>deuterostomes</u> have spiral cleavage.
3. Acoelomate animals are <u>protostomes</u>.
4. Budding is a form of <u>sexual</u> reproduction.
5. Malpighian tubules remove <u>urea</u>.
6. Insects have <u>open</u> circulatory systems.
7. The middle layer of cells in an animal embryo is called the <u>ectoderm</u>.
8. Nephridia are used in <u>respiration</u>.

Word Relationships

Replace the underlined definition with the correct vocabulary word.

1. The animal kingdom's <u>diagram that shows the evolutionary relationships between groups of organisms</u> indicates that animals evolved from protists.
2. <u>The waste product produced by the excretory system</u> contains concentrated nitrogenous wastes.
3. Sponges have <u>the type of digestion in which food is broken down inside food vacuoles within cells rather than in a digestive cavity.</u>

CONCEPT MASTERY

Use your understanding of the concepts developed in the chapter to answer each of the following in a brief paragraph.

1. Discuss the evolution of the body cavity in animals. Give specific examples of animals with each kind of body plan.
2. Explain why lungs tend to have a highly folded inner surface and gills are often feathery in appearance. (*Hint:* What features are common to all respiratory surfaces?)
3. What sorts of inferences can you make if you are told that an animal is a deuterostome?
4. How do crayfish show the evolutionary trends of cephalization, centralization, and specialization? (*Hint:* Refer to Figure 28–23 on page 621.)
5. Explain why sponges are able to eat only microscopic particles of food.
6. Why can internal fertilization be considered an adaptation to living on land?
7. Compare early development in protostomes and deuterostomes.

CRITICAL AND CREATIVE THINKING

Discuss each of the following in a brief paragraph.

1. **Summarizing information** Construct a table that compares the nine invertebrate phyla you have studied in this unit with regard to the seven essential life functions. Be sure to include at least two examples of each phylum and any other information that will help you see the relationships between invertebrates.
2. **Relating concepts** At one time, cnidarians and echinoderms were placed in the same classification group because they both have radial symmetry. Explain why echinoderms are now thought to be more closely related to chordates.
3. **Making generalizations** Ctenophores are marine animals that have radial symmetry, a digestive tract with a single opening, and long, branching tentacles that have special sticky cells used to capture prey. The thin, transparent body wall consists of three layers: epidermis, mesoglea, and gastroderm. Although the mesoglea contains muscle cells, ctenophores typically move by using combs of fused cilia. Ctenophores range in size from about that of a pea to that of a golf ball.
   a. Where would you expect ctenophores to fit on the phylogenetic tree? Explain.
   b. How would you expect a ctenophore to carry out the functions of respiration, internal transport, and excretion? Explain.
4. **Developing a hypothesis** Formulate a hypothesis to explain why slugs are slimy. How might you test your hypothesis?
5. **Evaluating theories** Deuterostomes are thought to have evolved from protostomes. Give two reasons explaining why this is a reasonable theory. What information would you need to make a more informed evaluation of this theory?
6. **Using the writing process** Pretend that you are the invertebrate of your choice. Prepare a résumé that will inform a potential employer of your specialized skills.

Reptile Farmer

Reptile farmers breed and capture reptiles such as snakes and tortoises for preservation, exhibition, meat, and venom. They raise the reptiles in cages that are similar to the animals' natural habitat.

Many reptile farmers are skilled in extracting venom from live snakes. This venom can be used by scientists to develop chemical treatments for people who have been bitten by poisonous snakes.

Reptile farmers usually learn about their trade through experience.

For additional information contact the National Council of Farmer Cooperatives, 1800 Massachusetts Ave., NW, Washington, DC 20036.

Chef

Chefs are responsible for the preparation, cooking, and presentation of foods. They plan menus, order food supplies, and follow or create recipes.

Many chefs specialize in a particular food group. For example, certain chefs prepare only seafoods such as shrimp, crab, lobster, scallops, and mussels. Other chefs prepare only meat dishes, or pastries.

Although a high school diploma is not required to become a chef, it is an asset to job applicants. Many chefs also complete training programs at cooking schools.

For more information write to the American Culinary Federation, P.O. Box 3466, St. Augustine, FL 32084.

Entomologist

Entomologists study insects and the relationships between insects and plants and animals. Their work involves collecting, observing, and classifying different insects, as well as determining the effects insects can have on other organisms.

Some entomologists do research on insects that are harmful to other organisms, such as those that destroy crops. They develop and improve pesticides and are interested in methods to prevent the spread of such insect pests.

To become an entomologist, a Bachelor's degree in the biological sciences and a Ph.D. in entomology are necessary.

For information write to the Entomological Society of America, 4603 Calvert Rd., College Park, MD 20740.

HOW TO WRITE A COVER LETTER

When you contact an employer through the mail, you should write a cover letter to introduce yourself. You must realize that the person receiving your letter probably reads many letters like yours every day. Therefore, your cover letter must be impressive, organized, and brief. Your letter must be an original copy, neatly typed without errors.

It is best to begin your letter with a statement explaining the kind of position you are seeking. The second paragraph is usually used to sum up your qualifications for the position. The third paragraph is used to close the letter and ask for an interview at a convenient time.

FROM THE AUTHORS

I never really liked hydras. They were small, didn't do much, and were usually half dead by the time my high school biology class got a chance to see them. Insects didn't turn me on much either, to tell the truth. Bees and mosquitoes bit me, ants pestered me at picnics, and flies kept me awake at night when I went camping. Worse yet, I had to memorize their names and body parts for school tests. "What are these things good for?" I'd ask myself. "Who cares about them anyway?"

I didn't change my mind about invertebrates for several years. Then, in one 24-hour period, everything I once thought about them changed.

I was visiting a tropical island. Not a resort, mind you, but a biological station on a tiny piece of rock in the middle of the Caribbean. The very first night, during dinner, a huge centipede crawled out of the garden and bit the resident dog on the nose. As the poor mutt ran away yelping, I thought, "This is something worth paying attention to." (I later found out that the centipede's bite was venomous and quite painful.)

The next morning I saw a living coral reef for the first time. Sure, I'd seen pictures of them, but they hadn't prepared me for the fantasyland of colors and shapes that drifted in front of my eyes. Most of the animals I saw were invertebrates, and I struggled to remember their names. There were corals, sea anemones, starfish, sea cucumbers, and more. And all of these animals played important roles in the living system of the reef. I was amazed. I was also hooked. I would never think poorly of animals without backbones again.

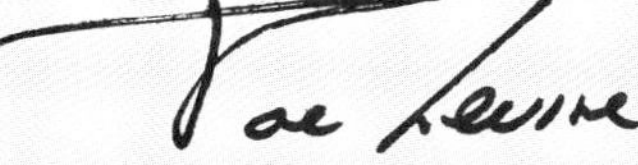

UNIT 8

Life on Earth: Vertebrate Animals

At first glance, fishes, amphibians, reptiles, birds, and mammals appear considerably different from one another. Some have feathers; others fins. Some fly; others swim. Some walk on land; others burrow beneath it. Some inhabit land environments; others call rivers and oceans their home. Indeed, such variations separate these animals into different classes.

All of these animals, however, have one important characteristic in common: They have special bones in their back that form a strong column that protects delicate nerve tissue and helps support their body. This vertebral column, which is a unique characteristic shared by many different animals, forms the basis for classifying them in the same phylum—the vertebrates, or animals with a backbone.

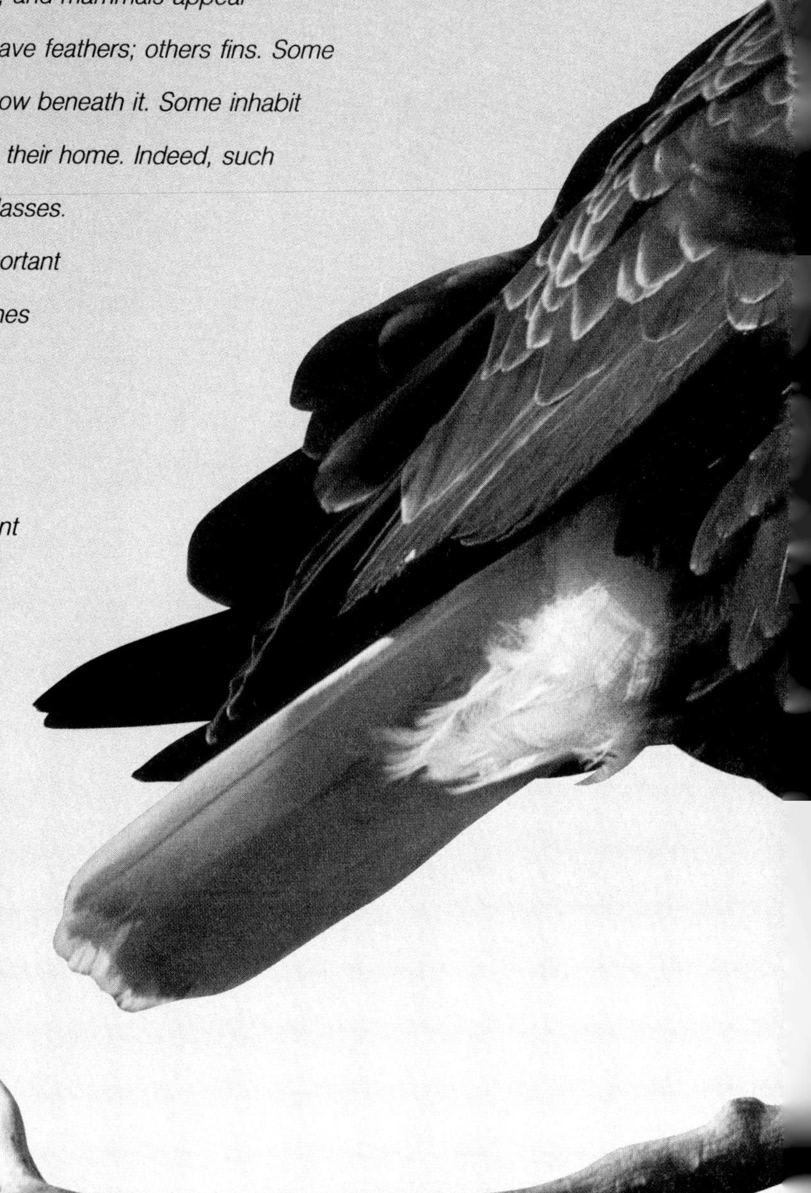

CHAPTERS

CHAPTER 31

Fishes and Amphibians

The lionfish is one of the most exotic, beautiful, and venomous marine fishes. Amphibians such as salamanders also protect themselves with their toxins.

Just off the shores of a tropical island, small reef fish dart among coral formations, creating dazzling, ever-changing patterns of brilliant colors. A shark swims by, its open mouth revealing several rows of sharp triangular teeth. On the other side of the world, the decks of a fishing ship are covered with wriggling silver bodies as nets filled with herring are hauled in from a cold gray ocean. Using its fins like stubby legs, a catfish drags itself out of the mud of a drying pond in Africa and scuttles off to find more suitable surroundings. Thousands of meters beneath the ocean surface, nightmarish fish—which seem to consist of nothing more than needlelike teeth, oversized jaws, and enormous eyes—flicker with ghostly lights produced by their own body.

Fishes are the most ancient and diverse group of vertebrates, or animals with backbones. In the pages that follow, you will learn more about fishes and their relatives the amphibians—the first groups of vertebrates to appear on Earth.

CHAPTER OUTLINE

31–1 Fishes

Section Objectives

- Describe the distinguishing characteristics of vertebrates.
- Explain how fishes carry out their essential life functions.
- Describe the three basic groups of fishes and give an example of each.

The name Earth is not particularly appropriate for the planet on which we live, for more than two thirds of its surface is water, not earth. And just about anywhere there is water, there are fishes. At the edge of the ocean, blennies jump from rock to rock and occasionally dunk themselves in tide pools. Beneath the arctic ice live fishes whose bodies contain a biological antifreeze that prevents them from freezing solid in sea water colder than 0°C. And in shallow desert streams in the southwestern United States, pupfish tolerate temperatures that would cook almost any other animal.

What Is a Fish?

To clearly understand what fishes are and how they are related to other vertebrates, it is necessary to know something about the characteristics that unite fishes, amphibians, reptiles, birds, and mammals into the subphylum Vertebrata. You may recall from Chapter 29 that vertebrates belong to the phylum Chordata. This means that fishes and other vertebrates have at some time during their development a notochord, a hollow dorsal nerve cord, and pharyngeal slits. In most vertebrates, the notochord is replaced during development by a backbone, or **vertebral column**, which encloses and protects much of the nerve cord. In addition, most vertebrates have two sets of paired appendages, a closed circulatory system with a ventral heart, and either gills or lungs for breathing.

Fishes can be defined as aquatic vertebrates that are characterized by scales, fins, and pharyngeal gills. However, fishes are so varied that for almost every general statement

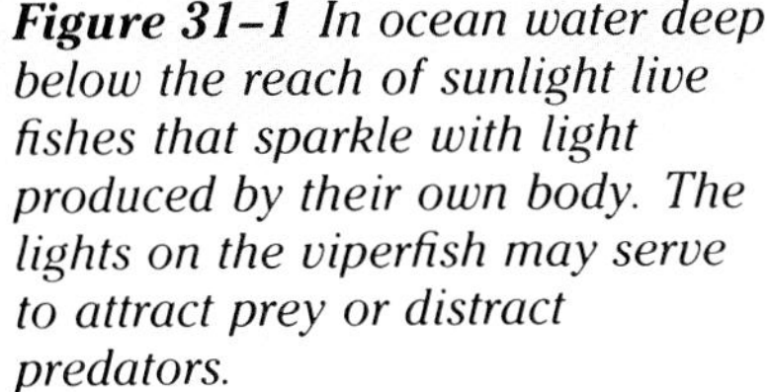

Figure 31–1 *In ocean water deep below the reach of sunlight live fishes that sparkle with light produced by their own body. The lights on the viperfish may serve to attract prey or distract predators.*

Figure 31–2 *Representatives of the three main groups of living fishes are shown here. The lamprey is a parasitic jawless fish (bottom). The blue-spotted stingray is a venomous bottom-dwelling cartilaginous fish (right). The Potter's angelfish, which is found only in Hawaiian coral reefs, is a bony fish (left).*

made about them there are exceptions. For example, some fishes do not have scales. One reason for the many differences among fishes is that four living classes of vertebrates make up the group of animals we know as fishes. Thus many fishes—sharks and lampreys, for example—are no more closely related to one another than humans are to frogs.

There are so many fishes, living and extinct, that their correct scientific classification is complicated. For our purposes, we can say that the living fishes fall into three main groups: **jawless fishes**, sharks and their relatives, and **bony fishes**. Sharks and their relatives are also known as **cartilaginous fishes** because their skeletons are made up of soft, flexible cartilage rather than bone.

Evolution of Fishes

Fishes are considered to be the most primitive living vertebrates. (This means that fishes were the first vertebrates to evolve and that they have many characteristics that are thought to have existed in their earliest ancestors. It does not mean that they are somehow inferior to other types of vertebrates.) Fishes did not evolve from such organisms as living lancelets or tunicates. But similarities in structure and embryological development show that fishes and modern invertebrate chordates probably did evolve from common invertebrate ancestors that lived many millions of years ago.

The first fishes—which are also the first vertebrates—were odd-looking jawless creatures whose bodies were covered with bony plates. They lived in the oceans of the late Cambrian Period, about 540 million years ago. For over 100 million years, fishes retained the basic armored jawless body plan. Then

Figure 31–3 *Early jawless fishes, unlike modern jawless fishes, had bones and were often heavily armored. Most early jawed fishes also had bony armor.*

during the Ordovician and Silurian periods, fishes underwent a major adaptive radiation. Some of the groups that emerged from this adaptive radiation were jawless fishes that had very little armor—the ancestors of modern lampreys and hagfish. Others were armored jawless fishes in a variety of new forms. These fishes were ultimately evolutionary dead ends that became extinct around the end of the Devonian Period, about 350 million years ago. Still others were armored fishes that possessed a feeding adaptation that would revolutionize vertebrate evolution: These fishes had jaws.

Jaws are extremely important evolutionary innovations. Jawless fishes are limited to eating small particles of food that they can filter out of the water or suck up like a vacuum cleaner. Jaws made it possible for vertebrates to nibble on plants, munch on other animals, and defend themselves by biting.

Another evolutionary innovation seen in the early jawed fishes were paired pectoral (anterior) and pelvic (posterior) fins that were attached to girdles of cartilage or bone. These fins gave the fishes more control over their movement in the water. See Figure 31–4. In addition, the pectoral fins and girdle provided the raw material from which evolution shaped the forelimbs and shoulder bones of terrestrial vertebrates. Similarly, the pelvic fins and girdle were the origins of the hindlimbs and hip bones.

Although the early jawed fishes soon disappeared, they left behind two major classes that continued to evolve and still survive today. The first of these classes is the cartilaginous fishes, an old and successful group that includes sharks and rays. The second class is the bony fishes, a large and diverse assemblage that contains more than 97 percent of all living fish species.

Figure 31–4 *The blackbar soldierfish has a typical assortment of fins for a bony fish. In this fish, the dorsal fin is divided into two distinct parts: a spiny anterior region and a relatively soft posterior region. Not all fins are present in all kinds of fishes.*

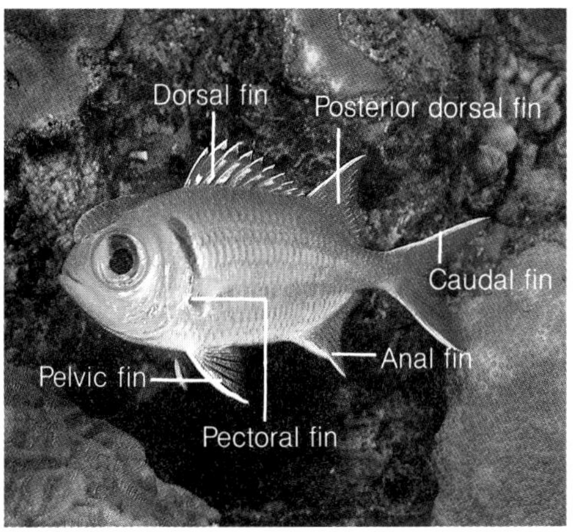

Form and Function in Fishes

Fishes have entered many environments and evolved adaptations that enable them to survive a tremendous variety of conditions. Here we can give only a brief survey of the many ways fishes accomplish the basic functions of life.

FEEDING Every mode of feeding is seen in fishes—herbivore, carnivore, parasite, filter feeder, and detritus feeder. In fact, a single fish may exhibit several modes of feeding, depending on what kind of food happens to be available. Certain carp, for example, eat just about anything—algae, water plants, worms, mollusks, arthropods, dead fish, and detritus. Some fishes—such as great white sharks, tunas, and barracuda—are carnivores. A few fishes are parasites. For example, pencil catfish live and lay their eggs in the gills of larger fishes. And the male in certain species of anglerfish attaches permanently to the much larger female and obtains nutrients from her blood. Still other fishes, such as lamprey larvae and manta rays, are filter feeders. Although their prey are tiny, many filter feeders are not—the filter-feeding whale shark, which grows as long as 18.5 meters, is the largest fish in the world.

The adaptations for feeding in fishes are often remarkable. The sawfish (a relative of sharks) kills and stuns prey by slashing into a school of small fish with a long snout edged with sharp teeth. The parrotfish has teeth fused into a short beak

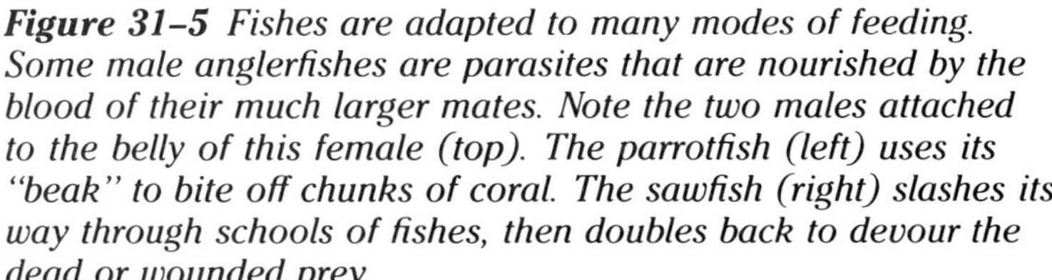

Figure 31–5 *Fishes are adapted to many modes of feeding. Some male anglerfishes are parasites that are nourished by the blood of their much larger mates. Note the two males attached to the belly of this female (top). The parrotfish (left) uses its "beak" to bite off chunks of coral. The sawfish (right) slashes its way through schools of fishes, then doubles back to devour the dead or wounded prey.*

that it uses to bite off chunks of living coral and additional teeth in its throat that grind the chunks of coral into sand. The archerfish shoots down insects by spitting drops of water at them. Anglerfish have wormlike or lighted lures that they use to entice prey. And some deep-sea fishes have enormous jaws that allow them to swallow prey larger than themselves!

Although some fishes have strong blunt teeth adapted for crushing clam and other mollusk shells, most fishes do not really chew their food. Instead, they tear their food into conveniently sized chunks or swallow their prey whole. The digestive system of a typical fish is shown in Figure 31–6.

From the mouth, the food passes through a short tube called the esophagus to the stomach, where it is partially broken down. In many fishes, the food is further processed in fingerlike pouches called pyloric ceca (pigh-LOR-ihk SEE-kah; singular: cecum), which are located at the point where the stomach and the intestine meet. The pyloric ceca secrete digestive enzymes and absorb nutrients from the digested food. The intestine receives partially digested food from the stomach and pyloric ceca and completes the process of digestion and nutrient absorption. In the intestine, the digestive enzymes from several other organs, such as the liver and pancreas, are added to the food. Any materials that remain undigested after passing through the intestine are eliminated through the anus.

The structure of a fish's intestine is adapted in ways that help fishes meet their nutritional needs. For example, herbivores typically have a much longer intestine than carnivores. (Incidentally, this is true of most types of animals.) This gives the animal more time and space to break down plant matter, which is difficult to digest. Lampreys, cartilaginous fishes, and a few bony fishes have a flap of tissue that spirals around the inside of part of the intestine, thus increasing the surface area for nutrient absorption.

Figure 31–6 *The internal organs of a typical bony fish are shown here. What bones do the muscles in a fish pull against?*

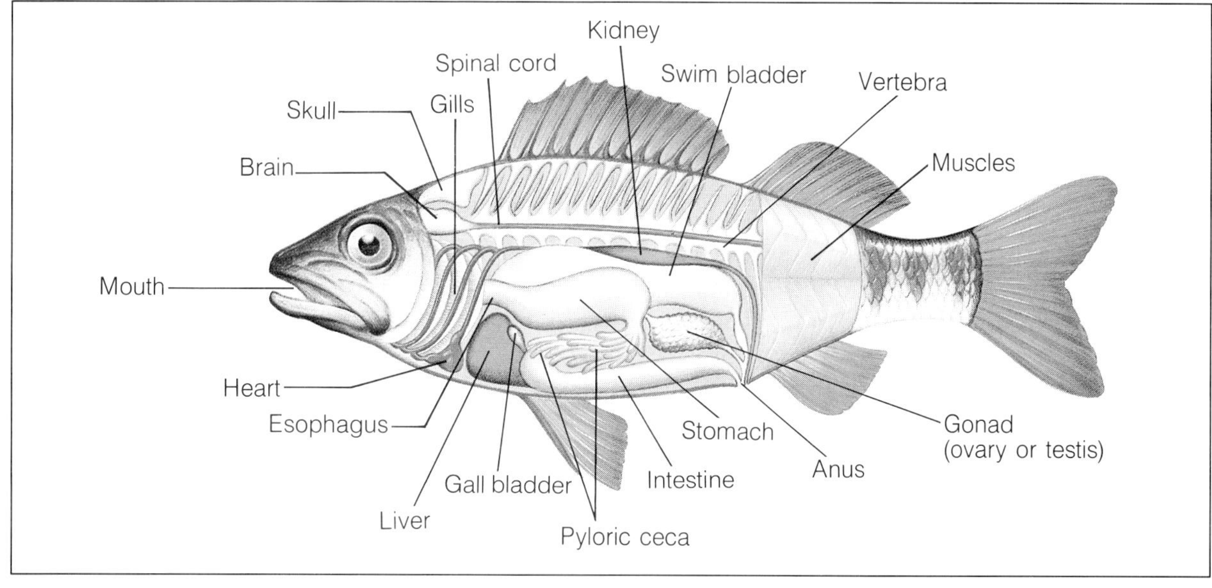

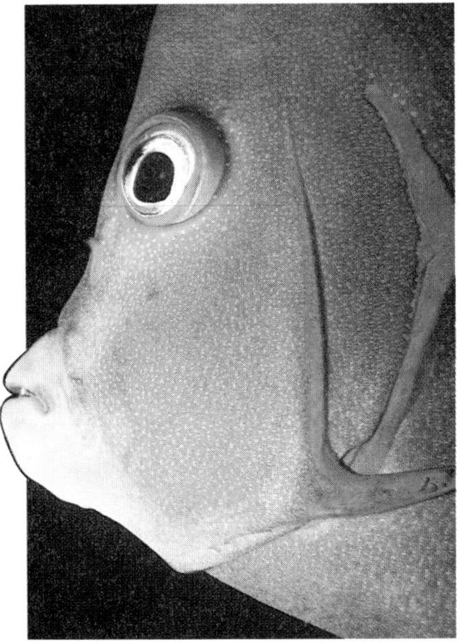

Figure 31–7 In some fishes, such as sharks, the gill chambers open to the outside through a number of slits (top). In other fishes, the gill chambers empty through a single opening that is covered by a protective flap. The curved blue stripe on this angelfish runs along the edge of the protective flap (bottom).

RESPIRATION Most fishes breathe with gills that are located on either side of the pharynx. The feathery gill filaments contain many capillaries and provide a large surface area for exchange of oxygen and carbon dioxide. Most fishes breathe by pumping water through the mouth, over the gill filaments, and out through slits in the sides of the pharynx. Some fishes, such as lampreys and sharks, have several gill slits on either side of the pharynx. Other fishes, such as almost all bony fishes, have a single opening through which water is "exhaled." This opening is usually hidden beneath a protective gill cover.

In many fishes the basic respiratory setup has been modified by evolutionary processes. For example, skates and rays are able to breathe while lying on the ocean floor even though their mouth is located on the underside of their body. Instead of taking in water (and gill-clogging mud and sand) through their mouth, they "inhale" water through special openings on the upper surface of their body.

A number of fishes—such as lungfish, gars, Siamese fighting fish, and kissing gouramis—have a special adaptation that allows them to survive in oxygen-poor water or in areas where bodies of water often dry up. They have specialized organs that serve as lungs by obtaining oxygen from the air. In most air-breathing fishes, this organ is actually a modified swim bladder. A swim bladder, which is found in most bony fish, is a gas-filled sac that lies at the top of the body cavity just beneath the backbone. The majority of fishes use the swim bladder to regulate their buoyancy: Dissolved gases in the blood diffuse into and out of the swim bladder and permit the fish to swim at lesser or greater depths, respectively. Unlike typical fishes, fishes that use the swim bladder as a lung have a tube that connects the swim bladder to the mouth. Some air-breathing fishes are so dependent on getting part of their oxygen from the air that they will suffocate if prevented from reaching the surface of the water.

INTERNAL TRANSPORT Fishes typically have closed circulatory systems with a heart that pumps blood around the body. The heart consists of two muscular pumping chambers: an **atrium** (AY-tree-uhm; plural: atria) and a **ventricle** (VEHN-trihk-uhl). Blood from the body collects in the atrium, which pumps blood into the ventricle. The ventricle pumps blood out of the heart into a muscular vessel called the **aorta** (ay-OR-tah). Blood goes directly from the aorta into the fine capillary networks in the gills, where gas exchange occurs. From the gills, blood travels throughout the rest of the body tissues and internal organs. As blood leaves muscles and organs, it collects in veins that gather in a thin-walled sac called the sinus venosus (SIGH-nuhs veh-NOH-suhs). From this sinus, blood enters the atrium once again. See Figure 31–8.

EXCRETION Like many other aquatic animals, most fishes get rid of nitrogenous wastes in the form of ammonia.

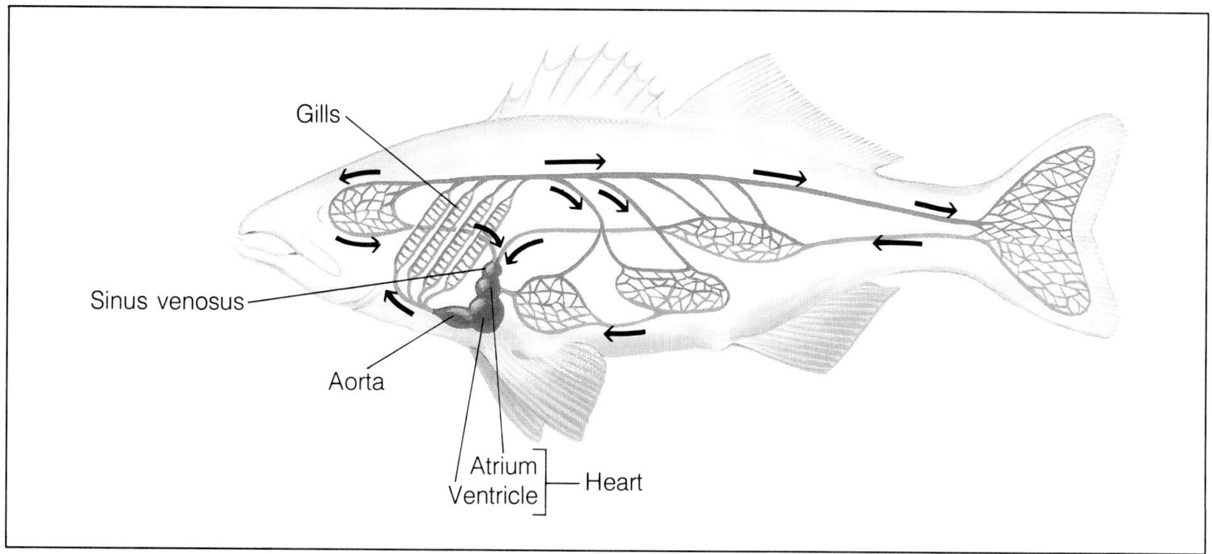

Figure 31–8 *Almost all fishes have a closed circulatory system in which a two-chambered heart pumps oxygen-poor blood from the body to the gills. Oxygen-rich blood then travels from the gills to all parts of the body.*

Some wastes diffuse through the gills into the surrounding water. Others are removed by the kidneys, which are excretory organs composed of many tubules that filter nitrogenous wastes from the blood and concentrate them.

Kidneys help fishes control the amount of water in their body. Because fishes in salt water tend to lose water by osmosis, the kidneys of marine fishes concentrate nitrogenous wastes and return as much water as possible to the body. The kidneys of freshwater fishes, on the other hand, pump out lots of dilute urine because in fresh water, a great deal of water continually enters by osmosis. One of the factors that determines which fishes are able to move from fresh to salt water (as salmon do) is their ability to control kidney function.

RESPONSE Fishes have a fairly well-developed nervous system organized around a brain. Fish brains, like those of other vertebrates, have several clearly visible parts. Refer to Figure 31–9 as you read about the parts of a fish's brain.

The most anterior parts of a fish's brain are the **olfactory bulbs**, which are connected by stalks to the two lobes of the **cerebrum** (suh-REE-bruhm). In fishes, the cerebrum is primarily involved with the sense of smell, although it also seems to be involved in such behaviors as taking care of young and exploring the environment. The **optic lobes** process information from the eyes. The **cerebellum** (ser-uh-BEHL-uhm) coordinates body movements. The **medulla** (mih-DUL-ah) controls many internal organ functions and maintains balance.

Posterior to the brain is the spinal cord, which is in fact the hollow dorsal nerve cord that characterizes chordates. In cartilaginous and bony fishes, the spinal cord is enclosed and protected by the vertebral column. Between each set of vertebrae, a pair of spinal nerves exits the cord and connects with internal organs and muscles.

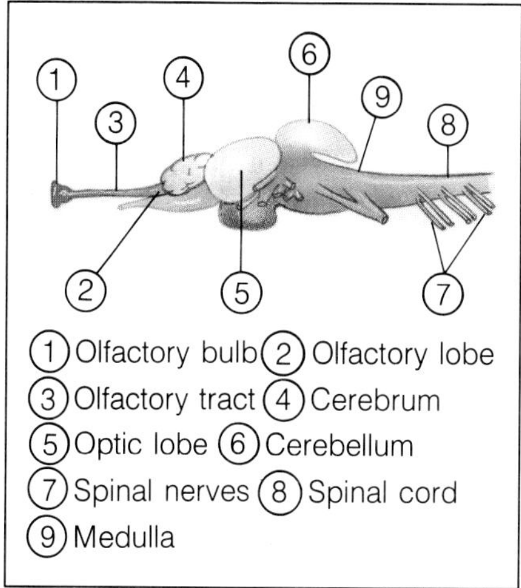

Figure 31–9 *The brain of a typical fish has several clearly visible parts. How might the sizes of the various parts of the brain differ in a blind cave fish that relies primarily on its sense of smell?*

Figure 31–10 *The sense organs in fishes are highly developed. A chimaera's huge silvery eyes enable it to see in the permanent dark of its deep-water home (left). The lateral line, which appears as a series of tiny dots in the pink stripe of the rainbow trout, detects water movements (right). Some fishes, such as the elephantfish (bottom), are able to detect electricity.*

Most fishes have superbly designed sense organs that collect information about their environment. Almost all fishes active in daylight have well-developed eyes and color vision at least as good as our own. Fishes active only at night or in cloudy water have large eyes with big pupils that gather as much light as possible. These species do not see color well, but they see in the dark as well as cats do.

Many fishes possess extraordinary senses of taste and smell. Special cells called chemoreceptors (*chemo-* means chemical) are located all over the head and much of the rest of the body surface as well as in the nose and mouth. Many species, such as catfish, also carry chemoreceptors on their "whiskers." Salmon can distinguish between the odor of their own home stream and that of another stream while they are still far out at sea. And sharks can detect the presence of a drop of blood in 115 liters of sea water!

Most fishes have ears inside their head, but they cannot hear sounds well. They can, however, easily detect gentle currents and vibrations in the water. All around their head and down the sides of their body are a series of pores connected to canals beneath the skin that form a sensitive motion detector called the lateral line system. Fishes use their lateral lines to detect other fishes or prey swimming nearby.

In addition to having the senses that we are familiar with, some fishes—electric eels, catfish, and sharks, for example—are able to detect electricity. These electrical detectors are extremely sensitive: A shark can detect one millionth of a volt, which is less than the charge produced by the nerves in an animal's body. Electric eels and electric catfish produce a strong electrical field around their bodies that responds to the presence of nearby objects. Thus electric fishes can locate prey and avoid obstacles in murky water. In addition, electric fishes can produce jolts of electricity (up to 650 volts!) that stun or kill prey and strongly discourage predators.

REPRODUCTION In most species of fishes, there are separate males and females. A number of fishes, however, are born as males but change to females as they grow older. Others start as females and later change into males. Unlike many invertebrates, few fishes function as both a male and a female at the same time.

Many fishes are **oviparous** (oh-VIHP-ah-ruhs), which means they lay eggs. Most oviparous fishes have external fertilization. However, a few oviparous fishes—certain species of sharks and rays, for example—have internal fertilization and thus lay fertilized eggs.

Some oviparous fishes, such as cod, do not take care of their young. Such fish typically release hundreds or even millions of eggs, which increases the chances that a few offspring will survive to adulthood. Other oviparous fishes care for their offspring. For example, Siamese fighting fish build nests of bubbles, and sticklebacks build nests of twigs. Some cichlids and catfish hold their eggs and young in their mouths. And male seahorses hold fertilized eggs in a pouch until the eggs are ready to hatch. These species lay fewer eggs because the parental care means more of the young are likely to survive.

Figure 31–11 *Some newly hatched fishes, such as salmon, are nourished by a yolk sac on their belly.*

In some species of fishes that have internal fertilization, such as guppies, the eggs develop inside the female. The developing embryos, like those of oviparous fishes, are nourished by food stored in an attached yolk sac. Thus the young do not receive food directly from the mother's body. The young are typically "born" after they have absorbed the yolk sac and are ready to swim on their own. Species with this pattern of reproduction are **ovoviviparous** (oh-voh-vigh-VIP-ah-ruhs). In other species, including several sharks, the young are actually nourished by the mother's body as they develop. These fishes are said to be **viviparous**, or truly live-bearing.

Many fishes, including several species you can keep in a home aquarium, exhibit fascinating mating behaviors. Guppy males dance up and down in front of females, trying to get the females interested in them. Cichlids often display beautiful colors to one another and build elaborate nests to attract a mate. A male stickleback will build a nest, drive all other males away, and perform an elaborate dance that shows passing females where his nest is.

Figure 31–12 *Modern jawless fishes are divided into two classes: lampreys (top) and hagfishes (bottom).*

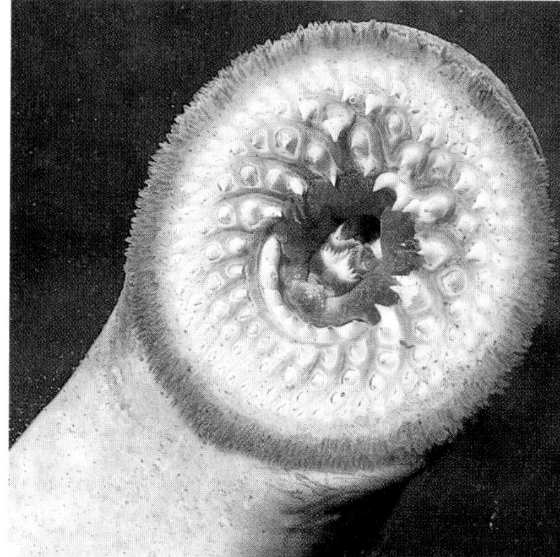

Jawless Fishes

The jawless fishes alive today are divided into two classes: lampreys and hagfishes. Although modern jawless fishes are thought to have evolved from heavily armored, bony ancestors, both lampreys and hagfishes have no bones at all. In fact, they are the only vertebrates that do not have backbones as adults! Instead, their long, snakelike bodies are supported by a notochord.

LAMPREYS Lampreys are typically filter feeders as larvae and parasites as adults. An adult lamprey's head is taken up almost completely by a circular sucking disk with a round jawless mouth in the center. Adult lampreys live by attaching themselves to fishes (and occasionally whales and porpoises) and scraping away at the skin with their large teeth and a strong, rasping tongue. Lampreys then suck up the tissues and body fluids of their host. Lampreys rarely kill their host, but they leave it in a weakened condition with a large open wound that is easily infected.

HAGFISHES Hagfishes are probably the most primitive vertebrates alive today. They have pinkish-gray wormlike bodies and four or six short tentacles around the mouth. Hagfishes lack eyes, although they do have light-detecting regions scattered around their body. They feed on dead and dying fish by using a toothed tongue to scrape a hole into the fish's side. Hagfishes have some peculiar traits: They secrete incredible amounts of slime, have six hearts, possess an open circulatory system, and regularly tie themselves into half-knots!

Sharks and Their Relatives

The class Chondrichthyes (cahn-DRIHK-theez)—which contains sharks, rays, skates, and a few uncommon fishes such as sawfish and chimaeras—is an ancient and successful group. The name of this class (*chondros* means cartilage; *ichthys* means fish) refers to the fact that all members have an endoskeleton built entirely out of cartilage. Most of them also have toothlike scales covering the skin. These scales make sharkskin so rough that it is possible to use it as sandpaper.

Most of the 225 living shark species have large curved tails, torpedo-shaped bodies, and rounded snouts with a mouth underneath. One of the most noticeable characteristics of sharks is their enormous number of teeth. A typical shark has about 3000 teeth arranged in 6 to 20 rows. As teeth in the front rows are worn out or lost, new teeth are continually replacing them. A shark goes through about 20,000 teeth in its lifetime!

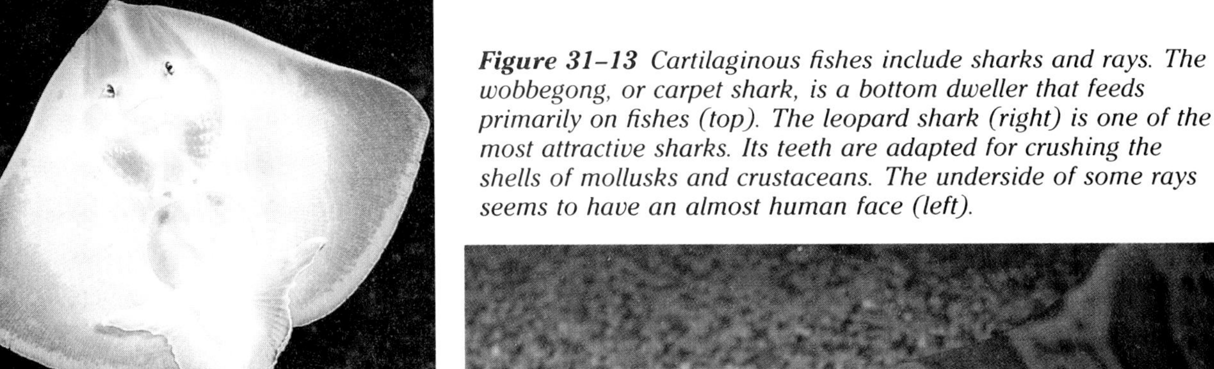

Figure 31–13 *Cartilaginous fishes include sharks and rays. The wobbegong, or carpet shark, is a bottom dweller that feeds primarily on fishes (top). The leopard shark (right) is one of the most attractive sharks. Its teeth are adapted for crushing the shells of mollusks and crustaceans. The underside of some rays seems to have an almost human face (left).*

You have probably heard a lot about shark feeding habits. But contrary to what you may have heard, not all sharks are man-eaters. Some sharks are filter feeders; others have flat teeth adapted for crushing the shells of mollusks and crustaceans. And although there are a number of carnivorous sharks large enough to prey on humans, each year more people are killed by lightning than by sharks.

Unlike sharks, which are adapted for swimming rapidly through the water, rays and skates are adapted for living on the ocean floor. Rays and skates are flattened from top to bottom (you can think of them as squashed sharks), and they swim by flapping their large winglike pectoral fins. Most rays and skates reach a maximum length of about 1 meter, but some, such as manta rays, are up to 7 meters in length.

Bony Fishes

Bony fishes make up the class Osteichthyes (ahs-tee-IHK-theez) (*oste-* means bone). There are more species in this class than in any of the other vertebrate classes. About 40 percent of all vertebrates are bony fishes. Experts estimate that there are somewhere between 15,000 and 40,000 species alive today.

Almost all bony fishes belong to the enormous group called the ray-finned fishes. This group includes everything from guppies to groupers, salmon, and eels. The name ray-finned refers to the thin bony spines, or rays, that are connected by a thin layer of skin to form the fins. These fins are adapted to a wide variety of functions. Stonefishes, scorpionfishes, and lionfishes have fin rays that are modified into poison spines. Flying fishes, on leaping from the water, can glide with winglike pectoral fins. Mudskippers, which spend a lot of time out of the

Figure 31–14 *Bony fishes come in a wide variety of forms and colors. The porcupine fish can inflate itself into a prickly ball when threatened (top). The moray eel has a narrow snakelike body (center). The bright colors of angelfish may be a means of communication within its species (right). The hawkfish's narrow snout enables it to pluck bits of food from crevices (left).*

Figure 31–15 *A few fishes manage quite nicely out of water for brief periods of time. African lungfishes (top) get most of their oxygen from the air, which they gulp into a simple sac that serves as a lung. Mudskippers (bottom) climb out of the water onto logs and rocks. As you can see, the mudskipper's bulging eyes are quite mobile, enabling it to appear as if it has eyes on the back of its head.*

water, have fins that have evolved into a suction cup that the fish uses in climbing. Triggerfishes have dorsal fins that are usually folded but can be locked in an upright position to help wedge the fish into a hiding place.

Only seven living species of bony fishes are not classified as ray-finned fishes. These are the lungfishes and the coelacanth. These fishes are of interest because they give us an idea of what the lungs and limbs may have been like in the ancestors of terrestrial vertebrates.

The six species of lungfishes alive today are found in Australia, Africa, and South America. The African and South American species live in areas that are flooded during the rainy season but are practically baked during the dry season. When water is available, lungfish use their gills to eliminate carbon dioxide, but they get most of their oxygen by gulping air into a simple sac that functions as a lung. During the dry season, lungfish burrow in the mud and enter a dormant state.

The single species of coelacanth (SEE-lah-kanth) alive today, *Latimeria*, is the only surviving member of the lobe-finned fishes, which were quite common in Devonian times. Unlike ray-finned fishes, which have many bones in the bases of their fins, coelacanths have few bones in their fin bases. Several of these bones are clearly homologous to the limb bones of terrestrial vertebrates. Attached to those bones are a few large rays that form the fins. Ancient lobe-finned fishes seemed to have lived in swampy areas where shallow pools alternated with mud flats and sand bars. Like some of the "walking catfishes" alive today, those lobe-finned species probably used their pelvic and pectoral appendages to move from pool to pool. Unlike its predecessors, the modern coelacanth lives in water about 70 to 400 meters deep in a relatively small area of ocean off the western coast of Africa. However, scientists have observed captive coelacanths "walking" on the bottom of their tank, moving their stubby fins in the same way terrestrial vertebrates move their legs.

Coelacanths were thought to have disappeared with the dinosaurs about 70 million years ago. In 1938, however, fishermen sailing in the ocean off the coast of South Africa caught a strange blue fish that was 1.5 meters long and had stubby fins and a triple tail. The coelacanth was not extinct after all! Scientists were enormously excited to find living coelacanths because these animals represent a fascinating piece of evolutionary history: Coelacanths are the closest thing we know of to the ancestors of all land vertebrates.

SCIENCE, TECHNOLOGY, AND SOCIETY APPLICATION

Catfish Slime

Catfish! The word alone can cause mouths to water and visions of fish fries to dance through people's heads. But recently, scientists working in the Arabian Gulf near Saudi Arabia discovered a new and unusual use for catfish.

Dr. Richard S. Criddle, professor of biology at the University of California, noticed that catfish secrete a gellike slime that covers their entire body. Dr. Criddle also observed that Arab fishermen rubbed this slime on any cuts and scratches they had on their body. When Dr. Criddle himself used the slime on a minor wound, the wound healed quickly. Although this use of folk medicine had been practiced in the area for many years, it had never before been documented by a scientist.

Dr. Criddle ordered a detailed chemical analysis of the catfish slime. The results indicated that the slime contains about 60 different proteins, each of which helps heal wounds in humans and other animals. Some of the proteins block the growth of bacteria that might infect the wound. Others promote the production of substances that speed the growth of new tissue near the wound. Still other substances in the slime aid in the clotting process, which keeps the wound from bleeding profusely.

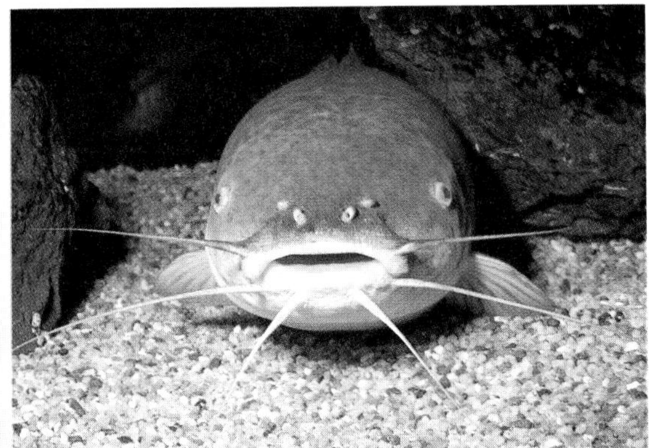

Catfish have a place in medical research—as well as on a dinner plate!

It must seem strange to you that such chemicals appear in catfish slime. Actually, the slime is a useful adaptation. A wounded, bleeding fish attracts predators. So a substance that helps the catfish heal quickly aids in its survival.

Several pharmaceutical companies have already become interested in the potential uses of the chemicals in catfish slime. They realize that substances that promote healing would benefit many people, especially those who do not heal well, such as burn victims. So it now seems likely that catfish will provide more than just a tasty tidbit.

How Fishes Fit into the World

With representatives in almost every body of water on our planet, fishes are vital parts of many biological systems. For many birds and mammals—including seagulls, raccoons, dolphins, and humans—fishes are important foods. As predators and herbivores, fishes help control the populations of the organisms they eat. Humans have learned to take advantage of this aspect of fish biology. Mosquito fish have been introduced into ponds and lakes in places far from their native home in North America because they consume large amounts of insect larvae. And grass carp and cichlids are used to keep waterways

Figure 31–16 For centuries, people have kept fishes for food and for pets. Selective breeding has resulted in strange-looking varieties of goldfish, such as bubble-eyes and lionheads.

clear of plant growth. Since prehistoric times, humans have caught fishes for food (and for recreation). For at least 4000 years, humans have also raised fishes in artificial ponds. Today we are still trying to find the best ways to cultivate food fishes in underwater farms. And we still keep captive fishes to admire their bright colors and exotic forms.

31–1 SECTION REVIEW

1. What are the distinguishing characteristics of vertebrates?
2. Discuss ways in which fishes are adapted for three different modes of feeding.
3. Name and describe three different reproductive strategies in fishes.
4. Describe the three basic groups of fishes. Give an example of a member of each group.
5. Why are lobe-finned fishes and lungfishes important to evolutionary biologists?

Section Objectives

- Describe how a typical amphibian carries out its essential life functions.
- Compare the two major living orders of amphibians.

31–2 Amphibians

With about 4000 living species, **amphibians** are the smallest major group of vertebrates. Despite their small numbers, amphibians are a varied group. They range in size from tiny tropical tree frogs 1 centimeter long to enormous salamanders 170 centimeters long. Some amphibians, such as salamanders and newts, have long tails and scuttle about on four legs. Others, such as frogs and toads, have no tails and leap from one place to another with large hind legs. Still others have no legs at all and burrow in soil like giant worms.

Amphibians are to the animal kingdom what mosses and ferns are to the plant kingdom. They are descendants of ancestral organisms that evolved some—but not all—of the adaptations necessary for life on land. Although many of these animals spend a great deal of time on land, nearly all of them are restricted to moist areas, and most of them must return to water to breed.

What Is an Amphibian?

The name amphibian refers to the double life that most amphibians lead (*amphi-* means both; *bio-* means life). Amphibian larvae are fishlike aquatic animals that breathe through gills, whereas adult amphibians are terrestrial carnivores that breathe through lungs and skin. Of course, there are exceptions: Some amphibians are completely terrestrial; others are

Figure 31–17 *Representatives of the three orders of living amphibians—salamanders, frogs and toads, and legless amphibians—are shown in these photographs. The tree salamander, which lives in the rain forests of Central America, can cling to branches with its prehensile tail (left). The leaf frog, an inhabitant of the Amazon rain forest, is as good at climbing trees as it is at hopping (right, top). Legless amphibians (right, bottom), which are found in the tropics, prey on insects and other small animals they encounter as they tunnel through fallen leaves and under ground.*

Figure 31–18 *Most amphibians spend the first part of their life in water as gilled larvae (top). As adults, they usually live on land (bottom).*

completely aquatic. But the majority of amphibians live in water for the first part of their life and on land as adults.

The aquatic larva is one reason that most amphibians must live in moist areas. However, it is not the only reason. Another reason amphibians are strongly tied to water is that their eggs do not have a shell. Thus they tend to dry out unless they are laid in water or in very moist places. Yet another reason is that amphibian skin does not bear scales, fur, or any other protective covering that would help prevent drying out. (However, the skin does contain mucous glands whose secretions help keep the skin moist.) In addition, the skin of almost all adult amphibians is used in respiration and thus must remain moist. If the skin dries out, most amphibians will suffocate.

Amphibians can be defined as vertebrates that are aquatic as larvae and terrestrial as adults, breathe with lungs as adults, have a moist skin that contains many glands, and lack scales and claws. This functional definition is not perfect. As you will soon discover, there are exceptions to almost every "rule" about amphibians.

Evolution of Amphibians

Amphibians first appeared around the end of the Devonian Period, about 360 million years ago. They probably evolved from lobe-finned fishes, similar to the modern coelacanth, that had bones in their fin bases and lungs.

Making the transition from water to land is no easy task. Gills are useless. Lungs that expand easily when the body is supported by water tend to collapse under the weight of other organs. Appendages that work fine under water are too weak to hold much weight on land. The result is inefficient movement and a tendency to scrape and damage the skin of the belly when traveling over rough surfaces. Because vibrations in air are weaker than those in water, it becomes difficult to detect sound and movement. And loss of water from the body is a constant danger.

Because natural selection favored individuals that were better able to live on land, early amphibians evolved in ways that surmounted these problems. For example, the bones of the limbs and limb girdles became stronger, permitting the first amphibians to move around on land more efficiently than lobe-finned fishes. The ribs formed a bony cage to support and protect the internal organs. Many early amphibians had scales that protected the skin on their undersides. Ears, which use a membrane to translate sound waves in the air into pressure waves in body fluid, were added to the lateral-line systems. And it is probable that mucous glands, eyelids, and other structures that protect sense organs and other parts of the body from drying out also developed in early amphibians.

Soon after they first appeared, amphibians underwent an adaptive radiation. Some of these ancient amphibians were huge—the largest is thought to have been about 4 meters long. Amphibians became so numerous that the Carboniferous Period (345 to 285 million years ago) is sometimes called the Age of Amphibians. Why were amphibians so successful?

When amphibians started crawling onto land, they entered an environment nearly empty of animal life. Land plants

Figure 31–19 *On a spring day during the early Permian Period (about 270 million years ago), ancient amphibians may have swum in streams and basked in the sun much as modern amphibians do today.*

appeared early in the Silurian Period. By the time amphibians appeared during the Devonian, there were well-established forests of mosses and ferns. Arthropods too had gone ashore, and many species of insects had already evolved. This meant that any vertebrates whose legs and lungs allowed them to spend time on land had lots of food and no competitors. The first land dwellers had at their disposal an environment full of empty niches!

The heyday of the amphibians was short-lived, however. Climate changes ultimately caused many of the low, swampy amphibian habitats to disappear. Most of the amphibian groups became extinct by the end of the Permian Period (about 245 million years ago), leaving behind four groups of land vertebrates—reptiles, which evolved from amphibians early in the Carboniferous Period, and three orders of small amphibians.

Form and Function in Amphibians

Living amphibians have evolved many adaptations that help them overcome the problems of living both in water and on land. As we examine the essential life functions in amphibians, we will focus our attention on the structures found in frogs. Keep in mind that although the majority of amphibians perform their life functions in ways that are similar to that of a typical frog, there are a number of species that function in unusual ways.

FEEDING Tadpoles, the larvae of frogs and toads, are typically filter feeders, which devour tiny floating plants and bits of organic matter, or herbivores, which use teeth on their lower jaw to graze on attached algae. Some tadpoles eat so much so quickly that up to half of their body mass is in their guts! Tadpoles are mostly herbivorous, so their long, coiled intestines are extremely important in helping them break down their hard-to-digest plant food. Tadpoles, of course, have to grow quickly, for those that lag behind may starve or die if their puddle dries out.

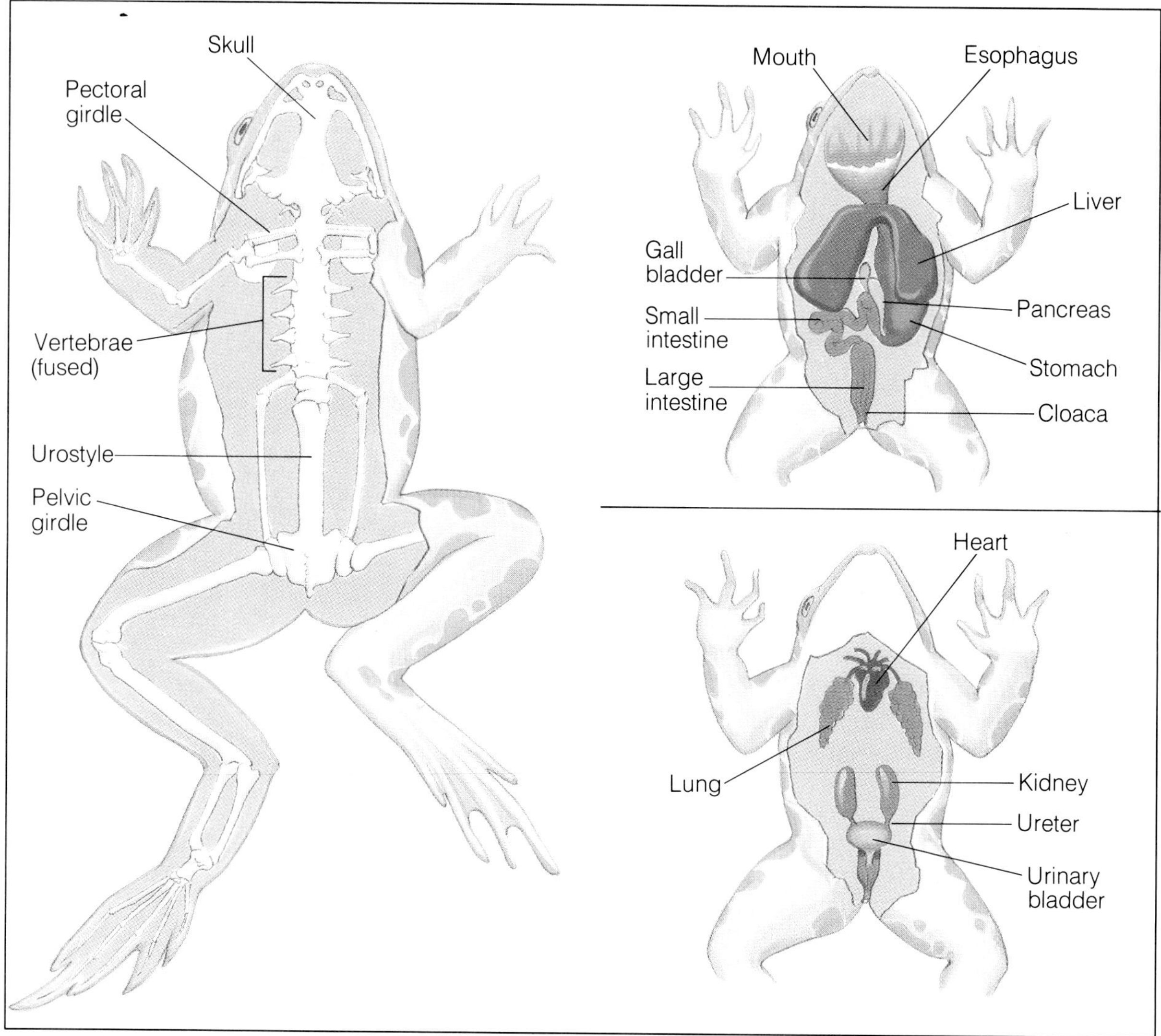

Figure 31–20 *The skeleton and major internal organs of a frog are shown in this illustration. In some cases, organs have been removed or cut away so that as many internal structures as possible can be shown. For example, part of the liver and one of the lungs have been removed.*

Adult amphibians are almost entirely carnivorous. Salamanders and legless amphibians can only snap their jaws open and shut to catch prey, but many frogs have a long sticky tongue specialized to capture insects. Figure 31–20 shows the digestive system of a frog.

From the mouth, food slides down the esophagus into the stomach. The stomach connects with the small intestine, where digestive enzymes are manufactured and dissolved food is absorbed. Tubes connect the intestine with organs that also produce digestive enzymes, such as the liver, pancreas, and gall bladder. The small intestine leads to the large intestine, or colon. At the end of the large intestine is a muscular cavity called the cloaca (kloh-AY-kah), which stores wastes until they are expelled.

RESPIRATION Adult amphibians typically breathe using lungs, mouth cavities, and skin. In many amphibians, such as frogs and toads, the lungs are reasonably well developed: Their internal surfaces are richly supplied with capillaries, as well as with folds that increase their surface area. In other amphibians, the lungs are not as well developed. In fact, many terrestrial salamanders have no lungs at all!

The lining of the mouth cavity and the body skin of many adult amphibians are thin and richly supplied with blood vessels. Thus they can serve as a gas-exchange organ whenever these animals are under water or in extremely moist places. The skin is an important respiratory organ in amphibians—most carbon dioxide is removed through it. And in salamanders and frogs, a large percentage of oxygen is taken in through it. Tadpoles, salamander larvae, and a few types of adult salamanders breathe primarily through their gills. However, they can get rid of excess carbon dioxide through their skin.

Because they do not have the necessary chest and stomach muscles, frogs cannot inhale and exhale as we do. Instead, they fill their mouth cavity with air, close their mouth, and force air back through an opening called the glottis into the lungs. The glottis then closes to keep the air in the lungs for a short time.

Frogs can also direct some of the air they take in to a pair of expandable vocal sacs in the rear of their mouth. Frogs croak by forcing air from these sacs over vocal cords in their throat. By directing air back and forth through the throat between the vocal sacs and the lungs, frogs can even croak under water!

Figure 31–21 *As air moves between the vocal sac and mouth in male toads it causes the vocal cords to vibrate. Although the resulting sounds may not be music to human ears, a female toad finds them quite attractive.*

INTERNAL TRANSPORT The circulatory system in adult amphibians is closely linked to the development of lungs. In adult amphibians and other air-breathing vertebrates, the circulatory system forms what is known as a double loop. The first loop carries oxygen-poor blood from the heart to the lungs and takes oxygen-rich blood from the lungs back to the heart. The second loop transports oxygen-rich blood from the heart to the rest of the body and oxygen-poor blood from the body back to the heart.

The amphibian heart has three separate chambers: left atrium, right atrium, and ventricle. Blood returning from most of the body collects in a large vein called the vena cava. The vena cava and other veins draining the head and skin empty into the sinus venosus. The sinus venosus, in turn, empties into the right atrium. Blood returning from the lungs in the pulmonary vein enters into the left atrium.

When the atria contract, they empty their blood into a single ventricle. The ventricle then pumps blood into a single large vessel called the bulbus cordus. The bulbus cordus quickly divides into a series of aortic arches that lead to the major body arteries.

Tadpoles have two-chambered hearts and single-loop circulatory systems, much like bony fishes. In a single-loop system, blood travels from the heart to the gills to the rest of the body and back to the heart. When tadpoles mature into adults, the circulatory system changes into a double-loop system.

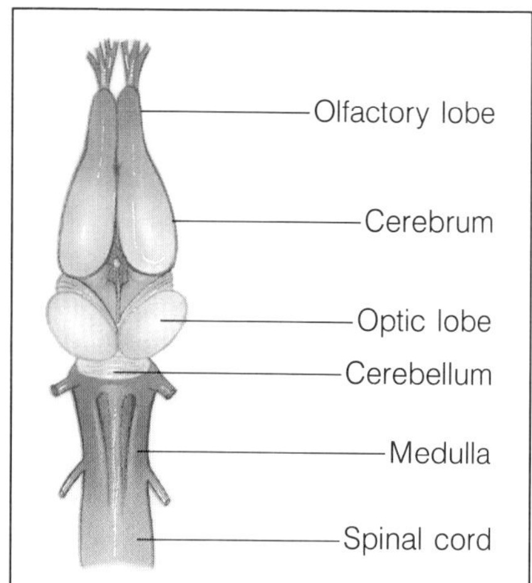

Figure 31–22 *The brain of a frog has the same basic parts as that of other vertebrates, such as fish.*

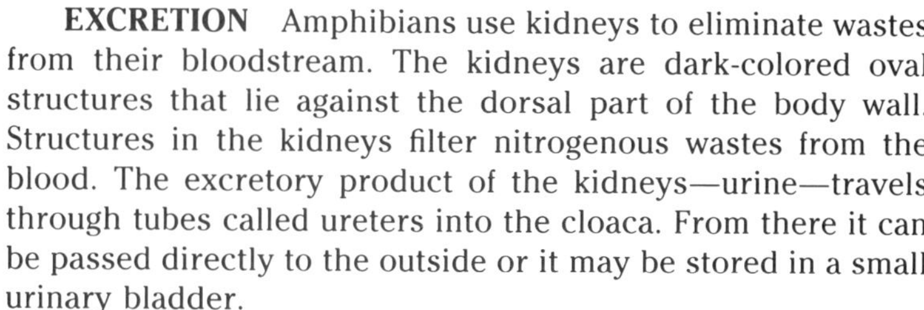

EXCRETION Amphibians use kidneys to eliminate wastes from their bloodstream. The kidneys are dark-colored oval structures that lie against the dorsal part of the body wall. Structures in the kidneys filter nitrogenous wastes from the blood. The excretory product of the kidneys—urine—travels through tubes called ureters into the cloaca. From there it can be passed directly to the outside or it may be stored in a small urinary bladder.

RESPONSE Amphibians have well-developed nervous and sensory systems. Their eyes are large and often bulge outward from the sides of the head. Amphibians can move their eyes around in their sockets quite well. The surface of the eye is protected from damage under water and kept moist on land by a transparent nictitating (NIHK-tih-tayt-ihng) membrane. This membrane is located inside the regular eyelid, which can also be closed over the eye. Frogs have keen vision for spotting moving insects, but they probably do not see color as well as fishes do.

Although amphibian ears have no external sound collectors, they are often very sensitive. Many frogs and toads use croaks, peeps, and a variety of other calls to find a mate, so hearing is vital to their survival and reproduction. Many amphibian larvae and adults also have a lateral line system like that of fishes that detects water movements.

Amphibians respond to adverse conditions in their environment in a number of ways. Because amphibians do not have an internal mechanism for regulating their body temperature, they deal with seasons that are too hot or too cold by hiding

Figure 31–23 *Frogs escape predators in many ways. The Amazon horned frog is almost invisible as it hides among dead leaves (top). Bullfrogs have long muscular hind legs that enable them to quickly leap away from enemies (right). Tree frogs live among the concealing leaves of plants (left). The miniature suction cups on the ends of their toes make them excellent climbers.*

in a sheltered spot, such as an underground burrow, and entering a dormant state.

Predators might seem to be a major problem for clawless, soft-skinned amphibians. However, amphibians have many ways of protecting themselves. Some amphibians hide; others run away quickly; still others are well-camouflaged. Many produce distasteful or toxic chemicals that are secreted in their mucous coatings. The more toxic amphibians usually have warning coloration—bright patterns that tell potential predators that the brilliantly colored animal is poisonous or otherwise dangerous. In addition, some poisonous amphibians respond to a threat by waving their tail or freezing in a pose that shows off their warning colors.

REPRODUCTION When frogs reproduce, the male climbs onto the female's back and squeezes. In response to this stimulus, the female releases as many as 200 eggs, which the male then fertilizes. The embryos are surrounded with a sticky, transparent jelly that attaches the egg mass to underwater plants and nourishes the developing embryos. The eggs typically hatch into tadpoles after one to three weeks.

Not all amphibians have external fertilization and are oviparous like frogs. Many have internal fertilization and are either oviparous, ovoviviparous, or viviparous. Some salamanders have an unusual form of internal fertilization in which the male never needs to come into direct contact with the female! Instead, the male deposits a packet of sperm on the ground and through an elaborate courtship dance persuades the female to pick up the sperm packet with her cloaca.

Figure 31–24 *Frogs typically go through an aquatic and a terrestrial phase during their life cycle. Frog eggs are fertilized externally (left) and generally develop in water (right). In most species the fertilized eggs hatch into aquatic larvae, or tadpoles (center). The tadpoles gradually grow limbs and lose their tails as they develop into terrestrial adults (top).*

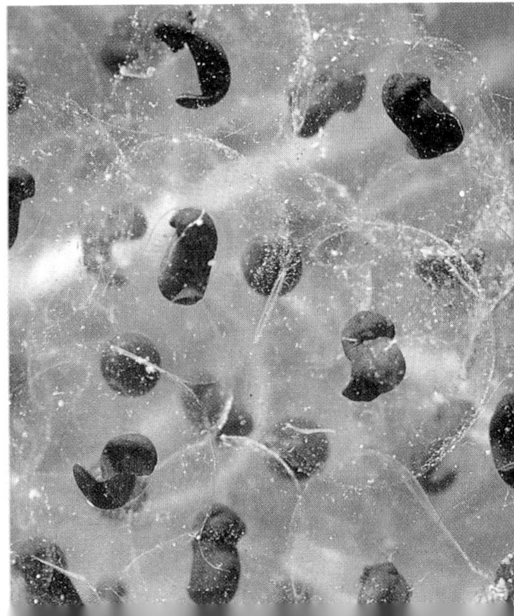

__Figure 31–25__ Salamanders are usually terrestrial as adults (left). However, certain species of salamanders, known as newts, are terrestrial only during an immature phase known as a red eft (right).

Parental care in amphibians varies even more than their methods of fertilizing eggs. As in other animals, parental care is a way of ensuring that more young will survive. In many amphibians, it may also be an adaptation to a lack of suitable bodies of water in which aquatic larvae can develop. Some frogs incubate their young in their mouth, vocal sac, or stomach. Male midwife toads wrap sticky strings of fertilized eggs around their hind legs and carry them about until the eggs are ready to hatch. The Surinam toad and marsupial frog have special structures on their back in which the young develop. And in certain tree frogs, tadpoles cling to their parent's back with a suckerlike mouth and are carried between pools of rainwater that collect among the leaves of certain plants.

Salamanders

These amphibians keep their tails even as adults. Both adults and larvae are carnivores. Although many fossil salamanders were more than 3 meters long, most modern salamanders are about 15 centimeters long. Most hatch as fully aquatic larvae with gills. As adults they live in moist woods, where they tunnel under rocks and rotting logs.

Some salamanders, such as the mud puppy and the axolotl (AK-soh-laht'l), never lose their gills and live in water all their life. Some newts, like the crimson-spotted newt, switch back and forth between water and land. Starting as aquatic larvae, they emerge and live entirely on land in a form called the red eft. After a year or two, the red eft changes its colors to green with red spots and returns to the water to breed.

Frogs and Toads

Most of us are familiar with the frogs and toads that live all over the United States. Their mating calls fill the night air in many parts of the country. Of these animals, frogs are more closely tied to water. Even adult frogs spend much of their time in or near ponds and streams. Adult toads, on the other hand, often live in moist woods. Some toads have even managed to invade relatively dry places by using the water permeability of their skin to good advantage. These animals burrow deep into moist soil and press their skin against the walls of their burrows. Their skin then functions just like the root hairs of plants. Because of osmotic pressure, water moves out of the soil into the toad.

Many toads and frogs produce potent toxins. For example, from glands behind its head, the marine toad can squirt toxins up to 1 meter, blinding or otherwise injuring predators. Some tropical tree frogs make a poison so powerful that it can kill humans and other large animals. Native tribes in the tropics often poison their arrow tips by rubbing them on these frogs. For this reason, these brightly colored amphibians are called poison arrow frogs. See Figure 31–26. One species of poison arrow frog produces a toxin so powerful that 0.00001 gram can kill an adult human.

Figure 31–26 *Toads are better adapted to life on land than frogs, primarily because their warty skin helps conserve water (top). Although water is plentiful in the tropical forests where poison arrow frogs live, puddles formed by rain last only briefly. Thus, the frogs occasionally give their tadpoles a piggyback ride to a new puddle (bottom).*

How Amphibians Fit into the World

Adult amphibians throughout the world today prey on animals that have been most abundant for millions of years: insects. As tadpoles, amphibians also devour large quantities of algae, powerfully affecting the energy balance of many bodies of water.

Humans do not often interact with amphibians, although frog legs are considered a delicacy by some. In tropical rain forests, native hunters tip their arrows with the toxic secretions of the poison arrow frogs. This enables them to kill large animals such as jaguars and deer with small weapons. In laboratories, researchers are studying the action of poison arrow frog toxins for clues to the way in which the nervous system works. Amphibians have also been the subject of studies on regeneration. It is still a mystery why salamanders can regenerate lost limbs, but closely related frogs cannot. By solving that mystery, researchers hope to develop new ways of treating humans who have lost limbs due to accidents or birth defects.

31–2 SECTION REVIEW

1. In what ways are amphibians adapted to life on land? What characteristics restrict most of them to water?
2. How does a frog carry out its essential life functions?
3. How are frogs and toads similar to salamanders? How are they different?
4. Major changes take place in a tadpole's digestive and circulatory systems during metamorphosis. Why do you think these changes are necessary?
5. Some frogs never go through a free-swimming tadpole stage. Instead, they hatch as tiny frogs. What kind of conditions might have brought about this adaptation?

LABORATORY INVESTIGATION

OBSERVING RESPIRATION IN A FISH

PROBLEM

How does temperature affect the breathing rate of a goldfish?

MATERIALS *(per group)*

600-mL beaker	graph paper
fish net	timer
goldfish in an aquarium	Celsius thermometer

PROCEDURE 

1. Fill the 600-mL beaker about halfway with water from the aquarium containing the goldfish. Remove a goldfish from the aquarium with a fish net and place it in the beaker of water. **CAUTION:** *Be careful when handling live animals.*
2. Place the thermometer in the beaker with the fish. Leave the fish undisturbed for 5 minutes to allow it to get used to its new surroundings. After this 5-minute period, record the water temperature.
3. With the aid of the timer, count the number of times the fish exhales per minute at room temperature. **Note:** *The gill covers at the side of the fish's head open each time the fish exhales.* Record your results.
4. Repeat step 3 for a total of four trials. Calculate the fish's average breathing rate. Record this number.
5. Gently place the beaker containing the goldfish in the ice-water bath your teacher has prepared. This will help simulate the cooler water that a goldfish encounters while swimming in its natural environment. Watch the temperature of the water in the beaker closely. When it is 3 degrees lower than room temperature, remove the beaker from the ice-water bath.
6. Measure the fish's breathing rate at the lower temperature for four trials, calculate the average breathing rate, and record.
7. Gently place the beaker containing the goldfish in the warm-water bath your teacher has prepared. This will help simulate the warm water that a goldfish encounters while swimming in its natural environment. Watch the temperature of the water closely. When it is 3 degrees higher than room temperature, remove the beaker from the warm water bath.
8. Measure the fish's breathing rate at the higher temperature for four trials, calculate the average breathing rate, and record.
9. When the water in the beaker has returned to room temperature, return the goldfish to the aquarium.

OBSERVATIONS

1. Describe how a goldfish breathes.
2. What is the average breathing rate of a goldfish at room temperature? At the lower temperature? At the higher?

ANALYSIS AND CONCLUSIONS

1. Prepare a graph of your results in which temperature is on the horizontal *(x)* axis and average breathing rate is on the vertical *(y)* axis.
2. How does temperature affect the breathing rate of a goldfish?
3. According to your graph, is a goldfish's breathing rate affected to the same extent by a 3-degree rise in temperature as by a 3-degree drop in temperature? Explain.
4. What are some possible sources of error in this investigation? Explain.

STUDENT STUDY GUIDE

SUMMARIZING THE CONCEPTS

The key concepts in each section of this chapter are listed below to help you review the chapter content. Make sure you understand each concept and its relationship to other concepts and to the theme of this chapter.

31–1 Fishes

- Vertebrates have at some time during their development a notochord, a hollow dorsal nerve cord, and pharyngeal slits. In almost all vertebrates, the notochord is replaced by a vertebral column.
- Fishes are aquatic vertebrates that typically have scales, fins, and pharyngeal gills.
- The first fishes were armored and jawless. Later fishes evolved jaws and paired fins.
- Fishes may be oviparous (egg-laying), ovoviviparous (eggs are incubated inside the mother's body), or viviparous (embryos develop inside the mother and are nourished directly by the mother's body).
- Jawless fishes—lampreys and hagfishes—are eellike parasites and scavengers that lack paired fins, scales, and a vertebral column.
- Members of class Chondrichthyes have a skeleton of cartilage. Cartilaginous fishes include sharks, rays, sawfish, and chimaeras.
- Members of class Osteichthyes, or bony fishes, have skeletons of bone. Almost all living bony fishes are ray-finned fishes.

31–2 Amphibians

- Amphibians are vertebrates that have a moist skin with many glands, lack scales and claws, and are typically aquatic as larvae and terrestrial as adults. Most adult amphibians breathe with lungs.
- Amphibian adults and young are typically carnivores. However, tadpoles are herbivores and filter feeders.
- Adult amphibians usually use a combination of lungs, skin, and mouth cavities to breathe, whereas amphibian larvae usually use gills and their skin.
- Adult amphibians have a three-chambered heart and a double-loop circulatory system.
- Fertilization in amphibians may be internal or external. Amphibians may be oviparous, ovoviviparous, or viviparous.
- Salamanders have a tail even after they undergo metamorphosis into the adult form.
- Frogs and toads have large hind legs adapted for jumping. Adult frogs and toads usually lack tails.

REVIEWING KEY TERMS

Vocabulary terms are important to your understanding of biology. The key terms listed below are those you should be especially familiar with. Review these terms and their meanings. Then use each term in a complete sentence. If you are not sure of a term's meaning, return to the appropriate section and review its definition.

31–1 Fishes

vertebral column
jawless fish
bony fish
cartilaginous fish
atrium
ventricle
aorta
olfactory bulb
cerebrum
optic lobe
cerebellum
medulla
oviparous
ovoviviparous
viviparous

31–2 Amphibians

amphibian

CHAPTER REVIEW

CONTENT REVIEW

Multiple Choice

Choose the letter of the answer that best completes each statement.

1. Sharks can detect a drop of blood in a large pool of water using their
   a. lateral lines. c. optic lobes.
   b. pyloric cecae. d. chemoreceptors.
2. Animals in which the young are nourished by the mother's body as they develop are
   a. ovoviviparous. c. viviparous.
   b. oviparous. d. externally fertilized.
3. At the end of the large intestine of a frog is a muscular cavity called the
   a. cloaca. c. gall bladder.
   b. pancreas. d. colon.
4. In most aquatic vertebrates, the notochord is replaced during development by
   a. pharyngeal gills. c. a vertebral column.
   b. fins. d. cartilage.
5. Bony fishes make up the class
   a. Osteichthyes. c. Chordata.
   b. Chondrichthyes. d. Latimeria.
6. An adult amphibian's heart typically has
   a. one chamber. c. three chambers.
   b. two chambers. d. four chambers.
7. Information from a fish's eyes is processed by the part of the brain called the
   a. olfactory bulbs. c. cerebrum.
   b. optic lobes. d. cerebellum.
8. Which of the following statements about excretion in a freshwater fish is true?
   a. The kidneys remove salt.
   b. Water is lost from the gills by osmosis.
   c. Wastes are excreted as urea.
   d. The urine is dilute.

True or False

Determine whether each statement is true or false. If it is true, write "true." If it is false, change the underlined word or words to make the statement true.

1. Members of the class Chondrichthyes are also known as jawless fishes.
2. Amphibians are considered to be the most primitive living vertebrates.
3. The cerebrum in the brain of a fish controls many internal organs and maintains balance.
4. Tadpoles are typically filter feeders or carnivores.
5. Viviparous animals lay eggs.
6. Adult amphibians are typically herbivores.
7. Olfactory bulbs are used to detect motion in the water.
8. The coelacanth is a ray-finned fish.

Word Relationships

In each of the following sets of terms, three of the terms are related. One term does not belong. Determine the characteristic common to three of the terms and then identify the term that does not belong.

1. pelvic fin, girdle, cloaca, pectoral fin
2. atrium, glottis, bulbus cordus, aortic arch
3. lamprey, shark, salamander, salmon
4. pyloric ceca, olfactory bulbs, cerebrum, medulla
5. catfish, electricity, shark, bullfrog

CONCEPT MASTERY

Use your understanding of the concepts developed in the chapter to answer each of the following in a brief paragraph.

1. Compare double-loop and single-loop circulatory systems.
2. Pacific salmon die soon after spawning (releasing reproductive cells into the water). Certain catfish incubate their eggs and young in their mouth. Female porbeagle sharks produce infertile eggs that are eaten by the young developing inside their body. Identify each of these fishes as oviparous, viviparous, or ovoviviparous. Which of these fishes probably produces the most offspring in its lifetime? Explain.
3. Give the common name for each of the four living classes of fishes. Briefly describe a specific example of each class.
4. Explain how a tadpole's digestive, respiratory, and circulatory systems must be modified when it undergoes metamorphosis.
5. Some fishes, such as salmon, live in both fresh and salt water. Explain how the excretory systems of such fishes must be adapted to cope with this kind of lifestyle.

CRITICAL AND CREATIVE THINKING

Discuss each of the following in a brief paragraph.

1. **Making inferences** Members of the amphibian order Apoda are typically blind, wormlike, brightly colored, and viviparous. They have two rows of needlelike inward-curving teeth on the upper jaw and one or two rows on the lower. They do not have gills. The head is shaped like a spade; the bones of the skull are thick and sturdy.
   a. Where would you expect to find apodans?
   b. What do apodans probably eat? Would you expect their intestine to be long or short? Explain.
   c. Describe the processes of fertilization and embryo development in apodans. How are the ways apodans reproduce an adaptation to their environment?
   d. What other inferences can you make about the habits of apodans? Explain.
2. **Relating concepts** When threatened, a certain harmless salamander stands on tiptoe, touches the tip of its tail to the top of its head to display a bright red underside, and remains perfectly still. Explain this behavior.
3. **Relating cause and effect** Certain deep-sea fishes "explode" if they are rapidly brought up from the depths at which they usually live. Using your knowledge of fish anatomy, explain why the fishes explode. (*Hint:* Pressure increases one atmosphere for every 10 meters of sea water.)
4. **Applying concepts** Explain why even the best-camouflaged prey cannot escape detection by a predator that can sense electricity.
5. **Relating concepts** A scuba diver notices that the surface of the water overhead seems light in color, whereas the water below seems quite dark. How might this observation relate to the fact that most fish have countershading (they are dark-colored on the dorsal side and light-colored on the ventral side)?
6. **Using the writing process** Humans depend mostly on vision. Sharks depend mostly on smell and electric sense. Describe a place you know as a shark might sense it.

CHAPTER 32

Reptiles and Birds

The fossil remains of the huge dinosaurs provide overwhelming evidence of their existence.

In the heart of a great forest during the late Carboniferous Period, almost 300 million years ago, giant tree ferns and mosses were everywhere. Amphibians were common.

But the Earth became drier, and as a result, new and different kinds of environments became available. Other animals evolved and filled the new niches. The most successful of these animals were the reptiles, which included the awesome dinosaurs. For more than 200 million years, the dinosaurs were masters of the Earth.

In time, however, the dinosaurs became extinct. They left behind fossil evidence of their passing—evidence that never ceases to amaze those who view the silent testimony of the largest animals ever to walk on Earth. But dinosaurs not only left fossils: They also left several evolutionary lines that were to develop into modern reptiles and birds. In this chapter you will learn more about reptiles and birds: how and why they have been able to survive on Earth long after their giant relatives became extinct.

CHAPTER OUTLINE

32–1 Reptiles

Section Objectives

- Describe several characteristics of reptiles.
- Explain reasons for the great adaptive radiation of reptiles that occurred during the late Triassic and Jurassic periods.
- Relate the form and function of reptiles to their success in dry environments.

When you think of reptiles, you probably think of snakes slithering through tall grass or lizards scurrying up the trunk of a tree. You may think of a tortoise slowly eating a meal of plant leaves or a crocodile floating noiselessly in a pool of dark water. All these animals are reptiles, and they represent three of the four surviving orders of reptiles. The fourth order is represented by a single species, the tuatara. You will learn more about these orders of reptiles later in this chapter.

What Is a Reptile?

Reptiles are vertebrate animals that have lungs, a scaly skin, and a special type of egg—adaptations that enable them to live their entire life out of water. Today **reptiles** are widely distributed over much of the Earth. The temperate and tropical areas on Earth contain populations of reptiles that are remarkably diverse in appearance and lifestyle. The only places on Earth that lack reptiles are very cold areas. This is due to an important reason that will soon become apparent.

In some ways, reptiles resemble amphibians. However, reptiles are better adapted to life on land. For example, reptilian skin is dry and leathery and is often covered with thick, protective scales. This body covering helps prevent loss of body water in dry environments. But the dry, waterproof skin

Figure 32–1 *The chameleon, a modern reptile, moves slowly and deliberately, creeping up to its insect prey. Its eyes are able to move independently of each other, so that one eye can guide its movements and the other can sight the unwitting victim.*

Figure 32–2 Unlike most amphibians, reptiles are able to survive quite well in dry environments, as this snake in a cactus patch shows (right). Their survival is due in part to their dry, scaly skin, which must be shed periodically (left).

can also be a disadvantage to reptiles. The tough, scaly layer of skin does not grow when the rest of the reptile grows, so it must be shed periodically when a reptile increases in size.

Perhaps the most important adaptation of reptiles to life on land is the type of egg they produce. Unlike amphibian eggs, which almost always need to develop in water, reptilian eggs are surrounded by a shell and several membranes that together create a protected environment in which the embryo can develop. See Figure 32–3. In fact, we named these eggs **amniotic** (am-nee-AHT-ihk) **eggs** for one of those membranes. Amniotic eggs are as important to the survival of land animals as the evolution of seeds was to the survival of land plants. In addition to a shell and membranes, amniotic eggs also contain a substantial yolk. The yolk is rich in nutrients that the developing embryo uses until it is ready to hatch. The legacy of an egg adapted to life on land was passed on from early reptiles to their descendants—modern reptiles, birds, and mammals. (Although few mammals lay eggs, they all use the membranes of the amniotic egg, in modified form, in the development of the embryo.)

Another important reason for the success of reptiles on land is the development of a more efficient respiratory system. Remember that most amphibians take in oxygen and give off waste gases primarily through their moist skin. This method of respiration works only as long as the amphibian's skin remains damp. In dry land environments, breathing through moist skin is not an option. The dry skin of reptiles, which prevents water loss, also prevents gases from moving through. To exchange gases with the environment, reptiles have two efficient lungs—or, in the case of certain species of snakes, one lung. All these adaptations contribute to the success of reptiles on land.

Figure 32–3 The reptile egg shows adaptations to survive the dryness of life on land. This tiny turtle has just hatched and is breaking free of its shell.

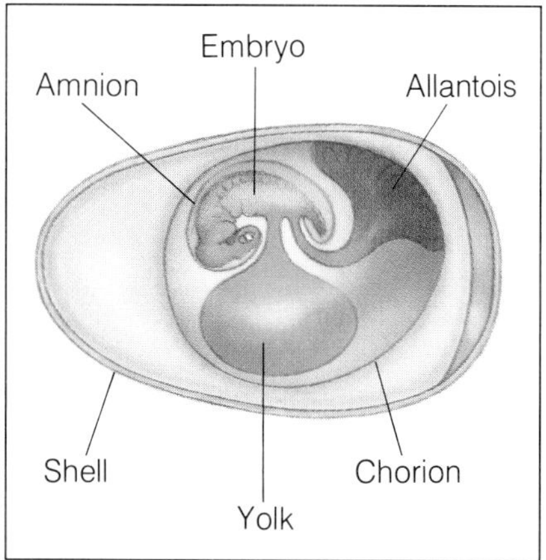

Evolution of Reptiles

Because several fossils show characteristics of both amphibians and reptiles, it is difficult to say exactly when the first true reptiles appeared on Earth. As you have just read, one determining factor that separates living reptiles from amphibians is the type of eggs they produce. But, unfortunately, there are no fossil eggs around for paleontologists to study. Because we cannot tell what kind of eggs these fossil animals laid, they must remain on the amphibian-reptilian borderline—at least for the present time. These animals are often called **transition fossils.** These transition fossils document the slow and steady evolutionary change of amphibianlike ancestors into reptiles over time.

Throughout most of the Carboniferous Period, amphibians greatly outnumbered reptiles. But during the Permian Period, which began about 285 million years ago, the Earth's surface and climate changed dramatically. Mountain ranges such as the Appalachians were formed. The climate became cooler and less humid. Many of the great swamps dried up. These changes made life difficult for a large number of water-dependent amphibians. But such was not the case with the reptiles. It was during this time that they began their great period of adaptive radiation.

One early reptile line developed into a fascinating group of mammallike reptiles that displayed a mix of reptilian and mammalian characteristics. Although these animals were extremely successful at first, they became extinct in just a few million years—nearly overnight on a geological time scale. Toward the end of the Triassic Period, about 195 million years ago, the mammallike reptiles were suddenly replaced in the fossil record by another group of reptiles that had remained in the background for millions of years—the dinosaurs.

__Figure 32–4__ Although they survived for many millions of years, dinosaurs eventually became extinct. One theory suggests that a meteor struck the Earth, causing the climate to cool. The dinosaurs could not survive this change in temperature.

During the late Triassic and Jurassic periods, a great adaptive radiation of the dinosaurs, or "terrible lizards," took place. The Triassic Period also saw the appearance of crocodiles and alligators, as well as the first birds.

At the end of the Cretaceous Period, about 65 million years ago, something happened to cause a worldwide mass extinction. Within a few million years, dinosaurs and most other animal and plant groups became extinct. Exactly why this mass extinction occurred is not known for certain. Some biologists think it was caused by the slow process of climatic change that resulted from movements of the continents into their present positions. Other biologists believe that the change in climate that produced the mass extinction occurred more suddenly. Some evidence suggests that a huge meteor struck the Earth, causing an explosion that produced enormous clouds of airborne dust. The explosion may also have caused worldwide forest fires. The smoke from the fires, as well as the clouds of dust, may have blocked the sun's rays, causing Earth's temperature to drop.

Whatever happened at the end of the Cretaceous Period resulted in the death of virtually all the great and terrible lizards. The disappearance of the dinosaurs left open many niches for animals, both on land and in the sea.

Form and Function in Reptiles

Because they have adapted to many different ways of life, reptiles exhibit numerous variations in structure and behavior. Some—for example, turtles, crocodiles, and lizards—move about on four legs. Others move about without legs. Snakes and certain lizards are two examples.

FEEDING There is remarkable diversity in the foods eaten by reptiles and in their modes of feeding. Some reptiles, such as the iguana, are herbivores. Other reptiles are carnivores. Certain carnivorous snakes prey on small animals by grabbing them with their jaws and swallowing them whole. See Figure 32–5. Other snakes live on a diet of birds' eggs. After

Figure 32–5 *All reptiles are carnivores. Many snakes eat small mammals. Because they are able to stretch their jaws wide, snakes swallow their prey whole. A chameleon obtains its food by flicking out its sticky tongue over a great distance. Any insects within striking range are greedily gobbled up.*

swallowing an egg whole, these snakes crack the egg in their throat by piercing the shell with bony projections of their vertebrae. The snakes swallow the liquid content of the egg, spitting out the cracked shell. Still other snakes, such as the huge king cobra, eat other snakes. Crocodiles and alligators eat fish and land animals, provided they can catch them. If they are successful in snaring a land animal, they pull it under water and drown it, eating what they want by tearing huge chunks off the corpse. Crocodiles and alligators often store the remains of their prey under water by anchoring the rotting body under a tree or rock and returning to it when hunger once again moves them to eat.

Carnivorous reptiles other than snakes feed in similarly unusual ways. Monitor lizards kill their prey with sharp teeth and powerful jaws. Chameleons have sticky tongues as long as their bodies, which flip out to catch insects on the wing. Iguanas tear plant material into shreds with the force of their teeth and jaws. Because herbivorous reptiles do not chew their food, they must swallow large pieces of material. Their long digestive system, however, enables them to digest these large tough, fibrous pieces of food.

Figure 32–6 *This anole, a type of lizard, is holding onto the downward hanging flower of a banana. Anoles are quite common in tropical and semitropical areas.*

RESPIRATION The lungs of reptiles are better developed than those of amphibians. Because they have muscles around their ribs, many reptiles are able to expand their chest cavity to inhale and collapse the cavity to force air out. Several species of crocodiles also have flaps of skin that can separate the mouth from the nasal passages, thus allowing them to breathe through their nostrils while their mouth remains open.

Although most reptiles have two lungs, some species of snakes have only one. This single lung functions quite well, and fits neatly into their long, thin body. Snakes have another important adaptation that allows them to breathe at the very same time they are swallowing their prey. You know from experience that it is impossible for a person to breathe and swallow simultaneously. This is true for snakes as well. But snakes have a special tube in the floor of their mouth through which they breathe, so they don't suffocate in the time it takes them to swallow their prey. This tube can be extended out of a snake's mouth while it is dining.

INTERNAL TRANSPORT Reptiles have a well-developed double-loop circulatory system. One of the two loops brings blood to and from the lungs, and the other loop brings blood to and from the rest of the body. Reptile hearts contain two atria and either one or two ventricles. Among reptiles, crocodiles and alligators have the most well-developed heart. Their heart consists of two atria and two ventricles. (This four-chambered heart is found in all birds and mammals.) However, most reptiles have a single ventricle with partial internal walls that help keep oxygenated and deoxygenated blood separate during the pumping cycle.

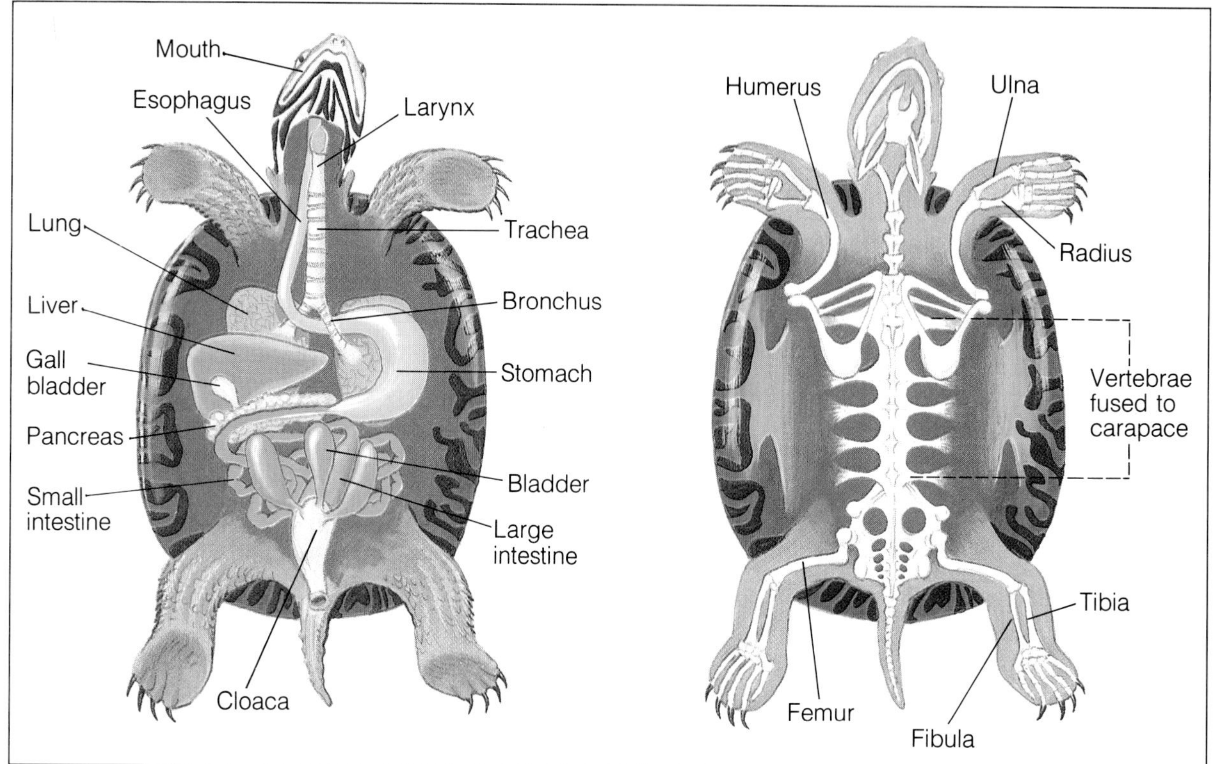

Figure 32–7 This illustration shows the internal organs of a turtle. The turtle's top shell is actually fused to its vertebrae. Other reptiles differ slightly from this body plan.

The circulatory system of reptiles is more well-developed than the circulatory system of amphibians. Because amphibians exchange gases through their moist skin, they do not need to have an efficient circulatory system to deliver oxygen to and remove waste gases from their cells. In reptiles, however, the development of efficient lungs necessitated the development of a more efficient circulatory system—a system that moves blood to and from the lungs in one loop and around the rest of the body in another, completely separate, loop.

EXCRETION Reptiles eliminate liquid wastes in the form of urine, which is produced in their kidneys. In some reptiles, urine flows through tubes directly into a cloaca similar to that of amphibians. In other reptiles, a urinary bladder stores urine before it is expelled. In many reptiles, especially desert-dwelling snakes, a large amount of water is removed from the urine in the cloaca and returned to body tissues.

Many reptiles excrete nitrogen-containing wastes in the form of uric acid rather than ammonia. Ammonia is extremely toxic and must be excreted in dilute form to avoid self-poisoning. Excreting dilute ammonia means excreting considerable amounts of water. This is not a problem for aquatic and semiaquatic animals like fishes and amphibians. But it is a problem for terrestrial animals that must conserve water. Uric acid is less toxic to cells than ammonia is and thus does not have to be diluted to the same extent that ammonia does. In addition, uric acid does not remain dissolved in urine but rather crystallizes out as a solid precipitate. When extra water is removed in the cloaca, urine is reduced to a pasty white material that can be excreted without much water loss. This represents another successful adaptation of reptiles to a land environment.

RESPONSE The reptilian brain shows the same basic pattern as the amphibian brain, although the reptile cerebrum and cerebellum are somewhat larger. Most reptilian sense organs are well-developed, although there are exceptions. Snakes, for example, cannot hear.

Most reptiles that are active during the day have complex eyes that contain several types of photoreceptor cells. Many reptiles can see color quite well. In fact, some turtles can probably see colors better than humans can.

Many snakes have an extremely good sense of smell. Snakes have a pair of nostrils that open near the mouth. They also have a pair of special organs in the roof of the mouth that aid the nose in smelling. Have you ever seen a snake constantly flicking its tongue in and out of its mouth? The tongue picks up molecules from the air and carries them into the mouth and onto this pair of special organs. In this way, the snake gathers information about its environment by "tasting" molecules in the air.

Some reptiles, including most lizards, have simple ears—much like those of amphibians. These ears have an external eardrum, or tympanum, and a single bone that conducts sound to the inner ear. But many other reptiles do not have an eardrum and are completely deaf to sounds carried in the air. Snakes are one example. However, snakes are able to pick up vibrations in the ground through bones in their skull. Tortoises also lack an eardrum, but a thick patch of skin on their head serves the same sound-conducting function.

Some reptiles are able to gather heat information from their environment. Snakes such as rattlesnakes have the extraordinary ability to detect the warmth given off by the body of the small animals they eat. Many vipers prey almost exclusively on small mammals such as mice and rats that have a high body temperature. Some pit vipers have heat-sensitive pits on both sides of their head. Using these pits, vipers obtain a temperature picture of the world around them. Mammals stand out as warm spots in that temperature picture, making them easier for vipers to locate and strike at. This method of locating prey is extremely valuable at night, when low levels of light make it difficult for a reptile to see its prey.

MOVEMENT The reptilian muscle and skeletal systems exhibit many advances over those of amphibians. Compared with amphibians, reptiles with legs have larger, stronger limbs whose movements are well-controlled. For example, the legs of many reptiles are well-adapted to walking, burrowing, swimming or climbing. Snakes, which lost their legs in the course of evolution, move by pressing large ventral scales against the ground. By expanding and contracting the muscles around

Figure 32–8 *Unlike certain snakes, the gila monster does not have fangs to inject its venom. Instead, it bites its prey and lets its venom flow into the open wound.*

Figure 32–9 *The fangs of this rattlesnake are so long they must fold in order for the snake to close its mouth. Note the position of the animal's venom glands.*

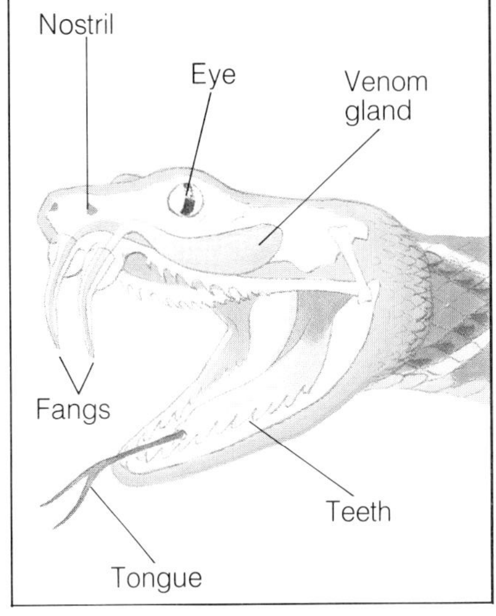

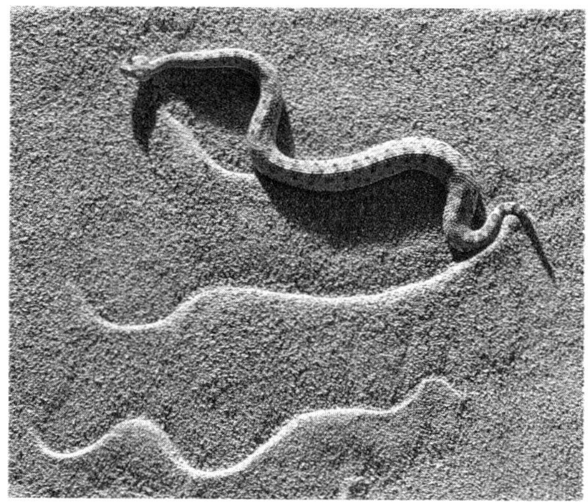

Figure 32–10 *Although much more at home in trees and shrubs, this chameleon walks gingerly along the ground (top, left). The sidewinder, a type of rattlesnake, is able to move along shifting desert sands quite quickly (top, right). Tiny flaps of skin on its toes enable the gecko to cling to surfaces as smooth as glass (bottom).*

their ribs in waves, snakes dig these ventral scales into the ground and push themselves forward. Because this kind of movement is slow and quiet, it makes snakes masters at stalking prey.

REPRODUCTION As you have already learned, the reptile egg is an important contributing factor to the success of these animals in a land environment. The leathery outer shell protects the delicate tissues inside the egg, and pores in the shell allow oxygen and carbon dioxide to pass through.

Reptiles lay eggs that hatch into animals that resemble small adults. Virtually all reptiles reproduce through **internal fertilization**, which means that a male reptile deposits sperm into the body of the female. In reptiles, as in amphibians, the male and female reproductive systems open into the cloaca. From the outside, it is extremely difficult to tell the sex of a reptile. Almost all male reptiles have a penis that allows them to deliver sperm into the female's cloaca. (Lizards and some snakes have two reproductive structures called hemipenes.) This internal fertilization makes it possible for the female's reproductive system to cover the embryos with protective membranes and a shell after fertilization has occurred.

Once fertilization occurs, reptile species treat their eggs very differently. Many species are **oviparous**, laying eggs that develop outside the mother's body. Some species, such as sea turtles, come ashore to bury their eggs in sand. After they have covered the eggs, the sea turtles move back into the sea, deserting the eggs and leaving the young turtles without parental care. Other reptiles provide minimal care for their eggs and young. Certain snakes, for example, bask in the sun to warm their bodies and then wrap themselves around their eggs to incubate them. Once the young hatch, however, they are on their own and must catch their own food. Baby cobras are born looking like miniature copies of their parents. They even have fully functioning fangs that produce the venom with which they kill their prey.

Figure 32–11 *Although reptiles rarely fight, conflicts do occur. Tortoises fight until one is flipped onto its back (left). If neither of the male chameleons retreats from the face-off, a fight will begin (right).*

Reptiles such as alligators build nests in which they lay their eggs and guard them until they hatch. At that point, alligators provide their young with a certain amount of care. When a female alligator hears her babies squeaking, she bites open the nest, picks up the babies in her mouth, and carries them to the water for protection. Some baby crocodiles and alligators stay with their mother for as long as two years after they hatch.

A number of female snakes and lizards hold their eggs inside their body until the eggs hatch. Thus the young are born alive. During the incubation period, an embryo grows and develops within the egg, using the yolk of the egg as a source of nutrients. Having the eggs carried within the female's body provides several important advantages. The mother snake can protect her young. She can also keep the eggs warm by basking in the sun. Snakes that bear living young are **ovoviviparous**.

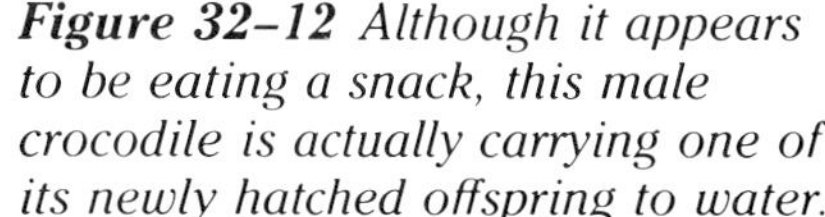

Figure 32–12 *Although it appears to be eating a snack, this male crocodile is actually carrying one of its newly hatched offspring to water.*

Tuataras

The tuatara (too-uh-TAH-ruh) is the only surviving member of the order Rhynchocephalia (rihng-koh-suh-FAY-lee-uh). This reptile resembles reptiles that lived during the dinosaur age. The tuatara is of interest to paleontologists because it retains features of the ancient reptiles from which it evolved.

Tuataras, which are found only on a few small islands off the coast of New Zealand, lead a leisurely life. Unlike many reptiles, they are active at night, hunting the small animals they eat. In tuataras, the part of the brain called the pineal gland is located on the top of the skull in a place where several skull bones meet. This type of pineal gland is sometimes called the "third eye" because it contains cells that are sensitive to light. However, tuataras do not actually see with the pineal gland. Instead, they use it to detect changes in day length.

Figure 32–13 *The tuatara is a rare lizard that lives in New Zealand. As you can see, it retains many of the features of its prehistoric ancestors.*

Figure 32–14 *This male anole is displaying the bright blue patch below its chin (top, left). The Komodo dragon is one of the largest lizards in the world, reaching a length of about 3 meters (top, right). The frilled dragon gets its name from a frill of skin around its neck that it can extend, thus making itself appear larger and more fearsome to other animals (bottom).*

Lizards and Snakes

Modern lizards and snakes belong to the order Squamata (skwah-MAH-tuh). Most lizards have legs, clawed toes, external ears, and movable eyelids. Lizards range in size from tiny geckos a few centimeters long to giant monitor lizards that can be more than 3 meters in length.

Some lizards have evolved into highly specialized forms. See Figure 32–14. For example, African chameleons live exclusively in trees and bushes, eating insects they catch with their incredibly long, coiled tongue. They flick their tongue out of their mouth, and, with unerring aim, they are usually able to catch their insect meal. Gila monsters, large, stocky lizards of the American Southwest and Mexico, have glands in their jaws that produce the venom with which they paralyze small prey. Gila monsters do not inject venom with fangs. Instead, they bite their prey and hold onto it with their teeth while the venom they produce flows into the wound. Another kind of lizard, the iguana, looks ferocious but is almost exclusively herbivorous.

The world's largest living lizards, the monitors, are the only reptiles alive today that provide some idea of what small dinosaurs may have been like. Monitors are quite intelligent and active for reptiles. Many eat birds and mammals. The largest monitor lizards are the Komodo dragons. With a length of as many as 3 meters and a mass of up to 75 kilograms, Komodo dragons can kill and devour animals as large as water buffalo!

Snakes are lizards that have lost both pairs of legs during their evolution into burrowing forms. Millions of years ago, some lizards began to live below ground level. In burrows and cracks, these relatively harmless lizards were safe from predators. Over time, the lizards with smaller legs or with no legs at all were able to burrow most efficiently. These lizards survived,

evolving into the legless snakes alive on Earth today. Although being legless may seem to be a disadvantage, snakes are efficient and effective predators in the niches they occupy, In fact, the distribution of snakes on Earth is limited only by temperature.

Snakes vary considerably in size. Some are so small they look like earthworms. Others are so large they're scary. Pythons, for example, can reach lengths of about 10 meters. But perhaps the most fascinating snakes are the venomous snakes —the ones that produce poisonous chemicals they inject into their prey. The ability of certain types of snakes to produce lethal poisons has caused some people to harbor an unjustified fear of all snakes. Actually, more people in the United States die from bee stings than snake bites. And most snakes are happier avoiding people than confronting them!

Figure 32–15 *Although they inspire fear in many, most snakes are not aggressive toward people. One can admire the exotic colors and patterns of their scales—and respect their ability to survive in a world where even their shape appears to be a handicap.*

Crocodilians

Members of the order Crocodilia—such as alligators, crocodiles, caimans, and gavials—split off from the ancient reptiles around the time dinosaurs did, probably at the beginning of the Triassic Period. In the 200 million years since then, alligators and crocodiles have changed little.

Crocodilians are among the largest living reptiles. Some species grow up to 7 meters in length. These animals live only in the tropics and subtropics, where the climate remains warm all year long. Alligators, and their relatives the caimans, live only in fresh water and are found almost exclusively in the Western Hemisphere. Crocodiles, on the other hand, may live in either fresh or salt water and are native to Africa, India, and Southeast Asia.

Figure 32–16 This painted turtle is one of our most colorful native species. Here you can see the rounded top shell and the flat bottom shell.

Turtles

Turtles and tortoises, members of the order Chelonia (kigh-LOH-nee-uh), also evolved a successful way of life during the Triassic Period and have changed little in the 200 million years since then. The word turtle usually refers to members of this order that live in water; the word tortoise, to those that live on land. All turtles and tortoises have some sort of shell covering their bodies, although in a few species, such as the American soft-shelled turtle, the shell is not very bony. The turtle shells consist of two parts: a dorsal part, or **carapace**, and a ventral part, or **plastron**. The animal's backbone is fused to the inside of the carapace, and its head, legs, and tail stick out through holes where carapace and plastron join.

Tortoises usually have a high, domed carapace and stubby, elephantlike legs. Tortoises pull into their shells to protect their more delicate body parts. In some species, the front end of the plastron is hinged and folds up to further seal out predators.

Turtles are adapted to life in freshwater ponds and lakes or the open sea. The legs and feet of many aquatic turtles have developed into flippers. Certain aquatic species cannot pull back into their shells completely, but they do have powerful jaws that are capable of giving a nasty bite.

Figure 32–17 This tortoise moves quite well, although slowly, on its strong stubby legs (left). The flipper-shaped feet of this sea turtle enable it to swim gracefully in its watery home (right).

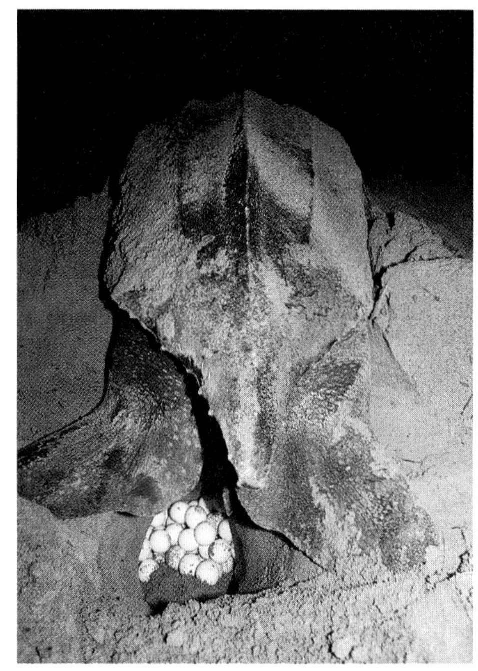

Figure 32–18 *After they hatch, sea turtles scurry into the water. Male sea turtles will never again walk on land; female sea turtles will return to the shore from which they hatched to lay their own eggs. Although they move effortlessly through water, sea turtles expend a great deal of effort to heave their large bodies along on land.*

How Reptiles Fit into the World

The reptiles alive today represent only a few survivors of a group of animals that once ruled the land. They are found in many habitats—from the temperate zone to the tropics and from the tops of rain forest trees to the open ocean.

Reptiles are important predators in many ecosystems. On farms, for example, snakes keep down the large numbers of rats and mice normally attracted to grains. Without snakes, most farms would be overrun by mice and rats. Small lizards eat insects; large lizards eat other small animals. Thus reptiles limit the populations of other animal species.

Sea turtles, once numerous in both the Atlantic and Pacific oceans, are now in danger of extinction for several reasons. Turtle soup and turtle eggs are eaten in many parts of the world. Tortoise shell was once commonly used to manufacture jewelry and as an inlay in furniture. Another reason for the decline in the number of sea turtles is the development of their nesting sites. Sea turtles always return to shore to lay their eggs in sand. They return, however, not to just any patch of beach but to the same spot where they hatched many years before. Seaside development (the construction of houses, hotels, and shopping centers) in many tropical areas threatens the ancient spawning sites of these animals. Today, however, most species of sea turtles are protected by law. This protection may lead to an increase in their dwindling numbers.

32–1 SECTION REVIEW

1. Describe four characteristics of reptiles.
2. How does the form of reptiles equip them for a life on dry land?
3. How did conditions during the Permian Period favor the adaptive radiation of reptiles?
4. Describe the structure of an amniotic egg. Why was the evolution of the amniotic egg critical to the survival of vertebrate life on land?
5. What four orders are found in the reptile class? Give an example of an animal in each order.
6. What might happen to reptiles if conditions on Earth became permanently warmer and much more damp?

Section Objectives

- Define ectothermic and endothermic.
- Compare ectothermic and endothermic strategies for surviving in different environments.

32–2 The Evolution of Temperature Control

On a spring morning after a cold night, a turtle lies on a rock basking in the sun. Nearby, a snake crawls out of its burrow beneath a rotting stump. In a tree overhead, a young robin puffs up its feathers into a ball. And as you walk out of the water after an early swim, your skin gets goose bumps, and you shiver. All these activities are examples of the strategies vertebrates use to control their body temperature.

Control of body temperature is important for animals, particularly in habitats where temperature varies widely with time of day and with season. Each animal species has its own preferred "operating range" of temperatures. For example, in order for muscles to move quickly, they must be kept at a certain minimum temperature. Yet if an animal's body gets too hot, muscles tire easily and other body systems are stressed.

In terms of how they generate and control their body heat, animals can be classified into two basic groups: **ectotherms** and **endotherms**. Turtles, snakes, and other modern reptiles are ectotherms, which literally means heat from outside. As a group, these animals have relatively low metabolic rates when they are resting. Thus they do not generate much heat inside their bodies. Because they also lack effective insulation, any heat they do generate is lost to their surroundings. In order to control their body temperature, therefore, these animals must pick up heat from the environment.

Birds and mammals, on the other hand, are endotherms, which literally means heat from inside. Birds and mammals have relatively high metabolic rates that generate a significant amount of heat, even when they are resting. Endotherms can move around at night and during cool, cloudy weather more easily than ectotherms can because endotherms do not have to warm up their muscles to operating temperature by basking in the sun.

Ectothermic animals are often incorrectly thought of as coldblooded, and endothermic animals, as warmblooded. These names give the wrong impression of the body temperature of these animals. Coldblooded animals may have a body temperature higher than their surroundings, whereas warmblooded animals may have a temperature lower than their

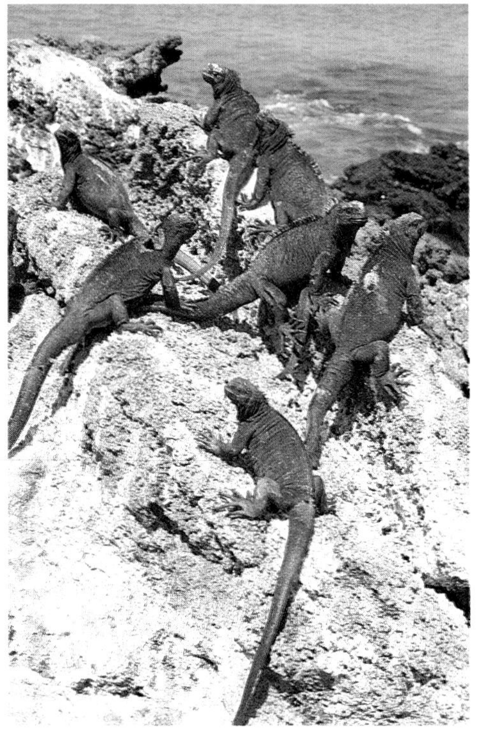

Figure 32–19 *These iguanas position themselves so that they are warmed by the heat of the sun. Then they dive into the cold water to eat algae. They must return to the land again when the water chills their body temperature. Penguins are able to generate their own body heat. They live in cold Antarctic climates, where their feathers act as insulation.*

Figure 32–20 *Remaining in the sun for a long period of time would cause the body temperature of a desert tortoise to climb too high. Thus a tortoise spends much of the hot desert days hiding in a shady spot, such as beneath a rock.*

surroundings. It was also long assumed that the body temperature of ectotherms varied much more than that of endotherms. However, a careful study of animal body temperatures shows that these assumptions are incorrect for many animals.

In nature, lizards and snakes warm up when they need to by basking in the sun. When their body reaches the right temperature, they go about their business. The right temperature for reptiles is often higher than that of their surroundings. While they are active, reptile muscles generate heat (just as ours do). If they get too hot during the day, reptiles duck into a cool burrow or under a rock to lose heat. When the sun goes down and the air gets cold, they head for a warm place in which they can conserve their heat overnight. Scientists have implanted radio thermometers inside certain lizards and monitored body temperature as the animals were allowed to be free in their natural habitat. The results showed that these lizards' body temperature was always higher than that of the environment and remained relatively constant as well!

In an absolute sense, neither endothermy nor ectothermy is superior. For different animals in different environments, each strategy has its advantages and disadvantages. For example, ectotherms cannot remain active for long periods. If you watch modern reptiles, you will see that they alternate periods of intense activity with periods of rest. A snake will expend energy in catching a meal, but it will remain relatively inactive while digesting it. And if the meal is large enough, the snake may remain inactive for several weeks. Endotherms, by comparison, remain active for a long time. Think about the amount of energy that is expended by a cheetah as it chases down its prey, or the amount of energy that is expended by a bird during its annual migration.

In climates that remain warm all the time, ectothermy is a way of conserving energy. Ectotherms remain at operating temperature fairly easily by basking in the sun and burrowing in the ground. This is why most of the world's large lizards and amphibians (and many of the largest insects) are today found in the tropics and subtropics. In these warm places, ectothermy is a perfectly adequate way to regulate body temperature. Endotherms, on the other hand, burn lots of calories to generate body heat. Therefore, endotherms need a lot more food than ectotherms of the same size. The amount of food needed to sustain a single cow would be enough to sustain a dozen cow-sized lizards!

Large ectotherms run into trouble, however, in temperate zone habitats where temperature varies a great deal. It takes a

Dinosaurs: New Light on Old Bones

Until recently, dinosaurs were thought to be lumbering dim-witted beasts scarcely able to support their own weight, let alone move. But more evidence indicates that these animals were probably both more intelligent and more active than was once believed.

New studies of fossil bones show that some dinosaur species stood up on their hind legs and were able to run at reasonable speeds to escape large predators. Scores of fossil footprints indicate that large herbivores such as *Apatosaurus* lived in herds much like some large herbivore species of animals alive today. Other evidence indicates that dinosaurs displayed the same sorts of mating and territorial behaviors seen among large mammals today. Nests containing fossil dinosaur eggs indicate that at least some dinosaur species cared for their young after hatching, not unlike modern-day birds.

A more hotly disputed hypothesis concerns endothermy. Some paleontologists believe that dinosaurs were endothermic. Supporters of this hypothesis point to certain features of dinosaur bones that make them quite similar to mammalian bones. Supporters also rely on an analysis of the ratio of predator to prey animals for evidence. They note that there seems to have been many more prey animals than predators among dinosaurs. Because endotherms require more food than ectotherms do, these researchers argue, a large population of prey animals would be needed to support a small population of endothermic predators. And since this is what the evidence shows, dinosaurs must have been endotherms. If dinosaurs were ectothermic, they argue, a different ratio of predator to prey animals would be expected.

The Tyrannosaurus rex *was one of the largest carnivores that ever lived. Its fearsome teeth made short work of its hapless prey.*

Today most paleontologists believe that dinosaurs had higher body temperatures than modern reptiles. They do not necessarily believe, however, that dinosaurs were endotherms. Instead, these researchers point out that dinosaurs lived during periods when climates were constantly warm. In fact, during the reign of the dinosaurs, much of what is now Europe and North America had a climate similar to that found in the tropics today. For this reason, dinosaurs could grow large and still regulate their body temperature as today's lizards do.

Even as more evidence is being collected, the debate about endothermy in ancient reptiles continues. In the meantime, it is easier to explain the extinction of dinosaurs if it is assumed they really were ectotherms. Large ectotherms, able to survive quite nicely in warm climates, would have been at a disadvantage in the cooler, more variable climates that ended the dinosaur era. Thus they would have disappeared from Earth. Smaller ectotherms, such as modern lizards, would have been better off than their much larger cousins, however.

long time for a large animal to warm up in the sun after a cold night. It is also much more difficult for a large animal to find cool shelter during a scorching-hot day. (Can you imagine a burrow big enough for a gigantic dinosaur?) Small ectotherms have much less trouble dealing with hot days and cool nights than large ones do. But even small ectotherms cannot cope with long cold, cloudy winters. They either hibernate or lay resting eggs and die. In certain parts of the United States and Canada, snake dens with many thousands of snakes can be found. These huge numbers of snakes cluster together in the winter in warm dens. Like birds, snakes also migrate. In spring, many snakes leave their winter dens and crawl hundreds of kilometers to return to the area they normally live in during the summer months.

Figure 32–21 *Some species of snakes migrate to special dens during cold winter weather. In these dens, many thousands of snakes keep one another warm. In the spring, the snakes leave the dens and migrate to summer feeding areas—only to return to the dens once again in the fall when air temperatures begin to drop.*

There is little doubt that the first terrestrial vertebrates were ectotherms. But there is some doubt as to when and how endothermy evolved. Some biologists believe that dinosaurs were endotherms, not ectotherms like modern reptiles. Most biologists, however, believe that endothermy evolved much later than the appearance of the dinosaurs. Putting these two hypotheses together means that endothermy evolved two separate times—once among the line of small dinosaurs that ultimately led to *Archaeopteryx*, an extinct ancestor of modern birds, and once again among the mammallike reptiles or their descendants.

32–2 SECTION REVIEW

1. What is endothermy? Give an example of an endothermic animal.
2. What is ectothermy? Give an example of an ectothermic animal.
3. How does a lizard control its body temperature?
4. Why would you not find a large lizard living in North Dakota?

32–3 Birds

Section Objectives

- Identify characteristics of birds.
- Describe ways the form of birds shows adaptations for flight.
- Explain how birds fit into the natural world.

You have probably observed many different kinds of birds during your lifetime. Colorful birds fill woods with song. Flocks of birds fly to backyard feeders. Exotic birds with fanciful feathers inhabit zoological gardens. Yes, there are many birds: about 8700 living species belonging to more than 160 families. And there were even more kinds of birds in the past. Paleontologists estimate that more than 100,000 species of birds have become extinct since the Jurassic Period.

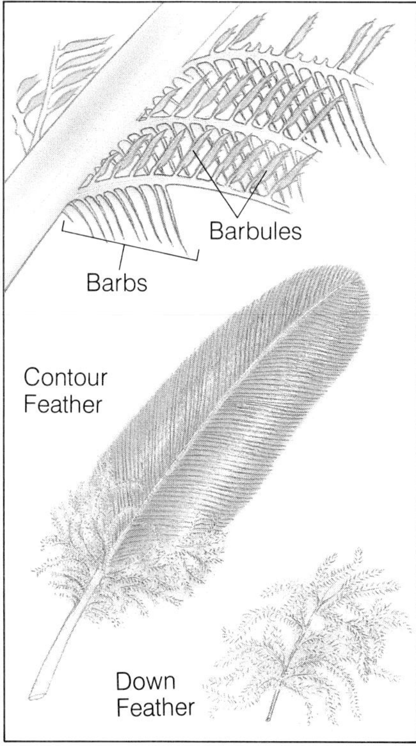

Figure 32–22 Baby owls are covered with a coat of down feathers. The air spaces in these fluffy feathers help insulate the birds from temperature changes. Most of the down feathers will later be shed and a new coat of contour feathers will grow in.

What Is a Bird?

In a group this diverse, it is difficult to find many characteristics that are shared by all members. But we can identify several features **birds** have in common. **Birds are endothermic reptilelike animals with an outer covering of feathers, two legs used for walking or perching, and front limbs modified into wings that usually do not have useful claws.**

The single most important characteristic that separates birds from reptiles is feathers. Feathers help birds fly and also keep them warm. Birds have several different kinds of feathers. Because many feathers are hollow, they are both light and strong.

Contour feathers are large feathers that cover a bird's body and wings. Certain contour feathers, known as flight feathers, are long and stiff. Flight feathers on the wings and tail provide the lifting force and balance needed for flight. From both sides of the long, stiff quill of a flight feather grow side branches called barbs. From the barbs, in turn, grow still smaller structures called barbules. The hooks on a barbule catch on the hooks of nearby barbules, holding the barbs together in flat vanes. Although the barbule hooks can be pulled apart, they can easily be lined up again. You may have seen a bird grooming its feathers by pulling them through its beak. This grooming is called preening. One of the reasons birds preen themselves after each flight is to realign any vanes whose barbules may have been split apart during use. Other contour feathers, known as general body feathers, have fluffy barbules at their base and are not as long and stiff as flight feathers. General body feathers are often brightly colored and help determine the shape of a bird's body.

Down feathers grow underneath and between the contour feathers. Down feathers are short, soft, and fluffy. These feathers trap warm air close to a bird's body, insulating the bird. Baby birds of many species are covered with down feathers for a period of time after they hatch.

Powder feathers are important to birds that live on or in water. As they grow, these feathers release a fine white powder that repels water and keeps it from penetrating the layer of down feathers. Birds also produce a waterproof oil in special glands near their tail. When ducks, geese, or other water birds preen themselves, they rub this oil over their feathers. The oil actually makes water "roll off a duck's back."

Evolution of Birds

Ask many paleontologists what a bird is and they'll reply with a grin, "a hot-blooded dinosaur with feathers." Although that answer may sound odd, there really is reason for it. The first fossil ever found of an early birdlike animal is called *Archaeopteryx* and dates from late in the Jurassic Period. Its skeleton looks much like a small running dinosaur. Unlike modern birds, *Archaeopteryx* had teeth in its beak. It also had toes and claws on its wings. In fact, *Archaeopteryx* would be classified as a dinosaur except for one important feature: It had well-developed feathers covering its entire body. More recently, another transitional fossil—a fossil with both dinosaur features and bird features—has been found. This species, called *Protoavis*, is older than *Archaeopteryx*. *Protoavis* confirms that birds are related to dinosaurs. Although these fossils leave many questions about bird evolution unanswered, they do document the evolution of birds from ancient reptiles.

Figure 32–23 *This photograph shows the remains of the first recognizable bird,* Protoavis.

Form and Function in Birds

Many characteristic features of birds—for example, feathers, wings, bones, beaks, and legs—differ dramatically among species adapted to different ways of life. In order to appreciate these differences in features, it is important to study birds that live in different habitats and examine the adaptations they show.

FEEDING Birds have high metabolic rates and burn many calories just to keep warm. For that reason, birds need to eat large amounts of food. They have evolved many specialized organs and behaviors that help them feed in a variety of ways.

Figure 32–24 *The huge talons of this soaring eagle help the bird catch fish (bottom, left). Woodpeckers hear insects chewing beneath the bark of a tree. The beak of the woodpecker is strong enough to pierce the bark, revealing the bug beneath it (top, right). The featherless head of this vulture gives the bird a sinister look, but a lack of head feathers serves a useful function: A featherless head is easy to keep clean (bottom, right). Because vultures often put their head into the carcass of dead animals, cleanliness is important.*

Carnivorous birds, such as hawks and eagles, catch prey in razor-sharp talons and slice them to pieces with pointed beaks. Insect-eating birds do everything from picking insects off leaves and branches to catching them on the fly. Some insect eaters, such as woodpeckers, have a complex set of adaptations for drilling into wood and pulling out the insects that live there. Pollen and nectar feeders, such as hummingbirds, have long, probing beaks with which they reach deep into flowers. Their tongues are often equipped with a brushlike structure at the tip for lapping up nectar and fruit juices. Fruit-eating and seed-eating birds may have short, stout beaks or long, sharp ones, depending on the fruits or seeds they commonly eat. Filter feeders such as ducks and flamingoes have broad beaks with strainers built into the upper and side parts of the bill. These birds sift through murky water to filter out plankton a mouthful at a time.

The digestive system of birds, much like that of reptiles, shows specializations for carnivorous and herbivorous diets. Many birds have organs called **crop** and **gizzard**. The crop is an enlarged area of the esophagus, where food can be stored and moistened before it enters the stomach. In some species, the crop stores food that is later regurgitated for feeding to a bird's young. In still other species, the crop actually produces food that is fed to young chicks.

The gizzard is a specialized muscular part of the stomach that often contains small bits of gravel swallowed by a bird. The muscular walls grind the gravel and food together, thus crushing food particles and making them easier to digest. Both a crop and a gizzard are highly developed structures in seed-eating birds.

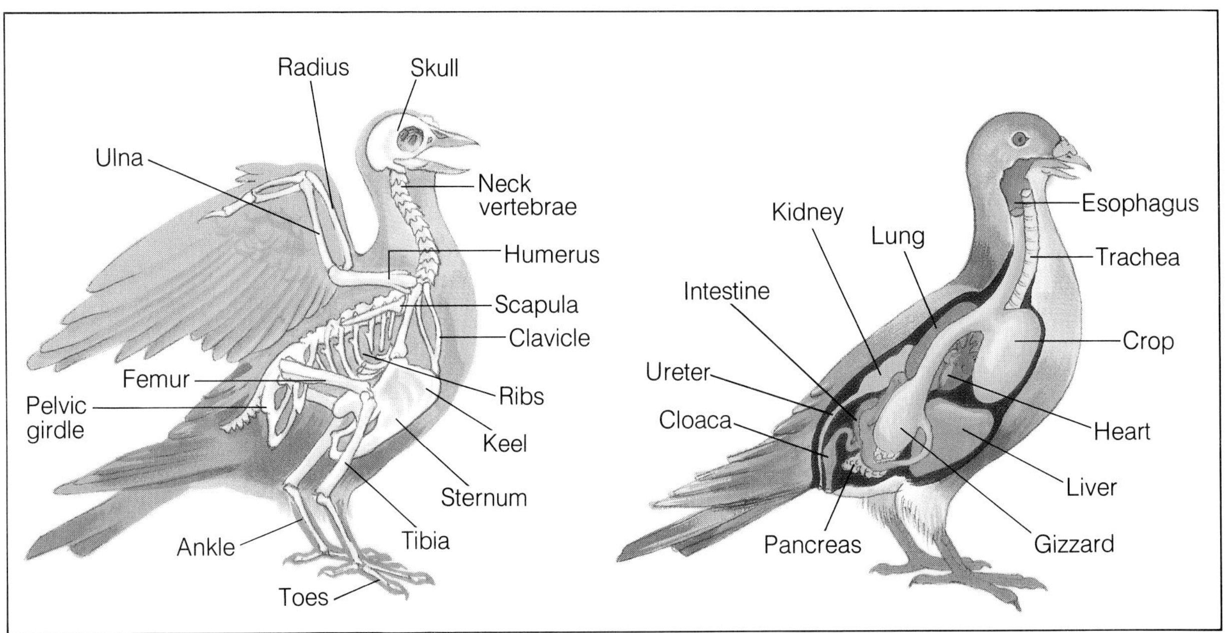

Figure 32–25 *The internal organs of a pigeon are shown here. You might be surprised to learn that there are fewer bones in the long neck of a giraffe than there are in the neck of a bird.*

RESPIRATION The respiratory system of birds is extremely efficient at taking in oxygen and eliminating carbon dioxide. This fact should not surprise you, as the high metabolic rate of birds demands an efficient gas exchange system.

The reason for this efficiency is that bird lungs are connected at both the anterior and posterior to large **air sacs** in the body cavity and bones. When a bird inhales, air travels through passageways that lead into the lungs. Some of this air remains in the lungs, where gas exchange occurs. Most of the air, however, goes through the lungs into posterior air sacs. When a bird exhales, air from the posterior air sacs passes into the lungs for gas exchange. Thus birds are able to remove oxygen from air when they inhale as well as when they exhale. For this reason, gas exchange in birds is more efficient than in other animals. The air sacs serve an additional function. They make a bird's body more buoyant, allowing the bird to fly more easily.

INTERNAL TRANSPORT Birds have a four-chambered heart and two separate circulatory loops. One half of the heart receives oxygen-poor blood from the body and pumps this blood to the lungs. Oxygen-rich blood returns to the other side of the heart to be pumped throughout the rest of the body. This dual-loop system ensures that oxygen collected by the lungs is distributed with maximum efficiency to the tissues that need it. To keep blood moving rapidly, a bird's heart beats quickly—from 150 to more than 1000 beats per minute.

EXCRETION Birds eliminate nitrogenous wastes by filtering them from the blood in the kidneys. Urine, which contains wastes in the form of uric acid, flows to the cloaca through the ureters. Most water is reabsorbed in the cloaca, leaving uric acid crystals in a white pastelike form. These crystals are the familiar "bird droppings."

Bird species that live far from shore or on small islands surrounded by sea water have no source of fresh water. Their diets contain larger amounts of salt than they need. For this reason, many of these species have evolved special salt glands near their eyes. These salt glands work like an extra pair of kidneys, except they specialize in excreting salt.

RESPONSE Despite the derogatory term "bird brain," birds are quite intelligent animals. The bird cerebrum, which controls such behaviors as flying, nest building, care of young, courtship, and mating, is quite large. The cerebellum is also well-developed, as might be expected in an animal in need of precisely coordinated movement. The medulla and spinal cord are much like those of reptiles.

Birds have extraordinarily well-developed eyes. Their excellent eyesight is reflected in a pair of sizable optic lobes in the brain. Birds see color very well—in many cases, better than

Figure 32–26 *The huge forward-facing eyes of an owl help this great bird hunt at night. Its eyes are able to spot a tiny mouse foraging among the leaves on the dark floor of a forest.*

Figure 32–27 *Birds have a unique respiratory system. Air sacs allow a bird to exchange oxygen and carbon dioxide when it inhales and when it exhales. The air sacs also make birds more buoyant.*

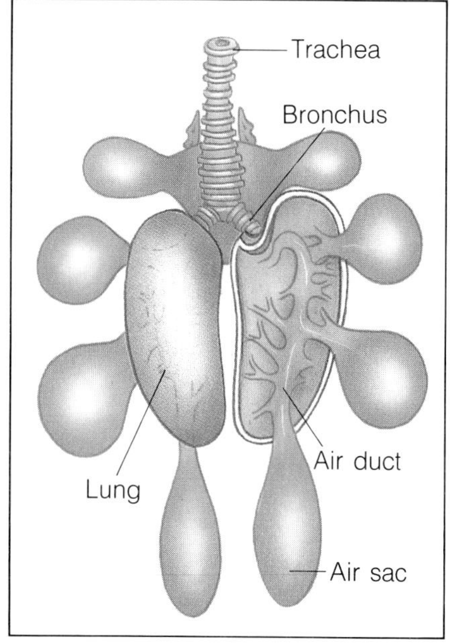

humans. Predatory birds such as hawks and eagles flying high in the air can spot mice on the ground with sight far keener than ours. The senses of taste and smell, however, are not well-developed. The olfactory lobes in a bird's brain are quite small.

Although birds lack external ears, they have ear openings in their head. Many bird species can hear quite well. For example, owls have an extremely acute sense of hearing that they use to find prey at night. Owls can so accurately hear mice crawling through dead leaves that they can swoop down and catch them in total darkness. Many migratory birds can hear the pounding of waves on the shore even when they are many kilometers away.

Some migratory birds use a magnetic sense to navigate. This magnetic sense, located somewhere in the head, operates like a built-in compass, responding to the Earth's magnetic field. Many other migratory birds use a combination of keen eyesight, instinct, and a built-in clock to navigate by the sun and stars.

MOVEMENT The many and diverse species of birds travel through different environments with wings, bodies, legs, and feet adapted for various types of locomotion. Some of the most impressive adaptations in birds involve flight. There are many variations in bird wings, depending on whether the animals soar like eagles, flap their wings steadily as robins do, or hover in place like hummingbirds.

Although the bones in a bird's wing are homologous to the bones in a human's arms, they have changed shape drastically to serve in flight. In flying birds, many large bones are nearly hollow. Hollow bones are not weak, however, because they are strengthened by internal struts similar to those used in the framework of tall buildings and bridges. The air sacs used in respiration extend inside certain bones, making the bones lighter. These air sacs also seem to help "air-condition" a bird's body by getting rid of excess heat generated by the flight muscles. Flying birds have other adaptations that decrease the weight they carry. One example is the shrinking in size of the sex organs during the time the birds are not breeding. As the birds prepare to mate, ovaries and testes grow larger until they reach functioning size.

To power the downward wing stroke necessary for flight, birds have large chest muscles. These muscles attach to a long keel that runs down the front of an enlarged breastbone, or sternum. The sternum, in turn, is firmly attached to the rib cage. In strong flying birds such as pigeons, the chest muscles may account for as much as 30 percent of the animal's mass.

Figure 32–28 *This roadrunner comes by its name honestly. It can often be seen running along roads and highways in search of the small snakes and lizards that are a main part of its diet.*

Many birds use their flying ability to migrate, or travel long distances, between summer breeding grounds in the North and winter resting grounds in the South or the tropics. You might be surprised to learn that many of the birds common to North American summers spend their winters in cozy tropical forests side by side with parrots and other exotic species.

A number of birds, however, have lost the ability to fly. Some species, such as ostriches, spend their time walking or running on a powerful pair of hind legs. Their feet usually have three strong toes that make contact with the ground. Their wings are usually much reduced in size and are incapable of lifting them off the ground. These birds can get quite large, as they have no need to minimize their mass. Still other birds have given up flying in favor of swimming. Penguins are a familiar example. Their wings, legs, and feet are so reduced in size that they look quite comical on land. In water, however, their feet and wings are powerful flippers that enable them to "fly" through the water.

REPRODUCTION The reproductive system of birds is similar to that of reptiles. Both male and female reproductive tracts open into the cloaca. In many female birds, only one side of the reproductive tract develops, apparently to minimize body weight. The single functioning ovary, however, is sufficient to provide enough eggs. Male birds have no external reproductive organs. Instead, mating birds press the lips of their cloacas close together to transfer sperm from male to female.

Although bird eggs have hard outside shells, their internal structure and membranes are similar to those of reptiles. Most birds incubate their eggs until the eggs hatch. The time between laying and hatching varies among species from 13 days

Figure 32–29 *In birds, sperm produced by males and eggs produced by females pass through the cloaca. An egg is fertilized before the shell is formed around it.*

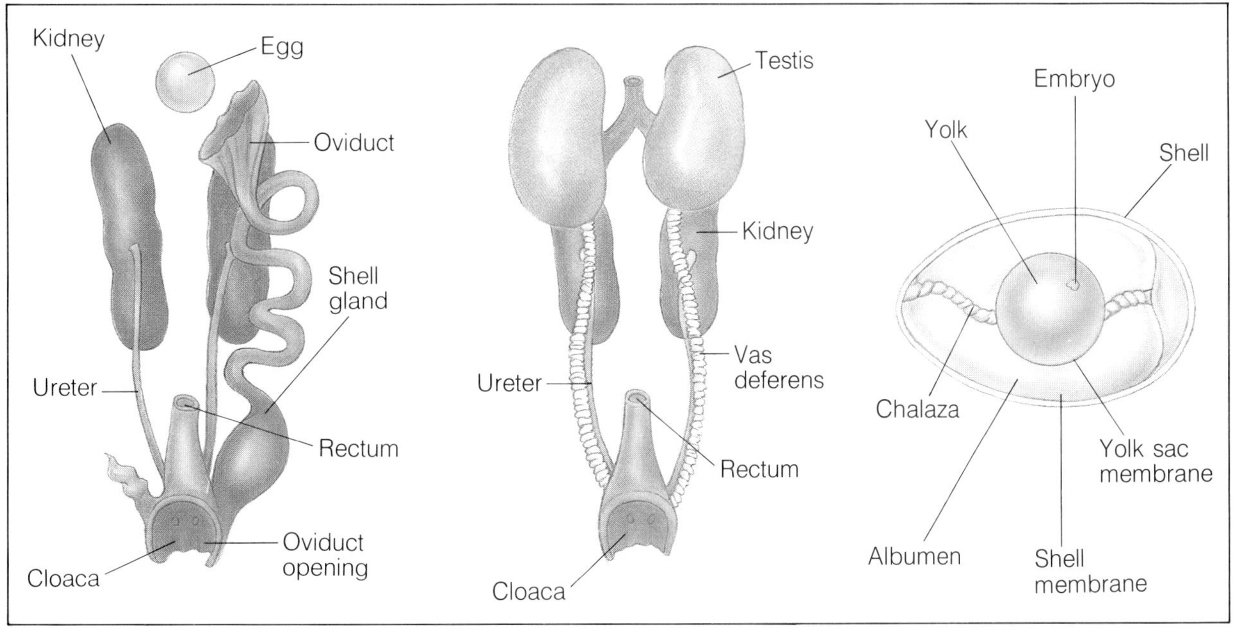

to more than 50 days. (The incubation period for chickens is usually about 20 to 22 days.) When a chick is ready to hatch, it uses a small egg tooth on its bill to make a hole in the shell. After much pushing, poking, and prodding by the chick, the eggshell breaks open. After it hatches, the exhausted bird collapses for a while and allows its feathers to dry.

Some birds, such as chickens and ducks, are able to take care of themselves as soon as they hatch. Within hours or a day, they walk on their own and feed themselves. They stay close to their mother for protection, but she rarely feeds them. Other newly hatched birds, such as robins and sparrows, are blind and totally helpless when they hatch. For days or even weeks, they sit in the nest with mouth wide open, screaming for food. Both male and female parents are kept busy providing food for their hungry offspring.

Birds have fascinating courtship and mating behaviors. Some species, such as swans, mate for life. Others pair up only briefly to mate. In such cases, the female wanders off by herself after fertilization to nest and lay her eggs. The male, however, may continue to mate with many other females. In species such as peacocks, the males use brightly colored feathers to attract females and warn off other males during the breeding season. Male canaries and similar species sing to attract females and keep other males out of their territory.

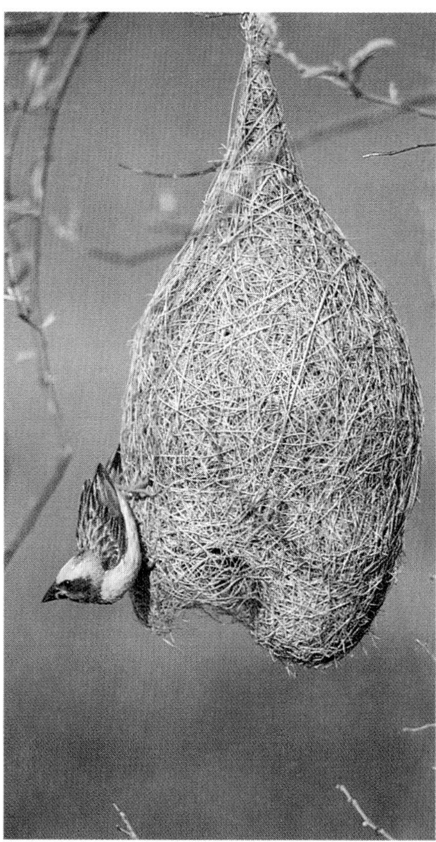

Figure 32–30 *Nests are supreme examples of the weavers' art. Birds often make complex nests of straw and other plant materials in which they lay their eggs and raise their young (left and right). Some birds, like the barn swallow, make their nest of mud, which they often attach to a building (center).*

How Birds Fit into the World

Imagine how dull a walk in the country would be without birds in the woods. No chirping. No singing. No graceful forms with brightly colored feathers. Humans the world over have always admired birds for their beauty and their powers of flight. But birds' contributions go far beyond their beauty.

In the course of a long evolutionary relationship with flowering plants, many bird species have come to serve vital functions in fields and forests. Hummingbirds serve as pollinators for a number of temperate and tropical plants. Fruit-eating birds disperse plant seeds when the seeds pass through their digestive tract unharmed.

Birds eat extraordinary numbers of insects. In some parts of the United States, chimney swifts begin their daily hunt for food at twilight. They zoom through the air, flitting back and forth, eating thousands of night-flying mosquitoes. Birds also eat caterpillars. Many bird species nest in the tundra, where huge insect "blooms" occur every spring at about the time baby birds hatch. The insect bloom, coming at hatching time, makes it easy for adult birds to find enough food for their young.

Humans use birds for many purposes. People in cold climates discovered long ago that in addition to being soft and comfortable, down feathers are good insulators. Down feathers are frequently used in making comforters and jackets. Many birds are favorite foods the world over, and raising them is part of the economy in many countries. With its low fat content, bird meat is a healthful source of protein in a balanced human diet. Birds such as chickens and turkeys have been specially bred for their meat. Because domestic strains of chickens and turkeys do not fly, their chest muscles are seldom used, making this part of the bird the juicy and tender "white meat." The leg and thigh muscles of these birds, used constantly for walking and running, are the "dark meat."

Figure 32–31 *This yellow warbler is feeding a group of hungry mouths. Because baby birds do not move from the nest, they use most of the nutrients in their food to grow.*

32–3 SECTION REVIEW

1. What are four characteristics of modern birds?
2. Describe the three different types of bird feathers.
3. In what two ways are a bird's bones adapted for flight?
4. How is a bird's respiratory system adapted to its high metabolic rate?
5. Penguin bones are not hollow like those of other birds. What is a logical explanation for this?
6. In what three ways would life on Earth be different if there were no birds?

LABORATORY INVESTIGATION

OBSERVING TERRESTRIAL ADAPTATIONS OF A CHICKEN EGG

PROBLEM

How are birds adapted to reproduction on land?

MATERIALS *(per group)*

400-mL beaker	petri dish
chicken egg (raw)	dissecting needle
hot plate	tongs

PROCEDURE

1. Hold a raw chicken egg in the palm of your hand. Gently close your fingers around the egg. Begin to squeeze the egg slowly, increasing the pressure until you are squeezing quite firmly. Note how much force the egg can withstand.
2. Gently shake the egg back and forth in your hand. Note whether you feel anything moving inside the egg.
3. Place the egg in the 400-mL beaker. Add enough water to barely cover the egg. Heat the water slowly on a hot plate just enough to make the water quite warm but still comfortable to the touch. **CAUTION:** *Do not touch the surface of the hot plate.* Watch the blunt end of the egg to see if tiny bubbles of air escape from the shell. Use the tongs to gently remove the egg from the beaker.
4. Gently crack open the egg over a petri dish. Carefully pour the contents of the egg into the petri dish.
5. Examine the structure and texture of the shell. Look in the blunt end of the shell. Locate the membrane and the air space.
6. Examine the contents of the egg in the petri dish. Refer to Figure 32-29 on page 729 as you work. The germinal disk is a small white spot on the top of the yolk. This is the spot where fertilization and the development of the embryo occur.
7. Find the whitish strands attached to both sides of the yolk. These are the chalazas. When the egg is intact, the chalazas stretch from the yolk to the membrane located just beneath the shell. The chalazas twist when the egg rolls, keeping the germinal disk and the embryo at the top of the egg.
8. The clear fluid in the petri dish is the albumin. In an intact egg, the albumin completely fills the space between the yolk and the membrane beneath the shell.
9. The yolk is the yellow material. Note how the yolk appears to form a slightly flattened sphere. The yolk is surrounded by a membrane that helps it maintain its shape. Puncture the membrane surrounding the yolk with the dissecting needle. Observe what happens.

OBSERVATIONS

1. What happened when you squeezed the intact egg?
2. What did you observe when you shook the egg back and forth?
3. What did you observe when you heated the egg?
4. What are the characteristics of the egg shell?
5. What happened to the yolk when you pierced the membrane?

ANALYSIS AND CONCLUSIONS

1. What characteristics of the egg shell help the egg survive on land?
2. Based on your observations, how does a developing chick get oxygen?
3. Using knowledge of the structures you observed in the egg, explain what happened when you shook the egg back and forth.
4. For what purpose do people use egg yolks? For what purpose do developing chicks use egg yolks?
5. How are birds' eggs adapted to reproduction on land?

SUMMARIZING THE CONCEPTS

The key concepts in each section of this chapter are listed below to help you review the chapter content. Make sure you understand each concept and its relationship to other concepts and to the theme of this chapter.

32–1 Reptiles

- Reptiles are vertebrate animals that have adaptations such as amniotic eggs, dry skin, and efficient respiratory and circulatory systems that enable them to live their entire lives out of water.
- Reptiles eliminate liquid wastes in the form of urine produced in their kidneys. Many reptiles conserve water by excreting nitrogen-containing wastes in the form of uric acid.
- The tuatara retains many features of the ancient reptiles from which it evolved.
- All lizards have legs, clawed toes, external ears, and movable eyelids. Snakes are lizards that have lost both pairs of legs during their evolution. Crocodilians live in tropic climates and are among the largest living reptiles. Turtles and tortoises are reptiles that have a shell consisting of a carapace and a plastron.

32–2 The Evolution of Temperature Control

- Control of body temperature is important for animals, particularly in habitats where temperature varies widely.
- Modern reptiles are ectotherms; they obtain heat from outside their body. Birds and mammals are endotherms.

32–3 Birds

- Birds are endothermic reptilelike animals with an outer covering of feathers, two legs used for walking or perching, and front limbs modified into wings. Fossils confirm the evolution of birds from ancient reptiles.
- Bird feathers are generally of three different types: contour, down, and powder.
- Because of their high metabolic rates, birds need to eat large amounts of food. The digestive system of many birds contains a crop and a gizzard. Birds eliminate nitrogenous wastes in the form of uric acid.
- Birds have an extremely efficient respiratory system because of the presence of air sacs. These sacs also make a bird's body more buoyant. Birds have a four-chambered heart and two circulatory loops.

REVIEWING KEY TERMS

Vocabulary terms are important to your understanding of biology. The key terms listed below are those you should be especially familiar with. Review these terms and their meanings. Then use each term in a complete sentence. If you are not sure of a term's meaning, return to the appropriate section and review its definition.

32–1 Reptiles

reptile
amniotic egg
transition fossil
internal fertilization
oviparous
ovoviviparous
carapace
plastron

32–2 The Evolution of Temperature Control

ectotherm
endotherm

32–3 Birds

bird
contour feather
down feather
powder feather
crop
gizzard
air sac

CHAPTER REVIEW

CONTENT REVIEW

Multiple Choice

Choose the letter of the answer that best completes each statement.

1. Reptiles that lay eggs that develop outside the mother's body are
   a. extinct. c. oviparous.
   b. ovoviviparous. d. externally fertilized.
2. A reptile that flips out its sticky tongue to catch insects is the
   a. chameleon. c. iguana.
   b. monitor lizard. d. crocodile.
3. A type of grooming in which a bird pulls its feathers through its beak is called
   a. shedding. c. preening.
   b. contouring. d. perching.
4. An animal that generates most of its heat inside its body is a (an)
   a. ectotherm. c. reptile.
   b. endotherm. d. tuatara.
5. The pineal gland of the tuatara is sensitive to
   a. touch. c. heat.
   b. vibration. d. light.
6. The single most important characteristic that separates birds from reptiles is
   a. endothermy. c. two legs.
   b. feathers. d. wings.
7. Feathers on the wings and tail of a bird that provide a lifting force and balance are
   a. down feathers. c. flight feathers.
   b. barbs. d. powder feathers.
8. The muscular part of a bird's stomach that contains gravel used to crush food particles is the
   a. cloaca. c. crop.
   b. barbule. d. gizzard.

True or False

Determine whether each statement is true or false. If it is true, write "true." If it is false, change the underlined word or words to make the statement true.

1. Reptilian eggs are <u>amniotic eggs</u> that are named after one of the membranes that surround the embryo.
2. The changes in the Earth's surface and climate during the Permian Period made life difficult for <u>reptiles</u>.
3. A mass extinction of dinosaurs and many other animals and plants occurred at the end of the <u>Triassic Period</u>.
4. <u>Birds</u> warm up by basking in the sun.
5. <u>Endothermy</u> is a way of conserving energy in warm climates.
6. <u>Down feathers</u> are soft, fluffy feathers that trap warm air close to a bird's body.
7. The <u>air sacs</u> help make a bird more buoyant during flight.
8. Some migratory birds have a <u>magnetic sense</u> that helps them find their way.

Word Relationships

Replace the underlined definition with the correct vocabulary word.

1. Birds have <u>large feathers that cover their bodies and wings.</u>
2. The digestive system of a bird contains a <u>structure where food is moistened before it enters the stomach.</u>
3. <u>Vertebrate animals that have lungs, scaly skin, and amniotic eggs</u> have evolved from amphibians.
4. When a bird inhales, most of the air goes through the lungs into <u>posterior structures</u> that also make a bird's body more buoyant.

CONCEPT MASTERY

Use your understanding of the concepts developed in the chapter to answer each of the following in a brief paragraph.

1. What are three adaptations that enable reptiles to live entirely out of water?
2. Discuss two possible explanations for the mass extinction that occurred about 65 million years ago.
3. Identify the three main types of bird feathers.
4. Explain why the excretion of nitrogen-containing wastes in the form of uric acid is another successful adaptation to a land environment shown by reptiles.
5. Describe the special adaptations that have developed in bird species that have no source of fresh water.

CRITICAL AND CREATIVE THINKING

Discuss each of the following in a brief paragraph.

1. **Applying concepts** Reptiles developed efficient respiratory systems after they evolved from water-dependent amphibians. They then developed a more efficient circulatory system. Explain why these systems evolved in this order.
2. **Relating cause and effect** Most of the various species of modern reptiles have changed little since their great period of adaptive radiation about 200 million years ago. Explain why drastic changes have not occurred in reptiles since then.
3. **Making predictions** Suppose you came upon the shore of a tropical island. Predict the method of regulating body temperature that you would expect to find in the animals that live on the island. Explain how this method is an adaptation to this environment.
4. **Drawing conclusions** You are given the description of a certain animal and told that it is endothermic, has two legs, and modified front limbs. You are also told that it has a four-chambered heart, two separate circulatory loops, and a well-developed cerebellum. Describe at least three more characteristics you can add to this description.
5. **Making comparisons** Compare and contrast the characteristics of reptiles with those of amphibians. Explain how each is suited to a particular environment.
6. **Summarizing information** Discuss some of the characteristics of birds that enable them to fly.

7. **Using the writing process** Pretend you are a visitor to Earth from the fictitious planet Chillee. Your ancestors visited planet Earth about 300 million years ago and then again about 55 million years ago. Describe the changes that would have occurred on Earth from the details recorded in the logbook your people maintained on their voyages.

CHAPTER 33

Mammals

Fleet of foot and mind, mammals began to evolve while dinosaurs roamed the Earth. Today, mammals, such as the elephant, rule the Earth they inherited from their now extinct relatives, the mastodons.

Although they continued to evolve, early mammals lived for 150 million years in the shadow of the dinosaurs and other reptiles. Then at the end of the Cretaceous Period, Earth's climate changed dramatically. The Rocky Mountains and other major mountain ranges formed, creating a barrier that blocked the flow of oceanic air over large land areas. Inland seas on the side of the mountain ranges away from the ocean dried up. All over the world, climates became more variable.

The mammals, by now expert endotherms, were able to survive the cooler temperatures and variable climates. So as the dinosaurs vanished, the great mammalian radiation began. What made these mammals so successful? And why have so many diverse kinds survived? These questions will be answered in this chapter.

CHAPTER OUTLINE

33–1 Mammals

Section Objectives

- Describe the characteristics of mammals.
- Discuss the importance of endothermy in the evolution of mammals.

The group of animals called mammals includes many diverse species that vary greatly in appearance. Mammals range in size from a tiny mouse nibbling its way along a corn cob several times its size to a huge elephant uprooting a gigantic tree with its tusks and trunk. Mammals can be found flying in the air, running along the ground, and swimming in the sea. Although they differ in size and habits, however, all members of the class Mammalia share certain characteristics.

What Is a Mammal?

Mammals are endothermic animals, which means they are able to generate substantial body heat internally. Most species are experts at maintaining a constant body temperature. Mammals use various combinations of fur, hair, and subcutaneous fat to conserve body heat. Subcutaneous fat is fat located under the skin (*sub-* means under; *cutaneous* refers to the skin). (We may not always appreciate having a layer of subcutaneous fat, but it is there for a reason!) Many mammals also have sweat glands that help cool the body. Sweat produced by sweat glands evaporates from the skin, lowering body temperature whenever necessary.

Figure 33–1 *One characteristic that unites all mammals is hair. This brown bear and her cubs can sleep through winter's cold insulated by their thick coats and a layer of fat beneath their skin.*

Figure 33–2 All female mammals nurse their young, feeding them milk they produce in mammary glands. These glands are the source of the class Mammalia's name.

Figure 33–3 Be they lions or whales, all mammals breathe air. Breathing is easy for land mammals, but sea mammals must return to the surface to breathe.

With the exception of several very primitive species that lay eggs, all mammals are viviparous. This means that young mammals develop within the mother for a time and then are born alive. Female mammals have **mammary glands**, which produce milk to nourish the young for some time after they are born. **Mammary glands, which give mammals their name, are probably the most important characteristic that scientists use to include an animal in class Mammalia.**

Mammals have several kinds of teeth. Combined with their jaws, the teeth of mammals bite, chew, and grind food efficiently. The teeth and jaws of various mammalian species take many forms, depending upon the species' feeding habits. Scientists use the teeth of a mammal to classify it in one of the mammalian orders. You will read about these different orders in the next section.

Mammals have well-developed breathing muscles, including a diaphragm that separates the chest cavity from the abdomen. The diaphragm, along with other muscles in the chest, pulls air into the lungs by expanding the chest cavity. Mammals have a four-chambered heart consisting of two atria and two ventricles. Each side of the heart, consisting of an atrium and a ventricle, is part of a completely separate circulatory circuit. One circuit moves blood to and from the lungs, and the other circuit moves blood to and from cells in the rest of the body. The two circuits make up an efficient system for the transfer of gases with the environment and for the delivery and removal of gases and other materials to and from body cells.

Evolution of Mammals

The first mammals were very small and, according to fossil evidence, resembled species of tree shrews alive today. They were probably nocturnal, which means they were active primarily at night. Because they were endotherms, they did not need to obtain heat from the environment in order to remain active—thus making them able to function well after dark. The ectothermic dinosaurs, on the other hand, would probably have been rather sluggish after sunset. (Even today there are very few nocturnal lizards, and those that do exist live only in the tropics.)

By the end of the Cretaceous Period, the mammals had split into three groups. The first group, and the most primitive, is the **monotremes**. Today only six species of monotremes survive. The most familiar species are the duckbill platypus and the spiny anteater.

The second group, the **marsupials**, include opossums, kangaroos, wombats, and koala bears. Each of these species has a pouch in which its young live for a time.

The third group, the **placental mammals**, include the mammals you are most familiar with. Mice, cats, whales, elephants, and humans are just a few examples of placental mammals.

Because the fossil record of the earliest mammals is incomplete, it is hard to say precisely where and when each of these three groups appeared. However, we do know that placental mammals experienced a period of adaptive radiation in North America and Europe. Marsupials experienced a period of adaptive radiation in Australia, South America, and Antarctica (which was a good deal warmer then than it is today).

Figure 33–4 *The fossil record shows that the first mammals resembled this tree shrew. Tree shrews are omnivores; they eat both plants and animals.*

Form and Function in Mammals

Mammals have limbs and organ systems that have evolved many shapes to serve many functions in different environments. The specialized adaptations are far too numerous to explore here, so we shall mention only a few of the more interesting ones.

FEEDING Carnivorous mammals, such as cats and dogs, have strong, sharp teeth called incisors and canines that are used for biting and ripping flesh from their prey. Some extinct carnivores, such as saber-toothed cats, had enormous canines. Even the molars of carnivorous mammals are sharp, for they are used to slice meat into small pieces to speed digestion. Carnivores use an up-and-down chopping movement of their jaws to chew their food.

The behavioral and physical characteristics of many mammals allow them to capture prey. For example, some carnivores have sharp claws on their feet with which they grab onto prey. Their bodies are built to produce the quick bursts of speed

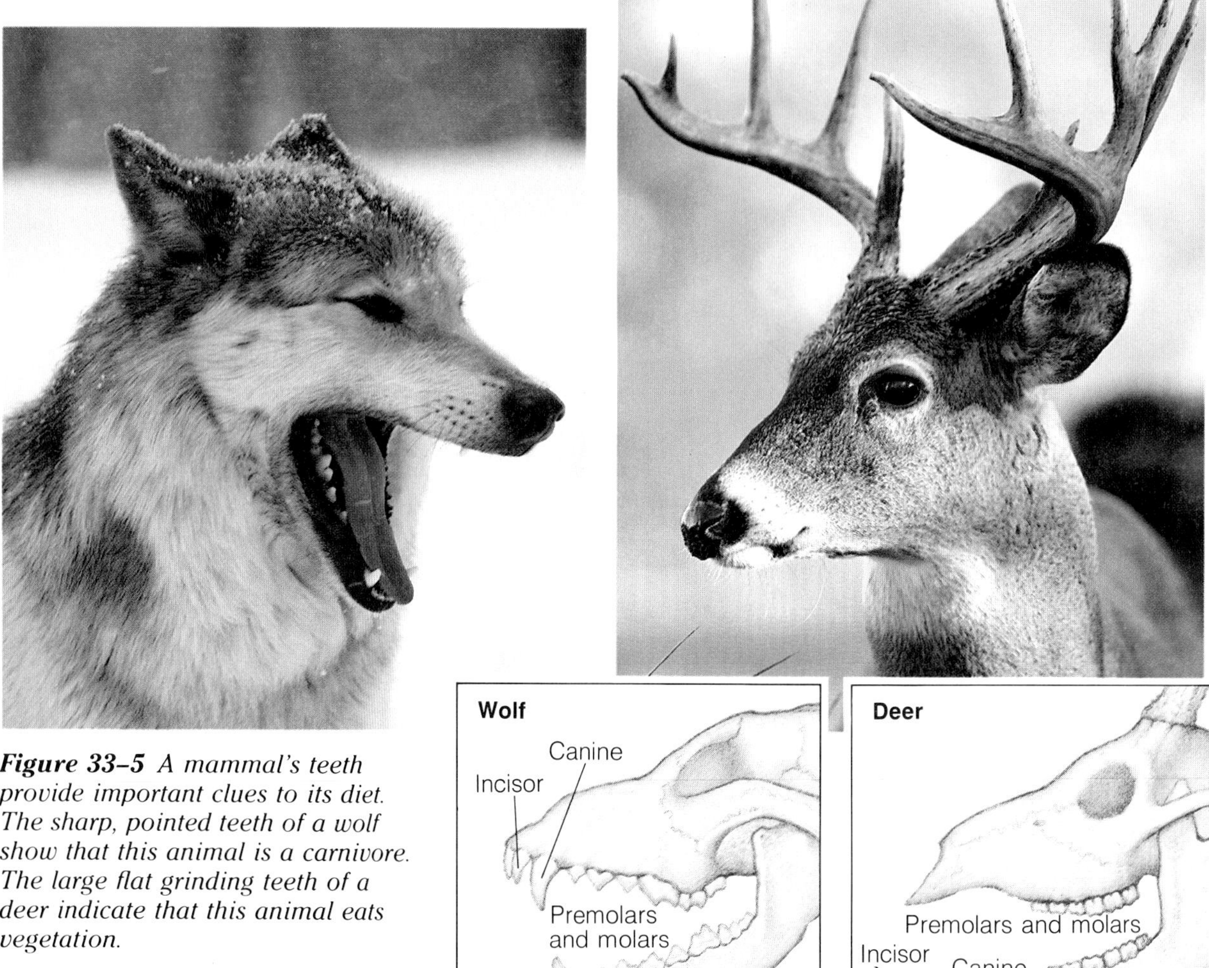

Figure 33–5 *A mammal's teeth provide important clues to its diet. The sharp, pointed teeth of a wolf show that this animal is a carnivore. The large flat grinding teeth of a deer indicate that this animal eats vegetation.*

they need to chase prey. Fish-eating mammals such as dolphins and killer whales have many sharp teeth to grasp and hold onto their slippery prey. Some whales and dolphins can produce loud bursts of sound that may stun nearby fish, thus making it easier for the fish to be caught.

Herbivorous mammals, from cows to giraffes, eat plants that are tough and require thorough chewing in order to be digested. Herbivorous animals have evolved strong lips and flat-edged incisors that grasp and tear this tough vegetation. They chew by moving their jaws from side to side, using flattened molars to grind the plant food into a pulp.

Despite this efficient chewing, the cellulose that most plant tissues contain is impossible for mammals to digest on their own. The vertebrate digestive system has never evolved the ability to produce enzymes that digest cellulose. To help in the digestion of plant material, many grazing mammals have a chamber in their digestive tract called the **rumen**, in which newly swallowed plant food is stored and processed for a time.

The rumen contains thriving colonies of symbiotic bacteria that produce enzymes needed to break down cellulose. After a certain amount of time, the mammal regurgitates the plant food from the rumen into its mouth. There the partially digested food is again chewed and mixed with saliva. This is the process being described when mammals such as cows, goats, and deer "chew their cud." The second time the food is swallowed, it moves through the rest of the digestive tract, where digestion is completed and nutrients are absorbed.

Some herbivores, such as rabbits, lack a rumen but have a large dead-end sac, or **cecum** (SEE-kuhm), forming part of their intestines. Many of the same kinds of microorganisms that digest cellulose are found in the cecum. The ancestors of modern humans had a cecum, but over time it has shrunk to the small, sometimes troublesome pouch we call the appendix.

Various other mammals have strange ways of harvesting food. Blood drinkers, such as vampire bats, have razor-sharp incisors that easily slice through the skin of larger mammals. Vampire bats also have a chemical in their saliva that keeps blood from clotting as they feed on it. Filter feeders, such as the giant blue whale, have teeth that do not resemble those we are familiar with. Their teeth are modified into huge stiffened plates called baleen, which act like giant filters. Baleen whales swallow huge mouthfuls of water that contains zooplankton and small fishes. They then force the water out of their mouth through the baleen plates, which strain out small organisms. When all the water is completely expelled, the whale swallows the small organisms that remain in its mouth.

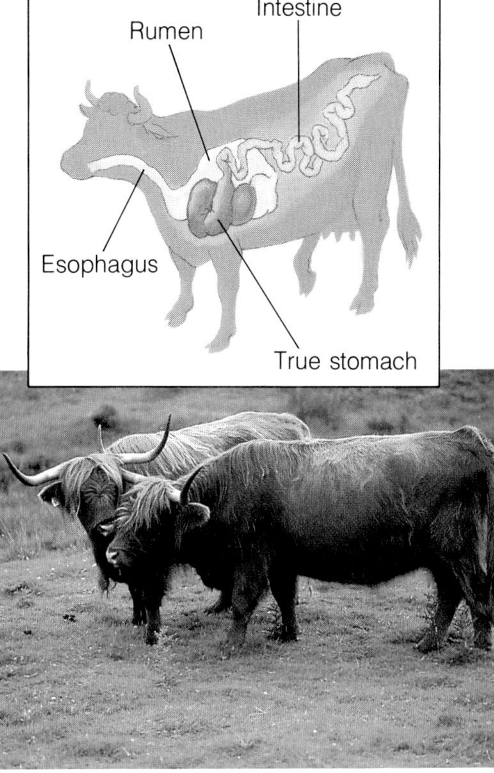

Figure 33–6 *It is difficult for a mammal to digest plant material. A cow has several stomachs through which its food must pass in order for the nutrients it needs to be extracted.*

RESPIRATION All mammals, even sea mammals, use lungs powered by two sets of muscles. Chest muscles pull air in and push air out by moving the ribs up and down to increase and decrease the size of the chest cavity. When the large muscle known as the diaphragm contracts, it pulls the bottom of the chest cavity downward, further increasing the cavity size and causing air to rush into the lungs. Many mammals are able to use exhaled air to vibrate their vocal cords and produce a variety of sounds, such as a roar, a bark, or even a song.

INTERNAL TRANSPORT The mammalian circulatory system is a wondrous arrangement of pumps and blood vessels. The main pump, a four-chambered heart, sends deoxygenated blood to the lungs. After it leaves the lungs, the now oxygenated blood returns to the heart and is pumped throughout the rest of the body via blood vessels. The two separate circuits—one to and from the lungs, the other to and from the rest of the body— efficiently transport gases and nutrients to every cell of a mammal's body.

EXCRETION Mammals have the most highly developed kidneys of all vertebrates, an important feature since the kidneys control the composition of all body fluids. Mammalian

Figure 33–7 This desert fox survives in areas that have scant supplies of water. Mammals that live in desert regions have very efficient kidneys. Thus their urine contains little water.

kidneys extract nitrogenous wastes from the blood in the form of urea. Urea, water, and other wastes form urine. From the kidneys, urine flows to a urinary bladder, where it is stored until it is eliminated. But mammalian kidneys do more than just filter urea from blood. Under the control of several hormones, the kidneys can excrete excess liquid or retain it. They can also retain salts, sugars, and other compounds the body cannot afford to lose. Because they are so efficient at controlling the composition and levels of body fluids, the mammalian kidneys have allowed mammals to live in many habitats they could not otherwise have inhabited (such as deserts).

RESPONSE Mammals have the most highly developed brains of any animals. The brain consists of three parts: cerebrum, cerebellum, and medulla. The large mammalian cerebrum makes such complicated behaviors as thinking, learning, and even understanding a textbook possible. The cerebellum coordinates movements such as the flight of a bat, the dive of a dolphin, and the wondrous somersaults of a human gymnast. The medulla regulates body functions such as breathing and heart rate, which are not under conscious control.

Mammals depend on highly developed senses to provide themselves with information about their external environment. Certain mammal species have well-developed senses of sight, hearing, and smell.

Eyes vary a great deal from one mammal species to another. With the exception of apes, monkeys, and humans, most mammals do not see color well. Biologists believe this is because the first mammals were nocturnal. Monkeys and humans, however, are active during the day and have accurate color vision. Most Old World apes, such as chimpanzees and gorillas, seem to have color vision much like our own.

Although all mammalian ears are built on the same basic plan, they also vary a great deal in their abilities. For example, human ears are not very sensitive when compared with those

Figure 33–8 Compared with other animals, a mammal has a large brain. Each antelope, alert to danger, is processing a great deal of information about the environment in its brain. If there is real danger, a delay of a fraction of a second could mean that the antelope will not survive.

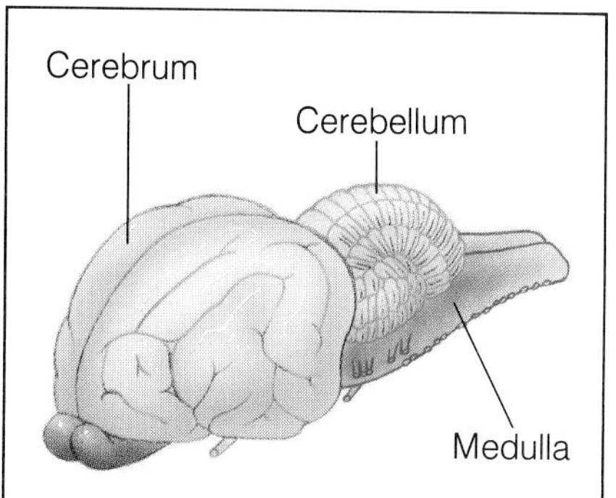

of dogs, cats, and bats—all of which can detect sounds of much higher frequencies than humans can. Other mammals, such as elephants, can hear sounds of much lower frequencies.

The senses of smell and taste are also often more highly developed in other mammals than in humans. You probably know that dogs and cats can easily identify people by recognizing their particular body odor. Some mammal species seem to use a combination of smell and hearing to obtain information they cannot get through their sight. For example, antelopes can detect the scent and sounds of a predator from afar.

More than any other animal group, mammals depend on complex behaviors for protection. Many herbivores are able to run long distances to escape a predator. When cornered, or when their young are threatened, some herbivores use horns and hooves to strike their attackers. Others band together in herds or groups and work to repel an attack by predators.

Figure 33–9 *This baby monkey swinging from a tree branch shows only some of the movements mammals are capable of. Its long tail is useful in maintaining balance as it moves through the trees.*

MOVEMENT From the four limbs they inherited from their ancestors, mammals have evolved different structures for movement. Running mammals such as horses and antelope can achieve great speeds on level ground. Climbing mammals such as monkeys have hands and feet with flexible digits that can grasp vines and branches. Some monkeys and other mammals also use a strong flexible tail as an additional hand for grasping branches. Flying mammals such as bats have arms modified to support flaps of skin that form wings. Aquatic mammals such as dolphins have arms modified into flippers, which they use to control their speed and direction in the water.

REPRODUCTION The three groups of mammals differ greatly in their methods of reproduction. These differences illustrate how mammals are linked with their reptilian ancestors

Figure 33–10 *A platypus is a strange animal indeed. A female platypus feeds milk to her young—but only after the young have hatched from eggs laid by the mother.*

Figure 33–11 The baby kangaroo, safely hitching a ride in its mother's pouch, views the world around it with amusement. If danger threatens, mother and baby can quickly hop away.

Figure 33–12 This orangutan mother will care for her baby for some time. Rarely setting foot on the ground, the baby clings tightly to its mother's fur.

through a series of stages in the evolution of reproductive techniques.

Egg-laying mammals, the monotremes, are the most primitive mammals and reproduce much like reptiles. Monotremes such as the duckbill platypus are oviparous. A female platypus lays eggs that are incubated outside the mother's body. Once the young hatch, however, they nurse on milk provided by the mother. Thus the platypus and its relatives show both reptilian and mammalian reproductive habits.

Marsupials are viviparous and bear their young alive. The fertilized egg grows into an embryo inside the mother's reproductive tract. The embryo is supplied with nourishment by a yolk sac on the egg. But because this yolk is not large enough to nourish the embryo through its entire developmental period, the embryo must leave its mother's womb very early. At such an early stage of development, the embryo is unable to survive alone. Instinctively, it crawls across its mother's fur into a pouch called the **marsupium** (mahr-SOO-pee-uhm). Inside the marsupium, the young quickly locates a nipple and grabs onto it with its jaws. It spends the next several months attached there, growing sufficiently large and independent so that it can leave the pouch.

The early stages of placental embryos are much like those of marsupials. But in placental mammals, the embryo's chorion, amnion, and allantois develop differently. Tissues from these membranes join with tissues from the mother's uterus to form an organ called the **placenta**. Nutrients, oxygen, carbon dioxide, and wastes are exchanged between embryo and mother through the placenta. The placenta allows the embryo to develop for a much longer time inside the mother. During this time the mother is free to move about and feed while still protecting the developing embryo. The time the embryo spends inside the uterus is called the gestation period. The gestation period of mammals ranges from a few weeks in mice and rats to as long as two years in elephants. The gestation period in humans is nine months.

After birth, most placental mammals provide their young with a period of care. The duration of this parental care varies among different species. For example, a newborn fawn is awkward and barely able to stand. Within a few hours, however, it can see well and walk around. Despite this, the mother protects its fawn and feeds it milk for some time. The young of mammals such as monkeys and humans are helpless at birth and for quite some time thereafter. These infants depend on their mother for food and protection, and they often spend several years growing up before they are able to live on their own. During the time infant and mother live together, the infant learns a great deal about its surroundings from its mother. Many biologists believe that this long learning period is one of the most important benefits of the prolonged childhood of many mammals. It may also be an important reason for the evolutionary success of these animals.

SCIENCE, TECHNOLOGY, AND SOCIETY **APPLICATION**

The Smallest Paleontologists

Many early mammals are known from their fossilized teeth. Because teeth are the hardest and most durable body part, they fossilize better than any other body part, including bones. As you might imagine, collecting teeth and bones from fossil animals not much bigger than mice is no easy job. Farish Jenkins of Harvard University, who has found many important early mammal fossils, must often search long and hard. Over kilometers of badlands in the Midwest, he and his research team choose rocks that seem likely to contain fossils. They pick these rocks apart with needles, cleaning the pieces with toothbrushes in order to expose tiny fossil teeth and bones.

Sometimes paleontologists enlist thousands of unusually tiny helpers for this tedious job. It just so happens that one ant species often dig large nests in places that are rich in early mammal fossils. As these ants tunnel, they uncover fossil teeth and sometimes entire jaws of early mammals. When the ants encounter such items, they treat them as they would anything that blocks their way—they dig them out and carry them to the surface. There, in a mound around the nest entrance, humans can sift through them easily!

Ants are remarkable excavators, moving material to the surface when they enlarge their underground living quarters. Sometimes they bring small fossils to the surface, making the job of paleontologists easier.

33–1 SECTION REVIEW

1. What are three important characteristics of all mammals?
2. What are two adaptations of mammals that enable them to live in many more different kinds of environments than reptiles do?
3. What changes occurred in the Earth's climate that finally allowed the mammalian adaptive radiation to occur?
4. In what three ways have well-developed senses contributed to the success of mammals?
5. How do the reproductive methods of monotremes, marsupials, and placental mammals differ? In what ways are they similar?
6. The big cats of Africa are known to sleep between kills. In fact, lions sleep up to 20 hours out of every 24! Large herbivores, on the other hand, seem to eat all the time. What characteristics of the foods eaten by these animals might be responsible for these differences in carnivore and herbivore behaviors?

Section Objectives

- Compare methods of mammalian reproduction.
- Identify the most important orders of placental mammals.
- Recognize the importance of mammals in the world.

33–2 Important Orders of Living Mammals

Scientists use several important characteristics to classify mammals. The structure of teeth and the number and kinds of bones in the head are two important features by which mammals are classified. But perhaps the most important characteristic used to classify mammals is the method of reproduction. As you have already learned, mammal species show three different methods of reproduction. Some mammals lay eggs. Some mammals give birth to young that are not well developed at birth and must therefore spend time developing in a special pouch in their mother's body. Some mammals—in fact, most—retain embryos within the mother's body, where the embryos grow and develop, nourished by the mother. At birth, these young are more well developed than the young of mammals that spend time in their mother's pouch.

Figure 33–13 *The echidna is known as the spiny anteater (top). Its spines protect it from enemies. Its long sticky tongue laps up the ants it eats. These baby opossums are hitching a ride on their mother's back, where they are safe (bottom). When their mother locates food, the babies climb off to eat.*

Monotremes

Monotremes, or egg-laying mammals, are very rare. In fact, only six species of monotremes exist today, living in isolated parts of Australia and New Guinea. You have already learned about the duckbill platypus, the most familiar monotreme. The spiny anteater, or echidna, is another monotreme. It has a jaw shaped like a bird's bill, strong clawed feet with which it can dig quickly, and long sharp spines among its body hairs.

Marsupials

Marsupials are pouched mammals. A number of fascinating marsupials, such as kangaroos and koala bears, are found in Australia. Kangaroos and their close relatives, the wallabies, are herbivores that feed primarily on range grasses. Koala bears spend most of their time in trees and eat only the leaves of eucalyptus trees.

Opossums are the only marsupials found in North America today. Active mostly at night, opossums spend the day sleeping in protected spots. These animals eat a variety of insects, birds, and small mammals. A newborn opossum is about the size of a bee. Just after birth, it uses its tiny hands and feet to grasp onto its mother's hair and crawl to the safety of her pouch.

In the past, many other marsupials lived in South America. These included many species similar in form to wolves, bears, camels, and moles (none of which are actually marsupials).

Placentals

Living placental mammals are placed in sixteen orders, most of which contain animals familiar to you. In addition to having different reproductive habits than marsupials, placental mammals also have slightly higher metabolic rates. Placental mammals are much more abundant today than their marsupial cousins. The most important orders of placental mammals are briefly described here.

ORDER INSECTIVORA This order, whose name means insect eaters, includes tree shrews, hedgehogs, shrews, and moles. Shrews, several of which are about the size of a mouse, have extremely high metabolic rates and must eat almost constantly to stay alive. Biologists believe that the first mammals looked and behaved much like certain modern tree shrews. Remember, however, that this does not mean that mammals evolved from tree shrews as we know them today. It simply means that living tree shrews have many characteristics of primitive mammals.

ORDER CHIROPTERA This order contains the many different species of bats, which in fact account for one quarter of all mammal species. Bats are closely related to insectivores, although different types of bats eat many different kinds of foods. Some bats eat only insects, whereas others eat only fruits. Still others, such as vampire bats, feed on the blood of other mammals. Many bats are active only at night. Night-flying bats use echolocation to help them navigate while in flight. By emitting high-pitched sounds that bounce off objects, the bats can calculate distances and determine locations of tiny insect prey. Some fruit-eating bats, like the giant flying foxes, feed during the day. Colonies of these bats sleep together in trees, hanging upside down and wrapping their wings around their body.

Figure 33–14 *Moles dig tunnels under ground (left). In the subterranean darkness, these animals eat the insect larvae that live in the soil. Bats are the only true flying mammals (right). They glide along, effortlessly flapping their delicate wings. Like moles, many species of bats also eat insects, which they catch in the air. The bats in this photograph, however, eat frogs.*

Figure 33–15 Common in certain parts of the United States, armadillos are in the order Edentata (top). The porcupine depends upon its many sharp quills for protection (center). One function of the huge ears of a rabbit is to give off excess body heat to the environment through the many blood vessels in these organs (bottom).

ORDER EDENTATA The name of this order means without teeth, although some of the mammals included here have small teeth. The edentates include such odd animals as sloths, anteaters, and armadillos. Sloths are South American animals that live most of their life hanging upside down in trees. Many sloths move so slowly that at times they scarcely seem alive. Anteaters have long tapered snouts and powerful front legs with sharp claws. They feed by ripping open ant nests and collecting the scurrying insects with a long and sticky tongue.

ORDER RODENTIA This order includes many amusing mammals, as well as many destructive ones. Mice, rats, squirrels, beavers, porcupines, and gophers are all rodents. Rodents have two long front teeth, which they use for chewing wood and other tough plant material. These two front teeth continue to grow during a rodent's life. The constant gnawing on tough plant material wears the teeth down. Most rodents are small and have a short gestation period. Rats and mice are very adaptable animals that eat a wide variety of foods. Long ago, both these rodents moved in with humans and have traveled with us all over the world.

ORDER LAGOMORPHA The familiar rabbits and hares comprise this order. In many ways, lagomorphs resemble rodents. They have sharp front teeth and eat plant material. Their gestation period is short, and the number of young they produce is high. Many of these animals compete with humans for food. Several species, such as jack rabbits and cottontails, are widely distributed across the United States.

ORDER CARNIVORA Carnivores are meat eaters. Many familiar animals—including cats, dogs, wolves, bears, weasels, hyenas, and seals—are in this order. Most are terrestrial, stalking and chasing their prey by running and pouncing, and then killing them with sharp teeth and claws. Carnivores such as seals and walruses had ancestors that at one time lived on land, but these mammals have since returned to the ocean, where they feed on fish, mollusks, and sea birds. Although quite agile in water, aquatic carnivores return to land to breed and bear their young. On land these animals move with difficulty. Their appendages, so useful in the sea, are not very effective at moving their body from place to place on land.

ORDER CETACEA This order contains truly aquatic mammals: whales, dolphins, and porpoises. Although they still breathe air, these mammals have lungs and a circulatory system designed to permit long, deep dives. Their thick layer of subcutaneous fat, called blubber, keeps them warm in even the coldest water. Cetaceans have lost both their external ears and their hind legs. These animals mate and bear their young in the water. On land, they are completely helpless. All cetaceans are carnivores. A few, such as the great blue whale and the humpback whale, are filter feeders and live by eating plankton.

Figure 33–16 Carnivores such as the walrus (left) and the hyena (right) are placed in the same order. The walrus moves along the ocean bottom, using its tusks to find the clams and other shellfish it eats. The hyena is an efficient hunter and often kills small antelopes.

ORDER SIRENIA These strange aquatic mammals are related to elephants. They are peaceful, slow-moving herbivores that live in rivers and streams in parts of Africa, South America, and Florida. Some species are also found in tropical oceans and the Caribbean. The manatee, or sea cow, lives in quiet waters in southern Florida, where it is often injured by careless boaters. The propellers of boat engines cut the manatee's back as it swims along just below the surface of the water.

ORDER ARTIODACTYLA This order contains the large grazing animals: cattle, sheep, goats, hippopotami, giraffes, and pigs. For mammals in this order, the original five toes on each foot have been reduced to two. Thus artiodactyls are called even-toed ungulates. The word ungulate means hoofed mammal.

ORDER PERISSODACTYLA Horses, zebras, tapirs, and rhinoceroses—the odd-toed ungulates—make up this order. Many grazing animals with habits similar to those of even-toed mammals are included in this order. Some odd-toed ungulates have hooves formed from the center toe of each foot.

ORDER PROBOSCIDEA These are the mammals with trunks, the great elephants. Some time ago, this order had a reasonably large adaptive radiation that produced about thirty species. Included in those species were the mammoths and mastodons, which today are extinct. Only two species, the Indian elephant and the African elephant, presently survive. Both species are in danger of becoming extinct.

ORDER PRIMATES This order, which includes our own species, is closely related to the ancient insectivores. Of all the animals, primates have the most highly developed cerebrum and the most complicated behaviors. The most primitive living primates, the lemurs, are small tree dwellers. The primates most people call monkeys or apes represent two main branches within this order.

Figure 33–17 Manatees live in tropical water, often floating. Their diet consists of water plants.

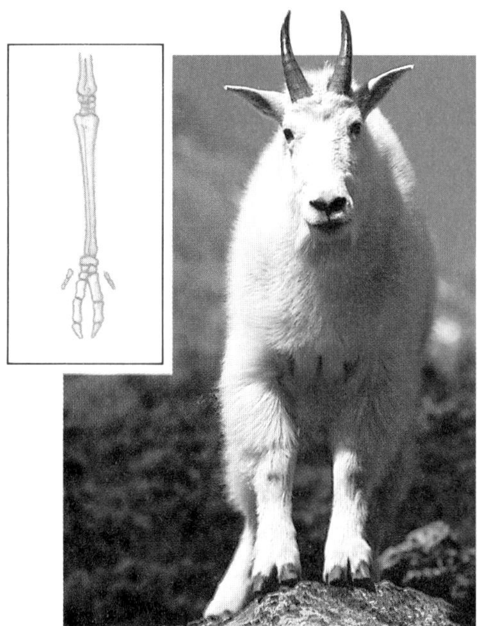

Figure 33–18 The mountain goat (left) has two toes and is included with other two-toed mammals in the order Artiodactyla. The tapir (right) has three toes and is grouped with other animals that have an odd number of toes.

Very early in their evolutionary history, primates (as a group) were split apart by the moving continents. One branch, the New World monkeys, includes the squirrel monkey and the spider monkey. These monkeys live almost entirely in trees. They have long arms for swinging from branch to branch and long **prehensile tails**, which they use for grasping while climbing.

The other branch, the Old World monkeys, include chimpanzees, gorillas, and the ancestors of humans. Many Old World monkeys still spend much of their time in trees, but they all lack prehensile tails.

How Mammals Fit into the World

Mammals evolved from early reptile ancestors during the Mesozoic Era about two hundred million years ago. During this era, and later during the Cenozoic Era, mammals underwent massive adaptive radiations. Today mammals are distributed throughout the world. Humans, one of the important mammalian species, inhabit areas that range from the very cold polar

Figure 33–19 Among the most intelligent animals, the black lemur (left) and the chimpanzee (right) are both primates. Today, chimpanzees and many species of lemurs are endangered.

regions to the warmest equatorial regions. And in all these regions, other mammal species live alongside humans.

In many parts of the world, herbivorous mammals are major consumers of plant material. For example, huge herds of grazing zebras and wildebeests eat their way across the savannas of Africa. Herds of reindeer and musk oxen move across the tundra, eating small plants and lichens. These peaceful grazers are, in turn, food for carnivorous mammals. Lions, leopards, cheetahs, wild dogs, wolves, and other carnivores hunt and kill plant eaters for food.

In the air, flying bats and gliding squirrels move gracefully in search of food. Bats eat enormous numbers of mosquitoes and other insects. Gliding squirrels feed on nuts and seeds.

Mammals also inhabit the oceans. Whales, the largest animals to have lived on Earth, are probably the most familiar example. Despite their huge size, many species are today in danger of becoming extinct.

Domesticated mammals such as dogs, cows, sheep, and goats have a significant influence on human culture. Many of these animals provide food in the form of meat and dairy products such as milk, butter, and cheese. Others help humans find food. Dogs are used to hunt, and monkeys are used to harvest coconuts and other fruits.

Some mammals have a negative impact on human life. Carnivores prey on domesticated animals. Rodents such as rats and mice damage crops and eat stored food. Some mammals carry diseases that can affect humans. For example, rats harbor fleas that can spread the plague. Dogs, squirrels, and other wild animals can transmit the virus that causes rabies.

Mammals can have a profound effect on the environment. Elephants destroy huge numbers of trees as they feed. Overgrazing by cattle and rabbits can turn an area of prime farmland into a virtual dust bowl. Beavers flood areas and can create ponds when they build their dams. Humans in particular are capable of altering the environment in many ways—both good and bad.

Figure 33–20 *People used natural fibers and fur to weave cloth long before synthetic fibers were developed. In this photograph, sheep are being shorn of their fine wool.*

Figure 33–21 *Animals often make profound changes to the natural environment. This beautiful dam was constructed by beavers, not by engineers. The pond that formed behind the dam provides safety for the beavers and a home for many other kinds of animals.*

33–2 SECTION REVIEW

1. What is a placental mammal? How does a placental mammal differ from a pouched mammal?
2. How do monotremes provide evidence for the evolution of mammals from ancient reptiles?
3. Name five different orders of placental mammals and give an example of each.
4. In what four ways do mammals influence human life?
5. How could you predict the diet of a mammal from an examination of its teeth?

LABORATORY INVESTIGATION

EXAMINING THE TYPICAL MAMMALIAN BODY COVERING

PROBLEM

What are the characteristics of hair?

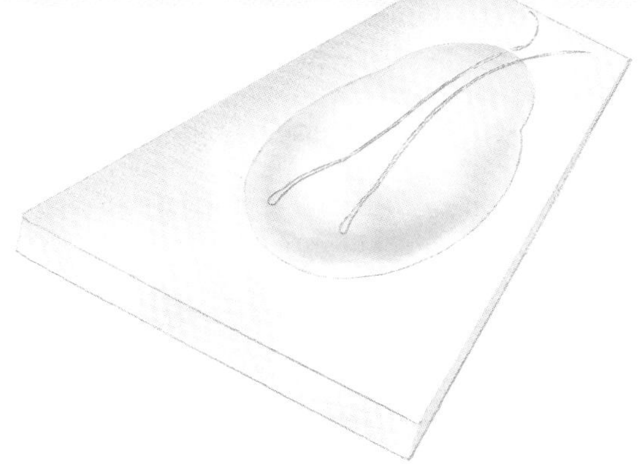

MATERIALS *(per group)*

comb or brush	methylene blue
glass slide	microscope
coverslip	scissors
electric light or bright sunlight	toothpick
medicine dropper	hand lens

PROCEDURE 

1. Using a medicine dropper, put two drops of methylene blue in the center of a clean glass slide.
2. Comb or brush your hair vigorously to remove a few loose hairs.
3. From your comb or brush, select two hairs that each have a root attached. Look for a small bulb-shaped swelling at one end of the hair. This is the root.
4. Using the scissors, trim the other end of the hairs so they will be short enough to fit on the slide. Place the trimmed hairs in the drops of methylene blue on the slide.
5. Gently rub the inside of your cheek with a toothpick.
6. Stir the material from the inside of your cheek in the methylene blue between the hairs on the glass slide. Cover the specimens with a coverslip.
7. Use the low-power objective to locate the hairs and some of the material from the inside of your cheek. Then switch to the high-power objective and focus with the fine adjustment.
8. When the hair appears to be in perfect focus, you are looking at the inside of the hair strand. The inside of the hair is made of keratin, a secretion of epidermal cells in the hair follicles of your scalp. Make a sketch of the hair strand.
9. Turn the fine adjustment toward you (counterclockwise) to focus on the upper surface of the hair. At one point in your focusing, the hair will appear to be covered by overlapping structures that look like shingles. Draw these structures, which are actually cells.
10. Locate some of the epidermal cells scraped from the inside of your cheek. Compare the size and shape of these cells to the overlapping cells on the hair strand. (Remember the layers of overlapping cells on the strand of hair are only partially visible.)
11. Under bright light, use the hand lens to examine a portion of your skin that does not seem to be covered with hair. (Do not examine the palms of your hands or the soles of your feet.)

OBSERVATIONS

1. Describe the appearance of a strand of hair under magnification.
2. How does the appearance of the epidermal cells from your cheek compare to the cells covering the strand of hair?
3. What did you observe when you examined the surface of your skin under bright light?

ANALYSIS AND CONCLUSIONS

1. What covers the surface of your body and the body of most mammals?
2. Based on your observations, what is hair?

STUDENT STUDY GUIDE

SUMMARIZING THE CONCEPTS

The key concepts in each section of this chapter are listed below to help you review the chapter content. Make sure you understand each concept and its relationship to other concepts and to the theme of this chapter.

33–1 Mammals

- The group of mammals includes a variety of endothermic animals.
- Monotremes—the egg-laying mammals—are oviparous and show both reptilian and mammalian reproduction habits.
- Marsupials are viviparous animals whose young are born in an immature state.
- Mammals have well-developed breathing muscles that include a diaphragm that changes the size of the chest cavity to pull air in and push air out.
- Mammalian circulatory systems consist of a four-chambered heart that moves blood through the rest of the body.
- The digestive system of herbivorous mammals contains either a rumen or cecum that houses symbiotic bacteria that produce enzymes that break down cellulose.
- Mammals have highly developed kidneys that function to extract nitrogenous wastes from the blood.
- The mammalian brain consists of a cerebrum, cerebellum, and medulla. Mammals depend on highly developed senses to provide information about their external environment.

33–2 Important Orders of Living Mammals

- Mammals are classified by structure of teeth, number and kinds of head bones, and methods of reproduction.
- Members of the order insectivora are relatively small mammals with high metabolic rates. The order Chiroptera contains the many species of bats. The order Edentata includes mammals that lack teeth or have very small teeth. Small mammals with long front teeth and short gestation periods belong to the order Rodentia. Rabbits and hares belong to the order Lagomorpha. Mostly terrestrial meat-eaters belong to the order Carnivora. Whales and dolphins, truly aquatic animals, belong in the order Cetacea. Slow-moving herbivorous aquatic mammals belong in the order Sirenia. Even-toed ungulates are in the order Artiodactyla, whereas odd-toed ungulates are in the order Perissodactyla. Mammals with trunks are found in the order Proboscidea. The order Primates contains mammals with the most developed cerebrum, including our own species.

REVIEWING KEY TERMS

Vocabulary terms are important to your understanding of biology. The key terms listed below are those you should be especially familiar with. Review these terms and their meanings. Then use each term in a complete sentence. If you are not sure of a term's meaning, return to the appropriate section and review its definition.

33–1 Mammals

mammary gland
monotreme
marsupial
placental mammal
rumen
cecum
marsupium
placenta

33–2 Important Orders of Living Mammals

prehensile tail

CHAPTER REVIEW

CONTENT REVIEW

Multiple Choice

Choose the letter of the answer that best completes each statement.

1. Certain whales have teeth modified into huge stiffened plates called
   a. rumen. c. cecums.
   b. baleen. d. monotremes.
2. Carnivorous mammals have strong
   a. sharp incisors. c. flat-edged incisors.
   b. baleens. d. flattened molars.
3. In humans, the cecum has evolved into the
   a. appendix. c. kidney.
   b. small intestine. d. liver.
4. The mammalian circulatory system sends deoxygenated blood to the
   a. heart. c. brain.
   b. internal organs. d. lungs.
5. The duckbill platypus and other egg-laying mammals are
   a. monotremes. c. placental mammals.
   b. marsupials. d. extinct.
6. Many biologists believe that mammals alive today do not see color well because early mammals
   a. lacked eyes.
   b. lived in cold regions.
   c. were nocturnal.
   d. were blind.
7. Bacteria in the digestive tracts of grazing animals produce enzymes that
   a. speed digestion.
   b. break down cellulose.
   c. break down fats.
   d. digest food for a second time.
8. In humans, nutrients, oxygen, carbon dioxide, and wastes are exchanged between embryo and mother through the
   a. rumen. c. marsupium.
   b. uterus. d. placenta.

True or False

Determine whether each statement is true or false. If it is true, write "true." If it is false, change the underlined word or words to make the statement true.

1. Old World monkeys, such as the squirrel monkey, have long prehensile tails used in climbing.
2. The odd-toed ungulates belong to the order Perissodactyla.
3. Night-flying bats use echolocation to calculate distances from objects.
4. The great blue whale and the humpback whale are carnivores.
5. Aquatic mammals such as whales and dolphins have a thick layer of skin called blubber.
6. The duckbill platypus is an example of a marsupial.
7. Elephants can hear sounds of higher frequencies than humans can.
8. Cottontail rabbits are in the order Lagomorpha.

Word Relationships

Replace the underlined definition with the correct vocabulary word.

1. Female mammals have structures that produce milk for their young.
2. Grazing animals have a chamber in their digestive tract that contains bacteria that break down cellulose.
3. Koala bears are an example of a pouched mammal.

CONCEPT MASTERY

Use your understanding of the concepts developed in the chapter to answer each of the following in a brief paragraph.

1. Describe three important characteristics used to classify mammals.
2. Explain how night-flying bats find tiny insect prey in total darkness.
3. How does a four-chambered heart add to the efficiency of the circulatory system of mammals?
4. What are the three parts of a mammal's brain and what functions does each control?
5. Describe the different types of teeth that have evolved in carnivorous and herbivorous mammals. How is each adapted to the animal's particular diet?
6. The digestive system of cows does not produce enzymes that break down cellulose. Explain how cows digest plant tissues that contain large amounts of cellulose.

CRITICAL AND CREATIVE THINKING

Discuss each of the following in a brief paragraph.

1. **Making comparisons** Compare and contrast the embryos of marsupials with those of placental mammals.
2. **Relating cause and effect** Explain how the change in world climate at the end of the Cretaceous Period led to the great mammalian radiation.
3. **Making inferences** In what ways have well-developed senses contributed to the success of mammals?
4. **Relating facts** Explain the relationship between a human's ability to speak and the movement of the diaphragm.

5. **Classifying organisms** You are given the following descriptions of three placental mammals. A is a flying mammal that has sharp teeth and a liquid diet. B is a mammal that has sharp front teeth and eats plant material. It has a short gestation period and produces many offspring. C is a carnivorous mammal that has a layer of subcutaneous fat. It lacks external ears and hind legs, and it mates and bears its young in water. Using your knowledge of mammals, classify each organism in its proper order. Give your reasoning for each classification.
6. **Identifying relationships** Early humans had a functioning appendix. Describe how the appendix changed over time. What reasons can you give to explain this change?
7. **Using the writing process** You are a writer for a small wildlife magazine. Your boss tells you that he has decided not to feature mammals any longer because he finds them dull. Write a memo to him in order to change his mind. Include the characteristics that separate mammals from organisms in other classes and describe the diversity that exists within the class.

CHAPTER 34

Humans

From the creation of stone tools to a trip through space, it is the nature of humans to question and wonder.

Humans are unique on this planet. No other organism lives in as many different habitats and does as many different things. No other organism has written and spoken language and keeps records of the past. We as a species have created art, music, philosophy, and science. Where did we come from? What were our ancestors like? How did we come to be as we are today?

There are few chapters of evolutionary history that are more fascinating (and more controversial) than the origin of our own species. More than a century before Darwin, Carolus Linnaeus realized that he should classify Homo sapiens *in the same group of mammals into which he placed the apes. He did not do so, however, primarily because he feared that such an act would cause a great furor. Darwin himself shied away from the topic at first. But after the success of* On the Origin of Species*, he wrote two books dealing with human evolution. In the years since Darwin's work, our understanding of our species' history has come a long way.*

CHAPTER OUTLINE

34–1 Primates and Human Origins

Section Objectives

- Describe the characteristics of primates.
- Compare New World monkeys with Old World monkeys.

The study of human origins is an exciting, almost frantic, search for our past. To piece together this complicated story in detail requires the skills of many kinds of scientists. Paleontologists study fossil primates and compare them with living forms. Archaeologists and anthropologists study ancient human tools and cultures, trying to piece together a story of human history. Molecular biologists examine the DNA of different species, looking for similarities and differences that show whether or not the species are closely related. All of these kinds of scientists and the methods they use—as you have read in Chapters 13 and 14—have made important contributions to the study of human evolution.

Research into human origins has always been spiced with competition among scientists, many of whom have different interpretations of the data gathered on our species' past. But all researchers agree on certain basic facts. We know, for example, that humans evolved from common ancestors we share with other living primates such as chimpanzees and apes. Our species almost certainly evolved in Africa and then spread around the world. We know that the first *Homo sapiens* appeared around 500,000 years ago, practically the day before yesterday on an evolutionary time scale. This means that humans did not appear until dinosaurs had been extinct for more than 60 million years (TV shows such as *The Flintstones* to the contrary).

Figure 34–1 *One adaptation of primates are eyes that point forward, as you can see in the ring-tailed lemur (left) and the orangutan (right).*

Figure 34–2 *Flexible primate fingers permit this gibbon to swing from branch to branch (top). Primates such as this chimpanzee have large cerebrums and complex social behaviors, including play (center). This loris, like other prosimian primates, is nocturnal and has large eyes that are well-adapted to seeing in the dark (bottom).*

What Are Primates?

As a group, primates share several important adaptations, many of which are extremely suitable to a life spent mainly in trees. In general, primates have faces that are much flatter than those of other mammals. Primate eyes point forward, and their snout is very much reduced. (Compare your nose to that of your favorite dog.) These features together allow both eyes to inspect the same area at the same time. Information gathered by those eyes is processed by highly developed visual centers in the brain to produce what is known as **binocular vision**, or stereoscopic vision. Binocular vision equips primates with a three-dimensional view of the world (a handy adaptation when trying to judge accurately the locations of tree branches, from which many primates swing).

All primates have flexible fingers (and some have flexible toes) that can curl around objects. This allows many primates to hold objects in either their hands or their feet. It also enables many of them to run along branches and swing from branch to branch with ease. Primates' arms also are well-adapted to swinging and climbing because they can rotate in broad circles around the shoulder.

Finally, primates have a large and complicated cerebrum. For that reason, they display far more complex behaviors than other animals. For example, primate mothers take care of their young for a much longer time than most other mammalian species. Many primate species also have complicated social behaviors that include friendships, protective relationships among relatives, adoption of orphans, and—unfortunately—warfare between rival primate troops.

How Did Primates Evolve?

Very early in their history, primates split into several evolutionary lines. Those that evolved from two of the earliest branches look very little like typical "monkeys" and are called prosimians. Living prosimians, which are odd but interesting animals, include lemurs, lorises, and aye-ayes. With a few exceptions, prosimians are almost entirely nocturnal and have large eyes adapted for seeing in the dark. Members of the more familiar primate group that includes monkeys, apes, and humans are called **anthropoids**, or humanlike primates. This group, in turn, has given rise over time to several major primate branches.

Two anthropoid branches—the two major groups of monkeys and apes—separated around 45 million years ago when the continents on which they lived moved apart and were no longer connected by land bridges. One anthropoid group, known as New World monkeys, evolved into the monkeys found today in Central and South America. (The term New World comes from the days of Columbus when the Americas were called the New World.) These animals are virtually all tree

Figure 34–3 Many New World monkeys spend their entire lives among the branches of trees. This spider monkey uses its prehensile tail like a fifth hand (left). Old World monkeys, such as this macaque, do not have prehensile tails and may spend much of their time on the ground (right).

dwellers, and many of them have grasping (prehensile) tails that aid in balance while moving through tree branches. The other anthropoid group evolved into the Old World monkeys and the great apes that are found today in areas that extend from Africa all the way across Asia to Indonesia and Japan. The Old World monkeys, which do not have prehensile tails, include baboons and macaques (muh-KAHKS). Some of these animals live in trees, whereas others spend a good deal of time on the ground. The great apes, also called **hominoids**, include gorillas, gibbons, orangutans, chimpanzees, and *Homo sapiens*.

34–1 SECTION REVIEW

1. What characteristics are shared by all primates?
2. Compare New World with Old World monkeys.
3. How did the separation of the continents contribute to the development of New World and Old World monkeys?

34–2 Hominid Evolution: Human Ancestors and Relatives

Section Objectives

- Describe the importance of various hominid adaptations.
- Discuss the evolutionary trends in hominids that led to *Homo sapiens*.

Some time between 4 and 9 million years ago, the hominoid line in Africa gave rise to a small group of species that we now recognize as our closest relatives. These species, called **hominids**, were not yet human, but they showed several evolutionary trends that distinguish them from other hominoids.

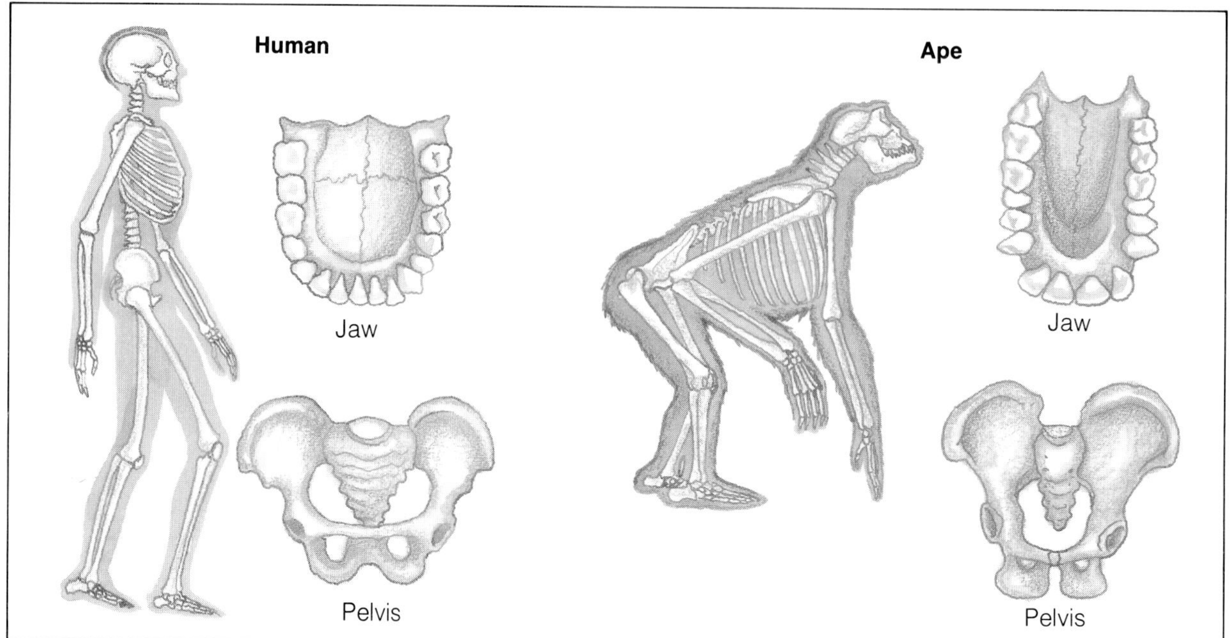

Figure 34–4 *Compare the skeletal system in a human and an ape. Note the shape of the jaws, the pelvic structure, and the way the spine enters the skull.*

What Are Hominids?

Hominids were omnivores that ate both meat and vegetable foods, as modern humans do. As time progressed, the spinal column, hip bones, and leg bones of these animals changed shape in ways that made it easier for them to walk upright on two legs. The evolution of this **bipedal**, or two-foot, **locomotion** was very important. Because our ancestors could walk erect, their hands were free to use tools more often. At the same time, the thumb of the hominid hand became more and more independent from the other fingers. The evolution of an **opposable thumb** enabled ancient hominids to grasp objects and use them as tools more effectively than other primates.

Hominids also displayed a remarkable increase in brain size. Hominid brains are exceptionally large, even for primates. Chimpanzees, our closest living relatives among the apes, have a brain size of about 280 to 450 cubic centimeters. The brain of *Homo sapiens*, on the other hand, ranges in size from 1200 to 1600 cubic centimeters! Most of the difference in brain size results from the enormously expanded human cerebrum. The cerebrum is the "thinking" area of the brain.

How Did Hominids Evolve?

To follow the story of human evolution, we need fossils of human ancestors. Much of our most recent evidence for hominid evolution comes from a small area in eastern Africa between Tanzania and Ethiopia. There, several researchers have found fossils of several species of hominids dating from about 4 million to about 1.5 million years ago.

***AUSTRALOPITHECUS:* THE FIRST HOMINIDS** The first hominid fossil to be found, a nearly complete skull of a young child, was discovered in South Africa in 1924. This specimen was placed in a new genus called *Australopithecus* (aw-stray-loh-PIHTH-uh-kuhs), or Southern Ape. Because the skull belonged to a child, it could not be used to determine how adults of the species looked. But 12 years later, investigators in Africa found fossils of adult australopithecines. One of these fossils was part of a hip bone, indicating that *Australopithecus* walked upright. Walking erect was an essential step in the evolution of our species from an apelike ancestor.

Since those discoveries, researchers have found many more complete hominid fossils. In 1974, a team led by Donald Johanssen and Tim White made a truly exciting find—a nearly complete *Australopithecus* skeleton. From the shape of the pelvic bone, it was clear that this skeleton had been that of a female, and the fossil has since been called Lucy. (They took the name, by the way, from the Beatles' song "Lucy in the Sky with Diamonds," which they had listened to in their camp the night before the discovery.)

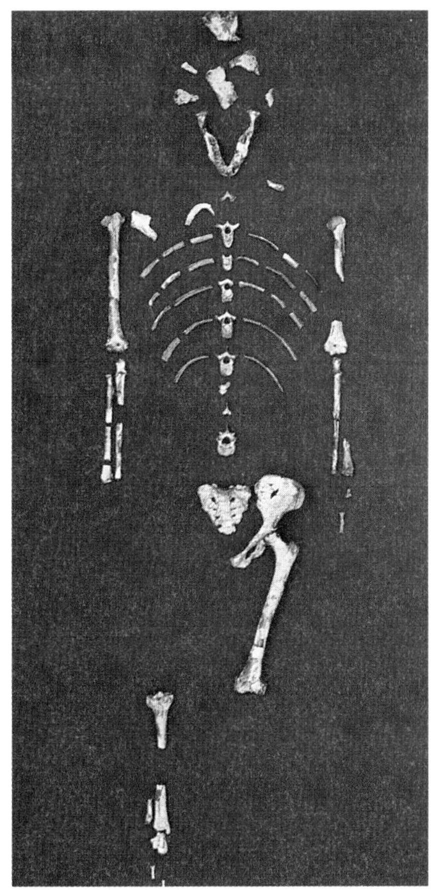

Figure 34–5 This nearly complete Australopithecus *skeleton was nicknamed Lucy.*

In 1977, anthropologist Mary Leakey made an equally exciting discovery: a set of fossil hominid footprints. The mud in which the prints were preserved has been dated at 4 million years old! Those footprints formed a fossilized record of two hominids walking together. From the size of the prints, they were probably a parent and an offspring. This record is clear evidence that the animals that made the footprints walked erect on two legs, as humans do. No stone tools have been found among *Australopithecus* fossils, but they may have used twigs and stones as tools in a way similar to that of chimpanzees today.

In recent years, other hominid fossils have been placed in the genus *Australopithecus*. Most current studies suggest that there were at least four species of *Australopithecus*: *A. boisei*, *A. robustus*, *A. afarensis*, and *A. africanus*. (The letter *A.* represents the genus name.) These species all lived between 4 and 1.5 million years ago, walked upright, and had much smaller brains than present-day humans. Many questions as to how these species were related to one another, as well as to human evolution, still remain to be answered.

HOMO HABILIS For a while, australopithecines were the only known links in the chain of human evolution. Then anthropologist Richard Leakey found another hominid fossil with a smaller face and significantly larger brain than the australopithecines. Leakey felt this species was similar enough to humans to be placed in our own genus, *Homo*. Fossils of this hominid were found along with tools made of stone and bone. As if to emphasize that fact, scientists have called these hominids *Homo habilis* (HAB-ih-lihs), which, appropriately, means handy man.

Figure 34–6 This skull of Homo habilis *was found in Kenya and is about 1.8 million years old.*

Near one of these fossil finds, in a valley in Kenya called Olduvai Gorge, is the oldest human settlement yet discovered. The settlement was found at a level in the rock dated at 1.9 million years ago. The main site is a circular stone structure about 4 meters in diameter. Inside, the floor is littered with animal bones and stone tools. Just what *Homo habilis* used these tools for is not clear. Some scientists think this species ate meat and the tools were used for hunting prey. More recent evidence indicates that *Homo habilis* was basically a vegetarian species that may have followed in the paths of other carnivores, stealing whatever parts of the kill they could find. Although not quite so glorious a past, it is one that seems to be real.

HOMO ERECTUS Evidence suggests that within a few hundred thousand years *Homo habilis* disappeared and was replaced by a larger brained species called *Homo erectus* (ee-REHK-tuhs). By 1 million years ago, this species had spread over most of the Old World, from Africa to Europe to Asia.

With a cranial capacity of more than 800 cubic centimeters, *Homo erectus* was an excellent toolmaker. Carefully chipped and balanced hand axes have been found with *Homo erectus* fossils throughout the world. In caves in China that are at least half a million years old, charred animal bones have been found around fire sites. This shows that *Homo erectus* must have used fire for cooking. From a site in France dated at about 400,000 years old, the remains of primitive huts have been discovered —huts not too different from some still in use in parts of the world today.

Figure 34–7 Homo erectus *replaced* Homo habilis, *spreading throughout Europe, Africa, and Asia by about 1 million years ago. Evidence strongly suggests that* Homo erectus *used and controlled fire.*

PROBLEM SOLVING IN BIOLOGY

ANALYZING *HOMO ERECTUS* BEHAVIOR

Scientists have found fossils of *Homo erectus* in many places on Earth. In one fossil find in Spain, a puzzling event seems to have occurred. On top of a cliff, the remains of ancient brush fires have been unearthed. At the base of the cliff, the bones of an entire herd of elephants have been found. Scattered among the elephant bones were stone tools.

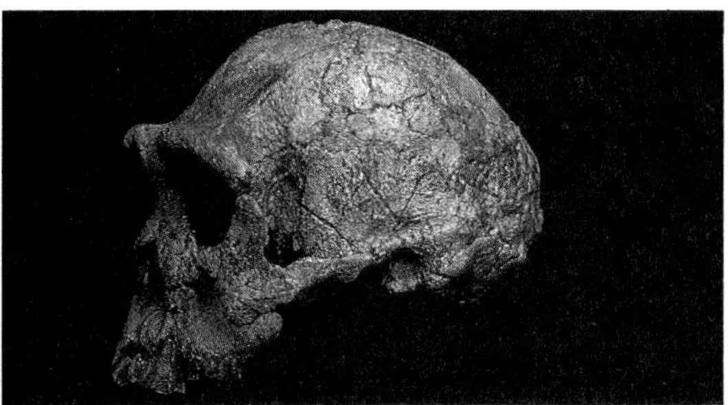

Analysis: Using the information in this chapter, formulate a hypothesis that would explain this event in ancient history. Then explain how your hypothesis can be used to make some logical assumptions about the behavior of *Homo erectus.*

HOMO SAPIENS About 500,000 years ago, the first hominids assigned to our own species (*Homo sapiens*) appeared. These hominids, often called archaic *Homo sapiens*, would not be easily recognizable as modern humans. Little is known about this species.

Around 150,000 years ago, a new hominid walked on Earth. First discovered in the Neander valley in Germany, this species was called Neanderthal man, or *Homo neanderthalensis*, for many years. Now, based on more complete fossil evidence, Neanderthals have been placed in our own species and are called *Homo sapiens neanderthalensis.* Although you have probably seen movies in which Neanderthal man is depicted as primitive looking, hunched over, and covered with hair, this depiction is totally inaccurate. Neanderthal man could probably walk down a busy street today and not be noticed (assuming he was dressed in modern clothes)! These early members of our species were quite successful for a time and became common throughout Europe and the Middle East by 70,000 years ago.

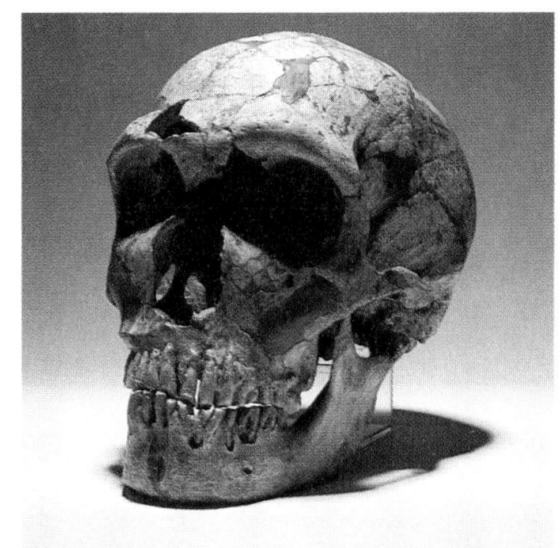

Figure 34–8 *This Neanderthal skull is between 35,000 and 50,000 years old.*

The first hominids truly identical to modern humans appeared in locations scattered throughout the Old World roughly 100,000 years ago. These large-brained people, called Cro-Magnon (kroh-MAG-nuhn), were more slender than the Neanderthals and had a more complex culture. They made a wide

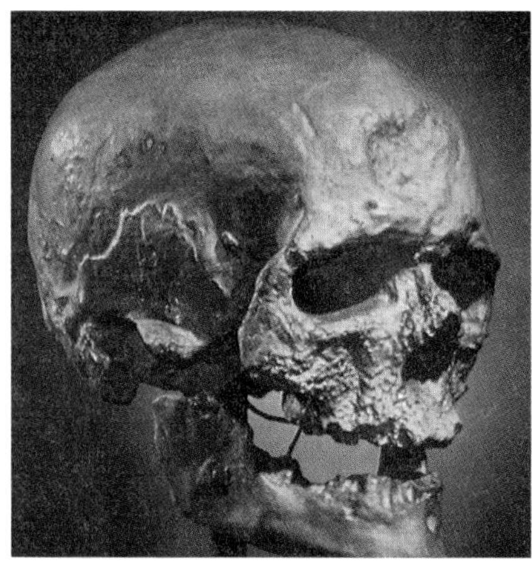

Figure 34–9 Cro-Magnon was the first hominid truly identical to modern humans.

variety of stone and bone tools, including spear points, knives, chisels, and needles. They were also talented artists. Fossils of Cro-Magnon are now classified as modern humans, *Homo sapiens sapiens.*

Most paleontologists interpret the dates of Cro-Magnon fossils found throughout the world as indicating that modern humans originated in Africa and from there spread out over the rest of the world. However, there are those who argue that modern humans evolved from Neanderthals in several regions, including Europe, the Middle East, and Asia. At this time, there is no clear resolution to this complex debate.

However and wherever Cro-Magnons originated, there is ample fossil evidence that they lived side by side with Neanderthals in several locations for some time. Then, around 30,000 years ago, the Neanderthals disappeared. Some scientists believe that Cro-Magnons interbred with Neanderthals, blending their characteristics. Others believe that the more intelligent newcomers slaughtered their older relatives. In either case, only *Homo sapiens sapiens* remained to populate the rest of the world.

34–2 SECTION REVIEW

1. What is the importance of the evolution of bipedal locomotion? Of the opposable thumb?
2. Why is *Homo habilis* aptly named?
3. Which genus was the first hominid to walk erect?
4. Based on your knowledge of evolution, why is it more likely that the ancestors of *Homo sapiens sapiens* evolved in a single area rather than in many places throughout the world?

Figure 34–10 Neanderthal buried their dead with tools, animal bones, and even flowers, probably indicating some sort of belief in an afterlife. In several caves around the world, animal skulls and bones were laid out on piles of stone and in nooks in the walls, which may have been altars to primitive gods.

Women and the Development of Human Society

Until recently, the study of human evolution has been a male-dominated science. A simple look at fossil names tells you that. We learn, after all, about Neanderthal man and Cro-Magnon man. But where are the Neanderthal and Cro-Magnon women in all this? Equally important to this concept of male domination are older studies of primates and early hominids that constantly place males in positions superior to those of females. By studying the social groups of other living primates, such as baboons and chimpanzees, biologists often try to infer the sorts of behaviors australopithecines might have displayed. And by examining certain isolated "stone age" human tribes, researchers try to imagine what the first human societies were like.

Both of these research techniques are useful, but they must be applied with caution. Male researchers, it seems, have found an overwhelming body of evidence that points toward universal male superiority among primates and early humans. It was male hunting, they say, that led to civilization. Another interpretation places males in control of most primate groups because "man the hunter" is strong, aggressive, and intelligent. "Woman the gatherer" is weaker, less coordinated, and always busy caring for infants.

But the old story is not necessarily the true story. For as more and more female researchers have entered the field of anthropology and other related fields (and, to be fair, as more open-minded males have joined in the pursuit), new information has come to light. It now seems likely that early hominids depended more on vegetable material than on meat. If this is true, the women who gathered vegetable foods would have been in powerful positions! The ability of females to cooperate in gathering and distributing food may have been a vital ingredient in the founding of the earliest civilizations. Women's skills might well have led to the development of agriculture, a cultural innovation that made large permanent human settlements possible. At the very least, women's contributions were just as important as men's ability to organize hunting parties.

It is also true that females of other primate species are not nearly as male dominated as researchers once reported them to be. Females, it appears, often control the length of time certain primate troops spend in particular feeding areas. In some species, a dominant male's position often depends on the support of female allies, even if he "rules the roost." And in several species, newborn infants inherit their rank within the troop not from their father, but from their mother.

These and many other studies remind us that the story of our species involves the evolution of both men and women, for neither could have survived alone.

LABORATORY INVESTIGATION — COMPARING PRIMATES, FROM GORILLAS TO HUMANS

PROBLEM

What changes occurred as humans evolved from earlier hominids?

MATERIALS *(per group)*

metric ruler	protractor
clean paper	scissors

PROCEDURE 

1. After reading the investigation, prepare a data table to record your observations.
2. Use the scissors to cut a strip of clean paper about 6-cm wide and 9-cm long.
3. Insert the strip of paper lengthwise into your mouth. Place the paper over your tongue so that it covers all your teeth, including your back molars. Bite down hard enough to make an impression of your teeth on the paper. Remove the paper from your mouth.
4. Draw a line on the paper from the center of the impression of the left back molar to the center of the right back molar. Mark the midpoint of this line. Use the protractor to draw a perpendicular line from the midpoint of the line connecting the back molars to the front teeth.
5. Measure the width of the jaw by measuring the length of the line between the back molars. Measure the length of the jaw by measuring the line from the back of the mouth to the front teeth. Record your measurements.

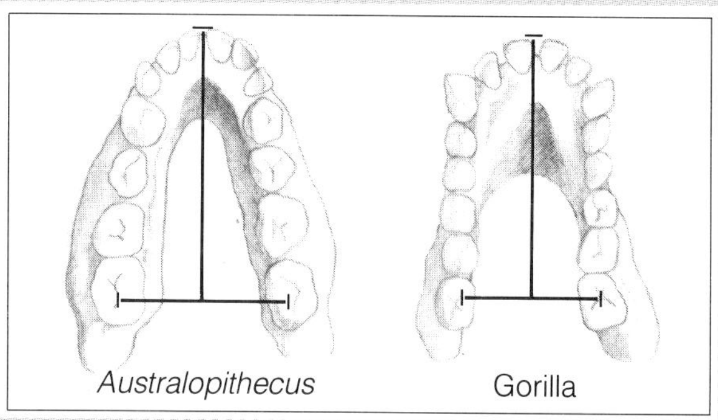
Australopithecus Gorilla

6. Calculate the jaw index by multiplying the width of the jaw by 100 and then dividing this number by the length of the jaw. Record the jaw index.
7. Repeat steps 5 and 6 using the drawings of the gorilla jaw and the *Australopithecus* jaw. Record your results.
8. Find the indentation at the bottom of your palm at the ball of your thumb. Measure the length of your thumb from the indentation to the tip. Measure the length of your index finger from the indentation to its tip. Record your measurements.
9. Calculate the thumb index by multiplying the length of the thumb by 100 and dividing by the length of the index finger. Record the thumb index.
10. Repeat steps 8 and 9 using the drawings of the thumb and index finger.

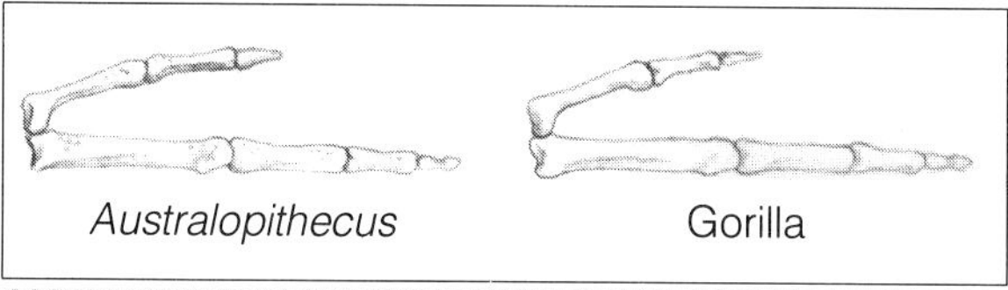
Australopithecus Gorilla

OBSERVATIONS

1. What trend did you observe regarding the relative length of the jaw? The relative length of the thumb and index fingers?

ANALYSIS AND CONCLUSIONS

1. What evidence is there that *Australopithecus* was an organism with characteristics intermediate to gorillas and humans?
2. Based on the thumb index, what adaptive change occurred in the evolution of humans? What was the advantage of this change?
3. Based on your observations, what other change occurred as humans evolved?

STUDENT STUDY GUIDE

SUMMARIZING THE CONCEPTS

The key concepts in each section of this chapter are listed below to help you review the chapter content. Make sure you understand each concept and its relationship to other concepts and to the theme of this chapter.

34–1 Primates and Human Origins

- Humans (*Homo sapiens*) evolved from common ancestors we share with other living primates such as chimpanzees and apes.
- Primates share certain characteristics: flat faces, reduced snouts, eyes that face forward and allow for binocular vision, flexible fingers and toes, arms that can rotate in broad circles around the shoulders, and a large cerebrum.
- Anthropoid primates include monkeys, apes, and humans.
- Two anthropoid branches separated around 45 million years ago when the continents shifted and were no longer connected by land bridges.
- One anthropoid branch evolved into the New World monkeys, which are primarily tree dwellers and, in general, have tails.
- The other anthropoid branch evolved into the Old World monkeys, which include baboons and the great apes.
- The great apes, also called hominoids, include gibbons, orangutans, chimpanzees, and *Homo sapiens.*

34–2 Hominid Evolution: Human Ancestors and Relatives

- Hominid adaptations include changes in the spinal column, hip bones, and leg bones that allow bipedal (two-foot) locomotion. Hominids also have a much larger brain than other primates.
- The first recognized hominids were the australopithecines, all of which walked erect.
- The first species to be classifed in the genus *Homo* was *Homo habilis,* or handy man.
- *Homo habilis* was replaced by *Homo erectus,* which spread throughout much of the world by around 1 million years ago.
- The first species to resemble modern humans seems to have evolved around 150,000 years ago and is called *Homo sapiens neanderthalensis.*
- The first fossils of modern humans date to about 100,000 years ago. These humans, called Cro-Magnons, are in the genus *Homo sapiens sapiens,* as are modern humans.
- Cro-Magnons probably evolved in Africa and spread throughout most of the world.

REVIEWING KEY TERMS

Vocabulary terms are important to your understanding of biology. The key terms listed below are those you should be especially familiar with. Review these terms and their meanings. Then use each term in a complete sentence. If you are not sure of a term's meaning, return to the appropriate section and review its definition.

34–1 Primates and Human Origins

binocular vision
anthropoid
hominoid

34–2 Hominid Evolution: Human Ancestors and Relatives

hominid
bipedal locomotion
opposable thumb

CHAPTER REVIEW

CONTENT REVIEW

Multiple Choice

Choose the letter of the answer that best completes each statement.

1. Modern humans are included in the genus
   a. *sapiens.* c. hominid.
   b. *Homo.* d. hominoid.
2. Old World monkeys include
   a. baboons. c. lemurs.
   b. prosimians. d. lorises.
3. Great apes do not include
   a. chimpanzees. c. orangutans.
   b. macaques. d. gibbons.
4. Hominids were
   a. carnivores. c. herbivores.
   b. omnivores. d. saprophytes.
5. The first hominid known to use tools was
   a. *Australopithecus boisei.* c. *Homo habilis.*
   b. Cro-Magnon. d. *Homo erectus.*
6. The first species to be considered *Homo sapiens* is believed to have evolved
   a. 100,000 years ago.
   b. 150,000 years ago.
   c. 1.3 to 4 million years ago.
   d. 500,000 years ago.
7. All of these are hominids except
   a. *Homo habilis.* c. hominoids.
   b. *Australopithecus afarensis.* d. *Homo sapiens.*
8. Which of these is not a characteristic of hominids?
   a. spinal cord
   b. bipedal locomotion
   c. opposable thumb
   d. enlarged cerebrum

True or False

Determine whether each statement is true or false. If it is true, write "true." If it is false, change the underlined word or words to make the statement true.

1. Binocular vision is an adaptation found in most primates.
2. Two hominoid branches split off around 45 million years ago when the continents separated.
3. Gibbons, chimpanzees, and baboons are all New World monkeys.
4. Hominids were primarily carnivores.
5. The first toolmakers were *Homo erectus.*
6. Cro-Magnon is included in the species *Homo sapiens sapiens.*
7. Primitive huts have been found in *Homo erectus* campsites.
8. Modern humans probably originated in Africa and spread out over the rest of the world from there.

Word Relationships

In each of the following sets of terms, three of the terms are related. One term does not belong. Determine the characteristic common to three of the terms and then identify the term that does not belong.

1. gibbon, chimpanzee, lemur, orangutan
2. hominid, *Homo sapiens*, *Homo erectus*, hominoid
3. *H. erectus*, Lucy, *A. boisei*, *A. robustus*
4. Cro-Magnon, Neanderthal, archaic *Homo sapiens*, *Homo habilis*

CONCEPT MASTERY

Use your understanding of the concepts developed in the chapter to answer each of the following in a brief paragraph.

1. Describe how various primate adaptations made them successful tree dwellers.
2. Compare *Homo habilis* and *Homo erectus*.
3. Explain why, in biological terms, Neanderthal was not a successful species.
4. Choose three different fields of biology and explain how each field can contribute to the study of human origins.
5. Why might *Homo erectus* be considered more advanced than *Homo habilis*?
6. Compare anthropoids, hominoids, and hominids.
7. Discuss possible reasons for the disappearance of Neanderthal.

CRITICAL AND CREATIVE THINKING

Discuss each of the following in a brief paragraph.

1. **Making inferences** Suggest some reasons for the fact that Cro-Magnon buried their dead in a ritualistic manner.
2. **Making predictions** Describe how society might have evolved if hominids had not developed an opposable thumb.
3. **Interpreting data** There are many theories regarding the specifics of human evolution and our common ancestors, two of which are shown in the accompanying illustration. Use the illustration to describe the major differences between these two versions of human evolutionary trends.
4. **Distinguishing fact and opinion** People often say that humans evolved from monkeys and apes. Explain why such a statement does not conform with modern evolutionary theory.
5. **Relating concepts** Most scientists agree that language did not develop prior to the appearance of Cro-Magnon. Describe some of the benefits language provides society.
6. **Using the writing process** With the exception of modern humans, choose a hominid and write a short story entitled "A Day in the Life of a Hominid."

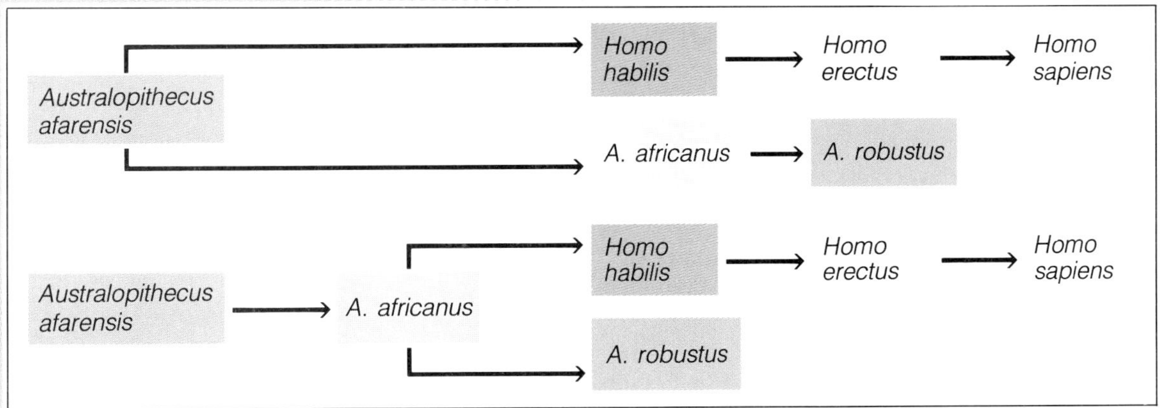

CHAPTER 35

Animal Behavior

Using every muscle in its body, this salmon strains to leap over a waterfall. The waterfall is one of several obstacles that make it difficult for the salmon to reach the stream in which it was born several years ago. Once there, it will reproduce and die. Later its offspring will swim to the sea, and the natural cycle of salmon journeys will continue.

In a freshwater marsh in Massachusetts, male redwing blackbirds perch on the tips of tall marsh reeds. There they sit for hours, singing loudly and flashing their red wing patches at other birds.

In the ice-cold waters of an Oregon stream, a meter-long salmon fights its way upstream. After living for several years in the vast Pacific Ocean, this salmon—and countless others like it—has returned to the very stream in which it hatched several years before.

Why do birds sing? And how do they know what songs to sing? How do salmon find the right stream to return to? In other words, how can the behaviors of animals—puzzling and often bizarre—be explained? The answers to these questions and a look at the fascinating field of animal behavior lie in the pages that follow.

35–1 Elements of Behavior

Section Objectives

- Describe the adaptive value of certain behaviors.
- Contrast instincts and learned behavior.

Animals are able to do some amazing things: Some bats fly in total darkness, navigating by means of high-pitched sounds, much as submarines do using sonar. Sea turtles spend many years swimming vast distances in the open sea, far from the beach on which they hatched. But when they are mature and able to reproduce, the sea turtles return to their birthplace to lay their eggs. Chimpanzees have a complex social system in which they love, tease, and help their friends and relatives—but fight, cheat, steal from, and even kill their enemies.

Behavior and Survival

Bats, turtles, chimpanzees, and other animals behave as they do for the same reasons that birds have feathers, frogs have sticky tongues, and giraffes have long necks. **The behavior of an animal is just as important to its survival and reproduction as any of its physical characteristics. For that reason, animal behaviors have evolved in many different ways, just as animal physical characteristics have.** All animal behaviors have their roots in the genetic makeup of the individual animal. Just as certain characteristics can enhance an animal's ability to survive, so can behaviors. Behaviors, like physical characteristics, can have adaptive value. For example, the fangs and sharp claws of a lion would have little survival value if a lion did not have clever hunting strategies.

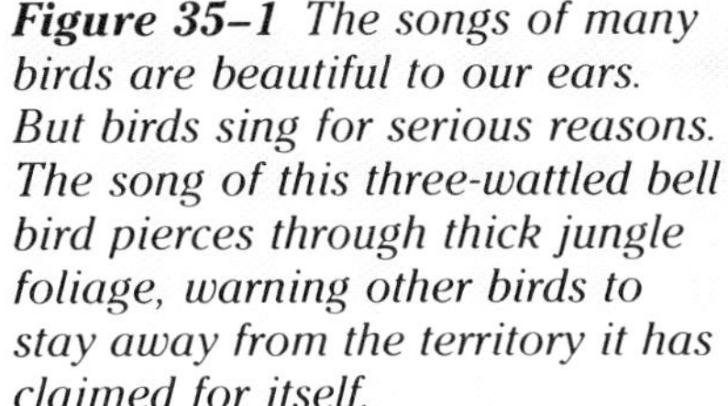

Figure 35–1 *The songs of many birds are beautiful to our ears. But birds sing for serious reasons. The song of this three-wattled bell bird pierces through thick jungle foliage, warning other birds to stay away from the territory it has claimed for itself.*

Figure 35–2 *This yawning lioness reveals one reason for her hunting success—huge fangs. Although male lions are well-fed, they rarely hunt. Relying on the hunting abilities of the females, the males grow fat on the efforts of others.*

There are some behaviors that animals must perform automatically in order to survive. For example, many carnivorous animals must "know" how to hunt soon after they are born. They have no chance to learn basic hunting techniques, for if they do not catch some food, they will starve. And newborn dolphins must know in advance that they have to hold their breath under water, or they will no doubt drown!

Other behaviors must be more flexible and capable of being changed by experience. Flexible behaviors allow animals to adjust to a changing environment. For example, hummingbirds must learn to find food in different kinds of flowers at different times of the year. For if they insisted on feeding on just a single type of flower that blooms only in May, they would starve when those flowers disappear in June.

A variety of automatic and flexible behaviors exist in the animal kingdom. Scientists separate these behaviors into two main categories: instincts and learning.

Instincts

Instincts are behaviors that can be called inborn. Instincts are built into an animal's nervous system and cannot be changed during the animal's lifetime, even by learned experiences. For example, newly hatched birds beg for food instinctively within moments after hatching. Similarly, all newborn mammals instinctively suckle at their mother's breast. Because animals perform these behaviors without any previous experience, the behaviors must be controlled by the "wiring" in the animal's nervous system. And because the nervous system is "assembled" under the instructions contained in an animal's DNA, instinctive behaviors are genetically controlled.

Figure 35–3 *Baby birds beg for food automatically when one of their parents approaches, and their pleadings rarely go unanswered (left). Nurturing and protecting its infant, this monkey makes an excellent parent (right).*

Many instinctive behaviors consist of actions that always continue in a certain order once they have begun. An example of this kind of fixed instinctive behavior is shown by the graylag goose. A graylag goose makes its nest on the ground. If a graylag goose sitting on her eggs sees an egg outside her nest, she stares at it closely. Instinctively, she slowly stands up, stretches out her neck, and carefully uses her beak to roll the egg back into the nest. This routine is always performed in the same way. By performing a simple experiment, researchers have proved that this sort of behavior is completely automatic: Just as a goose started to stretch out her neck to reach an egg placed outside her nest, the researchers pulled the egg away. To their amazement, the goose still went through all the motions of retrieving an egg—rolling it closer and closer to the nest and then settling down to incubate it—even though the egg had been taken away and was no longer there! It is interesting to note that further studies show nesting graylag geese will perform the same egg-rolling behavior even if the object outside the nest only barely resembles an egg. Employing the same techniques used to retrieve an errant egg, these geese have tried to roll objects as large as volleyballs to their nest.

Although some instinctive behaviors are relatively simple, others can be very complex. Web-building behavior in spiders is a complex fixed instinctive behavior. Other examples of fixed instinctive behaviors are seen in many of the complicated courtship and nest-building behaviors found in insects, fishes, birds, and mammals.

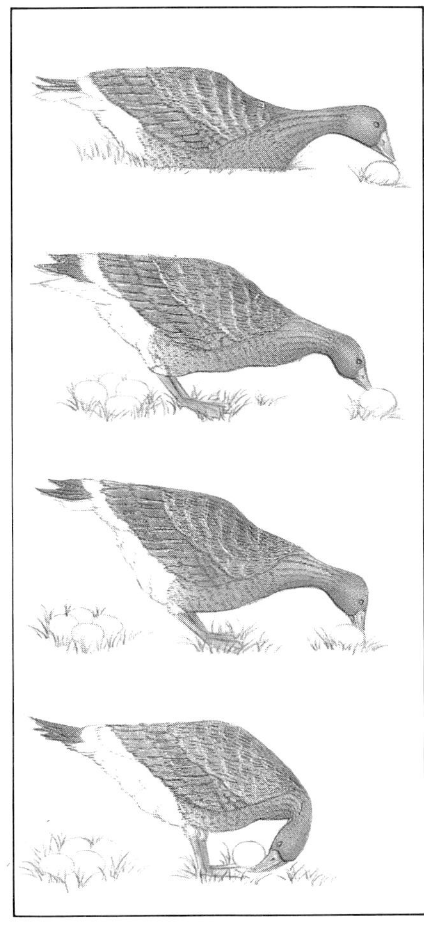

Figure 35–4 *This graylag goose carefully rolls an egg back to her nest. So instinctive is this behavior that she will continue her rolling actions even if the egg is removed from her sight.*

Learning

Unlike instinctive behaviors, learned behaviors are shaped by experience. Animals would not survive in the world if they were unable to modify their behavior. **Learning** is the way animals change their behavior as a result of experience. In invertebrates such as insects, little learning occurs. The things these animals can learn are strongly determined by their genetic makeup. For example, bees can learn to tell certain colors apart but only if those colors are associated with food such as sugar water. In vertebrate animals, however, learning is much less controlled by genetic makeup. Humans, for example, can learn to differentiate many colors under a wide variety of circumstances.

Learning is valuable to an animal because it may enhance the animal's chances of survival and, thus, its chances of reproducing and passing on its genes to another generation. Today, biologists who study learning recognize several different ways in which animals learn: habituation, classical conditioning, operant conditioning, and insight learning.

Habituation is a decrease in response to a stimulus that neither rewards nor harms an animal. It is one of the simplest ways in which animals learn. An example of habituation is

Figure 35–5 Bright colors often provide a warning of danger. This brightly colored poison arrow frog warns potential predators that a hasty meal may prove fatal.

Figure 35–6 Animals exhibit complicated behaviors when choosing a mate. These two courting penguins are grooming each other. Other penguins bring small pebbles as a "gift" to a potential mate.

found in certain young birds. Very young ducks and geese are frightened of any shadow that moves overhead. Within a few days of hatching, however, the young birds find that some shadows moving overhead—for example, the shadows of adult geese and ducks—mean nothing. They soon habituate to these shadows and no longer try to escape from them.

Classical conditioning occurs when an animal makes a mental connection between a stimulus and some kind of good or bad event. One famous example of classical conditioning is the work of the Russian biologist Ivan Pavlov. Pavlov discovered that if he always switched on a light before he fed his dogs, the dogs would begin to salivate whenever he turned on the light. The dogs had learned to associate the light (stimulus) with the arrival of food (good event). In a similar manner, newly hatched ducks and geese learn to associate one kind of overhead shadow with fear. When eagles or hawks fly overhead, adult ducks and geese become terrified and try to find a safe place to hide. The young birds quickly learn to respond to the overhead shadows of eagles and hawks by scurrying to find a safe place to hide. The ducklings and goslings learn which shadows to avoid by observing the actions of the adults.

Operant conditioning is sometimes called trial-and-error learning. In operant conditioning, an animal learns to behave in a certain way in order to receive a reward or to avoid punishment. There are many examples of operant conditioning in nature. Recall that many insects and amphibians carry bad-tasting chemicals or poisons in their bodies. Remember also that most of these bad-tasting animals are brightly colored. If a bird eats a brightly colored butterfly and gets sick soon afterward, it will avoid those butterflies in the future. In this example of operant conditioning, a predator learns not to eat a particular prey in order to avoid an unpleasant experience.

In **insight learning**, an animal applies something it has already learned to a new situation—without a period of trial and error. Insight learning is rare among most animals, including many mammals. Insight learning is common only in primates and is found most often among humans.

A dog on a long leash will often accidentally wrap the leash around a tree or a pole. In such a situation, the dog is usually completely helpless. Running in circles and tugging on the leash, the dog is not able to free itself by retracing its steps in the opposite direction. A chimpanzee in the same predicament, however, may be able to apply insight learning to unwind the leash and get free.

Instinct and Learning Combined

Some behaviors, although primarily instinctive, cannot occur without some learning on the part of the animal. For example, newborn ducks and geese have a built-in urge to follow their mother. But this instinct to follow does not include a

Figure 35–7 These geese, swimming with the famous animal behaviorist Konrad Lorenz, have decided that he is their mother. They have even followed him around on land—trailing along behind him in single file.

picture of what their mother looks like. This picture must be provided by experience in a process called **imprinting.** The newborn bird will follow the first large slowly moving object it sees. In nature, birds will almost always imprint on their mother, for it is she who is usually closest at the critical time during which imprinting takes place. In the laboratory, however, birds can be imprinted on humans, on wooden models, or even on a slow-moving watering can! See Figure 35–7. It is an important characteristic of imprinting that once the built-in circuitry of the nervous system is given a picture, the behavior cannot be changed. Once a baby bird decides who or what its mother is, it will follow "her"—even if a more appropriate mother appears on the scene.

35–1 SECTION REVIEW

1. What is an instinct? Why do newborn animals show many instinctive behaviors?
2. Name three kinds of learning and give an example of each.
3. How does imprinting combine instinct and learning?

35–2 Communication: Signals for Survival

Section Objectives

- Relate communication to animal behavior.
- Describe ways animals communicate with each other.
- Recognize the importance of communication to survival.

Any time animal behavior involves more than one individual, some form of **communication** is involved. **Communication is the passing of information from one animal to another. Animals use many varied techniques to communicate with one another**. Some of these methods are quite different from anything humans are familiar with.

Figure 35–8 *The clear, piercing eyes of an eagle enable this animal to see a fish swimming beneath the surface of a mountain lake (top). This grass snake gathers information about its environment by tasting it. Its tongue carries molecules from the air to special sensory organs in its mouth (bottom).*

Sensing the Natural World

No two animal species sense the world in the same way. Each animal species has a unique way of gathering and transmitting information. Because animals perceive the world in different ways through different senses, each obtains a different image of the world. Understanding the differences between our sensory world and that of animals is important in the study of animal behavior. Unless scientists understand the sorts of events an animal can detect, they will not be able to understand its behavior. Today, many scientists study animals under natural conditions. These scientists are called ethologists, and the study of animal behavior under natural conditions is called ethology. It is important to keep in mind that because animals react to stimuli in the natural world in different ways, they may also communicate using signals that human senses cannot detect.

Why Animals Communicate

Scientists have found that animals communicate with one another for a variety of reasons. For example, correctly choosing a mate is essential to species survival. Thus, courtship behavior is one of the most important types of communication in almost all animal species. Animals have developed a fairly complicated system of signals between males and females to make certain that the choice is correct. Penguins carry tiny rocks to potential mates, offering the pebbles as a choice bit of nesting material. Other birds have elaborate courtship displays that may occur over a considerable period of time as potential mates indicate their desire to pair. Because choosing a mate is so important, many birds, like the mute swan, pair for life.

Food is another reason why animals communicate. Parents and offspring often need to communicate about the location and availability of food. Parents also warn offspring about potential dangers. Adult animals, too, often warn one another of danger. Many animals, such as lions, communicate with one another when they band together in packs to hunt and kill prey. Animals that live in groups have developed complex and efficient ways to communicate with one another.

How Animals Communicate

Animals communicate with other members of their species and with other species. The ways in which they communicate are limited only by the kinds of stimuli their senses can detect.

Animals with good eyesight often use **visual signals** such as movement and color to communicate. For example, wolves raise their ears and arch their back to communicate anger. The males of many bird and fish species use brightly colored body parts as signals to attract females during courtship and to warn potential rivals to keep away.

Some animals use **sound signals** to communicate. Crickets, frogs, and birds are all able to make sounds to attract mates. Dolphins and other marine mammals signal to one another by making special sounds under water. Scientists have recorded many fascinating songs made by whales as they communicate over vast distances in the oceans.

Some animals with a well-developed sense of smell use **chemical signals** to communicate. These animals produce special chemicals called **pheromones** that transmit information. For example, when an ant finds food some distance from the nest, she walks back to the nest dragging her abdomen on the ground. As she does so, she releases a trail pheromone. Other ants quickly follow the scent of the trail pheromone to reach the food.

Some fishes can generate and detect **electrical signals**. These fishes communicate with other members of their school by changing the electrical signal they produce.

Language

Some forms of animal communication, such as the dance language of the bees, are more complicated than any of the signals just described. The dance developed by honeybees can pinpoint a food source with a great degree of accuracy.

Chimpanzees, one of the most intelligent of the great apes, have a reasonably complicated language composed of sounds, gestures, and facial expressions. However, human language is the most complicated form of communication. Some researchers feel they can teach chimpanzees to communicate with humans. Chimpanzees cannot talk, but chimpanzees do seem able to learn a language composed of hand signs. Some scientists believe the chimps are really intelligent and actually learn to communicate by using these signals. Other scientists insist the chimps are just learning which signs they need to use to get food and attention. According to these researchers, the chimps do not really understand the signs. The debate continues as both sides argue about this fascinating topic.

35-2 SECTION REVIEW

1. What is communication? Why is communication between animals important?
2. What are four ways in which animals communicate with one another? How do these methods of communication depend upon an animal's sensory abilities?
3. Suppose that you visited a planet populated by people very different in appearance from humans. How could an observation of the sense organs of these people help you to communicate with them?

Figure 35–9 *Animals often use sound to communicate with each other. This frog has filled special sacs in its throat with air (top). The air is then expelled, causing sounds to be produced when tissues in the frog's throat vibrate. The naked mole rat spends its life in dark underground tunnels (bottom). The society of mole rats is similar in some ways to insect societies. The "queen" mole rat is the only individual that reproduces. She excretes pheromones in her urine that control the behavior of other mole rats in the colony.*

Section Objectives

- Explain how behaviors are controlled by an animal's DNA.
- Describe how social behavior can increase the survival of a species.

35–3 The Evolution of Behavior

As you have learned in Chapters 9 and 10, the physical structures in organisms develop according to a program contained in their DNA. Different characteristics are coded in different genes or groups of genes. Variations in these genes lead to inheritable variations in the characteristics of the animals that carry them. This genetic variation is the raw material of evolutionary change. Natural selection increases the relative frequency of the most beneficial genes in the population.

Although it may be difficult to believe, genes code for behaviors as well as for physical characteristics. Thus a series of base pairs on a DNA molecule can cause a newborn goose to follow a watering can or a bee to perform a waggle dance. You have seen that genetic control of characteristics can be demonstrated by crossing individuals with different physical traits. In the same way, evidence for genetic control of behavior can be demonstrated by crossing closely related animals that show different behaviors.

Figure 35–10 *This male hornbill has sealed his mate within a hollow tree. Inside the tree, the female lays her eggs and tends her young. The male supplies food for both mother and babies. Later, when the babies have matured, the male frees mother and babies from their tree prison.*

A good example of hybrid behavior is found in lovebirds. A researcher studied two closely related species of lovebirds that build nests of leaves they rip into shreds and carry back to their roosts. One species of lovebird instinctively carries the leaf strips in its beak. The other species tucks the strips neatly between its tail feathers. In the laboratory, a lovebird that normally carries the strips in its beak was crossed with a lovebird that normally carries the strips in its tail. The nest-building attempts of the resulting hybrid birds were quite comical to watch. Hybrid birds were totally unable to build a nest! First they would try to carry the leaf strips in their beak. Then, failing that and acting quite confused, they would try to tuck the strips into their tail feathers. This attempt also met with failure. The birds spent a great deal of time trying to decide how to carry the strips, and when they finally took action, they wound up dropping the strips. Other examples of genetically controlled behaviors have been studied in laboratories in breeding experiments that involved crickets, bees, and fruit flies.

In some situations the fitness of an individual is not affected by cooperation with other members of its species. In such species, social behavior would not be favored by natural selection.

For some species, however, social behavior offers great survival advantages. The evolutionary fitness of an individual is increased if it forms some type of social group with others of its kind. Natural selection would favor the evolution of social behavior in such species. There are many ways that social behavior can increase an individual's fitness. Some animals, such as wolves, hunt together in groups much more successfully than they can as individuals. Other animals, such as many grazing animals, band together because they are safer from predators when they are part of a group than when alone.

SCIENCE, TECHNOLOGY, AND SOCIETY **BREAKTHROUGH**

The Benefits of Living with Relatives

Over the last twenty years, researchers studying animal societies have made some interesting discoveries. They have found that in many animal societies, all or most members of each social group are related to one another. And in many social groups of insects, birds, and mammals (including lions, elephants, and monkeys), all members are either parents, brothers, or sisters.

The theory of kin selection offers an explanation of the phenomena. Evolutionary fitness is now defined as the number of copies of an individual's genes that are inherited by the next generation. Kin selection theory states that it makes no difference whether those genes are provided by a particular individual itself or by that individual's relatives.

Think about this for a moment. A bird receives half of its genes from each parent. Therefore it shares many genes with its brothers and sisters. If for some reason a particular bird is unable to mate, that bird can still ensure that extra copies of some of its genes get into the next generation by helping its parents, brothers, or sisters raise more offspring. The bird's fitness is thus improved by becoming what is called a helper at the nest. Such helpers are, in fact, commonly found among birds such as Florida scrub jays.

Similarly, prides of lions and groups of many primate species are composed of close relatives that help one another. By helping related members of a group to survive, an individual animal, even if it is unable to breed, can contribute to the evolutionary fitness of the group. Thus natural selection can favor the evolution of behaviors that help other individuals.

All the lions in this photograph are closely related. Because they are, each young lion has many similar genes.

35–3 SECTION REVIEW

1. Describe animal behavior that is under genetic control.
2. How does social behavior contribute to the survival of an individual animal?
3. What do you predict would happen to a social animal that was driven from its group? Explain your answer.

LABORATORY INVESTIGATION

EXPLORING MEALWORM BEHAVIOR

PROBLEM

How do mealworms respond to their environment?

MATERIALS *(per person)*

aluminum foil	lamp (or sunlight)
150-mL beaker	10 mealworms
dry cereal	petri dish
small paintbrush	ruler
compass	scissors
cellophane tape	sheet of unlined paper
dissecting tray	

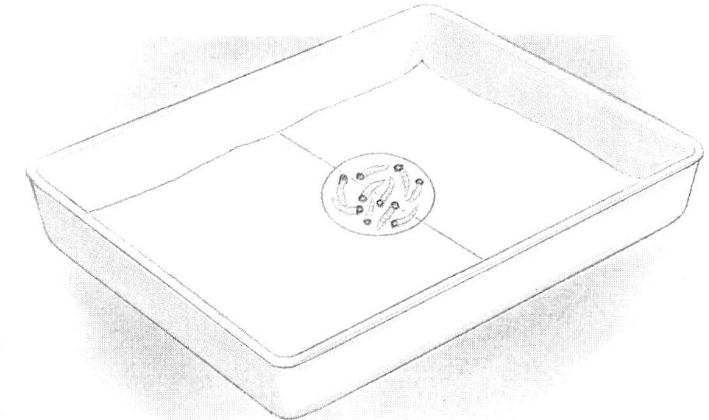

PROCEDURE 

1. Use the scissors to cut a sheet of paper to fit into the bottom of the dissecting tray.
2. Find the exact center of the paper. Use a compass to draw a circle with a 2.5-cm radius at the center of the sheet of paper. Use the ruler to find the centers of the two longest edges of the paper. Mark these two points. Connect the points with a straight line.
3. Place the sheet of paper in the bottom of the dissecting tray. Tape the sheet of paper to the tray along all edges of the paper.
4. Place 10 mealworms into a 150-mL beaker.
5. Put a petri dish under one edge of the dissecting tray to raise it about 1 cm. Place the mealworms into the circle in the center of the tray.
6. Observe the mealworms' behavior for 10 minutes. Note whether they crawl uphill or downhill. Observe what they do when they reach the edge of the tray. Record your observations. Remove the mealworms from the tray.
7. Place a piece of aluminum foil over half of the tray. Line up one edge of the foil with the line you drew down the center of the paper. Shine the lamp directly over the tray. Place the mealworms back in the circle. Observe the mealworms' behavior for 10 minutes. Record your observations.
8. Remove the aluminum foil. Place a small handful of dry cereal in one corner of the tray. Brush the mealworms back into the circle. Observe the mealworms' behavior for 10 minutes. Record your observations.

OBSERVATIONS

1. How many mealworms remained within the circle in the tilted dissecting tray? How many climbed uphill? How many climbed downhill?
2. In response to light, how many mealworms remained within the circle? How many crawled under the aluminum foil? How many crawled into the light?
3. When cereal was placed in the dissecting tray, how many mealworms remained within the circle? How many crawled into the cereal? How many did not?
4. What did the mealworms do when they reached the edge of the tray?

ANALYSIS AND CONCLUSIONS

1. Do mealworms prefer to climb uphill or downhill? How might this behavior be adaptive?
2. Do mealworms prefer to be in light or in shade? How might this be adaptive behavior?
3. Do mealworms prefer to be in or out of the cereal? How might this behavior be adaptive?
4. How is the mealworms' behavior at the edge of the tray adaptive?

STUDENT STUDY GUIDE

SUMMARIZING THE CONCEPTS

The key concepts in each section of this chapter are listed below to help you review the chapter content. Make sure you understand each concept and its relationship to other concepts and to the theme of this chapter.

35–1 Elements of Behavior

- The behavior of an animal is just as important to its survival and reproduction as any of its physical characteristics.
- Instincts are behaviors that are built into an animal's nervous system and cannot be changed during the animal's lifetime.
- Learning is the way animals change their behavior as a result of experience. Animals learn in several different ways.
- Some behaviors, although primarily instinctive, cannot occur without some learning on the part of the animal. In the process of imprinting, for example, newborn ducks and geese combine their natural instinct to follow their mother with an image obtained by experience.

35–2 Communication: Signals for Survival

- Communication is the passing of information from one animal to another. Animals use many varied techniques to communicate with each other.
- Animals communicate with each other for many reasons. For example, animals communicate in order to choose a mate, transmit information about the location and availability of food, and to warn others about potential dangers.
- The ways in which animals communicate is only limited by the kinds of stimuli their senses can detect.

35–3 The Evolution of Behavior

- The DNA in genes codes for behaviors as well as for physical characteristics. Like physical characteristics, variations in the genetic material that codes for behavior can be inherited if the behavior contributes to the animal's survival.
- In some species, the fitness of an individual is affected by cooperating with other members of its species. When social behavior offers great survival advantage, natural selection favors the evolution of such behavior.

REVIEWING KEY TERMS

Vocabulary terms are important to your understanding of biology. The key terms listed below are those you should be especially familiar with. Review these terms and their meanings. Then use each term in a complete sentence. If you are not sure of a term's meaning, return to the appropriate section and review its definition.

35–1 Elements of Behavior

instinct
learning
habituation
classical conditioning
operant conditioning
insight learning
imprinting

35–2 Communication: Signals for Survival

communication
visual signal
sound signal
chemical signal
pheromone
electrical signal

CHAPTER REVIEW

CONTENT REVIEW

Multiple Choice

Choose the letter of the answer that best completes each statement.

1. The fact that many carnivorous animals know how to hunt soon after they are born is an example of a (an)
   a. learned behavior.
   b. automatic behavior.
   c. flexible behavior.
   d. conditioned behavior.
2. The ability of an animal to make a mental connection between a stimulus and some kind of good or bad event is
   a. classical conditioning.
   b. operant conditioning.
   c. habituation.
   d. insight learning.
3. Crossing individuals with different behavioral characteristics demonstrates evidence for
   a. imprinting.
   b. conditioned learning.
   c. habituation.
   d. genetic control of behavior.
4. Behaviors that are naturally built into an animal's nervous system are
   a. imprints. c. instincts.
   b. habits. d. insights.
5. A newborn duck may decide that a wooden object or a human is its mother through the process of
   a. insight learning. c. habituation.
   b. communication. d. imprinting.
6. Scientists who study animals in their natural environments are called
   a. ornithologists. c. ethologists.
   b. imprinters. d. entomologists.
7. The use of pheromones to transmit information is an example of a (an)
   a. sound signal. c. electrical signal.
   b. chemical signal. d. visual signal.
8. An animal that can gather information from electric currents is a
   a. shark. c. dog.
   b. bat. d. goose.

True or False

Determine whether each statement is true or false. If it is true, write "true." If it is false, change the underlined word or words to make the statement true.

1. Physical characteristics of an animal are <u>more</u> important than its behavior to its survival and reproduction.
2. <u>Automatic</u> behaviors can be altered by experience and allow animals to adjust to a changing environment.
3. <u>Instinctive</u> behaviors cannot be changed and are said to be genetically controlled.
4. <u>Learning</u> is the way in which animals change their behavior as a result of experience.
5. <u>Classical conditioning</u> is a decrease in response to an unimportant stimulus that neither rewards nor harms an animal.
6. Trial-and-error learning is also known as <u>habituation</u>.
7. In humans, <u>sugar molecules</u> code for behaviors as well as for physical characteristics.
8. Genes code for <u>behaviors</u> as well as for physical characteristics.

Word Relationships

In each of the following sets of terms, three of the terms are related. One term does not belong. Determine the characteristic common to three of the terms and then identify the term that does not belong.

1. flexible behavior, learning, instinct, habituation
2. movement and color, songs of whales, imprints, pheromones
3. insight learning, training a pet, operant conditioning, trial and error

CONCEPT MASTERY

Use your understanding of the concepts developed in the chapter to answer each of the following in a brief paragraph.

1. What is behavior?
2. What is habituation? How does habituation contribute to an animal's survival?
3. How does behavior contribute to the survival of an individual?
4. How does social behavior contribute to the survival of a group of animals?
5. How do an animal's genes influence its behavior?
6. What is an instinct? Give an example of instinctive behavior in an animal.
7. What is learning? Give an example of a learning behavior shown by an animal.
8. What is insight learning? What group of animals commonly shows insight learning?
9. What is communication? What are two reasons why animals communicate with each other?

CRITICAL AND CREATIVE THINKING

Discuss each of the following in a brief paragraph.

1. **Applying concepts** In the past, zoos often exhibited a single social animal, like a wolf, in a cage. People observing the actions of this animal came away with a distorted view of a wolf's behavior. Today, most zoos exhibit social animals in a group. How does this present a more accurate picture of wolf behavior in the wild?
2. **Applying concepts** A pride of lions consists of several males, many females, and their offspring. About every two years new male lions drive the old males from the pride. One of the first acts of the new males is to kill all of the lion cubs. How could you explain the action of the new male lions?
3. **Relating concepts** Birds often build nests near outdoor bird feeders. What kinds of behaviors are shown by this action?
4. **Designing an experiment** Some people train a dog by giving the animal a treat every time it performs a trick successfully. Other people provide a treat occasionally. Design an experiment to determine which method is more effective.
5. **Using the writing process** You have been placed in charge of a program that hopes to wipe out drug abuse in the United States. Prepare a guidebook that details ways in which the behaviors of people who abuse drugs can be changed.

CHAPTER 36

Comparing Vertebrates

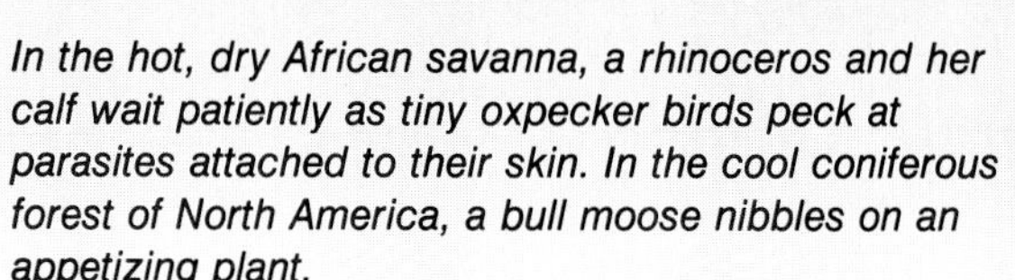

In the hot, dry African savanna, a rhinoceros and her calf wait patiently as tiny oxpecker birds peck at parasites attached to their skin. In the cool coniferous forest of North America, a bull moose nibbles on an appetizing plant.

Along the floor of the Atlantic Ocean, a rattail fish slithers through ice-cold water. In Brazil, a brightly colored tree frog peeps its mating song. In the South Pacific, a three-meter-long Komodo dragon dashes from its hiding place to ambush its prey. High above a New England forest, a bald eagle soars majestically. And atop a sheer cliff in Oregon, a mountain goat hops nimbly from rock to rock.

Each of these animals represents a major vertebrate group. Although each is visibly different from the others, they all share many features inherited from common ancestors that lived hundreds of millions of years ago. The ways in which the similarities and differences among vertebrates have evolved provide some of the most fascinating stories in biology . . . stories that you will read in the pages that follow, as you compare the systems that carry out essential life functions in vertebrates.

CHAPTER OUTLINE

36–1 Evolution of the Vertebrates

Section Objectives

- Describe two basic evolutionary trends.
- Compare techniques of body temperature control in vertebrates.

Ever since the first vertebrates appeared more than 500 million years ago, they have been evolving. During this continual process of change, vertebrates have developed many new and unusual features. Some of these features—sharper claws or longer hair, for example—were relatively simple. Others—such as paired front and rear limbs or an amniotic egg—were far more complex. All these features were tested and shaped by natural selection in a constantly changing world.

The Vertebrate Family Tree

The evolutionary relationships between different groups of vertebrates are shown graphically as a phylogenetic tree in Figure 36–2 on page 786. This tree represents just one hypothesis about how vertebrates are related. Although most (but not all) scientists will agree that amphibians evolved from lobe-finned fish ancestors, reptiles evolved from amphibian ancestors, and birds and mammals evolved from reptile ancestors, there is still much debate about the exact details of vertebrate evolution. For example, some experts think that birds are direct descendants of early dinosaurs, whereas others think that birds are descended from relatives of dinosaurs.

__Figure 36–1__ Taking its first look at the world, the hatching green snake pushes its head through the leathery shell of the amniotic egg in which it developed.

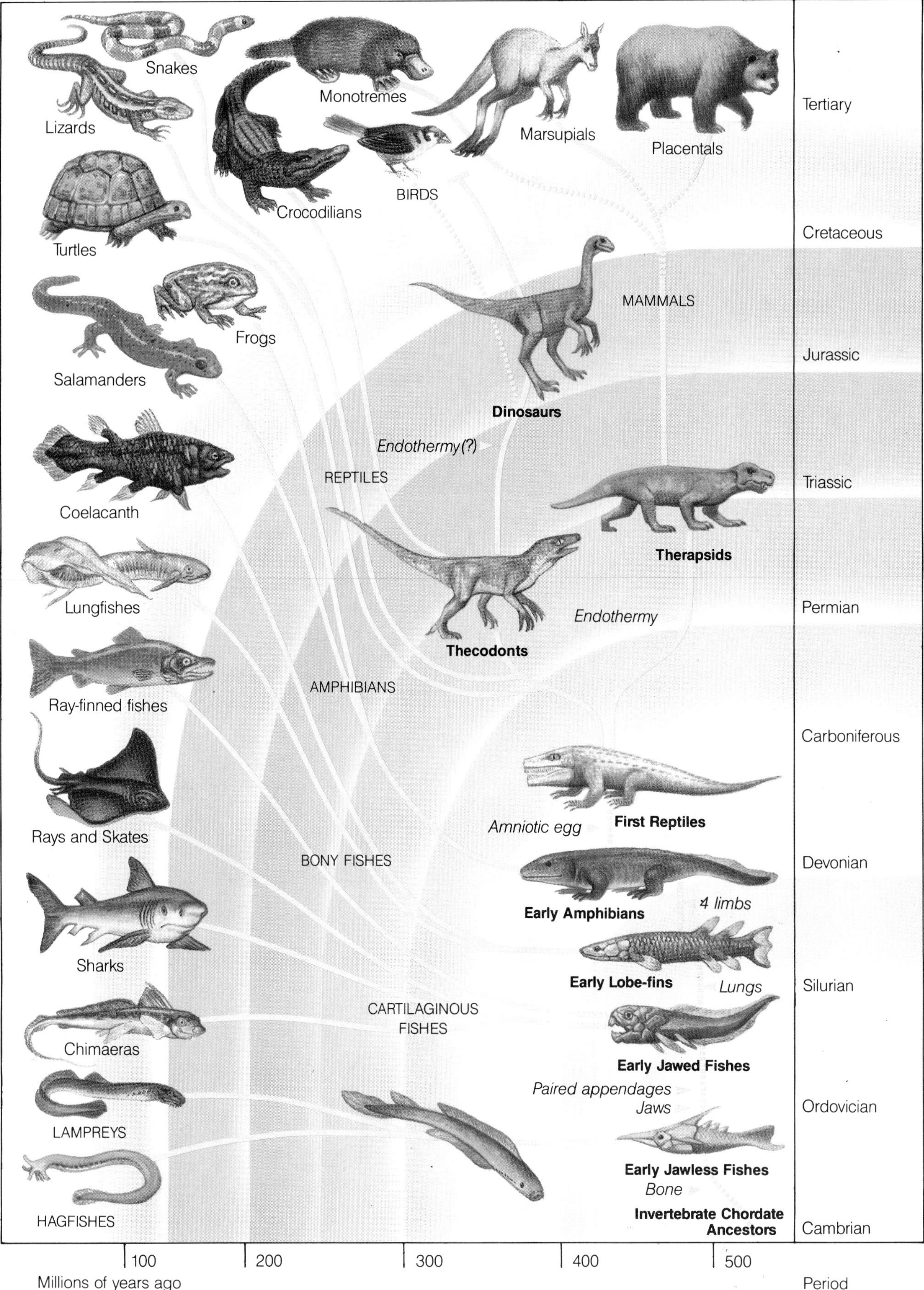
Snakes
Lizards
Monotremes
Marsupials
Placentals
Tertiary
Turtles
Crocodilians
BIRDS
Cretaceous
MAMMALS
Frogs
Salamanders
Jurassic
Dinosaurs
Endothermy(?)
REPTILES
Coelacanth
Triassic
Therapsids
Lungfishes
Endothermy
Permian
Thecodonts
Ray-finned fishes
AMPHIBIANS
Carboniferous
Amniotic egg
First Reptiles
Rays and Skates
BONY FISHES
Devonian
Early Amphibians
4 limbs
Sharks
Early Lobe-fins
Lungs
Silurian
CARTILAGINOUS
FISHES
Chimaeras
Early Jawed Fishes
Paired appendages
Jaws
Ordovician
LAMPREYS
Early Jawless Fishes
Bone
HAGFISHES
Invertebrate Chordate
Ancestors
Cambrian
100
200
300
400
500
Millions of years ago
Period

Trends in Vertebrate Evolution

Two general trends appear repeatedly during the course of vertebrate evolution. The first trend can be stated as follows: **If closely related evolutionary lines are subjected to different forces of natural selection, they tend to become more dissimilar as they evolve.** The second trend is related to the first: **If evolutionary lines encounter extremely similar forces of natural selection, they tend to become more similar to one another as they evolve.**

The animals represented by the vertebrate family tree have branched off into an enormous diversity of habitats and lifestyles. Although the animals produced by the vertebrate adaptive radiation may look incredibly different from the outside, they are remarkably similar inside. For as different vertebrate groups evolved, they utilized the same basic sets of body parts for many uses. The pattern of evolution known as adaptive radiation is also known as **divergent evolution.**

Convergent evolution is the opposite of divergent evolution. When animals from different groups evolve in ways that cause them to resemble one another, we say that they have experienced convergent evolution. One of the many examples of convergent evolution among vertebrates is illustrated in Figure 36-3. As you can see, as certain marsupials and placentals adapted to similar environmental conditions over time, many came to resemble one another a great deal.

Figure 36–3 *Many examples of convergent evolution can be seen between marsupials from Australia and placentals from elsewhere in the world. The ocelot, flying squirrel, groundhog, and giant anteater are placentals.*

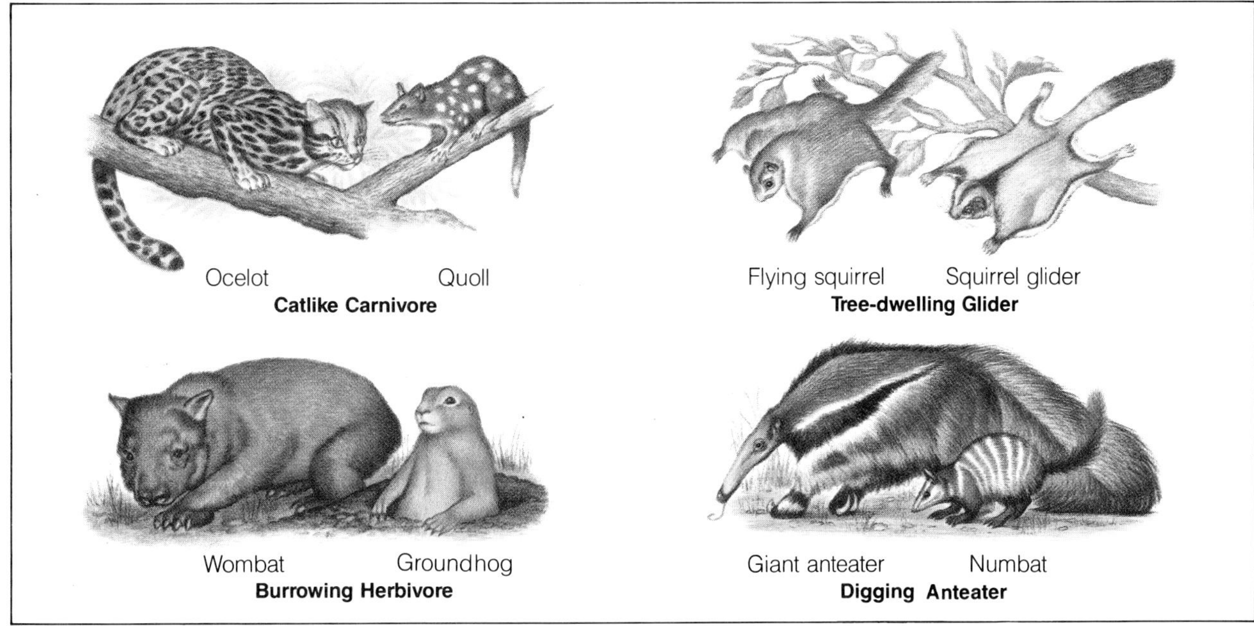

Figure 36–2 *(Opposite page) In addition to illustrating one hypothesis about the evolutionary relationships among vertebrate groups, this phylogenetic tree also shows approximately when important evolutionary innovations occurred. When did lungs appear? Which groups are endothermic?*

Body Temperature Control

The ability to control body temperature is an enormous asset in the struggle for existence. Why? Recall from Chapter 4 that many chemical reactions, including those important to living things, work better at certain temperatures. And essential life functions can be carried out smoothly and efficiently when an animal's internal body temperature is within its preferred "operating range." When the body temperature is too low, animals slow down or become immobile. (This is why ectotherms such as snakes and frogs are easier to catch in the early morning, before they have had a chance to warm up. It is also the reason that such animals necessarily enter a dormant state during cold winters.) When the body temperature is too high, body systems are stressed and fail to function properly. Thus it is not surprising that many techniques of temperature control have appeared in vertebrates. All these techniques incorporate three important features: a source of heat for the body, a way to conserve that heat, and a method of eliminating excess heat when necessary.

As you may recall from Chapter 32, ectotherms must obtain the heat they need from their environment. Endotherms, on the other hand, generate all the heat they need through metabolic activity.

Ectotherms usually rely on specific behaviors to conserve heat and to avoid overheating. For example, lizards bask in the

Figure 36–4 *A horned lizard (right) is an ectotherm that regulates its body temperature in an unusual way. When its body temperature is low, it changes color to a heat-absorbing dark brown. When its body temperature is high, it changes to a heat-reflecting light brown. A snow monkey (left) is an endotherm. Thick gray fur helps conserve heat produced in metabolic processes and allows the monkey to frolic in the snow without lowering its body temperature.*

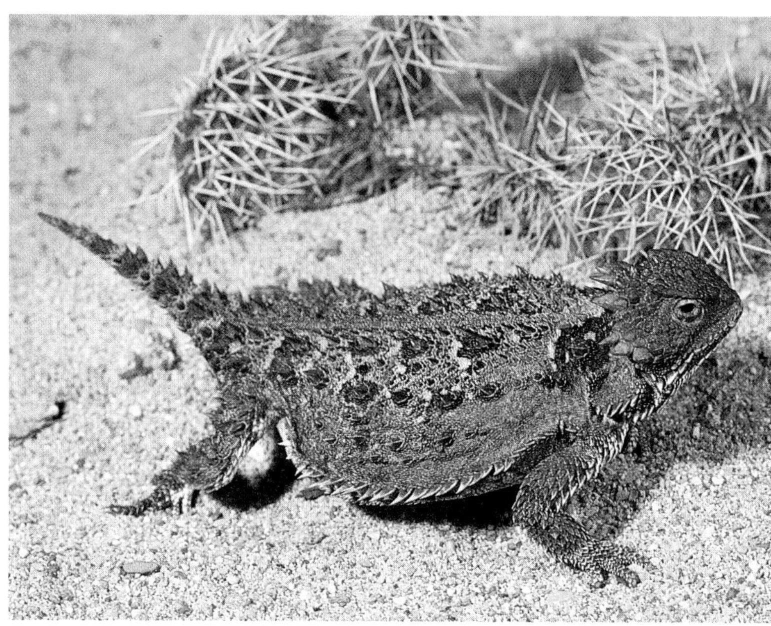

sun to heat their body and hide in the shade or in an underground burrow to cool themselves. A few ectotherms have body structures that enable them to conserve the heat they produce as a result of muscle movement. For example, in fishes such as sharks and tunas the blood vessels are arranged in a way that helps keep warmed blood deep inside the body.

Endotherms, on the other hand, tend to rely on body structures and physiological functions to regulate their internal temperature. Birds and mammals generate body heat internally through metabolic activity. Birds conserve that heat primarily through the use of insulating feathers; mammals use fat and fur as insulation. Mammals can get rid of excess heat either by panting (as dogs do) or by sweating (as humans do). Because it is difficult to get rid of excess heat, many endotherms also employ behaviors that keep their body from overheating when the outside temperature is greater than their body temperature. Some animals rest in the shade, swim in cool water, or retreat to cool underground burrows (or, in the case of many humans, to air-conditioned buildings).

36–1 SECTION REVIEW

1. What is divergent evolution? Give an example of this pattern in vertebrate evolution.
2. Give three examples of convergent evolution among mammals.
3. Compare the ways in which body temperature is controlled in a turtle and in a mouse.
4. People suffering from hypothermia, or low body temperature, often have slurred speech and uncoordinated movements. Explain this observation.

36–2 Form and Function in Vertebrates

Section Objectives

- Describe trends in the evolution of vertebrate systems.
- Compare the ways in which vertebrates carry out their essential life functions.

As you learned in previous chapters, vertebrates perform the essential functions of life with a variety of body structures. In this section you will compare those structures and examine how evolutionary processes have modified certain basic structures over time. As you examine form and function in vertebrates, keep this general evolutionary trend in mind: **As you move through the vertebrate classes from fishes to mammals, organ systems tend to become increasingly complex.** Note that the term increasingly complex does not mean better. The various organs and systems, with their varying degrees of complexity, are simply different ways of performing the functions essential to life.

Movement

As you may recall, all vertebrates except jawless fishes have a vertebral column, or backbone, made of numerous individual bones called vertebrae. These vertebrae are connected to one another by tough ligaments that allow the vertebral column to bend to a certain extent. Two pairs of limbs are attached to this basic supporting structure by sets of bones called limb girdles. Most of the bones in the body can be made to move through the contraction of muscles that are attached to the bones.

In certain vertebrates, such as many fishes and snakes, the main body muscles are arranged into blocks that are positioned on either side of the vertebral column. These muscle blocks contract in waves, one after another, first on one side of the body and then on the other. Because the vertebral column cannot be compressed, these contractions make the body bend rapidly back and forth. This is how many fishes and snakes develop the forward thrust they need to move.

In many (though not all) amphibians, reptiles, birds, and mammals, the muscles and bones of the limbs are the most important body structures involved in movement. There are two interesting evolutionary trends that can be seen as we move from amphibians to mammals. First, the position of the limbs relative to the body shifts toward the center. Second, the movement of the vertebral column when the animal runs changes from a predominantly side-to-side motion to an up-and-down motion. Refer to Figure 36–5 as you read about movement in some representative vertebrates.

Figure 36–5 *The positions of the pectoral and pelvic girdles and the limb bones differ among vertebrates. More primitive vertebrates such as salamanders have limbs that stick out from the sides of their body (top). The limbs of reptiles such as marine iguanas allow the body to be lifted off the ground more (left). In mammals such as lions, the limbs are positioned directly beneath the body (right).*

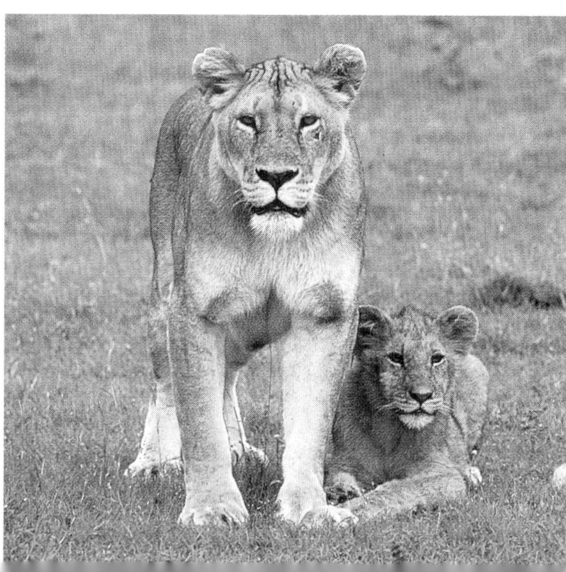

In many amphibians, such as salamanders, the limbs stick out sideways from the body, making it difficult for them to support much weight on land. This gives amphibians their characteristic sprawl. Although the limb muscles in these animals can create some movement, salamanders bend their bodies from side to side (fishlike) to help themselves move farther with each step. In many reptiles, the limbs point more directly down to the ground, allowing them to support weight more efficiently. The body curves somewhat during walking, but not as much as it does in amphibians. Many mammals can stand erect with their legs straight under them, whether they walk on two legs or on four. When walking, most mammals make minimal side-to-side movements with their body. But when running, many flex their backbones up and down a great deal.

Feeding

The heads of vertebrates show many adaptations for feeding. For example, the long bill of the hummingbird and the narrow snout of the honey possum are both adaptations to feeding

Figure 36–6 *As the shape of their jaws and teeth indicate, mammals have adapted to many different feeding habits during the course of evolution. How do the jaws and teeth of a filter feeder compare with those of a gnawing herbivore? How is a walrus specialized for its feeding habits?*

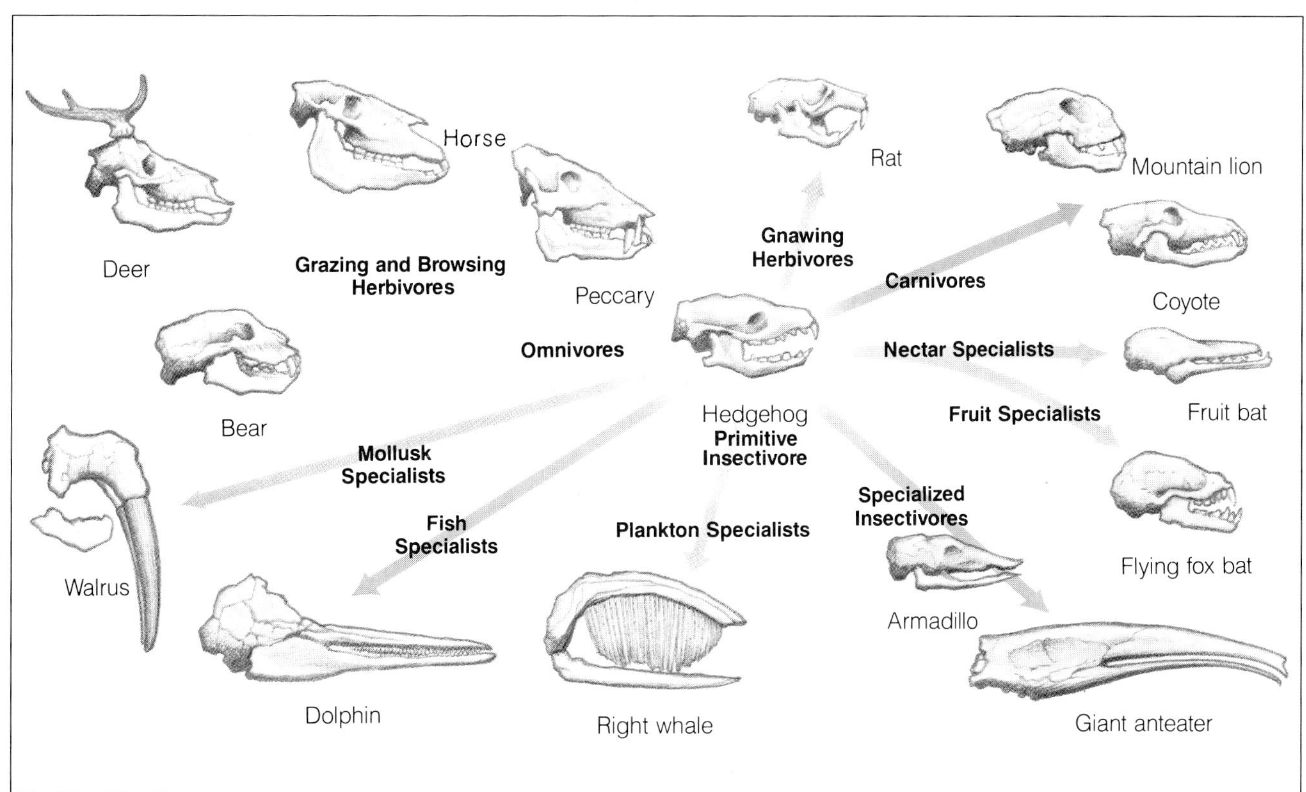

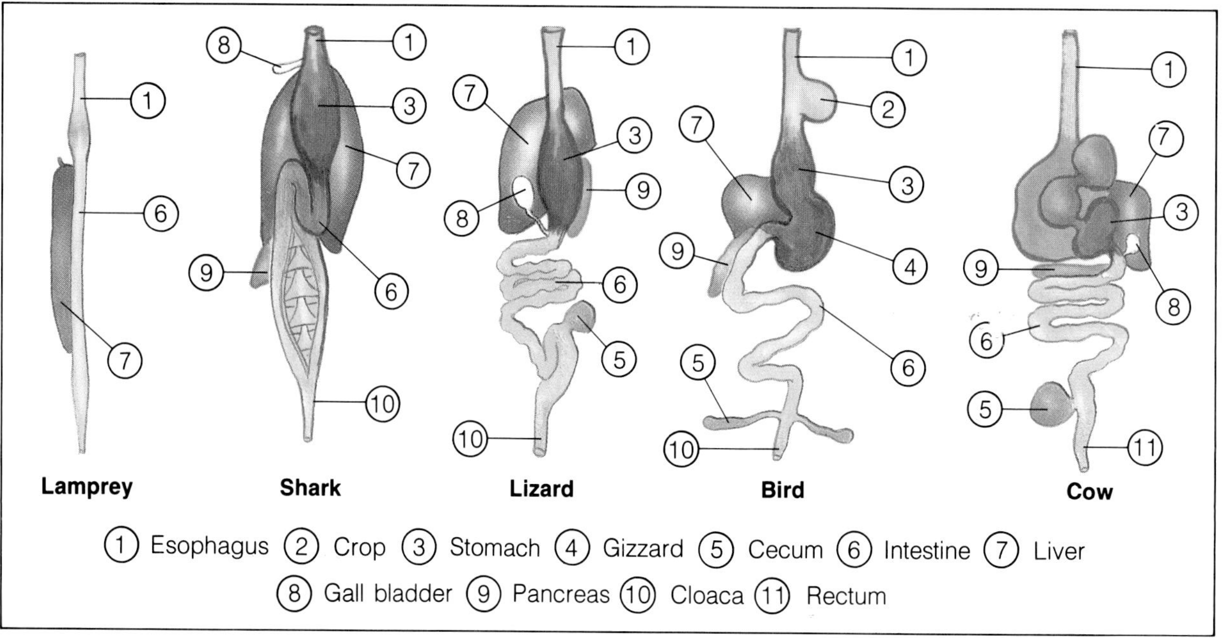

Figure 36–7 *The digestive systems of vertebrates vary in their complexity and are adapted for a variety of modes of feeding. Which vertebrate has the most primitive digestive system? Why does a cow require four "stomachs" to digest its food?*

on nectar. These animals also have long tongues, the better to sip the sweet liquid from flowers. Filter feeders—such as baleen whales, flamingoes, and manta rays—have sievelike structures that enable them to strain food from the water. And carnivores—such as sharks, eagles, and leopards—have sharp mouthparts that help them tear chunks of meat from the body of their prey.

The organs of the digestive systems of vertebrates are equally well adapted for different feeding habits. For example, carnivores typically have short digestive tracts that produce enzymes that are specially adapted to the rapid digestion of meat. Herbivores, on the other hand, often have long intestines and stomachs that harbor colonies of bacteria or protozoans helpful in the digestion of the tough cellulose fibers in plant tissues.

Respiration

Aquatic vertebrates such as fishes and amphibian larvae typically use gills for respiration. As water passes over the gill filaments, oxygen diffuses into the blood in the capillaries and carbon dioxide diffuses from the blood into the water.

Terrestrial vertebrates—and a few aquatic vertebrates such as porpoises and sea turtles—typically use lungs to breathe. When the animals inhale, oxygen-rich air enters the lungs. The

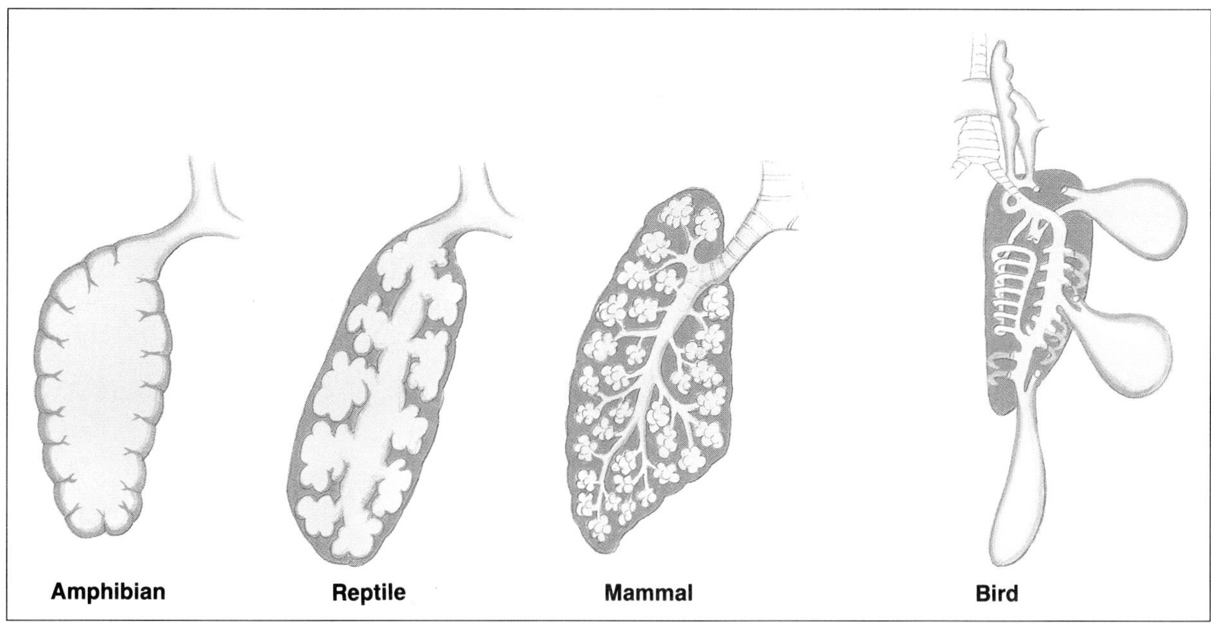

Figure 36–8 *As you move from amphibians to mammals, the branching of the bronchi, or air tubes, increases. In birds, the air tubes do not terminate in "dead-end" alveoli. Instead, tiny one-way tubes carry a continuous flow of fresh air past the respiratory tissues.*

oxygen in the air diffuses into the blood contained within the capillaries of the lungs; the carbon dioxide diffuses into the space within the lungs. When the animals exhale, carbon dioxide-rich air is expelled. Refer to Figure 36–8 as you read about the evolution of the lungs in terrestrial vertebrates.

The typical amphibian lung is little more than a sac with some ridges that increase its surface area slightly. The simplicity of amphibian lungs is not surprising. Because amphibians are ectothermic and not normally very active, their oxygen requirements are fairly low. In addition, many amphibians can also use their moist skin and the linings of their mouth and pharynx in respiration.

Although reptiles are also ectotherms and thus have fairly low oxygen requirements, their lungs are better developed than those of amphibians. Because lungs are typically the only structures used for gas exchange, it is important that their structure ensures efficiency. In more complex reptiles—such as turtles, crocodilians, and certain lizards—the lungs are divided into many large chambers that are in turn divided into smaller chambers. This greatly increases the surface area available for gas exchange.

In mammals, bronchi branch extensively, and the entire volume of the lungs is filled with many thousands of bubblelike structures called alveoli. These alveoli provide an enormous surface for gas exchange. The structure of the lungs allows endotherms to obtain the large amounts of oxygen required by their metabolism. However, the structure of the lungs is still somewhat inefficient. Because air must move in and out of the same passageways, there is always some old air trapped in the lungs after each breath.

The lungs of birds are even more efficient than those of humans and other mammals. A system of tubes within the lungs and air sacs attached to the lungs ensures that air is moved through the lung tissues in only one direction. Thus gas exchange surfaces constantly come in contact with fresh air. Unlike other vertebrates, birds never have old air sitting in their lungs.

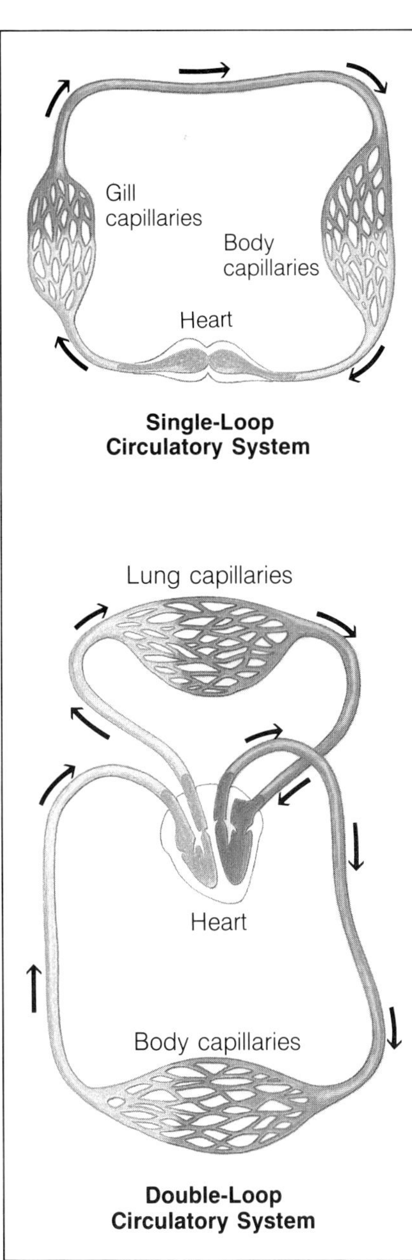

Figure 36–9 *Most vertebrates that use gills for respiration have a single-loop circulatory system. Vertebrates that use lungs have a double-loop system.*

Internal Transport

Vertebrates that use gills for respiration, such as fishes and larval amphibians, have a **single-loop circulatory system**. Blood travels from the heart to the gills to the body and back to the heart. The heart in a single-loop circulatory system is simple. It consists of two chambers: an atrium that receives blood and a ventricle that pumps blood to the body.

Vertebrates that use lungs for respiration have a **double-loop circulatory system**. The first loop carries blood between the heart and the lungs. Oxygen-poor blood from the heart is pumped to the lungs; oxygen-rich blood from the lungs returns to the heart. The second loop carries blood between the heart and the body. Oxygen-rich blood from the heart is pumped to the body; oxygen-poor blood from the body returns to the heart. During the course of vertebrate evolution, the heart developed chambers and partitions that help separate the blood traveling in the two loops of the circulatory system. See Figure 36–10.

In lungfishes, which rely both on gills and on primitive lungs, we can see the first step toward the development of a separate circulatory loop for the lungs. Blood from the lungs has a direct connection back to the heart, and there are partial partitions in the atrium and ventricle. Despite these partitions, a great deal of mixing of oxygen-rich and oxygen-poor blood takes place in the chambers of the heart.

In frogs and toads there are two atria. This means that oxygen-rich and oxygen-poor blood cannot mix in the atria. However, oxygen-rich and oxygen-poor blood can mix in the ventricle. Thus the concentration of oxygen in the blood traveling to the body is not as high as it could be.

Unlike frogs and toads, most reptiles have a partial partition in their ventricle. This partial partition minimizes the mixing of oxygen-rich and oxygen-poor blood, but it does not completely eliminate it.

Birds, mammals, and crocodilian reptiles have hearts that are completely partitioned into four chambers. This means that the lung loop and the body loop of the circulatory system are

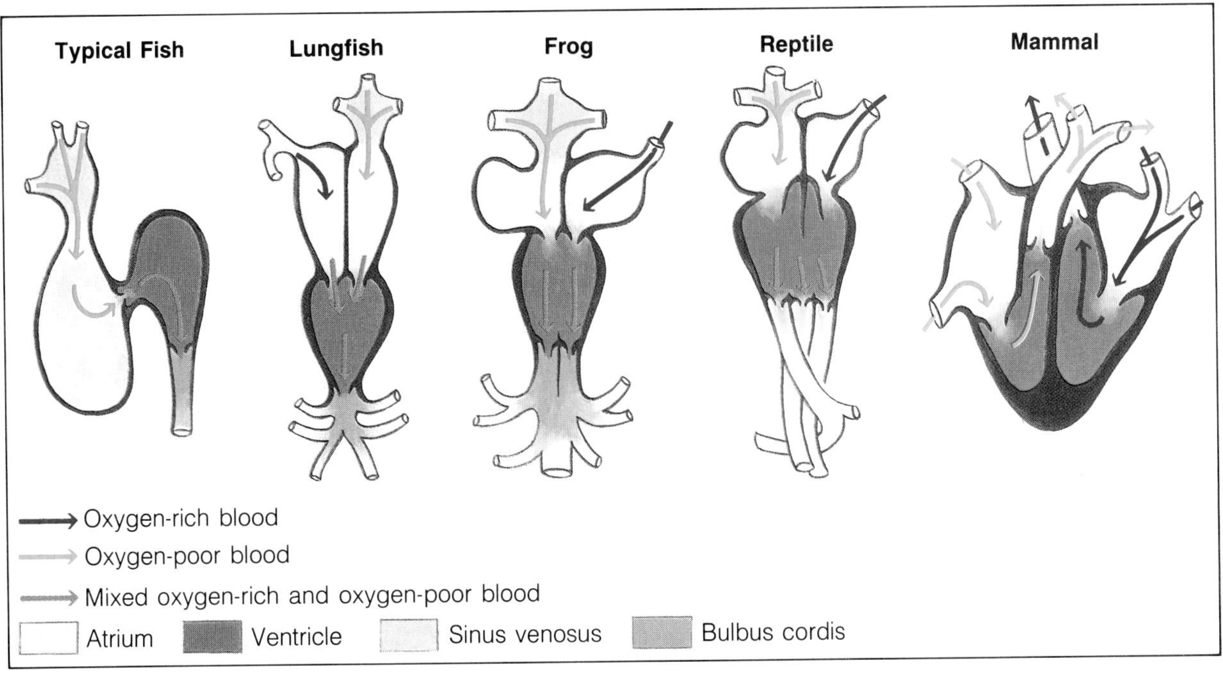

Figure 36–10 *In most fishes, the atrium and ventricle act as a single pump that forces blood around the body. An examination of the hearts of vertebrates that use lungs for respiration reveals various stages in the evolution of a double-pump (four-chambered) heart. Note that oxygen-rich and oxygen-poor blood do not mix in a four-chambered heart.*

completely separated: There is no mixing of oxygen-rich and oxygen-poor blood in the heart. The four-chambered heart is sometimes described as a double pump. One pump moves blood through the lung loop. The other pump moves blood through the body loop.

Excretion

Excretory systems eliminate nitrogenous wastes and regulate the amount of water in the body. In fishes, the gills play an important role in excretion. However, most vertebrates rely on kidneys to carry out the process of excretion. (Recall that a kidney is an excretory organ that is made up of tubules that filter nitrogenous wastes from the blood.)

Nitrogenous wastes are first produced in the form of ammonia, a highly toxic compound that must quickly be either eliminated from the body or changed into a less poisonous form. In aquatic amphibians and most fishes, ammonia diffuses from the gills into the surrounding water, which dilutes the ammonia and carries it away. In mammals, terrestrial amphibians, and cartilaginous fishes, the ammonia is changed into urea before it is excreted. In reptiles and birds, the ammonia is changed into uric acid.

The production of urea or uric acid is an adaptation to marine and terrestrial environments—environments in which the

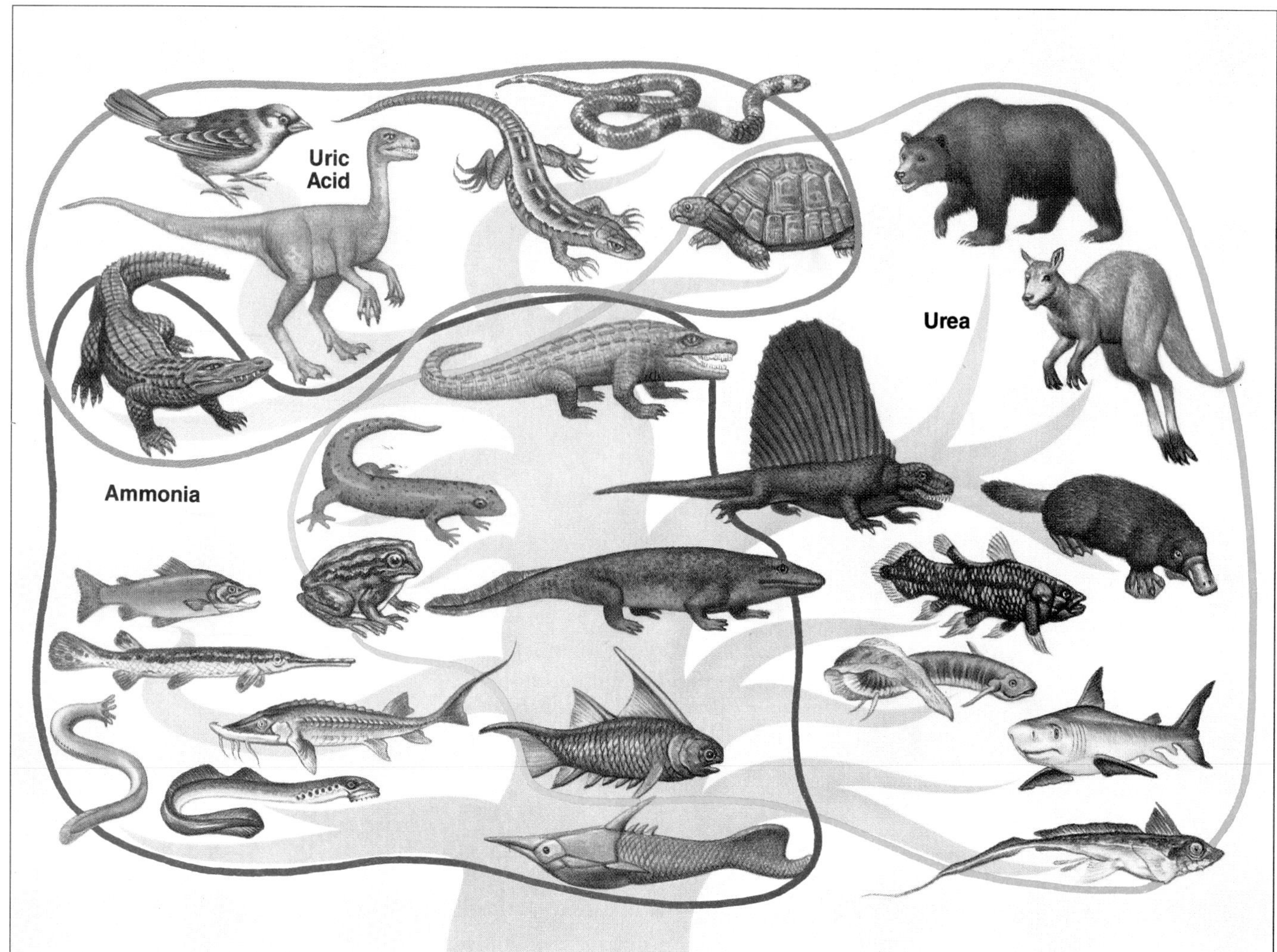

Figure 36–11 The phylogenetic distribution of nitrogenous wastes is shown in this illustration. Which modern-day animals excrete more than one kind of nitrogenous waste?

body tends to lose water through osmosis. Because urea and uric acid are less toxic than ammonia, they can be concentrated. Thus it takes less water to flush these forms of nitrogenous waste from the body. This helps conserve water.

Response

All vertebrates display a high degree of cephalization—their head contains a well-developed brain and bears many sense organs. Refer to Figure 36–12 on page 798 as you read about the evolution of the brain in vertebrates.

Note that the size and complexity of the cerebrum and cerebellum increase as you move through the vertebrate classes from fishes to mammals. The cerebrum can be thought of as the "thinking" region of the brain. It receives, interprets, and determines the response to sensory information. It is also involved in learning, memory, and conscious thought. In fishes, amphibians, and reptiles, the cerebrum is relatively small. In birds and mammals—especially primates—the cerebrum is enormously enlarged and may contain many folds that increase its area. The cerebellum, which coordinates movement and controls balance, is also best-developed in birds and mammals.

SCIENCE, TECHNOLOGY, AND SOCIETY APPLICATION

The Third Eye

Some parts of the brain have taken on a variety of forms and functions in different vertebrate groups. One such part is the pineal gland, a structure that controls the secretion of the hormone melatonin. Under normal conditions in most animals, the pineal gland seems to secrete melatonin at night but not during the day.

In some fishes and reptiles, the pineal gland is located at the top of the brain in a place where several skull bones meet. In some of these animals, such as the tuatara, the pineal gland is sometimes called the "third eye" because it contains cells that are sensitive to light. Despite this name, animals do not see with their pineal gland. Instead, they use it to detect the amount of time they are exposed to either light or darkness. When days are long, the pineal gland secretes less melatonin than when days are short. By reacting to the amount of melatonin secreted by the pineal gland, an animal's body somehow manages to determine changes in season and to prepare itself for such seasonal activities as breeding or hibernation.

Birds and mammals also have a pineal gland, although the gland is buried deep in the brain where it could not possibly be exposed to light. Yet in these animals—including humans—the pineal gland still secretes differing amounts of melatonin in response to changes in day length. Just how the pineal gland receives this information at its position deep in the brain is not certain. But it is clear that changes in melatonin levels from one season to another can have profound effects on human mood. For example, some people become extremely depressed during the long dark months of winter. By exposing such people to extremely bright light, physicians can simulate the effects of spring and cure the depression.

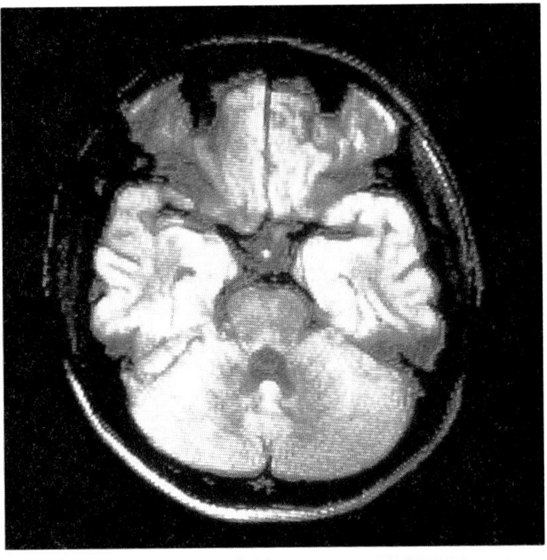

The pineal gland appears as a tiny white dot in the center of this NMR (nuclear magnetic resonance) image of a human brain.

Because humans are considered to have the best developed brain of all animals, people often tend to think that humans can see, hear, and generally detect the world around them better than most animals can. But nothing could be further from the truth. Fishes, certain turtles, and many birds can see colors and patterns much better than humans can. Dogs, bats, and dolphins all can hear sounds of much higher pitch than humans can; and elephants can hear very low-pitched sounds. Humans have an extremely poor sense of smell compared to dogs, cats, and, in fact, most other mammals. As well as having senses that are more keenly developed than ours,

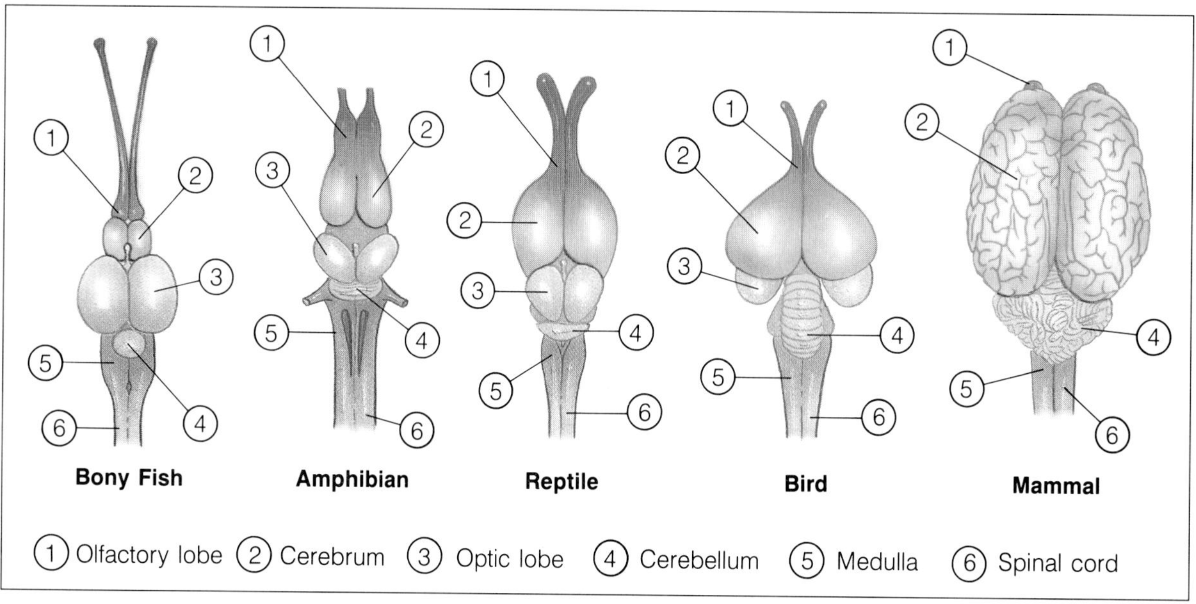

Figure 36–12 *Compare the relative sizes of the parts of the brain in the fish, amphibian, bird, reptile, and mammal.*

animals also possess senses that we lack. For example, rattlesnakes can detect infrared radiation (heat). And certain fishes and the duck-billed platypus can detect the presence of extremely weak electric fields!

Reproduction

Almost all vertebrates reproduce sexually. (However, there are a few species of lizards, fishes, and amphibians that develop from unfertilized eggs.) In some vertebrates, such as codfish and frogs, fertilization is external. In others—reptiles, birds, mammals, cartilaginous fishes, and certain amphibians, for example—fertilization occurs inside the body of the female. As you move through the vertebrate classes from fishes to mammals, there is a general trend from external fertilization to internal fertilization, although there are some exceptions.

Figure 36–13 *The reproductive systems in an amphibian, a bird, and a mammal are shown here. What adaptations to requirements of flight are shown by a female bird's reproductive system?*

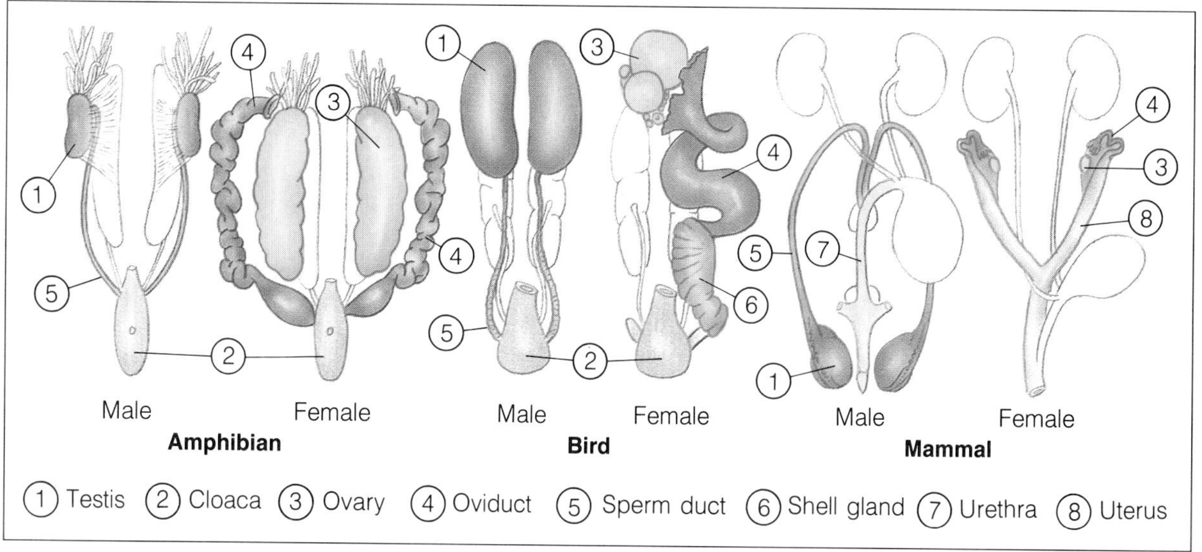

Vertebrates show three different modes of development: They may be oviparous, ovoviviparous, or viviparous. In oviparous species, the eggs develop outside the mother's body. In ovoviviparous species, the eggs develop inside the mother's body but the embryos receive the nutrients they need from the yolk that surrounds them, not from the mother directly. In viviparous species, the developing embryos obtain nutrients directly from the mother's body.

36–2 SECTION REVIEW

1. Describe two evolutionary trends involving the function of movement in vertebrates.
2. Compare the respiratory systems of a frog, a human, and a bird.
3. Compare the circulatory systems of a typical fish and a crocodile.
4. Explain why aquatic animals can eliminate wastes in the form of ammonia whereas land animals cannot.
5. Some biologists say that they can tell more about an animal by looking at certain of its teeth than they can by looking at almost any other bone. Why do you think this could be so?

Figure 36–14 *Many vertebrates care for their offspring. The fuzzy gray chinstrap penguin chick is begging for food. Its taps on the parent's beak signal the parent to release food stored in its crop.*

PROBLEM SOLVING IN BIOLOGY

IDENTIFYING VERTEBRATES

Read the following descriptions of animals and identify the vertebrate class to which each animal belongs. (*Hint:* The vertebrate classes are hagfishes, lampreys, cartilaginous fishes, bony fishes, amphibians, reptiles, birds, and mammals.)

a. Two-chambered heart; single-loop circulatory system; excretes ammonia; herbivore; vertebral column

b. Endothermic; one-way respiratory system; excretes uric acid; single ovary; oviparous

c. Endothermic; limbs located directly beneath the body; excretes urea; highly developed cerebrum

d. Parasite; ectothermic; gills; two-chambered heart; closed circulatory system; no vertebral column

e. Ectothermic; well-developed lungs; excretes uric acid; three-chambered heart; no limbs

f. Four-chambered heart; feet not directly beneath the body when standing; oviparous; ectothermic

g. Three-chambered heart; breathes through the lungs, the lining of the mouth, and the skin; excretes urea; carnivore

h. Single-loop circulatory system; excretes urea; internal fertilization; viviparous

LABORATORY INVESTIGATION

COMPARING VERTEBRATES

PROBLEM

What similarities and differences are there among the classes of vertebrates?

MATERIALS *(per group)*

assorted vertebrates

PROCEDURE

1. Your teacher will provide you with pictures and/or specimens of vertebrates. Each vertebrate will have an identification number.
2. Examine one vertebrate at a time. Determine to which class each vertebrate belongs by using the key below.
3. To use the key, start at step 1 and read descriptions A and B. Only one of the two descriptions correctly describes the vertebrate. At the end of the correct description is either the class to which the vertebrate belongs or directions to go to another step.
4. All steps work the same as step 1. Continue following the directions in each step until you find the proper classification of each vertebrate.
5. Record its identification number and classification. Repeat this procedure for all the vertebrates.

OBSERVATIONS

1. What did the vertebrates you examined have in common?
2. How were the classes of vertebrates you examined different from one another?
3. Did any two vertebrates with visible differences belong to the same class?

ANALYSIS AND CONCLUSIONS

1. How many classes of organisms are generally called fish? Why are they usually grouped together? Why are they placed in separate classes?
2. Why does a snake belong to the same class as a lizard even though it looks more like an eel? What problems does this present in devising a classification key?
3. Although a salamander looks more like a lizard than a frog, frogs and salamanders are in the same vertebrate class. What does this tell you about their ancestry?

Classification Key

1 A. Adult has gills and gill openings .... Go to 2
B. Adult has no gills or gill openings .... Go to 5
2 A. Has no jaw .... Go to 3
B. Has a jaw .... Go to 4
3 A. Wormlike with no eyes .... Hagfish
B. Snakelike with a circular mouth .... Lamprey
4 A. Mouth on ventral surface .... Chondrichthyes
B. Mouth in front .... Osteichthyes
5 A. No covering on skin, no claws on toes .... Amphibians
B. Skin covered with scales, feathers, or fur .... Go to 6
6 A. Scaly skin .... Reptiles
B. Skin not scaly .... Go to 7
7 A. Skin covered with feathers .... Birds
B. Skin covered with hair or fur .... Mammals

STUDENT STUDY GUIDE

SUMMARIZING THE CONCEPTS

The key concepts in each section of this chapter are listed below to help you review the chapter content. Make sure you understand each concept and its relationship to other concepts and to the theme of this chapter.

36–1 Evolution of the Vertebrates

- In divergent evolution, related evolutionary lines become more dissimilar as they are subjected to different forces of natural selection. Divergent evolution is also known as adaptive radiation.
- In convergent evolution, evolutionary lines that are subjected to similar forces of natural selection become more similar to one another as they evolve.
- Ectotherms must obtain the heat they need from their environment. They typically rely primarily on behavior to regulate their body temperature.
- Endotherms generate all the heat they need through metabolic activity. They typically rely on physiological mechanisms to regulate their body temperature. They also use a number of behaviors to prevent overheating.

36–2 Form and Function in Vertebrates

- As you move through the vertebrate classes from fishes to mammals, organ systems tend to become increasingly complex.
- In more primitive vertebrates, the limbs stick out from the sides of the body. In more advanced vertebrates, the limbs tend to be positioned directly beneath the body.
- Some vertebrates use gills for respiration; others use lungs. Lungs increase in efficiency as you move from amphibians to reptiles to mammals. Birds have the most advanced respiratory system of all vertebrates.
- Vertebrates that have a single-loop circulatory system also have a two-chambered heart. Double-loop circulatory systems are associated with lungs.
- Fishes have a two-chambered heart. Frogs and toads have a three-chambered heart. Most reptiles have a three-chambered heart that has a partial partition in the ventricle. Birds, mammals, and crocodilians have a four-chambered heart.
- Most fishes and aquatic amphibians excrete nitrogenous wastes in the form of ammonia. Mammals and cartilaginous fishes excrete urea. Birds and reptiles excrete uric acid.
- As you move through the vertebrate classes, the relative size and complexity of the cerebrum and cerebellum increase.
- Vertebrates may be oviparous, ovoviviparous, or viviparous.

REVIEWING KEY TERMS

Vocabulary terms are important to your understanding of biology. The key terms listed below are those you should be especially familiar with. Review these terms and their meanings. Then use each term in a complete sentence. If you are not sure of a term's meaning, return to the appropriate section and review its definition.

36–1 Evolution of the Vertebrates

divergent evolution
convergent evolution

36–2 Form and Function in Vertebrates

single-loop circulatory system
double-loop circulatory system

CHAPTER REVIEW

CONTENT REVIEW

Multiple Choice

Choose the letter of the answer that best completes each statement.

1. Flying squirrels and flying lizards have flaps of skin that help them glide from tree to tree. This is an example of
   a. phylogenetic evolution.
   b. convergent evolution.
   c. divergent evolution.
   d. adaptive radiation.
2. How many chambers are in a bird's heart?
   a. one c. two
   b. three d. four
3. Adaptive radiation is also known as
   a. endothermy.
   b. ectothermy.
   c. convergent evolution.
   d. divergent evolution.
4. If a vertebrate has lungs, it probably
   a. has single-loop circulation.
   b. has double-loop circulation.
   c. has a four-chambered heart.
   d. excretes ammonia.
5. If a terrestrial animal's limbs stick out from the sides of its body, it probably
   a. is viviparous.
   b. has a two-chambered heart.
   c. is endothermic.
   d. excretes urea.
6. Seals have flippers, bats have wings, and zebras have legs. This is an example of
   a. divergent evolution.
   b. convergent evolution.
   c. phylogenetic evolution.
   d. ectothermy.
7. Animals that generate all the body heat they need through metabolic activity are
   a. oviparous. c. viviparous.
   b. endothermic. d. ectothermic.
8. Which term is not associated with life functions in a typical mammal?
   a. large cerebrum c. endotherm
   b. urea d. oviparous

True or False

Determine whether each statement is true or false. If it is true, write "true." If it is false, change the underlined word or words to make the statement true.

1. Evolutionary lines subjected to similar forces of natural selection tend to become more dissimilar as they evolve.
2. According to the phylogenetic tree, birds are most closely related to mammals.
3. Endotherms rely on behavior to regulate body temperature.
4. All birds are ovoviviparous.
5. Most reptiles excrete urea.
6. Mammals have the most advanced respiratory systems of all vertebrates.
7. Most reptiles have a heart with three chambers.
8. Herbivores have relatively short intestines and special enzymes for digesting meat.

Word Relationships

A. *Replace the underlined definition with the correct vocabulary word.*

1. The part of the brain involved with learning, memory, making decisions, and interpreting information is well developed in mammals.
2. Fishes have a type of circulatory system in which blood travels from the heart to the gills to the body and then back to the heart.

B. *An analogy is a relationship between two pairs of words or phrases generally written in the following manner: a:b::c:d. The symbol : is read "is to," and the symbol :: is read "as." For example, cat:animal::rose:plant is read "cat is to animal as rose is to plant."*

In the analogies that follow, a word or phrase is missing. Complete each analogy by providing the missing word or phrase.

3. internal:external::convergent:____________

4. gills:single-loop circulation::lungs:____________

5. shark:urea::chicken:____________

6. crocodile:frog::four-chambered heart:____________

CONCEPT MASTERY

Use your understanding of the concepts developed in the chapter to answer each of the following in a brief paragraph.

1. Describe the evolution of the vertebrate heart.
2. How is a vertebrate's excretory product related to its environment?
3. Discuss the trends in the evolution of the vertebrate brain.
4. Compare movement in a salamander, an alligator, and a leopard.

CRITICAL AND CREATIVE THINKING

Discuss each of the following in a brief paragraph.

1. **Applying concepts** North American hummingbirds and Hawaiian honeycreepers have long, thin bills adapted for drinking nectar from flowers. How would you go about determining whether their similarities were the result of convergent evolution?

2. **Applying concepts** While traveling along a muddy stream bank, you notice the trail of a small animal. This trail consists of a wide squiggly groove located between footprints that are to either side. To which group of vertebrates does the trail-making animal belong? Explain.
3. **Assessing concepts** Suppose some friends tell you that they have discovered a new evolutionary trend in vertebrates: As you move from fishes to mammals, the body coverings of animals go from scales to fur. Explain whether or not you consider this a useful concept. What kind of information would you need to better evaluate this concept?
4. **Using the writing process** Write a humorous story in which an endotherm and an ectotherm debate the advantages and disadvantages of their particular lifestyles.

Nature Photographer

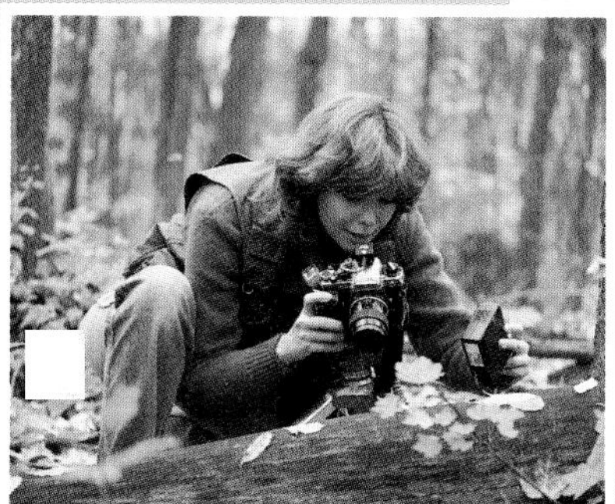

The wide variety of nature photographs that you see in magazines, books, and research articles does more than simply catch your attention. The photographs help you visualize and understand the subject matter. These pictures are the work of nature photographers.

Although no formal education is required to become a nature photographer, a knowledge of photographic techniques and equipment is essential. A strong background in biology or ecology would also be helpful in understanding the subjects being photographed.

To receive information write to the Professional Photographers of America, 1090 Express Way, Des Plaines, IL 60018.

Marine Biologist

Marine biologists study organisms that live in water—from the smallest marine bacteria to the largest whales. On sea expeditions marine biologists collect samples that are later identified and analyzed. Their conclusions provide information about how marine life is affected by environmental conditions. Most marine biologists specialize in either plants or animals, and many select a particular species to study.

Marine biologists are required to have a Bachelor's degree in the biological sciences or chemistry.

For additional information write to the Virginia Institute of Marine Science, Gloucester Point, VA 23062.

Veterinarian

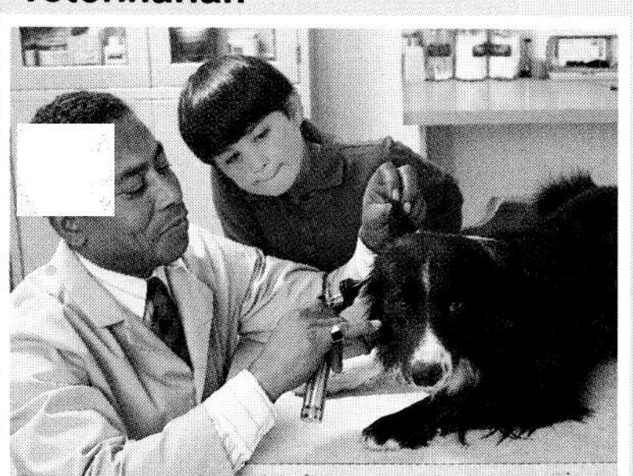

Veterinarians diagnose animal illnesses, treat diseased or injured animals, and give advice on animal care and breeding. Some veterinarians work exclusively with large animals, mostly in rural areas. Other veterinarians work in small animal hospitals, where they specialize in domestic animals.

Veterinarians must complete a four-year course of study after college to receive a Doctor of Veterinary Medicine degree. A state license is also required for private practice.

For information write to the American Veterinary Medical Association, 930 N. Meacham Rd., Schaumburg, IL 60196.

HOW TO WRITE A RÉSUMÉ

A résumé is a short summary of your background and accomplishments. Whether or not you will be granted an interview is dependent upon how you present yourself in your résumé. Your résumé, therefore, must highlight your skills in a clear and impressive manner.

Your résumé must first include your name, address, and telephone number. Your high school and the major courses you took as well as your past employers and the positions you held should be listed next. You can also include any personal accomplishments such as awards or scholarships. Any organizations to which you belong that might be of importance to an employer should be added.

Your résumé, like your cover letter, must be neatly typed without errors. If possible, your résumé should not exceed one page.

FROM THE AUTHORS

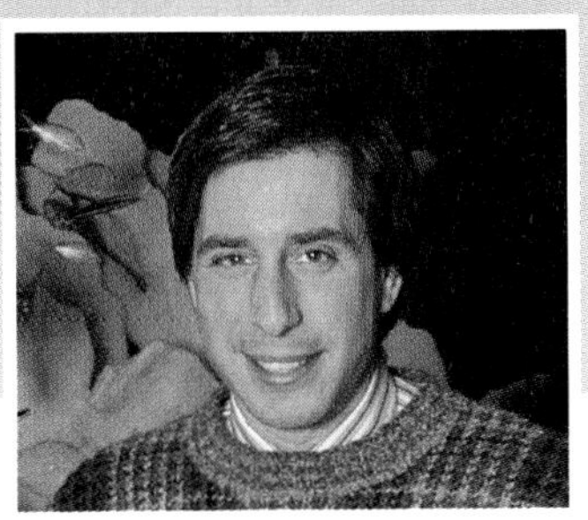

As a biologist, I am extremely fond of just about all the plants and animals I've ever met—with the possible exception of mosquitoes and slugs, which I think the world could do very well without. But I admit that I particularly like vertebrates and am unusually fond of fish. Perhaps that's because my love affair with the animal kingdom really began at the age of nine when I won a goldfish in a little glass jar with a lucky toss of a coin at the county fair. When I showed up on my parents' doorstep carrying "Oscar" in a plastic bag, my folks were kind enough—or perhaps foolish enough—to allow us both to stay. You see, we lived in an apartment building that didn't allow any other sorts of pets, so I could never have a dog, cat, or even a bird. But in less than a year, Oscar's bowl had grown into a ten-gallon aquarium, and things soon got out of control.

Later on, when my parents sent me off to college, they thought I was planning to go to medical school. Instead, several globe-trotting expeditions and two advanced degrees in biology later, I finally received my Ph.D. from the Fish Department at Harvard University. Along the way, I have managed to develop a liking for lots of other living things, many of which I have either worked with in my research or kept as pets. And to this day, some of my most enjoyable working days are spent designing exhibits for really big fish tanks—the kind they have in major public aquariums. Care to feed the sharks, anyone?

Joe Levine

UNIT 9

Human Biology

The music resounds as the beautifully clad figure skaters glide along the ice, turning and twisting to every beat. Their combination of delicate balance, precise timing, and graceful strength creates a wondrous display with seemingly effortless ease. Yet hidden from the outward performance is the amazing network of complex organ systems that enables the skaters to move as they do. Their muscles allow them to move their skeletal bones to the choreographed patterns of their routine. Their senses enable them to hear the music and to see each other and the arena. Their bodies use nutrient resources to provide them with a constant supply of energy throughout their act. And all of this is coordinated by the brain. Now that's quite a performance!

The internal performance is not limited to professional skaters. In fact, it is taking place in your own body at this very moment. And it is required for every single action you perform—from tying your shoes to skating on ice. It is the interaction of our various systems, the rhythm of the human body, that defines life as we know it and enables us to grow, develop, and reproduce.

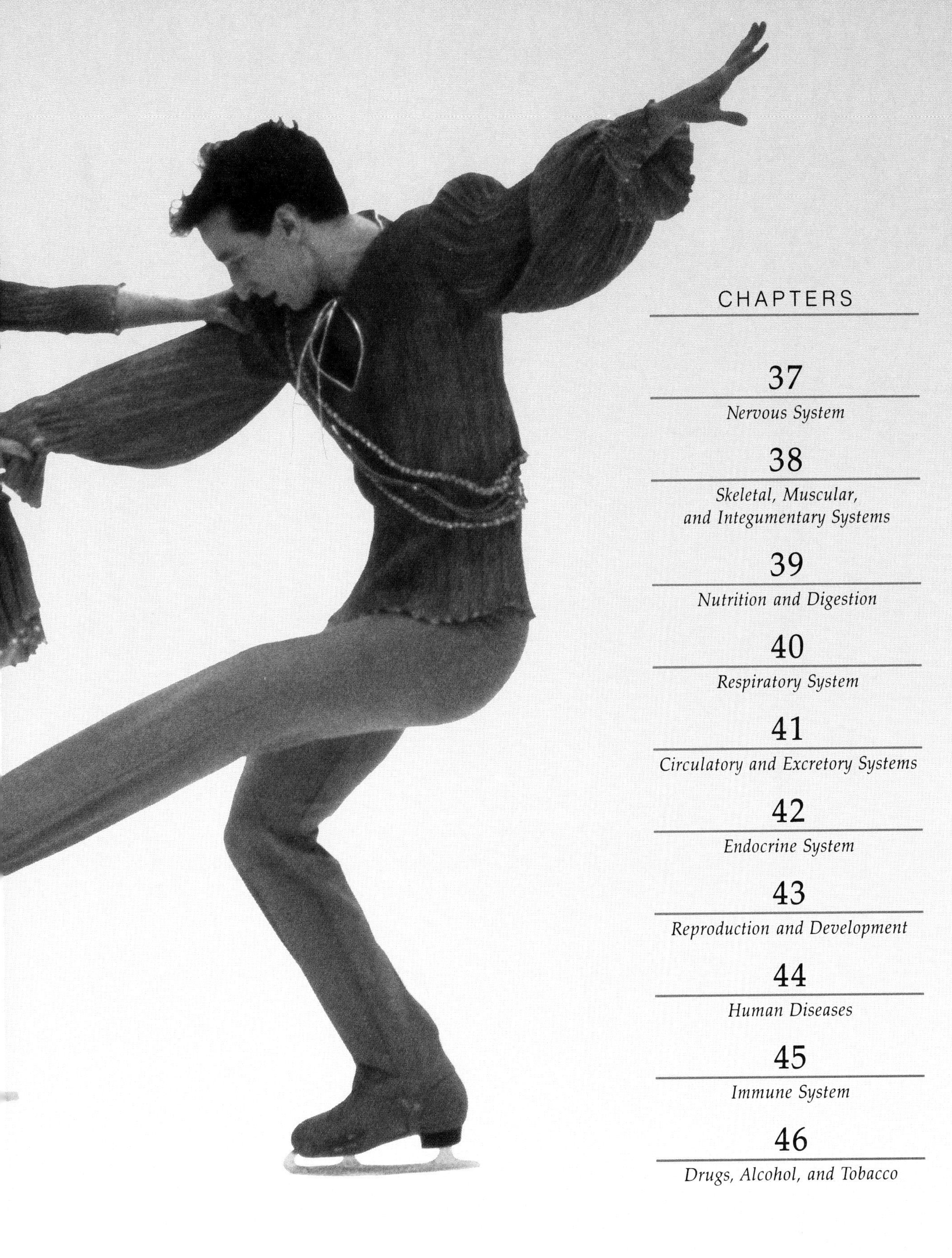

CHAPTERS

CHAPTER 37

Nervous System

The human nervous system contains billions of nerve cells. Each nerve cell, such as the one growing on an integrated circuit (right) and the one from the spinal cord (left), performs more complicated tasks than a computer.

Because it's such a beautiful summer day, you decide to visit one of your favorite places: the beach, a park, a woods, or a favorite spot in your own yard. Suddenly, while engrossed in reading a book, you feel a tingle on your shoulder. Quickly you place your book down next to you and swat at a mosquito just as it flies away.

What has happened? You and the mosquito have just engaged in combat. Fortunately for the mosquito, it got away. (It usually does.)

But how did you know the mosquito was there? And how were you able to coordinate the actions of thousands of your cells in order to react and respond to the presence of the mosquito? In this chapter you will find the answers to these questions. You will also learn how one of the systems of the human body—the nervous system—responds to, monitors, interprets, regulates, and adjusts to changes in the environment in a matter of milliseconds.

CHAPTER OUTLINE

37–1 The Nervous System

Section Objectives

- Describe the function of the nervous system.
- Relate the structure of a neuron to its function.
- Explain the changes that occur across a neuron during the transmission of a nerve impulse.

Most of us have played softball—a game that requires not only athletic skill but also control and communication. The catcher and the pitcher must agree on the pitch before it is thrown. The batter must be alert for the signal to bunt, take a pitch, or swing away. On-base runners must know if they are expected to steal a base. From the dugout, the coaches send in signals about these and other important matters. Communication is vital to a team's success.

Communication is also vital to the survival of living organisms. In order to interact with their environment, multicellular organisms have developed a communication system at the cellular level. Within these organisms, specialized cells allow messages to be carried from one cell to another so that communication among all body parts is smooth and efficient. In humans, these cells make up the **nervous system.** The nervous system controls and coordinates all the essential functions of the human body. **The nervous system receives and relays information about activities within the body and monitors and responds to internal and external changes.**

Figure 37–1 *Athletes such as Kathy Johnson have raised their coordinated movement to an art form. Their movements, like the hundreds we make every day, are made possible by the nervous system, with its intricate network of nerves (inset).*

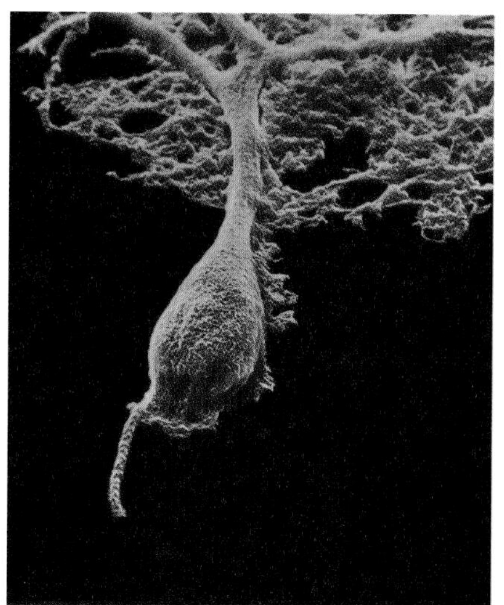

Figure 37–2 *One of the body's billions of neurons can be seen in this electron micrograph. Note the ropelike axon at the bottom of the photograph.*

The Neuron

The cells that carry messages throughout the nervous system are called **neurons**. Because the messages take the form of electrical signals, they are known as **impulses**. Neurons can be classified into three types according to the directions in which these impulses move. **Sensory neurons** carry impulses from the sense organs to the brain and spinal cord. **Motor neurons** carry impulses from the brain and spinal cord to muscles or glands. And **interneurons** connect sensory and motor neurons and carry impulses between them.

Although neurons come in all shapes and sizes, they have enough features in common that we can draw a typical neuron. See Figure 37–3. The largest part of the neuron is the **cell body**. The cell body contains the nucleus and much of the cytoplasm. Most of the metabolic activity of the cell, including the generation of ATP and the synthesis of proteins, takes place in the cell body. Spreading out from the cell body are short branched extensions called **dendrites**. Dendrites carry impulses from the environment or from other neurons toward the cell body. The long fiber that carries impulses away from the cell body is called the **axon**. The axon ends in a series of small swellings called **axon terminals**, which are located some distance from the cell body. Neurons may have dozens or even hundreds of dendrites but usually only one axon.

Figure 37–3 *In a typical neuron, the dendrite and cell body receive the stimulus, which then travels through the axon to the axon terminals.*

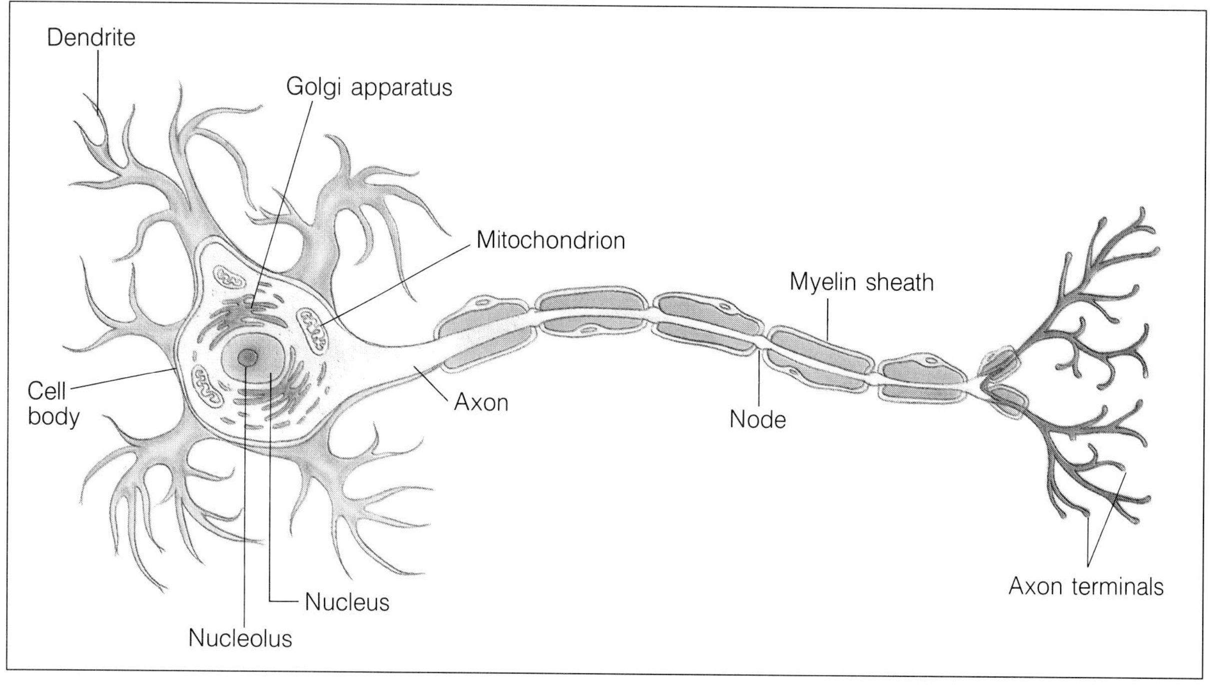

The Nerve Impulse

More than 150 years ago, the Italian scientist Luigi Galvani, a pioneer in the study of electricity, found that nervous tissue (groups of cells that conduct impulses) displays electrical activity. This electrical activity is in the form of a nerve impulse, which is a flow of electrical charges along the cell membrane of a neuron. This flow is due to movement of ions across the membrane.

RESTING POTENTIAL As shown in Figure 37–4, a nerve cell has an electrical potential (also known as a voltage) across its cell membrane because of a difference in the number of positively and negatively charged ions on each side of the cell membrane. This potential is approximately 70 millivolts (mV). One millivolt is equal to 0.001 volt. (By contrast, the potential between the poles of a flashlight battery is 1500 millivolts, or 1.5 volts.) What is the source of this potential? Proteins in the neuron known as sodium-potassium pumps move sodium ions (Na^+) out of the cell and actively pump potassium ions (K^+) into the cell.

As a result of this active transport, the cytoplasm of the neuron contains more K^+ ions and fewer Na^+ ions than the surrounding medium. The cytoplasm also contains many negatively charged protein molecules and ions. However, K^+ ions leak back out across the cell membrane more easily than Na^+ ions leak in, and the negatively charged protein molecules and ions do not leak in or out. The net result of the leakage of positively charged ions out of the cell is a negative charge on the inside of the neuron's cell membrane. This charge difference is known as the **resting potential** of the neuron's cell membrane. The neuron, of course, is not actually resting because it must produce a constant supply of ATP to fuel the sodium-potassium pump.

As a result of its resting potential, the neuron is said to be polarized: that is, negatively charged on the inside of the cell membrane, and positively charged on the outside. See Figure 37–4. A neuron maintains this polarization until it is stimulated.

Figure 37–4 *The resting potential across the neuron cell membrane is established when the protein pump in the cell membrane pumps potassium ions (K^+) in one direction and sodium ions (Na^+) in the other (A). As the protein pump continues to work for a while, a large number of K^+ ions enter the cell and a large number of Na^+ ions leave the cell (B). The cell membrane, however, is more leaky to K^+ ions than it is to Na^+ ions. As a result, more K^+ ions leak out of the cell, and fewer Na^+ ions leak into the cell. This leakage causes an excess of positive charges on the outside of the membrane and an excess of negative charges on the inside (C).*

Key
- Protein pump
- Sodium ion (Na^+)
- Potassium ion (K^+)
- Leakage of small amount of Na^+ into cell
- Leakage of large amount of K^+ out of cell

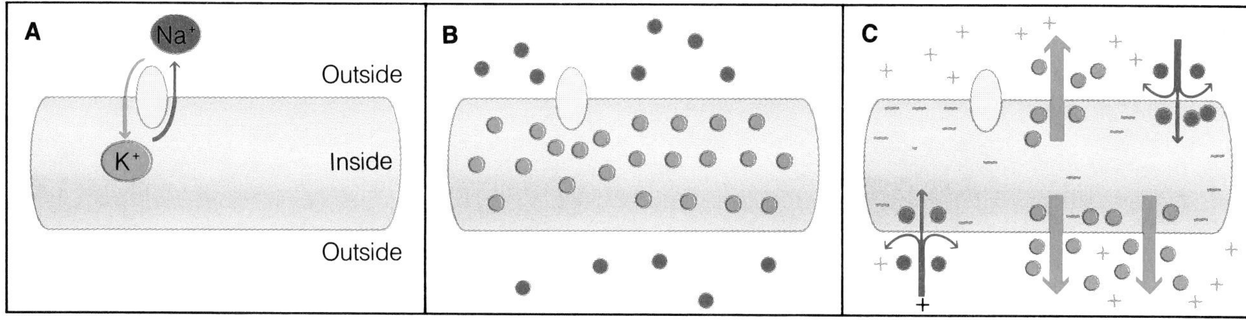

THE MOVING IMPULSE A nerve impulse is similar to a ripple passing along the surface of a pond. Instead of a splash, the impulse causes a movement of ions across the cell membrane of a neuron. How does this movement occur?

The cell membrane of a neuron contains thousands of tiny molecules, known as gates, that allow either sodium or potassium ions to pass through. Generally, the gates are closed. At the leading edge of an impulse, however, the sodium gates open, allowing positively charged Na^+ ions to flow inside the cell membrane. The inside of the membrane temporarily becomes more positive than the outside. The membrane is now said to be depolarized. As the impulse passes, the potassium gates open, allowing positively charged K^+ ions to flow out. The membrane is now said to be repolarized, which means that it is once again negatively charged on the inside of the cell membrane and positively charged on the outside.

The depolarization and repolarization of a membrane produce an **action potential**. The nerve impulse can be defined as an action potential traveling along the membrane.

There are several important facts about impulses (action potentials) that you should keep in mind. First, an impulse is not an electric current. Instead, it is a wave of depolarization and repolarization that passes along the neuron. Second, an impulse is much slower than an electric current. Electric currents move almost instantaneously, whereas action potentials usually travel at speeds ranging from 10 centimeters per second to 1 meter per second. Third, unlike an electric current, the strength of an impulse is always the same—there is either an impulse in response to a stimulus or there is not.

Figure 37–5 *When the inside of a neuron's cell membrane is negatively charged with respect to the outside, it is said to be polarized. If a stimulus is applied to the membrane, electrical changes occur across the cell membrane and may result in an impulse (A). At the leading edge of the impulse, a small part of the membrane becomes depolarized. When this happens, sodium gates open, the membrane becomes more permeable to Na^+ ions, and an action potential occurs (B). As the action potential passes, potassium gates open, allowing K^+ ions to flow out. This outward flow of K^+ ions restores the resting potential, and the membrane is said to be repolarized (C). The action potential continues to move along the axon in the direction of the nerve impulse (D).*

Key
— Closed sodium and potassium gates
⌣⌣ Opened sodium gates

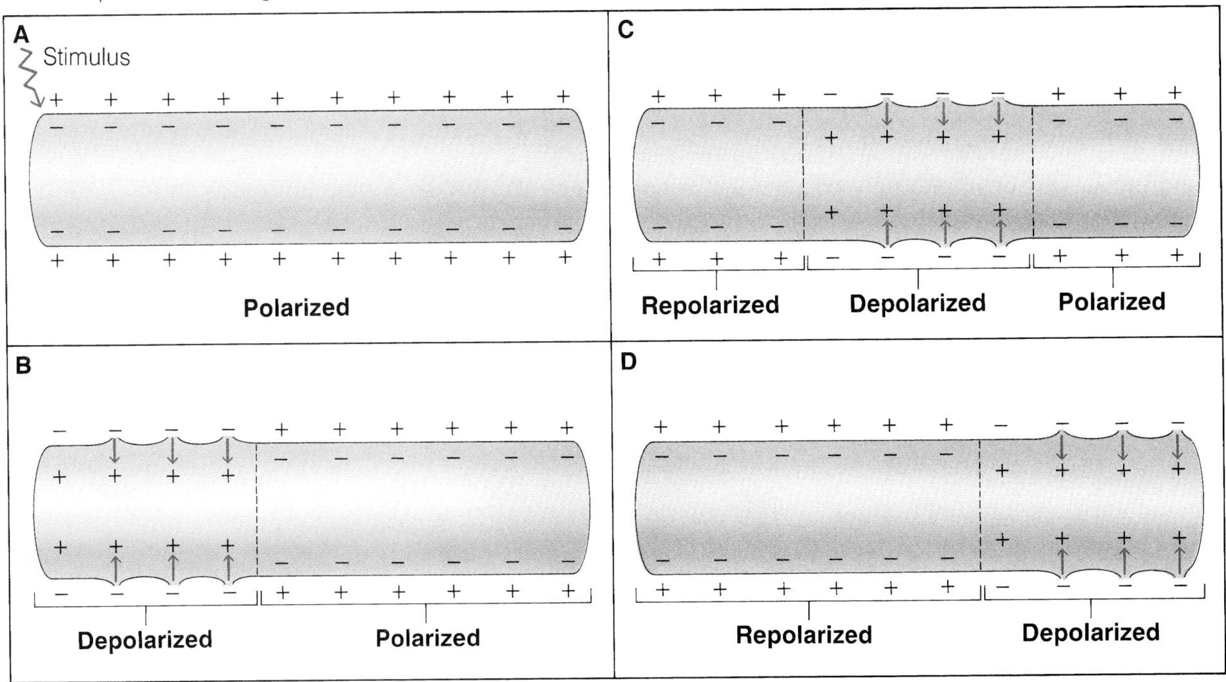

PROPAGATION OF THE IMPULSE Until now, we have discussed the nerve impulse as if it occurs in only one place on the membrane. However, an impulse is self-propagating. That is, an impulse at any point on the membrane causes an impulse at the next point along the membrane. We might compare the flow of an impulse to the fall of a row of dominoes. As each domino falls, it causes its neighbor to fall. Unlike dominoes, however, the impulse can restore itself. Imagine dominoes that can set themselves back up and wait to fall again!

Although the nerve impulse is self-propagating, it can move in only one direction. This is because the part of the membrane behind the impulse has a brief period during which its sodium gates will not open. As a result, the impulse cannot go backward.

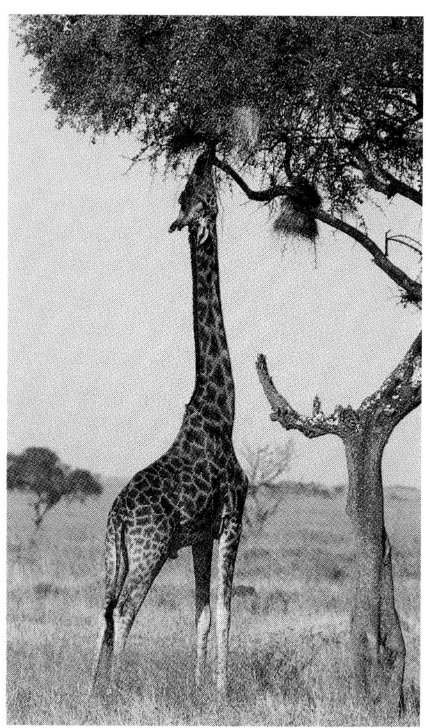

Figure 37–6 Because many of the axons of vertebrates, such as the giraffe, are wrapped in myelin, nerve impulses travel more rapidly than they do in invertebrates.

THE ROLE OF MYELIN As you just read, impulses can move along the membrane of a neuron at rates as fast as 1 meter per second. Although this rate is impressive, it is not practical for large animals. For example, a giraffe might have to wait three or four seconds for impulses to travel from its feet to its brain. Such delays would make large animals hopelessly uncoordinated. But as you probably know, giraffes are graceful and efficient in their movements.

What improves the rate of impulses along an axon? The answer is a substance known as **myelin**. Myelin, which is composed of 80 percent lipid and 20 percent protein, forms an insulated sheath, or wrapping, around the axon.

The most important feature of myelin is that there are small nodes, or gaps, between adjacent sheaths along the axon. As an impulse moves down a myelinated (covered with myelin) axon, the impulse jumps from node to node instead of moving continuously along the membrane. This jumping greatly increases the speed of the impulse. Some large myelinated axons conduct impulses as rapidly as 200 meters per second. This speed is significant when compared with speeds of only a few millimeters per second in small unmyelinated axons.

The formation of myelin around axons can be thought of as a crucial event in evolution. Because of myelin, the propagation of the nerve impulse is faster in vertebrates than in invertebrates.

Figure 37–7 Most nerve fibers, such as the human auditory nerve (right), are wrapped in myelin, which forms a thick outer covering. In myelinated fibers, the action potential jumps from node to node (left).

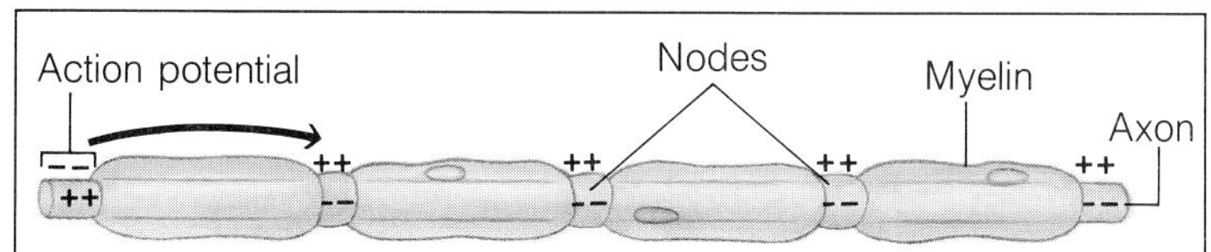

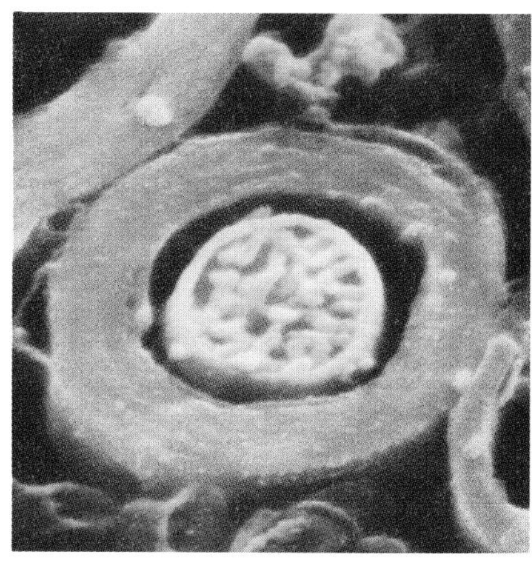

THE THRESHOLD Recall that the strength of an impulse is always the same—either there is an impulse in response to a stimulus or there is not. In other words, a stimulus must be of adequate strength to cause a neuron to conduct an impulse. The minimum level of a stimulus that is required to activate a neuron is called the **threshold**. Any stimulus that is weaker than the threshold will produce no impulse; any stimulus that is stronger than the threshold will produce an impulse. Thus a nerve impulse follows the all-or-none principle.

We can illustrate the all-or-none principle by again using a row of dominoes. Suppose we were to give the first domino in the row a slight push. If the push was really slight, the domino would not move at all. If we were to push a little harder, the domino would teeter back and forth a bit, touching the next domino. A slightly stronger push would cause the domino to fall, hitting the next domino. We have succeeded in reaching the domino's threshold and the row of dominoes would continue to fall.

It is important to mention that the all-or-none principle is not restricted to impulses as they travel along neurons. It also occurs when impulses move from one neuron to another and when information from the environment causes a nerve impulse to occur.

The Synapse

As you may recall, the axon ends with many small swellings called axon terminals. At these terminals the neuron may make contact with the dendrites of another neuron, with a **receptor**, or with an **effector**. Receptors are special sensory neurons in sense organs that receive stimuli from the external environment. Effectors are muscles or glands that bring about a coordinated response. The points of contact at which impulses are passed from one cell to another are known as **synapses**.

The axon terminals at a synapse contain tiny vesicles, or sacs. These tiny vesicles are filled with chemicals known as **neurotransmitters**. A neurotransmitter is a substance that is used by one neuron to signal another.

When an impulse moves down the axon and arrives at the axon terminal, dozens of vesicles fuse with the cell membrane and discharge the neurotransmitter into the small gap between the two cells. See Figure 37–8. The molecules of the neurotransmitter diffuse across the gap and attach themselves to special receptors on the membrane of the neuron receiving the impulse.

When the neurotransmitter becomes attached to the cell membrane of the adjacent nerve cell, it changes the permeability of that membrane. As a result, Na^+ ions diffuse through the membrane into the cell. This process continues for only a few milliseconds, stopping when the neurotransmitter detaches from the membrane. However, if enough neurotransmitter is

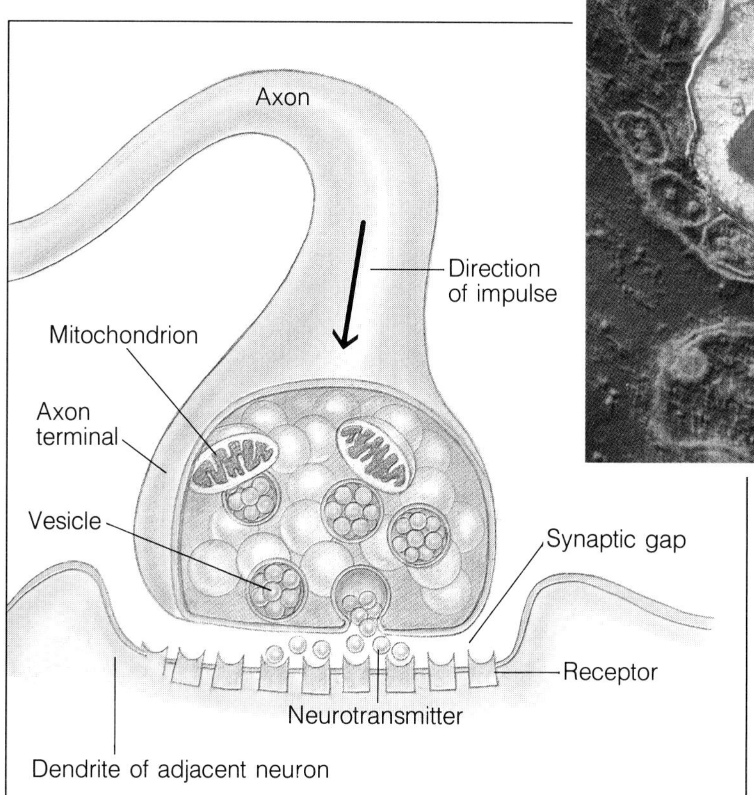

Figure 37–8 *When an impulse arrives at the axon terminal, dozens of vesicles fuse with the axon membrane, releasing neurotransmitter molecules into the synaptic gap. These molecules diffuse across the gap and combine with receptors on the membrane of the adjacent neuron. Compare the structures in the diagram with those in the electron micrograph.*

released by the axon terminal, so many Na^{+} ions diffuse into the neuron that the neuron becomes depolarized. A threshold is reached and an impulse (action potential) begins in the second cell.

After the neurotransmitter detaches from the membrane of the cell, it is rapidly removed or destroyed, thus halting its effect. The molecules of the neurotransmitter may be broken down by specific enzymes, taken up again by the axon terminal and recycled, or they may simply diffuse away.

37–1 SECTION REVIEW

1. What is the function of the nervous system?
2. Describe the structure of a typical neuron.
3. Describe a nerve impulse in terms of an action potential.
4. What is a neurotransmitter? How is its release controlled by a nerve impulse?
5. Why is the rapid removal or destruction of neurotransmitters important in controlling the activities of the nervous system?

Section Objective

- Identify the two major divisions of the nervous system.

37–2 Divisions of the Nervous System

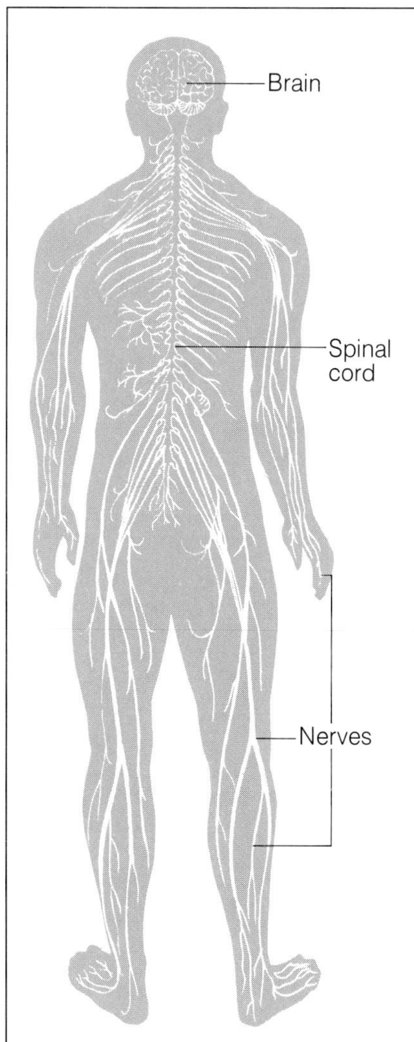

Figure 37–9 The human nervous system is made up of the central nervous system and the peripheral nervous system. The central nervous system contains the brain and the spinal cord. The peripheral nervous system contains all the nerves that carry information to and from the central nervous system.

Neurons, which are the functional units of the nervous system, do not act alone as individual cells. Instead, they are joined together to form a complicated communication network that gives rise to the human nervous system. **The human nervous system is divided into two major divisions: the central nervous system and the peripheral nervous system.**

The **central nervous system**, which serves as the control center of the body, consists of the brain and the spinal cord. Both the brain and the spinal cord are encased in and protected by bone. The functions of the central nervous system are similar to those of the central processing unit of a computer. The central nervous system relays messages, processes information, and compares and analyzes information. But the central nervous system does not come in contact with the environment. This job is left to the other major division of the nervous system—the **peripheral nervous system**.

The peripheral nervous system lies outside of the central nervous system. This means that it consists of all the nerves (bundles of axons) and associated cells that are not part of the brain and the spinal cord. Included here are all the cranial (pertaining to the brain) and spinal nerves and ganglia (GANG-glee-uh; singular: ganglion). Ganglia are a collection of nerve cell bodies. You will read more about the two major divisions of the nervous system in the following sections.

Figure 37–10 The human nervous system is divided into many subdivisions. What are the two major subdivisions of the nervous system?

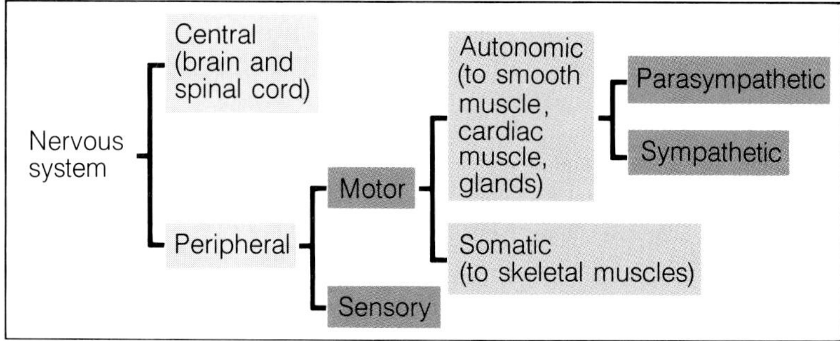

37–2 SECTION REVIEW

1. What are the two major divisions of the nervous system? What structures make up each of these systems?
2. What are the functions of the two major divisions of the nervous system?

37–3 The Central Nervous System

Section Objectives

- Describe the parts of the brain.
- Discuss the functions of the brain and the spinal cord.

As you have just read, the central nervous system consists of the brain and the spinal cord. **The brain is the main switching unit of the central nervous system; it is the place to which impulses flow and from which impulses originate. The spinal cord provides the link between the brain and the rest of the body.**

The brain is a highly organized organ that contains approximately 35 billion neurons and has a mass of 1.4 kilograms. In addition to being protected by a bony covering called the skull, the brain is also wrapped in three layers of connective tissue known as the meninges (muh-NINH-jeez). Connective tissue, as its name implies, connects one tissue to another. The innermost layer, which covers and is bound to the surface of the brain, is called the pia mater. It is a fibrous layer made up of many blood vessels, which help to carry food and oxygen to the spinal cord. The outermost layer, called the dura mater, is composed of thick connective tissue. The arachnoid (uh-RAK-noid) is the thin, cobweblike layer between the pia mater and the dura mater. Between the pia mater and the arachnoid is a space that is filled with cerebrospinal fluid. The cerebrospinal fluid protects the brain from mechanical injury by acting as a shock absorber.

In order for the brain to perform its functions, it must have a constant supply of food and oxygen. If the oxygen supply to the brain is cut off even for a few minutes, the brain will usually suffer enormous damage. Such damage may result in death.

The spinal cord is continuous with the brain and emerges from the opening at the base of the skull. The spinal cord stretches downward for approximately 42 to 45 centimeters. Like the brain, the spinal cord is protected by bone (vertebral column), by the meninges, and by cerebrospinal fluid.

Figure 37–11 *The brain and the spinal cord are wrapped in three layers of connective tissue called the meninges. The innermost layer is called the pia mater; the outermost layer is called the dura mater; the middle layer is called the arachnoid. The photograph shows the intricate network of blood vessels that constantly supply the brain with food and oxygen.*

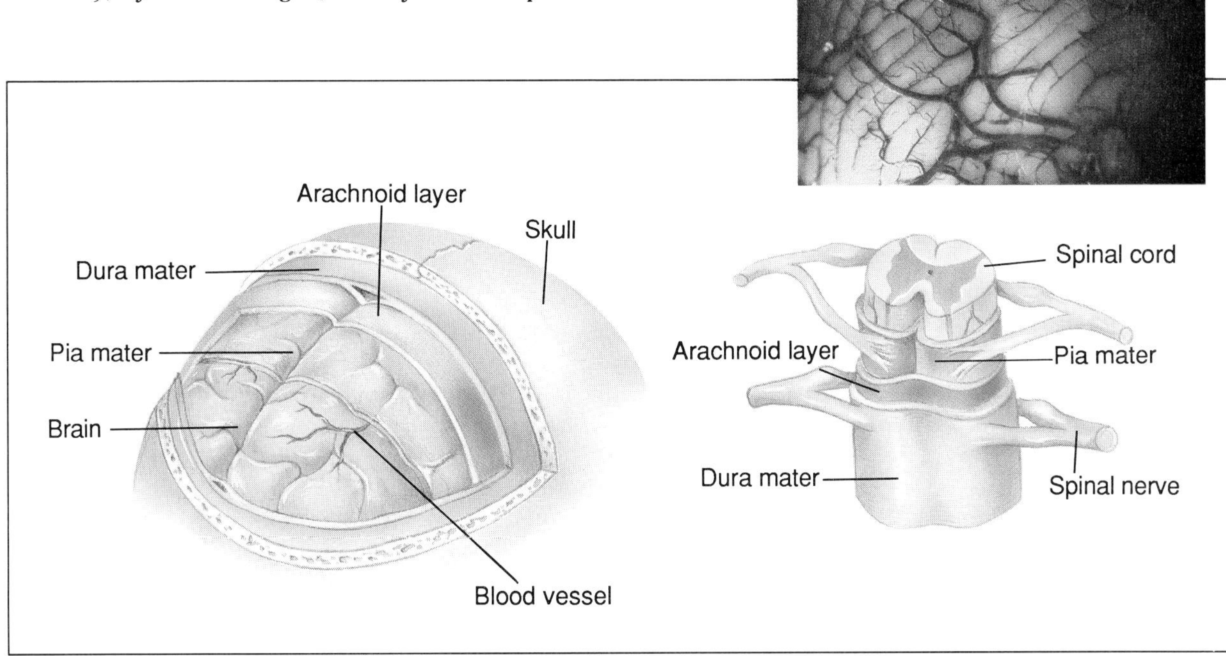

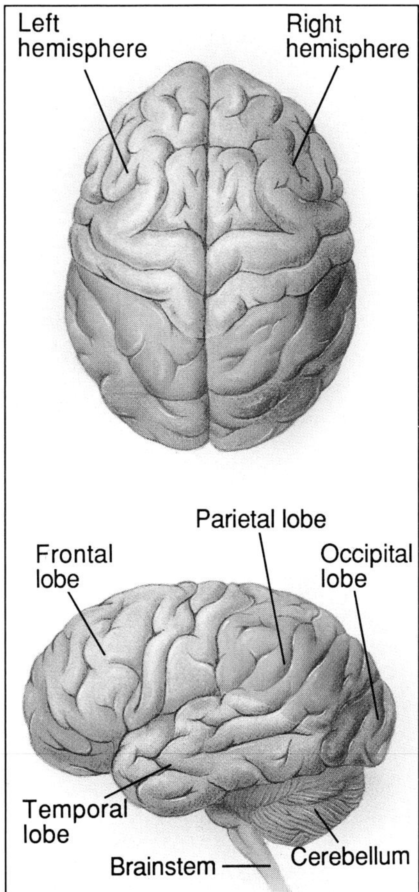

Figure 37–12 *The cerebrum is divided into the left and right hemispheres. Each hemisphere contains four lobes: frontal, parietal, temporal, and occipital.*

The Cerebrum

The largest and most prominent part of the human brain is the **cerebrum**. The cerebrum is responsible for all of the voluntary (conscious) activities of the body. In addition, it is the site of intelligence, learning, and judgment. The cerebrum takes up most of the space in the cavity that houses the brain. The cerebrum is divided into two hemispheres—the left hemisphere and the right hemisphere—by a deep groove. The hemispheres are connected in a region known as the corpus callosum (KOR-puhs kuh-LOH-suhm).

The most obvious feature on the surface of each hemisphere are the numerous folds. These folds and the grooves associated with them greatly increase the surface area of the cerebrum. The increased surface area permits the large number of neurons contained in the cerebrum to fit easily within the confines of the skull. Each hemisphere of the cerebrum is divided into regions called lobes. These lobes are named for the skull bones that cover them.

As a result of much research, scientists have discovered that the left side of the body sends its sensations to the right hemisphere of the cerebrum, and the right side of the body sends its sensations to the left hemisphere. Commands to move muscles are generated in the same way—the left hemisphere controls the right side of the body and the right hemisphere controls the left side of the body.

There is another remarkable aspect to the way in which the two hemispheres of the cerebrum function. The right hemisphere is associated with creativity and artistic ability, whereas the left hemisphere is associated with analytical and mathematical ability.

The Cerebral Cortex

The cerebrum consists of two surfaces. The outer surface is called the **cerebral cortex** and consists of gray matter. The gray matter is composed of densely packed nerve cell bodies that make it gray in appearance. The cerebral cortex is an extremely important part of the brain. Its functions will be discussed in more detail later in the section. The inner surface is called the **cerebral medulla**. The cerebral medulla consists of white matter, which is made up of bundles of myelinated axons. The myelin gives the white matter its white color.

The Cerebellum

The **cerebellum**, the second largest part of the brain, is located at the back of the skull. Although the commands to move muscles come from the cerebral cortex, the cerebellum coordinates and balances the actions of the muscles so that the body can move gracefully and efficiently. People with a damaged cerebellum suffer muscle weakness, lack of coordination, and difficulty in performing simple tasks such as walking and running.

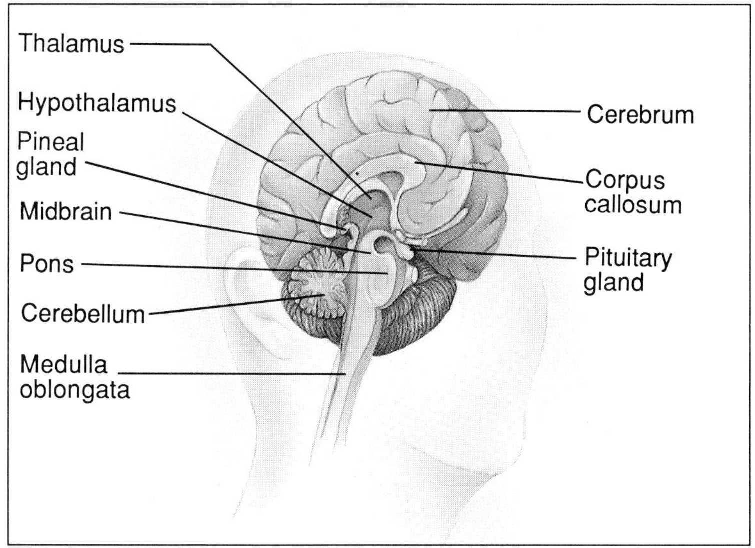

Figure 37–13 *The human brain consists of the cerebrum, cerebellum, and brainstem.*

A major part of learning how to perform physical activities seems to be related to training the cerebellum to coordinate the proper muscles. When you practice throwing a football, performing a pirouette, or executing a difficult dive, you are helping to develop connections in the cerebellum that will make the activity easier to do the next time. Because the functioning of the cerebellum is involuntary (not under conscious control), learning a completely new physical activity can be very difficult.

The Brainstem

The **brainstem** connects the brain to the spinal cord. The brainstem not only coordinates and integrates all incoming information, it also serves as the place of entry or exit for ten of the twelve cranial nerves.

The lowest part of the brainstem is the **medulla oblongata** (sometimes just called the medulla). It contains white matter that conducts impulses between the spinal cord and brain. The medulla controls involuntary functions that include breathing, blood pressure, heart rate, swallowing, and coughing.

Another important part of the medulla is a group of cells known as the reticular activating system. The reticular activating system actually helps to alert, or awaken, the upper parts of the brain, including the cerebral cortex. Such action keeps the brain alert and conscious.

Just above the medulla oblongata, the brainstem enlarges to form the **pons**. Pons means bridge, and this area of the brainstem contains mostly white matter that provides a link between the cerebral cortex and the cerebellum.

Above the pons and continuous with it is the **midbrain**, the smallest division of the brainstem. Areas in the midbrain are involved in hearing and vision.

Figure 37–14 *The reticular activating system, which passes through the brainstem, is a network of neurons that is concerned with general alertness.*

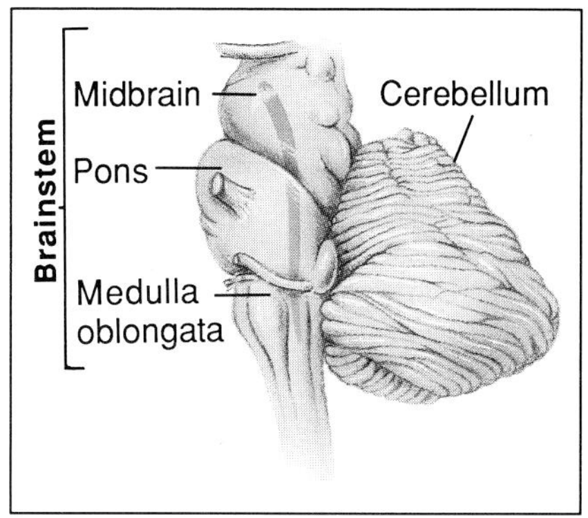

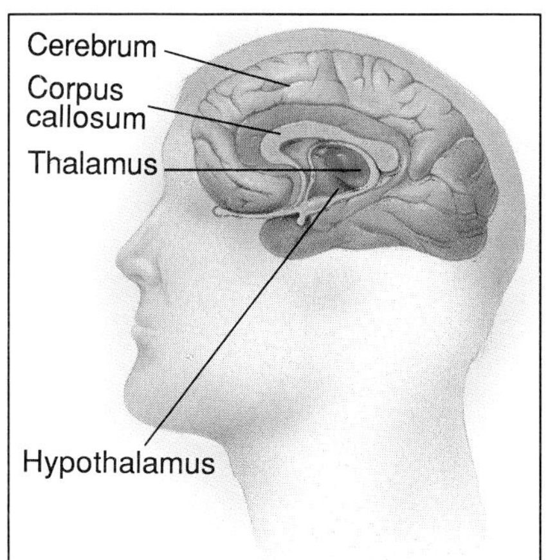

Figure 37–15 *The thalamus, located within the cerebrum, is the main relay center between the brainstem and the cerebrum. Lying below the thalamus is the hypothalamus, which coordinates the activities associated with hunger, thirst, fatigue, anger, and body temperature.*

The Thalamus and Hypothalamus

The **thalamus** and **hypothalamus** are found in the part of the brain between the brainstem and the cerebrum. See Figure 37–15. The thalamus, which is composed of gray matter, serves as a switching station for sensory input. With the exception of smell, each sense channels its sensory nerves through the thalamus. The thalamus seems to pass information to the proper region of the cerebrum for further processing. Immediately below the thalamus is the hypothalamus, which is the control center for hunger, thirst, fatigue, anger, and body temperature.

Functions of the Brain

Many of the functions that we associate with the brain are performed in the gray matter of the cerebral cortex. Figure 37–16 shows the various regions of the cerebral cortex and the parts of the body that they control. Some regions of the cerebral cortex are associated with sensory input; others, with motor output. Still other regions in the cerebral cortex are responsible for specific skills, such as the complex series of movements necessary for speech and the understanding of speech itself.

For some time, scientists believed that many functions of the body were controlled by specific regions of the cerebral cortex. They had good reasons for their belief. In the 1940s and

Figure 37–16 *This cutaway view of the cerebrum shows the motor cortex of one hemisphere and the sensory cortex of the other. The large areas devoted to the face and hands explain why these body parts are so sensitive.*

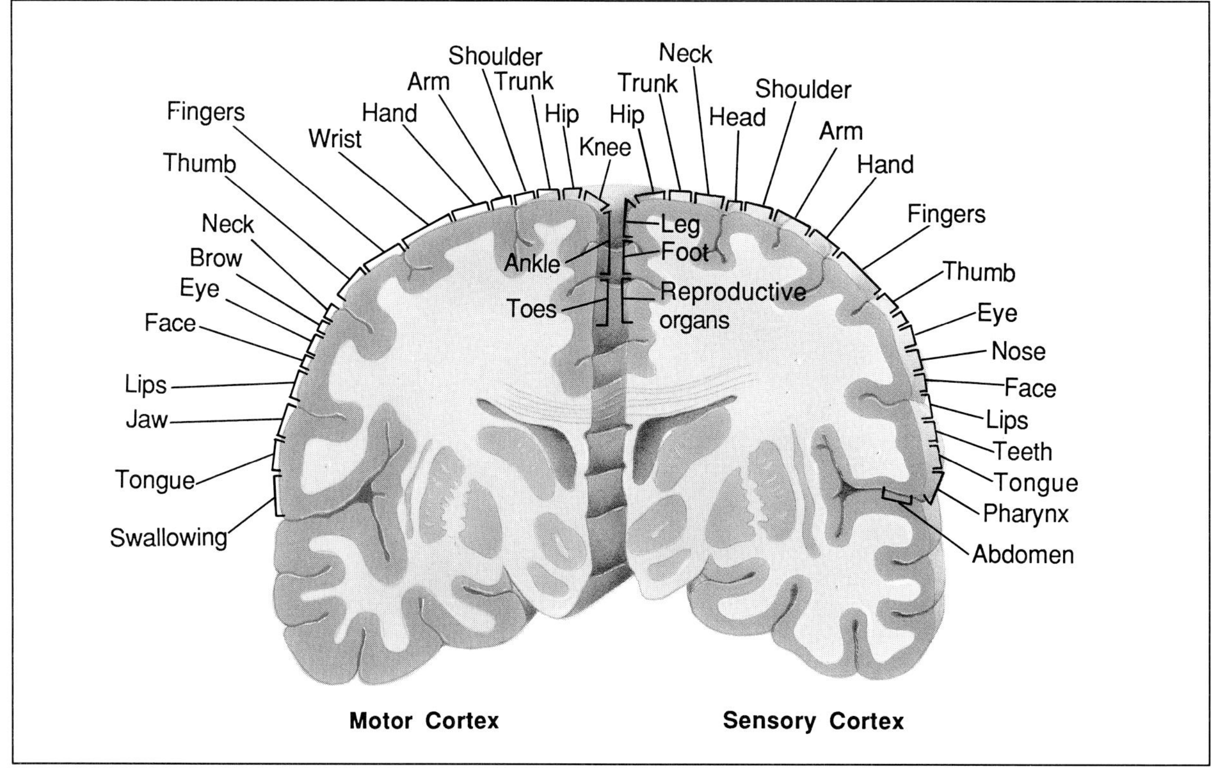

1950s, the Canadian neurosurgeon Wilder Penfield, along with other scientists, began to perform delicate experiments in which the brain of a patient was surgically exposed and different regions of the cerebral cortex were stimulated with weak electric currents. Experiments such as Penfield's are possible because of an interesting reason: Although the brain is packed with neurons, it does not have any pain receptors on its surface. Thus the brain cannot sense pain!

Using local anesthetics (pain killers), Penfield was able to perform surgery on his patients while they were awake. Stimulating one part of the cortex at a time, Penfield asked his patients to describe the sensations they experienced. In some places, stimulations caused muscles to contract. These areas, Penfield concluded, form a motor cortex that controls movement. In other places, stimulations caused the sensations of taste, touch, and sound. These regions of the brain form the sensory cortex. In still other places, stimulations caused his wide-awake patients to have vivid memories of past events, scenes, people, and places. These were the physical locations of memory, he concluded.

In recent years, the actual story has turned out to be quite a bit more complex. You might think from this brief discussion that sensory neurons are connected directly to the appropriate part of the sensory cortex. Unfortunately, this is not the case. There is no direct connection. Instead, sensory neurons synapse in the spinal cord, and neurons located in the spinal cord carry the impulses to the thalamus. The thalamus then relays the impulses to the sensory cortex. This is not the whole story, however. If it were, then in cases where parts of the spinal cord have been destroyed due to injury or surgery, sensation to certain parts of the body would be lost as well. But sometimes sensation is not affected—even though there seem to be no cells to carry the impulses to the cortex.

As you might imagine, the picture of the brain that is emerging is not a simple one. Scientists argue that information and control may be shared between different regions of the cerebral cortex in a complex way, but many more experiments will be required to understand more fully the workings of this vital part of the brain.

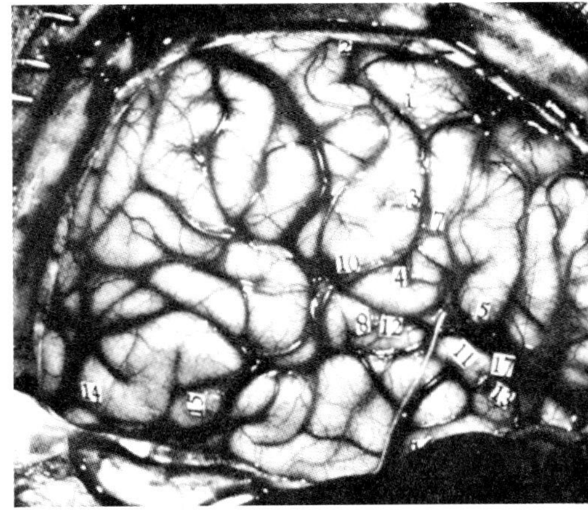

Figure 37–17 *During one of his operations, Doctor Penfield used numbered tags to mark the different areas of the cerebral cortex that were being electrically stimulated. When the area marked 13 was stimulated, the person recalled a circus.*

BRAIN WAVES Because the brain contains so many neurons, each one capable of maintaining an action potential, it is a source of electrical activity. If voltage-sensitive electrodes are placed on the scalp, a weak electrical signal can be recorded.

When a recording of electrical activity is made at a number of places on the scalp, the result is a record called an electroencephalogram (EEG). Although EEGs show the average activities of thousands of neurons, they cannot provide the specifics about any one cell. The EEGs can, however, give a general idea of the activity of the brain.

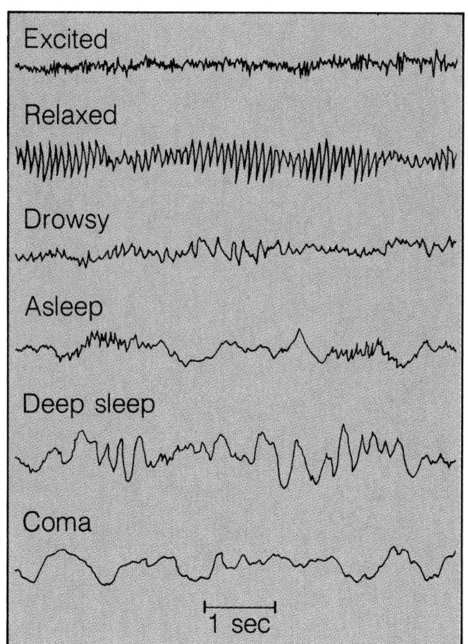

Figure 37–18 *The electrical activity of the brain is recorded as an electroencephalogram, or EEG. Notice the differences in the waves during excitement through coma.*

Brain-wave recordings, as EEGs are sometimes called, are shown in Figure 37–18. As you can see, brain waves vary during sleep and consciousness.

SLEEP When the activity of the cerebral cortex falls to the lowest possible level, a person becomes unconscious. Forms of unconsciousness can range from a deep, unresponsive state to a light sleep. Sleep is a state of unconsciousness in which a person can be awakened by normal sensory stimulation, such as a gentle nudge.

As you read earlier in this chapter, the network of neurons in the brainstem, known as the reticular activating system, helps to control consciousness. When sleep begins, the level of activity in the reticular activating system drops off. A special group of neurons in the brainstem seems to activate light sleep, as when we first close our eyes and lose consciousness. During deep sleep, other groups of neurons cause a decline in heart rate, blood pressure, respiratory rate, and use of energy. During rapid eye movement (REM) sleep, active dreaming occurs.

MEMORY In a computer, information is coded in numerical form and stored as bits in a special memory region of the circuit system. We might wonder whether the same thing happens in the brain. Interestingly, the answer is both yes and no.

Scientists now believe that there are at least two different kinds of memory: short-term (primary) and long-term. Each kind is stored in the brain in a different way. Short-term memories contain small amounts of information, such as a person's name or a telephone number. When you memorize a list of spelling words just before a test, you are making use of short-term memory. Short-term memory, as its name implies, is not permanent—you can easily forget some of the details of your last class or a story you read yesterday. There is some evidence that short-term memory is stored as a pattern of nerve impulses in the cerebral cortex. Generally, short-term memories vanish within a few days, except for the interesting ones we make an effort to remember.

Long-term memories are more permanent memories. Some may last for a lifetime. Some may fade with time and require considerable effort to recall. And some seem to be part of a person's consciousness, such as one's name. Is there a special place in the brain where long-term memories are stored? Probably not. Many patients with severe brain injuries suffer no loss of long-term memory, even when parts of the cerebral cortex have been destroyed. Some scientists have proposed that long-term memories are stored in the structure of the brain itself, not in any one place at any one time. This is an unusual proposal, but one that makes the following fact all too obvious: The human brain has, as yet, failed to figure itself out completely.

Figure 37–19 *Because the Egyptians thought the brain was an unimportant organ, they discarded it during the embalming process.*

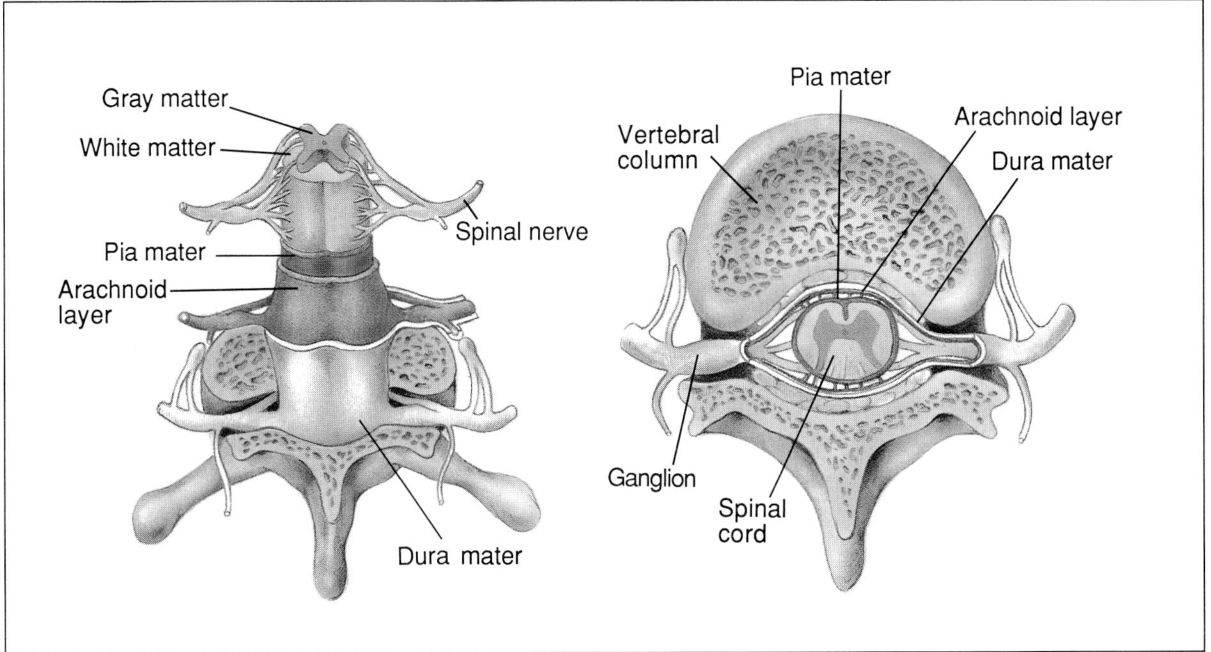

Figure 37–20 The spinal cord, which provides the critical link between the brain and the rest of the body, is protected by the vertebral column and the meninges. The butterfly-shaped gray matter within the spinal cord is composed mainly of interneurons.

The Spinal Cord

The spinal cord acts as a communications link between the brain and the peripheral nervous system. In addition to carrying impulses to and from the brain, the spinal cord regulates **reflexes**. A reflex is the simplest response to a stimulus. Sneezing and blinking are two examples of reflexes. Thirty-one pairs of spinal nerves originate in the spinal cord and branch out to both sides of the body. These nerves carry messages to and from the spinal cord.

Figure 37–20 shows a cross section of the spinal cord. Notice that it consists of two types of nerve tissue. The central portion of the cord is H-shaped and is made up of gray matter. Gray matter, as you may recall, consists of nerve cell bodies and unmyelinated axons. The outer portion of the cord consists of white matter, which is made up of myelinated axons. Sensory neurons carry impulses from receptors to the spinal cord, and motor neurons carry impulses from the spinal cord to the effectors. Within the spinal cord, motor and sensory neurons are connected by interneurons.

37–3 SECTION REVIEW

1. Describe the parts of the brain.
2. What are the functions of the brain and the spinal cord?
3. Explain why the cerebrum is more developed in humans than it is in any other vertebrate.

Mapping the Brain to Cure Epilepsy

Epilepsy is a disorder of certain neurons in the brain that results in periodic seizures, during which there is a loss of some brain activity. Epileptic seizures are classified into three types depending on the characteristics of the seizure. In a grand mal seizure, a person suddenly loses consciousness and the muscles jerk uncontrollably. During a petit mal seizure, the person has a blank look and loses awareness of his or her surroundings for a few seconds. In a psychomotor seizure, the person acts withdrawn and behaves strangely for a short period of time.

In the United States, approximately 2 million people suffer from some form of epilepsy. In many cases, epilepsy is caused by irregular activity in certain regions of the brain. In order to help people who suffer from epilepsy, physicians must first locate the area of the brain that is responsible for the abnormal activity. Until recently, this task was next to impossible.

Today, however, physicians can obtain a tremendous amount of information about brain activity. They can map the brain, in a sense. By attaching a large number of electrodes at predetermined positions over a person's entire scalp, the electrical activity of the brain can be recorded. A computer processes the recordings of this activity and then produces moving images on a map of the head. The maps are generated in such a way that they can show the brain's electrical activity at the exact time it is occurring in the person's brain. Normally, neurons in the brain produce small bursts of electrical impulses in a constantly changing pattern. But in epilepsy, large clusters of neurons fire simultaneously.

In many cases physicians treat epilepsy with antiepileptic drugs that either reduce the number of seizures or stop them entirely. In cases where only one area of the brain initiates the epileptic seizures, that area can be surgically removed. In this type of treatment, it is important for the physician to know the exact location of the area of the brain that is responsible for the abnormal activity. Equipped with such information, physicians are able to treat people with epilepsy so that they are able to lead normal lives.

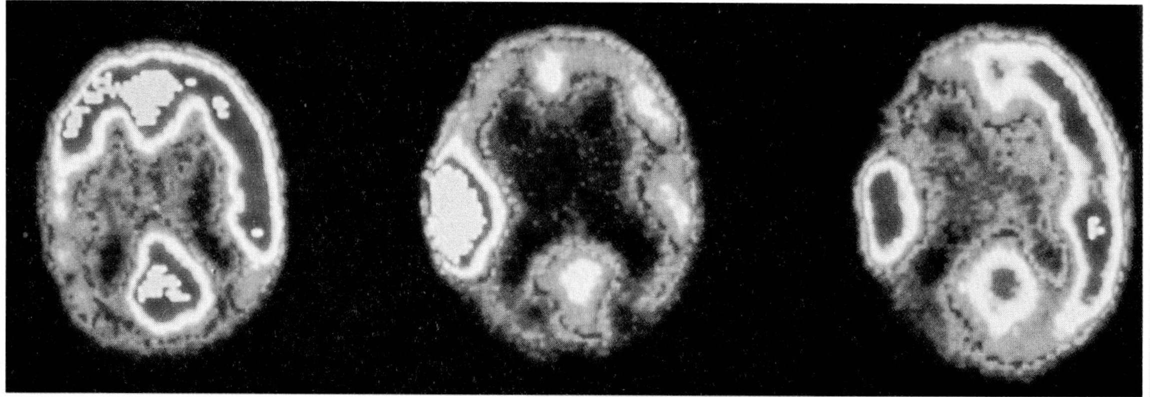

This PET scan shows the human brain during stages of an epileptic seizure. The middle image is that of the most severe stage.

37–4 The Peripheral Nervous System

Section Objective

- Describe the function and structure of the peripheral nervous system.

The peripheral nervous system, the link between the central nervous system and the rest of the body, consists of the cranial and spinal nerves and ganglia. The peripheral nervous system can be divided into two divisions: the sensory division and the motor division. **The sensory division of the peripheral nervous system transmits impulses from sense organs—such as the ears and taste buds—to the central nervous system. The motor division transmits impulses from the central nervous system to the muscles or glands (effectors).** The motor division is further divided into the **somatic nervous system** and the **autonomic nervous system**.

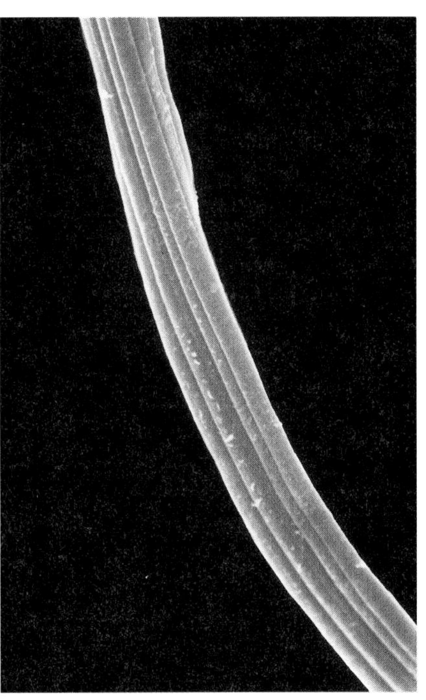

Figure 37–21 *Axons of the peripheral nervous system form cables that bring information to and from the brain.*

The Somatic Nervous System

The somatic nervous system regulates activities that are under conscious control, such as the movement of the skeletal muscles. Every time you lift your finger or wiggle your toes, you are using the motor neurons of the somatic nervous system. However, many nerves within this system are parts of reflexes and as such can act automatically.

If you accidentally step on a tack with your bare foot, your leg may recoil before you are aware of the pain. This rapid reflex is possible because receptors in the skin stimulate the sensory neurons to carry the impulse to the spinal cord. Even before the information is relayed to your brain, a group of neurons in the spinal cord automatically activates motor neurons. These motor neurons cause the muscles (effectors) in your leg to contract, pulling your foot away. The receptor, sensory neuron, motor neuron, and effector that are involved in this quick response are together known as a **reflex arc**.

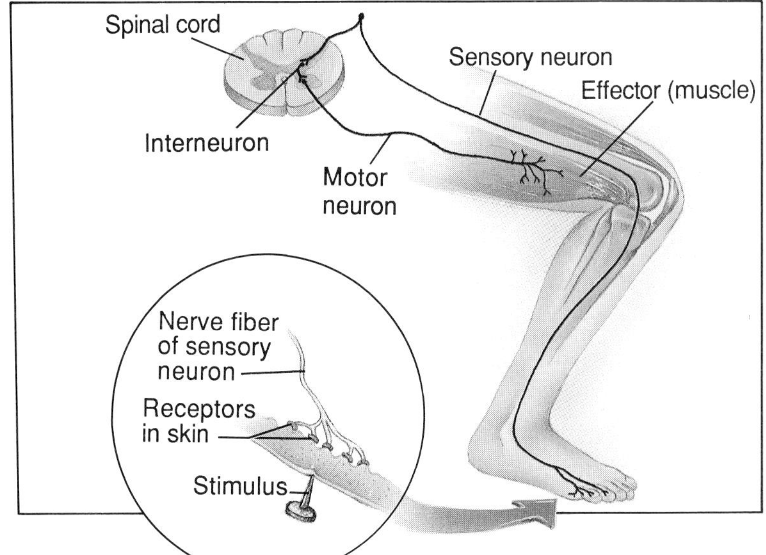

Figure 37–22 *In a reflex arc, sensory receptors stimulate a sensory neuron, which relays the signal to an interneuron within the spinal cord. The signal is then sent to a motor neuron, which in turn stimulates an effector.*

Part of Body	Effect of Sympathetic Nervous System	Effect of Parasympathetic Nervous System
Pupil of eye	Dilated	Constricted
Liver	Glucose released	None
Urinary bladder muscle	Relaxed	Contracted
Muscle of heart	Increased rate and force	Slowed rate
Bronchi of lungs	Dilated	Constricted

Figure 37–23 *The autonomic nervous system consists of the sympathetic and the parasympathetic nervous systems, which usually have complementary functions. In general, the sympathetic nervous system is involved in fight-or-flight reactions and the parasympathetic nervous system stimulates calmer functions, such as digestion.*

The Autonomic Nervous System

The autonomic nervous system regulates activities that are automatic, or involuntary. The nerves of the autonomic nervous system control functions of the body that are not under conscious control, such as the contractions in the heart and the movement of smooth muscles surrounding the blood vessels and the digestive system.

The autonomic nervous system is further subdivided into two parts that have opposite effects on the organs they control. The two parts are known as the **sympathetic nervous system** and the **parasympathetic nervous system**. Most organs controlled by the autonomic nervous system are under the control of both sympathetic and parasympathetic neurons. For example, heart rate is speeded up by the sympathetic nervous system, whereas it is slowed down by the parasympathetic nervous system.

Why is it important to have two systems that have opposite effects on the organs they control? Wouldn't one system make more sense? To answer this question, imagine a situation in which a single system could increase the rate of activity of an organ by releasing a single type of neurotransmitter. This system would be much like a car that had an accelerator pedal but no brake pedal. Getting the car to move would be easy, but stopping it would present a problem! The same would be true of an organ regulated by a single nervous system. The dual-control system puts an on-off switch on every organ and thus ensures precise control of a dozen organs or more.

37–4 SECTION REVIEW

1. What is the role of the peripheral nervous system?
2. What are the parts of the peripheral nervous system?
3. Describe the parts of a reflex arc. Is a reflex arc completely within the peripheral nervous system? Explain your answer.

37–5 The Senses

Section Objectives

- Describe the major parts of the eye and their function.
- Identify the parts of the ear responsible for hearing and balance.
- Compare the senses of smell and taste.
- Identify the various sense receptors in the skin.

There are millions of neurons in the body that do not receive impulses from other neurons. Instead, these neurons, which are called sensory receptors, react directly to stimulation from the environment. Examples of stimulation include light, sound, motion, chemicals, pressure, or changes in temperature. Once these sensory receptors are stimulated, they transform one form of energy from the environment (light, sound) into another form of energy (action potential) that can be transmitted to other neurons. Eventually these action potentials (impulses) reach the central nervous system.

The sensory receptors are contained in the sense organs. **Each of the five senses (sight, hearing, smell, taste, and touch) has a specific sense organ associated with it.** Specialized cells within each **sense organ** enable it to respond to particular stimuli.

Vision

The world around us is bathed in light. The sense organs that we use to sense light are the eyes. Each eye is composed of three layers. The outer layer consists of the sclera and the cornea. The middle layer contains the choroid, ciliary body, and iris. The inner layer consists of the retina.

The sclera, or white of the eye, consists of tough white connective tissue. The sclera helps maintain the shape of the eye and also provides a means of attachment for the muscles that move the eye. In the front of the eye, the sclera forms a transparent layer called the cornea. The cornea is the part of the eye through which light enters.

__Figure 37–24__ The eye is a complicated sense organ composed of three layers of tissue: sclera, choroid, and retina (left). As light enters the eye, it passes through the thin transparent cornea (right).

Conjunctiva
Cornea
Iris
Pupil
Lens
Suspensory ligaments
Ciliary body
Optic nerve
Vitreous humor
Retina
Choroid
Sclera

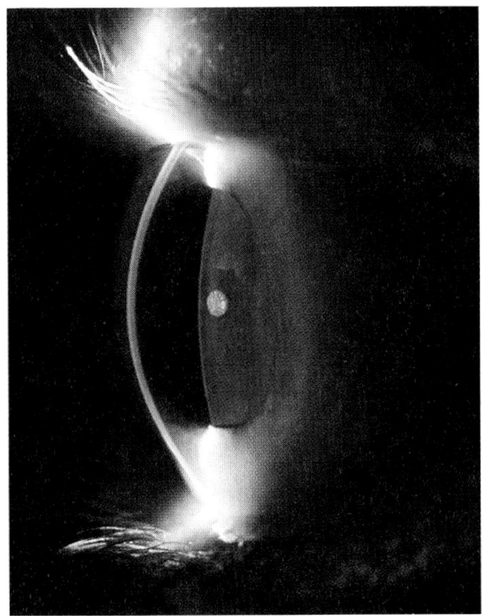

Just inside the cornea is a small chamber (anterior chamber) filled with a fluid known as the aqueous humor. (The word humor means any fluid within the body.) At the back of this chamber, the pigmented choroid, which contains the blood vessels of the eye, becomes the disklike structure called the iris. The iris is the portion of the eye that gives your eye its color. In the middle of the iris is a small opening called the pupil, through which light enters the eye. The pupil appears as the small black disk in the center of the eye. Tiny muscles in the iris regulate the size of the pupil and thus the amount of light that enters. In dim light the pupil opens to increase the amount of light entering the eye. In bright light the pupil closes to decrease the amount of light entering the eye, thus preventing damage to the delicate structures within the eye.

Just behind the iris is the lens. The cells that form the lens contain a special protein called crystalin. Crystalin is almost transparent and thus allows light to pass through. Small muscles attached to the lens cause it to bend slightly. This bending enables the normal eye to focus on close and distant objects. Behind the lens is a large chamber (posterior chamber) filled with a transparent jellylike fluid called vitreous humor.

Special light-sensitive receptor cells, or photoreceptors, are arranged in a layer in the retina, which is located at the back of the eye. The photoreceptors convert light energy into impulses that are carried to the central nervous system. There are two types of photoreceptors: rods and cones.

Photoreceptors contain a pigment called rhodopsin (also called visual purple) that can respond to most wavelengths of light. Rods are extremely sensitive to all colors of light, but they do not distinguish different colors. Cones are less sensitive than rods, but they do respond differently to light of different colors, producing color vision. In very dim light, when only rods are activated, objects may be clearly seen but their colors may not be distinguishable. As the amount of light increases, the cones are stimulated and the colors become clear.

The impulses assembled by this complicated layer of interconnected cells leave each eye by way of an optic nerve. The optic nerves then carry the impulses to a part of the brain known as the optic lobe. Here the brain interprets the visual images and provides information about the external world.

Figure 37–25 The retina, which is the innermost layer of the eye, contains the photoreceptor cells called rods and cones (bottom). Notice the upside-down image that was superimposed on a photograph of the retina taken through an ophthalmoscope (top).

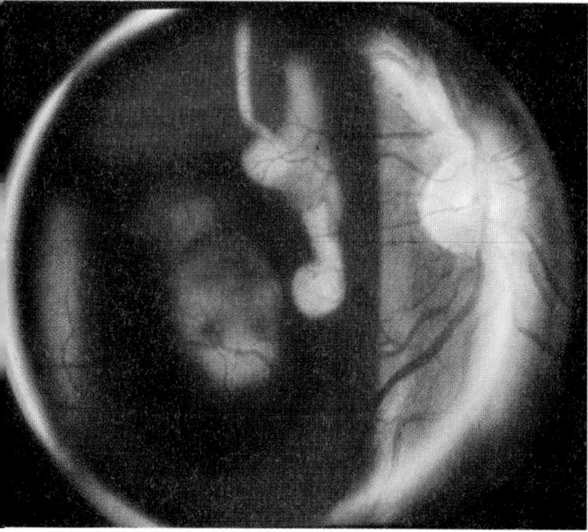

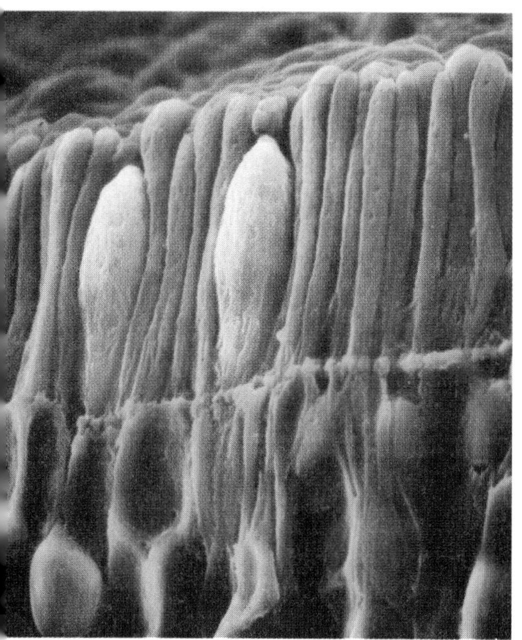

Hearing and Balance

Sound is nothing more than vibrations in the air around us. Deep, low-pitched sounds result from slow vibrations—100 to 500 vibrations per second. High-pitched sounds are caused by faster vibrations—1000 to 5000 vibrations per second. In addition to pitch, sounds differ from one another by their loudness, or volume. The sense organs that can distinguish both the pitch and loudness of sounds are the ears.

The external ear consists of the visible fleshy part that helps to collect sounds and funnel them into the auditory

PROBLEM SOLVING IN BIOLOGY

THE "EYES" HAVE IT!

Color Vision

The retina contains two types of photoreceptors: rods and cones. Rods are responsible for black-and-white vision; cones are responsible for color vision. In humans, there are three types of cones: blue cones, red cones, and green cones. Each type of cone is sensitive to a specific portion of the visible spectrum. The combined stimulation of these cones produces all the colors you see.

As the accompanying graph shows, the sensitivities of blue, red, and green cones overlap to some degree. Because their sensitivities overlap, we are able to distinguish all colors. For example, red light stimulates red cones and leaves the other cones unaffected. Thus we see the color red. Green light stimulates all three cones, but each to a certain degree. Depending upon the combinations, we see many other colors.

To determine the type of cone(s) stimulated and the percentage of stimulation produced by a certain light, you can analyze the graph. For example, if orange light were to strike the retina, about 99 percent of the red cones and about 40 percent of the green cones would be stimulated. No blue cones would be stimulated.

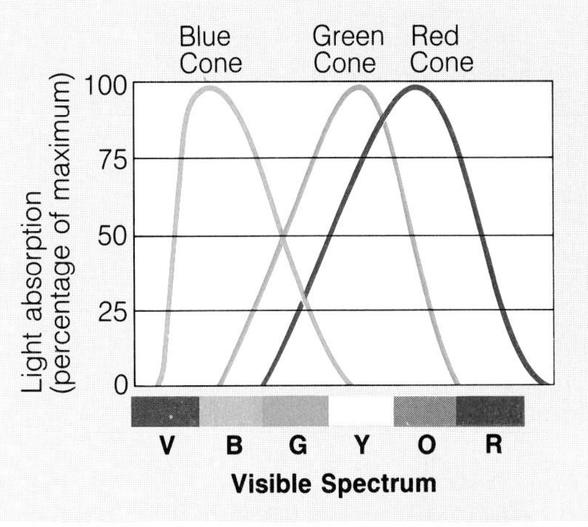

Now try your hand at a few problems.

1. In order to see the color green, what cone(s) must be stimulated?
2. What type of cone(s) and approximately what percentage of the cone(s) is (are) stimulated when blue light strikes the retina?
3. What cone(s) must be stimulated in order to see the color yellow?
4. What type of cone(s) and approximately what percentage of the cone(s) is (are) stimulated when red light strikes the retina?

canal. The auditory canal contains tiny hairs and wax-producing glands that prevent foreign objects from entering the ear.

The auditory canal extends into the bones of the head but stops at the eardrum, or tympanum. The eardrum is the beginning of the middle ear. Sound vibrations strike the eardrum and are then transmitted through three tiny bones: the malleus (hammer), incus (anvil), and stapes (stirrup).

The stapes vibrates against a thin membrane covering an opening called the oval window. This membrane transmits the vibrations to the cochlea, which begins the inner ear. The cochlea is a snail-shaped fluid-filled cavity. When the fluid vibrates, tiny hair cells lining the cochlea are pushed back and forth, providing stimulation that is turned into nerve impulses. These impulses are carried to the brain by the acoustic nerve.

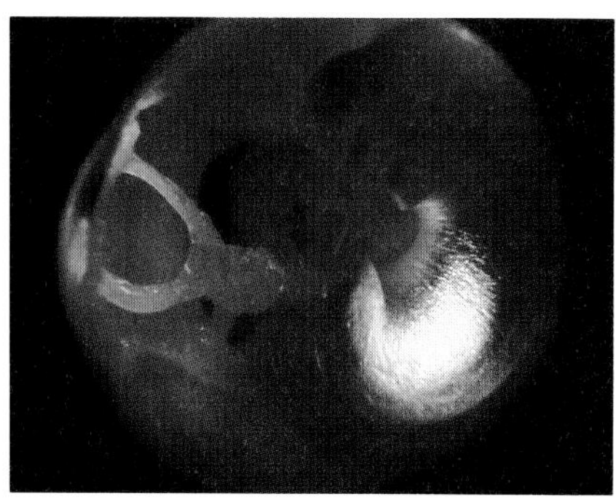

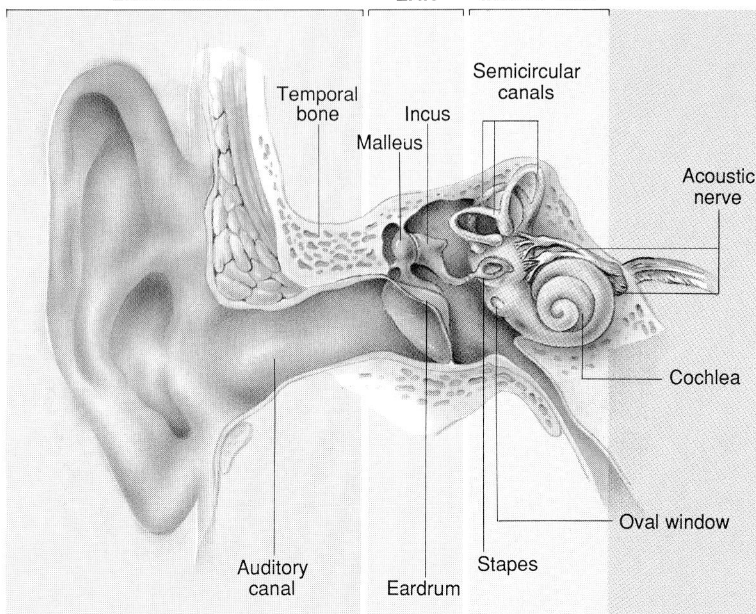

Figure 37–26 Sound waves enter the ear and are converted into impulses that are carried to the brain. The photograph of the middle ear shows the eardrum, which is tinted yellow, and the three small ear bones.

Figure 37–27 The semicircular canals (top) are set at right angles to one another so that they react to up-and-down, side-to-side, and tilting motions. Tiny crystals called otoliths (bottom) also play a part in maintaining balance.

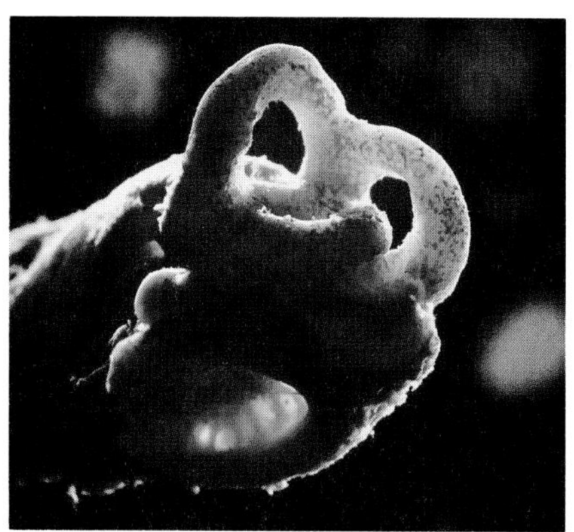

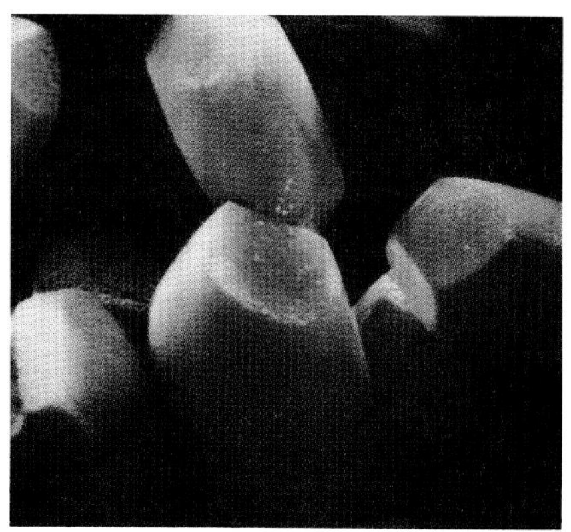

In addition to enabling us to hear, the ears contain structures for detecting stimuli that make us aware of our movements and allow us to maintain our balance. Located within the inner ear just above the cochlea are three tiny canals that lie at right angles to each other. They are called the semicircular canals because each makes half a circle. The semicircular canals and the two tiny sacs located behind them help us sense balance, or equilibrium.

The semicircular canals and the sacs are both filled with fluid and lined with hair cells (ciliated cells). The hair cells of each sac, however, are embedded in a gelatinlike substance that contains tiny grains of calcium carbonate and protein called otoliths (hearing stones). Otoliths roll back and forth in response to gravity, acceleration, and deceleration. Together, the movement of fluid and the otoliths bend the hair on the hair cells. This action, in turn, sends impulses to the brain that enable it to determine body motion and position.

Smell

Because the sense of smell is a chemical sense, the cells that are responsible for smell are called chemoreceptors. These cells are located in the upper part of the nasal (pertaining to the nose) cavity. See Figure 37-28. These chemoreceptors contain cilia that extend into the air passageways of the nose and react to chemicals in the air. Chemicals that come into contact with these chemoreceptors stimulate them, causing impulses to be sent to the brain.

Unfortunately, relatively little is known about the sense of smell. Although tens of thousands of different odors can be distinguished, it is not understood how one odor is distinguished from another. A challenge for biologists who study the sensory systems is to determine the basis of scent discrimination.

Taste

Like the sense of smell, the sense of taste is a chemical sense. And the cells that are stimulated by the chemicals are also called chemoreceptors. The sense organs that detect taste are the taste buds. Most taste buds are located between small projections on the tongue. However, taste buds are also found on the roof of the mouth and on the lips and throat (especially in children).

The tastes detected by taste buds are of four main kinds: sweet, salty, sour, and bitter. Each taste bud shows a particular sensitivity to one of these tastes.

Because many of the sensations associated with taste are actually smell sensations, humans depend upon both senses to detect flavors in food. Perhaps you are already aware of this fact. When you have a cold and your smell receptors are covered by mucus, food seems to have little, if any, flavor.

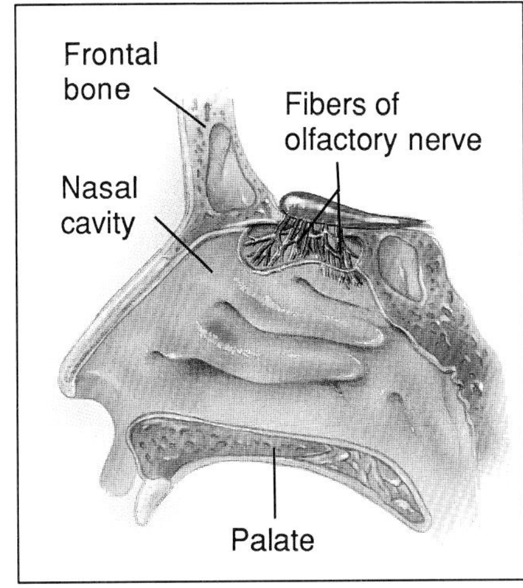

Figure 37–28 A tiny patch of specialized tissue located over the top of each nasal cavity is responsible for the sense of smell.

Touch and Related Senses

The sense of touch, unlike the other senses you have just read about, is not found in one particular place. All regions of the skin are sensitive to touch. In this respect, your largest sense organ is your skin.

There are several distinct types of sensory receptors that are present just below the surface of the skin. Two types of sensory receptors respond to heat and cold; two other types respond to touch; one type responds to pain. See Figure 37–29.

Sensory receptors for heat and cold are scattered directly below the surface of the skin. In general, there are three to four warm receptors for every cold receptor. Sensory receptors for touch are much more concentrated in some areas of the body than in others. For example, the most touch-sensitive areas are located on the fingers, toes, and lips. Pain receptors are located throughout the skin. Depending upon what type of sensory neurons are stimulated, the sensation of pain can be experienced as either prickling pain (fast pain) or burning and aching pain (slow pain).

Figure 37–29 The skin contains many types of sensory receptors that provide information about the external environment.

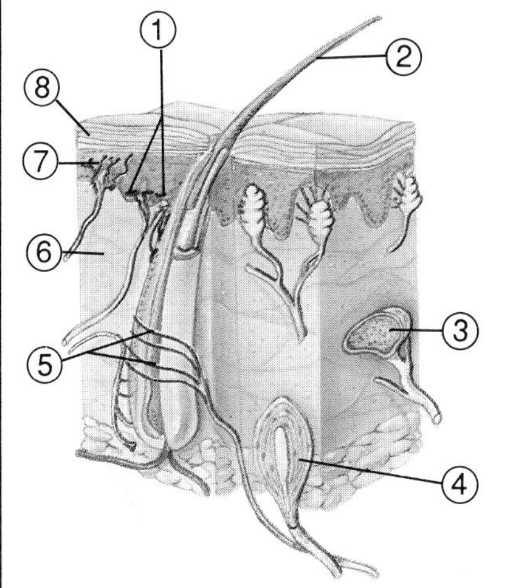

37–5 SECTION REVIEW

1. Identify the parts of the eye and the function of each.
2. What are the parts of the ear that are responsible for hearing? For balance?
3. Compare the senses of smell and taste.
4. Describe the location and function of sensory receptors in the skin.
5. Explain why it is sometimes helpful to inhale slowly and deeply through the nose when trying to identify an odor.

LABORATORY INVESTIGATION

MEASURING REACTION TIME

PROBLEM

How can reaction time be measured? What factors affect reaction time?

MATERIALS *(per pair of students)*

meterstick
biology textbook

PROCEDURE

1. On a separate sheet of paper, construct a data table similar to the one shown here.
2. While you hold the 100-centimeter end of the meterstick, have your partner position his or her thumb and forefinger around the zero end. Make sure that your partner does not touch the meterstick.
3. Instruct your partner to concentrate on catching the meterstick as soon as you drop it. Your partner should move only the thumb and forefinger to catch the meterstick.
4. When you are ready, drop the meterstick between your partner's fingers.
5. Note the measurement on the meterstick at the point at which your partner's fingers caught the meterstick. Record this distance in centimeters in the data table.
6. Repeat steps 1 through 5 four more times.
7. Switch roles with your partner and repeat steps 1 through 6.
8. Now work with another pair of students to determine whether reaction rate is affected by distractions. Have the other pair of students select a chapter from your biology textbook that your class has already studied.
9. Repeat steps 1 through 6, but this time have the distractors ask the student who is trying to catch the meterstick questions from the Chapter Review section at the end of the selected chapter.
10. Switch roles and repeat step 9 until all four students have caught the meterstick.

OBSERVATIONS

Trial	Distance Ruler Falls (cm)	
	Without Distractions	With Distractions
1		
2		
3		
4		
5		
Average		

1. Did your distances vary in the trials without distractions? With distractions? Describe the variations in each case, if any.
2. How did your average distance without distractions compare with your average distance with distractions?
3. How did your distances without and with distractions compare with those of your partner? With those of the other pair of students?

ANALYSIS AND CONCLUSIONS

1. Why did measuring the distance the meterstick falls give a relative measure of reaction time?
2. Why was it necessary to have each person perform five trials?
3. What might account for variations in your reaction time without distractions? With distractions?
4. How did the distractions affect your reaction times?
5. Explain why your reaction times might be different from the reaction times of your partner and the other pair of students?

STUDENT STUDY GUIDE

SUMMARIZING THE CONCEPTS

The key concepts in each section of this chapter are listed below to help you review the chapter content. Make sure you understand each concept and its relationship to other concepts and to the theme of this chapter.

37–1 The Nervous System

- The nervous system receives and relays information about activities within the body and monitors and responds to internal and external changes.
- Neurons transmit messages in the form of electrical signals known as impulses. A neuron consists of a cell body, dendrites, an axon, and axon terminals.

37–2 Divisions of the Nervous System

- The human nervous system is divided into two major divisions: the central nervous system and the peripheral nervous system.

37–3 The Central Nervous System

- The brain is the main switching unit of the central nervous system. The spinal cord provides the link between the brain and the rest of the body.

37–4 The Peripheral Nervous System

- The peripheral nervous system is made up of the sensory division and the motor division.

37–5 The Senses

- Each of the five senses (sight, hearing, smell, taste, and touch) has a specific sense organ associated with it.

REVIEWING KEY TERMS

Vocabulary terms are important to your understanding of biology. The key terms listed below are those you should be especially familiar with. Review these terms and their meanings. Then use each term in a complete sentence. If you are not sure of a term's meaning, return to the appropriate section and review its definition.

37–1 The Nervous System

nervous system
neuron
impulse
sensory neuron
motor neuron
interneuron
cell body
dendrite
axon
axon terminal
resting potential
action potential
myelin
threshold
receptor
effector
synapse
neurotransmitter

37–2 Divisions of the Nervous System

central nervous system
peripheral nervous system

37–3 The Central Nervous System

cerebrum
cerebral cortex
cerebral medulla
cerebellum
brainstem
medulla oblongata
pons
midbrain
thalamus
hypothalamus
reflex

37–4 The Peripheral Nervous System

somatic nervous system
autonomic nervous system
reflex arc
sympathetic nervous system
parasympathetic nervous system

37–5 The Senses

sense organ

CHAPTER REVIEW

CONTENT REVIEW

Multiple Choice

Choose the letter of the answer that best completes each statement.

1. Which type of neuron is responsible for transmitting impulses to the central nervous system?
   a. sensory neuron c. interneuron
   b. motor neuron d. receptor neuron
2. The central nervous system consists of the
   a. somatic system and the autonomic system.
   b. brain and the spinal cord.
   c. cerebrum, cerebellum, and medulla.
   d. spinal cord and the peripheral nerves.
3. Coordination and balance are controlled principally in the
   a. spinal cord. c. cerebellum.
   b. medulla. d. cerebrum.
4. The autonomic nervous system controls
   a. thinking. c. digestion.
   b. walking. d. hearing.
5. Which is not usually involved in a simple reflex?
   a. receptor c. spinal cord
   b. cerebrum d. effector
6. The outer layer of the eye consists of the
   a. choroid, ciliary body, and iris.
   b. cochlea.
   c. retina.
   d. sclera and the cornea.
7. The malleus, incus, and stapes conduct vibrations from the eardrum to the
   a. outer ear. c. brain.
   b. inner ear. d. middle ear.
8. The largest sense organ is the
   a. skin. c. eyes.
   b. ears. d. nose.

True or False

Determine whether each statement is true or false. If it is true, write "true." If it is false, change the underlined word or words to make the statement true.

1. Impulses are a flow of electrical charges along the cell membrane of a neuron.
2. A nerve impulse is the resting potential traveling along the membrane.
3. The minimum level of stimulus that is required to activate a neuron is called the conductor.
4. Axon terminals contain tiny vesicles that are filled with molecules of myelin.
5. The central nervous system and the sympathetic nervous system are the two main divisions of the human nervous system.
6. The largest and most prominent part of the brain is the cerebellum.
7. The brainstem connects the spinal cord to the brain.
8. The iris is the colored portion of the eye.

Word Relationships

A. *In each of the following sets of terms, three of the terms are related. One term does not belong. Determine the characteristic common to three of the terms and then identify the term that does not belong.*

1. dendrite, synapse, axon, cell body
2. sclera, ciliary body, iris, choroid
3. cerebrum, cranial nerves, spinal nerves, ganglia
4. malleus, ganglion, stapes, incus

B. *An analogy is a relationship between two pairs of words or phrases generally written in the following manner: a:b::c:d. The symbol : is read "is to," and the symbol :: is read "as." For example, cat:animal::rose:plant is read "cat is to animal as rose is to plant."*

In the analogies that follow, a word or phrase is missing. Complete each analogy by providing the missing word or phrase.

5. receptor:sensory neuron::effector:________________

6. ear:acoustic nerve::eye:________________

7. anterior chamber:aqueous humor::posterior chamber:________________

8. intelligence:cerebrum::breathing:________________

CONCEPT MASTERY

Use your understanding of the concepts developed in the chapter to answer each of the following in a brief paragraph.

1. Describe the structure and function of a neuron.
2. What is the relationship between receptors and effectors?
3. What changes occur in the neuron during the resting potential? During an action potential?
4. What is the function of the sodium-potassium pump?
5. Explain what happens when a nerve is stimulated.
6. How does the all-or-none principle relate to the transmission of a nerve impulse?
7. How is the central nervous system protected?
8. Describe the structure and function of the cerebrum.
9. Describe the structure of the spinal cord.
10. Trace the path of light through the eye.
11. What are the functions of the rods and cones?
12. Trace the path of sound through the ear.

CRITICAL AND CREATIVE THINKING

Discuss each of the following in a brief paragraph.

1. **Making predictions** If a portion of an axon is cut so that it is no longer connected to its nerve cell body, predict the effect this would have on the transmission of impulses.
2. **Applying concepts** What might happen if the cornea becomes inflamed so that fluid accumulates there?
3. **Relating concepts** Constant exposure to loud noises may cause loss of hearing. What part of the ear may be damaged?
4. **Relating cause and effect** Explain why you feel dizzy after spinning around for a few seconds.
5. **Relating facts** Hydrocephalus is a condition in which there is an abnormal increase of cerebrospinal fluid on the brain, causing the head to enlarge. How might this condition interfere with the proper functioning of the brain?
6. **Relating facts** Can a person who has normally functioning eyes still be blind? Explain your answer.
7. **Using the writing process** Imagine that you have to do without one of your sense organs for one day. Which one would you choose to give up? In an essay, describe how the absence of this sense organ would affect your life.

CHAPTER 38

Skeletal, Muscular, and Integumentary Systems

The actions involved in playing tennis require the combined use of the bones, joints, and muscles.

Compared to animals that have claws, sharp teeth, and armor plating, humans appear to be somewhat fragile. But you need only observe a group of people playing football, a rider taking a horse over a jump, dancers leaping through the air, a pole vaulter clearing the bar, or a swimmer moving through the water and the image of fragile humans begins to fade. In truth, we are large and strong and remarkably agile for our species.

The basis for all this flexibility is the way in which the human body is organized. This organization makes it possible for humans to perform a variety of physical activities that is truly astonishing. In this chapter you will discover how the body's foundation—its bones, muscles, and skin—provides structural support, mobility, and protection.

CHAPTER OUTLINE

38–1 The Skeletal System
- Structure of Bones
- Development of Bones
- Joints: Where Two Bones Meet

38–2 The Muscular System
- Types of Muscle Tissue
- Mechanism of Muscle Contraction
- Control of Muscle Contraction
- How Muscles and Bones Interact

38–3 The Integumentary System
- Epidermis
- Dermis
- Hair and Nails

38–1 The Skeletal System

Section Objectives

- List the parts and functions of the skeletal system.
- Describe the structure and development of bone.
- Identify the three classes of joints and describe the action of each.

In order to retain their shape and form, living things need some type of support. In single-celled organisms, this support is provided by the cell membranes. In multicellular animals, the support is provided by some form of skeleton. Among multicellular animals, skeletons range from the exoskeletons (outside skeletons) of arthropods to the endoskeletons (inside skeletons) of vertebrates.

Like that of all vertebrates, the skeleton of humans is composed of a special type of connective tissue (tissue that joins other tissues together) called bone. **Bones and their associated tissues—cartilage, tendons, and ligaments—make up the skeletal system.**

The bones that make up the **skeletal system** serve several important functions. They support and shape the body much as the internal wooden frame does a house. Just as the house could not stand without its wooden frame, the human body would collapse without its bony skeleton. Bones protect the delicate internal organs of the body. For example, the bones of the cranium form a protective shell around the brain, and the ribs form a basketlike cage that protects the heart and lungs.

Bones also provide a system of levers (rigid rods that can be moved about a fixed point) on which a group of specialized

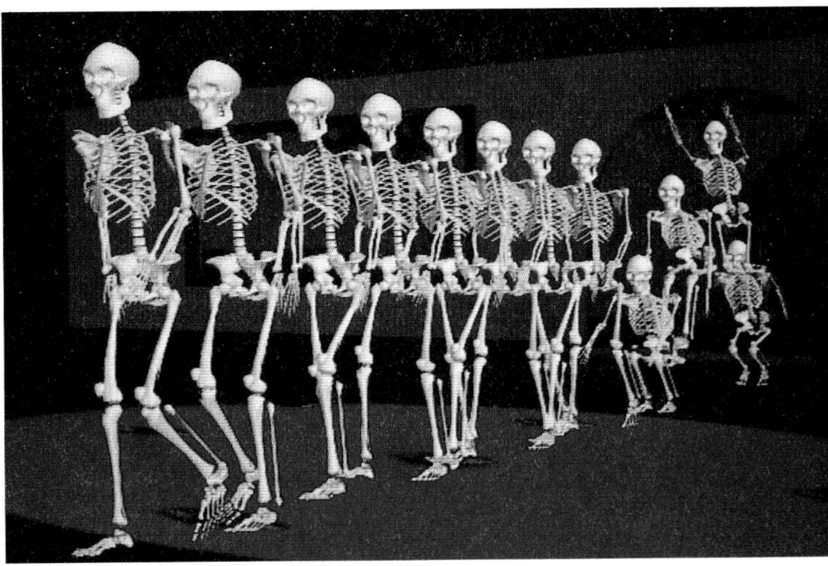

Figure 38–1 *The step-by-step movements of the human skeleton during jumping and walking have a ghostly appearance in this computer image.*

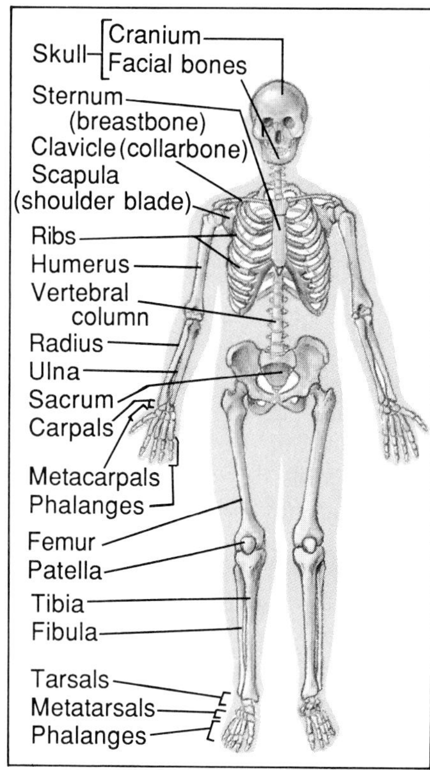

Figure 38–2 *The human skeleton consists of 206 bones.*

tissues act to produce movement. The movements produced range from the gentle motion of a fingertip to the powerful actions that cause a change in the position of the entire body.

In addition, bones contain enormous reserves of minerals, especially calcium and phosphorus, which are important to many body processes. Finally, bones are the sites of blood-cell formation. Most blood cells are produced within the soft tissue that fills the internal cavities in bones.

Structure of Bones

It is easy to think of bones as nonliving. After all, most of the mass of bone is mineral—largely calcium and phosphorus. But bones are living tissue. Bones are a solid network of living cells and fibers that are supported by deposits of calcium salts.

Each bone is surrounded by a tough membrane called the **periosteum** (per-ee-AHS-tee-uhm). Blood vessels pass through the periosteum, carrying oxygen and nutrients to the bone. Beneath the periosteum is a thick layer of compact bone. Although compact bone is dense and similar in texture to ivory, it is far from being solid. Running through compact bone is a network of tubes called **Haversian** (huh-VER-zhuhn) **canals** that contain blood vessels and nerves.

Inside the layer of compact bone is spongy bone. Spongy bone is not soft and spongy, as its name implies, but actually quite strong. Near the ends of bones where force is applied, spongy bone is organized into structures that resemble the supporting girders in a bridge. This structure of spongy bone helps to add strength to bone without adding mass.

Embedded in compact and spongy bone are cells known as **osteocytes** (AHS-tee-oh-sights) that can either deposit the calcium salts in bone or absorb them again. Osteocytes are responsible for bone growth and changes in the shapes of bones. Within bones are cavities that contain a soft tissue called **bone marrow**. There are two types of bone marrow: yellow and red. Most bone contains yellow marrow, which is made up of blood vessels, nerve cells, and fat cells. Red marrow produces red blood cells as well as special white blood cells (lymphocytes) and other elements of blood (platelets).

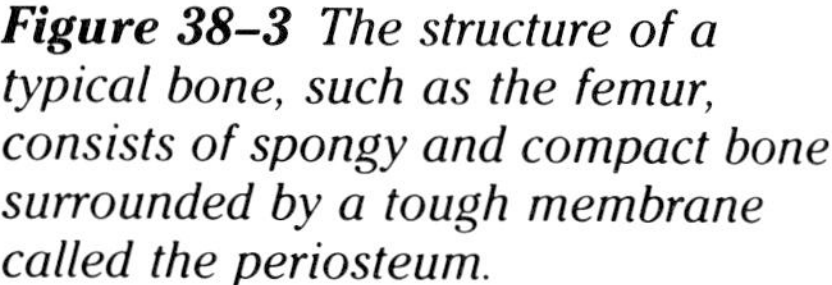

Figure 38–3 *The structure of a typical bone, such as the femur, consists of spongy and compact bone surrounded by a tough membrane called the periosteum.*

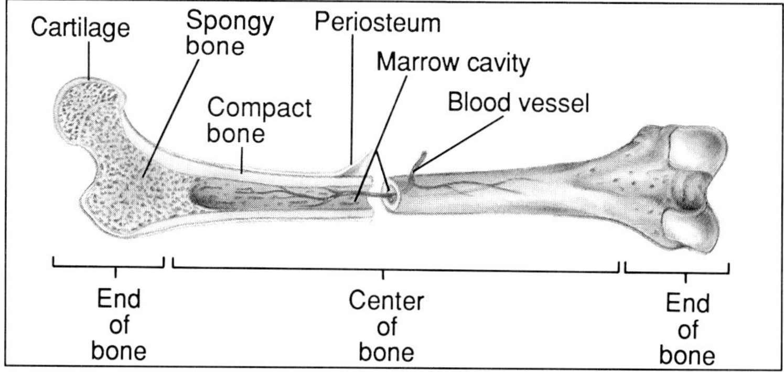

Development of Bones

Many bones are formed from the cells of a type of connective tissue called **cartilage**. Unlike bone, cartilage does not contain blood vessels. Cartilage cells must rely on the diffusion of nutrients from the tiny blood vessels (capillaries) in surrounding tissues. The cells that make up cartilage are scattered in a network of fibers composed of an elastic protein called collagen. Cartilage is dense and fibrous, can support weight, but is still extremely flexible.

Many bones in the skeleton of a newborn baby are composed almost entirely of cartilage. The cartilage is replaced by bone during **ossification** (ahs-uh-fih-KAY-shuhn), or the process of bone formation. Ossification begins to take place up to seven months before birth as mineral (calcium and phosphorus) deposits are laid down near the center of the bone. Gradually, bone tissue forms as osteocytes secrete mineral deposits that replace the cartilage.

Many long bones, such as those of the arms and legs, have growth (epiphyseal) plates at either end in which the growth of cartilage causes the bones to lengthen. Gradually, this new growth of cartilage is ossified (replaced by bone), and the bones become larger and stronger. This process usually continues until a person reaches the age of 18 or 20. At that time the growth plates disappear, the bones become completely ossified, and the person "stops growing."

In adults, cartilage is found in those parts of the body where flexibility is needed. Such places include the tip of the

__Figure 38–4__ The illustration shows the structures of compact and spongy bone. The opening in the center of the electron micrograph of compact bone is a single Haversian canal.

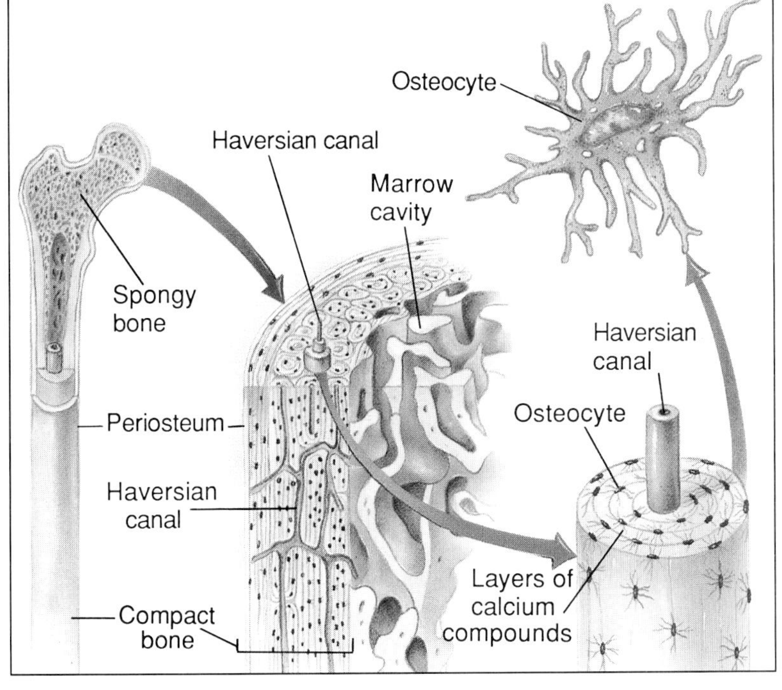

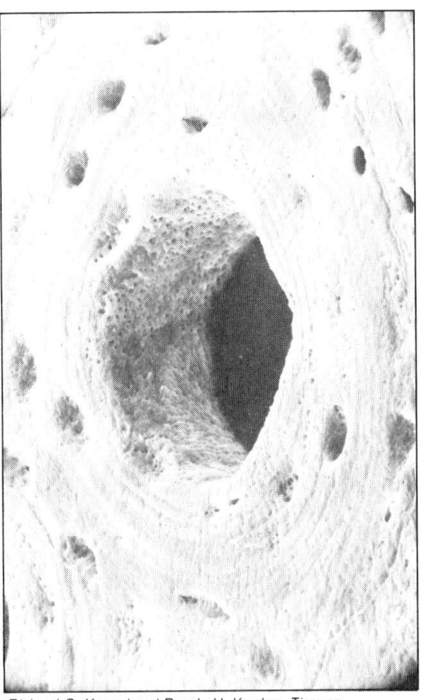

Richard G. Kessel and Randy H. Kardon. *Tissues and Organs: A Text Atlas of Scanning Electron Microscopy.* W. H. Freeman & Co. © 1979.

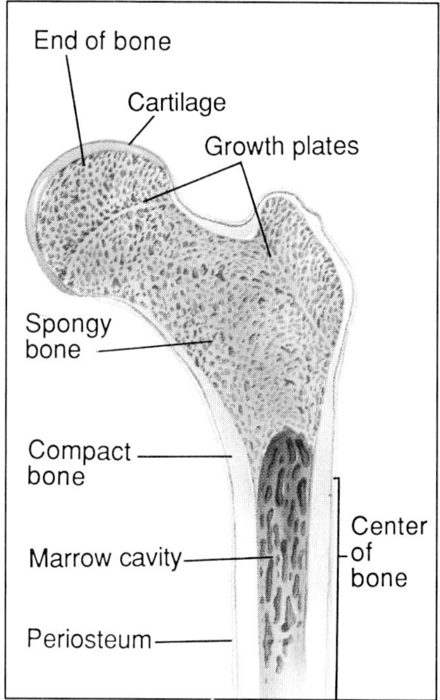

Figure 38–5 *A growth plate, which is located between the end and the center of a long bone, is a site at which a bone grows in length.*

nose, the external ears, the voice box (larynx) and walls of the windpipe (trachea), and the ends of the bones where joints are formed. Cartilage is also found where the ribs are attached to the breastbone (sternum), thus allowing the rib cage to move during breathing. In all these places, cartilage provides an important combination of strength and flexibility. You may recall from Chapter 31 that animals such as sharks and rays have skeletons composed entirely of cartilage.

Joints: Where Two Bones Meet

Joints, or places where two bones come together, permit the bones to move without damaging each other. In other words, joints are responsible for keeping the bones far enough apart so they do not rub against each other as they move. At the same time, joints hold the bones in place.

Because of the presence of joints, the human body is capable of a wide variety of movements, ranging from extensive movement (at the shoulder joint) to no movement at all (at the joints of the skull). Depending on their type of movement, joints are classified as either immovable, slightly movable, or freely movable.

IMMOVABLE JOINTS These joints, often called fixed joints, allow no movement between bones. This is because the bones at an immovable joint are interlocked and held together by connective tissue, or they are fused. The places where the bones in the skull meet are examples of immovable joints. Skull bones do not need to move because their main function is to protect the brain and the sense organs located in the head.

Figure 38–6 *Of the 28 bones that make up the skull, 8 of them form the cranium, or bony covering surrounding the brain. The photograph shows an interlocking immovable joint between two bones in the cranium.*

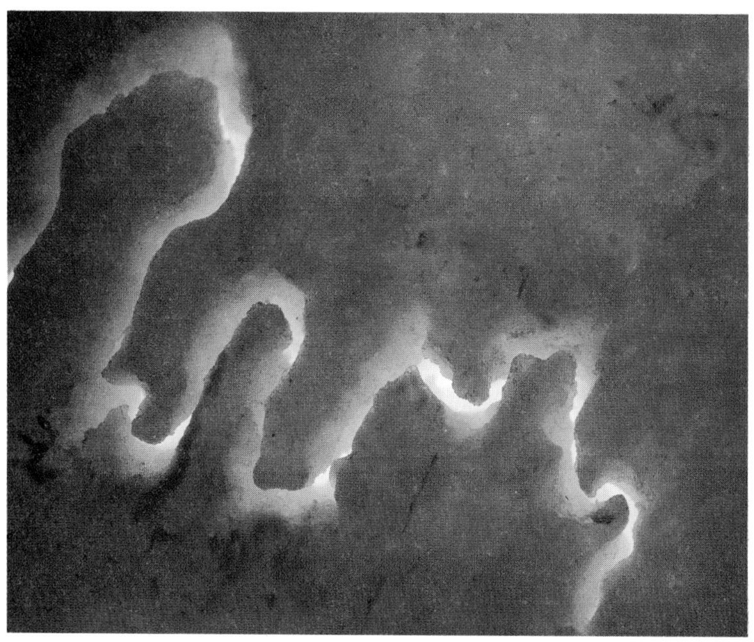

SLIGHTLY MOVABLE JOINTS These joints permit a small amount of movement. Unlike the bones of immovable joints, the bones of slightly movable joints are farther apart from each other. The joints between the two bones of the lower leg (tibia and fibula) and the joints of the vertebrae (bones of the spinal column) are examples of slightly movable joints.

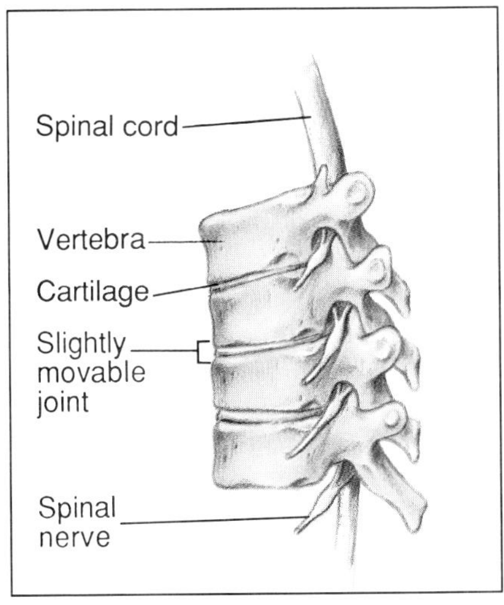

Figure 38–7 Slightly movable joints are found between the vertebrae, or bones that make up the spinal column.

FREELY MOVABLE JOINTS Most of the joints of the body are freely movable joints. In freely movable joints, the ends of the bones are covered with a layer of cartilage that provides a smooth surface at the joint. The joints are also surrounded by a fibrous joint capsule that helps hold the bones together and at the same time allows for movement. The joint capsule consists of two layers.

One of the layers of the joint capsule may thicken to form strips of tough connective tissue called **ligaments**. Ligaments are attached to the membranes that surround bones and hold the bones together. The other layer of the joint capsule produces synovial (sih-NOH-vee-uhl) fluid, which forms a thin lubricating film over the surface of a joint. This lubricating film enables the cartilage found on the ends of the bones to slip past each other more smoothly as the joint moves.

In some freely movable joints, small pockets of synovial fluid called bursae (BER-see; singular: bursa) form. A bursa reduces the friction between the bones of a joint and also acts as a tiny shock absorber. Sometimes when a joint is injured, too much fluid moves into the bursa, causing it to swell and become painful. When this happens at a joint, a condition called bursitis results.

A more serious disorder that affects the joints is arthritis, or inflammation of the joint. There are at least 20 different types of arthritis that affect approximately 10 percent of the world's population. You will learn more about arthritis in Chapter 45.

Freely movable joints are grouped according to the shapes of the surfaces of the adjacent bones. There are six types of freely movable joints. Refer to Figure 38–9 on page 842 as you read about each type of joint. Locate each joint on your body and duplicate its movement as you read about it.

A ball-and-socket joint permits circular movement—the widest range of movement. The shoulder joint and the hip joint are examples of a ball-and-socket joint. A hinge joint permits a back-and-forth motion, much like the opening and closing of a door. Examples of a hinge joint are the knee and the elbow. A pivot joint allows for rotation of one bone around another. Examples of this type of joint are found between the first two neck vertebrae and between the bones of the lower arm (ulna and radius).

A gliding joint permits a sliding motion of one bone over another. Gliding joints are found at the ends of the collarbones (clavicles), between wrist bones (carpals), and between ankle

Figure 38–8 A hinge joint, such as the knee, allows for movement in one plane only.

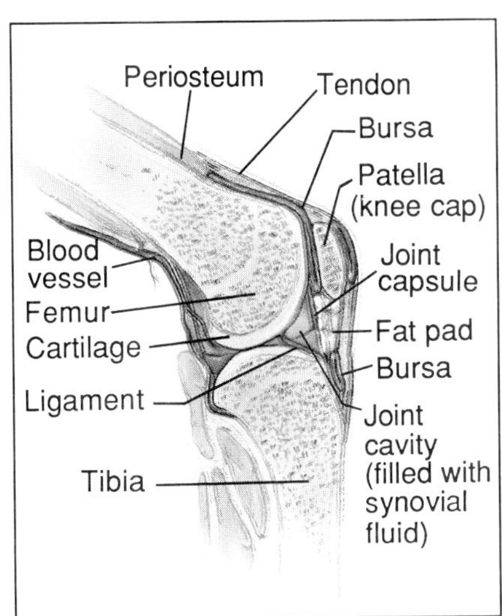

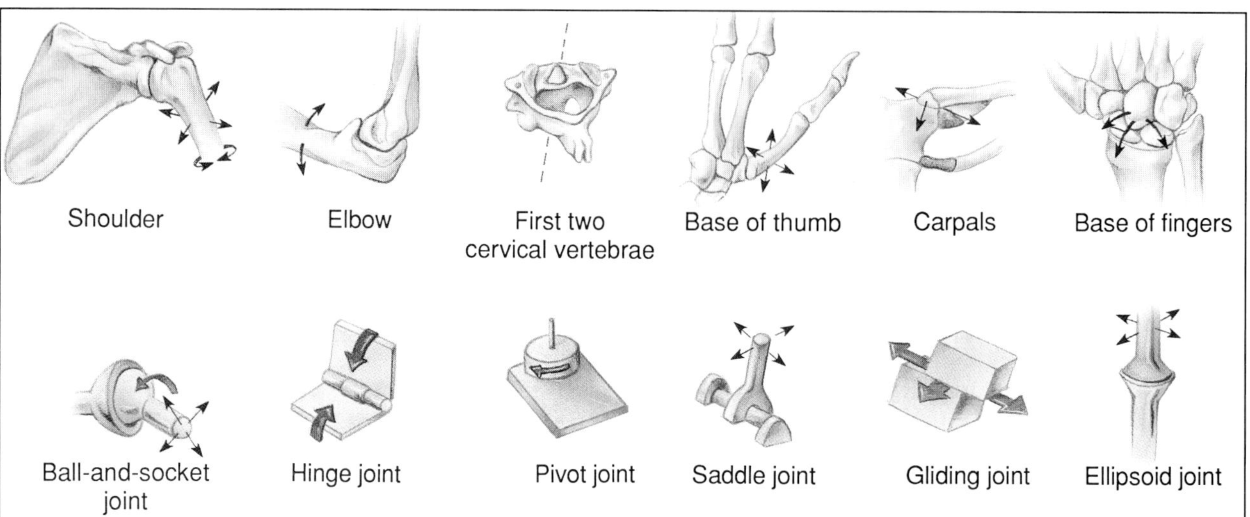

Figure 38–9 *Freely movable joints permit a wide range of motion. Notice the movements of six types of freely movable joints.*

bones (tarsals). A saddle joint permits movements in two planes. This type of joint is found at the base of the thumb. An ellipsoid (ee-LIHP-soid) joint allows for a hinge-type movement in two directions. The joints that connect the fingers with the palms of the hands and the toes with the soles of the feet are examples of ellipsoid joints.

38–1 SECTION REVIEW

1. Identify the parts of the skeletal system.
2. What are the functions of the skeletal system?
3. Describe the structure and development of bone.
4. What is a joint? List the three types of joints.
5. Describe and give an example of the six types of freely movable joints.
6. Explain why a bone that fractures, or breaks, is painful.

Section Objectives

- Describe the function and composition of the muscular system.
- Discuss the mechanism of muscle contraction.
- Explain the relationship among muscles, bones, and joints.

38–2 The Muscular System

As you have just read, the skeleton and its joints support, protect, and provide flexibility for the body. But the skeleton cannot move by itself. That job is performed by the muscle tissue that makes up the **muscular system**. Muscle tissue consists of groups of cells that are specialized for contraction. Approximately 40 to 50 percent of the mass of the human body is composed of muscle tissue—and that is true whether or not one is an athlete. **The muscular system is composed of muscle tissue that is highly specialized to contract, or shorten, when stimulated.** The word muscle is derived from the Latin word *mus,* meaning mouse. The Greeks and Romans, fascinated by the distribution of muscles in the body, compared the contractions of muscles to the movements of mice beneath the skin.

Muscle tissue is found everywhere within the body—not only beneath the skin but deep within the body, surrounding many internal organs and blood vessels. The size and location of muscle tissue helps determine the shape of our body, the way we move, and even the way we smile!

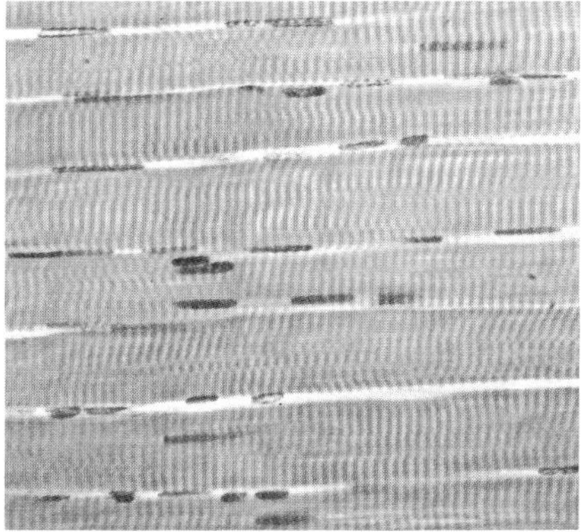

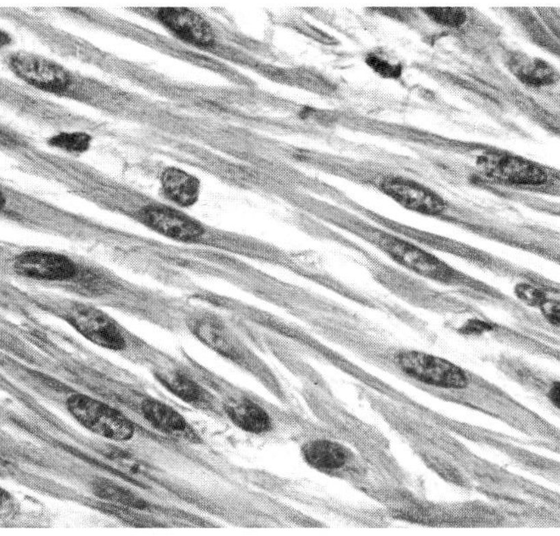

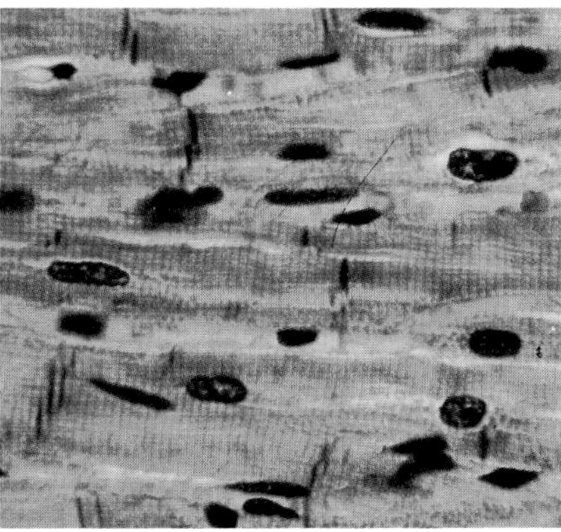

Figure 38–10 Muscle tissue is specialized for contraction. There are three types of muscle tissue: skeletal muscle (top), smooth muscle (center), and cardiac muscle (bottom).

Types of Muscle Tissue

There are three different types of muscle tissue, or muscles: skeletal, smooth, and cardiac. Each type of muscle has a different structure and plays a different role in the body.

SKELETAL MUSCLES **Skeletal muscles** are generally attached to bones and are at work every time we lift a finger, wink an eye, chew something, or stand up. Skeletal muscles are responsible for voluntary (conscious) movement. When viewed under a microscope, skeletal muscles appear to have striations (bands or stripes). For these reasons, skeletal muscles are also known as voluntary or striated muscles. Most skeletal muscles are consciously controlled by the central nervous system.

Skeletal muscle cells are large, have more than one nucleus, and vary in length from 1 millimeter to as many as 30 to 60 centimeters. Because skeletal muscle cells are long and slender, they are often called muscle fibers rather than muscle cells. The muscle fibers together with the connective tissues, blood vessels, and nerves associated with them form a skeletal muscle such as a leg muscle.

SMOOTH MUSCLES **Smooth muscles** are usually not under voluntary control. Smooth muscle cells are spindle-shaped, have individual nuclei, and are not striated. Smooth muscles are found in many internal organs and in the walls of many blood vessels. Most smooth muscle cells can contract

Figure 38–11 *This drawing shows the structure of the deltoid in the upper arm, a skeletal muscle. Notice that skeletal muscle is made up of bundles of muscle fibers.*

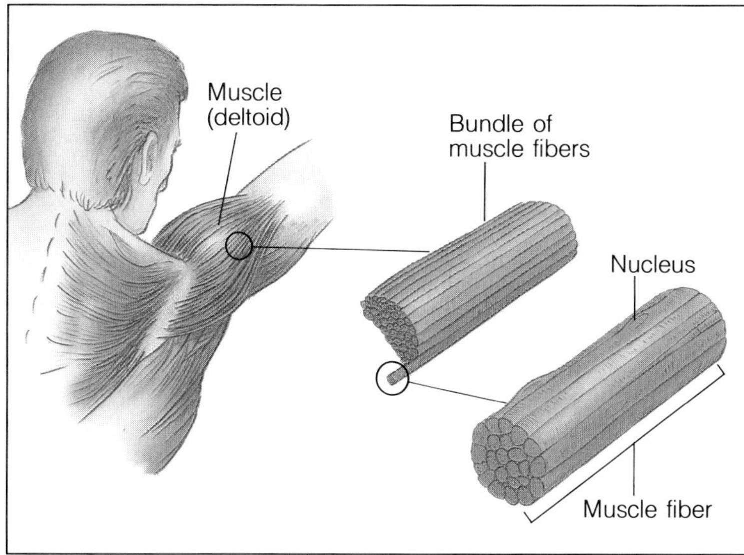

without nervous stimulation. These contractions in smooth muscles move food through our digestive tract, control the way blood flows through our circulatory system, and decrease the size of the pupils of our eyes in bright light.

CARDIAC MUSCLES The only place in the body where **cardiac muscles** are found is in the heart. Although cardiac muscle cells are striated, they are not under voluntary control. Unlike skeletal muscles, cardiac muscles contract without direct stimulation by the nervous system. The cardiac muscle cells contain one nucleus located near the center of the cell. Adjacent cells form branching fibers that allow nerve impulses to pass from cell to cell.

Mechanism of Muscle Contraction

Muscle contraction is one of the best-understood processes in the human body. We know as much as we do about muscle contraction because the regular structure of striated muscle cells has made them easy to study. When viewed through the electron microscope, the muscle cells are seen to contain both thick and thin filaments. The overlapping patterns of the thick and thin filaments are responsible for the light and dark bands seen in skeletal (striated) muscle. See Figure 38–12.

In the 1950s, the British scientist Hugh Huxley noted that when a muscle cell contracts, the light and dark bands contained in the muscle cell get closer together. We now know that the thick filaments are made up of a protein called **myosin**, and the thin filaments are composed of a protein called **actin**. When myosin filaments and actin filaments come near each other, many knoblike projections in each myosin filament form **cross-bridges** with an actin filament. When the muscle is stimulated to contract, the cross-bridges move, pulling the two filaments

__Figure 38–12__ Each muscle fiber is a single cell. The individual myofibrils, or cylindrical structures, within the cell contain thick filaments made up of myosin and thin filaments made up of actin. The electron micrograph shows a section of a myofibril.

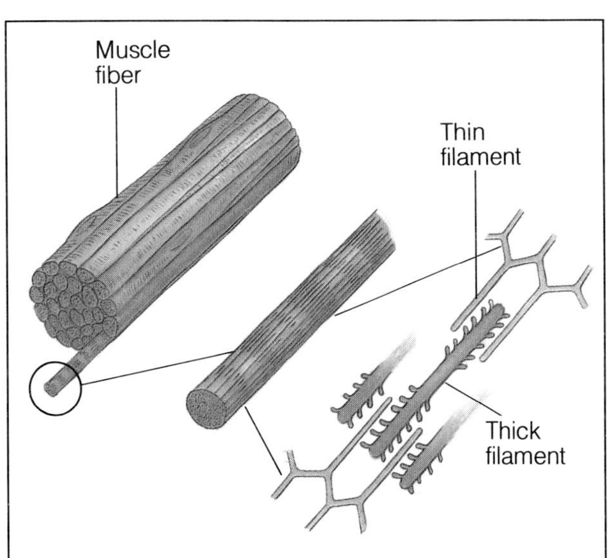

past each other. After each cross-bridge has moved as far as it can, it releases the actin filament and returns to its original position. The cross-bridge then attaches to the actin filament at another place and the cycle is repeated. When thousands of actin and myosin filaments interact in this way, the entire muscle cell shortens. This concept is the **sliding filament theory**.

ATP provides the energy necessary to make and break connections between actin and myosin filaments. ATP also powers the movement of the cross-bridges by attaching a molecule of itself to each myosin cross-bridge. Each time a cross-bridge goes through the cycle, the ATP is broken down to ADP and inorganic phosphate.

When a muscle cell contracts in the manner just described, large amounts of ATP are used up as the thick and thin filaments slide past each other. What is the source of all this ATP? Cells have two methods by which they make ATP from carbohydrates (glucose): by the aerobic process of cellular respiration and by the anaerobic process of fermentation. Muscle cells use both these methods to generate the ATP they need.

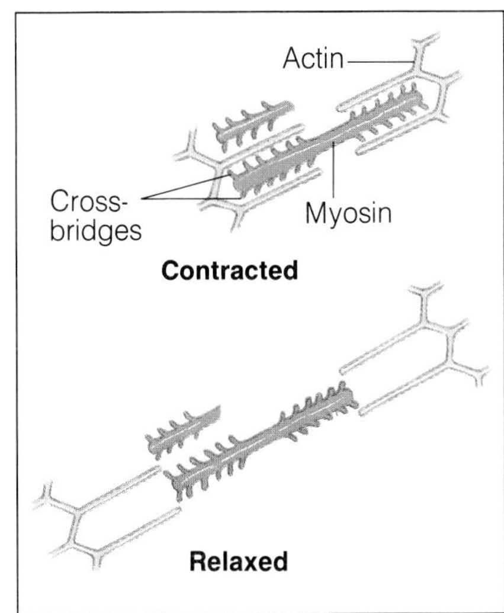

Figure 38–13 *When the muscle is stimulated to contract, cross-bridges on the myosin filaments move and pull the actin filaments past each other. These actions cause the muscle cells to shorten. When there is no stimulation, the cross-bridges let go and the muscle relaxes.*

Control of Muscle Contraction

Muscles are useful only if they contract in a controlled fashion. In Chapter 37 you learned that motor neurons connect the central nervous system to skeletal muscle cells (effectors). Impulses (action potentials) from motor neurons control the contraction of skeletal muscle cells.

Figure 38–14 shows how a motor neuron makes contact with a typical skeletal muscle cell. The point of contact is called the neuromuscular junction. Vesicles, or pockets, in the axon terminals of the motor neuron release molecules of the neurotransmitter acetylcholine (as-ih-tihl-KOH-leen). These molecules diffuse across the synapse, producing an impulse in the cell membrane of the muscle cell. The impulse causes the release of calcium ions (Ca^{2+}) within the cell. The calcium ions affect regulatory proteins that allow actin and myosin filaments to interact and form cross-bridges. From the time a nerve impulse reaches a muscle cell, it is only a matter of a few milliseconds before this series of events takes place and the muscle cell contracts.

Figure 38–14 *The threadlike structures in this electron micrograph are the axon terminals that form neuromuscular junctions.*

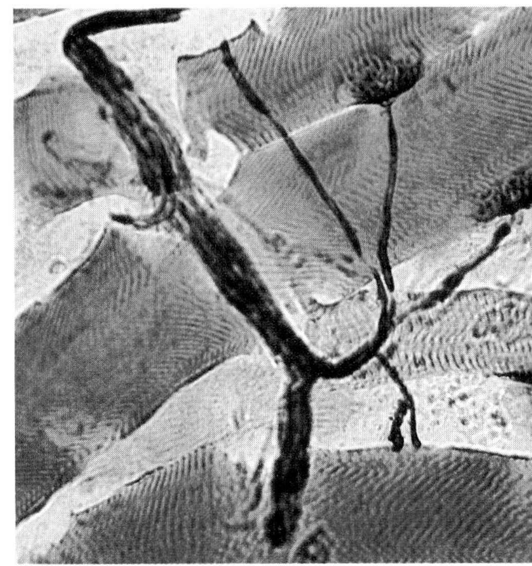

A muscle cell will remain in a state of contraction until the production of acetylcholine stops. An enzyme called acetylcholinesterase (as-ih-tihl-koh-leen-EHS-ter-ayz), also produced at the neuromuscular junction, destroys acetylcholine, permits the reabsorption of calcium ions into the muscle cell, and terminates the contraction.

Is there a difference between a strong contraction and a weak contraction? Recall that each muscle contains hundreds of muscle cells. When your brain sends a message for a weak contraction, such as blinking the eyes, only a few muscle cells are stimulated. When you exert maximum effort, trying to lift a heavy weight perhaps, most muscle cells are stimulated.

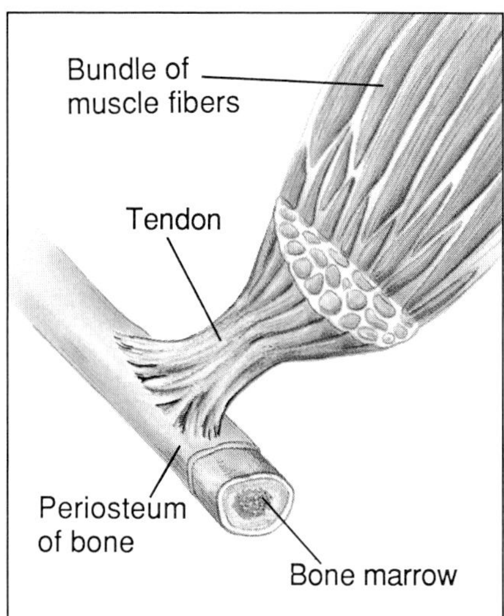

Figure 38–15 *Muscles are attached to bones by tough connective tissue called tendons. Tendons pull on bones and make them work like levers.*

How Muscles and Bones Interact

You have just learned that skeletal muscles generate force and produce movement only by contracting, or pulling on body parts. Individual muscles can only pull; they cannot push. Yet you know from experience that your arms and legs can push when you want them to. How is this possible?

Skeletal muscles are joined to bones by tough connective tissues called **tendons**. Tendons are attached in such a way that they pull on the bones and make them work like levers. The movements of the muscles and joints enable the bones to act as levers. The joint functions as a fulcrum (fixed point around which the lever moves), and the muscles provide the force to move the lever. See Figure 38–15. Usually there are several muscles surrounding each joint that pull in different directions.

Most skeletal muscles work in pairs. When one muscle or set of muscles contracts, the other relaxes. The muscles of the upper arm are a good example of this dual action. When the biceps muscle (on the front of the upper arm) contracts, it bends, or flexes, the elbow joint. When the triceps muscle (on the back of the upper arm) contracts, it opens, or extends, the elbow joint. A controlled movement, however, requires contraction by both muscles. To hold a tennis racket or a violin, for example, both the biceps and triceps must contract in balance. This is why the training of athletes and musicians is so difficult. The brain must learn how to work opposing muscle groups to just the right degree to get the joint to move precisely.

A normal characteristic of all skeletal muscles is that they remain in a state of partial contraction. At any given time, some muscles are being stimulated while others are not. This causes a tightened, or firmed, muscle and is known as muscle tone. Muscle tone is responsible for keeping the back and legs straight and the head upright even when you are relaxed. Regular exercise is good for your body because it increases your muscle tone. Muscles that are exercised regularly stay firm and increase in size by adding more materials to the inside of the muscle fibers. Muscles that are not used at all get weak, flabby, and actually decrease in size.

38–2 SECTION REVIEW

1. What is the function of the muscular system?
2. Name and describe the three types of muscles.
3. Describe the mechanism of muscle contraction. How is muscle contraction controlled?
4. How do muscles, bones, and joints work together to produce movement?
5. Do the number of bands in a striated muscle cell increase or decrease during contraction? Explain.

38–3 The Integumentary System

Section Objectives

- Identify the structures that make up the integumentary system.
- List the functions of the skin.
- Describe the structure of the skin, hair, and nails.

"Good fences make good neighbors," wrote the American poet Robert Frost, as he explained the importance of property boundaries. Living things have their own "fences," and none is as important as the skin—the boundary that separates the human body from the outside world.

Skin, the single largest organ in the body, is part of the **integumentary** (ihn-tehg-yoo-MEHN-ter-ee) **system**. The word integument comes from a Latin word that means to cover, reflecting the fact that the skin and its accessory structures form a covering over the entire body. **Skin and its accessory organs—the hair, nails, and a variety of glands—make up the integumentary system.**

The most important function of the integumentary system is protection. It performs this function by serving as a barrier against infection and injury; helping to regulate body temperature; removing waste products from the body; and providing protection against ultraviolet radiation from the sun. Because the main component of the integumentary system, the skin, contains several types of sensory receptors, it serves as the gateway through which sensations such as pressure, heat, cold, and pain are transmitted to the nervous system.

Epidermis

The skin consists of two main layers. The outermost layer is known as the **epidermis**. Most of the cells of the epidermis undergo rapid cell division (mitosis). As new cells are produced, they push older cells to the surface of the skin. Here the older cells become flattened, lose their cellular contents, and begin making keratin, a tough fibrous protein. In humans, keratin forms the basic structure of hair, nails, and calluses. In

Figure 38–16 The skin is the body's largest organ, covering an area of almost 2 square meters. About 6.5 square centimeters of skin may contain 20 blood vessels, 650 sweat glands, and more than 1000 nerve endings. Grooves and ridges formed by epidermal cells on the fingertips cause fingerprint patterns, as seen in the electron micrograph.

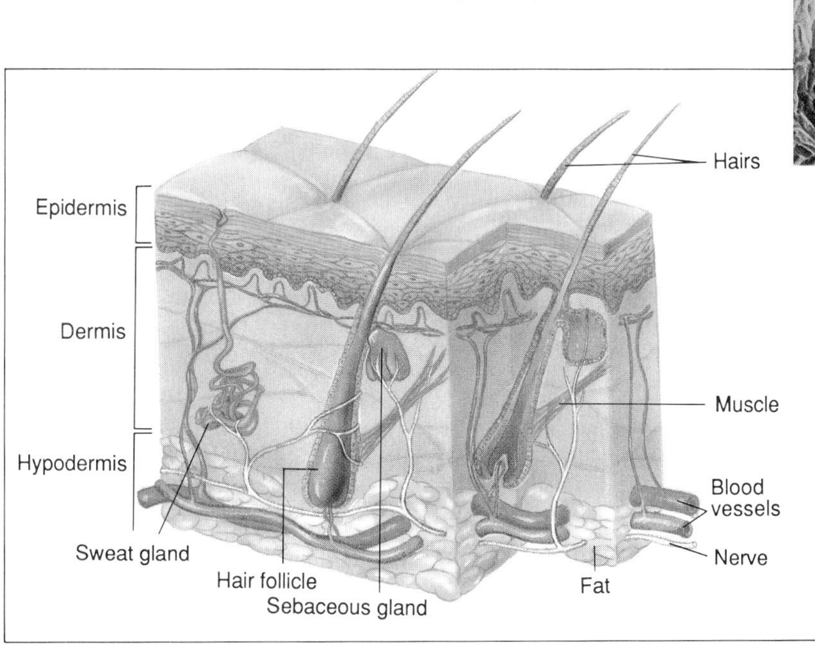

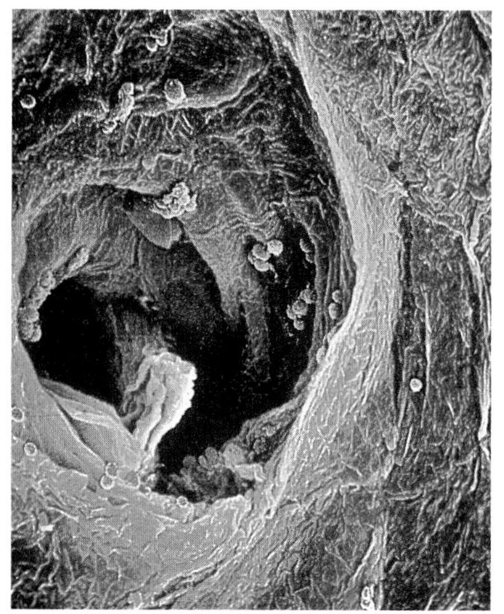

Figure 38–17 *The skin of an adult contains approximately 3 million sweat glands, one of which is shown in this photograph. The tiny green circular objects inside this sweat gland are bacteria.*

Figure 38–18 *In humans, hair is found almost everywhere in skin. Hair is produced in tubelike structures called hair follicles.*

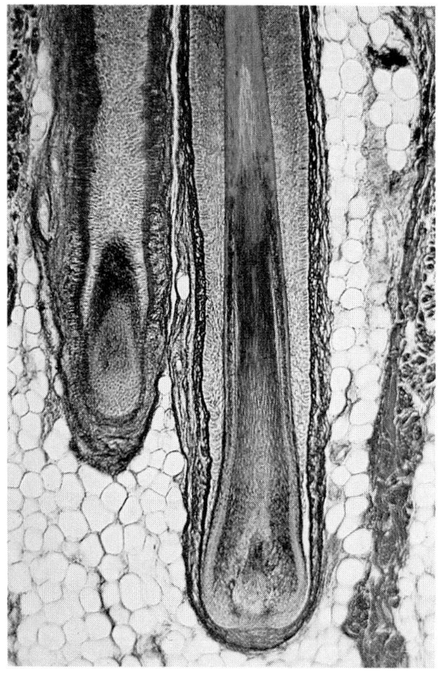

other animals, keratin is more versatile—forming cow horns, reptile scales, bird feathers, and porcupine quills.

Eventually, the keratin-producing cells (keratinocytes) die and form a tough, flexible waterproof covering on the surface of the skin. This outer layer of dead cells is shed or washed away at a surprising rate—once every 14 to 28 days.

The epidermis also contains melanocytes, or cells that produce melanin, a dark pigment. Although light-skinned and dark-skinned people have roughly the same number of melanocytes, the difference in their skin color is caused by the amount of melanin the melanocytes produce and distribute. There are no blood vessels in the epidermis, which explains why a slight scratch will not cause bleeding.

Dermis

The **dermis** is the innermost layer of the skin. It lies beneath the epidermis and contains blood vessels, nerve endings, glands, sense organs, smooth muscles, and hair follicles. When the body needs to conserve heat on a cold day, the blood vessels in the dermis narrow, helping to limit heat loss. On hot days, the blood vessels widen, warming the skin and increasing heat loss. Beneath the dermis is the hypodermis, a layer of fat and loose connective tissue that insulates the body.

The dermis contains two major types of glands: sweat glands and sebaceous (suh-BAY-shuhs), or oil, glands. These glands pass through the epidermis and release their products at the surface of the skin. Sweat glands produce the watery secretion known as sweat, which contains salts, water, and other compounds. These secretions are stimulated by nerve impulses that cause the production of sweat when the temperature of the body is raised. Sebaceous glands produce an oily secretion known as sebum that spreads out along the surface of the skin and keeps the keratin-rich epidermis flexible and waterproof.

Hair and Nails

Hair is produced by cells at the base of structures called **hair follicles**. Hair follicles are tubelike pockets of epidermal cells that extend into the dermis. Individual hairs are actually large columns of cells that have filled with keratin and then died. Rapid cell growth at the base of the hair follicle causes the hair to grow longer. Hair follicles are in close contact with sebaceous glands. The oily secretions of these glands help maintain the condition of each individual hair.

Nails grow from an area of rapidly dividing cells known as the **nail matrix**. The nail matrix is located near the tips of the fingers and toes. During cell division, the cells of the nail matrix fill with keratin and produce a tough, strong platelike nail that covers and protects the tips of the fingers and toes. Nails grow at an average rate of 0.5 to 1.2 millimeters per day, with fingernails growing more rapidly than toenails.

SCIENCE, TECHNOLOGY, AND SOCIETY **BREAKTHROUGH**

Finding the Gene for Duchenne Muscular Dystrophy

Muscular dystrophy (MD) is a serious genetic disorder that results in a gradual wasting away of muscle tissue. The most common severe form of the disorder is Duchenne muscular dystrophy. Duchenne MD is a sex-linked disorder that occurs in 1 out of 3500 male babies in the United States. Males who carry the gene for Duchenne MD begin to suffer its first symptoms in early childhood. By the time these males reach early adulthood, the gradual degeneration of muscle tissue causes paralysis and then death.

Using the techniques of molecular biology, a group of researchers, led by Louis Kunkel of Harvard University, announced in 1987 that they had found the location of the Duchenne MD gene on the X chromosome. This gene codes for an unknown protein that was soon to bear the name dystrophin. In healthy people, dystrophin is a tiny fraction, less than 0.002 percent, of the total protein in muscle tissue. But in people with Duchenne MD, dystrophin is completely absent or nonfunctional. Genetic studies now explain this phenomenon: MD sufferers are missing portions of the dystrophin gene.

Before the discovery of the MD gene, the existence of dystrophin was unknown. At present, scientists are trying to determine what role dystrophin plays in normal muscle. Their first experiments show that dystrophin can bind actin, the protein found in thin filaments. Far more work needs to be done, however, before the function of dystrophin is known with certainty. Scientists hope that a complete understanding of dystrophin may soon lead to a treatment for MD. In the meantime, the studies on MD have led to a new understanding of the proteins contained in normal muscle cells.

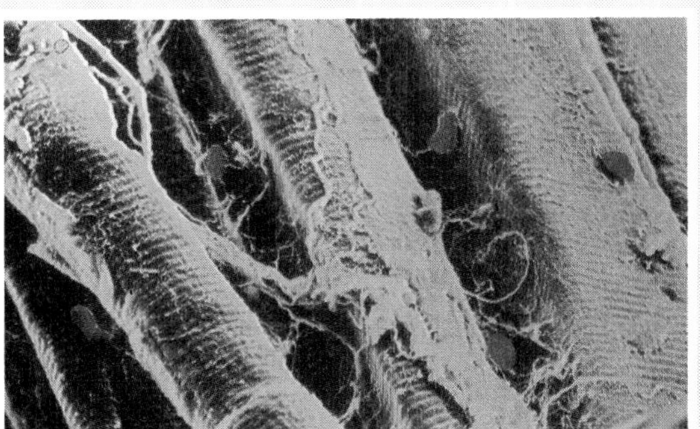

Normal skeletal muscle

38–3 SECTION REVIEW

1. What structures make up the integumentary system?
2. What are the functions of the skin?
3. Describe the epidermis and the dermis.
4. In what way is the growth of hair and nails similar?
5. Explain why your nose and ears turn red on cold winter days.

LABORATORY INVESTIGATION

EXAMINING SKELETAL MUSCLE

PROBLEM

How are muscle cells suited to their function?

MATERIALS *(per group)*

small piece of raw beef	toluidine blue
dissecting tray	clock with second hand
dissecting needle	coverslip
glass slide	microscope
2 medicine droppers	paper towels

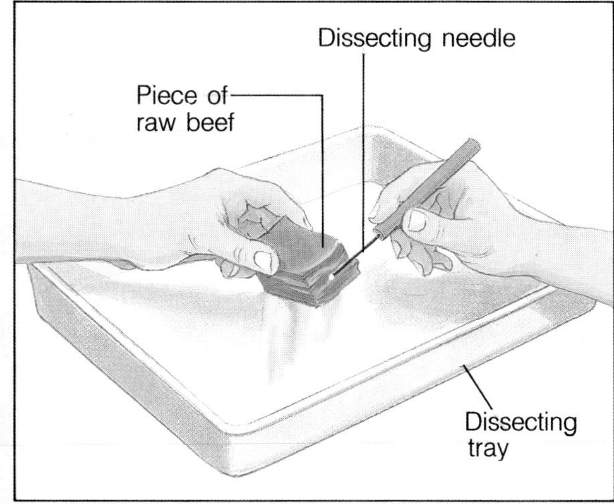

PROCEDURE   

1. Place the piece of beef in the dissecting tray.
2. To remove a muscle fiber from the beef, pass the tip of the dissecting needle over the beef's surface a few times. **CAUTION:** *Be careful when using a dissecting needle.*
3. Transfer the muscle fiber to a glass slide.
4. Using one of the medicine droppers, place two drops of toluidine blue on top of the muscle fiber. Allow the muscle fiber to remain in the toluidine blue for two minutes.
5. After two minutes, use a piece of paper towel to absorb the excess toluidine blue.
6. Using the second medicine dropper, place two drops of water on the muscle fiber. Allow the muscle fiber to remain in the water for two minutes.
7. After two minutes, use a piece of paper towel to absorb the excess water.
8. Place two additional drops of water on the muscle fiber and cover with a coverslip.
9. With the low-power objective of the microscope, locate a transparent, lightly stained section of the muscle fiber.
10. Switch to the high-power objective to focus on a few muscle cells.
11. Note the general shape of the muscle cells. Observe the light and dark patterns, the number of nuclei, and the arrangement of the muscle cells with respect to one another. Make a labeled sketch of the structures that you see.

OBSERVATIONS

1. What is the general shape of a muscle cell?
2. Describe the appearance of a muscle cell.
3. How many nuclei does a muscle cell have?
4. How are the muscle cells arranged with respect to one another?

ANALYSIS AND CONCLUSIONS

1. What microscopic evidence do you have that shows muscle cells contract by the overlapping of actin and myosin filaments?
2. How should the muscle fibers be arranged in order to provide for their movement in the same direction?
3. How are muscle cells suited to their function?

STUDENT STUDY GUIDE

SUMMARIZING THE CONCEPTS

The key concepts in each section of this chapter are listed below to help you review the chapter content. Make sure you understand each concept and its relationship to other concepts and to the theme of this chapter.

38–1 The Skeletal System

- Bones and their associated tissues—cartilage, tendons, and ligaments—make up the skeletal system.
- Bones of the skeletal system support and shape the body, provide a system of levers on which muscle tissues act to produce movement, contain reserves of minerals and are sites of blood-cell formation.
- During ossification, or bone formation, cartilage is replaced by bone.
- Joints, or places where two bones come together, permit bones to move without damaging each other.

38–2 The Muscular System

- The muscular system is composed of muscle tissue that is highly specialized to contract, or shorten, when stimulated.
- There are three different types of muscle tissue: skeletal, smooth, and cardiac.

38–3 The Integumentary System

- Skin and its accessory organs—the hair, nails, and a variety of glands—make up the integumentary system.
- The integumentary system has many functions: It protects the body by serving as a barrier against infection and injury, regulates body temperature, removes waste products, provides protection against ultraviolet radiation, and serves as a gateway through which sensations are sent to the nervous system.
- The outermost layer of the skin is the epidermis. The innermost layer is the dermis.
- Hair is produced by cells at the base of hair follicles. The nail matrix produces a tough, strong platelike nail.

REVIEWING KEY TERMS

Vocabulary terms are important to your understanding of biology. The key terms listed below are those you should be especially familiar with. Review these terms and their meanings. Then use each term in a complete sentence. If you are not sure of a term's meaning, return to the appropriate section and review its definition.

38–1 The Skeletal System

skeletal system
periosteum
Haversian canal
osteocyte
bone marrow
cartilage
ossification
joint
ligament

38–2 The Muscular System

muscular system
skeletal muscle
smooth muscle
cardiac muscle
myosin
actin
cross-bridge
sliding filament theory
tendon

38–3 The Integumentary System

integumentary system
epidermis
dermis
hair follicle
nail matrix

CHAPTER REVIEW

CONTENT REVIEW

Multiple Choice

Choose the letter of the answer that best completes each statement.

1. Which is not found in the human skeleton?
   a. calcium c. phosphorus
   b. cellulose d. living tissue
2. Bone cells are called
   a. melanocytes. c. osteocytes.
   b. lymphocytes. d. keratinocytes.
3. During ossification, cartilage is replaced by
   a. ligament. c. tendon.
   b. bone. d. muscle.
4. Bones are connected to muscles by
   a. ligaments. c. cartilage.
   b. skin. d. tendons.
5. Which serves as a lever for muscles?
   a. bones c. spinal cord
   b. ligaments d. tendons
6. Cardiac muscle tissue is located in the
   a. brain. c. arms.
   b. heart. d. digestive tract.
7. The outermost layer of skin is called the
   a. dermis. c. hypodermis.
   b. melanin. d. epidermis.
8. Melanocytes are located in the
   a. bones. c. epidermis.
   b. dermis. d. muscles.

True or False

Determine whether each statement is true or false. If it is true, write "true." If it is false, change the underlined word or words to make the statement true.

1. Bone is <u>nonliving</u> tissue.
2. The <u>Haversian canal</u> is a tough membrane that surrounds bone.
3. The elbow is a <u>pivot</u> joint.
4. An example of a <u>hinge</u> joint is the shoulder.
5. <u>Tendons</u> attach bones to bones.
6. Two types of striated muscle are <u>cardiac</u> and skeletal.
7. The thick filaments in a muscle cell are made up of <u>actin</u>.
8. Individual hairs are actually large columns of cells that have filled with <u>collagen</u>.

Word Relationships

A. *In each of the following sets of terms, three of the terms are related. One term does not belong. Determine the characteristic common to three of the terms and then identify the term that does not belong.*

1. striated, voluntary, skeletal, smooth
2. digestive tract, blood vessel, arm, pupil
3. hip, vertebrae, elbow, knee
4. muscle, hair, skin, nail

B. *An analogy is a relationship between two pairs of words or phrases generally written in the following manner: a:b::c:d. The symbol : is read "is to," and the symbol :: is read "as." For example, cat:animal::rose:plant is read "cat is to animal as rose is to plant."*

In the analogies that follow, a word or phrase is missing. Complete each analogy by providing the missing word or phrase.

5. skin:melanocyte::bone:____________
6. bone to bone:ligament::muscle to bone:____________
7. elbow:hinge::hip:____________

CONCEPT MASTERY

Use your understanding of the concepts developed in the chapter to answer each of the following in a brief paragraph.

1. Explain why bone is considered living.
2. Compare compact bone and spongy bone.
3. Describe a freely movable joint.
4. Compare the structure, function, and location of the three types of muscles.
5. Describe the sliding filament theory.
6. Describe a tendon and a ligament.
7. Using the terms fulcrum, lever, and force, explain how the contraction of a muscle results in movement.
8. What happens to the biceps and triceps when the arm is extended? When the arm is flexed?
9. Explain how the integumentary system provides protection for the body.
10. What is the importance of the sweat glands? Of sebaceous glands?
11. Explain why you are able to move the bones of your finger but not the bones of your skull.

CRITICAL AND CREATIVE THINKING

Discuss each of the following in a brief paragraph.

1. **Applying concepts** Suggest a reason why there are more joints in the hands and feet than in most other parts of the body.
2. **Making generalizations** People usually have more calluses, pads of thickened skin, on the soles of their feet or the palms of their hands. Explain the reason for this.
3. **Relating facts** Examine the photograph of coarse and fine hairs. Is hair alive or dead? Explain your answer.

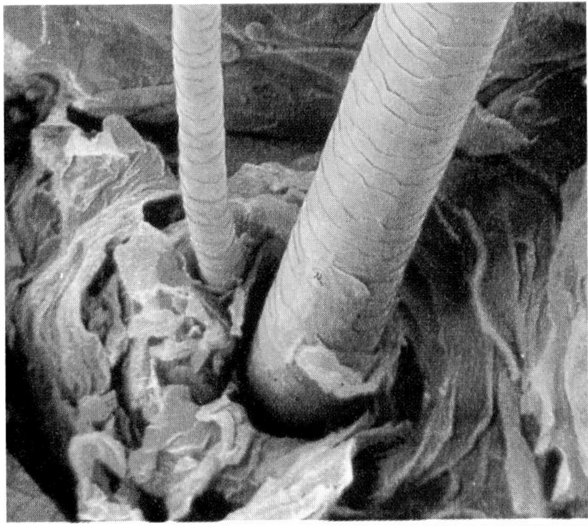

4. **Making comparisons** Why do bones heal faster in children than they do in adults?
5. **Developing a hypothesis** You have a habit of leaning on your elbow while reading. As a result, you have developed a noticeable swelling at your elbow. Explain what has happened.
6. **Identifying relationships** Few nerves and blood vessels enter a tendon or a ligament. Therefore, the supply of nutrients to these tissues is poor. Explain why injured tendons and ligaments take a long time to heal.
7. **Identifying patterns** Osteoporosis is a disease that usually occurs in older women. It involves a loss and weakening of bone tissue. Doctors recommend that women over the age of 45 eat more foods that contain calcium. How is this helpful in preventing osteoporosis?
8. **Using the writing process** Develop an advertising campaign for the dairy industry based on the relationship between milk and healthy bone development. Make it a full media blitz!

CHAPTER 39

Nutrition and Digestion

Eating, necessary to maintain life, can also be one of life's great pleasures. Eating a meal that contains a variety of nutrients is important for good health.

Most of us would agree that eating can be one of life's great pleasures. After all, what can compare with the delight of drinking an ice-cold glass of orange juice on a hot summer afternoon or savoring a turkey leg on Thanksgiving Day?

But just because eating is an enjoyable activity doesn't mean it is one to be taken lightly. You have probably been told many times that proper eating habits and good nutrition are important to your health. But what is good nutrition? And why aren't candies and snack foods as beneficial to you as a well-balanced meal? In order to answer these and other questions about healthful eating, you need to know what food is and how your body processes food through digestion. These are the subjects on the pages that follow.

CHAPTER OUTLINE

39–1 Food and Nutrition

Section Objectives
- Explain why we need to eat.
- Identify the main nutrients and how they are used by the body.
- Define balanced diet and tell why it is important.

Humans, like most other animals, are heterotrophs. Heterotrophs eat other organisms for food. But why must living things eat food? **Food contains nutrients, or molecules that provide energy and material for growth. Nutrients include water, minerals, carbohydrates, fats, proteins, and vitamins.** Although these nutrients are available in food, we cannot always be certain that the foods we eat will supply us with the nutrients we need. That's where the science of **nutrition** comes in. Nutrition is the study of how our bodies obtain energy, build tissue, and control body functions using materials supplied in the food we eat.

Why Food Is Important

Like an automobile or other machine that does work, our body needs fuel to supply energy. Food is our body's fuel. It supplies us with energy. We need energy not only to do work but to generate the heat that maintains our body temperature. As you may remember from Chapter 6, animals obtain energy primarily by oxidizing food to make ATP. To measure the amount of energy that can be obtained from food, biologists and chemists use the unit known as a **calorie**. A calorie is the amount of energy needed to raise the temperature of 1 gram of water by 1 degree Celsius. Because the energy needs of the body are great, nutritionists usually refer to the energy content of food in terms of the kilocalorie, which is 1000 calories. When books on diet and nutrition refer to food energy, they substitute the unit Calorie for kilocalorie. Notice that the Calorie used in place of the kilocalorie is spelled with a capital C and thus means 1000 of the calories spelled with a small c.

Figure 39–1 *Doing work requires energy. These kayakers expend a great deal of energy keeping their canoes on course in the white water of the river.*

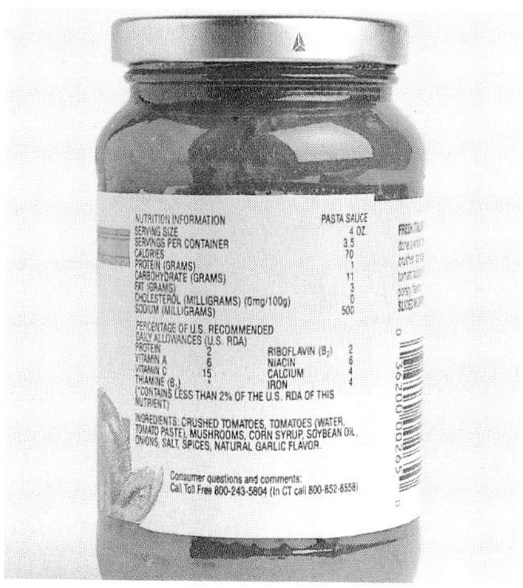

Figure 39–2 *Food labels provide valuable information for consumers.*

The basic energy needs of an average-sized adult human are about 1500 Calories per day. But energy needs vary depending upon the kind of work you do, how active you are, and your gender. Men generally have higher energy needs than women.

In addition to energy, food supplies building materials—the substances required by the cells in our body for proper growth and development. Even after we have reached adult size, tissues throughout the body must be repaired and replaced. Proteins and nucleic acids cannot be synthesized unless key compounds are supplied by a complete diet.

In the first part of this chapter you will learn about the kinds of food we need to eat to guarantee a supply of the vital nutrients. In the second part of the chapter you will see how the design of the digestive system ensures the proper delivery of those nutrients to the tissues that require them.

Water

Water is one of the simplest of the essential nutrients and also the most important. Animals will die from a lack of water long before they will starve from a lack of food. Most of the weight of the human body is water. So although a popular saying tells you that "you are what you eat," it would be closer to the truth if it were "you are as long as you drink."

Blood plasma—the liquid part of blood—is more than 90 percent water. Water is the solvent in which food and enzymes are dissolved in the digestive system. Water dissolves the waste materials that are eliminated in urine. On hot days, or when you take part in strenuous exercise, sweat glands remove

Figure 39–3 *Animals that live in dry environments get the water they need from the foods they eat, as this tortoise is doing by eating a piece of cactus.*

water from your tissues and use it to moisten the surface of your body. As the water in sweat evaporates, it cools the body.

Each time you take a breath, you lose water from the inner surfaces of the lungs. (That's why a mirror fogs up if you hold it in front of your nose and mouth.) Because water is constantly being lost from the body, a steady supply of this vital liquid is required. If the water lost from the body is not replaced, essential functions will slow down, the blood will begin to thicken, and a serious medical crisis will develop.

Although most of the water lost from the body is replaced by drinking liquids, we do obtain small quantities of water in two other ways. The foods we eat contain water. And water is released in cellular respiration when carbohydrates are broken down to produce energy ($C_6H_{12}O_6 + O_2 \rightarrow CO_2 + H_2O$).

Minerals

Minerals are inorganic substances required by the body. Some of the most important molecules in the body contain minerals. For example, hemoglobin, the protein in red blood cells that carries oxygen, contains four atoms of the mineral iron. DNA, RNA, and ATP all contain the mineral phosphorus. Calcium, another important mineral, is a major component of bones and teeth. It is also important for the normal functioning of nerves and muscles and for the normal clotting of blood. Without magnesium, another mineral, neither nerves nor muscle tissue will function properly.

Although the body does not destroy the minerals it takes in, it does lose many of them in sweat, urine, and other waste

Figure 39–4 *Minerals, which make up an important part of our diet, are used by the body in many ways. For example, your bones contain the mineral calcium; your red blood cells, the mineral iron. What is a good source of each of these minerals?*

MINERALS

Mineral	Source	Use
Calcium	Milk products, green leafy vegetables	Important component of bones and teeth; needed for normal blood clotting and for normal cell functioning
Chlorine	Table salt, many foods	Important for fluid balance
Magnesium	Milk products, meat, many foods	Needed for normal muscle and nerve functioning; metabolism of proteins and carbohydrates
Potassium	Grains, fruits, many foods	Normal muscle and nerve functioning
Phosphorus	Meats, nuts, whole grains, many foods	Component of DNA, RNA, ATP, and many proteins; part of bone tissue
Sodium	Many foods, table salt	Nerve and muscle functioning; water balance in body
Iron	Liver, red meats, grains, raisins, nuts	Important part of hemoglobin molecule
Fluorine	Water (natural and added)	Part of bones and teeth
Iodine	Seafood, iodized table salt	Part of hormones that regulate rate of metabolism

products. How then are these important chemicals replaced? Obviously, nibbling on automobiles to replenish the supply of iron or swallowing chalk dust to obtain calcium is not a reasonable solution. Luckily, most of these elements are found in the living tissues of plants and other animals. Plants absorb minerals from the soil and incorporate them into their tissues. Herbivores take in these minerals when they eat plants. Fruits, whole grains, meats, and vegetables contain iron, phosphorus, calcium, and magnesium. These foods also contain a wide range of other "trace elements" that the body needs in small amounts.

The minerals sodium and chlorine make up the compound commonly known as table salt and are also found in familiar foods such as milk, cheese, meat, and canned vegetables. Because the body loses sodium, potassium, and chlorine in sweat, athletes and people who perform hard physical work on hot days often need to supplement their diet with extra salt. Iodine, another mineral, is a natural component of seafood and of the drinking water in many areas. In the past, iodine deficiency, or goiter, was a serious problem in certain parts of the United States. Today, the addition of small amounts of iodine to table salt has all but eliminated this problem.

Carbohydrates

In Chapter 6 you learned that cells obtain energy from glucose in a process known as respiration. We get most of our glucose from carbohydrates: organic compounds composed entirely of carbon, hydrogen, and oxygen. Carbohydrates are the body's fuel.

Glucose is a simple sugar molecule that contains 6 carbon atoms, 12 hydrogen atoms, and 6 oxygen atoms ($C_6H_{12}O_6$). Glucose is a monosaccharide, or single sugar. Single sugars like glucose, fructose, and galactose are found in fruit juices, honey, and vegetables. Because they can be used directly by the body's cellular respiratory machinery, these simple sugars do not have to be digested, or broken down. They are therefore good sources of quick energy.

Many naturally occurring sugars are composed of two simple sugars that are linked together. These double sugars are called disaccharides. Maltose, or malt sugar, is a disaccharide made up of two glucose molecules. Another common disaccharide is sucrose, or table sugar, which is the sugar obtained from sugar cane. The disaccharide lactose is the sugar found in milk. In order for a disaccharide to be used for energy, enzymes must break the bond that holds the two simple sugars together.

Plants and animals store sugars as polysaccharides, long chains of monosaccharides. Polysaccharides are complex carbohydrates that are part of many foods. Two important polysaccharides found in plants are starch and cellulose.

Figure 39–5 *Sucrose is another name for table sugar, the sugar used to sweeten coffee, lemonade, pies, and cakes. In order to be used by the body, sucrose must be broken down into two molecules of the single sugar glucose.*

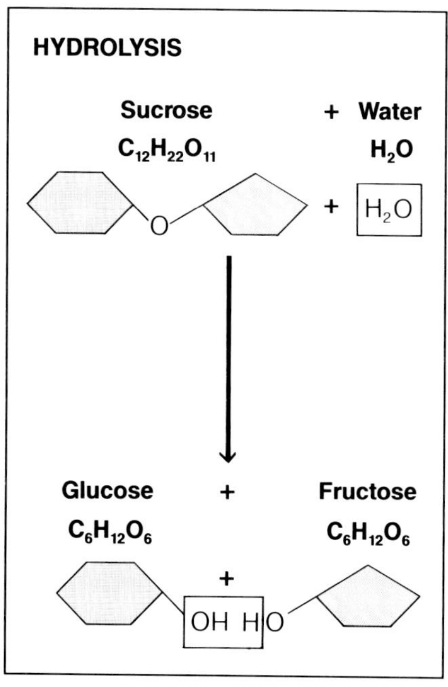

Starches have always been the most important carbohydrate in the diets of humans. The starch in grains used to make bread has nourished civilizations in Europe and the Middle East. Corn provided starch to Native Americans in the United States and in Central and South America. Starch in rice provides needed energy to billions of people in Asia. Potatoes, an important crop plant throughout the world, are another important source of starch in the diets of many people.

Before starches can be used in cellular respiration, however, they must be broken down. This is accomplished by our digestive system, which first breaks the long polysaccharide chain into disaccharides. The disaccharides are then broken apart to yield simple sugars such as glucose.

In plants, starch is usually found in the form of rather large granules that do not dissolve in water. Because enzymes in the digestive system are water soluble and work only on molecules in solution, it is difficult for them to break down insoluble starch granules. Fortunately, when starch granules are treated with hot water they swell and burst, releasing water-soluble starch molecules. This is one reason why many vegetables are more easily digested after they have been cooked.

Cellulose, another important polysaccharide, is part of the cell wall of plants. However, the sugar molecules in cellulose are hooked together in such a way that humans (and many other animals) cannot take them apart. For humans, cellulose is indigestible. Our digestive system cannot extract the energy contained in wood or blades of grass. But even though the body cannot digest cellulose, we need to include a substantial amount of it in our diets. Cellulose provides our digestive system with bulk, or roughage. Roughage stimulates the muscles of the stomach and intestines. This stimulation causes our digestive system to work more efficiently. Foods such as lettuce, celery, whole grain breads, and bran are rich in cellulose.

Figure 39–6 *Sugars and starches are an important part of the human diet. The source of these nutrients, however, varies in different parts of the world. These Peruvian natives eat some foods you would recognize and probably many more that you would not.*

Figure 39–7 *Like this beaver, many animals are herbivores. Their digestive systems show adaptations for removing nutrients from leaves and other plant materials that the human digestive system cannot easily break down.*

PROBLEM SOLVING IN BIOLOGY

READING A FOOD LABEL

Most of the packaged food products that are sold today are required by law to list the ingredients on their labels. About half of these food products also include nutrition labeling. To become a health-conscious, well-informed consumer, you should read the list of ingredients and the nutrition labeling. This information will enable you to compare similar foods on the basis of their proportion of nutrients to Calories. When you choose a food, it should be high in nutrition and low in Calories.

In order to burn up 1 gram of carbohydrate or protein, your body needs to use up 4 Calories. For 1 gram of fat, your body needs to use up 9 Calories. You can see that it takes more than twice the number of Calories to burn up 1 gram of fat than 1 gram of carbohydrate or protein. This is one reason why you should limit your intake of fats.

As you have learned, an ideal diet should derive no more than 30 percent of its Calories from fats. Of the remaining Calories, 15 to 20 percent should come from proteins and 50 to 55 percent from carbohydrates. The carbohydrates should be in the form of starches rather than sugars.

Now that you are on your way to becoming a more-informed consumer, look at the typical cereal box label and determine if it is high in nutrition and low in Calories:

1. To determine the percentage of fat Calories, multiply the grams of fat (in this case 1) by 9 (the number of Calories in 1 gram of fat). Then divide the result (9 Calories) by the total number of Calories (100). The resulting percentage of fat Calories is 9, which is to be expected because grains are low in fat.
2. To determine the percentage of carbohydrate Calories, multiply the grams of carbohydrate (22) by 4 (the number of Calories in 1 gram of carbohydrate). Then divide the result (88 Calories) by the total number of Calories (100). The resulting percentage of

NUTRITION INFORMATION

SERVING SIZE: 1 OZ. (28.4 g, about ⅔ cup)
SERVINGS PER PACKAGE: 16

	CEREAL	WITH ½ CUP VITAMINS A&D SKIM MILK
CALORIES	100	140*
PROTEIN	4 g	8 g
CARBOHYDRATE	22 g	28 g
FAT	1 g	1 g*
CHOLESTEROL	0 mg	0 mg*
SODIUM	270 mg	330 mg
POTASSIUM	115 mg	320 mg
PERCENTAGE OF U.S. RECOMMENDED DAILY ALLOWANCES (U.S. RDA)		
PROTEIN	6	15
VITAMIN A	15	20
VITAMIN C	**	2
THIAMIN	25	30
RIBOFLAVIN	25	35
NIACIN	25	25
CALCIUM	**	15
IRON	25	25
VITAMIN D	10	25
VITAMIN B_6	25	25
FOLIC ACID	25	25
VITAMIN B_{12}	25	35
PHOSPHORUS	15	25
MAGNESIUM	10	15
ZINC	25	30
COPPER	8	10

*WHOLE MILK SUPPLIES AN ADDITIONAL 30 CALORIES, 4 g FAT, AND 15 mg CHOLESTEROL.

**CONTAINS LESS THAN 2% OF THE U.S. RDA OF THIS NUTRIENT.

INGREDIENTS: OAT BRAN, WHEAT BRAN WITH OTHER PARTS OF WHEAT, SUGAR, WHOLE WHEAT FLOUR, CORN SYRUP, SALT, MALT FLAVORING, BAKING SODA,

VITAMINS AND MINERALS: NIACINAMIDE, ZINC (OXIDE), IRON, VITAMIN B_6 (PYRIDOXINE HYDROCHLORIDE), VITAMIN B_2 (RIBOFLAVIN). VITAMIN A (PALMITATE; PROTECTED WITH BHT), VITAMIN B_1 (THIAMIN HYDROCHLORIDE), FOLIC ACID, VITAMIN B_{12}, AND VITAMIN D.

CARBOHYDRATE INFORMATION

	CEREAL	WITH ½ CUP VITAMINS A&D SKIM MILK
STARCH AND RELATED CARBOHYDRATES	14 g	14 g
SUCROSE & OTHER SUGARS	5 g	11 g
DIETARY FIBER	3 g	3 g
TOTAL CARBOHYDRATES	22 g	28 g

carbohydrate Calories is 88, which is normal for a cereal because grains are high in carbohydrates and well above the 50 to 55 percent recommended as the maximum in a healthful diet.

3. To determine the percentage of protein Calories, multiply the grams of protein (4) by 4 (the number of Calories in 1 gram of protein). Then divide the result (16 Calories) by the total number of Calories (100). The resulting percentage of protein Calories is 16, which is within the recommended 15 to 20 percent.

Now it is your turn to play consumer. You can use a calculator or a computer to help with your calculations.

1. Determine the percentage of fat, carbohydrate, and protein Calories in the cereal to which one-half cup of skim milk has been added.
2. Determine the percentage of fat, carbohydrate, and protein Calories in the cereal to which one-half cup of whole milk has been added.
3. Based on your results, is it more healthful to use skim milk or whole milk?
4. In the dry cereal, how many grams of carbohydrates were in the form of starches? In the form of sugars?

Fats

Because our society places great emphasis on a trim physical appearance, the word fat has come to have a negative connotation. But fats in reasonable quantities are important to good health—just as important as other nutrients. Fats perform several vital functions in the body. Fats protect vital organs and joints and help keep the skin from drying out. Lipids, which are a kind of fat, are important parts of cell membranes. A layer of fat just beneath the skin helps insulate the body against changes in environmental temperature.

THE STRUCTURE OF FATS Fats, like carbohydrates, are organic compounds composed of carbon, oxygen, and hydrogen. But fats contain those elements in different proportions. Many fat molecules have a glycerol backbone to which are attached up to three fatty acid molecules. Depending upon the type of bond between adjacent carbon atoms and on the number of hydrogen atoms they contain, fatty acid molecules may be classified as either saturated or unsaturated. Fatty acids that contain single bonds and thus the maximum number of hydrogen atoms are saturated. Saturated fatty acids are usually solid at room temperature. Typical saturated fats include butter, lard, and other animal fats. Unsaturated fats have fatty acid molecules that contain one or more double bonds and thus have fewer hydrogen atoms. Unsaturated fats are usually liquid at room temperature. Most vegetable oils contain unsaturated fatty acid molecules that have multiple double bonds between adjacent carbon atoms and thus the fewest hydrogen atoms.

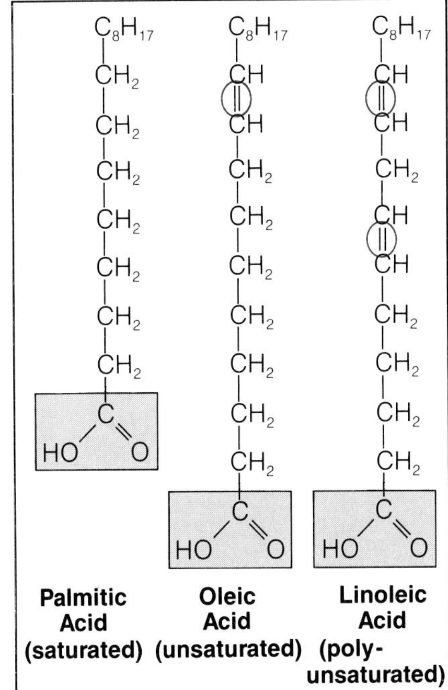

Figure 39–8 *Fats are an important nutrient found in many foods. Most people should restrict the amount, as well as the kinds, of fat they eat. Physicians recommend eating limited amounts of unsaturated or polyunsaturated fats.*

Figure 39–9 *One reason to limit the amount and kinds of fat you eat is dramatically illustrated in this photograph of fat deposits in an artery. Fat buildup can cause the opening in the blood vessel to narrow, restricting the flow of blood.*

These are polyunsaturated fatty acid molecules. The fats that contain them, such as many vegetable oils, are called polyunsaturated fats.

According to nutritionists, the diets of most Americans include too high a proportion of fats. A high level of dietary fats and cholesterol (a fatty sterol) can produce fatty deposits in the arteries. Physicians therefore recommend limiting the total amount of fats eaten and replacing saturated fats with unsaturated fats in the diet whenever possible. Unsaturated and polyunsaturated fats are not considered to be as harmful to the body's circulatory system as saturated fats.

FATS AND ENERGY Fats provide twice as many calories per gram as carbohydrates. For that reason, fats are an excellent way to store energy for future use. When a person eats more food than is needed, the body stores the extra energy by producing fat. This fat is deposited in a layer under the skin. When the body needs more energy than its glucose and glycogen supply can provide, it relies on the energy stored in that fat. Many mammals (bears, for example) prepare for long winters when their normal food supply is unavailable by purposely overeating during the late summer and autumn. These animals convert the energy in the extra food to fat. They use the stored fat during their long winter sleep.

Proteins

The organic nutrients we have discussed so far are important because they provide the body with energy. They do not, however, provide the body with the building materials it needs for growth and repair. That is the job of proteins. As you learned in Chapter 4, proteins are the complex macromolecules that make up critical parts of muscles, skin, and internal organs. Proteins also make up the enzymes that keep cell processes going.

ESSENTIAL AMINO ACIDS Amazingly enough, the thousands of different proteins in our body are built from only 20 or so different amino acids. Your body can manufacture 12 of these amino acids; the other 8 must be obtained from your diet. These 8 are called the **essential amino acids**—not because they are any more important in making up proteins than the other amino acids, but because it is essential that they are included in the food you eat.

Amino acids are released in the body when protein-rich food is digested. The proteins in meat and dairy products usually contain all 8 essential amino acids and are called complete proteins. Most plant proteins lack one or more essential amino acids and are called incomplete proteins. If any essential amino acids are missing from the diet, synthesis of important proteins stops completely. For this reason, the diets of vegetarians must include a careful balance of different plant foods so that all of the essential amino acids are obtained.

Figure 39–10 *In order to develop the large masses of muscles needed to lift heavy weights, weight lifters must eat large amounts of protein.*

PROTEINS AND ENERGY The amino acids obtained from the digestion of proteins may be used by the body as a source of energy. However, before most cells can do this, the amino acids the proteins contain must be converted into carbohydrates. This conversion is accomplished in the liver as an amino group (NH_2) is removed from the amino acid in a process called deamination. Deamination produces ammonia, which is poisonous to cells. The ammonia is immediately converted by the liver to urea, a compound that is much less poisonous. Urea then enters the bloodstream and is later removed by the kidneys.

Vitamins

The organic nutrients you have read about so far are compounds needed by the body in large amounts. **Vitamins** are complex molecules that are needed in small amounts and that usually cannot be synthesized by the body. Under certain conditions, however, some vitamins can be manufactured by the body. For example, vitamin D can be made in the skin under direct sunlight.

There is nothing magical about vitamins. If you are tired, vitamins will not make you feel wide awake. By themselves vitamins cannot make you grow bigger or stronger. Taking vitamins cannot substitute for a well-balanced diet. With a few exceptions, taking enormous doses of vitamins will not make a healthy person any healthier. In fact, taking large doses of certain vitamins can actually make you ill.

What then do vitamins do? And if they are so important, why do we need only tiny quantities of them? The answers are not simple, for different vitamins have different functions. Many vitamins are cofactors for enzyme-catalyzed chemical reactions. Cofactors are organic catalysts that assist enzymes in

VITAMINS

Vitamin	Source	Use
A (carotene)	Yellow and green vegetables, fish-liver oil, liver, butter, egg yolks	Important for growth of skin cells; important for vision
D (calciferol)	Fish oils, liver, made by body when exposed to sunlight, added to milk	Important for the formation of bones and teeth
E (tocopherol)	Green leafy vegetables, grains, liver	Proper red blood cell structure
K	Green leafy vegetables, made by bacteria that live in human intestine	Needed for normal blood clotting
B_1 (thiamine)	Whole grains, liver, kidney, heart	Normal metabolism of carbohydrates
B_2 (riboflavin)	Milk products, eggs, liver, whole grain cereal	Normal growth; part of electron transport chain
Niacin	Yeast, liver, milk, whole grains	Important in energy metabolism
B_6 (pyridoxine)	Whole grains, meats, poultry, fish, seeds	Important for amino acid metabolism
Pantothenic acid	Many foods, yeast, liver, wheat germ, bran	Needed for energy release
Folic acid	Meats, leafy vegetables	Proper formation of red blood cells
B_{12} (cyanocobalamin)	Liver, meats, fish, made by bacteria in human intestine	Proper formation of red blood cells
C (ascorbic acid)	Citrus fruits, tomatoes, green leafy vegetables	Strength of blood vessels; important in the formation of connective tissue; important for healthy gums

Figure 39–11 *There are two main kinds of vitamins: water-soluble vitamins and fat-soluble vitamins. Which vitamins are soluble in fat? Which are soluble in water?*

catalyzing reactions. If we think of growth as a building process, we can say that vitamins are some of the tools needed to piece together amino acids and the body's other building materials. So although vitamins are essential, they are needed in only very small amounts.

Because they can be stored in the fatty tissues of the body, vitamins A, D, E, and K are known as fat-soluble vitamins. The body can build up small stores of these vitamins for future use. The water-soluble vitamins, which include vitamin C and the B vitamins, cannot be stored. Therefore they should be included in a balanced diet every day.

Like other essential nutrients, most vitamins can be obtained naturally by eating a balanced diet that includes fresh fruits, vegetables, and meats. However, when the body does not receive a sufficient supply of vitamins, it can develop vitamin-deficiency diseases. One such disease is scurvy, a painful disease whose victims suffer bleeding gums, loss of teeth, aching muscles, and even death. Scurvy was once common among sailors. Many years before the discovery of vitamins, the British naval surgeon James Lind found that a supply of fresh fruit or fruit juice would prevent scurvy. (In fact, it was because of the lime juice they had to drink that British sailors came to be called "limeys.") We now know that citrus fruits and tomatoes prevent scurvy because they supply the body with large quantities of vitamin C.

Health and a Balanced Diet

How can you make sure that you get all the nutrients you need? The answer is relatively simple. You should select a variety of food from the four basic food groups:

- Meat, fish, and beans
- Milk and milk products
- Fruits and vegetables
- Bread, rice, and cereals

By selecting a variety of food from the four basic food groups, you should be able to satisfy all of your nutritional requirements. The typical American diet contains food selected from the four basic food groups. But for many people, too many of the calories they eat are derived from fats contained in foods in the first two food groups (meat and milk products). Nutritionists suggest that an ideal diet would derive no more than 30 percent of the calories from fats; that of the average American derives nearly 40 percent of the calories from fats. The key word here is balance: Increasing the amount of fruits, vegetables, and grains in your diet is a simple step that can result in better nutrition and health.

Figure 39–12 *You should select foods from each of the four food groups. A variety of foods chosen from these groups will provide a diet that supplies all of the nutrients needed for good health.*

SCIENCE, TECHNOLOGY, AND SOCIETY **BREAKTHROUGH**

Fat Mice

The simplest answer to the problem of obesity has been around for years: Lose weight by decreasing the amount of food eaten (without sacrificing essential nutrients and vitamins) and increasing the amount of exercise (to burn up energy stored in the form of fat). Even while following these guidelines, certain people seem to have a tendency toward being obese. Researchers have wondered why these people seem predisposed to gain weight. Although a theory that explains obesity in humans has still not been completely formulated, scientists are studying obesity in other animals with interesting results.

This genetically obese rat (left) is much larger than a normal one (right).

Scientists have developed strains of "genetically" obese laboratory rats—rats that inherit the tendency to become extremely overweight. In all rats, fat cells release a protein called adipsin into the bloodstream. In normal rats, as well as in rats that have been force-fed to gain weight, the levels of adipsin are relatively high. But in genetically obese rats, there is as little as 1 percent of the normal level of this protein. What exactly does adipsin do? Although there is little direct evidence as yet, speculation centers around adipsin's effects on the appetite and/or metabolism—both of which are controlled by the brain. High levels of adipsin in the blood may suppress appetite; low levels may increase appetite.

We cannot be sure that an identical system works in humans, but researchers recently have discovered a crucial link with the rodent system: Human fat cells also produce adipsin. Future research will attempt to link the problem of obesity in humans with the production of adipsin. In time, this research may lead to a treatment for obesity.

39–1 SECTION REVIEW

1. What is a nutrient? What family of nutrients does the body use for energy? For growth and repair?
2. What are the four major food groups and how do they help to produce a balanced diet?
3. When proteins are used for energy, the amount of urea released from the body increases. Why?

39–2 The Process of Digestion

Section Objectives

- Compare mechanical and chemical digestion.
- Identify the organs of the digestive system and explain their functions.

Digestion is the breakdown of food into simpler molecules that can be absorbed by the body. As you can see from Figure 39–13, the digestive system is actually a long, hollow tube called the **gastrointestinal tract,** or GI tract. **The digestive system includes the mouth, pharynx, esophagus, stomach, small intestine, and large intestine. Several major glands, including the salivary glands, the pancreas, and the liver, add their secretions to the digestive system.**

The first task of the digestive system is to break down food into a fine pulp. When food is in the form of a fine pulp, its surface area is increased and more food molecules are exposed to the action of digestive chemicals. The next task of the digestive system is to chemically act on the food, breaking it down into smaller and smaller molecules. For example, starches must be reduced to simple sugars before the cells of the body can oxidize them for energy. Proteins must be broken down into amino acids before they can be used to build new proteins. The

Figure 39–13 *The human digestive system is made up of a number of different organs. These organs work together to break down food and absorb the resulting nutrients into the blood for distribution throughout the body.*

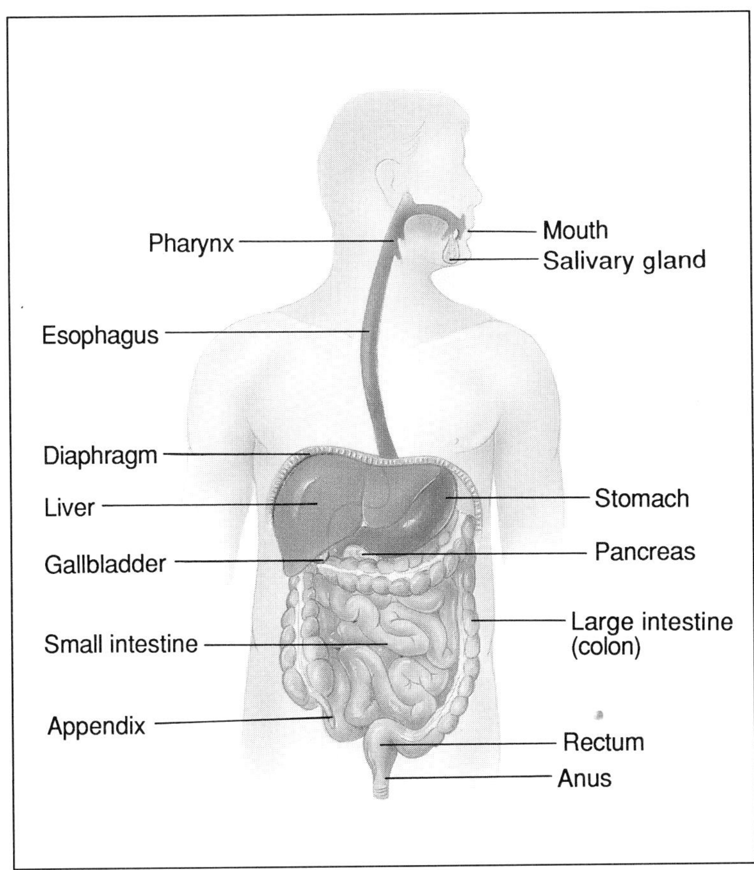

last task of the digestive system is to absorb these small molecules and pass them along to the bloodstream for distribution to the rest of the body.

In our survey of the animal kingdom, we encountered many animals that we were able to classify as either herbivores (plant eaters) or carnivores (meat eaters). These animals have digestive systems that are well adapted to digest the particular food they eat. But humans do not fit neatly into either of these categories. Humans are omnivores who eat both plant and animal food. The human digestive system is adapted to process both vegetable and animal materials.

The Mouth

The mouth is the organ in which the process of digestion begins. The mouth prepares food for entry into the gastrointestinal tract. The remarkably well-adapted parts of the mouth give it a variety of abilities that most of us take for granted.

The lips, cheeks, and tongue work in a carefully coordinated manner to place food between the teeth for chewing. The teeth break up the food as part of the process known as mechanical digestion. Mechanical digestion is the physical breaking up of food by the teeth and other parts of the digestive system. The teeth themselves are composed of the hardest materials found in the body. The inside lining of the cheeks contains special mucous glands. The secretions of these glands help lubricate the food and make it easier to swallow.

Figure 39–14 ***Figure 39–14*** *Taste buds are scattered over different areas on the surface of the tongue. The taste of food is actually a combination of taste and smell. Thus foods lose much of their taste when the nose is blocked by a cold.*

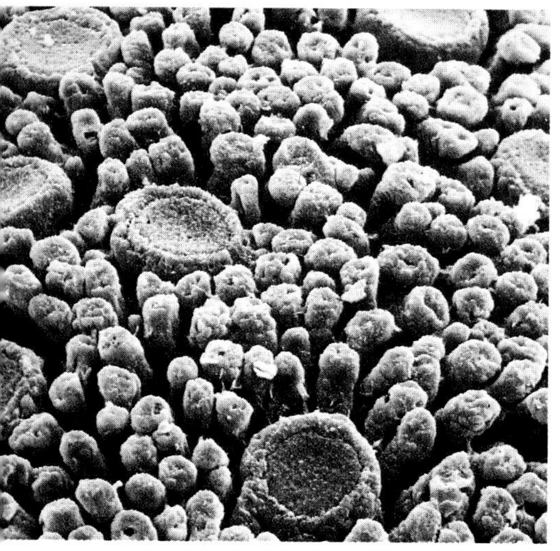

As food is passed back and forth in the mouth it comes in contact with a large number of taste buds located on the surface of the tongue. Taste buds send messages to the brain about the nature of the food being eaten. Taste buds can determine whether a food is sweet, sour, salty, or bitter. By passing this information to the nervous system, taste buds help us decide whether or not the contents of our mouth should be swallowed.

All mammals that eat solid food use their teeth to cut and grind the food. This prepares the food for chemical digestion. Carnivores have very sharp front teeth called incisors. These teeth can tear off pieces of meat. The sharp, pointed teeth at the front corners of their mouth are called canines. Carnivores use these teeth to catch, hold onto, and kill their prey. In a carnivore, the rear teeth, or molars, act like knives to help cut meat into pieces small enough to be swallowed. Herbivores, on the other hand, have teeth that are used primarily to grind the tough, fibrous plant food they eat into a fine pulp. Because humans are omnivores, eating both plant and animal materials, it is not surprising that some of their teeth look like the teeth of a carnivore and some look like the teeth of a herbivore.

Individually, each tooth is a wonder of biological design. Although teeth grow from the upper and lower jaw bones, they are constructed from material that is much harder than ordinary bone. During chewing, the jaw muscles close the mouth

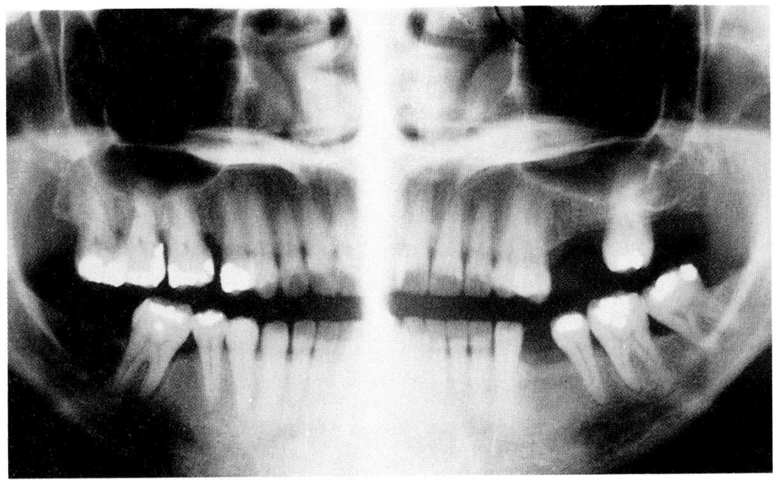

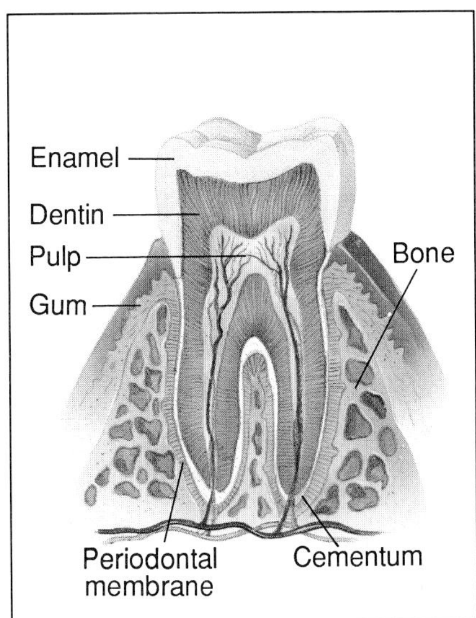

Figure 39–15 *A dentist uses X-rays to see parts of the teeth that cannot be seen with the unaided eye. The brighter areas in the teeth are fillings. You can also see spaces where teeth have been lost. The illustration shows a cross section of a tooth. A cavity occurs when places in the normally hard enamel decay. As an untreated cavity continues to increase in size, it may reach down into the pulp of the tooth, where nerves and blood vessels are located.*

with great force, pounding the teeth against the food and against one another with enough force to crack ordinary bones. To help in resisting this constant wear and tear, the crown, or top, of each tooth is covered by a layer of enamel, an extremely hard substance. Underneath the enamel is another hard material called dentin that makes up the bulk of the tooth. The enamel and dentin have no nerve cells in them.

Each tooth is anchored by long, pointed roots that extend into the jaw bone. A tough, fibrous periodontal membrane holds these roots in the jaw. The hollow center of the tooth, called the pulp cavity, contains the blood vessels and nerve cells that serve the tooth. If they are disturbed by heat, cold, or dental decay, it is these nerve cells that send the messages to the brain that signal "toothache."

While the teeth cut and grind the food into a pulp in preparation for swallowing, the salivary glands secrete the first digestive enzymes of the GI tract. The release of saliva is triggered by the nervous system. Often the mere sight or smell of food is enough to cause saliva to be secreted. Just think about your reaction to a whiff of bread baking in an oven or the sight of food at a holiday picnic!

Saliva has three important functions. One, saliva dissolves some foods and combines with mucus to speed the passage of food through the digestive system. Two, saliva contains enzymes that attack many of the potentially dangerous microorganisms that can enter the mouth. Three, saliva contains the

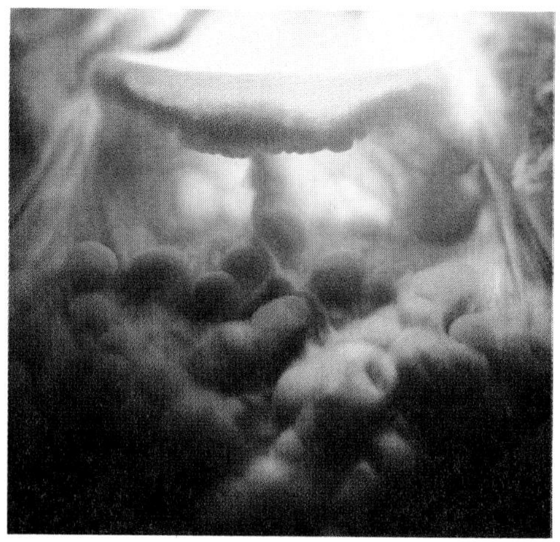

Figure 39–16 *The epiglottis is the flap of skin that folds over the trachea to prevent foods from moving down the "wrong pipe" when they are swallowed.*

enzyme salivary amylase, which breaks up long starch molecules into maltose. If you chew a soda cracker, which is made up of starches, for several minutes, it will begin to taste sweet. The starches in the cracker are broken down into sugars by the action of salivary amylase.

Once the teeth and salivary glands have completed the initial processing, the food is ready to be swallowed. Gathering the food together in a ball called a **bolus**, the tongue pushes it toward the back of the mouth. The back of the tongue sends the bolus down to the part of the throat called the **pharynx**.

In the pharynx, the GI tract and the respiratory tract cross each other. See Figure 39–16. At this point, food moving down the GI tract could enter the respiratory tract by mistake, causing a person to choke. However, as the tongue moves the food into the pharynx, it presses down on a small flap of cartilage called the **epiglottis**. When the epiglottis is depressed, it closes the entrance to the respiratory tract and guides the food down the GI tract.

Occasionally, if we try to talk and eat at the same time, the epiglottis does not have a chance to close properly. When that happens, we feel that "something went down the wrong pipe," which is an appropriate description. For some of the food we tried to swallow slipped into the passageway leading to the lungs instead of the one leading to the stomach. We usually begin coughing to clear the food out of the respiratory tract.

The Esophagus

The bolus next passes down the **esophagus**, a tube about 25 centimeters long that connects the pharynx with the stomach. The walls of the esophagus are made up of rings of muscles that circle the tube. As the bolus enters the tube, the circular muscles just above it begin to contract in waves that travel down the length of the esophagus. Each wave squeezes the bolus along ahead of it. These rhythmic muscular contractions are called **peristalsis**. See Figure 39–17. The esophagus passes through the diaphragm—the thick sheet of muscle that separates the chest cavity from the abdominal cavity—and empties into the stomach. A thick ring of muscle called a **sphincter** is found where the esophagus joins the stomach. The sphincter acts like a valve, allowing food to pass into the stomach but usually not letting it move back up into the esophagus.

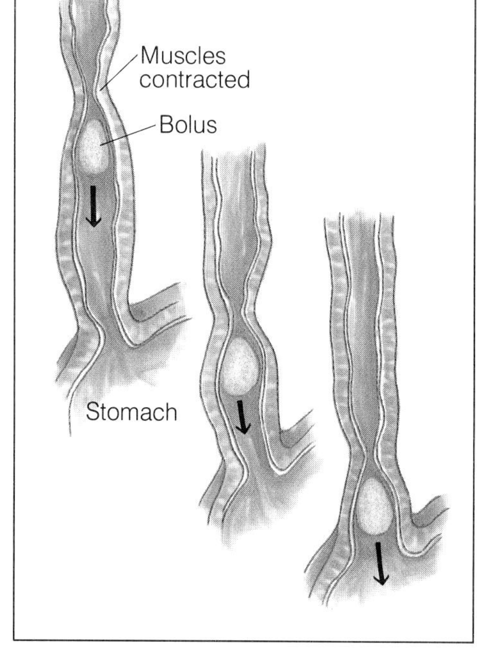

Figure 39–17 *Muscles in the walls of the esophagus contract in waves. Each wave pushes a bolus of food in front of it. Eventually the bolus is pushed into the stomach.*

The Stomach

The partially digested food is now in the **stomach**, a thick muscular sac located just below the diaphragm in the abdomen. Three sets of glands in the stomach lining produce secretions called gastric fluids. One set of stomach glands produces more mucus, keeping the food well lubricated and protecting the walls of the stomach from being digested by its own secretions. Another set of glands secretes hydrochloric acid, which makes the contents of the stomach very acidic. Yes, despite certain commercial messages to the contrary, the stomach is supposed to be acidic! The acid helps break down food. In fact, if all the acid in the stomach were to be completely neutralized, the stomach would not be able to digest food. The digestive enzyme pepsin, secreted by a third set of stomach glands, works best under the acidic conditions present in the stomach. Together with hydrochloric acid, pepsin in the stomach begins the complex process of protein digestion. Pepsin breaks proteins into smaller polypeptides.

As chemical digestion continues, the muscular walls of the stomach contract powerfully, churning and mixing food with the gastric fluids. After two or three hours of this action, the food has been changed into a pasty mixture called **chyme**. At this point, the **pyloric valve** between the stomach and the small intestine opens and the contents of the stomach are allowed to enter the small intestine, as peristalsis forces the mixture through the open valve.

By the time chyme leaves the stomach, most proteins have been broken down into smaller polypeptides. Sugars, however, have not yet been chemically altered, nor have fats. Some starch molecules have been broken down into disaccharides by the action of amylase, but other starch molecules have not been affected.

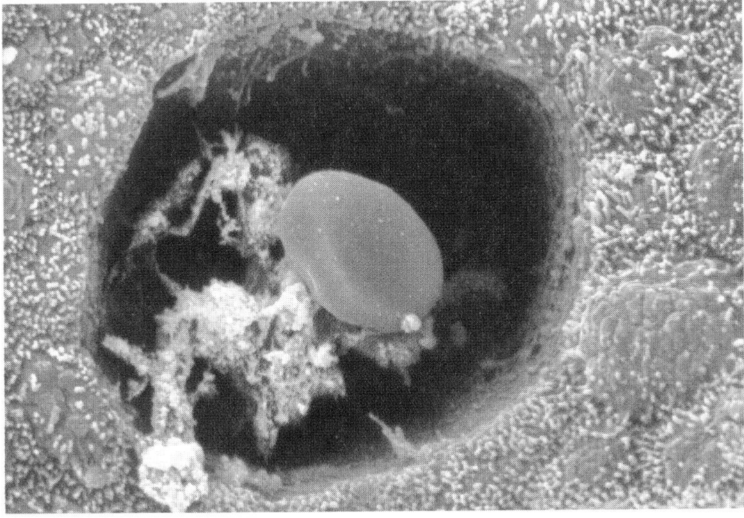

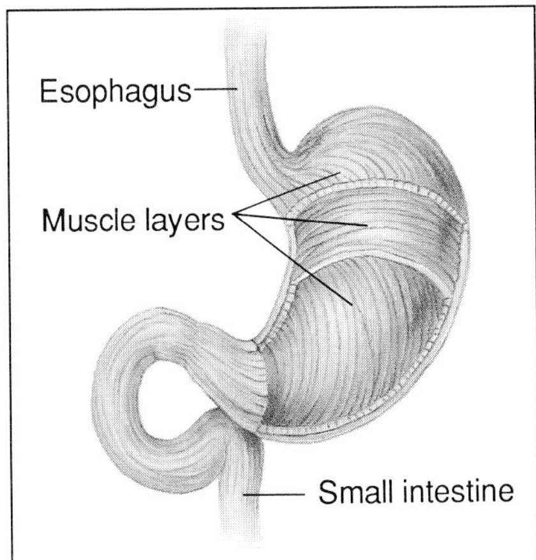

Figure 39–18 *Gastric pits are located in the lining of the stomach wall (left). Cells at the base of the gastric pits secrete enzymes, hydrochloric acid, and other substances that aid in digestion. Several layers of muscle make up the stomach wall (right). When these muscles contract, food and chemicals within the stomach are mixed together.*

The Small Intestine

As chyme is pushed through the pyloric valve, it enters the **duodenum** (doo-oh-DEE-nuhm). The duodenum is the first part of the **small intestine**. In the duodenum, chyme is flooded with a variety of enzymes and other digestive fluids that break down additional food molecules. The enzymes and digestive fluids that are active in the small intestine come from three separate sources: the intestine itself, the pancreas, and the liver.

Glands lining the duodenum release peptidases—enzymes that continue the process of protein digestion begun in the stomach. Other enzymes produced by intestinal glands attack complex carbohydrates, breaking them down into their component sugars. The enzyme maltase, for example, breaks the disaccharide maltose into two molecules of glucose. Lactase breaks down lactose (milk sugar) into glucose and galactose. Sucrase breaks down sucrose into fructose and glucose.

The **pancreas** is a long organ located behind the stomach. Most of the tissue in the pancreas consists of glands. When chyme enters the small intestine, glands in the pancreas are stimulated to release their secretions, called pancreatic fluid. Pancreatic fluid enters a duct that empties into the duodenum. Enzymes in pancreatic fluid are responsible for the digestion of carbohydrates, fats, and proteins. Amylases and proteases complete the breakdown of carbohydrates and proteins, respectively. At the same time, lipase begins to break down fats into glycerol and fatty acids.

Pancreatic fluid also contains sodium bicarbonate. This compound neutralizes the hydrochloric acid produced in the stomach, which entered the small intestine along with the chyme. Unlike enzymes that work in the stomach, pancreatic

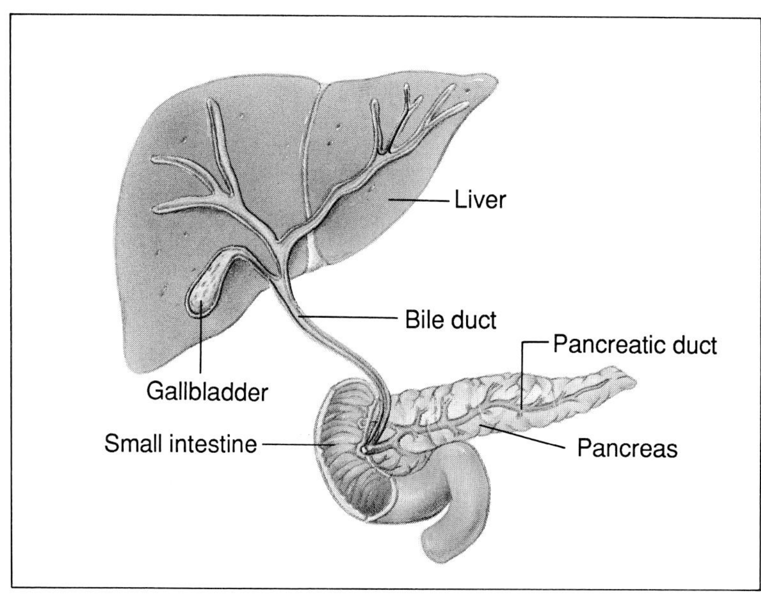

Figure 39–19 *Various organs of the body also add chemicals to the digestive system. The liver secretes bile, a chemical that breaks up large fat molecules. The pancreas secretes pancreatic fluid, which helps break down carbohydrates, proteins, and fats.*

enzymes work best near neutral pH, usually 7.0 to 8.0. In addition to secreting these enzymes, the pancreas also secretes a chemical that regulates the level of sugar in the blood. You will learn more about this action of the pancreas in Chapter 42.

The **liver** is a large brownish organ that lies above the stomach in the abdomen. The liver may weigh as much as 1500 grams. One of the functions of the liver is to secrete a yellow-brown liquid called bile. Bile is stored in a small sac called the **gallbladder**. The entrance of food into the small intestine stimulates the release of bile from the liver through the bile duct into the duodenum.

Although it is an extremely important digestive fluid, bile does not contain enzymes. Bile is a complicated mixture of cholesterol, colored pigments, and chemicals called bile salts. Bile salts play a major role in aiding the enzyme lipase to properly digest fats. Because fats do not dissolve in water, they tend to stick together in large globules—much like drops of oil in salad dressing. These fat globules are too large for lipase to work on them efficiently. Bile salts emulsify fats, or break them into smaller and smaller droplets. Bile salts act on fats in much the same way as a good dish-washing detergent would—it breaks them up into smaller and smaller particles. When fat particles are emulsified by bile salts, lipase can work on them more efficiently.

SOME DIGESTIVE ENZYMES

	Enzyme	Action
Proteins	Pepsin (produced by glands in stomach)	Breaks peptide bonds at NH_2 group
	Trypsin (pancreas)	Breaks peptide bonds
	Chymotrypsin (pancreas)	Breaks peptide bonds
	Carboxypeptidase (pancreas)	Breaks COOH terminal peptide bonds
Fats	Pancreatic lipase (pancreas)	Triacylglycerols
	Intestinal lipase (small intestine)	Tri-, di-, and monoglycerides
Carbohydrates	Ptyalin (saliva)	Starch
	Amylase (pancreas)	Starch
	Intestinal amylase (small intestine)	Starch
	Maltase (small intestine)	Maltose
	Sucrase (small intestine)	Sucrose
	Lactase (small intestine)	Lactose

Figure 39–20 *Many enzymes act in the digestive system to break down foods and make nutrients available to the body. Where in the body does the digestion of carbohydrates begin?*

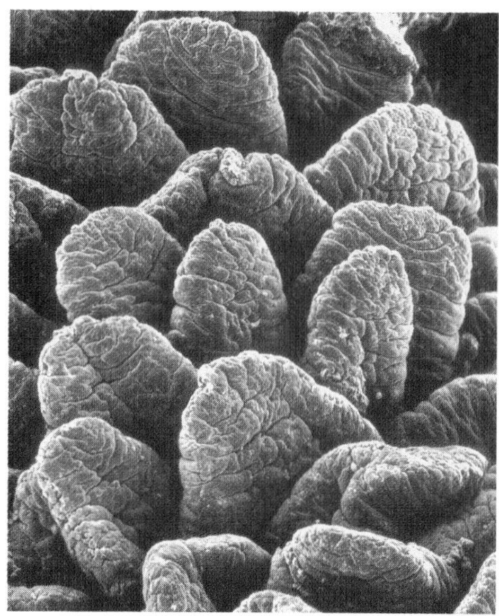

Figure 39–21 The villi that line the wall of the small intestine greatly increase its surface area, and thus the area over which food molecules are absorbed.

The small intestine is very long, often as long as 7 meters in an adult. Spending several hours traveling from one end to the other, food is pushed slowly through the small intestine by peristalsis. After leaving the duodenum, the now mostly digested food passes into the other parts of the small intestine, the jejunum and the illium. Here most digestive activities are completed, and many of the end products of digestion are absorbed into the bloodstream.

The inside walls of the small intestine are folded in such a way as to greatly increase their surface area. Under a microscope, the surface of the folds resembles wall-to-wall carpeting because of countless tiny fingerlike projections called **villi** (singular: villus). See Figure 39–21. The cells that make up the surfaces of the villi are folded into thousands of even tinier folds called microvilli.

What does all this folding accomplish? The folding increases the surface area of the small intestine, making the process of absorption proceed much more rapidly than it would if intestinal walls were smooth. The villi in the small intestine are richly supplied with blood vessels to absorb and carry away nutrients. Each tiny villus has its own set of arteries and veins with a dense network of capillaries connecting them. Among the capillaries are a number of very fine lymph vessels.

Figure 39–22 *Microvilli are the tiny projections that increase the surface area of the villi (right). Inside each microvilli are tiny blood vessels that begin the process in which nutrients are circulated to the rest of the body's cells (left).*

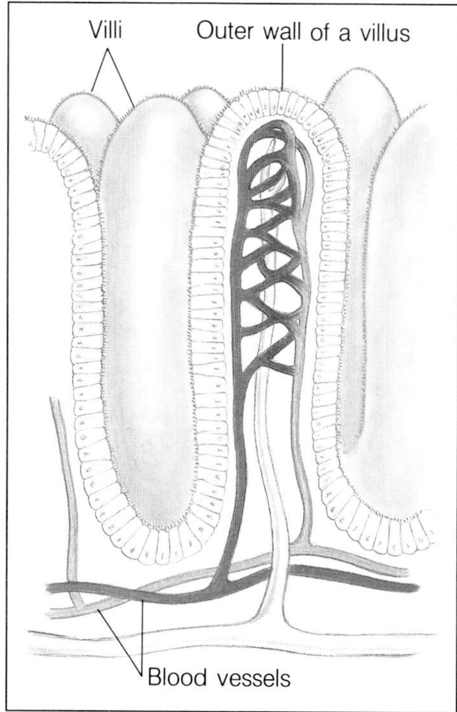

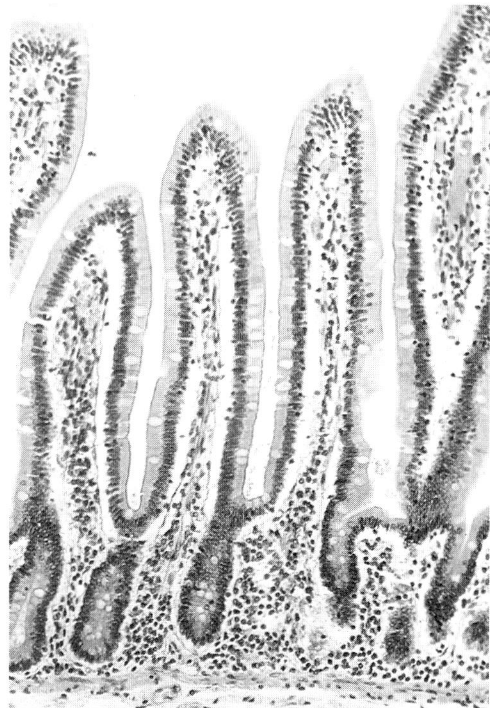

(You will learn more about lymph in Chapter 41.) Most of the products of carbohydrate and protein digestion are absorbed into the capillaries in the villi. Molecules of undigested fat and some fatty acids may enter the lymph vessels directly.

By the time it is ready to leave the small intestine, the food is basically nutrient-free. The complex organic molecules have been digested and absorbed, leaving only water, cellulose, and other undigestible substances behind. As this material leaves the small intestine, it passes by a small saclike organ called the appendix. The appendix is a vestigial organ in humans—it has virtually no function. In other mammals, the appendix is large and is used to store cellulose and other materials that the digestive enzymes cannot break down. But the only time we pay attention to the appendix is when it becomes clogged and inflamed, causing appendicitis. The only remedy for appendicitis is to remove the infected organ by surgery—as quickly as possible.

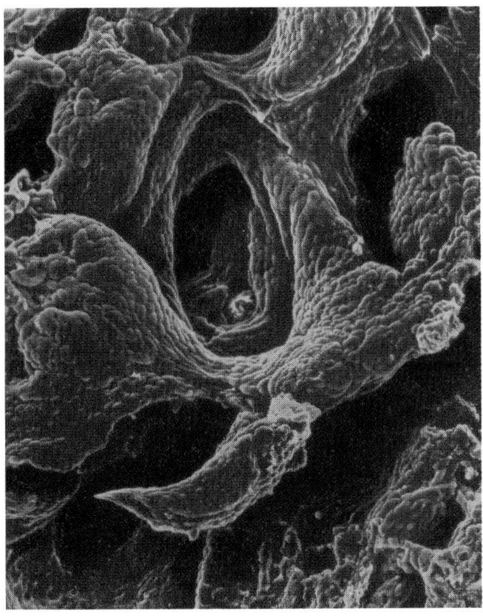

Figure 39–23 *This photograph shows the lining of the large intestine. By the time digested food reaches this organ, all the nutrients have been removed. The large intestine removes water from the remains of the digestive process.*

The Large Intestine

When food leaves the small intestine, it passes into the **large intestine**, or **colon**. The main job of the colon is to remove water from the undigested materials passing through it. Normally, the colon removes water efficiently and reduces the undigested materials to solid waste products called feces.

The feces move through the colon by peristalsis, finally collecting at the end of the colon in the rectum. Here valvelike anal sphincter muscles prevent the feces from being released until it is convenient for us to expel them through the anus.

Sometimes the normal function of the large intestine is disturbed and it does not absorb as much water as it should. This leaves a great deal of water in the feces and produces the condition known as diarrhea.

The colon also contains large amounts of bacteria that aid in the final stages of digestion. Some of the bacteria even manufacture vitamins, notably vitamin K. These vitamins are absorbed across the intestinal wall into the bloodstream.

39–2 SECTION REVIEW

1. What is mechanical digestion? Why is mechanical digestion an important part of the digestive process?
2. What is chemical digestion? How do mechanical and chemical digestion work together to break down foods?
3. How does bile aid in the digestion of fats? Where are fats absorbed from the GI tract?
4. What could you infer about the diet of an animal that has a large appendix?

LABORATORY INVESTIGATION

TESTING THE NUTRIENT CONTENT OF FOODS

PROBLEM

How can you be certain you are eating a balanced diet?

MATERIALS *(per group)*

starch suspension	400-mL beaker
Benedict's solution	10-mL graduated cylinder
Biuret reagent	glass-marking pencil
dextrose solution	hot plate
Lugol's iodine solution	medicine dropper
albumin solution	test tubes
assorted food items (milk, nuts, hard candy, and so on)	test tube holder
	test tube rack

PROCEDURE

1. Add 200 mL of water to the beaker. Place the beaker on the hot plate and heat to barely simmering. This is a water bath. Check the level of the water bath periodically, adding more water if necessary.
2. Use the clean graduated cylinder to measure 3 mL of tap water. Pour this into a clean test tube that has been labeled CONTROL. Pour about 3 mL of the starch suspension into another clean test tube. Label this test tube STARCH. Be sure to rinse the graduated cylinder well after each use.
3. Use the medicine dropper to add two or three drops of Lugol's iodine solution to these two test tubes. Record any changes you observe. Rinse out the test tubes.
4. Use the clean graduated cylinder to measure 3 mL of tap water. Pour this water into a clean test tube that has been labeled CONTROL. Pour about 3 mL of dextrose solution into another test tube. Label this test tube SUGAR.
5. Using the clean graduated cylinder, measure out and pour 3 mL of Benedict's solution into each test tube.
6. Use the test tube holder to place both test tubes in the water bath. **CAUTION:** *Use care in placing the test tubes in the water.* Record any changes you observe in the contents of the test tubes. Use the test tube holder to remove the test tubes from the water. Place them in the test tube rack to cool.
7. Use the clean graduated cylinder to pour 3 mL of tap water into another clean test tube labeled CONTROL. Use the graduated cylinder to pour 3 mL of albumin solution into a clean test tube labeled PROTEIN.
8. Using a clean graduated cylinder, measure out and pour 3 mL of Biuret reagent into these two test tubes. **CAUTION:** *Biuret reagent contains a strong base. Do not let this reagent come into contact with your skin or clothing.* Observe any changes that occur in the test tubes and record your observations.
9. Test a selection of foods for the presence of starch, sugar, and protein, following the same procedures you used in steps 2 through 9. Crush small pieces of each solid food and dissolve it in 3 mL of water. Record your observations.

OBSERVATIONS

1. What color change is a positive test for starch? For sugar? For protein?
2. Which of the nutrients tested are present in your food samples?

ANALYSIS AND CONCLUSIONS

1. Based on your observations, would eating only nuts or hard candies provide a balanced diet? Explain.
2. Would eating a diet of nuts and hard candy provide more nutrients than either food alone? Explain.
3. What nutrients are present in milk? Is milk a more complete food than nuts or hard candy?
4. How can you be sure you are eating a balanced diet?

STUDENT STUDY GUIDE

SUMMARIZING THE CONCEPTS

The key concepts in each section of this chapter are listed below to help you review the chapter content. Make sure you understand each concept and its relationship to other concepts and to the theme of this chapter.

39–1 Food and Nutrition

- Water, one of the simplest essential nutrients, is also the most important.
- Minerals are inorganic substances that are needed by the body to make many important compounds.
- Carbohydrates, sugars, and starches are organic nutrients the body uses for energy.
- In reasonable quantities, fats are an important nutrient for humans.
- Proteins provide the body with building materials needed for growth and repair. Proteins also make up the enzymes that keep cell processes going.
- Vitamins are complex molecules the body needs in small amounts. Vitamins are important cofactors for enzyme-catalyzed chemical reactions.

39–2 The Process of Digestion

- The teeth begin the process of digestion by breaking up food into small pieces. The pieces are mixed with the enzyme salivary amylase, which begins starch digestion.
- The esophagus connects the pharynx to the stomach. Rhythmic contractions of the muscular rings of the esophagus push the bolus of food down toward the stomach.
- The stomach is a muscular sac located in the abdomen. Glands in the wall of the stomach secrete gastric fluids, which include mucus, hydrochloric acid, and the enzyme pepsin. In the stomach, the food becomes a pasty mixture called chyme.
- Digestion continues in the small intestine as nutrients are absorbed through the villi and enter the bloodstream.
- The final stages of digestion occur in the large intestine, or colon, where water is removed from the materials that have passed through the small intestine.

REVIEWING KEY TERMS

Vocabulary terms are important to your understanding of biology. The key terms listed below are those you should be especially familiar with. Review these terms and their meanings. Then use each term in a complete sentence. If you are not sure of a term's meaning, return to the appropriate section and review its definition.

39–1 Food and Nutrition

nutrition
calorie
mineral
essential amino acid
vitamin

39–2 The Process of Digestion

digestion
gastrointestinal tract
bolus
pharynx
epiglottis
esophagus
peristalsis
sphincter
stomach
chyme
pyloric valve
duodenum
small intestine
pancreas
liver
gallbladder
villus
large intestine
colon

CHAPTER REVIEW

CONTENT REVIEW

Multiple Choice

Choose the letter of the answer that best completes each statement.

1. The body derives its energy from
a. fats. c. carbohydrates.
b. proteins. d. water.

2. The breakdown of a disaccharide results in the production of
a. fats. c. proteins.
b. monosaccharides. d. roughage.

3. Complex molecules our body usually cannot make that are needed in very small amounts are
a. minerals. c. proteins.
b. fats. d. vitamins.

4. Which one of the following vitamins is made in the large intestine?
a. A b. B c. C d. K

5. A balanced diet contains a variety of foods from the
a. complex proteins. c. essential amino acids.
b. complex sugars. d. four food groups.

6. The amount of energy in foods is measured in
a. ATP. c. calories.
b. disaccharides. d. carbohydrates.

7. Cellulose, an important part of plant cell walls, is made up of molecules of
a. water. c. starch.
b. amino acids. d. sugar.

8. The part of the digestive system in which digested materials are absorbed is the
a. mouth. c. esophagus.
b. stomach. d. small intestine.

True or False

Determine whether each statement is true or false. If it is true, write "true." If it is false, change the underlined word or words to make the statement true.

1. The surface area of the small intestine is increased by the presence of <u>villi</u>.
2. Bile helps the body digest <u>proteins</u>.
3. Digestion begins in the <u>stomach</u>.
4. Water is removed from digested food in the <u>large intestine</u>.
5. Humans are <u>omnivores</u>.
6. The body gets most of its energy from <u>maltose</u>.
7. <u>Lipids</u>, which are a kind of fat, are important parts of cell membranes.
8. <u>Saturated fatty acids</u> are usually solid at room temperature.

Word Relationships

A. *An analogy is a relationship between two pairs of words or phrases generally written in the following manner: a:b::c:d. The symbol : is read "is to," and the symbol :: is read "as." For example, cat:animal::rose:plant is read "cat is to animal as rose is to plant."*

In the analogies that follow, a word or phrase is missing. Complete each analogy by providing the missing word or phrase.

1. sugars:starches::amino acids:____________
2. mechanical digestion:mouth::chemical digestion:____________
3. water soluble:vitamin C::fat soluble:____________
4. pancreas:proteases::mouth:____________

B. *In each of the following sets of terms, three of the terms are related. One term does not belong. Determine the characteristic common to three of the terms and then identify the term that does not belong.*

5. proteins, roughage, fats, starches
6. pancreas, liver, small intestine, esophagus
7. incisors, enamel, canines, molars
8. produces acid, breaks down proteins, digests sugars, produces mucus

CONCEPT MASTERY

Use your understanding of the concepts developed in the chapter to answer each of the following in a brief paragraph.

1. What is a balanced diet? Why is a balanced diet important?
2. Briefly describe what happens to food in the stomach.
3. How do peristalsis and roughage help move food through the digestive tract?
4. What are the functions of the large intestine?
5. Explain the differences between saturated, unsaturated, and polyunsaturated fatty acids.
6. The respiratory and digestive systems meet in the area of the pharynx. How is food prevented from entering the respiratory system?
7. Why is water an important nutrient?

CRITICAL AND CREATIVE THINKING

Discuss each of the following in a brief paragraph.

1. **Applying concepts** Heartburn occurs when stomach acid enters the esophagus. Use your knowledge of the digestive system to explain how this might happen.
2. **Relating facts** Although the body gets most of its energy from glucose, it can also get energy from proteins and fats. Explain how this is so.
3. **Relating cause and effect** In what way is a Calorie, the unit of energy in food, related to an increase in body weight?
4. **Relating concepts** How is the pH of certain body organs important to digestion?
5. **Designing an experiment** Your friend tells you that the digestion of starches begins in the stomach. You suggest that starch digestion begins in the mouth. Design an experiment to show who is correct.
6. **Relating concepts** Some animals that live in the desert rarely drink water. How do they satisfy their need for this nutrient?
7. **Applying concepts** The diets of people in other parts of the world vary considerably from ours. Yet these people are for the most part healthy. How can you explain this?
8. **Using the writing process** A children's television workshop wants to make a movie that explains the process of digestion to young students. You have been asked to write a script that describes the travels of a hamburger and a glass of milk through the human digestive system. Write a brief but concise outline of your script, including information about what happens to each nutrient in each part of the digestive system.

CHAPTER 40

Respiratory System

The main job of the respiratory system is to get oxygen into the body and waste gases out of the body. Oxygen combines with food to produce energy, which is required for all life functions, including such activities as skiing. The respiratory tree (inset) contains the main organs of respiration.

Watch traffic on a crowded city street on a cold winter day and what do you see? Plumes of whitish steam rising from the exhausts of dozens of cars. Where does this exhaust come from? Your immediate thought might be that it comes from the engines. But there is more to it. For every liter of gasoline each car burns, hundreds of liters of air must enter the engine and hundreds of liters of warm, moist exhaust must be expelled. Burning even a small amount of fuel requires an enormous amount of oxygen.

Our bodies do not burn gasoline, but they do undergo a similar process. The constant idling of our metabolic "engines," which run in every cell of the body, requires an enormous amount of oxygen and produces large quantities of waste gases. How is oxygen efficiently supplied to all the cells of the body? And how are wastes effectively removed? Such questions are the subject of this chapter, for it is the respiratory system that performs these vital functions.

CHAPTER OUTLINE

40–1 The Importance of Respiration

Section Objectives

- Compare internal and external respiration.
- Define respiratory system and explain its importance to multicellular organisms.

Respiration is a vital function of all living things. We can think of respiration as a process that occurs at two different levels. One level is the level of the cell. Here, in the mitochondria of eukaryotic cells, respiration requires oxygen, releases carbon dioxide, and produces large amounts of ATP. This level of respiration is called **internal respiration,** or cellular respiration. Cellular respiration was discussed in detail in Chapter 6.

The other level at which respiration occurs is the level of the organism. Here, an organism must get oxygen into its cells (and thereby into the mitochondria) and carbon dioxide back out. This level of respiration is called **external respiration** because the exchange of gases takes place with the external environment. External respiration involves the **respiratory system.**

A respiratory system is a group of organs working together to bring about the exchange of oxygen and carbon dioxide with the environment. A single-celled organism living in sea water gets oxygen directly from its surroundings. There usually is plenty of dissolved oxygen in the sea water, and it diffuses easily across the cell membrane into the cell. Carbon dioxide diffuses out of the cell just as easily. Thus single-celled organisms do not need a respiratory system.

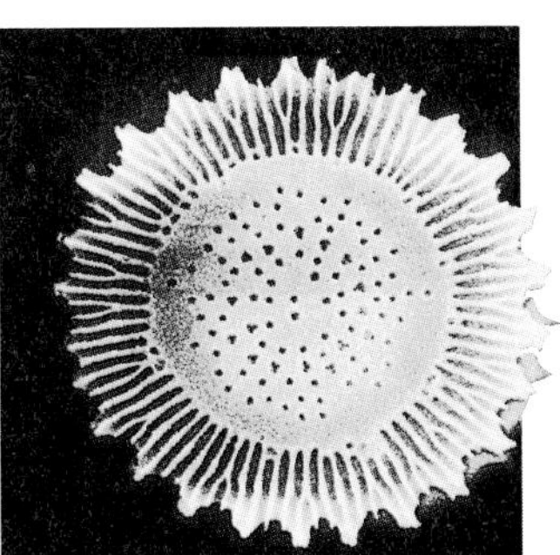

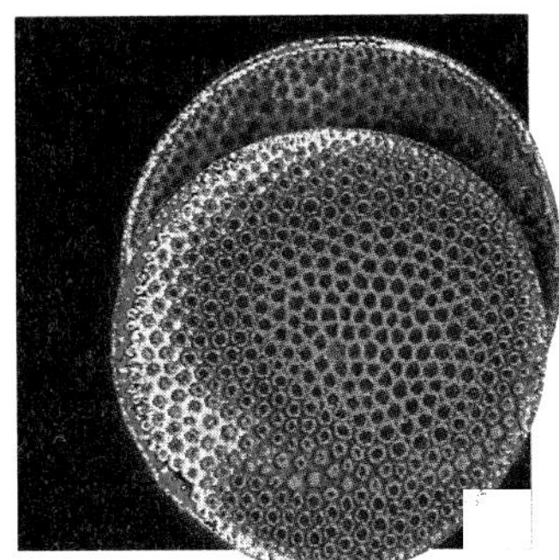

Figure 40–1 *Single-celled organisms, such as diatoms (right), respire through their cell membrane. They do not need a respiratory system, as do multicellular organisms, such as this grizzly bear (left).*

But this is not the case with most multicellular organisms. Within these organisms, each cell consumes oxygen and produces carbon dioxide. Without a system to exchange these gases with the atmosphere quickly and efficiently, large multicellular organisms could not survive. A respiratory system ensures the effective exchange of gases—and thus survival—every time an organism takes a breath.

40–1 SECTION REVIEW

1. What is a respiratory system?
2. Why do most multicellular organisms need a respiratory system?
3. What is the distinction between internal respiration and external respiration? How are they related?
4. Why are more complex respiratory systems found in larger animals?

Section Objectives

- Identify the parts of the human respiratory system and their functions.
- Explain the mechanics of inhalation and exhalation.
- Describe the process of gas exchange.

40–2 The Human Respiratory System

The atmosphere of planet Earth is approximately 78 percent nitrogen and 21 percent oxygen. The remaining 1 percent is made up of carbon dioxide, water vapor, argon, and other trace gases (neon, helium, krypton, hydrogen, and ozone are a few). Humans, like most animals, are air-breathers. Our respiratory system, as well as theirs, has adapted to these concentrations of gases in the atmosphere. Indeed, if the amount of available oxygen falls much below 15 percent, our respiratory system will be unable to provide enough oxygen to support cellular respiration.

***Figure 40–2** Which two gases comprise the largest percentage of the Earth's atmosphere?*

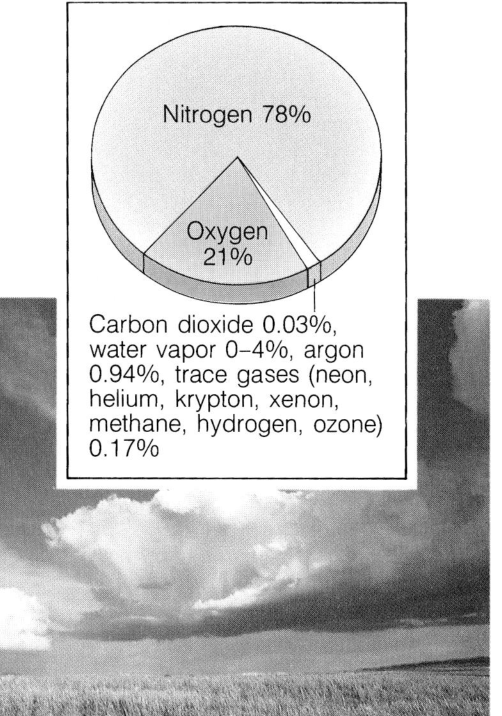

Respiratory Structures

The human respiratory system consists of the nose, nasal cavity, pharynx, larynx, trachea, smaller conducting passageways, and lungs. If we follow the passage of air from the time it enters the respiratory system to the time it leaves, you will be able to see how each structure of the system functions. Refer to Figure 40–3 often as you read.

Air enters the body through the mouth or nose. Air entering the nose passes into the nasal cavity. The nasal cavity is richly supplied with arteries, veins, and capillaries, which bring nutrients and water to its cells. As air passes back from the nasal cavity, it enters the **pharynx**. The pharynx is located in the back of the mouth and serves as a passageway for both air and food. From the pharynx, the air moves into the **trachea**

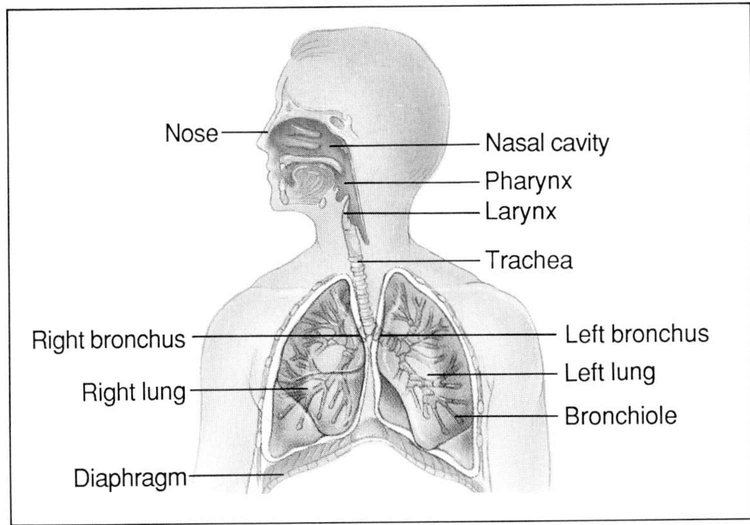

Figure 40–3 *Each component of the respiratory system has a specific function to perform. Working together, they ensure the exchange of oxygen and carbon dioxide with the environment. Why is oxygen required by the body?*

(windpipe), which leads directly into the lungs. All these passageways provide a direct connection between the outside air and some of the most delicate tissues in the body. Therefore, these passageways must filter out dust, dirt, smoke, bacteria, and a variety of other contaminants found in ordinary air.

The first filtering is done in the nose. The nasal airways are lined with hair and kept moist by mucous secretions. The combination of hair and mucus helps to filter out all sorts of solid particles from the air that passes through the nose. The moisture in the nose helps to humidify the air, increasing the amount of water vapor the air entering the lungs contains. This helps to keep the air that enters the nose from drying out the lungs and other parts of the respiratory system. When air enters the respiratory system through the mouth, much less filtering is done. Therefore, it is generally better to take in air through the nose.

At the top of the trachea is the **larynx**. The larynx is made up of several pieces of cartilage, the largest of which you can feel as your Adam's apple. Because the larynx produces sound, it is sometimes known as the voice box. Inside the larynx are two highly elastic folds of tissue called the **vocal cords**. Air being released from the lungs rushes past the vocal cords. When muscles cause the vocal cords to contract, the air passing between them vibrates and produces sound. The pitch of the sound produced by the vocal cords depends on the length of the vocal cords and their tension (how tightly stretched they are). Male and female children have short vocal cords and so produce high-pitched sounds. Adult males generally develop longer vocal cords than females and thus produce lower pitched sounds.

From the larynx, the air passes downward into the chest cavity through the trachea. The walls of the trachea are made up of C-shaped rings of tough, flexible cartilage. These rings of cartilage protect the trachea, make it flexible, and keep it from

Figure 40–4 *Cilia lining the nose, nasal passages, and trachea filter out dust, dirt, smoke, bacteria, and other contaminants found in ordinary air. As the particles get trapped, the nose and trachea often respond to the irritation by producing tiny explosions—sneezes and coughs!*

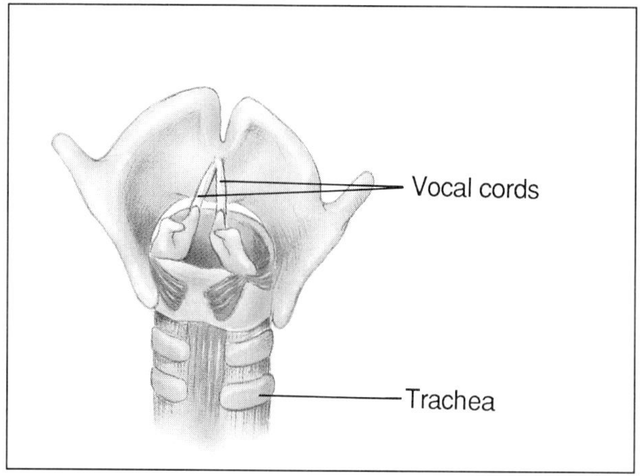

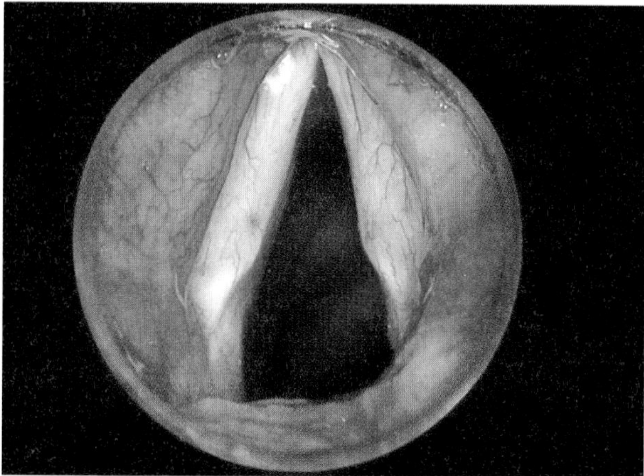

Figure 40–5 *The vocal cords are two highly elastic folds of tissue found inside the larynx. The larynx, which is made up of several pieces of cartilage, is located at the top of the trachea.*

collapsing or overexpanding. The cells that line the trachea produce mucus. This mucus is swept out of the air passageway by tiny cilia on other cells. In this way, particles trapped in the mucus are carried to the upper part of the trachea and swept down into the digestive system.

This means of protecting the respiratory system works quite well, except in those unfortunate cases in which people sabotage it! When tobacco smokers breathe in tobacco smoke, millions of tiny particles become lodged in the trachea. In time, the cilia of the trachea may actually become paralyzed and cease their cleansing action. When this happens, smokers begin to feel irritation in the chest and develop a persistent smokers' cough. Like the other problems associated with smoking, such coughs are self-induced and only the first sign of more serious problems to follow.

Figure 40–6 *It is through a bronchus (left) that air is conducted to bronchioles. The feathery appearance of the interior surface of a bronchus is due to the presence of cilia. From bronchioles, air passes into tiny alveoli (right).*

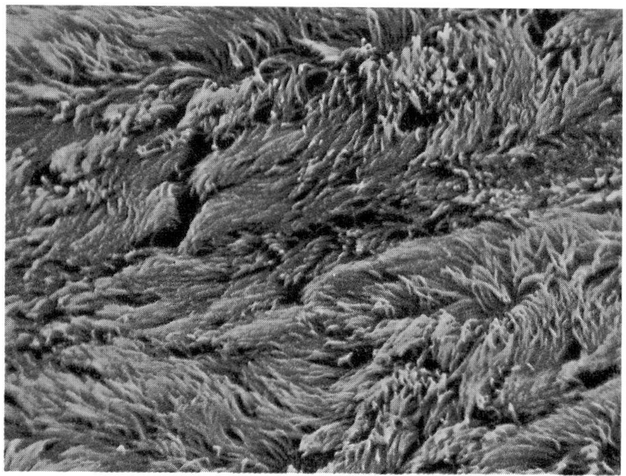

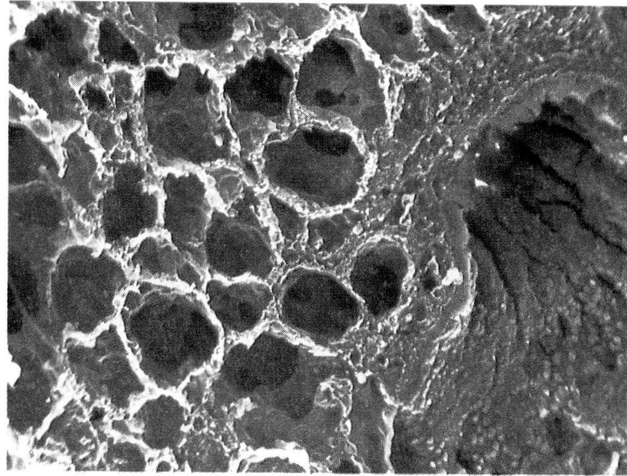

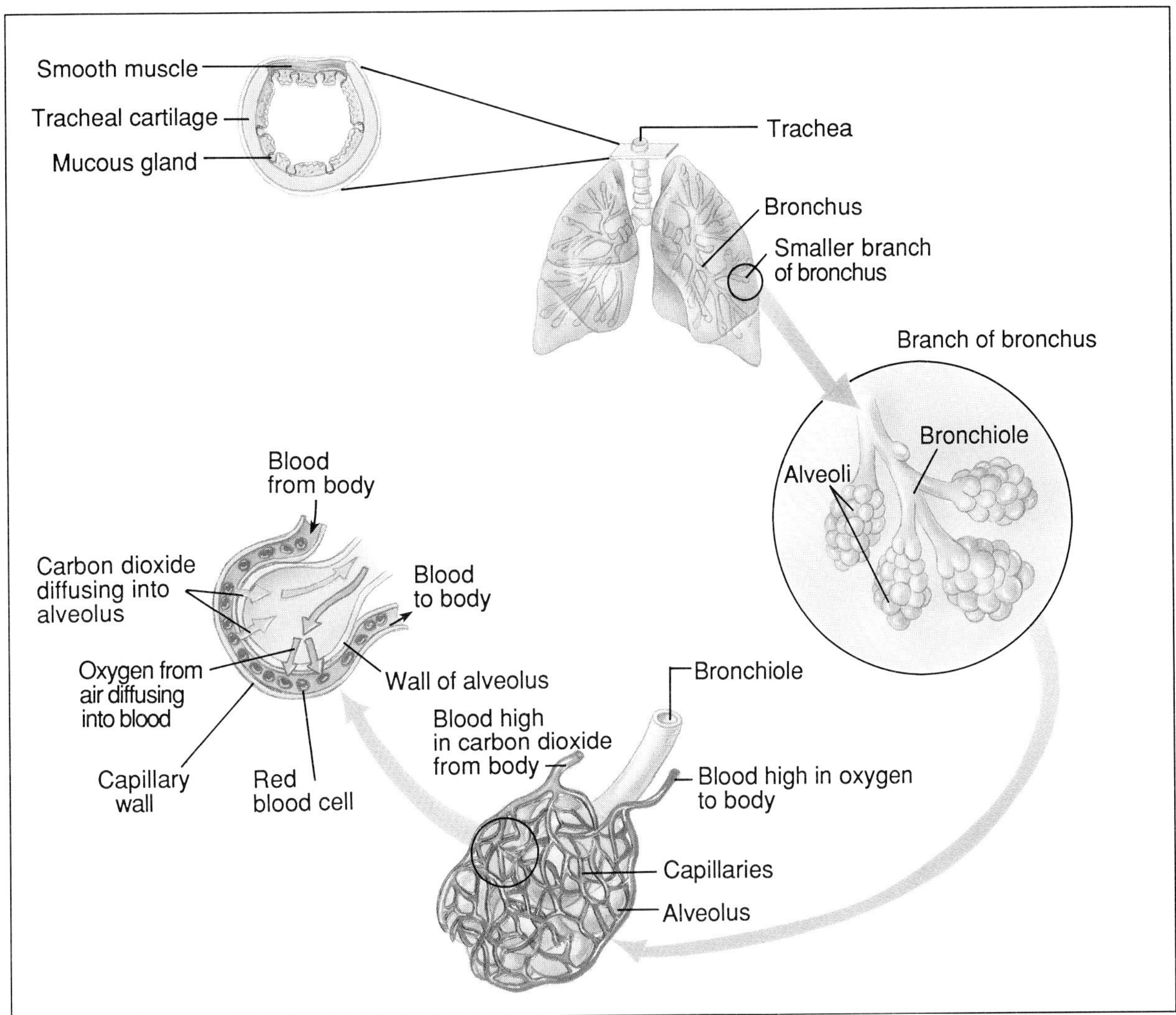

Figure 40–7 *Oxygen and carbon dioxide are exchanged with the blood in the tiny alveoli, or air sacs, of the lungs. Notice the extensive network of capillaries contained in the thin, flexible membrane of an alveolus.*

Within the chest cavity, the trachea divides into two branches, the right and left **bronchi** (singular: bronchus). Each bronchus enters the **lung** on its respective side. See Figure 40–7. The lungs are the main organs of the respiratory system. Like a superhighway splitting into smaller highways and eventually into country roads, the bronchi divide into smaller and smaller passageways. These passageways finally lead into even smaller passageways called **bronchioles**. Both bronchi and bronchioles contain smooth muscle tissue in their walls. This muscle tissue controls the size of the air passages.

The bronchioles continue to subdivide until they finally end in clusters of tiny hollow air sacs called **alveoli** (al-VEE-uh-ligh; singular: alveolus). As you can see from Figure 40–7, groups of alveoli look like bunches of grapes. The alveoli consist of thin, flexible membranes that contain an extensive network of capillaries. The membranes separate a gas from a liquid. The gas is the air that we take in through our respiratory system, and the liquid is blood. Oxygen and carbon dioxide must diffuse across these delicate membranes, so it follows that the membranes must be very thin. However, the fragile nature of the alveoli means that the air entering them must be thoroughly filtered and moistened. Thus the entire respiratory system—from the nose to the lungs—is a device for getting clean, fresh air into the alveoli. Each alveolus acts like a tiny loading station for gas exchange, a process we shall examine shortly.

The Mechanics of Breathing

Every single time you take a breath, or move air in and out of your lungs, two major actions take place. During **inhalation** (also called inspiration), air is pulled into the lungs. During **exhalation** (also called expiration), air is pushed out of the lungs. These two actions deliver oxygen to the alveoli and remove carbon dioxide. The continuous cycles of inhalation and exhalation are known as breathing. Most people breathe 10 to 15 times per minute.

Figure 40–8 *The mechanics of inhalation and exhalation are shown in this illustration. What does the flexible bottom of the bell-jar model represent? The balloon?*

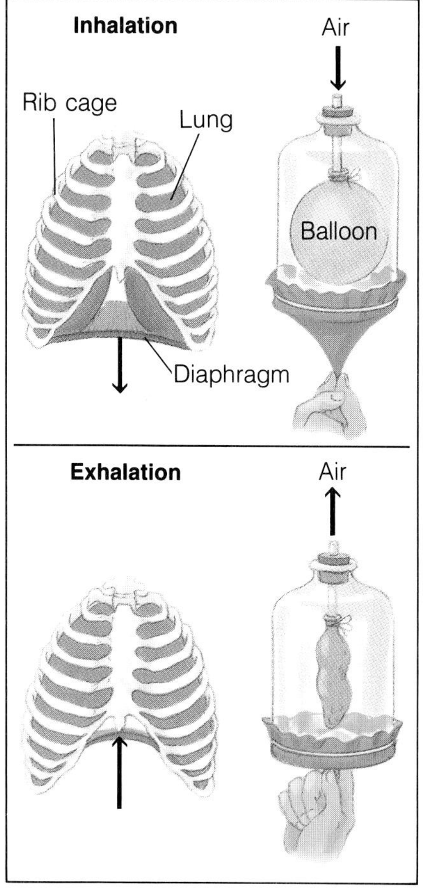

Exactly what happens when you breathe? Inhale deeply. Now exhale. Does it seem as if you are expanding and then contracting your lungs? Perhaps so, but the lungs are not directly attached to any muscles, so they cannot be expanded or contracted. Inhalation and exhalation are actually produced by the movements of the large flat muscle called the **diaphragm** and the intercostal (between the ribs) muscles. The diaphragm is located along the bottom of the rib cage and separates the chest cavity from the abdominal cavity.

The mechanics of inhalation and exhalation can be best illustrated by using the apparatus shown in Figure 40–8. A special jar called a bell jar has a flexible bottom and a balloon suspended from a glass tube inserted in a rubber stopper. Before inhalation, the diaphragm is curved upward into the chest cavity. During inhalation, the diaphragm contracts and moves down, causing the volume of the chest cavity to increase. Our bell-jar apparatus shows why this action causes the lungs to fill up with air. When the flexible bottom (diaphragm) moves down, the volume of the jar (chest cavity) increases and the pressure inside it decreases. The air outside the jar is still at atmospheric pressure, however. To equalize the pressure inside and out, the air rushes through the tubing (trachea) into the jar. This inflates the balloon (lungs). The lungs inflate in much the same way. Our lungs have a total capacity of about 6 liters. A normal breath exchanges only one tenth (about 600 milliliters) of this air volume.

When the diaphragm relaxes, it returns to its curved position. This action causes the volume of the chest cavity to decrease. As the volume decreases, the pressure in the chest cavity outside the lungs increases. This increased pressure causes the lungs to decrease in size. The air in the lungs is pushed out, or exhaled.

Although we generally breathe with the diaphragm and intercostal muscles, under extreme conditions we use other muscles to breathe. These muscles can be used to expand and forcibly contract the chest cavity. Both methods work just fine. The diaphragm and intercostal muscles are used most frequently at rest. Breathing by using accessory muscles occurs during vigorous activity for rapid and deep breathing.

The process of exhalation also involves the alveoli. The walls of these tiny air sacs contain many elastic fibers. During inhalation, the fibers are stretched. When inhalation ends and exhalation begins, the elastic fibers pull back to their original size, helping to force air out of the lungs.

The lungs can work properly only if the space around them is sealed. When the diaphragm contracts, the expanded volume in the chest cavity quickly fills as air rushes into the lungs. If there is a hole (even a small one) in the chest cavity, the system will not work. Air will rush into the cavity through the hole, upset the pressure relationship, and possibly cause the collapse of the lungs. This is one of the reasons why puncture wounds in the chest area are extremely serious, even if the lungs themselves are not damaged.

Gas Exchange

As you have read, the atmosphere of the Earth is about 78 percent nitrogen (N_2) and 21 percent oxygen (O_2). What happens to this air when we inhale? The results of a simple experiment provide some immediate answers. Chemical analysis of the gases that are inhaled and exhaled offers these data:

Gas	Inhaled	Exhaled
O_2 (oxygen)	20.71%	14.6%
CO_2 (carbon dioxide)	0.04%	4.0%
H_2O (water)	1.25%	5.9%

As you can see from these figures, three important things happen to the air we inhale: In the lungs, oxygen is removed from the inhaled air and carbon dioxide and water vapor are added to it. Let's take a close look at a single alveolus to understand how all this occurs.

There are nearly 300 million alveoli in a healthy lung, each alveolus similar to the one shown in Figure 40–9. Blood flowing from the heart enters the capillaries surrounding each alveolus. This blood contains a large amount of carbon dioxide and very little oxygen. It spreads around the surface of the alveolus like water streaming around a balloon. The alveolus is filled with fresh oxygen-rich inhaled air. The concentrations of the gases in the blood and in the alveolus are not equal.

Because there is much more carbon dioxide in the blood than in the alveolus, carbon dioxide diffuses out of the blood

Figure 40–9 *The membrane of each alveolus contains a network of capillaries. As blood flows through these capillaries, oxygen diffuses out of the alveolus and into the blood. Carbon dioxide diffuses in the opposite direction—out of the blood and into the alveolus. In the scanning electron micrograph of a section of the lung, you can see a capillary containing red blood cells surrounded by alveoli.*

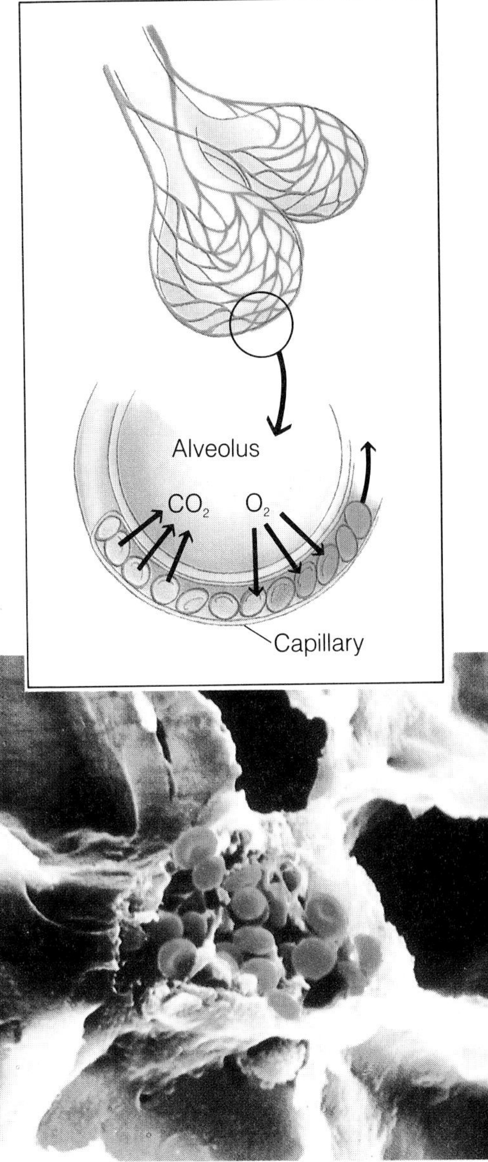

and into the alveolus. Because there is much more oxygen in the alveolus than in the blood, oxygen diffuses across the thin membrane of the sac and into the blood. Thus the blood that leaves the alveolus is oxygen-rich. In fact, it has nearly tripled the total amount of oxygen it originally carried.

Two special molecules help this process of gas exchange work effectively. One of the molecules has an action quite similar to that of soap when it mixes with water. Perhaps you have noticed that when soap is dissolved in water, the water does a much better job of coating surfaces and can even form intricate structures such as soap bubbles. Soaplike macromolecules, consisting of phospholipid and protein, coat the inner surface of each tiny alveolus. This coating keeps the membranes open and makes it easier for oxygen gas to diffuse into the blood.

The other molecule is a special oxygen-carrying molecule that is a natural component of the blood. Without this molecule the blood would be able to carry only about 2 percent of the oxygen needed by the body. This oxygen-carrying molecule is the red-colored protein **hemoglobin**, which is found in red blood cells. A single molecule of hemoglobin has four sites to which oxygen atoms can bind. As the blood flows through the capillaries surrounding an alveolus, oxygen diffusing into the blood is picked up by the hemoglobin in the red blood cells. This allows still more oxygen to diffuse into the blood.

To appreciate just how important hemoglobin is, imagine what the human body would be like without it. Without this oxygen-carrying protein, our lungs would have to be much larger and a far greater proportion of our body weight would have to be taken up by the blood required to deliver oxygen to the tissues. In fact, the body would have to contain about 50 times the blood volume it does now. Since a typical human contains approximately 6 liters of blood, this would mean an increase to 300 liters—with a mass of 300 kilograms!

Figure 40–10 *At altitudes much higher than sea level, atmospheric pressure drops. This means that the total amount of gases is much less, and it is more difficult to obtain the required amount of oxygen. Thus mountain climbers must use oxygen masks to help them breathe (right). At higher pressures below the ocean's surface, the story is quite different. Divers must carry oxygen tanks, which release a regulated amount of oxygen at a pressure that matches the pressure of the ocean water on the diver's body (left).*

SCIENCE, TECHNOLOGY, AND SOCIETY APPLICATION

An Invisible Poison

When a substance burns completely (that is, in a sufficient amount of oxygen), carbon dioxide (CO_2) is given off into the atmosphere. If burning occurs with only a limited oxygen supply, large amounts of a different gas are produced. This gas is carbon monoxide (CO). Carbon monoxide is produced when gasoline is burned in automobile engines, in charcoal fires, and in some wood-burning stoves.

Carbon monoxide is harmless to most cells. However, the carbon monoxide molecule can bind very tightly to the oxygen-carrying protein hemoglobin. When this happens, oxygen is prevented from attaching to hemoglobin. The carbon monoxide-hemoglobin combination is so stable that only a small amount of the gas is enough to inactivate much of the hemoglobin in the blood, making it unable to carry oxygen to all the parts of the body. As a result, the tissues of the body, deprived of oxygen, begin to suffocate and die. Death can occur after only a few minutes of carbon monoxide poisoning.

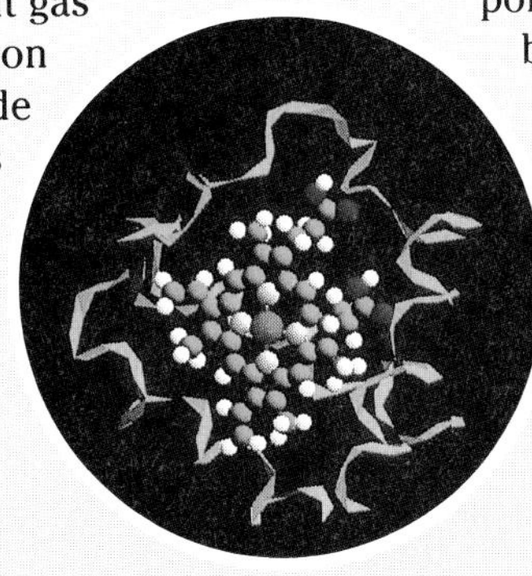

The protein hemoglobin is the oxygen- and carbon dioxide-transporting molecule in red blood cells. This computer representation of part of a hemoglobin molecule shows the binding site for oxygen, an iron atom, in red.

One of the symptoms of carbon monoxide poisoning is rather surprising. The carbon monoxide-hemoglobin combination is a more brilliant red than normal hemoglobin. Thus, victims of carbon monoxide poisoning often have a flushed, ruddy appearance—what might at first be taken for a healthy look. They should immediately be exposed to fresh air and given as much oxygen as possible in an effort to force oxygen into the blood.

Nearly 500 people die of carbon monoxide poisoning every year in the United States. Auto exhaust systems, stove pipes, and indoor heaters should be carefully checked to make sure they are not leaking dangerous carbon monoxide fumes into living spaces.

40–2 SECTION REVIEW

1. In the order in which air passes through, identify the parts of the respiratory system and their functions.
2. Describe what happens during an inhalation. An exhalation.
3. Explain the process of gas exchange in the lungs. What is the role of hemoglobin in this process?
4. When a blockage in the upper airways of the respiratory system cannot be removed, an emergency operation called a tracheotomy, which opens the trachea to the outside, is often performed. How does this operation solve the immediate problem of blockage?

Section Objectives

- Identify the conditions that regulate breathing.
- Relate exercise and lung capacity.

40–3 Control of the Respiratory System

Hold your breath for just a minute or so and then let it go. Did you notice that at first everything seemed just fine, but then you began to develop an urge to breathe. Your chest probably felt tight. Your throat burned. If you held your breath any longer, the pain would have been too much to bear—you just had to breathe!

Breathing is such an important function that your nervous system simply will not let you have complete control of it! **Breathing is an involuntary action under the control of the medulla oblongata in the lower part of the brain.** Sensory neurons (nerve cells) in this region control motor neurons in the spinal cord, and these motor neurons make direct connections with the diaphragm muscle. These neurons do not act alone, however. They are influenced by other nerve cells that detect the stretching action in the lungs. Although breathing can be consciously controlled to a limited extent—such as when you hold your breath or blow up a balloon—it cannot be consciously suppressed. The need to supply oxygen to the cells and remove carbon dioxide is a powerful one indeed.

Obviously, then, the nervous system must have a way of determining whether enough oxygen is getting into the blood. Two special sets of sensory neurons constantly check the levels of gases in the blood. One set is located in the carotid arteries in the neck, which carry blood to the brain. The other set is located near the aorta, the large artery that carries blood from the heart to the rest of the body. **These special sensory receptors are sensitive to the levels of gases in the blood, especially the level of carbon dioxide.** Perhaps this comes as a surprise to you, since you are accustomed to thinking it is the level of oxygen that is most important. Let's see why carbon dioxide is the determining factor.

When carbon dioxide dissolves in the blood, it forms an acid known as carbonic acid.

$$CO_2 + H_2O \rightarrow H_2CO_3$$

Carbonic acid is so unstable that it immediately breaks down into a hydrogen ion (H^+) and a bicarbonate ion (HCO_3^-).

$$H_2CO_3 \rightarrow H^+ + HCO_3^-$$

The hydrogen ions formed by this reaction change the acidity of the blood (its pH). It is to the change in acidity that the special sensory cells respond.

What happens when you hold your breath? The special sensory receptors begin to send messages to the breathing center in the brain. You can override the impulse to breathe at first. But as the messages become stronger due to rising carbon dioxide levels (and increased acidity of the blood), it becomes

Figure 40–11 Both the Weddell seal (right) and the gray whale (left) have a sophisticated way of holding their breath known as the diving reflex. The diving reflex enables these mammals to dive to great depths and remain submerged for long periods of time. As the animal dives, blood vessels in most parts of the body constrict, limiting the flow of blood to primarily the heart and the brain—the organs that need oxygen the most.

more difficult to hold your breath. Eventually the medulla oblongata sends such severe sensations to the conscious part of the brain that you are forced to yield—and gasp for air. Phew!

The lungs of an average person have a total air capacity of about 6.0 liters. Only about 0.6 liter is exchanged during normal breathing, however. That is about all the air we need when we are at rest. During vigorous exercise, the situation is considerably different. Deep breathing forces out much more of the total lung capacity. In normal people, as much as 4.5 liters of air can be inhaled and exhaled with effort. The maximum amount of air that can be moved into and out of the respiratory system is known as the **vital capacity** of the lungs. The vital capacity is always about 1 to 1.5 liters less than the total capacity because the lungs cannot be completely deflated without serious damage.

The extra capacity of the lungs allows us to exercise vigorously for long periods of time. Rather than breathing about 12 times a minute, as most of us do at rest, a runner may breathe as often as 50 times a minute.

40–3 SECTION REVIEW

1. What part of the brain controls breathing? How is this control regulated?
2. What gas has the greatest influence on the control of breathing? Explain why this is so.
3. What is vital capacity? Would you expect a trained athlete to have a greater or lesser vital capacity than an average person? Explain your answer.
4. Explain the importance of the location of each set of gas-monitoring sensory receptors.

LABORATORY INVESTIGATION

CONSTRUCTING A MODEL OF THE RESPIRATORY SYSTEM

PROBLEM

How do humans breathe?

MATERIALS *(per group)*

#2 one-hole rubber stopper
200-mL polyethylene bottle
round balloon (large)
round balloon (small)
scissors

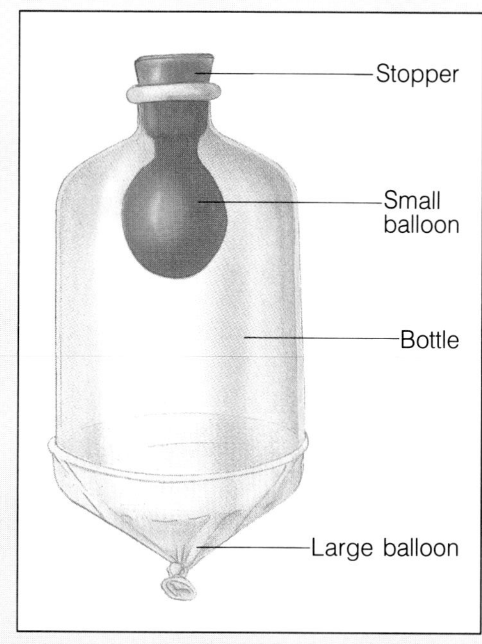

PROCEDURE

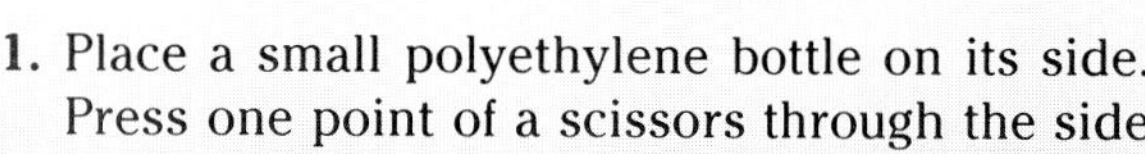

1. Place a small polyethylene bottle on its side. Press one point of a scissors through the side of the bottle about 1 cm from the bottom.
2. Using the scissors, cut off the bottom of the bottle by cutting all the way around.
3. Stretch a small balloon and blow it up several times to make it pliable.
4. Pull the lip of the small balloon over the bottom of a #2 one-hole rubber stopper.
5. Insert the balloon through the mouth of the polyethylene bottle. Press the stopper tightly into the bottle so it holds the lip of the balloon in place.
6. Stretch a large balloon and blow it up several times to make it pliable.
7. Using the scissors, cut off about 1 cm from the rounded closed end of the large balloon. Tie the other end closed.
8. Stretch the large balloon far enough over the cut end of the polyethylene bottle so it does not slip off. See the accompanying figure.
9. As you watch the small balloon, pull down on the knot of the large balloon. Then, still watching the small balloon, press up on the large balloon.

OBSERVATIONS

1. What happened to the small balloon when you pulled down on the large balloon?
2. What happened to the small balloon when you pressed up on the large balloon?

ANALYSIS AND CONCLUSIONS

1. What happened to the volume inside the bottle when the large balloon was moved up and down?
2. What caused the small balloon to expand and contract?
3. How is the model you constructed similar to the human respiratory system?
4. How do humans breathe?

STUDENT STUDY GUIDE

SUMMARIZING THE CONCEPTS

The key concepts in each section of this chapter are listed below to help you review the chapter content. Make sure you understand each concept and its relationship to other concepts and to the theme of this chapter.

40–1 The Importance of Respiration

- Internal respiration occurs at the level of cells. External respiration occurs at the level of the organism.
- A respiratory system is a group of organs working together to bring about the exchange of oxygen and carbon dioxide with the environment.

40–2 The Human Respiratory System

- Air enters the respiratory system through the nose and travels through the nasal cavity to the pharynx, the trachea, and the lungs.
- The larynx, located at the top of the trachea, contains the vocal cords.
- The trachea divides into the right bronchus and the left bronchus. Each bronchus enters a lung and further divides into bronchioles, finally ending in groups of alveoli.
- Breathing consists of inhalation and exhalation, which are both produced by movements of the diaphragm, a large flat muscle at the bottom of the rib cage.
- Due to unequal concentrations of gases, carbon dioxide diffuses out of the blood into the air in the alveoli and oxygen diffuses from the air in the alveoli into the blood. Hemoglobin in red blood cells increases the amount of oxygen that can diffuse into the blood.

40–3 Control of the Respiratory System

- Breathing is an involuntary action under the control of the medulla oblongata in the brain.
- The vital capacity of the lungs is the maximum amount of air that can be moved into and out of the respiratory system.

REVIEWING KEY TERMS

Vocabulary terms are important to your understanding of biology. The key terms listed below are those you should be especially familiar with. Review these terms and their meanings. Then use each term in a complete sentence. If you are not sure of a term's meaning, return to the appropriate section and review its definition.

40–1 The Importance of Respiration

internal respiration
external respiration
respiratory system

40–2 The Human Respiratory System

pharynx
trachea
larynx
vocal cord
bronchus
lung
bronchiole
alveolus
inhalation
exhalation
diaphragm
hemoglobin

40–3 Control of the Respiratory System

vital capacity

CHAPTER REVIEW

CONTENT REVIEW

Multiple Choice

Choose the letter of the answer that best completes each statement.

1. Internal respiration is at the level of the
   a. organism. c. lungs.
   b. cell. d. pharynx.
2. Sound is produced by vibrations of the
   a. notochords. c. vocal cords.
   b. bronchi. d. tracheal rings.
3. The passageway leading directly from the pharynx to the lungs is the
   a. esophagus. c. bronchus.
   b. trachea. d. larynx.
4. The order of air movement within the lungs is best described as
   a. bronchi to bronchioles to alveoli.
   b. bronchi to alveoli to bronchioles.
   c. bronchioles to bronchi to alveoli.
   d. trachea to bronchi to alveoli.
5. The substance in blood whose level regulates breathing is
   a. carbon monoxide. c. carbon dioxide.
   b. oxygen. d. nitrogen.
6. During inhalation, the contraction of the diaphragm and intercostal muscles causes the chest cavity's
   a. volume to decrease and pressure to increase.
   b. volume to increase and pressure to decrease.
   c. volume to increase and pressure to increase.
   d. volume to decrease and pressure to decrease.
7. Air in the alveoli following an inhalation has the highest concentration of which gas?
   a. nitrogen c. carbon dioxide
   b. water vapor d. oxygen
8. The two gases exchanged by the respiratory system are
   a. CO_2 and N_2. c. O_2 and N_2.
   b. CO and O_2. d. O_2 and CO_2.

True or False

Determine whether each statement is true or false. If it is true, write "true." If it is false, change the underlined word or words to make the statement true.

1. The part of the throat located behind the mouth is the pharynx.
2. The oxygen-carrying protein found in blood is mucus.
3. The large muscle whose movements control breathing is the trachea.
4. The cerebellum controls breathing.
5. Vital capacity refers to the maximum amount of air that can be inhaled and exhaled.
6. Respiration at the level of the organism is also called internal respiration.
7. The larynx is also known as the voice box.
8. Nitrogen and oxygen account for 99 percent of the Earth's atmosphere.

Word Relationships

In each of the following sets of terms, three of the terms are related. One term does not belong. Determine the characteristic common to three of the terms and then identify the term that does not belong.

1. carbon dioxide, oxygen, helium, water vapor
2. nose, pharynx, trachea, esophagus
3. rings of cartilage, alveoli, gas exchange, thin elastic membranes
4. filtering, humidifying, decomposing, warming

CONCEPT MASTERY

Use your understanding of the concepts developed in the chapter to answer each of the following in a brief paragraph.

1. Describe the passage of air through the respiratory system. Indicate the function of each structure of the system.
2. What process occurs during gas exchange in the alveoli? Explain why this process takes place.
3. What is breathing? Explain the mechanism of breathing by describing the relationship between movement of the diaphragm and volume-pressure changes.
4. What damage to the respiratory system is done by tobacco smoke? Why is this dangerous?
5. Explain how the concentration of carbon dioxide in the blood affects the rate of breathing.
6. How is the structure of the vocal cords related to their function?

CRITICAL AND CREATIVE THINKING

Discuss each of the following in a brief paragraph.

1. **Drawing conclusions** You exhale onto a cold surface and notice the condensation of water vapor. Where does this water vapor come from? Why?
2. **Identifying patterns** Emphysema is a disease of the respiratory system that mainly affects the alveoli. In the early stages, the elastic fibers in the walls of the tiny air sacs become damaged. In the later stages, the walls are destroyed. Describe the possible symptoms of a person suffering from this disease. Explain your reasoning.
3. **Relating cause and effect** The condition known as hypoxia is caused by a shortage of oxygen in the body tissues. Explain why the following two changes take place in a person who has hypoxia: (1) The bone marrow produces more red blood cells. (2) The respiratory center of the brain is stimulated.
4. **Relating facts** The air that patients who are breathing on a respirator (tube providing air directly into the trachea) receive must be filtered and humidified externally. Explain why this is so.
5. **Applying concepts** Drugs that artificially raise the pH of the blood can be dangerous. Explain this fact in light of the effects of pH on the breathing center.
6. **Drawing conclusions** Observing people in a crowded room shows that their breathing rates are elevated. Explain why this might be so.
7. **Identifying relationships** Metabolism is the sum of all the chemical activities carried out by a living organism, including cellular respiration. Explain why metabolism can be measured in terms of oxygen consumed.
8. **Relating facts** What physical problems can produce a cough? Why can coughing be considered a defensive action?
9. **Using the writing process** Reliable statistical and experimental evidence indicates that 85 to 90 percent of all lung cancers result directly from cigarette smoking. Write an advertising campaign in which you urge people, especially young people, to avoid smoking. Be sure to include information about smoking's effect on the respiratory system.

CHAPTER 41

Circulatory and Excretory Systems

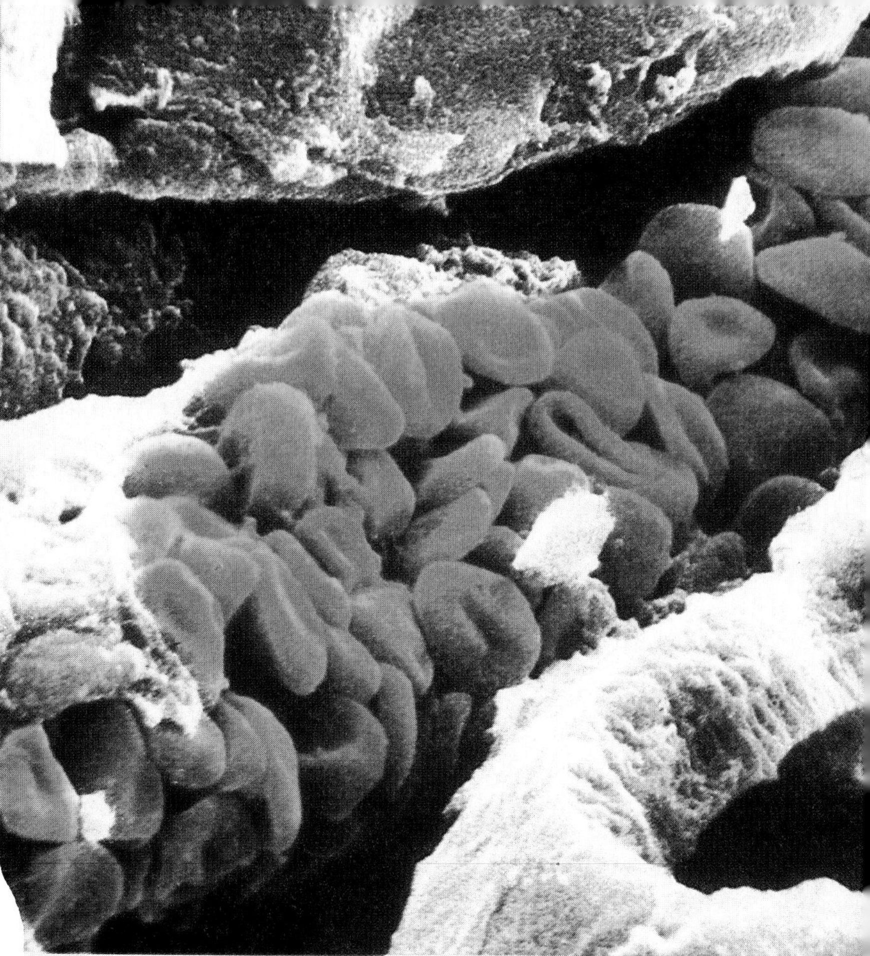

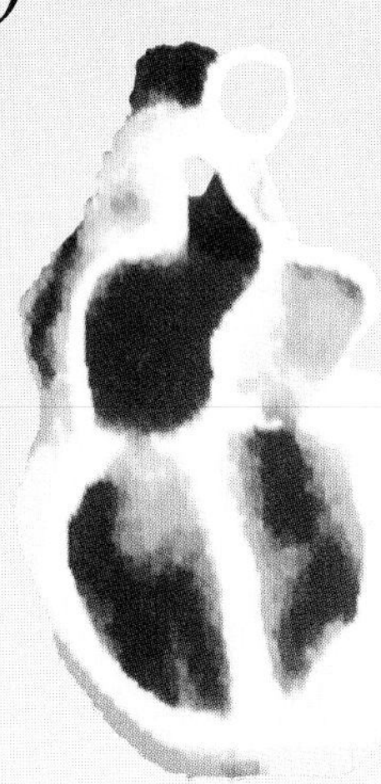

In the human body's great river—the circulatory system—blood, which is pumped by the heart (inset), flows through blood vessels.

Large cities are often located near rivers because rivers provide fresh water, food, and, most importantly, a means of transportation for people living there. A complex society cannot develop and thrive without a way to move raw materials, food, and finished products from one place to another. A flowing river provides the means of transportation that holds a society together.

Within the complex society of cells that make up the human body, the needs of living tissues are remarkably similar to those of a city. Each cell needs a steady supply of food and oxygen. That supply is provided by the body's great river—the circulatory system. The basic material of this system is a living tissue called blood.

In its travels, the circulatory system collects poisons and wastes from the cells of the body. These materials are removed by yet another system—the excretory system. You will now discover how these two systems allow billions of cells to live side by side in the most complex society ever constructed—the human body.

CHAPTER OUTLINE

41–1 The Circulatory System

Section Objectives

- List the parts of the circulatory system.
- Describe the structure and operation of the heart.
- Identify the three types of blood vessels and their functions.
- Compare pulmonary circulation and systemic circulation.

For thousands of years people have wondered about the nature of blood. The Roman physician Galen believed that blood was formed from food that passed from the stomach into the liver, then flowed through vessels to all parts of the body, returning slowly to the liver through the same vessels.

An accurate understanding of the nature of blood had to wait until 1628, when the English physician William Harvey showed that blood circulated throughout the body in one-way vessels. According to Harvey, blood was pumped out of the heart and into the tissues through one type of vessel and back to the heart through another type of vessel. The blood, in other words, moved in a closed cycle through the body.

Harvey was not sure why blood circulated in this way. Today we know the answer: Blood is the body's internal transportation system. Pumped by the heart, blood travels through a network of vessels, carrying materials such as oxygen, nutrients, and hormones to and waste products from each of the one hundred trillion cells in the human body. **Blood, the heart, and blood vessels make up the circulatory system.**

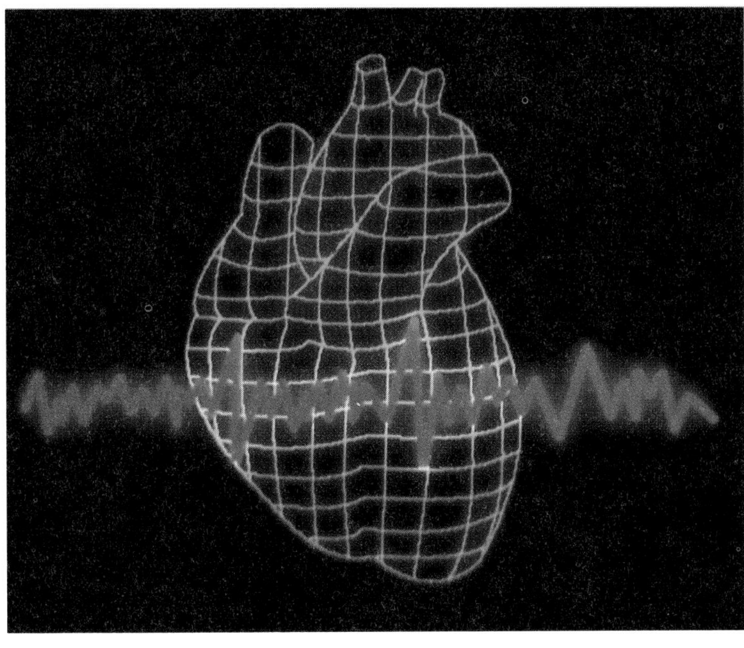

__Figure 41–1__ The red wavy line that is superimposed on a computer graphic grid of the human heart is a portion of an electrocardiogram (EKG). An electrocardiogram is a record of the electrical activities of the heart.

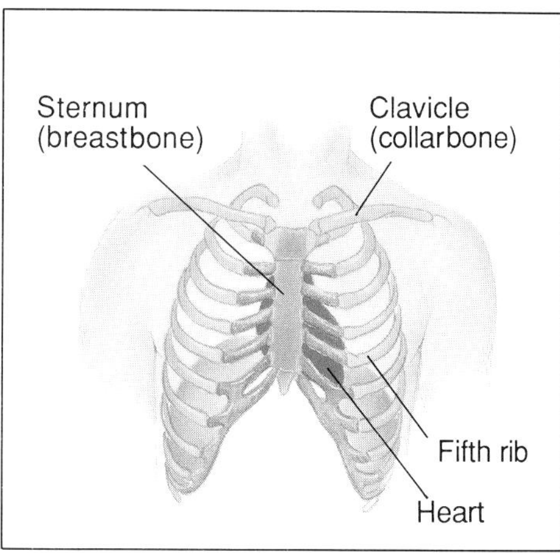

Figure 41–2 *The heart is located in the chest cavity and extends almost the length of the sternum (breastbone).*

The Heart

The **heart** is a hollow, muscular organ that contracts at regular intervals, forcing blood through the **circulatory system**. The walls of the heart are made up of three layers of tissue. The outer and inner layers are epithelial tissue, which covers and protects other tissue. The middle layer is cardiac muscle tissue.

As you may recall from Chapter 38, cardiac muscle tissue is not under conscious control of the nervous system. It can contract on its own. As you will soon see, this tendency is important in understanding how the heart works. Cardiac muscle tissue has a rich supply of blood, which ensures that it gets plenty of oxygen. It also has special connections between cells that allow impulses to travel from one cell to another. The cells that make up cardiac muscle tissue are loaded with mitochondria, guaranteeing that each cell has a constant supply of ATP. Whether you are asleep or awake, the heart contracts about once every second every day of your life. The only time the heart rests is between beats.

How the Heart Works

The heart can really be thought of as two pumps sitting side by side. The right side of the heart pumps blood from the body into the lungs, where oxygen-poor (deoxygenated) blood gives up carbon dioxide and picks up oxygen. The left side of the heart pumps oxygen-rich (oxygenated) blood from the lungs to the rest of the body.

The heart is enclosed in a protective sac of tissue called the pericardium (per-ih-KAHR-dee-uhm). Dividing the right side from the left side is a septum, or wall. The septum prevents the mixing of oxygen-poor and oxygen-rich blood.

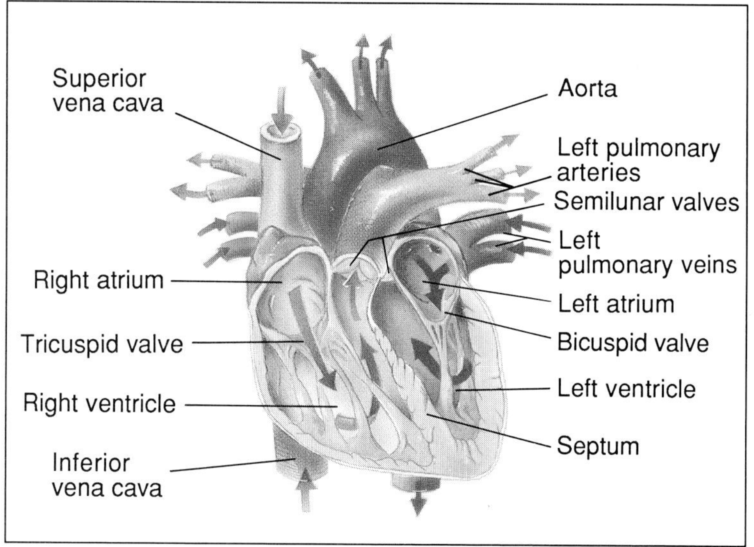

Figure 41–3 *The muscular heart is divided into halves by a septum, or wall. On each side of the septum are two chambers; the upper chambers are called atria and the lower chambers are called ventricles.*

On each side of the septum are two chambers. The upper chambers, which are called **atria** (AY-tree-uh; singular: atrium), receive blood coming into the heart. The lower chambers, which are called **ventricles**, pump blood out of the heart.

THE RIGHT SIDE OF THE HEART Blood from the body enters the right side of the heart through two large blood vessels called **venae cavae** (veh-nee KAY-vee; singular: vena cava). The superior (upper) vena cava brings blood from the upper part of the body to the heart. The inferior (lower) vena cava brings blood from the lower part of the body to the heart. Both venae cavae empty into the right atrium. When the heart relaxes (between beats), pressure in the circulatory system causes the atrium to fill up with blood. When the heart contracts, blood is squeezed from the right atrium into the right ventricle through an opening surrounded by flaps of tissue. These flaps of tissue form the tricuspid valve, which prevents blood from flowing back into the right atrium.

When the heart contracts a second time, blood in the right ventricle is sent through blood vessels (pulmonary arteries) into the lungs. At the base of these blood vessels is a valve that prevents the blood from traveling back into the right ventricle. Both this valve and the tricuspid valve ensure that blood flows in only one direction.

THE LEFT SIDE OF THE HEART Oxygen-rich blood leaves the lungs and returns to the heart by way of blood vessels (pulmonary veins). As the blood enters the left atrium, it passes through the bicuspid, or mitral, valve into the left ventricle. Powerful contractions force blood from the left ventricle into a large blood vessel (aorta) that carries it to every part of the body. At the base of this large blood vessel is another valve that prevents blood from flowing back into the left ventricle.

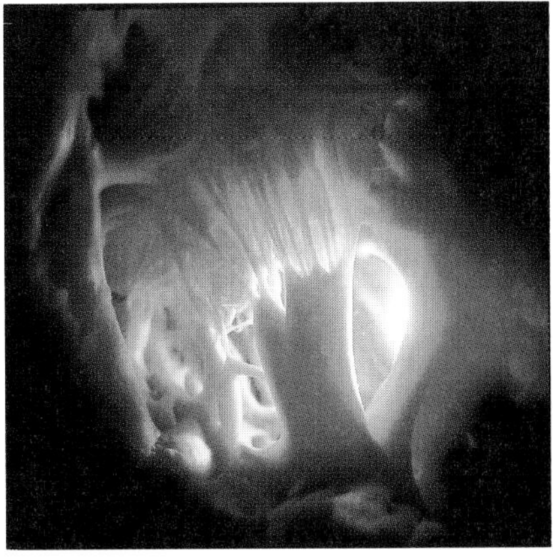

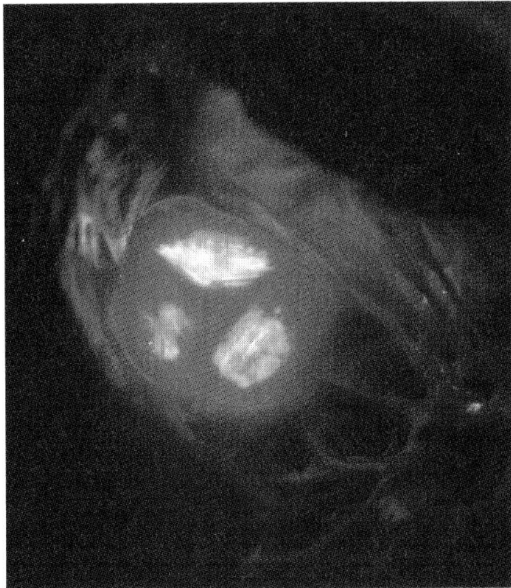

Figure 41–4 *Valves control the passage of blood through the heart. The tricuspid valve (top) is located between the right atrium and the right ventricle. The aortic valve (bottom) is found at the base of the aorta.*

The Heartbeat

Although the heart is a single muscle, it does not contract in a single motion. Instead, the contraction spreads out over the heart like a wave. This wave begins in a small bundle of cells embedded in the right atrium. Because this structure initiates each heartbeat, and thus sets the pace for the heart rate, it is called the pacemaker.

Figure 41–5 on page 900 shows how the impulse spreads from the pacemaker through the cardiac muscle cells in the right and left atria, causing both atria to contract almost simultaneously. When the impulse reaches the walls of the right and left ventricles, they too contract almost simultaneously. As the impulse spreads from one end of a chamber to the other, it stimulates the cardiac muscle cells to contract. This contraction causes the chambers to squeeze the blood, pushing it in the proper direction along its path.

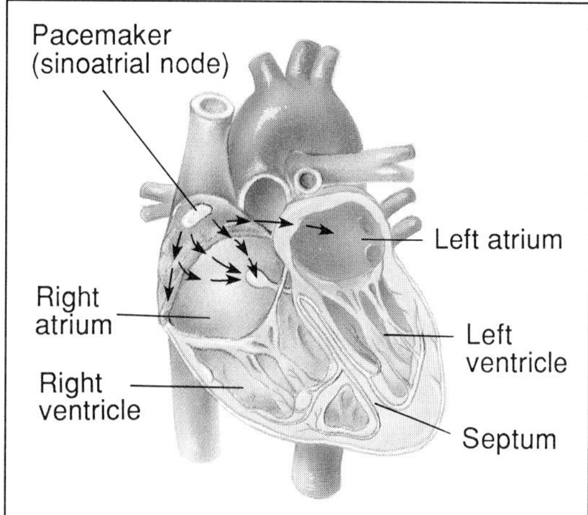

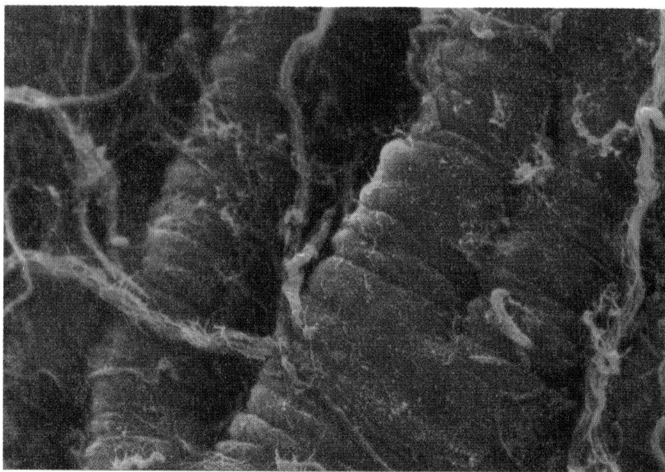

Figure 41–5 *The drawing shows the path an impulse takes as it spreads through the heart. The photograph shows a network of nerves that line a portion of the ventricle.*

You may recall from Chapter 38 that most muscles contract only when stimulated by a motor neuron. This is not the case with cardiac muscle, which initiates the stimulation by itself. However, the autonomic nervous system does influence heart rate. The sympathetic nervous system increases heart rate, and the parasympathetic system decreases it.

In most people at rest, the heart rate is between 60 and 80 beats per minute. During intense exercise, the rate can increase to as many as 200 beats per minute. In this way, the heart can pump oxygen-rich blood through the body more quickly.

Blood Vessels

After blood leaves the heart, it is pumped through a network of blood vessels to different parts of the body. The blood vessels that form this network and are part of the circulatory system are the arteries, capillaries, and veins.

With the exception of capillaries and tiny veins, blood vessels have walls made up of three layers of tissue. The inner layer is epithelial tissue. The middle layer is smooth muscle tissue and elastic fibers. The outer layer is connective tissue.

ARTERIES **Arteries** carry blood from the heart to all the tissues of the body. In general, the walls of arteries are thicker than those of veins. The smooth muscle cells and elastic fibers that make up these walls help make arteries tough and flexible. These characteristics enable arteries to withstand the high pressure of blood as it is pumped from the heart. Except for the pulmonary arteries, all arteries carry oxygen-rich blood.

The artery that carries oxygen-rich blood from the left ventricle to all parts of the body is the **aorta**. The aorta, with a diameter of 2.5 centimeters, is the largest artery in the body. As the aorta travels away from the heart, it branches into smaller and smaller arteries so that all parts of the body are supplied with blood. The smallest arteries are called arterioles.

CAPILLARIES Arterioles branch into networks of very small blood vessels called **capillaries.** It is in the thin-walled capillaries that the real work of the circulatory system is done. The walls of the capillaries consist of only one layer of cells, making it easy for oxygen and nutrients to diffuse from the blood into the tissues. The forces of diffusion drive carbon dioxide and waste products from the tissues into the capillaries. Capillaries are extremely narrow blood vessels—so narrow, in fact, that blood cells moving through them must pass in single file.

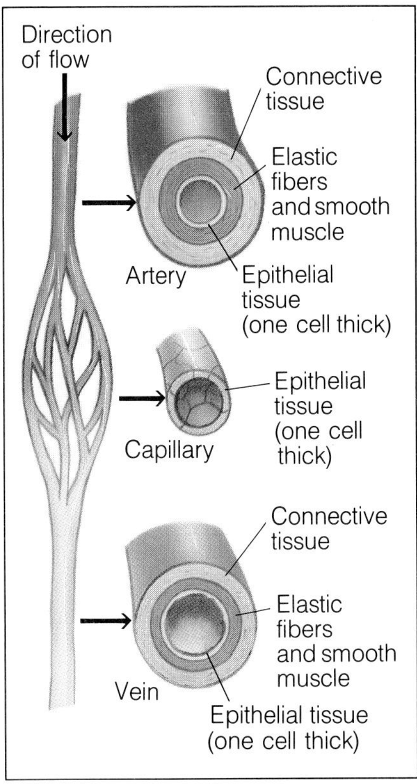

Figure 41–6 Although arteries, capillaries, and veins are all blood vessels, they each have a unique structure that helps them perform their particular function.

VEINS The flow of blood moves from capillaries into **veins.** Veins form a system that collects blood from every part of the body and carries it back to the heart. The smallest veins are called venules. Like arteries, veins are lined with smooth muscle. The walls of veins, however, are thinner and less elastic than those of arteries. Although the walls are less elastic, they are more flexible and are able to stretch out readily. This is important because it reduces the resistance the flow of blood encounters on its way back to the heart. Large veins contain valves that keep blood from flowing backward. These valves play an important role because blood must frequently flow against the force of gravity.

Blood flowing through veins gets quite a push from the contractions of skeletal muscles, especially those in the arms and the legs. When these muscles contract, they squeeze against veins and help force blood toward the heart. When these muscles are not used for long periods of time, this extra push is lost and blood accumulates in different parts of the body. This is what happens to people who are confined to bed for an extended period of time. In order to prevent this accumulation of blood, health-care workers often try to get these patients to walk— even for just a few minutes a day.

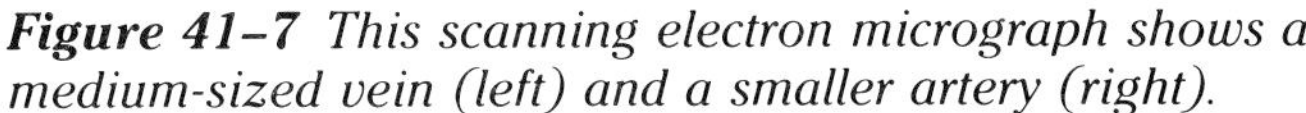

***Figure 41–7** This scanning electron micrograph shows a medium-sized vein (left) and a smaller artery (right).*

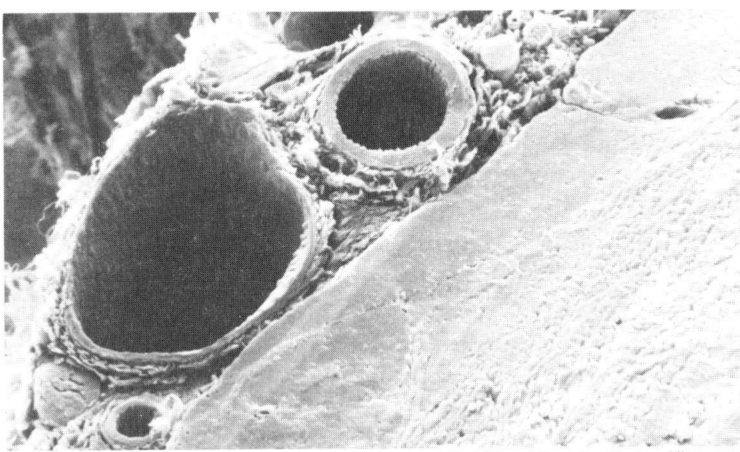

Pathways of Circulation

Blood moves through the body in a continuous pathway, of which there are two major parts. **Pulmonary circulation** carries blood between the heart and the lungs. This circulation begins at the right ventricle and ends at the left atrium. **Systemic circulation,** which starts at the left ventricle and ends at the right atrium, carries blood to the rest of the body.

PULMONARY CIRCULATION Oxygen-poor blood is pumped out of the right ventricle of the heart into the lungs through the pulmonary arteries. These are the only arteries in the body that carry deoxygenated blood. In fact, the blood in the pulmonary arteries contains the lowest percentage of oxygen of all other blood vessels. Blood returns to the heart through the pulmonary veins, which are the only veins in the body that carry oxygen-rich blood. The lungs are the only organs directly connected to both chambers of the heart.

SYSTEMIC CIRCULATION Oxygen-rich blood leaving the heart passes through the aorta and into a number of arteries that supply blood to every part of the body. Systemic circulation supplies each major organ with blood, including the heart.

You might think that the heart muscle can get oxygen and nutrients from the enormous amounts of blood that pass through it, but this is not the case. Instead, a pair of coronary arteries leading from the aorta carry blood through the tissues of the heart. These arteries branch into arterioles and then into capillaries, forming a lacy network throughout the heart. See Figure 41–9. The capillaries lead into veins through which blood returns to the right atrium.

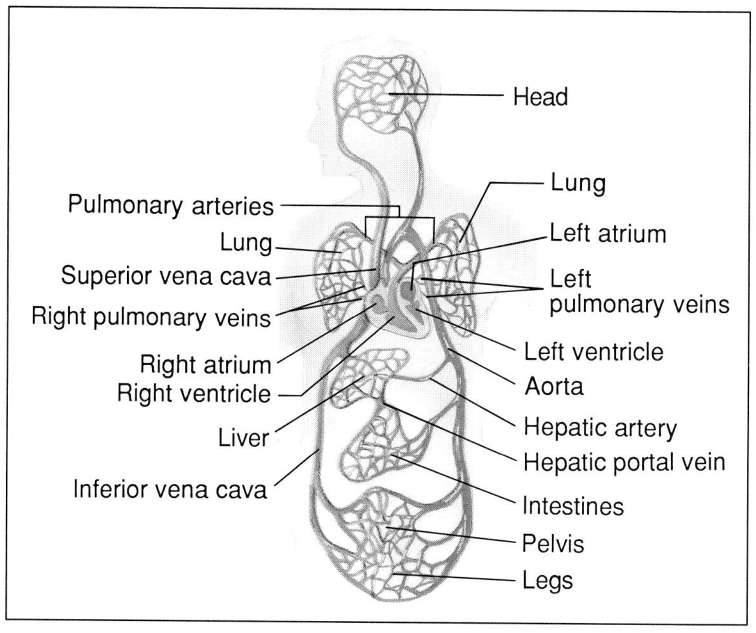

Figure 41–8 *Blood moves through the body in a continuous path. The path of oxygen-rich blood is shown in red; the path of oxygen-poor blood is shown in blue.*

In general, blood travels through only one set of capillaries before it returns to the heart. However, there is a special circulation known as the hepatic portal system that is an exception to this rule. Capillaries that line the walls of the digestive system absorb food, minerals, and water. Blood in these capillaries is collected into veins, but these veins do not lead directly to the heart. Instead, they are carried to the liver by the hepatic portal vein.

As it enters the liver, the hepatic portal vein divides into capillaries that deliver blood throughout the liver. Veins leading out of the liver collect the blood and return it to the general circulation through the heart. This unique circulation allows the liver to act as a gatekeeper, regulating the entry of food and nutrients into the circulatory system.

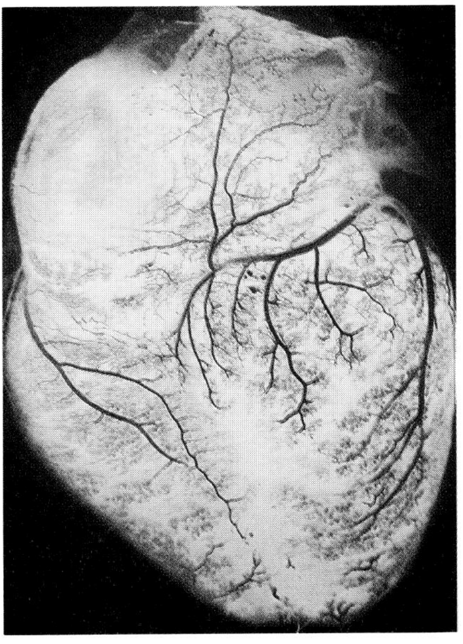

Figure 41–9 *The blood vessels covering the surface of the heart bring oxygen and nutrients to the heart muscle and carry wastes away.*

Blood Pressure

Blood moves through the vessels of the circulatory system because it is under pressure. The pressure is produced by the contraction of the heart and by the muscles that surround blood vessels. A measure of the force that blood exerts against a vessel wall is called **blood pressure**.

Blood pressure is regulated by the body in two ways. At several places in the body a special system of sensory neurons attached to blood vessels measures blood pressure. When blood pressure is too low, these sensory neurons stimulate the autonomic nervous system to increase the rate at which the heart pumps. When blood pressure is too high, the same system helps to slow the heart down. The kidneys are the other means by which blood pressure is regulated. When blood pressure is high, the kidneys remove more water from the blood, lowering the total amount of fluid in the circulatory system. The loss of fluid from the blood lowers the blood pressure, much like the loss of air from a balloon lowers the air pressure inside the balloon.

Problems can result when blood pressure is either too low or too high. Low blood pressure slows down the rate at which blood flows through the body. The parts of the body that are far away from the heart, such as the hands, feet, and the head, do not receive enough blood. If this happens in cold weather, these body parts may become easily chilled and injured.

Hypertension, or excessively high blood pressure, also has serious medical consequences. When blood pressure is high, the heart works much harder to pump blood, causing the heart muscle to weaken. People with high blood pressure are also more likely to develop problems in the arteries outside the heart. Like garden hoses under high pressure, the arteries are more likely to develop leaks.

Although scientists do not know all the causes of hypertension, they are sure of one—obesity. As fat tissue is added to the

Figure 41–10 *When arteries become narrowed by deposits of cholesterol, atherosclerosis results.*

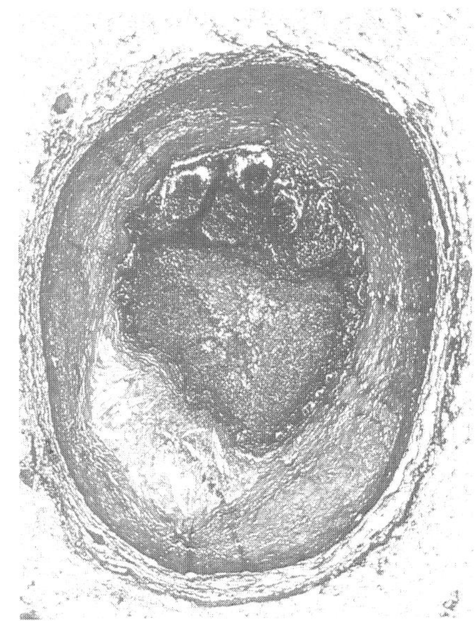

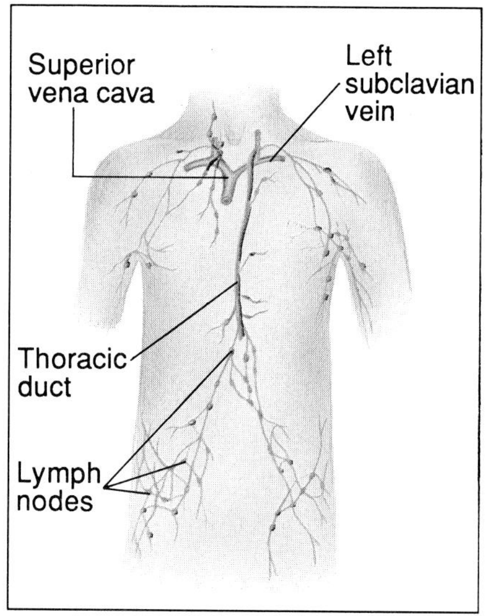

Figure 41–11 *The lymphatic system is made up of vessels, capillaries, nodes, and glands that recirculate any fluid that leaves the circulatory system.*

body, additional blood vessels are required in order to supply the tissues with oxygen and nutrients. The addition of more blood vessels causes the heart to work harder. As a result, blood pressure increases.

Scientists have developed a number of drugs to lower blood pressure and prevent some of its serious consequences. However, hypertension is easier to prevent than to cure. Exercising regularly, eating sensibly, watching one's weight, and avoiding smoking are the most sensible means of preventing hypertension.

The Lymphatic System

As blood circulates throughout the body, fluid from the blood leaks into the tissues. This action helps to maintain an efficient flow of nutrients and salts from the blood into the tissues. The total leakage of fluid from the circulatory system amounts to approximately 3 liters per day. If this leakage were to continue unchecked, the body would begin to swell with fluid—not a very pleasant prospect!

Fortunately this does not happen. A network of vessels known as the **lymphatic** (lihm-FAT-ihk) **system** collects the fluid that is lost by the blood and returns it to the circulatory system. This fluid, which is known as lymph (LIHMF), collects in lymphatic capillaries and slowly flows into larger and larger lymph vessels. Like veins, lymph vessels contain valves that prevent lymph from flowing backward.

The slowly moving fluid is returned to the circulatory system at an opening in a vein located under the left clavicle, or collarbone, just below the shoulder. Along the length of the lymph vessels are small bean-shaped enlargements called lymph nodes. Lymph nodes act as filters and producers of special white blood cells that prevent harmful material from invading the body cells.

41–1 SECTION REVIEW

1. What are the parts of the circulatory system?
2. Describe the structure of the heart and the circulation of blood through it.
3. How is the heartbeat controlled?
4. Identify the three types of blood vessels. What is the function of each?
5. What is blood pressure?
6. Describe the lymphatic system.
7. Why does regular exercise promote good circulation?

41–2 Blood

Section Objectives

- List the functions of blood.
- Describe the components of blood.
- Discuss the role of platelets in blood clotting.

The function of the circulatory system is to transport material in a fluid medium throughout the body. This fluid medium is called **blood.** Blood is a type of liquid connective tissue that has many functions. **Blood transports nutrients, dissolved gases (oxygen and carbon dioxide), enzymes, hormones, and waste products; blood regulates body temperature, pH, and electrolytes (ions in solution that conduct electric current); blood protects the body from invaders; and blood restricts the loss of fluid.**

Although blood is referred to as the river of life, the human body contains only 4 to 6 liters of this precious fluid—only 8 percent of the total mass of the body. Approximately 55 percent of blood is made up of a fluid portion called **plasma**. The remaining 45 percent consists of a cellular portion.

Blood Plasma

Plasma is a straw-colored fluid that is 90 percent water and 10 percent dissolved fats, salts, sugars, and proteins called plasma proteins. The plasma proteins, which perform a number of vital functions, are divided into three types: albumins, globulins, and fibrinogen. Albumins help regulate osmotic pressure. Globulins include antibodies that help fight off infection. Fibrinogen is responsible for the ability of blood to clot, a process that will be discussed in more detail later in the chapter. Nutrients, hormones, and waste products are also carried in the plasma.

Figure 41–12 *These packets of frozen plasma have been laid out to thaw so that a necessary clotting factor can be extracted from the plasma. This clotting factor is then used to treat hemophilia.*

Blood Cells

The cellular portion of the blood includes several types of highly specialized cells and cell fragments. They are red blood cells, white blood cells, and platelets.

RED BLOOD CELLS **Red blood cells**, or erythrocytes (eh-RIHTH-roh-sights), are the most numerous of the blood cells. One microliter of blood contains approximately 5 million red blood cells.

Red blood cells are biconcave, or shaped so that they are narrower in the center than along the edges. These cells are produced from cells in the bone marrow that gradually become filled with hemoglobin, forcing out their nucleus and other organelles. Thus mature red blood cells do not have a nucleus. Hemoglobin is the iron-containing protein that carries oxygen from the lungs to the tissues of the body. Hemoglobin gives the red blood cells their characteristic color.

Red blood cells normally stay in circulation for approximately 120 days before they are destroyed by special white

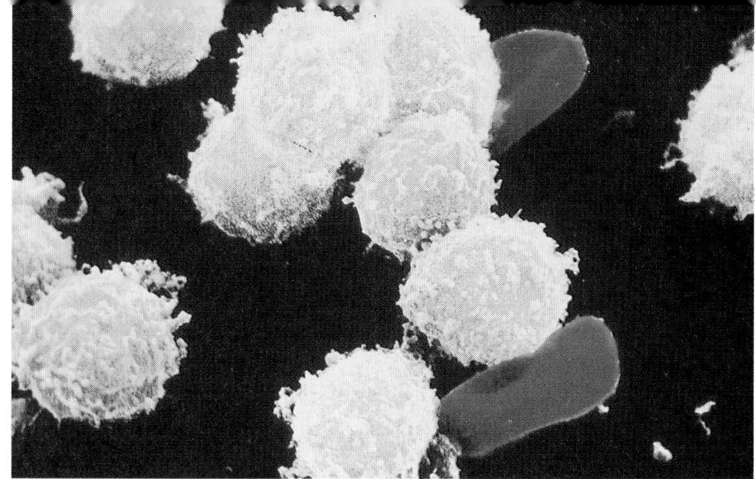

Figure 41–13 The large yellow objects in this photograph are the smallest types of white blood cells. The two red flattened objects are red blood cells.

blood cells in the liver and the spleen. At this moment, red blood cells in your body are dying at a rate of about 2 million per second. To replace them, new red blood cells are being formed in the bone marrow at the same rate.

WHITE BLOOD CELLS **White blood cells**, or leukocytes (LOO-koh-sights), are outnumbered by red blood cells almost 500 to 1. White blood cells are produced in the bone marrow, are larger than red blood cells, almost colorless, and do not contain hemoglobin. Unlike red blood cells, white blood cells have a nucleus and can live for many months or years.

The main function of white blood cells is to protect the body against invasion by foreign cells or substances. What enables white blood cells to do this job is, in part, their ability to move out into the surrounding tissue like amebas. Some white blood cells can destroy bacteria and foreign cells by phagocytosis (large particles are taken inside a cell and digested). Others make special proteins called antibodies (globulin-type plasma proteins). Still others release special chemicals that help the body fight off disease and resist infection.

Figure 41–14 When a red blood cell is about 120 days old, its life draws to a close. Here a special type of white blood cell engulfs and destroys an aging red blood cell.

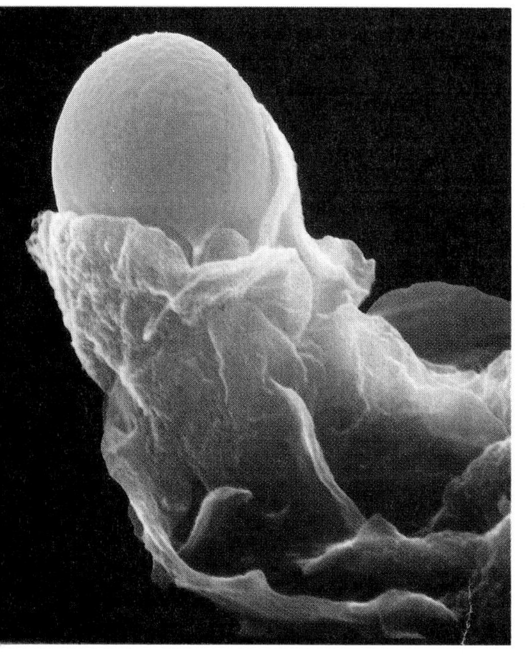

White blood cells respond quickly to infection. Physicians are often able to detect the presence of a serious infection by counting the number of white blood cells in the blood. When an infection such as appendicitis occurs, the number of white blood cells may increase from 10,000 to 30,000 per microliter.

PLATELETS AND BLOOD CLOTTING **Platelets** are not cells; rather, they are tiny fragments of other cells. Platelets are formed when small pieces of cytoplasm are pinched off the large cells called megakaryocytes (mehg-uh-KAHR-ee-oh-sights), which are found in the bone marrow. One microliter of blood contains between 250,000 and 400,000 platelets. The life span of a platelet is approximately 5 to 9 days.

Platelets play an important role in preventing the loss of blood by beginning a chain of reactions that result in blood clotting. When you cut or scratch yourself, blood will flow from the wound. Because of the action of platelets, the blood will clot and bleeding will stop after a short time.

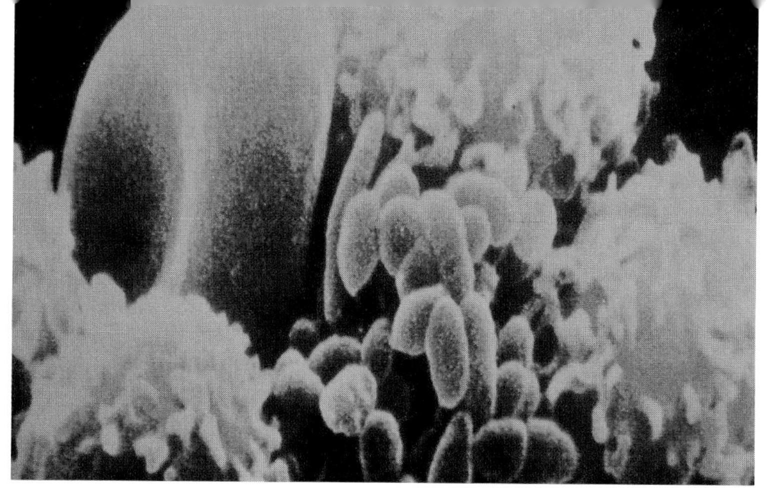

Figure 41–15 This electron micrograph shows the three types of blood cells that make up the cellular portion of the blood. The three large furry objects are white blood cells, the tiny spherical objects in the foreground are platelets, and the beret-shaped object is a red blood cell.

Platelets help the clotting process by clumping together and forming a plug at the site of a wound and then releasing proteins called clotting factors. These proteins start a series of chemical reactions that are extremely complicated. In one reaction, a clotting factor called thromboplastin (thrahm-boh-PLAS-tihn) converts prothrombin, which is found in the plasma of blood, into thrombin. Thrombin is an enzyme that converts the soluble plasma protein fibrinogen into a sticky meshwork of fibrin filaments that stop the bleeding by producing a clot.

The clotting process is extremely complex, and every step of it must go smoothly if a clot is to form. If one of the clotting factors is missing or defective, the clotting process does not work. A serious genetic disorder known as hemophilia results from defects in one of the clotting factor genes. Because they lack one of the clotting factors, hemophilia sufferers may bleed uncontrollably from even small cuts or scrapes. People suffering from hemophilia are given transfusions of clotting factors and platelets in order to treat their disorder.

The clotting of blood is not always a good thing. Sometimes a small clot will form in an unbroken blood vessel, blocking the flow of blood to the cells. If this happens in the brain, brain cells may begin to die, causing a stroke. A stroke may result in the loss of motor functions, such as speech or muscle control, or in death.

Figure 41–16 In the clotting process, a network of fibrin threads forms over a wound, trapping the blood cells.

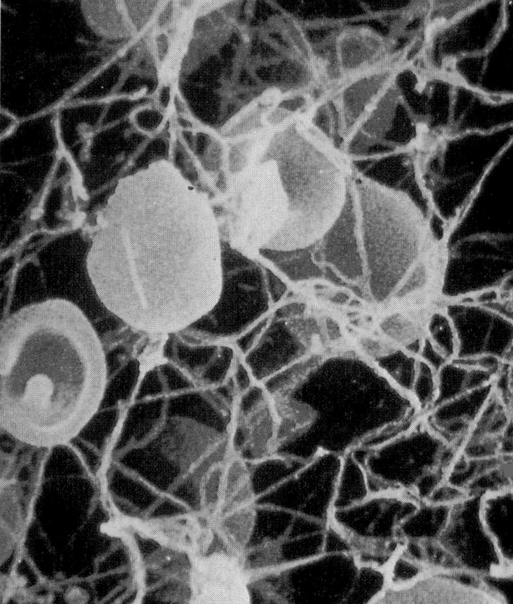

41–2 SECTION REVIEW

1. What are the functions of blood?
2. Describe the components of blood.
3. What role do platelets play in blood clotting?
4. Infections sometimes block the flow of fluid through the lymphatic system, causing severe swelling in the tissues. Explain why this happens.

Section Objectives

- List the parts of the excretory system.
- Describe the structure and function of the kidneys.
- Relate the parts of the nephron to their function.

41–3 The Excretory System

As a normal consequence of being alive, every cell in the body produces metabolic wastes. Examples of metabolic wastes include excess water and salts, carbon dioxide, and urea. Urea is a toxic compound that is produced when amino acids are used for energy. The process by which these metabolic wastes are removed from the body is called excretion.

You have already learned about two organs of excretion—the skin and the lungs. The skin excretes excess water and salts, as well as a small amount of urea. The lungs excrete carbon dioxide. The remaining organs of excretion are the kidneys. **Together, the skin, lungs, and kidneys—along with their associated organs—make up the excretory system.**

The Kidneys

The main organs of the **excretory system** are the **kidneys.** The kidneys are two bean-shaped organs, one located on either side of the spinal column near the lower back. Each kidney is about the size of a tightly clenched fist. Two blood vessels, the renal artery and the renal vein, enter and leave each kidney, respectively. A third vessel, the **ureter** (yoo-REET-er), leaves each kidney, carrying fluid to the **urinary bladder.**

The main functions of the kidneys can be summarized in terms of these three vessels. Waste-laden blood enters the kidney through the renal artery. Excess water, urea, and other waste products are removed from the blood and are collected in the ureter. The filtered blood exits through the renal vein.

Figure 41–17 *The main organs of the excretory system include the two kidneys, which in this X-ray are the green-colored bean-shaped organs located on either side of the spinal column. The tube that leaves each kidney is the ureter. It carries fluid to the urinary bladder, which is the round structure at the bottom of the X-ray.*

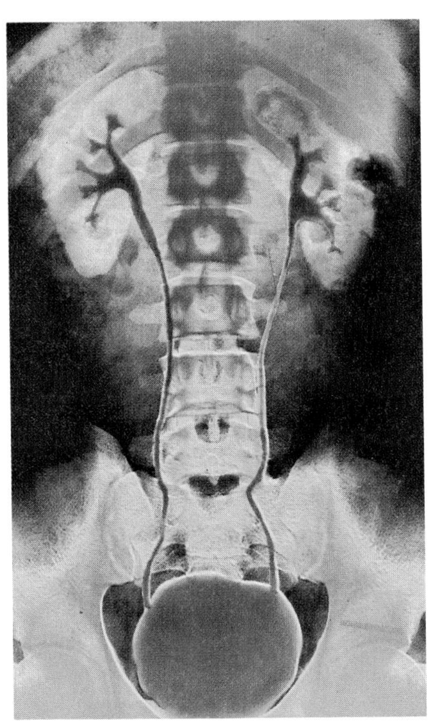

KIDNEY STRUCTURE If a kidney is cut in half, two distinct regions can be seen. The inner part is called the renal medulla; the outer part is called the renal cortex. The renal cortex contains the **nephrons** (NEHF-rahnz), the basic functional units of the kidneys. Each nephron is a small independent filtering unit. In each kidney there are about 1 million nephrons. Figure 41–19 shows the relationship of a single nephron to the two regions of the kidney.

Each nephron has its own blood supply: an arteriole, a venule, and a network of capillaries connecting them. In addition, each nephron has its own collecting tubule, which leads to the ureter. As blood enters a nephron through an arteriole, impurities are filtered out and emptied into the collecting tubule. Purified blood leaves the nephron through a venule. The actual mechanism of blood purification is rather complex, involving two separate processes—filtration and reabsorption.

FILTRATION As blood enters a nephron through an arteriole, it flows into a small network of 50 separate capillaries known as a **glomerulus** (gloh-MER-yoo-luhs). The glomerulus is encased in the upper end of the nephron by a cup-shaped structure called **Bowman's capsule.**

Because the blood is under pressure and the walls of the capillaries and Bowman's capsule are permeable, much of the fluid from the blood filters into Bowman's capsule. This process is known as **filtration**. The materials that are filtered from the blood are collectively called the filtrate. The filtrate contains water, urea, glucose, salts, amino acids, and some vitamins. Because plasma proteins, cells, and platelets are too large to pass through the membrane, they remain in the blood.

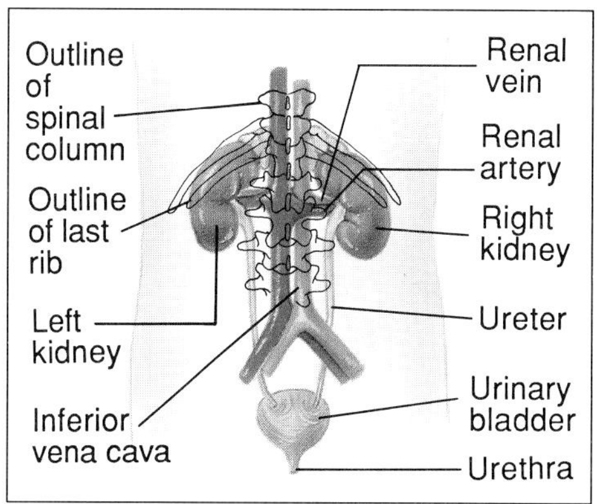

Figure 41–18 *This drawing shows the posterior, or back, view of the kidneys and their related structures.*

REABSORPTION Almost 180 liters of filtrate pass from the blood into the collecting tubules each day. This volume is equivalent to 90 2-liter bottles of soft drink! Needless to say, not all of the 180 liters is excreted. Most of the material removed from the blood at Bowman's capsule makes its way back into the blood by a process known as **reabsorption**.

A number of materials—including sodium and potassium salts, amino acids, fats, and sugars—are removed from the filtrate by active transport and reabsorbed by the capillaries. Active transport is the energy-requiring process that enables material to move across a membrane against a concentration difference. Water follows the active transport of these materials by osmosis. Approximately 99 percent of the water that is filtered into Bowman's capsule is reabsorbed into the blood.

The material that remains and is emptied into a collecting tubule is called urine. Urine consists of excess salts and water, and urea. These materials become concentrated in a section of the nephron, called the loop of Henle (HEHN-lee), by a specialized system that helps to conserve water and minimize the volume of urine.

As each kidney functions, purified blood is returned through the renal vein and urine is collected in the urinary bladder. Urine is stored in the urinary bladder until it can be released from the body through an opening called the **urethra**.

Figure 41–19 *Inside each kidney, more than one million nephrons function as filters. A nephron consists of a funnellike Bowman's capsule surrounding a tuft, or ball, of capillaries called a glomerulus. The electron micrograph shows a glomerulus.*

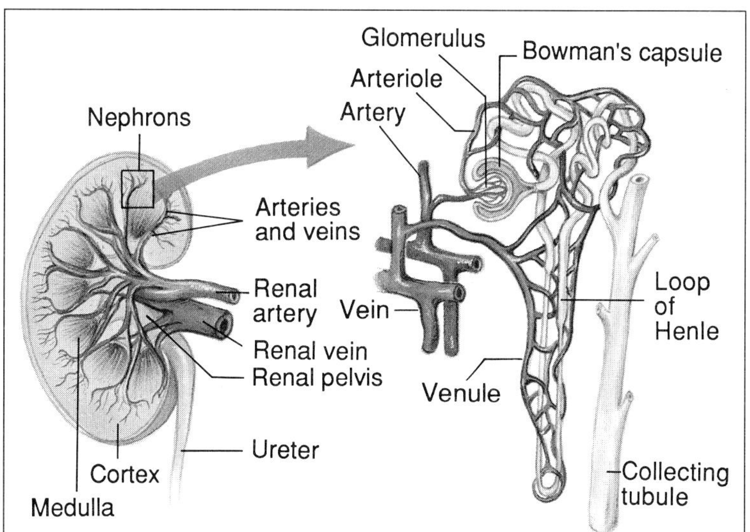

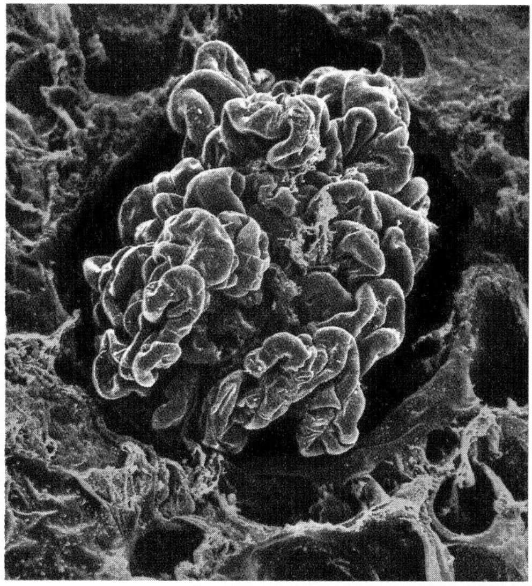

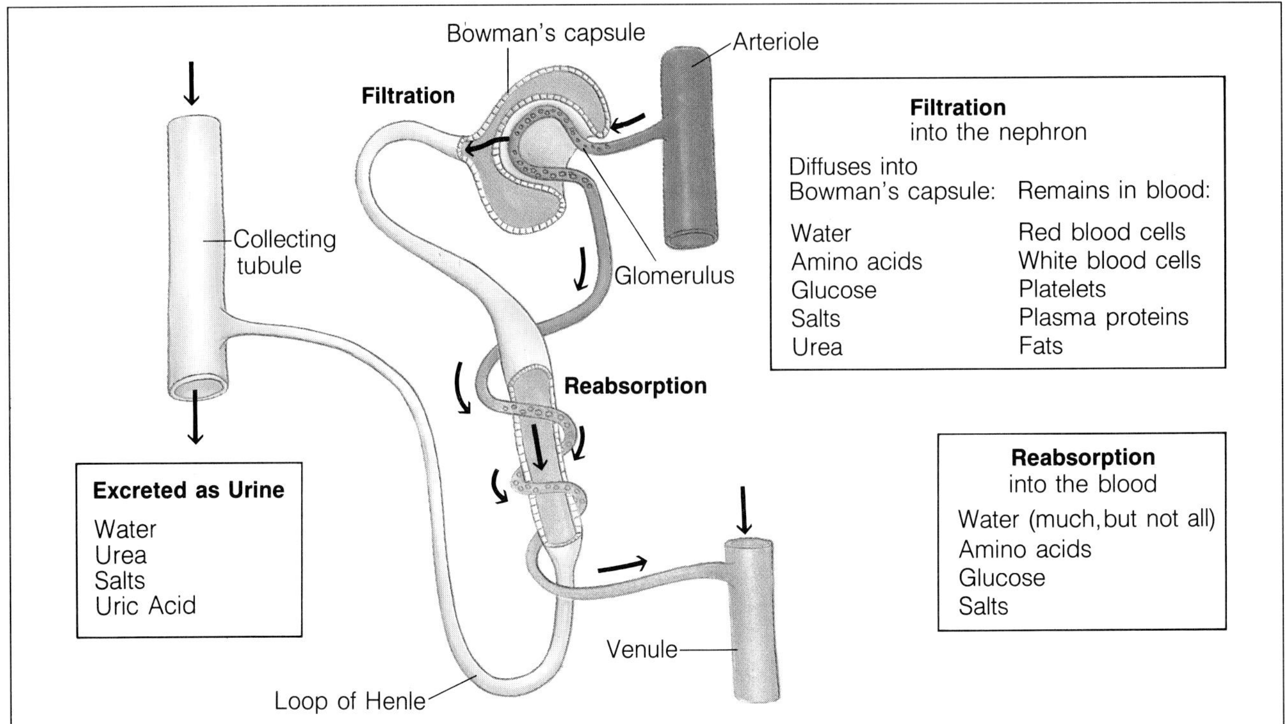

Figure 41–20 *The nephrons remove wastes from the blood through the processes of filtration and reabsorption. Filtration occurs in the glomerulus, and reabsorption occurs near the loop of Henle.*

Control of Kidney Function

The activity of the kidneys is controlled in a number of ways, one of which is the composition of blood itself. Another is the action of hormones that are released in response to the composition of blood. You will learn more about these hormones in Chapter 42. Both of these control mechanisms ensure that the kidneys will keep the composition of blood the same.

You have probably had the experience of occasionally drinking glass after glass of liquid. This liquid is quickly absorbed into the blood through the digestive system. As a result, the concentration of water in the blood increases. If it were not for your kidneys, this increased concentration of water in the blood would force water into cells and tissues by osmosis, causing the body to swell.

As the amount of water in the blood increases, the rate of water reabsorption in the kidneys decreases. Thus less water is returned to the blood, and the excess water is sent to the urinary bladder, to be excreted as urine.

If you eat salty food now and then, your kidneys will respond appropriately to the increased level of salt in your blood. As an increase in salt is detected by your kidneys, they will respond by returning less salt to the blood by reabsorption. The excess salt the kidneys keep is excreted in urine. The composition of the blood remains constant.

The kidneys are the master chemists of the blood supply. If anything goes wrong with the kidneys, serious medical problems soon follow. Fortunately, we have two kidneys and can survive with only one. Medical science is working rapidly to improve the efficiency of artificial kidneys and to develop alternate techniques of treating kidney problems.

SCIENCE, TECHNOLOGY, AND SOCIETY APPLICATION

Replacing a Kidney

A functioning kidney is absolutely essential to life. Fortunately, most of us have built-in insurance against a threat to our survival because of kidney damage. We have two kidneys —one more than is necessary to live a healthy, normal life. Thus you might think of the second kidney as a spare.

Unfortunately, many people develop severe kidney diseases that destroy both of their kidneys. Until recently, these people could not survive for more than a few weeks or months. Today, however, machines that purify blood by a process known as dialysis are reversing the situation and giving hope of a longer life.

Renal dialysis machines mimic some of the functions of the nephron. During dialysis, blood flows through a series of tubes composed of a selectively permeable membrane. Surrounding these tubes is a dialysis fluid that has a composition similar to that of blood, except that the concentration of waste products is low. The dialysis fluid flows in a direction opposite to that of blood. As a result, waste products such as urea diffuse from the blood into the dialysis fluid. Blood is usually taken from an artery, passed through the tubes of the dialysis machine, and then returned through a vein.

Patients experiencing kidney failure may visit a dialysis center several times a week to have their circulation cleansed by the machine. Although these machines work well, patients must use them nearly 20 hours per week, and the treatment often can be painful. Fortunately, a permanent cure for many people is available—a kidney transplant.

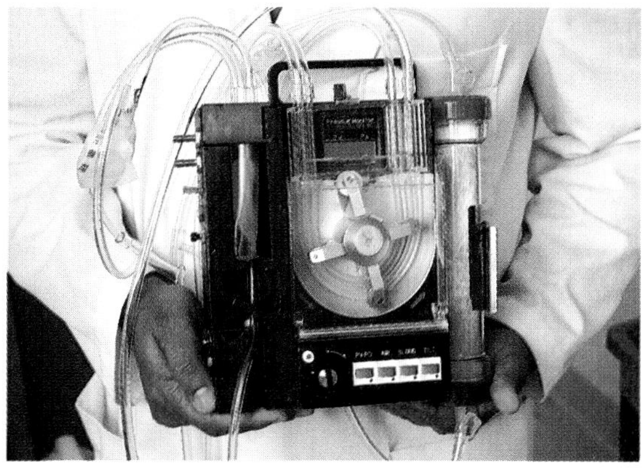

Recently designed dialysis machine

When trying to find a kidney donor, doctors must make sure that the donor's tissues are compatible with the patient's, so that the tissues of the donated kidney will not be attacked by the patient's immune system. Only then can the kidney from the donor be transplanted into the body of the patient. If the patient's body does not reject the donated kidney, the kidney will begin to function and both donor and recipient will live normal lives with only one kidney each.

41–3 SECTION REVIEW

1. What are the parts of the excretory system?
2. Describe the structure and function of the kidney.
3. What is a nephron? How does it function?
4. Describe the processes of filtration and reabsorption.
5. Explain why a person loses weight after changing to a low-salt diet even without reducing caloric intake.

LABORATORY INVESTIGATION

OBSERVING CIRCULATION IN A FISH TAIL

PROBLEM

How does blood flow in the tail of a goldfish?

MATERIALS *(per group)*

150-mL beaker	glass plate
goldfish in an aquarium	2 glass slides
medicine dropper	fish net
absorbent cotton	microscope
petri dish	

PROCEDURE 

1. Fill a 150-mL beaker almost full with water from the aquarium. Keep the water and medicine dropper near you at your laboratory table.
2. Using the medicine dropper, moisten two pieces of cotton with aquarium water.
3. Place one piece of moistened cotton in the petri dish and the other piece on the glass plate. Put the glass plate aside for now.
4. Place one of the glass slides on the side of the petri dish opposite the moistened cotton.
5. Using the fish net, remove a goldfish from the aquarium. **CAUTION:** *Be careful when handling live animals.* Gently place the head of the goldfish on the cotton in the petri dish. Be sure that the tail is on the glass slide.
6. Place the second piece of moistened cotton over the goldfish, leaving the mouth and tail uncovered. Place the other slide on top of the thin part of the tail. **Note:** *Be sure to keep the goldfish moist by adding aquarium water to the cotton as it begins to dry out.*
7. Remove the stage clips from the microscope and put them in a safe place.
8. When the goldfish has calmed down, place the petri dish on the stage of the microscope. Position the petri dish so the goldfish's tail is over the opening in the stage.
9. Examine the goldfish's tail under low power only. Move the petri dish around until you see blood moving in the blood vessels.

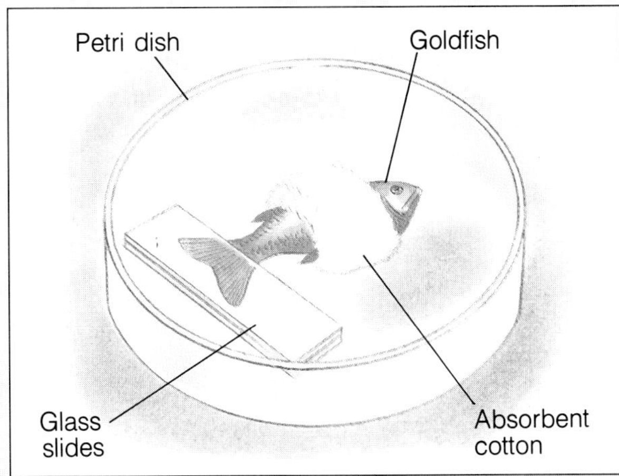

10. Locate a blood vessel in which blood cells are passing in single file. This is a capillary. Note the direction of the flow of blood.
11. Trace the capillary in the direction opposite the blood flow to where it joins a slightly larger vessel (arteriole). Then trace the capillary in the direction of blood flow until it joins a slightly larger vessel (venule). Draw and label the different types of blood vessels. Use arrows to show the direction of blood flow.
12. Return the goldfish to the aquarium as soon as you have completed the investigation. Replace the stage clips on the microscope.

OBSERVATIONS

1. Describe the blood cells' shape and color.
2. Describe the movement of blood through a capillary.
3. In which type of blood vessel does the blood seem to pulsate? In which type of blood vessel does the blood seem to flow smoothly and at a uniform rate?
4. Describe the appearance of the blood vessels.

ANALYSIS AND CONCLUSIONS

1. Explain why the capillaries are so small.
2. Why does blood in arterioles flow unevenly?
3. How does blood travel through capillaries, arterioles, and venules?

STUDENT STUDY GUIDE

SUMMARIZING THE CONCEPTS

The key concepts in each section of this chapter are listed below to help you review the chapter content. Make sure you understand each concept and its relationship to other concepts and to the theme of this chapter.

41–1 The Circulatory System

- Blood, the heart, and blood vessels make up the circulatory system.
- The heart, which pumps blood through the circulatory system, has four chambers: two atria and two ventricles.
- Arteries carry blood from the heart, and veins carry blood to the heart. Capillaries connect arteries and veins.
- Pulmonary circulation carries blood between the heart and the lungs. Systemic circulation carries blood between the heart and the rest of the body.
- The lymphatic system collects the fluid that is lost by blood and returns it to the circulatory system.

41–2 Blood

- Blood transports nutrients, dissolved gases, enzymes, hormones, and waste products; regulates body temperature, electrolytes, and pH; protects the body from invaders; and restricts the loss of fluid.
- Blood, which is a type of connective tissue, is made up of a liquid portion called plasma and a cellular portion composed of red blood cells, white blood cells, and platelets.

41–3 The Excretory System

- The skin, lungs, and kidneys—along with their associated organs—make up the excretory system, which removes metabolic wastes from the body.
- The kidneys, which are the main organs of the excretory system, regulate the fluid and salt balance in the body.
- The basic functional unit of the kidney is the nephron, which is composed of the glomerulus, Bowman's capsule, and tubules. Within the nephron, metabolic wastes are removed by the processes of filtration and reabsorption.

REVIEWING KEY TERMS

Vocabulary terms are important to your understanding of biology. The key terms listed below are those you should be especially familiar with. Review these terms and their meanings. Then use each term in a complete sentence. If you are not sure of a term's meaning, return to the appropriate section and review its definition.

41–1 The Circulatory System

heart
circulatory system
atrium
ventricle
vena cava
artery
aorta
capillary
vein
pulmonary circulation
systemic circulation
blood pressure
lymphatic system

41–2 Blood

blood
plasma
red blood cell
white blood cell
platelet

41–3 The Excretory System

excretory system
kidney
ureter
urinary bladder
nephron
glomerulus
Bowman's capsule
filtration
reabsorption
urethra

CHAPTER REVIEW

CONTENT REVIEW

Multiple Choice

Choose the letter of the answer that best completes each statement.

1. About 90 percent of plasma is composed of
   a. salts. c. water.
   b. proteins. d. tissues.
2. The color of red blood cells comes from a pigment called
   a. thrombin. c. hemoglobin.
   b. globulin. d. albumin.
3. Blood traveling to capillaries in the arm leaves the heart from the
   a. left atrium. c. left ventricle.
   b. right atrium. d. right ventricle.
4. If the blood flow in a vessel is toward the heart, then the vessel is known as a (an)
   a. atrium. c. artery.
   b. ventricle. d. vein.
5. Circulation to and from the lungs is
   a. lymphatic circulation.
   b. pulmonary circulation.
   c. coronary circulation.
   d. systemic circulation.
6. Which are excretory organs?
   a. skin and heart c. liver and pancreas
   b. lungs and kidneys d. lungs and heart
7. The kidney's basic functional unit is the
   a. nephron. c. ureter.
   b. Bowman's capsule. d. glomerulus.
8. Filtration of the blood in the kidney occurs at the
   a. urethra. c. Bowman's capsule.
   b. urinary bladder. d. loop of Henle.

True or False

Determine whether each statement is true or false. If it is true, write "true." If it is false, change the underlined word or words to make the statement true.

1. The liquid portion of the blood is called plasma.
2. The blood cell fragments that play a role in blood clotting are the leukocytes.
3. The largest artery in the body is the pulmonary artery.
4. Urine is carried from the kidneys to the urinary bladder by the urethras.
5. A network of capillaries in a Bowman's capsule is known as a nephron.
6. Urine is eliminated from the urinary bladder through the ureter.
7. The fluid that is lost by the blood is called lymph.
8. The blood vessels that contain valves are the capillaries.

Word Relationships

An analogy is a relationship between two pairs of words or phrases generally written in the following manner: a:b::c:d. The symbol : is read "is to," and the symbol :: is read "as." For example, cat:animal::rose:plant is read "cat is to animal as rose is to plant."

In the analogies that follow, a word or phrase is missing. Complete each analogy by providing the missing word or phrase.

1. away from the heart:artery::to the heart: ______________
2. left ventricle:aorta::right ventricle: ______________
3. hemoglobin:carrying oxygen::fibrinogen: ______________
4. pumping chamber:ventricle::receiving chamber: ______________

CONCEPT MASTERY

Use your understanding of the concepts developed in the chapter to answer each of the following in a brief paragraph.

1. How is the structure of an artery, a vein, and a capillary adapted to its function?
2. Explain how the lymphatic system protects the body.
3. Trace the path that blood follows in pulmonary circulation and in systemic circulation.
4. Explain why blood is considered a connective tissue.
5. Briefly describe the events of the clotting process.
6. Explain why red blood cells are the most numerous of the blood cells and why they have such a short life span.
7. Why is the blood pressure highest in the aorta and lowest in the venae cavae?
8. How is heartbeat rate controlled?
9. How does the lymphatic system differ from the circulatory system?
10. Trace the path of glucose and urea through the kidney.
11. Explain why it is important to replace the ventricles in a heart transplant.
12. Why does the left ventricle have a thicker wall than the right ventricle?
13. Explain why the tricuspid and bicuspid valves are also known as atrioventricular valves.

CRITICAL AND CREATIVE THINKING

Discuss each of the following in a brief paragraph.

1. **Applying concepts** Some infants are born with a small hole in the septum of the heart. Explain how this situation will affect the infant. How do you think this problem could be corrected?
2. **Relating facts** Atherosclerosis is a disorder in which deposits of cholesterol and fatty materials collect on the inner walls of the arteries. How does this disorder affect the circulatory system?
3. **Making inferences** Explain why it is possible that kidney failure can be fatal even though an individual's heart is still strong.
4. **Relating cause and effect** Would urine contain more or less water on a hot day? Explain your answer.
5. **Making predictions** Imagine that you are a medical student and your professor has asked you what would happen to a patient whose renal arteries have become greatly narrowed. How would you respond?

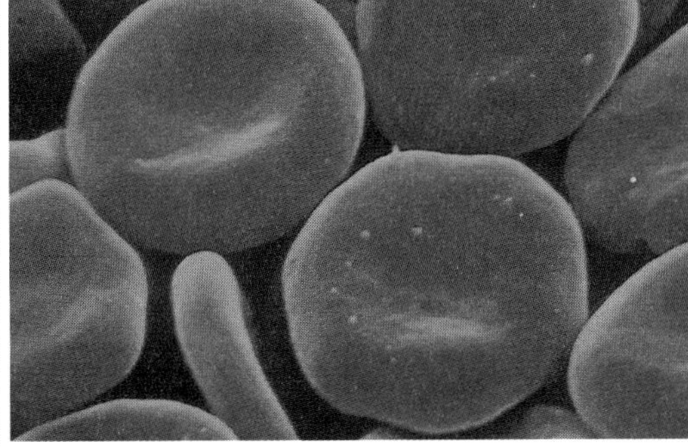

6. **Sequencing events** Trace the course of a single red blood cell from the right ventricle to the right atrium.
7. **Relating concepts** Could a person adrift on a life raft survive by drinking sea water? Explain your answer.
8. **Using the writing process** Pretend that you have hitched a ride on a red blood cell. Write a short description of your adventures through the circulatory system.

CHAPTER 42

Endocrine System

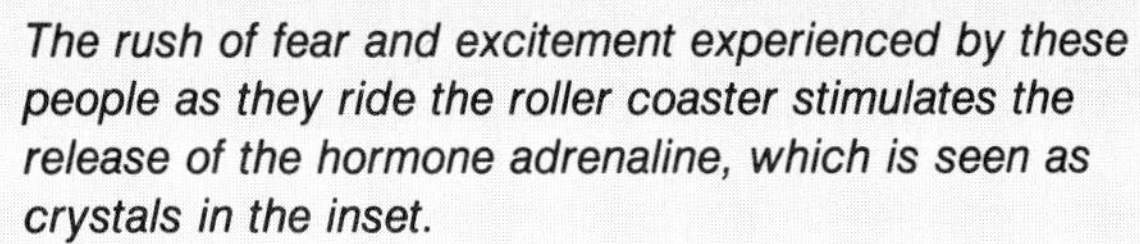

The rush of fear and excitement experienced by these people as they ride the roller coaster stimulates the release of the hormone adrenaline, which is seen as crystals in the inset.

Biological communications systems can be compared to those in human societies. We are all familiar with broadcast communications such as radio and television. The waves carrying the messages travel through the air to special receivers that tune in to the frequency of the messages. In this way, a radio or television broadcast can be sent to thousands or millions of homes at the same time.

The biological communications system that resembles a radio or television communications system is the endocrine system. Like broadcast signals, the messages sent by the endocrine system can affect millions of cells that are some distance away. How does the endocrine system "broadcast" its messages, and what effects do the messages have on the body's cells? Read on to find out the answers to these questions.

CHAPTER OUTLINE

42–1 Endocrine Glands

Section Objectives

- Describe the function of the endocrine system.
- Identify the major endocrine glands and the function of each.

As you may recall from Chapter 37, the nervous system regulates many of the body's activities. The nervous system, however, is only one of the body's regulatory systems. The **endocrine system** is the other regulatory system. **The endocrine system is composed of glands that secrete their products, called hormones, into the bloodstream.**

The endocrine system produces **hormones**, or chemical messengers, that travel through the bloodstream and exert their effects some distance from where they are produced. Hormones bind to receptors on the cells and affect the behavior of the cells. Cells that have receptors for a particular hormone are called **target cells**.

Although the endocrine system and the nervous system regulate the activities of the body, they do so in different ways. In general, the body's responses to hormones are slower and longer lasting than the responses to nerve impulses. For example, it may take several minutes, several hours, or even several days for a hormone to have its full effect on its target cells. A nerve impulse, on the other hand, may take only several seconds to reach and affect its target cells.

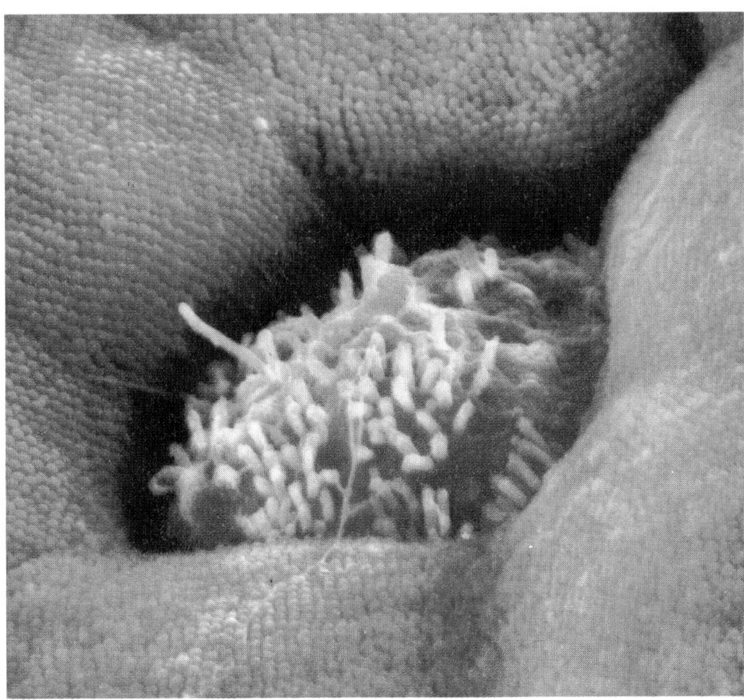

Figure 42–1 *The tiny rod-shaped filaments sticking out of this target cell in the stomach contain receptors to which the hormone gastrin binds. Gastrin stimulates the production of gastric juice.*

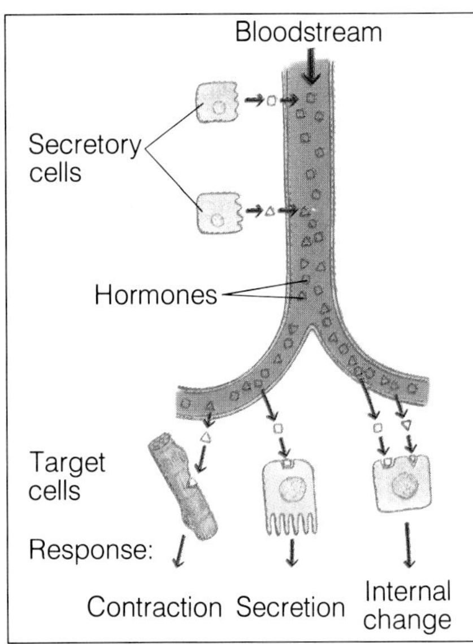

Figure 42–2 In the endocrine system, hormones diffuse into the bloodstream and are carried throughout the body to target cells.

The major hormone-producing organs of the endocrine system are the **endocrine glands**. A gland is an organ that produces a secretion, or a substance made inside a cell and released from that cell. Endocrine glands are only one group of glands that produce secretions. The other group is called the **exocrine glands**. Exocrine glands release their secretions through tubelike structures called ducts. For this reason, exocrine glands are also known as duct glands. Two examples of exocrine glands are the sweat glands and the digestive glands. Unlike exocrine glands, endocrine glands do not have ducts. Thus they are called ductless glands. Endocrine glands release their secretions (hormones) directly into the bloodstream.

Figure 42–3 shows the location of the major endocrine glands. As you can see, the endocrine glands are scattered throughout the body and generally do not have direct connections to one another. Like signals from a broadcast station that are beamed throughout the country, the hormones released from the endocrine glands travel throughout the body, reaching almost every cell.

Figure 42–3 According to this illustration, which hormone-producing gland of the endocrine system is located above each kidney?

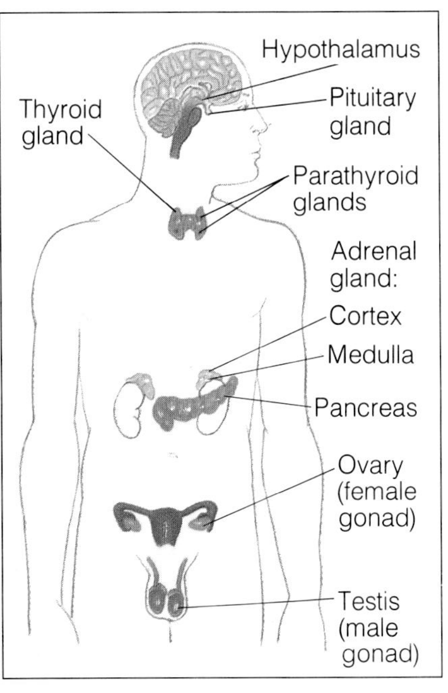

Thyroid Gland

The **thyroid gland** is located at the base of the neck and wraps around the upper part of the trachea just below the larynx. See Figure 42–4. The thyroid gland produces a hormone called thyroxine, which is an amino acid to which four iodine atoms are attached. Because iodine is needed for the production of thyroxine, it must be included in the diet. Fish and other seafood are good sources of iodine. But if these foods are not your favorites, do not worry. You can get the small amount of iodine your body needs from table salt, provided it is iodized salt, or salt to which small amounts of iodine have been added.

Thyroxine affects nearly all the cells of the body by regulating their metabolic rate. Increased levels of thyroxine cause an increase in the cellular respiration rate, which means the cells produce more energy and become more active. Decreased levels of thyroxine cause a decrease in the cellular respiration rate. Cells produce less energy and become less active.

If the thyroid gland produces too much thyroxine, a condition called hyperthyroidism (high-per-THIGH-roid-ihz-uhm) occurs. Hyperthyroidism results in nervousness, elevated body temperature, increased heart and metabolic rates, increased blood pressure, and weight loss. This condition can be treated by the surgical removal of part of the gland or by the use of certain drugs that slow down the production of thyroxine.

If the thyroid gland does not make enough thyroxine, a condition called hypothyroidism (high-poh-THIGH-roid-ihz-uhm) results. Lower metabolic rates and body temperature, lack of energy, and weight gain are characteristics of this

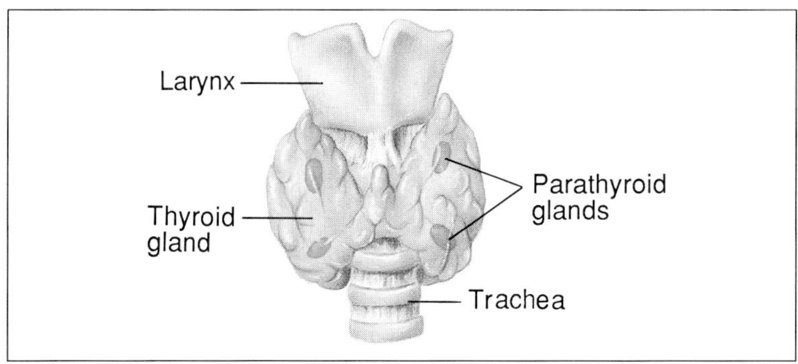

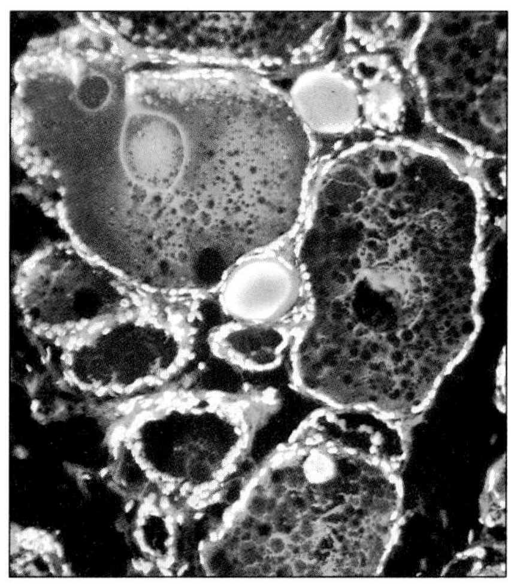

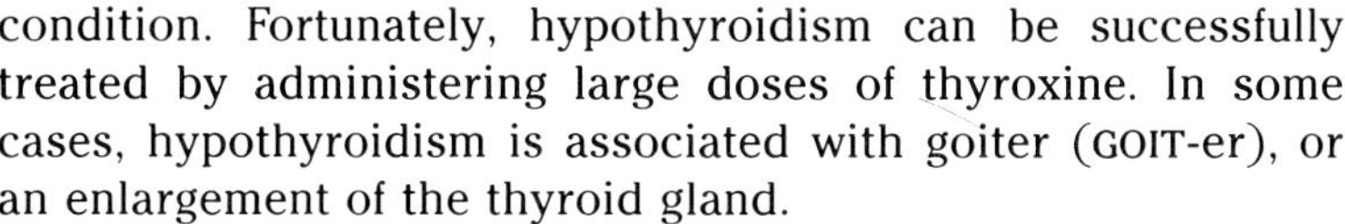

Figure 42–4 *The thyroid gland is a butterfly-shaped organ that wraps around the front of the trachea (windpipe). The electron micrograph shows a section of thyroid tissue in which the hormone thyroxine is formed.*

condition. Fortunately, hypothyroidism can be successfully treated by administering large doses of thyroxine. In some cases, hypothyroidism is associated with goiter (GOIT-er), or an enlargement of the thyroid gland.

The detection of hypothyroidism in infants is especially important. In infancy, hypothyroidism affects the normal development of the skeletal, muscular, and nervous systems and results in a condition called cretinism (KREET-'n-ihz-uhm). Cretinism is characterized by dwarfism and mental retardation. If detected in time, the most serious aspects of the disorder can be prevented by treatment with thyroxine.

In addition to thyroxine, the thyroid gland secretes a hormone called calcitonin (kal-sih-TOH-nihn). Calcitonin is produced by specialized cells (C cells) within the thyroid gland. The major action of calcitonin is to regulate the level of calcium in the blood.

Parathyroid Glands

The **parathyroid glands** are attached to or embedded in the back surface of the thyroid gland. See Figure 42–4. There are usually four parathyroid glands. These glands secrete a hormone called parathyroid hormone (PTH). PTH regulates the calcium levels in the blood by increasing the reabsorption of calcium in the kidneys (less calcium is excreted) and by increasing the uptake of calcium from the digestive system. Together with calcitonin and vitamin D, parathyroid hormone is important in promoting proper nerve and muscle function as well as maintaining bone structure.

As part of the treatment for hyperthyroidism, the parathyroid glands are sometimes surgically removed with the thyroid gland. This action causes a drop in the level of calcium in the blood, which may result in violent muscular spasms (tetany) and contractions. These symptoms can be relieved by the administration of large amounts of PTH and injections of calcium.

Figure 42–5 *Embedded within the thyroid gland, the parathyroids produce the parathyroid hormone that regulates the amount of calcium in the blood. What thyroid hormone has an effect opposite to that of the parathyroid hormone?*

Gland: Hormone	Action
Thyroid: Thyroxine, other thyroxinelike hormones	Stimulate and maintain metabolic activities
Thyroid: Calcitonin	Inhibits release of calcium from bone
Parathyroid: Parathyroid hormone (PTH)	Stimulates release of calcium from bone

Adrenal Glands

The **adrenal glands** are pyramid-shaped structures that sit on top of the kidneys, one gland on each kidney. The word adrenal, in fact, means near the kidneys. Because each adrenal gland is composed of two very different types of tissue, it is divided into two parts. The outer part is the adrenal cortex and the inner part is the adrenal medulla.

THE ADRENAL CORTEX The **adrenal cortex** makes up about 80 percent of the mass of the gland. It produces more than two dozen hormones called corticosteroids (kor-tih-koh-STIHR-oidz), which are essential for normal body function. One of these hormones is aldosterone (al-DAHS-tuh-rohn), which regulates the reabsorption of sodium and the excretion of potassium by the kidneys. Another hormone called cortisol (KORT-uh-sohl) helps to control the rate of metabolism of carbohydrates, fats, and proteins. In addition, cortisol helps people cope with stress.

A decrease in the activity of the adrenal cortex can result in a condition known as Addison disease. Some symptoms of this condition include weight loss, low blood pressure, and general weakness. In some cases, death may occur because of heart failure. Former President John F. Kennedy suffered from Addison disease and received regular doses of adrenal cortical hormones to control the symptoms.

An increase in the activity of the adrenal cortex can result in a condition called Cushing syndrome. Symptoms of this condition include obesity, increased blood sugar levels, high blood pressure, and weakening of bones. Treatment of Cushing syndrome involves decreasing the secretion of the hyperactive hormone, if possible.

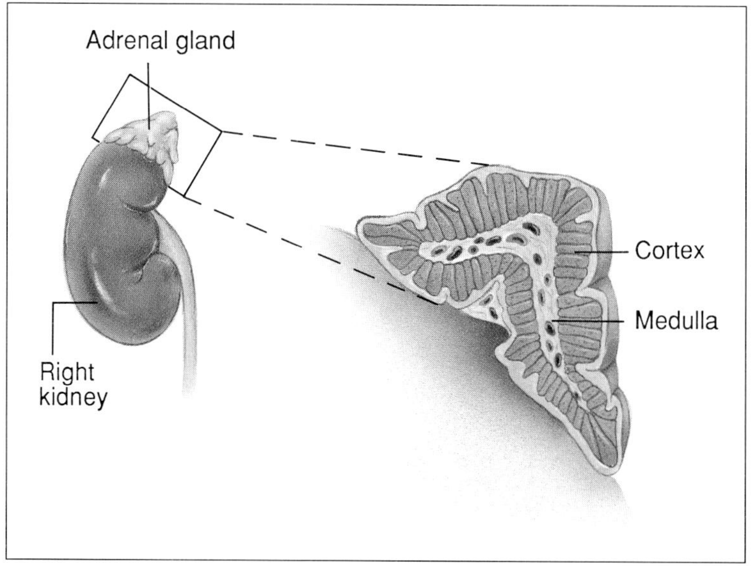

Figure 42–6 *The adrenal glands, each of which is located atop a kidney, are divided into an outer part called the adrenal cortex and an inner part called the adrenal medulla.*

THE ADRENAL MEDULLA The **adrenal medulla** is a specialized part of the sympathetic nervous system. For this reason, the adrenaline and noradrenaline it secretes are called neurohormones. Adrenaline is sometimes known as epinephrine (ehp-uh-NEHF-rihn). The words adrenaline and epinephrine are derived from Latin and Greek words, respectively, and mean "near the kidneys." Adrenaline, which is more powerful in its action than noradrenaline, makes up about 80 percent of the total secretion of the adrenal medulla.

When the body is confronted with a threatening "fight or flight" situation, nerve impulses from the sympathetic neurons enter and stimulate cells of the adrenal medulla. The result is an increase in the secretion of adrenaline and noradrenaline. Adrenaline increases heart rate, blood pressure, and blood supply to skeletal muscles. It also increases the conversion of glycogen to glucose and stimulates the rate of metabolism. Noradrenaline stimulates the heart muscle. These actions result in a general increase in body activity, which can serve as preparation for intense physical activity. The next time you take an exam, remember that your rapidly beating heart and perspiring hands are the results of your adrenal medulla at work!

Gland: Hormone	Action
Adrenal cortex: Aldosterone	Affects water and salt balance by the reabsorption of sodium and the excretion of potassium
Adrenal cortex: Cortisol, other corticosteroids	Affect carbohydrate, protein, and fat metabolism
Adrenal medulla: Adrenaline and noradrenaline	Increase blood glucose level, dilate or constrict specific blood vessels, increase rate and strength of heartbeat
Ovary: Estrogens	Develop and maintain female sex characteristics, initiate buildup of uterine lining
Ovary: Progesterone	Promotes continued growth of uterine lining
Testis: Androgens	Support sperm development, develop and maintain male sex characteristics

Figure 42–7 *The hormones secreted by the adrenal glands and reproductive glands (ovary and testis) regulate many of the body's activities.*

Reproductive Glands

The **gonads** are the body's reproductive glands. They serve two important functions. The female gonads, or **ovaries**, produce eggs (ova). The male gonads, or **testes** (TEHS-teez; singular: testis), produce sperm. The gonads also produce sex hormones that affect cells throughout the body.

The ovaries produce the female sex hormones, the estrogens (EHS-truh-jehnz) and progesterone (proh-JEHS-ter-ohn). Estrogens are required for the development of ova and for the formation of the physical characteristics associated with the female. These characteristics include the development of the female reproductive system, widening of the hips, and development of the breasts. Progesterone prepares the uterus for the arrival of a developing embryo.

The testes produce androgens, or the male sex hormones. Androgens are required for normal sperm production and the development of physical characteristics associated with the male. These characteristics include the growth of facial hair, increase in body size, and deepening of the voice.

The male and female sex hormones have important functions in the process of reproduction. For this reason they will be discussed in more detail in Chapter 43.

Pancreas

The **pancreas** is a most unusual gland. Located just behind the stomach, the pancreas seems to be a single gland—but its appearance is deceiving! You may recall from Chapter 39 that

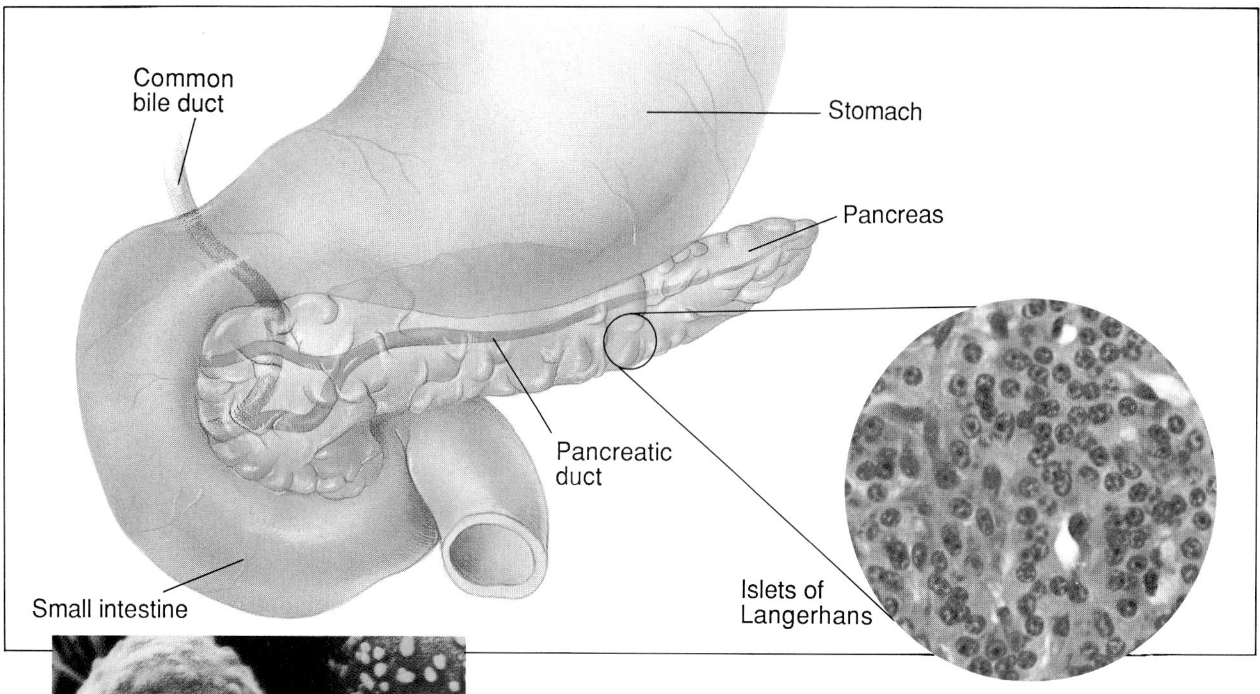

Figure 42–8 *Within the pancreas are groups of cells called the islets of Langerhans (inset). An islet of Langerhans can be seen as a large circular object in the electron micrograph. Each islet is composed of beta cells, which secrete insulin, and alpha cells, which secrete glucagon.*

the pancreas produces pancreatic fluid, which leaves the pancreas by means of a duct and empties into the digestive system. Once in the digestive system, the pancreatic fluid helps break down food. Because the pancreas has a duct, it is an exocrine gland. However, the pancreas also releases hormones into the blood. Therefore, it is also an endocrine gland.

The hormone-producing portion of the pancreas consists of clusters of cells that resemble islands. For this reason, their discoverer, the German anatomist Paul Langerhans, called them **islets of Langerhans.**

Each islet is composed of beta cells, which secrete insulin, and alpha cells, which secrete glucagon. Insulin and glucagon regulate the metabolism of blood glucose (sugar). Because these two hormones have opposite effects, it is vital that a proper balance between them is maintained by the body.

INSULIN When blood glucose levels rise, such as after eating a meal, beta cells release insulin. Insulin stimulates the ability of its target cells to take up and use glucose. Insulin's major target cells are those of the liver, skeletal muscles, and fat (adipose) tissue. Glucose molecules that are not immediately used as an energy source are stored as glycogen in the liver and skeletal muscles. In fat tissue, excess glucose molecules are converted to fat. Thus insulin prevents the level of glucose in the blood from rising immediately after a meal. It also ensures that excess glucose will be stored by the body for further use.

GLUCAGON Within one or two hours after eating, when the level of blood glucose drops, alpha cells release glucagon from the pancreas. In general, glucagon stimulates the cells of the liver and skeletal muscles to break down glycogen and increase glucose levels in the blood. Glucagon also causes fat cells to break down fats so that they can be used for the production of carbohydrates. These actions make more chemical energy available to the body and help raise the blood glucose level to normal.

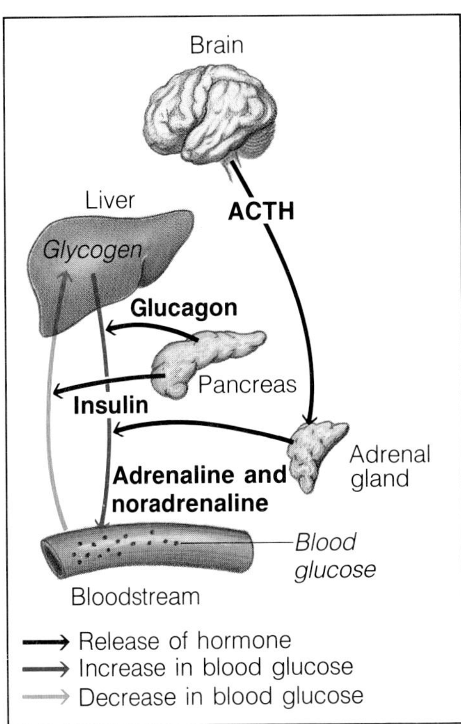

Figure 42–9 *This illustration shows the regulation of blood glucose by hormones. When blood glucose levels are low, the pancreas releases glucagon, which stimulates the breakdown of glycogen and the release of glucose from the liver. When blood glucose levels are high, the pancreas releases insulin, which removes glucose from the blood by increasing its uptake by cells and its conversion to glycogen.*

DIABETES MELLITUS When there is an undersecretion of insulin, a condition called diabetes mellitus (digh-uh-BEET-eez muh-LIGHT-uhs) occurs. In diabetes mellitus, the amount of glucose in the blood is so high that the kidneys cannot reabsorb all of the glucose. As a result, glucose is excreted in the urine. You may recall from Chapter 41 that glucose is not normally present in urine. Thus its presence is a symptom that is used by doctors to confirm diabetes mellitus.

There are two principal types of diabetes mellitus. Juvenile-onset diabetes, as its name implies, most commonly develops in people before the age of 25. In this type of diabetes, also known as Type I, there is little or no secretion of insulin. The treatment includes a combination of strict diet control and daily injections of insulin. Adult-onset, or Type II, diabetes, most commonly develops in people after the age of 40. Although people with adult-onset diabetes produce normal amounts of insulin, their cells are unable to respond to the hormone properly because the cells lack the necessary number of insulin receptors. Adult-onset diabetes, especially in its early stages, can be controlled by diet.

Pituitary Gland and Hypothalamus

The **pituitary gland** is a bean-sized structure that dangles on a slender stalk of tissue at the base of the skull. The gland is divided into two parts: the anterior pituitary and the posterior pituitary. See Figure 42–10. The pituitary gland secretes nine major hormones that directly regulate many body functions. It also controls the release of hormones by several other endocrine glands.

Figure 42–10 *The pituitary gland, which lies under the hypothalamus, is located at the base of the brain in the center of the skull.*

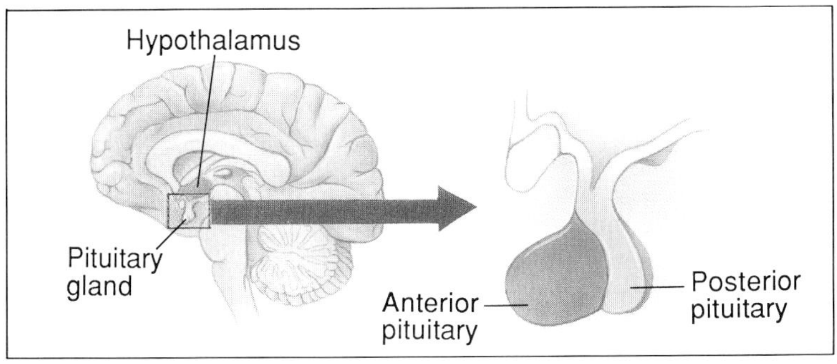

Pituitary: Hormone	Action
Posterior: Antidiuretic hormone (ADH)	Controls water excretion
Posterior: Oxytocin	Stimulates uterine contraction, milk release
Anterior: Follicle-stimulating hormone (FSH)	Stimulates follicle maturation in females and sperm production in males
Anterior: Luteinizing hormone (LH)	Stimulates ovulation and corpus luteum formation in females and androgen secretion in males
Anterior: Thyroid-stimulating hormone (TSH)	Stimulates and maintains metabolic activities
Anterior: Adrenocoticotrophic hormone (ACTH)	Stimulates adrenal cortex
Anterior: Growth hormone (GH) or somatotropin	Stimulates bone growth, inhibits glucose oxidation, promotes fatty acid breakdown
Anterior: Prolactin	Stimulates milk production
Anterior: Melanocyte-stimulating hormone (MSH)	Increases synthesis of melanin

Figure 42–11 *The pituitary gland is divided into the anterior pituitary and the posterior pituitary. What effect does ACTH have on the body?*

POSTERIOR PITUITARY The **posterior pituitary** secretes antidiuretic (an-tigh-digh-yoo-REHT-ihk) hormone (ADH) and oxytocin (ahks-ih-TOH-sihn). ADH stimulates the kidneys to reabsorb more water from the collecting tubules that comprise the organs. In females, oxytocin stimulates the contractions of smooth muscles in the uterus, which help push a baby out of the mother during childbirth. Oxytocin also causes the release of milk from the breasts of a nursing mother. Oxytocin is found in males, too, but its function is not known.

ANTERIOR PITUITARY The remaining seven hormones are produced by the **anterior pituitary**. Two of these—follicle-stimulating hormone (FSH) and luteinizing (LOOT-ee-ihn-ighz-ihng) hormone (LH)—control the growth, development, and functioning of the ovaries and testes (gonads).

The third hormone secreted by the anterior pituitary is thyroid-stimulating hormone (TSH). TSH stimulates the synthesis and release of thyroxine from the thyroid gland. Adrenocorticotropic (uh-dree-noh-kor-tih-koh-TROHP-ihk) hormone, also known as ACTH, is the fourth hormone secreted by the anterior pituitary. ACTH stimulates the release of hormones from the adrenal cortex.

Growth hormone (GH), the fifth anterior pituitary hormone, is also known as somatotropin (suh-maht-uh-TROHP-uhn). Growth hormone stimulates protein synthesis and growth in cells throughout the body. Although almost all cells respond to levels of GH, skeletal muscle cells and cartilage cells are particularly sensitive. As you might expect, GH is extremely important during the first 15 years of life, when its production ensures normal body growth.

The sixth hormone secreted by the anterior pituitary is prolactin, which plays an important role in the production of milk in pregnant females. Prolactin has no known function in males. As its name indicates, melanocyte-stimulating hormone (MSH), the seventh anterior pituitary hormone, stimulates the melanocytes of the skin, increasing their production of the dark pigment melanin.

PITUITARY GLAND DISORDERS The release of growth hormone (GH) from the anterior pituitary is associated with the normal growing years, from birth to age 15 or 16. If too much GH is produced, the body will grow too fast and a condition called giantism will result. If too little GH is produced, a condition known as pituitary dwarfism occurs. Although people who suffer from pituitary dwarfism are proportionately smaller than the average-sized person, the development of their nervous system is not affected. The symptoms of pituitary dwarfism can be treated in childhood by administering growth hormone. Prior to the advent of genetic engineering, growth hormone was in short supply. Today, however, genetically engineered bacteria are able to produce GH in large quantities.

Normally, the production of growth hormone decreases dramatically in the late teens, when body growth is complete. Sometimes, however, the anterior pituitary fails to stop producing GH and a disorder known as acromegaly (ak-roh-MEHG-uh-lee) results. In this disorder, there is no increase in height because the growth plates of bones have ossified. However, there is an increase in the diameter of fingers, toes, hands, and feet. There is also formation of bony ridges over the eyes and enlargement of the jaw. Treatment for acromegaly involves reducing the levels of growth hormone by surgery, radiation, or hormone therapy.

Other pituitary gland disorders can lead to underactivity of the adrenal cortex, problems with thyroid activity, or failure to produce sex hormones. Each of these disorders has serious medical consequences.

THE HYPOTHALAMUS Attached to the posterior pituitary is a portion of the brain called the **hypothalamus** (high-poh-THAL-uh-muhs). The hypothalamus controls the secretions of the pituitary gland. In turn, the activity of the hypothalamus is influenced by the levels of the hormones in the blood and by sensory information that enters the central nervous system. The hypothalamus and the pituitary gland are the major areas where the nervous system and the endocrine system interact. Indeed, a major portion of the pituitary gland is an extension of the hypothalamus.

In the hypothalamus, special neurons called neurosecretory cells extend their axons into the posterior pituitary. When the neurosecretory cells are stimulated, the vesicles located at the ends of the axon terminals release their contents (ADH and oxytocin). Following their release from the neurosecretory cells in the posterior pituitary, ADH and oxytocin diffuse into capillaries, thus entering the general circulation of blood.

The neurosecretory cells not only allow the hypothalamus to control the posterior pituitary, they also automatically coordinate its activity with the rest of the body. Does the anterior pituitary work in the same way?

For many years, scientists searched for a connection between the hypothalamus and the anterior pituitary. Their efforts were seemingly in vain, for they found no connection. About 30 years ago, however, some scientists remembered that there was a tiny blood vessel that passed through the hypothalamus on its way to the anterior pituitary. They hypothesized that the hypothalamus might control the anterior pituitary by releasing substances through this blood vessel into the anterior pituitary.

Today we know that the hypothalamus produces tiny amounts of special hormones called releasing hormones. The releasing hormones are secreted directly into capillaries and then into veins to yet another network of capillaries. Here the releasing hormones enter the anterior pituitary, where they affect the production of anterior pituitary hormones.

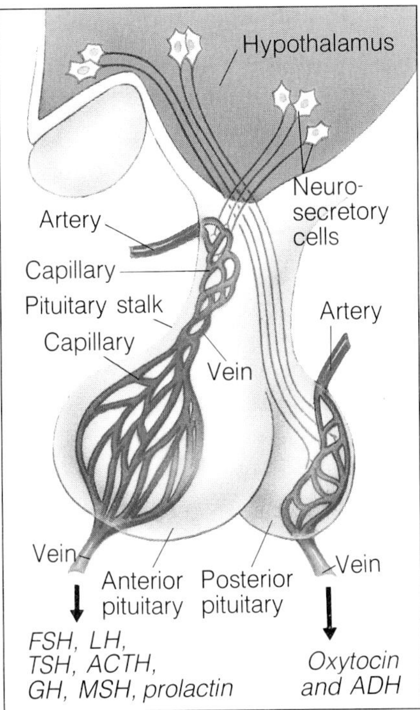

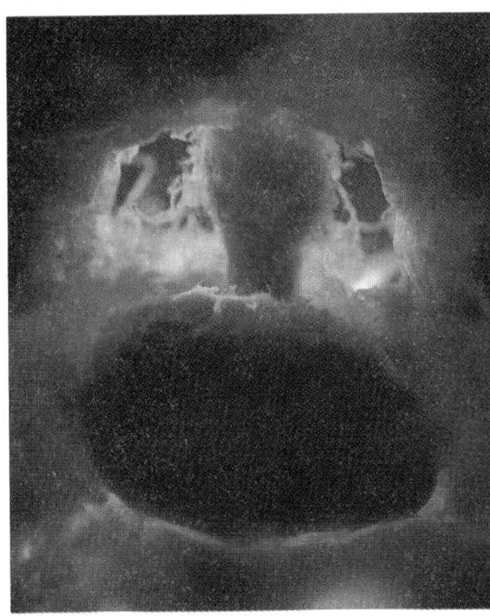

Figure 42–12 *The bean-shaped structure in the photograph is the pituitary gland, which is connected to the hypothalamus by a stalk. The hypothalamus coordinates the activities of the endocrine and nervous systems.*

Anabolic Steroids

Testosterone is a male sex hormone that promotes protein synthesis in most tissues of the body. As a result, skeletal muscle can increase in mass. Because this process stimulates growth and synthesis, it is said to be anabolic. Thus testosterone is known as an anabolic steroid.

Some athletes, especially weight lifters, believe that if normal levels of testosterone increase muscle mass, then increased levels will work even better. By ingesting synthetic anabolic steroids, these athletes have been risking their health and even their lives in the hope of gaining an edge over their competitors.

Taken in large quantities over long periods of time, anabolic steroids have grave side effects. In athletes of both sexes, anabolic steroids can stunt growth. They can damage the liver, and they may cause cancer. Their use is also linked to strokes and heart disease. In males, anabolic steroids sometimes stop the production of testosterone, resulting in a decrease in the size of the testes and the inability to produce sperm. In females, anabolic steroids can interfere with the menstrual cycle and may lead to the development of male sex characteristics, including a deep voice, excessive facial hair, and enlarged muscles.

Athletes who use anabolic steroids endanger their lives as well as their chances of winning. The sprinter Ben Johnson was stripped of his Olympic Gold Medal in 1988 when traces of anabolic steroids were found in his system.

42-1 SECTION REVIEW

1. What is the function of the endocrine system?
2. List the major endocrine glands and give the function of each.
3. How does an endocrine gland differ from an exocrine gland?
4. Describe how the hypothalamus regulates the anterior and posterior pituitary.
5. The heartbeat of a swimmer increases significantly both before and during a swim meet. Explain this.

42–2 Control of the Endocrine System

Section Objectives

- Describe the negative-feedback mechanism.
- Compare polypeptide and steroid hormones.
- Discuss the action of prostaglandins.

As powerful as they are, the concentrations of hormones must be closely monitored in order to keep the functions of different organs in balance. Even though we may think of the endocrine system as one of the master regulators of the body, it too must be controlled. **Like most systems of the body, the endocrine system is regulated by a negative-feedback mechanism that functions to maintain homeostasis, or the maintenance of a relatively constant internal environment.**

Negative-Feedback Mechanism

A **negative-feedback mechanism** occurs when an increase in a substance inhibits the process leading to the increase. Although this sounds complicated, it is actually rather simple.

Consider a thermostatically controlled heating and cooling system found in many homes. A thermostat controls the system in order to keep the temperature within acceptable limits. Suppose you set the thermostat to 20°C. If the temperature in your home rises above 20°C, the thermostat turns on the air-conditioner. The cooling effect produced by the air-conditioner brings the temperature back down to 20°C. Now the thermostat shuts the air-conditioner off. If the temperature falls below 20°C, the thermostat turns on the heater rather than the air-conditioner. The heater, which has a warming effect, remains on until the temperature again returns to the desired level (20°C). In this way, the thermostat controls the internal temperature of your home. In a manner similar to this, a negative-feedback mechanism automatically controls the levels of hormones in the body. The following example will help you understand exactly how this mechanism works.

Recall that the production of hormones in the anterior pituitary is regulated by the hypothalamus. One of the hormones, thyroid-stimulating hormone (TSH), stimulates the activity of the thyroid gland, causing it to release thyroxine into the bloodstream. An increase in the level of thyroxine in the blood stimulates cells throughout the body to increase their metabolic activity. When the level of thyroxine in the blood drops, the cells' metabolic activity decreases.

The hypothalamus is sensitive to body temperature as well as to the level of thyroxine in the blood. Body temperature decreases as metabolic activity decreases. When the hypothalamus is activated, either by lowered body temperature or lowered thyroxine level, it produces a releasing hormone, or factor, that acts on the anterior pituitary. The anterior pituitary, in turn, releases TSH into the bloodstream.

As the level of TSH in the blood increases, the thyroid gland is stimulated and steps up the rate at which it releases thyroxine into the bloodstream. Increasing levels of thyroxine

Figure 42–13 The production of many hormones is regulated by the complicated negative-feedback mechanism involving the pituitary gland and the hypothalamus.

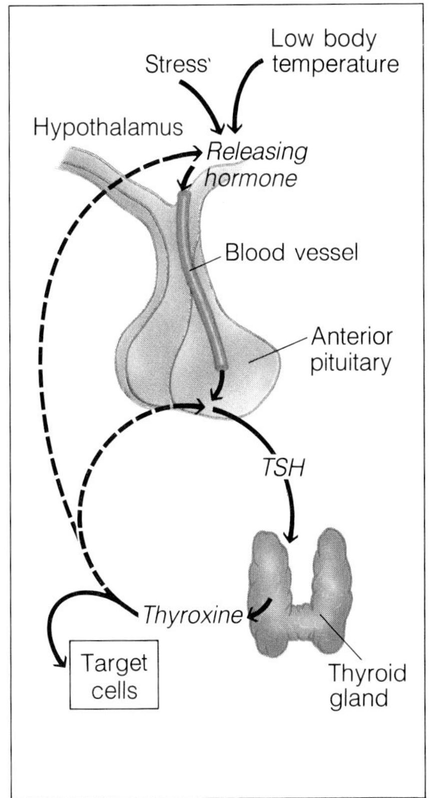

in the blood speed up metabolism in cells throughout the body. As a result, there is an increase in body temperature. These changes in the body cause the hypothalamus to react negatively by lowering the rate at which it sends releasing hormone to the anterior pituitary.

As you can see, the negative-feedback mechanism is automatic and self-regulating. Similar negative-feedback mechanisms exist to control the levels of other hormones.

Hormone Action

The hormones that are produced by the endocrine system fall into two general groups. Polypeptide hormones, such as glucagon and thyroxine, are large proteins composed of chains of amino acids. Steroid hormones, such as progesterone, are lipids that are produced from cholesterol. How do these two groups of hormones affect the functions of their target cells? There are two basic patterns of hormone action that we understand well enough to explain here.

Polypeptide hormones do not enter their target cells. Instead, they bind to receptors on the cell membrane. See Figure 42–14. The binding of these hormones activates enzymes attached to the inner surface of the cell membrane. Because the polypeptide hormones are the first substances to carry a signal to the cell membrane, they are called first messengers. The activated enzymes then convert ATP into molecules known as cyclic AMP (cAMP), which functions as a second messenger.

From the cell membrane, cAMP diffuses through the target cell's cytoplasm, binding to and activating other enzymes. As more hormones bind to their receptors on the cell membrane, the level of cAMP within the target cell increases. Because different target cells respond in different ways to the change in cAMP levels, cells may be stimulated to speed up or slow down certain cellular activities. For example, the binding of adrenaline to liver cell membranes causes an increase in cAMP. This increase activates the enzymes that break down glycogen to glucose and then release glucose into the bloodstream. As you can

Figure 42–14 *The hormones produced by the endocrine system fall into two groups, depending upon their mechanism of hormone action. In A, polypeptide hormones affect the target cell by means of receptor molecules embedded in the cell membrane. In B, steroid hormones pass through the cell membrane and combine with receptor molecules in the cytoplasm, forming a hormone-receptor complex.*

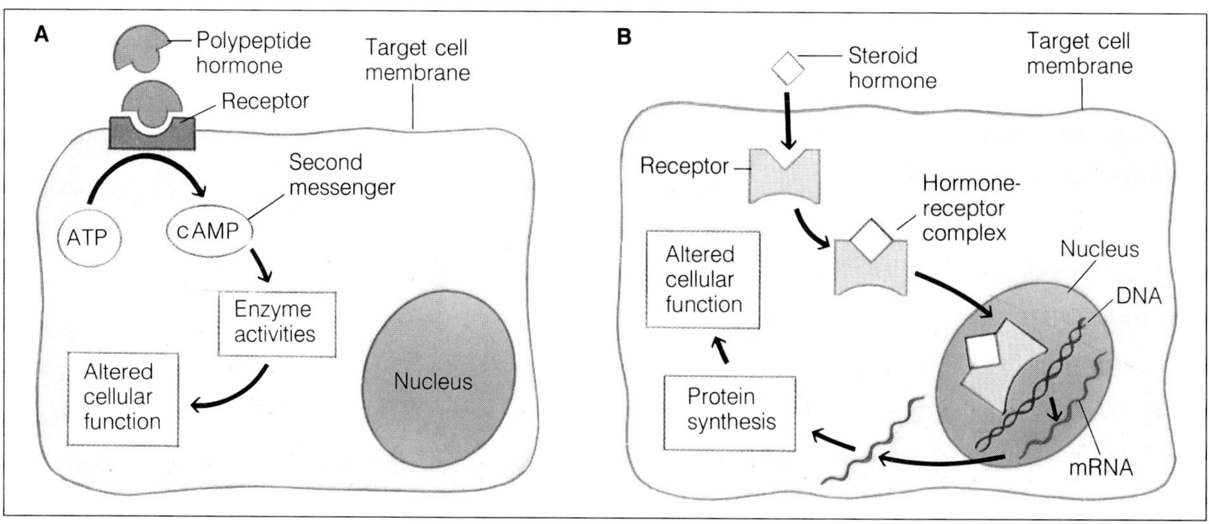

see, cAMP is one of the most important second messengers. Another one is the calcium ion.

Unlike polypeptide hormones, steroid hormones can easily diffuse through the lipid portion of the cell membrane and enter the cytoplasm of their target cells. Here they become attached to receptor molecules, which are usually proteins that float freely in the cytoplasm. The hormones then bind with the receptor molecules, forming a hormone-receptor complex. This complex drifts through the cell until it makes its way into the cell nucleus. Within the nucleus, the hormone-receptor complex can affect gene expression by attaching tightly to certain gene sequences. This action can cause the activation of genes that previously were not expressed.

Because they do not use second messengers, steroid hormones control gene expression directly. This causes steroid hormones to produce dramatic changes in cell behavior.

Prostaglandins: Local Hormones

Until recently, the endocrine system was thought to have a monopoly on the production of hormones. In the last decade this idea has changed. All sorts of cells and tissues have been shown to produce small amounts of hormonelike substances called **prostaglandins** (prahs-tuh-GLAN-dihnz).

Prostaglandins are so named because they were originally discovered in the secretions of the prostate gland, a structure in the male reproductive system. Prostaglandins, which are fatty acids, function only within the same cells in which they are produced. Thus prostaglandins are called "local hormones."

Among the many effects of prostaglandins is their ability to cause contractions in smooth muscles, such as those in the uterus, bronchioles, and walls of blood vessels. One group of prostaglandins was found to be involved in the sensation of pain. As it turns out, the discovery of these prostaglandins helped provide a solution to another puzzle. Although the pain-killing effect of aspirin was well-known, its action was not understood—at least not until it was discovered that aspirin stops the synthesis of the pain-causing prostaglandins.

42–2 SECTION REVIEW

1. Describe the negative-feedback mechanism.
2. Compare the actions of polypeptide hormones and steroid hormones.
3. What are prostaglandins?
4. Suppose the secretion of a certain hormone causes an increase in the concentration of substance X in the blood. What is the effect on the rate of hormone secretion if an abnormal condition causes the level of X in the blood to remain very low?

LABORATORY INVESTIGATION

SIMULATING THE NEGATIVE-FEEDBACK PROCESS

PROBLEM

How are hormone levels in the blood controlled?

MATERIALS *(per group)*

penny	scissors
3 sheets of unlined white paper	2 small boxes
	sheet of graph paper

PROCEDURE

1. On one sheet of paper, construct a data table similar to the one shown here.
2. Draw 22 circles on another sheet of white paper using the penny as a guide. With the scissors, cut out the circles.
3. Place the letters TSH on one side of 11 circles and the letter T on one side of the remaining 11 circles. The letters TSH and T represent thyroid-stimulating hormone and thyroxine, respectively. Each circle represents a level of that particular hormone.
4. Label one box ANTERIOR PITUITARY and the other THYROID. Place all the TSH circles in the ANTERIOR PITUITARY box and all the T circles in the THYROID box. Label the third sheet of white paper BLOODSTREAM. The boxes and the sheet of paper represent the anterior pituitary, the thyroid, and the bloodstream, respectively.
5. To represent the starting level of each hormone in the bloodstream, remove 5 TSH circles and 0 T circles from their boxes. Place the TSH circles in the "bloodstream." The starting number for each hormone has been recorded for you in the data table.
6. To adjust the level of thyroxine in the bloodstream, follow these directions:

   When the level of thyroxine in the blood is low, TSH production is stimulated and the level of TSH in the blood increases. To simulate this action, if the number of T's is below 5, remove 1 TSH from the anterior pituitary and place it in the bloodstream. When T = 5, there is no change in TSH. Record.

   When the level of thyroxine in the blood is high, TSH production is inhibited and the level of TSH in the blood decreases. To simulate this action, if the number of T's is above 5, remove 1 TSH from the bloodstream and place it back in the anterior pituitary. Record.
7. To adjust the level of TSH in the bloodstream, follow these directions:

   When the level of TSH in the blood is low, the production of thyroxine is inhibited and the level of thyroxine in the blood decreases. To simulate this action, if the number of TSH's is below 5, remove 1 T from the bloodstream and put it back in the thyroid. Record.

   When the level of TSH in the blood is high, thyroxine production is stimulated and the level of the thyroxine in the blood increases. To simulate this action, if the number of TSH's is above 5, remove 1 T from the anterior pituitary and place it in the bloodstream. When TSH = 5, there is no change in T. Record.
8. Repeat steps 6 and 7 for a total of 30 trials.
9. On the sheet of graph paper, construct a graph of your results.

OBSERVATIONS

Trial	Hormone Level in Bloodstream (number of circles)	
	TSH	Thyroxine (T)
0 (start)	5	0
30		

1. What happens to levels of thyroxine as TSH levels increase? As TSH levels decrease?
2. What happens to levels of TSH as thyroxine levels increase? As thyroxine levels decrease?

ANALYSIS AND CONCLUSIONS

1. What causes thyroxine levels to increase?
2. What causes TSH levels to decrease?
3. How are blood hormone levels controlled?

SUMMARIZING THE CONCEPTS

The key concepts in each section of this chapter are listed below to help you review the chapter content. Make sure you understand each concept and its relationship to other concepts and to the theme of this chapter.

42-1 Endocrine Glands

- The endocrine system is composed of glands that secrete their products, called hormones, into the bloodstream.
- The thyroid gland regulates the cells' rates of metabolism and the blood's calcium level.
- The parathyroid glands control the level of calcium in the blood.
- The adrenal cortex regulates reabsorption of sodium, excretion of potassium, and rate of metabolism of carbohydrates, fats, and proteins. The adrenal medulla increases heart rate, blood pressure, and blood supply to skeletal muscles, converts glycogen to glucose, and stimulates the heart muscle.
- The gonads—ovaries and testes—stimulate the development of the secondary sex characteristics in both females and males.
- The pancreas stimulates the uptake and use of glucose and the conversion of glycogen to glucose.
- The posterior pituitary gland stimulates the kidneys to reabsorb more water and the uterus to contract during childbirth.
- The anterior pituitary gland controls the growth, development, and functioning of the gonads, the functioning of the thyroid gland and adrenal glands, the growth of the body, the production of milk in females, and the production of melanin.
- The hypothalamus, a portion of the brain, controls the secretions of the pituitary gland.

42-2 Control of the Endocrine System

- Like most systems of the body, the endocrine system is regulated by a negative-feedback mechanism that functions to maintain homeostasis, or the maintenance of a relatively constant internal environment.
- Hormonelike substances called prostaglandins are synthesized and secreted by the tissues upon which they act.

REVIEWING KEY TERMS

Vocabulary terms are important to your understanding of biology. The key terms listed below are those you should be especially familiar with. Review these terms and their meanings. Then use each term in a complete sentence. If you are not sure of a term's meaning, return to the appropriate section and review its definition.

42-1 Endocrine Glands

endocrine system
hormone
target cell
endocrine gland
exocrine gland
thyroid gland
parathyroid gland
adrenal gland
adrenal cortex
adrenal medulla
gonad
ovary
testis
pancreas
islet of Langerhans
pituitary gland
posterior pituitary
anterior pituitary
hypothalamus

42-2 Control of the Endocrine System

negative-feedback mechanism
prostaglandin

CHAPTER REVIEW

CONTENT REVIEW

Multiple Choice

Choose the letter of the answer that best completes each statement.

1. Through the activity of which body system do cells receive hormones?
a. digestive c. excretory
b. respiratory d. circulatory

2. Secretions from ductless glands are called
a. enzymes. c. digestive fluids.
b. hormones. d. excretory fluids.

3. A high concentration of calcium in the blood suggests a disorder of the
a. thyroid gland. c. liver.
b. pancreas. d. parathyroid glands.

4. Which gland produces cortisol?
a. parathyroid c. thyroid
b. pancreas d. adrenal

5. If the amount of blood glucose is low, the islets of Langerhans will
a. secrete insulin. c. secrete GH.
b. become inactive. d. secrete glucagon.

6. Which hormone is not involved in the control of glucose metabolism?
a. adrenaline c. PTH
b. insulin d. glucagon

7. A type of self-regulation such as the relationship between the pituitary gland, TSH, the thyroid gland, and thyroxine is known as
a. cyclosis.
b. negative-feedback mechanism.
c. synapsis.
d. voluntary control.

8. Hormonelike substances that are secreted by all types of cells and are involved in the sensation of pain are called
a. prostaglandins. c. thyroxines.
b. adrenalines. d. insulins.

True or False

Determine whether each statement is true or false. If it is true, write "true." If it is false, change the underlined word or words to make the statement true.

1. <u>Calcitonin</u> is secreted by the thyroid gland.

2. Insulin and glucagon are both produced in the <u>liver</u>.

3. <u>Type I</u> diabetes most commonly develops in people over the age of 40.

4. The <u>hypothalamus</u> is a part of the brain that controls secretions of the pituitary gland.

5. The <u>anterior</u> pituitary gland produces oxytocin.

6. Another name for somatotropin is <u>prolactin</u>.

7. Giantism is caused by an excess of hormones from the <u>thyroid</u> gland.

8. <u>Steroid</u> hormones enter their target cells.

Word Relationships

In each of the following sets of terms, three of the terms are related. One term does not belong. Determine the characteristic common to three of the terms and then identify the term that does not belong.

1. estrogen, cortisol, androgen, progesterone

2. dwarfism, acromegaly, giantism, cretinism

3. pancreas, thyroid, pituitary, adrenal

4. prolactin, PTH, TSH, ACTH

CONCEPT MASTERY

Use your understanding of the concepts developed in the chapter to answer each of the following in a brief paragraph.

1. Distinguish between the conditions of hypothyroidism and hyperthyroidism.
2. How does the secretion of adrenaline prepare the body for emergencies?
3. Describe how prostaglandins work.
4. Describe the functions of the hormones of the anterior and posterior pituitary.
5. Why must the blood glucose level be kept fairly constant?
6. Explain the functions of the hormones secreted by the adrenal cortex.
7. Compare cretinism and acromegaly.
8. What are the functions of glucagon and insulin?
9. How may injury to the parathyroid glands affect the muscles?
10. Why has the pituitary gland often been called the master gland?
11. Explain how negative-feedback mechanisms help maintain homeostasis in the body.
12. How do the polypeptide hormones and steroid hormones affect the functions of their target cells?

CRITICAL AND CREATIVE THINKING

Discuss each of the following in a brief paragraph.

1. **Relating facts** Explain why the thyroid gland enlarges in response to a deficiency of iodine in the diet.
2. **Making predictions** Predict the effect of removing the pancreas from a person's body.
3. **Relating concepts** Suppose a person is not getting a sufficient amount of calcium in his or her diet. How does this affect the parathyroid hormone secretion and parathyroid hormone target cells?
4. **Making diagrams** Diagram a negative-feedback mechanism involving hormones that function to regulate the production of thyroid hormones.
5. **Relating cause and effect** Explain why some hormones may be taken orally whereas others, such as insulin, which is a protein, are injected directly into the body.
6. **Interpreting graphs** The graph shows the level of glucose in the blood of two people during a 5-hour period immediately following ingestion of a typical meal. Which line represents an average person? A person with diabetes? Explain.

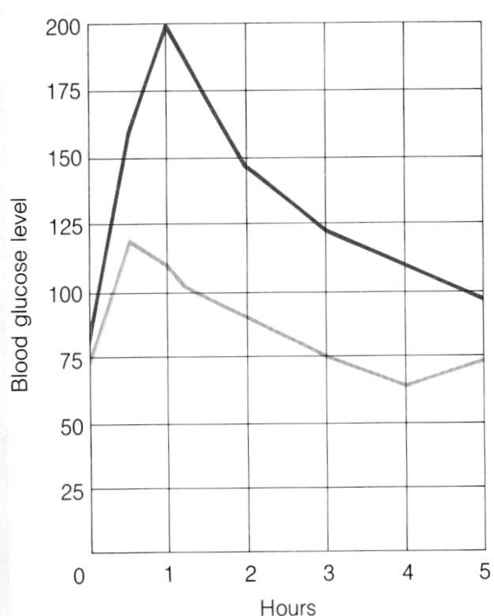

7. **Using the writing process** Recently athletes have been barred from participating in certain sports because they have tested positive for anabolic steroids. Although anabolic steroids have strength-enhancing properties, they can cause irreparable damage to the body. Design a poster in which you inform people of the harmful effects of these substances.

CHAPTER 43

Reproduction and Development

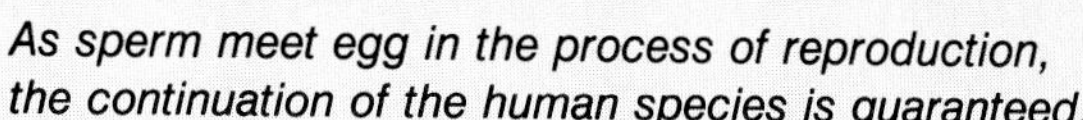

As sperm meet egg in the process of reproduction, the continuation of the human species is guaranteed.

The season of spring is synonymous with rebirth. Flowers burst from the soil, the songs of birds are heard after a long winter's absence, and many animals give birth to their young. The symbolism that we apply to this time of year comes, at least in part, from the importance of reproduction to living creatures—ourselves included. For every species of living thing, reproduction forms the next generation. It guarantees the continuation of every form of life. It gives us a personal stake in the world of the future. And it determines many aspects of our lives. How does this extraordinary process take place in humans? What systems interact to produce a new generation of living organisms? And how do single cells become complete human beings millions and millions of times every year? In this chapter you shall learn about the human reproductive system and the way in which new life begins.

CHAPTER OUTLINE

43-1 The Reproductive System

Section Objectives

- Describe the function and importance of the reproductive system.
- Compare sexual development in males and females.
- Identify the structures of the male and female reproductive systems.

Plants and animals produce new individuals through the process of reproduction. Reproduction involves special structures that make up the **reproductive system**. As you have learned from the preceding chapters, most of the systems of the body are essential to survival. The loss of the nervous system, the digestive system, or the circulatory system would be fatal in most animals. The reproductive system, however, is not essential to the survival of an individual. Organisms can survive and lead healthy lives without reproducing. What the reproductive system is important to is the survival of the species. Reproduction is absolutely essential to the continuation of the species. Without it, a species will cease to exist.

In humans, as in other vertebrates, the reproductive system produces, stores, nourishes, and releases specialized sex cells known as gametes. The ways in which the gametes are released make possible the fusion of sperm (male gamete) and egg (female gamete) in the process of fertilization. From a fertilized egg, or zygote, come all the cells in a human body.

Sexual Development

For the first six weeks after fertilization, human male and female embryos are identical in appearance. Then, during the

Figure 43-1 In generation after generation, similarities and differences between parents and offspring are identifiable. This unity and diversity result from the fact that humans reproduce sexually and genetic material from each parent is contributed to the offspring.

Figure 43–2 Puberty may occur anytime from age 9 to 15. During this growing period, adolescents display a wide variety of physical characteristics.

Figure 43–3 Sperm are produced within the testes in structures known as seminiferous tubules. In the photograph, the rounded cells just inside the rim of the tubule are immature sperm. As they journey to the center of the tubule, they develop into mature sperm whose tangled tails are visible in the center.

seventh week of development, major changes occur. The **testes** (singular: testis), which are the primary reproductive organs of a male embryo, begin to produce steroid hormones known as **androgens**. The tissues of the embryo respond to these hormones by developing into the male reproductive organs.

If the embryo is female, the **ovaries**, or the primary reproductive organs of a female embryo, produce steroid hormones known as **estrogens**. In response to these hormones, the tissues of the embryo develop in a pattern that produces the female reproductive organs. The male and female reproductive organs develop from exactly the same tissues in the embryo.

After birth the testes and the ovaries continue to produce small amounts of androgens and estrogens, respectively. These sex hormones continue to influence the development of the reproductive organs. However, neither testes nor ovaries are capable of producing active reproductive cells (gametes) until the onset of **puberty**. Puberty is a period of rapid growth and sexual maturation during which the reproductive system becomes fully functional. At the completion of puberty, the male and female **gonads**, or reproductive organs, are fully developed. The onset of puberty varies considerably among individuals. It may occur anytime from age 9 to 15. Generally, puberty begins about a year earlier in females than in males.

Puberty begins with a change in the hypothalamus, the part of the brain that regulates the secretions of the pituitary gland. This change causes the pituitary gland to produce increased levels of two hormones that affect the gonads. These hormones, named for their effects on the female, are follicle-stimulating hormone (FSH) and luteinizing hormone (LH).

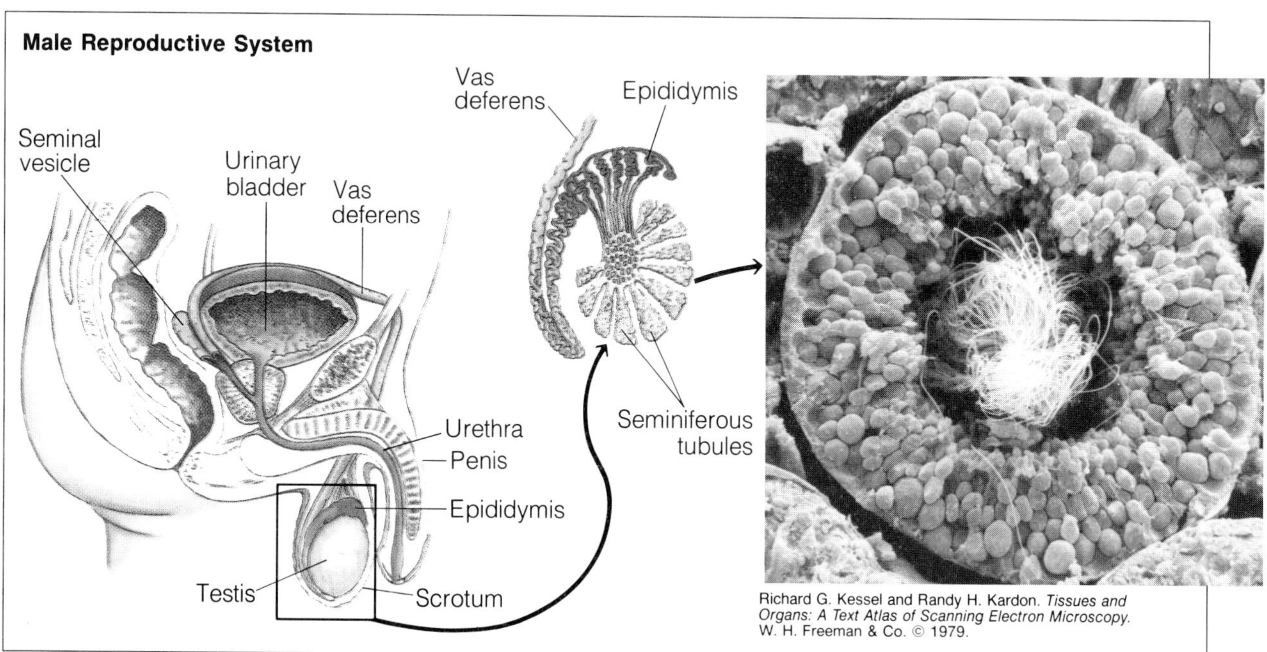

The Male Reproductive System

The primary male reproductive organs, the testes, develop within the abdominal cavity. Just before birth (and sometimes just after) the testes descend through a canal into an external sac called the **scrotum**. The testes remain in the scrotum, outside the body cavity, where the temperature is about 1° to 3°C lower than the internal temperature of the body (37°C). Sperm development in the testes requires the lower temperature.

The testes are clusters of hundreds of tiny tubules called **seminiferous** (sehm-uh-NIHF-er-uhs) **tubules**. The word seminiferous means seed-bearing, making it an appropriate name for these tubules because it is there that sperm are produced. The seminiferous tubules are tightly coiled and twisted together to form a compact organ. See Figure 43–3. As the pituitary gland begins to release FSH and LH, these hormones stimulate the testes to make the principal male sex hormone **testosterone** (tehs-TAHS-ter-ohn).

Cells that can respond to testosterone are found all over the body. Testosterone produces a number of **secondary sex characteristics** that appear in males at puberty. (The primary sex characteristics are those that pertain to the reproductive system itself—the reproductive tract and external features.) A boy's voice becomes deeper, he grows a beard and more body hair, his chest broadens, and he may find it easier to develop large muscles. He will continue to grow for several years after his female classmates have stopped growing.

FSH and testosterone stimulate the development of sperm. When large numbers of sperm have been produced in the testes, the developmental process of puberty is completed. The reproductive system is now functional, meaning that the male can produce and release active sperm.

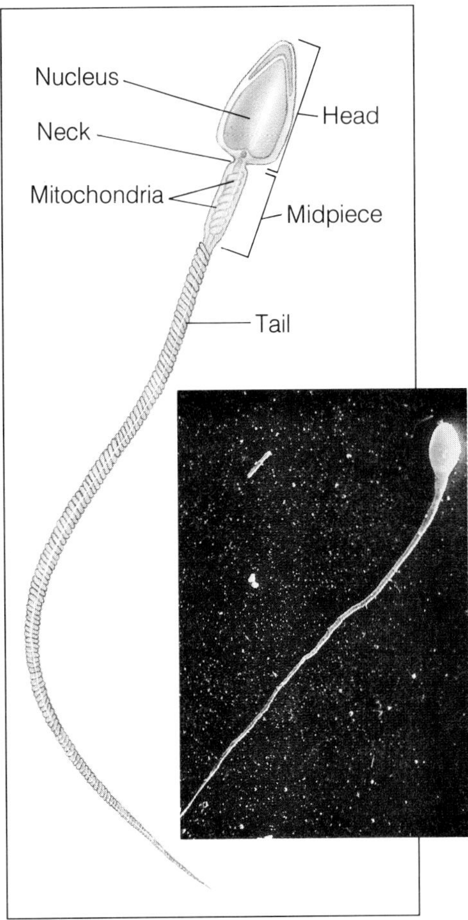

Figure 43–4 *A mature sperm cell consists of a head, a midpiece, and a tail. Millions of these male gametes are produced daily by the testes.*

SPERM DEVELOPMENT Sperm are derived from special cells within the testes that go through the process of meiosis to form the haploid nuclei found in mature sperm. A sperm cell consists of a head, which contains the highly condensed nucleus; a midpiece, which is packed with energy-releasing mitochondria; and a tail, or flagellum, which propels the cell forward. At the tip of the head is a small cap that contains an enzyme vital to the process of fertilization.

Developed sperm travel from the seminiferous tubules into the **epididymis** (ehp-uh-DIHD-ih-mihs), a comma-shaped structure in which they fully mature and are stored. After brief storage in the epididymis, the sperm are forced into a tube known as the **vas deferens** (vas DEHF-uh-rehnz). The vas deferens passes into the abdominal cavity where three glands produce **seminal fluid** in which the sperm are suspended. The combination of sperm and seminal fluid is known as **semen**.

The number of sperm present in even a few drops of semen is astonishing. Between 100 and 200 million sperm are present in 1 milliliter of semen. That's about 5 million sperm per drop! Eventually, the vas deferens merges with the **urethra**, the tube that leads to the outside of the body through the **penis**.

SPERM RELEASE When the male is sexually excited, the autonomic nervous system prepares the male organs to deliver sperm. Sperm are ejected from the penis by the contractions of smooth muscles lining the vas deferens. This process is called ejaculation. Because ejaculation is regulated by the autonomic nervous system, it is not completely voluntary. Approximately 2 to 3 milliliters of sperm are released in an ejaculation. If the 300 million or so sperm are released in the reproductive tract of a female, the chances of a single sperm fertilizing an ovum, if one is available, are quite good.

The Female Reproductive System

The primary reproductive organs in the female are the ovaries (singular: ovary). The ovaries are located in the abdominal cavity. Whereas the testes may produce several hundred million reproductive cells each day, the ovaries usually produce only one egg, or **ovum**, per month. But in addition to producing ova, the female reproductive system has another important job to perform. Each time an ovum is released, the body of the female must be prepared to nourish a developing embryo.

As in males, puberty in females starts with changes in the hypothalamus that cause the release of FSH and LH from the pituitary gland. These are the same kinds of hormones that are found in males, although their target cells and the effects they produce are quite different.

FSH (follicle-stimulating hormone) stimulates cells within the ovaries to produce the hormones known as estrogens. The estrogens cause the reproductive system to complete its development and also to produce the secondary sex characteristics that appear in females. These characteristics include enlargement of the breasts and reproductive organs, widening of the hips, and growth of hair in the armpits and pubic area.

OVA DEVELOPMENT Each ovary contains about 400,000 **primary follicles**, which are clusters of cells surrounding a single ovum. The function of a follicle is to prepare a single ovum for release into the part of the reproductive system where it can be fertilized.

Ova mature within their follicles. Although a female is born with about 400,000 immature ova (primary follicles) in her ovaries—and does not produce any new ova during her lifetime—fewer than 500 ova will actually be released. Under the influence of FSH, one (or more) ovum completes meiosis and increases in size as nutrients are added to its cytoplasm.

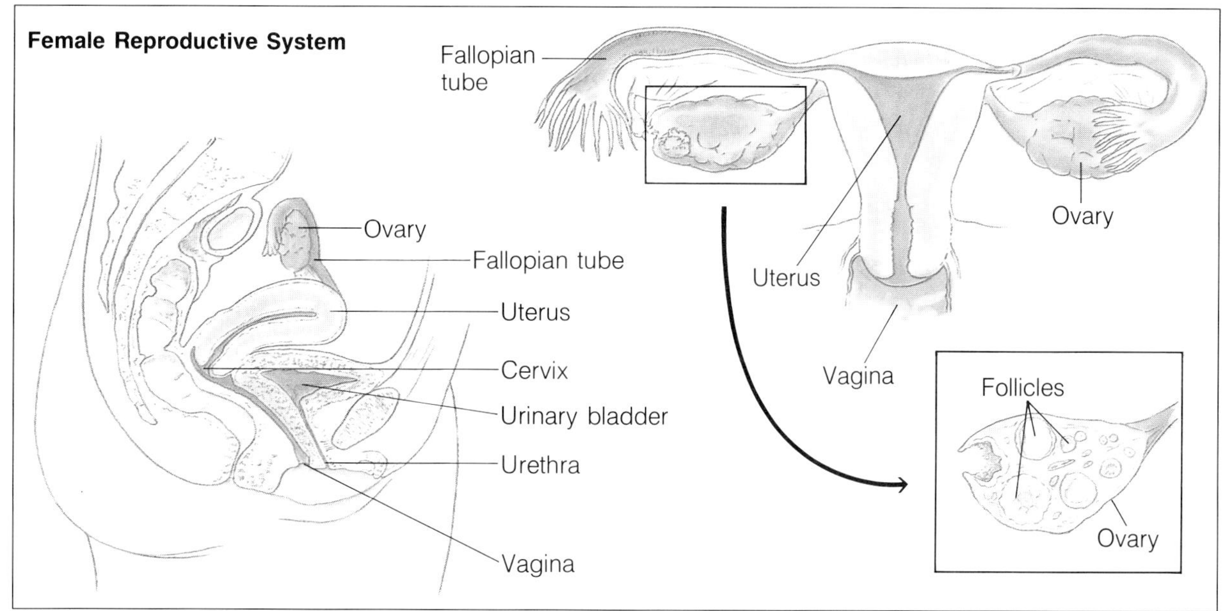

Figure 43–5 *Deep within the abdomen, the female reproductive organs perform their dual function. They produce the eggs that could be fertilized by sperm and they prepare a place in which a fertilized egg can grow and develop.*

OVULATION When a follicle has completely matured, the ovum is released. This process is called **ovulation**. The follicle literally ruptures, and the ovum is swept from the surface of the ovary into the opening of one of the two **Fallopian tubes**. The ovum moves through the fluid-filled Fallopian tube, pushed along by microscopic cilia attached to the cells that line the walls of the tube. It is during its journey through the Fallopian tube that an egg can be fertilized. After a few days, the ovum passes from the Fallopian tube into a larger cavity known as the **uterus**. The lining of the uterus is specially designed to receive a fertilized ovum, if fertilization has occurred. The uterus opens into a canal known as the **vagina**, which leads to the outside of the body.

Ovulation begins at puberty and usually continues until a female is in her late forties, when **menopause** occurs. After menopause, follicle development no longer occurs and a female is no longer capable of bearing a child.

The Menstrual Cycle

In females, the interaction of the reproductive system and the endocrine system takes the form of a complex series of periodic events called the menstrual cycle. This name is quite appropriate: The cycle takes an average of about 28 days, and the word menstrual comes from the Latin word *mensis*, meaning "month."

The **menstrual cycle**, which is controlled by hormones operating on a negative-feedback mechanism, involves the development and the release of an egg for fertilization and the

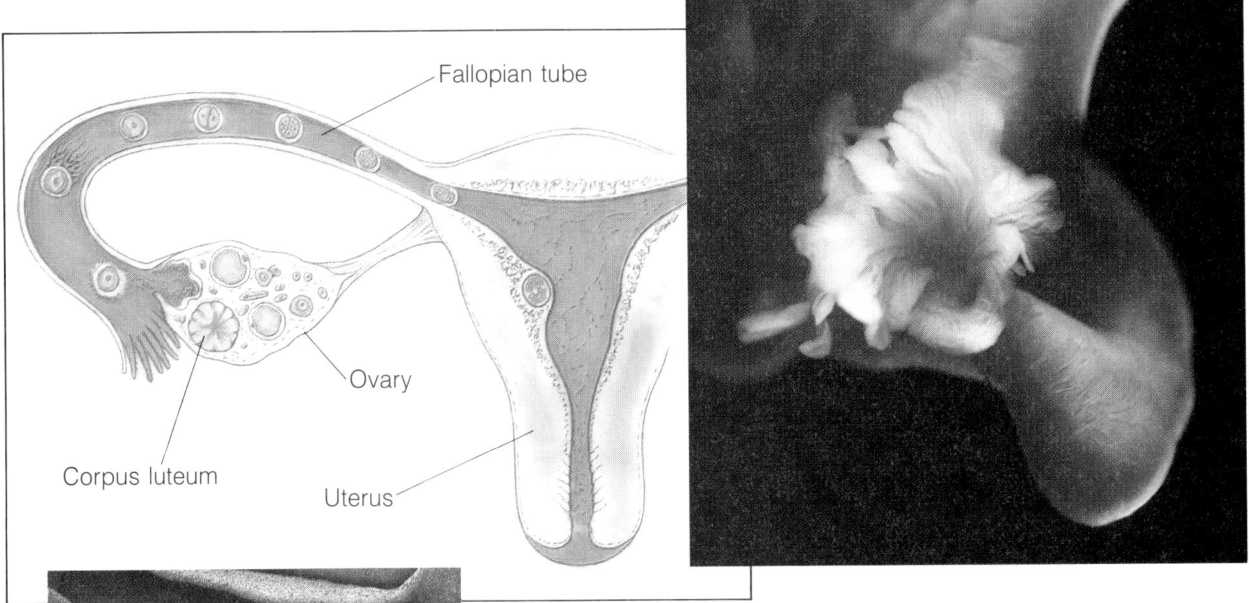

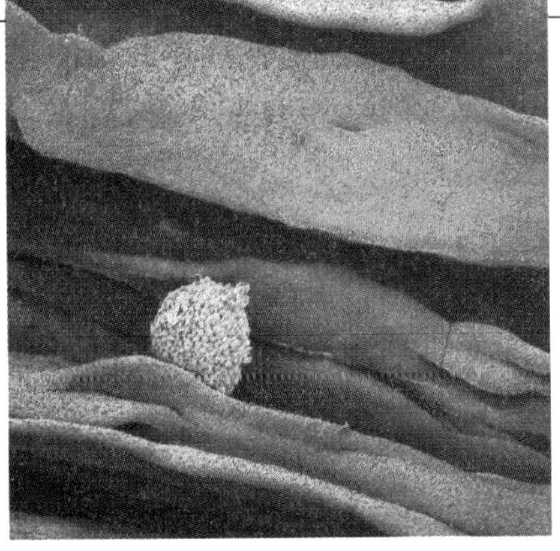

Figure 43–6 *During ovulation, an ovum bursts from a ruptured mature follicle (top, left). It is then swept into the funnel-shaped opening of a Fallopian tube by fringelike petals called fimbriae (top, right). The ovum journeys toward the uterus along the folds of the 11-cm-long tube (bottom). It is during this passage that the ovum can be fertilized by a sperm.*

preparation of the uterus to receive a fertilized egg. If an egg is not fertilized, it is discharged along with the lining of the uterus. The menstrual cycle has four phases: follicle phase, ovulation, luteal phase, and menstruation.

FOLLICLE PHASE The follicle phase begins when the level of estrogen in the blood is relatively low. The hypothalamus reacts to the low estrogen level by producing a releasing hormone that acts on the pituitary gland. The releasing hormone stimulates the pituitary gland to secrete FSH and LH into the blood. These two pituitary gland hormones travel through the circulatory system to the ovaries, where they cause a follicle to develop to maturity.

As the follicle develops, the cells surrounding the ovum enlarge and begin to produce increased amounts of estrogen. Estrogen levels in the blood rise dramatically as the follicle increases in size and produces more and more of the hormone. Estrogen causes the lining of the uterus to thicken in preparation for receiving a fertilized egg. The development of an ovum in this stage of the cycle takes about 10 days.

OVULATION This phase is the shortest in the cycle, occurring about midway through the cycle (14 days) and lasting about 3 to 4 days. During this phase, something (no one is certain what) causes the hypothalamus to send a large amount of releasing hormone to the pituitary gland. This in turn causes the pituitary gland to produce a sudden rush of FSH and LH. The release of these hormones has a dramatic effect on the follicle: it ruptures, and a mature ovum is released. This is the process known as ovulation.

LUTEAL PHASE The ruptured follicle, now known as the **corpus luteum** (KOR-puhs LOOT-ee-uhm), continues to release estrogen. Corpus luteum means yellow body in Latin, thus describing the color of the follicle after ovulation. Immediately following ovulation, the corpus luteum begins to release a new steroid hormone called **progesterone**. During the first 14 days of the cycle, rising estrogen levels have stimulated cell growth and tissue development in the lining of the uterus. Progesterone adds the finishing touches to that lining. Blood supply is increased, the tissue matures, and the lining is fully prepared to accept a fertilized ovum.

During the first two days of the luteal phase, immediately following ovulation, the chances of an egg being fertilized are greatest. This is usually from 10 to 14 days after the completion of the last menstrual cycle. If an ovum is fertilized by a sperm, the resulting zygote will start to divide. After several divisions, the ball of cells will implant itself in the lining of the uterus. Within a few days of implantation, the uterus and the growing embryo will release hormones that keep the corpus luteum functioning for several weeks. This allows the lining of the uterus to nourish and protect the developing embryo.

MENSTRUATION What happens if fertilization does not occur? Within 2 to 3 days of ovulation, the ovum passes through the uterus without implantation. The corpus luteum, left on the surface of the ovary, begins to disintegrate. As the old follicle breaks down it releases less and less estrogen and progesterone. The result is a decrease in the level of these hormones in the blood.

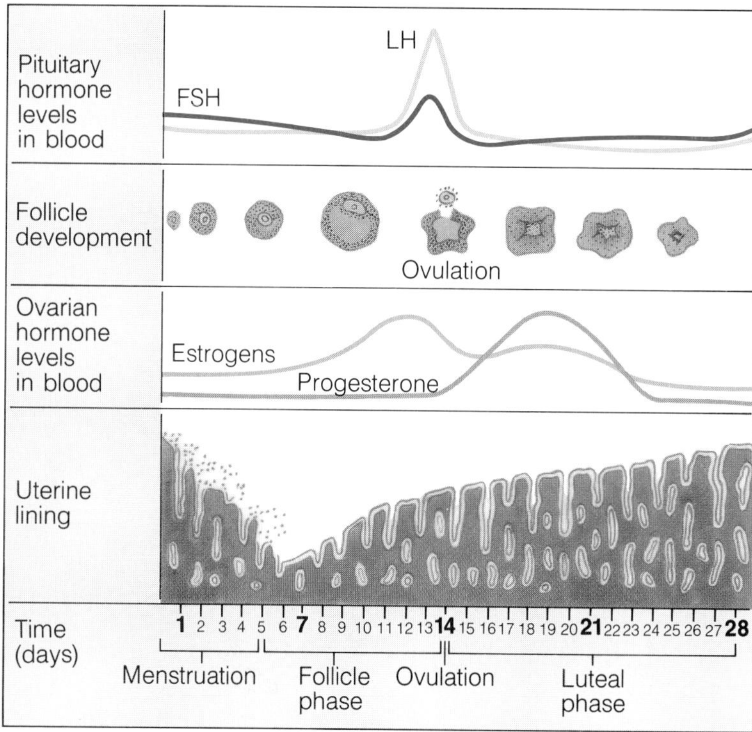

Figure 43–7 *The menstrual cycle involves the development and release of an ovum for fertilization and the preparation of the uterus to receive a fertilized ovum. Note the relative concentrations of the various hormones and the corresponding condition of the uterine lining and the follicle. What are the four phases of the menstrual cycle?*

When the level of estrogen falls below a certain point, the lining of the uterus begins to detach from the uterine wall. This tissue along with blood and the unfertilized ovum are sloughed off, or discharged, through the vagina in the last (and externally visible) phase of the cycle, which is called **menstruation**. Menstruation lasts from 3 to 7 days, with an average of 4 days. At the end of menstruation, a new cycle begins.

A few days after menstruation, levels of estrogen in the blood are once again low enough to stimulate the hypothalamus. The hypothalamus produces a releasing hormone that acts on the pituitary gland, which then starts to secrete FSH and LH, and the menstrual cycle begins anew.

Fertilization

In order for an ovum to become fertilized, sperm must be present in the female reproductive tract—more specifically, in a Fallopian tube. Sperm are released during sexual intercourse, when semen is ejaculated through the penis of the male into the vagina of the female. The penis generally enters the vagina to a point just below the cervix, which is the opening that connects the vagina to the uterus. Sperm swim actively through the uterus and up into the Fallopian tubes. Although hundreds of millions of sperm are released during an ejaculation, only a few will reach the ovum in a Fallopian tube. And only a single sperm cell will fertilize the ovum.

The ovum is surrounded by a dense protective layer that contains receptor sites to which sperm bind. This binding causes a vesicle in the sperm head to rupture and release enzymes that break down the protective layer and form a pathway through which the sperm nucleus can reach the ovum. Once the sperm nucleus enters the ovum, the cell membrane of the ovum changes, thereby preventing other sperm from entering the cell.

The fertilized ovum is properly called a **zygote** after the two haploid (N) nuclei (one from the sperm cell and one from the egg cell) fuse to form a single diploid (2N) nucleus. The zygote will go through several rounds of cell division, and the ball of cells formed by those divisions will attach itself to the wall of the uterus and begin to grow into an embryo.

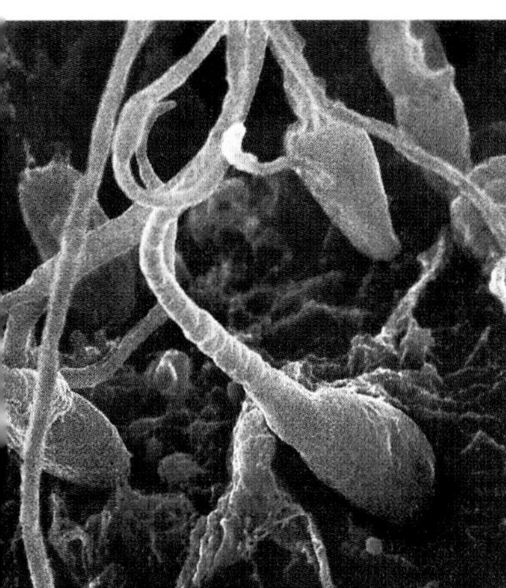
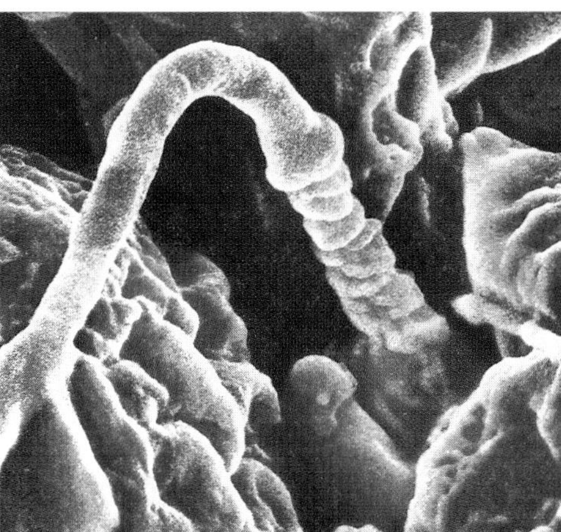
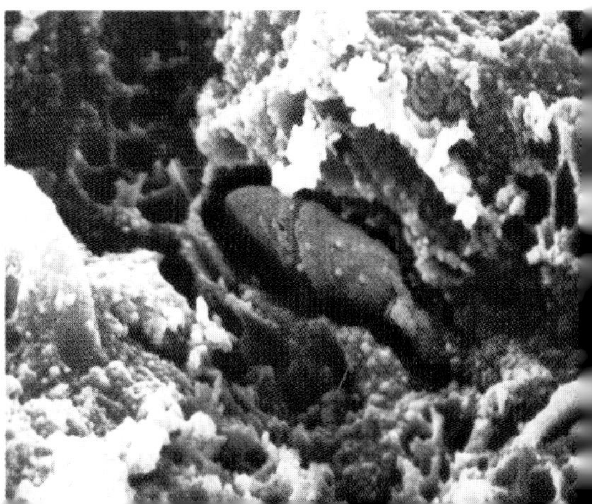

Figure 43–8 *Outnumbering an ovum by nearly 500 million to 1, fewer than 500 sperm survive their journey to the upper part of a Fallopian tube, where they attempt to penetrate the egg (left). Usually only 1 sperm fertilizes an ovum, plunging into its protective layer headfirst (center). As projections on the surface of the ovum pull the sperm inside, the sperm's tail disintegrates. Only the head and midpiece remain within the ovum (right).*

43-1 SECTION REVIEW

1. What is the function of the reproductive system?
2. At what point in development do male and female embryos begin to differ from each other? What is the nature of this difference? What causes it?
3. Describe the changes that occur in males during puberty. In females. In each case, what hormone causes these changes?
4. Describe the phases of the menstrual cycle.
5. How does fertilization occur?
6. Explain how the shape of a sperm cell helps its function.

43-2 Human Development

Section Objectives

- Trace the development of a fertilized ovum into a fetus.
- Describe the process of childbirth.

When an ovum is fertilized, the remarkable process of human development begins. In the course of this process, a single cell no larger than the period at the end of this sentence will undergo a series of cell divisions that will result in the formation of a new human being.

Early Development

The first few **cleavages**, or mitotic cell divisions of the zygote, take place while the zygote is still in a Fallopian tube. Four days after fertilization, the embryo consists of a solid ball of about 50 cells known as the **morula** (MOR-yoo-luh). As the embryo grows, a fluid-filled cavity forms in the center, transforming it into a hollow structure known as a **blastocyst**. About 6 or 7 days after fertilization, the blastocyst attaches itself to the wall of the uterus and begins to grow inward in a process known as **implantation**.

A cluster of cells gradually forms within the cavity of the blastocyst. This cluster sorts itself into two layers, which then produce a third layer, by a process of cell migration known as **gastrulation** (gas·troo-LAY-shuhn). See Figure 43-9. The result of gastrulation is the formation of three cell layers known as the **ectoderm, mesoderm,** and **endoderm**. These three layers are referred to as the primary germ layers because all of the organs and tissues of the embryo will be formed from them. See Figure 43-9.

During implantation, the outer layer of cells of the blastocyst produces two important membranes that surround, protect, and nourish the developing embryo. These membranes are the **amnion** and the **chorion**.

By the end of the third week of development, the nervous system has begun to form and so has a primitive tube that will

Figure 43-9 During gastrulation, the three primary germ layers, from which all the organs and tissues of the embryo will arise, form.

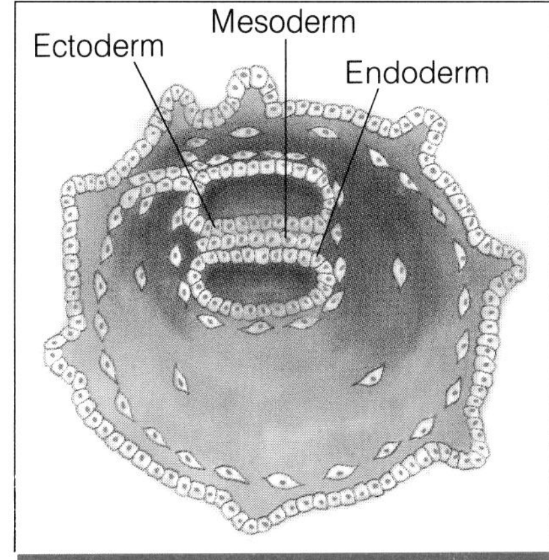

Primary Germ Layer	Develops into
Ectoderm	Epidermis of skin (hair and nails) Nervous system Tooth enamel Lining of nose and mouth
Mesoderm	Skeleton Muscles Excretory system Circulatory system Gonads
Endoderm	Digestive tract Respiratory system Liver and pancreas

give rise to the digestive system. The chorion has grown into the uterine tissue to form a vital organ called the **placenta.** The placenta is the connection between mother and developing embryo. The developing embryo needs a supply of nutrients and oxygen. It also needs a means of eliminating carbon dioxide and metabolic wastes. At first thought, it seems that this could be accomplished simply by having the blood supply of the embryo joined to that of the mother. But such an arrangement would allow disease to spread from mother to embryo and would cause problems with immunity if the mother and embryo had different blood types.

In actuality, the blood of mother and embryo flow past each other, but they do not mix. They are separated by a thin membrane similar in structure to the one shown in Figure 43–12. Across this thin barrier, gases exchange and food and waste products diffuse. The placenta is the embryo's organ of respiration, nourishment, and excretion.

After 8 weeks of development, the embryo is known as a **fetus**. By the end of 3 months of development, most of the major organs and tissues of the fetus are fully formed. During this time, a structure known as the **umbilical cord** forms. The umbilical cord, which contains two arteries and one vein, connects the fetus to the placenta. The muscular system of the fetus is by now well developed and the fetus may begin to move and show signs of reflexes. The fetus is about 9 centimeters long and has a mass of about 15 grams. The amnion has developed into a fluid-filled **amniotic sac**, which cushions and protects the developing fetus.

Later Development

During the fourth, fifth, and sixth months, the tissues of the fetus continue to become more complex and specialized. A skeleton begins to form, and the fetal heartbeat becomes strong enough to be heard with a stethoscope. A layer of soft

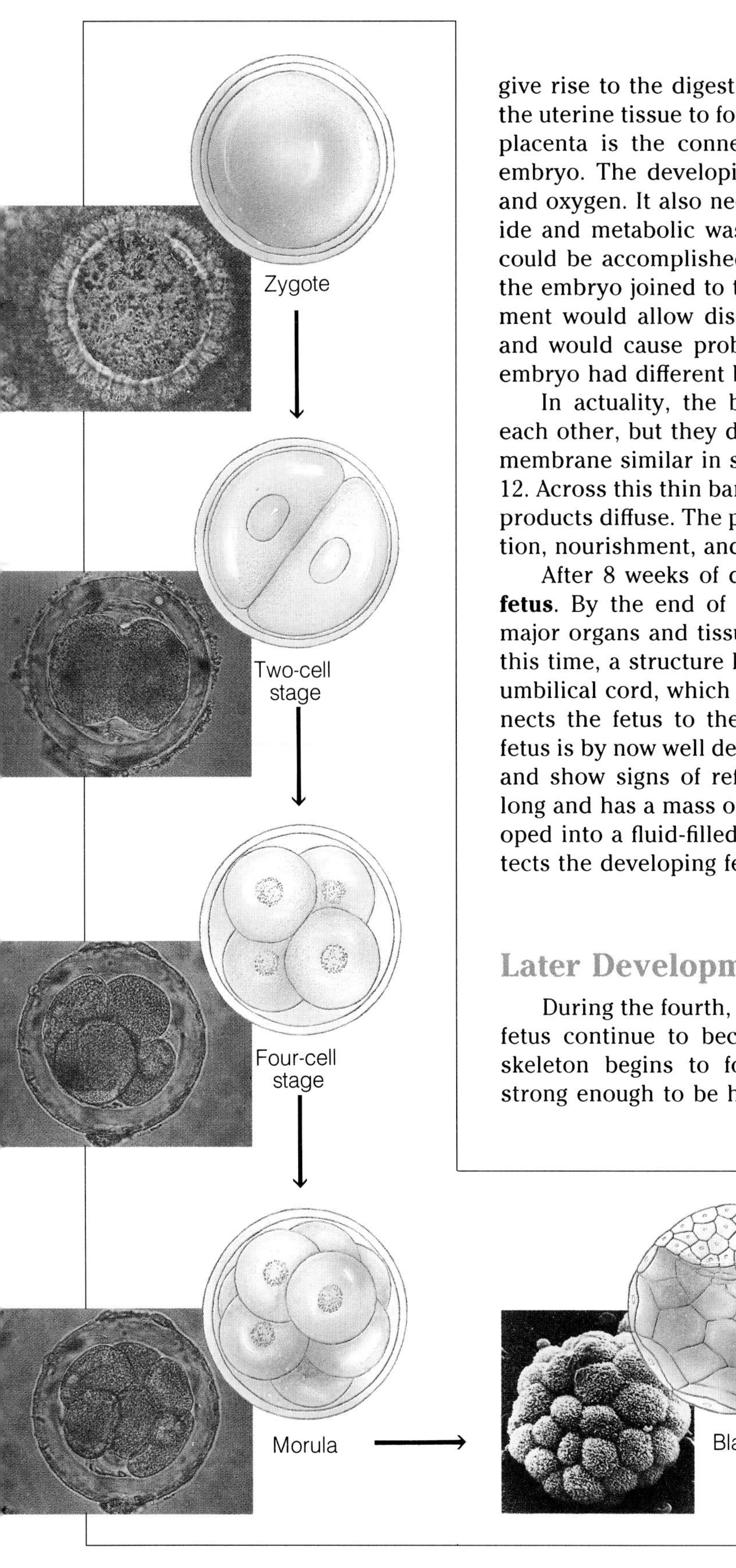

Figure 43–10 *As it develops into a fetus, a fertilized ovum, or zygote, goes through a series of mitotic cell divisions known as cleavages. At what stage does the developing embryo implant itself in the uterine wall?*

hair grows over the fetus's skin. As the fetus increases in size, the mother's abdomen swells to accommodate it. The developing fetus will be about 35 centimeters in length and have a mass of approximately 700 grams by the end of 6 months.

In many respects, the fetus is capable of leading a completely independent existence during the final 3 months it spends in the uterus. These months have an important purpose, however. The fetus actually doubles in mass, and the lungs and other organs undergo a series of changes that prepare them for life outside the mother. Premature babies, or those born before 8 months of development have been completed, have severe problems breathing because of incomplete lung development.

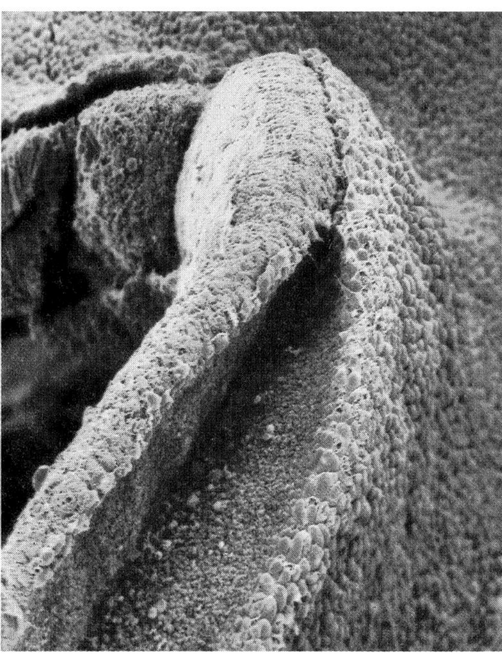

Figure 43–11 Within weeks of fertilization, a blastocyst no larger than a grain of rice begins to form specialized structures and take on shape. A groove that will develop into the nervous system is visible in this 3-week-old embryo.

Childbirth

About 9 months after fertilization, at the end of a full-term pregnancy, the fetus is ready for birth. Exactly how this process is triggered is not known for certain. However, when the time comes, a hormone known as oxytocin is released from the pituitary gland. As you learned in Chapter 42, oxytocin affects a group of large involuntary muscles that surround the uterus. As these muscles are stimulated, they begin a series of rhythmic contractions known as **labor** that expand the opening of the cervix so that it will be large enough (about 10 centimeters) to allow the baby to pass through it.

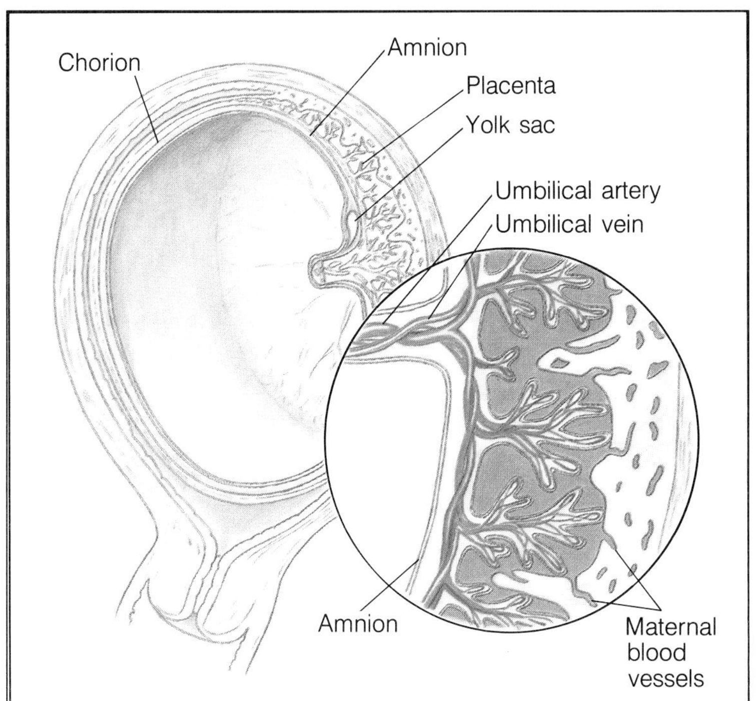

Figure 43–12 The placenta is the lifeline between mother and fetus. Through blood vessels in the umbilical cord, which connects the fetus to the placenta, food and oxygen from the mother and wastes from the fetus are exchanged.

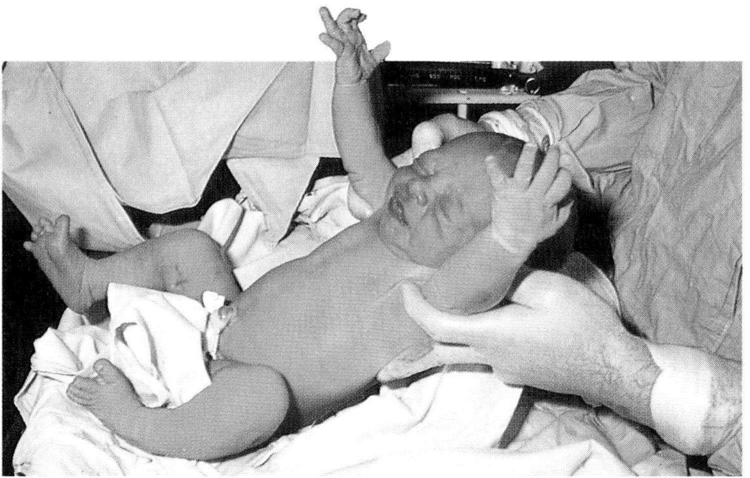

Figure 43–13 *Approximately 9 months after fertilization, the end product of reproduction emerges. Fresh to the world, this newborn is experiencing its first "weighing-in."*

As the contractions continue, they become more powerful and more frequent, occurring once every minute or two. Little by little, in a process that lasts from 2 to 16 hours, the baby is forced toward the vagina as labor continues. The amniotic sac breaks, and the fluid it contains rushes out of the vagina. The baby is finally forced out of the uterus and the vagina, usually head first, still attached to its mother by the umbilical cord.

As the baby meets the outside world, it may begin to cough or cry in order to rid its lungs of the fluid with which they have been filled. Breathing starts almost immediately, and the blood supply to the placenta begins to dry up. The umbilical cord is clamped and cut, leaving a small piece attached to the baby. This piece will soon dry and fall off, leaving a scar known as the navel—or in its more familiar term, the belly button. In a final series of uterine contractions, the placenta itself and the now-empty amniotic sac are expelled from the uterus as the afterbirth. The baby now begins to lead an independent existence.

After Childbirth

The interaction of the reproductive and endocrine systems in the creation of a human life does not end at childbirth, however. Within a few hours, a pituitary hormone known as prolactin stimulates the production of milk in the breast tissues of the mother. If a mother breastfeeds her baby regularly, several remarkable things happen: The milk is always ready when needed, it seldom runs dry, yet it stops whenever the mother decides to end breastfeeding. Exactly how does the mother's body "know" when to release milk and when to stop making it?

Upon stimulation, a series of nerve cells in the breast transmit impulses to the hypothalamus. The hypothalamus causes the pituitary gland to release nearly ten times the normal amount of prolactin. The increased level of prolactin enables milk production to keep up with demand.

Just think about it: The nervous system causes the endocrine system to produce a hormone that is important to the reproductive system. Remarkable!

SCIENCE, TECHNOLOGY, AND SOCIETY

Infant Formula in the Third World

A number of substitutes for human milk, known as infant formulas, are on the shelves of most supermarkets. These products are important and useful to those mothers who cannot be with their baby all day long or who have chosen not to breastfeed. Infant formulas have caused controversy in developing countries throughout the world, however. In many poorer nations, mass-marketing campaigns have stressed a connection between an image of sophistication and infant formulas, encouraging women to use these products in preference to breastfeeding.

In many cultures, however, mass-marketing of infant formula has actually decreased the health of the infant population. Poorly educated families may not prepare a formula correctly, thereby depriving an infant of the proper balance of nutrients. Once prepared, the formula may often be stored without refrigeration, resulting in spoilage and increased incidence of disease. Concerned about this situation, the World Health Organization has asked the formula manufacturers to emphasize the benefits of breastfeeding.

Mother's milk contains everything an infant needs for the first several months of its life: minerals, vitamins, fats, proteins, and carbohydrates, all in a perfect balance. It also contains antibodies, which help protect the nursing baby from infections. Compared to canned or powdered formulas, mother's milk has several additional advantages: It is available on a moment's notice, never has to be sterilized or warmed (it's always the right temperature!), travels well, and does not have to be purchased at a store.

Both methods of infant feeding have advantages. How do you feel about this issue?

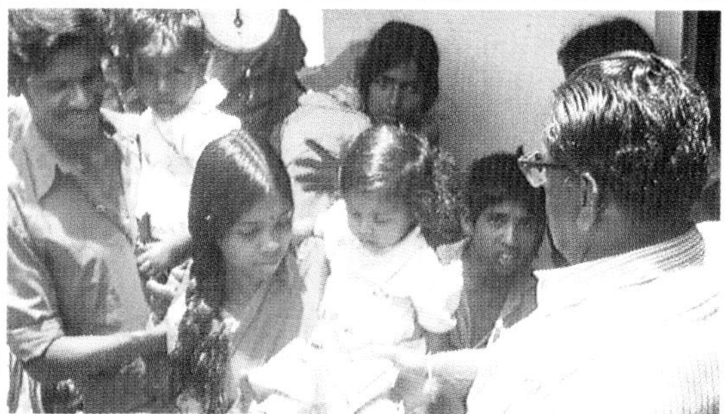

43-2 SECTION REVIEW

1. Describe the development of a blastocyst.
2. What is gastrulation? What forms as a result of this process?
3. What is the placenta? From what does it form? Why is it important?
4. Why is it important to separate the blood supplies of mother and fetus?
5. What is oxytocin? What role does it play in childbirth?
6. Explain why it is important for a pregnant woman to have good health practices.

LABORATORY INVESTIGATION

EXAMINING MAMMALIAN GAMETES

PROBLEM

How are mammalian gametes suited to their functions?

MATERIALS *(per group)*

microscope
transparent plastic metric ruler
prepared slides of a mammalian ovary and of mammalian sperm cells

PROCEDURE 

1. Record the magnification of the microscope's low-power and high-power objectives.
2. Place the clear plastic metric ruler on the stage of the microscope. Using the low-power objective, focus on the ruler's millimeter marks. Measure the diameter of the low-power field of view. Record this measurement in decimal form.
3. Calculate the diameter of the high-power field of view according to the procedure described by your teacher. Record this value.
4. Calculate the diameter of the field of view for each objective in micrometers (μm) by multiplying each diameter in millimeters by 1000. Record the results.
5. Examine the slide of the ovary under low power. Notice the many round cavities in the ovary. These are maturing follicles that are swollen with fluid. Note the varying sizes of the ova (eggs) inside the follicles. In the mature follicles, the ovum is toward one side of the follicle and is surrounded by a layer of follicle cells.
6. Locate a mature follicle. Switch to high power and focus with the fine adjustment. Draw a diagram of the mature follicle and ovum.
7. Using the procedure described by your teacher, estimate the size of an ovum. Record the result under your diagram of the ovum.
8. Examine the slide of sperm cells under low power. When you locate some sperm cells, switch to high power and focus with the fine adjustment. Draw a diagram of a sperm cell.
9. Estimate the length of a sperm cell and the width of a sperm head. Record the results under your diagram.

OBSERVATIONS

Power of Objective	Magnification of Objective	Diameter of Field of View	
		Millimeters	Micrometers
Low			
High			

1. Describe the appearance of the ovum. What is the approximate diameter of a mature ovum?
2. How does the size of a mature ovum compare to that of an immature ovum?
3. Describe the appearance of a sperm cell. What is its approximate length? Width?

ANALYSIS AND CONCLUSIONS

1. Why do developing ova come in different sizes? (*Hint:* What is contained inside an ovum?)
2. Why are sperm cells and ova different in size?
3. How does the unique shape of a sperm cell help it perform its function?
4. How are mammalian gametes suited to their functions?

STUDENT STUDY GUIDE

SUMMARIZING THE CONCEPTS

The key concepts in each section of this chapter are listed below to help you review the chapter content. Make sure you understand each concept and its relationship to other concepts and to the theme of this chapter.

43–1 The Reproductive System

- The reproductive system produces, stores, nourishes, and releases gametes.
- The testes are the primary male reproductive organs. The primary female reproductive organs are the ovaries.
- The menstrual cycle involves the development and release of an egg for fertilization and the preparation of the uterus to receive a fertilized egg. The menstrual cycle has four phases: follicle phase, ovulation, luteal phase, and menstruation.
- For an ovum to be fertilized, sperm must be present in the Fallopian tube of the female. The fertilized ovum is called a zygote.

43–2 Human Development

- Human development begins when an ovum is fertilized and commences a series of mitotic divisions, or cleavages.
- The placenta supplies the embryo with nutrients and oxygen and eliminates carbon dioxide and metabolic wastes.
- The embryo is known as a fetus after 8 weeks of development. The fetus is ready for birth about 9 months after fertilization.
- Within a few hours of childbirth, a pituitary hormone known as prolactin stimulates the production of milk in the breast tissues of the mother.

REVIEWING KEY TERMS

Vocabulary terms are important to your understanding of biology. The key terms listed below are those you should be especially familiar with. Review these terms and their meanings. Then use each term in a complete sentence. If you are not sure of a term's meaning, return to the appropriate section and review its definition.

43–1 The Reproductive System

reproductive system
testis
androgen
ovary
estrogen
puberty
gonad
scrotum
seminiferous tubule
testosterone
secondary sex characteristic
epididymis
vas deferens
seminal fluid
semen
urethra
penis
ovum
primary follicle
ovulation
Fallopian tube
uterus
vagina
menopause
menstrual cycle
corpus luteum
progesterone
menstruation
zygote

43–2 Human Development

cleavage
morula
blastocyst
implantation
gastrulation
ectoderm
mesoderm
endoderm
amnion
chorion
placenta
fetus
umbilical cord
amniotic sac
labor

CHAPTER REVIEW

CONTENT REVIEW

Multiple Choice

Choose the letter of the answer that best completes each statement.

1. In male embryos, testes produce steroid hormones known as
   a. oxytocins. c. androgens.
   b. prolactins. d. estrogens.
2. A comma-shaped structure in which sperm mature and are stored is the
   a. epididymis. c. semen.
   b. urethra. d. vas deferens.
3. The hormone that stimulates cells within the ovaries to produce estrogen is
   a. progesterone. c. LH.
   b. oxytocin. d. FSH.
4. The cluster of cells that surrounds a single ovum and prepares it for ovulation is the
   a. ovary. c. Fallopian tube.
   b. primary follicle. d. uterus.
5. The development and release of an egg for fertilization and the preparation of the uterus to receive it is
   a. menopause. c. the menstrual cycle.
   b. puberty. d. implantation.
6. The chances of an egg being fertilized are greatest during
   a. ovulation. c. the follicle phase.
   b. menstruation. d. the luteal phase.
7. Four days after fertilization, the embryo consists of a ball of cells known as the
   a. morula. c. placenta.
   b. blastocyst. d. chorion.
8. Mitotic cell divisions of the zygote are
   a. implantations. c. cleavages.
   b. morulas. d. blastocysts.

True or False

Determine whether each statement is true or false. If it is true, write "true." If it is false, change the underlined word or words to make the statement true.

1. Menopause is a period of rapid growth and sexual maturation.
2. Male and female reproductive organs develop from the same embryonic tissues.
3. The principal male sex hormone is testosterone.
4. The vas deferens leads to the outside of the male body through the penis.
5. The ovaries consist of seminiferous tubules.
6. After childbirth, the production of milk in the breast tissues of the mother is stimulated by oxytocin.
7. In order for an ovum to become fertilized, sperm must be present in a Fallopian tube.
8. The cluster of cells within the blastocyst sorts itself into layers by implantation.

Word Relationships

In each of the following sets of terms, three of the terms are related. One term does not belong. Determine the characteristic common to three of the terms and then identify the term that does not belong.

1. ectoderm, ectotherm, mesoderm, endoderm
2. ovulation, follicle phase, gastrulation, menstruation
3. semen, FSH, estrogen, LH
4. testes, scrotum, follicles, seminiferous tubules
5. cleavage, blastocyst, implantation, menstruation

CONCEPT MASTERY

Use your understanding of the concepts developed in the chapter to answer each of the following in a brief paragraph.

1. Describe how the male and female reproductive organs develop from the same tissues in the embryo.
2. Describe the period known as puberty.
3. Discuss the importance of and the effects of the hormone testosterone on the male reproductive system.
4. Trace the path a sperm must travel from production to fertilization of an ovum.
5. How does the endocrine system affect the menstrual cycle?
6. Explain why the menstrual cycle is a negative-feedback mechanism.
7. Describe gastrulation and the importance of the primary germ layers.
8. Describe the development and importance of the amnion and chorion.
9. Why is reproduction important?

CRITICAL AND CREATIVE THINKING

Discuss each of the following in a brief paragraph.

1. **Drawing conclusions** The menstrual cycle is suppressed during pregnancy. Explain why this is important to the success of a full-term pregnancy.
2. **Making predictions** If a female does not produce sufficient amounts of FSH and LH, how will her ability to have a baby be affected?
3. **Forming a hypothesis** Two babies born at the same time are called twins. In the photos below, one set of twins is identical (they look exactly alike) and the other set is fraternal (they look as alike or as different as any two children of the same parents). Propose a hypothesis about the formation of each type of twins.

4. **Identifying relationships** Explain the importance of the luteal phase on a female's reproductive system.
5. **Identifying patterns** Although only a single sperm fertilizes an ovum, the presence of many sperm is beneficial to the process of fertilization. Based on what you know about a sperm's effects on an ovum, explain why this is true.
6. **Identifying relationships** Explain why it is important that the membrane of an ovum changes after a sperm has reached its nucleus.
7. **Relating concepts** Describe how each of the following represents an adaptation that helps to ensure successful fertilization: seminal fluid; production and release of millions of sperm; cilia lining the Fallopian tubes; small mass and long tail of a sperm.
8. **Drawing conclusions** Why is it that sperm can survive for only about 24 hours in the female body, whereas they can survive much longer in the male testes?
9. **Using the writing process** Prepare a poster that highlights the dangers of alcohol and drug abuse during pregnancy.

CHAPTER 44

Human Diseases

"Bring out your dead" was often heard throughout Europe as bubonic plague took its toll. Doctors frequently dressed in leather and filled the beaks of their outfits with perfumes and spices to ward off the disease (inset).

Ring-a-ring o'roses,
A pocket full of posies,
A-tishoo! A-tishoo!
We all fall down.

For all its apparent innocence and playfulness as a child's game, this rhyme originated from something fatally serious—the Black Death, or bubonic plague. This terrible disease ravaged London, England, from 1664 to 1665, killing more than 70,000 people—nearly one fourth of London's population.

In the rhyme, the "ring o' roses" relates to the round rosy rash that is one of the early symptoms of the disease. The phrase "pocket full of posies" stands for the spices or herbs people carried in their pockets to ward off the disease. The last lines, "A-tishoo! A tishoo! We all fall down," refer to the deadly sneeze that occurred as the victim fell dead.

CHAPTER OUTLINE

44–1 The Nature of Disease

Section Objectives

- Define disease and describe how diseases may spread.
- State the germ theory of infectious disease.
- List Koch's postulates.

Any change, other than an injury, that interferes with the normal functioning of the body is a disease. The oldest human documents, some religious and some purely historical, make reference to **disease** and to the burdens that it has placed on human life. Different diseases can be recognized by their **symptoms,** or the changes they produce in the body.

Diseases can be caused by many different things. **Infectious diseases** are produced by **pathogens.** Pathogens are disease-causing microorganisms—such as viruses, bacteria, rickettsiae, fungi, and protozoans. In this chapter we shall discuss several infectious diseases as well as one noninfectious disease —cancer.

What Is Disease?

When the body is successfully invaded by a pathogen, we say that an **infection** has occurred. The numbers of microorganisms in the world around us are so large that infection is a daily event. But sickness is not a daily event because not all infections produce disease. Infectious disease results only when the growth of a pathogen begins to injure the cells and tissues of an infected person.

The relationship between a pathogen and the organism it infects is essentially that of a parasite and its host. You may recall from Chapter 17 that a parasite is an organism that obtains nutrition from the body of a host organism in a way that harms the host. The parasitic lifestyle of the pathogen enables it to take advantage of the host and to ultimately become dependent upon the host organism for its survival.

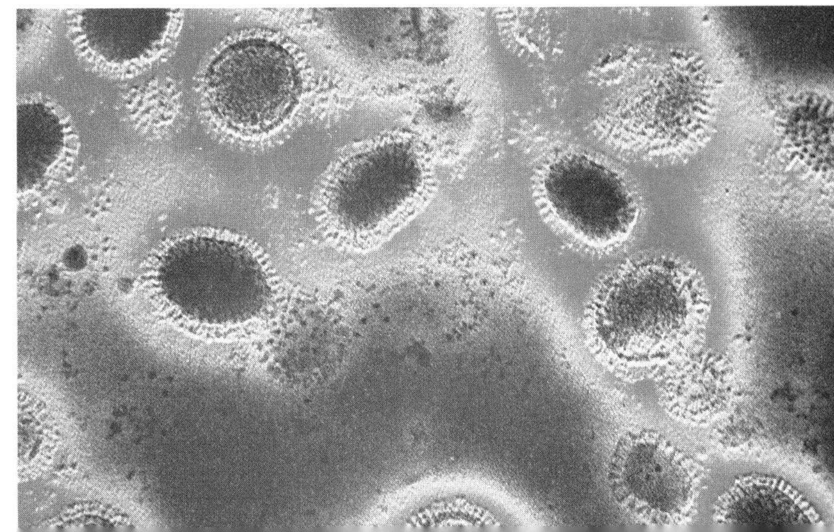

Figure 44–1 *The world we live in is full of microorganisms, most of which have little effect on us. Some, however, such as these influenza viruses can cause disease.*

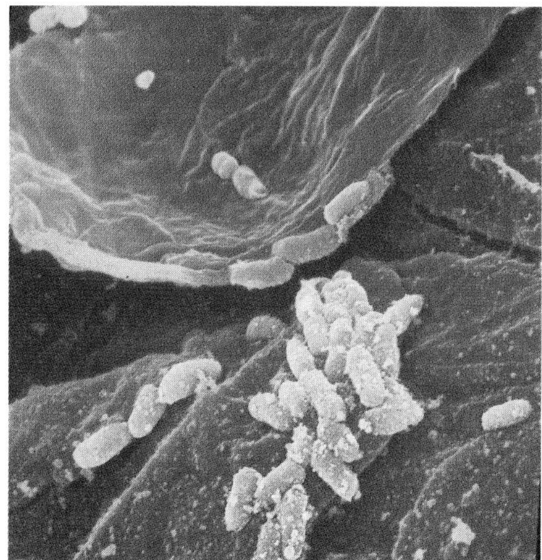

Figure 44–2 *Even when the skin is freshly washed with soap and then rinsed clean, some areas may be home to millions of harmless bacteria (green rod-shaped objects).*

How Is Disease Spread?

Many pathogens are present in the environment and require only the opportunity to enter the body to produce disease. For example, tetanus, often called lockjaw, is produced by the bacterium *Clostridium tetani,* which is present in soil. When the tetanus pathogen enters the body through a cut or puncture in the skin, it grows rapidly in the deepest parts of the wound, causing fever, muscle spasms, and sometimes death.

Some infectious diseases—such as the common cold, measles, mumps, and influenza—are spread from one person to another through coughing and sneezing. Other infectious diseases are spread through contaminated water supplies or through food that has been handled by people infected with a disease. Still other infectious diseases are spread by infected animals such as ticks and mosquitoes. Sexual contact is another way in which infectious diseases are spread.

The Germ Theory of Infectious Disease

Figure 44–3 *This drawing of Robert Koch shows him hard at work in his laboratory investigating rinderpest, a disease that infects cattle.*

For thousands of years people believed that diseases were caused by evil spirits, magic, or miasmas (vapors rising from marshes or decaying plant or animal matter). In fact, the word malaria is taken from the Italian words *mal aria,* meaning bad air. People feared that those who became ill were cursed or had brought bad luck with them.

Fortunately, a new idea developed in the nineteenth century that explained the origins of infectious diseases. Based on the work of the French chemist Louis Pasteur and the German bacteriologist Robert Koch, it was shown that infectious diseases were caused by microorganisms. This idea is now known as the **germ theory of infectious disease.**

Koch was a great pioneer in the study of disease. Not only did he help develop the germ theory of infectious disease, but he also discovered the bacteria that cause tuberculosis, a respiratory disease, and anthrax, a deadly disease that affects farm animals. As he investigated these diseases, Koch realized that the body of an infected person contains dozens of different microorganisms. Which of these microorganisms are responsible for the disease and which are not? Koch's experiments and observations led him to develop a series of rules for proving that a specific type of microorganism causes a specific disease. These rules are called **Koch's postulates:**

- **The microorganism should always be found in the body of the host organism and not in a healthy organism.**
- **The microorganism must be isolated and grown in a pure culture away from the host.**

SCIENCE, TECHNOLOGY, AND SOCIETY **APPLICATION**

The Magic Bullets

When Alexander Fleming discovered penicillin, he opened the door for scores of other scientists to discover weapons against infectious diseases. Penicillin is an antibiotic, or a substance produced by an organism that weakens or kills bacteria. Since Fleming's work in 1928, nearly a hundred different antibiotics have been discovered. Some of them, such as penicillin and tetracycline, are produced by fungi. Others, such as streptomycin, are produced by bacteria.

The action of all antibiotics is based on the differences that exist between bacteria and the cells of the body. For example, penicillin weakens the bacteria's cell walls, causing them to burst under osmotic pressure. Streptomycin and tetracycline, on the other hand, stop protein synthesis on bacterial ribosomes, yet these antibiotics do not affect the cytoplasmic ribosomes of body cells.

Although antibiotics are powerful and effective, they have two serious limitations. First, they act only against bacterial infections. Second, the widespread use of antibiotics has led to the evolution of strains of bacteria that are resistant to antibiotics. This development points out the fact that evolution is a continuing process. It also stresses the need to develop new bacterial-resistant antibiotics and to make wiser use of the ones we already have.

- **When the microorganisms grown in pure culture are injected into a new host organism, they produce disease.**
- **The same microorganisms should be reisolated from the second host and grown in a pure culture, after which the microorganisms should still be the same as the original microorganisms.**

Koch's postulates enable scientists to determine whether a particular microorganism causes a disease. These postulates are still used today in the study of infectious disease.

44–1 SECTION REVIEW

1. What is disease? How are diseases spread?
2. What is the germ theory of infectious disease? What are Koch's postulates?
3. Devise an experiment to determine whether a microorganism causes a certain infectious disease.

Section Objectives

- Explain how infectious diseases are grouped.
- List some diseases caused by viruses, bacteria, rickettsiae, fungi, and protozoans.

44–2 Agents of Disease

Most microorganisms have little interest in humans. A few microorganisms, however, find the human body an inviting home that is warm, protected, and chock-full of nutrients. These friendly microorganisms settle in certain parts of the body and live in harmony with it.

Unfortunately, some microscopic residents may invade body tissue and multiply within it or travel through the bloodstream to all parts of the body. If left unchecked, these invaders can cause serious, even fatal, illnesses.

Scientists group infectious diseases according to the kind of pathogen that causes them. The most common pathogens are viruses and bacteria. Rickettsiae, fungi, and protozoans also produce infections.

Viruses

As you may recall from Chapter 17, viruses are noncellular particles that invade living cells. Viruses contain genetic information in the form of RNA or DNA enclosed in a protein coat. Some viruses are also enclosed in a membrane. Nearly all living organisms, including bacteria, plants, insects, and mammals, can be infected by viruses.

Viruses show no lifelike activities unless they infect a living cell. In order to do so, a virus must become attached to the cell's surface and then insert its genetic material into the cell. Once inside, the viral genes may lie dormant for a period of time or they may go right to work producing new viruses and destroying the infected cell. Some serious diseases—such as AIDS (*A*cquired *I*mmune *D*eficiency *S*yndrome), poliomyelitis (polio), smallpox, and measles—are caused by viruses.

Figure 44–4 *According to this chart of common viral diseases, by what methods is the virus that causes German measles spread?*

SOME VIRAL DISEASES

Disease	Organism that Causes the Disease	Methods of Spreading the Disease
Chicken pox	One virus	Droplets in air; direct contact with infected person
Common cold	Many viruses	Droplets in air; direct contact with infected person
German measles (rubella)	One virus	Droplet spread; direct contact with infected person
Infectious mononucleosis	Probably one virus	Spread by droplets; may be spread by direct contact
Influenza	Two important types (A,B) of virus and many subtypes	Direct contact with infected person; droplet infection; also may be airborne
Measles (rubeola)	One virus	Droplets in air; direct contact with secretions of infected person
Mumps	One virus	Droplet spread; direct contact with infected person
Pneumonia (viral)	Several viruses	Droplets; oral contact with infected person
Poliomyelitis	Poliovirus types 1, 2, and 3	Direct contact with infected person

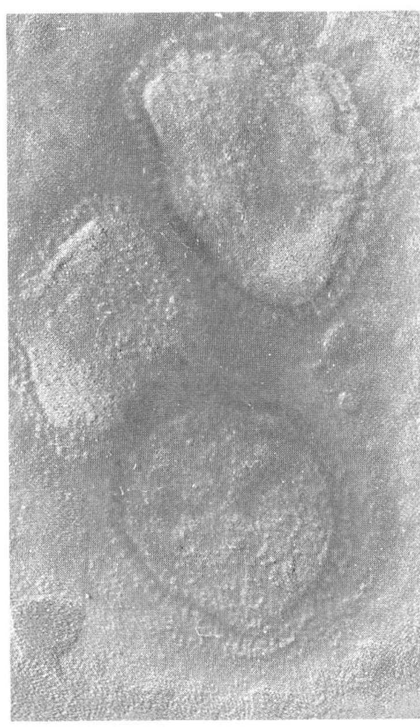

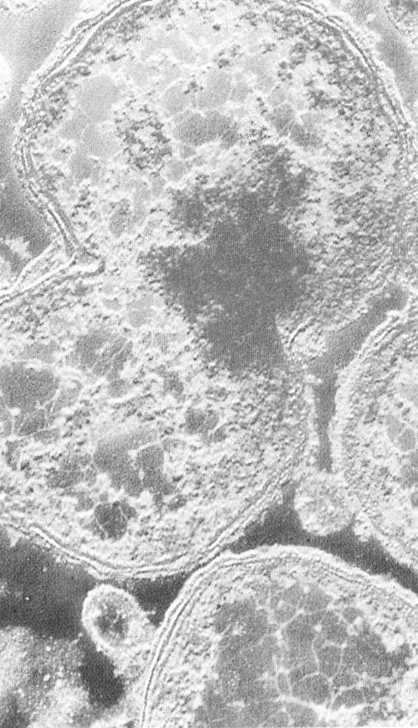

Figure 44–5 *Once inside their host, mumps viruses (left) cause the painful swelling of the salivary glands characteristic of the disease. The bacteria* Neisseria meningitidis *(right) are responsible for causing meningococcal meningitis, which is often more serious than meningitis.*

Bacteria

Contrary to popular belief, most bacteria are harmless to humans. The few bacteria that are pathogens produce disease in a variety of ways. Some bacteria infect the tissues of the body directly. For example, the bacterium that causes gonorrhea (*Neisseria gonorrhoeae*) grows in the tissues that line the male and female reproductive tracts. As the bacterium multiplies, it kills the cells in those passageways, causing irritation and bleeding (symptoms of the disease). Gonorrhea may also be transmitted from an infected mother to her child at birth.

Figure 44–6 *According to this chart of bacterial diseases, what organism causes whooping cough?*

SOME BACTERIAL DISEASES

Disease	Organism That Causes the Disease	Methods of Spreading the Disease
Diphtheriae	*Corynebacterium diphtheria*	Contact with a patient or carrier; contaminated raw milk
Meningitis	*Listeria monocytogenes*	Direct exposure to the organism
Pneumonia	*Diplococcus pneumoniae*	Droplets in air; direct oral contact with infected person
Scarlet fever	*Streptococcus pyogenes*	Droplets in air; direct contact with infected person or carrier; contaminated milk
Syphilis	*Treponema pallidum*	Sexual contact
Tetanus	*Clostridium tetani*	Dirty wound, usually a puncture wound
Tuberculosis	*Mycobacterium tuberculosis*	Droplets in air; contaminated milk and dairy products
Whooping cough	*Bordetella pertussis*	Droplets in air

Other bacteria cause disease by producing **toxins,** or poisons. In some cases the toxin itself may be enough to cause illness. For example, the bacterium *Clostridium botulinum* produces a toxin so powerful that just a few drops of it is enough to kill the population of a small city. Botulism, the illness produced by this toxin, attacks the nervous system and is often fatal.

Rickettsiae

Like bacteria, rickettsiae (rih-KEHT-see-ee) are prokaryotes. However, like viruses, they can grow only within a living cell. Rickettsiae can be transmitted to humans by arthropods (animals with jointed legs). Ticks sometimes carry a disease called Rocky Mountain spotted fever, which produces a high fever, muscle pains, and headaches. These symptoms may last for as long as three weeks. A disease more serious than Rocky Mountain spotted fever is typhus. Typhus is transmitted from person to person by body lice or fleas.

Figure 44–7 *African sleeping sickness is caused by the protozoan* Trypanosoma, *which is transmitted to humans by the bite of a tsetse fly (top). The discovery of these 35-million-year-old fossils of tsetse flies (bottom) in Colorado is evidence that the flies once existed in an area other than Africa.*

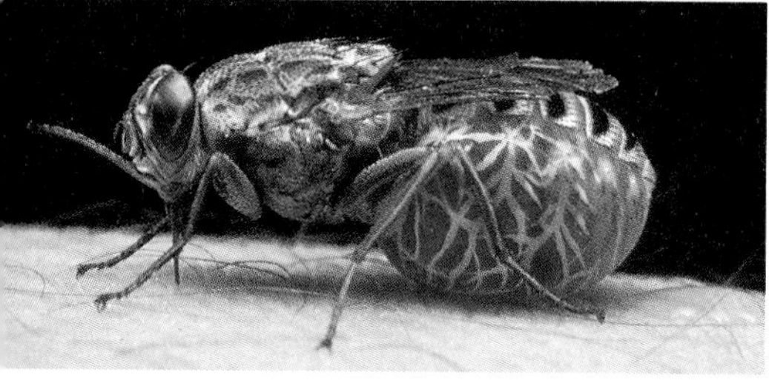

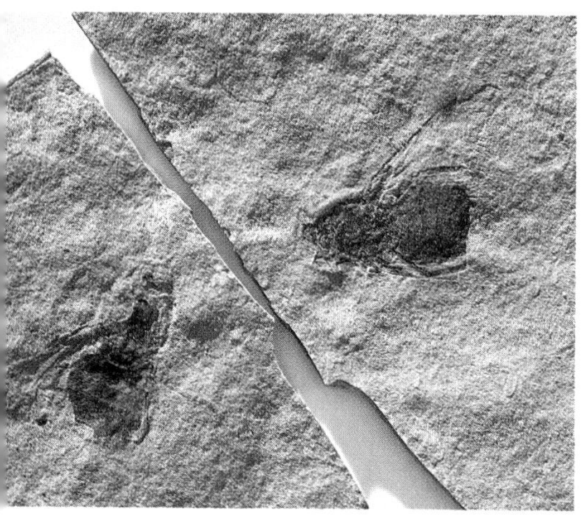

Fungi

Most fungi, which include the molds and mushrooms, do not cause disease. Occasionally, however, the fungi that are normally present on the skin grow so rapidly that they can cause serious infections. The most common fungal infections are those caused by the dermatophytes (skin plants). Dermatophytes include those organisms that produce the rough, irritated patches on the toes known as athlete's foot and the scaly scalp infection known as ringworm.

Protozoans

More than 30 different species of protozoans cause human disease. The most serious infections produced by these organisms are commonly found in the tropical regions of the world. There, the warm, moist surroundings provide the protozoans with ideal conditions for survival.

Because of the enormous numbers of people infected with malaria, this disease may be considered the most serious health problem affecting the human species. Malaria is caused by the protozoan *Plasmodium*, which lives in the bloodstream. Malaria is spread from one person to another by mosquitoes. The life cycle of the malaria parasite is discussed in Chapter 18.

The protozoan *Entamoeba histolytica* causes a disease known as amebic dysentery. Amebic dysentery affects the intestines and causes abdominal pain and fever. The disease-causing protozoan is found in contaminated water supplies.

African sleeping sickness is another disease caused by a protozoan—in this case, the flagellated protozoan known as *Trypanosoma*. African sleeping sickness is spread by the tsetse fly and is common in tropical regions of Africa. The disease results in an inflammation of the nervous system, including the brain. Once symptoms develop, the disease is usually fatal.

44–2 SECTION REVIEW

1. How are infectious diseases grouped?
2. Give two examples each of diseases caused by viruses, bacteria, rickettsiae, fungi, and protozoans.
3. Why is it not possible for viruses to grow on agar?

SCIENCE, TECHNOLOGY, AND SOCIETY BREAKTHROUGH

A New Disease

In 1975, Dr. Allen Steere of Yale University School of Medicine was faced with a puzzle. Close to 50 cases of rheumatoid arthritis, a painful swelling of the joints, had been reported in three townships in eastern Connecticut: Old Lyme, Lyme, and East Haddam. Although this form of arthritis is not rare, there was something odd about these cases. There were too many of them, they appeared too suddenly, and they were associated with reddish skin rashes.

Little by little, Dr. Steere and his colleagues began to put the pieces of the puzzle together. After a thorough study, Steere concluded that the disease was caused by a spirochete bacterium spread by the tiny deer tick. He named the condition Lyme disease after the town in which it was first observed.

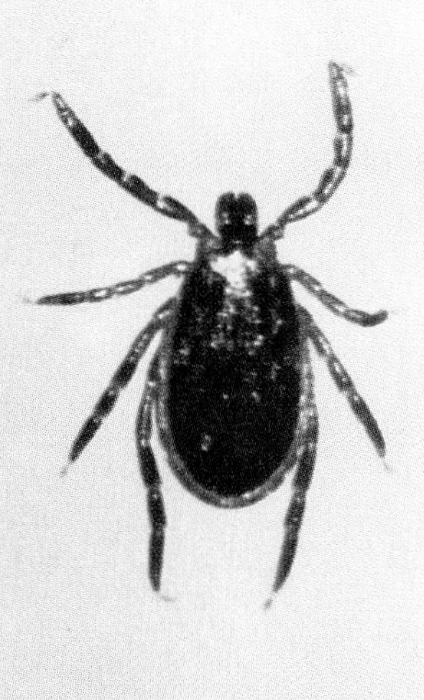

A female deer tick (Ixodes dammini)

Because the deer tick is barely larger than a pinhead, it is easily overlooked by its victims. Within a few days after being bitten by the deer tick, a bull's-eye-like rash appears in the area of the tick bite. The rash is frequently accompanied by fatigue, fever, chills, backache, and headache. In some cases these symptoms, including the rash, do not appear. Later, infections of the nervous system and musculoskeletal pain can result. Lastly rheumatoid arthritis occurs.

Fortunately, Lyme disease can be treated successfully if detected early. Orally administered antibiotics such as penicillin, tetracycline, and erythromycin are effective against the disease. Advanced cases, however, are more difficult to treat and require hospitalization and the intravenous administration of antibiotics.

Section Objectives

- Define cancer.
- Discuss three main causes of cancer.
- List three methods of cancer treatment.

44–3 Cancer

Cancer is a life-threatening disease in which cells multiply uncontrollably and destroy healthy tissue. Cancer is a unique disease because the cells that cause it are not foreign cells but rather the body's own cells. This fact has made **cancer** difficult to treat and to understand.

Cancer develops when something goes wrong with the normal controls that exist to regulate cell growth. A single cell or group of cells begins to grow and divide uncontrollably, often resulting in the formation of a **tumor.** A tumor is a mass of tissue. Some tumors are benign (bih-NIGHN), or noncancerous. A benign tumor does not spread to surrounding healthy tissue or to other parts of the body.

Cancerous tumors, on the other hand, are malignant. Malignant tumors invade and eventually destroy surrounding healthy tissue. In some cases, cells from a malignant tumor break away and are carried by blood and lymph to other parts of the body. As the cancer cells spread throughout the body, they absorb the nutrients needed by other cells, block nerve connections, and prevent the organs they invade from functioning properly. Soon the delicate balances that exist in the body are disrupted, and life-threatening illness results. There are many different forms of cancer, most of which take their name from the tissues in which cancer cells originate. Liver cancer, skin cancer, and bone cancer are some examples.

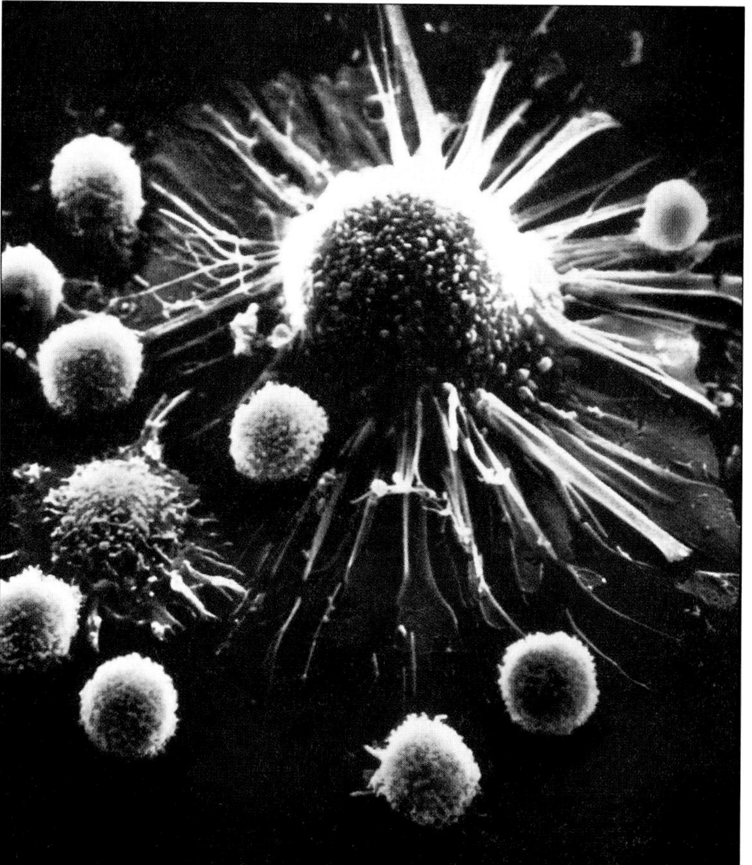

Figure 44–8 The crablike structure in this photograph is a cancer cell. The spherical objects surrounding the cancer cell are special white blood cells that are preparing to attack and destroy it.

Causes of Cancer

Although the basic cause of cancer is not known, scientists believe that cancer develops because of repeated or prolonged contact with a cancer-causing substance. In addition, scientists suspect that a person may inherit a tendency to develop certain types of cancer.

VIRUSES Because most cancers seem to arise spontaneously, the causes of cancer have baffled scientists for decades. In recent years, however, cancer research has made dramatic strides in identifying certain viruses as cancer-causing agents. A small number of cancers in animals were found to be caused by viruses. This discovery has led scientists to propose a viral theory of cancer. According to this theory, **oncogenes**, or cancer-causing genes, in certain viruses cause normal cells to be transformed into cancer cells. Exactly what are oncogenes?

Remarkably, viral oncogenes resemble normal cellular genes that regulate cell growth, cell division, and metabolic pathways. When oncogenic viruses infect normal cells, the altered or extra copies of oncogenes that they contain upset the normal balances that control cell growth. The infected cells begin to grow and produce tumors.

Despite the association between viruses and cancer, viruses are not a major cause of human cancer. Cancer, therefore, is not a disease that can be transmitted from one person to another. Thus there is no way of "catching" cancer from a person who has it.

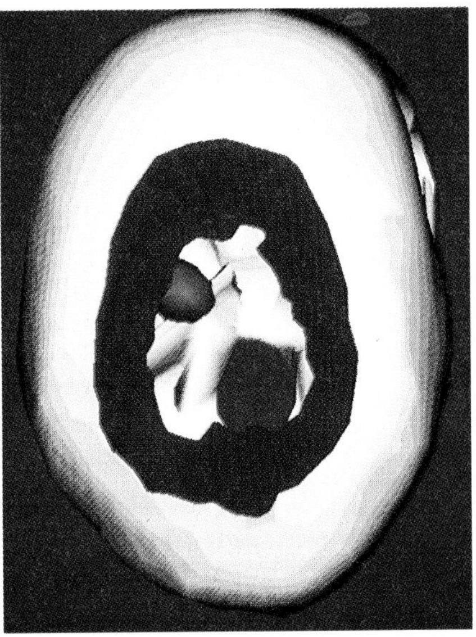

Figure 44–9 *The red area visible on this CAT (computerized axial tomography) image shows the location of a tumor within the skull. The yellow and black areas are parts of the skull, and the blue area is the opening through which the spinal cord joins with the brain.*

RADIATION Most forms of radiation—including sunlight, X-rays, and nuclear radiation—can cause cancer. The larger the amount of radiation, the greater the chance of developing cancer. Why does radiation cause cancer?

Radiation produces mutations, or changes in the structure of DNA, in living cells that are exposed to it. If these mutations occur in genes that control cell growth, a normal cell may be transformed into a cancer cell.

Figure 44–10 *Overexposure to the ultraviolet radiation of sunlight on a repeated basis can cause skin cancer.*

Most cases of skin cancer, for example, are caused by the ultraviolet radiation that is a normal part of sunlight. Over many years, constant exposure of the skin to this type of radiation can produce mutations in the DNA of skin cells. For this reason, it is important to avoid sunburn and excessive exposure to sunlight.

CHEMICALS Chemical **carcinogens**, or cancer-causing compounds, are some of the most important causes of cancer. Like radiation, carcinogens produce cancer by causing mutations in the DNA of normal cells. Some carcinogens, such as aflatoxin, are produced naturally by molds that grow on peanuts. Others, such as chloroform and benzene, are synthetic compounds. Some of these synthetic compounds may pollute the air or drinking water and therefore endanger entire communities. When this occurs, local, state, or federal agencies must step in to stop such practices.

Some of the most powerful chemical carcinogens are found in tobacco smoke. In the United States, cigarette smoking is responsible for nearly half the cancers that occur. Cigarette smoking causes most cases of lung cancer—the most fatal form of cancer.

Cancer Treatment

The most important weapon in the fight against cancer is early detection. If a cancer is detected early, the chances of treating it successfully are as high as 90 percent. **Physicians use three main methods to treat cancer: surgery, radiation**

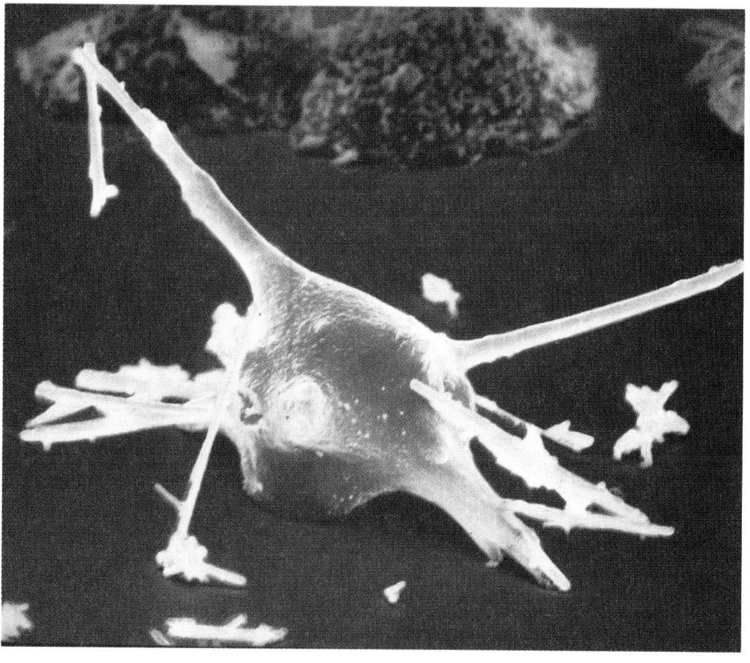

Figure 44–11 *Some chemicals, such as asbestos, are carcinogenic, or cancer-causing. The asbestos fibers visible in this photograph are being engulfed by a special white blood cell.*

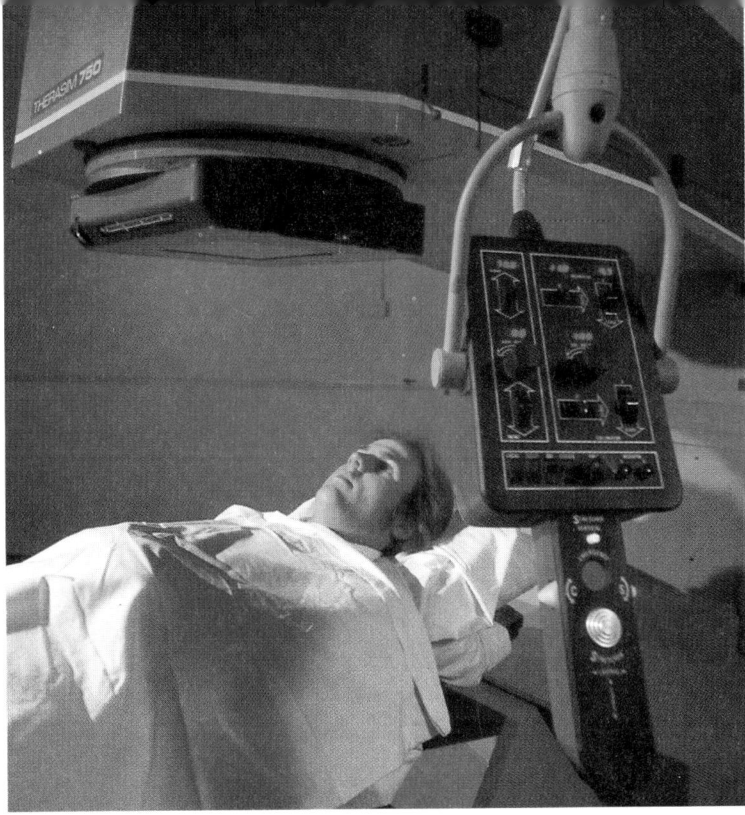

Figure 44–12 *Radiation therapy is one method of treating cancer.*

therapy, and drug therapy. In many cases, treatment is made up of two or sometimes all three of these methods.

Localized tumors, or those that do not spread, are often removed by surgery. If this can be done before the cancer has spread, the patient may be completely cured. Unfortunately, healthy tissue may also have to be removed to help prevent the disease from spreading.

Radiation therapy involves attacking cancer with radiation. Perhaps this seems confusing, as you just learned that radiation is also a cause of cancer. However, radiation destroys fast-growing cancer cells more quickly than normal cells, making this method a useful form of therapy.

Drug therapy, or chemotherapy, is the use of a combination of chemicals to destroy the fast-growing cancer cells. More than 50 drugs are used against a variety of cancers. Most of the anticancer drugs destroy cancer cells with as little harm to normal cells as possible. However, they do injure normal cells to some degree, producing some side effects such as nausea and high blood pressure.

44–3 SECTION REVIEW

1. What are the three main causes of cancer?
2. What are some methods of treating cancer?
3. Is cancer an infectious disease? Explain your answer.

LABORATORY INVESTIGATION

OBSERVING BACTERIAL GROWTH

PROBLEM

What conditions are needed for the growth of bacteria?

MATERIALS *(per group)*

2 nutrient agar plates	transparent tape
glass-marking pencil	refrigerator
hand soap	incubator
paper towel	

PROCEDURE 

1. Turn the nutrient agar plates upside down. With a glass-marking pencil, draw a line across the center of the plates dividing each in half. Label one half *WASHED* and the other half *UNWASHED.* Also label one plate *R* for refrigerator and the other *I* for incubator. Write the initials of a group member on each plate.
2. Slightly raise the cover of the agar plate labeled *R* and touch your thumb to the surface on the half labeled *UNWASHED.* **Note:** *Do not completely remove the cover from the plate.* Cover the plate immediately.
3. Repeat step 2 for the plate labeled *I.*
4. Thoroughly wash your hands with soap and water. Rinse and then dry your hands with a clean paper towel.
5. Repeat steps 2 and 3, touching your washed thumb to the surface of the agar on the half of each plate labeled *WASHED.*
6. Tape both plates closed with transparent tape. Place the plate labeled *R* in the refrigerator and the plate labeled *I* in the incubator at 37°C. Be sure that the plates are placed upside down. Allow them to remain undisturbed for 48 hours.
7. After 48 hours, examine both plates. Look for raised patches on the agar where you touched it. The raised patches are colonies of bacteria.
8. Examine the colonies of bacteria. Note the color and general appearance of individual colonies.

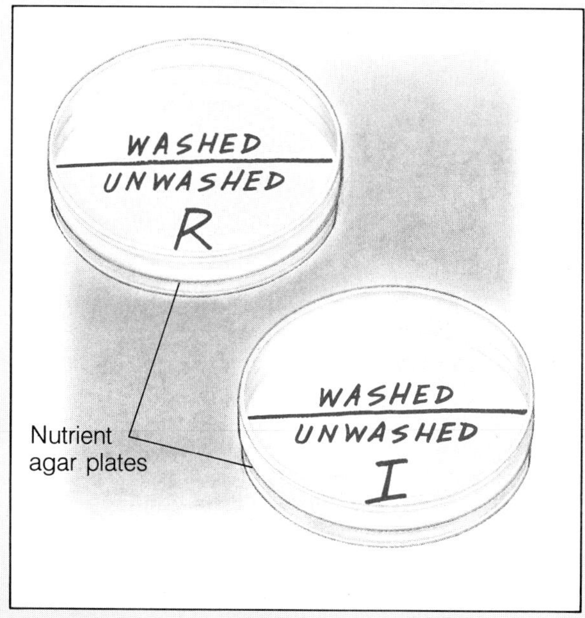

OBSERVATIONS

1. Which nutrient agar plate has more bacterial growth?
2. Based on color and general appearance, how many different types of bacteria appear to be growing on each agar plate?

ANALYSIS AND CONCLUSIONS

1. Why do you slightly raise the cover of the agar plate rather than remove it completely?
2. What evidence indicates the presence of bacteria on your skin?
3. Are conditions more favorable for the growth of bacteria inside or outside the body? Give evidence to support your answer.
4. In addition to food (which had been added to the agar), what other conditions are necessary for bacterial growth?
5. Describe some ways in which you might stop the growth of bacteria.

STUDENT STUDY GUIDE

SUMMARIZING THE CONCEPTS

The key concepts in each section of this chapter are listed below to help you review the chapter content. Make sure you understand each concept and its relationship to other concepts and to the theme of this chapter.

44–1 The Nature of Disease

- Any change other than an injury that interferes with the normal functioning of the body is a disease. Diseases can be recognized by their symptoms.
- The idea that infectious diseases are caused by microorganisms is known as the germ theory of infectious disease.
- Koch's postulates state: the microorganism should always be found in the body of the host organism and not in a healthy organism; the microorganism must be isolated and grown in a pure culture away from the host; when the microorganisms grown in pure culture are injected into a new host organism, they produce disease; and the same microorganisms should be reisolated from the second host and grown in a pure culture, after which the microorganisms should still be the same as the original microorganisms.

44–2 Agents of Disease

- Infectious diseases are grouped according to the kind of pathogen that causes them. Viruses, bacteria, rickettsiae, fungi, and protozoans are some examples of pathogens.
- Some examples of diseases caused by viruses are AIDS, poliomyelitis, smallpox, and measles. Gonorrhea and botulism are examples of bacterial diseases.
- Rocky Mountain spotted fever and typhus are diseases caused by rickettsiae.
- Common types of fungal infections include athlete's foot and ringworm.
- Malaria, amebic dysentery, and African sleeping sickness are caused by protozoans.

44–3 Cancer

- Cancer is a life-threatening disease in which cells multiply uncontrollably and destroy healthy tissue.
- Causes of cancer include viral oncogenes, radiation, and chemical carcinogens.
- Physicians use three main methods to treat cancer: surgery, radiation therapy, and drug therapy.

REVIEWING KEY TERMS

Vocabulary terms are important to your understanding of biology. The key terms listed below are those you should be especially familiar with. Review these terms and their meanings. Then use each term in a complete sentence. If you are not sure of a term's meaning, return to the appropriate section and review its definition.

44–1 The Nature of Disease

disease
symptom
infectious disease
pathogen
infection
germ theory of infectious disease
Koch's postulates

44–2 Agents of Disease

toxin

44–3 Cancer

cancer
tumor
oncogene
carcinogen

CHAPTER REVIEW

CONTENT REVIEW

Multiple Choice

Choose the letter of the answer that best completes each statement.

1. An infectious disease is caused by a (an)
a. pathogen. c. infection.
b. symptom. d. tumor.

2. What occurs when the body is invaded by a pathogen?
a. vaccine c. infection
b. toxin d. cancer

3. Which disease is caused by a virus?
a. botulism c. malaria
b. athlete's foot d. measles

4. The poisons produced by some bacteria are called
a. antibiotics. c. pathogens.
b. toxins. d. oncogenes.

5. Which disease is caused by a rickettsia?
a. AIDS c. typhus
b. cancer d. mumps

6. A mass of tissue in the body is called a (an)
a. tumor. c. infection.
b. pathogen. d. toxin.

7. Chemical compounds that are cancer-causing are called
a. oncogenes. c. carcinogens.
b. pathogens. d. toxins.

8. Which is used in the treatment of cancer?
a. carcinogens c. radiation
b. viruses d. antibiotics

True or False

Determine whether each statement is true or false. If it is true, write "true." If it is false, change the underlined word or words to make the statement true.

1. Diseases caused by microorganisms are called infectious diseases.
2. Tetanus is caused by a virus.
3. The idea that infectious diseases are caused by microorganisms is known as Koch's postulates.
4. Skin cancer often results from constant overexposure to carcinogens.
5. Smallpox is caused by a protozoan.
6. Ringworm is caused by a fungus.
7. Antibiotics are cancer-causing compounds.
8. Cancerous tumors are also called benign tumors.

Word Relationships

A. *An analogy is a relationship between two pairs of words or phrases generally written in the following manner: a:b::c:d. The symbol : is read "is to," and the symbol :: is read "as." For example, cat:animal::rose:plant is read "cat is to animal as rose is to plant."*

In the analogies that follow, a word or phrase is missing. Complete each analogy by providing the missing word or phrase.

1. tetanus:bacterium::athlete's foot: ________________
2. infectious disease:common cold::noninfectious disease: ________________
3. noncancerous:benign::cancerous: ________________
4. fungus:ringworm::rickettsia: ________________

B. *In each of the following sets of terms, three of the terms are related. One term does not belong. Determine the characteristic common to three of the terms and then identify the term that does not belong.*

5. polio, measles, gonorrhea, smallpox
6. cancer, botulism, AIDS, typhus
7. surgery, radiation, drugs, viruses
8. tetanus, malaria, botulism, gonorrhea

CONCEPT MASTERY

Use your understanding of the concepts developed in the chapter to answer each of the following in a brief paragraph.

1. Discuss the importance of Koch's postulates in explaining the origins of infectious disease.
2. Compare the transmission of African sleeping sickness and amebic dysentery.
3. Discuss the advantages and disadvantages of the three methods used to treat cancer.
4. Compare a benign and a malignant tumor.
5. Describe three ways in which infectious diseases are spread.
6. List five types of pathogens that are responsible for the spread of infectious disease. Describe each and give one example of a disease that the specific pathogen may cause.

CRITICAL AND CREATIVE THINKING

Discuss each of the following in a brief paragraph.

1. **Interpreting diagrams** The chart shows the incidence and survival rates of some cancers in the United States. Which type of cancer has the best survival rate? The worst? Why do you think the five-year survival rates increased between 1960 and 1963 and between 1977 and 1983?

	Five-Year Survival Rates	
Site of Cancer	**1960–63**	**1977–83**
Digestive tract		
Stomach	9.5%	16.0%
Colon and rectum	36.0%	46.0%
Respiratory tract		
Lung and bronchus	6.5%	12.0%
Urinary tract		
Kidney and other urinary structures	37.5%	51.0%
Reproductive system		
Breast	54.0%	68.0%
Ovary	32.0%	38.0%
Testis	63.0%	74.5%
Prostate gland	42.5%	63.0%
Skin (melanoma only)	60.0%	79.0%

2. **Applying concepts** Explain why you should not go to school with influenza.
3. **Developing a hypothesis** A doctor suspects that an apparently new disease is caused by a bacterium. Describe a set of procedures for proving this hypothesis.
4. **Making predictions** Some people think that it will be possible to wipe out all diseases some day. Do you think that this is possible? Explain your answer.
5. **Relating facts** Why is cancer more of a problem today than it was 100 years ago?
6. **Using the writing process** The incidence of sexually transmitted diseases in the United States is on the rise. Prepare an advertising campaign in which you alert people to the serious medical consequences of these diseases.

CHAPTER 45

Immune System

The virus that causes polio is only 28 billionths of a meter wide (inset). In 1954, a vaccine was developed that protected people from polio. These children, obviously filled with apprehension, were among the first to be vaccinated.

For parents, springtime had always been a time of mixed feelings: happiness in seeing their children out of doors but terror in knowing that the children could catch a terrible crippling disease called polio.

In 1954, the nation breathed a sigh of relief. Headlines around the country announced the results of an experimental vaccine that had been tested on more than 1 million children. Polio was beaten! Children were free to run and play at last, parents could sleep more easily, and many forgot why they had worried about the coming of springtime. In this chapter you will learn how this disease and many others were conquered. But you will also learn about new diseases that constantly challenge both our social and scientific skills and continue to take their toll in human lives.

CHAPTER OUTLINE

45–1 Nonspecific Defenses

Section Objectives

- Describe the function of the immune system.
- Identify three nonspecific defenses against infection.

Protective mechanisms are found in every living thing. An ameba pulls itself back when it is poked with a pin. Many algae grow thick cell walls to survive in the mud when the lake they live in dries up. A prairie dog dives into its burrow to hide from a hawk circling overhead.

One of our most basic protective devices is our nervous system. Using automatic reflexes and conscious decisions, we protect ourselves from physical injury in many ways. We close our eyelids when an object approaches our face, and we brace for a fall if we lose our balance. Other kinds of protection are built into the human body. Extremely delicate structures, such as the eye, are protected by a casing of bones. Vital organs, such as the lungs and heart, are located deep within the chest cavity. The spinal cord is surrounded by the vertebrae that make up the spinal column.

Skin, muscles, bones, and nerves all protect the body against obvious physical dangers—threats that we can see. But there is an unseen threat that each of us faces every day. It is the threat of infection. As you learned in Chapter 44, an infection occurs when the body is successfully invaded by a pathogen, or disease-causing microorganism. The living world teems with pathogens—viruses, bacteria, rickettsiae, fungi, and protozoans—all capable of producing infectious disease.

The immune system is our primary defense against disease-causing microorganisms. The **immune system** consists of nonspecific and specific defenses against infection. **Nonspecific defenses** are the body's first line against disease.

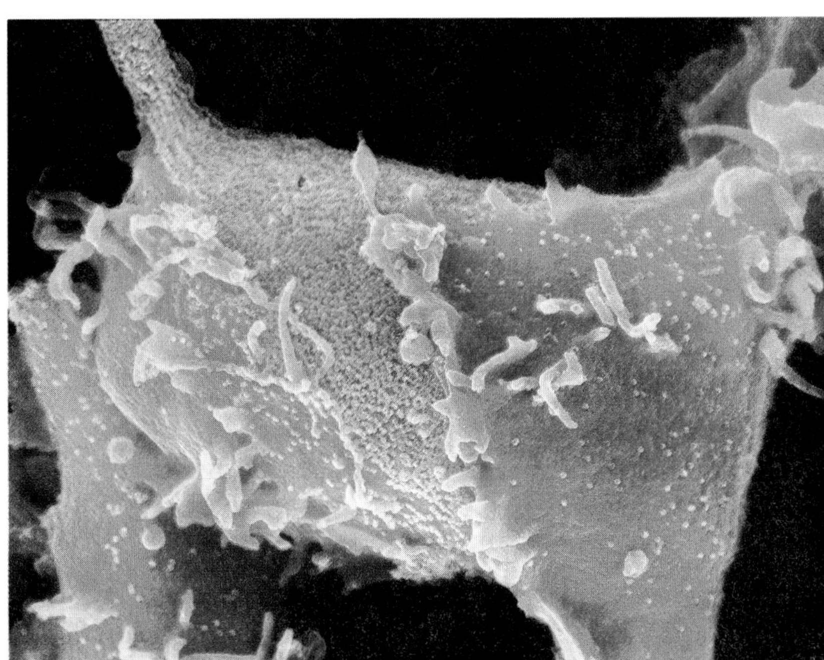

Figure 45–1 *When a virus infects a cell, it takes control of the genetic material of the cell and reproduces. In time, fully formed viruses burst from the cell, killing it. The new viruses are then able to infect other cells.*

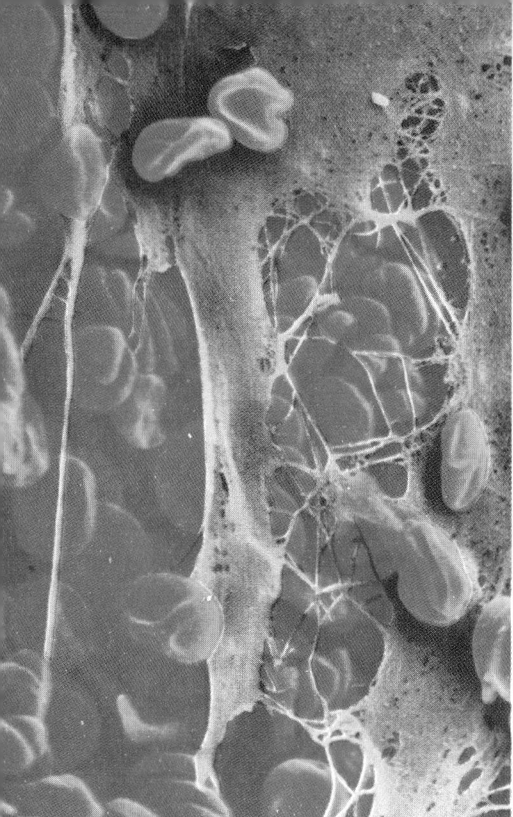

Figure 45–2 Unbroken skin is an effective barrier against most microorganisms. But any break in the skin—even the tiniest—will provide microorganisms with a means of entering the body quite easily. Here red blood cells are visible through broken skin.

Nonspecific defenses are not directed against a particular pathogen. Rather, nonspecific defenses guard against all infections, regardless of their cause. Specific defenses are attempts by the body to defend itself against particular pathogens. You will read more about specific defenses later in this chapter.

The Skin and Other Barriers

The body's most important nonspecific defense is the skin. As you learned in Chapter 38, skin is a tough, flexible layer that covers most of the body. Very few pathogens can penetrate the layers of dead cells at the skin's outer surface. Oil and sweat glands at the surface of the skin produce an acidic environment that kills many bacteria and other microorganisms. The importance of the skin as a barrier against infection becomes obvious when a small portion of skin is broken or scraped off: Infections almost always follow such cuts and scrapes. These infections are the result of the penetration of the broken skin by microorganisms normally present on the unbroken surface.

Pathogens also enter the body through the mouth and nose, but the body has other nonspecific defenses that protect those openings. For example, mucus and hairs in the nose and throat trap viruses and bacteria. Cilia in the trachea trap bacteria and dust and push them up toward the mouth. Many pathogens that make their way to the stomach are destroyed by stomach acid and digestive enzymes. Finally, many secretions of the body—including mucus, saliva, sweat, and tears—contain **lysozyme**, an enzyme that breaks down the cell wall of many bacteria.

Phagocytes and Inflammation

If large numbers of pathogens do enter the body, however, a second line of defense begins. This second line is called the **inflammatory response**. The bacteria within a wound cause fluid and white blood cells to leak from blood vessels into nearby tissue. Bacteria are attacked by **phagocytes**, which are white blood cells that engulf and destroy bacteria. If the infection remains small and in one place, a reddish swollen area develops just beneath the skin. The area is said to be **inflamed** (literally, "on fire"). Sometimes an infection spreads through the lymphatic system (Chapter 41) to the **lymph nodes**, where it causes swelling and tenderness of the nodes as the battle between pathogen and white blood cells continues.

Serious infections may allow pathogens to spread throughout the body. The immune system now responds in two ways. One, it produces more white blood cells. Two, it releases chemicals that stimulate the action of these white cells by increasing the body's temperature. Thus a **fever** is produced. Physicians know that fever and an increased number of white blood cells are two indications that the body is hard at work fighting infection. Fever also serves another important function: Many

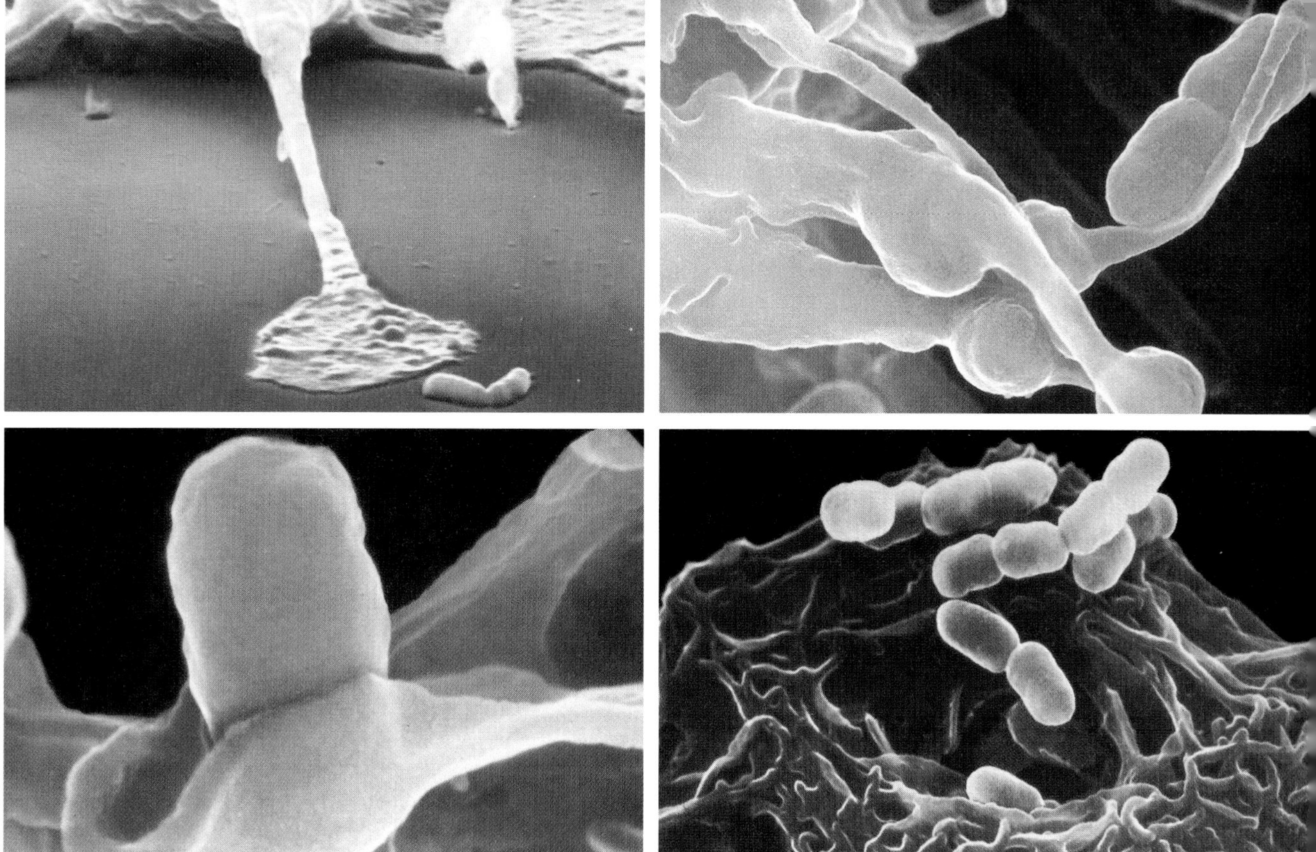

Figure 45–3 Macrophages are an extremely important defense against microorganisms. This remarkable sequence of photographs illustrates what happens when a macrophage encounters bacteria. The macrophage first reaches out toward two bacterial cells. Pseudopods from the macrophage then trap the bacteria. Digestive enzymes produced by the macrophage begin to digest one of the bacterial cells. The bacteria will eventually be digested, and their component chemicals will be absorbed by the macrophage.

disease-causing microorganisms can survive within only a narrow temperature range. A higher-than-normal temperature often slows down or stops the growth of such microorganisms.

Interferon

In 1957, scientists discovered that virus-infected cells produce a protein that helps other cells resist viral infection. This protein was named **interferon** because it "interferes" with the virus. Interferon inhibits the synthesis of viral proteins in infected cells and helps block viral replication. These effects on a virus slow down the progress of infection and often give the specific defenses of the immune system time to respond.

45–1 SECTION REVIEW

1. What is the function of the immune system?
2. Compare specific and nonspecific defenses.
3. Why is the skin considered a nonspecific defense?
4. In what two ways does fever help the body fight infection?
5. Why should people wash breaks in the skin with antiseptics?

Section Objectives

- Define antigen and antibody.
- List several specific defenses of the body.

45–2 Specific Defenses

If a pathogen is able to get past the body's nonspecific defenses, the immune system reacts with a series of specific defenses that attack the disease-causing agent. A substance that triggers the **specific defenses** of the immune system is known as an **antigen**. Carbohydrates, proteins, and lipids on the surfaces of viruses, bacteria, and other pathogens may serve as antigens that trigger responses by the immune system.

The Immune Response

The key cells of the immune system are **lymphocytes**, a type of white blood cell. **B-lymphocytes**, which mature in the bone marrow, are responsible for producing **antibodies**. Antibodies are special proteins that can bind to the antigens on the surfaces of a pathogen and help destroy it.

Figure 45–4 *An antibody molecule has two identical antigen-bonding sites. It is at these sites that one or two specific antigens bonds to the antibody.*

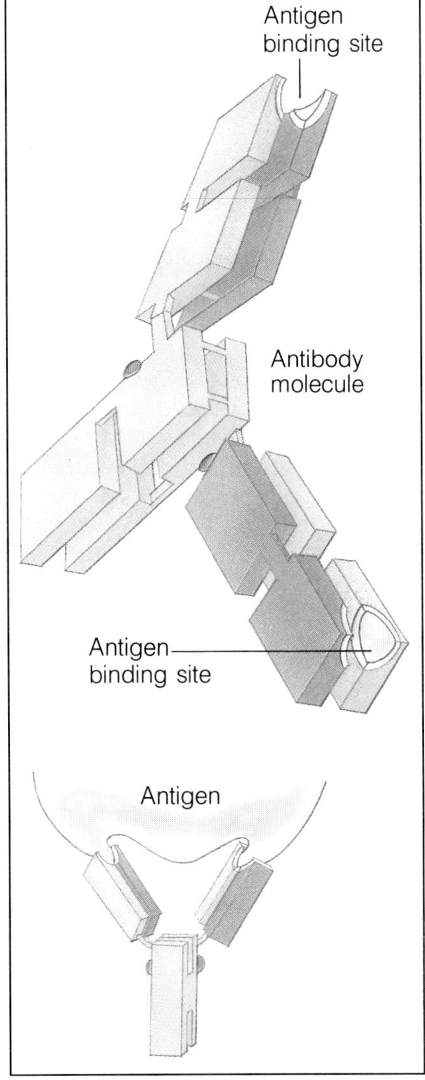

ANTIBODIES The antibody molecule is the basic functional unit of the immune response. An antibody molecule is shaped like the letter Y and has two identical **antigen-binding sites** that precisely fit the shape of a particular antigen. See Figure 45–4. These sites allow each antibody to bind to two antigens. Let's suppose that these antigens are proteins found on the surface of the flu virus. Each flu virus particle is covered with scores of such protein antigens. By attaching to the viral antigens, a group of antibody molecules can link the viruses together in a large mass. This process is called **agglutination**.

For a virus, agglutination is bad news. Agglutinated viruses cannot enter cells. In addition, the linked antibody molecules attract phagocytes, which engulf and destroy the entire mass—viruses and antibodies alike. Simply by binding to the correct antigens, antibodies can prevent viruses from infecting cells.

Antibodies can fight bacterial infections as well. Antibodies that bind to bacterial surface antigens can cause agglutination and mark the agglutinated bacteria for destruction by phagocytes and other white blood cells.

ANTIBODY PRODUCTION How does the immune system produce the specific antibodies that bind to antigens on the surfaces of pathogens? The answer involves a little bit of internal genetic engineering. As each B-cell (B-lymphocyte) develops, the genes that code for antibodies rearrange themselves in slightly different ways in each cell. Although each B-cell produces only one type of antibody, the body's population of B-cells can produce hundreds of thousands of different antibodies. This enables the immune system to respond with specific antibodies for almost any antigen.

When a pathogen invades the body, its antigens activate a small fraction of the body's B-cells. These activated B-cells grow and divide rapidly, producing a large population of specialized B-cells called **plasma cells** that release antibodies into the bloodstream to deal with the infection. The production of antibodies from the first exposure to an antigen is known as the **primary immune response**. Millions of plasma cells may form from just a few dozen B-cells as a result of exposure to an antigen. The activation process is assisted and regulated by lymphocytes that have matured in the thymus gland and are known as **T-lymphocytes** (T-cells).

Immunity

The growth of B-cells and T-cells in response to an infection has an important consequence—one that people have been aware of for more than 2000 years. The Greek physician Hippocrates noted that people who survived certain diseases, such as measles and smallpox, never developed those diseases again. They were permanently **immune**. Today we understand the nature of this immunity. Once the body has been exposed to a disease, a large group of B-cells and T-cells remains capable of producing a **secondary immune response** should the pathogen reappear in the body. A secondary immune response is more powerful than the primary response, producing antibodies so quickly that the disease never gets a chance to develop.

ACTIVE IMMUNITY Smallpox is a serious contagious disease caused by a virus that spreads through the air from one person to another. In 1796, the English country physician Edward Jenner wondered if he could make people immune to smallpox. He knew that there was a mild disease called cowpox that was often contracted by milkmaids. Jenner observed that people who contracted cowpox developed a permanent immunity to smallpox.

Jenner took fluid from one of the sores of a cowpox patient and mixed it into a small cut that he made on the arm of a young farm boy named Jamie Phipps. Jamie developed a mild cowpox infection. Later, to prove that the boy was now immune, Jenner inoculated him with fluid from a smallpox infection. Fortunately for Jamie, the experiment was a success—the boy was indeed immune to smallpox.

The injection of a weakened or mild form of a pathogen to produce immunity is known as **vaccination**. *Vacca* is the Latin word for cow, reflecting the history of Jenner's first vaccination experiment. The immunity produced by a vaccine is known as **active immunity** because the body has the ability to mount an active immune response against the pathogen.

PASTEUR AND THE ANTHRAX VACCINE A different approach was necessary for other diseases. Louis Pasteur, the great French scientist, reasoned that if a weakened or killed disease-causing microorganism was introduced into a person's

THE IMMUNE SYSTEM

Cell	Function
Macrophage	Removes foreign materials and dead and dying cells in the body; also attracts T-cells to foreign organisms
Helper T-cell	Identifies foreign cells in the body; stimulates other cells to fight infection
Killer T-cell	Kills cancerous cells in the body; also kills body cells that have been invaded by pathogenic organisms
Suppressor T-cell	Slows down or stops the activities of B-cells and other T-cells once the danger of infection has passed
B-cell	Produces antibodies; some "remember" the identity of foreign proteins
Antibody	Y-shaped protein molecule that rushes to a site of infection where it neutralizes the enemy or identifies it for attack by other cells or chemicals

Figure 45–5 *Each component of the immune system contributes to the defense of the body. What is the function of killer T-cells?*

body, it might be able to produce immunity without causing the disease. Following this reasoning, Pasteur isolated the bacterium responsible for anthrax, a serious disease that affects farm animals and humans. He grew the bacterium in his lab and treated it with heat in order to weaken it. He believed that the treated bacteria from which he would make his vaccine would not cause anthrax. Eager to prove that his approach could prevent disease, Pasteur arranged a public demonstration.

He placed 25 sheep in one pen and 25 in another. All of the animals in the first pen were injected with his vaccine. A week later, Pasteur injected the animals in both pens with anthrax bacteria. The next day every one of the unvaccinated animals was dead. But every vaccinated animal was alive! Pasteur had proved that successful vaccines could be prepared by weakening a pathogen.

RABIES Following his success with anthrax, Pasteur began to work on a vaccine for rabies, a deadly viral disease that can be transmitted by the bite of an infected animal. In 1885, a young boy named Joseph Meister was bitten by a rabid dog. Joseph's parents learned that Pasteur had been working on a vaccine for rabies, and they begged him to try to save their son. At first Pasteur refused. His vaccine was not ready, he argued, and he was afraid that the untested vaccine might be dangerous. The Meisters persisted, and Pasteur finally agreed to try the vaccine on Joseph. Rabies usually takes several weeks to develop, and Pasteur hoped that a series of injections would build up Joseph's immunity before the disease could firmly establish itself in the boy's body. After three desperate weeks, it became apparent that the vaccine had worked. Joseph Meister was the first of many people to be saved from rabies by the Pasteur vaccine.

Figure 45–6 *In 1885, Louis Pasteur developed a vaccine for rabies. In this photograph, he looks on as an assistant vaccinates a young boy against this serious and often fatal disease.*

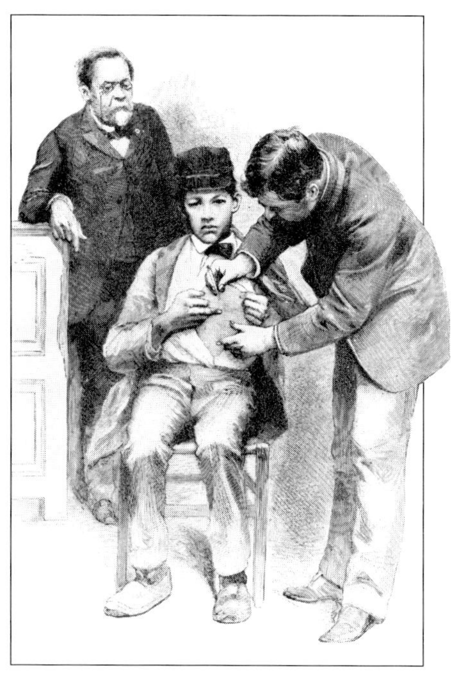

THE POLIO VACCINE Today, more than 20 serious human diseases can be prevented by vaccination. One of the most important vaccines was developed over 30 years ago by the American physician Jonas Salk. The target of this vaccine was polio, a crippling disease caused by a virus that attacks the nervous system, killing the nerves that carry messages to the muscles of the body. Although it infected people of all ages, polio was most common among children. In 1953, more than 60,000 Americans contracted polio. In some people, the disease destroyed the motor nerves leading to the legs, placing many people in wheelchairs for the rest of their life. In others, polio paralyzed the breathing muscles. Thousands of adults and children were placed in iron lungs—large artificial breathing machines that kept them alive after the ravages of polio.

Salk discovered that three slightly different viruses were responsible for polio. He developed a way to kill these viruses with the chemical compound formaldehyde. He used the killed viruses, which could not cause infection, as a vaccine. First he tested his experimental vaccine on animals to see if it produced immunity against the viruses. It did. Next he tested the vaccine for safety in humans. His experimental subjects were himself, his wife, and their three sons. The vaccine seemed safe. Then a large group of schoolchildren, potentially at risk for polio, were given the vaccine. The vaccine was nearly 100 percent effective. Finally, in 1955, the vaccine was released for general use. Schoolchildren throughout the country lined up to be vaccinated with Salk's polio vaccine. In 1961, Albert Sabin, another American researcher, developed a polio vaccine that could be taken orally, making polio vaccination even easier.

Figure 45–7 *Before the Salk polio vaccine was developed, many people with polio spent a great part of their life in this machine. Because polio often paralyzed the diaphragm, this "iron lung" breathed for the person.*

PASSIVE IMMUNITY As you just learned, in active immunity the body makes its own antibodies in response to an antigen. The body can also be protected from disease in another way. If antibodies produced by other animals against a pathogen are injected into the bloodstream, they produce a **passive immunity** against the pathogen as long as they remain in the circulation, usually for several weeks. Before the development of the Salk and Sabin vaccines, polio antibodies were used for temporary protection. Travelers are sometimes given antibodies against tropical diseases before they leave home.

Cell-Mediated Immunity

As you have learned, the function of certain T-cells is to regulate the production of antibodies by B-cells. However, other T-cells can attack antigen-bearing cells directly. The most effective attacking cells in the immune system are **killer T-cells.** These killer cells transfer special proteins into the cell membrane of a pathogen that make the membrane leak fluids from inside the cell. The rapid loss of material from the pathogen cell causes it to rupture and die. This immune response, which is called **cell-mediated immunity**, is particularly important in the case of diseases caused by eukaryotic pathogens, such as fungi and protozoa.

Killer T-cells are also responsible for the rejection of tissue transplants. The cells of your body have a special set of marker proteins on their surfaces that enable the immune system to identify them. If tissue from another individual is transplanted into the body, the immune system recognizes the transplanted tissue as foreign and attacks it. Gradually, the immune system damages and destroys the transplanted organ, a process known as **rejection**. To make rejection less likely, physicians search for an organ donor whose own proteins match the recipient's marker proteins as closely as possible. They may also administer drugs such as cyclosporine, which depress the cell-mediated immune response.

Figure 45–8 *Killer T-cells, normally round, become elongated when they are active. The killer T-cells shown here are destroying a cancer cell by breaking down the cancer cell's membrane.*

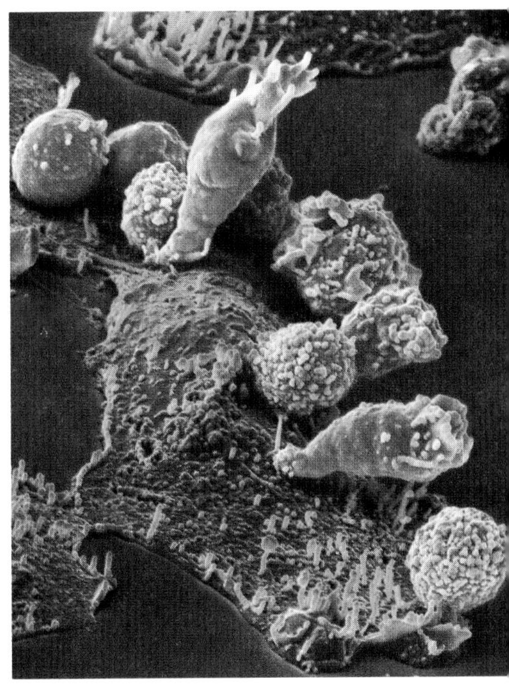

SCIENCE, TECHNOLOGY, AND SOCIETY **BREAKTHROUGH**

Activation of Immune Cells Against Cancer

One of the primary purposes of the immune system is to protect the body against cancer cells. Scientists believe that most potential cancer cells are destroyed by the immune system before they develop and produce a tumor. Only rarely do cancer cells evade the immune system and produce disease.

Now scientists are experimenting with a radical new treatment designed to boost the immune system and enlist killer T-cells against the most deadly forms of cancer. Led by Steven Rosenberg at the National Institutes of Health Laboratory in Maryland, researchers remove white blood cells from patients stricken with melanoma, a form of skin cancer that is incurable if not treated early. The white blood cells are grown outside the patient's body and treated with interleukin-2, a protein produced by the immune system. Interleukin-2 causes T-lymphocytes to develop into activated killer T-cells. The activated cells are then injected back into the patient in the hope that they will attack the tumor.

The treatment has side effects. The killer T-cells attack many of the body's own cells, producing severe fever and nausea. But tumors in some patients have shrunk by as much as 80 percent, and 10 percent of the patients may have been cured completely by the treatment. Still in its infancy, immune therapy is a promising new treatment for cancer.

The round killer T-cell has done its job. All that is left of the cancer cell are the golden fibers that are part of its cytoskeleton.

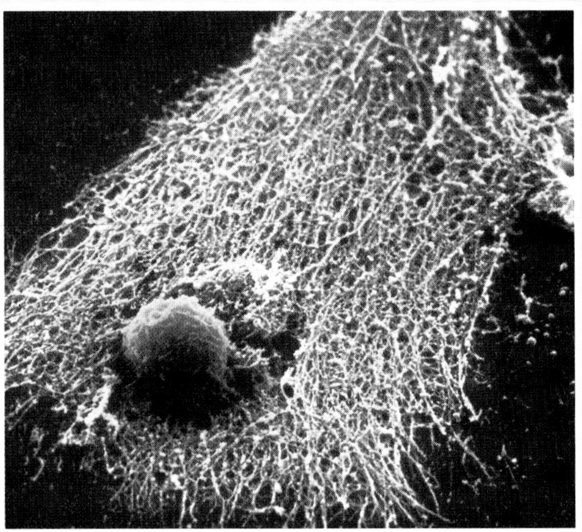

45–2 SECTION REVIEW

1. What is an antigen? Why are antigens important to the immune system?
2. What are the two major types of lymphocytes? What roles do they play in the immune response?
3. Compare active and passive immunity.
4. What is cell-mediated immunity? How does cyclosporine affect this immunity?
5. Why would a physician use techniques of passive immunity to protect someone from disease?

45–3 Immune Disorders

Section Objectives

- Recognize allergies and autoimmune disease as disorders of the immune system.
- Describe the effects of AIDS on the immune system.

The impressive power of the immune system to defend the body against a wide range of potential pathogens comes at a price. First, the immune system may overreact to an antigen, producing discomfort or even disease. Second, the cellular nature of the immune response is a potential weak point. What might happen if a disease attacked the lymphocytes that are the heart of the immune system? As we will learn shortly, the consequences are disastrous.

Allergies

The most common overreactions of the immune system are known as **allergies**. Allergies result when antigens bind to mast cells, which are a type of immune cell found throughout the body but especially in the linings of the nasal passages. When allergy-causing antigens attach themselves to mast cells, the activated mast cells release chemicals known as **histamines**. Histamines increase the flow of blood and fluids to the surrounding area. Histamines produce the sneezing, runny eyes and nose, and other irritations that make a person with allergies so miserable.

Antigens on plant pollen, dust, molds, and animal fur trigger allergies in as many as 20 percent of the population. One of the most serious allergic reactions is **asthma**, a condition in which smooth muscles contract around the passages leading to the lungs, making breathing difficult.

Scientists do not fully understand the reasons why some individuals become oversensitive to certain antigens. Fortunately, however, asthma and other allergies can usually be treated successfully with antihistamine drugs and other medicines.

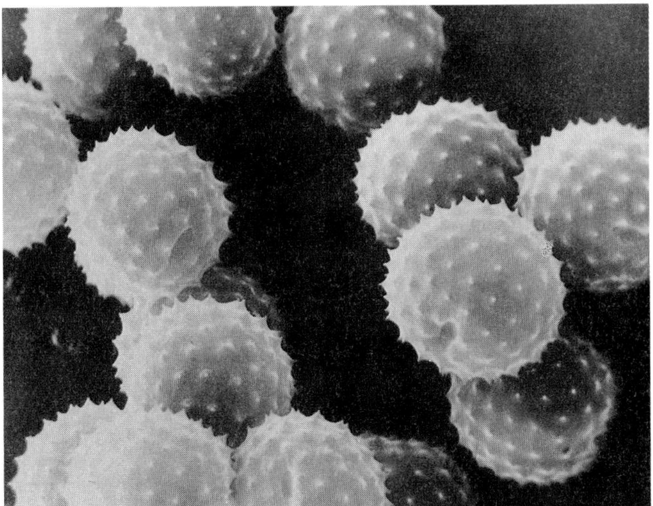

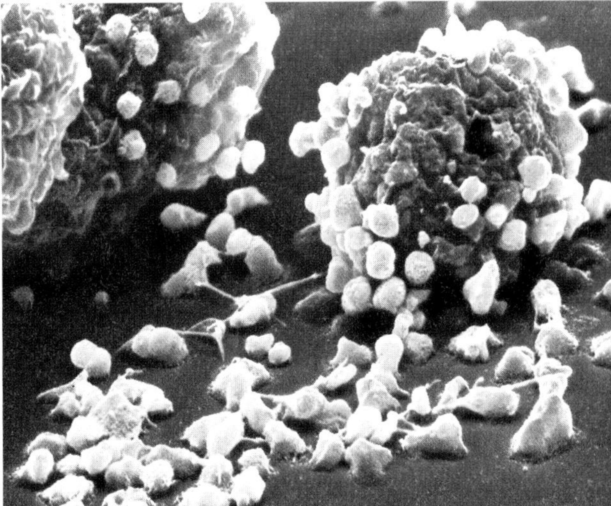

Figure 45–9 *These spheres, covered with spikes, are actually microscopic pollen grains produced by ragweed plants (left). Pollen grains often stimulate an allergic response in certain people. Mast cells, a type of immune cell common to the nasal passages, explode when allergy-causing antigens attach themselves (right). The histamine released by the mast cells causes the runny nose, watery eyes, and other unpleasant symptoms associated with allergies.*

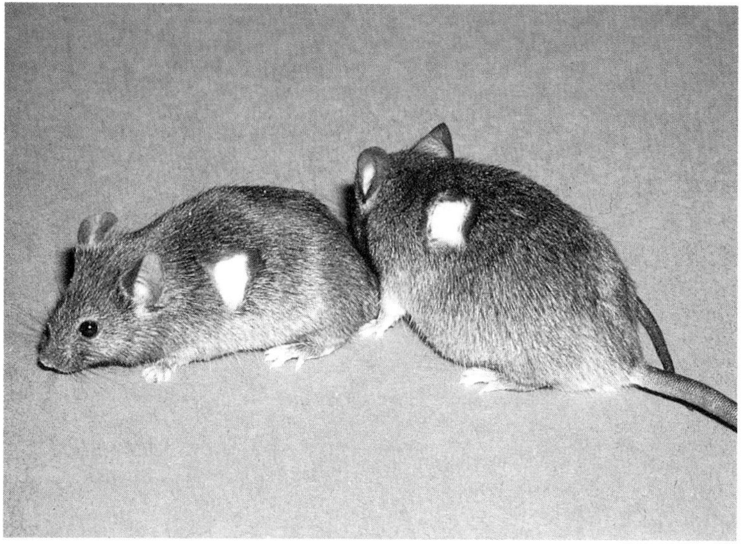

Figure 45–10 *The immune system is able to distinguish between the cells that make up an individual and the cells not normally found in the body. During an early stage in their development, these brown mice received an injection of cells from a white mouse. Now as adults, they accept a skin graft from a white mouse. The mice do not recognize the injected cells as "nonself."*

Autoimmune Disease

The immune system could not defend the body against a host of invading organisms unless it was able to distinguish those organisms from the cells and tissues that belong in the body. In other words, the immune system has the ability to distinguish "self" from "nonself." When this ability breaks down, the immune system may attack the body's own cells, producing an **autoimmune disease.**

Sometimes an infection can produce autoimmune disease by tricking the immune system. This can happen when streptococcus bacteria produce an infection known as strep throat. If the disease is left untreated, the immune system produces antibodies that destroy the bacteria. Because antigens on the surface of the bacteria are so similar to proteins on the surface of some cardiac cells, the immune system, in effect, attacks the heart as well. This results in a condition known as **rheumatic fever**. Antibodies and killer T-cells cause cell death and scarring of the heart lining and the heart valves. Rheumatic fever can be prevented if the streptococcus infection is promptly treated with antibiotics.

Rheumatoid arthritis is a destructive inflammation of the joints. This disease usually first appears between the ages of 30 and 40. The exact cause of rheumatoid arthritis is unknown, but there is clear evidence that the inflammation of the joints is produced by the actions of the immune system.

Juvenile-onset diabetes may be the result of an autoimmune reaction against the insulin-producing cells of the pancreas. **Multiple sclerosis** is a nerve disease that results from an autoimmune destruction of the myelin sheath that surrounds nerve fibers. The first symptoms of multiple sclerosis usually appear between the ages of 20 and 40. There is some evidence that suggests that this disease may result from a viral infection.

AIDS

A dramatic example of what happens when cells of the immune system are weakened by infection is the disease called **Acquired Immune Deficiency Syndrome**, or **AIDS**. The virus that causes AIDS was first discovered in 1984 and was named human immunodeficiency virus, or **HIV.** HIV is a retrovirus, or a virus whose genetic information is contained in RNA. Once HIV enters the body, it attaches to receptors on the surfaces of a type of T-cell known as **helper T-cells**. These cells are so named because they help other lymphocytes respond to the early stages of an infection. Once inside the helper T-cells, HIV replicates and eventually kills the infected cells. Although the body produces antibodies against HIV, the virus grows within cells of the immune system and is thus not affected by the antibodies. Gradually HIV kills off most of the helper T-cell population.

THE EFFECTS OF AIDS The death of the helper T-cells cripples the immune system, making it impossible for it to respond to infection by pathogens that rarely cause disease in healthy people. AIDS patients develop protozoan infections in

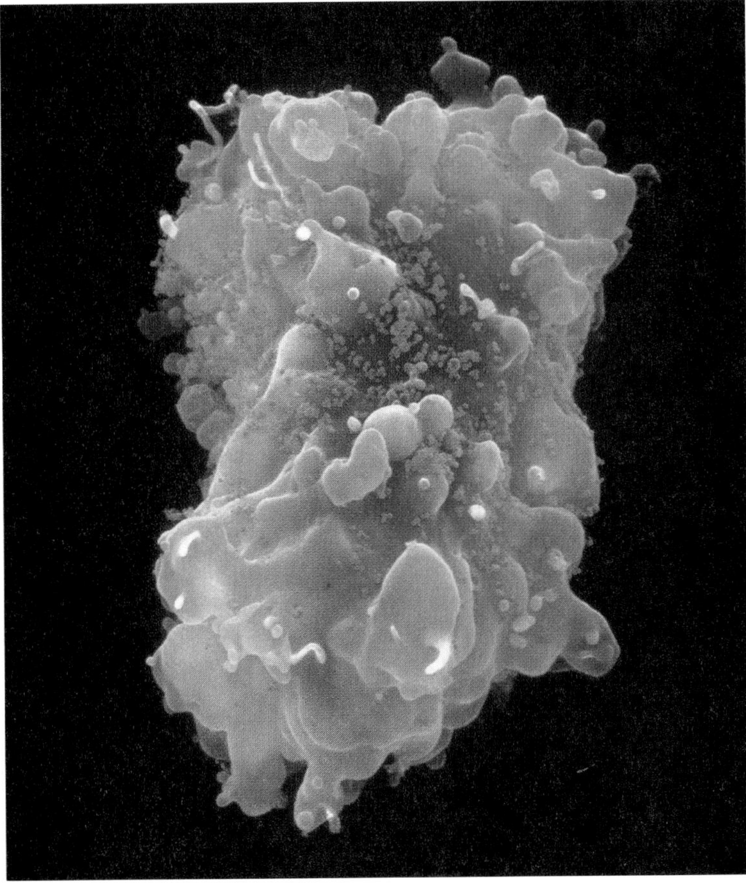

Figure 45–11 *The virus that causes AIDS, stained blue in this photograph, has infected a T-cell.*

the lungs, fungal infections of the mouth, and a rare form of cancer that is normally prevented by the immune system. It is these kinds of repeated, uncontrollable infections that eventually weaken and kill people with AIDS. Although AIDS may take 6 months to 10 years or more to develop from the time of the first HIV infection, no person who has developed the symptoms of AIDS has yet recovered from the disease. At the writing of this book, more than 50 percent of the people infected with HIV have died.

THE SPREAD OF AIDS HIV is present in the blood and body secretions of infected persons. Because it has been found in the semen and vaginal secretions, HIV can be spread during sexual intercourse. It can also be spread from one person to another by contaminated blood. Before 1985, some cases of AIDS were caused by blood that was unknowingly donated by infected individuals and used for transfusions. Since that time, however, all blood has been screened for AIDS. The incidence of AIDS is increasing in sexually active heterosexual teenagers. HIV is also spreading rapidly among intravenous drug users who share the needles used to inject drugs. HIV can pass through the placenta from mother to child, and an increasing number of newborn children have been infected with HIV while still in the womb.

Figure 45–12 *By killing T-cells, the AIDS virus increases the body's susceptibility to many infections that would not normally affect a person with a healthy, functioning immune system.*

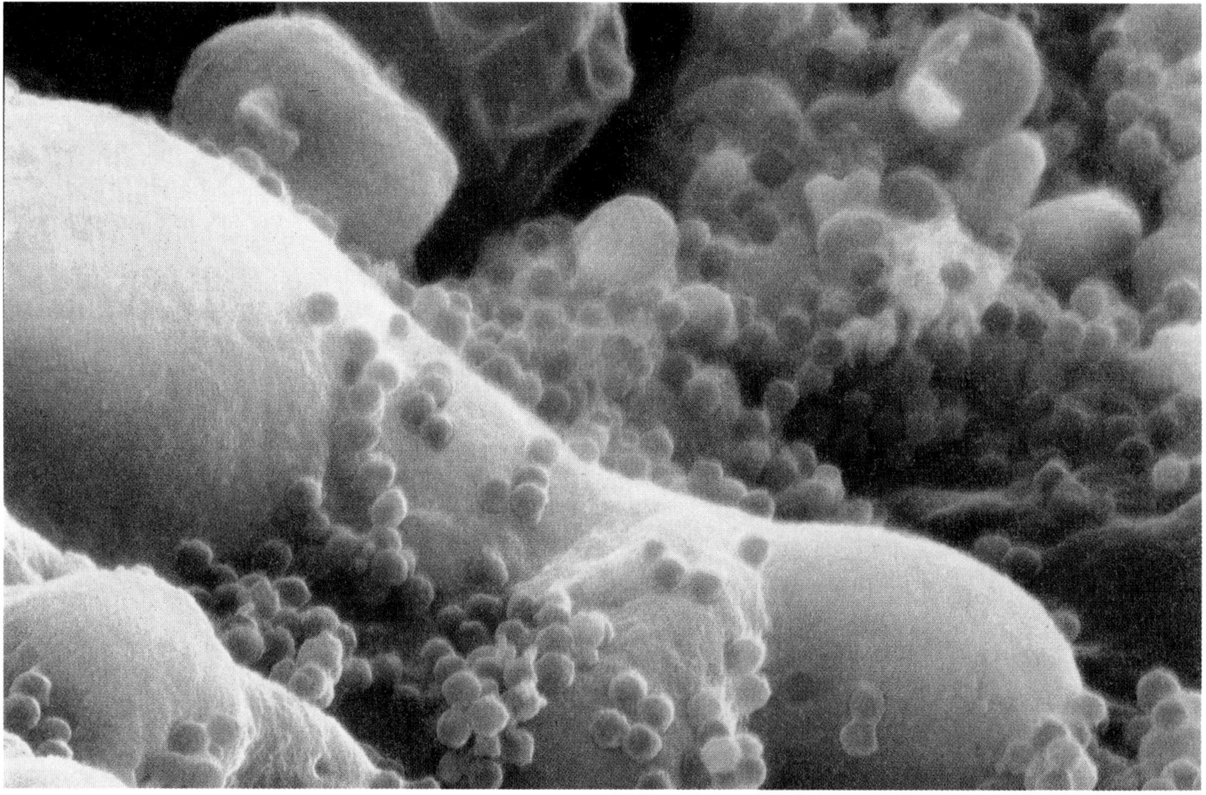

AIDS TREATMENT AND PREVENTION The rising number of AIDS cases in the United States has produced a genuine epidemic—by 1989 more than 100,000 cases of AIDS had been identified in the United States. At present there is no cure for AIDS, and experimental vaccines have not yet been proven to prevent HIV infection. Several promising drugs that slow the growth of the virus have been developed, thus enabling AIDS patients to survive longer. There is hope that some of these drugs will prevent the development of AIDS in individuals who have been infected with HIV but who have not yet shown symptoms of the disease. Unfortunately these medicines are extremely expensive. Intensive research in laboratories throughout the world is underway to find a cure for this killer.

Although we have not yet discovered a cure for AIDS, it is a fact that we do know how to prevent it. **YOU CAN PREVENT AIDS BY AVOIDING EXPOSURE TO HIV, THE VIRUS THAT CAUSES THE DISEASE.** AIDS is not spread by casual contact. AIDS is spread by intravenous drug use, and that alone is reason enough to avoid using such drugs. AIDS is also spread by sexual contact, and thus a sexual contact carries with it the risk of contracting an HIV infection. The safest course of conduct, as former Surgeon General of the United States C. Everett Koop pointed out in 1986, is to abstain from sexual intercourse before marriage. According to Dr. Koop, the next safest course is the use of a condom, a sheath that fits around the penis and prevents most sexually transmitted diseases from being passed during intercourse. A condom does not provide 100 percent protection, but it is safer than unprotected sexual intercourse. Every AIDS death is unnecessary. You should be sure that you, your friends, and your classmates understand how to prevent becoming infected with HIV—and how to end this deadly epidemic.

Figure 45–13 *Ryan White had hemophilia, a genetic disorder that interferes with the normal ability of the blood to form clots. Dependent upon transfusions, he contracted AIDS from contaminated blood and blood products he needed to treat his disease. Ryan White died on April 8, 1990, but his great courage is an inspiration to many. Today, blood and blood products are tested to ensure that they are free of HIV infection.*

45–3 SECTION REVIEW

1. What is an allergy? What are histamines? Name an example of an allergy.
2. What is an autoimmune disease? Name some examples of autoimmune diseases.
3. What is AIDS? What causes it? What happens to the immune system as a result of this disease?
4. What are the three principal ways in which HIV is transmitted from person to person?
5. In treating an asthmatic patient, the first thing that many physicians will do is to ask the patient to make a list of times and places they have experienced asthmatic reactions. Why do you suppose they do this?

LABORATORY INVESTIGATION

SIMULATING CLONAL SELECTION OF ANTIBODIES

PROBLEM

How do plasma cells form antibodies specific for each antigen?

MATERIALS *(per person)*

protractor	scissors
ruler	typing paper

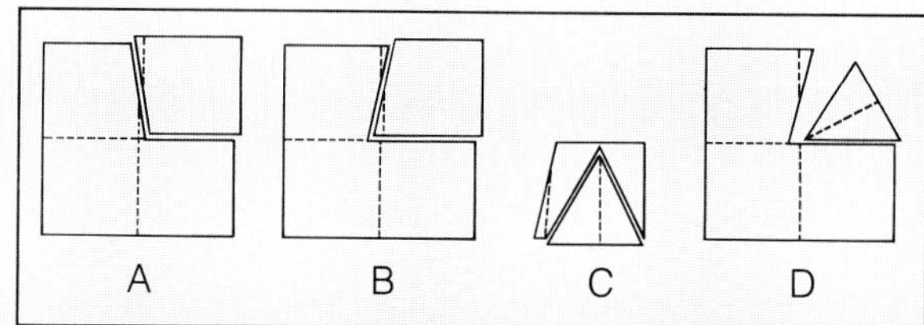

PROCEDURE

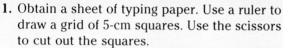

1. Obtain a sheet of typing paper. Use a ruler to draw a grid of 5-cm squares. Use the scissors to cut out the squares.
2. Fold two of the squares in half twice to produce four equal quarters. These two folded squares represent plasma cells.
3. Cut one of the folded squares as shown in Figure A. Make the first cut along the horizontal fold. Continue this cut to the vertical fold. Then make a second cut that begins just to the left of the top of the vertical fold and continues to just to the right of the vertical fold at the bottom.
4. Take the other folded square. Cut this square as shown in Figure B. Make the first cut along the horizontal fold. Continue this cut to the vertical fold. Then make a second cut that begins just to the right of the top of the vertical fold and continues to just to the left of the vertical fold at the bottom. The cut corners of the squares represent antigen receptor sites.
5. Take one of the cut-out corners and fold it in half. Cut diagonally from the top point of the fold to each of the opposite corners. This will form a triangle, as shown in Figure C. This triangle represents an antigen.
6. Place the antigen into the receptor site of one of the plasma cells as shown in Figure D. Use a protractor to measure the angle formed by the empty space between the antigen and the receptor site of the plasma cell. Write the angle measurement on the plasma cell. Repeat the procedure with the other plasma cell.
7. The receptor site that forms the smallest angle fits the antigen best. Select the plasma cell that fits best.
8. Take three other squares and fold them in half horizontally. Try to duplicate the receptor site of the plasma cell you selected by cutting partway along the fold. Then cut down toward the fold with scissors. Estimate the correct angle to cut. These three cells represent clones of the selected cell.
9. Insert the antigen into the receptor site of one of the three cells. Measure the angle formed, as you did in step 6. Repeat this procedure with the other two cells.
10. From the original cells or the clones select the plasma cell that fits the antigen best. Try to duplicate this cell using three new pieces of paper (step 8).
11. Repeat steps 9 and 10 until you have used all the cut squares or until the angle formed by the empty space between the antigen and the receptor site equals 0°.

OBSERVATIONS

1. What happened to the size of the angle with each new generation of cloned cells?

ANALYSIS AND CONCLUSIONS

1. What causes changes to occur in the fit between receptor sites and antigens over time?
2. How do plasma cells form antibodies for each antigen? (*Hint:* Antibodies are formed from receptor sites shed by plasma cell clones.)

STUDENT STUDY GUIDE

SUMMARIZING THE CONCEPTS

The key concepts in each section of this chapter are listed below to help you review the chapter content. Make sure you understand each concept and its relationship to other concepts and to the theme of this chapter.

45–1 Nonspecific Defenses

- The immune system is the body's primary defense against disease-causing microorganisms. It is composed of specific and nonspecific defense mechanisms. Specific defenses are attempts by the body to defend itself against particular pathogens. Nonspecific defenses guard against all infections.

45–2 Specific Defenses

- If a pathogen is able to get past the body's nonspecific defenses, the immune system reacts with a series of specific defenses that attack the disease-causing agent. A substance that triggers the specific defenses of the immune system is known as an antigen.

45–3 Immune Disorders

- Allergies result when antigens bind to mast cells. The activated mast cells release chemicals known as histamines.
- At present, there is no cure for AIDS, and experimental vaccines have not yet proven to prevent HIV infection. You can prevent AIDS by avoiding exposure to HIV.

REVIEWING KEY TERMS

Vocabulary terms are important to your understanding of biology. The key terms listed below are those you should be especially familiar with. Review these terms and their meanings. Then use each term in a complete sentence. If you are not sure of a term's meaning, return to the appropriate section and review its definition.

45–1 Nonspecific Defenses

immune system
nonspecific defense
lysozyme
inflammatory response
phagocyte
inflamed
lymph node
fever
interferon

45–2 Specific Defenses

specific defense
antigen
lymphocyte
B-lymphocyte
antibody
antigen-binding site
agglutination
plasma cell
primary immune response
T-lymphocyte
immune
secondary immune response
vaccination
active immunity
passive immunity
killer T-cell
cell-mediated immunity
rejection

45–3 Immune Disorders

allergy
histamine
asthma
autoimmune disease
rheumatic fever
rheumatoid arthritis
juvenile-onset diabetes
multiple sclerosis
Acquired Immune Deficiency Syndrome
AIDS
HIV
helper T-cell

CHAPTER REVIEW

CONTENT REVIEW

Multiple Choice

Choose the letter of the answer that best completes each statement.

1. Special proteins that can bind to antigens on the surfaces of a pathogen and help destroy it are
   a. lymphocytes. c. antibodies.
   b. plasma cells. d. phagocytes.
2. A vaccine produces a
   a. primary immune response.
   b. secondary immune response.
   c. passive immunity.
   d. active immunity.
3. Specialized B-cells that release antibodies into the bloodstream to deal with infection are
   a. plasma cells. c. T-cells.
   b. antigens. d. histamines.
4. HIV attaches to receptors on
   a. killer T-cells. c. helper T-cells.
   b. RNA. d. helper B-cells.
5. The type of immunity that is particularly important against diseases caused by eukaryotic pathogens is
   a. passive immunity.
   b. cell-mediated immunity.
   c. active immunity.
   d. autoimmunity.
6. A disease that results from an autoimmune destruction of the myelin sheath is
   a. multiple sclerosis. c. polio.
   b. smallpox. d. rheumatic fever.
7. Allergy-causing antigens cause activated mast cells to release
   a. insulin. c. antibiotics.
   b. antihistamines. d. histamines.
8. The oral polio vaccine was developed by
   a. Louis Pasteur. c. Albert Sabin.
   b. Edward Jenner. d. Jonas Salk.

True or False

Determine whether each statement is true or false. If it is true, write "true." If it is false, change the underlined word or words to make the statement true.

1. The process by which a group of antibody molecules links viruses together in a large mass is rejection.
2. Edward Jenner developed a rabies vaccine.
3. B-cells are responsible for the rejection of tissue transplants.
4. B-lymphocytes, which mature in the bone marrow, are responsible for producing antibodies.
5. The body's most important nonspecific defense is the skin.
6. HIV is present in the blood and body secretions of persons infected with AIDS.
7. Newborn children cannot be infected with HIV while still in the womb.
8. Once exposed to a disease, the body exhibits a secondary immune response if the pathogen reappears.

Word Relationships

Replace the underlined definition with the correct vocabulary word.

1. The secretions of the body contain an enzyme that breaks down the cell wall of many bacteria.
2. Virus-infected cells produce a protein that inhibits the synthesis of viral proteins in infected cells and helps block viral replication.
3. Carbohydrates, proteins, and lipids on the surfaces of pathogens may serve as substances that trigger the specific defenses of the immune system.

CONCEPT MASTERY

Use your understanding of the concepts developed in the chapter to answer each of the following in a brief paragraph.

1. What is AIDS? What causes AIDS? How does AIDS affect the body?
2. What role do B-cells play in the body's immune response?
3. How does the body recognize "self"?
4. What is a vaccine? How does a vaccination protect the body?
5. What contributions to human health care did Pasteur, Jenner, Salk, and Sabin make?
6. Differentiate between active and passive immunity.
7. What is a primary immune response? A secondary immune response?
8. What is the inflammatory response? How does the inflammatory response help the body fight infection?
9. List three nonspecific defenses of the body. Tell how each protects the body.

CRITICAL AND CREATIVE THINKING

Discuss each of the following in a brief paragraph.

1. **Relating cause and effect** The blood of a person with HIV infection often shows decreasing numbers of T-cells each time it is analyzed. How do you explain this observation?
2. **Applying concepts** This photograph shows a child who lives within a sterile environment, an environment free of pathogenic organisms. Offer a probable explanation to explain the way this child must live.
3. **Assessing concepts** The first vaccine was developed against smallpox, a serious and often fatal disease. Today, scientists for the World Health Organization claim that smallpox has been eradicated and the world is free of smallpox infection. What do you think is the basis for this claim? (*Hint:* Smallpox is exclusively a disease of humans.)
4. **Relating concepts** In the past, organ transplants were most effective when organs were transplanted from one close relative to another. Today, organs can be transplanted from one unrelated person to another with success. What is the most probable reason for the dramatic change in transplant success?

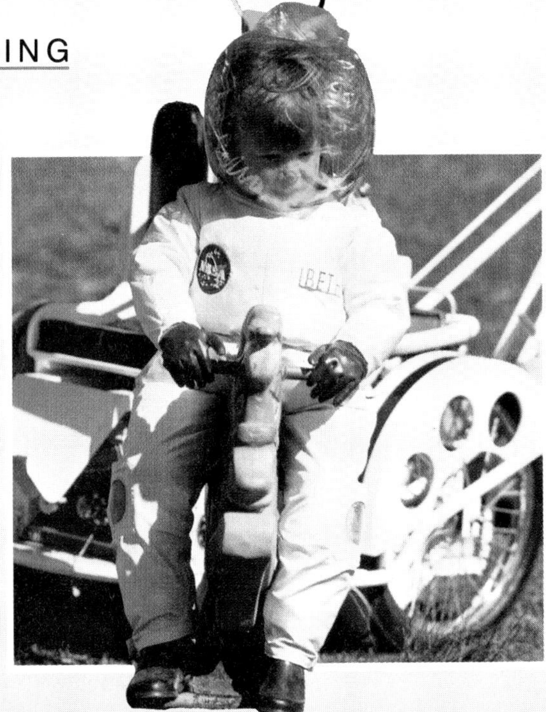

5. **Applying concepts** People often view slight fevers with alarm. However, many physicians do not. Why would a slight fever not be viewed with much alarm?
6. **Using the writing process** Pretend you are a kidney that has been transplanted into a person. Write a letter to the body you have been transplanted into explaining why you should not be "rejected."

CHAPTER 46

Drugs, Alcohol, and Tobacco

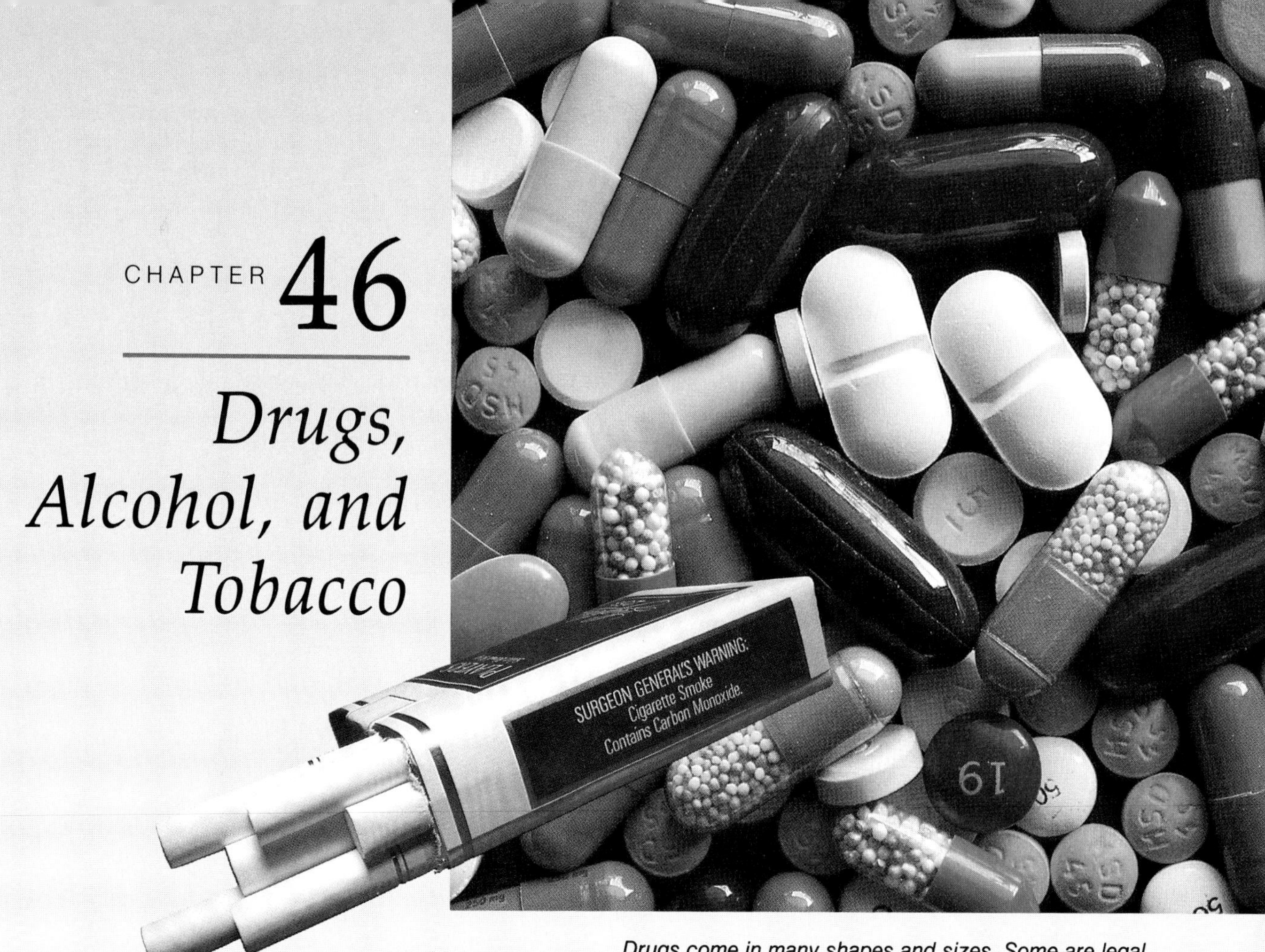

Drugs come in many shapes and sizes. Some are legal and others are not. But any drug, if used improperly, can be dangerous.

It was 1986 and Len Bias was on top of the world. The University of Maryland basketball star had just been drafted by the Boston Celtics. His parents beamed with pride at the success that their son had earned from years of athletic discipline and hard work. Boston sportswriters could barely contain their excitement over what this new star might mean to the team. But one evening, in the space of a few minutes, everything in Len Bias's young life came undone.

Len Bias attended a party with a few friends. Someone took out some cocaine. Bias took a couple of sniffs, moaned, and fell to the floor. A powerful surge of cocaine in his bloodstream had paralyzed his heart muscle. Len Bias was having a heart attack. Before morning, he was dead. Newspaper headlines reported the death of this star athlete. But no headlines were printed for dozens of others who died that same week in exactly the same way. Drug abuse kills!

What are drugs? How do drugs affect the body? And what is drug abuse? Read on to learn the answers.

CHAPTER OUTLINE

46–1 Drugs

Section Objectives

- Define the term drug and explain why any drug can be harmful.
- Describe the different ways in which drugs can affect the body.

By definition, a **drug** is any substance that causes a change in the body. Many substances fit that definition, including antibiotics that are used to fight infection and aspirin that is used to control pain.

All drugs affect the body in some ways. Some drugs, such as cocaine and heroin, are so powerful and dangerous that their possession is illegal. Other drugs, including penicillin and codeine, are prescription drugs and can be used only under the supervision of a doctor. Still other drugs, including cough and cold medicines, are sold over the counter.

All drugs (legal and illegal) have the potential to do harm if they are used improperly, or abused. In this section we will consider some of the most commonly abused drugs and the ways in which they affect the body.

How Drugs Affect the Body

Drugs differ in the ways in which they affect the body. Some drugs kill bacteria and are useful in treating disease. Other drugs affect a particular system of the body, such as the digestive or circulatory system. Among the most powerful drugs, however, are the ones that affect the nervous system in ways that can change behavior.

MARIJUANA Statistically, the most widely abused illegal drug is **marijuana.** Marijuana comes from a species of hemp plant known as *Cannabis sativa.* Marijuana is commonly called

Figure 46–1 *Artist Keith Haring described his attitude toward drug abuse in this anticrack mural.*

Figure 46–2 *Written on this clay tablet are the world's oldest known prescriptions, dating back to about 2000 BC. The prescriptions describe the medicinal uses of certain plants.*

grass or pot. Hashish, or hash, is a potent form of marijuana made from the flowering parts of the plant. The active ingredient in all forms of marijuana is tetrahydrocannabinol (THC). Smoking or ingesting THC can produce a temporary feeling of euphoria and disorientation.

Short-term use of marijuana does not seem to cause immediate physical damage to the body. However, the word *seem* here is deceiving. For there is clear evidence that smoking marijuana is bad for the lungs, although the damaging effects may not be immediate. In fact, smoking marijuana is even more destructive to the lungs than smoking tobacco.

Long-term use of marijuana can result in loss of memory, inability to concentrate, and reduced levels of the hormone testosterone in males. Heavy users develop a psychological dependence (need) on the drug, which can make constructive behavior—work, sports, study, and social activities—almost impossible.

HALLUCINOGENS Some drugs affect a user's view of reality so strongly that they are known as **hallucinogens** (from a Latin word meaning "to dream"). **LSD** (lysergic acid diethylamide) is the most powerful hallucinogen. Acid, as this drug is commonly called, interferes with the normal transmission of nerve impulses in the brain. Although its effects vary from person to person, virtually all people who use LSD regularly have had a "bad trip" in which their hallucinations became frighteningly real. Some LSD users have lost touch with reality after only a single dose of the drug.

In recent years, another hallucinogen has come into use. This powerful drug, called **PCP** (phencyclidine), produces feelings of strength and great power. Also known as angel dust, PCP can result in nightmarish illusions that may last for many days. High doses of PCP produce seizures and even heart attacks. And hospital workers in emergency wards know another side effect of PCP: Users often become extremely violent and are a danger to themselves and others.

Figure 46–3 *Using medication after the prescription has expired is one way that even legal drugs can be abused.*

STIMULANTS A number of drugs speed up the actions of the nervous system and are therefore known as **stimulants.** The most powerful stimulants are a group of drugs called **amphetamines.** Commonly known as speed or uppers, amphetamines chemically resemble natural neurotransmitters found in the body. You may recall from Chapter 37 that neurotransmitters are compounds that pass nerve impulses from one neuron (nerve cell) to another. When a person takes a dose of amphetamine, the drug floods the body with what the body assumes are natural neurotransmitters. This causes the nervous system to increase its activity, producing a feeling of strength and energy in the user. Fatigue seems to vanish. But there is a dark side to such drugs as well.

The nervous system cannot handle the overstimulation produced by amphetamines. When a dose of the drug wears off,

Figure 46–4 *Amphetamines are among the most powerful and dangerous drugs known. After it was given a small dose of amphetamine, this orb-weaver spider was unable to spin a normal web.*

the user suffers from fatigue and depression. Long-term use causes hallucinations, circulatory problems, and psychological difficulties. Heavy users become so dependent on amphetamines that they are unable to function without them. They have difficulty dealing with other people and fall into a pattern of speeding up and crashing (recovering from the rapid pace of their drug-induced activities).

DEPRESSANTS Drugs that reduce the rate of nervous system activity are called **depressants.** Among the most commonly used (and abused) depressants are the **barbiturates,** a group of compounds often found in sleeping pills. People who abuse downers, as these drugs are called, can quickly become dependent on them. When barbiturates are used with alcohol, the results are often fatal, as the nervous system can become so depressed even breathing stops.

Another danger of barbiturate abuse occurs when a user tries to stop. Unlike virtually all other abused drugs, cutting off the supply of barbiturates to the body can result in serious medical problems that must be treated immediately. Thus a barbiturate abuser needs medical attention when trying to quit.

COCAINE The leaves of the coca plant grown in South America contain a compound known as **cocaine.** In the nineteenth century cocaine was used as a local anaesthetic to deaden pain during surgery. Today, people who abuse cocaine may sniff it, smoke it, or inject it directly into the bloodstream.

Cocaine causes the release of a neurotransmitter in the brain called dopamine. Normally, dopamine release occurs when a basic need, such as hunger or thirst, is satisfied. The release of dopamine in the brain produces a feeling of pleasure (a feeling you have probably experienced after a particularly large Thanksgiving dinner). Cocaine fools the brain into releasing dopamine, producing an intense feeling of pleasure and satisfaction.

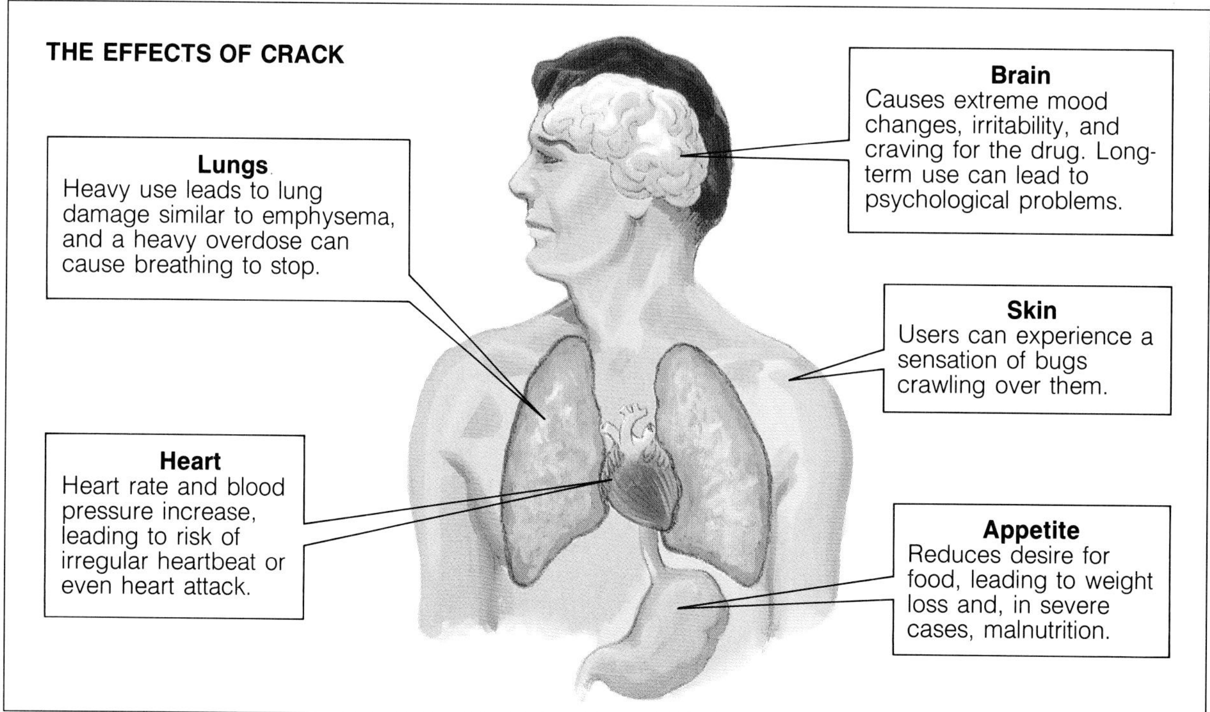

THE EFFECTS OF CRACK
Lungs
Heavy use leads to lung damage similar to emphysema, and a heavy overdose can cause breathing to stop.
Brain
Causes extreme mood changes, irritability, and craving for the drug. Long-term use can lead to psychological problems.
Skin
Users can experience a sensation of bugs crawling over them.
Heart
Heart rate and blood pressure increase, leading to risk of irregular heartbeat or even heart attack.
Appetite
Reduces desire for food, leading to weight loss and, in severe cases, malnutrition.

Figure 46–5 *Crack is an extremely powerful form of cocaine. What effect does crack have on the brain?*

The effects of cocaine can be so powerful that a long-term user makes obtaining the drug more important than anything else in life, including food, sleep, and career. So much dopamine is released when the drug is used that not enough is left when it wears off. As a result, users quickly discover that they feel sad and depressed without the drug and seek to use it again and again. Thus the psychological dependence that cocaine produces is particularly difficult to break.

When cocaine reaches the bloodstream, it acts as a powerful stimulant, increasing the heartbeat and blood pressure. The stimulation can be so powerful that the heart is damaged by the drug. In some cases, even a first-time user may experience a heart attack, as happened to basketball star Len Bias.

In the late 1980s cocaine abusers began to use a form of cocaine called **crack,** which can be smoked in a pipe. Crack is a particularly potent and dangerous form of cocaine that can become addictive after only a few doses. Read the Science, Technology, and Society feature in this chapter carefully, for it discusses in more detail the dangers of using crack.

OPIATES Some of the most powerful drugs are the **opiates,** a group of drugs produced from the opium poppy. The most common opiates are opium itself, which is derived directly from the opium poppy, and **morphine** and **heroin,** which are chemically refined forms of opium. All of the opiates, with the exception of heroin, can be used under a doctor's supervision to relieve severe pain. Morphine is particularly effective as a pain killer. However, all of the opiates can also result in death when taken in large doses (overdose).

SCIENCE, TECHNOLOGY, AND SOCIETY

Crack: A Cheap Way to Die

For many years, scientists were not certain if cocaine was a physically addictive drug. (Psychological dependence on cocaine is well established.) Cocaine is dangerous and potentially fatal, but true physical addiction to cocaine may take years to develop. However, the same cannot be said for crack, an inexpensive form of cocaine that first appeared in the 1980s. Crack is made by chemically treating cocaine. Crack, which is usually found in the form of small "rocks," can be melted and injected into the bloodstream. However, most users smoke crack. Smoking crack delivers the drug to the nervous system more quickly and in a more powerful form than sniffing even pure cocaine.

Crack is more powerful than ordinary cocaine because the drug's effect on the nervous system peaks just a few seconds after smoking. The brain is flooded with a concentrated dose of the drug, producing an intense high. The effect of the drug wears off quickly too, leaving the user to seek another dose. After a time, the intense pleasurable effects are no longer felt. Continued use briefly relieves the sense of craving. Crack is among the most addictive drugs known. Crack users can become hooked on the drug in as few as 6 to 10 weeks. (Some studies indicate even less time is required.) And even though an individual dose of crack is inexpensive, the fact that it wears off quickly and is extremely addictive means that continued use is expensive. Where do most crack users get the money to pay for their addiction? The answer is, unfortunately, from violent crime and other illegal acts. Crack also produces disturbed mental behavior in heavy users, which has led to a rash of drug-related murders and assaults.

Scientific work has shown that lab animals supplied with unlimited amounts of cocaine will take the drug again and again until they die from lack of food and water. We humans have the capacity to make better choices than that, and crack is just the latest drug to challenge our ability to say NO.

Knowing what we do about crack, why do people still try the drug—again and again?

Heroin, the most commonly abused opiate, is often injected directly into the bloodstream. Heroin produces a powerful sleepy feeling of well-being that users often crave. As you might expect, heroin can result in strong psychological dependence. Opiates can also cause a strong physical dependence in which the body actually requires the drug in order to function properly. (So can barbiturates, alcohol, and tobacco.) In addition to the many other dangers they face, heroin users run the risk of contracting AIDS from the use of shared needles. (See Chapter 45.)

Drug Abuse

Each of the drugs we have discussed presents a danger to users. **Drug abuse**—the misuse of either a legal or illegal drug—is a serious problem in modern society. **Drug abuse can be defined as using any drug in a way that most doctors would not approve.** With some drugs, such as cocaine, drug abuse causes serious physical damage to the body. With other drugs, such as marijuana, drug abuse produces psychological dependence that can be strong enough to disrupt family life and schoolwork. Workers under the influence of drugs are unreliable and may commit errors of judgment that place them and their co-workers at risk.

Figure 46–6 *The round yellow structure in the center of the opium poppy flower is the pod. Notice the sap, from which the opiates are derived, oozing out of the ripe poppy pod.*

DRUG ADDICTION An uncontrollable craving for a drug is known as a **drug addiction.** As you have read, some drugs cause a strong psychological dependence, or need, in the user, whereas other drugs cause a strong physical dependence. (Many cause both.) In general, the term drug addiction is used to describe a physical dependence on a drug. However, as you now know, even a psychological dependence can have a chemical basis.

Opiates, such as heroin, are examples of drugs that cause a strong physical dependence. All regular users of heroin will eventually become addicted. At that point, their nervous system will become dependent on a steady supply of the drug. Any attempt at **withdrawal,** or stopping the use of the drug, will cause severe pain, nausea, chills, and fever. You may have heard the terms kick-the-habit and cold turkey applied to people who quit using heroin. These terms have a basis in fact. For during heroin withdrawal, a person develops goose bumps that make the skin resemble the skin of a turkey (cold turkey). In addition, the leg muscles of the body may jerk uncontrollably (kicking the habit). The symptoms of withdrawal are so severe that users usually seek another dose of the drug to "cure" them of withdrawal sickness.

Casual users of opiates often believe that they can control their body's need for the drug. But they are nearly always wrong. And now we know the reason why!

In the 1970s, scientists began to look for a cellular basis for opiate addiction. They found that heroin and morphine would bind to special receptors on the surfaces of nerve cells. Why should human nerve cells have receptors for compounds derived from a poppy plant native to Asia?

A group of scientists led by Candace Pert at the National Institutes of Health found the answer: The brain produces its own opiates! These morphinelike chemicals produced by the brain are called **endorphins.** There are several classes of endorphins, and not all endorphin functions are understood. But what is very clear is that endorphins produced by the brain help to overcome pain and produce sensations of pleasure.

Now we can understand how opiate addiction occurs. By coincidence, compounds such as morphine and heroin bind to the same receptors as endorphins do, producing a feeling of pleasure and blocking sensations of pain. But the abnormally high levels of opiates reached during drug use upset the normal balance of endorphins and receptors in the brain. Once the body adjusts to the higher levels of opiates, it literally cannot do without them. If the drug is withdrawn, natural endorphins cannot be supplied by the body in large enough amounts to prevent the uncontrollable pain and sickness that are characteristic withdrawal symptoms. Addiction has a cellular basis that the addict simply cannot control!

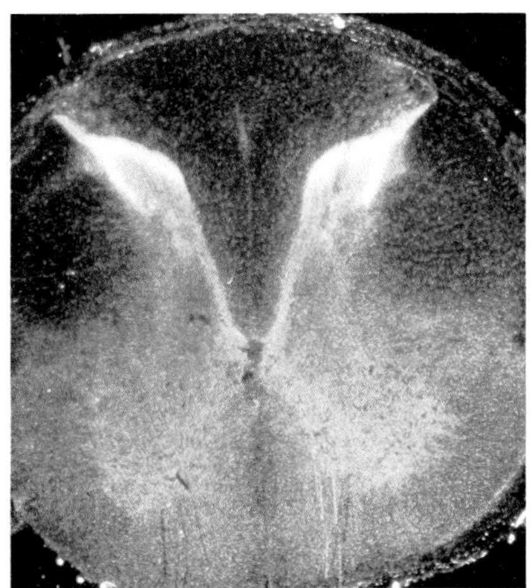

Figure 46–7 *The bright spots in this cross section of the spinal cord are some of the receptors in the nervous system to which opiates bind.*

46–1 SECTION REVIEW

1. Define the term drug.
2. Distinguish between drug abuse and drug addiction. Are they different? If so, how?
3. Compare the actions of stimulants and depressants on the nervous system.
4. Explain why withdrawing from an addictive drug is not simply a matter of willpower.

46–2 Alcohol

Section Objectives

- Describe the effects of alcohol on the body.
- Compare alcohol use and abuse.

Alcohol is a drug—the oldest drug known to human culture. Written records from Egypt and Babylon show that people have made alcoholic beverages for more than 3500 years. Alcohol is produced when yeast grow in a sugar-containing liquid in the absence of oxygen. The yeast ferment the sugar to obtain energy and release alcohol and carbon dioxide as byproducts.

Effects of Alcohol

Alcohol-containing drinks are popular in nearly all cultures. They include fermented drinks, such as beer and wine, and stronger drinks made by distillation, including whiskey, vodka, scotch, and gin. The strength of different drinks depends mainly on the percentage of alcohol. Regardless of the type of drink or its strength, the form of alcohol is always **ethyl alcohol** (C_2H_5OH).

Alcohol is a small molecule that passes through cell membranes easily and is quickly absorbed into the bloodstream. High concentrations of alcohol are toxic. However, very low concentrations of alcohol can be used by the body as a source of food. This is one reason why the effects of alcohol wear off within a few hours after it enters the body.

ALCOHOL'S EFFECTS ON THE BRAIN

BAC	Part of Brain Affected	Behavior
0.05%		Lack of judgment, lack of inhibition
0.1%		Reduced reaction time, difficulty walking and driving
0.2%		Saddened, weeping, abnormal behavior
0.3%		Double vision, inadequate hearing
0.45%		Unconscious
0.65%		Death

Figure 46–8 *BAC, or blood alcohol concentration, is a measure of the amount of alcohol in the bloodstream per 100 mL of blood. What happens if the BAC exceeds 0.45 percent?*

The most immediate effects of alcohol are on the nervous system. **Alcohol is a depressant.** Even small amounts of alcohol slow down the rate at which the nervous system functions. This means that any amount of alcohol slows down reflexes, disrupts coordination, and impairs judgment. Heavy drinking fills the blood with so much alcohol that the nervous system cannot function properly. People who have had three or four drinks in the span of an hour may feel relaxed and confident, but their blood contains as much as 0.10 percent alcohol, making them legally drunk in most states. They usually cannot walk or talk properly, and they are certainly not able to safely control an automobile.

Alcohol is used and accepted by cultures throughout the world. Because of this cultural acceptance, alcohol is the most dangerous and abused drug in the world. More than half of all Americans consume alcoholic beverages. Although many do so quite responsibly, a dangerously large number do not. Alcohol is the drug most commonly abused by teenagers. The abuse of alcohol has a frightening social price. One half of the 50,000 people who die on American highways in a typical year are victims of accidents in which at least one driver has been drinking. One third of all homicides are attributed to the effects of alcohol. At least $25 billion worth of damage is done to the economy in this country alone as a result of alcohol-related accidents that injure workers and damage property.

But the toll of alcohol abuse does not stop there! Women who are pregnant and drink on a regular basis run the risk of **fetal alcohol syndrome,** or damage to the developing baby due to the effects of alcohol. More than 50,000 babies are born in this country every year with alcohol-related birth defects.

Alcohol and Disease

People who have become addicted to alcohol suffer from a disease called **alcoholism.** Some alcoholics may need to have a drink before work or school—every day! They may drink so heavily that they black out and cannot remember what they have done while drinking. Other alcoholics, however, do not necessarily drink to the point where it is obvious that they have an alcohol-abuse problem. **If a person cannot function properly without satisfying the need or craving for alcohol, that person is considered to have an alcohol-abuse problem.**

Repeated bouts of heavy drinking damage the digestive system, through which the alcohol passes on its way into the bloodstream. Alcohol taken in excessive amounts can destroy neurons in the brain. Long-term alcohol use also destroys cells in the liver, where alcohol is broken down. As liver cells die, the liver becomes less able to handle large amounts of alcohol. The formation of scar tissue, known as cirrhosis of the liver, occurs next. The scar tissue blocks the flow of blood through the liver and interferes with its other important functions. Eventually, a heavy drinker may die from chronic liver failure.

You may be tempted to believe that deaths due to alcoholism are rare. If so, it might surprise you to learn that cirrhosis of the liver is the seventh leading cause of death in the United States! And although attempts have been made in the past to eliminate this drug from our society, alcohol remains with us today. Thus we must each find a way to deal with it.

As with other drugs, dealing with alcohol abuse is not simply a matter of willpower. Alcoholics often need special help and support to quit their drinking habit. Organizations such as Alcoholics Anonymous are available in most communities to help individuals and families deal with the problems created by alcohol abuse. There are even organizations for the relatives of the ten million or so alcoholics in this country. One such organization, Alateen, is for the children of people who have an alcohol problem.

"Before I'll ride with a drunk, I'll drive myself." —Stevie Wonder
Driving after drinking, or riding with a driver who's been drinking, is a big mistake. Anyone can see that.

Figure 46–9 *More than 25,000 Americans die in car accidents every year in which at least one driver was under the influence of alcohol.*

46–2 SECTION REVIEW

1. What type of drug is alcohol?
2. Distinguish an alcoholic from the millions of Americans who drink but do not have a drinking problem.
3. Prohibition was a period in our nation's history (1920–1933) during which alcohol was outlawed. Would Prohibition be any more effective today than it was then? Explain your answer.

46–3 Tobacco

Section Objectives

- Describe the main components of tobacco smoke.
- Discuss the health problems associated with smoking.

Tobacco is a plant native to North America. European explorers learned of the aromatic properties of the tobacco plant and helped to found an industry based on smoking the dried leaves. Today tobacco is used throughout the world. It may be smoked in pipes or in the form of cigarettes and cigars. Tobacco may also be used in the form of chewing tobacco or snuff.

Effects of Tobacco

Tobacco contains many substances that affect the body. **Nicotine** in tobacco smoke enters the bloodstream and causes the release of epinephrine, a stimulant that increases the pulse rate and blood pressure. Tobacco smoke also contains carbon monoxide, a poisonous gas that blocks the transport of oxygen by hemoglobin in the blood. (See Chapter 40.) Carbon monoxide decreases the body's supply of oxygen to its tissues, depriving the heart and other organs of the oxygen they need to function. **Tar**, a mixture of complex chemicals in tobacco products, includes a number of compounds that have been shown to cause cancer.

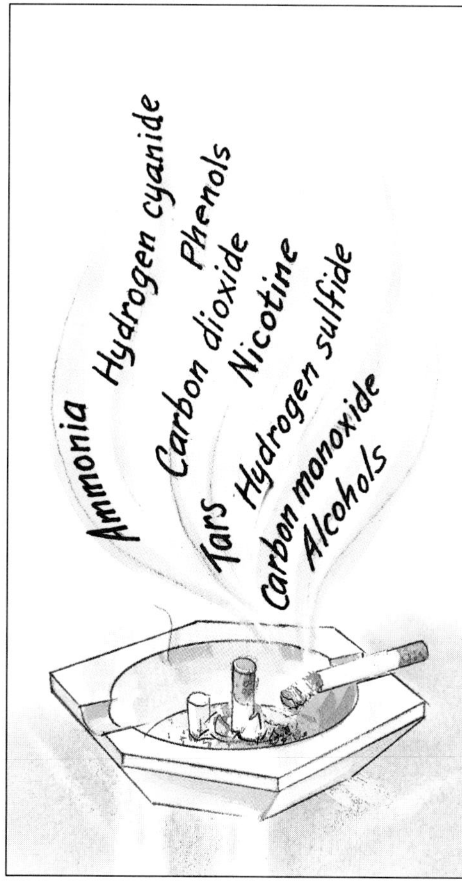

Figure 46–10 *In addition to these harmful substances, there are over 4000 other compounds given off when a cigarette burns.*

When tobacco products are used or smoked regularly, the body develops an addiction to nicotine. For this reason, long-term smokers find it extremely difficult to stop.

Tobacco and Disease

Tobacco is one of the leading causes of premature death in this country. **Lung cancer, the most common form of fatal cancer in the United States, has been directly linked to smoking.** Because lung cancer may take twenty years to develop, smokers may have a false sense of security about their habit. However, even in younger smokers the signs of destruction and illness are unmistakable.

LUNG DISORDERS By age 45, the death rate from lung cancer for smokers is four times that for nonsmokers. By age 65, it is more than ten times greater. For every smoker there is a serious risk of developing lung cancer. But lung cancer is not the only risk! There are other lung disorders associated with smoking. Smoke particles become trapped in the linings of the breathing passageways. At first these linings cleanse themselves. But as smoking continues, the cells of the linings are damaged. In time, smokers may develop a persistent cough as their lungs attempt to clear themselves. Smokers also suffer higher rates of respiratory infections than nonsmokers. They often develop chronic **bronchitis,** an inflammation of the large breathing tubes (bronchi) in the lungs. Long-term smoking can lead to **emphysema,** a stiffening of the normally elastic tissues of the lung.

Figure 46–11 *This photograph shows the bronchial walls in the lungs of a nonsmoker (left). Notice the cancer cells invading the bronchial wall of a smoker (right). As you can imagine, it was too late for this person to quit.*

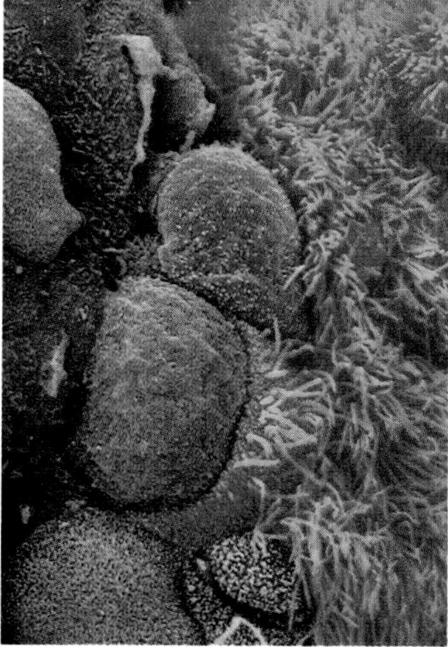

CIRCULATORY DISEASES The steady inhalation of carbon monoxide seems to cause a slow poisoning of the heart. Smoking also constricts, or narrows, blood vessels. Constriction of blood vessels causes blood pressure to rise and makes the heart work harder. It is no real surprise that statistics indicate that smoking doubles the risk of death from heart disease for men between the ages of 45 and 65. Moreover, for every age group and for both sexes, the risk of death from heart disease is greater among smokers than nonsmokers.

OTHER CANCERS Tobacco smokers also suffer from higher than normal levels of mouth and throat cancer, probably due to chemicals in tobacco tar. People who chew tobacco or inhale snuff should not be fooled into thinking these forms of tobacco are safe. Tobacco-chewers, for example, have extremely high rates of oral cancer and often fail to detect these cancers in time to prevent damage to the mouth and face.

SMOKING AND THE NONSMOKER In recent years evidence has clearly shown that the dangers of smoking are not restricted to the smoker. Tobacco smoke in the air is damaging to anyone who inhales it, not just the smoker. For this reason, many states require restaurants to have smoking and nonsmoking sections. And in many parts of the country, smoking in public places has been restricted, if not prohibited.

Passive smoking, or inhaling the smoke of others, is particularly damaging to young children. Studies now indicate that the children of smokers are twice as likely to develop respiratory problems as are children of nonsmokers.

DEALING WITH TOBACCO Only 30 percent of male smokers live to the age of 80. About 55 percent of male nonsmokers do. Clearly, smoking reduces expected life span. Moreover, whatever the age and no matter how long a person has smoked, a person's health can be improved by quitting. But tobacco is a powerful drug with strong addictive qualities that make it very difficult to give up. Thus, considering the cost, the medical dangers, and the chemical power of addiction, the best solution is not to begin smoking. Period!

46–3 SECTION REVIEW

1. Describe the main components of tobacco smoke and their effects on the body.
2. List and describe some of the disorders that can result from smoking.
3. What is the best advice you can give to a smoker who has not shown any ill effects, as yet, from the habit?

LABORATORY INVESTIGATION

OBSERVING THE EFFECT OF A STIMULANT ON THE HEART RATE

PROBLEM

How does caffeine affect the heart rate of a *Daphnia*?

MATERIALS *(per group)*

coffee (solution)	medicine dropper
coverslip	paper towel
Daphnia	stopwatch
microscope	calculator
depression slide	

PROCEDURE 

1. After reading the entire investigation, prepare a data table to record your observations.
2. Use the medicine dropper to withdraw a *Daphnia* from the container in which it is stored. Place the *Daphnia* and a few drops of water from the container in the center of a clean depression slide. Cover the *Daphnia* with a coverslip.
3. Examine the *Daphnia* under low power. Because the *Daphnia* is transparent, it is possible to observe its internal organs. Using the accompanying diagram, locate the labeled organs.
4. Set the stopwatch to zero. Locate the beating heart. Gently tap your finger on the table in time with the heartbeat. When you have found the rhythm of the heart, start the stopwatch. Count 20 beats and stop the stopwatch. Record the amount of time it took for the heart to beat 20 times.
5. Repeat step 4 for two more trials. Calculate the average time for 20 beats. Record your results.
6. Calculate the heart rate in beats per minute by dividing 1200 by the average time for 20 beats. Record the result.
7. Use the medicine dropper to put two drops of coffee at one edge of the coverslip. Place a small piece of paper towel at the other edge of the coverslip. As the paper towel soaks up liquid, the *Daphnia* will be exposed to the caffeine in the coffee.
8. Determine the effects of caffeine on the heartbeat by repeating steps 4 through 6.

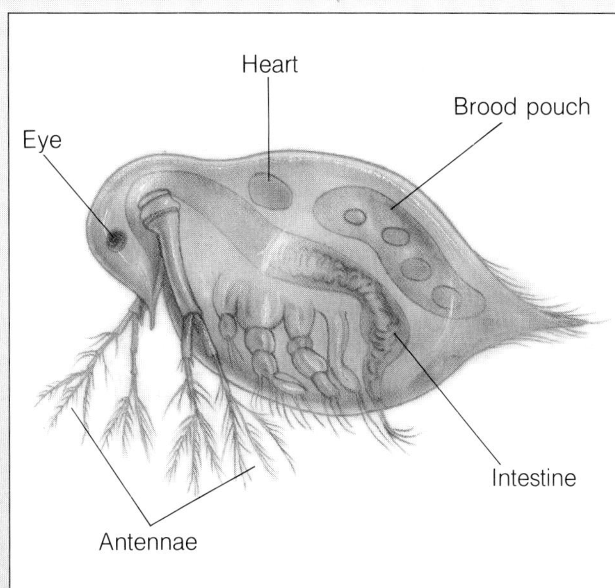

OBSERVATIONS

1. Describe the *Daphnia*'s heartbeat.
2. What was the *Daphnia*'s heart rate before exposure to caffeine? After exposure to caffeine?

ANALYSIS AND CONCLUSIONS

1. Why is the *Daphnia* an ideal organism to use in this type of investigation?
2. What effect did caffeine have on the *Daphnia*'s heart rate?
3. What type of drug is caffeine? How do you know?

STUDENT STUDY GUIDE

SUMMARIZING THE CONCEPTS

The key concepts in each section of this chapter are listed below to help you review the chapter content. Make sure you understand each concept and its relationship to the theme of this chapter.

46–1 Drugs

- A drug is any substance that causes a change in the body.
- All drugs, when used improperly, have the potential to do harm.
- The most widely abused illegal drug in the United States is marijuana.
- Hallucinogens, such as LSD and PCP, are powerful drugs that change the user's view of reality.
- Stimulants, such as amphetamines, speed up the actions of the nervous system.
- Depressants, such as barbiturates, slow down the actions of the nervous system.
- Cocaine, derived from the coca plant, is a stimulant that produces very strong psychological dependence. Use of cocaine can damage the heart and cause a heart attack. Crack is a form of cocaine that is highly addictive and has many serious effects on the body.
- Opiates, such as heroin and morphine, can be used to reduce pain. Opiates are addictive and lead to strong physical dependence.
- Drug abuse can be defined as using any drug in a way most doctors would not approve.
- People addicted to drugs may suffer withdrawal symptoms when cut off from their drug supply.

46–2 Alcohol

- Alcohol is a depressant that easily passes through cell membranes. Even a small amount of alcohol acts to slow down the actions of the nervous system.
- People who are addicted to alcohol are said to suffer from a disease called alcoholism.

46–3 Tobacco

- Several substances in tobacco—among them nicotine, tar, and carbon monoxide—can lead to serious health problems, including lung cancer, other cancers, respiratory problems, and circulatory problems.

REVIEWING KEY TERMS

Vocabulary terms are important to your understanding of biology. The key terms listed below are those you should be especially familiar with. Review these terms and their meanings. Then use each term in a complete sentence. If you are not sure of a term's meaning, return to the appropriate section and review its definition.

46–1 Drugs

drug
marijuana
hallucinogen
LSD
PCP
stimulant
amphetamine
depressant
barbiturate
cocaine
crack
opiate
morphine
heroin
drug abuse
drug addiction
withdrawal
endorphin

46–2 Alcohol

ethyl alcohol
fetal alcohol syndrome
alcoholism

46–3 Tobacco

nicotine
tar
bronchitis
emphysema

CHAPTER REVIEW

CONTENT REVIEW

Multiple Choice

Choose the letter of the answer that best completes each statement.

1. Over-the-counter drugs include
   a. amphetamines. c. aspirin.
   b. depressants. d. codeine.
2. Tetrahydrocannabinol is the active ingredient in
   a. opiates. c. alcohol.
   b. cocaine. d. marijuana.
3. Drugs that speed up the actions of the nervous system are
   a. prescription drugs. c. depressants.
   b. stimulants. d. opiates.
4. A drug that causes the release of dopamine in the brain is
   a. cocaine. c. tobacco.
   b. alcohol. d. marijuana.
5. Cirrhosis is a condition that affects the
   a. heart. c. lungs.
   b. liver. d. digestive system.
6. Alcohol is a
   a. depressant. c. hallucinogen.
   b. stimulant. d. prescription drug.
7. Which substance is found in tobacco smoke?
   a. PCP c. LSD
   b. tar d. THC
8. Morphine binds to the same receptor sites in the brain as
   a. cocaine. c. THC.
   b. endorphins. d. LSD.

True or False

Determine whether each statement is true or false. If it is true, write "true." If it is false, change the underlined word or words to make the statement true.

1. When opiate users stop using the drug, they undergo dependence.
2. Alcohol acts as a stimulant on the nervous system.
3. Barbiturates are examples of depressants.
4. Carbon dioxide is a poisonous gas found in cigarette smoke.
5. A drug is any substance that has an effect on the body.
6. The most powerful stimulants are the amphetamines.
7. Morphinelike chemicals produced by the brain are called receptors.
8. The form of alcohol used in beverages is methyl alcohol.

Word Relationships

A. *In each of the following sets of terms, three of the terms are related. One term does not belong. Determine the characteristic common to three of the terms and then identify the term that does not belong.*

1. cocaine, stimulant, barbiturate, amphetamine
2. alcohol, tobacco, barbiturate, depressant
3. ethyl alcohol, tar, nicotine, carbon monoxide
4. hallucinogen, opium, morphine, heroin

B. *Replace the underlined definition with the correct vocabulary word.*

5. Amphetamines are drugs that speed up the actions of the nervous system.
6. Cocaine causes the brain to release a chemical that produces a feeling of pleasure.
7. People who abuse heroin develop an uncontrollable craving for the drug.
8. Long-term smoking of tobacco can lead to stiffening of the elastic tissues in the lungs.

CONCEPT MASTERY

Use your understanding of the concepts developed in the chapter to answer each of the following in a brief paragraph.

1. Many people who drink alcohol state that it makes them more peppy. Explain why that is not the case.
2. Describe the physical effects of alcohol.
3. Compare psychological dependence and physical dependence.
4. Tobacco-chewers often think that their habit is much safer than tobacco smoking. Are they correct? Explain your answer.
5. Suggest some reasons why an ex-smoker should not start smoking again.
6. Not all alcoholics need to drink every day. Explain that statement.
7. Define drug abuse in your own words.
8. It has been said that no one can ever be cured of drug dependence. Explain why.
9. How is cigarette smoke related to respiratory and circulatory problems?

CRITICAL AND CREATIVE THINKING

Discuss each of the following in a brief paragraph.

1. **Relating cause and effect** Based on alcohol's effects on the nervous system, why is drinking and driving an extremely dangerous behavior?

2. **Making comparisons** Compare cocaine and crack.
3. **Expressing an opinion** How might you convince someone not to abuse drugs?
4. **Relating facts** Compare the actions on the nervous system of stimulants and depressants.
5. **Applying concepts** Explain the meaning of this ancient Japanese proverb: "First the man takes a drink, then the drink takes a drink, then the drink takes the man."
6. **Making inferences** In what ways are drug abuse and criminal acts related?
7. **Using the writing process** Choose any commonly abused drug and construct a poster designed to display the dangers of drug abuse.

Physical Therapist Assistant

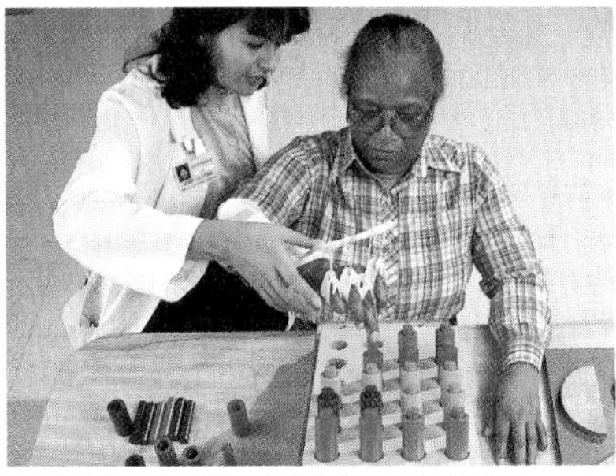

People who have lost partial or total use of a limb or joint due to surgery, injury, or disease can often regain their strength through careful exercise and therapy. Such therapy may be provided by a physical therapist assistant who works under the supervision of a physical therapist. Physical therapist assistants teach patients to exercise properly on different types of equipment. They also observe and record patients' progress.

High school courses in health, biology, and physical education along with some specialized training in physical therapy will help prepare a physical therapist assistant.

For more information write to the American Physical Therapy Association, 1111 N. Fairfax St., Alexandria, VA 22314.

Dietician

Dieticians study the chemical makeup of foods and the effects of foods on the human body. They use this knowledge to plan meals for groups and individuals. Some dieticians work in the management of food equipment and staff, others work directly with patients, and still others perform research on the nutritional needs of the human body.

A Bachelor's degree with a major in foods and nutrition or institutional management is necessary for a career as a dietician.

For more information write to the American Dietetic Association, 430 N. Michigan Ave., Chicago, IL 60611.

Biomedical Engineer

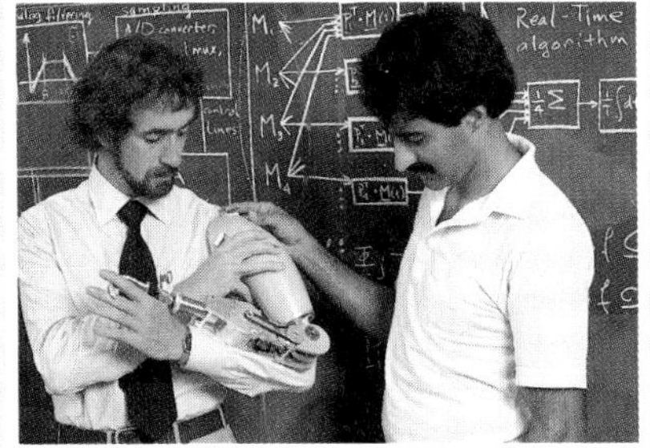

Biomedical engineers use a knowledge of engineering to solve problems in medicine and biology. They are involved in the design of technology used in and on the human body—for example, artificial organs, life support systems, and surgical lasers. Biomedical engineers often participate in research on life systems.

To become a biomedical engineer, a Bachelor's degree in a major field of engineering and an advanced degree in biomedical engineering is needed.

For more information write to the Biomedical Engineering Society, P.O. Box 2399, Culver City, CA 90231.

HOW TO PREPARE FOR A JOB INTERVIEW

A job interview gives you a chance to meet an employer and express your qualifications for a job. The interview is a deciding factor in whether or not you get the job.

You should first find out about the company at which you are having the interview. Information on the history, structure, and financial status of different companies can be found at your local library.

Before the interview, you might want to call to confirm the date and time of the interview. You should dress neatly and properly for any job interview, and you should take along any information that might be requested, such as a résumé. Be prepared to answer questions about yourself, your goals, your background, and why you want to work for that particular company.

FROM THE AUTHORS

I am always amazed at how many *facts* find their way into a book on biology, a book like this one. Charts, tables, diagrams, lists, and terms seem to occupy every page. It's easy to be overwhelmed. It's also possible to be convinced that biology is a closed science—to think that with so many facts crammed into one book that we must know just about everything. Of all the *mistakes* that you could make as a student, that would be the greatest—to believe that all the great scientists and great discoveries in biology are behind us. The great hidden truth is that we have barely begun to understand life.

Some of my friends who are experts in other subjects have told me that they would like to have lived at a different time. Philosophers sometimes wish that they could have lived in ancient Greece and talked with Plato and Socrates. Physicists wish that they could have worked with Einstein in the early part of the twentieth century when he developed his theories. An artist I know wishes that he could have been in France when the Impressionist movement began in the 1870s.

What time in history would have been the most exciting for a biologist? That's an easy question to answer. Recent history suggests that the greatest achievements for biology are still ahead of us. The last ten years of scientific research have produced one discovery after another that has revolutionized our understanding of living things. Despite all of this, some of the most fundamental questions about how life is produced, adapts to its surroundings, and is passed along to new generations are still unanswered. Right now we are closer to answering those great questions than at any time in human history, and *that* is exciting. As I said, it's easy to pick a favorite time in history. But the best time for a biologist to be alive is right now!

Ken Miller

UNIT 10

Ecological Interactions

Seemingly independent of one another, a great diversity of marine and terrestrial organisms has flourished in the pristine beauty of Alaska's Prince William Sound. The actual interrelationships among these organisms, however, became painfully obvious in March 1989 when the Exxon Valdez *polluted the waters with more than 240,000 barrels of crude oil.*

The effects were disastrous. Hundreds of thousands of organisms were killed by the thick black liquid. In addition, the toxic chemicals released by the spill spread throughout the environment. Some of the profound effects have already been observed; others remain to be seen in the years to come.

Like all living things, the organisms in Alaska are involved in delicately balanced interactions with one another and with their physical surroundings. Any disturbance that alters these interactions—such as pollution or natural disaster—can change the face of the Earth forever.

CHAPTERS

CHAPTER 47

The Biosphere

The Earth is a planet of striking beauty whose oceans and landmasses are home to a rich variety of life, including this caribou foraging for food in Denali National Park in Alaska.

When the first astronauts traveled beyond Earth and looked back to view their home planet, they were struck by its beauty. Great green continents and sparkling turquoise oceans stand out against the blackness of space. Compared to the other planets, Earth is a special sight.

But it is not appearance alone that makes our planet singular. Earth is different from the other planets because it is teeming with life. This life covers Earth like a huge web whose countless threads spread out and intertwine with one another.

Living things constantly interact with one another and with their surroundings. The invisible processes that occur deep within the cells of all living things form the basis of these interactions and affect the entire Earth. In this chapter you will explore these interactions, which are vital to the life of both the organism and the planet.

CHAPTER OUTLINE

47–1 Earth: A Living Planet

Section Objectives

- Define ecology, biosphere, and ecosystem.
- Describe the process of ecological succession.

During the last few years, people around the world have finally begun to understand that our remarkable planet is home not only to people but also to other forms of life. And the health of this life is essential to the health of human society.

In order to properly care for our planet, we must understand how the living world operates. To do so, we must study ecology. **Ecology is the study of the interactions of organisms with one another and with their physical surroundings.** The word **ecology** comes from the Greek word *oikos*, which means house. The "house" includes the environment in which organisms live, the interactions of organisms with one another, and the interactions of organisms with the nonliving environment. Scientists who study ecology are called ecologists.

From space, it is easy to see that Earth is a single living system that has been named the **biosphere**, or living globe. **The biosphere is that part of the Earth in which life exists.** It includes all the areas of land, air, and water on the entire planet, as well as all the life that populates these areas. The biosphere extends from about 8 kilometers above the Earth's surface to as far as 8 kilometers below the surface of the ocean. Living organisms are not distributed uniformly throughout the biosphere. For example, few organisms live in polar regions, whereas tropical rain forests swarm with life.

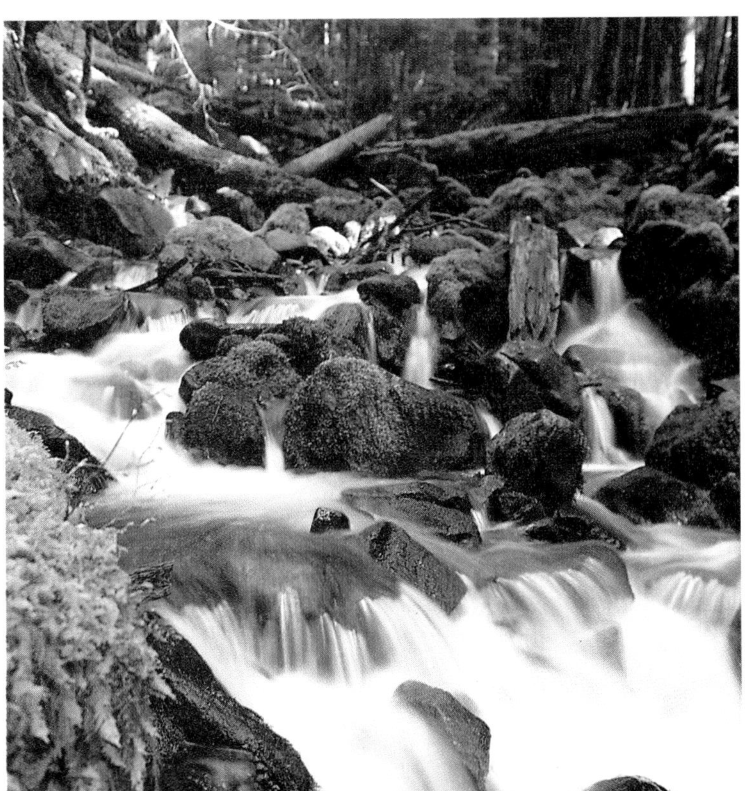

Figure 47–1 *A fast-moving stream in Olympic National Park in Washington is an example of how organisms interact with one another and with their physical surroundings. The spray from the stream made it possible for mosses to grow on the surfaces of nearby boulders.*

Ecosystems

Ecologists divide the biosphere into a variety of smaller units called **ecosystems.** Ecosystems consist of all the biotic (living) and abiotic (nonliving) factors that surround organisms and affect their way of life. Biotic factors are all the living organisms. Abiotic factors include soil type, rainfall, elevation, temperature, and location on the Earth. A pond ecosystem is made up of the pond itself and all the plants, animals, protists, and bacteria that live within it. A forest ecosystem is composed of everything from the soil to the fungi living in rotting leaves to the birds on the tips of the trees' tallest branches.

It is important for you to remember that although it may appear as if ecosystems are isolated from one another, they really are not. One ecosystem blends into another. For example, as water flows through a forest into a pond, frogs in the pond eat insects that fly through the woods and feed on plants and animals living near the pond. You should also remember that every organism in an ecosystem constantly changes the ecosystem. For example, leaves from trees near a pond fall onto the ground as well as into the pond. With the passage of time, the leaves decay, returning important nutrients to the forest floor and introducing new nutrients into the pond.

Figure 47–2 *Like all ecosystems, a stream ecosystem consists of all the biotic (living) and abiotic (nonliving) factors that surround organisms and affect their way of life.*

Ecological Succession

Because so many organisms alter their surroundings, environments are constantly changing in the process of **ecological succession.** In ecological succession, an existing community (organisms living in a common environment and interacting with one another) is gradually replaced by another community.

Ecological succession sometimes occurs in areas where there has been no previous living community. For example, when a new island rises out of the sea, the newly cooled lava rock is devoid of life. Soon, however, weathering by the wind, rain, and other agents creates a surface for the growth of lichens. The lichens produce organic acids that further help to dissolve the rock.

Eventually the lichens die and add their organic matter to the forming soil. Now the soil is fit for the growth of mosses, which break up the rock more and also add their remains to the soil. As the soil becomes more suitable for other organisms, new species move in and change the environment in their own ways. Ecological succession may take thousands of years and continues until a stable community becomes established.

Over long periods of time, ecological succession can produce dramatic changes in an ecosystem. For example, as a lake or pond ages, it may slowly fill up with silt and fallen leaves. Gradually the pond or lake turns into a marsh and then into dry land. See Figure 47–3. Eventually plants and animals from the surrounding communities colonize the area.

Ecological succession also occurs in areas where farmland is abandoned and forests are cut down or are destroyed by fire or other natural disasters and diseases. Often, ecological succession in these areas re-establishes the original community. For example, on an abandoned farm in New England, grasses are usually the first plants to grow, followed by weeds and small shrubs. Later, fast-growing trees, such as poplars and sumac, start to grow. Soon larger trees develop. Ecological succession continues until a forest develops.

Ecological succession often leads to a relatively stable collection of plants and animals called a **climax community.** In reality, a climax community is described by the major forms of plant life. However, the types of animals that live in a climax community depend directly or indirectly on the types of plants. Ecologists often describe different parts of the world in terms of their most common climax community. If, for example, you tell an ecologist that an area is a "temperate zone beech-maple forest" he will have a good idea of what the area is like. Tell a marine biologist that you visited a "South Pacific coral atoll" and she too will know what you are talking about.

Although we describe a climax community as relatively stable, it does not mean that it never changes. Fires, floods, or droughts can disturb a climax community and cause the area to undergo ecological succession again. Similarly, tsunamis (incorrectly called tidal waves) and hurricanes can upset climax

Figure 47–3 *Ecological succession can occur as a pond fills up with silt and fallen leaves. Over a period of time, the pond turns into a marsh and then into dry land, which soon becomes inhabited by a climax community.*

communities in many marine environments. In some cases, disasters can completely wipe out an entire climax community, causing ecological succession to begin.

47–1 SECTION REVIEW

1. Define ecology, biosphere, and ecosystem. How are they related to one another?
2. What are the abiotic factors in an environment? The biotic factors?
3. Describe the process of ecological succession.
4. What is a climax community?
5. How would the breakdown of large amounts of organic matter upset the natural balance of a lake ecosystem?

Section Objectives

- Explain how biomes are classified.
- Describe the characteristics of each land biome.

47–2 Land Biomes

Areas that are similar in climate and other physical factors develop similar types of climax communities. These areas are called biomes. **A biome is an environment that has a characteristic climax community.** The Earth is made up of two main types of **biomes**: land biomes and aquatic biomes. Aquatic biomes will be discussed in the next section.

Most land biomes are named for their climax community, or the dominant type of plant life. The major land biomes are the tundra, taiga, temperate deciduous forest, grassland, tropical rain forest, and desert.

Figure 47–4 *According to this illustration, what type of biome covers most of Europe?*

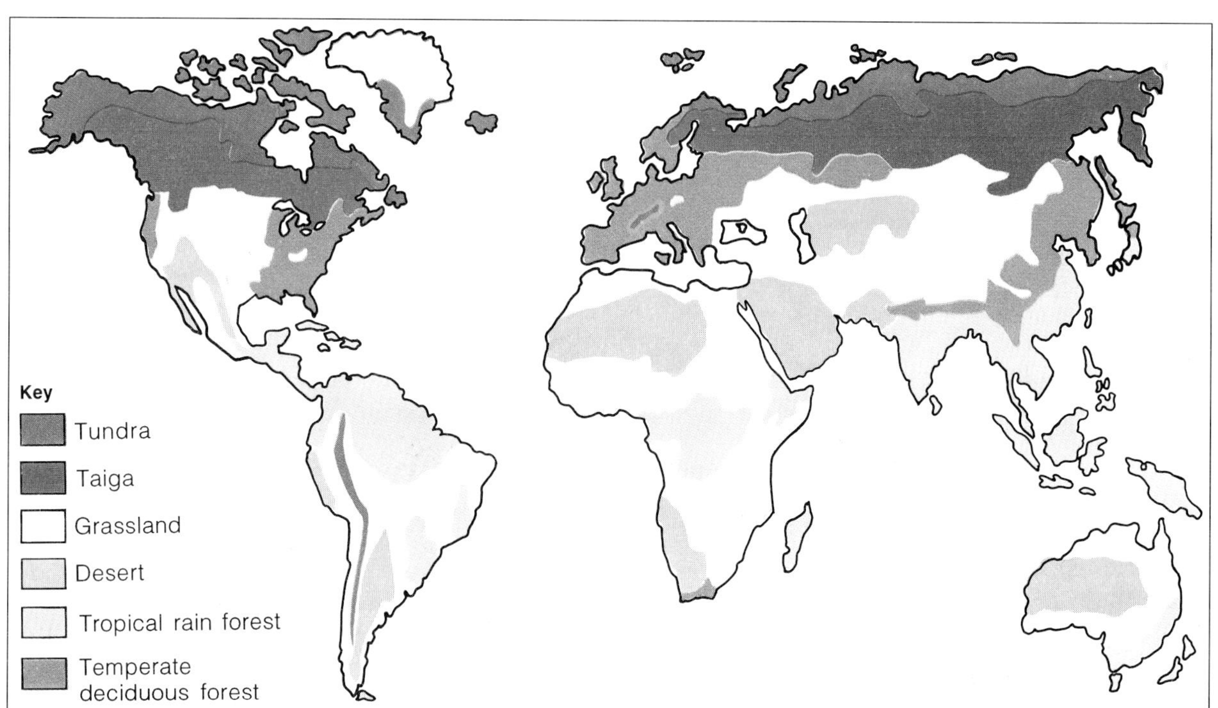

Figure 47–5 During the summer months, plants such as grasses and dwarf trees dominate the tundra. The caribou (left) and ptarmigan (right) are two types of animals that migrate to this biome in search of food.

Tundra

Northern North America, Asia, and Europe are covered by biomes called **tundra.** The tundra is the northernmost land biome. This nearly treeless biome is covered by mosses, lichens, and grasses. A few stunted trees survive here and there. Many animals migrate into the tundra during the summer to feed on the plants that grow there. Caribou and reindeer are two examples. In turn, wolves, foxes, and hordes of mosquitoes feed on these animals. A great many birds summer here, then fly south in early autumn.

The most characteristic feature of the tundra is permafrost, which is a layer of permanently frozen subsoil. During the summer the ground thaws to a depth of a few centimeters and becomes soggy and wet; in the winter it freezes again. This cycle of thawing and freezing, which rips and crushes plant roots, is what keeps the plants small and stunted.

Taiga

South of the tundra are biomes dominated by great coniferous, or cone-bearing, forests of fir, pine, and spruce. These biomes are called **taiga** (TIGH-guh). The term taiga comes from the Russian word that means primeval forest.

The taiga stretches across much of North America and Asia, with a narrow band reaching into Norway and Sweden (in Europe). The taiga rises to the higher elevations of many mountain ranges in the United States, including the Rocky and Appalachian mountains. The taiga also extends along the coasts of Washington, Oregon, and northern California, where it

Figure 47–6 Great horned owls and grizzlies are two examples of the animals that inhabit the taiga, which is dominated by coniferous, or cone-bearing, trees.

is home to the giant redwoods—some of the tallest trees in the world. Redwoods can reach heights of more than 60 meters.

Although winters in the taiga are cold, summers are mild enough and long enough to allow many animals and plants to reproduce. The ground thaws during the warmer months, although in some places the thawing does not last for long. Many rivers, ponds, lakes, and bogs provide homes for a variety of living things. Many small birds and mammals live in the taiga and either hibernate or move to warmer regions during the long, cold winters. Typical inhabitants of the taiga include black bears, grizzlies, wolves, moose, elk, and dozens of smaller animals such as voles, wolverines, and grouse.

Temperate Deciduous Forests

Covering the eastern coast of the United States, the southern coast of Canada, most of Europe, and parts of Japan, China, and Australia are biomes that are characterized by changing seasons and leaf fall. These biomes are called **temperate deciduous forests.** A temperate deciduous forest gets its name from its forests of oak, maple, beech, and birch—trees that are deciduous, or shed their leaves in autumn. Although rainfall is sufficient year round, cold winters halt plant growth for several months. Because deciduous trees shed their leaves every autumn, this biome goes through striking seasonal changes. In the spring, many small plants in the forest practically burst out of the ground and grow quickly so that they can flower and bear fruit before they are shaded by the trees.

Although a great number of animals once inhabited these forests, many have been hunted to near extinction. With careful

protection and hunting regulations, deer, moose, gray foxes, and several other species are beginning to reappear. An enormous variety of birds spend their summers in this biome, and chipmunks, raccoons, opossums, and squirrels make it their permanent home.

In the temperate deciduous forest biome, an abundance of organic matter and nutrients are stored in a layer of decaying leaves and twigs called humus (HYOO-muhs). Because humus enriches the soil, these forests make good farmland. And this has encouraged human activities that have greatly altered the biome. For example, forest land in New England was cleared of trees and used for farming. Fortunately, much of the original deciduous forest has since recovered.

Figure 47–7 *Because the trees in a temperate deciduous forest shed their leaves every autumn, this biome goes through striking seasonal changes. The mountain lion and mallard ducks are but two of the many species of animals that make this biome their home.*

Grasslands

Usually found in the interior portions of many continents, **grasslands** are vast areas covered with grasses and small leafy plants. Although this biome may receive significant rainfall (25 to 75 centimeters per year), most of it falls in one season. The grasslands of the world include the plains and prairies of North America, the steppes of the Soviet Union, the veld of South Africa, and the pampas of Argentina.

In the midwestern United States, grasslands are characterized by hot summers and cold winters. In some tropical grasslands, however, there is little seasonal change in temperature. Instead, the seasons change from wet to very dry. These tropical grasslands, which are dotted with groves of trees, are called savannas. See Figure 47–8 on page 1014.

Figure 47–8 *In Africa, grazing animals, such as these Thompson's gazelles, feast on the low-growing plants that make up a savanna, or tropical grassland. Notice the many acacia trees in the background.*

In grasslands, as in other biomes, interactions among animals and plants shape the environment. In fact, many grasslands do not undergo ecological succession and thus do not become forests primarily because of the grazing of large animals and periodic fires. On the Serengeti grasslands of Africa, impala, gazelles, wildebeests, and elephants graze.

Wheat, corn, and other grains are heavily farmed in the grasslands of the midwestern United States and in the Ukraine in the Soviet Union. In the past, these grasslands were almost destroyed by overfarming. Overfarming strips the grasslands of their protective layer of vegetation, thus allowing windstorms to blow away kilometers of topsoil. This is exactly what happened in the 1930s when windstorms carried away hundreds of millions of metric tons of rich topsoil, creating the great dust bowls.

Tropical Rain Forests

In parts of the world where the temperature stays warm and rain falls year round, **tropical rain forest** biomes are found. Typically, tropical rain forests receive 200 to 400 centimeters of rainfall each year. Temperatures remain constant at about 25°C throughout the year. This biome covers large areas of South America, Southeast Asia, Africa, and Central America.

The tropical rain forests are home to more species of plants and animals than can be found in all the rest of the land biomes combined! Here, many trees grow to a height of 70 meters, and their tops form a dense covering called a canopy. The tall trees also provide surfaces on which many other plants grow. Lianas (lee-AH-nuhz) are large woody vines that use the trees to support their rapid growth.

Animal life in the rain forests is rich and varied. Colorful insects and birds are particularly abundant. Reptiles, small mammals, and amphibians are common inhabitants of this biome. It is not surprising that many of the animals living here are tree dwellers, as the floor of tropical rain forests bristles with danger.

Figure 47–9 Tree ferns, tangled lianas, and towering, slender trees characterize this section of a tropical rain forest in Costa Rica. Most of the animal inhabitants—the sloth (left) and squirrel monkeys (right), for example—live high in the trees, where they stay out of the way of predators that roam the floor of the forest.

Many of the animals and plants that inhabit the rain forests produce chemicals that may be useful in fighting some types of diseases. Unfortunately, the world's tropical rain forests are being destroyed by the rapid growth of the human population. If the destruction continues at its present rate, almost all of the tropical rain forests will disappear by the end of this century! Along with the rain forests will go thousands of plant and animal species found only in this fascinating biome.

Deserts

Deserts are biomes that usually occur in areas where there is less than 25 centimeters of rainfall a year. There are many different kinds of deserts around the world. In deserts such as the Sahara in Africa—the world's largest desert—rain almost never falls, and the wind is hot and dry. Because almost nothing grows in this type of desert, the landscape looks as barren as the surface of the moon. Other deserts are home to many species of lizards, insects, scorpions, snakes, and birds.

In seasonal deserts there is some rainfall during the year. Rapidly growing plants soak up the water as quickly as possible, then grow, flower, fruit, and become dormant until the next rainfall. In the deserts of the southwestern United States and Mexico, rainfall is more even, but it is sparse. Here, sagebrush, cacti, and only a few types of trees survive. Another type of desert is found on mountains and plateaus where the high altitudes cause a decrease in temperature. These deserts are called cold deserts. Cold deserts have a brief rainy season that permits the growth of grasses and shrubs.

If modern science can find a way to bring water to the deserts, they can be made suitable for farming. Desert soil is often very fertile and, of course, receives plenty of sunlight. In parts of the Middle East, archaeologists have uncovered the ruins of waterworks that were used thousands of years ago by desert inhabitants to collect rainwater. In several areas these waterworks have been rebuilt, making farming possible again.

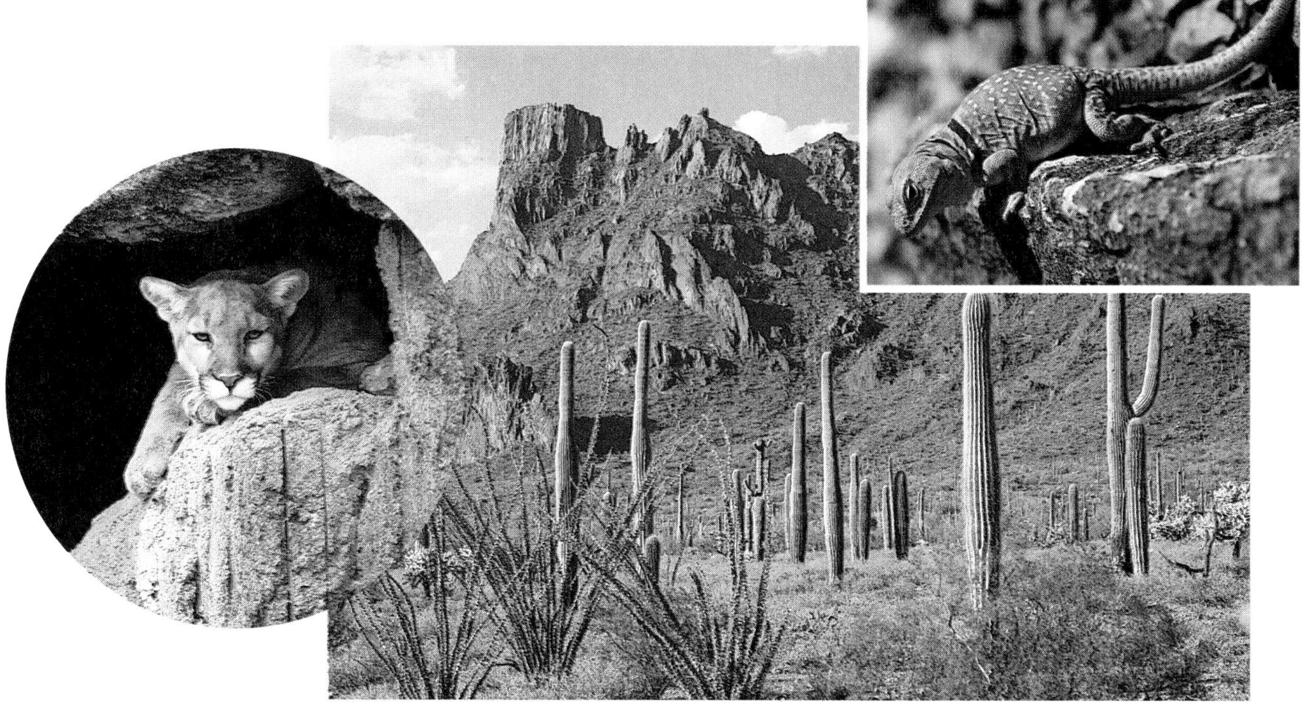

Figure 47–10 *In the Sonoran Desert, which stretches from southern California to western Arizona and down into Mexico, the dominant plant is the giant saguaro cactus. The collared lizard and cougar are examples of animals that inhabit the Sonoran Desert.*

47–2 SECTION REVIEW

1. How are biomes classified?
2. Describe the characteristics of each land biome.
3. What characteristics would you expect tundra-dwelling animals to have?

Section Objectives

- List some abiotic factors that affect aquatic biomes.
- Describe the three aquatic biomes.

47–3 Aquatic Biomes

The aquatic biomes are the water ecosystems. They include the freshwater biome, marine biome, and estuaries. These biomes support more organisms than do the land biomes.

Some of the abiotic factors that affect the kinds of organisms found in the aquatic biomes are light intensity, amounts of oxygen and carbon dioxide dissolved in the water, and the availability of organic and inorganic nutrients. The aquatic biomes do not vary in temperature as much as land biomes do.

Freshwater Biomes

Rivers, streams, and lakes are the lifeblood of our continents and are considered the **freshwater biomes** of the Earth. Not only do they provide much of our drinking water, but they are also an important source of food. Tiny floating plants and animals drift and swim through the water. These organisms are eaten by fishes and amphibians, which also eat the vegetation and insects that fall into the water from overhanging trees. Trout are typical of the fast-swimming fishes that live in mountain streams. Large rivers such as the Amazon in South America and the Nile in Africa are home to many species of insects, fishes, amphibians, reptiles, and mammals.

Unfortunately, people all over the world are using rivers and lakes as dumping grounds for wastes. The results of this carelessness are beginning to catch up with us. We will discuss the problems of water pollution in more detail in Chapter 49.

Figure 47–11 In swift-moving rivers, most organisms live in the shallows, where algae and mosses cling to the surfaces of rocks.

Marine Biomes

The vast habitats of the ocean, or the **marine biomes**, cover most of the surface of the Earth. Because sunlight penetrates only a short distance before it is absorbed by the water, photosynthesis can take place only in the uppermost region of a marine biome. This region is called the photic (FOHT-ihk) zone. The photic zone may be as shallow as 30 meters in the North Atlantic Ocean or as deep as 200 meters in the South Pacific Ocean. It is in this thin ocean layer that phytoplankton (tiny free-floating photosynthetic organisms) and algae grow.

Oceanographers have divided marine biomes into ecologically distinct zones depending on depth and distance from shore. Each of these zones contains organisms that are adapted to the conditions there.

INTERTIDAL ZONE The intertidal zone is the most difficult zone for organisms to live in. Those that live here must tolerate radical changes in their surroundings: Once or twice a day they are submerged in ocean water; the remainder of the time they are exposed to air and sunlight. Organisms in the intertidal zone have adapted in some way to the pounding and surging of waves. Some organisms, such as clams, burrow into

Figure 47–12 The intertidal zone (left), is characterized by organisms such as barnacles and starfish. The neritic zone (right) provides a home to brilliantly colored coral-reef fishes.

the sand to keep from being washed out to sea. Others, such as barnacles and seaweed, attach themselves to rocks. Still others, such as snails, sea urchins, and starfish, cling to rocks by their feet or suckers.

NERITIC ZONE The neritic zone is the part of a marine biome that extends from the low-tide line to the edge of the open sea. Large algae (seaweed) are abundant here because this part of the ocean is in the photic zone. For example, off the coast of California grow huge forests of giant kelp (brown algae). In shallow areas of tropical waters, meadows of turtle grass provide food for fishes, invertebrates, and turtles. And along the ocean floor, lobsters and crabs crawl while flounder and rays swim above them.

OPEN-SEA ZONE In the open-sea zone, phytoplankton are responsible for 80 to 90 percent of the Earth's photosynthetic activity. Phytoplankton are in turn eaten by larger animals. Thus the chain of life in the sea begins with these tiny organisms. Swimming rapidly through the open-sea zone are fishes of all shapes and sizes and mammals such as dolphins and whales. The open ocean is also home to sea birds such as albatrosses, which live most of their life at sea.

Because nutrients are scarce in most of the open sea, the growth of phytoplankton is relatively slow. This limits the number of animals that can live there. Closer to the shore, however, nutrients are more abundant, and countless fishes swim there to feed and reproduce. Unfortunately, these rich fishing areas are much more susceptible to pollution than is the open sea.

DEEP-SEA ZONE The deep-sea zone is an area of high pressure, cold temperature, and total darkness. Until recently, biologists thought the deep-sea zone was completely devoid of life. But it is now known that this area is home to some of the Earth's strangest creatures. Gulper eels with mouths that make up almost half of their body and giant squid with glowing spots along their sides inhabit the ocean depths.

Here, too, zooplankton (free-floating microscopic animals) wait for night in order to migrate to the ocean's surface and feed on phytoplankton. Herds of bottom-dwellers, such as sea cucumbers, crawl along the ocean floor. Hardly a day goes by that an interesting life form is not found in the deep-sea zone.

Estuaries

Estuaries (EHS-tyoo-er-eez) are found at the boundary between fresh water and salt water. Salt marshes, mangrove swamps, lagoons, and the mouths of rivers that empty into the ocean are examples of estuaries. These areas contain a mixture of fresh water and salt water.

Figure 47–13 *Estuaries are areas where fresh water and salt water meet. This salt marsh in Long Island, New York (top), and the mangrove swamp in Florida (bottom) are examples of estuaries.*

Estuaries support a variety of life forms. Because estuaries are usually shallow, sunlight is able to penetrate the water completely. Photosynthesis occurs at all levels, making estuaries a suitable environment for aquatic plants. The abundance of such plants, in turn, supports many types of fishes, shrimps, and crabs. In fact, many fishes and invertebrates spawn, hatch, and nurse their young in estuaries. As the young mature, they head for the open sea, then return to the estuaries to reproduce. Several species of birds use estuaries for nesting, feeding, and resting.

SCIENCE, TECHNOLOGY, AND SOCIETY **BREAKTHROUGH**

Life Without Sunlight at the Bottom of the Sea

In 1974, a group of scientists from the Woods Hole Oceanographic Institute were using the deep-sea submersible *Alvin* to explore the sea floor in the Pacific Ocean. At a distance of about 380 kilometers off the coast of the Galapagos Islands and at a depth of 2700 meters, they made two exciting discoveries: The near-freezing water, which is usually between 2° and 3°C, was getting warmer! And there was life in this usually uninhabitable place—giant tube worms nearly 9 meters long, huge clams measuring more than 20 centimeters in diameter, and eyeless, colorless crabs!

Here, as in several places on the sea floor, fissures open up and expose the Earth's molten crust to sea water. The water seeps into the volcanic rocks, becomes superheated, and rises—picking up minerals along the way. Finally, the water shoots out of the sea floor through vents, or "chimneys." How hot is this water? The first time the scientists on board the *Alvin* tried to measure the water temperature, the heat melted *Alvin*'s robot arm! When they finally did obtain a temperature reading, the scientists were amazed. The water was a very hot 300°C!

Excited by these discoveries, other scientists made subsequent trips to this area. They found that as the superheated water left the vents, it carried with it large amounts of hydrogen sulfide. As the water moved farther away from the vents, it began to cool enough for organisms to carry out their life activities. In this cooler water, scientists found a most interesting life form: chemosynthetic bacteria. Chemosynthetic bacteria capture the energy released by certain inorganic substances—in this case, hydrogen sulfide. They use this energy to build organic molecules, and in turn they become the energy source for the tube worms, huge clams, and eyeless crabs.

These discoveries have shown that entire ecosystems exist in which the producers are chemosynthetic bacteria. Such ecosystems are dependent not on energy from sunlight but on heat energy from deep within the Earth.

47–3 SECTION REVIEW

1. What are some abiotic factors that affect aquatic biomes?
2. Describe the freshwater biome, marine biome, and estuary.
3. Describe the four zones of the marine biome.
4. In parts of the deep-sea zone far below the depth to which sunlight penetrates, many types of species live. Suggest some special characteristics that would enable species to live in this zone.

47–4 Energy and Nutrients: Building the Web of Life

Section Objectives

- Explain how energy flows through an ecosystem.
- Discuss how water, nitrogen, carbon, and oxygen are recycled in the environment.
- Define limiting factor.
- Describe a food chain and a food web.

One of the most important factors in any ecosystem is the flow of energy through the ecosystem. Of all the sun's energy that reaches the Earth's surface, only a small amount—approximately 0.1 percent on a worldwide basis—is used by living things. Yet this amount, as small as it is, is responsible for the production of several thousand grams of organic matter per square meter of forest per year.

Approximately one half of the energy plants absorb from the sun is used immediately. The rest is stored in plant tissues in the form of energy-containing compounds (carbohydrates). Animals that eat the plants obtain this energy. But because the animals must use much of this energy to carry on their life activities, they store an even smaller amount. Energy cannot be recycled, or used again. Thus energy in an ecosystem is referred to as a flow rather than a cycle.

Nutrients, on the other hand, are generally recycled through an ecosystem. When an animal dies, its matter does not disappear. Rather, it decomposes and eventually gets used by another organism.

The Flow of Energy

You may recall from Chapter 6 that the sun is the ultimate source of energy for all living things. During photosynthesis, green plants and certain bacteria trap sunlight and use it to assemble carbon dioxide and water into carbohydrates. Because photosynthetic organisms are able to make their own food from inorganic substances, they are called **producers**.

Figure 47–14 *Organisms are classified as producers, consumers, or decomposers, depending on how they get their food. Because spruce bud worms feed directly on the jack pine, which is a producer, they are called primary consumers (left). Robins, which feed on the worms, are called secondary consumers (center). Decomposers, such as mushrooms, get their food from the remains of dead organisms (right).*

Animals, on the other hand, are **consumers.** Consumers get their energy either directly or indirectly from producers. Consumers that feed directly on producers are called primary consumers. Primary consumers are also called herbivores (plant-eating animals). Consumers that feed on primary consumers are called secondary consumers. There may be tertiary (third-level) or quaternary (fourth-level) consumers that feed on secondary and tertiary consumers, respectively. Secondary and higher level consumers are usually carnivores (flesh-eating animals). For example, an insect that eats plants is a primary consumer, a frog that eats the insect is a secondary consumer, a snake that eats the frog is a tertiary consumer, and so on. **Energy flows through an ecosystem from the sun to producers and then to consumers.**

When plants and animals in an ecosystem die, their remains do not build up because of the presence of **decomposers.** Decomposers are organisms that obtain their energy from nonliving organic matter. Some examples of decomposers are bacteria and fungi.

Each step in this series of organisms eating other organisms is called a trophic, or feeding, level. The term trophic comes from the Greek word *trophe* which means food. There is no limit to the number of trophic levels in a particular ecosystem. However, at each higher trophic level, less and less of the energy originally captured by the producers is available. This is because the energy obtained from digested food is used to maintain the metabolism of the organism and to power its daily activities. A small amount of the energy taken in by herbivores (primary consumers) is changed into new animal biomass. Biomass is the total mass of all the organisms in a trophic level.

As a rule, approximately 10 percent of the energy at one trophic level can be used by animals at the next trophic level. Thus 10 percent of the energy in plants becomes stored in the tissues of herbivores, and 10 percent of the energy in herbivores becomes stored in the tissues of carnivores. At each successive trophic level, less energy is available to an organism.

Ecological Pyramids

Ecologists use **ecological pyramids** to represent the energy relationships among trophic levels. There are three types of ecological pyramids. A pyramid of energy shows the total amount of incoming energy at each successive level. Notice in Figure 47–15 that energy (in the form of heat) is lost going from one trophic level to another.

The trophic levels of an ecosystem can also be represented by a pyramid of biomass, which shows the total mass of living tissue at each level. See Figure 47–15. This pyramid of biomass shows, for example, that a large amount of grass is needed to feed a single rabbit, and a large number of rabbits is needed to nourish a single hawk.

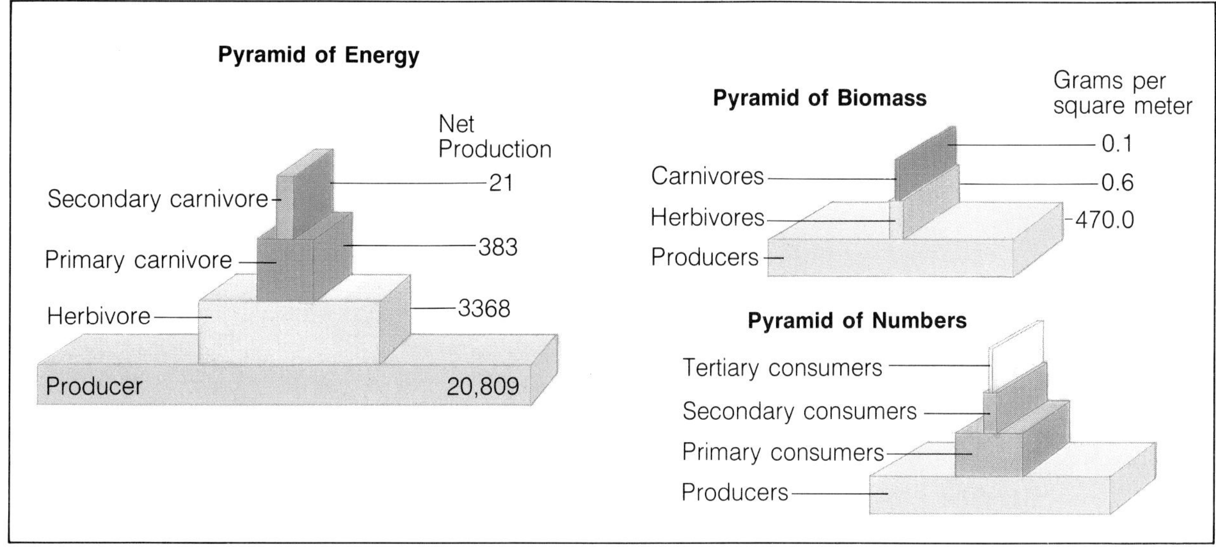

Figure 47–15 *A pyramid of energy shows that a small amount of energy in an ecosystem is transferred at each trophic level. A pyramid of biomass shows the mass present in each trophic level at any one time. A pyramid of numbers shows the number of organisms in a particular ecosystem.*

Relationships among trophic levels may also be represented by a pyramid of numbers. A pyramid of numbers illustrates the total number of organisms at each level. In a grassland, for example, a large amount of grass (producers) is needed to support the herbivores (primary consumers). Usually the number of organisms decreases at each successive level. Sometimes, however, this is not the case. In a temperate deciduous forest, one tree (producer) can support a large number of insects (primary consumers).

Like pyramids of biomass, pyramids of numbers show only the amount of organic material present at one time. They do not give the total amount of material produced or the rate at which it is produced, as do pyramids of energy.

Biogeochemical Cycles

Although energy moves in a one-way direction through an ecosystem, nutrients are recycled. All organisms require certain essential nutrients in order to grow. Plants need water, carbon dioxide, phosphorus, potassium, and many other elements. Animals require complex compounds (such as proteins and amino acids), several types of vitamins, and many of the same elements plants do.

As members of each trophic level eat members of the level beneath them, they acquire the complex organic molecules and elements they need in addition to energy. Although energy and nutrients move together from one trophic level to the next, they move through the biosphere differently.

Nutrients move through the biosphere in a series of physical and biological processes called **biogeochemical**, or nutrient, **cycles**. They are called cycles because nutrients, unlike energy, may be used over and over again by living systems.

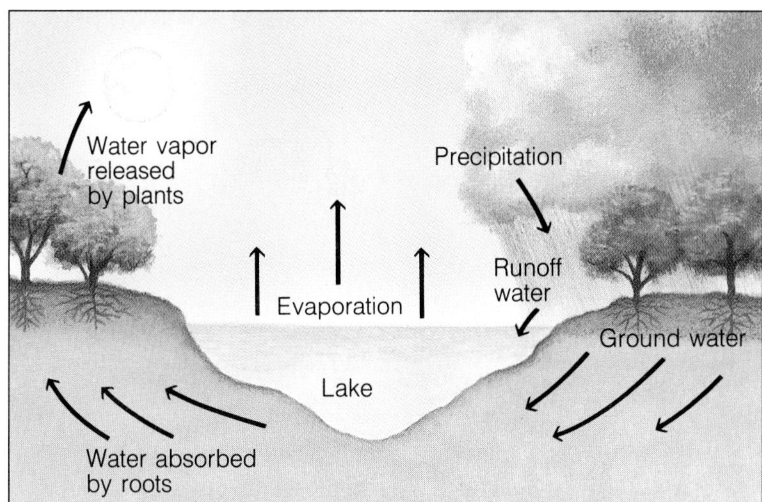

Figure 47–16 *The water cycle consists of an alternation of evaporation and condensation.*

THE WATER CYCLE The movement of water from the atmosphere to the Earth and back to the atmosphere is called the **water cycle**. The water cycle consists of an alternation of evaporation and condensation. Water molecules enter the air by evaporation from the ocean and other bodies of water. In the air, the water molecules condense (in clouds) and then return to the Earth in the form of precipitation (rain). On land, most of the rainwater runs along the surface of the ground until it enters a river or stream that carries it to a larger body of water. Some water sinks into the ground and is called ground water. The upper surface of ground water is known as the water table.

THE NITROGEN CYCLE All organisms require nitrogen to build proteins. Nitrogen is available to organisms in several ways. Free nitrogen gas makes up 78 percent of the atmosphere. Nitrogen is also found in the wastes produced by many organisms and in dead and decaying organisms. The movement of nitrogen through the biosphere is called the **nitrogen cycle**. However, most of this nitrogen cannot be directly used by living things. It must be converted into other forms.

Certain bacteria that live on roots of plants such as legumes (beans, peas, and peanuts) change free nitrogen in the

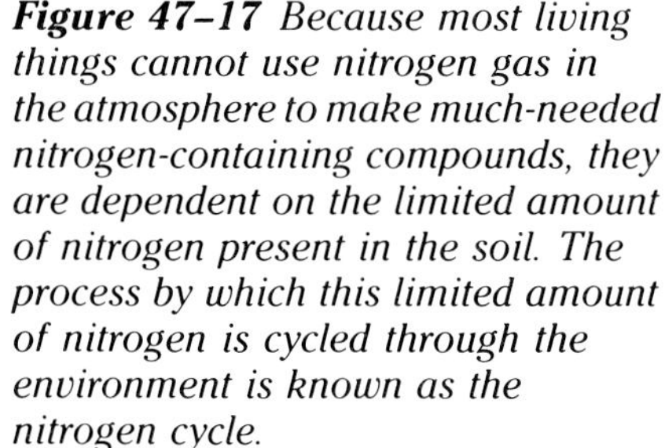

Figure 47–17 *Because most living things cannot use nitrogen gas in the atmosphere to make much-needed nitrogen-containing compounds, they are dependent on the limited amount of nitrogen present in the soil. The process by which this limited amount of nitrogen is cycled through the environment is known as the nitrogen cycle.*

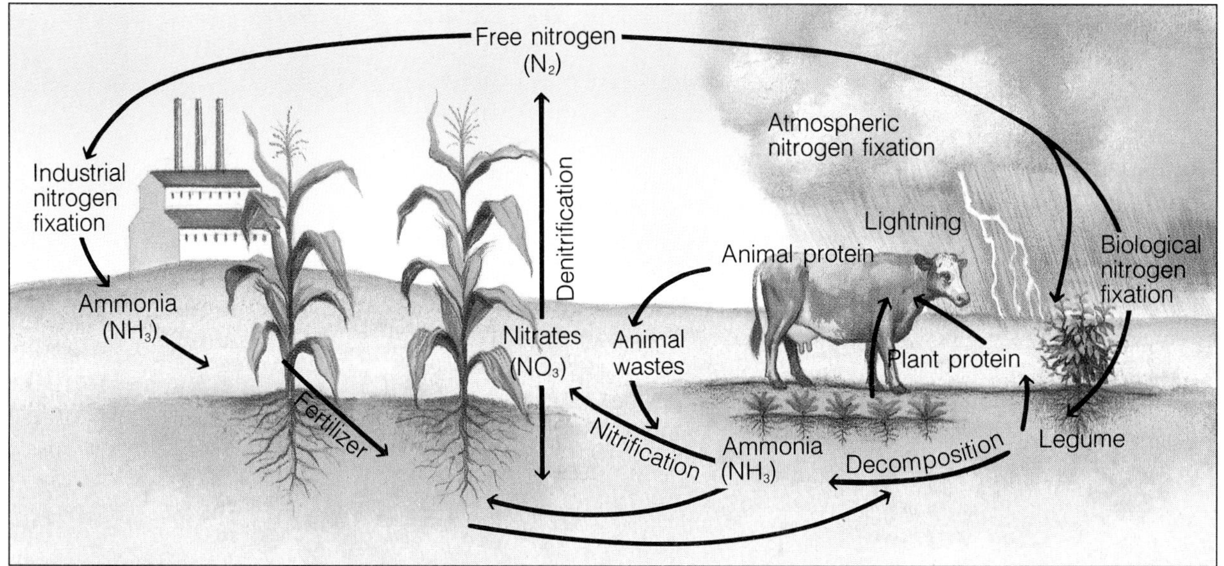

atmosphere into nitrogen compounds (nitrates and nitrites) that can be used by living things. This process is known as **nitrogen fixation**, and the bacteria are called nitrifying bacteria. Once the nitrogen compounds are available, plants use them to make plant proteins. Animals then eat the plants and use the proteins to make animal proteins. When the plants and animals die, the nitrogen compounds return to the soil.

Eventually other bacteria in the soil break down these nitrogen compounds into free nitrogen in a process called **denitrification** (dee-nigh-trih-fih-CAY-shuhn). These bacteria are called denitrifying bacteria. Through the process of denitrification, free nitrogen is returned to the atmosphere.

THE CARBON AND OXYGEN CYCLES The process by which carbon is moved through the environment is called the **carbon cycle**. During photosynthesis, green plants and algae use carbon dioxide from the atmosphere to form glucose. Consumers and decomposers use glucose in respiration, during which they produce carbon dioxide. Carbon dioxide is then released into the atmosphere, completing the carbon cycle.

The movement of oxygen through the environment is called the **oxygen cycle**. During photosynthesis, water molecules are split, releasing oxygen into the atmosphere. The oxygen is used by most organisms for respiration. During respiration, water is released. The water is absorbed by plants, and the cycle begins again.

Nutrient Limitation

The rate at which producers can capture energy and use it to produce living tissue is controlled by several factors, one of which is the amount of available nutrients. If a nutrient is in short supply—thus limiting an organism's growth—it is called a **limiting factor**.

For example, coastal ocean water often contains sufficient supplies of several nutrients to support much more plant

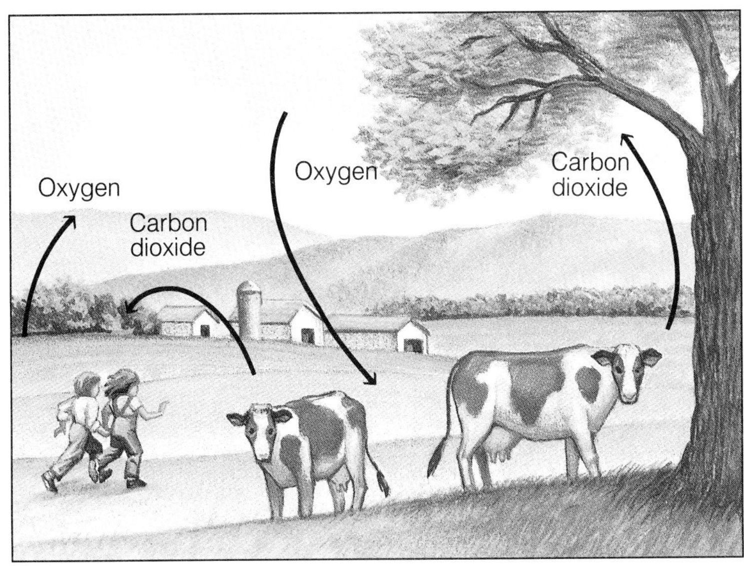

Figure 47–18 *Photosynthesis and respiration are the major biochemical events in the carbon and oxygen cycles.*

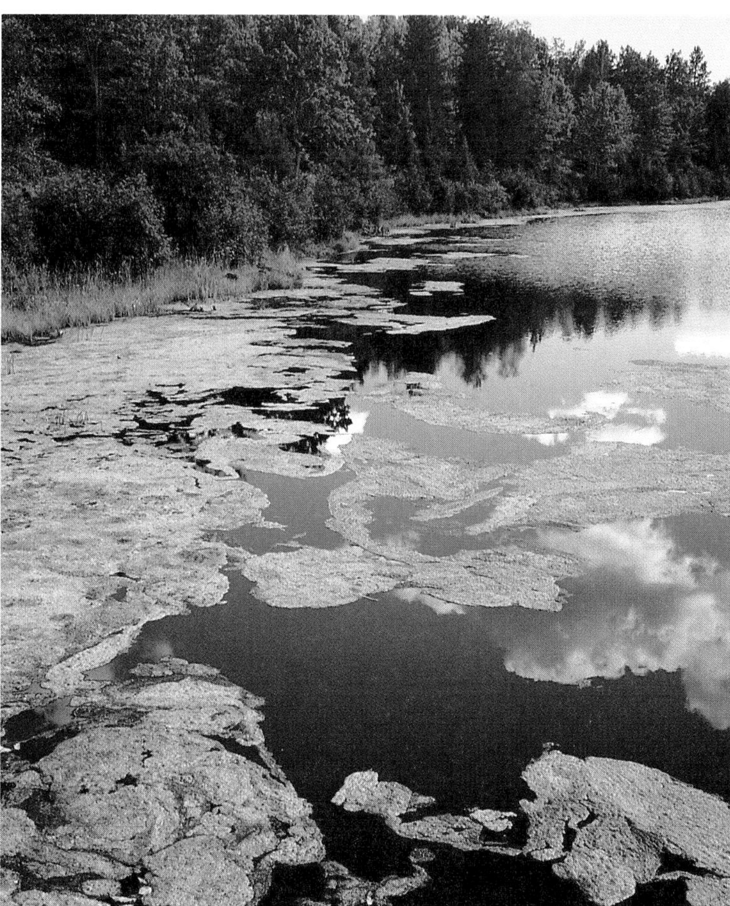

Figure 47–19 When an algal bloom in a pond begins to cover a large portion of the water's surface, the plants below the surface die from the lack of sunlight. Bacteria then grow at a rapid rate and use up much of the available oxygen. Eventually, the animals in the water suffocate.

growth than is normally present. The producers in these ecosystems, however, are slowed by the lack of sufficient nitrogen. If nitrogen is added to this system in large amounts, there is a tremendous growth, or bloom, of algae.

Sometimes adding nutrients does not hurt an ecosystem. A little extra fertilizer may even help the system produce more plants and animals for human food. But we must be very careful about tampering with natural ecosystems in this way. If an algal bloom in a lake or river gets too big, it may cover the surface of the water. If that happens, plants below die because they receive no sunlight. Bacteria grow and use up much of the available oxygen. Animals may then suffocate.

Feeding Relationships

Animals and plants in the biosphere are tied together in complicated networks of feeding relationships. The simplest feeding relationship is a **food chain**. In one food chain, a big fish eats little fishes that eat tiny fishes that eat plankton. But nature is almost never that simple.

In nature, plants absorb nutrients and grow. Herbivores eat plants. Carnivores eat herbivores and each other. Scavengers eat dead animals. Bacteria and fungi decompose dead tissue, returning essential elements to the environment. Filter feeders

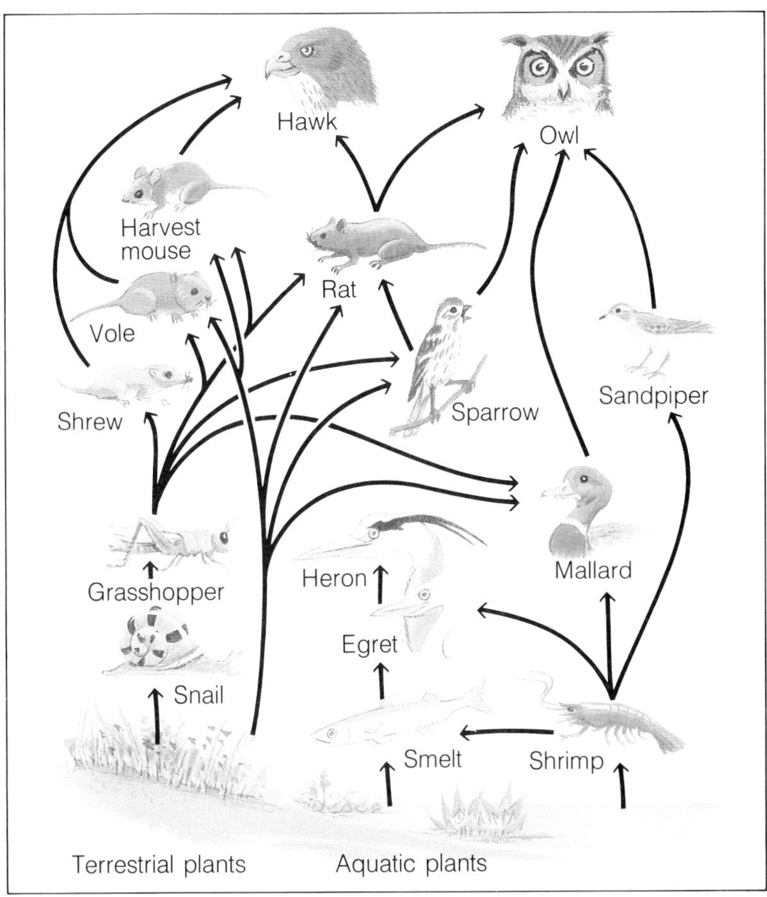

Figure 47–20 *In a food web, food chains are connected to one another. The arrows in this salt marsh food web show the movement of energy and matter as one organism eats another.*

strain floating organisms from the water. Detritus feeders eat bacteria and the wastes of other organisms. Parasites live at the expense of host organisms. All are connected to one another in many complex **food webs**. As Figure 47–20 shows, food webs have many crisscrossing strands.

In the next chapter you will learn that feeding relationships in food webs often contain a built-in system of checks and balances. These checks and balances regulate the number of individuals of each species in the food web. Because of this, many natural ecosystems are remarkably stable.

47–4 SECTION REVIEW

1. How does energy flow through an ecosystem?
2. Describe the three types of ecological pyramids.
3. How are water, nitrogen, carbon, and oxygen recycled in the environment?
4. What is a limiting factor? Give an example.
5. Compare a food chain and a food web.
6. Describe a food chain in which you are a member.

LABORATORY INVESTIGATION

OBSERVING SUCCESSION IN AGED TAP WATER

PROBLEM

What changes occur in a microscopic water community over time?

MATERIALS *(per group)*

sheet of white paper	4 coverslips
600-mL beaker	4 glass slides
1000-mL beaker or jar	medicine droppers
soil	microscope
grasses	reference books
leaves	

PROCEDURE 

1. On a separate sheet of paper, draw a data table similar to the one shown.
2. Fill a 600-mL beaker with tap water. Set the beaker aside and allow it to remain undisturbed for 48 hours so that any gases harmful to microscopic organisms can evaporate. After 48 hours, the water is called aged water.
3. Place enough soil in the 1000-mL beaker to cover the bottom. Fill the beaker with a loosely packed mixture of grasses, green leaves, and dried leaves. Pour the aged water over the leaves and the soil.
4. Set the beaker aside in a cool place where it should remain undisturbed for 24 hours.
5. After 24 hours, examine the beaker for signs of life. For example, a strong odor or cloudy water is proof of bacterial growth; fuzzy growths or threads indicate the presence of mold; and a greenish tint is caused by algae.
6. Using a medicine dropper, remove some water from the beaker. Place a drop of the water in the center of a clean glass slide and cover it with a coverslip.
7. Examine the slide under the microscope. Use the low-power objective to locate any microorganisms. If you do not find any microorganisms under low power, focus on some debris, which probably will contain bacteria and other microorganisms. Then switch to high power.
8. Use reference books to identify any microorganisms that you may find. Note the number, size, and complexity of these microorganisms. Record the date and your observations in the data table.
9. Repeat steps 6 through 8 using water samples from several different areas of the beaker.
10. Repeat steps 5 through 9 every day for two weeks. Note any changes in the number or types of organisms in the beaker.

OBSERVATIONS

Date	Observations

1. How do the number and variety of organisms that appear in the beaker change over the two-week period?
2. Describe the size and complexity of the organisms that appear in the beaker over the two-week period.
3. What other changes, if any, occur in the microscopic water community during this time period?

ANALYSIS AND CONCLUSIONS

1. What kind of organisms appeared first in the microscopic water community? Which appeared last? Explain your answers.
2. Explain why the population in the water community changes over time. What is this process of change called?

STUDENT STUDY GUIDE

SUMMARIZING THE CONCEPTS

The key concepts in each section of this chapter are listed below to help you review the chapter content. Make sure you understand each concept and its relationship to other concepts and to the theme of this chapter.

47–1 Earth: A Living Planet

- Ecology is the study of interactions of organisms with one another and with their physical surroundings.
- The biosphere is that part of the Earth in which life exists and is divided into environments that include biotic and abiotic factors.
- Ecological succession is a process by which an existing community is gradually replaced by another community.

47–2 Land Biomes

- A biome is a large area that has a characteristic climax community.
- The major land biomes are the tundra, taiga, temperate deciduous forest, grassland, tropical rain forest, and desert.

47–3 Aquatic Biomes

- The major aquatic biomes include the freshwater biome, marine biome, and estuaries.

47–4 Energy and Nutrients: Building the Web of Life

- Producers make their own food. Consumers feed directly or indirectly on producers. Decomposers break down organisms and organic matter and return them to the environment.
- Water, nitrogen, carbon, and oxygen are recycled within the ecosystem in biogeochemical cycles.
- Networks of feeding relationships called food chains are connected to one another in complex food webs.

REVIEWING KEY TERMS

Vocabulary terms are important to your understanding of biology. The key terms listed below are those you should be especially familiar with. Review these terms and their meanings. Then use each term in a complete sentence. If you are not sure of a term's meaning, return to the appropriate section and review its definition.

47–1 Earth: A Living Planet

ecology
biosphere
ecosystem
ecological succession
climax community

47–2 Land Biomes

biome
tundra
taiga
temperate deciduous forest
grassland
tropical rain forest
desert

47–3 Aquatic Biomes

freshwater biome
marine biome
estuary

47–4 Energy and Nutrients: Building the Web of Life

producer
consumer
decomposer
ecological pyramid
biogeochemical cycle
water cycle
nitrogen cycle
nitrogen fixation
denitrification
carbon cycle
oxygen cycle
limiting factor
food chain
food web

CHAPTER REVIEW

CONTENT REVIEW

Multiple Choice

Choose the letter of the answer that best completes each statement.

1. All the biotic and abiotic factors in a pond form a (an)
   a. biosphere. c. community.
   b. ecosystem. d. estuary.
2. Which climax community indicates a taiga?
   a. coniferous trees c. grasses
   b. cacti d. lichens and mosses
3. Which of the following biomes is the most stable?
   a. desert c. taiga
   b. marine d. tropical rain forest
4. A producer-consumer relationship is best illustrated by
   a. foxes eating mice.
   b. leaves growing on trees.
   c. tapeworms living in foxes.
   d. rabbits eating clover.
5. Which are usually the last type of plants to appear in the ecological succession of a forest?
   a. mosses c. grasses
   b. oaks d. shrubs
6. Free nitrogen in the atmosphere is converted to nitrogen compounds during
   a. nitrogen fixation. c. photosynthesis.
   b. denitrification. d. respiration.
7. Plant-eating animals are known as
   a. producers. c. decomposers.
   b. carnivores. d. herbivores.
8. In a food chain, herbivores are known as
   a. secondary consumers. c. primary consumers.
   b. producers. d. carnivores.

True or False

Determine whether each statement is true or false. If it is true, write "true." If it is false, change the underlined word or words to make the statement true.

1. The study of the interactions of organisms with one another and with their physical surroundings is called ecology.
2. The ecosystem is that part of the Earth in which life exists.
3. The land biome with the largest variety of plant and animal species is the taiga.
4. Permafrost is characteristic of the tropical rain forest.
5. Estuaries are found at the boundaries of fresh water and salt water.
6. The process by which nitrogen compounds are converted to free nitrogen by bacteria is called nitrogen fixation.
7. A limiting factor is a nutrient that can prevent the growth of organisms.
8. Bacteria act as producers in a food web.

Word Relationships

In each of the following sets of terms, three of the terms are related. One term does not belong. Determine the characteristic common to three of the terms and then identify the term that does not belong.

1. mosses, lichens, caribou, snakes
2. prairies, lianas, pampas, velds
3. estuary, tundra, desert, taiga
4. ecosystem, consumer, producer, decomposer

CONCEPT MASTERY

Use your understanding of the concepts developed in the chapter to answer each of the following in a brief paragraph.

1. Why is sunlight needed to maintain an ecosystem?
2. Explain why each trophic level in a food chain contains less energy than the level below it.
3. Why is it more energy efficient for people to eat plants instead of animals?
4. Discuss some of the limiting factors in the growth of a forest.
5. What factors account for the fact that tropical rain forests have the highest biomass of any biome?
6. Why are there no tall trees in the desert?
7. Describe the process of ecological succession in which a pond becomes a forest.
8. Describe what happens to the light energy striking a cornfield.
9. Trace the path of nitrogen through the nitrogen cycle.
10. What are some of the special adaptations that an animal might have in order to survive in areas that have large daily temperature fluctuations?
11. What conditions must be met by an ecosystem for it to be self-sustaining?

CRITICAL AND CREATIVE THINKING

Discuss each of the following in a brief paragraph.

1. **Relating concepts** Why can the tundra be considered a cold desert?
2. **Making predictions** By burning fossil fuels such as coal and oil, carbon dioxide is being added to the atmosphere. In addition, forests are being destroyed at a rapid rate. How do these actions affect the carbon cycle? The oxygen cycle?
3. **Drawing conclusions** Each year kilometers of mangrove swamps and salt marshes are destroyed, filled in, or paved over for commercial and recreational use. What effect could such development have on surrounding ecosystems?
4. **Expressing an opinion** A leading ecologist stated: "The plough is the most deadly weapon of extinction ever devised; not even thermonuclear weapons pose such a threat to the beauty and diversity of life on earth." Explain this statement.
5. **Applying concepts** Explain how it is possible to walk through several biomes as you climb up a mountain.

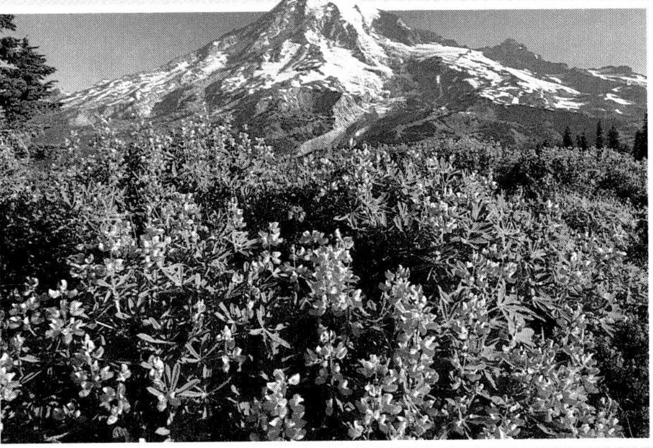

6. **Making diagrams** Draw a food web that includes organisms from a temperate deciduous forest. Identify each organism as a producer or a consumer.
7. **Using the writing process** Pretend that as a reporter for a major newspaper you have been assigned to interview farmers in South America who have cleared areas in tropical rain forests for farming. Prepare a list of questions that you will pose in your interview.

CHAPTER 48

Populations and Communities

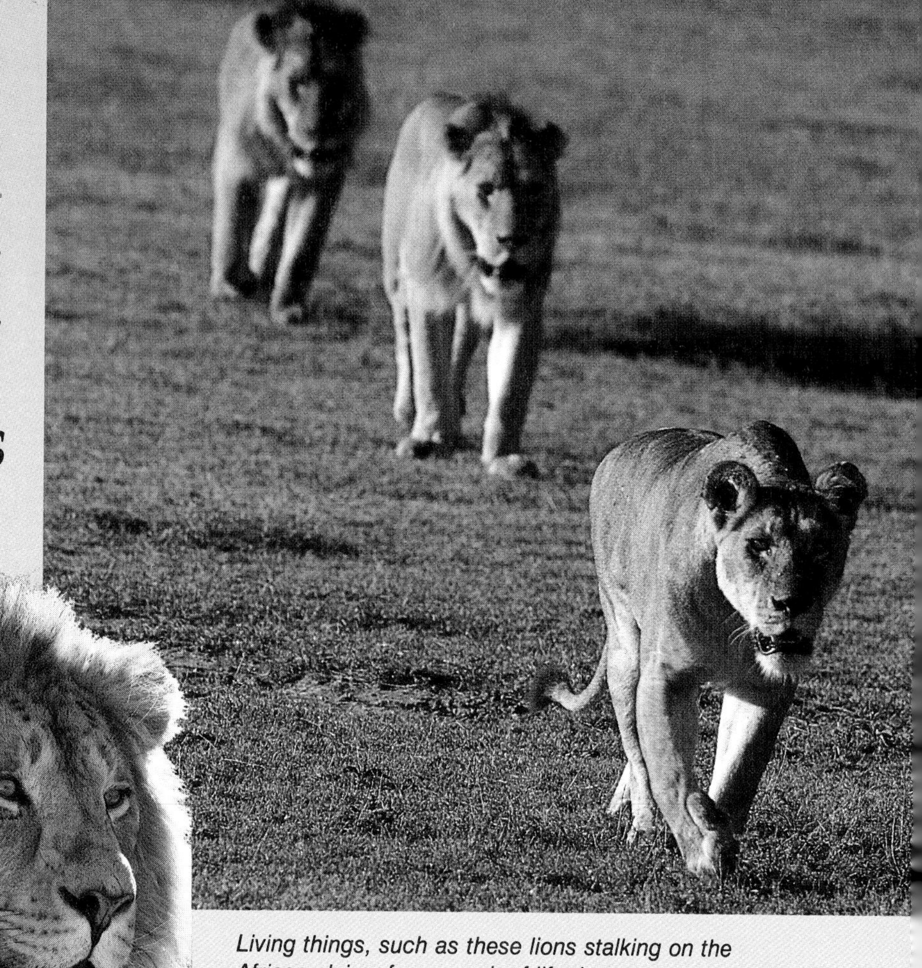

Living things, such as these lions stalking on the African plains, form a web of life that covers our entire planet.

Living things inhabit many different environments. From the poles to the equator, life can be found under ground, in air, in water, and on land. The web of life that covers our planet contains millions of species. Many of these species interact with one another in complicated ways.

How can we begin to understand the complex relationships among living things? There is no way we can look at the entire world—or even an entire biome—at once and understand the interactions that take place among organisms. So what we must do is first look at small pieces of the web of life. In this chapter the pieces we shall explore are called populations and communities.

CHAPTER OUTLINE

48–1 Population Growth

Section Objectives

- Compare exponential growth and logistic growth in a given population.
- Relate population growth to an environment's carrying capacity.

In order to study relationships between organisms, ecologists need to know how groups of organisms change over time. How many individuals are born? How many die? How many organisms live in an area at any given time? To answer these questions, ecologists study **populations**. A population is a group of organisms that all belong to the same species and that live in a given area.

Exponential Growth: A Baby Boom

Almost any organism provided with ideal conditions for growth and reproduction will experience a rapid increase in its population. What's more, the larger the population gets, the faster it grows. If nothing stops the population from growing, it will continue to expand faster and faster. The kind of curve this growth pattern produces on a graph is called an **exponential growth curve**. See Figure 48–2 on page 1034.

As you learned in Chapter 13, Charles Darwin realized that this tendency of populations to grow exponentially (rapidly) presented a puzzle to biologists of his time. Among other things, Darwin calculated that if all the offspring of a single elephant couple were to survive and reproduce, in less than 750 years one pair of elephants alone would produce 19 million offspring!

Obviously, exponential growth does not continue in natural populations for long. Most offspring of plants and animals do not survive long enough to reproduce. The question is . . . why?

Figure 48–1 A population is a group of organisms of the same species that live in a given area. These walruses, packed onto Round Island in Alaska, are a population.

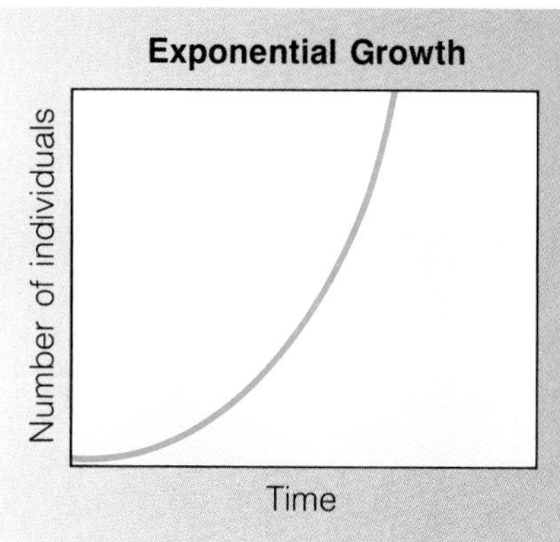

Figure 48–2 *Exponential growth is illustrated on this graph. How does the number of organisms change over time during exponential growth?*

Logistic Growth: A Step Closer to Reality

The population growth history of a particular species is a bit more complicated than simple exponential growth. **Most populations go through a number of growth phases, which can be represented on a logistic growth curve**. A **logistic growth curve** is shown on the graph in Figure 48–3.

Let's examine an example of logistic growth. Suppose a few animals are introduced into a new environment. At first their numbers will begin to grow slowly. This initial growth is shown by section A in Figure 48–3. Soon, however, the population will begin to grow very rapidly. Here, in section B of the same graph, the population grows exponentially. The population grows quickly because few animals are dying and a great many are being produced.

Exponential growth does not continue for long. Soon the population reaches point C on the graph. Here the speed at which the population grows begins to slow down. Think about this carefully. Notice we did not say that the size of the population drops. The population is still growing, but it is growing at a slower rate. From here on, the population grows more and more slowly, through section D on the curve. How might we explain what is happening?

A population grows when more organisms are produced in a given period of time than die during the same period. In this situation, an ecologist would say that the population's birthrate is greater than its deathrate. Population growth may slow down because either the birthrate decreases or because the deathrate increases or both.

When the birthrate and deathrate are the same, population growth will stop, or reach zero growth. Remember, when we say that population growth is zero, we mean that the number of

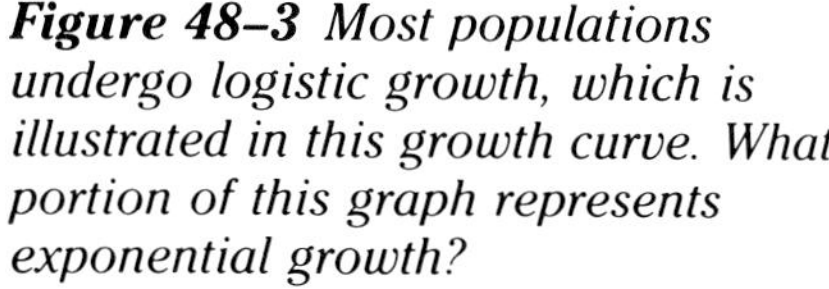

Figure 48–3 *Most populations undergo logistic growth, which is illustrated in this growth curve. What portion of this graph represents exponential growth?*

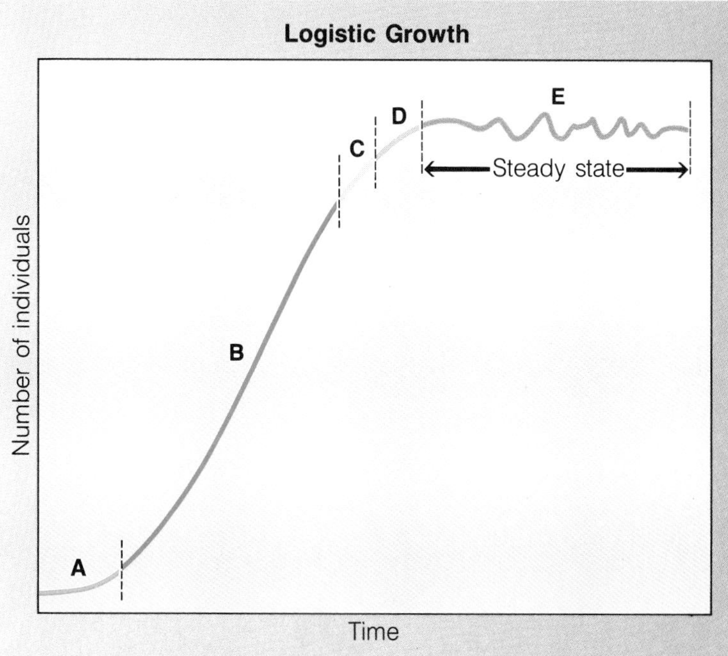

organisms in the population remains the same. Look again at the logistic growth curve in Figure 48–3. The portion of the curve labeled E is called the **steady state.** During the steady state, the average growth rate is zero. However, it is important to note that the steady state is not really all that steady. The population rises and falls somewhat. In fact, in some populations it rises and falls a great deal. But the rises and falls average out around a certain population size.

If we draw a horizontal line through the middle of the steady state region, as in Figure 48–4, that line will tell us how big the population is in the steady state. Ecologists say this line represents the **carrying capacity** of a particular environment for a particular species.

Once a population reaches the carrying capacity of its environment, certain factors keep the population from growing any further. These factors include a lack of food, overcrowding, and competition among the individuals in the population. If the population does grow larger, either the birthrate will fall or the deathrate will rise. (More individuals will die than will be born and the population will be reduced to the carrying capacity.) If the population falls, either the birthrate will rise or the deathrate will drop. (More individuals will be born than will die and the population will grow once again.)

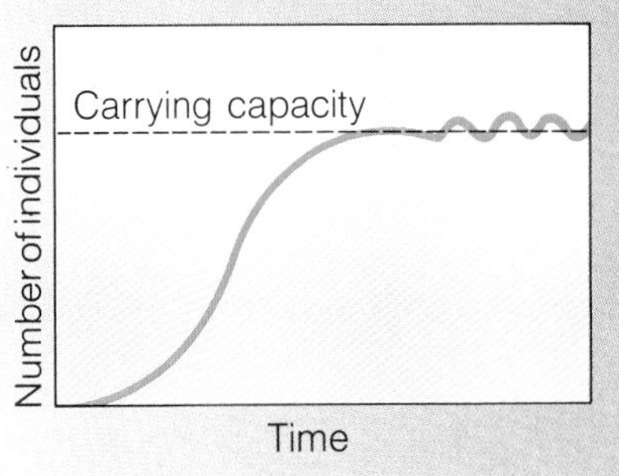

Figure 48–4 *Carrying capacity represents the optimum number of organisms of a particular species that can be supported by a particular environment.*

48–1 SECTION REVIEW

1. What is a population? Give three examples of a population in your area.
2. Describe the five stages of a logistic growth curve.
3. Use the concept of carrying capacity to explain the importance of conservation.

48–2 Factors That Control Population Growth

Section Objectives

- Compare density-dependent and density-independent limiting factors.
- Relate competition, predation, parasitism, overcrowding, and natural catastrophes to population growth.

Why, you might ask, don't populations grow indefinitely? Recall from the previous chapter that the growth of individuals can be controlled by limiting factors. Similarly, both plant and animal populations can be controlled by several factors. Although controls on natural populations do not keep those populations from changing in size, no single species has ever threatened to overpopulate the entire planet. (That is, not until *Homo sapiens* came along.) Let us examine the ways in which natural populations are kept between extinction and overpopulation of their environment.

Density-Dependent Limiting Factors

When factors that control population size operate more strongly on large populations than on small ones, they are called **density-dependent limiting factors.** Density-dependent limiting factors usually operate only when a population is large and crowded. They do not affect small, widely scattered populations much. **Density-dependent limiting factors include competition, predation, parasitism, and crowding.**

COMPETITION When populations become crowded, both plants and animals compete, or struggle, with one another for food, water, space, sunlight, and other essentials of life. It is easy to see why competition among members of the same species is a density-dependent limiting factor. The more individuals there are, the more of them there are to use up the available food, water, space, and other necessities. The fewer individuals around, the less they compete.

Competition between members of different yet similar species is a major force behind evolutionary change. As you learned in Chapter 14, no two organisms can occupy the same niche in the same place at the same time. When two species compete, both find themselves under pressure from natural selection to change in ways that decrease their competition. This idea is important because it ties ecology and evolution together. It is another example of the way in which all the biological sciences are interrelated when you look at them from an evolutionary point of view.

PREDATION Just about every species serves as food for some other species. In most situations, predators and prey coexist over long periods of time. Like tennis partners who have played together for years, predators and prey have become accustomed to each other's strengths and weaknesses.

Figure 48–5 *Perhaps the most important density-dependent limiting factor is predation. Both the leopard hunting the bush pig (left) and the European tree frog capturing its prey off a water lily (right) are examples of predation.*

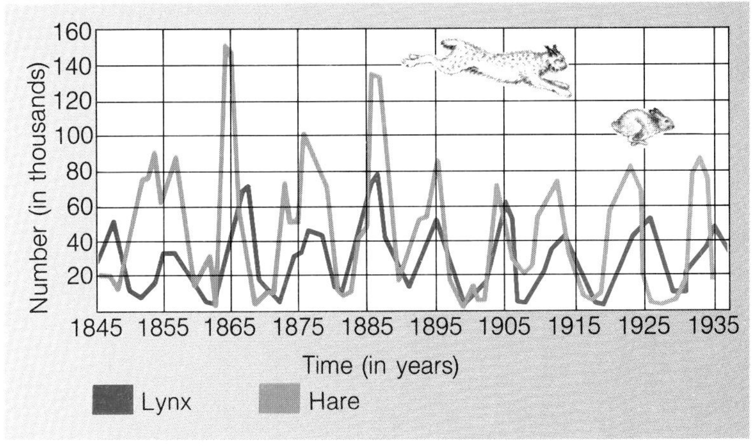

Figure 48–6 *This graph represents the relationship between populations of lynx (predator) and snowshoe hare (prey) over many years. What can you infer from the growth curves of each organism?*

Prey, for example, have evolved defenses against predators. Some plants may produce poisonous chemicals. Some animals may have shells, poisonous skins, or camouflage behaviors and colors that help them hide.

At the same time, predators have evolved counterdefenses. Some herbivores, such as monarch butterfly caterpillars, have evolved the ability to avoid the effects of certain plant poisons. Carnivores have evolved stronger jaws and teeth, powerful digestive enzymes, or extra-keen eyesight.

If we watch populations of predators and prey over time, we almost always find changes in their numbers. Typically, at some point the prey population grows so large that prey are numerous and easy to find. With such a large and available food supply to feast upon, there may soon be almost as many predators as prey. As you probably know by now, this situation cannot last because each predator needs many prey to satisfy its energy needs.

As predators become numerous, they eat more prey than are born. This means that the prey's deathrate becomes higher than its birthrate and the population decreases in size. But as the prey population drops, predators begin to starve, so the predator population drops too. When only a few predators are left, the prey begin reproducing and surviving in large numbers again, and the whole situation repeats itself.

For many years people did not truly understand (as we do now) that predator-prey relationships are important in controlling natural populations. Travelers and farmers took animals from one part of the world to another, releasing them into the wild. There, without a predator to keep their numbers down, the animals became serious pests. One famous example is the introduction of rabbits by Australians to their island continent a number of years ago. The collection of animals native to Australia is unique to that continent. Thus, rabbits had no natural predators. Within a relatively short time, the Australian rabbit population went into exponential growth and remained that way for a long time. Rabbits infested the countryside and devoured much of the natural vegetation. They have been a serious problem in Australia ever since.

PROBLEM SOLVING IN BIOLOGY

ANALYZING PREDATOR-PREY POPULATION MODELS

The relationships between predator and prey are often intertwined, particularly in an environment in which each prey has a single predator and vice versa. Examine the accompanying graph, which shows a computer model of the changes in predator and prey populations over time. After analyzing the graph, answer the following questions.

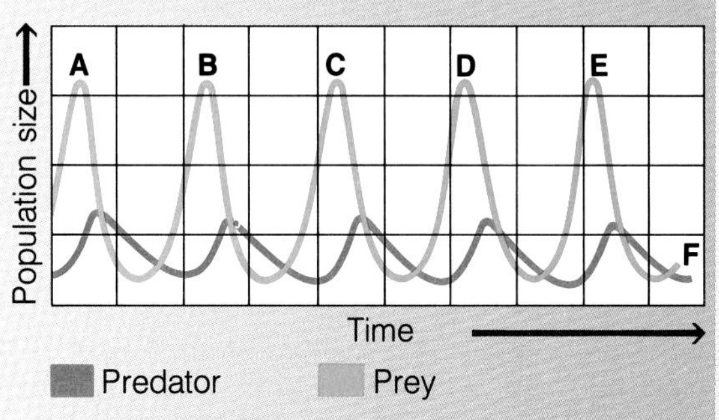

1. A sudden extended cold spell destroys almost the entire predator population at point F on the graph. What will happen to the prey population? How will the next cycle of prey population growth appear on the graph?
2. A bacterial infection kills off most of the prey at point B on the graph. How will this affect the predator and prey growth curves at point C? At point D?
3. A viral infection kills all of the prey at point D on the graph. What effect will this have on the predator and prey growth curves at point E? What will happen in future years to the predator population? How could ecologists ensure the continued survival of the predators in this ecosystem?

Figure 48–7 *The California dodder plant is a parasite that wraps itself around a host plant and uses the host for support and food.*

PARASITISM Parasites act like predators in many ways. Parasites live off their hosts, weakening them and causing disease. Like predators, parasites work most effectively if hosts are present in large numbers. Crowding helps parasites travel from one host to another. Stress related to crowding can also reduce a host's resistance to parasites. As a result, parasitism often affects large, concentrated populations more than small, scattered ones. Thus parasitism works as a density-dependent limiting factor on population growth. Note that few parasites kill their hosts—at least not right away. If a parasite kills its host too quickly, the parasite will have no chance to reproduce and spread. It is thus to the parasite's advantage not to be too deadly.

CROWDING AND STRESS Most animals have a built-in behavioral need for a certain amount of space. Both males and females, for example, may need room to hunt for food. They may need a certain amount of space for nesting. Or they may need a territory of a certain size. A number of fishes on coral reefs fit into this latter category. Many of these fishes are extremely territorial. Each male stakes out a territory and chases away all other males of his species. Young fish do not stand a chance of setting up a territory unless an older male dies or is eaten. In such cases, the number of suitable territories regulates population size in a density-dependent manner.

Certain species fight among themselves if they are overcrowded. Too much fighting can cause high levels of stress. This stress disturbs the finely tuned endocrine system you read about in Chapter 42. Large amounts of adrenaline secreted under conditions of stress upset the body's normal balance. Levels of several other hormones also change due to stress. As a result of these hormonal changes, animals fight more and breed less. Often the immune system is weakened as well. Hormonal changes can so upset a female's behavior that she neglects, kills, or even eats her own offspring. Extreme overcrowding among mice can affect the females' endocrine system so that pregnant females miscarry, or lose the fetus they are carrying. All these factors combine to lower birthrate.

Figure 48–8 *The wolverine is a carnivore that maintains a large territory. Except for the breeding season, wolverines will not allow another wolverine into their territory, thus preventing overpopulation in a given area.*

Density-Independent Limiting Factors

Not all populations are controlled by density-dependent limiting factors alone. Many species show what are called boom-and-bust growth curves. Their populations grow exponentially for some time and then suddenly crash. After the crash, the population may build right up again or it may stay low for some time.

Thrips, aphids, and other insects that feed on plant buds and leaves can be washed out by a rainstorm. They may also be harmed by long hot periods of dry weather. Frosts, too, can cause sudden drops in insect populations. For these species, storms, cold weather, dry weather, or other natural occurrences can nearly wipe out the population. Such wipeouts can happen regardless of how large the population is at the time. Because population density does not matter in such cases, these natural occurrences are called **density-independent limiting factors.** As you might expect, the growth of many species is controlled by some combination of density-dependent and density-independent limiting factors.

Figure 48–9 *Hurricanes such as Hurricane Hugo, which struck the southeastern United States, are examples of density-independent limiting factors.*

Human Population Growth

Human populations, like those of all other animals, tend to increase in size with time. If we examine the size of the human population over the course of history, we see that for a long time it grew slowly. Then, about 500 years ago, the world's human population started growing exponentially. See Figure 48–10 on page 1040.

Today, population growth in the United States and parts of Europe has slowed down. But most of the world's people do not live in these countries. Instead, they live in China, India,

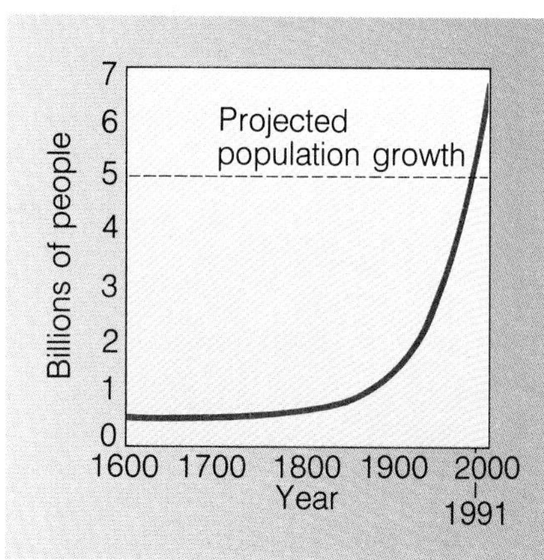

Figure 48–10 *This graph illustrates human population growth since 1600.*

and parts of Africa and Latin America—places where populations are still growing very rapidly. This population growth poses a serious threat to global ecology, as we shall see in the next chapter.

48–2 SECTION REVIEW

1. Describe three density-dependent limiting factors.
2. Compare density-dependent and density-independent limiting factors.
3. How does the evolution of a successful defense mechanism in a species of prey increase the chances of survival for a species of predator that uses the prey for food?

Section Objectives

- Describe the ways in which populations within a community interact.
- Compare parasitism, commensalism, and mutualism.
- Discuss the interrelationships between ecosystems.

48–3 Interactions Within and Between Communities

After populations, the next larger biological units studied by ecologists are **communities**. A community consists of all the populations of organisms living in a given area. **Populations in communities interact with one another in many ways.** Plant species, for example, compete for water, nutrients, and sunlight. At the same time, some plants have evolved defenses against herbivores.

Herbivores compete with one another for food and space. There are usually several different herbivore species in any community. Certain of these herbivores may have evolved counterdefenses for the protective mechanisms of one or more plant species.

While this is going on, carnivores are hunting the herbivores. Often there are several carnivores in a community, each of which is best at hunting a particular herbivore.

Symbiosis

Many of the interactions among organisms we have discussed so far involve predation. But there are several other relationships that play an important role in nature. These relationships between organisms are called **symbioses** (*sym-* refers to together; *-bios* refers to life; *symbiosis* means living together). Parasitism, which you read about earlier in this chapter, is a symbiosis in which one species benefits and the other is harmed.

There are also many relationships between organisms in which one member benefits and the other is not harmed. This

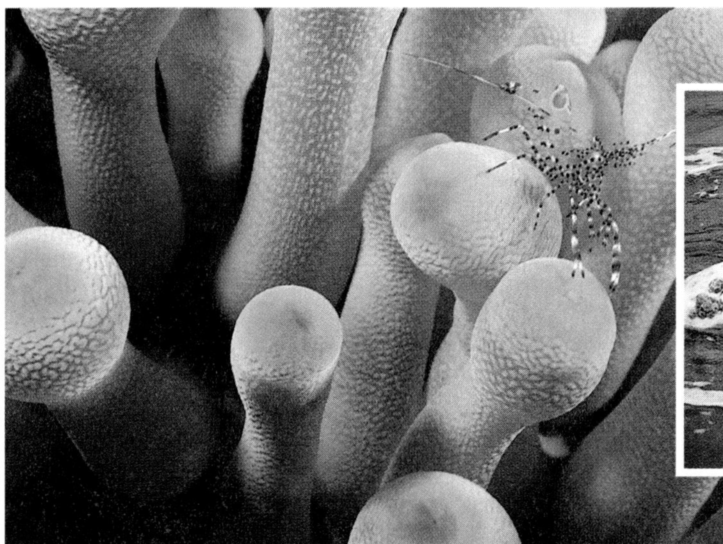

Figure 48–11 Commensalism is a form of symbiosis in which one organism is helped and another organism is neither helped nor harmed. The tiny shrimp living within the tentacles of this sea anemone (left) and the barnacles hitching a ride on the back of this gray whale (right) are examples of commensalism.

kind of symbiosis is called **commensalism** (kuh-MEHN-suhl-ihz-uhm). A good example of commensalism takes place on a coral reef where shrimp live within the stinging tentacles of sea anemones. The shrimp are not affected by the anemone's poison. As a result, the shrimp are protected from predators that cannot tolerate the anemone's stings. Anemones are not harmed by shrimp living on them, but they are not helped either, which is the definition of commensalism.

In still another kind of symbiosis, two species live together in such a way that both species benefit. This kind of symbiosis is called **mutualism.** Let's return to the coral reef to examine an example of mutualism. Right next to the sea anemone and the shrimp we might find clownfish. Clownfish form a mutualistic symbiosis with sea anemones. Clownfish benefit from living within the stinging tentacles of the sea anemones in the same way shrimp do. However, clownfish also help the anemones by chasing away several species of anemone-eating fish. In this case, both species benefit, which is the definition of mutualism.

Commensal and mutualistic symbioses are everywhere in nature. You may recall that lichens are a mutualistic symbiosis between a blue-green bacteria and a fungus. Many marine animals—such as corals—have symbiotic algae that live inside their tissues. Many land plants can live only with the help of symbiotic fungi on their roots. In fact, practically no organism can live in a world by itself. Each requires other organisms in some way.

Figure 48–12 This tiny fish survives on the bits of food it can find by cleaning the teeth of the larger fish. In this case, both organisms benefit, and their symbiotic relationship is known as mutualism.

Interactions Among Ecosystems

Not only do populations and communities interact, ecosystems also interact with one another in many ways. Consider, for example, a pond in the woods. Certainly that pond contains

Figure 48–13 What point was the photographer trying to make when putting together this dramatic shot of the Earth superimposed over a green plant?

populations of plants and animals that live only in the pond and not in the woods. But where does the water in the pond come from? Most likely from a stream that flows out of the woods. Where does extra water from the pond go? Probably into another stream or a nearby marsh. What about leaves and insects that fall into the pond from surrounding trees? How about raccoons, birds, and other animals that visit the pond from homes in the woods? What about air and rain that blow in from outside, carrying nutrients and possibly pollution into the pond? And don't forget about migrating birds that travel thousands of kilometers to summer in the pond.

Nearly every ecosystem is connected, either directly or indirectly, with other ecosystems. We can see how some of these connections work if we take an imaginary journey—a journey that begins when a farmer puts fertilizer on a corn field. Let's hitch a ride on a single nitrogen atom in that fertilizer and see where our travels take us.

Rain washes us into a stream. That stream flows through a pond and into a river. The river enters an estuary, where we are taken in by the roots of a plant. Later the plant dies, and its decaying remains are washed out into the coastal waters nearby. As we float along, we are eaten by a shrimp that in turn is eaten by a fish. The fish swims out into the open sea, dies, and sinks to the bottom. On the ocean floor the fish decays, and nutrients (including us) are released. Ocean currents carry us for hundreds of kilometers to a place where upwellings carry us back to the ocean surface. There we are taken in by phytoplankton, which are eaten by zooplankton, which are then eaten by fish. This time the fish is eaten by a bird that picks it up and flies to shore with it.

Are you beginning to get the picture? Our journey could continue indefinitely, taking us from one ecosystem to another all over the globe. Herein lies an important lesson for us all: Winds, rivers, and ocean currents tie Earth's ecosystems together in ways that we are just beginning to understand. That is why our growing human population must be ever more careful about how we dispose of wastes. Disposing of something in one ecosystem may just cause it to show up again somewhere else. We shall discuss this matter in more detail in the next chapter.

48–3 SECTION REVIEW

1. What is a community? How do populations in a community interact?
2. Define symbiosis. Compare parasitism, commensalism, and mutualism.
3. Do ecosystems operate independently of one another? Describe some ways in which ecosystems are interconnected.

Gypsy Moths: Nature to the Rescue

In many places around the world, people have unwittingly demonstrated the importance of natural population control mechanisms by introducing into an environment organisms that have no natural predators. Around the turn of the century, a few gypsy moth caterpillars were accidentally introduced into the Northeast. First detected in 1905 in Connecticut, the gypsy moths began chewing their way through the eastern states.

Gypsy moth caterpillars are leaf-eaters and can cause widespread destruction of trees. Without any natural predators, gypsy moths were unaffected by density-dependent limiting factors. The only real check on the gypsy moth population was their breeding cycle: Every 8 to 10 years gypsy moths begin a new breeding cycle, after which they remain to cause problems for about 4 years. Thus gypsy moth populations exhibit a boom-or-bust growth curve characterized by periods in which the gypsy moths present no danger.

The last outbreak of gypsy moths occurred between 1979 and 1983. So in the spring of 1989, scientists prepared themselves for the onset of another breeding cycle and another round of widespread destruction in eastern forests. But something quite unexpected began happening instead. Throughout the Northeast, gypsy moth caterpillars were dying—before they could destroy the trees. Something was killing the gypsy moth caterpillars.

When scientists at the Connecticut Agricultural Experiment Station in New Haven examined the dead caterpillars, they discovered that the animals had been infected by a fungus. It was the fungus that was killing the gypsy moth caterpillars. Researchers now believe that about 80 years ago the fungus was intentionally introduced into the environment by scientists who realized that a similar fungus controlled gypsy moth caterpillars in Japan. Why had it taken so long for the fungus to act?

Scientists now believe that the unusually heavy rains in the Northeast in 1988 and 1989 caused the fungus to suddenly thrive. The thriving fungus, in turn, has destroyed the gypsy moths in record numbers. Due to continued heavy rains, scientists expect the fungus to reduce the gypsy moth population even further in subsequent years.

Will the fungus end the cycle completely and eliminate the gypsy moth population from the northeastern states? Scientists cannot be sure, but they suspect it will not. They know that natural controls tend to keep a population in check rather than destroy it completely. But they do hope to use the fungus to help them develop a biological agent that will control the gypsy moths in future years. However, as Dr. Andreadis at the New Haven experimental station points out, biological controls will not eradicate gypsy moths. "The whole idea behind biological weaponry is to create a balance with nature so that the gypsy moth population will perhaps maintain itself at a very low level."

LABORATORY INVESTIGATION

EXAMINING PATTERNS OF POPULATION GROWTH IN BACTERIA

PROBLEM

What happens to the number of bacteria in a bean infusion over time?

MATERIALS *(per group)*

aluminum foil	2 lima beans
100-mL beaker	2 medicine droppers
coverslips	methylene blue
glass slides	microscope
10-mL graduated cylinder	test tube rack
100-mL graduated cylinder	4 test tubes

PROCEDURE 

1. Use a 100-mL graduated cylinder to pour 50 mL of water into a 100-mL beaker. Put two lima beans into the water in the beaker. Allow this bean infusion to sit for 48 hours.
2. After 48 hours, use a medicine dropper to transfer a drop of water from the beaker to the center of a clean glass slide. Use the other medicine dropper to add a drop of methylene blue to the drop of water. Cover the sample with a coverslip.
3. Use the low-power objective to examine the slide under a microscope. Switch to high power. Use the fine adjustment to locate some bacteria.
4. Try to count the number of bacteria in the field of view. If there are too many bacteria to count, proceed to step 5. If you are able to count the number of bacteria, do so, then go directly to step 7.
5. In order to reduce the number of bacteria, the bean infusion must be diluted. To do this, proceed as follows. Use a 10-mL graduated cylinder to put 9 mL of water into a test tube. With a medicine dropper, put 1 mL of the bean infusion into the 10-mL graduated cylinder. Pour the bean infusion into the test tube containing 9 mL of water. This procedure, which dilutes the infusion by a factor of 10, can be repeated as often as necessary until the infusion is dilute enough to make the bacteria easy to count. This procedure is known as a serial dilution. Each time you follow the procedure described, you increase the dilution by a factor of 10. If the infusion is not diluted, the dilution factor is 1. Rinse the graduated cylinders when you are finished.
6. Examine each dilution under the microscope. Stop making dilutions when you can count the bacteria in the field of view.
7. After counting the bacteria, record the data, dilution factor, and number of bacteria. To determine the actual number of bacteria present, multiply the number of bacteria observed by the dilution factor.
8. Cover the beaker with aluminum foil and set it aside overnight.
9. Repeat steps 2 through 8 every day for at least four more days.
10. Prepare a graph with the date on the X-axis and the number of bacteria present on the Y-axis.

OBSERVATIONS

1. Describe the appearance of the bacteria.
2. When did the size of the bacterial population change the least?
3. When did the bacterial population grow the fastest?
4. Describe the bacterial population during the course of the observation period.

ANALYSIS AND CONCLUSIONS

1. How can you explain the changes you observed in the bacterial population?
2. What lessons does this investigation have for humans regarding the use of resources?

STUDENT STUDY GUIDE

SUMMARIZING THE CONCEPTS

The key concepts in each section of this chapter are listed below to help you review the chapter content. Make sure you understand each concept and its relationship to other concepts and to the theme of this chapter.

48–1 Population Growth

- A population is a group of organisms that all belong to the same species and that live in a given area.
- Given ideal conditions for growth and reproduction, a population of organisms will grow very rapidly. This rapid growth is shown in an exponential growth curve.
- Most populations go through a series of growth phases, which can be represented on a logistic growth curve.
- On a typical logistic growth curve, a population of organisms grows slowly at first, then grows rapidly during exponential growth, then slows down before reaching a steady state.
- A population with zero growth has reached a steady state. This means the average population over time will not change markedly.
- A population usually achieves a steady state when it reaches the carrying capacity of the environment.

48–2 Factors That Control Population Growth

- Density-dependent limiting factors—which include predation, competition, parasitism, and crowding—operate strongly on large populations with high density.
- Factors that do not depend on population density to control population size are called density-independent limiting factors. Severe storms, dry weather, and other climate conditions that can reduce a species' population are density-independent limiting factors.

48–3 Interactions Within and Between Communities

- A community consists of all the populations of organisms living in an area.
- Although predation is the primary relationship between organisms in a community, symbioses are other important relationships.
- Symbioses include parasitism, commensalism, and mutualism.
- All ecosystems are interconnected.

REVIEWING KEY TERMS

Vocabulary terms are important to your understanding of biology. The key terms listed below are those you should be especially familiar with. Review these terms and their meanings. Then use each term in a complete sentence. If you are not sure of a term's meaning, return to the appropriate section and review its definition.

48–1 Population Growth

population
exponential growth curve
logistic growth curve
steady state
carrying capacity

48–2 Factors That Control Population Growth

density-dependent limiting factor
density-independent limiting factor

48–3 Interactions Within and Between Communities

community
symbiosis
commensalism
mutualism

CHAPTER REVIEW

CONTENT REVIEW

Multiple Choice

Choose the letter of the answer that best completes each statement.

1. During population growth
   a. birthrate increases.
   b. deathrate increases.
   c. birthrate decreases.
   d. birthrate and deathrate decrease.
2. A population that reaches the carrying capacity of its environment is said to have reached
   a. logistic growth. c. density dependence.
   b. exponential growth. d. a steady state.
3. Density-independent limiting factors include
   a. predation. c. crowding.
   b. hurricanes. d. parasitism.
4. All of the organisms living in a given area make up a (an)
   a. population. c. ecosystem.
   b. community. d. steady state.
5. A relationship in which one organism is helped and another organism is neither helped nor hurt is called
   a. mutualism. c. symbiosis.
   b. parasitism. d. commensalism.
6. A form of symbiosis in which both organisms benefit is called
   a. mutualism. c. commensalism.
   b. parasitism. d. the carrying capacity.
7. A type of symbiosis in which one organism benefits and the other is harmed is called
   a. mutualism. c. commensalism.
   b. parasitism. d. symbiosis.
8. On a logistic growth curve, the portion of the curve in which the population grows rapidly is called
   a. logistic growth. c. exponential growth.
   b. a steady state. d. the carrying capacity.

True or False

Determine whether each statement is true or false. If it is true, write "true." If it is false, change the underlined word or words to make the statement true.

1. A community is a group of organisms that belong to the same species and that live in a given area.
2. The rapid growth of a population is best shown by a logistic growth curve.
3. A horizontal line drawn through the middle of the steady state region on a growth curve represents the environment's carrying capacity.
4. Predation is a density-independent limiting factor.
5. Crowding is a density-dependent limiting factor.
6. The sea anemone and the clownfish are an example of commensalism.
7. In general, parasites kill their hosts.
8. When both organisms in a symbiotic relationship benefit, that relationship is called mutualism.

Word Relationships

In each of the following sets of terms, three of the terms are related. One term does not belong. Determine the characteristic common to three of the terms and then identify the term that does not belong.

1. parasitism, mutualism, predation, commensalism
2. exponential growth, steady state, carrying capacity, symbiosis
3. predation, tornado, crowding, competition
4. parasitism, crowding, hormonal imbalance, territoriality

CONCEPT MASTERY

Use your understanding of the concepts developed in the chapter to answer each of the following in a brief paragraph.

1. Explain how a population normally controlled by density-dependent limiting factors might be affected by a density-independent limiting factor.
2. Given ideal conditions, a population will grow exponentially. What limits does nature place on such exponential growth?
3. Why did biologists such as Darwin question the concept of exponential growth?
4. What is the relationship between steady state and carrying capacity?
5. How might the introduction of a toxic waste in a pond affect the carrying capacity of that pond?
6. Why are parasites considered a density-dependent limiting factor?
7. Describe and compare the three main types of symbiosis. What type of symbiosis is formed by the fungus that causes athlete's foot?

CRITICAL AND CREATIVE THINKING

Discuss each of the following in a brief paragraph.

1. **Applying concepts** Why might a communicable virus that causes a fatal disease be considered a density-dependent limiting factor? What about a virus that is not communicable?
2. **Developing formulas** Based on the information in this chapter, develop a mathematical formula for population growth rate. *Hint:* How are the two axes on a growth curve labeled?
3. **Interpreting graphs** Examine the growth curve shown in the illustration. What does the curve show? How might you interpret this data?
4. **Making comparisons** Describe the growth curve in a small town made up mainly of senior citizens. Compare this growth curve to a small town made up of newly married couples.
5. **Relating concepts** Using the concept of carrying capacity, explain how the growth of both predator and prey are interrelated.
6. **Making inferences** Would a density-independent limiting factor have more of an effect on population size in a large ecosystem or in a small ecosystem?
7. **Using the writing process** The union representing predators cannot reach a labor agreement with the union representing prey. Each side wants a large increase in their steady state population. You are the arbitrator hired to mediate the dispute. What is your learned decision?

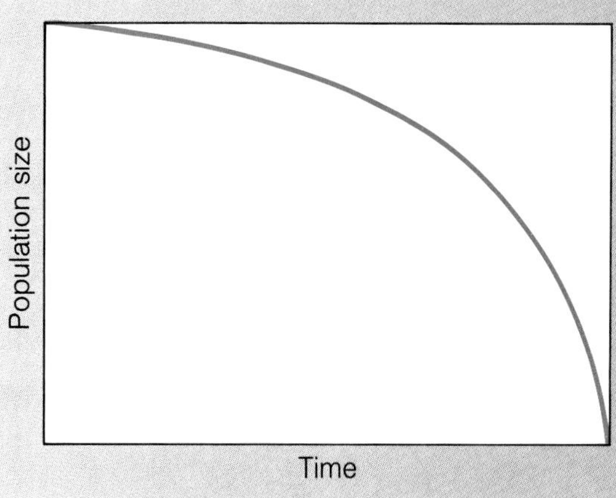

CHAPTER 49

People and the Biosphere

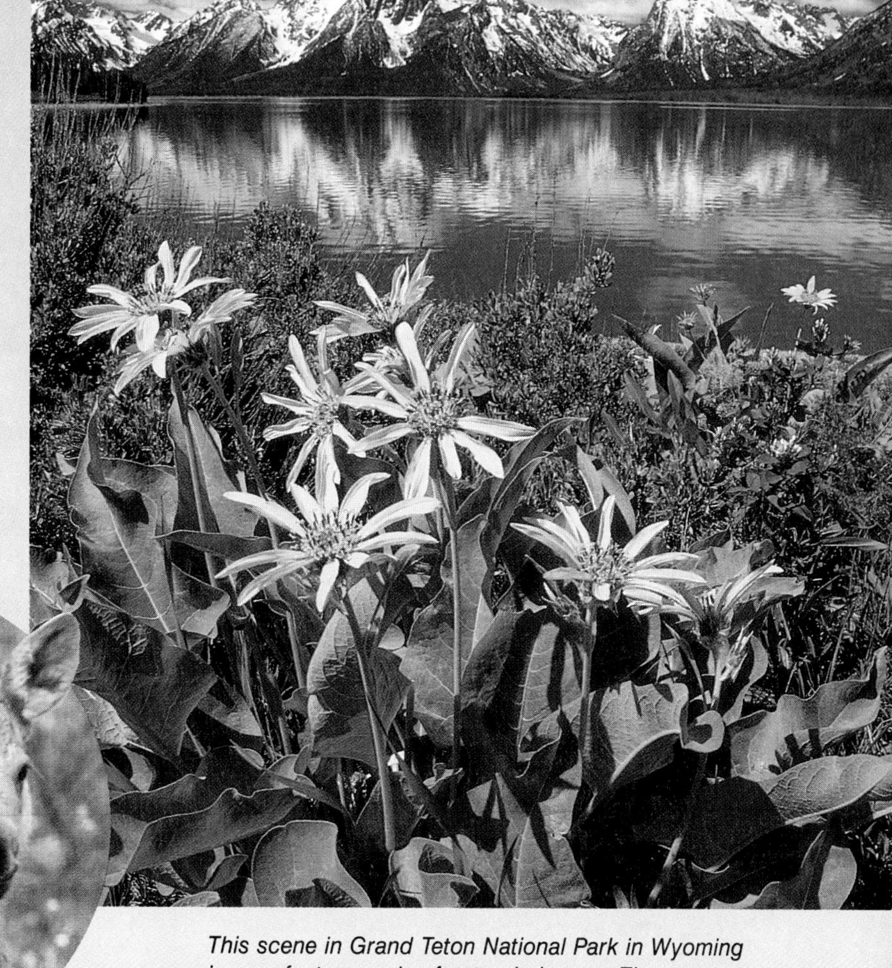

This scene in Grand Teton National Park in Wyoming is a perfect example of nature's beauty. The moose twins, animals that people travel to national parks to see, seem to be as interested in the photographer as he is in them.

Have you ever read Aesop's fables? Aesop used brief stories about animals to deliver a lesson. Here is a modern story that contains a lesson for those wise enough to learn it.

Songbirds work hard to raise a family. They build a soft nest for their babies. They return again and again to the nest with food. The adults keep the nest clean. They carefully remove the droppings produced by the young birds. Many even carry the droppings away from the nest. Thus songbirds do not soil their nest.

Can you see the moral of this story? If so, you are well on the way to understanding your role in preserving planet Earth. In this chapter you will learn about some of the ways in which people mistreat the biosphere. You will also learn how you and others can actively protect it.

CHAPTER OUTLINE

49–1 Human Population

Section Objectives

- Describe the effects of an increased human population on planet Earth.
- Relate the demands of our lifestyle to environmental problems on Earth.

In the very distant past, life on Earth was far different from what it is today. Most people lived in small tribes and family groups that hunted animals and gathered plants for food. Because these groups were small and almost always on the move, their effects on the environment were minimal. Natural processes could easily restore depleted food sources and break down wastes once the humans moved on.

When humans formed permanent settlements, however, they began a long history of profoundly affecting the environment. Not only did humans concentrate their effects on a small area for a long period of time, but they made changes in the environment that were not easily undone. For example, large numbers of trees were cut down to provide fuel for fires and lumber for buildings. Plants that were not useful were destroyed to make room for an unnatural number of food-producing plants. Dangerous animals were killed to protect humans and domesticated animals.

Because people did not really understand how the natural environments on Earth functioned, they could not assess the effects of their activities on the environment. For a long time, the human population was unaware that it was harming the world around it.

Figure 49–1 *Motorized vehicles of all types have made it easier for people to enjoy the beauty of our national parks. But the huge numbers of visitors have placed tremendous pressures on park capacity. On the busiest summer days, long lines of automobiles and recreational vehicles form outside many parks, causing traffic jams and huge delays.*

Figure 49–2 *The diverse human population brings richness to the human family. But a population that is ever-increasing places enormous demands on the resources of planet Earth.*

Over time, the human population has increased dramatically—as has our knowledge of the Earth's fragile environments. Today we are more aware of how our actions affect our world. But at the same time, we are also more capable of permanently damaging not just particular places on Earth but the entire biosphere itself.

Population Growth

Why is there all this environmental gloom and doom? Why have so many environmental disasters happened in our lifetime and not before? Why is quick action necessary? These questions, although they need to be asked, are not easy to answer.

Many environmental problems loom large and seem urgent today because of the rapid increase in human population. The huge numbers of humans on Earth are making enormous demands on the planet. We may, in fact, be reaching the limits of the Earth to support our needs.

Why has the human population grown so quickly? As you may recall from Chapter 48, a population grows when the birthrate is greater than the deathrate. Thus both birthrate and deathrate must be examined in order to understand the growth of the human population.

BIRTHRATE The birthrate varies dramatically from one country to another. In the United States and much of Europe, the birthrate has decreased. People in these countries are having fewer children. Populations are still growing, but they are growing much more slowly than they have in the past. If our current rate of growth is maintained, the population of the United States will double in just under a hundred years. In some European countries, the growth rate is so low that populations are actually declining.

The situation is quite different in other countries, however. More than two thirds of the world's population live in the tropical countries of Africa, South America, and Asia. In some of these countries, the population continues to grow at an annual rate of about 3 percent. Although this rate of growth appears to be low, it will double the present population in only 23 years!

DEATHRATE Another important factor in determining population growth is the deathrate, which has decreased worldwide. Over the past few hundred years, changes in agriculture have made more and better foods available throughout the world. Improvements in the quality and availability of medical care have wiped out many deadly diseases and contributed to an increase in the life span of the average person. Today physicians can effectively treat diseases that once killed hundreds of thousands of people. Better nutrition and health care have dramatically reduced infant mortality. For example, in the past, a woman in Kenya who gave birth to eight children could probably expect only four to survive beyond infancy. Today, a woman who has eight children will likely see most of them survive and produce families of their own!

EFFECTS OF HUMAN POPULATION GROWTH A high birthrate, a low infant deathrate, and a longer life span all contribute to population growth. But why is human population growth important? And what are its effects on Earth?

As human populations grow, their effects on the environment also grow. Countries with a rapidly growing population are often unable to produce enough food to satisfy the demand. In many parts of the world, all the land suitable for growing crops is already in use. In certain tropical areas, new fields are constantly being carved out of forests and mountains in an attempt to provide new areas for cultivation. Unfortunately, these lands do not remain productive for long. The constant rains characteristic of tropical areas quickly wash nutrients from the soil. After only a few growing seasons, the soil becomes barren.

Today, scientists worry about the destruction of tropical forests. Such devastation seems to be a high price to pay for farmland that is productive for only a few short years. In addition, many of these tropical forests are often cleared by burning. The burning produces large amounts of carbon dioxide, which is added to our atmosphere. As you will learn shortly, increased amounts of carbon dioxide in the air can have serious adverse effects. Many people mistakenly believe that leveling the rain forests produces only local effects. But, as scientists warn, the destruction of tropical forests may produce profound effects on the rest of the world—the world far removed from the rain forest.

__Figure 49–3__ A hungry population forces many countries to take drastic measures to increase farmable land. In some countries, huge forests are cleared by burning. The effects of forest burning may be felt far away from the burn site.

Effects of Lifestyles

It is not population growth alone that causes environmental problems. After all, the rate of population growth in many industrial countries has actually slowed. **The lifestyle of a population also contributes to the extraordinary environmental demands made on the Earth.**

The population of the United States is a good example. Although our population growth has stabilized at a low level, we use more energy and more natural resources than any other country in the world. We own many consumer goods. Most families in the United States have one or more automobiles. Radios, television sets, and labor-saving devices are staples of most modern homes. Consumers pay a price for these products —and the Earth does too! Natural resources are consumed in the production and use of such goods. And almost all of the factories in which the goods are manufactured produce wastes. In the past, industries could grow rapidly and cheaply because they simply threw their wastes out into the environment. Now we are learning that many of the wastes pollute our air and water, and may be changing the climate of the entire world. We are truly dirtying our nest! It is our responsibility to understand the effects of our actions on the global environment. We must be aware of what we are doing to our planet. And we must learn what we can do to solve the many environmental problems that face us.

49–1 SECTION REVIEW

1. What are three factors that have contributed to population overgrowth?
2. Describe the effects of increased human population on the Earth.
3. How can our way of life contribute to some of the environmental problems on Earth?
4. How could you change your lifestyle to lessen your demands on the environment?

Section Objectives

- Distinguish between biodegradable and nonbiodegradable wastes.
- Define biological magnification.
- Describe some of the harmful effects of air pollution on the biosphere.
- List ways in which the Earth's waters are polluted.

49–2 Pollution

You are aware of some of the serious problems that we are presently faced with. We need to make many difficult decisions, some of which will require us to change our way of life. We must learn to produce fewer wastes. We must learn to clean up the wastes we produce. To do these things, we may have to live with fewer of the familiar products we take for granted. As a nation, we may have to live with less economic growth. No one knows how to accomplish this; we only know we must. To help you understand why these difficult decisions are necessary, we shall examine some of our problems from an ecological viewpoint.

Materials released into the environment fall into two broad categories: biodegradable and nonbiodegradable. Materials that can be degraded, or broken down, by microorganisms into the essential nutrients from which they were made are **biodegradable**. Organic wastes such as sewage and scraps of food are biodegradable materials. **Nonbiodegradable** materials cannot be broken down by natural processes or are broken down only very slowly. Examples of nonbiodegradable materials are asbestos, glass, certain plastics and metals, radioactive wastes, and chemicals such as DDT, Dieldrin, and PCB's. Once these materials are released into the environment, they remain there for a long time—sometimes forever.

Figure 49–4 *A consumer society produces extremely large quantities of wastes. However, some wastes can prove useful. These automobiles are valuable for the scrap metal they contain. And some household wastes can be recycled for further use.*

Biological Magnification

Sometimes pollutants affect the biosphere in ways no one expects. Thus a minor environmental pollutant may develop into a serious threat to life.

Many primary producers (such as plants and algae) pick up nonbiodegradable pollutants from the water. They do not metabolize these compounds, nor do they get rid of them. Instead, they concentrate them and store them in their tissues. When herbivores eat producers, they too concentrate and store these nonbiodegradable compounds in their tissues. In fact, concentrations of these compounds in herbivores may be more than ten times the levels in producers. When carnivores eat herbivores, the compounds are further concentrated. At each step in a food chain, the compounds are concentrated more and more. In other words, the amount of the compounds in each organism in a food chain increases. This phenomenon is known as **biological magnification.** In some animals at the end of a food chain, the concentrations of nonbiodegradable compounds may be 10,000,000 times their original concentration in the environment as a result of biological magnification.

Biological magnification occurs with many pesticides and industrial waste products. The first, and perhaps the most famous case of biological magnification, involved the powerful insecticide DDT. From the outset, DDT was an extremely useful pesticide. It kills many kinds of insects and remains effective for a long period of time. The use of DDT rapidly became widespread. It was used to kill mosquitoes and to help control the diseases malaria and yellow fever in tropical areas. It was used to kill annoying insects around the home. In fact, people were often sprayed from head to foot with DDT to kill body lice. It was also sprayed over huge areas of farmland to control the spread of insect pests.

Figure 49–5 If the plants in the pond in which this moose is dining have been contaminated by toxic materials, they may actually poison the moose. The concentrations of toxic chemicals in the plants will increase in the tissues of the moose.

Figure 49–6 The toxic chemical DDT became part of many food chains when it was widely used as a pesticide. These two peregrine falcon eggs show the dramatic effect of DDT poisoning. The red egg is free of contamination; its shell is strong. The shell of the contaminated white egg is much more fragile. This egg will never hatch.

For a while everything seemed fine, and the use of DDT continued to increase. But then people began to notice several disturbing things. Fish in streams started dying. Fish-eating birds such as eagles, pelicans, and ospreys started laying eggs that never hatched. DDT was found in human body fat. And traces of DDT were found in the fat of penguins that lived as far away as Antarctica! What had happened? How had DDT managed to affect so many different organisms in so many diverse locations?

Aerial spraying and runoff from farmlands sprayed with the pesticide had allowed DDT to enter lakes and streams. There, DDT had been picked up by producers and had become part of various food chains. It had concentrated in the tissues of organisms in food chains as a result of biological magnification and had become widespread in food webs in many areas. Fortunately, the adverse effects of DDT were discovered before many people were harmed. Strict federal rules today control the use of insecticides such as DDT. But DDT lasts for a long time. It has entered the biosphere and will remain there for many years to come.

Unfortunately, the case of DDT is not an isolated one. Other compounds have created environmental disasters even worse than that of DDT. Dieldrin is an insecticide that was at one time used to control agricultural pests. Like DDT, Dieldrin builds up in food chains as a result of biological magnification.

PCB's are also dangerous chemical pollutants. PCB's are byproducts of several manufacturing processes. For a long time, PCB's were simply dumped into streams or other bodies of water near the factories that produced them. There they became concentrated in each step in a food chain, reaching dangerous levels in animals at the end of the food chain.

Air Pollution

We live in an ocean of air. The air supplies the oxygen our cells need to metabolize food and receives the waste products we give off as a result of our life processes. But the air also contains many other chemicals—chemicals that are not part of the natural composition of the atmosphere. The chemical pollution of the air, though it remains mostly invisible, poses very real problems. For with every breath we take, we are introducing these chemicals into our body.

SMOG If you live in a city, you may be familiar with the dirty-brown haze called **smog**. Smog, which gets its name from a combination of the words smoke and fog, contains different pollutants in different places. But regardless of its makeup, smog is unsightly, unpleasant, and harmful to life.

The causes of smog differ from one location to another. In Los Angeles, most of the smog comes from automobile exhausts. In industrial cities in the Midwest, most smog comes from factory smokestacks.

Weather conditions called **temperature inversions** can make smog a serious health hazard. Normally, cooler air is at higher altitudes than warmer air. The warmer air closer to the Earth's surface contains pollutants. But because it is warm, it is less dense than cool air and rises. As it rises, it slowly cools, and the pollutants it contains are carried away by winds. During an inversion, a layer of cool polluted air is trapped beneath a layer of warm air. Because the cool air is denser than the warm air above it, it cannot rise. As a result, the pollutants are

Figure 49–7 *The skyline of Los Angeles, California, is barely visible through a curtain of smog. This city and many others like it depend upon automobiles and buses to move people from place to place. The vehicles produce waste gases that contribute to the formation of smog.*

kept near the ground. In time, this air and the pollutants it contains are warmed enough so that they become lighter and rise.

Temperature inversions can last for hours, days, or even weeks. When a temperature inversion occurs over a large city, pollution levels can rise high enough to threaten human life. Elderly people and those with respiratory problems, such as emphysema or asthma, are especially vulnerable to this kind of air pollution.

ACID RAIN Certain pollutants in the air combine with water vapor to form droplets of acid. When these droplets fall to the Earth in rain, the rain is called **acid rain**. Actually, any form of precipitation—even snow—can contain droplets of acid. Where do the pollutants that form acid rain come from?

In many areas, the coal and oil burned in factories and power plants to generate energy contain large amounts of sulfur. When sulfur is burned, it forms sulfur dioxide (SO_2). The exhausts of gasoline-powered vehicles contain nitric oxide (NO). When sunlight strikes nitric oxide in the air, it causes the nitric oxide to combine with oxygen to form nitrogen dioxide (NO_2). Both SO_2 and NO_2 dissolve in water to form strong acids: SO_2 forms sulfuric acid and NO_2 forms nitric acid.

Often SO_2 and NO_2 are carried on prevailing winds far from where they are produced. Parts of Canada and the Northeast have been and continue to be especially hard hit by acid rain whose origin is pollutants produced by industry in the Midwest. Acid rain also affects parts of Europe and the Soviet Union.

The effects of acid rain on the environment are numerous and serious to life. Acid rain damages plants directly by

Figure 49–8 *The beauty of this photomicrograph of a drop of acid rain is somewhat misleading. Acid rain is a serious threat to the environment. Its effect on forest trees can be seen in this photograph of evergreens that are now never green. Their needles have been burned off the branches by caustic rains.*

destroying their leaves, which are the food-making organs. And it damages plants indirectly by making the already acidic soil in which they grow even more acidic. This is especially true of many regions in Canada and the Northeast. Plants cannot absorb necessary minerals from such acidic soil, and they eventually die. In addition, acid rain dissolves toxic elements, such as aluminum, found in the soil. Once dissolved, these toxic elements are absorbed by plants. Aluminum in the soil can stunt the growth of plant roots.

Rivers and lakes are also victims of acid rain. In areas plagued by acid rain, lakes have become more and more acidic. Increased acid levels place the entire living community under stress. For example, water with a low pH (low pH means high levels of acid) causes the skeletons of fishes to lose calcium. Fishes become humpbacked, dwarfed, or deformed from the loss of calcium. When the levels of acid become high, fishes and other aquatic organisms die.

The toxic metals dissolved by acid rain—aluminum and mercury, for example—can damage rivers and lakes as well as plant roots. These toxic metals accumulate in the food chain, reaching dangerous levels by biological magnification. Clams and snails are the first organisms to die from aluminum and mercury poisoning. They are followed by aquatic insects, fishes, and amphibians. Soon the entire lake is lifeless. But the destruction does not end there. Animals dependent on these organisms are no longer able to survive without a source of food. Thus an entire region becomes unable to support certain kinds of life. Perhaps this situation sounds a bit exaggerated. Unfortunately, it is not. Entire lakes in Canada, northern New York, and New England have already died from the effects of acid rain. Sadly, many continue to do so.

Mountain forests in areas of Maine and Vermont are dying too. Trees in these areas are surrounded by acid fog. The good health of forest areas is important in protecting the quality of the freshwater supply. When forest areas begin to die, trouble with streams and ground water often follows close behind. Thus acid rain indirectly threatens the water supply in these areas.

THE GREENHOUSE EFFECT You may be surprised to learn that carbon dioxide is considered a pollutant. After all, it is a naturally occurring gas. However, the amount of carbon dioxide in the atmosphere is increasing as a result of human activity in the biosphere. And this increased amount of carbon dioxide may have a major effect on the Earth's climate.

Carbon dioxide is produced when carbon-containing fuels are burned. Carbon-containing fuels include wood and charcoal as well as fossil fuels such as coal, oil, and natural gas. Over the years, the burning of trees and fossil fuels for energy has released vast quantities of carbon dioxide into the atmosphere. In addition, clearing land for farming and building destroys

Figure 49–9 *Venus (left), although much like the Earth in many ways, has an atmosphere that consists mostly of carbon dioxide. As a result, Venus is considerably hotter than Earth. Scientists are concerned that the temperature of Earth will increase as levels of carbon dioxide in the atmosphere increase. If this happens, the huge polar icecaps will melt and sea levels will rise, flooding many coastal regions.*

plants, which remove carbon dioxide from the air during photosynthesis.

How do increased amounts of carbon dioxide affect the atmosphere? Energy from the sun is absorbed by the Earth and changed into heat. Later, this energy is radiated back from the Earth to the atmosphere. Carbon dioxide and other gases in the atmosphere absorb this heat energy, forming a kind of "heat blanket" around the Earth. This process is called the **greenhouse effect** because the carbon dioxide holds in heat like the glass in a greenhouse. The greenhouse effect makes the Earth a warm, comfortable place to live.

As levels of carbon dioxide in the air increase, however, more heat is absorbed, and the temperature of the Earth increases. The effects of this global warming, which is occurring slowly at present, are unclear. Some scientists believe that if a global warming of even a few degrees occurs, it will cause the polar icecaps to melt. This will release enough water to raise sea levels and flood many coastal areas. A warming of the Earth's climate—by even a few degrees—will also cause major changes in human agriculture to occur. For example, corn grows best within a narrow temperature range. If the Earth's climate becomes warmer, the best areas in the United States for growing corn will shift farther north from the equator. Thus global warming will have a major impact on many farming states.

HOLES IN THE OZONE LAYER A layer of ozone exists far above the Earth in a part of the atmosphere called the stratosphere (16 to 48 kilometers above the Earth's surface). This ozone layer protects the Earth from harmful ultraviolet radiation from the sun. Without the protection of this ozone layer, few living things could survive.

Scientists have recently discovered that the ozone layer is becoming thinner in certain places around the poles—a phenomenon they have called **holes in the ozone layer**. Holes in the ozone layer are not actual holes but rather areas where little ozone is found. The thin spots in the ozone layer indicate that the Earth's protective layer of ozone is being depleted.

The major cause of ozone depletion is a form of chemical air pollution that results primarily from the addition of chlorofluorocarbons to the air. At one time these chemicals were used in most aerosol containers to force the contents from the container. Once the harmful effects of chlorofluorocarbons were known, the United States banned their use as an aerosol propellant. Many other countries did too. However, other sources of these chemicals—whose primary use is now in cooling and refrigeration equipment—continue to pose a threat to the protective ozone layer. If the ozone layer is depleted, more of the sun's harmful ultraviolet radiation will reach the Earth. Scientists predict that if the amount of ultraviolet radiation that reaches the Earth increases, the frequency of certain diseases—such as certain forms of skin cancer—will also increase.

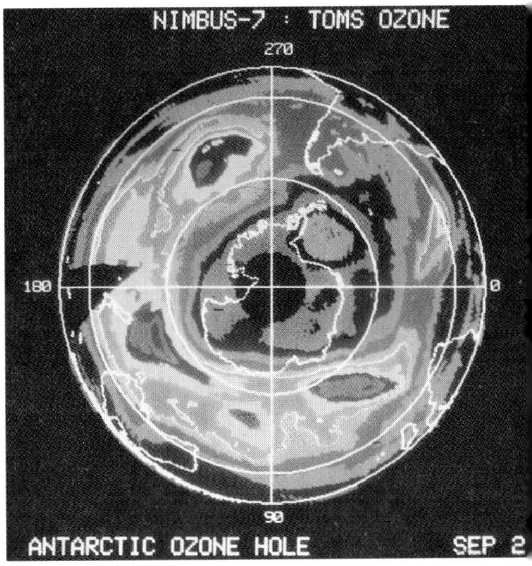

Figure 49–10 *In this computer-generated image of ozone levels over the southern hemisphere, the light-blue areas near the coast of Antarctica indicate ozone holes.*

Water Pollution

In the United States, billions of liters of fresh water are used daily. Water is used for drinking, cooking, bathing, and cleaning. It is also used for industrial processes and irrigation. Although water is a renewable resource, there is a limited amount of fresh water.

Although almost three fourths of the Earth is covered by water, only about 3 percent is fresh water—97 percent is salty ocean water. Of the 3 percent that is fresh water, only a small portion is available for use by living things. The greater portion is locked up in ice, mainly in the polar icecaps and in glaciers. Considering the fact that all living things depend upon water, the pollution of this very small available supply looms as an extremely serious problem facing us today.

Figure 49–11 *In many places in the world, the supply of drinkable water is severely limited. Here in Mali, people fill buckets with water that is pumped from a communal well. These heavy buckets of water must be carried to their home.*

CHEMICAL CONTAMINATION Water can be polluted in many ways. **The most common sources of water pollution are chemical wastes, raw sewage, and high temperatures.** Toxic chemicals can pollute water supplies in two ways. The chemicals can enter streams and rivers, which carry them first into lakes and then into oceans. There the toxic chemicals can kill aquatic plants and animals or they can enter the food chain and eventually pose a threat to human health. Even in lakes as large as the Great Lakes, the presence of several pollutants has made eating fishes from these waters dangerous to health. In addition, chemical wastes discarded on land can seep through the

Figure 49–12 *Although almost three quarters of the Earth is covered by water, the supply of fresh water that is available for human needs is limited. It is extremely important to protect this water from becoming polluted.*

ground and enter the underground water supply, through which they can be carried long distances. Toxic chemicals contaminate wells and the underground water supplies that serve many towns and cities. Because water moves through the ground slowly, toxic chemicals in underground water are difficult to remove.

SEWAGE CONTAMINATION Have you ever wondered what happens to the water after you flush the toilet? Or to the detergents used to wash dishes and clothes? These wastes, like chemical pollutants, are typically added to the Earth's waters. Although these domestic wastes are usually not poisonous to life as are chemical pollutants, they do pose environmental problems.

Sewage consists of large quantities of wastes that contain nitrogen compounds. These compounds are used by bacteria in a process that requires oxygen. If untreated sewage is added to rivers and streams, the number of bacteria increases dramatically. These bacteria use up most of the available oxygen as they break down the nitrogen compounds. Other organisms that live in the water may suffocate because their supply of oxygen is depleted.

In addition to nitrogen compounds, sewage often contains phosphates, or compounds that contain phosphorus. Both nitrogen compounds and phosphates are nutrients that stimulate the growth of plants. In rural areas, where homes are far apart, sewage is usually treated in septic systems. In a septic system, decay bacteria work on the sewage, reducing it to water that is nearly pure. This water, which still contains some dissolved nutrients, seeps out of the septic system and into the ground. This explains why plants near a septic system grow well.

Figure 49–13 *Many cities and towns have sewage-treatment plants that process household waste water. In huge outdoor tanks, water is treated by chemicals and microorganisms and then aerated.*

In cities, however, the large population makes the use of septic systems impossible. City sewage must be treated in sewage-treatment plants. In special ponds and tanks in these plants, some of the organic wastes in sewage are broken down by the actions of bacteria. Once the bacteria have decomposed the organic matter, chemicals that kill harmful microorganisms are added to the sewage and the treated water is released. But the treated water often still contains nutrients that can produce a rapid growth, or bloom, of algae in streams, lakes, coastal bays, and ocean waters. These algal blooms can disrupt the normal balance of organisms in a water community.

Human sewage also contains many potentially harmful microorganisms: bacteria, viruses, and protozoa. A few bacteria in the water usually pose no threat to people. But filter-feeding organisms, such as clams and mussels, ingest the microorganisms and concentrate them in their tissues. When these shellfish are eaten, diseases such as hepatitis, typhoid, and certain forms of dysentery can be spread.

THERMAL POLLUTION Many factories and power plants produce heat as a waste product. In the past, water from nearby rivers, lakes, or the ocean was used to cool such plants. The water was pumped through pipes in the cooling system, where it absorbed heat. The heated water was then pumped back into the environment. In some cases, heated water has no harmful effects on the ecosystem. But often, heated water kills aquatic plants and animals. This kind of water pollution is called **thermal pollution**. Thermal pollution also affects the larvae of many aquatic animals, which are more sensitive than the adults to temperature changes. So even if the adults are unharmed, the larvae may be killed.

Figure 49–14 *Water is often used by industries as a coolant. In this nuclear power plant, heated water is returned to the river from which it was pumped, causing a kind of pollution called thermal pollution. Thermal pollution is a danger to some forms of aquatic life.*

OCEAN POLLUTION Water pollution is not limited to the pollution of fresh water. For centuries, people have dumped their wastes into the oceans. Such a practice presented few problems when the number of people was small, the amount of waste was minimal, and the wastes were biodegradable. But today the situation is vastly different. Too many people produce too much waste, a great deal of which is nonbiodegradable. Plastics and other wastes dumped into the oceans may float around for months or even years. Large cities continue to dump so much sewage into the oceans that it cannot be degraded quickly enough. Often, some of this sewage washes up on beaches, offering ample proof that we do indeed foul our nest.

Pollution near the shore is a serious matter. Because so many people live in the great port cities, the sources of pollution are numerous and the problems posed are grave. Some wastes dumped into the oceans—such as containers of disposable medical items—wash back onto shore, threatening the health of beach-goers. Other wastes remain at sea, posing a hazard to ocean life. And along the continental shelves near shore, the oceans' most productive areas are threatened by pollution. Here, many of the world's important fisheries provide food for much of the world's population.

OIL SPILLS Oil pollution in the ocean, too, is serious. Even when oil companies are careful, accidents happen. For example, some oil spills occur when boats run aground. Others occur when oil tankers are damaged during storms. But regardless of the cause, oncc oil is spilled, it is difficult to remove.

Figure 49–15 *The solid wastes produced by consumer societies are often dumped into the oceans. The effects of ocean dumping have become painfully apparent: Washed up by ocean waves, these pollutants despoil once pristine beaches.*

Oil slicks are deadly to marine animals that swallow the toxic oil or become coated with it. Oil spilled in the ocean may also enter the estuaries that are the nurseries for the oceans. The larvae and young of many species spend time in estuaries before they move into the open sea. Many plants and animals are killed when oil pollutes estuaries. Toxic chemicals in oil often accumulate in those animals that are not killed immediately. In many cases, these chemicals make the animals sterile, or unable to reproduce. In addition, some of the chemicals that accumulate in animal tissue are potent carcinogens that may cause cancer in the people who eat them. We are still not certain what effects oil pollution has on the plankton that float in the ocean and form the basis of many food chains. Much more research is needed in this area.

Our continental shelves contain large and potentially valuable reserves of crude oil and natural gas. It is clear that precautions must be taken to protect these areas and their aquatic inhabitants if offshore drilling is to take place.

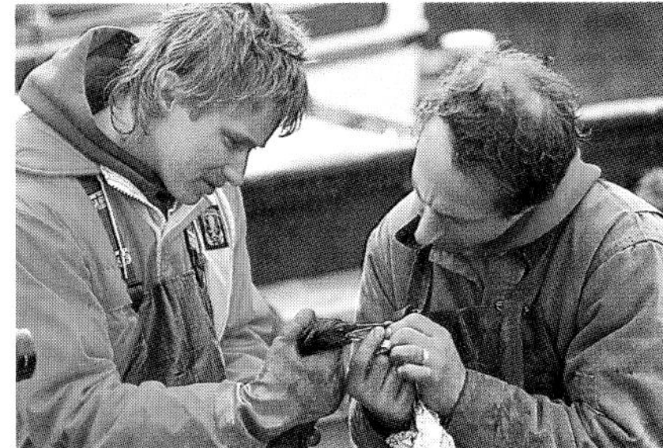

Figure 49–16 *The sea bird in the top photograph was an unlucky victim of a tragic accident. Its body was covered with heavy black oil that spilled when a tanker ran aground. The bird in the bottom photograph was more fortunate. It, too, was covered with oil, but it has been captured and will be washed with special detergents to remove the oil from its feathers. With luck, it will fly again.*

49–2 SECTION REVIEW

1. Compare a biodegradable waste with a nonbiodegradable waste. Give two examples of each kind of waste.
2. What is biological magnification? How does biological magnification increase the dangers posed by certain environmental pollutants?
3. What are two kinds of pollution? How does each pose a danger to human health?
4. How does acid rain threaten our water supply?
5. Lakes affected by acid rain often appear clear and blue. Why might this be so?

49–3 The Fate of the Earth

Section Objectives

- Explain the importance of tropical forests to the health of the biosphere.
- Define endangered species.
- List reasons why organisms should be protected.

People have always relied upon plants and animals for food, clothing, and shelter. **The survival of humans and human society depends upon the survival of other organisms in the biosphere.** Today, the survival of many of these organisms is threatened.

Forests

You probably do not live in a forest—few people do today. But wherever you live, your life is dependent upon forests in many ways. Trees provide us with many essential products. Wood is used to make everything from pencils to houses. The paper on which these words are printed is made from wood. Trees are an important source of charcoal used in cooking and in industrial processes.

Trees are also a vital part of many ecosystems. The roots of trees keep the soil loose and at the same time hold it in place, allowing rainwater to penetrate the soil without washing it away. Water that penetrates the ground often becomes part of the underground water table. If you drive through a forested area, you may see signs indicating that you are in a watershed area. This means that the forest is actually helping to gather water for use by people.

When forests are carelessly cut down, many important changes occur. The structure of the soil changes. Microorganisms die. Many small plants and animals can no longer survive. Without trees to hold the soil, heavy rains wash away the fertile topsoil, leaving behind only the less fertile subsoil. Essential nutrients are washed from the soil and carried into lakes, rivers, and streams. The water table drops. Rains bring sudden floods instead of steady streams. The soil cannot store moisture, and so it dries out quickly after each rain. In some cases, new plants cannot grow in what was once fertile soil.

Despite knowledge of these harmful outcomes, many of our country's few remaining old forests are being cut down at an alarming rate. And in tropical countries, rain forests are being destroyed so rapidly that they may disappear completely by the end of this century!

Figure 49–17 *This proud, tall tree is no match for a huge chainsaw. Once cut, it will be used to make many consumer products. A tiny tree will be placed in its stead. Varieties of trees that reach harvesting size in fewer years have been developed.*

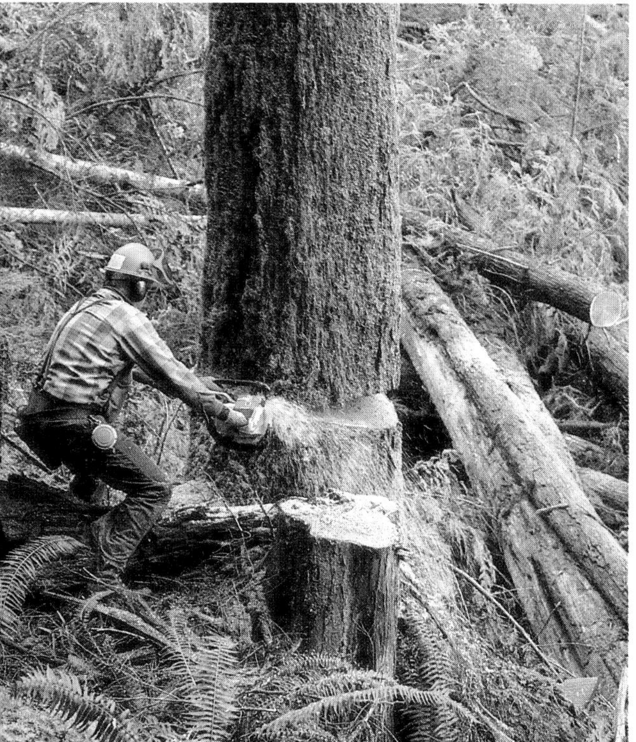

Fortunately, government officials became aware of the problems associated with forest destruction as long ago as 1905. The United States Forestry Service protects and manages our forest resources. Today there is increased awareness on the part of lumber companies to manage forest resources wisely.

Programs that plant new trees when old trees are cut down are called **reforestation** programs. Reforestation programs are vital to the health of the biosphere. But caring for forests while harvesting their wood is not an easy task. When a forest is cut, lumber companies often want to reforest by planting large numbers of a single tree species. However, such plantings cannot adequately replace a natural forest. One obvious reason is that in most natural forests there is a large variety of tree species. A less obvious reason is that the animal and plant communities that develop naturally in forests and help control harmful insects are not easily established in artificially planted forests. Wise planting of various species of trees may help save much former forest land from disaster.

Figure 49–18 *Huge herds of bison roamed the Great Plains until hunters brought these awesome animals to the verge of extinction. Today, protected by strict laws, herds of these animals once again roam.*

Endangered Species

When an animal or plant species becomes so rare that it is threatened with extinction, it is called an **endangered species**. Species become endangered in several ways. A species that was once quite common can be hunted until few remain. With so few individuals remaining, a harsh winter, a disease epidemic, or any other natural disaster can mean extinction. Some species can become endangered if they are able to survive in only one particular habitat. If that habitat is destroyed, the species may become extinct.

Today, one plant or animal species becomes extinct every hour! It is predicted that by the year 2000, many land animals will be extinct in their natural environment. Just imagine what it will be like for you and your children to live in a world without elephants, giraffes, tigers, or monkeys.

Why Save Endangered Species?

Extinction is forever. Once a species becomes extinct, it will never exist again. Many people feel that we have no right to cause the extinction of other species—as we are presently doing. Many biologists (including the authors of this book) feel this way. But human needs are great, as are the demands on the ecosystem. If someone were to ask you why we should be concerned about protecting other species, could you answer them?

USEFUL PRODUCTS In earlier sections of this textbook we mentioned why other species are important to us. It might

Figure 49–19 *Other animals have not been as lucky as the bison. The California condor (left) is close to extinction. Captive breeding programs aim to keep this species alive. The black-footed ferret hunts prairie dogs (center). The population of ferrets is so small that their actual location in the wild is a closely guarded secret. The desert pupfish lives in small desert pools (right). If anything happens to its delicate habitat, it too will be in real danger of becoming extinct.*

be useful to the discussion of saving endangered species to summarize a few important points here. Many everyday foods, medicines, and industrial compounds come from wild plant and animal species. Antibiotics, heart drugs, anticancer medications, painkillers, and other important medicines are derived from plants. Yet these plant species represent only a few that have been tested for useful compounds. No one knows the riches that might be hidden in yet unknown plants that grow in tropical rain forests. If these rain forests disappear, the potential contributions of their inhabitants to our society will also vanish.

Many animal species produce compounds that may prove important to human health. Sponges may contain chemical compounds useful in treating viral diseases such as herpes and encephalitis. Chemicals in sea cucumbers are currently being tested to see if they have potential anticancer uses. The blood of the horseshoe crab is presently collected and used in important medical tests.

Food from Plants

Most of the world's population obtains its food from crops grown on farms. But this does not mean that species of wild plants are unimportant in horticulture. They are, in fact, quite important. Here is why.

The crop plants grown in the United States today are the results of generations of selective breeding. When plant breeders develop a better variety, it is produced in enormous numbers and planted all over the country. But planting a single variety can prove dangerous.

Genetically similar plants are susceptible to the same diseases. If only a single variety is planted in huge numbers, entire croplands can be destroyed by a single disease. One famous example of such a disease is the great corn blight that occurred in 1970. This disease was resistant to all existing agricultural defenses. Nothing could save an infected field. That year about 15 percent of the total corn crop was destroyed. In the future, diseases that affect important crop plants could be even more devastating.

How can such situations be prevented? Crop breeders are constantly at work developing new disease-resistant strains of crop plants. In many cases, they cross crop plants with strains of wild plants that have more genetic variability. (The strains produced by selective breeding have little genetic variability.) So far, wild plants related to crop plants have provided the necessary "new genes" crop breeders want to introduce into already developed strains of crop plants. Scientists all over the world regularly search for new wild species related to food crops. But they face one serious problem: The destruction of natural habitats will surely destroy as yet undiscovered wild plants and thus make their job even harder.

Figure 49–20 *The tomato, eaten with relish by many people, was once thought to be poisonous. In the past, the tomato grew in the wild. Today, this plant is commonly grown in many gardens. Who can tell how many other wild plants will be found in remote areas and what uses these plants may serve?*

49–3 SECTION REVIEW

1. How does the destruction of a rain forest in South America affect a person living on a farm in South Dakota?
2. What is an endangered species? How does a species become endangered?
3. Why should we make an attempt to protect endangered species?
4. Planting huge fields of a single crop plant is often the most economical way to raise a good crop. How does planting a single variety make people who are dependent upon the crop more vulnerable?

Saving the World's Great Mammals

On the great plains of Africa, a mother elephant sprays her calf with a refreshing shower from a water hole. In the cold waters of the North Atlantic, a humpback whale calf launches herself out of the water and falls back with a giant splash. These magnificent animals have much in common. Both elephants and whales are mammals. Both species are among the largest animals ever to live on our planet. Both are peaceful animals by nature. Both live in close family groups and wander over large areas in search of food. And although both species were numerous at one time, today they are in danger of becoming extinct.

Ninety thousand elephants are killed every year for the ivory in their tusks, which is made into jewelry and other decorative objects. The total population of African elephants is about 650,000. You can see that if the killing of elephants continues at the present rate, elephants could become extinct within a few years. Elephant hunting is already illegal in several African states, but poachers have begun to hunt these animals with machine guns from airplanes to collect the valuable ivory. To help save the African elephant, the Convention on International Trade in Endangered Species added the species to their list of protected animals in October 1989.

Whales are killed for meat and for the oil made from their thick layers of fat. Although a few whales are hunted in traditional ways by native people, most of the whales killed today are taken by massive factory ships that process the whales while at sea. Most of the whale meat eaten today is a delicacy, not a staple food. Some whale species, such as the blue whale, may already be so rare that they cannot reproduce well. The International Whaling Commission sets limits on the number of whales that can be hunted. But some countries ignore these limits and continue to hunt more whales than are permitted.

Many people think that the killing of these inoffensive animals should stop. Other people think that in free societies it is a personal right to hunt animals and sell the products of the hunt. What do you think?

49–4 The Future of the Biosphere

Section Objectives

- Explain why the biosphere must be protected.
- Identify ways in which people are acting to protect the environment.
- Explain why protecting the environment is a difficult job.

At this point in your reading you might be concerned that we have painted a rather bleak picture of our planet's future. But do you remember the bird in the opening story of this chapter? It worked hard to keep its nest clean. The Earth is our nest. It supplies us with food, water, oxygen, and natural resources—all the things we need for life. And we too can work to keep our nest clean; that is, if we want to!

In the past, people have treated Earth with neglect. Today, however, attitudes are changing. Yet even if we are committed to saving endangered species and protecting the environment, we still face many problems in deciding how to go about it.

Actions for Conservation

Happily, there are people in the world who love wild places, wild plants, and wild animals. There are also many people who understand how important the health of the biosphere is to the health of all species, including humans. These people work together to protect the environment in many different ways.

Towns, counties, states, the federal government, and conservancy groups have all purchased land that is to be set aside for conservation purposes. In many locations this land can simultaneously serve as a watershed and as a home for wildlife. The preservation of land habitats is one of the most important responsibilities we shall assume in the years ahead.

It is more difficult to conserve the resources of the ocean. Ocean currents travel all over the world. Marine animals ignore national boundaries and maritime laws. They are carried along by ocean currents or swim wherever their instincts direct them. Fishing boats in international waters can catch an unlimited number of fish. There is little our government can do to prevent fishing boats from taking too many haddock or too many whales, for example. To conserve ocean species, the countries of the world must join together to protect the oceans and their inhabitants.

Sometimes people work together to protect a single species. For example, sportsfishermen on the east coast of the United States have formed a group called Stripers Unlimited. This group works to protect habitats important to the striped bass, an ocean game fish that is seriously threatened by pollution and by the destruction of estuaries. Striped bass lay eggs in estuaries. PCB's and other chemical pollutants make their way into estuaries and kill the delicate eggs. Members of Stripers Unlimited attend town meetings, support cleanup legislation, and raise money to reclaim estuaries. By these actions, other species that inhabit estuaries are also saved.

Figure 49–21 *At one time, the Arabian oryx, hunted for its beautiful horns, was close to extinction. Today, this animal is raised on ranches. Captive-bred animals are returned to their native habitat, where they are protected by strict laws that prohibit hunting. Captive breeding programs offer some hope that endangered animals will survive.*

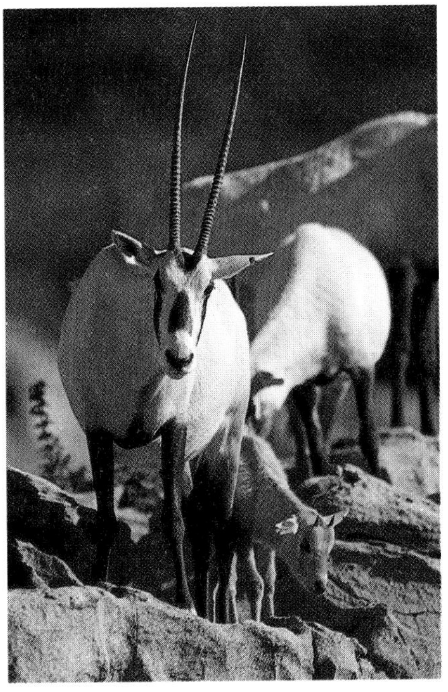

Larger organizations such as the Sierra Club, World Wildlife Fund, and Greenpeace work on a national and international level to protect the environment. The actions of these groups recognize the importance of protecting the biosphere. By backing political candidates who support environmental causes and by suing corporations and governments whose actions endanger the environment, these groups demonstrate their commitment to saving planet Earth.

Difficult Decisions

Cleaning up the environment and keeping it clean are not easy jobs. Some cities have realized that they can no longer continue to dump untreated sewage into their rivers and streams and harbors. In some coastal areas, cities have built sewage treatment plants and constructed pipelines to carry sewage far offshore. Other cities are repairing and replacing old-fashioned sewage systems that overflow after heavy rains. These projects are expensive, and all of us must pay for them. This means that the costs of using city water and sewer services will increase. Although no one likes to pay more for such services, increased fees will allow communities to make the environment cleaner. We, and future generations, will benefit in the end.

Figure 49–22 *La Guardia airport in New York City indicates how far humans have developed. But its past speaks volumes about how we developed. The land for this airport was once part amusement park and part landfill. Every time a plane takes off or lands, it does so on the wastes produced by other generations of New Yorkers.*

The problem of solid-waste disposal is probably one that few of us think about. But what happens to our trash after we throw it out? It must all be disposed of, usually by burying it in places called sanitary landfills. However, sanitary landfills, especially those near large cities, are almost filled to overflowing. One solution to the solid-waste problem is **recycling**. In the process of recycling, certain kinds of solid wastes—newspapers, bottles, and metal or plastic cans, for example—can be processed and used again. Recycling can make a big difference if enough people participate.

Controlling the dumping of toxic wastes by industry is also important. It is more expensive to clean up toxic wastes after they have been dumped into the environment than it is to dispose of them in a safe way. Once an area has become polluted with toxic chemicals, cleanup can cost millions of dollars.

Up until now, few companies have been willing to pay the costs of cleanup. But public opinion is making more and more companies aware of the need to protect the environment. Consumers should be aware, however, that protecting the environment is often accompanied by increases in the prices of products. So far, most people have not demonstrated that they are willing to pay these extra costs.

But attitudes are changing. A recent poll found that 93 percent of Americans are concerned about pollution of our lakes and rivers by toxic chemicals, and 92 percent are concerned about the disposal of hazardous wastes on land. More than 75

Figure 49–23 Planet Earth moves through space carrying its precious cargo of life. The Earth offers us a good home. But we must protect that home so future generations can enjoy their lives here as well.

percent of Americans are concerned about air pollution and the problems caused by acid rain.

In overwhelming numbers, Americans are expressing their fears for the future of planet Earth. But they are also expressing their hopes that a healthy biosphere will become a major priority for all the Earth's inhabitants. **You must decide how important the environment is and whether you are willing to pay to keep it healthy.** You must decide, because you are the stewards of the Earth.

49–4 SECTION REVIEW

1. Why must the biosphere be protected?
2. Describe three ways in which people are protecting the environment.
3. What are some of the obstacles that stand in the way of cleaning up the environment?
4. In what three ways can you protect the environment?

LABORATORY INVESTIGATION

SIMULATING THE EFFECTS OF ACID RAIN

PROBLEM

How do high-sulfur fuels affect the environment?

MATERIALS *(per group)*

2 100-mL beakers	pH paper
Bunsen burner	rubber stopper (#8 ½)
deflagrating spoon	safety goggles
filter paper	steel wool
1000-mL flask	stirring rod
glass-marking pencil	sulfur
100-mL graduated cylinder	test tube rack
100 mustard seeds	2 test tubes
2 petri dishes	tongs

PROCEDURE

1. Put on safety goggles. Use a graduated cylinder to measure 50 mL of water. Pour the water into a clean 1000-mL flask. Swirl the flask.
2. Use tongs to dip a piece of pH paper in the water. Record the pH of the water.
3. Fill a deflagrating spoon halfway with sulfur. Heat the sulfur with a Bunsen burner until it melts and ignites. **CAUTION:** *Work in a well-ventilated room or under a fume hood. Do not inhale the fumes.*
4. Immediately insert the deflagrating spoon and burning sulfur into the flask. **CAUTION:** *Be sure not to put them into the water.* When the flames fill the flask and begin to escape, insert the rubber stopper into the mouth of the flask so that the deflagrating spoon is held in place.
5. When the sulfur stops burning, remove the deflagrating spoon. Restopper the flask. Swirl the flask gently until the fumes dissolve.
6. Remove the stopper from the flask. Use tongs to dip another piece of pH paper in the water to measure the pH. Record the pH.
7. Label a test tube, a beaker, and a petri dish *WATER*. Label a second test tube, beaker, and petri dish *SULFUR WATER*. Put a piece of filter paper in each petri dish.
8. Pour 10 mL of water into the test tube labeled *WATER* and 30 mL of water into the beaker labeled *WATER*. Stand the test tube in the test tube rack. Repeat this procedure using the sulfur water in the flask, the test tube, and the beaker labeled *SULFUR WATER*.
9. Put 50 mustard seeds into each beaker. Set the beakers aside overnight.
10. Place a small piece of steel wool in each test tube. Note any color changes. Check the texture of each piece of steel wool with a stirring rod. Set the test tubes aside overnight. After 24 hours, repeat your observations.
11. Pour the contents of the beakers into the appropriately labeled petri dishes. Set the petri dishes aside overnight.
12. After another 24 hours, count the number of seeds that germinated in each petri dish. Calculate the percentage of seeds that germinated. Record the results.

OBSERVATIONS

1. What was the pH of the water? The pH of the sulfur water?
2. Describe the steel wool in each test tube.
3. How did the percentage of germinating seeds in the petri dishes compare?

ANALYSIS AND CONCLUSIONS

1. What effect does burning high-sulfur fuels have on the acidity of water?
2. Based on your observations, what effect would acid rain have on steel structures?
3. Based on your observations, what effect would acid rain have on living organisms?

STUDENT STUDY GUIDE

SUMMARIZING THE CONCEPTS

The key concepts in each section of this chapter are listed below to help you review the chapter content. Make sure you understand each concept and its relationship to other concepts and to the theme of this chapter.

49–1 Human Population

- The human population has increased dramatically over time. As human populations increase, their effects on the environment also increase. Changes in lifestyles also contribute to environmental problems.

49–2 Pollution

- Some materials that are released into the environment are biodegradable. They can be broken down by microorganisms into the essential elements from which they were made. Other wastes are nonbiodegradable, which means they cannot be broken down by natural processes.
- The ozone layer protects the Earth from the sun's harmful ultraviolet radiation. Scientists have discovered holes in this layer. The holes result mainly from the addition of chlorofluorocarbons to the air.
- Pollution of the Earth's water is another important problem. Industrial chemicals, sewage wastes, and thermal pollution are the three main causes of this problem.

49–3 The Fate of the Earth

- Forest destruction poses a danger to people living far from the forest area. When forests are cut, changes occur in the numbers and kinds of organisms that live in the forest.
- An endangered species is a species whose numbers are so small that the species is threatened with extinction.

49–4 The Future of the Biosphere

- Fortunately, there are people who understand how important the health of the biosphere is to the health of all species. Government agencies have purchased land to be set aside for conservation purposes. To conserve ocean species, the countries of the world must join together to protect the oceans. Sometimes people work together to protect a single species.
- Only an increasing awareness of the problems caused by pollution and the degradation of the environment can ensure that planet Earth will remain a planet full of promise for a better life for all organisms.

REVIEWING KEY TERMS

Vocabulary terms are important to your understanding of biology. The key terms listed below are those you should be especially familiar with. Review these terms and their meanings. Then use each term in a complete sentence. If you are not sure of a term's meaning, return to the appropriate section and review its definition.

49–2 Pollution

biodegradable
nonbiodegradable
biological magnification
smog
temperature inversion
acid rain
greenhouse effect
hole in the ozone layer
thermal pollution

49–3 The Fate of the Earth

reforestation
endangered species

49–4 The Future of the Biosphere

recycling

CHAPTER REVIEW

CONTENT REVIEW

Multiple Choice

Choose the letter of the answer that best completes each statement.

1. Which of the following is biodegradable?
a. glass c. DDT
b. orange peel d. mercury

2. If the United States maintains its current rate of population growth, in a hundred years the number of people will
a. decrease by half. c. remain the same.
b. increase by half. d. double.

3. Wastes that cannot be broken down into essential nutrients by natural processes are
a. nonbiodegradable. c. biodegradable.
b. water soluble. d. organic compounds.

4. A condition in which smog is trapped close to the surface of the Earth results from a
a. snowstorm.
b. temperature inversion.
c. hurricane.
d. hole in the ozone layer.

5. Sulfur dioxide and nitric oxide in the air combine with water to form
a. biological magnification.
b. smog.
c. PCB's.
d. acid rain.

6. The greenhouse effect causes an increase in
a. carbon dioxide. c. temperature.
b. ozone. d. sulfur.

7. Areas in the ocean where the larvae and young of many species dwell before they move into the open sea are called
a. sea nurseries. c. estuaries.
b. glaciers. d. tidal pools.

8. An area of a forest where water gathers for use by people is a (an)
a. rain forest. c. eroded area.
b. watershed area. d. water basin.

True or False

Determine whether each statement is true or false. If it is true, write "true." If it is false, change the underlined word or words to make the statement true.

1. DDT, asbestos, and Dieldrin are examples of <u>biodegradable</u> substances.

2. The burning of fossil fuels and wood can lead to a <u>greenhouse effect</u>.

3. <u>Chemical pollution</u> results when warm water is pumped from factories into the environment.

4. A species that is so rare that its survival is threatened with extinction is an <u>endangered species</u>.

5. The rate of population increase has <u>leveled off</u> in all countries on Earth.

6. <u>Biological magnification</u> occurs with many pesticides and industrial waste products.

7. <u>Smog</u> damages plant leaves, makes water and soil more acidic, and carries salts of aluminum and mercury into rivers and lakes.

8. Chlorofluorocarbons are a major source of the air pollution that depletes the <u>ozone layer</u>.

Word Relationships

A. *Replace the underlined definition with the correct vocabulary word.*

1. Some wastes are <u>materials that can be broken down by microorganisms into the essential nutrients from which they were made</u>.

2. One type of air pollution involves <u>a combination of smoke and fog</u>.

3. <u>Programs that plant new trees when old trees are cut</u> are vitally important.

B. *In each of the following sets of terms, three of the terms are related. One item does not belong. Determine the characteristic common to three of the terms and then identify the term that does not belong.*

4. food scraps, DDT, asbestos, Dieldrin
5. sulfur, acid rain, ozone, nitric oxide
6. industrial chemicals, sewage, thermal pollution, watershed area.

CONCEPT MASTERY

Use your understanding of the concepts developed in the chapter to answer each of the following in a brief paragraph.

1. Explain how water organisms may suffocate if sewage is added to the water.
2. Discuss some reasons why there has been increased population growth in the past few hundred years.
3. The trees of a forest play an important role in many ecosystems. Discuss the importance of trees and describe the changes that occur when forests are cut.
4. Explain the difference between the treatment of sewage in a septic system and in a sewage treatment plant.
5. How can a species become endangered?
6. What are some of the problems associated with the disposal of radioactive wastes?
7. What is acid rain? How does it affect lakes in upstate New York and in New England?
8. Why is it difficult to replace a forest?

CRITICAL AND CREATIVE THINKING

Discuss each of the following in a brief paragraph.

1. **Identifying relationships** Most people in the United States will never see a tropical rain forest. Why, then, is the destruction of tropical rain forests a global concern?
2. **Relating cause and effect** The owner of a local factory believes that he should be able to dump wastes into a nearby river. His argument is that water in the river will dilute any dangerous chemicals. Present several arguments to convince him that he should find another method to dispose of the wastes.
3. **Making inferences** Oil spills can become large-scale catastrophes that have a major impact on entire ecosystems. Explain how an oil spill can affect an ecosystem.
4. **Using the writing process** Developers have chosen to build a large factory in a remote area of your state. The land is uninhabited and little is known about the wildlife and plants that exist there. In order to build, the developers plan to clear the area completely. Write a letter to the governor. Explain the type of information that might be lost forever if the developers do not wait at least until the area has been explored and studied.

Wastewater-Treatment-Plant Operator

Waste materials enter our water supply so quickly that if they were not stopped, water would soon become unfit for any use. Wastewater-treatment-plant operators control the equipment and processes that remove wastes from water and restore the water to a condition safe for human consumption.

A high school education is required to work as a wastewater-treatment-plant operator. There are also some two-year programs leading to an associate degree in wastewater technology.

For more information write to the Water Pollution Control Federation, 2626 Pennsylvania Ave., NW, Washington, DC 20037.

Park Ranger

Park rangers enforce the laws and regulations in national, state, and county parks. They are responsible for protecting the park's natural resources and animal and plant life. In addition, rangers inform, guide, and ensure the safety of park visitors.

To become a park ranger, it is necessary to have a Bachelor's degree in park management, forestry, or a related field. Sometimes, however, rangers substitute work experience for part of their education.

To receive information write to the National Park Service, United States Department of the Interior, Washington, DC 21240.

Biogeographer

Biogeographers study the way in which plants and animals are distributed throughout the world. By observing different species and their habitats and then recording and interpreting the data, biogeographers help us understand why organisms exist where they do. Some biogeographers also study the influence of certain human activities on plant and animal life.

Biogeographers must have a Bachelor's degree in geography and a Ph.D. in biogeography. An interest in botany, zoology, and meteorology is also important.

For information write to the Association of American Geographers, Biogeography Specialty Group, 1710 16th St., NW, Washington, DC 20009.

HOW TO FOLLOW UP ON A JOB INTERVIEW

After you have had a job interview, you may have to wait several weeks to hear the results. During that period, however, you should send a letter to the interviewer thanking him or her for the time and consideration. You can also call the person to show your interest in working for that company and to provide any additional information that might be needed.

If you do not get the job that you interviewed for, ask the interviewer for comments or suggestions on how to improve your interviewing skills. Most employers are willing to discuss the interview with you and explain their impressions so that you can be better prepared for your next interview.

FROM THE AUTHORS

As a biologist, I've been lucky enough to travel around the world. I have seen coral reefs in the South Pacific. I have hiked across deserts in Israel. And I have climbed through forests in the mountains of Central America and India. I have worked long hours, studying plants and animals. But I have also sat quietly, drinking in the splendor of a sparkling dawn or a flaming sunset. And I have often taken a few moments to give thanks, in my own way, for the natural beauty that surrounds us.

Yet with all my traveling, one of my favorite places is a wildlife refuge only an hour's drive from my home. I go there when I'm happy. I go there when I'm sad. I go there whenever I have problems to think about or joyful things to celebrate.

This weekend I plan to visit that refuge and wander along its nature trails. I have been there at every season and at every time of day, so I know much of what I'll see. It is autumn, so ripening grasses on the marsh will look like a swirling golden sea in the afternoon sun. Maple trees will be dressing up in red and orange. Flocks of geese will drop in on their long trip south for the winter. Then, in a chorus of honks and squawks, they'll take wing to fly in formation across the sky.

But I also know that there will be something new, something different, to discover. A rare bird, perhaps. A white mushroom, glistening after a rain. Or a flower I've never seen in bloom. That's the way wild places are.

Because I've just finished writing these chapters, I'll be thinking about you—the young people who will inherit the world we older folks have prepared for you. The wildlife refuge I love so much exists thanks to the wisdom of people my parents' age. They realized that such places are important to our society and to our souls. They knew that in order to be sure we will always have wild places, we must protect them from people who are not so wise. I hope that enough people in my generation have the wisdom to protect the health of our planet for you and your children. And I hope that you, too, in your time will be wise enough to care for the living planet that shelters and protects us all.

For Further Reading

If you have an interest in a specific area of biology or simply want to know more about the topics you are studying, one of the following books may open the door to an exciting learning adventure.

CHAPTER 1 **The Nature of Science**

Kramer, Stephen P. *How to Think Like a Scientist: Answering Questions by the Scientific Method.* T.Y. Crowell, 1987.

Mannoia, V. James. *What Is Science? An Introduction to the Structure and Methodology of Science.* University Press of America, 1980.

Medawar, P.B. *Advice to a Young Scientist.* Harper, 1984.

Moravcsik, M.J. *How to Grow Science.* Universe Books, 1980.

Morrison, Philip and Phylis. *The Ring of Truth: An Inquiry into How We Know What We Know.* Random, 1987.

CHAPTER 2 **Biology as a Science**

Campbell, P.N., ed. *Biology in Profile: An Introduction to the Many Branches of Biology.* Pergamon, 1980.

Ford, Brian J. *Single Lens: The Story of the Simple Microscope.* Harper & Row, 1985.

Grave, Eric V. *Discover the Invisible: A Naturalist's Guide to Using the Microscope.* Prentice-Hall, 1984.

Johnson, Gaylord, and Maurice Bleifield. *Hunting with the Microscope*, 3rd ed. Arco, 1980.

Smith, John Maynard. *The Problems of Biology.* Oxford University Press, 1986.

CHAPTER 3 **Introduction to Chemistry**

Asimov, Isaac. *Asimov on Chemistry.* Doubleday, 1974.

Baker, J.J., and G.E. Allen. *Matter, Energy and Life: An Introduction to Chemical Concepts*, 4th ed. Addison-Wesley, 1981.

Brady, J.E., and G.E. Humiston. *General Chemistry: Principles and Structures*, 2nd ed. Wiley, 1980.

Bruckman, H. J., and A. Cruickshanks. *Understanding Chemistry.* Wiley, 1988.

Puddephatt, R.J., and P.K. Monaghan. *The Periodic Table of Elements.* 2nd ed. Oxford University Press, 1986.

CHAPTER 4 **The Chemical Basis of Life**

Berger, Jim. *Clear and Simple Chemistry.* Simon and Schuster, 1986.

Berman, W. *Beginning Biochemistry,* rev. ed. Arco, 1980.

Boikess, R.S. *Chemistry for Biologists.* Carolina Biology Reader. Carolina Biological Supply Co., 1987.

Breslow, Ronald. *Enzymes.* Carolina Biology Reader. Carolina Biological Supply Co., 1986.

Carroll, Harvey F. *Preview of General Chemistry.* Wiley, 1988.

Jenson, William B. *The Lewis Acid-Base Concepts: An Overview.* Wiley, 1980.

CHAPTER 5 **Cell Structure and Function**

Berns, M.W. *Cells.* Holt, Rinehart and Winston, 1977.

De Duve, Christian. *A Guided Tour of the Living Cell.* W.H. Freeman, 1985.

Moner, John. *The Animal Cell.* Carolina Biology Reader. Carolina Biological Supply Co., 1987.

Nachmias, Vivianne T. *Microfilaments.* Carolina Biology Reader. Carolina Biological Supply Co., 1984.

Sheeler, P., and D.E. Bianchi. *Cell Biology: Structure, Biochemistry, and Function.* Wiley, 1983.

CHAPTER 6 **Cell Energy: Photosynthesis and Respiration**

Amesz, J. *Photosynthesis.* Elsevier, 1987.

Foyer, Christine H. *Photosynthesis.* Wiley, 1984.

Miller, Kenneth. *Energy and Life.* Carolina Biology Reader. Carolina Biological Supply Co., 1988.

Nakatani, Herbert Y. *Photosynthesis.* Carolina Biology Reader. Carolina Biological Supply Co., 1988.

CHAPTER 7 **Nucleic Acids and Protein Synthesis**

Asimov, Isaac. *How Did We Find Out About DNA?* Walker, 1985.

Dickerson, R., and I. Geis. *The Structure and Action of Proteins,* 2nd ed. W.A. Benjamin, 1985.

Gribbon, John. *In Search of the Double Helix.* Bantam, 1987.

Rosenfield, Israel, Edward Ziff, and Borin Van Loon. *DNA for Beginners.* Writers and Readers, 1983.

CHAPTER 8 **Cell Growth and Division**

Baserga, Renato. *The Biology of Cell Reproduction.* Harvard University Press, 1985.

Becker, Wayne M. *The World of the Cell.* Benjamin-Cummings, 1986.

John, B., and K.R. Lewis. *Somatic Cell Division,* rev. Carolina Biology Reader. Carolina Biological Supply Co., 1980.

Kornberg, Warren, ed. National Science Foundation Staff. *DNA: The Master Molecule.* Avery Pub., 1982.

Zimmerman, A.M., and A. Forer, eds. *Mitosis/Cytokinesis.* Academic Press, 1981.

CHAPTER 9 *Introduction to Genetics*

Fincham, John R.S. *Genetics.* Jones and Bartlett, 1983.

Gerbi, Susan A. *From Genes to Proteins.* Carolina Biology Reader. Carolina Biological Supply Co., 1987.

John, Bernard, and Kenneth Lewis. *The Meiotic Mechanism,* rev. Carolina Biology Reader. Carolina Biological Supply Co., 1984.

Moens, Peter B. *Meiosis.* Academic Press, 1987.

Parker, Gary E., et al. *Mitosis and Meiosis,* 2nd ed. Longman Finan, 1979.

CHAPTER 10 *Genes and Chromosomes*

Arnold, Caroline. *Genetics: From Mendel to Gene Splicing.* Franklin Watts, 1986.

Dillon, Lawrence S. *The Gene: Its Structure, Function, and Evolution.* Plenum Pub., 1987.

Lewin, Benjamin. *Genes.* Wiley, 1987.

McCarty, Maclyn. *The Transforming Principle: Discovering That Genes Are Made of DNA.* Norton, 1986.

Snyder, Hartl F. *Basic Genetics.* Jones and Bartlett, 1987.

CHAPTER 11 *Human Heredity*

Carlson, Elof A. *Human Genetics.* Heath, 1983.

Cavalli-Sforza, L.L. *The Genetics of Human Races.* Carolina Biology Reader. Carolina Biological Supply Co., 1983.

Fox, L. Raymond, and Paul R. Elliott. *Heredity and You,* 2nd ed. Kendall-Hunt, 1983.

Gardner, Eldon J. *Human Heredity.* Wiley, 1983.

Singer, Sam. *Human Genetics: An Introduction to the Principles of Heredity.* W.H. Freeman, 1986.

Therman, E. *Human Chromosomes,* 2nd ed. Springer-Verlag, 1985.

CHAPTER 12 *Genetic Engineering*

Drlica, Karl. *Understanding DNA and Gene Cloning.* Wiley, 1984.

Lampton, Christopher. *DNA and the Creation of New Life.* Arco, 1985.

Nossal, G.J.V. *Reshaping Life. (Key Issues in Genetic Engineering).* Cambridge University Press, 1985.

Perbal, Bernard. *A Practical Guide to Molecular Cloning.* Wiley, 1988.

Sylvester, Edward, and Lynn Klotz. *The Gene Age,* rev. Scribner, 1987.

Watson, James D., and John Tooze. *The DNA Story.* W.H. Freeman, 1983.

Zimmerman, Burke K. *Biofuture: Confronting the Genetic Era.* Plenum Publishers, 1984.

CHAPTER 13 *Evolution: Evidence of Change*

Barrett, Paul H., et al., eds. *Charles Darwin's Notebooks, 1836–1844: Geology, Transmutation of Species, Metaphysical Enquiries.* Cornell University Press, 1987.

Berry, R.J., and A. Hallam, eds. *The Encyclopedia of Animal Evolution.* Facts on File, 1987.

Case, Gerald Ramon. *A Pictorial Guide to Fossils.* Van Nostrand Reinhold, 1982.

Darwin, Charles. *The Illustrated Origin of Species.* Hill and Wang, 1979.

Lambert, David, and the Diagram Group. *The Field Guide to Prehistoric Life.* Facts on File, 1985.

Steadman, David W., and Steven Zousmer. *Galapagos: Discovery on Darwin's Islands.* Smithsonian Institution Press, 1988.

Taylor, Kenneth N. *What High School Students Should Know About Evolution.* Tyndale, 1983.

CHAPTER 14 *Evolution: How Change Occurs*

Ayala, F.J. *Origin of Species.* Carolina Biology Reader. Carolina Biological Supply Co., 1983.

Eldredge, Niles, ed. *The Natural History Reader in Evolution.* Columbia University Press, 1987.

Fox, Sidney. *The Emergence of Life: Darwinian Evolution from the Inside.* Basic, 1988.

McMahon, Thomas, and John Bonner. *On Size and Life.* W.H. Freeman, 1983.

Miller, Jonathan. *Darwin for Beginners.* Pantheon, 1982.

Stebbins, G. Ledyard. *Darwin to DNA, Molecules to Humanity.* W.H. Freeman, 1982.

CHAPTER 15 *Classification Systems*

Hickman, Cleveland J., Jr., et al. *Biology of Animals,* 4th ed. Mosby, 1985.

Jones, Susan, et al. *Classification.* Sabbot-Natural History Books, 1983.

Margulis, Lynn, and Karlene Schwartz. *Five Kingdoms,* 2nd ed. W.H. Freeman, 1987.

CHAPTER 16 *The Origin of Life*

Asimov, Isaac. *Beginnings: The Story of Origins—of Mankind, Life, the Earth, the Universe.* Walker, 1987.

Bone, Q. *The Origin of Chordates,* 2nd ed. Carolina Biology Reader. Carolina Biological Supply Co., 1979.

Cairns-Smith, A.G. *Seven Clues to the Origin of Life.* Cambridge University Press, 1985.

Cattermole, Peter, and Patrick Moore. *The Story of the Earth.* Cambridge University Press, 1985.

Fisher, David E. *The Origin and Evolution of Our Own Particular Universe.* Macmillan, 1988.

Hagene, Bernard, and Charles Lenay. *The Origin of Life.* Barron, 1987.

Minelli, Giuseppe. *The Evolution of Life.* Facts on File, 1987.

Pellegrino, Charles. *Time Gate: Hurtling Backward Through Time.* TAB Books, 1985.

Woese, Carl R. *The Origin of Life.* Carolina Biology Reader. Carolina Biological Supply Co., 1984.

CHAPTER 17 *Viruses and Monerans*

Asimov, I. *How Did We Find Out About Germs?* Avon, 1981.

Eron, C. *The Virus That Ate Cannibals.* Macmillan, 1981.

Flint, S. Jane. *Viruses.* Carolina Biology Reader. Carolina Biological Supply Co., 1988.
Lappe, M. *Germs That Won't Die.* Anchor/Doubleday, 1982.
Nourse, Alan E., M.D. *Viruses.* Franklin Watts, 1983.

CHAPTER 18 *Protists*

Anderson, Dean A. *An Introduction to Microbiology.* Mosby, 1980.
Farmer, J.N. *The Protozoa.* Mosby, 1980.
Gortz, H.D., ed. *Paramecium.* Springer-Verlag, 1988.
Lee, John J., et al., eds. *The Illustrated Guide to the Protozoa.* Allen Press, 1985.
Teasdale, Jim. *Microbes.* Silver Burdett, 1985.

CHAPTER 19 *Fungi*

Arora, David. *Mushrooms Demystified.* Ten Speed Press, 1986.
Coldrey, Jennifer. *Discovering Fungi.* Bookwright, 1987.
Krieger, Louis C.C. *The Mushroom Handbook.* Dover, 1967.
Miller, Orson, and Hope Miller. *Mushrooms in Color.* Elsevier-Dutton, 1980.
Moore-Landecker, Elizabeth. *Fundamentals of Fungi,* 2nd ed. Prentice-Hall, 1982.
Pearson, Lorentz. *The Mushroom Manual.* Naturegraph, 1987.
Savonius, Moira. *All Color Book of Mushrooms and Fungi.* Octopus Books Limited, 1973.
Smith, Alexander, and Nancy S. Weber. *The Mushroom Hunter's Field Guide.* University of Michigan Press, 1980.

CHAPTER 20 *Multicellular Algae*

Bold, Harold C., and Michael J. Wynne. *Introduction to the Algae,* 2nd ed. Prentice-Hall, 1985.
Chapman, A.R.O. *Biology of Seaweeds: Levels of Organization.* University Park Press, 1979.
Humm, Harold J., and Susanne Wicks. *Introduction and Guide to the Marine Blue-green algae.* Wiley, 1980.
Kavaler, Lucy. *Green Magic; Algae Rediscovered.* Harper & Row Junior Books, 1983.
Pickett-Heaps, Jeremy. *New Light on the Green Algae.* Carolina Biology Reader. Carolina Biological Supply Co., 1982.
Vinyard, William. *Diatoms of North America.* Mad River, 1979.

CHAPTER 21 *Mosses and Ferns*

Conrad, Henry S., and Paul L. Redfearn, Jr. *How to Know the Mosses and Liverworts,* 2nd ed. William C. Brown & Co., 1979.
Ferns: A Natural History. The Stephen Green Press, 1981.
Lellinger, David B. *Field Manual of the Ferns and Fern-Allies of the United States and Canada.* Smithsonian, 1985.
Streams, John, ed. *Treasures of Nature: Ferns.* Crossing Press, 1987.
Wexler, Jerome. *From Spore to Spore: Ferns and How they Grow.* Dodd, Mead, 1985.

CHAPTER 22 *Plants with Seeds*

Bryant, John A. *Seed Physiology.* David R. Murray, ed. Academic Press, 1985.
Burn, Barbara. *North American Trees.* National Audubon Society Collection. Bonanza Books, dist. by Crown Pub., 1984.
———. *North American Wildflowers.* National Audubon Society Collection. Bonanza Books, dist. by Crown Pub., 1984.
Line, Les, Ann Line, and Myron Sutton. *The Audubon Society Book of Trees.* Abrams, 1981.
Meeuse, B.J.D. *Pollination.* Carolina Biology Reader. Carolina Biological Supply Co., 1984.

CHAPTER 23 *Roots, Stems, and Leaves*

Esau, K. *Plant Anatomy,* 3rd ed. Wiley, 1988.
Grimn-Lacy, Janice, and Peter Kaufman. *Botany Illustrated.* Van Nostrand Reinhold, 1984.
Jensen, W.A., and F.B. Salisbury. *Botany,* 2nd ed. Wadsworth, 1984.
Prance, Ghillean Tulmie. *Leaves.* Crown, 1985.
Raven, Peter, et al. *Biology of Plants,* 4th ed. Worth, 1986.
Stern, Kingsley R. *Introductory Plant Biology,* 4th ed. William C. Brown & Co., 1988.

CHAPTER 24 *Plant Growth and Development*

Art, Henry. *A Garden of Wildflowers: 101 Species and How to Grow Them.* Storey Communications, Inc., 1986.
Bender, Lionel. *Plants.* Franklin Watts Ltd., ed. Watts, 1988.
Gibbons, Bob. *How Flowers Work: A Guide to Plant Biology.* Blandford Press, 1984.
Hendricks, Sterling B. *Phytochrome and Plant Growth.* Carolina Biology Reader. Carolina Biological Supply Co., 1980.
Wareing, P.F., and I.D.J. Phillips. *Growth and Differentiation in Plants,* 3rd ed. Pergamon, 1981.
Wilkins, Malcolm. *Plantwatching: How Plants Remember, Tell Time, Form Partnerships, and More.* Facts on File, 1988.

CHAPTER 25 *Reproduction in Seed Plants*

Buckles, Mary Parker. *The Flowers Around Us.* University of Missouri Press, 1985
Hartman, Hudson T., and Dale E. Kester. *Plant Propagation.* Prentice-Hall, Inc., 1983.
Richards, A.J. *Plant Breeding Systems in Seed Plants.* Unwin Hyman, 1986.
Roland, J.C., and F. Roland. *Atlas of Flowering Plant Structure.* Longman, 1981
Stone, Doris. *The Lives of Plants.* Scribner, 1983.

CHAPTER 26 Sponges, Cnidarians, and Unsegmented Worms

Evslin, Bernard. *Thy Hydra (Monsters of Mythology).* Chelsea House, 1989.

Greenberg, Idan. *Field Guide to Marine Invertebrates.* Seahawk Press, 1980.

Simpson, T.L. *The Cell Biology of Sponges.* Springer-Verlag, 1984.

Walls, J.G., ed. *Encyclopedia of Marine Invertebrates.* TFH Publications, 1982.

CHAPTER 27 Mollusks and Annelids

Carstarphen, Dee. *The Conch Book.* Banyan Books, 1981.

Cousteau, Jacques-Yves, and Philippe Diole. *Octopus and Squid: The Soft Intelligence.* Doubleday, 1973.

Lee, Kenneth F. *Earthworms: Their Ecology Relationships with Soils and Land Use.* Academic Press, 1985.

Roberts, Mervin F. *Pearlmakers: The Tidemarsh Guide to Clams, Oysters, Mussels, and Scallops.* Roberts M.F. Enterprises, 1984.

Russell-Hunter, W.D., ed. *Mollusca: Ecology,* Vol 6. Academic Press, 1983.

CHAPTER 28 Arthropods

Carolina Arthropods Manual. Carolina Biological Supply Co., 1982.

Crompton, John. *Ways of the Ant.* Nick Lyons, 1988.

Evans, Howard. *The Pleasures of Entomology: Portraits of Insects and the People Who Study Them.* Smithsonian, 1985.

Headstrom, Richard. *All About Lobsters, Crabs, Shrimps, and Their Relatives.* Dover, 1985.

Nardi, James B. *Close Encounters with Insects and Spiders.* Iowa State University Press, 1988.

Pringle, J.W.S. *Insect Flight,* 2nd ed. Carolina Biology Reader. Carolina Biological Supply Co., 1983.

Saintsing, David. *The World of Butterflies.* Gareth Stevens, 1987.

Taylor, Herb. *The Lobster: Its Life Cycle.* Sterling Publishing Co., Inc., 1984.

Whalley, Paul and Mary. *The Butterfly in the Garden.* Gareth Stevens, 1987.

CHAPTER 29 Echinoderms and Invertebrate Chordates

Lawrence, John. *A Functional Biology of Echinoderms.* Johns Hopkins, 1987.

Lechman, H. Eugene. *Chordate Development,* 2nd ed. Hunter Textbooks, 1983.

Sumich, James L. *An Introduction to the Biology of Marine Life,* 3rd ed. William C. Brown & Co., 1984.

CHAPTER 30 Comparing Invertebrates

Barnes, R.D. *Invertebrate Zoology,* 5th ed. Saunders College Publishing, 1987.

Barth, Robert H., and Broshears, Robert. *The Invertebrate World.* Saunders College Publishing, 1982.

Buchsbaum, Mildred, et al. *Living Invertebrates.* Blackwell Publications, 1987.

Lutz, Paul E. *Invertebrate Zoology.* Benjamin-Cummings, 1985.

Pecknik, Jan A. *Biology of the Invertebrates.* Wadsworth Publications, 1985.

CHAPTER 31 Fishes and Amphibians

Binder, Lionel. *Fish to Reptiles.* Gloucester, 1988.

Dickerson, Mary C. *The Frog Book.* Dover, 1969.

Gibbons, Whit. *Their Blood Runs Cold: Adventures with Reptiles and Amphibians.* University of Alabama Press, 1985.

Mattison, Christopher. *Frogs & Toads of the World.* Facts on File, 1987.

Minelli, Giuseppe. *Amphibians.* Facts on File, 1987.

Nicholls, Richard E. *The Book of Turtles.* Running Press, 1977.

Pyrom, Jay. *Frogs and Toads: A Complete Introduction.* TFH Publications, 1987.

Shoemaker, Hurst, and Herbert S. Zim. *Fishes.* Western Pub., 1987.

CHAPTER 32 Reptiles and Birds

Anderson, Robert. *Snakes.* TFH Publications, 1987.

Burton, Robert. *Bird Behavior.* Knopf, 1985.

Halliday, Dr. Tim, and Dr. Kraig Adler, eds. *Encyclopedia of Reptiles and Amphibians.* Facts on File, 1986.

Mehrtens, John M. *Living Snakes of the World in Color.* Sterling Publishing Co., 1987.

Minelli, Giuseppe. *Reptiles.* Facts on File, 1987.

Sparks, John, and Tony Soper. *Penguins.* Facts on File, 1987.

Terres, John K. *Songbirds in Your Garden.* Harper & Row, 1987.

CHAPTER 33 Mammals

Alden, Peter. *Peterson's First Guide to Mammals.* Houghton Mifflin, 1987.

Bender, Lionel. *Birds and Mammals.* Watts, 1988.

Ferry, G., ed. *The Understanding of Animals.* Basil Blackwell, 1984.

Gallant, Roy A. *The Rise of Mammals.* Franklin Watts, 1986.

Leatherwood, Stephen, and Randall R. Reeves. *The Sierra Club Handbook of Whales and Dolphins.* Sierra Club Books, 1983.

MacDonald, D., ed. *The Encyclopedia of Mammals.* Facts on File, 1984.

Minelli, Giuseppe. *Mammals.* Facts on File, 1988.

Ricciuti, Edward. *Older Than the Dinosaurs: The Origin and Rise of the Mammals.* Harper & Row Junior Books, 1980.

Savage, R.J.G. *Mammal Evolution: An Illustrated Guide.* Facts on File, 1986.
Voelker, William. *The Natural History of Living Mammals.* Plexus Publishing, Inc., 1986.
Walker, Ernest P. *Walker's Mammals of the World* (2 vols.), 4th ed. Johns Hopkins, 1983.

CHAPTER 34 *Humans*

Asimov, Isaac. *Beginnings.* Walker and Co., 1987.
Day, M.H. *Fossil History of Man,* rev. ed. Carolina Biology Reader. Carolina Biological Supply Co., 1984.
Fossey, Dian. *Gorillas in the Mist.* Houghton Mifflin, 1983.
Goodall, Jane. *In the Shadow of Man.* Houghton Mifflin, 1983.
Johanson, Donald C., and Maitland A. Edey. *Lucy: The Beginnings of Human Kind.* Warner Books, 1982.
Kornberg, W., ed. National Science Foundation Staff. *Human Evolution.* Avery Pub. Group, Inc., 1982.
Leakey, Richard E. *The Making of Mankind.* E.P. Dutton, 1981.

CHAPTER 35 *Animal Behavior*

Christie, David, et al. *Remarkable Animals.* Sterling Publishing Co. Published by Guinness Superlatives, 1987.
Evans, Peter. *Ourselves and Other Animals.* Pantheon Books, 1987.
Penny, Malcolm. *Animal Homes.* Bookwright, 1987.
———. *Animals and Their Young.* Bookwright, 1987.
———. *Animal Migration.* Bookwright,1987.
Porter, Keith. *How Animals Behave.* Facts on File, 1987.
Seddon, Tony. *Animal Eyes.* Facts on File, 1988.
Tudge, Colin. *The Environment of Life.* Oxford University Press, 1987.

CHAPTER 36 *Comparing Vertebrates*

Colbert, Edwin H. *Evolution of the Vertebrates: A History of the Backboned Animals Through Time,* 3rd ed. Wiley, 1980.
Martin, Domm D. *Anatomy of Vertebrates.* William C. Brown, Inc., 1988.
Pough, F. Harvey, et al. *Vertebrate Life,* 3rd ed. Macmillan, 1989.
Rogers, E. *Looking at Vertebrates: A Practical Guide to Vertebrate Adaptations.* Wiley, 1986.
Romer, Alfred S., and Thomas S. Parsons. *The Vertebrate Body,* 6th ed. Saunders College Publishing, 1986.

CHAPTER 37 *Nervous System*

Bodanis, David. *The Body Book: A Fantastic Voyage to the World Within.* Little, 1984.
Kee, Leong S. *An Introduction to the Human Nervous System.* Ohio University Press, 1987.
Nilson, Lennart. *Behold Man.* Little, Brown, 1973.
Ralston, Diane D., and Henry J. Ralston III. *The Nerve Cell.* Carolina Biology Reader. Carolina Biological Supply Co., 1988.
Restak, Richard, M.D. *The Brain.* Bantam, 1985.
Stafford, Patricia. *Your Two Brains.* Atheneum, 1986.

CHAPTER 38 *Skeletal, Muscular, and Integumentary Systems*

Buller, A.J., and N.P. Buller. *Contractile Behavior of Mammalian Skeletal Muscle,* 2nd ed. Carolina Biology Reader. Carolina Biological Supply Co., 1980.
Harrington, W.F. *Muscle Contraction.* Carolina Biology Reader. Carolina Biological Supply Co., 1981.
Pritchard, J.J. *Bones,* 2nd ed. Carolina Biology Reader. Carolina Biological Supply Co., 1979.
Steele, D. Gentry, and Claude A. Bramblett. *The Anatomy and Biology of the Human Skeleton.* Texas A&M University Press, 1988.
Tiger, Steven. *Arthritis.* Messner, 1986.

CHAPTER 39 *Nutrition and Digestion*

Bolt, Robert J., et al. *The Digestive System.* Wiley, 1983.
Calloway, D.H., and K.O. Carpenter. *Nutrition and Health.* Saunders College Publishing, 1981.
Kirschmann, John D. *Nutrition Almanac,* rev. ed. McGraw-Hill, 1985.
Magee, D.F., and A.F. Dalley. *Digestion and the Structure and Function of the Gut.* S. Karger, 1986.
Sproule, Anna. *Bodywatch: Know Your Insides.* Facts on File, 1987.

CHAPTER 40 *Respiratory System*

Burkart, John, and Loretta Chiarenza. *Human Biology.* Avery Pub. Group, Inc., 1984.
Kittredge, Mary. *The Respiration System.* Chelsea House, 1989.
Nicholls, P. *The Biology of Oxygen.* Carolina Biology Reader. Carolina Biological Supply Co., 1982.
Sebel, Dr. Peter, et al. *The Human Body: Respiration: The Breath of Life.* Torstar Books, 1985.
Whipp, B.J., ed. *The Control of Breathing in Man.* University of Pennsylvania Press, 1987.

CHAPTER 41 *Circulatory and Excretory Systems*

Asimov, Isaac. *How Did We Find Out About Blood?* Walker and Co., 1986.
Guiness, Alma E., ed. *ABC's of the Human Body.* Random, 1987.
Moffat. *The Control of Water Balance by the Kidney,* 2nd ed. Carolina Biology Reader. Carolina Biological Supply Co., 1978.
Neil, Eric. *The Human Circulation.* Carolina Biology Reader. Carolina Biological Supply Co., 1979.
Nora, James J. *The Whole Heart Book.* Holt, Rinehart, and Winston, 1980.
Ross, Dennis W. *Blood.* Carolina Biology Reader. Carolina Biological Supply Co., 1988.
Tiger, Steven. *Heart Disease.* Messner, 1986.

CHAPTER 42 *Endocrine System*

Blake, Charles A. *The Pituitary Gland.* Carolina Biology Reader. Carolina Biological Supply Co., 1984.

Bloom, A. *Diabetes Explained.* Kluwer-Boston, Inc., 1982.

Crapo, Lawrence. *Hormones: The Messengers of Life.* W.H. Freeman, 1985.

Elting, Mary. *The Macmillan Book of the Human Body.* Aladdin (Macmillan), 1986.

Villee, Claude A. *Human Hormones.* Carolina Biology Reader. Carolina Biological Supply Co., 1987.

CHAPTER 43 *Reproduction and Development*

Parker, Gary. *Life Before Birth.* Master Books, 1987.

Smith, Anthony. *The Body,* rev. Viking, 1986.

CHAPTER 44 *Human Diseases*

Aaseng, Nathan. *The Disease Fighters: The Nobel Prize in Medicine.* Lerner, 1987.

Anderson, Madelyn Klein. *Environmental Diseases.* Watts, 1987.

Eagles, Douglas A. *Nutritional Diseases.* Watts, 1987.

Hughes, Barbara. *Drug-Related Diseases.* Watts, 1987.

Landau, Elaine. *Alzheimer's Disease.* Watts, 1987.

Metos, Thomas H. *Communicable Diseases.* Watts, 1987.

CHAPTER 45 *Immune System*

Arehart-Treichel, Joan. *Immunity: How Our Bodies Resist Disease.* Holiday House, 1976.

Desowitz, Robert S. *A Thorn in the Starfish: The Immune System and How It Works.* Norton, 1987.

Gershwin, M. Eric, et al. *Nutrition and Immunity.* Academic Press, 1985.

Greenberg, Sylvia. *Immunity and Survival: The Immune System at Work.* Human Sciences Press, 1989.

Nilsson, Lennart, with Jan Lindberg. *The Body Victorious.* Delacorte Press, 1987.

Vidic, Branislav, and Faustino R. Suarez. *Photographic Atlas of the Human Body.* Mosby, 1984.

CHAPTER 46 *Drugs, Alcohol, and Tobacco*

Alcohol: How it Affects Your Health. Do It Now Foundation, 1988.

Berger, Gilda. *Crack: The New Drug Epidemic.* Watts, 1987.

Chomet, Julian. *Cocaine and Crack.* Watts, 1987.

Cumming, G., and G. Bonsignore, eds. *Smoking and the Lung.* Plenum Publishers, 1985.

Jones, Helen C., and Paul W. Covinger. *The Marijuana Question and Science's Search for an Answer.* Dodd, Mead, 1985.

Stepney, Rob. *Alcohol.* Watts, 1987.

CHAPTER 47 *The Biosphere*

Bowen, E. *Grasslands and Tundra.* Silver, 1985.

Bramwell, Martyn. *Deserts.* Watts, 1988.

Durrell, Lee. *State of the Ark.* Doubleday, 1986.

Healy, Timothy, and Paul Houle. *Energy and Society.* Boyd and Fraser, 1983.

Perry, Donald. *Life Above the Forest Floor: A Biologist Explores a Strange and Hidden Treetop World.* Simon and Schuster, 1986.

Sagan, Dorion, and Lynn Margulis. *Biospheres: From Earth to Space.* Enslow Pubs., 1989.

CHAPTER 48 *Populations and Communities*

Begon, Michael, et al. *Ecology: Individuals, Populations and Communities.* Sinauer Associates, 1986.

Clapham, W.B., Jr. *Natural Ecosystems,* 2nd ed. Macmillan, 1983.

Moore, Peter D., ed. *The Encyclopedia of Animal Ecology.* Facts on File, 1987.

Smith, Howard E., Jr. *Small Worlds: Communities of Living Things.* Macmillan, 1987.

Van Lawick, Hugo. *Among Predators and Prey.* Sierra Club Books, 1986.

CHAPTER 49 *People and the Biosphere*

Albright, Horace M., Russell E. Dickerson, and William Penn Mott, Jr. *National Park Service: The Story Behind the Scenery.* KC Publications, 1987.

Fine, John Christopher. *Oceans in Peril.* Atheneum, 1987.

Lo Pinto, Richard W. *Pollution.* Carolina Biology Reader. Carolina Biological Supply Co., 1987.

Miller, Christina G., and Louise A. Berry. *Acid Rain.* Messner, 1987.

Milne, Louis, and Margery Milne. *A Shovelful of Earth.* Holt, 1987.

Pitt, David C., ed. *The Future of the Environment.* Chapman & Hall, 1988.

Pringle, Laurence. *Restoring Our Earth.* Enslow Pubs., 1987.

Stanley, Steven M. *Extinction.* Scientific American, 1987.

APPENDIX A The Metric System

The Metric System of measurement is used by scientists throughout the world. It is based on units of ten. Each unit is ten times larger or ten times smaller than the next unit. The most commonly used units of the metric system are given below. After you have finished reading about the metric system, try to put it to use. How tall are you in meters? What is your mass? What is your normal body temperature in degrees Celsius?

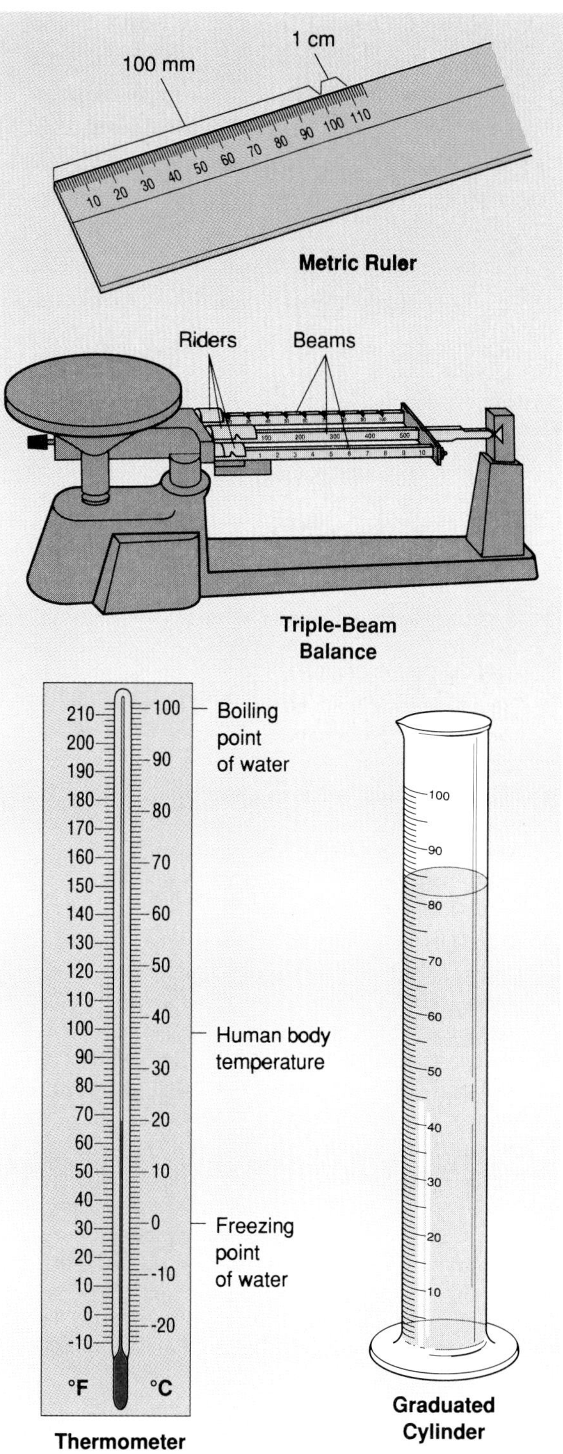

COMMONLY USED METRIC UNITS

Length The distance from one point to another

meter(m) A meter is slightly longer than a yard.
1 meter = 1000 millimeters (mm)
1 meter = 100 centimeters (cm)
1000 meters = 1 kilometer (km)

Volume The amount of space an object takes up

liter (L) A liter is slightly more than a quart.
1 liter = 1000 milliliters (mL)

Mass The amount of matter in an object

gram (g) A gram has a mass equal to about one paper clip.
1000 grams = 1 kilogram (kg)

Temperature The measure of hotness or coldness

degrees Celsius (°C) 0°C = freezing point of water
100°C = boiling point of water

METRIC — ENGLISH EQUIVALENTS

2.54 centimeters (cm) = 1 inch (in.)
1 meter (m) = 39.37 inches (in.)
1 kilometer (km) = 0.62 miles (mi)
1 liter (L) = 1.06 quarts (qt)
250 milliliters (mL) = 1 cup (c)
1 kilogram (kg) = 2.2 pounds (lb)
28.3 grams (g) = 1 ounce (oz)
°C = 5/9 x (°F−32)

APPENDIX B Science Safety Rules

One of the first things a scientist learns is that working in the laboratory can be an exciting experience. But the laboratory can also be quite dangerous if proper safety rules are not followed at all times. To prepare yourself for a safe year in the laboratory, read over the following safety rules. Then read them a second time. Make sure you understand each rule. If you do not, ask your teacher to explain any rules you don't understand.

DRESS CODE

1. Many materials in the laboratory can cause eye injury. To protect yourself from possible injury, wear safety goggles whenever you are working with chemicals, burners, or any substance that might get into your eyes. Never wear contact lenses in the laboratory.
2. Wear a laboratory apron or coat whenever you are working with chemicals or heated substances.
3. Tie back long hair to keep it away from any chemicals, burners and candles, or other laboratory equipment.
4. Before working in the laboratory, remove or tie back any article of clothing or jewelry that can hang down and touch chemicals and flames.

GENERAL SAFETY RULES

5. Read all directions for an experiment several times. Follow the directions exactly as they are written. If you are in doubt about any part of the experiment, ask your teacher for assistance.
6. Never perform investigations that are not authorized by your teacher. Obtain permission before "experimenting" on your own.
7. Never handle any equipment unless you have specific permission.
8. Take extreme care not to spill any material in the laboratory. If spills occur, ask your teacher immediately about the proper cleanup procedure. Never simply pour chemicals or other substances into the sink or trash container.
9. Never eat in the laboratory.

FIRST AID

10. Report all accidents, no matter how minor, to your teacher immediately.
11. Learn what to do in case of specific accidents, such as getting acid in your eyes or on your skin. (Rinse acids on your body with lots of water.)
12. Be aware of the location of the first-aid kit. Your teacher should administer any required first aid due to injury. Or your teacher may send you to the school nurse or call a physician.
13. Know where and how to report an accident or fire. Find out the location of the fire extinguisher, phone, and fire alarm. Keep a list of important phone numbers such as the fire department and school nurse near the phone. Report any fires to your teacher at once.

HEATING AND FIRE SAFETY

14. Again, never use a heat source such as a candle or burner without wearing safety goggles.
15. Never heat a chemical you are not instructed to heat. A chemicalthat is harmless when cool can be dangerous when heated.
16. Maintain a clean work area and keep all materials away from flames.
17. Never reach across a flame.
18. Make sure you know how to light a Bunsen burner. (Your teacher will demonstrate the proper procedure for lighting a burner.) If the flame leaps out of a burner toward you, turn the gas off immediately. Do not touch the burner. It may be hot. And never leave a lighted burner unattended!
19. When you are heating a test tube or bottle, point it away from yourself and others. Chemicals can splash or boil out of a heated test tube.
20. Never heat a liquid in a closed container. The expanding gases produced may blow the container apart, causing it to injure yourself or others.
21. Never pick up a container that has been heated without first holding the back of your hand near it. If you can feel the heat on the back of your hand, the container may be too hot to handle. Use a clamp or tongs when handling hot containers.

USING CHEMICALS SAFELY

22. Never mix chemicals for the "fun of it." You might produce a dangerous, possibly explosive substance.
23. Never touch, taste, or smell a chemical that you do not know for a fact is harmless. Many chemicals are poisonous. If you are instructed to note the fumes in an experiment, gently wave your hand over the opening of a container and direct the fumes toward your nose. Do not inhale the fumes directly from the container.

24. Use only those chemicals needed in the investigation. Keep all lids closed when a chemical is not being used. Notify your teacher whenever chemicals are spilled.
25. Dispose of all chemicals as instructed by your teacher. To avoid contamination, never return chemicals to their original containers.
26. Be extra careful when working with acids or bases. Pour such chemicals over the sink, not over your workbench.
27. When diluting an acid, pour the acid into water. Never pour water into the acid.
28. If any acids get on your skin or clothing, rinse them with water. Immediately notify your teacher of any acid spill.

USING GLASSWARE SAFELY

29. Never force glass tubing into a rubber stopper. A turning motion and lubricant will be helpful when inserting glass tubing into rubber stoppers or rubber tubing. Your teacher will demonstrate the proper way to insert glass tubing.
30. Never heat glassware that is not thoroughly dry. Use a wire screen to protect glassware from any flame.
31. Keep in mind that hot glassware will not appear hot. Never pick up glassware without first checking to see if it is hot.
32. If you are instructed to cut glass tubing, fire-polish the ends immediately to remove sharp edges.
33. Never use broken or chipped glassware. If glassware breaks, notify your teacher and dispose of the glassware in the proper trash container.
34. Never eat or drink from laboratory glassware. Thoroughly clean glassware before putting it away.

USING SHARP INSTRUMENTS

35. Handle scalpels or razor blades with extreme care. Never cut material toward you; cut away from you.
36. Notify your teacher immediately if you cut yourself when in the laboratory.

ANIMAL SAFETY

37. No experiments that will cause pain, discomfort, or harm to mammals, birds, reptiles, fishes, and amphibians should be done in the classroom or at home.
38. Animals should be handled only if necessary. If an animal is excited or frightened, pregnant, feeding, or with its young, special handling is required.
39. Your teacher will instruct you as to how to handle each animal species that may be brought into the classroom.
40. Clean your hands thoroughly after handling animals or the cage containing animals.

END-OF-EXPERIMENT RULES

41. When an experiment is completed, clean up your work area and return all equipment to its proper place.
42. Wash your hands before and after every experiment.
43. Turn off all burners before leaving the laboratory. Check that the gas line leading to the burner is off as well.

APPENDIX C Care and Use of the Microscope

THE COMPOUND MICROSCOPE

One of the most essential tools in the study of biology is the microscope. With the help of different types of microscopes, biologists have developed detailed concepts of cell structure and function. The type of microscope used in most biology classes is the compound microscope. It contains a combination of lenses and can magnify objects normally unseen with the unaided eye.

The eyepiece lens is located in the top portion of the microscope. This lens usually has a magnification of 10 X. A compound microscope usually has two other interchangeable lenses. These lenses, called objective lenses, are at the bottom of the body tube on the revolving nosepiece. By revolving the nosepiece, either of the objectives can be brought into direct line with the body of the tube.

The shorter objective is of low power in its magnification, usually 10 X. The longer one is of high power, usually 40 X or 43 X. The magnification is always marked on the objective. To determine the total magnification of a microscope, multiply the magnifying power of the eyepiece by the magnifying power of the objective being used. For example, the eyepiece magnifying power, 10 X, multiplied by the low-power objective, 10 X, equals 100 X. The total magnification is 100 X.

A microscope also produces clear contrasts to enable the viewer to distinguish between objects that lie very close together. Under a microscope the detail of objects is very sharp. The ability of a microscope to produce contrast and detail is called resolution, or resolving power. Although microscopes can have the same magnifying power, they can differ in resolving power.

Learning the name, function, and location of each of the microscope's parts is necessary for proper use. Use the following procedures when working with the microscope.

1. Remove the microscope from its storage area by placing one hand beneath the base and grasping the arm of the microscope with the other hand.
2. Gently place the microscope on the lab table with the arm facing you. The microscope's base should be resting evenly on the table, approximately 10 centimeters from the table's edge.
3. Raise the body tube by turning the coarse adjustment knob until the objective lens is about 2 centimeters above the opening of the stage.
4. Revolve the nosepiece so that the low-power objective (10 X) is directly in line with the body tube. A click indicates that the lens is in line with the opening of the stage.
5. Look through the eyepiece and switch on the lamp or adjust the mirror so that a circle of light can be seen. This is the field of view. Moving the lever of the diaphragm permits a greater or smaller amount of light to come through the opening of the stage.

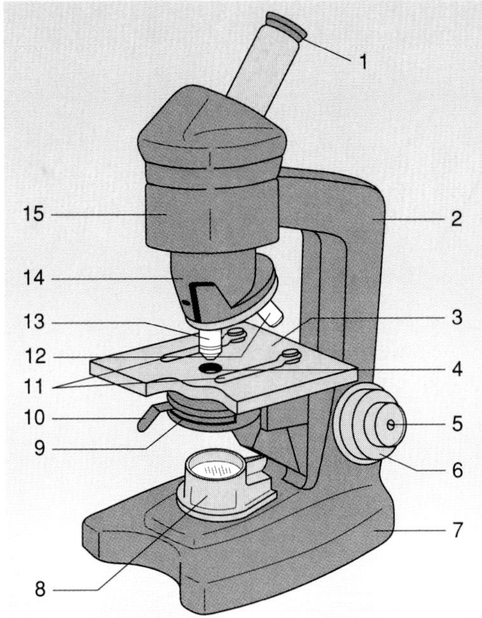

Microscope Parts and Their Function

1. **Eyepiece** Contains a magnifying lens
2. **Arm** Supports the body tube
3. **Stage** Supports the slide being observed
4. **Opening of the stage** Permits light to travel up to the eyepiece
5. **Fine adjustment** Moves the body tube slightly to sharpen the focus
6. **Coarse adjustment** Moves the body tube up and down for focusing
7. **Base** Supports the microscope
8. **Illuminator** Produces light or reflects light up through the body tube
9. **Diaphragm** Regulates the amount of light entering the body tube
10. **Diaphragm lever** Opens and closes the diaphragm
11. **Stage clips** Hold the slide in position
12. **Low-power objective** Provides a magnification of 10X and is the shorter of the objectives
13. **High-power objective** Provides a magnification of 43X and is the longer of the objectives
14. **Revolving nosepiece** Contains the low- and high-power objectives and can be rotated to change magnification
15. **Body tube** Maintains a proper distance between the eyepiece and the objective lenses

6. Place a prepared slide on the stage. Place the specimen over the center of the opening of the stage. Fasten the stage clips to hold the slide in position.
7. Look at the microscope from the side. Carefully turn the coarse adjustment knob to lower the body tube until the low-power objective almost touches the slide or until the body tube can no longer be moved. Do not allow the objective to touch the slide.
8. Look through the eyepiece and observe the specimen. If the field of view is out of focus, use the coarse adjustment knob to raise the body tube while looking through the eyepiece. When the specimen comes into view, use the fine adjustment knob to focus the specimen. Be sure to keep both eyes open when viewing a specimen. This helps prevent eyestrain.
9. Adjust the lever of the diaphragm to allow the right amount of light to enter.
10. To view the specimen under high power (43 X), revolve the nosepiece until the high-power objective is in line with the body tube and clicks into place.
11. Look through the eyepiece and use the fine adjustment knob to bring the specimen into focus.
12. After every use remove the slide. Clean the stage of the microscope and the lenses with lens paper. Do not use other types of paper to clean the lenses, as they may scratch the lenses.

PREPARING A WET-MOUNT SLIDE

1. Obtain a clean microscope slide and a coverslip. A coverslip is very thin, permitting the objective lens to be lowered very close to the specimen.
2. Place the specimen in the middle of the microscope slide. The specimen must be thin enough for light to pass through it.
3. Using a medicine dropper, place a drop of water on the specimen.
4. Lower one edge of the coverslip so that it touches the side of the drop of water at a 45° angle. The water will spread evenly along the edge of the coverslip. Using a dissecting needle or probe, slowly lower the coverslip over the specimen and water. Try not to trap any air bubbles under the coverslip. Air bubbles interfere with the view of the specimen. If air bubbles are present, gently tap the surface of the coverslip over the air bubble with a pencil eraser.
5. Remove any excess water at the edge of the coverslip with a paper towel. If the specimen begins to dry out, add a drop of water at the edge of the coverslip.

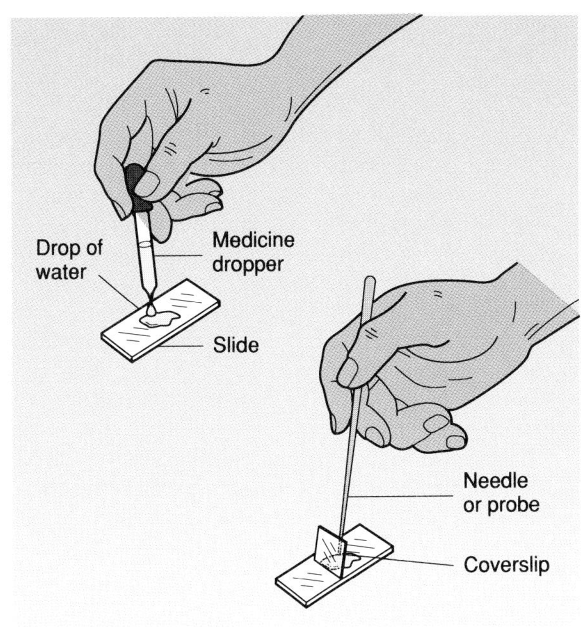

STAINING TECHNIQUES

1. Obtain a clean microscope slide and coverslip.
2. Place the specimen in the middle of the microscope slide.
3. Using a medicine dropper, place a drop of water on the specimen.
4. Place one edge of the coverslip so that it touches the side of the drop of water at a 45° angle. After the water spreads along the edge of the coverslip, use a dissecting needle or probe to lower the coverslip over the specimen.
5. Add a drop of stain at the edge of the coverslip. Using forceps, touch a small piece of lens paper or paper towel to the opposite edge of the coverslip. The paper causes the stain to be drawn under the coverslip and stain the cells. Some common stains are methylene blue, iodine, fuchsin, and Wright's.

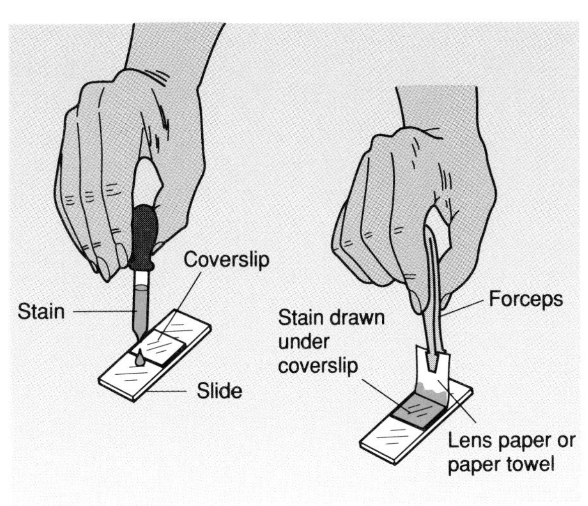

APPENDIX D The Laboratory Balance

The laboratory balance is an important tool in scientific investigations. You can use the balance to determine the mass of materials that you study or experiment with in the laboratory.

Different kinds of balances are used in the laboratory. One kind of balance is the double-pan balance. Another kind of balance is the triple-beam balance. The balance that you may use in your science class is probably similar to one of the balances illustrated in this Appendix. To use the balance properly, you should learn the name, function, and location of each part of the balance you are using.

THE DOUBLE-PAN BALANCE

The double-pan balance shown in this Appendix has two beams. Some double-pan balances have only one beam. The beams are calibrated, or marked, in grams. The upper beam is divided into 10 major units of 1 gram each. Each of these units is further divided into units of 1/10 of a gram. The lower beam is divided into 20 units, and each unit is equal to 10 grams. The lower beam can be used to find the mass of objects up to 200 grams. Each beam has a rider that is moved to the right along the beam. The rider indicates the grams used to balance the object in the left pan.

Before you begin using the balance, you should be sure that both riders are pointing to zero grams on their beams and that the pans are empty. The balance should be on a flat, level surface. The pointer should be at the zero point. If your pointer does not read zero, slowly turn the adjustment knob until it does.

The following procedure can be used to find the mass of an object with a double-pan balance:

1. Place the object whose mass is to be determined on the left pan.
2. Move the rider on the lower beam to the 10-gram notch.
3. If the pointer moves to the right of the zero point on the scale, the object has a mass less than 10 grams. Return the rider on the lower beam to zero. Slowly move the rider on the upper beam until the pointer is at zero. The reading on the beam is the mass of the object.
4. If the pointer did not move to the right of the zero, move the rider on the lower beam notch by notch until it does. Move the rider back one notch. Then move the rider on the upper beam until the pointer is at zero. The sum of the readings on both beams is the mass of the object.
5. If the two riders are moved completely to the right side of the beams and the pointer remains to the left of the zero point, the object has a mass greater than the total mass that the balance can measure.

The total mass that most double-pan balances can measure is 210 grams. If an object has a mass greater than 210 grams, return the riders to zero.

Double-Pan Balance

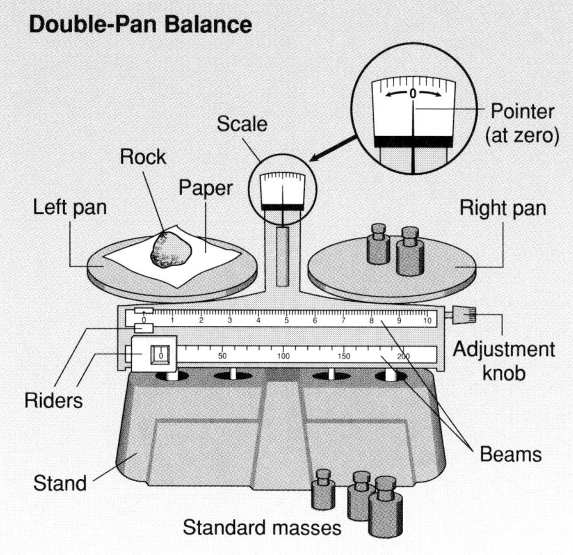

Scale Graduated instrument along which the pointer moves to show if the balance is balanced

Pointer Marker that indicates on the scale if the balance is balanced

Zero point Center line of the scale to which the pointer moves when the balance is balanced

Adjustment knob Knob used to balance the empty balance

Left pan Platform on which an object whose mass is to be determined is placed

Right pan Platform on which standard masses are placed

Beams Scales calibrated in grams

Riders Movable markers that indicate the number of grams needed to balance an object

Stand Support for the balance

The following procedure can be used to find the mass of an object greater than 210 grams.

1. Place the standard masses on the right pan one at a time, starting with the largest, until the pointer remains to the right of the zero point.
2. Remove one of the large standard masses and replace it with a smaller one. Continue replacing the standard masses with smaller ones until the pointer remains to the left of the zero point. When the pointer remains to the left of the zero point, the mass of the object on the left pan is greater than the total mass of the standard masses on the right pan.
3. Move the rider on the lower beam and then the rider on the upper beam until the pointer stops at the zero point on the scale. The mass of the object is equal to the sum of the readings on the beams plus the mass of the standard masses.

THE TRIPLE-BEAM BALANCE

The triple-beam balance is a single-pan balance with three beams calibrated in grams. The back, or 100-gram, beam is divided into 10 units of 10 grams each. The middle, or 500-gram, beam is divided into 5 units of 100 grams each. The front, or 10-gram, beam is divided into 10 major units of 1 gram each. Each of these units is further divided into units of 1/10 of a gram.

The following procedure can be used to find the mass of an object with a triple-beam balance:

1. Place the object on the pan.
2. Move the rider on the middle beam notch by notch until the horizontal pointer drops below zero. Move the rider back one notch.
3. Move the rider on the front beam notch by notch until the pointer again drops below zero. Move the rider back one notch.
4. Slowly slide the rider along the back beam until the pointer stops at the zero point.
5. The mass of the object is equal to the sum of the readings on the three beams.

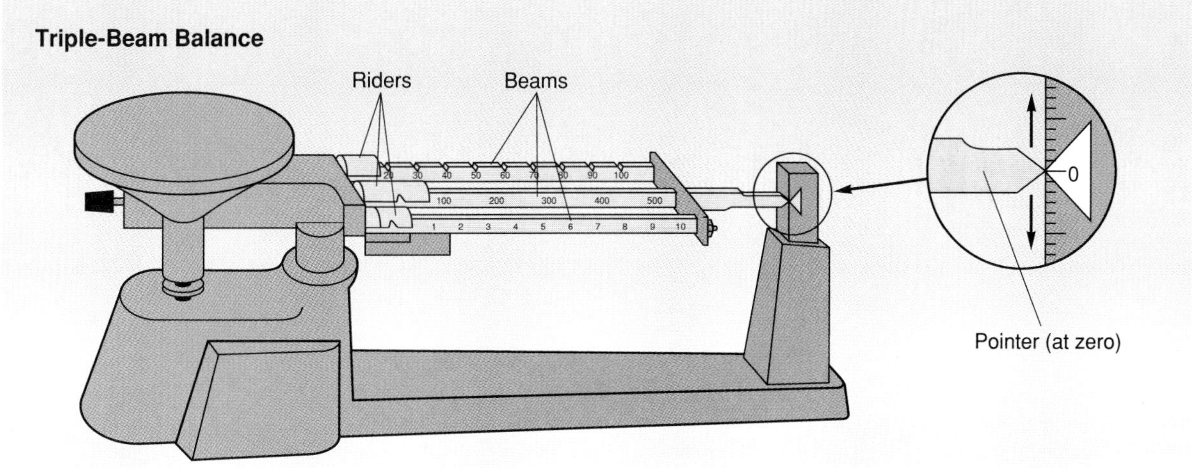

APPENDIX **E** *The Periodic Table of the Elements*

PERIODIC TABLE

1 —New designation
IA —Original designation

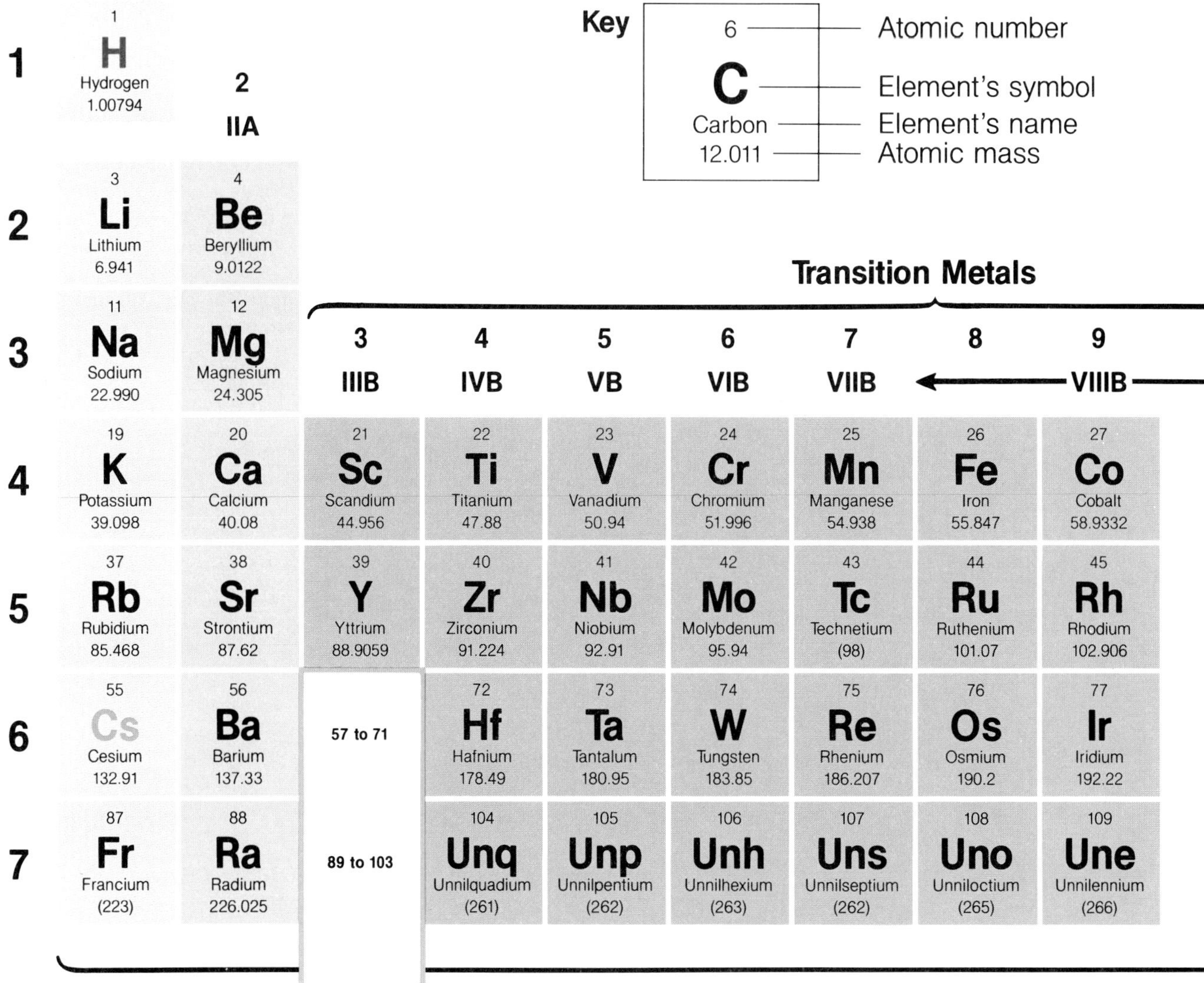

Key

6	Atomic number
C	Element's symbol
Carbon	Element's name
12.011	Atomic mass

Transition Metals

Period	1	2 IIA	3 IIIB	4 IVB	5 VB	6 VIB	7 VIIB	8 VIIIB	9 VIIIB
1	1 **H** Hydrogen 1.00794								
2	3 **Li** Lithium 6.941	4 **Be** Beryllium 9.0122							
3	11 **Na** Sodium 22.990	12 **Mg** Magnesium 24.305							
4	19 **K** Potassium 39.098	20 **Ca** Calcium 40.08	21 **Sc** Scandium 44.956	22 **Ti** Titanium 47.88	23 **V** Vanadium 50.94	24 **Cr** Chromium 51.996	25 **Mn** Manganese 54.938	26 **Fe** Iron 55.847	27 **Co** Cobalt 58.9332
5	37 **Rb** Rubidium 85.468	38 **Sr** Strontium 87.62	39 **Y** Yttrium 88.9059	40 **Zr** Zirconium 91.224	41 **Nb** Niobium 92.91	42 **Mo** Molybdenum 95.94	43 **Tc** Technetium (98)	44 **Ru** Ruthenium 101.07	45 **Rh** Rhodium 102.906
6	55 **Cs** Cesium 132.91	56 **Ba** Barium 137.33	57 to 71	72 **Hf** Hafnium 178.49	73 **Ta** Tantalum 180.95	74 **W** Tungsten 183.85	75 **Re** Rhenium 186.207	76 **Os** Osmium 190.2	77 **Ir** Iridium 192.22
7	87 **Fr** Francium (223)	88 **Ra** Radium 226.025	89 to 103	104 **Unq** Unnilquadium (261)	105 **Unp** Unnilpentium (262)	106 **Unh** Unnilhexium (263)	107 **Uns** Unnilseptium (262)	108 **Uno** Unniloctium (265)	109 **Une** Unnilennium (266)

The new Group designations are those assigned by IUPAC in 1984.

Rare-Earth Elements

Lanthanoid Series	57 **La** Lanthanum 138.906	58 **Ce** Cerium 140.12	59 **Pr** Praseodymium 140.908	60 **Nd** Neodymium 144.24	61 **Pm** Promethium (145)	62 **Sm** Samarium 150.36
Actinoid Series	89 **Ac** Actinium 227.028	90 **Th** Thorium 232.038	91 **Pa** Protactinium 231.036	92 **U** Uranium 238.029	93 **Np** Neptunium 237.048	94 **Pu** Plutonium (244)

OF THE ELEMENTS

C	Solid
Br	Liquid
H	Gas

Nonmetals

10	11 IB	12 IIB	13 IIIA	14 IVA	15 VA	16 VIA	17 VIIA	18 VIIIA
								2 **He** Helium 4.003
			5 **B** Boron 10.81	6 **C** Carbon 12.011	7 **N** Nitrogen 14.007	8 **O** Oxygen 15.999	9 **F** Fluorine 18.998	10 **Ne** Neon 20.179
			13 **Al** Aluminum 26.98	14 **Si** Silicon 28.086	15 **P** Phosphorus 30.974	16 **S** Sulfur 32.06	17 **Cl** Chlorine 35.453	18 **Ar** Argon 39.948
28 **Ni** Nickel 58.69	29 **Cu** Copper 63.546	30 **Zn** Zinc 65.39	31 **Ga** Gallium 69.72	32 **Ge** Germanium 72.59	33 **As** Arsenic 74.922	34 **Se** Selenium 78.96	35 **Br** Bromine 79.904	36 **Kr** Krypton 83.80
46 **Pd** Palladium 106.42	47 **Ag** Silver 107.868	48 **Cd** Cadmium 112.41	49 **In** Indium 114.82	50 **Sn** Tin 118.71	51 **Sb** Antimony 121.75	52 **Te** Tellurium 127.60	53 **I** Iodine 126.905	54 **Xe** Xenon 131.29
78 **Pt** Platinum 195.08	79 **Au** Gold 196.967	80 **Hg** Mercury 200.59	81 **Tl** Thallium 204.383	82 **Pb** Lead 207.2	83 **Bi** Bismuth 208.98	84 **Po** Polonium (209)	85 **At** Astatine (210)	86 **Rn** Radon (222)

The symbols shown here for elements 104-109 are being used temporarily until names for these elements can be agreed upon.

Metals

Mass numbers in parentheses are those of the most stable or common isotope.

63 **Eu** Europium 151.96	64 **Gd** Gadolinium 157.25	65 **Tb** Terbium 158.925	66 **Dy** Dysprosium 162.50	67 **Ho** Holmium 164.93	68 **Er** Erbium 167.26	69 **Tm** Thulium 168.934	70 **Yb** Ytterbium 173.04	71 **Lu** Lutetium 174.967
95 **Am** Americium (243)	96 **Cm** Curium (247)	97 **Bk** Berkelium (247)	98 **Cf** Californium (251)	99 **Es** Einsteinium (252)	100 **Fm** Fermium (257)	101 **Md** Mendelevium (258)	102 **No** Nobelium (259)	103 **Lr** Lawrencium (260)

APPENDIX F

The Five-Kingdom Classification System

KINGDOM MONERA

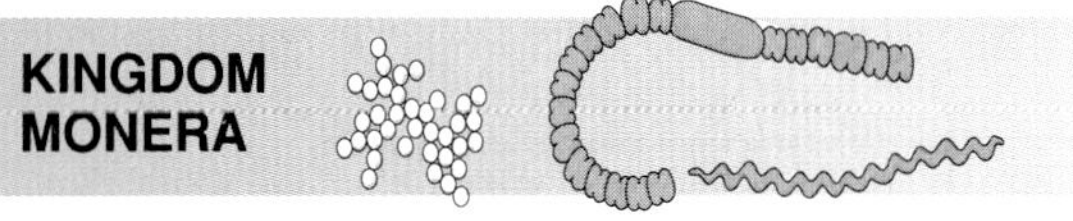

Single-celled prokaryotic organisms; sometimes form colonies of clumps or filaments.

PHYLUM ARCHAEBACTERIA ("ancient" bacteria)

Most live in harsh environments such as animal digestive tracts, hot springs, deep-sea vents, and extremely salty water; many, known as methanogens, produce methane gas. Example: *Thermoplasma.*

PHYLUM EUBACTERIA ("true" bacteria)

Outer cell wall contains complex carbohydrates; all species have at least one inner cell membrane (some have two); most are heterotrophs. Examples: *Escherichia coli, Streptococcus.*

PHYLUM CYANOBACTERIA (blue-green bacteria)

Photosynthetic autotrophs, once called blue-green algae; contain pigments phycocyanin and chlorophyll *a*; some fix atmospheric nitrogen. Examples: *Anabaena, Nostoc.*

PHYLUM PROCHLOROBACTERIA

Photosynthetic autotrophs containing chlorophylls *a* and *b*; strikingly similar to chloroplasts; few species identified to date. Example: *Prochloron.*

KINGDOM PROTISTA

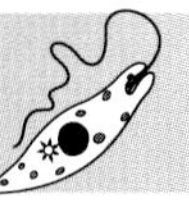

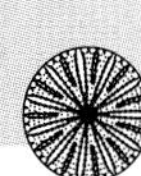

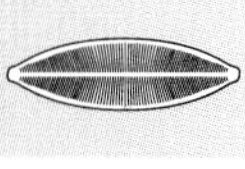

Eukaryotic; usually unicellular; some multicellular or colonial; heterotrophic or autotrophic organisms.

ANIMALLIKE PROTISTS Unicellular; heterotrophic; usually motile; also known as protozoa.

PHYLUM CILIOPHORA (ciliates)

All have cilia at some point in development; almost all use cilia to move; characterized by two types of nuclei: macronuclei and micronuclei; most have a sexual process known as conjugation. Examples: *Paramecium, Didinium, Stentor.*

PHYLUM ZOOMASTIGINA (animallike flagellates)

Possess one or more flagella (some have thousands); some are internal symbionts of wood-eating animals. Examples: trypanosomes, *Trichonympha.*

PHYLUM SPOROZOA

Nonmotile parasites; produce small infective cells called spores; life cycles usually complex, involving more than one host species; cause a number of diseases, including malaria. Example: *Plasmodium.*

PHYLUM SARCODINA

Use pseudopods for feeding and movement; some produce elaborate shells that contain silica or calcium carbonate; most free-living; a few parasitic; some involved in formation of sedimentary rock. Examples: *Amoeba,* foraminifers.

PLANTLIKE PROTISTS Mostly unicellular photosynthetic autotrophs that have characteristics similar to green plants or fungi. A few species are multicellular or heterotrophic.

PHYLUM EUGLENOPHYTA (plantlike flagellates)

Primarily photosynthetic; most live in fresh water; possess two unequal flagella; lack a cell wall. Example: *Euglena.*

PHYLUM PYRROPHYTA ("fire algae")

Two flagella; most live in salt water, are photosynthetic, and have a rigid cell wall that contains cellulose; some are luminescent; many are symbiotic. Examples: *Gonyaulux, Noctilucans scintillans.*

PHYLUM CHRYSOPHYTA ("golden algae")

Photosynthetic; aquatic; mostly unicellular; contain yellow-brown pigments; most are diatoms, which build a two-part cell covering that contains silica. Example: *Thallasiosira.*

PHYLUM ACRASIOMYCOTA (cellular slime molds)

Spores develop into independent free-living amebalike cells that may come together to form a multicellular structure; this structure, which behaves much like a single organism, forms a fruiting body that produces spores. Example: *Dictyostelium.*

PHYLUM MYXOMYCOTA (acellular slime molds)

Spores develop into haploid cells that can switch between flagellated and amebalike forms; these haploid cells fuse to form a zygote that grows into a plasmodium, which ultimately forms spore-producing fruiting bodies. Example: *Physarum.*

KINGDOM FUNGI

Eukaryotic; unicellular or multicellular; cell walls typically contain chitin; mostly decomposers; some parasites; some commensal or mutualistic symbionts; asexual reproduction by spore formation, budding, or fragmentation; sexual reproduction involving mating types; classified according to type of fruiting body and style of spore formation.

PHYLUM OOMYCOTA (water molds)

Unicellular or multicellular; mostly aquatic; cell walls contain cellulose or a polysaccharide similar to cellulose; form zoospores asexually and eggs and sperms sexually. Example: *Saprolegnia* (freshwater mold).

PHYLUM ZYGOMYCOTA (conjugation fungi)

Cell walls of chitin; hyphae lack cross walls; sexual reproduction by conjugation produces diploid zygospores; asexual reproduction produces haploid spores; most parasites; some decomposers. Example: *Rhizopus stolonifer* (black bread mold).

PHYLUM ASCOMYCOTA (sac fungi)

Cell walls of chitin; hyphae have perforated cross walls; most multicellular; yeasts unicellular; sexual reproduction produces ascospores; asexual reproduction by spore formation or budding; some cause plant diseases such as chestnut blight and Dutch elm disease. Examples: *Neurospora* (red bread mold), baker's yeast, morels, truffles.

PHYLUM BASIDIOMYCOTA (club fungi)

Cell walls of chitin; hyphae have cross walls; sexual reproduction involves basidiospores, which are borne on club-shaped basidia; asexual reproduction by spore formation. Examples: mushrooms, puffballs, shelf fungi, rusts.

PHYLUM DEUTEROMYCOTA (imperfect fungi)

Cell walls of chitin; sexual reproduction never observed; members resemble ascomycetes, basidiomycetes, or zygomycetes; most thought to be ascomycetes that have lost the ability to form asci. Examples: *Penicillium,* athlete's foot fungus.

KINGDOM PLANTAE

Eukaryotic; overwhelmingly multicellular and nonmotile; photosynthetic autotrophs; possess chlorophylls *a* and *b* and other pigments in organelles called chloroplasts; cell walls contain cellulose; food stored as starch; reproduce sexually; alternate haploid (gametophyte) and diploid (sporophyte) generations; botanists typically use the term division rather than phylum.

PHYLUM CHLOROPHYTA (green algae)

Live in fresh water and salt water; unicellular or multicellular; chlorophylls and accessory pigments similar to those in vascular plants; food stored as starch. Examples: *Ulva* (sea lettuce), *Chlamydomonas, Spirogyra, Acetabularia.*

PHYLUM PHAEOPHYTA (brown algae)

Live almost entirely in salt water; multicellular; contain brown pigment fucoxanthin; food stored as oils and carbohydrates. Examples: *Fucus* (rockweed), kelp, *Sargassum.*

PHYLUM RHODOPHYTA (red algae)

Live almost entirely in salt water; multicellular; contain red pigment phycoerythrin; food stored as carbohydrates. Examples: *Chondrus* (Irish moss), coralline algae.

PHYLUM BRYOPHYTA (bryophytes)

Generally small; multicellular green plants; live on land in moist habitats; lack vascular tissue; lack true roots, leaves, and stems; gametophyte dominant; water required for reproduction. Examples: mosses, liverwort, hornwort.

PHYLUM TRACHEOPHYTA (vascular plants)

Contain xylem and phloem; true roots; sporophyte dominant; in primitive forms, gametophyte independent of sporophyte; in advanced forms, gametophyte dependent on sporophyte.

Subphylum Psilopsida (whisk ferns) Primitive vascular plants; no differentiation between root and shoot; produce only one kind of spore; motile sperm must swim in water.

Subphylum Lycopsida (lycopods) Primitive vascular plants; usually small; sporophyte dominant; possess roots, stems, and leaves; water required for reproduction. Examples: club moss, quillwort.

Subphylum Sphenopsida (horsetails) Primitive vascular plants; stem comprises most of mature plant and contains silica; produce only one kind of spore; motile sperm must swim in water. Only one living genus: *Equisetum.*

Subphylum Pteropsida (ferns) Vascular plants well-adapted to live in predominantly damp or seasonally wet environments; sporophyte dominant and well-adapted to terrestrial life; gametophyte inconspicuous; reproduction still dependent on water for free-swimming gametes. Examples: cinnamon fern, Boston fern, tree fern, maidenhair fern.

Subphylum Spermopsida (seed plants) Vascular; use seeds for reproduction: nonmotile; cell walls contain cellulose; almost all photosynthetic; many can live in very wet places but others adapted to live and reproduce in dry environments; do not require water for reproduction.

Gymnosperms Four classes of seed plants—Cycadae, Ginkgoae, Coniferae, and Gnetalae—were once considered to be orders within the class Gymnospermae. Today, botanists realize that members of these groups differ from one another as much as they differ from angiosperms and are therefore not closely related enough to be placed in the same class.

Although the term gymnosperm no longer refers to a taxonomic category, it is still used casually. Gymnosperms are characterized by seeds that develop exposed or "naked" on fertile leaves—there is no ovary wall (fruit) surrounding the seeds. Gymnosperms lack flowers.

Class Cycadae (cycads) Evergreen, slow-growing, tropical and subtropical shrubs; many resemble small palm trees; palmlike or fernlike compound leaves; possess symbiotic cyanobacteria in special roots; sexes are separate—individuals have either male pollen-producing cones or female seed-producing cones.

Class Gingkoae Deciduous trees with fan-shaped leaves; sexes separate; outer skin of ovule develops into a fleshy, fruitlike covering. Only one living species: *Gingko biloba* (gingko).

Class Gnetalae Few species; mostly desert-living; functional xylem cells are alive; sexes separate. Examples: *Welwitschia,* joint fir (*Ephedra*).

Class Coniferae (conifers) Cones predominantly wind-pollinated; most are evergreen; most temperate and subarctic shrubs and trees; many have needlelike leaves; in most species, sexes are not separate. Examples: pine, spruce, cedar, cypress, yew, fir, larch, sequoia.

Angiosperms Unlike the term gymnosperm, the term angiosperm continues to refer to a taxonomic group. Nearly all familiar trees, shrubs, and garden plants are angiosperms.

Class Angiospermae Members of this class are commonly called flowering plants. Seeds develop enclosed within ovaries; fertile leaves modified into flowers; flowers pollinated by wind or by animals, including insects, birds, and bats; occur in many different forms; found in most land and freshwater habitats; a few species found in shallow saltwater and estuarine areas.

Subclass Monocotyledonae (monocots) Embryo with a single cotyledon; leaves with predominantly parallel veination; flower parts in threes or multiples of three; vascular bundles scattered throughout stem. Examples: lily, corn, grasses, iris, palms, tulip.

Subclass Dicotyledonae (dicots) Embryo with two cotyledons; leaves with veination in netlike patterns; flower parts in fours or fives (or multiples thereof); vascular bundles arranged in rings in stem. Examples: rose, maple, oak, daisy, apple.

KINGDOM ANIMALIA

Multicellular; eukaryotic; typical heterotrophs that ingest their food; lack cell walls; approximately 35 phyla; in most phyla cells are organized into tissues that make up organs; most reproduce sexually; motile sperm have flagella; nonmotile egg is much larger than sperm; development involves formation of a hollow ball of cells called a blastula.

Subkingdom Parazoa

Animals that possess neither tissues nor organs; most asymmetrical.

PHYLUM PORIFERA (sponges)

Aquatic; lack true tissues and organs; motile larvae and sessile adults; filter feeders; internal skeleton made up of spongin and/or spicules of calcium carbonate or silica. Examples: Venus' flower basket, bath sponge, tube sponge.

Subkingdom Metazoa

Animals with definite symmetry; definite tissues; most possess organs.

PHYLUM CNIDARIA

Previously known as coelenterates; aquatic; mostly carnivorous; two layers of true tissues; radial symmetry; tentacles bear stinging nematocysts; many alternate between polyp and medusa body forms; gastrovascular cavity.

Class Hydrozoa Polyp form dominant; colonial or solitary; life cycle typically includes a medusa generation that reproduces sexually and a polyp generation that reproduces asexually. Examples: hydra, Portuguese man-of-war.

Class Scyphozoa Medusa form dominant; some species bypass polyp stage. Examples: lion's mane jellyfish, moon jelly, sea wasp.

Class Anthozoa Colonial or solitary polyps; no medusa stage. Examples: reef coral, sea anemone, sea pen, sea fan.

PHYLUM PLATYHELMINTHES (flatworms)

Three layers of tissues (endoderm, mesoderm, ectoderm); bilateral symmetry; some cephalization; acoelomate; free-living or parasitic.

Class Turbellaria Free-living carnivores and scavengers; live in fresh water, in salt water, or on land; move with cilia. Example: planarians.

Class Trematoda (flukes) Parasites; life cycle typically involves more than one host. Examples: *Schistosoma,* liver fluke.

Class Cestoda (tapeworms) Internal parasites; lack digestive tract; body composed of many repeating sections (proglottids).

PHYLUM NEMATODA (roundworms)

Digestive system has two openings—a mouth and an anus; pseudocoelomates. Examples: *Ascaris lumbricoides* (human ascarid), hookworm, *Trichinella.*

PHYLUM MOLLUSCA (mollusks)

Soft-bodied; usually (but not always) posses a hard, calcified shell secreted by a mantle; most adults have bilateral symmetry; muscular foot; divided into seven classes; digestive system with two openings; coelomates.

Class Pelecypoda (bivalves) Two-part hinged shell; wedge-shaped foot; typically sessile as adults; primarily aquatic; some burrow in mud or sand. Examples: clam, oyster, scallop, mussel.

Class Gastropoda (gastropods) Use broad muscular foot in movement; most have spiral, chambered shell; some lack shell; distinct head; some terrestrial, others aquatic; many are cross-fertilizing hermaphrodites. Examples: snail, slug, nudibranch, sea hare, sea butterfly.

Class Cephalopoda (cephalopods) Foot divided into tentacles; live in salt water; closed circulatory system; sexes separate. Examples: octopus, squid, nautilus, cuttlefish.

PHYLUM ANNELIDA (segmented worms)

Body composed of segments separated by internal partitions; digestive system has two openings; coelomate; closed circulatory system.

Class Polychaeta (polychaetes) Live in salt water; pair of bristly, fleshy appendages on each segment; some live in tubes. Examples: sandworm, bloodworm, fanworm, feather-duster worm, plume worm.

Class Oligochaeta (oligochaetes) Lack appendages; few bristles; terrestrial or aquatic. Examples: *Tubifex,* earthworm.

Class Hirudinea (leeches) Lack appendages; carnivores or blood-sucking external parasites; most live in fresh water. Example: medicinal leech (*Hirudo medicinalis*).

PHYLUM ARTHROPODA (arthropods)

Exoskeleton of chitin; jointed appendages; segmented body; many undergo metamorphosis during development; open circulatory system; ventral nerve cord; largest animal phylum.

Subphylum Trilobita (trilobites) Two furrows running from head to tail divide body into three lobes; one pair of unspecialized appendages on each body segment; each appendage divided into two branches—a gill and a walking leg; all extinct.

Subphylum Chelicerata (chelicerates) First pair of appendages specialized as feeding structures called chelicerae; body composed of two parts—cephalothorax and abdomen; lack antennae; most terrestrial. Examples: horseshoe crab, tick, mite, spider, scorpion.

Subphylum Crustacea (crustaceans) Most aquatic; most live in salt water; two pairs of antennae; mouthparts called mandibles; appendages consist of two branches; many have a carapace that covers part or all of the body. Examples: crab, crayfish, pill bug, water flea, barnacle.

Subphylum Uniramia Almost all terrestrial; one pair of antennae; mandibles; unbranched appendages; generally divided into five classes.

Class Chilopoda (centipedes) Long body consisting of many segments; one pair of legs per segment; poison claws for feeding; carnivorous.

Class Diplopoda (millipedes) Long body consisting of many segments; two pairs of legs per segment; mostly herbivorous.

Class Insecta (insects) Body divided into three parts—head, thorax, and abdomen; three pairs of legs and usually one pair of wings attached to thorax; some undergo complete metamorphosis; approximately 25 orders. Examples: termite, ant, beetle, dragonfly, fly, moth, grasshopper.

PHYLUM ECHINODERMATA (echinoderms)

Live in salt water; larvae have bilateral symmetry; adults typically have five-part radial symmetry; endoskeleton; tube feet; water vascular system used in respiration, excretion, feeding, and locomotion.

Class Crinoidea (crinoids) Filter feeders; feathery arms; mouth and anus on upper surface of body disk; some sessile. Examples: sea lily, feather star.

Class Asteroidea (starfish) Star-shaped; carnivorous; bottom dwellers; mouth on lower surface. Examples: crown-of-thorns starfish, sunstar.

Class Ophiuroidea Small body disk; long armored arms; most have only five arms; lack an anus; most are filter feeders or detritus feeders. Examples: brittle star, basket star.

Class Echinoidea Lack arms; body encased in rigid, boxlike covering; covered with spines; most grazing herbivores or detritus feeders. Examples: sea urchin, sand dollar, sea biscuit.

Class Holothuroidea (sea cucumbers) Cylindrical body with feeding tentacles on one end; lie on their side; mostly detritus or filter feeders; endoskeleton greatly reduced.

PHYLUM CHORDATA (chordates)

Notochord and pharyngeal gill slits during at least part of development; hollow dorsal nerve cord.

Subphylum Urochordata (tunicates) Live in salt water; tough outer covering (tunic); display chordate features during larval stages; many adults sessile, some free-swimming. Examples: sea squirt, sea peach, salp.

Subphylum Cephalochordata (lancelets) Fishlike; live in salt water; filter feeders; no internal skeleton. Example: *Branchiostoma.*

Subphylum Vertebrata Most possess a vertebral column (backbone) that supports and protects dorsal nerve chord; endoskeleton; distinct head with a skull and brain.

Jawless Fishes Characterized by long eellike body and a circular mouth; two-chambered heart; lack scales, paired fins, jaws, and bones; ectothermic; possess a notochord as adults. Once considered a single class, Agnatha, jawless fishes are now divided into two classes: Myxini and Cephalaspidomorphi. Although the term agnatha no longer refers to a true taxonomic group, it is still used informally.

Class Myxini (hagfishes) Mostly scavengers; live in salt water; short tentacles around mouth; rasping tongue; extremely slimy; open circulatory system.

Class Cephalaspidomorphi (lampreys) Larvae filter feeders; adults are parasites whose circular mouth is lined with rasping toothlike structures; many live in both salt water and fresh water during the course of their lives.

Class Chondrichthyes (cartilaginous fishes) Jaw; fins; endoskeleton of cartilage; most live in salt water; typically several gill slits; tough small scales with spines; ectothermic; two-chambered heart; males possess structures for internal fertilization. Examples: shark, ray, skate, chimaera, sawfish.

Class Osteichthyes (bony fishes) Bony endoskeleton; aquatic; ectothermic; well-developed respiratory system, usually involving gills; possess swim bladder; paired fins; divided into two groups—ray-finned fishes (Actinopterygii), which include most living species, and fleshy-finned fishes (Sarcopterygii), which include lungfishes and the coelacanth. Examples: salmon, perch, sturgeon, tuna, goldfish, eel.

Class Amphibia (amphibians) Adapted primarily to life in wet places; ectothermic; most carnivorous; smooth, moist skin; typically lay eggs that develop in water; usually have gilled larvae; most have three-chambered heart; adults either aquatic or terrestrial; terrestrial forms respire using lungs, skin, and/or lining of the mouth.

ORDER URODELA (salamanders) Possess tail as adults; carnivorous; usually have four legs; usually aquatic as larvae and terrestrial as adults.

ORDER ANURA (frogs and toads) Adults in almost all species lack tail; aquatic larvae called tadpoles; well-developed hind legs adapted for jumping.

ORDER APODA (legless amphibians) Wormlike; lack legs; carnivorous; terrestrial burrowers; some undergo direct development; some viviparous.

Class Reptilia (reptiles) As a group adapted to fully terrestrial life, although some live in water; dry, scale-covered skin; ectothermic; most have three-chambered hearts; internal fertilization; amniotic eggs typically laid on land; extinct forms include dinosaurs and flying reptiles.

ORDER RHYNCOCEPHALIA (tuatara) "Teeth" formed by serrations of jawbone; found only in New Zealand; carnivorous. One species: *Sphenodon punctatus.*

ORDER SQUAMATA (lizards and snakes) Most carnivorous; majority terrestrial; lizards typically have legs; snakes lack legs. Examples: iguana, gecko, skink, cobra, python, boa.

ORDER CROCODILIA (crocodilians) Carnivorous; aquatic or semiaquatic; four-chambered heart. Examples: alligator, crocodile, caiman, gharial.

ORDER CHELONIA (turtles) Bony shell; ribs and vertebrae fused to upper part of shell; some terrestrial, others semiaquatic or aquatic; all lay eggs on land. Examples: snapping turtle, tortoise, hawksbill turtle, box turtle.

Class Aves (birds) Endothermic; feathered over much of body surface; scales on legs and feet; bones hollow and lightweight in flying species; four-chambered heart; well-developed lungs and air sacs for efficient air exchange; about 27 orders. Examples: owl, eagle, duck, chicken, pigeon, penguin, sparrow, stork.

Class Mammalia (mammals) Endothermic; subcutaneous fat; hair; most viviparous; suckle young with milk produced in mammary glands; four-chambered heart; four legs; use lungs for respiration.

Monotremes (egg-laying mammals)

ORDER MONOTREMATA (monotremes) Exhibit features of both mammals and reptiles; possess a cloaca; lay eggs that hatch externally; produce milk from primitive nipplelike structures. Examples: duck-billed platypus, short-beaked echidna.

Marsupials (pouched mammals)

ORDER MARSUPALIA (marsupials) Young develop in the female's uterus but emerge at very early state of development; development completed in mother's pouch. Examples: opossum, kangaroo, koala.

Placentals Young develop to term in uterus; nourished through placenta; some born helpless, others able to walk within hours of birth; about 17 orders.

ORDER INSECTIVORA (insectivores) Among the most primitive of living placental mammals; feed primarily on small arthropods. Examples: shrew, mole, hedgehog.

ORDER CHIROPTERA (bats) Flying mammals, with forelimbs adapted for flight; most nocturnal; most navigate by echolocation; most species feed on insects, nectar, or fruits; some species feed on blood. Examples: fruit bat, flying fox, vampire bat.

ORDER PRIMATES (primates) Highly developed brain and complex social behavior; excellent binocular vision; quadrupedal or bipedal locomotion; five digits on hands and feet. Examples: lemur, monkey, chimpanzee, human.

ORDER EDENTATA (edentates) Teeth reduced or absent; feed primarily on social insects such as termites and ants. Examples: anteater, armadillo.

ORDER LAGOMORPHA (lagomorphs) Small herbivores with chisel-shaped front teeth; generally adapted to running and jumping. Examples: rabbit, pika, hare.

ORDER RODENTIA (rodents) Mammalian order with largest number of species; mostly herbivorous but some omnivorous; sharp front teeth. Examples: rat, beaver, guinea pig, hamster, gerbil, squirrel.

ORDER CETACEA (cetaceans) Fully adapted to aquatic existence; feed, breed, and give birth in water; forelimbs specialized as flippers; external hindlimbs absent; many species capable of long, deep dives; use echolocation to navigate; communicate using complex auditory signals. Examples: whale, porpoise, narwhale, dolphin.

ORDER CARNIVORA (carnivores) Mostly carnivorous; live in salt water or on land; aquatic species must return to land to breed. Examples: dog, seal, cat, bear, raccoon, weasel, skunk, panda.

ORDER PROBOSCIDEA (elephants) Herbivorous; largest land animal; long, flexible trunk.

ORDER SIRENIA (sirenians) Aquatic herbivores; slow-moving; front limbs modified as flippers; hindlimbs absent; little body hair. Examples: manatee, sea cow.

ORDER PERISSODACTYLA (odd-toed ungulates) Hooved herbivores; hooves derived from middle digit on each foot; teeth, jaw, and digestive system adapted to plant material. Examples: horse, donkey, rhinoceros, tapir.

ORDER ARTIODACTYLA (even-toed ungulates) Hooved herbivores; hooves derived from two digits on each foot; digestive system adapted to thoroughly process tough plant material. Examples: sheep, cow, hippopotamus, antelope, camel, giraffe, pig.

Glossary

PRONUNCIATION KEY

When difficult names or terms first appear in the text, a pronunciation key follows in parentheses. A syllable in small capital letters receives the most stress. The key below lists the letters used in the pronunciations. It includes examples of words using each sound and shows how those words would be written.

Symbol	Example	Pronunciation
a	hat	(hat)
ay	pay; late	(pay); (layt)
ah	star; hot	(stahr); (haht)
ai	air; dare	(air); (dair)
aw	law; all	(law); (awl)
eh	met	(meht)
ee	bee; eat	(bee); (eet)
er	learn; sir; fur	(lern); (ser); (fer)
ih	fit	(fiht)
igh	mile; sigh	(mighl); (sigh)
oh	no	(noh)
oi	soil; boy	(soil); (boi)
oo	root; rule	(root); (rool)
or	born; door	(born); (dor)
ow	plow; out	(plow); (owt)

Symbol	Example	Pronunciation
u	put; book	(put); (buk)
uh	fun	(fuhn)
yoo	few; use	(fyoo); (yooz)
ch	chill; reach	(chihl); (reech)
g	go; dig	(goh); (dihg)
j	jet; gently; bridge	(jeht); (JENT-lee); (brihj)
k	kite; cup	(kight); (kuhp)
ks	mix	(mihks)
kw	quick	(kwihk)
ng	bring	(brihng)
s	say; cent	(say); (sehnt)
sh	she; crash	(shee); (krash)
th	three	(three)
y	yet; onion	(yeht); (UHN-yuhn)
z	zip; always	(zihp); (AWL-wayz)
zh	treasure	(TREH-zher)

A

abscission layer: band formed when the cells that join leaf petioles to a stem become weak

absolute dating: method of measuring rates of decay of radioactive materials to determine how long ago an event occurred or an organism lived

accessory pigment: compound other than chlorophyll that absorbs light energy and passes it on to the primary photosynthetic pigment (chlorophyll)

acid: compound that releases hydrogen ions in solution

acid rain: rain that contains droplets of acid formed when certain pollutants in the air combine with water vapor

acoelomate: animal that lacks a body cavity

Acquired Immune Deficiency Syndrome: condition in which certain cells of the immune system are killed by infection with HIV

Acrasiomycota (uh-kras-ee-oh-migh-KOH-tuh): phylum containing cellular slime molds

actin: protein that makes up the thin filaments in a muscle cell

action potential: changes in membrane potential that characterize a nerve impulse; essentially the depolarization and repolarization of a neuron

active immunity: type of immunity produced by the body when stimulated by a vaccine or by exposure to a pathogen

active site: region on an enzyme that can bind with a specific substrate or substrates

active transport: energy-requiring process that moves material across a cell membrane against a concentration difference

adaptation: process that enables organisms to become better suited to their environments

adaptive radiation: process, also known as divergent evolution, in which one species gives rise to many species that appear different externally but are similar internally

adenine (AD-uh-neen): nitrogenous base in nucleic acids, belonging to the purines; base pairs with thymine or uracil

adenine triphosphate (ATP): compound that stores energy in cells

adrenal cortex: outer portion of the adrenal gland that produces more than two dozen hormones called corticosteroids

adrenal gland: pyramid-shaped endocrine gland located on top of each kidney that secretes hormones such as adrenaline, noradrenaline, cortisol, and other corticosteroids

adrenal medulla: inner portion of the adrenal gland that secretes adrenaline and noradrenaline and is considered part of the sympathetic nervous system

aerobic: any process that requires oxygen

agglutination: process in which viruses are linked together in a large mass by a group of antibody molecules

AIDS: Acquired Immune Deficiency Syndrome; condition in which certain cells of the immune system are killed by infection with HIV

air sac: one of several sacs attached to a bird's lungs that allow for the one-way flow of air through the respiratory system and make a bird's body more buoyant

alcoholic fermentation: fermentation that produces alcohol

alcoholism: disease in which a person becomes addicted to alcohol

allele (uh-LEEL): one of a number of different forms of the same gene for a specific trait

allergy: reaction of the immune system that results when antigens bind to mast cells

alternation of generations: the switching back and forth between the production of diploid and haploid cells

alveolus (al-VEE-oh-luhs): air sac at the end of a bronchiole where gas exchange occurs

ameba: flexible active cell without cell walls, flagella, or cilia that moves by means of pseudopods, reproduces by binary fission, and belongs to the phylum Sarcodina

amino acid: substance that has an amino group ($-NH_2$) on one end and a carboxyl group ($-COOH$) on the other; makes up the building blocks for proteins

amniocentesis (am-nee-oh-sehn-TEE-sihs): prenatal diagnostic technique that requires the removal of a small amount of fluid from the sac surrounding the embryo

amnion: membrane that surrounds and protects a developing embryo; in placental mammals such as humans, develops into the amniotic sac

amniotic sac: fluid-filled structure that cushions and protects the developing fetus in placental mammals such as humans

amphetamine: stimulant chemically resembling the body's neurotransmitters that causes the nervous system to increase its activity

amphibian: vertebrate that typically is aquatic in the larval stage and terrestrial as an adult; breathes with lungs as an adult, has a moist skin that contains many glands, and lacks scales and claws

anabolism (uh-NAB-uh-lihz-uhm): process in a living thing that involves synthesizing complex substances from simpler substances

anaerobe: organism that does not require oxygen to survive

anaerobic: any process that does not require oxygen

anal pore: structure in paramecia and certain other protists through which waste materials are emptied into the environment

analogous structures: structures that are similar in appearance and function but have different origins and usually different internal structures

anaphase: third phase of mitosis in which paired chromatids separate

androgen: steroid hormone in males involved in the development of male reproductive structures

angiosperm: flowering plant whose seeds develop within ovaries

Animalia: kingdom that contains multicellular heterotrophic organisms whose cells lack cell walls

annelid: round wormlike animal that has a long segmented body and belongs to the phylum Annelida

annual: plant that grows from seed to maturity, flowers, produces seeds, and dies, all in the course of one growing season

annual ring: tree ring formed by the growth of xylem cells; often indicates the age of a tree

anterior: front end of a bilaterally symmetrical organism

anterior pituitary: part of the pituitary gland that secretes seven hormones: FSH, LH, TSH, GH, prolactin, and MSH

anther: structure in which the male gametophytes are produced in flowering plants

antheridium (an-ther-IHD-ee-uhm): male reproductive structure in some plants, including mosses and liverworts

anthropoid: humanlike primate

antibiotic: drug or natural compound that can attack and destroy certain microorganisms

antibody: special protein that can bind to an antigen on the surface of a pathogen and help destroy it

anticodon: three-nucleotide sequence in transfer RNA that base pairs with a complementary sequence in messenger RNA during protein synthesis

antigen: foreign substance that induces an immune response and interacts with specific antibodies

antigen-binding site: area on an antibody molecule that allows it to bind to an antigen

aorta (ay-OR-tah): large artery in mammals that carries oxygen-rich blood from the left ventricle of the heart to all parts of the body except the lungs

apical meristem: plant structure containing meristematic tissue that divides, allowing stems and roots to grow in length

arachnid: chelicerate arthropod that has four pairs of legs on its cephalothorax and no antennae

archegonium (ahr-kuh-GOH-nee-uhm): female reproductive structure in some plants, including mosses and liverworts

artery: tough, flexible blood vessel that carries blood away from the heart to the tissues of the body

arthropod: animal having a segmented body, an exoskeleton containing chitin, and a series of jointed appendages; belongs to the phylum Arthropoda.

artificial selection: technique in which the intervention of humans allows only selected organisms to produce offspring

ascospore: haploid spore produced within the ascus of ascomycetes

ascus: tiny sac in which fungal spores develop for sexual reproduction in ascomycetes

asexual reproduction: process in which a single organism produces a new organism or organisms identical to itself

asthma: allergic reaction in which smooth muscles contract around the passages leading to the lungs

atom: smallest particle of matter that can exist and still have the properties of a particular kind of matter

atomic number: number of protons in the nucleus of an atom; identifies each element

atrium (AY-tree-uhm): chamber of the heart that receives incoming blood

autoimmune disease: condition in which the immune system attacks the body's own cells

autonomic nervous system: division of the peripheral nervous system that regulates involuntary activities

autosome: chromosome that is not a sex chromosome

autotroph (AW-toh-trahf): organism that is able to use a source of energy to produce its food from inorganic raw materials

auxin: plant hormone that can stimulate elongation of stem cells and inhibit elongation in root cells

axon: long fiber that carries impulses away from the cell body of a neuron

axon terminal: small swelling in a neuron at the end of an axon

B

B-lymphocyte: white blood cell responsible for producing antibodies

bacillus (buh-SIHL-uhs): rod-shaped bacterium

bacteriophage: virus that invades bacteria and consists of a core of nucleic acid, a capsid, and a tail

bacterium: one-celled prokaryote; chiefly parasitic or saprophytic

barbiturate: depressant often found in sleeping pill medications; can be fatal when combined with alcohol and can result in serious medical problems when supply to the body is discontinued

base: compound that releases hydroxide ions in solution

base pairing: attraction between complementary nitrogenous bases that produces a force that holds the two strands of the DNA double helix together

basidiospore: spore in basidiomycetes that germinates to produce haploid primary mycelia

basidium (buh-SIHD-ee-uhm): specialized reproductive structure in basidiomycetes

biennial: plant that grows roots, stems, and leaves in its first growing season, then flowers and dies in its second season

bilateral symmetry: arrangement of an organism's body parts so that if an imaginary line were drawn down the longitudinal middle of the body, the body's parts would repeat on either side of the line

binary fission: type of asexual reproduction in which an organism divides to produce two identical daughter cells

binocular vision: stereoscopic vision that provides primates with a three-dimensional view of the world

binomial nomenclature (bigh-NOH-mee-uhl NOH-muhn-klay-cher): classification system in which each organism is given a two-part scientific name

biodegradable: description of a substance that can be broken down by microorganisms into the essential nutrients from which it was made

biogeochemical cycle: series of physical and biological processes by which nutrients move through the biosphere

biological magnification: phenomenon in which the concentration of certain compounds in each organism in a food chain increases

biome: environment that has a characteristic climax community

biosphere: part of the Earth in which life exists

bipedal locomotion: upright movement on two legs

bivalve: mollusk that lives within a shell made of two sections that are hinged together

blastocyst: hollow structure in early human embryonic development that results after the morula forms a fluid-filled cavity in the center

blood: fluid medium of transport of the circulatory system

blood pressure: measure of the force that blood exerts against a vessel wall

bloom: enormous growth of algae, protists, and other organisms that results if too much waste is present in a body of water

bolus: ball of partially digested food formed in the mouth after the initial digestive processes of the teeth and salivary glands have acted upon it

bone marrow: soft tissue in the cavities of bones
bony fish: fish whose skeleton is made up of bone; belongs in the class Osteichthyes
Bowman's capsule: cup-shaped structure in the upper end of a nephron that encases the glomerulus and is involved in filtration in the kidneys
brainstem: structure that connects the brain with the spinal cord and is composed of the medulla oblongata, pons, and midbrain; coordinates and integrates all information coming into the brain
bronchiole: one of the finest branches of the bronchial tubes; ends in an air sac
bronchitis: inflammation of the bronchi
bronchus: ringed tube that branches from the trachea and enters each lung
bud scale: thick, waxy structure that wraps around an apical meristem to protect the terminal bud
bulb: modified stem with most of its food stored in layers of short, thick leaves that wrap around the stem

C

calorie: amount of heat energy required to raise the temperature of 1 gram of water 1 degree Celsius
Calvin cycle: name given to the cycle of dark reactions in photosynthesis
calyx: ring of sepals at the base of a flower
capillary: small thin-walled blood vessel that allows materials to diffuse between the blood and the tissues
carapace: in turtles, the dorsal part of the shell; in crustaceans, the part of the exoskeleton that covers the cephalothorax
carbohydrate: organic compound containing carbon, hydrogen, and oxygen in a 1:2:1 ratio; human body's main source of energy
carbon cycle: movement of carbon between organic compounds that make up living tissues and carbon dioxide in the air
carcinogen: cancer-causing compound
cardiac muscle: tissue made up of striated cells not under voluntary control; found only in the heart
carnivore: organism that eats meat
carpel: structure produced from fertile leaves that have rolled up to comprise the centermost circle of flower parts
carrying capacity: size of a population during the steady state portion of a logistic growth curve
cartilage: dense, fibrous connective tissue whose cells are scattered in a network of fibers composed of collagen
cartilaginous fish: fish, such as a shark or one of its relatives, whose skeleton is made up of soft, flexible cartilage instead of bone; belongs to the class Chondrichthyes
Casparian strip: waterproof strip that surrounds each endodermal cell in a root and is involved in the one-way passage of materials into the vascular cylinder in plant roots
catabolism (kuh-TAB-uh-lihz-uhm): breakdown of complex substances into simpler substances
catalyst: substance that speeds up the rate of a chemical reaction without being changed or used up by the reaction
cecum (SEE-kuhm): long sac that forms part of the intestines of some herbivores; contains microorganisms that digest cellulose
cell: basic unit of structure and function in living things
cell body: part of a neuron that contains the nucleus and much of the cytoplasm
cell cycle: period from the beginning of one mitosis to the beginning of the next
cell division: process by which a cell divides into two daughter cells
cell-mediated immunity: immune response in which killer T-cells cause the cells of pathogenic organisms to rupture and die
cell membrane: cell structure that regulates the passage of materials between the cell and its environment; aids in the protection and support of the cell
cell specialization: characteristic of certain cells that makes them uniquely suited to perform a particular function within an organism
cell theory: understanding that all living things are composed of cells and that all cells come from preexisting cells
cell wall: cell structure that surrounds the cell membrane for protection and support in plants, algae, and some bacteria
Celsius (SEHL-see-uhs) (C): metric temperature scale on which water freezes at 0° and boils at 100°
central nervous system: division of the nervous system that consists of the brain and spinal cord
centriole (SEHN-tree-ohl): structure involved in mitosis that contains a microtubule protein called tubulin
centromere (SEHN-troh-mihr): structure that holds together each pair of chromatids
cephalization: gathering of sense organs and nerve cells into the head region
cephalopod (SEHF-uh-loh-pahd): marine mollusk whose head is attached to its foot, which is divided into tentacles
cerebellum (ser-uh-BEHL-uhm): part of the brain that coordinates and balances the actions of muscles
cerebral cortex: outer surface of the cerebrum associated with sensory input, motor output, and the complex movements associated with speech
cerebral medulla: inner surface of the cerebrum; composed of bundles of myelinated axons
cerebrum (suh-REE-bruhm): part of the brain responsible for all voluntary activities of the body; largest part of the brain

chelicerate (keh-LIHS-er-ayt): arthropod characterized by a two-part body and mouthparts called chelicerae
chemical bonding: process by which atoms of elements combine to achieve stability
chemical properties: properties that describe a substance's ability to change into a new substance as a result of a chemical reaction
chemical reaction: any process in which a chemical change occurs
chemical signal: stimulus used for communication among animals that involves the sense of smell
chemotrophic autotroph: organism that can obtain energy from inorganic molecules
chemotrophic heterotroph: organism that can obtain energy by taking in organic molecules and then breaking them down
chitin (KIGH-tihn): protein that makes up much of an arthropod's exoskeleton and the cell wall in most fungi
chlorophyll: principal pigment in the cells of photosynthetic autotrophs that captures light energy
chloroplast: organelle that converts sunlight into chemical energy in plants
cholesterol: compound found in animal fats, meats, and dairy products that can build cells but, in excess, can be a risk factor in heart disease
chordate: animal that possesses a notochord, a hollow dorsal nerve cord, and pharyngeal slits at some point in its development
chorion: outermost membrane surrounding a developing reptile, bird, or mammal embryo; forms the placenta in placental mammals
chorionic villus biopsy (kor-ee-AHN-ihk VIHL-uhs BIGH-ahp-see): prenatal diagnostic method in which a sample of embryonic cells is removed from the sac surrounding the embryo
chromatid (KROH-muh-tihd): one of two distinct strands that make up each chromosome
chromatin (KROH-muh-tihn): material in chromosomes that is composed of DNA and protein
chromosomal mutation: change in the number or structure of chromosomes in a cell
chromosome: threadlike structure in a cell that contains the genetic information that is passed on from one generation of cells to the next
chromosome theory of heredity: theory that states that genes are located on chromosomes and that each gene occupies a specific place on a chromosome
Chrysophyta (krihs-uh-FIGHT-uh): phylum containing yellow-green algae, golden-brown algae, and diatoms
chyme: pasty mixture that results after food is partially digested in the stomach
ciliate (SIHL-ee-iht): protist that has many hairlike structures that aid in movement; belongs to the phylum Ciliophora
Ciliophora (sihl-ee-AHF-uh-ruh): phylum containing solitary and colonial ciliates
cilium: short hairlike projection that produces movement in many cells
circulatory system: group of organs including the heart and blood vessels that transports blood to all the body cells
class: group of closely related orders
classical conditioning: type of learning that occurs when an animal makes a mental connection between a stimulus and some kind of positive or negative event
cleavage: mitotic cell division of a zygote or early embryo
climax community: relatively stable collection of plants and animals that results from ecological succession
clone: large population of genetically identical cells derived from one original cell
closed circulatory system: system in which blood always moves inside blood vessels
Cnidaria (nigh-DAIR-ee-ah): phylum that contains soft-bodied animals with stinging tentacles arranged in circles around their mouth
cocaine: addictive drug that causes the brain to release dopamine
coccus (KAHK-uhs): spherical bacterium
codominance: condition in which both alleles of a gene are expressed
codon (KOH-dahn): three-nucleotide sequence on messenger RNA that codes for an amino acid
coelom (SEE-lohm): body cavity that is completely lined with mesoderm
coelomate: animal that has a body cavity that is completely lined with mesoderm
coevolution: process by which two organisms evolve structures and behaviors in response to changes in each other over time
colon: digestive organ, also known as the large intestine, that removes water from the undigested materials that pass through it
colony: group of cells that are joined together and show few specialized structures
commensalism: symbiosis in which one member benefits and the other is not harmed
common descent: idea that species have descended from common ancestors
communication: passing of information from one animal to another
community: all the populations of organisms living in a given area
companion cell: special type of phloem cell that is found near a sieve tube element
compound: matter composed of two or more elements chemically bonded
compound light microscope: microscope with more than one lens that uses a beam of light to magnify objects
conidiophore (koh-NIHD-ee-uh-for): specialized hypha that produces asexual spores in ascomycetes

conidium: asexual spore produced in an ascomycete

conjugation: process in bacteria and protists that involves an exchange of genetic information

consumer: organism that gets its energy either directly or indirectly from producers

contour feather: one of the large feathers that cover the body and wings of a bird

contractile vacuole: structure in some protists that collects water and discharges it from the cell

control setup: part of an experiment that does not contain the variable

convergent evolution: phenomenon in which adaptive radiations among different organisms produce species that are similar in appearance and behavior; opposite of divergent evolution

cork cambium: meristematic tissue that produces the outer covering of stems

corm: round underground stem that stores food and is surrounded with thin leaves for protection

corolla: combined petals of a flower

corpus luteum (KOR-puhs LOOT-ee-uhm): name given to the follicle after ovulation because of its yellow appearance

cortex: root tissue that transports water and nutrients inward through the root; may store sugar and starches

covalent bond: chemical bond formed by the sharing of electrons

crack: potent and dangerous form of cocaine that can be smoked in a pipe

crop: enlarged area of the esophagus of a bird where food can be stored and moistened before it enters the stomach; or a food-storing organ in an earthworm

cross-bridge: knoblike projection of a myosin filament that connects with an actin filament during muscle contraction

cross-pollination: transfer of pollen from the flower of one plant to the flower of another plant

crossing-over: process by which homologous chromosomes exchange portions of their chromatids during meiosis

crustacean (kruhs-TAY-shuhn): arthropod characterized by a stony exoskeleton, two pairs of antennae, and mandibles

cubic centimeter (cc or cm^3): basic metric unit of volume for solids; equal to a milliliter

cuticle: noncellular protective coating on the exterior surface of an organism, such as the waxy covering on leaves and insect exoskeletons that helps prevent water loss through evaporation

cytokinesis (sight-oh-kih-NEE-sihs): process by which a cell's cytoplasm divides to form two distinct cells

cytokinin: hormone manufactured in plant roots that stimulates cell division and causes dormant seeds to sprout

cytoplasm: area between the nucleus and cell membrane of a cell

cytosine (SIGHT-oh-seen): nitrogenous base in nucleic acids belonging to the pyramidines; base pairs with guanine

cytoskeleton: framework of the cell composed of a variety of filaments and fibers that support cell structure and drive cell movement

D

dark reactions: reactions of photosynthesis that do not require light but use energy produced and stored during light reactions to make glucose

data: recorded observations and information

decomposer: organism that breaks down and obtains energy from dead organic material

dehydration synthesis: reaction in which small molecules join to form a large molecule, removing water in the process

dendrite: extension from the cell body of a neuron that carries impulses from the environment toward the cell body

denitrification (dee-nigh-trih-fih-KAY-shuhn): process in which bacteria in the soil break down nitrogen compounds into free nitrogen

density-dependent limiting factor: factor that controls population size and operates more strongly on large populations than on small ones

density-independent limiting factor: factor that controls population size regardless of how large the population is at the time

Deoxyribonucleic Acid (DNA): nucleic acid that stores and transmits genetic information from one generation of an organism to the next by coding for the production of a cell's proteins

depressant: drug that reduces the rate of nervous system activity

dermis: innermost layer of skin beneath the epidermis

desert: biome that receives less than 25 centimeters of rainfall a year

detritus feeder: animal that feeds on tiny bits of decaying plants and animals

deuterostome: organism whose anus formed from its blastopore during early embryonic development

diaphragm: large flat muscle involved in the mechanics of breathing that lies at the bottom of the rib cage

diatom: photosynthetic cell belonging to the phylum Chrysophyta that produces intricate cell walls rich in silicon

dicot: angiosperm whose seed has two cotyledons

diffusion (dih-FYOO-zhuhn): process by which molecules of a substance move from areas of higher concentration of that substance to areas of lower concentration

digestion: breakdown of food into simple molecules that can be absorbed by the body

dinoflagellate: protist belonging to the phylum Pyrrophyta that typically is photosynthetic, moves by means of two flagella, and reproduces by binary fission

diploid: description of a cell that contains a double set of chromosomes, one from each parent

disaccharide: double sugar formed from the combination of two simple sugars

disease: any change, other than an injury, that interferes with the normal functioning of the body

divergent evolution: pattern of evolution, also known as adaptive radiation, in which one species gives rise to many species that appear different externally but are similar internally

division of labor: phenomenon in which groups of specialized cells carry out different tasks in an organism

DNA: nucleic acid that stores and transmits genetic information from one generation of an organism to the next by coding for the production of a cell's proteins

DNA fingerprinting: technique for identifying individuals using repeated sequences in the human genome that produce a pattern of bands that is unique for every individual

dominance: principle that recognizes that some alleles are dominant and some are recessive

dominant: form of a gene that is expressed even if present with a contrasting recessive allele

dormancy: period during which an organism's growth and activity decrease or stop, usually during unfavorable environmental conditions

dorsal: upper side of an organism that has bilateral symmetry

double fertilization: process that occurs in angiosperms, in which one sperm nucleus fuses with the egg nucleus to form the zygote and one sperm nucleus fuses with the two nuclei that flank the egg nucleus to form the endosperm

double-loop circulatory system: system of internal transport in which one loop carries blood between the heart and the lungs and a second loop carries blood between the heart and the body

down feather: short, fluffy feather that traps warm air close to a bird's body

drug: any substance that causes a change in the body

drug abuse: misuse of either a legal or illegal drug

drug addiction: uncontrollable craving for a drug

duodenum (doo-oh-DEE-nuhm): first part of the small intestine

E

echinoderm: spiny-skinned animal that belongs to the phylum Echinodermata and is an invertebrate characterized by five-part radial symmetry, an internal skeleton, a water vascular system, and tube feet

ecological pyramid: diagram used to represent the energy relationships among trophic levels of an ecosystem

ecological succession: process through which an existing community is gradually replaced by another community

ecology: study of the interactions of organisms with one another and with their physical surroundings

ecosystem: division of the biosphere consisting of all the biotic and abiotic factors that surround organisms and affect their way of life

ectoderm: outermost primary germ layer in an animal embryo

ectotherm: animal that does not generate much internal heat and must rely on its external environment for the heat it requires

effector: muscle or gland that brings about a coordinated response to a stimulus

egg: female gamete

egg nucleus: nucleus in the embryo sac of angiosperms that locates itself close to the opening of the ovule and enlarges to become the female gamete

electrical signal: stimulus used for communication among certain fishes involving electrical impulses sent through water

electron: negatively charged subatomic particle located outside the atomic nucleus

electron transport: process in which high-energy electrons are transferred along a series of electron-carrier molecules in a membrane

element: substance consisting entirely of one type of atom

embryo: organism at an early stage of development

embryo sac: female gametophyte within the ovule of a flower

emphysema: stiffening of the normally elastic tissues of the human lung

endangered species: animal or plant that is so rare it is threatened with extinction

endocrine gland: hormone-producing organ of the endocrine system

endocrine system: body system composed of glands that secrete hormones into the bloodstream

endoderm: innermost primary germ layer in an animal embryo

endoplasmic reticulum (ehn-doh-PLAZ-mihk rih-TIHK-yuh-luhm): complex network that transports materials throughout the inside of a cell

endorphin: morphinelike chemical produced by the brain

endoskeleton: skeletal system in which a rigid framework is located inside the body of an animal

endosperm: triploid structure resulting from the fusion of a sperm nucleus with the two nuclei that flank the egg nucleus in the embryo sac of an angiosperm; provides food for the embryo

endospore: type of spore formed when a bacterium produces a thick internal wall that encloses its DNA and a portion of its cytoplasm

Endosymbiont Hypothesis: theory proposed by Lynn Margulis that states that the first eukaryotic cell was formed from a symbiosis among several prokaryotes

endotherm: animal that generates a significant amount of internal heat and has a relatively high metabolic rate

energy level: one of a series of "orbits" in which electrons travel around the nucleus of an atom

enzyme: one of a number of special protein catalysts contained in living organisms

epicotyl: portion of a shoot's stem above the cotyledon(s)

epidermis: in animals, outermost layer of skin; in plants, thin layer of root tissue that takes in water and nutrients

epididymis (ehp-uh-DIHD-ih-mihs): structure in the male reproductive system attached to the seminiferous tubules in which sperm mature and are stored

epiglottis: small flap of cartilage in the back of the mouth that closes the entrance to the respiratory tract when depressed by food

epoch: interval of time in a geologic time scale

equilibrium (ee-kwih-LIHB-ree-uhm): state in which no net change occurs

era: largest interval of time in a geologic time scale

esophagus: tube that connects the pharynx with the stomach

essential amino acid: amino acid that is needed but cannot be manufactured by the body

estrogen: steroid hormone in females involved in the development of the reproductive organs

estuary (EHS-tyoo-er-ee): area between fresh water and salt water

ethyl alcohol: form of alcohol present in alcohol-containing drinks

euglena: cell belonging to the phylum Euglenophyta that contains chlorophyll and has a pouch that contains two flagella at its front end

Euglenophyta (yoo-glee-nuh-FIGHT-uh): phylum that contains plantlike protists that move by means of flagella and have chloroplasts

eukaryote (yoo-KAHR-ee-oht): organism made up of cells that have a nucleus

evolution: process by which modern organisms have descended from ancient organisms; any change in the relative frequencies of alleles in the gene pool of a population

excretory system: group of organs, including the skin, lungs, and kidneys, that removes metabolic wastes from the body

exhalation: action in which air is pushed out of the lungs

exocrine gland: gland that releases secretions through tubelike structures called ducts

exon: expressed segment of a gene that is separated from similar segments by unexpressed sequences called introns

exoskeleton: system of supporting structures covering the outside of the body

experimental setup: part of an experiment that contains the variable being tested

exponential growth curve: graph that shows the phase of population growth during which the size of the population doubles regularly within a certain time period

external fertilization: process in which eggs are fertilized outside the body

external respiration: respiration that occurs at the level of the organism in which oxygen is obtained from and carbon dioxide is released to the external environment

extracellular digestion: process in which food is broken down outside the cells

F

facilitated diffusion: diffusion of materials across a cell membrane assisted by carrier molecules

facultative anaerobe: organism that can survive with or without oxygen

Fallopian tube: one of two fluid-filled tubes in human females through which an ovum passes after its release from an ovary; location of fertilization

family: group of closely related genera

fetal alcohol syndrome: damage to a developing baby due to the effects of alcohol in the mother's body

fermentation: process that enables cells to carry out energy production in the absence of oxygen; breakdown of glucose and release of energy in which organic substances are the final electron acceptors

fetus: unborn young of an animal during the later stages of development; in humans, the name given to embryo after eight weeks of development

fever: human body's response to an infection that results in increased body temperature in an effort to kill pathogens with heat

fibrous root: threadlike, branched root developing from a secondary root in some plants

filament: in a plant, the long, thin structure that supports the anther; in algae, a threadlike colony formed by many green algae

filter feeder: aquatic animal that feeds by straining tiny floating plants and animals from the water around it

filtration: process by which fluid from the blood filters into Bowman's capsule in the kidneys

fitness: combination of physical traits and behaviors that help an organism survive and reproduce in its environment

flagellate: organism that has taillike structures that aid in movement

flagellum: long, whiplike projection that aids in movement in some cells

flatworm: simple animal with bilateral symmetry belonging to the phylum Platyhelminthes

flower: reproductive structure in an angiosperm

food chain: series of organisms through which food energy is passed in an ecosystem

food vacuole: membrane-enclosed cavity in protists in which food is digested

food web: complex relationship formed by interconnecting and overlapping food chains

foot: muscular structure in mollusks that usually contains the mouth and other structures associated with feeding

fossil: preserved remains or evidence of an ancient organism

fossil record: collection of fossils that represents the preserved collective history of the Earth's organisms

frameshift mutation: gene mutation involving an addition or deletion that alters every codon from the point of the mutation on; can completely change the polypeptide product produced by a gene

freshwater biome: rivers, streams, and lakes that provide drinking water and food

frond: large leaf of a fern

fruit: protective structure formed from an enlarged, thickened ovary wall that contains angiosperm seeds

Fungi: kingdom that includes heterotrophic organisms that build cell walls that typically do not contain cellulose

fungus: organism made of eukaryotic cells with cell walls that gets its food by absorbing organic substances

G

gallbladder: small sac in which bile is stored

gametangium (gam-uh-TAN-jee-uhm): gamete-forming structure produced when the hyphae of opposing mating types of fungi meet

gamete (GAM-eet): specialized reproductive cell involved in sexual reproduction

gametophyte (guh-MEET-uh-fight): haploid plant that produces gametes

ganglion: small cluster of nerve cells

gastrointestinal tract: long, hollow tube that makes up the digestive system

gastropod (GAS-troh-pahd): mollusk that moves by means of a broad, muscular foot located on its ventral side; usually has a one-piece shell for protection

gastrovascular cavity: digestive cavity in cnidarians with only one opening

gastrulation (gas-troo-LAY-shuhn): process of cell migration during which the primary germ layers are formed in an embryo

gene: segment of DNA that codes for a particular protein

gene mutation: change involving the nucleotides of DNA

gene pool: common group of genes shared by members of a population

generative nucleus: nucleus that results from the mitotic division of the nucleus of the pollen grain in angiosperms; divides to form the two sperm cells involved in double fertilization

genetic code: manner in which cells store the program that they pass from one generation to the next

genetic drift: random change in the frequency of a gene

genetic engineering: technique that directly alters an organism's DNA; altering the structure of a DNA molecule is altered by substituting genes from other DNA molecules

genetics: branch of biology that studies heredity

genome: all the genes possessed by an organism

genotype: genetic makeup of an organism

genus: group of closely related species

geologic time scale: record of the history of life determined by the positions of layers of rock

germ theory of infectious disease: idea that infectious diseases are caused by microorganisms

gibberellin (jihb-er-EHL-ihn): plant hormone that stimulates growth

gill: filamentous respiratory structure in an aquatic animal

gizzard: muscular part of a reptile's or bird's stomach that contains bits of gravel that mix with food in order to make the food easier to digest; organ posterior to the crop in earthworms that is used to grind food

glomerulus (glom-MER-yoo-luhs): small network of capillaries surrounded by Bowman's capsule in the nephrons of the kidneys

glucose: sugar with formula $C_6H_{12}O_6$ that is a product of photosynthesis; can be broken down for energy

glycolysis (gligh-KAHL-ih-sihs): production of ATP by the conversion of glucose to pyruvic acid

Golgi apparatus: organelle that modifies, collects, packages, and distributes molecules made at one location of the cell and used at another

gonad: reproductive gland that produces gametes and sex hormones

gradualism: theory that evolutionary change occurs slowly and gradually

grassland: biome consisting of a vast area covered with grasses and small leafy plants

gravitropism: organism's response to gravity

greenhouse effect: condition in which carbon dioxide in the atmosphere absorbs heat radiated from the Earth, forming a kind of heat blanket around the Earth

guanine (GWAH-neen): nitrogenous base in nucleic acids belonging to the purines; base pairs with cytosine

guard cell: specialized epidermal cell that controls the opening and closing of the stomata by responding to changes in water pressure

gullet: indentation on one side of a paramecium that brings food from the outside to the interior of the cell

gymnosperm: plant known as a naked seed plant because its seeds do not develop within ovaries

H

habituation: decrease in response to a stimulus that neither rewards nor harms an animal

hair follicle: tubelike pocket of epidermal cells that extends into the dermis and produces hair

half-life: length of time required for half of the radioactive atoms in a sample to decay

hallucinogen: drug that affects a user's view of reality

haploid: description of cells that contain a single set of chromosomes

Haversian (huh-VER-zhuhn) **canal**: one of a network of tubes containing blood vessels and nerves that supply blood to bones

heart: hollow muscular organ that contracts at regular intervals, forcing blood through the circulatory system

heartwood: xylem tissue that no longer conducts water but gives strength and support to a stem

helper T-cell: cell of the immune system that helps other lymphocytes respond to the early stages of an infection

hemoglobin: red iron-containing pigment in red blood cells of vertebrates that increases the oxygen-carrying capacity of the blood

herbaceous (her-BAY-shuhs): description of a plant whose stem has little or no woody tissue

herbivore: organism that eats plants

heredity: passing of traits from parents to their young

hermaphrodite: individual that has both male and female reproductive organs

heroin: opiate that is injected directly into the bloodstream, resulting in strong physical and psychological dependence

heterogamy: production of two different kinds of gametes within the same species

heterotroph (HEHT-er-oh-trahf): organism that cannot produce its own food but obtains energy from the foods it eats

heterozygous (heht-er-oh-ZIGH-guhs): organism that has two different alleles for the same trait and is said to be hybrid for that particular trait

histamine: chemical released from mast cells when allergy-causing antigens attach themselves to mast cells; responsible for producing allergy symptoms

HIV: human immunodeficiency virus; virus that causes AIDS

holdfast cell: specialized cell that attaches an algal filament to the bottom of a lake or pond

hole in the ozone layer: area where little ozone is found

hollow dorsal nerve cord: cord that runs along the dorsal surface of a chordate and is connected by nerves to internal organs, muscles, and sense organs

homeostasis (hoh-mee-oh-STAY-sihs): process by which organisms keep internal conditions constant despite changes in their external environments

hominid: member of the evolutionary line that produced humans; classified in the family Hominidae; characterized by omnivory, bipedal locomotion, opposable thumbs, and a large brain

hominoid: great ape, such as a gorilla, gibbon, orangutan, chimpanzee, and Homo sapien

homologous: description of chromosomes that occur in pairs; having a corresponding structure

homologous structures: parts of different organisms, often quite dissimilar, that developed from the same ancestral body parts

homozygous (hoh-moh-ZIGH-guhs): organism that has two identical alleles for a particular trait

hormone: chemical substance produced in one part of an organism that affects another part of the organism

hybrid: organism with two different alleles for a particular trait, heterozygous; organism resulting from a cross between dissimilar parents

hybridization: breeding technique that involves a cross between dissimilar individuals

hydrolysis: catabolic reaction that splits apart molecules with the consumption of water

hydrostatic skeleton: skeletal system in which muscles surround and are supported by a water-filled body cavity

hypha (HIGH-fuh): branching filament that makes up a fungus

hypocotyl: portion of a stem below the cotyledon(s) in a newly germinated seed

hypothalamus (high-poh-THAL-uh-muhs): portion of the brain that controls the secretions of the pituitary gland; control center for hunger, thirst, fatigue, anger, and body temperature

hypothesis: possible explanation or conclusion about some event in nature; proposed solution to a scientific problem

I

immune: condition in which a body is able to permanently fight a disease using B-cells and T-cells produced the first time the body was exposed to the disease

immune system: body's primary defense against disease-causing microorganisms

implantation: process in early embryonic development in which the blastocyst attaches itself to the wall of the uterus and begins to grow inward

imprinting: process in which newborn birds add to their natural instinct to follow their mother with an image obtained by experience, usually the first slow-moving object they see
impulse: message carried by the nervous system that takes the form of an electrical signal
inbreeding: method of maintaining desirable characteristics by crossing individuals with similar characteristics who are often closely related
incomplete dominance: inheritance in which an active allele does not entirely compensate for an inactive allele
independent assortment: process by which genes segregate independently
inducer: chemical substance that causes the production of enzymes
infection: condition that results when the body is invaded by a pathogen
infectious disease: disease produced by a pathogen that affects the cells and tissues of the body
inflamed: reddish swollen area of the skin at the site of an infection
inflammatory response: defense mechanism that begins when a number of pathogens enter the body, causing fluid and white blood cells to leak from blood vessels into tissue
inhalation: action in which air is pulled into the lungs
inorganic compounds: compounds that do not contain carbon
insight learning: type of learning in which an animal applies something it has already learned to a new situation
instinct: behavior that is built into an animal's nervous system and cannot be changed
integumentary (ihn-tehg-yoo-MEHN-ter-ee) **system**: protective system formed by the skin and its accessory organs
interferon: protein that helps other cells resist viral infection
internal fertilization: process in which eggs are fertilized inside the female's body
internal respiration: respiration that occurs at the level of the cell
interneuron: cell that connects sensory and motor neurons and carries impulses between them
interphase: period of the cell cycle between cell divisions
intracellular digestion: process in which food is broken down inside the cells
intron: intervening sequence of DNA that does not code for a protein
invertebrate: animal that does not have a backbone
ion: charged particle
ionic bond: chemical bond that involves the transfer of electrons
islet of Langerhans: cluster of cells in the pancreas that produces insulin and glucagon
isogamy (igh-SAHG-uh-mee): condition in which the gametes of a species appear identical
isotope: atom of an element that has a different number of neutrons than other atoms of the same element

J

jawless fish: fish, such as a lamprey or hagfish, that lacks a jaw
joint: place where two bones come together
juvenile-onset diabetes: diabetes that appears in childhood; may be the result of an autoimmune reaction against the insulin-producing cells of the pancreas

K

kidney: organ that filters excess water, urea, and other waste products from the blood and excretes them out of the body
killer T-cell: special type of immune cell that transfers proteins into the cell membrane of a pathogen, causing the pathogen to rupture and die
kilogram (kg): basic metric unit of mass
kingdom: group of closely related phyla
Koch's postulates: series of rules for proving that a specific type of microorganism causes a particular disease
Krebs cycle: continuing series of reactions in cellular respiration that produces carbon dioxide, NADH, and $FADH_2$

L

labor: series of rhythmic contractions that cause the opening of the cervix of the uterus to expand so that it will be large enough to allow the baby to pass through
lactic acid fermentation: anaerobic process of glucose breakdown that produces lactic acid
large intestine: organ, also known as the colon, that removes water from the undigested materials that pass through it
larva: immature stage of an organism that is unlike the adult form in appearance
larynx: structure at the top of the trachea that contains the vocal cords
lateral bud: meristematic area on the side of a stem that gives rise to side branches
learning: way animals change their behavior as a result of experience
leech: annelid worm that typically exists as an external parasite that drinks the blood and body fluids of its host
lichen (LIGH-kuhn): symbiotic partnership between a fungus and a photosynthetic organism
ligament: strip of tough connective tissue in a joint that surrounds bones and holds them together

light reactions: reactions of photosynthesis that require light

limit of resolution: point of magnification in a microscope beyond which images become blurry and lose detail

limiting factor: condition that limits the rate at which energy is produced in an ecosystem by preventing a species from growing to its potential

linkage group: genes that are inherited in a group

linked genes: genes that are inherited together and do not undergo independent assortment

lipid: waxy or oily organic compound that stores energy in its bonds

liter (L): basic metric unit of volume for liquids

liver: large organ that lies above the stomach, secretes bile, and stores excess glucose in the form of glycogen

logistic growth curve: graph of a curve that shows the various growth phases experienced by a given population

LSD: powerful hallucinogen that interferes with the normal transmission of nerve impulses in the brain

lung: organ of respiration specialized for the exchange of gases between the blood and the atmosphere

lymph node: structure in the lymphatic system that acts as a filter and produces special white blood cells

lymphatic (lihm-FAT-ihk) **system**: network of vessels that collects fluid lost by the blood and returns it to the circulatory system

lymphocyte: white blood cell that responds to the presence of antigens

lysogenic (ligh-soh-JEHN-ihk) **infection**: process in which viral DNA is inserted into the DNA of a host cell where it can remain for many generations before becoming active

lysosome (LIGH-suh-sohm): organelle that contains chemicals and enzymes necessary for digesting certain materials in the cell

lysozyme: enzyme that breaks down the cell walls of many bacteria

lytic infection: process in which a host cell is invaded, lysed, and destroyed by a virus

M

macromolecule: large polymer

macronucleus: larger of two types of nuclei in ciliates, which controls the life process of the cell

mammary gland: gland in female mammals that produces milk to nourish the young for some time after they are born

mandible: mouthpart designed for biting and grinding food

mantle: thin, delicate layer of tissue that covers most of a mollusk's body and secretes the shell when one is present

marijuana: drug that comes from a species of hemp plant known as Cannabis sativa

marine biome: ocean habitat

marsupial: nonplacental mammal in which the fetus is born at a very immature stage and completes its development in a pouch on the mother's body

marsupium (mahr-SOO-pee-uhm): pouch in marsupials where the young embryos complete development

mass: measure of the amount of matter in an object

mass extinction: phenomenon in which many species suddenly vanish

mass number: total number of protons and neutrons in the nucleus of an atom

medulla (mih-DUL-ah): part of the brain that controls internal organ functions and maintains balance

medulla oblongata: part of the brainstem that controls involuntary functions that include breathing, blood pressure, heart rate, swallowing, coughing, and keeping the brain alert

medusa (meh-DOO-sah): motile bell-shaped cnidarian

meiosis: process that produces haploid gametes from diploid cells

menopause: period after which follicle development no longer occurs and a female is no longer capable of bearing a child

menstrual cycle: process that involves the development and release of an egg for fertilization and the preparation of the uterus to receive a fertilized egg

menstruation: last phase of the menstrual cycle during which the lining of the uterus along with blood and the unfertilized ovum are discharged through the vagina

meristematic (mer-uh-stuh-MAT-ihk) **tissue**: plant tissue that produces new cells by mitosis

mesoderm: middle primary germ layer in an animal embryo

mesophyll: layer of cells that contains chloroplasts and performs most of a plant's photosynthesis

messenger RNA (mRNA): type of RNA that carries genetic information from the DNA in the nucleus out to the ribosomes in the cytoplasm

metabolism: sum of all chemical reactions in the body; balance of anabolism and catabolism

metamorphosis: series of dramatic changes in body form in the life cycle of some animals

metaphase: second phase of mitosis in which the chromosomes line up across the equator of the cell

meter (m): basic metric unit of length

methanogen: bacterium that produces methane gas

metric system: universal system of measurement scaled on the multiples of ten

microfossil: preserved remains of an ancient microscopic organism

micronucleus: small nucleus in ciliates that undergoes meiosis and mitosis during conjugation and contains more genes than the macronucleus

midbrain: part of the brainstem that is involved in hearing and vision

mineral: inorganic substance required by the body

mitochondrion (might-oh-KAHN-dree-uhn): organelle that changes chemical energy stored in food into compounds that can be used by the cell

mitosis (migh-TOH-sihs): process by which the nucleus of a cell is divided into two nuclei, each with the same number and kinds of chromosomes as the parent cell

mixture: substance composed of two or more elements or compounds that are mixed together but not chemically combined

molecule: collection of two or more atoms covalently bonded

mollusk: soft-bodied invertebrate animal that is characterized by an internal or external shell, a foot, a mantle, and visceral mass; member of the phylum Mollusca

molt: to shed an exterior layer of skin, feathers, or an exoskeleton

Monera: kingdom that includes prokaryotic organisms

monocot: angiosperm whose seeds have one cotyledon

monomer: small compound that can be joined together with other small compounds to form polymers

monosaccharide: simple carbohydrate, also known as single sugar

monotreme: egg-laying mammal that belongs to the order Monotremata

morphine: chemically refined form of opium that is effective as a painkiller in small supervised doses

morula (MOR-yoo-luh): solid ball of cells that makes up an embryo; in humans, this stage occurs four days after fertilization

motor neuron: neuron that carries impulses from the brain and spinal cord to muscles and glands

multicellular: description of an organism consisting of many cells, some of which are typically specialized for particular functions

multiple alleles: three or more alleles of the same gene that code for a single trait

multiple sclerosis: nerve disease that results from autoimmune destruction of the myelin sheath that surrounds nerve fibers

muscular system: system that provides movement to the body and is composed of tissues that contract when stimulated

mutagen: substance or agent that can cause a mutation

mutation: change in the genetic material of a cell

mutualism: symbiosis in which two species live together in such a way that both benefit from the relationship

mycelium (migh-SEE-lee-uhm): thick mass of tangled filaments that make up the body of a fungus

mycorrhiza (migh-koh-RIGH-zuh): symbiotic relationship between a fungus and the roots of a green plant

myelin: substance composed of lipids and protein that forms an insulated sheath around an axon

myosin: protein that makes up the thick filaments of a muscle cell

Myxomycota (mihks-uh-migh-KOH-tuh): phylum containing acellular slime molds

N

nail matrix: area of rapidly dividing cells located at the tips of the fingers and toes that produces nails

natural selection: process in nature that results in the most fit organisms producing offspring

negative-feedback mechanism: control mechanism whereby an increase in a substance inhibits the process leading to the increase

nematocyst (neh-MAT-oh-sihst): stinging structure on the tentacles of cnidarians that is used to paralyze or kill prey

Nematoda (nee-mah-TOHD-ah): phylum containing roundworms

nephridium (neh-FRIHD-ee-uhm): simple tube-shaped excretory organ used to remove ammonia from the blood and release it from the body

nephron (NEHF-rahn): basic functional unit of the kidneys that filters out impurities from the blood

nervous system: system that receives and relays information about activities within the body and monitors and responds to internal and external changes

neuron: cell that carries impulses throughout the nervous system

neurotransmitter: substance used by one neuron to signal another

neutralization reaction: chemical reaction that occurs when the hydrogen ions of a strong acid react with the hydroxide ions of a strong base to form water and a salt

neutron: subatomic particle that is electrically neutral and is located in the atomic nucleus

niche (NIHCH): combination of an organism's habitat and its role in that habitat

nicotine: poisonous substance in tobacco that enters the bloodstream and causes the release of epinephrine

nitrogen cycle: movement of nitrogen through the biosphere between organisms and the atmosphere

nitrogen fixation: process by which nitrogen in the atmosphere is converted into a form that can be used by living things

nonbiodegradable: description of material that cannot be broken down by natural processes or is broken down extremely slowly

nondisjunction: failure of homologous chromosomes to separate normally during meiosis

nonspecific defense: defense mechanism of the body that guards against all infections rather than a particular pathogen

notochord: flexible supporting rod that runs along the dorsal surface of the body and is found in all chordates at some point in their development

nuclear envelope: membrane that surrounds the nucleus of a cell

nucleic acid: large, complex organic molecule that stores and transmits genetic information

nucleolus (noo-KLEE-uh-luhs): cell structure that contains RNA and proteins

nucleotide: unit of a nucleic acid that is made up of a 5-carbon sugar, a phosphate group, and a nitrogenous base

nucleus: in atoms, the center, which contains neutrons and protons and accounts for 99.9 percent of the atom's mass; in cells, the organelle that controls the cell's activities and contains DNA

nutrition: study of how bodies obtain energy, build tissue, and control body functions using materials supplied in food

O

obligate aerobe: organism that requires a constant supply of oxygen in order to live

obligate anaerobe: organism that lives only in the absence of oxygen

olfactory bulb: most anterior part of a fish's or amphibian's brain, involved in the sense of smell

oligochaete (AHL-ih-goh-keet): annelid worm belonging to the class that contains common earthworms and related species that live in soil and in water

oncogene: cancer-causing gene

open circulatory system: system in which blood does not always travel inside blood vessels

operant conditioning: trial-and-error learning in which an animal learns to behave in a certain way in order to receive a reward or avoid punishment

operator: region of chromosome near the cluster of genes in an operon to which the repressor binds when the operon is "turned off"

operon: genes and regions of DNA that operate together; consists of a gene cluster and regions involved in the regulation and expression of that cluster

opiate: powerful drug produced from the opium poppy

opposable thumb: thumb that is independent from the rest of the fingers, enabling hominids to grasp objects

optic lobe: in some animals, the part of the brain that processes information from the eyes

order: group of closely related families

organ: group of tissues that work together to perform a specific function

organ system: group of organs that work together to perform a specific function

organelle (or-guh-NEHL): cell structure that performs a specialized function within the cell

organic compounds: primarily those compounds that contain carbon

osmosis (ahs-MOH-sihs): diffusion of water molecules through a selectively permeable membrane from an area of higher water concentration to an area of lower water concentration

ossification (ahs-uh-fih-KAY-shuhn): process in which cartilage is replaced by bone

osteocyte (AHS-tee-oh-sight): cell in compact and spongy bone that is responsible for bone growth and changes in the shape of bones

ovary: in animals, female gonad that produces ova and estrogens; in plants, base of the pistil that contains ovules and developing gametophytes

oviparous (oh-VIHP-ah-ruhs): description of species that lay eggs that develop outside the mother's body

ovoviviparous (oh-voh-vigh-VIHP-ah-ruhs): description of species whose young develop inside the mother's body but are not nourished directly by the mother's body

ovulation: process that involves the release of a mature ovum from the ovary

ovule: specialized reproductive structure in seed plants

ovum: egg produced in an ovary; animal egg cell

oxygen cycle: movement of oxygen through the environment

P

paleontologist: scientist who studies fossils

palisade layer: layer of tall, column-shaped mesophyll cells just beneath the epidermal covering of a leaf

pancreas: organ that is both an exocrine gland and an endocrine gland; secretes digestive fluids and the hormones insulin and glucagon

paramecium: unicellular slipper-shaped ciliate protist

parasite: organism that survives by living and feeding either inside of or attached to outer surfaces of another organism, thus doing harm to that host organism

parasympathetic nervous system: portion of the autonomic nervous system that controls the internal organs during routine activities

parathyroid gland: gland that produces parathyroid hormone (PTH) and is attached to or embedded in the thyroid gland

parenchyma (puh-REHNG-kuh-muh): tissue composed of thin-walled cells found in roots, stems, and leaves

passive immunity: type of immunity that results when antibodies produced by other animals against a pathogen are injected into the bloodstream

pathogen: disease-causing microorganism

PCP: hallucinogen, also known as angel dust, that produces feelings of strength and power as well as nightmarish illusions and seizures; has been known to produce heart attacks

pellicle: complex living outer layer of certain protists

penis: external male reproductive organ; the organ through which the urethra connects to the outside of the body in humans and certain other animals

peptide bond: covalent bond that joins two amino acids

perennial: plant that grows and reproduces for an indefinite number of years

pericycle: type of cambium that enables roots to grow thicker and branch

period: interval in a geologic time scale that is composed of epochs

periosteum (per-ee-AHS-tee-uhm): tough membrane that surrounds bone

peripheral nervous system: division of the nervous system that lies outside the central nervous system and contains the cranial and spinal nerves and ganglia

peristalsis: rhythmic muscular contractions that move food through the digestive system

petal: structure located in the second circle of flower parts just inside the sepals

petiole: structure that attaches the leaf blade to the stem

pH scale: measurement system that ranges from 0 to 14 and indicates the relative concentrations of hydrogen ions and hydroxide ions in a substance

phagocyte: white blood cell that engulfs and destroys microorganisms

pharyngeal slit: structure that appears in pairs in the throat region of a chordate's body

pharynx (FAR-ihnks): muscular tubelike structure located at the back of the mouth that connects the mouth with the rest of the digestive tract

phase: physical property of matter that describes one of a number of different states of the same substance

phenotype: physical characteristics of an organism

pheromone: specific chemical messenger produced by an organism that affects the behavior and/or development of other individuals of the same species

phloem: vascular tissue responsible for the transport of nutrients and the products of photosynthesis throughout the plant

photoperiodicity (foht-oh-pihr-ee-uh-DIHS-uh-tee): plant's response to the period of darkness to which it is exposed

photosynthesis: process in which autotrophs make their own food using the energy in light and CO_2 and H_2O

photosynthetic membrane: chlorophyll-containing membrane in chloroplasts that serves as the site of the light reactions

photosystem: cluster of pigment molecules within a photosynthetic membrane

phototrophic autotroph: organism that can trap the energy of sunlight and convert it to organic nutrients

phototrophic heterotroph: organism that is able to use sunlight for energy but also requires organic compounds for nutrition

phototropism: plant's growth responses to light

phylogenetic (figh-loh-juh-NEHT-ihk) **tree**: diagram that shows evolutionary relationships among different groups of organisms

phylum: group of closely related classes

physical property: characteristic of matter that can be observed and measured without permanently changing the identity of the matter

phytoplankton: any small photosynthetic organism found in great numbers near the surface of the ocean

pigment: colored substance that absorbs or reflects light

pistil: female reproductive structure in a flower formed from one or more carpels; consists of the ovary, style, and stigma

pituitary gland: endocrine gland at the base of the skull that secretes hormones that regulate body functions and control other endocrine glands

placenta: organ in placental mammals through which nutrients, oxygen, carbon dioxide, and wastes are exchanged between embryo and mother

placental mammal: mammal in which a placenta forms during development of the embryo

Plantae: kingdom that includes multicellular autotrophic organisms

plasma: liquid portion of the blood that contains water, dissolved fats, salts, sugars, and proteins

plasma cell: specialized B-lymphocyte that releases antibodies into the bloodstream to deal with an infection

plasmid: small circular piece of DNA in some bacterial cells that is often used in genetic engineering

plasmodium: mass of cytoplasm that contains many nuclei, such as the structure produced by acellular slime molds that contains thousands of nuclei enclosed in a single cell membrane

plastid: plant cell organelle involved in the storage of food and pigments

plastron: ventral part of a turtle's shell

platelet: tiny fragment of a cell that plays a part in the process of blood clotting

Platyhelminthes (pla-tee-hehl-MIHN-theez): phylum consisting of acoelomate flatworms such as tapeworms, flukes, and planarians

point mutation: gene mutation that affects a single nucleotide

polar nucleus: one of the two nuclei in the embryo sac of angiosperms that locate themselves in the center of the sac during fertilization

pollen chamber: structure in anther that produces microspore mother cells

pollen cone: male cone in gymnosperms that produces male gametophytes in the form of pollen grains

pollen grain: structure that contains the male gametophyte in seed plants

pollen tube: structure that grows once a pollen grain has landed on the stigma in order to bring the sperm cells to the egg nucleus

pollination: transfer of pollen from the anther of a stamen to the stigma of a pistil

polychaete (PAHL-ee-keet): segmented worm, usually marine, characterized by paired paddlelike appendages on its body segments and a bristly body

polygenic (pahl-uh-JEHN-ihk) **trait**: trait that is controlled by a number of genes

polymer: large compound formed by combinations of monomers

polymerization: process by which large compounds are constructed by joining smaller compounds

polyp (PAH-lihp): sessile flowerlike cnidarian

polyploidy: condition in which an organism has extra sets of chromosomes

polysaccharide: large molecule formed when many monosaccharides link together

pons: part of brainstem that provides a link between the cerebral cortex and the cerebellum

population: collection of individuals of the same species in a given area whose members can breed with one another

posterior: back end of a bilaterally symmetrical organism

posterior pituitary: part of the pituitary gland that secretes antidiuretic hormone (ADH) and oxytocin

powder feather: bird feather that releases a fine white powder that repels water and keeps it from penetrating the layer of down feathers

prehensile tail: tail found in New World monkeys that is used for grasping while climbing

primary follicle: cluster of cells that surround an ovum and prepare it for release from the ovary

primary immune response: production of antibodies from the first exposure to an antigen

primary tissue: tissue produced by the apical meristem

probability: likelihood that a particular event will occur

producer: organism that is able to make its own food from inorganic substances

progesterone: steroid hormone released by the corpus luteum

prokaryote (pro-KAHR-ee-oht): single-celled organism whose cells do not have a nucleus

promoter: region of a chromosome next to the operator in an operon to which RNA polymerase binds at the beginning of transcription

prophage: viral DNA attached to a bacterial chromosome

prophase: first phase of mitosis in which chromosomes become visible

prostaglandin (prahs-tuh-GLAN-dihn): hormonelike substance that functions only within the same cell in which it is produced

protein: complex polymer of amino acids that builds and repairs cells

prothallium (proh-THAL-ee-uhm): thin heart-shaped structure formed from the gametophyte of a fern

protist: unicellular eukaryotic organism belonging to the kingdom Protista

Protista: kingdom that includes all single-celled eukaryotic organisms

proton: positively charged subatomic particle located in the nucleus

protonema: tangled mass of green filaments in moss that forms during germination

protostome: organism whose mouth was formed from its blastopore during early embryonic development

pseudocoelomate: animal that has a body cavity that is partially lined with mesoderm

pseudopod (SOO-doh-pahd): fingerlike projection of cytoplasm used for movement and feeding

puberty: period of rapid growth and sexual maturation during which the reproductive system becomes fully functional

pulmonary circulation: division of the circulatory system in which blood flows between the heart and the lungs

punctuated equilibria: pattern of long stable periods interrupted by brief periods of change

Punnett square: chart showing the possible combinations of genes in the offspring of a cross

pupa (PYOO-pah): resting stage of metamorphosis in which the tissues of an insect are organized into the adult form

purebred: belonging to a group of organisms that can produce offspring having only one form of a trait in each generation

pyloric valve: valve between the stomach and the small intestine

Pyrrophyta (pigh-roh-FIGHT-uh): phylum containing protists known as dinoflagellates

R

radial symmetry: arrangement of the body parts of an organism in such a way that they repeat around an imaginary line drawn through the center of the organism's body

radicle: region at the base of the hypocotyl of a stem that contains an apical meristem and becomes the primary root

radioactive element: unstable element that decays into a stable element at a steady rate

radula (RAJ-oo-lah): in some mollusks, layer of flexible skin with hundreds of tiny teeth used for feeding

reabsorption: process by which most of the material removed from the blood at Bowman's capsule makes its way back into the blood

receptor: special sensory neuron in a sense organ that receives stimuli from the external environment

recessive: description of a form of a gene (allele) that is only expressed in the homozygous state

recombinant: individual organism with new combinations of genes

recombinant DNA: DNA molecule that forms from the combination of portions of two different DNA molecules

recycling: process by which certain kinds of solid wastes can be processed and used again

red blood cell: blood cell, also known as an erythrocyte, produced in bone marrow and filled with hemoglobin to transport oxygen; in humans, erythrocytes lack a nucleus

reflex: simplest response to a stimulus

reflex arc: receptor, sensory neuron, motor neuron, and effector that are involved in a quick response to a stimulus

reforestation: planting of new trees where old trees have been cut down or burned

rejection: process in which the immune system damages and destroys a transplanted organ

relative dating: technique used to determine the age of fossils by comparing them with other fossils in different layers of rock

relative frequency: number of times an event (allele) occurs compared with the number of times another event (other alleles for the same gene) occurs

replication (rehp-luh-KAY-shuhn): process by which DNA is duplicated before a cell divides

repressor: special protein that binds to the operator and thus turns off an operon

reproductive isolation: separation of populations so that they do not interbreed to produce fertile offspring

reproductive system: body system that produces, stores, nourishes, and releases gametes

respiration: process that involves oxygen and breaks down food molecules to release energy

respiratory system: group of organs working together to bring about the exchange of oxygen and carbon dioxide with the environment

resting potential: difference in charge across a nerve cell membrane resulting from the negative charge on the inside and the positive charge on the outside

restriction enzyme: protein capable of cutting genes at specific DNA sequences

retrovirus: type of virus that contains RNA as its genetic information

rheumatic fever: autoimmune disease that results when antibodies produced to destroy untreated streptococcus bacteria attack cardiac cells as well

rheumatoid arthritis: destructive inflammation of the joints produced by the actions of the immune system

rhizoid: in fungi, small branching hypha growing downward from the stolons that anchors the fungus, releases digestive enzymes, and absorbs digested organic material; in bryophytes, rootlike structure that anchors the plant to the ground

rhizome: thick, fleshy creeping stem that grows either on or just beneath the surface of the ground

ribonucleic acid (RNA): nucleic acid made of a single chain of nucleotides that acts as a messenger between DNA and the ribosome and carries out the process by which proteins are made from amino acids

ribosomal RNA (rRNA): type of RNA that makes up the major part of the ribosomes

ribosome: organelle in which proteins are made

root cap: structure that protects the root as it forces its way through the soil

roundworm: pseudocoelomate animal with a digestive system with two openings that belongs to the phylum Nematoda

rumen: chamber in the digestive tract of some herbivorous animals that contains symbiotic bacteria that produce enzymes needed to break down cellulose

S

saprophyte: organism that uses the complex molecules of a once-living organism as its source of energy and nutrition

sapwood: area in plants that contains water-conducting xylem tissue

Sarcodina (sahr-kuh-DIGH-nuh): phylum that contains protists that use pseudopods to move and feed

scale: specialized reproductive structure in gymnosperms that forms male or female cones; tough protective structure on the skin of animals such as certain fishes, reptiles, and birds

scanning electron microscope (SEM): microscope that uses a beam of electrons to scan the surface of a specimen and produce a three-dimensional image of the surface by recording the electrons that bounce off

science: process whose goal is to understand the natural world

scientific method: systematic approach to problem solving that involves observation and experimentation

scion: piece of a stem or a lateral bud that is cut from a parent plant and attached to another plant

sclerenchyma (sklih-REHNG-kuh-muh): cell with a tough, thick cell wall that strengthens and supports plant tissues

scrotum: external sac in which the testes are located

secondary immune response: defense mechanism that occurs when a pathogen reappears in the body involving B-cells and T-cells produced the first time the body was exposed to the disease

secondary phloem: new phloem cells formed on the surface of the vascular cambium that faces the outside of the stem

secondary sex characteristic: sex characteristic that appears at puberty

secondary xylem: new xylem cells formed on the surface of the vascular cambium that faces the center of the stem

sedimentary rock: rock that forms when grains of eroded rock and other materials are carried to the bottom of a body of water and build up under pressure into layers

seed coat: structure that surrounds a plant embryo and protects it and its food supply from drying out

seed dispersal: process of distributing seeds away from the parent plant

segregation: separation; in genetics, the separation of alleles during gamete formation

selective breeding: method of improving a species by choosing animals or plants that have desirable characteristics to produce offspring that have the parents' desirable traits

selectively permeable: description of a biological membrane that allows some substances to pass through but not others

self-pollination: process in which pollen falls from the anther to the stigma of the same flower or between flowers of the same plant

semen: combination of sperm and seminal fluid

seminal fluid: substance in which sperm are suspended that is produced by three glands in the abdominal cavity

seminiferous (sehm-uh-NIHF-er-uhs) **tubule**: one of thousands of tiny tubules that make up the testes

sense organ: structure that contains sensory receptors

sensory neuron: neuron that carries impulses from the sense organs to the brain and spinal cord

sepal: structure in the outermost circle of flower parts that encloses a bud before it opens and protects the flower while it is developing

sex chromosome: chromosome that is different in males and females; often involved in sex determination

sex-influenced: description of a trait that is caused by a gene whose expression differs in males and females

sex-linked: description of a trait that is determined by a gene located on one of the sex chromosomes

sexual reproduction: process in which two cells, normally from different individuals, unite to produce the first cell of a new organism

shell: structure in mollusks made by glands in the mantle that secrete calcium carbonate

sieve tube element: phloem cell that is joined with similar cells end to end to form a continuous tube throughout the plant

single-loop circulatory system: system of internal transport in which blood travels from the ventricle in the heart to the gills to the body to the atrium of the heart

skeletal muscle: tissue, also known as striated muscle, that is attached to bones and is responsible for voluntary movement

skeletal system: system consisting of the bones and their associated tissues that supports, protects, and provides flexibility to the body of humans and many other animals

sliding filament theory: concept in which actin and myosin filaments slide over one another during muscle contraction

slime mold: protist that is amebalike at one stage of its life and at other stages produces moldlike masses that give rise to spores

small intestine: digestive organ in which chyme from the stomach is flooded with enzymes and digestive fluids

smog: air pollutant consisting of a combination of smoke and fog

smooth muscle: tissue made up of spindle-shaped cells that control involuntary activities; found in internal organs and in blood vessel walls

solute: substance that is dissolved in a mixture

solution: homogeneous mixture in which one substance is dissolved in another

solvent: substance in which a solute is dissolved to produce a solution

somatic nervous system: division of the peripheral nervous system that regulates activities that are under conscious control

sorus: large cluster of sporangia on the underside of fern fronds

sound signal: stimulus used for communication among animals that involves the sense of hearing

species: group of organisms that share similar characteristics and can interbreed with one another to produce fertile offspring

specific defense: defense mechanism directed toward a specific disease-causing agent

sperm: male gamete

sperm nucleus: nucleus in angiosperms that results when the generative nucleus within the pollen grain divides

spindle: meshlike structure of microtubules that appears to guide the movements of chromosomes during mitosis

spirillum (spigh-RIHL-uhm): spiral-shaped bacterium

spongy mesophyll: layer of cells in leaves, arranged in a network with spaces between them, that connect with the stomata

spontaneous generation: hypothesis that life arises from nonlife

sporangium (spoh-RAN-jee-uhm): structure in ferns, some protists, and some fungi that contains spores

sporophyte: diploid plant that produces spores

Sporozoa (spohr-oh-ZOH-uh): phylum containing nonmotile parasitic protists

stamen: male reproductive structure of a flower belonging to the first circle of fertile leaves located just inside the petals

steady state: portion of a logistic growth curve in which the average growth rate is zero

stigma: upper part of a pistil upon which pollen grains are deposited

stimulant: drug that speeds up the actions of the nervous system

stock: plant to which a scion is grafted

stolon: stemlike hypha that grows parallel to a fungus's growth medium

stoma: opening in the leaf epidermis through which water vapor and oxygen pass out of the leaf and carbon dioxide passes into it

stomach: thick muscular sac in which food is partially digested; located just below the diaphragm in humans

style: stalk between the stigma and the ovary in a flower

substrate: reactant affected by an enzyme

survival of the fittest: principle that states that only individuals with characteristics best suited to their environment survive the struggle for existence

suspension: mixture containing nondissolved particles distributed within a solid, liquid, or gas

symbiosis (sihm-bigh-OH-sihs): close relationship between two species in which at least one species benefits from the other

sympathetic nervous system: portion of the autonomic nervous system that controls the internal organs during stressful situations and increased activity

symptom: change in the body as a result of a disease

synapse: point of contact at which an impulse is passed from one cell to another

syngamy (SIHNG-guh-mee): the fusing of algal gametes

systemic circulation: division of the circulatory system in which blood flows between the heart and all the tissues of the body other than the lungs

T

T-lymphocyte: lymphocyte that matures in the thymus gland

taiga (TIGH-guh): biome dominated by great coniferous forests

taproot: primary plant root that grows longer and thicker than other roots

tar: mixture of complex chemicals in tobacco products

target cell: cell that has receptors for a particular hormone

target organ: part of an organism affected by a hormone

taxon: group into which organisms are classified

taxonomy: science of naming organisms and assigning them to groups

telophase: final phase of mitosis, during which chromosomes uncoil, a nuclear envelope reforms around the chromatin, and a nucleolus becomes visible in each daughter nucleus

temperate deciduous forest: biome characterized by changing seasons and leaf fall

temperature inversion: condition in which a layer of cool air becomes trapped beneath a layer of warm air, keeping pollutants near the ground

tendon: tough connective tissue that joins skeletal muscle to bone

test cross: cross between an organism of unknown genotype and an organism that is homozygous recessive for a particular trait

testis (TEHS-tihs): male gonad that produces sperm and androgens

testosterone (tehs-TAHS-ter-ohn): principal male sex hormone that stimulates the development of many male sex characteristics

thalamus: structure in the vertebrate brain that serves as a switching station for sensory input

theory: time-tested concept that makes useful and dependable predictions about the natural world

thermal pollution: type of water pollution in which heated water is pumped into the environment, often killing aquatic plants and animals

thigmotropism: response to touch

threshold: minimum level of a stimulus required to activate a neuron

thymine (THIGH-meen): nitrogenous base found in DNA but not in RNA; base pairs with adenine

thyroid gland: gland located at the base of the neck that produces thyroxine and calcitonin

tissue: group of similar cells that perform a particular function

toxin: poison

trachea: tube through which air passes from the pharynx to the lungs; windpipe

tracheid: cell in xylem tissue that conducts water and gives strength to the plant

trait: characteristic that a living thing can pass on to its young

transcription: process by which a molecule of DNA is copied into a complementary strand of RNA

transfer RNA (tRNA): type of RNA that carries amino acids to the ribosomes where the amino acids are joined together to form polypeptides

transformation: process by which genetic material absorbed from the environment is added to or replaces part of a bacterium's DNA

transgenic: description of an organism that contains foreign genes

translation: process in which a message carried by messenger RNA is decoded into a polypeptide chain (protein)
transmission electron microscope (TEM): microscope that uses a beam of electrons to magnify an image onto a fluorescent screen
transpiration: evaporation of water from plant leaves
transpiration pull: force that pulls water from the roots to the leaves as a result of the evaporation of water from the leaves
trichocyst (TRIHK-oh-sihst): flask-shaped structure in the pellicles of some protists used to defend and anchor the organism
trilobite (TRIGH-loh-bight): sea-dwelling organism belonging to the oldest, now extinct, subphylum of arthropods
tropical rain forest: biome in which the temperature stays warm and rain falls year round
tropism (TROH-pihz-uhm): response of an organism to an environmental stimulus
tube foot: suction-cuplike structure connected to the water vascular system of an echinoderm
tube nucleus: nucleus that results from the mitotic division of the nucleus of a pollen grain during the pollination of a flower
tuber: modified underground stem swollen with stored food
tumor: mass of tissue
tundra: northernmost land biome covered by mosses, lichens, and grasses and characterized by permafrost

U

unicellular: description of an organism consisting of only a single cell
uniramian (yoo-nih-RAY-mee-ahn): member of the largest subphylum of arthropods; contains centipedes, millipedes, and insects
unsegmented worm: worm whose body is not divided into special sections by internal partitions; flatworms and roundworms
uracil (YOOR-uh-sihl): nitrogenous base found only in RNA; base pairs with adenine
ureter (yoo-REET-er): tube that carries fluid from the kidney to the urinary bladder or cloaca
urethra: tube through which urine is released from the body
urinary bladder: saclike organ where urine is stored before being excreted
uterus: organ lying between the Fallopian tubes and the vagina in which a fertilized ovum can develop

V

vaccination: injection of a weakened or mild form of a pathogen used to produce immunity
vacuole (VAK-yoo-ohl): organelle that stores materials such as water, salts, proteins, and carbohydrates
vagina: canal that leads from the uterus to the outside of the female body
variable: single factor that is isolated and tested in an experiment
vas deferens (VAS DEHF-uh-rehnz): tube that carries sperm from the epididymis to the urethra
vascular bundle: strand of xylem and phloem cells
vascular cambium: meristematic area that produces vascular tissues and increases the thickness of stems over time
vascular cylinder: central area of a plant root where xylem and phloem tissues are gathered
vascular tissue: specialized tissue that transports water and the products of photosynthesis throughout a plant; xylem and phloem tissue
vector pollination: pollination by the actions of animals
vein: in animals, blood vessel that collects blood from the body and carries it back to the heart; in plants, area in leaves containing one or more bundles of vascular tissue
vena cava (VEE-nah KAY-vah): large blood vessel that brings blood from all parts of the body except the lungs to the heart
ventral: lower side of an organism with bilateral symmetry
ventricle (VEHN-trihk-uhl): muscular chamber that pumps blood out of the heart
vertebral column: backbone, which encloses and protects the nerve cord
vertebrate: animal that has a backbone
vessel element: xylem cell in angiosperms that forms part of a continuous tube through which water can move
vestigial organ: structure that serves no useful purpose or function in an organism
villus: folded projection that increases the surface area of the walls of the small intestine
virus: noncellular particle made up of genetic material and protein that can invade living cells
visceral mass: structure in mollusks that contains the internal organs
visual signal: stimulus used for communication among animals that involves the sense of sight
vital capacity: maximum amount of air that can be moved into and out of the respiratory system
vitamin: complex molecule needed by the body in small amounts that usually cannot be synthesized by the body
viviparous: species that bears living young and in which the unborn young are directly nourished by the mother's body
vocal cord: elastic fold of tissue in the larynx that produces sound when exhaled air is passed by it, causing it to vibrate

W

water cycle: movement of water from the atmosphere to the Earth and back to the atmosphere

water vascular system: internal network of fluid-filled canals involved in feeding, respiration, internal transport, elimination of wastes, and movement in echinoderms

weight: measure of the pull of gravity on a mass

white blood cell: blood cell produced in bone marrow that protects the body against invasion by foreign cells or substances

withdrawal: stopping the use of a drug

X

X chromosome: sex chromosome; in humans, fruit flies, and certain other organisms, females have two X chromosomes and males have only one

xylem: vascular tissue that provides support to a plant and conducts water from the roots to all parts of the plant

Y

Y chromosome: male sex chromosome in humans, fruit flies, and certain other organisms

Z

zone of elongation: area where cell enlargement occurs in plants

zone of maturation: region in plants in which newly lengthened cells differentiate

Zoomastigina (zoh-oh-mas-tuh-GIGH-nuh): phylum consisting of animallike protists that move through the water by means of flagella

zoospore (ZOH-oh-spohr): haploid cell involved in asexual reproduction in algae

zygospore: in fungi, thick-walled zygote formed during sexual reproduction in zygomycetes; in green algae, diploid cells resulting from conjugation

zygote (ZIGH-goht): fertilized egg cell

Index

A

B

C

D

H

I

J

K

L

M

N

O

P

R

S

T

U

V

Z

Credits

Cover Art: Joseph Cellini

Photo Research: Natalie Goldstein, Yvonne Gerin, Barbara Scott

Design and Layout: Function Thru Form Inc.

Contributing Artists: Joel Ito **817** bottom; **818**; **819** top left, bottom right; **820** top left, bottom; **823** top; **825** bottom left; **827** bottom left; **830** top right; **831** top right, bottom right; **838** top left, bottom right; **839** bottom left; **840** top left, **841** top right, bottom right; **842** top; **846**; **847** bottom left; **867**; **869** top right; **871** bottom right; **872**; **883** top left; **884** top left; **885**;**898** top left, bottom right; **900** top left; **902**; **904**; **909** top right, bottom left; **919** top left; **920**; **922** top; **923** bottom left. John Rowe **178**; **179**. Raymond Smith **246**; **264**; **265**; **268** top; **273**; **281** top left; **309**; **312**; **342**; **706**; **709**; **722**; **736**; **786**; **787**; **791**; **796**; **1024**; **1025**. All other art by Lee Ames & Zak Ltd.

Photographs: i Stephen J. Krasemann/DRK Photo; **vi** left: John Gerlach/Tom Stack & Associates; right: Wolfgang Kaehler; **vii** top: Eric V. Grave/Phototake; bottom: DPI; **viii** top: Wayne Lynch/DRK Photo; left: Hans Reinhard/Bruce Coleman Inc.; **ix** top: Dr. E.R. Degginger; center: Eric V. Grave/Phototake; bottom: Manfred Kage/Peter Arnold; **x** top: Harvey Lloyd/The Stock Market; bottom: Kjell B. Sandved; **xi** top: F. Stuart Westmorland/Tom Stack & Associates; left: J.H. Robinson/Photo Researchers; right: Denise Tackett/Tom Stack & Associates; **xii** top: Jeff Rotman; bottom: Leonard Lee Rue III/Animals Animals; **xiii** left top: Ronn Maratea/International Stock Photography; bottom: Brian Brake/Photo Researchers; right: David M. Phillips/Visuals Unlimited; **xiv** top: NASA/Science Source/Photo Researchers; left: Don Carroll/The Image Bank; right: Doug Perrine/DRK Photo; **xv** top: Brian Parker/Tom Stack & Associates; bottom: Dean Cornwell/The Bettmann Archive; inset: Dwight Kuhn/DRK Photo; **xvi** top: W.H. Hodge/Peter Arnold; bottom: Larry Lefever/Grant Heilman; **xvii**: Zig Leszczynski/Animals Animals; **2** D. McCoy/R. Feldman/Rainbow; **2** and **3** Wolfgang Kaehler; **4** Laurent Chana/The Image Bank; **5** Michael Coyne/The Image Bank; **6** top: Suzanne & Nick Geary/TSW-Click/Chicago; bottom: Wolfgang Kaehler; **7** Giuliano Colliva/The Image Bank; **12** left: John Gerlach/DRK Photo; right: CNRI/Science Photo Library/Photo Researchers; **13** left: Willi Dolder/TSW-Click/Chicago; right: J.F. Preedy/TSW-Click/Chicago; bottom: Kim Taylor/Bruce Coleman, Inc.; **15** The Granger Collection; **16** left: Co Rentmeester/The Image Bank; top right: Mitch Reardon/TSW-Click/Chicago; bottom right: Warren & Genny Garst/Tom Stack & Associates;**17** left: Will McIntyre/Photo Researchers; right: Sepp Seitz/Woodfin Camp & Associates; **18** John Lei/OMNI-Photo Communications; **20** St. Mary's Hospital Medical School/Photo Researchers; **21** clockwise: Chris Bjornberg/Photo Researchers; F.S. Mitchell/Tom Stack & Associates; Dick Durrance/Woodfin Camp & Associates; Jeffrey D. Smith/Woodfin Camp & Associates; Steve Niedorf/The Image Bank; **26** Rod Planck/TSW-Click/Chicago; inset: Susan McCartney/Photo Researchers; **27** left: Runk/Schoenberger/Grant Heilman; right: K.H. Switak/Photo Researchers; **28** top left: Eric V. Grave/Photo Researchers; top right: Wolfgang Kaehler; bottom: David Smart/DRK Photo; **29** left: Breck P. Kent; right: Breck P. Kent; **30** top: James H. Carmichael/The Image Bank; bottom: Merlin B. Tuttle; **31** Belinda Wright/DRK Photo; **33** top: Frans Lanting; bottom: Fred Ward/Black Star; **35** top: Howard Sochurek/Woodfin Camp & Associates; left: M.I. Walker/Photo Researchers; center: M.I. Walker/Photo Researchers; right: M.I. Walker/Photo Researchers; **36** top: Ted Horowitz/The Stock Market; center: CNRI/Science Photo Library/Photo Researchers; bottom: CNRI/Science Photo Library/Photo Researchers; **37** top left: Dr. J.A.L. Cooke; top right: David Scharf/Peter Arnold, Inc.; bottom: Manfred Kage/Peter Arnold, Inc.; **38** Peter J. Kaplan/Medichrome/The Stock Shop; **39** top: Dean Cornwell/The Bettmann Archive; inset: Dwight Kuhn/DRK Photo; **44** top: Kjell B. Sandved/Photo Researchers; inset: D. McCoy/R. Feldman/Rainbow; **45** left: John Blaustein/Woodfin Camp & Associates; right: Jeff Foott/Tom Stack & Associates; **46** top: Paul Silverman/Fundamental Photographs; left: Richard Megna/Fundamental Photographs; center: David Sutherland/TSW-Click/Chicago; right: GJ Images/The Image Bank; **47** top: Fundamental Photographs; bottom: Dr. Mitsuo Ohtsuki/Science Photo Library/Photo Researchers; **48** top: Photo Researchers; **50** top: CEA-ORSAY/CNRI/Science Photo Library/Photo Researchers; bottom: Howard Sochurek; **56** top: Paul Silverman/Fundamental Photographs; bottom: Dwight Kuhn; **57** Chemical Design Ltd/Science Photo Library/Photo Researchers; **62** top: Will McIntyre/Photo Researchers; inset: Science Photo Library/Photo Researchers; **63** top: DPI; center: Tobias Heldt/The Image Bank; bottom: Dan Budnik/Woodfin Camp & Associates; **64** top: Dr. E.R. Degginger; center: Dr. E.R. Degginger; bottom: Dr. E.R. Degginger; right: Paul Silverman/Fundamental Photographs; **65** Science Photo Library/Photo Researchers; **67** left: Kip Peticolas/Fundamental Photographs; right: Dr. Tony Brain/Science Photo Library/Photo Researchers; **71** top: J. Litvay/Visuals Unlimited; bottom: Larry Ulrich/DRK Photo; **72** right: Kristen Brochmann/Fundamental Photographs; **73** Wayne Lynch/DRK Photo; **75** top left: Jan Cobb/The Image Bank; top right: John Gerlach/Tom Stack & Associates; bottom left: Wolfgang Kaehler; bottom right: Jan Cobb/The Image Bank; **77** Dave Umberger/Perdue News; **82** top: Robert Frerck/Odyssey; center: Robert Frerck/Odyssey; bottom: A. Boccaccio/The Image Bank; **84** and **85** DPI; **85** Len Rue, Jr./DRK Photo; **86** top: David M. Phillips/Visuals Unlimited; inset: Runk/Schoenberger/Grant Heilman; **87** inset: Eric V. Grave/Phototake; bottom: Dr. Jean Lorre/SPL/Science Source/Photo Researchers; **88** Leonard Lessin/Peter Arnold, Inc.; **92** top: M.R.J. Salton/Visuals Unlimited; bottom: S. Elems/Visuals Unlimited; **93** K.G. Murti/Visuals Unlimited; **94** left: CNRI/Science Photo Library/Photo Researchers; **95** right: Kenneth Miller; **96** top: Dr. Gopal Murti/Science Photo Library/Photo Researchers; bottom: David M. Phillips/Visuals Unlimited; **97** top: K.G. Murti/Visuals Unlimited; bottom: Biophoto Associates/Photo Researchers; **98** K.G. Murti/Visuals Unlimited; **99** left: David M. Phillips/Visuals Unlimited; right: David M. Phillips/Visuals Unlimited; **101** left, center, and right: M. Sheetz/University of Connecticut Health Center/J. Cell Biol.; **103** left: M. Abbey/Visuals Unlimited; **105** Drs. Haim Gamliel & Harvey M. Golomb/Dept. of Medicine, University of Chicago; **112** top: F. Bergemann/The Image Bank; bottom: Luis Castaneda/The Image Bank; **113** bottom: Wes Thompson Photography/The Stock Market; **114** left: Pat O'Hara/DRK Photo; right: Larry Ulrich/DRK Photo; **115** left: Luis Villota/The Stock Market; right: Runk/Schoenberger/Grant Heilman; **122** University of California, Lawrence Berkeley Laboratory; **129** right: Paul J. Sutton/Duomo; **130** left: David Madison/Duomo; **131** top left: Dr. Jeremy Burgess/Science Photo Library/Photo Researchers; top right: Dario Perla/After Image; bottom right: Roy Morsch/The Stock Market; **136** top: Oxford Molecular Biophysics Lab/SPL/Photo Researchers; inset: R. Langridge/D. McCoy/USCF Computer Grap/Rainbow; **137** bottom: Science Photo Library/Photo Researchers; **139** bottom: Lee Simon/Stammers/Science Photo Library/Photo Researchers; **141** right: Philippe Plailly/Science Photo Library/Photo Researchers; **142** Franklin & Gosling B-DNA, *Nature*/Franklin, Rosalind; **143** top: J.D. Watson/Cold Spring Harbor Laboratory; bottom: AP/Wide World Photos; **151** O.L. Miller, Jr., B.A. Hamkalo & C.A. Thomas/O.L. Miller; **158** top: Lennart Nilsson; inset: Ed Reschke/Peter Arnold, Inc.; (a) Ed Reschke/Peter Arnold, Inc.; (b) Ed Reschke/Peter Arnold, Inc.; (c) Ed Reschke/Peter Arnold, Inc. (d) Ed Reschke/Peter Arnold, Inc.; **159** Miriam Austerman/Animals Animals; **161** David M. Phillips/Visuals Unlimited; **162** top: Brownie Harris/The Stock Market; bottom: David M. Phillips/Visuals Unlimited;**164** bottom: K.G. Murti/Visuals Unlimited; **165** inset: S.L. McKnight and O.L. Miller, Jr./University of Virginia; **166** bottom: Science VU/Visuals Unlimited; **167** bottom: Ed Reschke/Peter Arnold, Inc.; **168** top left: Carolina Biological Supply Company; bottom left: Dr. Richard Linck/University of Minnesota, Department of Cell Biology and Neuroanatomy; top right: Ed Reschke/Peter Arnold, Inc.; **169** top left: Carolina Biological Supply Company; top right: Ed Reschke/Peter Arnold, Inc.; bottom left: Carolina Biological Supply Company; bottom right: Ed Reschke/Peter Arnold, Inc.; **170** top left: Carolina Biological Supply Company; top right: Ed Reschke/Peter Arnold, Inc., bottom: B.A. Palevitz/Tom Stack & Associates; **171** G.I. Bernard/Earth Scenes; **176** top: Ted Horowitz/The Stock Market; center: Gabe Palmer/The Stock Market; bottom: Steve Dunwell/The Image Bank; **177** left: Will & Deni McIntyre/Photo Researchers; right: Will & Deni McIntyre/Photo Researchers; **178** top: CNRI/Science Photo Library/Photo Researchers; bottom: Karl Aufderhelde/Visuals Unlimited; **179** top left: Rod Planck/Tom Stack & Associates; bottom left: DPI; right: Wayne Lynch/DRK Photo; **180** top: MV Cooke; inset: Gary S. Chapman/The Image Bank; **181** Hans Reinhard/Bruce Coleman, Inc.; **182** left: Dr. Jeremy Burgess/Science Photo Library/Photo Researchers; **189** Dr. E.R. Degginger; **190** left: Myrleen Ferguson/PhotoEdit; **192** Walter Chandoha; **193** right: Runk/Schoenberger/Grant Heilman; **204** top: Ron Kimball; bottom: Darwin Dale/Photo Researchers; **205** David M. Phillips/Visuals Unlimited; **208** Breck P. Kent; **212** Runk/Schoenberger/Grant Heilman; **214** W.H. Hodge/Peter Arnold, Inc.; **215** top and bottom: Erick Greene/Dept. of Avian Sciences; University of

California; **217** Hans Reinhard/Bruce Coleman, Inc.; **220** Dr. Bert O'Malley/PNAS 76:2253-2257,1979.FIG #5; **221** Nik Kleinberg/Picture Group; **226** top: Michel Tcherevkoff; **227** Lennart Nilsson/The Incredible Machine; **228** top: John Giannicchi/Science Source/Photo Researchers; center: David M. Phillips/Visuals Unlimited; bottom: Mary Kate Denny/PhotoEdit; **229** Technique des.in J. Lawrence et al/Jeanne B. Lawrence, Robert Singer, & Lisa Marselle; **230** Runk/Schoenberger/Grant Heilman; **231** Dr. E.R. Degginger; **232** top left: Stanley Flegler/ Visuals Unlimited; top right: Stanley Flegler/ Visuals Unlimited; bottom: Ed Reschke/Peter Arnold, Inc.; **233** Lennart Nilsson/The Incredible Machine; **234** Frank Siteman/Taurus Photos; **236** John Lei/Omni Photo Communications; **238** Robert Brenner/PhotoEdit; **240** top: Grace Moore/Imagery; inset: Mario Ruiz/Picture Group; **247** R. Van Nostrand/Photo Researchers; **248** top: Wolfgang Kaehler; bottom: Hans Reinhard/Bruce Coleman, Inc.; **249** top left: Courtesy of Kenneth Miller; bottom left; Sven-Olaf Lindblad/Photo Researchers; top right: Barry L. Runk/Grant Heilman; bottom right; Dwight Kuhn; **250** Larry Lefever/Grant Heilman; **251** Phil Harrington/Peter Arnold, Inc.; **252** K.G. Murti/Visuals Unlimited; **254** Dr. Barbara Stebbins-Boaz; **255** top: Hank Morgan/ Photo Researchers; left: Eli Lilly Company; right: Dr. Steven Howell/University of California, San Diego, La Jolla; **256** Jackson Lab/Visuals Unlimited; **264** top: Hank Morgan/Rainbow; center: Robert Frerck/Odyssey; bottom: Lawrence Migdale/Photo Researchers; **269** left to right: Breck Kent; George D. Dodge/Tom Stack & Associates; Norman Owen Tomalin/ Bruce Coleman, Inc.; Brian Parker; **270** top: Chip Clark; bottom: Stephen Dalton/NHPA; **271** top left: E.R. Degginger/Bruce Coleman, Inc.; top right: D. Cavagnaro/DRK Photo; bottom: Gary Milburn/Tom Stack & Associates; **272** Timothy Eagan/Woodfin Camp & Associates; **275** top and inset: Kal Muller/Woodfin Camp & Associates; **278** left: Dr. E.R. Degginger; center: Dr. David Schwimmer/Bruce Coleman, Inc.; right: Jane Burton/Bruce Coleman, Inc.; **279** Jeff Gnass/The Stock Market; **280** left: George Polinar, Jr./University of California at Berkeley; right: M.D. Maser/Visuals Unlimited; **282** Tom Bean/ DRK Photo; **284** Frans Lanting; **285** top: Don & Pat Valenti/DRK Photo; bottom: Douglas Kirkland/Woodfin Camp & Associates; **290** top: Down House & The Royal College of Surgeons; inset: The Granger Collection; **291** bottom: Breck P. Kent; inset: Julie Habel/Woodfin Camp & Associates; **292** left: Gerard Lacz/NHPA; **293** bottom: Solarfilma; **294** top: Larry Lefever/Grant Heilman; center: Jane Grushow/Grant Heilman; bottom: John Colwell/Grant Heilman; right: Lewis Kemper/DRK Photo; **295** top: Dwight Kuhn; bottom: A. Upitis/ The Image Bank; 296 Dwight Kuhn; **297** top and bottom: Breck P. Kent; **298** top left: Joe McDonald/Tom Stack & Associates; top right: Breck P. Kent; bottom left: James H. Carmichael/The Image Bank; **299** Frans Lanting; **300** New York Public Library; **301** M. Philip Kahl/DRK Photo; **302** Nancy Adams/Tom Stack & Associates; **303** Hans Wolf/The Image Bank; **304** left and right; Aaron Norman; **305** top: Photo—R.E. Logan/American Museum of Natural History; bottom: C.B. & D.W. Frith/Bruce Coleman, Inc.; **307** center: Bruce Coleman, Inc.; right: Jessica Anne Ehlers/ Bruce Coleman, Inc.; **310** left: Merlin B. Tuttle; right: G.I. Bernard/NHPA; **311** top: Jeffrey Hutcherson/DRK Photo; bottom left: Belinda Wright/DRK Photo; bottom right: Stephen J. Krasemann/DRK Photo; **318** top: Brian Parker/ Tom Stack & Associates; bottom: George Holton/Photo Researchers; **319** Kevin Schaefer/ Tom Stack & Associates; **320** left: Jeanne White/ Photo Researchers; center: Larry Lipsky/DRK Photo; right: Jeff Rotman; **321** from top to bottom: Virginia P. Weinland/Photo Researchers; Michael P. Gadomski/Bruce Coleman, Inc.; Michael P. Gadomski/Photo Researchers; Marcia Stevens/New York Botanical Garden; **323** left: Belinda Wright/DRK Photo; top center: Tom McHugh/Photo Researchers; bottom center: Lee Green/West Light; top right: Stan Osolinski/TSW-Click/ Chicago; bottom right: Dick Candy/DRK Photo; **324** top left: Tom McHugh/Photo Researchers; top right: Peter Veit/DRK Photo; bottom: Peter Scoones/Seaphot; **326** Asa C. Thoresen/Photo Researchers; **327** top: Dr. Tony Brain/David Parker/SPL/Photo Reseachers; bottom: Runk/ Schoenberger/Grant Heilman; **328** top left: Larry Ulrich/DRK Photo; top right: Wolfgang Kaehler; bottom left: Breck P. Kent; bottom right: Steve Powell/All-Sport; **334** top: Robert Frerck/Odyssey; center: Dan Guravich/Photo Researchers; bottom: Robert Frerck/Odyssey; **335** Jack Dermid; **336** and **337** A. B. Dowsett/ Science Photo Library/Photo Researchers; **337** inset: M. Abbey/Visuals Unlimited; **338** top and inset: NASA; **341** L. West/Bruce Coleman, Inc.; **343** top: J.G. Paren/Science Photo Library/ Photo Researchers; bottom: Lynn Margulis, Dept. of Botany/University of Massachusetts; **344** top: Roger Ressmeyer/Starlight; **345** top left: Science VU/Sidney Fox/Visuals Unlimited: top right: Science VU/Sidney Fox/Visuals Unlimited; bottom right: Science VU-WHO/ Visuals Unlimited; **346** top: Breck P. Kent; bottom: William E. Ferguson; **347** CNRI/Science Photo Library/Photo Researchers; **348** top: CNRI/Science Photo Library/Photo Researchers; bottom: Dan McCoy/Rainbow; **349** Dan McCoy/Rainbow; **354** top: R. Feldman/ D. McCoy/Rainbow; inset: Oxford Molecular Biophysics Lab/SPL/Photo Researchers; **355** left: Norm Thomas/Photo Researchers; right: Dennis Kunkel—color by David Wacner/ Phototake; **356** bottom: B. Heggeler/ Biozentrum, University of Basel/SPL/Photo Researchers; **358** bottom: Lee D. Simon/ Science Source/Photo Researchers; **360** SIU/ Photo Researchers; **361** David M. Phillips/ Visuals Unlimited; **362** J.H. Robinson/Science Source/Photo Researchers; **363** Ralph Robinson/Visuals Unlimited; **364** left: Dr. Tony Brain & David Parker/SPL/Photo Researchers; center: David M. Phillips/Visuals Unlimited; right: David M. Phillips/Visuals Unlimited; bottom: David M. Phillips/Visuals Unlimited; **365** Barry Dowsett/Science Photo Library/Photo Researchers; **366** A.B. Dowsett/Science Photo Library/Photo Researchers; **367** George J. Wilder/Visuals Unlimited; **368** left: David Scharf/ Peter Arnold, Inc.; right: David M. Phillips/Visuals Unlimited; **369** top: Tom Stack & Associates; bottom: Biophoto Associates/Photo Researchers; **370** Thomas Kitchin/Tom Stack & Associates; **371** Corale L. Brierley/Visuals Unlimited; **372** top: Runk/Schoenberger/Grant Heilman; bottom: C.P. Vance/Visuals Unlimited; **373** top left: Tektoff-RM/CNRI/Science Photo Library/Photo Researchers; top right: CNRI/ Science Photo Library/Photo Researchers; bottom: NCI/Science Source/Photo Researchers; **374** top: Department of Zoology/ University of California; bottom: Department of Zoology/University of California; **375** CNRI/ Science Photo Library/Photo Researchers; **380** top: Manfred Kage/Peter Arnold, Inc.; inset: Eric V. Grave/Photo Researchers; **381** left: Manfred Kage/Peter Arnold, Inc.; right: Walker/ Photo Researchers; **382** top: Dr. E.R. Degginger; bottom: Biophoto Associates/Photo Researchers; **384** top: John D. Cunningham/ Visuals Unlimited; bottom: Eric V. Grave/Photo Researchers; **385** top: Eric V. Grave/Photo Researchers; bottom: Michael Abbey/Photo Researchers; **386** top: Brian Parker/Tom Stack & Associates; bottom: Eric V. Grave/ Photo Researchers; **387** top left: David M. Phillips/ Visuals Unlimited; top right: Jerome Paulin/ Visuals Unlimited; bottom: CNRI/Science Photo Library/Photo Researchers; **388** Lennart Nilsson/Bonnier Fakta; **389** M. Abbey/Visuals Unlimited; **390** top: Manfred Kage/Peter Arnold, Inc.; bottom left: Manfred Kage/Peter Arnold Inc.; bottom right: Eric V. Grave/Phototake; **392** Arthur M. Siegelman/Visuals Unlimited; **393** left: Eric V. Grave/Photo Researchers; right: Dwight Kuhn; **395** Biophoto Associates/Photo Researchers; **396** top: Biophoto Associates/ Photo Researchers; bottom: Terry Hazen/ Visuals Unlimited; **397** top: David M. Phillips/ Visuals Unlimited; bottom: Biophoto Associates/ Photo Researchers; **398** top left and right: Manfred Kage/Peter Arnold, Inc.; bottom: David M. Phillips/Visuals Unlimited; **399** top: CBS/ Visuals Unlimited; bottom left: B. Beatty/Visuals Unlimited; bottom right: John Shaw/Tom Stack & Associates; **400** top: Kevin Schaefer/Peter Arnold, Inc.; bottom: David M. Phillips/Visuals Unlimited; **401** top: Daniel W. Gotshall/Visuals Unlimited; center: Fred McConnaughey/Photo Researchers; bottom: Roland Birke/Peter Arnold, Inc.; **402** Manfred Kage/Peter Arnold, Inc.; **406** top: John Shaw/Tom Stack & Associates; inset: John Eastcott/Yva Momatiuk/ DRK Photo; **407** E.R Degginger/Bruce Coleman, Inc.; **410** top: R.C. Baye/Photo Researchers; **411** top: Fletcher W.K./Photo Researchers; bottom: Richard H. Thom/Tom Stack & Associates; **413** top left: C.B. & D.W. Frith/Bruce Coleman,Inc.; bottom left: J.L. Lepore/Photo Researchers; right: RIchard Kolar/Earth Scenes; **414** top: Kerry T. Givens/ Tom Stack & Associates; **415** top: David M. Phillips/Visuals Unlimited; bottom: David Scharf/Peter Arnold, Inc.; **416** left and right: R. Wenger/Sandoz Pharmaceutical; **417** Dick Canby/DRK Photo; **418** top left: Noble Proctor/ Photo Researchers; bottom left: A. Davies/ Bruce Coleman, Inc.; top right: Michael Fogden/ Bruce Coleman, Inc.; bottom right: CBS/Visuals Unlimited; **419** top: Dr. E.R. Degginger; center: Jack Dermid; bottom: L. West/Photo Researchers; **420** top left: Fred Mayer/Woodfin Camp & Associates; top right: Adam Woolfitt/ Daily Telegraph Magazine/Woodfin Camp & Associates; bottom: Lee Foster/Bruce Coleman, Inc.; **421** Biophoto Associates/Photo Researchers; **423** Dr. Charles Brewer Carias; **427** Dr. E.R. Degginger; **428** top: Bill Varie/The Image Bank; center: Pete Saloutos/The Stock Market; bottom: Dan McCoy/Rainbow; **429** Peter Parks/Oxford Scientific Films; **430** and **431** Wolfgang Kaehler; **431** Harvey Lloyd/The Stock Market; **432** top: Frans Lanting; inset: Dr. E.R. Degginger; **433** left: Scott Blackman/Tom Stack & Associates; right: D.P. Wilson/Eric & David Hosking/Photo Researchers; **434** Hal Clason, M. Photog/Tom Stack & Associates; **435** D.P. Wilson/Eric & David Hosking/Photo Researchers; **436** left: G.I. Bernard/Oxford

Scientific Films/Animals Animals; right: Doug Wechsler/Animals Animals; center: L. Sims/ Visuals Unlimited; bottom: Jeff Foott; **437** M.I. Walker/Photo Researchers; **438** center: MIchael Abbey/Science Source/Photo Researchers; left: John D. Cunningham/Visuals Unlimited; right: James Bell/Science Source/ Photo Researchers; bottom: Dwight Kuhn; **439** Jeff Foott; **442** top: B. & C. Alexander; center: DPI; bottom: R. Calentine/Visuals Unlimited; **443** Brad Hess/Black Star; **444** A.M. Siegelman/Visuals Unlimited; **448** top: D. Cavagnaro/DRK Photo; inset: L. West/Bruce Coleman, Inc.; **449** Jack Dermid; **450** top: Kjell B. Sandved; bottom: Stephen J. Krasemann/ DRK Photo; **452** left and right: Runk/ Schoenberger/Grant Heilman; **453** Dwight Kuhn; **455** Kjell B. Sandved; **456** G.R. Roberts; **457** top left: Addison-Wesley Biology Text; top right: Kevin Schaefer/Tom Stack & Associates; bottom: Kjell B. Sandved; **458** top: Kjell B. Sandved; bottom left: Jeff Foott/DRK Photo; bottom right: Kjell B. Sandved; **459** Stan Elems/ Visuals Unlimited; **460** Kjell B. Sandved; **461** top left: Rod Planck/Tom Stack & Associates; top right: Derek Fell; bottom: Pat O'Hara/DRK Photo; **465** Kjell B. Sandved; **466** top: Hans Pfletschinger/Peter Arnold, Inc.; inset: Jeff Lepore/Photo Researchers; **467** top: Wendy Shattil/Bob Rozinski/Tom Stack & Associates; inset: Wil Blanche/DPI; **468** top: G.R. Roberts; bottom left: Jack Dermid; bottom right: Wolfgang Kaehler; **469** Larry Ulrich/DRK Photo; **470** Tom Algire; **471** Dr. E.R. Degginger; **472** top left: Derek Fell; top right: John Trager/Visuals Unlimited; bottom: G.R. Roberts; **473** top: Doug Sokell/Tom Stack & Associates; bottom: Breck P. Kent/Earth Scenes; **474** top left: D. Cavagnaro/DRK Photo; top right: Wolfgang Kaehler; bottom: Kjell B. Sandved; **475** Dwight Kuhn; **476** left: Merlin B. Tuttle/Photo Researchers; right: Paul Skelcher/Rainbow; **477** Bob & Clara Calhoun/Bruce Coleman, Inc.; **478** top and bottom: Dr. E.R. Degginger; **479** top: John D. Cunningham/Visuals Unlimited; bottom left: John Gerlach/Tom Stack & Associates; bottom right: Coco McCoy/Rainbow; **480** William James Warren/West Light; **481** top: Ken W. Davis/Tom Stack & Associates; bottom: John Serrao/Photo Researchers; **485** Kjell B. Sandved; **486** top: Dr. E.R. Degginger; inset: Janice Travia/TSW-Click/Chicago; **487** Peter Katsaros/Photo Researchers; **488** top right: F.C. Earney/Visuals Unlimited; **489** top: Holt Studios, Ltd./Earth Scenes; bottom: Hans Christian Heap; **490** right: Hugh Spencer/Photo Researchers; **492** left: Dwight Kuhn; right: E.J. Cable/Tom Stack & Associates; **493** top: Biophoto Associates/Photo Researchers; bottom: P. Dayanandan/Photo Researchers; **494** top: Runk/Schoenberger/Grant Heilman; bottom: Dwight Kuhn; **495** left: P. Dayanandan/ Photo Researchers; right: J.F. Gennaro/NY Cellular Biology/Photo Researchers; **499** top: Dwight Kuhn; bottom: Dr. E.R. Degginger; **500** Breck P. Kent; **501** top left: Dwight Kuhn; bottom left: W.H. Hodge/Peter Arnold, Inc.; top right: Dwight Kuhn; bottom right: Jerome Wexler/ Photo Researchers; **502** top: Jane Burton/Bruce Coleman, Inc.; inset: Joe McDonald/Tom Stack & Associates; **503** John D. Cunningham/Visuals Unlimited; **504** top and bottom: Dr. Jeremy Burgess/Science Photo Library/Photo Researchers; **507** Jack Dermid; **508** Alan Pitcairn/Grant Heilman; **509** top: Tom Algire; center: Dr. E.R. Degginger; bottom: Richard Weiss/Peter Arnold, Inc.; **510** John D. Cunningham/Visuals Unlimited; **511** top left: Breck P. Kent; top right: Nundsany & Perennou/ Photo Researchers; bottom: Ed Reschke/Peter Arnold, Inc.; **516** top: D. Cavagnaro/DRK Photo; bottom: Steve Solum/Bruce Coleman, Inc.; **517** left: James H. Carmichael, Jr./The Image Bank; right: J. Castner; **518** left: Derek Fell; right: Lucy Jones/Visuals Unlimited; **519** left: DPI; right: Dr. William M. Harlow/Photo Researchers; **520** top: Bill Beatty/Visuals Unlimited; center and bottom: Wolfgang Kaehler; **522** top and bottom: Runk/ Schoenberger/Grant Heilman; **523** E.J. Cable/ Tom Stack & Associates; **524** Runk/ Schoenberger/Grant Heilman; **525** Biophoto Associates/Science Source/Photo Researchers; **526** John Sohlden/Visuals Unlimited; **527** top and bottom: Hans Pfletschinger/Peter Arnold, Inc.; **531** left and right: Tovah Martin; **532** top: Tom Bledsoe/DRK Photo; inset: D.M. Phillips/ Visuals Unlimited; **533** left: John Gerlach/Tom Stack & Associates; right: Breck P. Kent; **535** Brian Parker/Tom Stack & Associates; **536** top: B. Ormerod/Visuals Unlimited; bottom: James L. Castner; **538** top: Holt Studios/Earth Scenes; bottom left: James L. Castner; bottom right: T. Kitchin/Tom Stack & Associates; **539** top left: Gabriella Bergamini Mulcahy/University of MA —Amherst; top right: Runk/Schoenberger/ Grant Heilman; bottom: Dwight Kuhn; **541** top: Breck P. Kent; bottom: C.C. Lockwood/Earth Scenes; **543** top: Breck P. Kent; bottom: Runk/ Schoenberger/Grant Heilman; **544** top, center, and bottom: D. Cavagnaro/DRK Photo; **545** Runk/Schoenberger/Grant Heilman; **549** William E. Ferguson; **550** top: Gary Gladstone/ The Image Bank; center: Benn Mitchell/The Image Bank; bottom: Sepp Seitz/Woodfin Camp & Associates; **551** inset: Sydney Thompson/ Earth Scenes; bottom: Nicholas Foster/The Image Bank; **552** and **553**: Heather Angel **553** inset: CBS/Visuals Unlimited; **554** top: C.C. Lockwood/DRK Photo; inset: Denise Tackett/ Tom Stack & Associates; **555** left: Fran Allan/ Animals Animals; right: Jack Dermid; **556** top left: Robert Maier/Animals Animals; top right: Breck P. Kent; bottom: Polaroid-R. Oldfield/ Visuals Unlimited; **557** top left: Richard Matthews/Seaphot Limited/Planet Earth Pictures; top right: Georgette Douwma/Seaphot Limited/Planet Earth Pictures; bottom: Jeff Rotman; **558** top: David Maitland/Plant Earth Pictures; center: William E. Ferguson; bottom left: Robert Arnold/Planet Earth Pictures; bottom right: Doug Perrine; **559** Jeff Rotman; **560** Breck P. Kent; **561** left: Charles Seaborn/Odyssey/ Frerck; center: Jeff Rotman; right: Charles Seaborn/Odyssey/Frerck; **562** top: Oxford Scientific Films/Animals Animals; bottom: Doug Perrine; **563** Chris Howes: Seaphot Limited/ Planet Earth Pictures; **564** top: Breck P. Kent; bottom left: Charles Seaborn/Odyssey/Frerck; bottom right: Jeff Rotman; **566** top: Dwight Kuhn; bottom: John D. Cunningham/Visuals Unlimited; **567** top and bottom: Dave B. Fleetham/Tom Stack & Associates; **568** top left: Charles Seaborn/Odyssey/Frerck; top right: Jeff Rotman; bottom: Oxford Scientific Films/ Animals Animals; **569** Denise Tackett/Tom Stack & Associates; **570** Scott Johnson/Animals Animals; **571** Michael Abbey/Photo Researchers; **572** top: T.E. Adams/Visuals Unlimited; bottom left: Charles Seaborn/ Odyssey/Frerck; bottom right: Jeff Foott; **574** top: George J. Wilder/Visuals Unlimited; bottom: CNRI/Science Photo Library/Photo Researchers; **575** CNRI/Science Photo Library/ Photo Researchers; **577** CNRI/Science Photo Library/Photo Researchers; **578** top: R. Calentine/Visuals Unlimited; bottom: Edward Gray/Science Photo Library/Photo Researchers; **579** Eugene Richards/Magnum Photos; **584** top: Dick Clarke/Seaphot Limited/ Planet Earth Pictures; inset: E.R. Degginger/ Animals Animals; **585** left: Ken Lucas/Seaphot Limited; right: Richard LaVal/Animals Animals; **587** G. Alan Solem; **588** top left: David Maitland/ Seaphot Limited/Planet Earth Pictures; top right: W. Gregory Brown/Animals Animals; bottom: Mark Mattock/Planet Earth Pictures; **589** top left: Leo Collier/Seaphot Limited/Planet Earth Pictures; inset: Jim Doran/Animals Animals; bottom: Heather Angel; **590** top: Breck P. Kent/ Animals Animals; bottom left: F. Stuart Westmorland/Tom Stack & Associates; bottom right: Leo Collier/Seaphot LImited/Planet Earth Pictures; **591** top: Heather Angel; center: John Lythgoe/Planet Earth Pictures; bottom: Kjell B. Sandved; **592** top: P. Herring/Biofotos; center: Jack Wilburn/Animals Animals; bottom: A. Kerstitch; **594** Raymond A. Mendez/Animals Animals; **595** left: Kjell B. Sandved; right: Larry Lipsky/Tom Stack & Associates; **597** J.G. James/Planet Earth Pictures; **598** left: Kjell B. Sandved; right: David George/Seaphot Limited/ Planet Earth Pictures; **599** top: A. Kerstitch; bottom: Hans Pfletschinger/Peter Arnold, Inc.; **600** top: Oxford Scientific Films/Animals Animals; bottom: Oxford Scientific Films/ Animals Animals; **601** Geoff Tompkinson/ Aspect Picture Library; **605** Jeff Rotman; **606** top: J. Carmichael/The Image Bank; inset: Stanley Breeden/DRK Photo; **607** left: Gary A. Polis/Vanderbilt University; right: Don & Pat Valenti/DRK Photo; **608** top: Richard K. LaVal/ Animals Animals; bottom: John Cancalosi/Tom Stack & Associates; **609** top left: Jeff Foott/DRK Photo; top right: Catherine Ellis/Photo Researchers; center: Ken Lucas/Planet Earth Pictures; bottom: David Maitland/Planet Earth Pictures; **610** top: G.I. Bernard/Animals Animals; bottom left: Dwight Kuhn/DRK Photo; bottom right: James H. Carmichael/The Image Bank; **611** top: Joe McDonald/Tom Stack & Associates; **612** left: Kjell D. Sandved; right: Jeff Rotman; **613** top: Kjell B. Sandved; center: John Lythgoe/Planet Earth Pictures; bottom left: Raymond A. Mendez/Animals Animals; bottom right: J.H. Robinson/Photo Researchers; **614** left: L. & D. Klein/Photo Researchers; center: Stephen J. Krasemann/DRK Photo; right: Dwight Kuhn; **615** K.G. Preston-Mafham/ Premaphotos Wildlife; **616** Dwight Kuhn; **617** Dwight Kuhn; **618** top: David Maitland/Seaphot Limited/Planet Earth Pictures; bottom left: C.A. Henley; bottom right: Tom McHugh/Photo Researchers; **619** top: John Gerlach/DRK Photo; bottom left: Raymond A. Mendez/ Animals Animals; bottom right: L. West/Photo Researchers; **620** Donald Specker/Animals Animals; **621** top: Steinhart Aquarium/Photo Researchers; bottom: Dan Guravich/Photo Researchers; **622** top: Tom McHugh/Photo Researchers; bottom: Ken Lucas/Planet Earth Pictures; **624** left: Stephen Dalton/Photo Researchers; **625** top: Richard K. LaVal/ Animals Animals; bottom: Kjell B. Sandved; **626** Dwight Kuhn/DRK Photo; **628** Dwight Kuhn; **629** top: Ken W. Davis/Tom Stack & Associates; bottom: Doug Perrine/DRK Photo; **630** top: Catherine Ellis/Photo Researchers; bottom: Stephen Dalton/Photo Researchers; **631** left: Rod Planck/Tom Stack & Associates; center: Brian Parker/Tom Stack & Associates; top right and bottom right: Dr. E.R. Degginger; **632** John

Lei/Omni-Photo Communications; **636** Jeff Rotman/Jeff Rotman; inset: Roessler/Animals Animals; **637** top: A. Kerstitch/A. Kerstitch; bottom: Robert A. Ross/Dr. E.R. Degginger, FPSA; **638** Tom Stack/Tom Stack & Associates; **640** left: Herwarth Voightmann/Planet Earth Pictures; right: Doug Wechsler/Animals Animals; **641** Dave Woodward/Tom Stack & Associates; **642** left: Jeff Rotman/Jeff Rotman; right: Linda Pitkin/Planet Earth Pictures; **643** left: Jeff Rotman/Jeff Rotman; top right: Oxford Scientific Films/Animals Animals; bottom right: Kjell B. Sandved/Kjell B. Sandved; **644** top: Bill Wood/Planet Earth Pictures; center: Charles Seaborn/Odyssey/Frerck/Chicago; bottom: Leo Collier/Planet Earth Pictures; **646** top: Carl Roessler/Planet Earth Pictures; center: Dick Clarke/Planet Earth Pictures; bottom: M. Laverack/Planet Earth Pictures; **647** Larry Madin/Planet Earth Pictures; **651** Jeff Rotman/Jeff Rotman; **652** top: Nancy Sefton/Planet Earth Pictures; inset: James H. Carmichael, Jr./The Image Bank; **653** James L. Castner/James L. Castner; **654** Jeff Rotman/Jeff Rotman; **656** top: Photo Researchers; center: Photo Researchers; bottom: Photo Researchers; bottom left: Chuck Nicklin/Sea Library; bottom right: Oxford Scientific Films/Animals Animals; **659** Chuck Nicklin/Chuck Nicklin; **660** G.I. Bernard/Oxford Scientific Films/Animals Animals; **661** top: Robert Frerck/Robert Frerck; bottom: W. Gregory Brown/Animals Animals; **663** Kjell B. Sandved/Kjell B. Sandved; **665** top: Planet Earth Pictures; bottom: James M. King/Planet Earth Pictures; **667** top left: Dwight Kuhn/DRK Photo; top right: Chris Prior/Seaphot Limited/Planet Earth Pictures; bottom: J.H. Robinson/Photo Researchers; **668** top: C.A. Henley/C.A. Henley; bottom: C.A. Henley/C.A. Henley; **670** Zig Leszczynski/Animals Animals; **674** top: Ira Block/Woodfin Camp & Associates; center: Ed Wheeler/The Stock Market; bottom: Dan McCoy/Rainbow; **675** Jeff Rotman; left: Gary Milburn/Tom Stack & Associates; center: Robert Frerck/Odyssey; right: Doug Perrine/DRK Photo; **676** and **677** Leonard Lee Rue III/Animals Animals; **677** inset: Jeff Rotman; **678** top: Herwarth Voightmann/Planet Earth Pictures; inset: David M. Dennis/Tom Stack & Associates; **679** P. Herring/Biofotos; **680** top left: Animals Animals; top right: Jeff Rotman; bottom left: Breck P. Kent; **681** Charles Seaborn/Odyssey; **682** top: Peter David/Planet Earth Pictures; bottom left: Dave B. Fleetham/Tom & Stack Associates; bottom right: Norbert Wu/Planet Earth Pictures; **684** top: Doug Perrine/DRK Photo; bottom: Walter Deas/Seaphot Unlimited/ Planet Earth Pictures; **686** top left, top right, and bottom: Ken Lucas/ Planet Earth Pictures; **687** top : Jeff Foott/DRK Photo; center: Breck P. Kent; bottom: Ken Lucas/Planet Earth Pictures; **688** top: Carl Roessler/Planet Earth Pictures; bottom left: G.I. Bernard/Oxford Scientific Films/Animals Animals; bottom right: Ken Lucas/Planet Earth Pictures; **689** top: Charles Seaborn/Odyssey; center: Larry Lipsky/Tom Stack & Associates; bottom left: Charles Seaborn/Odyssey; bottom right: Kjell B. Sandved; **690** top: Breck P. Kent; bottom: Dwight Kuhn/DRK Photo; **691** Ken Lucas/Planet Earth Pictures; **692** Robert Frerck/Odyssey; **693** left: Raymond Mendez/Animals Animals; right: from top to bottom: Michael Fogden/DRK Photo; Juan M. Reujito/Animals Animals; Dwight Kuhn; Dwight Kuhn/DRK Photo; **697** Richard Thom/Tom Stack & Associates; **698** top: Zig Leszczynski/Animals Animals; center: David M. Dennis/Tom Stack & Associates; right: Stephen Dalton/Animals Animals; **699** left: Michael Fogden/Animals Animals; right, from top to bottom: Dwight Kuhn; E.R. Degginger/Animals Animals; P.J. Palmer/Planet Earth Pictures; **700** left and right: Breck P. Kent; **701** top: Don and Esther Phillips/Tom Stack & Associates; bottom: Michael Fogden/DRK Photo; **707** Breck P. Kent; **708** top left; Dwight Kuhn; top right: Wayne Lynch/DRK Photo; bottom: David M. Dennis/Tom Stack & Associates; **710** left: Breck P. Kent; right: Dwight Kuhn; **711** Heather Angel; **713** top and bottom: Tom McHugh/Photo Researchers; **714** top left: Kim Taylor/Bruce Coleman, Inc.; top right: Tom McHugh/Photo Researchers; center: Gary Milburn/Tom Stack & Associates; bottom: Breck P. Kent; **715** top left: Paul Kuhn/Tom Stack & Associates; top right: Frans Lanting/Minden Pictures; center: Wolfgang Bayer/Bruce Coleman, Inc.; bottom: Zig Leszczynski/Breck P. Kent; **716** top left: Jany Sauvanet/Photo Researchers; top right: Breck P. Kent; bottom: Belinda Wright/DRK Photo; **717** top left: Kjell B. Sandved; top right: Breck P. Kent; bottom: Michael Fogden/DRK Photo; **718** top: S. Nielsen/DRK Photo; center: Wayne Lynch/DRK Photo; bottom left: Stephen J. Krasemann/DRK Photo; bottom right: Dave B. Fleetham/Tom Stack & Associates; **719** Frans Lanting/Minden Pictures; **720** top: Breck P. Kent; bottom: Kjell B. Sandved; **721** Jeff Foott; **723** Jeff Lepore/Photo Researchers; **724** Chuck J. Lamphiear/DRK Photo; **725** top: Barbara Laing/Black Star; center: S. Nielsen/DRK Photo; bottom: Tom McHugh/ Photo Researchers; left: Johnny Johnson/DRK Photo; **727** Jeff Lepore/Photo Researchers; **728** John Cancalosi/Tom Stack & Associates; **730** left: John Shaw/Tom Stack & Associates; center: John Gerlach/DRK Photo; right: Belinda Wright/DRK Photo; **731** Michael Gadomski/Photo Researchers; **735** Johnny Johnson/DRK Photo; **737** Kennan Ward/DRK Photo; **738** top: Stephen J. Krasemann/DRK Photo; center: Dieter Blum/Peter Arnold, Inc.; bottom: Francois Gohier/Photo Researchers; **739** Rod Williams/Bruce Coleman, Inc.; **740** left: Gary Milburn/Tom Stack & Associates; right: Thomas Kitchin/Tom Stack & Associates; **741** Weinberg/Clark/The Image Bank; **742** top: Stephen J. Krasemann/DRK Photo; bottom: Frans Lanting/Minden Pictures; **743** top: Gregory G. Dimijian/Photo Researchers; bottom: Tom McHugh/Photo Researchers; **744** top: John Cancalosi/Peter Arnold, Inc.; bottom: Brian Parker/Tom Stack & Associates; **745** S.J. Krasemann/DRK Photo; **746** top: C.B. & B.W. Frith/Bruce Coleman, Inc.; bottom: Yeager & Kay/Photo Researchers; **747** left: Stephen Dalton/Photo Researchers; right: Merlin Tuttle/Photo Researchers; **748** top: Jeff Foott/Bruce Coleman, Inc.; center: Brian Parker/Tom Stack & Associates; bottom: John Shaw/Bruce Coleman, Inc.; **749** top left: Carleton Ray/Photo Researchers; top right: Stephen J. Krasemann/DRK Photo; bottom: Jeff Foott; **750** top left: Harry Engels/Photo Researchers; top right: Kevin Schaefer/Tom Stack & Associates; bottom left: Frans Lanting/Minden Pictures; bottom right: C.Allan Morgan/Peter Arnold, Inc.; **751** top: Melinda Berge/DRK Photo; bottom: Charlie Ott/Photo Researchers; **755** Kevin Schaefer/Peter Arnold, Inc.; **756** top: NASA; inset: From British Museum/Michael Holford; **757** left: Gary Milburn/Tom Stack & Associates; right: John Cancalosi/Peter Arnold, Inc.; **758** top: Tom McHugh/Photo Researchers; center: Dieter & Mary Plage/Bruce Coleman, Inc.; bottom: Stanley Breeden/DRK Photo; **759** left: Jack Swenson/Tom Stack & Associates; right: Nancy Adams/Tom Stack & Associates; **761** Cleveland Museum of Natural History; **762** Margo Crabtree; **763** top and bottom: Margo Crabtree; **764** American Museum of Natural History; **770** Johnny Johnson/DRK Photo; **771** Michael Fogden/DRK Photo; **772** top: Jonathan Scott/Planet Earth Pictures; bottom left: Breck P. Kent/Breck P. Kent; bottom right: Nancy Adams/Tom Stack & Associates; **774** top: Breck P. Kent; bottom: Frans Lanting; **775** Nina Leen/Life Magazine, Time, Inc.; **776** top: Tom & Pat Leeson/DRK Photo; bottom: Philip Chapman/Planet Earth Pictures; **777** top: Michael Fogden/DRK Photo; bottom: Raymond Mendez/Animals Animals; **778** Bruce Davidson/Animals Animals; **779** PH Powers/Sandved & Coleman; **784** top: Stephen J. Krasemann/DRK Photo; inset: Johnny Johnson/DRK Photo; **785** Kerry T. Givens/Tom Stack & Associates; **788** left: Steve Kaufman/Peter Arnold, Inc.; right: Breck P. Kent; **790** top: Breck P. Kent; bottom left: Wolfgang Kaehler; bottom right: Stephen J. Krasemann/DRK Photo; **797** CNRI/Science Photo Library/Photo Researchers; **799** Wolfgang Kaehler; **803** left: J.A. Hancock/Photo Researchers; right: Bob & Clara Calhoun/Bruce Coleman, Inc.; **804** top: Stephen J. Krasemann/DRK Photo; center: Robert Frerck/Odyssey; bottom: Dan McCoy/Rainbow; **805** top left: Ken Lucas/Planet Earth Pictures; bottom left: Breck P. Kent; right: Peter Scoones/Planet Earth Pictures; **806–807** Duomo/Dan Helms: inset: The Image Bank/J.L.Stage; **808** top: Library Science Source/Photo Researchers; inset: Eric V. Grave/Phototake; **809** left: Steven E. Sutton/Duomo; inset: Francis Leroy/Photo Researchers; **810** Lennart Nilsson/Lennart Nilsson; **813** top: Stephen J. Krasemann/DRK Photo; bottom: Lennart Nilsson/The Incredible Machine; **815** CNRI/Science Photo Library/Photo Researchers; **817** Lennart Nilsson; **821** "The Excitable Cortex in Conscious Man"/W. Penfield; **822** Brian Brake/Photo Researchers; **824** Science Source/Photo Researchers; **825** The Incredible Machine/Lennart Nilsson; **827** Lennart Nilsson/Lennart Nilsson; **828** top: Lennart Nilsson; bottom: Lennart Nilsson/Lennart Nilsson; **830** top: Lennart Nilsson/Lennart Nilsson; center: Lennart Nilsson; bottom: Lennart Nilsson/The Incredible Machine; **836** Globus Brothers/The Stock Market; **837** Dan McCoy/David Seltzer/Rainbow; **840** Lennart Nilsson/The Incredible Machine; **843** top: Eric Grave/Phototake; center: Biophoto Associates/Photo Researchers; bottom: John D. Cunningham/Visuals Unlimited; **844** Clara Franzini-Armstrong/Photo Researchers; **845** F. Hossler/Visuals Unlimited; **847** Veronica Burmeister/Visuals Unlimited; **848** top: Lennart Nilsson; bottom: John D. Cunningham/Visuals Unlimited; **849** CNRI/Phototake; **853** CNRI/Science Photo Library/Photo Researchers; **854** top and bottom: Ken Karp/Omni-Photo Communications; **855** Duomo; **856** top: John Lei/Omni-Photo Communications; bottom: Jerry L. Ferrara/Photo Researchers; **859** top: Wolfgang Kaehler; bottom: Wayne Lankinen/DRK Photo; **862** The Incredible Machine/Lennart Nilsson; **863** David Madison/Duomo; **865** USDA; **866** Yoav/Phototake; **868** Omikron/Science Source/Photo Researchers; **869** Howard Sochurek; **870** The Incredible Machine/Lennart Nilsson; **871** Lennart Nilsson-The Incredible Machine/

Boehringer Ingelheim International GmbH; **874** Lennart Nilsson/The Incredible Machine; **875** Lennart Nilsson/The Incredible Machine; **880** top: Bob Winsett/Jeff Andrew/Tom Stack & Associates; inset: Art Siegel/Art Siegel; **881** left: Mark Newman/Tom Stack & Associates; top right: Veronica Burmeister/Visuals Unlimited; bottom right: Dr. Dennis Kunkel/Phototake; **882** Stephen J. Krasemann/DRK Photo; **883** Lennart Nilsson/Boehringer Ingelheim International GmbH; **884** top: Chet Childs/TSW Click/ Chicago; bottom left: CNRI/Science Photo Library/Photo Researchers; bottom right: CNRI/ Science Library/Photo Researchers; **887** CNRI/ Scince Library/Photo Researchers; **888** left: Peter Scoones/Planet Earth Pictures; right: Keith Gunnar/Bruce Coleman, Inc.; **889** Chemical Design/Science Photo Library/Photo Researchers; **891** left: Jeff Foott/DRK Photo; right: M.A. Chappell/Animals Animals; **896** top: CNRI/Science Photo LIbrary/Photo Researchers; inset: Mallinckrodt Institute of Radiology; **897** David Wagner/Phototake; **899** top: Lennart Nilsson/Lennart Nilsson; bottom: Lennart Nilsson/Lennart Nilsson; **900** Lennart Nilsson/Boehringer Ingelheim International GmbH; **903** top: Photo Researchers; bottom: Biophoto Associates/Science Source/Photo Researchers; **905** Nathan Benn/Woodfin Camp & Associates; **906** top: CNRI/Science Photo Library/Photo Researchers; bottom: Lennart Nilsson/Lennart Nilsson; **907** top: Visuals Unlimited; bottom: Veronica Burmeister/Visuals Unlimited; **908** CNRI/Science Photo Library/ Photo Researchers; **909** Lennart Nilsson/ Lennart Nilsson; **911** Dan McCoy/Rainbow; **915** David M. Phillips/Visuals Unlimited; **916** top: Co Rentmeester/The Image Bank; bottom: David Parker/Photo Researchers; **917** Lennart Nilsson/Boehringer Ingelheim International GmbH; **919** Jan Hinsch/Science Photo Library/ Photo Researchers; **922** top right: Bruce Iverson/Visuals Unlimited; bottom left: Lennart Nilsson/The Incredible Machine; **925** Lennart Nilsson; **926** David Madison/Duomo; **934** top: Lennart Nilsson; bottom: Ronn Maratea/ International Stock Photography; **935** Tom Hollyman/Photo Researchers; **936** top: PH; **937** Dr. G. Schatten/Science Photo Library/Photo Researchers; **940** left: Lennart Nilsson; right: Lennart Nilsson/The Incredible Machine; **942** left, center and right: Lennart Nilsson; **944** all photos: Petit Format/Nestle/Science Source/ Photo Researchers; **945** Lennart Nilsson; **946** David Leah/Science Photo Library/Photo Researchers; **947** CARE; **951** left: Andree Abecassis/The Stock Market; right: George Ancona/International Stock Photography; **952** top and inset: The Mansell Collection; **953** CNRI/Science Photo Library/Photo Researchers; **954** top: The Incredible Machine/ Lennart Nilsson; bottom: drawing, 1897/The Granger Collection; **955** Robert Isear/Photo Researchers; **957** left: CNRI/Science Photo Library/Photo Researchers; right: Tektoff-Merieux, CNRI/Science Photo Library/Photo Researchers; **958** top: Martin Dohrn/Photo Researchers; bottom: Georg Gerster/ Comstock; **959** Willy Burgdorfer & Stanley F. Haynes/Rocky Mountain Laboratories; **960** Lennart Nilsson/Boehringer Ingelheim International GmbH; **961** top: Dan McCoy/ Rainbow; bottom: G.V. Faint/The Image Bank; **962** Lennart Nilsson/Boehringer Ingelheim International GmbH; **963** Bill Pierce/Rainbow; **968** top: UPI/Bettmann Newsphotos; inset: Science VU/Visuals Unlimited; **969** Lennart Nilsson/Boehringer Ingelheim International GmbH; **970** Lennart Nilsson/Boehringer Ingelheim International GmbH; **971** top left, top right, bottom left, bottom right: Lennart Nilsson/ Boehringer Ingelheim International GmbH; **974** The Bettmann Archive; **975** top: National Library of Medicine; bottom: Lennart Nilsson/ Boehringer Ingelheim International GmbH; **976** Lennart Nilsson/Boehringer Ingelheim International GmbH; **977** left: David M. Phillips/ Visuals Unlimited; right: Lennart Nilsson/ Boehringer Ingelheim International GmbH; **978** Prof. L. Brent/St. Mary's Hospital Medical School; **979** Lennart Nilsson/Boehringer Ingelheim International GmbH; **980** Lennart Nilsson/Boehringer Ingelheim International GmbH; **981** Brian Reynolds/Sygma; **985** NASA/ Science Source/Photo Researchers; **986** top: Gary Cralle/The Image Bank; inset: Michael P. Gadomski/Photo Researchers; **987** R.B. Sanchez/The Stock Market; **988** top: Nippur, Iraq/The University Museum, University of Pennsylvania; bottom: John Lei/Omni-Photo Communications; **989** left: Howard Sochurek; inset: J.H. Robinson/Photo Researchers; **991** Wesley Bocxe/Photo Researchers; bottom: Michael Hardy/Woodfin Camp & Associates; **992** inset: Dr. Jeremy Burgess/Science Photo Library/Photo Researchers; bottom: Michael Hardy/Woodfin Camp; **993** Bobby Holland/ Reader's Digest Foundation; **995** Bobby Holland/Readers Digest Foundation; **996** left: Lennart Nilson/Boehringer Ingelheim International GmbH; right: The Incredible Machine/Lennart Nilsson; **1001** Ted Russell/ The Image Bank; **1002** top: Kay Chernush/The Image Bank; center: Don Klumpp/The Image Bank; bottom: Dan McCoy/Rainbow; **1003** left: Gary Cralle/The Image Bank; center: Michael Hardy/Woodfin Camp & Associates; right: Mark Newman/Tom Stack & Associates; **1004** and **1005** Charles Mason/Black Star; **1005** inset: Michael Baytoff/Black Star; **1006** top: John Johnson/DRK Photo; inset: NASA; **1007** Wolfgang Kaehler; **1011** left center, and right: Stephen J. Krasemann/DRK Photo; **1012** left: Charles Krebs/The Stock Market; center: Michael Giannechini/Photo Researchers; right: Jeff Foott/Jeff Foott; **1013** left: Viviane Moos/ The Stock Market; top: Jeff Foott/Jeff Foott; bottom: Cs. Nielsen/DRK Photo; **1014** Stephen Krasemann/DRK Photo; **1015** left and right: Wolfgang Kaehler/Wolfgang Kaehler; center: Michael Fogden/DRK Photo; **1016** left: Nancy Adams/Tom Stack & Associates; center: Robert Jureit/The Stock Market; right: Jeff Foott/Jeff Foott; **1017** top: DPI; bottom left: Wolfgang Kaehler/Wolfgang Kaehler; bottom right: Planet Earth Pictures; **1019** top: Roy Morsch/The Stock Market; bottom: James R. Fisher/DRK Photo; **1020** J. Frederick Grassle/Woods Hole Oceanographic Institution; **1021** left: Wayne Lynch/DRK Photo; center: S. Nielsen/DRK Photo; right: Wolfgang Kaehler/Wolfgang Kaehler; **1026** Don & Pat Valenti/DRK Photo; **1031** Pat O'Hara/DRK Photo; **1032** top: Stephen J. Krasemann/DRK Photo; inset: G.C. Kelley/Photo Researchers; **1033** Dan Guravich/Photo Researchers; **1036** left: Warren Garst/Tom Stack & Associates; right: Kim Taylor/Bruce Coleman, Inc.; **1038** Stephen J. Krasemann/DRK Photo; **1039** top: Erwin & Peggy Bauer/Bruce Coleman, Inc.; bottom: Philippe Giraud/Sygma; **1041** top left: Doug Perrine/DRK Photo; top right: Jeff Foott; bottom: Bill Wood/Bruce Coleman, Inc.; **1042** Don Carroll/The Image Bank; **1043** Norman Owen Tomalin/Bruce Coleman, Inc.; **1048** top: Pat O'Hara/DRK Photo; inset: Stephen J. Krasemann/DRK Photo; **1049** Jack Willburn/ Earth Scenes; **1050** Richard Hutchings/Photo Researchers; **1051** Frans Lanting/Minden Pictures; **1053** top: John Bryson/The Image Bank; bottom: Jack Swenson/Tom Stack & Associates; **1054** top: Stephen J. Krasemann/ DRK Photo; bottom: Frans Lanting/Minden Pictures; **1055** bottom: Ted Spiegel/Black Star; inset: Melchior DiGiacomo/The Image Bank; **1056** right: Breck P. Kent/Breck P. Kent; inset Roger Cheng; **1058** left: NASA; right: Mark Newman/Earth Images; **1059** top: NASA; bottom: Wolfgang Kaehler/Wolfgang Kaehler; **1060** top: Tom Stack/Tom Stack & Associates; bottom: David Smart/DRK Photo; **1061** Leif Skoogfors/Woodfin Camp & Associates; **1062** Ken Sakamoto/Black Star; **1063** top: Michael Baytoff/Black Star; bottom: B. Nation/Sygma; **1064** left: Thomas Kitchin/Tom Stack & Associates; right: Thomas Kitchin/Tom Stack & Associates; **1065** Jeff Foott/Jeff Foott; **1066** left: Tom McHugh/Photo Researchers; center and right: Jeff Foott/Jeff Foott; **1067** Larry Lefever/Grant Heilman, Inc.; **1068** left: Steve Jackson/Black Star; right: Terry G. Murphy/ Animals Animals; **1069** James Balog/Black Star; **1070** Joe Azzara/The Image Bank; **1071** top left: G. Brimacombre/The Image Bank; bottom left: John Kelly/The Image Bank; top right: Denis Valentine/The Stock Market; bottom right: DPI; center: NASA; **1075** Holt Conter/DRK Photo; **1076** top: David Smart/DRK Photo; center: C.C. Lockwood/DRK Photo; bottom: Robert Frerck/ Odyssey; **1077** NASA.

All photographs of Ken Miller by Jody Miller.

All photographs of Joe Levine by Paula Chandoha.